Student's Solution Manual

Brian Hons
San Antonio College

Beginning and Intermediate Algebra:
Building a Foundation

Paula McKenna
San Antonio College

Honey Kirk
Palo Alto College

Addison-Wesley
is an imprint of

PEARSON

D0166066

Copyright ©2010 Pearson Education, Inc.
Publishing as Pearson Addison-Wesley, 75 Arlington Street, Boston, MA 02116.

ISBN-13: 978-0-321-59404-4
ISBN-10: 0-321-59404-5

3 4 5 6 CRS 12 11 10 09

Addison-Wesley
is an imprint of

www.pearsonhighered.com

Table of Contents

Chapter 1

1.1 Exercises

1. A <u>set</u> is a collection of well-defined objects.

3. The <u>roster</u> <u>notation</u> of a set includes set braces and elements offset by commas.

5. The <u>set-builder</u> <u>notation</u> of a set includes set braces, a variable, and reads like a sentence.

7. Set intersection is a set operation denoted by <u>$\cap$</u>.

9. The union of A and B, denoted <u>$A \cup B$</u>, means the set of all those elements in <u>A</u>, all of those elements in <u>B</u>, or all of those elements they <u>share</u>.

11. $\{$Alabama, Alaska, Arizona, ..., Wyoming$\}$

13. Answers will vary; for example: The set C whose elements are all the men in my math class.

15. False, $6 \notin A$

17. True

19. True

21. False, $111 \in A$

23. False, $9 \in B$

25. True

27. False, rational numbers can always be written as a quotient of integers.

29. False, every integer is a fraction with a denominator of 1.

31. False, $Q \cup M = R$

33. True

35. True

37. $\left\{ 0, 1, \sqrt{36}, 18, \dfrac{40}{2} \right\}$

39. $\left\{ -120, -23\dfrac{1}{4}, -\sqrt{13}, -1, 0, 1, \pi, \sqrt{36}, \dfrac{26}{3}, 18, \dfrac{40}{2}, \right.$
$\left. 32.121121112..., 43.36 \right\}$

41. $\left\{ 1, \sqrt{36}, 18, \dfrac{40}{2} \right\}$

43. $B = \{..., -2, -1, 0, 1\}$

45. $C \cup D = \{1, 2, 3, 4, 6, 7, 8, 9, 10, ...\}$

47. $A \cap C = \{1, 2, 3\}$

49. $C \cap D = \{\ \}$ or $\varnothing$

51. $B \cup C = \{..., -5, -4, -3, -2, -1, 0, 1, 2, 3, 4\}$

53. True

55. True

57. False, possible answers include: If $a < b$, and $a, b \in R$, then $a \neq b$.

59. False, possible answers include: If $a = b$, and $a, b \in R$, then $a \geq b$.

61. A verbal description is a sentence describing the elements of a set. Roster notation lists the elements in a set. Set-builder notation is a shorthand way of defining a set using a variable and mathematical symbols.

63. $\{..., -8, -6, -4, -2\}$

1.2 Exercises

1. The process of writing a natural number as a product of only prime numbers is called <u>prime factorization</u>.

3. A number is divisible by 2 if it is an <u>even</u> <u>number</u>.

5. A number is divisible by 3 if the <u>sum</u> of its digits is divisible by <u>three</u>.

7. An <u>improper</u> fraction has a value greater than or equal to 1 or less than or equal to -1.

9. The <u>sum</u> of a whole number and a <u>proper</u> <u>fraction</u> may be written as a mixed number.

11. The <u>Fundamental</u> Principle of Fractions gives us the tool we need to <u>simplify (or reduce)</u> fractions.

13. The fraction $\dfrac{5}{5}$ is an example of an <u>improper</u> fraction.

15. The fraction $\dfrac{8}{0}$ has an <u>undefined</u> value.

17. $68 = 2 \cdot 2 \cdot 17$

19. $120 = 2 \cdot 2 \cdot 2 \cdot 3 \cdot 5$

21. $270 = 2 \cdot 3 \cdot 3 \cdot 3 \cdot 5$

23. $250 = 2 \cdot 5 \cdot 5 \cdot 5$

25. $320 = 2 \cdot 2 \cdot 2 \cdot 2 \cdot 2 \cdot 2 \cdot 5$

27. $456 = 2 \cdot 2 \cdot 2 \cdot 3 \cdot 19$

29. $945 = 3 \cdot 3 \cdot 3 \cdot 5 \cdot 7$

31. $8 = 2 \cdot 2 \cdot 2$
    $20 = 2 \cdot 2 \cdot 5$
    $$\text{LCM}(8, 20) = 2 \cdot 2 \cdot 2 \cdot 5$$
    $$= 40$$

33. $12 = 2 \cdot 2 \cdot 3$
    $15 = 3 \cdot 5$
    $$\text{LCM}(12, 15) = 2 \cdot 2 \cdot 3 \cdot 5$$
    $$= 60$$

35. $10 = 2 \cdot 5$
    $12 = 2 \cdot 2 \cdot 3$
    $14 = 2 \cdot 7$
    $$\text{LCM}(10, 12, 14) = 2 \cdot 2 \cdot 3 \cdot 5 \cdot 7$$
    $$= 420$$

37. $240 = 2 \cdot 2 \cdot 2 \cdot 2 \cdot 3 \cdot 5$
    $360 = 2 \cdot 2 \cdot 2 \cdot 3 \cdot 3 \cdot 5$
    $$\text{LCM}(240, 360) = 2 \cdot 2 \cdot 2 \cdot 2 \cdot 3 \cdot 3 \cdot 5$$
    $$= 720$$

39. $125 = 5 \cdot 5 \cdot 5$
    $250 = 2 \cdot 5 \cdot 5 \cdot 5$
    $$\text{LCM}(125, 250) = 2 \cdot 5 \cdot 5 \cdot 5$$
    $$= 250$$

41. $25 = 5 \cdot 5$
    $125 = 5 \cdot 5 \cdot 5$
    $200 = 2 \cdot 2 \cdot 2 \cdot 5 \cdot 5$
    $$\text{LCM}(25, 125, 200) = 2 \cdot 2 \cdot 2 \cdot 5 \cdot 5 \cdot 5$$
    $$= 1000$$

43. $\dfrac{1}{2}$

45. $\dfrac{5}{8}$

47. $\dfrac{13}{5},\ 2\dfrac{3}{5}$

49. $\dfrac{4}{12} = \dfrac{\overset{1}{\cancel{4}} \cdot 1}{\underset{1}{\cancel{4}} \cdot 3}$
    $$= \dfrac{1}{3}$$

51. $\dfrac{28}{42} = \dfrac{2 \cdot \overset{1}{\cancel{14}}}{3 \cdot \underset{1}{\cancel{14}}}$
    $$= \dfrac{2}{3}$$

53. $\dfrac{90}{195} = \dfrac{6 \cdot \overset{1}{\cancel{15}}}{13 \cdot \underset{1}{\cancel{15}}}$
    $$= \dfrac{6}{13}$$

55. $\dfrac{230}{65} = \dfrac{\overset{1}{\cancel{5}} \cdot 46}{\underset{1}{\cancel{5}} \cdot 13}$

$\qquad = \dfrac{46}{13}$

57. $\dfrac{1,224}{2,244} = \dfrac{\overset{1}{\cancel{12}} \cdot 102}{\underset{1}{\cancel{12}} \cdot 187}$

$\qquad = \dfrac{102}{187}$

59. $\dfrac{1,013}{0}$ is undefined.

61. $\dfrac{1}{2} \cdot \dfrac{3}{5} = \dfrac{1 \cdot 3}{2 \cdot 5}$

$\qquad = \dfrac{3}{10}$

63. $8 \cdot \dfrac{3}{4} = \dfrac{8}{1} \cdot \dfrac{3}{4}$

$\qquad = \dfrac{2 \cdot \overset{1}{\cancel{4}} \cdot 3}{1 \cdot \underset{1}{\cancel{4}}}$

$\qquad = \dfrac{2 \cdot 3}{1}$

$\qquad = 6$

65. $\dfrac{2}{5} \cdot \dfrac{10}{3} = \dfrac{2 \cdot 2 \cdot \overset{1}{\cancel{5}}}{\underset{1}{\cancel{5}} \cdot 3}$

$\qquad = \dfrac{2 \cdot 2}{3}$

$\qquad = \dfrac{4}{3}$

67. $3\dfrac{1}{2} \cdot 5\dfrac{1}{3} = \dfrac{7}{2} \cdot \dfrac{16}{3}$

$\qquad = \dfrac{7 \cdot \overset{1}{\cancel{2}} \cdot 8}{\underset{1}{\cancel{2}} \cdot 3}$

$\qquad = \dfrac{7 \cdot 8}{3}$

$\qquad = \dfrac{56}{3}$

69. $11\dfrac{7}{8} \cdot 10 = \dfrac{95}{8} \cdot \dfrac{10}{1}$

$\qquad = \dfrac{95 \cdot \overset{1}{\cancel{2}} \cdot 5}{\underset{1}{\cancel{2}} \cdot 4}$

$\qquad = \dfrac{95 \cdot 5}{4}$

$\qquad = \dfrac{475}{4}$

71. $\dfrac{213}{7} \cdot \dfrac{23}{3} = \dfrac{\overset{1}{\cancel{3}} \cdot 71 \cdot 23}{7 \cdot \underset{1}{\cancel{3}}}$

$\qquad = \dfrac{71 \cdot 23}{7}$

$\qquad = \dfrac{1,633}{7}$

73. $\dfrac{12}{13} \div \dfrac{11}{26} = \dfrac{12}{13} \cdot \dfrac{26}{11}$

$\qquad = \dfrac{12 \cdot 2 \cdot \overset{1}{\cancel{13}}}{\underset{1}{\cancel{13}} \cdot 11}$

$\qquad = \dfrac{24}{11}$

75. $\dfrac{180}{220} \div \dfrac{210}{154} = \dfrac{180}{220} \cdot \dfrac{154}{210}$

$\qquad = \dfrac{\overset{1}{\cancel{4}} \cdot 3 \cdot \overset{1}{\cancel{3}} \cdot \overset{1}{\cancel{5}} \cdot \overset{1}{\cancel{2}} \cdot \overset{1}{\cancel{7}} \cdot \overset{1}{\cancel{11}}}{\underset{1}{\cancel{4}} \cdot 5 \cdot \underset{1}{\cancel{11}} \cdot \underset{1}{\cancel{2}} \cdot \underset{1}{\cancel{3}} \cdot \underset{1}{\cancel{5}} \cdot \underset{1}{\cancel{7}}}$

$\qquad = \dfrac{3}{5}$

77. $6 \div \dfrac{9}{8} = \dfrac{6}{1} \cdot \dfrac{8}{9}$

$\qquad = \dfrac{2 \cdot \overset{1}{\cancel{3}} \cdot 8}{1 \cdot \underset{1}{\cancel{3}} \cdot 3}$

$\qquad = \dfrac{16}{3}$

79. $1\dfrac{3}{4} \div 5 = \dfrac{7}{4} \div \dfrac{5}{1}$

$\qquad = \dfrac{7}{4} \cdot \dfrac{1}{5}$

$\qquad = \dfrac{7 \cdot 1}{4 \cdot 5}$

$\qquad = \dfrac{7}{20}$

81. $\dfrac{3}{5} \div 0$ is undefined.

83. $0 \div \dfrac{11}{5} = 0$

85. $1\dfrac{5}{21} \div \dfrac{55}{42} = \dfrac{26}{21} \div \dfrac{55}{42}$

$\qquad = \dfrac{26}{21} \cdot \dfrac{42}{55}$

$\qquad = \dfrac{26 \cdot 2 \cdot \overset{1}{\cancel{3}} \cdot \overset{1}{\cancel{7}}}{\underset{1}{\cancel{3}} \cdot \underset{1}{\cancel{7}} \cdot 55}$

$\qquad = \dfrac{52}{55}$

87. $\dfrac{2}{5} + \dfrac{1}{5} = \dfrac{2+1}{5}$

$\qquad = \dfrac{3}{5}$

89. $\dfrac{4}{5} + \dfrac{11}{5} = \dfrac{4+11}{5}$

$\qquad = \dfrac{15}{5}$

$\qquad = 3$

91. $\dfrac{8}{9} - \dfrac{2}{9} = \dfrac{8-2}{9}$

$\qquad = \dfrac{6}{9}$

$\qquad = \dfrac{2}{3}$

93. $\dfrac{78}{150} - \dfrac{18}{150} = \dfrac{78-18}{150}$

$\qquad = \dfrac{60}{150}$

$\qquad = \dfrac{2}{5}$

95. $\dfrac{127}{49} - \dfrac{113}{49} = \dfrac{127-113}{49}$

$\qquad = \dfrac{14}{49}$

$\qquad = \dfrac{2}{7}$

97. $\dfrac{2}{3} = \dfrac{2}{3} \cdot 1 \qquad\qquad \dfrac{4}{5} = \dfrac{4}{5} \cdot 1$

$\qquad = \dfrac{2}{3} \cdot \dfrac{20}{20} \qquad\qquad = \dfrac{4}{5} \cdot \dfrac{12}{12}$

$\qquad = \dfrac{40}{60} \qquad\qquad\quad = \dfrac{48}{60}$

99. $\dfrac{1}{2} = \dfrac{1}{2} \cdot 1 \qquad \dfrac{2}{3} = \dfrac{2}{3} \cdot 1 \qquad \dfrac{10}{7} = \dfrac{10}{7} \cdot 1$

$\quad = \dfrac{1}{2} \cdot \dfrac{42}{42} \qquad = \dfrac{2}{3} \cdot \dfrac{28}{28} \qquad = \dfrac{10}{7} \cdot \dfrac{12}{12}$

$\quad = \dfrac{42}{84} \qquad\quad = \dfrac{56}{84} \qquad\quad = \dfrac{120}{84}$

101. $\dfrac{11}{18} = \dfrac{11}{18} \cdot 1 \qquad\qquad \dfrac{7}{36} = \dfrac{7}{36} \cdot 1$

$\qquad = \dfrac{11}{18} \cdot \dfrac{12}{12} \qquad\qquad = \dfrac{7}{36} \cdot \dfrac{6}{6}$

$\qquad = \dfrac{132}{216} \qquad\qquad\quad = \dfrac{42}{216}$

103. $\quad 6 = 2 \cdot 3$

$\qquad 15 = 3 \cdot 5$

$\qquad\qquad \text{LCD}(6,15) = 2 \cdot 3 \cdot 5$

$\qquad\qquad\qquad\qquad = 30$

105. $\quad 12 = 2 \cdot 2 \cdot 3$

$\qquad 18 = 2 \cdot 3 \cdot 3$

$\qquad\qquad \text{LCD}(12,18) = 2 \cdot 2 \cdot 3 \cdot 3$

$\qquad\qquad\qquad\qquad = 36$

107. $\quad 9 = 3 \cdot 3$

$\qquad 45 = 3 \cdot 3 \cdot 5$

$\qquad 15 = 3 \cdot 5$

$\qquad\qquad \text{LCD}(9,45,15) = 3 \cdot 3 \cdot 5$

$\qquad\qquad\qquad\qquad = 45$

109. $\text{LCD}(10,35) = 70$

$\qquad \dfrac{3}{10} + \dfrac{4}{35} = \dfrac{3 \cdot 7}{10 \cdot 7} + \dfrac{4 \cdot 2}{35 \cdot 2}$

$\qquad\qquad = \dfrac{21}{70} + \dfrac{8}{70}$

$\qquad\qquad = \dfrac{21+8}{70}$

$\qquad\qquad = \dfrac{29}{70}$

111. $\text{LCD}(8,10) = 40$

$$\frac{7}{8} - \frac{3}{10} = \frac{7 \cdot 5}{8 \cdot 5} - \frac{3 \cdot 4}{10 \cdot 4}$$

$$= \frac{35}{40} - \frac{12}{40}$$

$$= \frac{35 - 12}{40}$$

$$= \frac{23}{40}$$

113. $\text{LCD}(8,6) = 24$

$$\frac{7}{8} - \frac{5}{6} = \frac{7 \cdot 3}{8 \cdot 3} - \frac{5 \cdot 4}{6 \cdot 4}$$

$$= \frac{21}{24} - \frac{20}{24}$$

$$= \frac{21 - 20}{24}$$

$$= \frac{1}{24}$$

115. $\text{LCD}(21,15) = 105$

$$\frac{4}{21} - \frac{2}{15} = \frac{4 \cdot 5}{21 \cdot 5} - \frac{2 \cdot 7}{15 \cdot 7}$$

$$= \frac{20}{105} - \frac{14}{105}$$

$$= \frac{20 - 14}{105}$$

$$= \frac{6}{105}$$

$$= \frac{2 \cdot \overset{1}{\cancel{3}}}{\underset{1}{\cancel{3}} \cdot 35}$$

$$= \frac{2}{35}$$

117. $\text{LCD}(35,15) = 105$

$$\frac{1}{35} + \frac{8}{15} = \frac{1 \cdot 3}{35 \cdot 3} + \frac{8 \cdot 7}{15 \cdot 7}$$

$$= \frac{3}{105} + \frac{56}{105}$$

$$= \frac{3 + 56}{105}$$

$$= \frac{59}{105}$$

119. $\text{LCD}(10,18) = 90$

$$\frac{9}{10} - \frac{5}{18} = \frac{9 \cdot 9}{10 \cdot 9} - \frac{5 \cdot 5}{18 \cdot 5}$$

$$= \frac{81}{90} - \frac{25}{90}$$

$$= \frac{81 - 25}{90}$$

$$= \frac{56}{90}$$

$$= \frac{\overset{1}{\cancel{2}} \cdot 28}{\underset{1}{\cancel{2}} \cdot 45}$$

$$= \frac{28}{45}$$

121. $\text{LCD}(9,6) = 18$

$$7\frac{2}{9} + \frac{1}{6} = \frac{65}{9} + \frac{1}{6}$$

$$= \frac{65 \cdot 2}{9 \cdot 2} + \frac{1 \cdot 3}{6 \cdot 3}$$

$$= \frac{130}{18} + \frac{3}{18}$$

$$= \frac{133}{18}$$

123. $\text{LCD}(4,3) = 12$

$$4\frac{3}{4} + 6\frac{2}{3} = \frac{19}{4} + \frac{20}{3}$$

$$= \frac{19 \cdot 3}{4 \cdot 3} + \frac{20 \cdot 4}{3 \cdot 4}$$

$$= \frac{57}{12} + \frac{80}{12}$$

$$= \frac{137}{12}$$

125. $\text{LCD}(7,5) = 35$

$$14\frac{3}{7} - 9\frac{2}{5} = \frac{101}{7} - \frac{47}{5}$$

$$= \frac{101 \cdot 5}{7 \cdot 5} - \frac{47 \cdot 7}{5 \cdot 7}$$

$$= \frac{505}{35} - \frac{329}{35}$$

$$= \frac{176}{35}$$

127. $\text{LCD}(12,9)=36$

$$10\frac{1}{12}-6\frac{7}{9}=\frac{121}{12}-\frac{61}{9}$$

$$=\frac{121\cdot3}{12\cdot3}-\frac{61\cdot4}{9\cdot4}$$

$$=\frac{363}{36}-\frac{244}{36}$$

$$=\frac{119}{36}$$

129. $13.04+8.123=21.163$

131. $200.56+128.04=328.60$

133. $12+0.87=12.87$

135. $54-0.13=53.87$

137. $47.8-22.59=25.21$

139. $1,200.006-850=350.006$

141. $(0.004)(0.02)=0.00008$

143. $(5.6)(12.08)=67.648$

145. $(1,000)(123.28)=123,280$

147. $120\div(0.03)=4,000$

149. $21.065\div(0.05)=421.3$

151. $\dfrac{0.12}{1,000}=0.00012$

153. 127

155. 101

157. a) prime factorization

$$18=2\cdot3\cdot3$$
$$30=2\cdot3\cdot5$$
$$42=2\cdot3\cdot7$$
$$\text{LCM}(18,30,42)=2\cdot3\cdot3\cdot5\cdot7=630$$

b) listing multiples

$18:36,54,72,90,108,...,630,648$

$30:60,90,120,150,...,600,630,660$

$42:84,126,168,210,...,630,672$

157. c) Make a factor tree.

159. The answer is incorrect because Omar forgot to "borrow" $\frac{5}{5}$ from 24 in the first term before attempting the subtraction. This mistake would have been avoided had Omar converted each mixed number to an improper fraction before subtracting.

161.
$$8\frac{1}{2}+8\frac{1}{2}+9\frac{3}{5}+9\frac{3}{5}=\frac{17}{2}+\frac{17}{2}+\frac{48}{5}+\frac{48}{5}$$

$$=\frac{17+17}{2}+\frac{48+48}{5}$$

$$=\frac{34}{2}+\frac{96}{5}$$

$$=\frac{170+192}{10}$$

$$=\frac{362}{10}$$

$$=\frac{181}{5}\text{ inches}$$

163.
$$27\frac{5}{12}+3\frac{7}{8}+7+\frac{27}{5}+18+\frac{25}{4}+3\frac{7}{8}=\frac{329}{12}+\frac{31}{8}+\frac{7}{1}+\frac{27}{5}+\frac{18}{1}+\frac{25}{4}+\frac{31}{8}$$

$$=\frac{329\cdot10}{12\cdot10}+\frac{31\cdot15}{8\cdot15}+\frac{7\cdot120}{1\cdot120}+\frac{27\cdot24}{5\cdot24}+\frac{18\cdot120}{1\cdot120}+\frac{25\cdot30}{4\cdot30}+\frac{31\cdot15}{8\cdot15}$$

$$=\frac{8,618}{120}$$

$$=\frac{4,309}{60}$$

$$=71\frac{49}{60}\text{ feet}$$

165. $\mathrm{LCD}(24,36,72) = 72$

$$\frac{5}{24} + \frac{7}{36} + \frac{1}{72} = \frac{5 \cdot 3}{24 \cdot 3} + \frac{7 \cdot 2}{36 \cdot 2} + \frac{1}{72}$$

$$= \frac{15}{72} + \frac{14}{72} + \frac{1}{72}$$

$$= \frac{15 + 14 + 1}{72}$$

$$= \frac{30}{72}$$

$$= \frac{5}{12}$$

167. $\mathrm{LCD}(16,24) = 48$

$$25\frac{11}{16} - 18\frac{7}{24} = \frac{411}{16} - \frac{439}{24}$$

$$= \frac{411 \cdot 3}{16 \cdot 3} - \frac{439 \cdot 2}{24 \cdot 2}$$

$$= \frac{1,233}{48} - \frac{878}{48}$$

$$= \frac{1,233 - 878}{48}$$

$$= \frac{355}{48}$$

1.3 Exercises

1. The absolute value of a real number x is the number of <u>units</u> x lies from <u>zero</u> on the number line.

3. To add two real numbers with different signs, we subtract their absolute values and attach the <u>sign</u> of the number with the larger <u>absolute</u> <u>value</u>.

5. Another name for additive inverse is <u>opposite</u>.

7. g, f

9. h, d

11. d

13. $|-27| = 27$

15. $|145| = 145$

17. $|0| = 0$

19. $\left|\dfrac{-1}{2}\right| = \dfrac{1}{2}$

21. $\left|17\dfrac{5}{6}\right| = 17\dfrac{5}{6}$

23. $|0.03| = 0.03$

25. $|-121.05| = 121.05$

27. $27 + (-35) = -8$

29. $-18 + (-40) = -58$

31. $\left(-\dfrac{2}{3}\right) + \left(-\dfrac{1}{2}\right) = \left(-\dfrac{2 \cdot 2}{3 \cdot 2}\right) + \left(-\dfrac{1 \cdot 3}{2 \cdot 3}\right)$

$= \left(-\dfrac{4}{6}\right) + \left(-\dfrac{3}{6}\right)$

$= -\dfrac{7}{6}$

33. $\dfrac{-10}{7} + 6\dfrac{1}{3} = -\dfrac{10}{7} + \dfrac{19}{3}$

$= -\dfrac{10 \cdot 3}{7 \cdot 3} + \dfrac{19 \cdot 7}{3 \cdot 7}$

$= -\dfrac{30}{21} + \dfrac{133}{21}$

$= \dfrac{103}{21}$

35. $62.5 + (-103.01) = -40.51$

37. $(-17.23) + (-45.087) = -62.317$

39. $-1035 - 805 = -1035 + (-805)$

$= -1,840$

41. $(-37) - (-54) = -37 + 54$

$= 17$

43. $\dfrac{24}{35} - \left(-\dfrac{7}{15}\right) = \dfrac{24}{35} + \dfrac{7}{15}$

$= \dfrac{24 \cdot 3}{35 \cdot 3} + \dfrac{7 \cdot 7}{15 \cdot 7}$

$= \dfrac{72}{105} + \dfrac{49}{105}$

$= \dfrac{121}{105}$

45. $\dfrac{9}{10} - \dfrac{45}{14} = \dfrac{9}{10} + \left(-\dfrac{45}{14}\right)$

$= \dfrac{9 \cdot 7}{10 \cdot 7} + \left(-\dfrac{45 \cdot 5}{14 \cdot 5}\right)$

$= \dfrac{63}{70} + \left(-\dfrac{225}{70}\right)$

$= -\dfrac{162}{70}$

$= -\dfrac{81}{35}$

47. $-18.02 - 4.8 = -18.02 + (-4.8)$

$= -22.82$

49. $-37.881 - (-40.28) = -37.881 + 40.28$

$= 2.399$

51. $54 - 115 = 54 + (-115)$
$$= -61$$

53. $-1,005 + (-23) = -1,028$

55. $-17 + 107 = 90$

57. $-48 - (-49) = -48 + 49$
$$= 1$$

59. $\dfrac{7}{33} + \left(-\dfrac{40}{33}\right) = \dfrac{7 + (-40)}{33}$
$$= \dfrac{-33}{-33}$$
$$= -1$$

61. $\dfrac{25}{42} - \dfrac{105}{42} = \dfrac{25}{42} + \left(-\dfrac{105}{42}\right)$
$$= \dfrac{25 + (-105)}{42}$$
$$= -\dfrac{80}{42}$$
$$= -\dfrac{40}{21}$$

63. $-\dfrac{17}{90} - \left(-\dfrac{5}{18}\right) = -\dfrac{17}{90} + \dfrac{5}{18}$
$$= -\dfrac{17}{90} + \dfrac{5 \cdot 5}{18 \cdot 5}$$
$$= -\dfrac{17}{90} + \dfrac{25}{90}$$
$$= \dfrac{8}{90}$$
$$= \dfrac{4}{45}$$

65. $-10 + \left(-\dfrac{9}{8}\right) = -\dfrac{10}{1} + \left(-\dfrac{9}{8}\right)$
$$= -\dfrac{10 \cdot 8}{1 \cdot 8} + \left(-\dfrac{9}{8}\right)$$
$$= -\dfrac{80}{8} + \left(-\dfrac{9}{8}\right)$$
$$= -\dfrac{89}{8}$$

67. $-0.03 - 2.7 = -0.03 + (-2.7)$
$$= -2.73$$

69. $-138.71 + 140 = 1.29$

71. $20.9 - (-12.6) = 20.9 + 12.6$
$$= 33.5$$

73. $(-33.27) + (-74.7) = -107.97$

75. Answers will vary; one example is: To add two real numbers with opposite signs, subtract the absolute values of the two numbers and keep the sign of the number with the larger absolute value.

    a) $2 + (-8) = -6$

    b) $-\dfrac{4}{3} + \dfrac{5}{3} = \dfrac{1}{3}$

    c) $2.361 + (-4.852) = -2.491$

    d) $5\dfrac{1}{2} + \left(-3\dfrac{2}{3}\right) = \dfrac{11}{6} = 1\dfrac{5}{6}$

77. No. For example, $2 - 3 \neq 3 - 2$ because $-1 \neq 1$.

79. $9 + (-12) + 24 + (-3) = 18$
The total gain is 18 yards.

81. $733 - 633 = 100$
The total gain is 100 employees.

83. $20,320 - 14,433 = 5,887$
Mt McKinley is 5,887 feet higher.

85. $825.32 - 143.25 - 48.15 + 250 - 154.46 - 47.45 = 682.01$
The ending balance is $682.01.

1.4 Exercises

1. The multiplicative identity element is <u>1</u>.

3. The product of zero with any real number is <u>zero</u>. This is called the <u>multiplication</u> property of zero.

5. The sign of a product of two positive real numbers is <u>positive</u>.

7. The number 0 is called the <u>additive</u> identity element.

9. Within the associative property, the <u>grouping</u> of the numbers change.

11. c

13. i

15. b

17. a

19. e

21. f

23. d

25. h

27. g

29. $2 + x = x + 2$

31. $5(x+3) = 5x + 15$

33. $5(x+3) = (x+3) \cdot 5$

35. $5 + (7y + 3) = (5 + 7y) + 3$

37. $\left(\dfrac{2}{3}\right) + 0 = \dfrac{2}{3}$

39. $\left(\dfrac{x}{3}\right) \cdot 1 = \dfrac{x}{3}$

41. $3y + (x+4) = y \cdot 3 + (x+4)$

43. $3y + 4x = 4x + 3y$

45. $(-135) \cdot (42) = -5,670$

47. $0(-15) = 0$

49. $\dfrac{-138}{-6} = 23$

51. $\left(-5\dfrac{2}{3}\right) \div 1\dfrac{1}{5} = \left(-\dfrac{17}{3}\right) \div \left(\dfrac{6}{5}\right)$

$= -\dfrac{17 \cdot 5}{3 \cdot 6}$

$= -\dfrac{85}{18}$

53. $(-56.22) \div (-0.3) = 187.4$

55. $\left(\dfrac{-125}{3}\right) \cdot \left(\dfrac{-4}{15}\right) = \dfrac{500}{45}$

$= \dfrac{100}{9}$

57. $\dfrac{-5}{0}$ is undefined

59. $0\left(-4\dfrac{2}{3}\right) = 0$

61. $1.5314 \div (-0.124) = -12.35$

63. $(-12.01)(-0.03) = 0.3603$

65. $\left(\dfrac{1}{2}\right)(-22.6) = (0.5)(-22.6)$

$= -11.3$

67. $5\left(22\dfrac{1}{3}\right) = \dfrac{5}{1}\left(\dfrac{67}{3}\right)$

$= \dfrac{335}{3}$

69. $\left(-\dfrac{26}{5}\right) \div (-10) = -\dfrac{26}{5} \div \left(-\dfrac{10}{1}\right)$

$= \dfrac{26 \cdot 1}{5 \cdot 10}$

$= \dfrac{26}{50}$

$= \dfrac{13}{25}$

71. $18 \div \left(\dfrac{-2}{7} \right) = \dfrac{18}{1} \div \left(-\dfrac{2}{7} \right)$

$$= -\dfrac{18 \cdot 7}{1 \cdot 2}$$

$$= -\dfrac{126}{2}$$

$$= -63$$

73. Answers will vary; one example is: An additive inverse is an element for which, when added to a number, the result is zero; for multiplication, the result is one. An identity element, when added to or multiplied by a number, returns the same number.

75. Answers will vary; one example is: $2 + 3(xy) = 2 + (3x)y$.

77. Answers will vary; one example is: The multiplication property of zero states that zero multiplied by any number results in zero.

1.5 Exercises

1. In the expression 2^3, 2 is the <u>base</u> and 3 is the <u>exponent</u>.

3. A numerical term without a variable is called a <u>constant</u> term.

5. In the order of operations, we perform multiplication and division from <u>left</u> to <u>right</u>.

7. $5^4 = 5 \cdot 5 \cdot 5 \cdot 5$
$\quad = 625$

9. $-1^5 = -1 \cdot 1 \cdot 1 \cdot 1 \cdot 1$
$\quad\quad = -1$

11. $\left(\dfrac{2}{3}\right)^3 = \dfrac{2}{3} \cdot \dfrac{2}{3} \cdot \dfrac{2}{3}$
$\quad\quad\quad = \dfrac{8}{27}$

13. $(-0.2)^4 = (-0.2) \cdot (-0.2) \cdot (-0.2) \cdot (-0.2)$
$\quad\quad\quad = 0.0016$

15. $-10^2 = -10 \cdot 10$
$\quad\quad\quad = -100$

17. $(3.5)^0 = 1$

19. $(-1)^4 = (-1) \cdot (-1) \cdot (-1) \cdot (-1)$
$\quad\quad\quad = 1$

21. $(-8)^2 = (-8) \cdot (-8)$
$\quad\quad\quad = 64$

23. $\left(\dfrac{-1}{2}\right)^4 = \left(\dfrac{-1}{2}\right) \cdot \left(\dfrac{-1}{2}\right) \cdot \left(\dfrac{-1}{2}\right) \cdot \left(\dfrac{-1}{2}\right)$
$\quad\quad\quad = \dfrac{1}{16}$

25. $4 + 6(-2 - 7) = 4 + 6(-9)$
$\quad\quad\quad\quad = 4 + (-54)$
$\quad\quad\quad\quad = -50$

27. $1.2 + 2.4 \div 1.2 = 1.2 + 2$
$\quad\quad\quad\quad = 3.2$

29. $3 + \sqrt{9 + 16} = 3 + \sqrt{25}$
$\quad\quad\quad\quad = 3 + 5$
$\quad\quad\quad\quad = 8$

31. $5 - 3(-4 - 6)^2 = 5 - 3(-10)^2$
$\quad\quad\quad\quad = 5 - 3(100)$
$\quad\quad\quad\quad = 5 - 300$
$\quad\quad\quad\quad = -295$

33. $-15 \div 5(-3) = -3(-3)$
$\quad\quad\quad\quad = 9$

35. $6^2 \cdot 2 + 2(-3) = 36 \cdot 2 + 2(-3)$
$\quad\quad\quad\quad = 72 + 2(-3)$
$\quad\quad\quad\quad = 72 + (-6)$
$\quad\quad\quad\quad = 66$

37. $\left|-5 - 3^2\right| + 6^0 = |-5 - 9| + 6^0$
$\quad\quad\quad\quad = |-14| + 6^0$
$\quad\quad\quad\quad = 14 - 6^0$
$\quad\quad\quad\quad = 14 - 1$
$\quad\quad\quad\quad = 13$

39. $\dfrac{12 + 2(-14 - 2 \cdot 3)}{-6^2 + 30} = \dfrac{12 + 2(-14 - 6)}{-36 + 30}$
$\quad\quad\quad\quad = \dfrac{12 + 2(-20)}{-6}$
$\quad\quad\quad\quad = \dfrac{12 + (-40)}{-6}$
$\quad\quad\quad\quad = \dfrac{-28}{-6}$
$\quad\quad\quad\quad = \dfrac{14}{3}$

41. $\dfrac{2}{3} \cdot 12 \div (-6) = 8 \div (-6)$
$\quad\quad\quad\quad = -\dfrac{8}{6}$
$\quad\quad\quad\quad = -\dfrac{4}{3}$

43.
$$-14 \cdot 2 \div 7 + 3 \div 3(-1) = -28 \div 7 + 3 \div 3(-1)$$
$$= -4 + 3 \div 3(-1)$$
$$= -4 + 1(-1)$$
$$= -4 + (-1)$$
$$= -5$$

47.
$$\frac{14 - 4(-20+5)}{\sqrt{49-40}} = \frac{14 - 4(-15)}{\sqrt{9}}$$
$$= \frac{14 - (-60)}{3}$$
$$= \frac{14 - (-60)}{3}$$
$$= \frac{74}{3}$$

49.
$$1.5 + 6.45 \div 0.5 + (-2.4)^2 (0.24)^0$$
$$= 1.5 + 6.45 \div 0.5 + (5.76)(0.24)^0$$
$$= 1.5 + 6.45 \div 0.5 + (5.76)(1)$$
$$= 1.5 + 12.9 + (5.76)(1)$$
$$= 1.5 + 12.9 + 5.76$$
$$= 14.4 + 5.76$$
$$= 20.16$$

51.
$$\frac{2(a-b)}{3c-d} = \frac{2((2)-(-4))}{3(0)-(3)}$$
$$= \frac{2(6)}{0-(3)}$$
$$= \frac{12}{-3}$$
$$= -4$$

53.
$$-6a^2 - 5b + c - 12 = -6(2)^2 - 5(-5) + (-1) - 12$$
$$= -6(4) - 5(-5) + (-1) - 12$$
$$= -24 - 5(-5) + (-1) - 12$$
$$= -24 - (-25) + (-1) - 12$$
$$= 1 + (-1) - 12$$
$$= 0 - 12$$
$$= -12$$

55.
$$\left| a^2 - b^2 \right| + c = \left| (-4)^2 - (3)^2 \right| + (-11)$$
$$= \left| 16 - (3)^2 \right| + (-11)$$
$$= \left| 16 - 9 \right| + (-11)$$
$$= \left| 7 \right| + (-11)$$
$$= 7 + (-11)$$
$$= -4$$

57.
$$\frac{a(2c-b)^2}{-c+5a} = \frac{(2)(2(-2)-(4))^2}{-(-2)+5(2)}$$
$$= \frac{(2)(-4-(4))^2}{2+5(2)}$$
$$= \frac{(2)(-8)^2}{2+10}$$
$$= \frac{(2)(64)}{12}$$
$$= \frac{128}{12}$$
$$= \frac{32}{3}$$

59.
$$6x - 15x = (6-15)x$$
$$= -9x$$

61.
$$\frac{1}{2}y + 3y = \left(\frac{1}{2} + 3 \right) y$$
$$= \frac{7}{2}y$$

63.
$$4t - 5 + 2t = 4t + 2t - 5$$
$$= (4+2)t - 5$$
$$= 6t - 5$$

65.
$$17x - x + 5x = (17 - 1 + 5)x$$
$$= (16+5)x$$
$$= 21x$$

67.
$$8.1a - a + b = (8.1 - 1)a + b$$
$$= 7.1a + b$$

69.
$$-24 - 9w + 12 - 10w = -9w - 10w12 - 24$$
$$= (-9 - 10)w - 12$$
$$= -19w - 12$$

71. $2.5b - 65 + 3.8b + 92 = 2.5b + 3.8b + 92 - 65$
$$= (2.5 + 3.8)b + 27$$
$$= 6.3b + 27$$

73. $x^2 - 3y - 2x^2 + 4y = x^2 - 2x^2 + 4y - 3y$
$$= (1 - 2)x^2 + (4 - 3)y$$
$$= -x^2 + y$$

75. $2a^2 - 3a + 5 = 2a^2 - 3a + 5$

77. $\dfrac{2}{3}y + \dfrac{1}{4}x - 4y + \dfrac{2}{5}x = \dfrac{1}{4}x + \dfrac{2}{5}x + \dfrac{2}{3}y - 4y$
$$= \left(\dfrac{1}{4} + \dfrac{2}{5}\right)x + \left(\dfrac{2}{3} - 4\right)y$$
$$= \dfrac{13}{20}x - \dfrac{10}{3}y$$

79. $5 + 2(x - 8) = 5 + 2x - 16$
$$= 2x + 5 - 16$$
$$= 2x - 11$$

81. $8 + 4(9 + 3w) = 8 + 36 + 12w$
$$= 12w + 44$$

83. $13x - 5(2x + 7) = 13x - 10x - 35$
$$= 3x - 35$$

85. $4y - 10(8 - 6y) = 4y - 80 + 60y$
$$= 4y + 60y - 80$$
$$= 64y - 80$$

87. $-2x^2 + 15(-3x^2 + 2) = -2x^2 - 45x^2 + 30$
$$= -47x^2 + 30$$

89. $2(6x^2 - 3x + 1) + 9x^2 + 4 = 12x^2 - 6x + 2 + 9x^2 + 4$
$$= 12x^2 + 9x^2 - 6x + 2 + 4$$
$$= 21x^2 - 6x + 6$$

91. $7a - (3a + 4) - 4a = 7a - 3a - 4 - 4a$
$$= 7a - 3a - 4a - 4$$
$$= 0 - 4$$
$$= -4$$

93. $-6.2s^2 + 0.5s - 1.1 - 2(4s^2 + 6.2s - 3)$
$$= -6.2s^2 + 0.5s - 1.1 - 8s^2 - 12.4s + 6$$
$$= -6.2s^2 - 8s^2 + 0.5s - 12.4s + 6 - 1.1$$
$$= -14.2s^2 - 11.9s + 4.9$$

95. $-\dfrac{2}{3}a + \dfrac{4}{5}b - 3\left(\dfrac{5}{9}a + \dfrac{1}{5}b\right) - \dfrac{7}{3}a + \dfrac{1}{5}b$
$$= -\dfrac{2}{3}a + \dfrac{4}{5}b - \dfrac{5}{3}a - \dfrac{3}{5}b - \dfrac{7}{3}a + \dfrac{1}{5}b$$
$$= -\dfrac{2}{3}a - \dfrac{5}{3}a - \dfrac{7}{3}a + \dfrac{4}{5}b - \dfrac{3}{5}b + \dfrac{1}{5}b$$
$$= -\dfrac{14}{3}a + \dfrac{2}{5}b$$

97. $3x - 10(2x + 4) - (7 - 6x) = 3x - 20x - 40 - 7 + 6x$
$$= 3x - 20x + 6x - 40 - 7$$
$$= -11x - 47$$

99. Answers will vary; one example is: The quantities are not equal because of order of operations. -3^2 is taking the opposite sign of three squared; $(-3)^2$ is squaring the opposite of 3.

101. Answers will vary; one example is: $5^4 = 625$, $\dfrac{5^4}{5} = 5^3 = 125$, $\dfrac{5^3}{5} = 5^2 = 25$, $\dfrac{5^2}{5} = 5^1 = 5$, $\dfrac{5^1}{5} = 5^0 = 1$

103. $5n + n$

105. $\dfrac{3n}{17}$

107. $2n(n - 5)$

109. $\dfrac{1}{2}n - 9$

111. $0.16(n + 12)$

113. $n - 45$

115. $19 + \dfrac{6}{n}$

117. $(18.75 + 18.75(0.15)) \div 4 = (18.75 + 2.8125) \div 4$
$$= 21.5625 \div 4$$
$$= 5.390625$$

Each student paid about $5.39.

119. $-4(7-19) + \sqrt{6^2 - 3^2} = -4(-12) + \sqrt{6^2 - 3^2}$
$$= -4(-12) + \sqrt{36 - 3^2}$$
$$= -4(-12) + \sqrt{36 - 9}$$
$$= -4(-12) + \sqrt{27}$$
$$= 48 + \sqrt{27}$$
$$= 48 + 3\sqrt{3}$$

121. $\left|(-4)^2 - 5^2\right| + 8 \div 2(3) = \left|16 - 5^2\right| + 8 \div 2(3)$
$$= \left|16 - 25\right| + 8 \div 2(3)$$
$$= \left|-9\right| + 8 \div 2(3)$$
$$= 9 + 8 \div 2(3)$$
$$= 9 + 4(3)$$
$$= 9 + 12$$
$$= 21$$

123. $\dfrac{3}{4}\left(\dfrac{16}{9} - 1\right) + \dfrac{1}{2} = \dfrac{3}{4}\left(\dfrac{7}{9}\right) + \dfrac{1}{2}$
$$= \dfrac{7}{12} + \dfrac{1}{2}$$
$$= \dfrac{13}{12}$$

125. $\dfrac{11}{5}a^2 - \dfrac{7}{8}a + \dfrac{1}{2}\left(\dfrac{3}{5}a - 9a^2\right)$
$$= \dfrac{11}{5}a^2 - \dfrac{7}{8}a + \dfrac{3}{10}a - \dfrac{9}{2}a^2$$
$$= \dfrac{11}{5}a^2 - \dfrac{9}{2}a^2 - \dfrac{7}{8}a + \dfrac{3}{10}a$$
$$= -\dfrac{23}{10}a^2 - \dfrac{23}{40}a$$

127. $2.1\left(3x^2 - 4.2x + 1\right) - 3\left(-7.8x^2 + 10.9\right)$
$$= 6.3x^2 - 8.82x + 2.1 + 23.4x^2 - 32.7$$
$$= 6.3x^2 + 23.4x^2 - 8.82x + 2.1 - 32.7$$
$$= 29.7x^2 - 8.82x - 30.6$$

1.6 Exercises

1. A <u>bar</u> <u>graph</u> represents data using bars and both a vertical and horizontal axis.

3. A line graph uses a <u>line</u> and a <u>vertical</u> and <u>horizontal</u> axis to show a trend in data.

5. A <u>circle</u> <u>graph</u> represents data as part of a whole and is drawn using a circle.

7. The origin, $(0,0)$, does not lie in a <u>quadrant</u>.

9. Quadrant: IV

11. The point lies on the x-axis.

13. Quadrant: I

15. Quadrant: III

17. The point lies on the y-axis.

19. Quadrant: II

Graph for 9 – 19

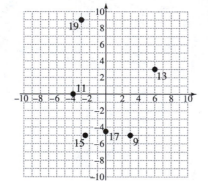

21. 900

23. 300

25. $31,500

27. $117,000

29. 26%

31. Approximately 75

33. Approximately 20

35. Approximately 21%

37. 10%

39. 167.2 square miles

41. 999.3 or approximately 1,000 persons per square mile

43. a) 3.2%

    b) 33.44 square miles

45. 41 million

47. Hong Kong

49. France and the United States

51. Approximately 36.5 million

53. Quadrant: II

55. Quadrant: III

57. The origin.

1.7 Exercises

1. Prepare: What am I looking for?
    Plan: How will I find what I am looking for?
    Process: This is where I do the math.
    Ponder: Does my answer make sense?

3. Draw a picture strategy. Apply this strategy when it is helpful to visualize an area or an object that is not given in the problem.

5. Answers will vary; one example is: Reading and studying examples in the text and doing problems from the exercise set will increase my problem-solving ability.

7. Answers will vary; one example is: If a strategy is unsuccessful I should try another approach to the problem. If that doesn't work I should seek help from a classmate, tutor, or my instructor.

9. **Prepare** We are asked to determine what coins Aditya has on his dresser.

    Plan Let's try a guess and test strategy using the given information that the sum of the 12 coins is 91 cents.

    Process Let's organize our guesses in a table.

	No. of Pennies	No. of Nickels	No. of Dimes	Value of Pennies	Value of Nickels	Value of Dimes	Total Value of 12 Coins
1st Guess	1	2	9	$0.01	$0.10	$0.90	$1.01 (too much)
2nd Guess	1	3	8	$0.01	$0.15	$0.80	$0.96 (too much)
3rd Guess	1	4	7	$0.01	$0.20	$0.70	$0.91 (correct amount)

    There are 7 dimes, 4 nickels, and 1 penny.

    Ponder Does the answer seem reasonable? Is it the only possible solution? Yes, the answer is reasonable because it gives us 12 total coins that yield 91 cents, as stated in the problem. Continuing the chart of guesses would prove that this is the only possible solution to the problem.

11. **Prepare** We are asked to determine what animals are in Dr. Doolittle's office.

    Plan Let's try a guess and test strategy using the given information that there are 22 animals and 72 animal feet.

    Process Let's organize our guesses in a table.

	No. of Dogs	No. of Birds	Number of Dog Feet	Number of Bird Feet	Total Number of Animal Feet
1st Guess	11	11	44	22	66 (too little)
2nd Guess	12	10	48	20	68 (too little)
3rd Guess	14	8	56	16	72 (correct amount)

    There are 14 dogs and 8 birds.

    Ponder Does the answer seem reasonable? Is it the only possible solution? Yes, the answer is reasonable because it gives us 72 total animal feet, as stated in the problem. Continuing the chart of guesses would prove that this is the only possible solution to the problem.

13. Prepare We are asked to determine two unknown numbers.

Plan Let's try a guess and test strategy using the given information that the sum of the two numbers is 138 and the product of the two numbers is 4,437.

Process Let's organize our guesses in a table.

	First Number	Second Number	Sum	Product
1st Guess	85	53	138	4,505 (too large)
2nd Guess	86	52	138	4,472 (too large)
3rd Guess	87	51	138	4,437 (correct product)

The two numbers are 87 and 51.

Ponder Does the answer seem reasonable? Is it the only possible solution? Yes, the answer is reasonable because the two numbers have a sum of 138 and a product of 4,437. Continuing the chart of guesses would prove that this is the only possible solution to the problem.

15. Prepare We are asked to determine who came in third in the foot race.

Plan Let's try analyzing the data.

Process Ross finished behind Chandler but ahead of Monica, therefore, the order of these three must be: Chandler, Ross, and Monica. Finally, because Phoebe came in second, the order of the four must be: Chandler, Phoebe, Ross, and Monica, therefore, Ross came in third.

Ponder Does the answer seem reasonable? Yes, it fits all the conditions of the problem.

17. Prepare We are asked to determine the total number of bricks.

Plan We simply need to add the number of bricks in each layer to determine the total. The bottom layer has 11 bricks, the next layer has 9 bricks, and so on. It is apparent that we need to add the numbers 11, 9, 7, 5, 3, and 1.

Process The sum is $11+9+7+5+3+1=36$, therefore, there are 36 bricks.

Ponder Does the answer seem reasonable? Yes, it satisfies all the conditions of the problem.

19. Prepare We are asked to determine the next three terms of the sequence.

Plan Let's try to determine the pattern of the sequence.

Process Each term is 8 more than the previous term, therefore the term following 147 will be 155. The next term will be 163, and the last term will be 171.

Ponder Does the answer seem reasonable? Yes, these three terms fit the pattern of the sequence.

21. Prepare We are asked to determine the next three terms of the sequence.

Plan Let's try to determine the pattern of the sequence.

Process Each term is one-third the previous term, therefore the term following 3 will be 1. The next term will be $\frac{1}{3}$, and the last term will be $\frac{1}{9}$.

Ponder Does the answer seem reasonable? Yes, these three terms fit the pattern of the sequence.

23. Prepare We are asked to determine the next three terms of the sequence.

Plan Let's try to determine the pattern of the sequence.

Process The second term is 7 more than the first, and the third term is 11 less than the second. This pattern continues throughout the rest of the sequence, therefore the term following 50 will be 57. The next term will be 46, and the last term will be 53.

Ponder Does the answer seem reasonable? Yes, these three terms fit the pattern of the sequence.

25. Prepare We must draw a bar graph that represents the information given in the table.

Plan The horizontal axis will be labeled with the sport and the vertical axis will be labeled with the number of injuries. Mark the vertical axis by 10 starting at 0 and ending at 120. Write a title for the graph; "Total Injuries by Sport".

Process

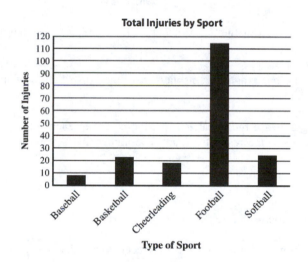

Ponder Does our answer seem reasonable? Yes. However, we should keep in mind that the number of injuries represented on the graph is only for the years 1982 to 2002.

27. Prepare We must draw a bar graph that represents the information given in the table.

Plan The horizontal axis will be labeled with the food and the vertical axis will be labeled with the number of carbohydrates. Mark the vertical axis by 2.5 starting at 0 and ending at 40.0. Write a title for the graph; "Carbohydrate Content of Select Food".

Process

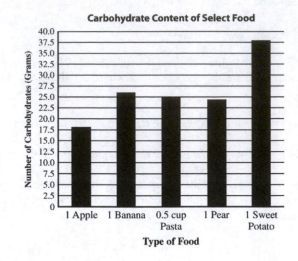

Ponder Does our answer seem reasonable? Yes. Double check to make sure that the bars are the correct height.

29. **Prepare** We will analyze the bar graph that displays that grade distribution of the final exam grades to answer the questions stated in the problem.

Plan To analyze the bar graph, we must realized that the height of each bar represents the number of students that received the grade labeled below the respective bar. The higher the bar, the more student there were that made the grade below that bar.

Process

a) There were 12 students that received a C.

b) $7 - 3 = 4$ There were 4 more students that received a B than received a D.

c) $\dfrac{4}{28} \times 100\% \approx 14.3\%$

Ponder Do our answers seem reasonable? Yes. A quick double check of the graph and arithmetic should show that our answers are correct.

Chapter 1 Review Problem Set

1. True

2. True

3. True

4. False, every element of A is also an element of N.

5. True

6. False, $A \cap B = \{1,5\}$.

7. True

8. True

9. $W = \left\{0, \sqrt{49}, 15\right\}$

10. $Q = \left\{-76, -40\frac{1}{2}, -2, 0, \sqrt{49}, \frac{35}{4}, 15, 38.51\right\}$

11. $R = \left\{-76, -40\frac{1}{2}, -2, 0, \sqrt{2}, \pi, \sqrt{49},\right.$
    $\left. \frac{35}{4}, 15, 21.13113111..., 38.51\right\}$

12. $Z = \left\{-76, -2, 0, \sqrt{49}, 15\right\}$

13. $N = \left\{\sqrt{49}, 15\right\}$

14. $M = \left\{\sqrt{2}, \pi, 21.13113111...\right\}$

15. $C = \{2, 1, 0, -1, ...\}$

16. $D = \{6, 7, 8, 9, ...\}$

17. $A \cup D = \{1, 2, 3, 4, 6, 7, ...\}$

18. $B \cup C = \{3, 2, 1, 0, -1, ...\}$

19. $B \cap C = \{-3, -2, -1, 0\}$

20. $A \cap D = \varnothing$

21. True

22. False, if $a > b$ and $a, b \in R$, then $a \neq b$.

23. False, $15 = 15$.

24. True

25. $88 = 2 \cdot 2 \cdot 2 \cdot 11$

26. $124 = 2 \cdot 2 \cdot 31$

27. $270 = 2 \cdot 3 \cdot 3 \cdot 3 \cdot 5$

28. $645 = 3 \cdot 5 \cdot 43$

29. $12 = 2 \cdot 2 \cdot 3$
    $20 = 2 \cdot 2 \cdot 5$
    $$\text{LCM}(12, 20) = 2 \cdot 2 \cdot 3 \cdot 5$$
    $$= 60$$

30. $18 = 2 \cdot 3 \cdot 3$
    $24 = 2 \cdot 2 \cdot 2 \cdot 3$
    $$\text{LCM}(18, 24) = 2 \cdot 2 \cdot 2 \cdot 3 \cdot 3$$
    $$= 72$$

31. $10 = 2 \cdot 5$
    $18 = 2 \cdot 3 \cdot 3$
    $24 = 2 \cdot 2 \cdot 2 \cdot 3$
    $$\text{LCM}(10, 18, 24) = 2 \cdot 2 \cdot 2 \cdot 3 \cdot 3 \cdot 5$$
    $$= 360$$

32. $16 = 2 \cdot 2 \cdot 2 \cdot 2$
    $20 = 2 \cdot 2 \cdot 5$
    $32 = 2 \cdot 2 \cdot 2 \cdot 2 \cdot 2$
    $$\text{LCM}(16, 20, 32) = 2 \cdot 2 \cdot 2 \cdot 2 \cdot 2 \cdot 5$$
    $$= 160$$

33. $\dfrac{5}{8}$

34. $\dfrac{7}{3}$

35. $\dfrac{28}{36} = \dfrac{\overset{1}{\cancel{4}} \cdot 7}{\underset{1}{\cancel{4}} \cdot 9}$
    $$= \dfrac{7}{9}$$

36. $\dfrac{80}{165} = \dfrac{\,{}^1\!\!\not{5}\cdot 16}{{}_1\!\not{5}\cdot 33}$

$\qquad = \dfrac{16}{33}$

37. $\dfrac{140}{100} = \dfrac{\,{}^1\!\!\not{20}\cdot 7}{{}_1\!\not{20}\cdot 5}$

$\qquad = \dfrac{7}{5}$

38. $\dfrac{1,422}{2,244} = \dfrac{\,{}^1\!\!\not{6}\cdot 237}{{}_1\!\not{6}\cdot 374}$

$\qquad = \dfrac{237}{374}$

39. $\dfrac{3}{4}\cdot\dfrac{3}{5} = \dfrac{3\cdot 3}{4\cdot 5}$

$\qquad = \dfrac{9}{20}$

40. $8\cdot\dfrac{2}{3} = \dfrac{8}{1}\cdot\dfrac{2}{3}$

$\qquad = \dfrac{8\cdot 2}{1\cdot 3}$

$\qquad = \dfrac{16}{3}$

41. $\dfrac{3}{5}\cdot\dfrac{10}{7} = \dfrac{3\cdot 2\cdot{}^1\!\not{5}}{{}_1\!\not{5}\cdot 7}$

$\qquad = \dfrac{3\cdot 2}{7}$

$\qquad = \dfrac{6}{7}$

42. $\dfrac{63}{49}\cdot\dfrac{21}{12} = \dfrac{9\cdot{}_1\!\not{7}\cdot{}_1\!\not{3}\cdot{}_1\!\not{7}}{{}_1\!\not{7}\cdot{}_1\!\not{7}\cdot{}_1\!\not{3}\cdot 4}$

$\qquad = \dfrac{9}{4}$

43. $3\dfrac{1}{2}\cdot 6\dfrac{2}{3} = \dfrac{7}{2}\cdot\dfrac{20}{3}$

$\qquad = \dfrac{7\cdot{}_1\!\not{2}\cdot 10}{{}_1\!\not{2}\cdot 3}$

$\qquad = \dfrac{7\cdot 10}{3}$

$\qquad = \dfrac{70}{3}$

44. $\dfrac{44}{3}\cdot 5\dfrac{3}{8} = \dfrac{44}{3}\cdot\dfrac{43}{8}$

$\qquad = \dfrac{\,{}^1\!\!\not{4}\cdot 11\cdot 43}{3\cdot 2\cdot{}_1\!\not{4}}$

$\qquad = \dfrac{11\cdot 43}{3\cdot 2}$

$\qquad = \dfrac{473}{6}$

45. $\dfrac{1}{2}\div\dfrac{6}{7} = \dfrac{1}{2}\cdot\dfrac{7}{6}$

$\qquad = \dfrac{1\cdot 7}{2\cdot 6}$

$\qquad = \dfrac{7}{12}$

46. $\dfrac{7}{8}\div\dfrac{11}{16} = \dfrac{7}{8}\cdot\dfrac{11}{16}$

$\qquad = \dfrac{7\cdot 2\cdot{}_1\!\not{8}}{{}_1\!\not{8}\cdot 11}$

$\qquad = \dfrac{14}{11}$

47. $6\div\dfrac{8}{7} = \dfrac{6}{1}\div\dfrac{8}{7}$

$\qquad = \dfrac{6}{1}\cdot\dfrac{7}{8}$

$\qquad = \dfrac{\,{}_1\!\not{2}\cdot 3\cdot 7}{1\cdot{}_1\!\not{2}\cdot 4}$

$\qquad = \dfrac{21}{4}$

48. $1\dfrac{2}{3}\div 4 = \dfrac{5}{3}\div\dfrac{4}{1}$

$\qquad = \dfrac{5}{3}\cdot\dfrac{1}{4}$

$\qquad = \dfrac{5\cdot 1}{3\cdot 4}$

$\qquad = \dfrac{5}{\cdot 12}$

49. $4\dfrac{3}{5}\div\dfrac{7}{65} = \dfrac{23}{5}\div\dfrac{7}{65}$

$\qquad = \dfrac{23}{5}\cdot\dfrac{65}{7}$

$\qquad = \dfrac{23\cdot{}_1\!\not{5}\cdot 13}{1\not{5}\cdot 7}$

$\qquad = \dfrac{299}{7}$

50. $\dfrac{2}{3} \div 0$ is undefined

51. $0 \div \dfrac{8}{5} = 0$

52. $2\dfrac{2}{3} \div 3\dfrac{4}{5} = \dfrac{8}{3} \div \dfrac{19}{5}$

$= \dfrac{8}{3} \cdot \dfrac{5}{19}$

$= \dfrac{8 \cdot 5}{3 \cdot 19}$

$= \dfrac{40}{57}$

53. $\dfrac{5}{6} + \dfrac{5}{6} = \dfrac{5+5}{6}$

$= \dfrac{10}{6}$

$= \dfrac{5}{3}$

54. $\dfrac{48}{65} - \dfrac{30}{65} = \dfrac{48-30}{65}$

$= \dfrac{18}{65}$

55. $6\dfrac{23}{50} - 4\dfrac{13}{50} = \dfrac{323}{50} - \dfrac{213}{50}$

$= \dfrac{110}{50}$

$= \dfrac{11}{5}$

56. $\text{LCD}(8,7) = 56$

$\dfrac{5}{8} + \dfrac{2}{7} = \dfrac{5 \cdot 7}{8 \cdot 7} + \dfrac{2 \cdot 8}{7 \cdot 8}$

$= \dfrac{35}{56} + \dfrac{16}{56}$

$= \dfrac{35+16}{56}$

$= \dfrac{51}{56}$

57. $\text{LCD}(8,5) = 40$

$\dfrac{7}{8} - \dfrac{3}{5} = \dfrac{7 \cdot 5}{8 \cdot 5} - \dfrac{3 \cdot 8}{5 \cdot 8}$

$= \dfrac{35}{40} - \dfrac{24}{40}$

$= \dfrac{35-24}{40}$

$= \dfrac{11}{40}$

58. $\text{LCD}(9,6) = 18$

$5\dfrac{2}{9} + \dfrac{1}{6} = \dfrac{47}{9} + \dfrac{1}{6}$

$= \dfrac{47 \cdot 2}{9 \cdot 2} + \dfrac{1 \cdot 3}{6 \cdot 3}$

$= \dfrac{94}{18} + \dfrac{3}{18}$

$= \dfrac{94+3}{18}$

$= \dfrac{97}{18}$

59. $\text{LCD}(7,3) = 21$

$14\dfrac{2}{7} + \dfrac{1}{3} = \dfrac{100}{7} + \dfrac{1}{3}$

$= \dfrac{100 \cdot 3}{7 \cdot 3} + \dfrac{1 \cdot 7}{3 \cdot 7}$

$= \dfrac{300}{21} + \dfrac{7}{21}$

$= \dfrac{300+7}{21}$

$= \dfrac{307}{21}$

60. $\text{LCD}(9,3) = 9$

$12\dfrac{4}{9} - 8\dfrac{1}{3} = \dfrac{112}{9} - \dfrac{25}{3}$

$= \dfrac{112}{9} - \dfrac{25 \cdot 3}{3 \cdot 3}$

$= \dfrac{112}{9} - \dfrac{75}{9}$

$= \dfrac{112-75}{9}$

$= \dfrac{37}{9}$

61. $24.06 + 9.213 = 33.273$

62. $34 + 0.67 = 34.67$

63. $65.3 - 22.49 = 42.81$

64. $145 - 0.18 = 144.82$

65. $(0.005)(0.03) = 0.00015$

66. $(3.4)(11.09) = 37.706$

67. $(100)(245.37) = 24,537$

68. $540 \div (0.06) = 9,000$

69. $0.861 \div 12.3 = 0.07$

70. $1.6 \div 32 = 0.05$

71. $6\dfrac{5}{8} \cdot 4 = \dfrac{53}{8} \cdot \dfrac{4}{1}$

$\qquad = \dfrac{53 \cdot {}_1\cancel{4}}{2 \cdot {}_1\cancel{4} \cdot 1}$

$\qquad = \dfrac{53}{2}$

The perimeter is $\dfrac{53}{2}$ feet or $26\dfrac{1}{2}$ feet.

72. $28\dfrac{2}{3} + 3\dfrac{1}{4} + \dfrac{19}{2} + 12 + \dfrac{25}{6} + 8 + 3\dfrac{1}{4}$

$= \dfrac{86}{3} + \dfrac{13}{4} + \dfrac{19}{2} + \dfrac{12}{1} + \dfrac{25}{6} + \dfrac{8}{1} + \dfrac{13}{4}$

$= \dfrac{86 \cdot 4}{3 \cdot 4} + \dfrac{13 \cdot 3}{4 \cdot 3} + \dfrac{19 \cdot 6}{2 \cdot 6} + \dfrac{12 \cdot 12}{1 \cdot 12} + \dfrac{25 \cdot 2}{6 \cdot 2} + \dfrac{8 \cdot 12}{1 \cdot 12} + \dfrac{13 \cdot 3}{4 \cdot 3}$

$= \dfrac{344}{12} + \dfrac{39}{12} + \dfrac{114}{12} + \dfrac{144}{12} + \dfrac{50}{12} + \dfrac{96}{12} + \dfrac{39}{12}$

$= \dfrac{344 + 39 + 114 + 144 + 50 + 96 + 39}{12}$

$= \dfrac{826}{12}$

$= \dfrac{413}{6}$

The perimeter is $\dfrac{413}{6}$ meters or $68\dfrac{5}{6}$ meters.

73. $|-18| = 18$

74. $\left| 64\dfrac{2}{3} \right| = 64\dfrac{2}{3}$

75. $|0| = 0$

76. $|-1| = 1$

77. $62 - 110 = 62 + (-110)$

$\qquad\qquad = -48$

78. $-42 + (-12) = -54$

79. $49 + (-12) = 37$

80. $-14 - (-23) = -14 + 23$

$\qquad\qquad\quad = 9$

81. $\dfrac{16}{9} - \dfrac{22}{9} = \dfrac{16}{9} + \left(\dfrac{-22}{9} \right)$

$\qquad\quad = \dfrac{16 + (-22)}{9}$

$\qquad\quad = \dfrac{-6}{9}$

$\qquad\quad = -\dfrac{2}{3}$

82. $\dfrac{5}{8} + \left(-\dfrac{7}{8} \right) = \dfrac{5 + (-7)}{8}$

$\qquad\qquad\quad = \dfrac{-2}{8}$

$\qquad\qquad\quad = -\dfrac{1}{4}$

83. $4\dfrac{2}{3} + \left(-5\dfrac{1}{6} \right) = \dfrac{14}{3} + \left(-\dfrac{31}{6} \right)$

$\qquad\qquad\qquad = \dfrac{14 \cdot 2}{3 \cdot 2} + \left(-\dfrac{31}{6} \right)$

$\qquad\qquad\qquad = \dfrac{28}{6} + \left(-\dfrac{31}{6} \right)$

$\qquad\qquad\qquad = \dfrac{28 + (-31)}{6}$

$\qquad\qquad\qquad = \dfrac{-3}{6}$

$\qquad\qquad\qquad = -\dfrac{1}{2}$

82. $25 + \left(\dfrac{-16}{5} \right) = \dfrac{25}{1} + \left(\dfrac{-16}{5} \right)$

$\qquad = \dfrac{25 \cdot 5}{1 \cdot 5} + \left(\dfrac{-16}{5} \right)$

$\qquad = \dfrac{125}{5} + \left(\dfrac{-16}{5} \right)$

$\qquad = \dfrac{125 + (-16)}{5}$

$\qquad = \dfrac{109}{5}$

85. $-8.2 - 5.7 = -8.2 + (-5.7)$

$\qquad = -13.9$

86. $-23.05 + 18.7 = -4.35$

87. $331.9 - 316.5 = 15.4$

The total increase was \$15.4 million.

88. $41.692 - 14.269 = 27.423$

Florida residents spent \$27.423 million more.

89. Commutative Property of Multiplication

90. Associative Property of Addition

91. Multiplicative Property of Zero

92. Additive Identity

93. Multiplicative Identity

94. Commutative Property of Addition

95. $9(x+4) = 9(4+x)$

96. $9(x+4) = (x+4)9$

97. $9(x+4) = 9x + 36$

98. $9 + (x+4) = (9+x) + 4$

99. $(-26)(-5) = 130$

100. $0(-16) = 0$

101. $\dfrac{-54}{-3} = 18$

102. $-6\dfrac{2}{3} \div 1\dfrac{1}{2} = -\dfrac{20}{3} \div \dfrac{3}{2}$

$\qquad = -\dfrac{20}{3} \cdot \dfrac{2}{3}$

$\qquad = -\dfrac{20 \cdot 2}{3 \cdot 3}$

$\qquad = -\dfrac{40}{9}$

103. $\left(-\dfrac{123}{5} \right)\left(-\dfrac{10}{66} \right) = \dfrac{123 \cdot 10}{5 \cdot 66}$

$\qquad = \dfrac{{}_1\cancel{3} \cdot 41 \cdot {}_1\cancel{2} \cdot {}_1\cancel{5}}{{}_1\cancel{5} \cdot {}_1\cancel{3} \cdot {}_1\cancel{2} \cdot 11}$

$\qquad = \dfrac{41}{11}$

104. $\left(-2\dfrac{2}{3} \right) \cdot 0 = 0$

105. $\dfrac{-15}{0}$ is undefined

106. $0.492 \div (-1.23) = -0.4$

107. $-5^3 = -5 \cdot 5 \cdot 5$

$\qquad = -125$

108. $16^0 = 1$

109. $\left(\dfrac{-2}{3} \right)^4 = \left(\dfrac{-2}{3} \right)\left(\dfrac{-2}{3} \right)\left(\dfrac{-2}{3} \right)\left(\dfrac{-2}{3} \right)$

$\qquad = \dfrac{16}{81}$

110. $(1.5)^3 = (1.5)(1.5)(1.5)$

$\qquad = 3.375$

111. $(-1)^7 = (-1)(-1)(-1)(-1)(-1)(-1)(-1)$

$\qquad = -1$

112. $-16 + 2 \cdot 3^2 = -16 + 2 \cdot 9$

$\qquad = -16 + 18$

$\qquad = 2$

113. $14+2(6-8)^2 = 14+2(-2)^2$
$$= 14+2(4)$$
$$= 14+8$$
$$= 22$$

114. $2\cdot3+8\div(-2)^2 = 2\cdot3+8\div4$
$$= 6+8\div4$$
$$= 6+2$$
$$= 8$$

115. $\dfrac{2\sqrt{9+16}\div5(2)}{-1^2} = \dfrac{2\sqrt{25}\div5(2)}{-1}$
$$= \dfrac{2(5)\div5(2)}{-1}$$
$$= \dfrac{10\div5(2)}{-1}$$
$$= \dfrac{2(2)}{-1}$$
$$= \dfrac{4}{-1}$$
$$= -4$$

116. $\dfrac{8^2-4(1-4)}{-3(5)^2-1} = \dfrac{8^2-4(-3)}{-3(25)-1}$
$$= \dfrac{64-4(-3)}{-75-1}$$
$$= \dfrac{64-(-12)}{-76}$$
$$= \dfrac{76}{-76}$$
$$= -1$$

117. $\left[\dfrac{3|5-12|+6}{-3-6}\right]^2 = \left[\dfrac{3|-7|+6}{-9}\right]^2$
$$= \left[\dfrac{3(7)+6}{-9}\right]^2$$
$$= \left[\dfrac{21+6}{-9}\right]^2$$
$$= \left[\dfrac{27}{-9}\right]^2$$
$$= [-3]^2$$
$$= 9$$

118. $3a^2-10b-c = 3(-3)^2-10(5)-(-1)$
$$= 3(9)-10(5)-(-1)$$
$$= 27-10(5)-(-1)$$
$$= 27-50-(-1)$$
$$= -23-(-1)$$
$$= -22$$

119. $5|2a-b|+c^2 = 5|2(0)-(-4)|+(-10)^2$
$$= 5|0-(-4)|+(-10)^2$$
$$= 5|4|+(-10)^2$$
$$= 5(4)+(-10)^2$$
$$= 5(4)+100$$
$$= 20+100$$
$$= 120$$

120. $3x+5-4x+15 = 3x-4x+5+15$
$$= -x+20$$

121. $\dfrac{1}{2}x-3(x-5) = \dfrac{1}{2}x-3x+15$
$$= -\dfrac{5}{2}x+15$$

122. $-5x^2+2x-11-\left(-6x^2+17x+9\right)$
$$= -5x^2+2x-11+6x^2-17x-9$$
$$= -5x^2+6x^2+2x-17x-11-9$$
$$= x^2-15x-20$$

123. $1.8ab-0.03a+2b = 1.8ab-0.03a+2b$

124. $-\dfrac{2}{3}x^2y+y+\dfrac{1}{4}x^2y-2y$
$$= -\dfrac{2}{3}x^2y+\dfrac{1}{4}x^2y+y-2y$$
$$= -\dfrac{5}{12}x^2y-y$$

125. $2(0.1x-2.04)-3.5x+12.1$
$$= 0.2x-4.08-3.5x+12.1$$
$$= 0.2x-3.5x-4.08+12.1$$
$$= -3.3x+8.02$$

126. $2n-3$

127. $14(n+6)$

128. $\dfrac{3n}{8}$

129. $0.65(n+8)$

130. 80

131. 8

132. 16

133. 168

134. 16,000

135. $\dfrac{2,000}{27,038} \times 100\% = 7.4\%$

136. Heart-Lung

137. $6,000 - 1,100 = 4,900$

138. 47%

139. $0.13(3,313) = 430.69$ million

140. $0.28(3,313) - 0.06(3,313) = 728.86$ million

141. Approximately 41 million

142. Approximately 22 million

143. $62 - 16 = 46$ million

144. $62 + 41 + 16 + 22 + 18 + 21 = 180$ million

145. **Prepare** We are asked to determine what coins Jared found on his dad's desk.

Plan Let's try a guess and test strategy using the given information that the sum of the 13 coins is $1.27.

Process Let's organize our guesses in a table.

	No. of Pennies	No. of Dimes	No. of Quarters	Value of Pennies	Value of Dimes	Value of Quarters	Total Value of 12 Coins
1st Guess	0	13	0	$0.00	$1.30	$0.00	$1.30 (too much)
2nd Guess	1	11	1	$0.01	$1.10	$0.25	$1.36 (too much)
3rd Guess	2	10	1	$0.02	$1.00	$0.25	$1.27 (correct amount)

There are 10 dimes, 2 pennies, and 1 quarter.

Ponder Does the answer seem reasonable? Is it the only possible solution? Yes, the answer is reasonable because it gives us 13 total coins that yield $1.27, as stated in the problem. Continuing the chart of guesses would prove that this is the only possible solution to the problem.

146. **Prepare** We are asked to determine animals are in the petting zoo.

Plan Let's try a guess and test strategy using the given information there are 28 animals and 90 animal feet.

Process Let's organize our guesses in a table.

	No. of Ostriches	No. of Gazelles	Number of Ostrich Feet	Number of Gazelle Feet	Total Number of Animal Feet
1st Guess	9	19	18	76	94 (too many)
2nd Guess	10	18	20	72	92 (too many)
3rd Guess	11	17	22	68	90 (correct number)

There are 11 ostriches and 17 gazelles.

Ponder Does the answer seem reasonable? Is it the only possible solution? Yes, the answer is reasonable because it gives us a total of 28 animals and 90 animal feet, as stated in the problem. Continuing the chart of guesses would prove that this is the only possible solution to the problem.

147. Prepare We are asked to determine two unknown numbers.

Plan Let's try a guess and test strategy using the given information that the difference of the two numbers is 11 and the product of the two numbers is 782.

Process Let's organize our guesses in a table.

	First Number	Second Number	Difference	Product
1st Guess	32	21	11	672 (too small)
2nd Guess	33	22	11	726 (too small)
3rd Guess	34	23	11	782 (correct product)

The two numbers are 34 and 23.

Ponder Does the answer seem reasonable? Is it the only possible solution? Yes, the answer is reasonable because the two numbers have a difference of 11 and a product of 782. Continuing the chart of guesses would prove that this is the only possible solution to the problem.

148. Prepare We are asked to determine who was the second one through the door.

Plan Let's try analyzing the data.

Process Lisa went into the house before Bart but after Homer, therefore, the order of these three must be: Homer, Lisa, and Bart. Finally, because Marge entered the house third, the order of the four must be: Homer, Lisa, Marge, and Bart, therefore, Lisa was the second one through the door.

Ponder Does the answer seem reasonable? Yes, it satisfies all the conditions of the problem.

149. Prepare We are asked to determine how many new floor tiles there are.

Plan We simply need to add the number of tiles in each pile to determine the total. The first stack has 24 tiles, the second stack has 23 tiles, the third stack has 22 tiles, and so on. It is apparent that we need to add the numbers; 24, 23, 22, 21, 20, 19, 18, and 17.

Process The sum is $24 + 23 + 22 + 21 + 20 + 19 + 18 + 17 = 164$, therefore, there are 164 tiles.

Ponder Does the answer seem reasonable? Yes, it satisfies all the conditions of the problem.

150. Prepare We are asked to determine the next three terms of the sequence.

Plan Let's try to determine the pattern of the sequence.

Process 16 is one-half of 32, 8 is one-half of 16, and 4 is one-half of 8. It seems that each term is half the term before it. One-half of 4 is 2, one-half of 2 is 1, and one-half of 1 is ½. Therefore, the next three terms are 2, 1, and ½.

Ponder Does the answer seem reasonable? Yes, these three terms fit the pattern of the sequence.

151. Prepare We are asked to determine the next three terms of the sequence.

Plan Let's try to determine the pattern of the sequence.

Process 77 is six more that 71, 65 is twelve less that 77, 71 is six more than 65, and 59 is twelve less than 71. Therefore, the term after 53 should be six more than 53, or 59, the term after 59 should be twelve less than 59, or 47, and finally the last term should be six more than 47, or 53. The next three terms are 59, 47, and 53.

Ponder Does the answer seem reasonable? Yes, these three terms fit the pattern of the sequence.

152. **Prepare** We must draw a bar graph that represents the information given in the table.

Plan The horizontal axis will be labeled with the favorite type of movie and the vertical axis will be labeled with the number of student responses. Mark the vertical axis by 10 starting at 0 and ending at 40.

Process

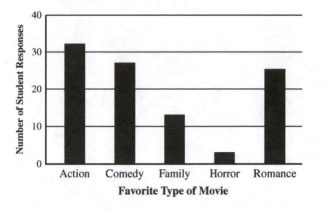

Ponder Does our answer seem reasonable? Yes. However, we should keep in mind that the numbers, and therefore the graph, could differ with each different sample of 100 students.

153. **Prepare** We will analyze the bar graph that displays that grade distribution of the final exam grades to answer the questions stated in the problem.

Plan To analyze the bar graph, we must realized that the height of each bar represents the number of students that received the grade labeled below the respective bar. The higher the bar, the more student there were that made the grade below that bar.

Process

      a)   E.T. the Extra-Terrestrial

      b) $\$435,000,000 + \$285,000,000 = \$720,000,000$

      c)   E.T. the Extra-Terrestrial and Shrek; $\$435,000,000 - \$260,000,000 = \$175,000,000$

Ponder Do our answers seem reasonable? Yes. A quick double check of the graph and arithmetic should show that our answers are correct.

CHAPTER 1 TEST

1. d

2. c, j

3. e, l

4. h

5. b, f

6. $A \cap B = \{x \mid x \in Z \text{ with } x > -3\} \cap \{-6, -3, -1, 4, 7\}$
   $= \{-2, -1, 0, 1, 2, 3, \ldots\} \cap \{-6, -3, -1, 4, 7\}$
   $= \{-1, 4, 7\}$

7. $B \cup C = \{-6, -3, -1, 4, 7\} \cup \{0, 2, 4, 6\}$
   $= \{-6, -3, -1, 0, 2, 4, 6, 7\}$

8. False
   $\dfrac{-2}{3} \in Q$

9. True

10. False
    Every whole number is also an integer.

11. Commutative Property of Multiplication
    The order of the factors is changed.

12. $\left\{-\sqrt{25},\ -3,\ 0,\ 1\right\}$

13. $\left\{-\sqrt{25},\ -3,\ \dfrac{-9}{4},\ 0,\ 1,\ 6\dfrac{1}{2}\right\}$

14. $\left\{-\sqrt{25},\ -3,\ \dfrac{-9}{4},\ 0,\ 1,\ 2.34345\ldots,\ \pi,\ 6\dfrac{1}{2}\right\}$

15. $a^2 + 3(b - c) = (-4)^2 + 3\big[(6) - (-2)\big]$
    $= (-4)^2 + 3[8]$
    $= 16 + 3[8]$
    $= 16 + 24$
    $= 40$

16. $x \div y (z + 3)^2 = (-20) \div (5)\big[(-1) + 3\big]^2$
    $= (-20) \div (5)[2]^2$
    $= (-20) \div (5)[4]$
    $= -4[4]$
    $= -16$

17. $\dfrac{6 + 3\left(\dfrac{2}{3} - 1\right)}{\left|-20 + 6\right|} = \dfrac{6 + 3\left(\dfrac{2}{3} - \dfrac{3}{3}\right)}{\left|-14\right|}$

    $= \dfrac{6 + 3\left(-\dfrac{1}{3}\right)}{14}$

    $= \dfrac{6 + \dfrac{3}{1}\left(-\dfrac{1}{3}\right)}{14}$

    $= \dfrac{6 + (-1)}{14}$

    $= \dfrac{5}{14}$

18. $5x^3 + 27x - 2\left(-3x^3 + 12x - 5\right)$
    $= 5x^3 + 27x - 2\left(-3x^3\right) - 2(12x) - 2(-5)$
    $= 5x^3 + 27x + 6x^3 - 24x + 10$
    $= 5x^3 + 6x^3 - 24x + 27x + 10$
    $= 11x^3 + 3x + 10$

19. $\dfrac{11}{12} + \dfrac{7}{20} - \dfrac{13}{30} = \dfrac{11 \cdot 5}{12 \cdot 5} + \dfrac{7 \cdot 3}{20 \cdot 3} - \dfrac{13 \cdot 2}{30 \cdot 2}$

    $= \dfrac{55}{60} + \dfrac{21}{60} - \dfrac{26}{60}$

    $= \dfrac{76}{60} - \dfrac{26}{60}$

    $= \dfrac{50}{60}$

    $= \dfrac{\overset{1}{\cancel{2}} \cdot 5 \cdot \overset{1}{\cancel{5}}}{2 \cdot \underset{1}{\cancel{2}} \cdot 3 \cdot \underset{1}{\cancel{5}}}$

    $= \dfrac{5}{6}$

20. $(-19.12)^0 + (2.5 - 0.07) = (-19.12)^0 + (2.43)$
    $= 1 + 2.43$
    $= 3.43$

21.
$$-\frac{165}{15} \div \frac{143}{273} = -\frac{165}{15} \cdot \frac{273}{143}$$

$$= -\left(\frac{165}{15} \cdot \frac{273}{143}\right)$$

$$= -\left(\frac{165 \cdot 273}{15 \cdot 143}\right)$$

$$= -\left(\frac{\overset{1}{\cancel{3}} \cdot \overset{1}{\cancel{5}} \cdot \overset{1}{\cancel{11}} \cdot 3 \cdot 7 \cdot \overset{1}{\cancel{13}}}{\underset{1}{\cancel{3}} \cdot \underset{1}{\cancel{5}} \cdot \underset{1}{\cancel{11}} \cdot \underset{1}{\cancel{13}}}\right)$$

$$= -21$$

22. The record low for Dallas, Texas, for the month of April was $30°F$. The variation in temperature from the highest record low to the lowest record low is $(40-4)°\,F = 36°F$.

23. Let n be the unknown number.

$$\frac{3}{4}n + 6$$

24. Let P represent the perimeter of the geometric figure.

$$
\begin{array}{r}
12.040 \\
13.200 \\
8.450 \\
9.003 \\
14.270 \\
12.040 \\
+31.500 \\
\hline
100.503
\end{array}
$$

The perimeter of the geometric figure is $P = 100.503$ cm.

25. Prepare We are asked to determine the total number of rabbits Max will have.

Plan We will make a chart to keep track of all the rabbits.

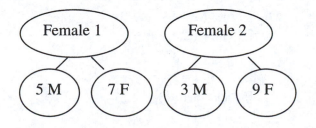

According to this chart, Max now has a total of 18 females. Max then breeds all 18 females and each has 6 babies for a total of $18 \cdot 6 = 108$ babies.

Process We now need to add up all the rabbits. There are 8 males, 18 females, and 108 babies from the second breeding. This gives a total of $8 + 18 + 108 = 134$ rabbits.

Ponder Is the answer of 134 rabbits reasonable? A simple check of arithmetic should ensure that the answer is yes.

Chapter 2

2.1 Exercises

1. A conditional linear equation in one variable is characterized by an <u>exponent</u> of <u>positive</u> <u>one</u> on the variable.

3. To solve a linear equation of the form $a + bx = cx$, where x is the variable, we must first <u>gather</u> the variables to one side.

5. This is a linear equation in one variable because the exponent on x is positive one.

7. This is a linear equation in one variable because the highest power of x is one.

9. This is not a linear equation in one variable because the equation contains both x and y. The power of y is three.

11. $3x - 5 = 2$

$3(1) - 5 = 2$

$3 - 5 = 2$

$-2 = 2$

No, 1 is not a solution.

13. $2(s-1) + 5 = s + 3(2s - 4)$

$2((3) - 1) + 5 = (3) + 3(2(3) - 4)$

$2(2) + 5 = 3 + 3(6 - 4)$

$4 + 5 = 3 + 3(2)$

$9 = 3 + 6$

$9 = 9$

Yes, 3 is a solution.

15. $\frac{1}{2}(n + 4) = \frac{2}{3}n - \frac{5}{6}$

$\frac{1}{2}((17) + 4) = \frac{2}{3}(17) - \frac{5}{6}$

$\frac{1}{2}(21) = \frac{34}{3} - \frac{5}{6}$

$\frac{21}{2} = \frac{63}{6}$

$\frac{21}{2} = \frac{21}{2}$

Yes, 17 is a solution.

17. $0.1x - 0.03 = 2.1x - 1.03$

$0.1(2) - 0.03 = 2.1(2) - 1.03$

$0.2 - 0.03 = 4.2 - 1.03$

$0.17 = 3.17$

No, 2 is not a solution.

19. $x + 17 = -10$

$x + 17 - 17 = -10 - 17$

$x + 0 = -27$

$x = -27$

Solution Set: $\{-27\}$

21. $m - 42 = 10$

$m - 42 + 42 = 10 + 42$

$m + 0 = 52$

$m = 52$

Solution Set: $\{52\}$

23. $168 + p = 3$

$168 - 168 + p = 3 - 168$

$0 + p = -165$

$p = -165$

Solution Set: $\{-165\}$

25. $28 = t - \frac{2}{3}$

$28 + \frac{2}{3} = t - \frac{2}{3} + \frac{2}{3}$

$28\frac{2}{3} = t + 0$

$28\frac{2}{3} = t$

Solution Set: $\left\{ 28\frac{2}{3} \right\}$

27. $1.5 + x = 4.5$

$1.5 - 1.5 + x = 4.5 - 1.5$

$0 + x = 3$

$x = 3$

Solution Set: $\{3\}$

29.
$$-\frac{2}{3} = x - \frac{4}{5}$$
$$-\frac{2}{3} + \frac{4}{5} = x - \frac{4}{5} + \frac{4}{5}$$
$$\frac{2}{15} = x + 0$$
$$\frac{2}{15} = x$$

Solution Set: $\left\{\frac{2}{15}\right\}$

31.
$$3x = -18$$
$$\frac{1}{3}(3x) = \frac{1}{3}(-18)$$
$$1 \cdot x = -6$$
$$x = -6$$

Solution Set: $\{-6\}$

33.
$$3.5w = 10.5$$
$$\frac{3.5w}{3.5} = \frac{10.5}{3.5}$$
$$1 \cdot w = 3$$
$$w = 3$$

Solution Set: $\{3\}$

35.
$$\frac{x}{15} = -20$$
$$\frac{15}{1}\left(\frac{x}{15}\right) = 15(-20)$$
$$1 \cdot x = -300$$
$$x = -300$$

Solution Set: $\{-300\}$

37.
$$\frac{2}{7}x = -\frac{3}{14}$$
$$\frac{7}{2}\left(\frac{2}{7}x\right) = \frac{7}{2}\left(-\frac{3}{14}\right)$$
$$1 \cdot x = -\frac{3}{4}$$
$$x = -\frac{3}{4}$$

Solution Set: $\left\{-\frac{3}{4}\right\}$

39.
$$-6x = 3\frac{1}{2}$$
$$-\frac{1}{6}(-6x) = -\frac{1}{6}\left(3\frac{1}{2}\right)$$
$$1 \cdot x = -\frac{1}{6}\left(\frac{7}{2}\right)$$
$$x = -\frac{7}{12}$$

Solution Set: $\left\{-\frac{7}{12}\right\}$

41.
$$0 = \frac{t}{7}$$
$$7(0) = \frac{7}{1}\left(\frac{t}{7}\right)$$
$$0 = 1 \cdot t$$
$$0 = t$$

Solution Set: $\{0\}$

43.
$$8d + 5 = 29$$
$$8d + 5 - 5 = 29 - 5$$
$$8d = 24$$
$$\frac{8d}{8} = \frac{24}{8}$$
$$d = 3$$

Solution Set: $\{3\}$

45.
$$32 = 2x - 22$$
$$32 + 22 = 2x - 22 + 22$$
$$54 = 2x$$
$$\frac{54}{2} = \frac{2x}{2}$$
$$27 = x$$

Solution Set: $\{27\}$

47.
$$-4x + 1.6 = 3.2$$
$$-4x + 1.6 - 1.6 = 3.2 - 1.6$$
$$-4x = 1.6$$
$$\frac{-4x}{-4} = \frac{1.6}{-4}$$
$$x = -0.4$$

Solution Set: $\{-0.4\}$

49.
$$3x + 15 = 15$$
$$3x + 15 - 15 = 15 - 15$$
$$3x = 0$$
$$\frac{3x}{3} = \frac{0}{3}$$
$$x = 0$$
Solution Set: $\{0\}$

51.
$$-51 - 7d = 5$$
$$-51 + 51 - 7d = 5 + 51$$
$$-7d = 56$$
$$\frac{-7d}{-7} = \frac{56}{-7}$$
$$d = -8$$
Solution Set: $\{-8\}$

53.
$$-102 = 14 - 2x$$
$$-102 - 14 = 14 - 14 - 2x$$
$$-116 = -2x$$
$$\frac{-116}{-2} = \frac{-2x}{-2}$$
$$58 = x$$
Solution Set: $\{58\}$

55.
$$\frac{1}{2}x - 18 = 52$$
$$\frac{1}{2}x - 18 + 18 = 52 + 18$$
$$\frac{1}{2}x = 70$$
$$2\left(\frac{1}{2}x\right) = 2(70)$$
$$x = 140$$
Solution Set: $\{140\}$

57.
$$30 = \frac{9}{2}x + 12$$
$$30 - 12 = \frac{9}{2}x + 12 - 12$$
$$18 = \frac{9}{2}x$$
$$\frac{2}{9}(18) = \frac{2}{9}\left(\frac{9}{2}x\right)$$
$$4 = x$$
Solution Set: $\{4\}$

59.
$$-14h + 42 = 0$$
$$-14h + 42 - 42 = 0 - 42$$
$$-14h = -42$$
$$\frac{-14h}{-14} = \frac{-42}{-14}$$
$$h = 3$$
Solution Set: $\{3\}$

61.
$$21x + 5 = 13x + 53$$
$$21x - 13x + 5 = 13x - 13x + 53$$
$$8x + 5 = 53$$
$$8x + 5 - 5 = 53 - 5$$
$$8x = 48$$
$$\frac{8x}{8} = \frac{48}{8}$$
$$x = 6$$
Solution Set: $\{6\}$

63.
$$6x + 3 - x = 15x - 8 + x$$
$$5x + 3 = 16x - 8$$
$$5x - 16x + 3 = 16x - 16x - 8$$
$$-11x + 3 = -8$$
$$-11x + 3 - 3 = -8 - 3$$
$$-11x = -11$$
$$\frac{-11x}{-11} = \frac{-11}{-11}$$
$$x = 1$$
Solution Set: $\{1\}$

65.
$$6.2x + 0.6 = 5.6 - 3.8x$$
$$6.2x + 3.8x + 0.6 = 5.6 - 3.8x + 3.8x$$
$$10x + 0.6 = 5.6$$
$$10x + 0.6 - 0.6 = 5.6 - 0.6$$
$$10x = 5$$
$$\frac{10x}{10} = \frac{5}{10}$$
$$x = \frac{1}{2}$$
Solution Set: $\left\{\frac{1}{2}\right\}$

67. $8x - 3x = -20$

$5x = -20$

$\dfrac{5x}{5} = \dfrac{-20}{5}$

$x = -4$

Solution Set: $\{-4\}$

69. $\dfrac{x}{3} + 5 = -9$

$\dfrac{x}{3} + 5 - 5 = -9 - 5$

$\dfrac{x}{3} = -14$

$\dfrac{3}{1}\left(\dfrac{x}{3}\right) = 3(-14)$

$x = -42$

Solution Set: $\{-42\}$

71. $14x + \dfrac{5}{6} = -\dfrac{2}{6}$

$14x + \dfrac{5}{6} - \dfrac{5}{6} = -\dfrac{2}{6} - \dfrac{5}{6}$

$14x = -\dfrac{7}{6}$

$\dfrac{1}{14}(14x) = \dfrac{1}{14}\left(-\dfrac{7}{6}\right)$

$x = -\dfrac{1}{12}$

Solution Set: $\left\{-\dfrac{1}{12}\right\}$

73. $n - 18 = 3n - 18$

$n - 3n - 18 = 3n - 3n - 18$

$-2n - 18 = -18$

$-2n - 18 + 18 = -18 + 18$

$-2n = 0$

$\dfrac{-2n}{-2} = \dfrac{0}{-2}$

$n = 0$

Solution Set: $\{0\}$

75. $-10 = -105x + 35 + 20x$

$-10 = -85x + 35$

$-10 - 35 = -85x + 35 - 35$

$-45 = -85x$

$\dfrac{-45}{-85} = \dfrac{-85x}{-85}$

$\dfrac{9}{17} = x$

Solution Set: $\left\{\dfrac{9}{17}\right\}$

77. $2.4x - 16 = 8$

$2.4x - 16 + 16 = 8 + 16$

$2.4x = 24$

$\dfrac{2.4x}{2.4} = \dfrac{24}{2.4}$

$x = 10$

Solution Set: $\{10\}$

79. $-66 = -33x + 231$

$-66 - 231 = -33x + 231 - 231$

$-297 = -33x$

$\dfrac{-297}{-33} = \dfrac{-33x}{-33}$

$9 = x$

Solution Set: $\{9\}$

81. $-x - 0.35 + 0.5x = -4$

$-0.5x - 0.35 = -4$

$-0.5x - 0.35 + 0.35 = -4 + 0.35$

$-0.5x = -3.65$

$\dfrac{-0.5x}{-0.5} = \dfrac{-3.65}{-0.5}$

$x = 7.3$

Solution Set: $\{7.3\}$

83. Answers will vary; one example is: $x^2 + 3x = 6$ (the exponent does not equal one).

85. Answers will vary; one example is: $23x - 7 = 16$ (one variable) and $2x - 3y = 6$ (two variables).

87. Answers will vary; one example is: $3x = 9$. $x = 3$

89.
$$x + x - 14 + x + 1 = 59$$
$$3x - 13 = 59$$
$$3x - 13 + 13 = 59 + 13$$
$$3x = 72$$
$$\frac{3x}{3} = \frac{72}{3}$$
$$x = 24$$

The sides are 10m, 24m, and 25m.

91.
$$8x = 162.4$$
$$\frac{8x}{8} = \frac{162.4}{8}$$
$$x = 20.3$$

Each side is 20.3cm.

93. Prepare We must solve the linear equation for s to determine how much Lucinda Smeeds must sell at L & C Electronics so that she earns as much as her current $12.50 per hour wage.

Plan Solve the linear equation for s by using the Strategy for Solving Linear Equations.

Process
$$0.05s + 350 = 500$$
$$0.05s + 350 - 350 = 500 - 350$$
$$0.05s = 150$$
$$\frac{0.05s}{0.05} = \frac{150}{0.05}$$
$$s = 3000$$

Therefore, Lucinda would have to sell $3000 worth of electronics per week to make the same salary she makes earning $12.50 per hour based on a 40-hour week.

Ponder Does our answer seem reasonable? We can check our answer. The hourly wage for one week would be $12.50(40) = $500. The commission plus $350 would be $(0.05)(3,000) + 350 = 500.

95.
$$6x + \left[-15x - 3(x - 1)\right] = 11$$
$$6\left(-\frac{2}{3}\right) + \left[-15\left(-\frac{2}{3}\right) - 3\left(\left(-\frac{2}{3}\right) - 1\right)\right] = 11$$
$$-4 + \left[10 - 3\left(-\frac{5}{3}\right)\right] = 11$$
$$-4 + [10 + 5] = 11$$
$$-4 + 15 = 11$$
$$11 = 11$$

Yes, $-\dfrac{2}{3}$ is a solution.

97.
$$-2x + \left[-6x + 2(x - 3)\right] = -15$$
$$-2\left(\frac{3}{2}\right) + \left[-6\left(\frac{3}{2}\right) + 2\left(\left(\frac{3}{2}\right) - 3\right)\right] = -15$$
$$-3 + \left[-9 + 2\left(-\frac{3}{2}\right)\right] = -15$$
$$-3 + [-9 - 3] = -15$$
$$-3 + [-12] = -15$$
$$-15 = -15$$

Yes, $\dfrac{3}{2}$ is a solution.

99.
$$-\frac{1}{3}x + 0.05 = -0.2$$
$$-\frac{1}{3}x + 0.05 - 0.05 = -0.2 - 0.05$$
$$-\frac{1}{3}x = -0.25$$
$$-3\left(-\frac{1}{3}x\right) = -3(-0.25)$$
$$x = 0.75$$

Solution Set: $\{0.75\}$

101.
$$0.6x - \frac{1}{4} = 3.2$$
$$0.6x - 0.25 = 3.2$$
$$0.6x - 0.25 + 0.25 = 3.2 + 0.25$$
$$0.6x = 3.45$$
$$\frac{0.6x}{0.6} = \frac{3.45}{0.6}$$
$$x = 5.75$$

Solution Set: $\{5.75\}$

2.2 Exercises

1. When solving a linear equation involving fractions, if clearing fractions is necessary, we <u>multiply</u> both sides of the equation by the <u>least</u> <u>common</u> <u>denominator</u> of all the denominators present.

3. An equation that does not have a solution is called an <u>inconsistent</u> equation.

5. The equation $5(x-1) = 5(x+2)$ is an <u>inconsistent</u> equation.

7. Yes, because there are three different denominators.

9. No, because the constant terms combine to become a whole number.

11.
$$5(x+2) = 45$$
$$5x + 10 = 45$$
$$5x + 10 - 10 = 45 - 10$$
$$5x = 35$$
$$\frac{5x}{5} = \frac{35}{5}$$
$$x = 7$$
Solution Set: $\{7\}$

13.
$$6(4-w) = 12$$
$$24 - 6w = 12$$
$$24 - 24 - 6w = 12 - 24$$
$$-6w = -12$$
$$\frac{-6w}{-6} = \frac{-12}{-6}$$
$$w = 2$$
Solution Set: $\{2\}$

15.
$$18 = 4(d-2)$$
$$18 = 4d - 8$$
$$18 + 8 = 4d - 8 + 8$$
$$26 = 4d$$
$$\frac{26}{4} = \frac{4d}{4}$$
$$\frac{13}{2} = d$$
Solution Set: $\left\{\frac{13}{2}\right\}$

17.
$$x - 5(2x+1) = 58$$
$$x - 10x - 5 = 58$$
$$-9x - 5 = 58$$
$$-9x - 5 + 5 = 58 + 5$$
$$-9x = 63$$
$$\frac{-9x}{-9} = \frac{63}{-9}$$
$$x = -7$$
Solution Set: $\{-7\}$

19.
$$60 = 5 - (2x+9)$$
$$60 = 5 - 2x - 9$$
$$60 = -2x - 4$$
$$60 + 4 = -2x - 4 + 4$$
$$64 = -2x$$
$$\frac{64}{-2} = \frac{-2x}{-2}$$
$$-32 = x$$
Solution Set: $\{-32\}$

21.
$$12(3x-5) = 10x - 8$$
$$36x - 60 = 10x - 8$$
$$36x - 10x - 60 = 10x - 10x - 8$$
$$26x - 60 = -8$$
$$26x - 60 + 60 = -8 + 60$$
$$26x = 52$$
$$\frac{26x}{26} = \frac{52}{26}$$
$$x = 2$$
Solution Set: $\{2\}$

23.
$$-12 + 5(2s-1) = 20s + 3$$
$$-12 + 10s - 5 = 20s + 3$$
$$10s - 17 = 20s + 3$$
$$10s - 20s - 17 = 20s - 20s + 3$$
$$-10s - 17 = 3$$
$$-10s - 17 + 17 = 3 + 17$$
$$-10s = 20$$
$$\frac{-10s}{-10} = \frac{20}{-10}$$
$$x = -2$$
Solution Set: $\{-2\}$

25.
$$-7(m-1) = 11(2m-2)$$
$$-7m+7 = 22m-22$$
$$-7m-22m+7 = 22m-22m-22$$
$$-29m+7 = -22$$
$$-29m+7-7 = -22-7$$
$$-29m = -29$$
$$\frac{-29m}{-29} = \frac{-29}{-29}$$
$$m = 1$$
Solution Set: $\{1\}$

27.
$$4.5+0.1x = 1.5$$
$$10(4.5+0.1x) = 10(1.5)$$
$$45+x = 15$$
$$45-45+x = 15-45$$
$$x = -30$$
Solution Set: $\{-30\}$

29.
$$2.3x-0.11 = 0.8x+34.39$$
$$100(2.3x-0.11) = 100(0.8x+34.39)$$
$$230x-11 = 80x+3439$$
$$230x-80x-11 = 80x-80x+3439$$
$$150x-11 = 3439$$
$$150x-11+11 = 3439+11$$
$$150x = 3450$$
$$\frac{150x}{150} = \frac{3450}{150}$$
$$x = 23$$
Solution Set: $\{23\}$

31.
$$0.25x+0.1(x+5) = 2.25$$
$$0.25x+0.1x+0.5 = 2.25$$
$$0.35x+0.5 = 2.25$$
$$100(0.35x+0.5) = 100(2.25)$$
$$35x+50 = 225$$
$$35x+50-50 = 225-50$$
$$35x = 175$$
$$\frac{35x}{35} = \frac{175}{35}$$
$$x = 5$$
Solution Set: $\{5\}$

33.
$$6x+0.8(2x-0.1) = 151.92$$
$$6x+1.6x-0.08 = 151.92$$
$$7.6x-0.08 = 151.92$$
$$100(7.6x-0.08) = 100(151.92)$$
$$760x-8 = 15192$$
$$760x-8+8 = 15192+8$$
$$760x = 15200$$
$$\frac{760x}{760} = \frac{15200}{760}$$
$$x = 20$$
Solution Set: $\{20\}$

35.
$$-\frac{7}{6}-3x = \frac{1}{6}+x$$
$$\frac{6}{1}\left(-\frac{7}{6}-3x\right) = \frac{6}{1}\left(\frac{1}{6}+x\right)$$
$$-7-18x = 1+6x$$
$$-7-18x-6x = 1+6x-6x$$
$$-7-24x = 1$$
$$-7+7-24x = 1+7$$
$$-24x = 8$$
$$\frac{-24x}{-24} = \frac{8}{-24}$$
$$x = -\frac{1}{3}$$
Solution Set: $\left\{-\frac{1}{3}\right\}$

37.
$$x+\frac{2}{3} = 3x-\frac{5}{6}$$
$$\frac{6}{1}\left(x+\frac{2}{3}\right) = \frac{6}{1}\left(3x-\frac{5}{6}\right)$$
$$6x+4 = 18x-5$$
$$6x-18x+4 = 18x-18x-5$$
$$-12x+4 = -5$$
$$-12x+4-4 = -5-4$$
$$-12x = -9$$
$$\frac{-12x}{-12} = \frac{-9}{-12}$$
$$x = \frac{3}{4}$$
Solution Set: $\left\{\frac{3}{4}\right\}$

39.

$$\frac{x}{2}+\frac{x}{3}=6-\frac{x}{6}$$

$$\frac{6}{1}\left(\frac{x}{2}+\frac{x}{3}\right)=\frac{6}{1}\left(6-\frac{x}{6}\right)$$

$$3x+2x=36-x$$

$$5x=36-x$$

$$5x+x=36-x+x$$

$$6x=36$$

$$\frac{6x}{6}=\frac{36}{6}$$

$$x=6$$

Solution Set: $\{6\}$

41.

$$\frac{2}{3}x+40=\frac{x}{2}-\frac{x}{6}-\frac{2x}{9}$$

$$\frac{18}{1}\left(\frac{2}{3}x+40\right)=\frac{18}{1}\left(\frac{x}{2}-\frac{x}{6}-\frac{2x}{9}\right)$$

$$12x+720=9x-3x-4x$$

$$12x+720=2x$$

$$12x-2x+720=2x-2x$$

$$10x+720=0$$

$$10x+720-720=0-720$$

$$10x=-720$$

$$\frac{10x}{10}=\frac{-720}{10}$$

$$x=-72$$

Solution Set: $\{-72\}$

43.

$$\frac{x-5}{3}=\frac{3x+1}{6}$$

$$\frac{6}{1}\left(\frac{x-5}{3}\right)=\frac{6}{1}\left(\frac{3x+1}{6}\right)$$

$$2x-10=3x+1$$

$$2x-3x-10=3x-3x+1$$

$$-x-10=1$$

$$-x-10+10=1+10$$

$$-x=11$$

$$\frac{-x}{-1}=\frac{11}{-1}$$

$$x=-11$$

Solution Set: $\{-11\}$

45.

$$\frac{x-3}{3}+\frac{x+2}{4}=\frac{11}{6}$$

$$\frac{12}{1}\left(\frac{x-3}{3}+\frac{x+2}{4}\right)=\frac{12}{1}\left(\frac{11}{6}\right)$$

$$4x-12+3x+6=22$$

$$7x-6=22$$

$$7x-6+6=22+6$$

$$7x=28$$

$$\frac{7x}{7}=\frac{28}{7}$$

$$x=4$$

Solution Set: $\{4\}$

47.

$$5x+3(x+2)=2x+6(3x-3)$$

$$5x+3x+6=2x+18x-18$$

$$8x+6=20x-18$$

$$8x-20x+6=20x-20x-18$$

$$-12x+6=-18$$

$$-12x+6-6=-18-6$$

$$-12x=-24$$

$$\frac{-12x}{-12}=\frac{-24}{-12}$$

$$x=2$$

Solution Set: $\{2\}$

49.

$$-3(a+2)+7(-2a-1)=6a-6(3a+5)$$

$$-3a-6-14a-7=6a-18a-30$$

$$-17a-13=-12a-30$$

$$-17a+12a-13=-12a+12a-30$$

$$-5a-13=-30$$

$$-5a-13+13=-30+13$$

$$-5a=-17$$

$$\frac{-5a}{-5}=\frac{-17}{-5}$$

$$a=\frac{17}{5}$$

Solution Set: $\left\{\frac{17}{5}\right\}$

51. $14m - 2\{3 + 5m - [6 - (m-2)]\} = -10$

$\qquad 14m - 2\{3 + 5m - [6 - m + 2]\} = -10$

$\qquad 14m - 2\{3 + 5m - [-m + 8]\} = -10$

$\qquad 14m - 2\{3 + 5m + m - 8\} = -10$

$\qquad 14m - 2\{6m - 5\} = -10$

$\qquad 14m - 12m + 10 = -10$

$\qquad 2m + 10 = -10$

$\qquad 2m + 10 - 10 = -10 - 10$

$\qquad 2m = -20$

$\qquad \dfrac{2m}{2} = \dfrac{-20}{2}$

$\qquad m = -10$

Solution Set: $\{-10\}$

53. $-\dfrac{1}{2}x + 5(x-3) = x-1$

$\qquad -\dfrac{1}{2}x + 5x - 15 = x - 1$

$\qquad \dfrac{9}{2}x - 15 = x - 1$

$\qquad \dfrac{9}{2}x - x - 15 = x - x - 1$

$\qquad \dfrac{7}{2}x - 15 = -1$

$\qquad \dfrac{7}{2}x - 15 + 15 = -1 + 15$

$\qquad \dfrac{7}{2}x = 14$

$\qquad \dfrac{2}{7}\left(\dfrac{7}{2}x\right) = \dfrac{2}{7}\left(\dfrac{14}{1}\right)$

$\qquad x = 4$

Solution Set: $\{4\}$

55. $-9\left(2x - \dfrac{1}{3}\right) = 4\left(-\dfrac{1}{2}x + \dfrac{1}{4}\right)$

$\qquad -18x + 3 = -2x + 1$

$\qquad -18x + 2x + 3 = -2x + 2x + 1$

$\qquad -16x + 3 = 1$

$\qquad -16x + 3 - 3 = 1 - 3$

$\qquad -16x = -2$

$\qquad \dfrac{-16x}{-16} = \dfrac{-2}{-16}$

$\qquad x = \dfrac{1}{8}$

Solution Set: $\left\{\dfrac{1}{8}\right\}$

57. $5 - 2a = 8 - 6a + 4a$

$\qquad 5 - 2a = 8 - 2a$

$\qquad 5 - 2a + 2a = 8 - 2a + 2a$

$\qquad 5 = 8$

This equation is inconsistent.   Solution Set: $\{\ \}$ or $\varnothing$

59. $6 + 2(3x - 3) = 6x$

$\qquad 6 + 6x - 6 = 6x$

$\qquad 6x = 6x$

$\qquad 6x - 6x = 6x - 6x$

$\qquad 0 = 0$

This equation is an identity.   Solution Set: $\{x \mid x \in R\}$

61. $\dfrac{3}{5} + x = x - \dfrac{2}{7}$

$\qquad \dfrac{3}{5} + x - x = x - x - \dfrac{2}{7}$

$\qquad \dfrac{3}{5} = -\dfrac{2}{7}$

This equation is inconsistent.   Solution Set: $\{\ \}$ or $\varnothing$

63. $2 + 3(4x - 1) = 6(2x - 5) + 29$

$\qquad 2 + 12x - 3 = 12x - 30 + 29$

$\qquad 12x - 1 = 12x - 1$

$\qquad 12x - 12x - 1 = 12x - 12x - 1$

$\qquad -1 = -1$

This equation is an identity.   Solution Set: $\{x \mid x \in R\}$

65. $4(5x + 2) - 3(x - 2) = 10x + (7x + 9)$

$\qquad 20x + 8 - 3x + 6 = 17x + 9$

$\qquad 17x + 14 = 17x + 9$

$\qquad 17x - 17x + 14 = 17x - 17x + 9$

$\qquad 14 = 9$

This equation is inconsistent.   Solution Set: $\{\ \}$ or $\varnothing$

67. $0.3 + 0.85x = 0.5(1.7x + 4) - 1.7$

$\qquad 0.3 + 0.85x = 0.85x + 2 - 1.7$

$\qquad 0.3 + 0.85x = 0.85x + 0.3$

$\qquad 0.3 + 0.85x - 0.85x = 0.85x - 0.85x + 0.3$

$\qquad 0.3 = 0.3$

This equation is an identity.   Solution Set: $\{x \mid x \in R\}$

69. An equation that has all real numbers as its solutions is an identity.

71. We clear fractions from an equation by multiplying every term by the LCD of all the denominators. The Multiplication Property of Equality allows us to do this step.

73.
$$3(x-2)+5 = 2x-(5-x)$$
$$3x-6+5 = 2x-5+x$$
$$3x-1 = 3x-5$$
$$3x-3x-1 = 3x-3x-5$$
$$-1 = -5$$

This equation is inconsistent.   Solution Set: $\{\ \}$ or $\varnothing$

75.
$$12x-7(x+2) = 10(x-1)-(5x+4)$$
$$12x-7x-14 = 10x-10-5x-4$$
$$5x-14 = 5x-14$$
$$5x-5x-14 = 5x-5x-14$$
$$-14 = -14$$

Solution Set: $\{x \mid x \in R\}$ This equation is an identity.

77.   Let x represent the number.
$$0.5x = 0.24$$
$$\frac{0.5x}{0.5} = \frac{0.24}{0.5}$$
$$x = 0.48$$
The number is 0.48.

79.   Let x represent the number.
$$4x = -\frac{3}{4}$$
$$\frac{1}{4}(4x) = \frac{1}{4}\left(-\frac{3}{4}\right)$$
$$x = -\frac{3}{16}$$
The number is $-\frac{3}{16}$.

81. Let x represent the number.
$$\frac{1}{2}x+7 = \frac{2}{3}x$$
$$\frac{6}{1}\left(\frac{1}{2}x+7\right) = \frac{6}{1}\left(\frac{2}{3}x\right)$$
$$3x+42 = 4x$$
$$3x-4x+42 = 4x-4x$$
$$-x+42 = 0$$
$$-x+42-42 = 0-42$$
$$-x = -42$$
$$\frac{-x}{-1} = \frac{-42}{-1}$$
$$x = 42$$
The number is 42.

83. Let x represent the number.
$$\frac{2x+3}{5} = -\frac{17}{5}$$
$$\frac{5}{1}\left(\frac{2x+3}{5}\right) = \frac{5}{1}\left(-\frac{17}{5}\right)$$
$$2x+3 = -17$$
$$2x+3-3 = -17-3$$
$$2x = -20$$
$$\frac{2x}{2} = \frac{-20}{2}$$
$$x = -10$$
The number is -10.

85.   a)   Let t represent the sales tax on the vehicle.
$$\text{sales tax} = (\text{retail price})(\text{tax rate})$$
$$t = (15{,}350)(0.065)$$
$$t = 997.75$$
The sales tax on the vehicle is $997.75.

   b)   Let p represent the total purchase price of the vehicle.
$$\binom{\text{purchase}}{\text{price}} = \binom{\text{retail}}{\text{price}} + \binom{\text{sales}}{\text{tax}} + (\text{title}) + (\text{license})$$
$$p = 15{,}350+997.75+150+35$$
$$p = 16{,}532.75$$
The purchase price of the vehicle is $16,532.75.

87. Let p represent the original price of the boots.

$$\begin{pmatrix} \text{Original} \\ \text{Price} \end{pmatrix} - \begin{pmatrix} \text{Amount of} \\ \text{Discount} \end{pmatrix} = \text{Sale Price}$$

$$p - 0.3p = 73.50$$
$$0.7p = 73.50$$
$$\frac{0.7p}{0.7} = \frac{73.50}{0.7}$$
$$p = 105$$

The original price of the boots was \$105.

89. Let s represent the sale price of the blouse.

$$\begin{pmatrix} \text{Original} \\ \text{Price} \end{pmatrix} - \begin{pmatrix} \text{Amount of} \\ \text{Discount} \end{pmatrix} = \text{Sale Price}$$

$$40 - (0.15)(40) = s$$
$$40 - 6 = s$$
$$34 = s$$

The sale price of the blouse is \$34.

91. Let x be the measure of the first angle $(m\angle 1)$.

Then, the measure of the second angle $(m\angle 2)$ is $3x - 4.2$.

$$m\angle 1 + m\angle 2 = 90$$
$$x + 3x - 4.2 = 90$$
$$4x - 4.2 = 90$$
$$4x - 4.2 + 4.2 = 90 + 4.2$$
$$4x = 94.2$$
$$\frac{4x}{4} = \frac{94.2}{4}$$
$$x = 23.55$$

The measure of the first angle is $m\angle 1 = 23.55°$, and the measure of the second angle is $m\angle 2 = 66.45°$.

93.   Let x be the measure of the first angle $(m\angle 1)$.

Then, the measure of the second angle $(m\angle 2)$ is $\frac{3}{5}x + 4$.

$$m\angle 1 + m\angle 2 = 180$$
$$x + \frac{3}{5}x + 4 = 180$$
$$\frac{8}{5}x + 4 = 180$$
$$\frac{8}{5}x + 4 - 4 = 180 - 4$$

$$\frac{8}{5}x = 176$$
$$\frac{5}{8}\left(\frac{8}{5}x\right) = \frac{5}{8}\left(\frac{176}{1}\right)$$
$$x = 110$$

The measure of the first angle is $m\angle 1 = 110°$, and the measure of the second angle is $m\angle 2 = 70°$

95. Prepare We are asked to solve the linear equation for x in order to determine the number of microwaves Harlow Builders should purchase from L & C in order for the cost to be equal.

Plan Solve the linear equation for x by using the Strategy for Solving Linear Equations.

Process

$$580 + 130x = 950 + 75(x - 2)$$
$$580 + 130x = 950 + 75x - 150$$
$$580 + 130x = 800 + 75x$$
$$580 + 130x - 75x = 800 + 75x - 75x$$
$$580 + 55x = 800$$
$$580 - 580 + 55x = 800 - 580$$
$$55x = 220$$
$$\frac{55x}{55} = \frac{220}{55}$$
$$x = 4$$

Harlow Builders should purchase 4 microwaves from L & C in order for the cost to be equal.

Ponder Does our answer seem reasonable? Yes, because we can check that the purchase of 4 microwaves does indeed give the same cost.

97. Prepare We are asked to determine the lengths of the three pieces of the board.

Plan Let x represent the length of the first piece. Then the length of the second piece of wood is $\frac{1}{3}x + 2$ and the length of the third piece of wood is $x + 4$. We can use these expressions and the fact that the total length of the three pieces is 20 feet to set up an equation.

Process

$$x + \frac{1}{3}x + 2 + x + 4 = 20$$

$$\frac{7}{3}x + 6 = 20$$

$$\frac{7}{3}x + 6 - 6 = 20 - 6$$

$$\frac{7}{3}x = 14$$

$$\frac{3}{7}\left(\frac{7}{3}x\right) = \frac{3}{7}(14)$$

$$x = 6$$

The first piece of wood is 6 feet long, the second piece is 4 feet long, and the third piece is 10 feet long.

Ponder Does our answer seem reasonable? Yes, because the sum of the lengths of the three boards is 20.

99.

$$-\frac{5}{3}x + 0.2 = \frac{1}{2} - 0.4x$$

$$\frac{6}{1}\left(-\frac{5}{3}x + 0.2\right) = \frac{6}{1}\left(\frac{1}{2} - 0.4x\right)$$

$$-10x + 1.2 = 3 - 2.4x$$

$$-10x + 2.4x + 1.2 = 3 - 2.4x + 2.4x$$

$$-7.6x + 1.2 = 3$$

$$-7.6x + 1.2 - 1.2 = 3 - 1.2$$

$$-7.6x = 1.8$$

$$\frac{-7.6x}{-7.6} = \frac{1.8}{-7.6}$$

$$x = -\frac{9}{38}$$

Solution Set: $\left\{-\dfrac{9}{38}\right\}$

2.3 Exercises

1. An equation involving more than one variable is a literal equation.

3. Ohm's Law, $I = \dfrac{E}{R}$, is an example of a formula.

5. The first step in solving $3a + 2b = 7x$ for b is to isolate the term $2b$.

7.
$$x + 4y = 12$$
$$x + 4y - 4y = 12 - 4y$$
$$x = 12 - 4y$$

9.
$$-5x + y = 25$$
$$-5x + y - y = 25 - y$$
$$-5x = 25 - y$$
$$\dfrac{-5x}{-5} = \dfrac{25 - y}{-5}$$
$$x = \dfrac{25 - y}{-5}$$
$$x = -5 + \dfrac{y}{5}$$

11.
$$8x - 8y = -16$$
$$8x - 8x - 8y = -16 - 8x$$
$$-8y = -16 - 8x$$
$$\dfrac{-8y}{-8} = \dfrac{-16 - 8x}{-8}$$
$$y = x + 2$$

13.
$$-12x + 8y = 36$$
$$-12x + 12x + 8y = 36 + 12x$$
$$8y = 36 + 12x$$
$$\dfrac{8y}{8} = \dfrac{36 + 12x}{8}$$
$$y = \dfrac{3}{2}x + \dfrac{9}{2}$$

15.
$$\dfrac{5}{6}x - 7y = 2$$
$$\dfrac{5}{6}x - 7y + 7y = 2 + 7y$$
$$\dfrac{5}{6}x = 2 + 7y$$
$$\dfrac{6}{5}\left(\dfrac{5}{6}x\right) = \dfrac{6}{5}(2 + 7y)$$
$$x = \dfrac{12}{5} + \dfrac{42}{5}y$$

17.
$$-\dfrac{2}{5}x + \dfrac{1}{3}y = 1$$
$$-\dfrac{2}{5}x + \dfrac{2}{5}x + \dfrac{1}{3}y = 1 + \dfrac{2}{5}x$$
$$\dfrac{1}{3}y = 1 + \dfrac{2}{5}x$$
$$\dfrac{3}{1}\left(\dfrac{1}{3}y\right) = \dfrac{3}{1}\left(1 + \dfrac{2}{5}x\right)$$
$$y = 3 + \dfrac{6}{5}x$$

19.
$$D = RT$$
$$\dfrac{D}{R} = \dfrac{RT}{R}$$
$$\dfrac{D}{R} = T$$

21.
$$A = lw$$
$$\dfrac{A}{w} = \dfrac{lw}{w}$$
$$\dfrac{A}{w} = l$$

23.
$$V = lwh$$
$$\dfrac{V}{lw} = \dfrac{lwh}{lw}$$
$$\dfrac{V}{lw} = h$$

25.
$$P = 2l + 2w$$
$$P - 2l = 2l - 2l + 2w$$
$$P - 2l = 2w$$
$$\dfrac{P - 2l}{2} = \dfrac{2w}{2}$$
$$\dfrac{P - 2l}{2} = w$$

27.
$$A = \frac{1}{2}h(a+b)$$
$$2A = 2\left(\frac{1}{2}h(a+b)\right)$$
$$2A = h(a+b)$$
$$\frac{2A}{h} = \frac{h(a+b)}{h}$$
$$\frac{2A}{h} = a+b$$
$$\frac{2A}{h} - b = a+b-b$$
$$\frac{2A}{h} - b = a$$

29.
$$A = P(1+rt)$$
$$A = P + Prt$$
$$A - P = P - P + Prt$$
$$A - P = Prt$$
$$\frac{A-P}{Pt} = \frac{Prt}{Pt}$$
$$\frac{A-P}{Pt} = r$$

31.
$$ax + x = 5$$
$$(a+1)x = 5$$
$$\frac{(a+1)x}{a+1} = \frac{5}{a+1}$$
$$x = \frac{5}{a+1}$$

33.
$$S = P + Prt$$
$$S = (1+rt)P$$
$$\frac{S}{1+rt} = \frac{(1+rt)P}{1+rt}$$
$$\frac{S}{1+rt} = P$$

35.
$$S = 2wh + 2lw + 2lh$$
$$S - 2lw = 2wh + 2lw - 2lw + 2lh$$
$$S - 2lw = 2wh + 2lh$$
$$S - 2lw = (2w + 2l)h$$
$$\frac{S-2lw}{2w+2l} = \frac{(2w+2l)h}{2w+2l}$$
$$\frac{S-2lw}{2w+2l} = h$$

37. Answers will vary; one example is: I have $10,000 to invest and want to earn $1000 in interest in two years. What rate do I need?

39.
$$C = \frac{5}{9}(F-32)$$
$$\frac{9}{5}C = \frac{9}{5}\left(\frac{5}{9}(F-32)\right)$$
$$\frac{9}{5}C = F - 32$$
$$\frac{9}{5}C + 32 = F - 32 + 32$$
$$\frac{9}{5}C + 32 = F$$

41.
$$F = \frac{9}{5}C + 32$$
$$F - 32 = \frac{9}{5}C + 32 - 32$$
$$F - 32 = \frac{9}{5}C$$
$$\frac{5}{9}(F-32) = \frac{5}{9}\left(\frac{9}{5}C\right)$$
$$\frac{5}{9}(F-32) = C$$

43.

P	l	w
24 ft.	3 ft.	$w = \dfrac{P-2l}{2}$ $w = \dfrac{24-2(3)}{2}$ $w = 9$ ft.
8½ in.	3¼ in.	$w = \dfrac{8\frac{1}{2} - 2\left(3\frac{1}{4}\right)}{2}$ $w = \dfrac{8\frac{1}{2} - 6\frac{1}{2}}{2}$ $w = 1$ in.
6.48 cm	1.15 cm	$w = \dfrac{P-2l}{2}$ $w = \dfrac{6.48-2(1.15)}{2}$ $w = 2.09$ cm

45. $I = Prt$

$I = (1200)(0.035)(1)$

$I = 42$

You would earn \$42 in interest.

47. $I = Prt$

$(945) = (13500)(0.07)t$

$945 = 945t$

$\dfrac{945}{945} = \dfrac{945t}{945}$

$1 = t$

It would take 1 year to earn \$945 in interest.

49. $I = Prt$

$1620 = (12000)(0.0675)t$

$1620 = 810t$

$\dfrac{1620}{810} = \dfrac{810t}{810}$

$2 = t$

It would take 2 years to earn \$1,620 in interest.

51. $I = Prt$

$273.6 = (2280)(r)(1.5)$

$273.6 = 3420r$

$\dfrac{273.6}{3420} = \dfrac{3420r}{3420}$

$0.08 = r$

You would need to invest at a rate of 8%.

53. $I = Prt$

$269.5 = P(0.055)(2)$

$269.5 = 0.11P$

$\dfrac{269.5}{0.11} = \dfrac{0.11P}{0.11}$

$2450 = P$

You would have to invest \$2,450.

55. $D = rt$

$D = (620)\left(2\dfrac{1}{2}\right)$

$D = 1550$

The plane can travel 1,550 miles.

57. $D = rt$

$7.5 = r(0.75)$

$7.5 = 0.75r$

$\dfrac{7.5}{0.75} = \dfrac{0.75r}{0.75}$

$10 = r$

The woman is jogging at 10 miles per hour.

59. $D = rt$

$0.8 = 4t$

$\dfrac{0.8}{4} = \dfrac{4t}{4}$

$0.2 = t$

It takes Jasmine 0.2 hours or 12 minutes.

61.   **Prepare** We are asked to determine the details of purchasing a home theater projector on a 12 month no interest plan.

Plan We will use the sales receipt and the advertisement to answer the questions.

Process

a)

Standard APR $=$ Prime $+ 12.6\%$

Standard APR $= 7.75\% + 12.6\%$

Standard APR $= 20.35\%$

Default APR $=$ Prime $+ 16.4\%$

Default APR $= 7.75\% + 16.4\%$

Defalut APR $= 24.15\%$

Let m represent the minimum monthly payment.

$m = (1\%)(\text{Principal Balance})$

$m = (0.01)(\$1364.99)$

$m \approx \$13.65$

The minimum monthly payment would be \$13.65.

b)

$I = Prt$

$I = (\$1,364.99)(0.2035)(1)$

$I \approx \$277.78$

The interest on the initial balance is \$277.78. The first month's interest would be $\$277.78 \div 12 \approx \$23.15$.

c) Helaku would owe the first month's payment, the second month's payment and the late fee,

which would come to
$\$13.65 + \$13.65 + \$35 = \$62.30$.

Ponder Do our answers seem reasonable? It seems reasonable that the minimum monthly payment would be considerably less than the payment needed to pay off the principal balance in 12 months, which would be $\$1,364.99 \div 12 \approx \$113.75$.

63. Prepare We are to find the height of a right circular cylinder after first solving the surface area formula for h.

Plan We will first solve the surface area formula $S = 2\pi r^2 + 2\pi rh$ for h and then substitute the given information into the new formula to find the height.

Process

$$S = 2\pi r^2 + 2\pi rh$$
$$S - 2\pi r^2 = 2\pi r^2 - 2\pi r^2 + 2\pi rh$$
$$S - 2\pi r^2 = 2\pi rh$$
$$\frac{S - 2\pi r^2}{2\pi r} = \frac{2\pi rh}{2\pi r}$$
$$\frac{S - 2\pi r^2}{2\pi r} = h$$

$$h = \frac{S - 2\pi r^2}{2\pi r}$$
$$h = \frac{48\pi - 2\pi(3)^2}{2\pi(3)}$$
$$h = \frac{48\pi - 18\pi}{6\pi}$$
$$h = \frac{30\pi}{6\pi}$$
$$h = 5$$

The height of the cylinder is 5 feet.

Ponder Does our answer seem reasonable? Yes, we can substitute 3 and 5 for the radius and height, respectively, in the surface area formula and verify that we get a surface area of 48π square feet.

65.
$$a(y+8) = 10$$
$$ay + 8a = 10$$
$$ay + 8a - 8a = 10 - 8a$$
$$ay = 10 - 8a$$
$$\frac{ay}{a} = \frac{10 - 8a}{a}$$
$$y = \frac{10 - 8a}{a}$$

67.
$$\frac{x}{2} + \frac{y}{3} = 1$$
$$\frac{6}{1}\left(\frac{x}{2} + \frac{y}{3}\right) = 6(1)$$
$$3x + 2y = 6$$
$$3x + 2y - 2y = 6 - 2y$$
$$3x = 6 - 2y$$
$$\frac{3x}{3} = \frac{6 - 2y}{3}$$
$$x = \frac{6 - 2y}{3}$$

69.
$$\frac{x}{a} + \frac{y}{b} = 1$$
$$\frac{ab}{1}\left(\frac{x}{a} + \frac{y}{b}\right) = ab(1)$$
$$bx + ay = ab$$
$$bx - bx + ay = ab - bx$$
$$ay = ab - bx$$
$$\frac{ay}{a} = \frac{ab - bx}{a}$$
$$y = \frac{ab - bx}{a}$$

71.
$$y = mx + b$$
$$y - b = mx + b - b$$
$$y - b = mx$$
$$\frac{y - b}{m} = \frac{mx}{m}$$
$$\frac{y - b}{m} = x$$

73.

$$\frac{y-2}{3} = \frac{x+5}{2}$$

$$\frac{6}{1}\left(\frac{y-2}{3}\right) = \frac{6}{1}\left(\frac{x+5}{2}\right)$$

$$2y-4 = 3x+15$$

$$2y-4+4 = 3x+15+4$$

$$2y = 3x+19$$

$$\frac{2y}{2} = \frac{3x+19}{2}$$

$$y = \frac{3x+19}{2}$$

75.

$$(y-2)(x-5) = a+3$$

$$\frac{(y-2)(x-5)}{(y-2)} = \frac{a+3}{y-2}$$

$$x-5 = \frac{a+3}{y-2}$$

$$x-5+5 = \frac{a+3}{y-2}+5$$

$$x = \frac{a+3}{y-2}+5$$

77.

$$D = rt$$

$$10 = 40t$$

$$\frac{10}{40} = \frac{40t}{40}$$

$$\frac{1}{4} = t$$

It will take Manuel ¼ hour or 15 minutes to travel from the restaurant to the theater, therefore, he must leave the restaurant no later than 7:45 pm.

79.

$$I = Prt$$

$$500 = (19800)(0.0775)t$$

$$500 = 1534.5t$$

$$\frac{500}{1534.5} = \frac{1534.5t}{1534.5}$$

$$0.33 \approx t$$

It will be almost 4 months before Koki has her down payment.

2.4 Exercises

1. When we <u>multiply</u> or <u>divide</u> an inequality by a <u>negative</u> quantity, we must reverse the inequality symbol.

3. If the solution set to an inequality is given by the interval $[-4,\infty)$, the number -4 <u>is</u> a solution to the inequality.

5. $(-\infty, 2]$

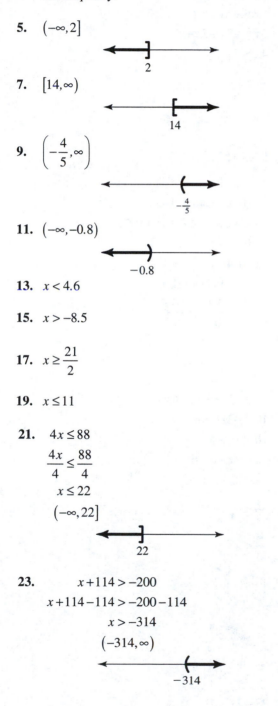

7. $[14,\infty)$

9. $\left(-\dfrac{4}{5},\infty\right)$

11. $(-\infty,-0.8)$

13. $x < 4.6$

15. $x > -8.5$

17. $x \geq \dfrac{21}{2}$

19. $x \leq 11$

21. $4x \leq 88$

$$\dfrac{4x}{4} \leq \dfrac{88}{4}$$

$$x \leq 22$$

$$(-\infty, 22]$$

23. $\qquad x+114 > -200$

$$x+114-114 > -200-114$$

$$x > -314$$

$$(-314,\infty)$$

25. $\qquad -7x \geq 49$

$$\dfrac{-7x}{-7} \leq \dfrac{49}{-7}$$

$$x \leq -7$$

$$(-\infty, -7]$$

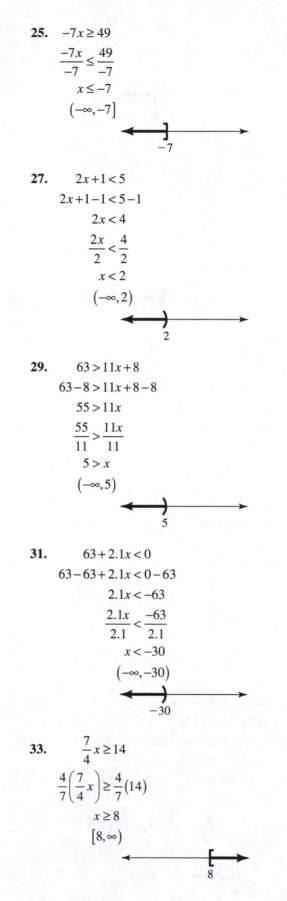

27. $\qquad 2x+1 < 5$

$$2x+1-1 < 5-1$$

$$2x < 4$$

$$\dfrac{2x}{2} < \dfrac{4}{2}$$

$$x < 2$$

$$(-\infty, 2)$$

29. $\qquad 63 > 11x+8$

$$63-8 > 11x+8-8$$

$$55 > 11x$$

$$\dfrac{55}{11} > \dfrac{11x}{11}$$

$$5 > x$$

$$(-\infty, 5)$$

31. $\qquad 63+2.1x < 0$

$$63-63+2.1x < 0-63$$

$$2.1x < -63$$

$$\dfrac{2.1x}{2.1} < \dfrac{-63}{2.1}$$

$$x < -30$$

$$(-\infty, -30)$$

33. $\qquad \dfrac{7}{4}x \geq 14$

$$\dfrac{4}{7}\left(\dfrac{7}{4}x\right) \geq \dfrac{4}{7}(14)$$

$$x \geq 8$$

$$[8,\infty)$$

35. $-x \le 11$

$$\frac{-x}{-1} \ge \frac{11}{-1}$$

$$x \ge -11$$

$$[-11, \infty)$$

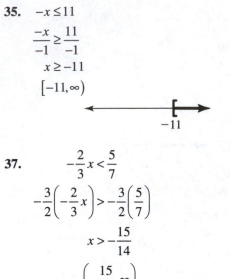

37. $-\dfrac{2}{3}x < \dfrac{5}{7}$

$$-\frac{3}{2}\left(-\frac{2}{3}x\right) > -\frac{3}{2}\left(\frac{5}{7}\right)$$

$$x > -\frac{15}{14}$$

$$\left(-\frac{15}{14}, \infty\right)$$

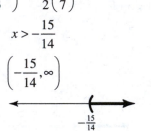

39. $5 - x \ge -16$

$$5 - 5 - x \ge -16 - 5$$

$$-x \ge -21$$

$$\frac{-x}{-1} \le \frac{-21}{-1}$$

$$x \le 21$$

$$(-\infty, 21]$$

41. $7x + 7 < 3 + 9x$

$$7x - 9x + 7 < 3 + 9x - 9x$$

$$-2x + 7 < 3$$

$$-2x + 7 - 7 < 3 - 7$$

$$-2x < -4$$

$$\frac{-2x}{-2} > \frac{-4}{-2}$$

$$x > 2$$

$$(2, \infty)$$

43. $-6x + 2 \ge 2(5 - x)$

$$-6x + 2 \ge 10 - 2x$$

$$-6x + 2x + 2 \ge 10 - 2x + 2x$$

$$-4x + 2 \ge 10$$

$$-4x + 2 - 2 \ge 10 - 2$$

$$-4x \ge 8$$

$$\frac{-4x}{-4} \le \frac{8}{-4}$$

$$x \le -2$$

$$(-\infty, -2]$$

45. $15 \le 1 - 7x$

$$15 - 1 \le 1 - 1 - 7x$$

$$14 \le -7x$$

$$\frac{14}{-7} \ge \frac{-7x}{-7}$$

$$-2 \ge x$$

$$(-\infty, -2]$$

47. $x > -3x + 5$

$$x + 3x > -3x + 3x + 5$$

$$4x > 5$$

$$\frac{4x}{4} > \frac{5}{4}$$

$$x > \frac{5}{4}$$

$$\left(\frac{5}{4}, \infty\right)$$

49. $0.3x + 1.4 \ge -0.4x$

$$0.3x + 0.4x + 1.4 \ge -0.4x + 0.4x$$

$$0.7x + 1.4 \ge 0$$

$$0.7x + 1.4 - 1.4 \ge 0 - 1.4$$

$$0.7x \ge -1.4$$

$$\frac{0.7x}{0.7} \ge \frac{-1.4}{0.7}$$

$$x \ge -2$$

$$[-2, \infty)$$

51. $10 < -3(x - 2) + 6x$

$$10 < -3x + 6 + 6x$$

$$10 < 3x + 6$$

$$10 - 6 < 3x + 6 - 6$$

$$4 < 3x$$

$$\frac{4}{3} < \frac{3x}{3}$$

$$\frac{4}{3} < x$$

$$\left(\frac{4}{3}, \infty\right)$$

53. $\dfrac{x}{2} - \dfrac{x}{3} \le \dfrac{7}{6}$

$$\frac{6}{1}\left(\frac{x}{2} - \frac{x}{3}\right) \le \frac{6}{1}\left(\frac{7}{6}\right)$$

$$3x - 2x \le 7$$

$$x \le 7$$

$$(-\infty, 7]$$

50

55.
$$-2(x+5)<3(2x-7)$$
$$-2x-10<6x-21$$
$$-2x-6x-10<6x-6x-21$$
$$-8x-10<-21$$
$$-8x-10+10<-21+10$$
$$-8x<-11$$
$$\frac{-8x}{-8}>\frac{-11}{-8}$$
$$x>\frac{11}{8}$$
$$\left(\frac{11}{8},\infty\right)$$

57. $7(x+2)+3(2x-1)>0$
$$7x+14+6x-3>0$$
$$13x+11>0$$
$$13x+11-11>0-11$$
$$13x>-11$$
$$\frac{13x}{13}>\frac{-11}{13}$$
$$x>-\frac{11}{13}$$
$$\left(-\frac{11}{13},\infty\right)$$

59.
$$8x+4\le13+8x$$
$$8x-8x+4\le13+8x-8x$$
$$4\le13$$
$$(-\infty,\infty)$$

61.
$$3(2x-8)>6x$$
$$6x-24>6x$$
$$6x-6x-24>6x-6x$$
$$-24>0$$
$$\varnothing$$

63.
$$-6h<2(4-3h)$$
$$-6h<8-6h$$
$$-6h+6h<8-6h+6h$$
$$0<8$$
$$(-\infty,\infty)$$

65. $2(4m-2)+m<11+9m$
$$8m-4+m<11+9m$$
$$9m-4<11+9m$$
$$9m-9m-4<11+9m-9m$$
$$-4<11$$
$$(-\infty,\infty)$$

67.
$$1.2x+3\ge0.6(2x+5)$$
$$1.2x+3\ge1.2x+3$$
$$1.2x-1.2x+3\ge1.2x-1.2x+3$$
$$3\ge3$$
$$(-\infty,\infty)$$

69. a) $6<2x$; answers will vary
Six is less than twice a number.

b) $2x-6$; answers will vary
six less than twice a number

71. Answers will vary; one example is: Sandra needs to take a cab from the airport. She can spend at most $20. If one company charges a flat rate of $9.75 and an additional $1.50 per mile, and she lives 4.3 miles away, can she afford to take the cab home?

73. Let x represent the number.
$$\frac{3}{4}+5x>x-3$$
$$\frac{3}{4}+5x-x>x-x-3$$
$$\frac{3}{4}+4x>-3$$
$$\frac{3}{4}-\frac{3}{4}+4x>-3-\frac{3}{4}$$
$$4x>-\frac{15}{4}$$
$$\frac{1}{4}(4x)>\frac{1}{4}\left(-\frac{15}{4}\right)$$
$$x>-\frac{15}{16}$$
$$\left(-\frac{15}{16},\infty\right)$$

75. Let x represent Priscilla's score on the third game.

$$\frac{115+88+x}{3} \geq 110$$

$$\frac{203+x}{3} \geq 110$$

$$\frac{3}{1}\left(\frac{203+x}{3}\right) \geq 3(110)$$

$$203+x \geq 330$$

$$203-203+x \geq 330-203$$

$$x \geq 127$$

She must score 127 points or higher on her third game.

77. Prepare We are asked to determine what Hector must score on his final exam in order to make a B in his math course.

Plan To average the scores we must add them together and divide by 5. This average must be greater than or equal to 80 in order to earn a B.

Process Let x represent Hector's score on the final exam.

$$\frac{77+83+x+70+x}{5} \geq 80$$

$$\frac{230+2x}{5} \geq 80$$

$$\frac{5}{1}\left(\frac{230+2x}{5}\right) \geq 5(80)$$

$$230+2x \geq 400$$

$$230-230+2x \geq 400-230$$

$$2x \geq 170$$

$$\frac{2x}{2} \geq \frac{170}{2}$$

$$x \geq 85$$

Hector must score 85% to 100% on the final exam in order to earn at least a B.

Ponder Does our answer seem reasonable? We can verify our answer by averaging the grades.

79. Prepare We are to determine which meal plans Candelle can afford.

Plan We must set up an inequality using the given information. Candelle's expenses cannot exceed $13,800 for the year.

Process Let x be the amount that Candelle can spend on a meal plan for one semester.

$$2(2,600)+2(2,300)+2(1,200)+2x \leq 13,800$$

$$12,200+2x \leq 13,800$$

$$12,200-12,200+2x \leq 13,800-12,200$$

$$2x \leq 1,600$$

$$\frac{2x}{2} \leq \frac{1,600}{2}$$

$$x \leq 800$$

Candelle must spend no more than $800 per semester on a meal plan. Therefore, Candelle can afford plans A or B.

Ponder Does our answer seem reasonable? Yes, We can verify our answer by adding up Candelle's expenses using $800 for a meal plan.

81.
$$\frac{3x-1}{9}+\frac{3x}{2} \leq \frac{7}{6}$$

$$\frac{18}{1}\left(\frac{3x-1}{9}+\frac{3x}{2}\right) \leq \frac{18}{1}\left(\frac{7}{6}\right)$$

$$6x-2+27x \leq 21$$

$$33x-2 \leq 21$$

$$33x-2+2 \leq 21+2$$

$$33x \leq 23$$

$$\frac{33x}{33} \leq \frac{23}{33}$$

$$x \leq \frac{23}{33}$$

$$\left(-\infty, \frac{23}{33}\right]$$

83.
$$\frac{7}{8}x+\frac{11}{8}x \leq 6.5-x$$

$$\frac{18}{8}x \leq 6.5-x$$

$$2.25x \leq 6.5-x$$

$$2.25x+x \leq 6.5-x+x$$

$$3.25x \leq 6.5$$

$$\frac{3.25x}{3.25} \leq \frac{6.5}{3.25}$$

$$x \leq 2$$

$$(-\infty, 2]$$

85. $4(3x-2)-3(7x-4)>-14$

$12x-8-21x+12>-14$

$-9x+4>-14$

$-9x+4-4>-14-4$

$-9x>-18$

$\dfrac{-9x}{-9}<\dfrac{-18}{-9}$

$x<2$

$(-\infty,2)$

87. $-15\le 11x-7(-2x+5)$

$-15\le 11x+14x-35$

$-15\le 25x-35$

$-15+35\le 25x-35+35$

$20\le 25x$

$\dfrac{20}{25}\le \dfrac{25x}{25}$

$\dfrac{4}{5}\le x$

$\left[\dfrac{4}{5},\infty\right)$

89. $-5(2x+4)<16x-(5-4x)$

$-10x-20<16x-5+4x$

$-10x-20x-20<20x-20x-5$

$-30x-20<-5$

$-30x-20+20<-5+20$

$-30x<15$

$\dfrac{-30x}{-30}>\dfrac{15}{-30}$

$x>-\dfrac{1}{2}$

$\left(-\dfrac{1}{2},\infty\right)$

2.5 Exercises

1. A compound inequality may be connected by either the word <u>and</u> or <u>or</u>.

3. The <u>closed</u> interval $[-3,7]$ as a solution set tells us that both -3 and 7 are <u>solutions</u> to the original inequality.

5. The goal when solving a double inequality is to <u>isolate</u> the variable in the <u>center</u>.

7. In the interval $\left[-\frac{1}{2},15\right)$, the number <u>15</u> is not a solution to the inequality, but the number $-\frac{1}{2}$ is a solution.

9. $(-\infty,-5)\cup[23,\infty)$

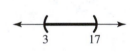

11. $(3,17)$

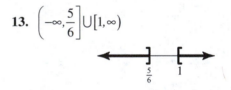

13. $\left(-\infty,\frac{5}{6}\right]\cup[1,\infty)$

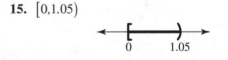

15. $[0,1.05)$

17. $\{\ \}$

18. <!-- blank -->

19. $(-\infty,\infty)$

21. $-2.3 \le x \le 11.57$

23. $-\frac{2}{3} < x < \frac{25}{4}$

25. $0 \le x < 5$

27. $-2 < x \le 75$

29. $x \le -2$ or $x > -1$

31. $x < 8$ or $x > 12$

33. $x \le -2.2$ or $x \ge 5.8$

35. $-\dfrac{12}{5} < x < 0$ or $x \ge 3$

37. $x > 12.5$ or $0.25x < 2.5$
$$\frac{0.25x}{0.25} < \frac{2.5}{0.25}$$
$$x < 10$$
$$(-\infty,10)\cup(12.5,\infty)$$

39. $x \le 5.06$ and $10x > 21$
$$\frac{10x}{10} > \frac{21}{10}$$
$$x > 2.1$$
$$(2.1,5.06]$$

41. $-6x < -36$ and $\dfrac{2}{3}x < 16$
$$\frac{-6x}{-6} > \frac{-36}{-6} \quad\text{and}\quad \frac{3}{2}\left(\frac{2}{3}x\right) < \frac{3}{2}(16)$$
$$x > 6 \qquad\text{and}\qquad x < 24$$
$$(6,24)$$

43. $3x-6 \le 2$ or $2x-1 < 0$
$$3x \le 8 \qquad\text{or}\qquad 2x < 1$$
$$\frac{3x}{3} \le \frac{8}{3} \quad\text{or}\quad \frac{2x}{2} < \frac{1}{2}$$
$$x \le \frac{8}{3} \quad\text{or}\quad x < \frac{1}{2}$$
$$\left(-\infty,\frac{8}{3}\right]$$

45. $17-6x \ge 65$ or $45x+4 < 14$
$$-6x \ge 48 \qquad\text{or}\qquad 45x < 10$$
$$\frac{-6x}{-6} \le \frac{48}{-6} \quad\text{or}\quad \frac{45x}{45} < \frac{10}{45}$$
$$x \le -8 \qquad\text{or}\qquad x < \frac{2}{9}$$
$$\left(-\infty,\frac{2}{9}\right)$$

47. $-7x+2>5$ or $-8x\le-32$

$\quad\quad -7x>3$ or $\dfrac{-8x}{-8}\ge\dfrac{-32}{-8}$

$\quad\quad \dfrac{-7x}{-7}<\dfrac{3}{-7}$ or $x\ge4$

$\quad\quad\quad x<-\dfrac{3}{7}$

$\quad\quad\left(-\infty,-\dfrac{3}{7}\right)\cup[4,\infty)$

49. $x+3<-7$ or $2x-1\ge9$

$\quad\quad x<-10$ or $\quad 2x\ge10$

$\quad\quad\quad\quad\quad\quad\quad \dfrac{2x}{2}\ge\dfrac{10}{2}$

$\quad\quad\quad\quad\quad\quad\quad\quad x\ge5$

$\quad\quad(-\infty,-10)\cup[5,\infty)$

51. $-(x+45)>3x+41$ and $6(x-5)<42$

$\quad -x-45>3x+41$ and $\quad 6x-30<42$

$\quad\quad -4x>86$ and $\quad\quad 6x<72$

$\quad\quad \dfrac{-4x}{-4}<\dfrac{86}{-4}$ and $\quad \dfrac{6x}{6}<\dfrac{72}{6}$

$\quad\quad x<-21.5$ and $\quad\quad x<12$

$\quad\quad\quad\quad (-\infty,-21.5)$

53. $5x+6\le2(x-7)$ or $-10x-3<3(6-x)$

$\quad 5x+6\le2x-14$ or $-10x-3<18-3x$

$\quad\quad 3x\le-20$ or $\quad\quad -7x<21$

$\quad\quad \dfrac{3x}{3}\le\dfrac{-20}{3}$ or $\quad \dfrac{-7x}{-7}>\dfrac{21}{-7}$

$\quad\quad x\le-\dfrac{20}{3}$ or $\quad\quad x>-3$

$\quad\quad\left(-\infty,-\dfrac{20}{3}\right]\cup(-3,\infty)$

55. $\quad 24<x+6<32$

$\quad 24-6<x+6-6<32-6$

$\quad\quad 18<x<26$

$\quad\quad (18,26)$

57. $\quad -15\le3x\le24$

$\quad \dfrac{-15}{3}\le\dfrac{3x}{3}\le\dfrac{24}{3}$

$\quad\quad -5\le x\le8$

$\quad\quad [-5,8]$

59. $\quad -235<5-2x\le-115$

$\quad -235-5<5-5-2x\le-115-5$

$\quad\quad -240<-2x\le-120$

$\quad \dfrac{-240}{-2}>\dfrac{-2x}{-2}\ge\dfrac{-120}{-2}$

$\quad\quad 60\le x<120$

$\quad\quad [60,120)$

61. $\quad \dfrac{1}{3}<\dfrac{x}{4}\le\dfrac{2}{3}$

$\quad \dfrac{4}{1}\left(\dfrac{1}{3}\right)<\dfrac{4}{1}\left(\dfrac{x}{4}\right)\le\dfrac{4}{1}\left(\dfrac{2}{3}\right)$

$\quad\quad \dfrac{4}{3}<x\le\dfrac{8}{3}$

$\quad\quad \left(\dfrac{4}{3},\dfrac{8}{3}\right]$

63. $\quad 0\le\dfrac{x-3}{4}\le4$

$\quad 4(0)\le\dfrac{4}{1}\left(\dfrac{x-3}{4}\right)\le4(4)$

$\quad\quad 0\le x-3\le16$

$\quad 0+3\le x-3+3\le16+3$

$\quad\quad 3\le x\le19$

$\quad\quad [3,19]$

65. $\quad -14<-11-x\le-3$

$\quad -14+11<-11+11-x\le-3+11$

$\quad\quad -3<-x\le8$

$\quad \dfrac{-3}{-1}>\dfrac{-x}{-1}\ge\dfrac{8}{-1}$

$\quad\quad -8\le x<3$

$\quad\quad [-8,3)$

67. $\quad 35.1<0.3x<124.2$

$\quad \dfrac{35.1}{0.3}<\dfrac{0.3x}{0.3}<\dfrac{124.2}{0.3}$

$\quad\quad 117<x<414$

$\quad\quad (117,414)$

69. $x<17$ and $x>-18$. $-18<x<17$. Answers will vary; one example is: I prefer the second form because it is easier to visualize that x is between -18 and 17 because it is physically written between the two numbers.

71. $\dfrac{2}{3}x - 4 \le 12 \qquad$ or $\quad \dfrac{1}{5}x + 10 > 15$

$\qquad \dfrac{2}{3}x \le 16 \qquad$ or $\qquad \dfrac{1}{5}x > 5$

$\dfrac{3}{2}\left(\dfrac{2}{3}x\right) \le \dfrac{3}{2}(16) \quad$ or $\quad \dfrac{5}{1}\left(\dfrac{1}{5}x\right) > 5(5)$

$\qquad x \le 24 \qquad$ or $\qquad x > 25$

$\qquad (-\infty, 24] \cup (25, \infty)$

73. $\dfrac{5}{9}(-69 - 32) \le C \le \dfrac{5}{9}(117 - 32)$

$\qquad \dfrac{5}{9}(-101) \le C \le \dfrac{5}{9}(85)$

$\qquad \dfrac{-505}{9} \le C \le \dfrac{425}{9}$

This is approximately the double inequality $-56° \le C \le 47°$.

75. a) $6,000 \le 55x + 4,625 \le 7,980$

b)

$\qquad 6,000 \le 55x + 4,625 \le 7,980$

$6,000 - 4,625 \le 55x + 4,625 - 4,625 \le 7,980 - 4,625$

$\qquad 1,375 \le 55x \le 3,355$

$\qquad \dfrac{1,375}{55} \le \dfrac{55x}{55} \le \dfrac{3,355}{55}$

$\qquad 25 \le x \le 61$

The Hudsons can afford between 25 and 61 hours of labor.

77. Prepare Felix wishes to determine the September sales his department needs in order to beat the record low and meet the high for the quarter.

Plan Write a double inequality with the record low as the lowest value, the record high as the greatest value, and the expression that represents the average sales for the third quarter of Felix's department in the middle.

Process Let x represent the sales for September.

$34,000 < \dfrac{38,790 + 56,235 + x}{3} < 75,000$

$34,000 < \dfrac{95,025 + x}{3} < 75,000$

$3(34,000) < \dfrac{3}{1}\left(\dfrac{95,025 + x}{3}\right) < 3(75,000)$

$102,000 < 95,025 + x < 225,000$

$102,000 - 95,025 < 95,025 - 95,025 + x < 225,000 - 95,025$

$\qquad 6,975 < x < 129,975$

The July sales should be between \$6,775 and \$129,975.

Ponder Does our answer make sense? Yes. We can easily compute the average for the three months to see that the conditions are satisfied.

79. $\dfrac{x}{3} + \dfrac{x}{4} > \dfrac{x}{6} + 1 \qquad$ or $\qquad \dfrac{x}{5} - \dfrac{x}{2} < 1$

$\dfrac{12}{1}\left(\dfrac{x}{3} + \dfrac{x}{4}\right) > \dfrac{12}{1}\left(\dfrac{x}{6} + 1\right) \quad$ or $\quad \dfrac{10}{1}\left(\dfrac{x}{5} - \dfrac{x}{2}\right) < 10(1)$

$\quad 4x + 3x > 2x + 12 \qquad$ or $\qquad 2x - 5x < 10$

$\qquad 7x > 2x + 12 \qquad$ or $\qquad -3x < 10$

$7x - 2x > 2x - 2x + 12 \quad$ or $\qquad \dfrac{-3x}{-3} > \dfrac{10}{-3}$

$\qquad 5x > 12 \qquad$ or $\qquad x > -\dfrac{10}{3}$

$\qquad \dfrac{5x}{5} > \dfrac{12}{5}$

$\qquad x > \dfrac{12}{5}$

$\qquad \left(-\dfrac{10}{3}, \infty\right)$

81. $\quad -4x - 15 > 5 + x \qquad$ and $\qquad 2(x+3) > 2(3 - 2x)$

$-4x - x - 15 > 5 + x - x \quad$ and $\qquad 2x + 6 > 6 - 4x$

$\qquad -5x - 15 > 5 \qquad$ and $\quad 2x + 4x + 6 > 6 - 4x + 4x$

$-5x - 15 + 15 > 5 + 15 \quad$ and $\qquad 6x + 6 > 6$

$\qquad -5x > 20 \qquad$ and $\quad 6x + 6 - 6 > 6 - 6$

$\qquad \dfrac{-5x}{-5} < \dfrac{20}{-5} \qquad$ and $\qquad 6x > 0$

$\qquad x < -4 \qquad$ and $\qquad \dfrac{6x}{6} > \dfrac{0}{6}$

$\qquad \qquad \qquad \qquad \qquad \qquad x > 0$

$\qquad \qquad \qquad \qquad \{ \ \}$

83.

$$2(x+7)+1 < 15 \qquad \text{or} \qquad -4(x-6) < -3$$
$$2x+14+1 < 15 \qquad \text{or} \qquad -4x+24 < -3$$
$$2x+15 < 15 \qquad \text{or} \quad -4x+24-24 < -3-24$$
$$2x+15-15 < 15-15 \quad \text{or} \qquad -4x < -27$$
$$2x < 0 \qquad \text{or} \qquad \frac{-4x}{-4} > \frac{-27}{-4}$$
$$\frac{2x}{2} < \frac{0}{2} \qquad \text{or} \qquad x > \frac{27}{4}$$
$$x < 0$$

$$(-\infty, 0) \cup \left(\frac{27}{4}, \infty\right)$$

85.

$$-\frac{2}{3}x+\frac{1}{4} > \frac{1}{2} \qquad \text{or} \qquad 15x+10 \le 32$$
$$\frac{12}{1}\left(-\frac{2}{3}x+\frac{1}{4}\right) > \frac{12}{1}\left(\frac{1}{2}\right) \quad \text{or} \quad 15x+10-10 \le 32-10$$
$$-8x+3 > 6 \qquad \text{or} \qquad 15x \le 22$$
$$-8x+3-3 > 6-3 \qquad \text{or} \qquad \frac{15x}{15} \le \frac{22}{15}$$
$$-8x > 3 \qquad \text{or} \qquad x \le \frac{22}{15}$$
$$\frac{-8x}{-8} < \frac{3}{-8}$$
$$x < -\frac{3}{8}$$

$$\left(-\infty, \frac{22}{15}\right]$$

87.

$$\frac{29}{2} \le \frac{15x-6}{2} < 21$$
$$\frac{2}{1}\left(\frac{29}{2}\right) \le \frac{2}{1}\left(\frac{15x-6}{2}\right) < 2(21)$$
$$29 \le 15x-6 < 42$$
$$29+6 \le 15x-6+6 < 42+6$$
$$35 \le 15x < 48$$
$$\frac{35}{15} \le \frac{15x}{15} < \frac{48}{15}$$
$$\frac{7}{3} \le x < \frac{16}{5}$$
$$\left[\frac{7}{3}, \frac{16}{5}\right)$$

89.

$$\frac{3}{2}x < -15 \qquad \text{and} \qquad 7x+13 \ge -15$$
$$\frac{2}{3}\left(\frac{3}{2}x\right) < \frac{2}{3}(-15) \quad \text{and} \quad 7x+13-13 \ge -15-13$$
$$x < -10 \qquad \text{and} \qquad 7x \ge -28$$
$$\frac{7x}{7} \ge \frac{-28}{7}$$
$$x \ge -4$$

$$\{\ \}$$

2.6 Exercises

1. When solving an absolute value equation, the first thing we should do is <u>isolate</u> the absolute value on the left-hand side. Then, check to see if the constant on the right-hand side is strictly <u>positive</u>.

3. If the constant on the right-hand side is zero, and absolute value equation may have <u>one</u> solution.

5. An absolute value inequality involving "greater than" may have <u>infinite</u> real numbers as its solution, if the constant on the right-hand side is negative.

7. An absolute value equation may have <u>two</u> solutions, if the constant on the right-hand side is positive.

9. $|x| = 23$
   $x = -23$ or $x = 23$
   $\{-23, 23\}$

11. $|x + 1| = 109$
   $x + 1 = -109$ or $x + 1 = 109$
   $x = -110$ or $x = 108$
   $\{-110, 108\}$

13. $|5x| = 55$
   $5x = -55$ or $5x = 55$
   $x = -11$ or $x = 11$
   $\{-11, 11\}$

15. $|-8x| = 64$
   $-8x = -64$ or $-8x = 64$
   $x = 8$ or $x = -8$
   $\{-8, 8\}$

17. $\left|\dfrac{x}{2}\right| = \dfrac{3}{4}$
   $\dfrac{x}{2} = -\dfrac{3}{4}$ or $\dfrac{x}{2} = \dfrac{3}{4}$
   $\dfrac{2}{1}\left(\dfrac{x}{2}\right) = \dfrac{2}{1}\left(-\dfrac{3}{4}\right)$ or $\dfrac{2}{1}\left(\dfrac{x}{2}\right) = \dfrac{2}{1}\left(\dfrac{3}{4}\right)$
   $x = -\dfrac{3}{2}$ or $x = \dfrac{3}{2}$
   $\left\{-\dfrac{3}{2}, \dfrac{3}{2}\right\}$

19. $\left|-\dfrac{2}{3}x\right| = \dfrac{4}{5}$
   $-\dfrac{2}{3}x = -\dfrac{4}{5}$ or $-\dfrac{2}{3}x = \dfrac{4}{5}$
   $-\dfrac{3}{2}\left(-\dfrac{2}{3}x\right) = -\dfrac{3}{2}\left(-\dfrac{4}{5}\right)$ or $-\dfrac{3}{2}\left(-\dfrac{2}{3}x\right) = -\dfrac{3}{2}\left(\dfrac{4}{5}\right)$
   $x = \dfrac{6}{5}$ or $x = -\dfrac{6}{5}$
   $\left\{-\dfrac{6}{5}, \dfrac{6}{5}\right\}$

21. $\left|\dfrac{7 - x}{3}\right| = 110$
   $\dfrac{7 - x}{3} = -110$ or $\dfrac{7 - x}{3} = 110$
   $\dfrac{3}{1}\left(\dfrac{7 - x}{3}\right) = 3(-110)$ or $\dfrac{3}{1}\left(\dfrac{7 - x}{3}\right) = 3(110)$
   $7 - x = -330$ or $7 - x = 330$
   $-x = -337$ or $-x = 323$
   $\dfrac{-x}{-1} = \dfrac{-337}{-1}$ or $\dfrac{-x}{-1} = \dfrac{323}{-1}$
   $x = 337$ or $x = -323$
   $\{-323, 337\}$

23. $|17 - 3x| = 12$
   $17 - 3x = -12$ or $17 - 3x = 12$
   $-3x = -29$ or $-3x = -5$
   $\dfrac{-3x}{-3} = \dfrac{-29}{-3}$ or $\dfrac{-3x}{-3} = \dfrac{-5}{-3}$
   $x = \dfrac{29}{3}$ or $x = \dfrac{5}{3}$
   $\left\{\dfrac{5}{3}, \dfrac{29}{3}\right\}$

25. $|3x - 2| = 6$
   $3x - 2 = -6$ or $3x - 2 = 6$
   $3x = -4$ or $3x = 8$
   $\dfrac{3x}{3} = \dfrac{-4}{3}$ or $\dfrac{3x}{3} = \dfrac{8}{3}$
   $x = -\dfrac{4}{3}$ or $x = \dfrac{8}{3}$
   $\left\{-\dfrac{4}{3}, \dfrac{8}{3}\right\}$

27.
$$|5x-3|+11=23$$
$$|5x-3|=12$$
$$5x-3=-12 \quad \text{or} \quad 5x-3=12$$
$$5x=-9 \quad \text{or} \quad 5x=15$$
$$\frac{5x}{5}=\frac{-9}{5} \quad \text{or} \quad \frac{5x}{5}=\frac{15}{5}$$
$$x=-\frac{9}{5} \quad \text{or} \quad x=3$$
$$\left\{-\frac{9}{5},3\right\}$$

29.
$$\left|\frac{1}{2}x-1\right|=3$$
$$\frac{1}{2}x-1=-3 \quad \text{or} \quad \frac{1}{2}x-1=3$$
$$\frac{1}{2}x=-2 \quad \text{or} \quad \frac{1}{2}x=4$$
$$\frac{2}{1}\left(\frac{1}{2}x\right)=2(-2) \quad \text{or} \quad \frac{2}{1}\left(\frac{1}{2}x\right)=2(4)$$
$$x=-4 \quad \text{or} \quad x=8$$
$$\{-4,8\}$$

31.
$$|4x+2|-12=-12$$
$$|4x+2|=0$$
$$4x+2=0$$
$$4x=-2$$
$$\frac{4x}{4}=\frac{-2}{4}$$
$$x=-\frac{1}{2}$$
$$\left\{-\frac{1}{2}\right\}$$

33.
$$|6-5x|+8=10$$
$$|6-5x|=2$$
$$6-5x=-2 \quad \text{or} \quad 6-5x=2$$
$$-5x=-8 \quad \text{or} \quad -5x=-4$$
$$\frac{-5x}{-5}=\frac{-8}{-5} \quad \text{or} \quad \frac{-5x}{-5}=\frac{-4}{-5}$$
$$x=\frac{8}{5} \quad \text{or} \quad x=\frac{4}{5}$$
$$\left\{\frac{4}{5},\frac{8}{5}\right\}$$

35.
$$\left|\frac{1}{2}-x\right|+22=12$$
$$\left|\frac{1}{2}-x\right|=-10$$
$$\{\ \}$$

37.
$$\left|\frac{3}{4}x+\frac{1}{4}\right|+6=6$$
$$\left|\frac{3}{4}x+\frac{1}{4}\right|=0$$
$$\frac{3}{4}x+\frac{1}{4}=0$$
$$\frac{3}{4}x=-\frac{1}{4}$$
$$\frac{4}{3}\left(\frac{3}{4}x\right)=\frac{4}{3}\left(-\frac{1}{4}\right)$$
$$x=-\frac{1}{3}$$
$$\left\{-\frac{1}{3}\right\}$$

39.
$$|0.2x+3|-4.2=0$$
$$|0.2x+3|=4.2$$
$$0.2x+3=-4.2 \quad \text{or} \quad 0.2x+3=4.2$$
$$0.2x=-7.2 \quad \text{or} \quad 0.2x=1.2$$
$$\frac{0.2x}{0.2}=\frac{-7.2}{0.2} \quad \text{or} \quad \frac{0.2x}{0.2}=\frac{1.2}{0.2}$$
$$x=-36 \quad \text{or} \quad x=6$$
$$\{-36,6\}$$

41.
$$6+|2x+1|=2$$
$$|2x+1|=-4$$
$$\{\ \}$$

43.
$$|x-6|=|5-3x|$$
$$x-6=5-3x \quad \text{or} \quad x-6=-(5-3x)$$
$$4x=11 \quad \text{or} \quad x-6=-5+3x$$
$$x=\frac{11}{4} \quad \text{or} \quad -2x=1$$
$$x=-\frac{1}{2}$$
$$\left\{-\frac{1}{2},\frac{11}{4}\right\}$$

45.
$$|-3x-14|=|9+11x|$$
$$-3x-14=9+11x \quad \text{or} \quad -3x-14=-(9+11x)$$
$$-14x=23 \quad\quad\quad \text{or} \quad -3x-14=-9-11x$$
$$x=-\frac{23}{14} \quad\quad \text{or} \quad\quad 8x=5$$
$$x=\frac{5}{8}$$
$$\left\{-\frac{23}{14},\frac{5}{8}\right\}$$

47.
$$|x+3|=|x-15|$$
$$x+3=x-15 \quad \text{or} \quad x+3=-(x-15)$$
$$0=-18 \quad\quad \text{or} \quad x+3=-x+15$$
$$\text{or} \quad 2x=12$$
$$x=6$$
$$\{6\}$$

49.
$$|3x+5|=|7+3x|$$
$$3x+5=7+3x \quad \text{or} \quad 3x+5=-(7+3x)$$
$$5=7 \quad\quad\quad \text{or} \quad 3x+5=-7-3x$$
$$6x=-12$$
$$x=-2$$
$$\{-2\}$$

51. $|x|<6$
$$-6<x<6$$
$$(-6,6)$$

53. $|6x|\le 12$
$$-12\le 6x\le 12$$
$$\frac{-12}{6}\le\frac{6x}{6}\le\frac{12}{6}$$
$$-2\le x\le 2$$
$$[-2,2]$$

55. $|x-6|<78$
$$-78<x-6<78$$
$$-78+6<x-6+6<78+6$$
$$-72<x<84$$
$$(-72,84)$$

57.
$$|12x+5|\le 65$$
$$-65\le 12x+5\le 65$$
$$-65-5\le 12x+5-5\le 65-5$$
$$-70\le 12x\le 60$$
$$\frac{-70}{12}\le\frac{12x}{12}\le\frac{60}{12}$$
$$-\frac{35}{6}\le x\le 5$$
$$\left[-\frac{35}{6},5\right]$$

59.
$$|17-2x|<19$$
$$-19<17-2x<19$$
$$-19-17<17-17-2x<19-17$$
$$-36<-2x<2$$
$$\frac{-36}{-2}>\frac{-2x}{-2}>\frac{2}{-2}$$
$$-1<x<18$$
$$(-1,18)$$

61.
$$\left|\frac{x-8}{5}\right|\le 6$$
$$-6\le\frac{x-8}{5}\le 6$$
$$5(-6)\le\frac{5}{1}\left(\frac{x-8}{5}\right)\le 5(6)$$
$$-30\le x-8\le 30$$
$$-30+8\le x-8+8\le 30+8$$
$$-22\le x\le 38$$
$$[-22,38]$$

63.
$$|5x - 13| + 16 < 18$$
$$|5x - 13| + 16 - 16 < 18 - 16$$
$$|5x - 13| < 2$$
$$-2 < 5x - 13 < 2$$
$$-2 + 13 < 5x - 13 + 13 < 2 + 13$$
$$11 < 5x < 15$$
$$\frac{11}{5} < \frac{5x}{5} < \frac{15}{5}$$
$$\frac{11}{5} < x < 3$$
$$\left(\frac{11}{5}, 3\right)$$

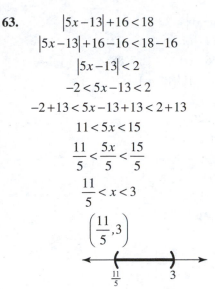

65.
$$\left|\frac{2x}{5} - \frac{2}{3}\right| \leq \frac{1}{15}$$
$$-\frac{1}{15} \leq \frac{2x}{5} - \frac{2}{3} \leq \frac{1}{15}$$
$$\frac{15}{1}\left(-\frac{1}{15}\right) \leq \frac{15}{1}\left(\frac{2x}{5} - \frac{2}{3}\right) \leq \frac{15}{1}\left(\frac{1}{15}\right)$$
$$-1 \leq 6x - 10 \leq 1$$
$$-1 + 10 \leq 6x - 10 + 10 \leq 1 + 10$$
$$9 \leq 6x \leq 11$$
$$\frac{9}{6} \leq \frac{6x}{6} \leq \frac{11}{6}$$
$$\frac{3}{2} \leq x \leq \frac{11}{6}$$
$$\left[\frac{3}{2}, \frac{11}{6}\right]$$

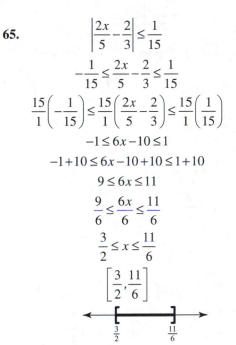

67.
$$|12x + 5| + 27 < 17$$
$$|12x + 5| + 27 - 27 < 17 - 27$$
$$|12x + 5| < -10$$
$$\{\ \}$$

69.
$$|x| \geq 26$$
$$x \leq -26 \quad \text{or} \quad x \geq 26$$
$$(-\infty, -26] \cup [26, \infty)$$

71.
$$|10x| > 130$$
$$10x < -130 \quad \text{or} \quad 10x > 130$$
$$\frac{10x}{10} < \frac{-130}{10} \quad \text{or} \quad \frac{10x}{10} > \frac{130}{10}$$
$$x < -13 \quad \text{or} \quad x > 13$$
$$(-\infty, -13) \cup (13, \infty)$$

73.
$$|x - 18| \geq 26$$
$$x - 18 \leq -26 \quad \text{or} \quad x - 18 \geq 26$$
$$x \leq -8 \quad \text{or} \quad x \geq 44$$
$$(-\infty, -8] \cup [44, \infty)$$

75.
$$|8x + 5| > 69$$
$$8x + 5 < -69 \quad \text{or} \quad 8x + 5 > 69$$
$$8x < -74 \quad \text{or} \quad 8x > 64$$
$$\frac{8x}{8} < \frac{-74}{8} \quad \text{or} \quad \frac{8x}{8} > \frac{64}{8}$$
$$x < -\frac{37}{4} \quad \text{or} \quad x > 8$$
$$\left(-\infty, -\frac{37}{4}\right) \cup (8, \infty)$$

77.
$$|16 - 4x| \geq 28$$
$$16 - 4x \leq -28 \quad \text{or} \quad 16 - 4x \geq 28$$
$$-4x \leq -44 \quad \text{or} \quad -4x \geq 12$$
$$\frac{-4x}{-4} \geq \frac{-44}{-4} \quad or \quad \frac{-4x}{-4} \leq \frac{12}{-4}$$
$$x \geq 11 \quad \text{or} \quad x \leq -3$$
$$(-\infty, -3] \cup [11, \infty)$$

61

79.
$$|5x-10|-12>34$$
$$|5x-10|>46$$
$$5x-10<-46 \quad \text{or} \quad 5x-10>46$$
$$5x<-36 \quad \text{or} \quad 5x>56$$
$$\frac{5x}{5}<\frac{-36}{5} \quad \text{or} \quad \frac{5x}{5}>\frac{56}{5}$$
$$x<-\frac{36}{5} \quad \text{or} \quad x>\frac{56}{5}$$
$$\left(-\infty,-\frac{36}{5}\right)\cup\left(\frac{56}{5},\infty\right)$$

81.
$$\left|\frac{x-5}{4}\right|+4\geq6$$
$$\left|\frac{x-5}{4}\right|\geq2$$
$$\frac{x-5}{4}\leq-2 \quad \text{or} \quad \frac{x-5}{4}\geq2$$
$$\frac{4}{1}\left(\frac{x-5}{4}\right)\leq4(-2) \quad \text{or} \quad \frac{4}{1}\left(\frac{x-5}{4}\right)\geq4(2)$$
$$x-5\leq-8 \quad \text{or} \quad x-5\geq8$$
$$x\leq-3 \quad \text{or} \quad x\geq13$$
$$(-\infty,-3]\cup[13,\infty)$$

83. $\left|\frac{5x}{3}+1\right|+24\geq18$
$$\left|\frac{5x}{3}+1\right|\geq-6$$
$$(-\infty,\infty)$$

85. a) $\{\ \}$ The absolute value of any number is always greater than or equal to zero and cannot be a negative number. Thus the solution set is the empty set.

b) $\{\ \}$ The absolute value of any number is always greater than or equal to zero, thus the solution set is the empty set.

c) $(-\infty,\infty)$ The absolute value of any number is always greater than a negative number, thus the solutions set is the set of all real numbers.

87.
$$|x-16|>72$$
$$x-16<-72 \quad \text{or} \quad x-16>72$$
$$x<-56 \quad \text{or} \qquad x>88$$
$$(-\infty,-56)\cup(88,\infty)$$

89.
$$|100x|\leq400$$
$$-400\leq100x\leq400$$
$$\frac{-400}{100}\leq\frac{100x}{100}\leq\frac{400}{100}$$
$$-4\leq x\leq4$$
$$[-4,4]$$

91.
$$\left|\frac{7-3x}{5}\right|-3=-1$$
$$\left|\frac{7-3x}{5}\right|=2$$
$$\frac{7-3x}{5}=-2 \quad \text{or} \quad \frac{7-3x}{5}=2$$
$$\frac{5}{1}\left(\frac{7-3x}{5}\right)=5(-2) \quad \text{or} \quad \frac{5}{1}\left(\frac{7-3x}{5}\right)=5(2)$$
$$7-3x=-10 \quad \text{or} \quad 7-3x=10$$
$$-3x=-17 \quad \text{or} \quad -3x=3$$
$$\frac{-3x}{-3}=\frac{-17}{-3} \quad \text{or} \quad \frac{-3x}{-3}=\frac{3}{-3}$$
$$x=\frac{17}{3} \quad \text{or} \quad x=-1$$
$$\left\{-1,\frac{17}{3}\right\}$$

93.
$$|6-4x|=|4x-7|$$
$$6-4x=4x-7 \quad \text{or} \quad 6-4x=-(4x-7)$$
$$-8x=-13 \quad \text{or} \quad 6-4x=-4x+7$$
$$\frac{-8x}{-8}=\frac{-13}{-8} \quad \text{or} \qquad 6=7$$
$$x=\frac{13}{8}$$
$$\left\{\frac{13}{8}\right\}$$

95.
$$\left|-2x+\frac{4}{5}\right|<14$$

$$-14<-2x+\frac{4}{5}<14$$

$$5(-14)<\frac{5}{1}\left(-2x+\frac{4}{5}\right)<5(14)$$

$$-70<-10x+4<70$$

$$-74<-10x<66$$

$$\frac{-74}{-10}>\frac{-10x}{-10}>\frac{66}{-10}$$

$$-\frac{33}{5}<x<\frac{37}{5}$$

$$\left(-\frac{33}{5},\frac{37}{5}\right)$$

97. $\left|-18x+1\right|+6=4$

$\left|-18x+1\right|=-2$

$\{\ \}$

99.
$$6+\left|x-18\right|\geq13$$

$$\left|x-18\right|\geq7$$

$$x-18\leq-7\quad\text{or}\quad x-18\geq7$$

$$x\leq11\quad\text{or}\quad x\geq25$$

$$(-\infty,11]\cup[25,\infty)$$

101.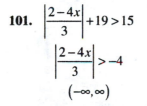

$$\left|\frac{2-4x}{3}\right|+19>15$$

$$\left|\frac{2-4x}{3}\right|>-4$$

$$(-\infty,\infty)$$

2.7 Exercises

1. If we are kayaking upstream, <u>against</u> the current, we would be <u>decreasing</u> the rate of the kayak in still water by the current's rate.

3. When setting up an equation for a mixture problem involving pure acid, the percentage of acid would be <u>100%</u>.

5. When setting up a mixture problem involving 100% boric acid, 35% boric acid, and 50% boric acid, the two percentages we are mixing together would be <u>35%</u> and <u>100%</u>.

7. **Prepare** We are to determine how long it will take Johanna to catch Katherine.

   Plan We will set up a chart to organize the information given in the problem. We will then use this information to write and solve a linear equation with one variable.

   Process Let t represent the amount of time it takes Johanna to catch Katherine.

	Rate •	Time	=	Distance
Katherine	4mph	$t+1.5$ (in hours)		$D_1 = 4(t+1.5)$ (in miles)
Johanna	16mph	t (in hours)		$D_2 = 16t$ (in miles)

   $$D_1 = D_2$$
   $$4(t+1.5) = 16t$$
   $$4t + 6 = 16t$$
   $$6 = 12t$$
   $$\frac{1}{2} = t$$

   It will take Johanna ½ hour to catch Katherine.

   Ponder Does our answer seem reasonable? Yes. We can check to see if they traveled the same distance.

9. **Prepare** We are to determine how long it will take the military jet to overtake the subsonic airplane.

   Plan We will set up a chart to organize the information given in the problem. We will then use this information to write and solve a linear equation with one variable.

   Process Let t represent the amount of time it takes the military jet to overtake the subsonic airplane.

	Rate •	Time	=	Distance
Military Jet	1,476mph	t (in hours)		$D_1 = 1,476t$ (in miles)
Subsonic Airplane	492mph	$t+4$ (in hours)		$D_2 = 492(t+4)$ (in miles)

$$D_1 = D_2$$
$$1,476t = 492(t+4)$$
$$1,476t = 492t + 1,968$$
$$984t = 1,968$$
$$t = 2$$

It will take the military jet 2 hours to overtake the subsonic airplane.

Ponder Does our answer seem reasonable? Yes. We can check to see if they traveled the same distance.

11. **Prepare** We are to determine how long it will take for the O'Connells and the Smiths to be 5 miles apart.

Plan We will set up a chart to organize the information given in the problem. We will then use this information to write and solve a linear equation with one variable.

Process Let t represent the amount of time the O'Connells drive after the stop at the railroad crossing.

	Rate	•	Time	=	Distance
O'Connells	75mph		t (in hours)		$D_1 = 75t$ (in miles)
Smiths	65mph		$t + 0.25$ (in hours)		$D_2 = 65(t+0.25)$ (in miles)

$$D_2 - D_1 = 5$$
$$65(t+0.25) - 75t = 5$$
$$-10t + 16.25 = 5$$
$$-10t = -11.25$$
$$t = 1.125$$

It will take the O'Connells 1.125 or $1\frac{1}{8}$ hours to be within talking distance of the Smiths.

Ponder Does our answer seem reasonable? Yes. We can check to see if their difference between their distances is 5 miles.

13. **Prepare** We are to determine the speed of the blimp in still air.

Plan We will set up a chart to organize the information given in the problem. We will then use this information to write and solve a linear equation with one variable.

Process Let r represent the speed of the blimp in still air.

	Rate	•	Time	=	Distance
Tailwind	$r + 15$ mph		6 hours		$D_1 = (r+15)6$ (in miles)
Headwind	$r - 5$ mph		10 hours		$D_2 = (r-5)10$ (in miles)

65

$$D_1 + D_2 = 600$$
$$(r+15)6 + (r-5)10 = 600$$
$$6r + 90 + 10r - 50 = 600$$
$$16r + 40 = 600$$
$$16r = 560$$
$$r = 35$$

The speed of the blimp in still air is 35 miles per hour.

Ponder Does our answer seem reasonable? Yes. It seems reasonable that a blimp could travel 35 miles per hour in still air.

15. **Prepare** We are to determine how much Aneesa invested in each of the two simple interest accounts.

Plan We will set up a chart to organize the information given in the problem. We will then use this information to write and solve a linear equation with one variable.

Process Let p represent the amount invested at 2% interest.

$P \cdot r \cdot t = I$			
3% Investment	$p + 3,000$	0.03	1	$I_1 = 0.03(p + 3,000)$
2% Investment	p	0.02	1	$I_2 = 0.02p$

$$I_1 + I_2 = 690$$
$$0.03(p + 3,000) + 0.02p = 690$$
$$0.03p + 90 + 0.02p = 690$$
$$0.05p = 600$$
$$p = 12,000$$

Aneesa invested $12,000 at 2% interest and $15,000 at 3% interest.

Ponder Does our answer seem reasonable? Yes. The interest earned at 3% is $0.03(15,000) = \$450$, and the interest earned at 2% is $0.02(12,000) = \$240$. The sum of the interest from the two investments is $\$450 + \$240 = \$690$.

17. **Prepare** We are to determine how much the honor society invested at 8% interest.

Plan We will set up a chart to organize the information given in the problem. We will then use this information to write and solve a linear equation with one variable.

Process Let p represent the amount invested at 7% interest.

$P \cdot r \cdot t = I$			
7% Investment	p	0.07	1	$I_1 = 0.07p$
8% Investment	$500 - p$	0.08	1	$I_2 = 0.08(500 - p)$

$$I_1 + I_2 = 38$$
$$0.07p + 0.08(500 - p) = 38$$
$$0.07p + 40 - 0.08p = 38$$
$$-0.01p = -2$$
$$p = 200$$

The honor society invested $300 at 8% interest.

Ponder Does our answer seem reasonable? Yes. The interest earned at 7% is $0.07(200) = \$14$, and the interest earned at 8% is $0.08(300) = \$24$. The sum of the interest from the two investments is $\$14 + \$24 = \$38$.

19. **Prepare** We are to determine how much Professor Cadena invested at each of two simple interest rates.

Plan We will set up a chart to organize the information given in the problem. We will then use this information to write and solve a linear equation with one variable.

Process Let p represent the amount invested at 7% interest.

$P \cdot r \cdot t = I$				
7% Investment	p	0.07	1	$I_1 = 0.07p$
8% Investment	$p + 6,000$	0.08	1	$I_2 = 0.08(p + 6,000)$

$$I_1 + I_2 = 780$$
$$0.07p + 0.08(p + 6,000) = 780$$
$$0.07p + 0.08p + 480 = 780$$
$$0.15p = 300$$
$$p = 2,000$$

Professor Cadena invested $2,000 at 7% interest and $8,000 at 8% interest.

Ponder Does our answer seem reasonable? Yes. The interest earned at 7% is $0.07(2,000) = \$140$, and the interest earned at 8% is $0.08(8,000) = \$640$. The sum of the interest from the two investments is $\$140 + \$640 = \$780$.

21. **Prepare** We are to determine how much Tiffany invested at each of two simple interest rates.

Plan We will set up a chart to organize the information given in the problem. We will then use this information to write and solve a linear equation with one variable.

Process Let p represent the amount invested at 5.5% interest.

$P \cdot r \cdot t = I$				
5.5% Investment	p	0.055	1	$I_1 = 0.055p$
7.7% Investment	$p + 2,500$	0.077	1	$I_2 = 0.077(p + 2,500)$

$$I_1 + 275 = I_2$$
$$0.055p + 275 = 0.077(p + 2,500)$$
$$0.055p + 275 = 0.077p + 192.5$$
$$-0.022p = -82.5$$
$$p = 3,750$$

The honor society invested $3,750 at 5.5% interest and $6,250 at 7.7% interest.

Ponder Does our answer seem reasonable? Yes. The interest earned at 5.5% is $0.055(3,750) = \$206.25$, and the interest earned at 7.7% is $0.077(6,250) = \$481.25$. The difference between the interest from the two investments is $\$481.25 - \$206.25 = \$275$.

23. **Prepare** We want to determine how much 100% pineapple juice Olaf should mix with 50 cups of 10% pineapple juice liquid to make a punch containing 20% pineapple juice.

Plan We will set up a chart to organize the information given in the problem. We will then use this information to write and solve a linear equation with one variable.

Process Let x represent the number of cups of 100% pineapple juice needed for the mixture.

	100% Pineapple Juice	10% Pineapple Juice	20% Pineapple Juice
# of cups	x	50	$x+50$
% pineapple juice	1	0.10	0.20

$$x + 0.10(50) = 0.20(x + 50)$$
$$x + 5 = 0.20x + 10$$
$$0.80x = 5$$
$$x = 6.25$$

Olaf will need 6.25 cups of 100% pineapple juice.

Ponder Does our answer seem reasonable? Yes. There are $6.25(100\%) = 6.25$ cups of pineapple juice in the first container and $50(10\%) = 5$ cups of pineapple juice in the second container. Therefore, there are $6.25 + 5 = 11.25$ cups of pineapple juice in the two containers combined. In the final mixture, there are $(6.25 + 50)(20\%) = 11.25$ cups of pineapple juice. Since this is equal to the amount we obtained from both containers, our answer is correct.

25. **Prepare** We want to determine how much 60% acid solution the chemist should mix with some 100% acid solution to make an 80% acid solution.

Plan We will set up a chart to organize the information given in the problem. We will then use this information to write and solve a linear equation with one variable.

Process Let x represent the number of liters of 60% acid solution needed for the mixture.

	60% Acid Solution	100% Acid Solution	80% Acid Solution
# of liters	x	$6.3 - x$	6.3
% acid	0.60	1	0.80

$$0.60x + 1(6.3 - x) = 6.3(0.80)$$
$$0.60x + 6.3 - x = 5.04$$
$$-0.40x = -1.26$$
$$x = 3.15$$

The chemist will need 3.15 liters of 60% acid solution.

Ponder Does our answer seem reasonable? Yes. There are $3.15(60\%) = 1.89$ liters of acid in the first container and $(6.3 - 3.15)(100\%) = 3.15$ liters of acid in the second container. Therefore, there are $3.15 + 1.89 = 5.04$ liters of acid in the two containers combined. In the final mixture, there are $6.3(80\%) = 5.04$ liters of acid. Since this is equal to the amount we obtained from both containers, our answer is correct.

27. **Prepare** We want to determine how much 40% salt solution Josie should mix with some 70% salt solution to make a 50% salt solution.

Plan We will set up a chart to organize the information given in the problem. We will then use this information to write and solve a linear equation with one variable.

Process Let x represent the number of gallons of 40% salt solution needed for the mixture.

	40% Salt Solution	70% Salt Solution	50% Salt Solution
# of gallons	x	$12-x$	12
% salt	0.40	0.70	0.50

$$0.40x+0.70(12-x)=0.50(12)$$
$$0.40x+8.4-0.7x=6$$
$$-0.3x=-2.4$$
$$x=8$$

Josie will need 8 gallons of 40% salt solution.

Ponder Does our answer seem reasonable? Yes. There are $8(40\%)=3.2$ gallons of salt in the first container and $(12-8)(70\%)=2.8$ gallons of salt in the second container. Therefore, there are $3.2+2.8=6$ gallons of salt in the two containers combined. In the final mixture, there are $12(50\%)=6$ gallons of salt. Since this is equal to the amount we obtained from both containers, our answer is correct.

29. **Prepare** We want to determine the number of pounds of cashews the Athletic Club will be able to purchase at $12 per pound to mix with peanuts that cost $4 per pound in order to make a mixture that costs $6 per pound.

    Plan We will set up a chart to organize the information given in the problem. We will then use this information to write and solve a linear equation with one variable.

    Process Let x represent the number of pounds of cashews the club will be able to purchase.

	Cashews	Peanuts	Mixture
# of pounds	x	3	$x+3$
price per pound	$12	$4	$6

$$12x+3(4)=6(x+3)$$
$$12x+12=6x+18$$
$$6x=6$$
$$x=1$$

The Athletic Club will be able to purchase 1 pound of cashews.

Ponder Does our answer seem reasonable? Yes. The total cost of the cashews is $1(\$12)=\$12$ and the total cost of the peanuts is $3(\$4)=\$12$. Therefore, the total cost for the nuts is $\$12+\$12=\$24$. The cost of the mix is $(1+3)(\$6)=\$24$. Since the cost for the mix is the same as the total cost of the nuts, our answer is correct.

31. **Prepare** We want to determine the number of quarts of creamy peanut butter that Mrs. Humphries need to purchase to mix with some 20% smooth peanut butter to make 2 quarts of 50% smooth peanut butter.

    Plan We will set up a chart to organize the information given in the problem. We will then use this information to write and solve a linear equation with one variable.

    Process Let x represent the number of quarts of creamy peanut butter that Mrs. Humphries will need to purchase.

	100% Smooth Peanut Butter	20% Smooth Peanut Butter	50% Smooth Peanut Butter
# of quarts	x	$2-x$	2
% smooth	1	0.20	0.50

$$x + 0.20(2 - x) = 2(0.50)$$
$$x + 0.40 - 0.20x = 1$$
$$0.80x = 0.60$$
$$x = 0.75$$

Mrs. Humphries must purchase 0.75 quarts of creamy peanut butter.

Ponder Does our answer seem reasonable? Yes. There is $0.75(100\%) = 0.75$ quart of creamy peanut butter in the first container and $(2 - 0.75)(20\%) = .25$ quart of smooth peanut butter in the second container. Therefore, there is $0.75 + 0.25 = 1$ quart of smooth peanut butter in the two containers combined. In the final mixture, there is $2(50\%) = 1$ quart of smooth peanut butter. Since this is equal to the amount we obtained from both containers, our answer is correct.

Chapter 2 Review Problem Set

1. Yes, because the exponent on x is positive one.

2. No, because the highest power of x is two.

3. No, because there are two variables.

4. No, because the power of x in the first term is negative one.

5. $$5x+1=12$$
$$5\left(\frac{11}{5}\right)+1=12$$
$$11+1=12$$
$$12=12$$
Yes, $\frac{11}{5}$ is a solution.

6. $$-14=3x-2$$
$$-14=3(-3)-2$$
$$-14=-9-2$$
$$-14=-11$$
No, -3 is not a solution.

7. $$4a-2-a=5a+10$$
$$4(-4)-2-(-4)=5(-4)+10$$
$$-16-2+4=-20+10$$
$$-14=-10$$
No, -4 is not a solution.

8. $$-2(y-4)-(3y-1)=-2+(2y-1)$$
$$-2\left(\left(\frac{12}{7}\right)-4\right)-\left(3\left(\frac{12}{7}\right)-1\right)=-2+\left(2\left(\frac{12}{7}\right)-1\right)$$
$$-2\left(-\frac{16}{7}\right)-\left(\frac{36}{7}-1\right)=-2+\left(\frac{24}{7}-1\right)$$
$$\frac{32}{7}-\left(\frac{29}{7}\right)=-2+\left(\frac{17}{7}\right)$$
$$\frac{3}{7}=\frac{3}{7}$$
Yes, $\frac{12}{7}$ is a solution.

9. $$x+15=-10$$
$$x+15-15=-10-15$$
$$x=-25$$
Solution Set: $\{-25\}$

10. $$2.5-x=3.5$$
$$2.5-2.5-x=3.5-2.5$$
$$-x=1$$
$$\frac{-x}{-1}=\frac{1}{-1}$$
$$x=-1$$
Solution Set: $\{-1\}$

11. $$x+\frac{2}{3}=-\frac{4}{5}$$
$$x+\frac{2}{3}-\frac{2}{3}=-\frac{4}{5}-\frac{2}{3}$$
$$x=-\frac{22}{15}$$
Solution Set: $\left\{-\frac{22}{15}\right\}$

12. $$-5x=2\frac{1}{2}$$
$$-5x=\frac{5}{2}$$
$$-\frac{1}{5}(-5x)=-\frac{1}{5}\left(\frac{5}{2}\right)$$
$$x=-\frac{1}{2}$$
Solution Set: $\left\{-\frac{1}{2}\right\}$

13. $$\frac{x}{10}=-15$$
$$\frac{10}{1}\left(\frac{x}{10}\right)=10(-15)$$
$$x=-150$$
Solution Set: $\{-150\}$

14. $$\frac{1}{2}=\frac{2}{3}y$$
$$\frac{3}{2}\left(\frac{1}{2}\right)=\frac{3}{2}\left(\frac{2}{3}y\right)$$
$$\frac{3}{4}=y$$
Solution Set: $\left\{\frac{3}{4}\right\}$

15.
$$3c - 12 = 18$$
$$3c - 12 + 12 = 18 + 12$$
$$3c = 30$$
$$\frac{3c}{3} = \frac{30}{3}$$
$$c = 10$$
Solution Set: $\{10\}$

16.
$$45 = 12 - 11w$$
$$45 - 12 = 12 - 12 - 11w$$
$$33 = -11w$$
$$\frac{33}{-11} = \frac{-11w}{-11}$$
$$-3 = w$$
Solution Set: $\{-3\}$

17.
$$\frac{2}{3}x - 8 = 0$$
$$\frac{2}{3}x - 8 + 8 = 0 + 8$$
$$\frac{2}{3}x = 8$$
$$\frac{3}{2}\left(\frac{2}{3}x\right) = \frac{3}{2}(8)$$
$$x = 12$$
Solution Set: $\{12\}$

18.
$$12x + 5 = 5$$
$$12x + 5 - 5 = 5 - 5$$
$$12x = 0$$
$$\frac{12x}{12} = \frac{0}{12}$$
$$x = 0$$
Solution Set: $\{0\}$

19.
$$12 = 8m - 10m$$
$$12 = -2m$$
$$\frac{12}{-2} = \frac{-2m}{-2}$$
$$-6 = m$$
Solution Set: $\{-6\}$

20.
$$\frac{x}{4} + 5 = -2$$
$$\frac{x}{4} + 5 - 5 = -2 - 5$$
$$\frac{x}{4} = -7$$
$$\frac{4}{1}\left(\frac{x}{4}\right) = 4(-7)$$
$$x = -28$$
Solution Set: $\{-28\}$

21.
$$-10x + \frac{1}{6} = -\frac{2}{3}$$
$$-10x + \frac{1}{6} - \frac{1}{6} = -\frac{2}{3} - \frac{1}{6}$$
$$-10x = -\frac{5}{6}$$
$$-\frac{1}{10}(-10x) = -\frac{1}{10}\left(-\frac{5}{6}\right)$$
$$x = \frac{1}{12}$$
Solution Set: $\left\{\frac{1}{12}\right\}$

22.
$$-x + 0.25 + 0.5x = -4$$
$$-0.5x + 0.25 = -4$$
$$-0.5x + 0.25 - 0.25 = -4 - 0.25$$
$$-0.5x = -4.25$$
$$\frac{-0.5x}{-0.5} = \frac{-4.25}{-0.5}$$
$$x = 8.5$$
Solution Set: $\{8.5\}$

23.
$$4a - 3 + 2a = 8a - 3 - a$$
$$6a - 3 = 7a - 3$$
$$6a - 7a - 3 = 7a - 7a - 3$$
$$-a - 3 = -3$$
$$-a - 3 + 3 = -3 + 3$$
$$-a = 0$$
$$\frac{-a}{-1} = \frac{0}{-1}$$
$$a = 0$$
Solution Set: $\{0\}$

24.
$$6x-4-3x = 3x+10+4x$$
$$3x-4 = 7x+10$$
$$3x-7x-4 = 7x-7x+10$$
$$-4x-4 = 10$$
$$-4x-4+4 = 10+4$$
$$-4x = 14$$
$$\frac{-4x}{-4} = \frac{14}{-4}$$
$$x = -\frac{7}{2}$$

Solution Set: $\left\{-\dfrac{7}{2}\right\}$

25. Let x represent the unknown number.

$$\frac{1}{4}x = 0.12$$
$$0.25x = 0.12$$
$$\frac{0.25x}{0.25} = \frac{0.12}{0.25}$$
$$x = 0.48$$

The number is 0.48.

26. Let x represent the unknown number.

$$x+250 = 84$$
$$x+250-250 = 84-250$$
$$x = -166$$

The number is -166.

27. Let x represent the length of the first side of the triangle.

$$x+x+2+x-2 = 24$$
$$3x = 24$$
$$\frac{3x}{3} = \frac{24}{3}$$
$$x = 8$$

The length of the first side is 8 inches, the second side is 10 inches, and the third side is 6 inches.

28. Prepare We are to determine the difference between the body shop price and the retail price of the front-end grill.

Plan We can set up and solve a linear equation in one variable.

Process Let x represent the difference between the body shop price and the retail price of the front-end grill.

$$x = (\text{body shop price}) - (\text{retail price})$$
$$x = 799+799(0.20)-799$$
$$x = 159.8$$

The difference in price is \$159.80.

Ponder Does our answer seem reasonable? Yes. A simple check of arithmetic will validate the result.

29.
$$4(3x+1) = 40$$
$$12x+4 = 40$$
$$12x+4-4 = 40-4$$
$$12x = 36$$
$$\frac{12x}{12} = \frac{36}{12}$$
$$x = 3$$

Solution Set: $\{3\}$

30.
$$16 = 8(n-10)$$
$$16 = 8n-80$$
$$16+80 = 8n-80+80$$
$$96 = 8n$$
$$\frac{96}{8} = \frac{8n}{8}$$
$$12 = n$$

Solution Set: $\{12\}$

31.
$$26 = 7x-(2x+9)$$
$$26 = 7x-2x-9$$
$$26 = 5x-9$$
$$26+9 = 5x-9+9$$
$$35 = 5x$$
$$\frac{35}{5} = \frac{5x}{5}$$
$$7 = x$$

Solution Set: $\{7\}$

32. $18x - 2(6x + 1) = -10$

$18x - 12x - 2 = -10$

$6x - 2 = -10$

$6x - 2 + 2 = -10 + 2$

$6x = -8$

$\dfrac{6x}{6} = \dfrac{-8}{6}$

$x = -\dfrac{4}{3}$

Solution Set: $\left\{ -\dfrac{4}{3} \right\}$

34. $5 + 2(3a - 1) = -3a - 15$

$5 + 6a - 2 = -3a - 15$

$6a + 3 = -3a - 15$

$6a + 3a + 3 = -3a + 3a - 15$

$9a + 3 = -15$

$9a + 3 - 3 = -15 - 3$

$9a = -18$

$\dfrac{9a}{9} = \dfrac{-18}{9}$

$a = -2$

Solution Set: $\{-2\}$

35. $-2(x - 4) - (3x - 1) = -2 + (2x - 1)$

$-2x + 8 - 3x + 1 = -2 + 2x - 1$

$-5x + 9 = 2x - 3$

$-5x - 2x + 9 = 2x - 2x - 3$

$-7x + 9 = -3$

$-7x + 9 - 9 = -3 - 9$

$-7x = -12$

$\dfrac{-7x}{-7} = \dfrac{-12}{-7}$

$x = \dfrac{12}{7}$

Solution Set: $\left\{ \dfrac{12}{7} \right\}$

36. $4m - 2\left\{ 3 + 2m - \left[5 - (m + 1) \right] \right\} = -24$

$4m - 2\left\{ 3 + 2m - \left[5 - m - 1 \right] \right\} = -24$

$4m - 2\left\{ 3 + 2m - \left[-m + 4 \right] \right\} = -24$

$4m - 2\left\{ 3 + 2m + m - 4 \right\} = -24$

$4m - 2\left\{ 3m - 1 \right\} = -24$

$4m - 6m + 2 = -24$

$-2m + 2 = -24$

$-2m + 2 - 2 = -24 - 2$

$-2m = -26$

$\dfrac{-2m}{-2} = \dfrac{-26}{-2}$

$m = 13$

Solution Set: $\{13\}$

37. $x + \dfrac{2}{3} = 3x - \dfrac{5}{4}$

$\dfrac{12}{1}\left(x + \dfrac{2}{3} \right) = \dfrac{12}{1}\left(3x - \dfrac{5}{4} \right)$

$12x + 8 = 36x - 15$

$12x - 36x + 8 = 36x - 36x - 15$

$-24x + 8 = -15$

$-24x + 8 - 8 = -15 - 8$

$-24x = -23$

$\dfrac{-24x}{-24} = \dfrac{-23}{-24}$

$x = \dfrac{23}{24}$

Solution Set: $\left\{ \dfrac{23}{24} \right\}$

38. $\dfrac{x - 4}{2} = \dfrac{3x - 10}{5}$

$\dfrac{10}{1}\left(\dfrac{x - 4}{2} \right) = \dfrac{10}{1}\left(\dfrac{3x - 10}{5} \right)$

$5x - 20 = 6x - 20$

$5x - 6x - 20 = 6x - 6x - 20$

$-x - 20 = -20$

$-x - 20 + 20 = -20 + 20$

$-x = 0$

$\dfrac{-x}{-1} = \dfrac{0}{-1}$

$x = 0$

Solution Set: $\{0\}$

39.
$$\frac{x}{2}+\frac{x-3}{4}=\frac{10}{3}$$
$$\frac{12}{1}\left(\frac{x}{2}+\frac{x-3}{4}\right)=\frac{12}{1}\left(\frac{10}{3}\right)$$
$$6x+3x-9=40$$
$$9x-9=40$$
$$9x-9+9=40+9$$
$$9x=49$$
$$\frac{9x}{9}=\frac{49}{9}$$
$$x=\frac{49}{9}$$

Solution Set: $\left\{\dfrac{49}{9}\right\}$

40.
$$1.2x-0.66=0.3x+1.14$$
$$1.2x-0.3x-0.66=0.3x-0.3x+1.14$$
$$0.9x-0.66=1.14$$
$$0.9x-0.66+0.66=1.14+0.66$$
$$0.9x=1.80$$
$$\frac{0.9x}{0.9}=\frac{1.80}{0.9}$$
$$x=2$$

Solution Set: $\{2\}$

41.
$$\frac{2}{3}x-0.3=\frac{1}{15}x+\frac{9}{30}$$
$$\frac{30}{1}\left(\frac{2}{3}x-0.3\right)=\frac{30}{1}\left(\frac{1}{15}x+\frac{9}{30}\right)$$
$$20x-9=2x+9$$
$$20x-2x-9=2x-2x+9$$
$$18x-9=9$$
$$18x-9+9=9+9$$
$$18x=18$$
$$\frac{18x}{18}=\frac{18}{18}$$
$$x=1$$

Solution Set: $\{1\}$

42.
$$8+4w=9w-5w+2$$
$$8+4w=4w+2$$
$$8+4w-4w=4w-4w+2$$
$$8=2$$

The equation is inconsistent.
Solution Set: $\{\ \}$ or $\varnothing$

43.
$$20+4(3v-5)=12v$$
$$20+12v-20=12v$$
$$12v=12v$$
$$12v-12v=12v-12v$$
$$0=0$$

The equation is an identity.
Solution Set: $\{v\,|\,v\in R\}$

44.
$$2.2(4x+6)-0.8x=4(3.3+2x)$$
$$8.8x+13.2-0.8x=13.2+8x$$
$$8x+13.2=13.2+8x$$
$$8x-8x+13.2=13.2+8x-8x$$
$$13.2=13.2$$

The equations is an identity.
Solution Set: $\{x\,|\,x\in R\}$

45.
$$\frac{3}{7}+x=x+\frac{7}{3}$$
$$\frac{3}{7}x-x=x-x+\frac{7}{3}$$
$$\frac{3}{7}=\frac{7}{3}$$

The equation is inconsistent.
Solution Set: $\{\ \}$ or $\varnothing$

46. Let x represent the unknown number.

$$\frac{3}{4}x=32+\frac{1}{8}x$$
$$\frac{8}{1}\left(\frac{3}{4}x\right)=\frac{8}{1}\left(32+\frac{1}{8}x\right)$$
$$6x=256+x$$
$$6x-x=256+x-x$$
$$5x=256$$
$$\frac{5x}{5}=\frac{256}{5}$$
$$x=\frac{256}{5}$$

The number is $\frac{256}{5}$.

47. Let x represent the original price of the car battery.

$$x - 0.20x = 68.50$$
$$0.80x = 68.50$$
$$\frac{0.80x}{0.80} = \frac{68.50}{0.80}$$
$$x = 85.625$$

The original price of the car battery was $85.63.

48. Prepare We must solve the linear equation for x to determine how many miles a customer would have to travel with each company for the cost of his rides to be equal.

Plan Solve the linear equation for x by using the Strategy for Solving Linear Equations.

Process
$$2.50 + 0.75x = 3.70 + 0.90(x - 2)$$
$$2.50 + 0.75x = 3.70 + 0.90x - 1.8$$
$$2.50 + 0.75x = 0.90x + 1.9$$
$$2.50 + 0.75x - 0.90x = 0.90x - 0.90x + 1.9$$
$$2.50 - 0.15x = 1.9$$
$$2.50 - 2.50 - 0.15x = 1.9 - 2.50$$
$$-0.15x = -0.6$$
$$x = 4$$

Therefore, a customer would have to travel 4 miles for the cost of his rides to be equal.

Ponder Does our answer seem reasonable? We can check our answer. The cost of travel with the first cab is $\$2.50 + \$0.75(4) = \$5.50$. The cost of travel with the second cab is $\$3.70 + \$0.90(4 - 2) = \$5.50$. Because the cost is the same for both cabs, the answer is correct.

49. Prepare We must find the measures of two unknown supplementary angles.

Plan We will write and solve a linear equation in one variable using the given information.

Process Let x represent the first angle.

$$x + \frac{2}{3}x + 5 = 180$$
$$\frac{5}{3}x + 5 - 5 = 180 - 5$$
$$\frac{5}{3}x = 175$$
$$\frac{3}{5}\left(\frac{5}{3}x\right) = \frac{3}{5}(175)$$
$$x = 105$$

The first angle is $105°$, and the second angle is $\frac{2}{3}(105) + 5 = 75°$.

Ponder Does our answer seem reasonable? Yes. Because the sum of the angles is $180°$, the result is reasonable.

50. Prepare We are to find the three lengths that the board must be cut into.

Plan We will set up and solve a linear equation in one variable.

Process Let x represent the length of the first piece.

$$x + \frac{1}{2}x + 1 + x - 3 = 32$$
$$\frac{5}{2}x = 34$$
$$\frac{2}{5}\left(\frac{5}{2}x\right) = \frac{2}{5}(34)$$
$$x = 13.6$$

The length of the first board is 13.6 feet, the length of the second board is 7.8 feet, and the length of the third board is 10.6 feet.

Ponder Does our answer seem reasonable? Yes. Because the lengths of the three pieces add up to 32, our answer is reasonable.

51.
$$8x - 5y = 2$$
$$8x - 5y + 5y = 2 + 5y$$
$$8x = 5y + 2$$
$$\frac{8x}{8} = \frac{5y + 2}{8}$$
$$x = \frac{5y + 2}{8}$$

52.
$$-\frac{1}{2}x+\frac{2}{3}y=5$$
$$\frac{6}{1}\left(-\frac{1}{2}x+\frac{2}{3}y\right)=6(5)$$
$$-3x+4y=30$$
$$-3x+3x+4y=30+3x$$
$$4y=30+3x$$
$$\frac{4y}{4}=\frac{3x+30}{4}$$
$$y=\frac{3x+30}{4}$$

53.
$$D=RT$$
$$\frac{D}{T}=\frac{RT}{T}$$
$$R=\frac{D}{T}$$

54.
$$P=2l+2w$$
$$P-2w=2l+2w-2w$$
$$P-2w=2l$$
$$\frac{P-2w}{2}=\frac{2l}{2}$$
$$l=\frac{P-2w}{2}$$

55.
$$A=\frac{1}{2}h(a+b)$$
$$2A=2\left(\frac{1}{2}h(a+b)\right)$$
$$2A=h(a+b)$$
$$\frac{2A}{h}=\frac{h(a+b)}{h}$$
$$\frac{2A}{h}=a+b$$
$$\frac{2A}{h}-a=a-a+b$$
$$b=\frac{2A}{h}-a$$

56.
$$cx+x=0$$
$$(c+1)x=0$$
$$\frac{(c+1)x}{c+1}=\frac{0}{c+1}$$
$$x=0$$

57.
$$\frac{x}{2}+\frac{y}{3}=1$$
$$\frac{6}{1}\left(\frac{x}{2}+\frac{y}{3}\right)=6(1)$$
$$3x+2y=6$$
$$3x-3x+2y=6-3x$$
$$2y=6-3x$$
$$\frac{2y}{2}=\frac{6-3x}{2}$$
$$y=\frac{6-3x}{2}$$

58.
$$F=kx$$
$$120=k(8)$$
$$\frac{120}{8}=\frac{8k}{8}$$
$$k=15$$

59.
$$C=\frac{5}{9}(F-32)$$
$$C=\frac{5}{9}((-40)-32)$$
$$C=-40°$$

60.
$$F=\frac{9}{5}C+32$$
$$F=\frac{9}{5}(20)+32$$
$$C=36+32$$
$$C=68$$

61.
$$I=Prt$$
$$1,543.50=(6,300)(r)\left(3\frac{1}{2}\right)$$
$$1,543.50=22,050r$$
$$\frac{1,543.50}{22,050}=\frac{22,050r}{22,050}$$
$$r=0.07$$
The interest rate is 7%.

62.
$$I=Prt$$
$$1,237.50=(7,500)(0.055)t$$
$$1,237.50=412.5t$$
$$\frac{1,237.50}{412.5}=\frac{412.5t}{412.5}$$
$$t=3$$
It will take 3 years.

63. $D = RT$

$$D = (40)\left(3\frac{1}{4}\right)$$

$D = 130$

The blimp can travel 130 miles.

64. $D = RT$

$42 = R(0.75)$

$$\frac{42}{0.75} = \frac{0.75R}{0.75}$$

$R = 56$

Erin drove at a rate of 56 miles per hour.

65. $\left(-\infty, -\dfrac{2}{5}\right)$

$-\dfrac{2}{5}$

66. $x \geq 3.5$

67. $x - 92 < 12$

$x - 92 + 92 < 12 + 92$

$x < 104$

$(-\infty, 104)$

68. $-3x > 8$

$$\frac{-3x}{-3} < \frac{8}{-3}$$

$$x < -\frac{8}{3}$$

$$\left(-\infty, -\frac{8}{3}\right)$$

69. $6x \geq -24$

$$\frac{6x}{6} \geq \frac{-24}{6}$$

$x \geq -4$

$[-4, \infty)$

70. $12 - x \leq 5$

$12 - 12 - x \leq 5 - 12$

$-x \leq -7$

$$\frac{-x}{-1} \geq \frac{-7}{-1}$$

$x \geq 7$

$[7, \infty)$

71. $x > -4x + 20$

$x + 4x > -4x + 4x + 20$

$5x > 20$

$$\frac{5x}{5} > \frac{20}{5}$$

$x > 4$

$(4, \infty)$

72. $-5x - 2 < 3(x + 2)$

$-5x - 2 < 3x + 6$

$-5x - 3x - 2 < 3x - 3x + 6$

$-8x < 8$

$$\frac{-8x}{-8} > \frac{8}{-8}$$

$x > -1$

$(-1, \infty)$

73. $0 \leq -2(x - 3) + 6x$

$0 \leq -2x + 6 + 6x$

$0 \leq 4x + 6$

$0 - 4x \leq 4x - 4x + 6$

$-4x \leq 6$

$$\frac{-4x}{-4} \geq \frac{6}{-4}$$

$$x \geq -\frac{3}{2}$$

$$\left[-\frac{3}{2}, \infty\right)$$

74. $0.8x + 9.1 < 0.1x$

$0.8x - 0.1x + 9.1 < 0.1x - 0.1x$

$0.7x + 9.1 < 0$

$0.7x + 9.1 - 9.1 < 0 - 9.1$

$0.7x < -9.1$

$$\frac{0.7x}{0.7} < \frac{-9.1}{0.7}$$

$x < -13$

$(-\infty, -13)$

75.
$$\frac{x}{3}-\frac{x}{2}\geq\frac{5}{6}$$
$$\frac{6}{1}\left(\frac{x}{3}-\frac{x}{2}\right)\geq\frac{6}{1}\left(\frac{5}{6}\right)$$
$$2x-3x\geq 5$$
$$-x\geq 5$$
$$\frac{-x}{-1}\leq\frac{5}{-1}$$
$$x\leq-5$$
$$(-\infty,-5]$$

76.
$$\frac{x-3}{5}+\frac{x}{4}>3$$
$$\frac{20}{1}\left(\frac{x-3}{5}+\frac{x}{4}\right)>20(3)$$
$$4x-12+5x>60$$
$$9x-12>60$$
$$9x-12+12>60+12$$
$$9x>72$$
$$\frac{9x}{9}>\frac{72}{9}$$
$$x>8$$
$$(8,\infty)$$

77.
$$7p+27\geq 15+7p$$
$$7p-7p+27\geq 15+7p-7p$$
$$27\geq 15$$
$$(-\infty,\infty)$$

78.
$$-24t<8(5-3t)$$
$$-24t<40-24t$$
$$-24t+24t<40-24y+24t$$
$$0<40$$
$$(-\infty,\infty)$$

79.
$$8(6-x)+10x\leq 2x+6$$
$$48-8x+10x\leq 2x+6$$
$$48+2x\leq 2x+6$$
$$48+2x-2x\leq 2x-2x+6$$
$$48\leq 6$$
$$\{\ \}\text{ or }\varnothing$$

80.
$$3.2x-5<6x-(2.8x+5)$$
$$3.2x-5<6x-2.8x-5$$
$$3.2x-5<3.2x-5$$
$$3.2x-3.2x-5<3.2x-3.2x-5$$
$$-5<-5$$
$$\{\ \}\text{ or }\varnothing$$

81. Let x represent the unknown number.

$$4x-\frac{2}{3}<x+1$$
$$4x-x-\frac{2}{3}<x-x+1$$
$$3x-\frac{2}{3}<1$$
$$3x-\frac{2}{3}+\frac{2}{3}<1+\frac{2}{3}$$
$$3x<\frac{5}{3}$$
$$\frac{1}{3}(3x)<\frac{1}{3}\left(\frac{5}{3}\right)$$
$$x<\frac{5}{9}$$
$$\left(-\infty,\frac{5}{9}\right)$$

82. Let x represent the score Danita needs in her third game to average at least 110.

$$\frac{120+96+x}{3}\geq 110$$
$$\frac{216+x}{3}\geq 110$$
$$\frac{3}{1}\left(\frac{216+x}{3}\right)\geq 3(110)$$
$$216+x\geq 330$$
$$216-216+x\geq 330-216$$
$$x\geq 114$$
$$[114,\infty)$$

Danita needs to score at least 114.

83. $(-\infty,-3]\cup(20,\infty)$

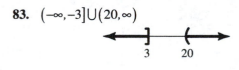

84. $\{\ \}$

79

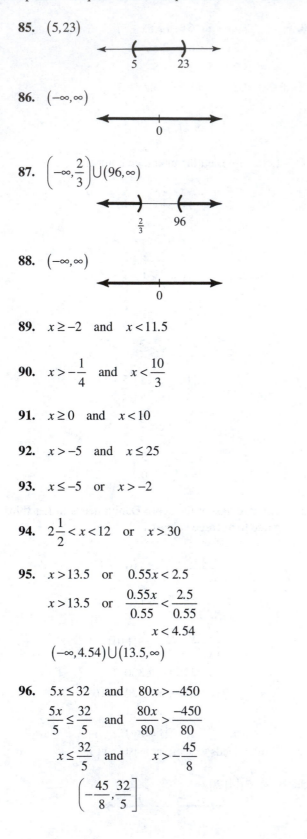

85. $(5, 23)$

86. $(-\infty, \infty)$

87. $\left(-\infty, \dfrac{2}{3}\right) \cup (96, \infty)$

88. $(-\infty, \infty)$

89. $x \ge -2$ and $x < 11.5$

90. $x > -\dfrac{1}{4}$ and $x < \dfrac{10}{3}$

91. $x \ge 0$ and $x < 10$

92. $x > -5$ and $x \le 25$

93. $x \le -5$ or $x > -2$

94. $2\dfrac{1}{2} < x < 12$ or $x > 30$

95. $x > 13.5$ or $0.55x < 2.5$

$x > 13.5$ or $\dfrac{0.55x}{0.55} < \dfrac{2.5}{0.55}$

$x < 4.54$

$(-\infty, 4.54) \cup (13.5, \infty)$

96. $5x \le 32$ and $80x > -450$

$\dfrac{5x}{5} \le \dfrac{32}{5}$ and $\dfrac{80x}{80} > \dfrac{-450}{80}$

$x \le \dfrac{32}{5}$ and $x > -\dfrac{45}{8}$

$\left(-\dfrac{45}{8}, \dfrac{32}{5}\right]$

97. $-3x < -18$ and $\dfrac{2}{3}x < 16$

$\dfrac{-3x}{-3} > \dfrac{-18}{-3}$ and $\dfrac{3}{2}\left(\dfrac{2}{3}x\right) < \dfrac{3}{2}(16)$

$x > 6$ and $x < 24$

$(6, 24)$

98. $-(x + 20) > 2x + 15$ and $3(x + 2) < -10$

$-x - 20 > 2x + 15$ and $3x + 6 < -10$

$-3x > 35$ and $3x < -16$

$\dfrac{-3x}{-3} < \dfrac{35}{-3}$ and $\dfrac{3x}{3} < \dfrac{-16}{3}$

$x < -\dfrac{35}{3}$ and $x < -\dfrac{16}{3}$

$\left(-\infty, -\dfrac{35}{3}\right)$

99. $\dfrac{x}{3} - \dfrac{x}{4} \le 5$ or $\dfrac{x}{6} + \dfrac{x}{3} > \dfrac{3x}{2}$

$\dfrac{12}{1}\left(\dfrac{x}{3} - \dfrac{x}{4}\right) \le 12(5)$ or $\dfrac{6}{1}\left(\dfrac{x}{6} + \dfrac{x}{3}\right) > \dfrac{6}{1}\left(\dfrac{3x}{2}\right)$

$4x - 3x \le 60$ or $x + 2x > 9x$

$x \le 60$ or $-6x > 0$

$\dfrac{-6x}{-6} < \dfrac{0}{-6}$

$x < 0$

$(-\infty, 60]$

100. $2(x + 3) + 5 < 10$ and $7(x - 2) + 5 > -9$

$2x + 6 + 5 < 10$ and $7x - 14 + 5 > -9$

$2x < -1$ and $7x > 0$

$\dfrac{2x}{2} < \dfrac{-1}{2}$ and $\dfrac{7x}{7} > \dfrac{0}{7}$

$x < -\dfrac{1}{2}$ and $x > 0$

$\{\,\}$

101. $0 < 2x + 8 < 36$

$0 - 8 < 2x + 8 - 8 < 36 - 8$

$-8 < 2x < 28$

$\dfrac{-8}{2} < \dfrac{2x}{2} < \dfrac{28}{2}$

$-4 < x < 14$

$(-4, 14)$

102.
$$-10 < 3 - 2x \le 14$$
$$-10 - 3 < 3 - 3 - 2x \le 14 - 3$$
$$-13 < -2x \le 11$$
$$\frac{-13}{-2} > \frac{-2x}{-2} \ge \frac{11}{-2}$$
$$-\frac{11}{2} \le x < \frac{13}{2}$$
$$\left[-\frac{11}{2}, \frac{13}{2} \right)$$

103.
$$-5 \ge -18 - x > -20$$
$$-5 + 18 \ge -18 + 18 - x > -20 + 18$$
$$13 \ge -x > -2$$
$$\frac{13}{-1} \le \frac{-x}{-1} < \frac{-2}{-1}$$
$$-13 \le x < 2$$
$$[-13, 2)$$

104.
$$-10 \le \frac{-12x + 5}{2} \le 25$$
$$2(-10) \le \frac{2}{1}\left(\frac{-12x + 5}{2} \right) \le 2(25)$$
$$-20 \le -12x + 5 \le 50$$
$$-20 - 5 \le -12x + 5 - 5 \le 50 - 5$$
$$-25 \le -12x \le 45$$
$$\frac{-25}{-12} \ge \frac{-12x}{-12} \ge \frac{45}{-12}$$
$$-\frac{15}{4} \le x \le \frac{25}{12}$$
$$\left[-\frac{15}{4}, \frac{25}{12} \right]$$

105.
$$|x| = 16$$
$$x = -16 \quad \text{or} \quad x = 16$$
$$\{-16, 16\}$$

106. $|x + 4| = -96$
$$\{\ \}$$

107.
$$|-5x| = 75$$
$$-5x = -75 \quad \text{or} \quad -5x = 75$$
$$\frac{-5x}{-5} = \frac{-75}{-5} \quad \text{or} \quad \frac{-5x}{-5} = \frac{75}{-5}$$
$$x = 15 \quad \text{or} \quad -15$$
$$\{-15, 15\}$$

108.
$$|4 - 2x| - 18 = -6$$
$$|4 - 2x| = 12$$
$$4 - 2x = -12 \quad \text{or} \quad 4 - 2x = 12$$
$$-2x = -16 \quad \text{or} \quad -2x = 8$$
$$\frac{-2x}{-2} = \frac{-16}{-2} \quad \text{or} \quad \frac{-2x}{-2} = \frac{8}{-2}$$
$$x = 8 \quad \text{or} \quad x = -4$$
$$\{-4, 8\}$$

109.
$$|4 - x| = 25$$
$$4 - x = -25 \quad \text{or} \quad 4 - x = 25$$
$$-x = -29 \quad \text{or} \quad -x = 21$$
$$\frac{-x}{-1} = \frac{-29}{-1} \quad \text{or} \quad \frac{-x}{-1} = \frac{21}{-1}$$
$$x = 29 \quad \text{or} \quad x = -21$$
$$\{-21, 29\}$$

110.
$$\left| \frac{a}{2} \right| = \frac{7}{8}$$
$$\frac{a}{2} = -\frac{7}{8} \quad \text{or} \quad \frac{a}{2} = \frac{7}{8}$$
$$\frac{2}{1}\left(\frac{a}{2} \right) = \frac{2}{1}\left(-\frac{7}{8} \right) \quad \text{or} \quad \frac{2}{1}\left(\frac{a}{2} \right) = \frac{2}{1}\left(\frac{7}{8} \right)$$
$$a = -\frac{7}{4} \quad \text{or} \quad a = \frac{7}{4}$$
$$\left\{ -\frac{7}{4}, \frac{7}{4} \right\}$$

111. $|5x - 1| - 6 = -6$
$$|5x - 1| = 0$$
$$5x - 1 = 0$$
$$5x = 1$$
$$\frac{5x}{5} = \frac{1}{5}$$
$$x = \frac{1}{5}$$
$$\left\{ \frac{1}{5} \right\}$$

112. $\left| \frac{1-y}{3} \right| + 40 = 22$
$$\left| \frac{1-y}{3} \right| = -18$$
$$\{\ \}$$

113.
$$|x-2| = |4-2x|$$
$$x-2 = -(4-2x) \quad \text{or} \quad x-2 = 4-2x$$
$$x-2 = -4+2x \quad \text{or} \quad 3x = 6$$
$$-x = -2 \quad \text{or} \quad \frac{3x}{3} = \frac{6}{3}$$
$$\frac{-x}{-1} = \frac{-2}{-1} \quad \text{or} \quad x = 2$$
$$x = 2$$
$$\{2\}$$

114.
$$|-3x-10| = |9+2x|$$
$$-3x-10 = -(9+2x) \quad \text{or} \quad -3x-10 = 9+2x$$
$$-3x-10 = -9-2x \quad \text{or} \quad -5x = 19$$
$$-x = 1 \quad \text{or} \quad \frac{-5x}{-5} = \frac{19}{-5}$$
$$\frac{-x}{-1} = \frac{1}{-1} \quad \text{or} \quad x = -\frac{19}{5}$$
$$x = -1$$
$$\left\{-\frac{19}{5}, -1\right\}$$

115.
$$|x| \leq 5$$
$$-5 \leq x \leq 5$$
$$[-5,5]$$

116.
$$|16-2x| < 18$$
$$-18 < 16-2x < 18$$
$$-34 < -2x < 2$$
$$\frac{-34}{-2} > \frac{-2x}{-2} > \frac{2}{-2}$$
$$-1 < x < 17$$
$$(-1,17)$$

117.
$$\left|\frac{x-12}{4}\right| \leq 10$$
$$-10 \leq \frac{x-12}{4} \leq 10$$
$$4(-10) \leq \frac{4}{1}\left(\frac{x-12}{4}\right) \leq 4(10)$$
$$-40 \leq x-12 \leq 40$$
$$-28 \leq x \leq 52$$
$$[-28,52]$$

118.
$$|2x-4| + 6 < 18$$
$$|2x-4| < 12$$
$$-12 < 2x-4 < 12$$
$$-8 < 2x < 16$$
$$\frac{-8}{2} < \frac{2x}{2} < \frac{16}{2}$$
$$-4 < x < 8$$
$$(-4,8)$$

119.
$$|8x+3| + 15 < 12$$
$$|8x+3| < -3$$
$$\{\ \}$$

120.
$$|2x| > 8$$
$$2x < -8 \quad \text{or} \quad 2x > 8$$
$$\frac{2x}{2} < \frac{-8}{2} \quad \text{or} \quad \frac{2x}{2} > \frac{8}{2}$$
$$x < -4 \quad \text{or} \quad x > 4$$
$$(-\infty,-4) \cup (4,\infty)$$

121.
$$|4x+16| - 10 \geq 34$$
$$|4x+16| \geq 44$$
$$4x+16 \leq -44 \quad \text{or} \quad 4x+16 \geq 44$$
$$4x \leq -60 \quad \text{or} \quad 4x \geq 28$$
$$\frac{4x}{4} \leq \frac{-60}{4} \quad \text{or} \quad \frac{4x}{4} \geq \frac{28}{4}$$
$$x \leq -15 \quad \text{or} \quad x \geq 7$$
$$(-\infty,-15] \cup [7,\infty)$$

122.

$$\left|\frac{x-2}{4}\right| + 6 > 8$$

$$\left|\frac{x-2}{4}\right| > 2$$

$$\frac{x-2}{4} < -2 \quad \text{or} \quad \frac{x-2}{4} > 2$$

$$\frac{4}{1}\left(\frac{x-2}{4}\right) < 4(-2) \quad \text{or} \quad \frac{4}{1}\left(\frac{x-2}{4}\right) > 4(2)$$

$$x - 2 < -8 \quad \text{or} \quad x - 2 > 8$$

$$x < -6 \quad \text{or} \quad x > 10$$

$$(-\infty, -6) \cup (10, \infty)$$

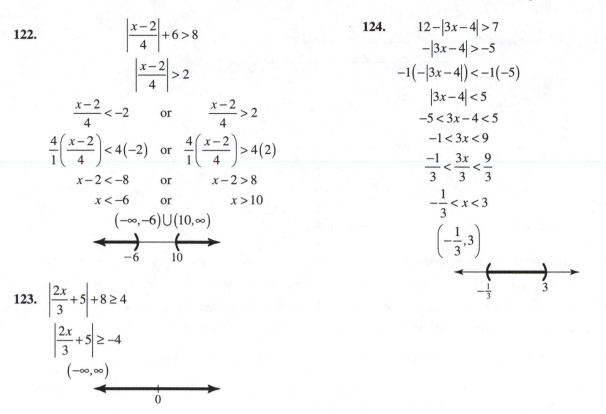

123. $\left|\frac{2x}{3} + 5\right| + 8 \geq 4$

$$\left|\frac{2x}{3} + 5\right| \geq -4$$

$$(-\infty, \infty)$$

124.

$$12 - |3x - 4| > 7$$

$$-|3x - 4| > -5$$

$$-1(-|3x - 4|) < -1(-5)$$

$$|3x - 4| < 5$$

$$-5 < 3x - 4 < 5$$

$$-1 < 3x < 9$$

$$\frac{-1}{3} < \frac{3x}{3} < \frac{9}{3}$$

$$-\frac{1}{3} < x < 3$$

$$\left(-\frac{1}{3}, 3\right)$$

125. Prepare We are to determine the speed of the helicopter in still air.

Plan We will set up a chart to organize the information given in the problem. We will then use this information to write and solve a linear equation with one variable.

Process Let r represent the speed of the helicopter in still air.

	Rate	• Time	=	Distance
headwind	$r - 15$ mph	2 (in hours)		$D_1 = 2(r - 15)$ (in miles)
tailwind	$r + 5$ mph	$1\frac{1}{2}$ (in hours)		$D_2 = 1.5(r + 5)$ (in miles)

$$D_1 + D_2 = 240$$

$$2(r - 15) + 1.5(r + 5) = 240$$

$$2r - 30 + 1.5r + 7.5 = 240$$

$$3.5r - 22.5 = 240$$

$$3.5r = 262.5$$

$$r = 75$$

The helicopter can travel 75 miles per hour in still air.

Ponder Does our answer seem reasonable? Yes. We can check to see that the total distance traveled at this speed is 240 miles.

126. Prepare We want to determine how many milliliters of the mixture the curator makes from 150 ml of a 3% acid solution and some 100% acid solution.

Plan We will set up a chart to organize the information given in the problem. We will then use this information to write and solve a linear equation with one variable.

Process Let x represent the number of milliliters in the final mixture.

	40% Acid Solution	3% Acid Solution	100% Acid Solution
# of milliliters	x	150	$x-150$
% acid	0.40	0.03	1

$$0.03(150)+x-150=0.40x$$
$$4.5+x-150=0.40x$$
$$0.60x=145.5$$
$$x=242.5$$

The curator makes 242.5 milliliters of the 40% acid solution.

Ponder Does our answer seem reasonable? Yes. There are $150(3\%)=4.5$ milliliters of acid in the first container and $(242.5-150)(100\%)=92.5$ milliliters of acid in the second container. Therefore, there are $4.5+92.5=97$ milliliters of acid in the two containers combined. In the final mixture, there are $242.5(40\%)=97$ milliliters of acid. Since this is equal to the amount we obtained from both containers, our answer is correct.

127. **Prepare** We want to determine the number of pounds of cashews and peanuts that Sayem purchased.

Plan We will set up a chart to organize the information given in the problem. We will then use this information to write and solve a linear equation with one variable.

Process Let x represent the number of pounds of cashews that Sayem purchased.

	Cashews	Peanuts	Mixture
# of pounds	x	$x+2$	$2x+2$
price per pound	$7.50	$2.50	$4.50

$$7.5x+2.5(x+2)=4.5(2x+2)$$
$$7.5x+2.5x+5=9x+9$$
$$x=4$$

Sayem purchased 4 pounds of cashews and 6 pounds of peanuts.

Ponder Does our answer seem reasonable? Yes. The total cost of the cashews is $4(\$7.50)=\$30$ and the total cost of the peanuts is $6(\$2.50)=\$15$. Therefore, the total cost for the nuts is $\$30+\$15=\$45$. The cost of the mix is $(2(4)+2)(\$4.50)=\$45$. Since the cost for the mix is the same as the total cost of the nuts, our answer is correct.

128. **Prepare** We are to determine how much Shannon invested at each of two simple interest rates.

Plan We will set up a chart to organize the information given in the problem. We will then use this information to write and solve a linear equation with one variable.

Process Let p represent the amount invested at 8% interest.

$P \cdot r \cdot t = I$				
8% Investment	p	0.08	1	$I_1=0.08p$
9% Investment	$8,000-p$	0.09	1	$I_2=0.09(8,000-p)$

$$I_1 + I_2 = 690$$
$$0.08p + 0.09(8{,}000 - p) = 690$$
$$0.08p + 720 - 0.09p = 690$$
$$-0.01p = -30$$
$$p = 3{,}000$$

Shannon invested \$3,000 at 8% interest and \$5,000 at 9% interest.

Ponder Does our answer seem reasonable? Yes. The interest earned at 8% is $0.08(3{,}000) = \$240$, and the interest earned at 9% is $0.09(5{,}000) = \$450$. The sum of the interest from the two investments is $\$240 + \$450 = \$690$.

CHAPTER 2 TEST

1. c, e, j

2. e

3. h

4. a, f, g, i

5. b, d

6. $-3(x+4)+7=5x+11$
$-3x-12+7=5x+11$
$-3x-5=5x+11$
$-3x-5x-5=5x-5x+11$
$-8x-5=11$
$-8x-5+5=11+5$
$-8x=16$
$\dfrac{-8x}{-8}=\dfrac{16}{-8}$
$x=-2$
$\{-2\}$

7. $\dfrac{3}{2}t+\dfrac{1}{5}=-\dfrac{2}{5}$
$10\left(\dfrac{3}{2}t+\dfrac{1}{5}\right)=10\left(-\dfrac{2}{5}\right)$
$15t+2=-4$
$15t+2-2=-4-2$
$15t=-6$
$\dfrac{15t}{15}=\dfrac{-6}{15}$
$t=-\dfrac{2}{5}$
$\left\{-\dfrac{2}{5}\right\}$

8. $\dfrac{x-2}{3}-\dfrac{x+5}{2}=\dfrac{1}{6}$
$6\left(\dfrac{x-2}{3}-\dfrac{x+5}{2}\right)=6\left(\dfrac{1}{6}\right)$
$2x-4-3x-15=1$
$-x-19=1$
$-x-19+19=1+19$
$-x=20$
$\dfrac{-x}{-1}=\dfrac{20}{-1}$
$x=-20$
$\{-20\}$

9. $|3x+5|=26$

$3x+5=26$ or $3x+5=-26$
$3x+5-5=26-5$ $3x+5-5=-26-5$
$3x=21$ $3x=-31$
$\dfrac{3x}{3}=\dfrac{21}{3}$ $\dfrac{3x}{3}=\dfrac{-31}{3}$
$x=7$ $x=-\dfrac{31}{3}$

$\left\{-\dfrac{31}{3},7\right\}$

10. $\left|6-\dfrac{1}{2}x\right|+8=0$

$\left|6-\dfrac{1}{2}x\right|+8-8=0-8$

$\left|6-\dfrac{1}{2}x\right|=-8$

$\{\ \}$

11. $0.05x+0.25(3x-5)=10.75$
$0.05b+0.75b-1.25=10.75$
$0.8b-1.25=10.75$
$100(0.8b-1.25)=100(10.75)$
$80b-125=1075$
$80b-125+125=1075+125$
$80b=1200$
$\dfrac{80b}{80}=\dfrac{1200}{80}$
$b=15$
$\{15\}$

12.
$$5x - 8y = 16$$
$$5x - 5x - 8y = 16 - 5x$$
$$-8y = 16 - 5x$$
$$\frac{-8y}{-8} = \frac{16 - 5x}{-8}$$
$$y = \frac{16 - 5x}{-8}$$
$$\text{or} \quad y = \frac{16}{-8} - \frac{5x}{-8}$$
$$y = \frac{5}{8}x - 2$$

13.
$$A = \frac{1}{2}h(a+b)$$
$$2A = 2\left(\frac{1}{2}h(a+b)\right)$$
$$2A = h(a+b)$$
$$2A = ah + bh$$
$$2A - bh = ah + bh - bh$$
$$2A - bh = ah + 0$$
$$2A - bh = ah$$
$$\frac{2A - bh}{h} = \frac{ah}{h}$$
$$\frac{2A - bh}{h} = a$$
$$a = \frac{2A - bh}{h}$$
$$a = \frac{2A}{h} - \frac{bh}{h}$$
$$a = \frac{2A}{h} - b$$

14.
$$-\frac{7}{5}x > \frac{14}{25}$$
$$-\frac{5}{7}\left(-\frac{7}{5}x\right) < -\frac{5}{7}\left(\frac{14}{25}\right)$$
$$x < -\frac{2}{5}$$
$$\left(-\infty, -\frac{2}{5}\right)$$

15.
$$-5(x+7) - 4 \geq 3x - (x+4)$$
$$-5x - 35 - 4 \geq 3x - x - 4$$
$$-5x - 39 \geq 2x - 4$$
$$-5x - 2x - 39 \geq 2x - 2x - 4$$
$$-7x - 39 \geq -4$$
$$-7x - 39 + 39 \geq -4 + 39$$
$$-7x \geq 35$$
$$\frac{-7x}{-7} \leq \frac{35}{-7}$$
$$x \leq -5$$
$$(-\infty, -5]$$

16.
$$-410 \leq 80x - 10 < 230$$
$$-410 + 10 \leq 80x - 10 + 10 < 230 + 10$$
$$-400 \leq 80x < 240$$
$$\frac{-400}{80} \leq \frac{80x}{80} < \frac{240}{80}$$
$$-5 \leq x < 3$$
$$[-5, 3)$$

17.
$$7x + 3 > 9 \qquad \text{and} \qquad -5x \geq -25$$
$$7x + 3 - 3 > 9 - 3 \qquad \frac{-5x}{-5} \leq \frac{-25}{-5}$$
$$7x > 6 \qquad\qquad x \leq 5$$
$$\frac{7x}{7} > \frac{6}{7}$$
$$x > \frac{6}{7} \qquad\qquad \left(\frac{6}{7}, 5\right]$$

18.
$$3x + 5 < -7 \qquad \text{or} \qquad 6 > -2(x-3)$$
$$3x + 5 - 5 < -7 - 5 \qquad 6 > -2x + 6$$
$$3x < -12 \qquad\qquad 6 + 2x > -2x + 2x + 6$$
$$\frac{3x}{3} < \frac{-12}{3} \qquad\qquad 6 + 2x > 6$$
$$x < -4 \qquad\qquad 6 - 6 + 2x > 6 - 6$$
$$\qquad\qquad\qquad 2x > 0$$
$$(-\infty, -4) \cup (0, \infty) \qquad \frac{2x}{2} > \frac{0}{2}$$
$$x > 0$$

19.
$$|7-8x| < 21$$
$$-21 < 7-8x < 21$$
$$-21-7 < 7-7-8x < 21-7$$
$$-28 < -8x < 14$$
$$\frac{-28}{-8} > \frac{-8x}{-8} > \frac{14}{-8}$$
$$\frac{7}{2} > x > -\frac{7}{4}$$
$$-\frac{7}{4} < x < \frac{7}{2}$$
$$\left(-\frac{7}{4}, \frac{7}{2}\right)$$

20.

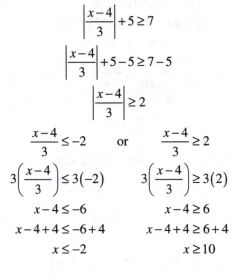

$$\left|\frac{x-4}{3}\right| + 5 \geq 7$$
$$\left|\frac{x-4}{3}\right| + 5 - 5 \geq 7 - 5$$
$$\left|\frac{x-4}{3}\right| \geq 2$$

$$\frac{x-4}{3} \leq -2 \quad \text{or} \quad \frac{x-4}{3} \geq 2$$
$$3\left(\frac{x-4}{3}\right) \leq 3(-2) \qquad 3\left(\frac{x-4}{3}\right) \geq 3(2)$$
$$x-4 \leq -6 \qquad\qquad x-4 \geq 6$$
$$x-4+4 \leq -6+4 \qquad x-4+4 \geq 6+4$$
$$x \leq -2 \qquad\qquad\qquad x \geq 10$$

$$(-\infty, -2] \cup [10, \infty)$$

21.
$$\left|\frac{3}{5}x+1\right| + 4 > 2$$
$$\left|\frac{3}{5}x+1\right| + 4 - 4 > 2 - 4$$
$$\left|\frac{3}{5}x+1\right| > -2$$
$$(-\infty, \infty)$$

22. Let x represent the unknown number.

$$2x-5 = 3(x+2)$$
$$2x-5 = 3x+6$$
$$2x-3x-5 = 3x-3x+6$$
$$-x-5 = 6$$
$$-x-5+5 = 6+5$$
$$-x = 11$$
$$\frac{-x}{-1} = \frac{11}{-1}$$
$$x = -11$$
$$\{-11\}$$

The number is -11.

23. Use the formula $D = RT$.

$$D = 56\frac{1}{4} \text{ miles}$$

$$R = 75 \text{ miles per hour}$$

$$T = \text{ unknown hours}$$

$$D = RT$$
$$56\frac{1}{4} = 75T$$
$$\frac{225}{4} = 75T$$
$$\frac{225}{4} \div 75 = 75T \div 75$$
$$\frac{3}{4} = T$$
$$\left\{\frac{3}{4}\right\}$$

Sheila drove for $\frac{3}{4}$ of an hour or 45 minutes.

24. Prepare   We are to find the amount of money invested in each of two mutual funds, given the total amount to be invested and the interest rate of each mutual fund.

Plan   We must understand how to calculate the interest earned from each mutual fund. This is accomplished by multiplying the amount invested in the account by the interest rate (which must first be converted into decimal form).

Process   Make a chart using the formula, $I = \text{Pr}t$.

Investment	P	r	t	I
7.5%	x	0.075	1	$0.075x$
5%	$8000 - x$	0.05	1	$0.05(8000 - x)$

The total interest earned from both accounts is the sum of the interest earned from each account. We can now write the equation and solve.

$$0.075x + 0.05(8000 - x) = 537.5$$
$$0.075x + 400 - 0.05x = 537.5$$
$$0.025x + 400 = 537.5$$
$$0.025x + 400 - 400 = 537.5 - 400$$
$$0.025x = 137.5$$
$$\frac{0.025x}{0.025} = \frac{137.5}{0.025}$$
$$x = 5500$$

The amount invested at 7.5% is $5,500.
The amount invested at 5% is $2,500.

Ponder Are the amounts reasonable, that is, is their sum $8,000 and is the total interest earned $537.50? The sum of the two amounts, $5500 + 2500$ is $8,000. The interest earned at 7.5% interest is $(0.075)(5500)$ which is $412.50 and the interest earned at 5% is $(0.05)(2500)$ which is $125. The sum of the interest is $412.50 + 125$ which is equal to $537.50.

25. Prepare We are to find the grade that Ignacio must make on his final exam in order to make an A for the semester, given the scores for exams 1, 2, and 4 and given that the final exam will replace the grade from exam 3.

Plan We must understand how to calculate the average grade for the semester and that this average must be large enough to receive an A for the course.

Process Let $x =$ the grade that Ignacio must receive on the final exam in order to receive an A for the semester. Since all the exam grades will weigh equally, we simply add up all the exam grades and divide the sum by 5. In order for Ignacio to receive an A, this average must equal at least 90.

$$\frac{84 + 92 + x + 88 + x}{5} \geq 90$$
$$\frac{2x + 264}{5} \geq 90$$
$$5\left(\frac{2x + 264}{5}\right) \geq 5(90)$$
$$2x + 264 \geq 450$$
$$2x + 264 - 264 \geq 450 - 264$$
$$2x \geq 186$$
$$\frac{2x}{2} \geq \frac{186}{2}$$
$$x \geq 93$$

Ignacio must make a 93 or better on the final exam in order to earn an A for the semester.

Ponder Is this grade reasonable? We simply need to use this grade to compute Ignacio's average. We must also remember that the final exam grade will also replace the grade for exam 3.

$$\frac{84 + 92 + 93 + 88 + 93}{5} = \frac{450}{5}$$
$$= 90$$

Since the average of the 5 exam grades is 90, Ignacio will receive an A for the semester.

Chapter 3

3.1 Exercises

1. $3x - 2y = 6$ is the standard form of a <u>linear</u> <u>equation</u> in <u>two</u> <u>variables</u>.

3. The set of solutions to a linear equation is represented by a <u>straight</u> <u>line</u> in the coordinate plane.

5. This is not a linear equation because it cannot be rewritten in standard form.

7. This is a linear equation.
$$x = \frac{1}{2}y + 3$$
$$x - \frac{1}{2}y = \frac{1}{2}y - \frac{1}{2}y + 3$$
$$x - \frac{1}{2}y = 3$$

9. This is a linear equation.
$$5x = -3y + 1$$
$$5x + 3y = -3y + 3y + 1$$
$$5x + 3y = 1$$

11. This is not a linear equation because the exponent on y is 2.

13.
$$x + y = 0$$
$$(-5) + (5) = 0$$
$$0 = 0$$
a

15.
$$-3x + 2y = 0$$
$$-3(-4) + 2(-6) = 0$$
$$12 + (-12) = 0$$
$$0 = 0$$
b

17.
$$4x + 6y = -10$$
$$4(-1) + 6(-1) = -10$$
$$-4 + (-6) = -10$$
$$-10 = -10$$
d

19.
$$3x - y = 3$$
$$3(0) - (-3) = 3$$
$$0 + 3 = 3$$
$$3 = 3$$
The ordered pair $(0, -3)$ is a solution.

21.
$$x - 3y = -2$$
$$(4) - 3(-2) = -2$$
$$4 + 6 = -2$$
$$10 = -2$$
The ordered pair $(4, -2)$ is not a solution.

23.
$$6y = 4x - 2$$
$$6\left(\frac{1}{3}\right) = 4(1) - 2$$
$$2 = 4 - 2$$
$$2 = 2$$
The ordered pair $\left(1, \frac{1}{3}\right)$ is a solution.

25.
$$3y = 2x + 6.6$$
$$3(-3) = 2(1.2) + 6.6$$
$$-9 = 2.4 + 6.6$$
$$-9 = 9$$
The ordered pair $(1.2, -3)$ is not a solution.

27.a.
$$4x + 2y = -8$$
$$4(-1) + 2y = -8$$
$$-4 + 2y = -8$$
$$2y = -4$$
$$y = -2$$
The ordered pair $(-1, -2)$ is a solution.

27.b.
$$4x + 2y = -8$$
$$4(0) + 2y = -8$$
$$0 + 2y = -8$$
$$2y = -8$$
$$y = -4$$
The ordered pair $(0, -4)$ is a solution.

27.c.
$$4x + 2y = -8$$
$$4x + 2(2) = -8$$
$$4x + 4 = -8$$
$$4x = -12$$
$$x = -3$$
The ordered pair $(-3, 2)$ is a solution.

29.a.
$$-2x = y - 12$$
$$-2\left(-\frac{1}{2}\right) = y - 12$$
$$1 = y - 12$$
$$13 = y$$
The ordered pair $\left(-\frac{1}{2}, 13\right)$ is a solution.

29.b.
$$-2x = y - 12$$
$$-2(0) = y - 12$$
$$0 = y - 12$$
$$12 = y$$
The ordered pair $(0, 12)$ is a solution.

29.c.
$$-2x = y - 12$$
$$-2x = (-8) - 12$$
$$-2x = -20$$
$$x = 10$$
The ordered pair $(10, -8)$ is a solution.

31.a.
$$y = \frac{2}{3}x - 6$$
$$y = \frac{2}{3}(-6) - 6$$
$$y = -4 - 6$$
$$y = -10$$
The ordered pair $(-6, -10)$ is a solution.

31.b.
$$y = \frac{2}{3}x - 6$$
$$y = \frac{2}{3}(0) - 6$$
$$y = 0 - 6$$
$$y = -6$$
The ordered pair $(0, -6)$ is a solution.

31.c.
$$y = \frac{2}{3}x - 6$$
$$(6) = \frac{2}{3}x - 6$$
$$12 = \frac{2}{3}x$$
$$18 = x$$
The ordered pair $(18, 6)$ is a solution.

33.a.
$$x + 0.3y = 7.2$$
$$(1.2) + 0.3y = 7.2$$
$$0.3y = 6$$
$$y = 20$$
The ordered pair $(1.2, 20)$ is a solution.

33.b.
$$x + 0.3y = 7.2$$
$$(0) + 0.3y = 7.2$$
$$0.3y = 7.2$$
$$y = 24$$
The ordered pair $(0, 24)$ is a solution.

33.c.
$$x + 0.3y = 7.2$$
$$x + 0.3(4) = 7.2$$
$$x + 1.2 = 7.2$$
$$x = 6$$
The ordered pair $(6, 4)$ is a solution.

35.

$x = 0$	$x = 1$	$x = 2$
$x - y = 5$	$x - y = 5$	$x - y = 5$
$(0) - y = 5$	$(1) - y = 5$	$(2) - y = 5$
$-y = 5$	$-y = 4$	$-y = 3$
$y = -5$	$y = -4$	$y = -3$
$(0, -5)$	$(1, -4)$	$(2, -3)$

37.

$x = 2$	$x = 3$	$x = 4$
$-x + y = -6$	$-x + y = -6$	$-x + y = -6$
$-(2) + y = -6$	$-(3) + y = -6$	$-(4) + y = -6$
$y = -4$	$y = -3$	$y = -2$
$(2, -4)$	$(3, -3)$	$(4, -2)$

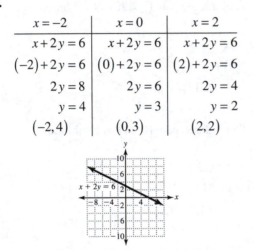

39.

$x = -2$	$x = 0$	$x = 2$
$x + 2y = 6$	$x + 2y = 6$	$x + 2y = 6$
$(-2) + 2y = 6$	$(0) + 2y = 6$	$(2) + 2y = 6$
$2y = 8$	$2y = 6$	$2y = 4$
$y = 4$	$y = 3$	$y = 2$
$(-2, 4)$	$(0, 3)$	$(2, 2)$

41.

$x = -1$	$x = 0$	$x = 1$
$-2x + y = 4$	$-2x + y = 4$	$-2x + y = 4$
$-2(-1) + y = 4$	$-2(0) + y = 4$	$-2(1) + y = 4$
$2 + y = 4$	$0 + y = 4$	$-2 + y = 4$
$y = 2$	$y = 4$	$y = 6$
$(-1, 2)$	$(0, 4)$	$(1, 6)$

43.

$x = -3$	$x = 0$	$x = 3$
$2x + 3y = -6$	$2x + 3y = -6$	$2x + 3y = -6$
$2(-3) + 3y = -6$	$2(0) + 3y = -6$	$2(3) + 3y = -6$
$-6 + 3y = -6$	$0 + 3y = -6$	$6 + 3y = -6$
$3y = 0$	$3y = -6$	$3y = -12$
$y = 0$	$y = -2$	$y = -4$
$(-3, 0)$	$(0, -2)$	$(3, -4)$

45.

$x = 0$	$x = 2$	$x = 4$
$3x - 4y = 12$	$3x - 4y = 12$	$3x - 4y = 12$
$3(0) - 4y = 12$	$3(2) - 4y = 12$	$3(4) - 4y = 12$
$0 - 4y = 12$	$6 - 4y = 12$	$12 - 4y = 12$
$-4y = 12$	$-4y = 6$	$-4y = 0$
$y = -3$	$y = -\frac{3}{2}$	$y = 0$
$(0, -3)$	$(2, -\frac{3}{2})$	$(4, 0)$

47.

$x = -4$	$x = 0$	$x = 4$
$\frac{1}{4}x + y = 6$	$\frac{1}{4}x + y = 6$	$\frac{1}{4}x + y = 6$
$\frac{1}{4}(-4) + y = 6$	$\frac{1}{4}(0) + y = 6$	$\frac{1}{4}(4) + y = 6$
$-1 + y = 6$	$0 + y = 6$	$1 + y = 6$
$y = 7$	$y = 6$	$y = 5$
$(-4, 7)$	$(0, 6)$	$(4, 5)$

49.

$x=-1$	$x=0$	$x=1$
$3x=y+2$	$3x=y+2$	$3x=y+2$
$3(-1)=y+2$	$3(0)=y+2$	$3(1)=y+2$
$-3=y+2$	$0=y+2$	$3=y+2$
$-5=y$	$-2=y$	$1=y$
$(-1,-5)$	$(0,-2)$	$(1,1)$

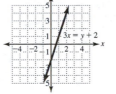

51.

$x=-1$	$x=0$	$x=1$
$y=2x-1$	$y=2x-1$	$y=2x-1$
$y=2(-1)-1$	$y=2(0)-1$	$y=2(1)-1$
$y=-2-1$	$y=0-1$	$y=2-1$
$y=-3$	$y=-1$	$y=1$
$(-1,-3)$	$(0,-1)$	$(1,1)$

53.

$x=-1$	$x=0$	$x=1$
$y=3x$	$y=3x$	$y=3x$
$y=3(-1)$	$y=3(0)$	$y=3(1)$
$y=-3$	$y=0$	$y=3$
$(-1,-3)$	$(0,0)$	$(1,3)$

55.

$x=-2$	$x=0$	$x=2$
$1.5x-y=3$	$1.5x-y=3$	$1.5x-y=3$
$1.5(-2)-y=3$	$1.5(0)-y=3$	$1.5(2)-y=3$
$-3-y=3$	$0-y=3$	$3-y=3$
$-y=6$	$-y=3$	$-y=0$
$y=-6$	$y=-3$	$y=0$
$(-2,-6)$	$(0,-3)$	$(2,0)$

57. Answers will vary; one example is: It would not be an equation in two variables if A or B is zero; it would reduce to an equation in one variable.

61. Answers will vary; one example is: A line graph is a set of partial solutions (line segments) of several equations in two variables.

59. Answers will vary; one example is: It is necessary to plot at least three points because that makes for a straighter and more accurate graph.

63. Prepare We must determine the y values that are related to each of the given x values and then use these values to make a T table.

Plan We will use the given equation to substitute the given x values and solve for the corresponding y values.

Process

$-0.03x+y=120$	$-0.03x+y=120$
$-0.03(550)+y=120$	$-0.03(725)+y=120$
$-16.5+y=120$	$-21.75+y=120$
$y=136.5$	$y=141.75$
$-0.03x+y=120$	$-0.03x+y=120$
$-0.03x+(135)=120$	$-0.03x+(132.75)=120$
$-0.03x=-15$	$-0.03x=-12.75$
$x=500$	$x=425$

x	y
550	136.5
725	141.75
500	135
425	132.75

Ponder Are our results correct? A quick check of the arithmetic will show that the answers are correct.

65. **Prepare** We must determine the y values that are related to each of the given x values and then use these values to make a T table.

Plan We will use the given equation to substitute the given x values and solve for the corresponding y values.

Process

$$-0.04x + y = 500$$
$$-0.04(15,000) + y = 500$$
$$-600 + y = 500$$
$$y = 1,100$$

$$-0.04x + y = 500$$
$$-0.04(8,000) + y = 500$$
$$-320 + y = 500$$
$$y = 820$$

$$-0.04x + y = 500$$
$$-0.04x + (960) = 500$$
$$-0.04x = -460$$
$$x = 11,500$$

x	y
15,000	1,100
8,000	820
11,500	960

Ponder Are our results correct? A quick check of the arithmetic will show that the answers are correct.

67.

$x = -3$	$x = 0$	$x = 3$
$\frac{2}{3}x + \frac{1}{6}y = 1$	$\frac{2}{3}x + \frac{1}{6}y = 1$	$\frac{2}{3}x + \frac{1}{6}y = 1$
$\frac{2}{3}(-3) + \frac{1}{6}y = 1$	$\frac{2}{3}(0) + \frac{1}{6}y = 1$	$\frac{2}{3}(3) + \frac{1}{6}y = 1$
$-2 + \frac{1}{6}y = 1$	$0 + \frac{1}{6}y = 1$	$2 + \frac{1}{6}y = 1$
$\frac{1}{6}y = 3$	$\frac{1}{6}y = 1$	$\frac{1}{6}y = -1$
$y = 18$	$y = -3$	$y = -6$
$(-3, 18)$	$(0, -3)$	$(3, -6)$

3.2 Exercises

1. The solution where the graph of an equation crosses the *x*-axis is called the _x-intercept_.

3. To find the *y*-intercept, we set _x_ equal to zero and solve for _y_.

5. When *y* is constant and there is no *x* variable, we have a _horizontal_ line.

7. Let $x = 0$, and solve for *y*.
$$3x + 2y = 6$$
$$3(0) + 2y = 6$$
$$2y = 6$$
$$y = 3$$
The *y*-intercept is $(0, 3)$.
Let $y = 0$, and solve for *x*.
$$3x + 2y = 6$$
$$3x + 2(0) = 6$$
$$3x = 6$$
$$x = 2$$
The *x*-intercept is $(2, 0)$.

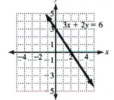

9. Let $x = 0$, and solve for *y*.
$$2x - 6y = 6$$
$$2(0) - 6y = 6$$
$$-6y = 6$$
$$y = -1$$
The *y*-intercept is $(0, -1)$.
Let $y = 0$, and solve for *x*.
$$2x - 6y = 6$$
$$2x - 6(0) = 6$$
$$2x = 6$$
$$x = 3$$
The *x*-intercept is $(3, 0)$.

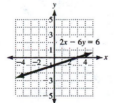

11. Let $x = 0$, and solve for *y*.
$$4x - y = 2$$
$$4(0) - y = 2$$
$$-y = 2$$
$$y = -2$$
The *y*-intercept is $(0, -2)$.
Let $y = 0$, and solve for *x*.
$$4x - y = 2$$
$$4x - (0) = 2$$
$$4x = 2$$
$$x = \frac{1}{2}$$
The *x*-intercept is $\left(\frac{1}{2}, 0\right)$.

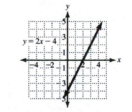

13. Let $x = 0$, and solve for *y*.
$$y = 2x - 4$$
$$y = 2(0) - 4$$
$$y = -4$$
The *y*-intercept is $(0, -4)$.
Let $y = 0$, and solve for *x*.
$$y = 2x - 4$$
$$(0) = 2x - 4$$
$$4 = 2x$$
$$2 = x$$
The *x*-intercept is $(2, 0)$.

15. Let $x = 0$, and solve for *y*.
$$y = -3x + 1$$
$$y = -3(0) + 1$$
$$y = 1$$
The *y*-intercept is $(0, 1)$.

Let $y = 0$, and solve for x.

$$y = -3x + 1$$
$$(0) = -3x + 1$$
$$3x = 1$$
$$x = \frac{1}{3}$$

The x-intercept is $\left(\frac{1}{3}, 0\right)$.

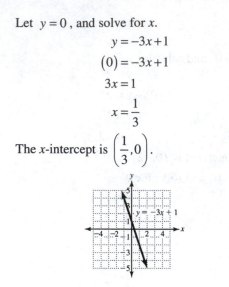

17. Let $x = 0$, and solve for y.

$$6y = 3x - 12$$
$$6y = 3(0) - 12$$
$$6y = -12$$
$$y = -2$$

The y-intercept is $(0, -2)$.

Let $y = 0$, and solve for x.

$$6y = 3x - 12$$
$$6(0) = 3x - 12$$
$$0 = 3x - 12$$
$$12 = 3x$$
$$4 = x$$

The x-intercept is $(4, 0)$.

19. Let $x = 0$, and solve for y.

$$\frac{1}{2}x + \frac{1}{5}y = 1$$
$$\frac{1}{2}(0) + \frac{1}{5}y = 1$$
$$\frac{1}{5}y = 1$$
$$y = 5$$

The y-intercept is $(0, 5)$.

Let $y = 0$, and solve for x.

$$\frac{1}{2}x + \frac{1}{5}y = 1$$
$$\frac{1}{2}x + \frac{1}{5}(0) = 1$$
$$\frac{1}{2}x = 1$$
$$x = 2$$

The x-intercept is $(2, 0)$.

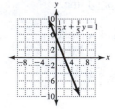

21. Let $x = 0$, and solve for y.

$$\frac{1}{2}x + \frac{1}{4}y = 8$$
$$\frac{1}{2}(0) + \frac{1}{4}y = 8$$
$$\frac{1}{4}y = 8$$
$$y = 32$$

The y-intercept is $(0, 32)$.

Let $y = 0$, and solve for x.

$$\frac{1}{2}x + \frac{1}{4}y = 8$$
$$\frac{1}{2}x + \frac{1}{4}(0) = 8$$
$$\frac{1}{2}x = 8$$
$$x = 16$$

The x-intercept is $(16, 0)$.

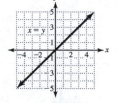

23. Let $x = 0$, then $y = 0$. The x- and y-intercept are $(0,0)$. Let $x = 1$, then $y = 1$. Plot the point $(1,1)$.

25. Let $x = 0$, then $y = 0$. The x- and y-intercept are $(0,0)$. Let $x = 1$, then $y = 2$. Plot the point $(1,2)$.

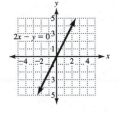

27. Let $x = 0$, and solve for y.
$$1.2x + 3y = 6$$
$$1.2(0) + 3y = 6$$
$$3y = 6$$
$$y = 2$$
The y-intercept is $(0,2)$.
Let $y = 0$, and solve for x.
$$1.2x + 3y = 6$$
$$1.2x + 3(0) = 6$$
$$1.2x = 6$$
$$x = 5$$
The x-intercept is $(5,0)$.

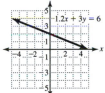

29. The graph of $x = -3$ is a vertical line with x-intercept $(-3,0)$.

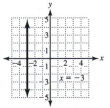

31. The graph of $x = \dfrac{2}{3}$ is a vertical line with x-intercept $\left(\dfrac{2}{3}, 0\right)$.

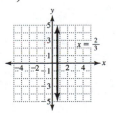

33. The graph of $y = -2$ is a horizontal line with y-intercept $(0,-2)$.

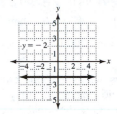

35. The graph of $y - 3.5 = 0$ is a horizontal line with y-intercept $(0,3.5)$.

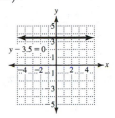

37. vertical

39. horizontal

41. neither

43. horizontal

45. neither

47. vertical

49. neither

51. horizontal

53. vertical

55. Answers will vary; one example is: Given the equation of a line, set one variable to zero to get the intercept of the other variable.

57. Answers will vary; one example is: You could make a T table.

59. Prepare We are asked to use the given linear equation, representing the number bird houses and planters that can be made in one 1,200 work week, to answer problems a) through d).

Plan We will answers the questions by using the techniques learned in this section concerning the intercepts of a line.

Process

a) Let $x = 0$, then $y = 300$. The y-intercept is $(0,300)$. Let $y = 0$, then $x = 400$. The x-intercept is $(400,0)$.

b) Answers will vary; one example is: If they make no planters, they can make 400 birdhouses; if they make no birdhouses, then they can make 300 planters.

c)

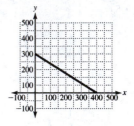

d)

$$3x + 4y = 1,200$$
$$3(200) + 4y = 1,200$$
$$600 + 4y = 1,200$$
$$4y = 600$$
$$y = 150$$

They build 150 planters.

Ponder   Does our answer seem reasonable? Yes. It seems reasonable that as the number of birdhouses produced goes up, that the number of planters produced would go down, and vice versa.

3.3 Exercises

1. If the graph of a line rises from left to right, then the slope of the line must be <u>positive</u>.

3. The slope of a line is determined by finding the difference in the <u>rise</u>, divided by the difference in the <u>run</u>.

5. The slope of any vertical line is <u>undefined</u>.

7. negative

9. undefined

11. zero

13. positive

15. $m = \dfrac{\text{rise}}{\text{run}}$

$= \dfrac{3}{2}$

17. $m = \dfrac{\text{rise}}{\text{run}}$

$= \dfrac{2}{2}$

$= 1$

19. $m = \dfrac{\text{rise}}{\text{run}}$

$= \dfrac{7}{0}$

undefined

21. $m = \dfrac{\text{rise}}{\text{run}}$

$= \dfrac{-3}{2}$

$= -\dfrac{3}{2}$

23. $m = \dfrac{\text{rise}}{\text{run}}$

$= \dfrac{0}{3}$

$= 0$

25. $m = \dfrac{\text{rise}}{\text{run}}$

$= \dfrac{-2}{2}$

$= -1$

27. $m = \dfrac{y_2 - y_1}{x_2 - x_1}$

$= \dfrac{4-1}{7-5}$

$= \dfrac{3}{2}$

29. $m = \dfrac{y_2 - y_1}{x_2 - x_1}$

$= \dfrac{-3-0}{6-7}$

$= \dfrac{-3}{-1}$

$= 3$

31. $m = \dfrac{y_2 - y_1}{x_2 - x_1}$

$= \dfrac{-7-1}{1-4}$

$= \dfrac{-8}{-3}$

$= \dfrac{8}{3}$

33. $m = \dfrac{y_2 - y_1}{x_2 - x_1}$

$= \dfrac{-16-(-16)}{-3-3}$

$= \dfrac{0}{-6}$

$= 0$

35. $m = \dfrac{y_2 - y_1}{x_2 - x_1}$

$= \dfrac{\dfrac{1}{2}-(-2)}{3-3}$

$= \dfrac{\dfrac{5}{2}}{0}$

undefined

37. $m = \dfrac{y_2 - y_1}{x_2 - x_1}$

$= \dfrac{-5 - (-3)}{-5 - 0}$

$= \dfrac{-2}{-5}$

$= \dfrac{2}{5}$

39. $m = \dfrac{y_2 - y_1}{x_2 - x_1}$

$= \dfrac{\dfrac{1}{2} - \dfrac{3}{2}}{\dfrac{2}{5} - \left(-\dfrac{3}{5}\right)}$

$= \dfrac{-1}{1}$

$= -1$

41. $m = \dfrac{y_2 - y_1}{x_2 - x_1}$

$= \dfrac{-10 - (-5)}{-1 - (-2)}$

$= \dfrac{-5}{1}$

$= -5$

43. $m = \dfrac{y_2 - y_1}{x_2 - x_1}$

$= \dfrac{-25 - (-13)}{15 - 15}$

$= \dfrac{-12}{0}$

undefined

45. $m = \dfrac{y_2 - y_1}{x_2 - x_1}$

$= \dfrac{0 - 7}{2.5 - (-3.5)}$

$= \dfrac{-7}{6}$

$= -\dfrac{7}{6}$

47. $m = \dfrac{y_2 - y_1}{x_2 - x_1}$

$= \dfrac{\dfrac{1}{3} - \dfrac{1}{3}}{10 - 8}$

$= \dfrac{0}{2}$

$= 0$

49. $m = \dfrac{y_2 - y_1}{x_2 - x_1}$

$= \dfrac{24 - (-6)}{-3 - (-18)}$

$= \dfrac{30}{15}$

$= 2$

51. Slope: $m = 2$

y-intercept: $(0, 3)$

53. Slope: $m = \dfrac{2}{3}$

y-intercept: $(0, 5)$

55. Slope: $m = -2$

y-intercept: $(0, 0)$

57. Slope: $m = 0$

y-intercept: $(0, 4)$

59. Slope: $m = \dfrac{1}{4}$

y-intercept: $(0, 0)$

61. The slope is undefined.

There is no y-intercept.

63. Slope: $m = \dfrac{2}{3}$

y-intercept: $(0, 0)$

65. $2x - 3y = 6$

$-3y = -2x + 6$

$y = \dfrac{2}{3}x - 2$

Slope: $m = \dfrac{2}{3}$

y-intercept: $(0, -2)$

67.
$$3y = 15$$
$$y = 5$$
Slope: $m = 0$
y-intercept: $(0, 5)$

69.
$$4y - 3x = 0$$
$$4y = 3x$$
$$y = \frac{3}{4}x$$
Slope: $m = \frac{3}{4}$
y-intercept: $(0, 0)$

71. The slope is undefined.
There is no y-intercept.

73.   Slope: $m = 3$
y-intercept: $(0, 0)$

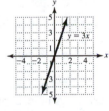

75.   Slope: $m = -1$
y-intercept: $(0, 4)$

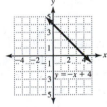

77.   Slope: $m = \frac{2}{3}$
y-intercept: $(0, 1)$

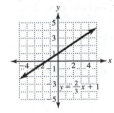

79.   Slope: $m = 0$
y-intercept: $(0, 4)$

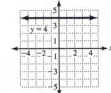

81.
$$3x + y = 4$$
$$y = -3x + 4$$
Slope: $m = -3$
y-intercept: $(0, 4)$

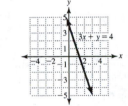

83.
$$2x - 4y = 8$$
$$-4y = -2x + 8$$
$$y = \frac{1}{2}x - 2$$
Slope: $m = \frac{1}{2}$
y-intercept: $(0, -2)$

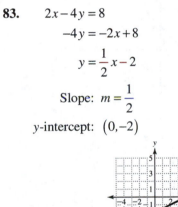

85. $x = -3$
The slope is undefined.
The x-intercept is $(-3, 0)$.

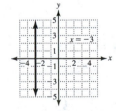

87.
$$2x - 3y = 3$$
$$-3y = -2x + 3$$
$$y = \frac{2}{3}x - 1$$

Slope: $m = \frac{2}{3}$

y-intercept: $(0, -1)$

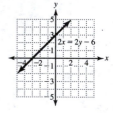

89.
$$2x = 2y - 6$$
$$2x + 6 = 2y$$
$$y = x + 3$$

Slope: $m = 1$

y-intercept: $(0, 3)$

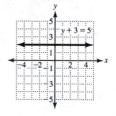

91.
$$y + 3 = 5$$
$$y = 2$$

Slope: $m = 0$

y-intercept: $(0, 2)$

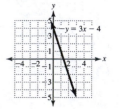

93.
$$-y = 3x - 4$$
$$y = -3x + 4$$

Slope: $m = -3$

y-intercept: $(0, 4)$

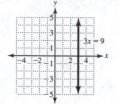

95.
$$3x = 9$$
$$x = 3$$

The slope is undefined.

The x-intercept is $(3, 0)$.

97. Answers will vary; one example is: Slope can be defined as Rise over Run; a vertical line only rises; it does not run. Because division by zero is undefined and the run for a vertical line is zero, the slope is undefined.

99. Answers will vary; one example is: If y increases as x increases, then the line has a positive slope. If y decreases as x increases, then the line has a negative slope.

101. a) April to May, May to June, and June to July

b) July to August, August to September

c) April-May: 15, May-June: 10, June-July: 7, July-August: -7, August-September: -10

d) April to May,   Answers will vary; one example is: The temperature change was the most severe.

e) Answers will vary; one example is: The slopes are additive inverses of each other; the change from May to June increased by the same amount that the temperature decreased from August to September.

103. Prepare   We will use the information in the problems to answer questions a) through e).

Plan   We will use the techniques learned in this section to answer the questions.

Process

a) $(1, 5)$ and $(12, 38)$

b)

$$m = \frac{y_2 - y_2}{x_2 - x_1}$$

$$= \frac{38 - 5}{12 - 1}$$

$$= \frac{33}{11}$$

$$= 3$$

c) Yes, because the slope of the equation is three and the two ordered pairs from part a) satisfy the equation.

d) Let $x = 0$.

$$y = 3x + 2$$

$$y = 3(0) + 2$$

$$y = 2$$

The y-intercept is $(0, 2)$. The y-intercept represents the company's initial cost of $2.

e)

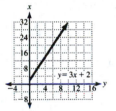

Ponder Do our answers seem reasonable? Yes. It is reasonable that the cost will continue to increase and the number of birdhouses produced increases.

105.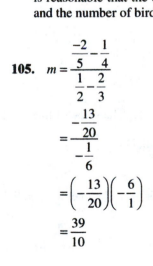

3.4 Exercises

1. The graph of the line given by $y = -6$ is a <u>horizontal</u> line.

3. Two nonvertical lines are parallel if their slopes are <u>equal</u> and their y-intercepts are <u>different</u>.

5. The slope of the graph of a line parallel to $x = 10$ is <u>undefined</u>.

7. The slope of the graph of a line perpendicular to $x = -3$ is <u>0</u>.

9. c

11. f

13. a

15. $y = mx + b$

$y = \left(\dfrac{2}{3}\right)x + (3)$

$y = \dfrac{2}{3}x + 3$

17. $y = mx + b$

$y = (-3)x + (4)$

$y = -3x + 4$

19. $y = mx + b$

$y = (0)x + (-1)$

$y = -1$

21. $y = mx + b$ $\qquad$ $y = mx + b$

$5 = (3)(-1) + b$ $\qquad$ $y = (3)x + (8)$

$5 = -3 + b$ $\qquad$ $y = 3x + 8$

$8 = b$

23. $y = mx + b$ $\qquad$ $y = mx + b$

$0 = \left(\dfrac{-3}{4}\right)(-4) + b$ $\qquad$ $y = \left(\dfrac{-3}{4}\right)x + (-3)$

$0 = 3 + b$ $\qquad$ $y = -\dfrac{3}{4}x - 3$

$-3 = b$

25. $x = -3$

27. $m = \dfrac{y_2 - y_1}{x_2 - x_1}$ $\qquad$ $y = mx + b$

$ = \dfrac{-2-2}{0-3}$ $\qquad$ $y = \left(\dfrac{4}{3}\right)x + (-2)$

$ = \dfrac{-4}{-3}$ $\qquad$ $y = \dfrac{4}{3}x - 2$

$ = \dfrac{4}{3}$

29. $m = \dfrac{y_2 - y_1}{x_2 - x_1}$ $\qquad$ $y = mx + b$

$ = \dfrac{-3-5}{3-(-3)}$ $\qquad$ $(5) = \left(-\dfrac{4}{3}\right)(-3) + b$

$ = \dfrac{-8}{6}$ $\qquad$ $5 = 4 + b$

$ = -\dfrac{4}{3}$ $\qquad$ $1 = b$

$y = mx + b$

$y = \left(-\dfrac{4}{3}\right)x + (1)$

$y = -\dfrac{4}{3}x + 1$

31. $m = \dfrac{y_2 - y_1}{x_2 - x_1}$ $\qquad$ $x = 2$

$ = \dfrac{-6-5}{2-2}$

$ = \dfrac{-11}{0}$

undefined

33. The slope of line L_1 is -4. The slope of line L_2 is $\dfrac{1}{4}$. The lines are perpendicular.

35. The slope of L_1 and L_2 is $\dfrac{3}{2}$. The lines are parallel.

37. The slope of L_1 and L_2 is $-\dfrac{1}{2}$. The lines are parallel.

39. The slope of L_1 is $-\dfrac{2}{3}$. The slope of L_2 is $\dfrac{2}{3}$. The lines are neither parallel nor perpendicular.

41. The slope of L_1 is $-\dfrac{1}{5}$. The slope of L_2 is -5.

The lines are neither parallel nor perpendicular.

43. The slope of line L_1 is $\dfrac{1}{3}$. The slope of line L_2 is

-3. The lines are perpendicular.

45. Line L_1 is horizontal. Line L_2 is vertical. The lines are perpendicular.

47. $m = 0$

$y = -3$

49. $m = -\dfrac{1}{2}$ and $b = -3$

$y = mx + b$

$y = \left(-\dfrac{1}{2}\right)x + (-3)$

$2y = -x - 6$

$x + 2y = -6$

51. $m = -\dfrac{2}{5}$ $\qquad$ $y = mx + b$

$(-1) = \left(-\dfrac{2}{5}\right)(5) + b$

$-1 = -2 + b$

$1 = b$

$y = mx + b$

$y = \left(-\dfrac{2}{5}\right)x + (1)$

$5y = -2x + 5$

$2x + 5y = 5$

53. $y = mx + b$ $\qquad$ $y = mx + b$

$-5 = (3)(-2) + b$ $\qquad$ $y = (3)x + (1)$

$-5 = -6 + b$ $\qquad$ $y = 3x + 1$

$1 = b$ $\qquad$ $3x - y = -1$

55. $x = \dfrac{1}{2}$

57. $y = mx + b$

$y = \left(-\dfrac{2}{3}\right)x + (-4)$

$y = -\dfrac{2}{3}x - 4$

$3y = -2x - 12$

$2x + 3y = -12$

59. $m = \dfrac{y_2 - y_1}{x_2 - x_1}$ $\qquad$ $b = 10$ $\qquad$ $y = mx + b$

$= \dfrac{10 - 0}{0 - (-5)}$ $\qquad$ $y = (2)x + (10)$

$= \dfrac{10}{5}$ $\qquad$ $y = 2x + 10$

$= 2$ $\qquad$ $2x - y = -10$

61. $y = -2$

63. $x = -\dfrac{5}{6}$

65. $m = \dfrac{y_2 - y_1}{x_2 - x_1}$ $\qquad$ $y = mx + b$

$= \dfrac{-2 - (-3)}{-6 - 5}$ $\qquad$ $(-3) = \left(-\dfrac{1}{11}\right)(5) + b$

$= \dfrac{1}{-11}$ $\qquad$ $-3 = -\dfrac{5}{11} + b$

$= -\dfrac{1}{11}$ $\qquad$ $-\dfrac{28}{11} = b$

$y = mx + b$

$y = \left(-\dfrac{1}{11}\right)x + \left(-\dfrac{28}{11}\right)$

$11y = -x - 28$

$x + 11y = -28$

67. $m = \dfrac{y_2 - y_1}{x_2 - x_1}$ $\qquad$ $x = -5$

$= \dfrac{1 - 18}{-5 - (-5)}$

$= \dfrac{-17}{0}$

undefined

69. $y = mx + b$ $\qquad$ $y = mx + b$

$(0) = (-4)(-2) + b$ $\qquad$ $y = (-4)x + (-8)$

$0 = 8 + b$ $\qquad$ $y = -4x - 8$

$-8 = b$ $\qquad$ $4x + y = -8$

71. $y = -12$

73. $m = \dfrac{y_2 - y_1}{x_2 - x_1}$ $\qquad y = mx + b$

$\quad = \dfrac{-25 - 0}{0 - 5}$ $\qquad y = (5)x + (-25)$

$\quad = \dfrac{-25}{-5}$ $\qquad y = 5x - 25$

$\quad = 5$ $\qquad 5x - y = 25$

75. $m = -\dfrac{1}{2}$ $\qquad y = mx + b$

$\qquad (1) = \left(-\dfrac{1}{2}\right)(-2) + b$

$\qquad 1 = 1 + b$

$\qquad 0 = b$

$\quad y = mx + b$

$\quad y = \left(-\dfrac{1}{2}\right)x + (0)$

$\quad 2y = -x$

$\quad x + 2y = 0$

77. $m = \dfrac{3}{2}$ $\qquad y = mx + b$

$\qquad y = \left(\dfrac{3}{2}\right)x + (10)$

$\qquad 2y = 3x + 20$

$\qquad 3x - 2y = -20$

79. Find the equation of the line and any solution to the equation $2x + 3y = -14$, such as $(-7, 0)$, is a point on the line.

81. a) The parallel line is also horizontal, so the equation is $y = c,\ c \neq -3$.

b) The perpendicular line is vertical, so the equation is $x = a,\ a \in R$.

83. The graphs of the lines are parallel because they have equal slopes and different y-intercepts.

85. a) If we consider sea level to be zero feet high, then at time $x = 0$, the plane is 5,280 feet high. Therefore, the ordered pair is $(0, 5280)$. If the plane climbs at a rate of 500 feet per minute, then after 2 minutes, the plane has risen 1,000 feet, making its total altitude 6,280 feet. Therefore, the ordered pair is $(2, 6280)$.

b) The rate at which the plane is climbing is 500 feet per minute, so the slope is $m = 500$. The initial altitude of the plane is 5,280 feet, so the y-intercept is $(0, 5280)$.

c) $y = 500x + 5,280$

d) Let $y = 30,000$.

$$y = 500x + 5,280$$
$$30,000 = 500x + 5,280$$
$$24,720 = 500x$$
$$49.44 = x$$

It will take approximately 49.44 minutes.

87. a) If we consider sea level to be zero feet high, then at time $x = 0$, the trap is zero feet high. Therefore, the ordered pair is $(0, 0)$. If the trap descends at a rate of 30 feet per minute, then after 2 minutes, the trap is at a depth of 60 feet. Therefore, the ordered pair is $(2, -60)$.

b) The rate at which the trap is descending is 30 feet per minute, so the slope is $m = -30$. The initial depth of the trap is zero feet, so the y-intercept is $(0, 0)$.

c) $y = -30x$

d) Let $x = 3$.

$$y = -30x$$
$$y = -30(3)$$
$$y = -90$$

The trap is at a depth of 90 feet.

89. a) The first year the profits were \$175,000, which can be written as the ordered pair $(1, 175000)$. The third year the profits were \$300,000, which can be written as the ordered pair $(3, 300000)$.

b)

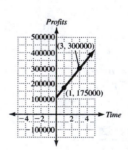

c)
$$m = \frac{y_2 - y_1}{x_2 - x_1}$$
$$= \frac{300,000 - 175,000}{3 - 1}$$
$$= \frac{125,000}{2}$$
$$= 62,500$$

$$y = mx + b$$
$$(175,000) = (62,500)(1) + b$$
$$112,500 = b$$
y-intercept: $(0, 112500)$

d)
$$y = mx + b$$
$$y = (62,500)x + (112,500)$$
$$62,500x - y = -112,500$$

e) $y = 62,500x + 112,500$
$$y = 62,500(5) + 112,500$$
$$= 425,000$$
The profit after 5 years would be $425,000.

91. $m = \frac{y_2 - y_1}{x_2 - x_1}$
$$= \frac{-3 - (-3)}{-5 - 2}$$
$$= \frac{0}{-7}$$
$$= 0$$

$x = a, \ a \in R$

93. $m = \frac{3}{2}$

$$y = mx + b$$
$$(-4) = \left(\frac{3}{2}\right)(2) + b$$
$$-4 = 3 + b$$
$$-7 = b$$

$$y = mx + b$$
$$y = \frac{3}{2}x - 7$$
$$2y = 3x - 14$$
$$3x - 2y = 14$$

3.5 Exercises

1. A linear inequality in two variables can be written in the form $Ax + By > C$.

3. When graphing the solutions for a linear inequality in two variables, in order to determine which region to shade, we use a <u>test</u> point that does not line on the line.

5. The graph of the line for an inequality is <u>dotted</u> if the inequality symbol is either $<$ or $>$.

7. Graph the line $y = \dfrac{2}{5}x + 2$ using a solid line. Choose the test point $(0, 0)$.

    $$y \le \frac{2}{5}x + 2$$

    $$(0) \le \frac{2}{5}(0) + 2$$

    $$0 \le 2$$

    True

    Shade the region that contains the point $(0, 0)$.

    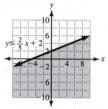

9. Graph the line $x - y = 1$ using a dashed line. Choose the test point $(0, 0)$.

    $$x - y > 1$$

    $$(0) - (0) > 1$$

    $$0 > 1$$

    False

    Shade the region that does not contain the point $(0, 0)$.

    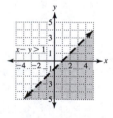

11. Graph the line $4y = 5x + 20$ using a solid line. Choose the test point $(0, 0)$.

    $$4y \ge 5x + 20$$

    $$4(0) \ge 5(0) + 20$$

    $$0 \ge 20$$

    False

    Shade the region that does not contain the point $(0, 0)$.

    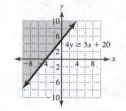

13. Graph the line $y = x$ using a dashed line. Choose the test point $(0, 1)$.

    $$y < x$$

    $$(1) < (0)$$

    $$1 < 0$$

    False

    Shade the region that does not contain the point $(0, 1)$.

    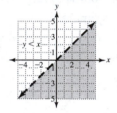

15. Graph the line $-3y = 2x$ using a dashed line. Choose the test point $(0, 1)$.

    $$-3y < 2x$$

    $$-3(1) < 2(0)$$

    $$-3 < 0$$

    True

    Shade the region that contains the point $(0, 1)$.

    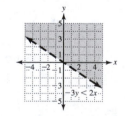

17. Graph the line $x = 4$ using a solid line. Choose the test point $(0, 0)$.

    $$x \le 4$$

    $$(0) \le 4$$

    $$0 \le 4$$

    True

    Shade the region that contains the point $(0, 0)$.

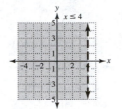

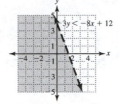

19. Graph the line $y = -4$ using a dashed line. Choose the test point $(0,0)$.

$$y < -4$$
$$(0) < -4$$
$$0 < -4$$

False

Shade the region that does not contain the point $(0,1)$.

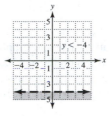

21. Graph the line $7 - y = 7x$ using a dashed line. Choose the test point $(0,0)$.

$$7 - y < 7x$$
$$7 - (0) < 7(0)$$
$$7 < 0$$

False

Shade the region that does not contain the point $(0,0)$.

23. Graph the line $3y = -8x + 12$ using a dashed line. Choose the test point $(0,0)$.

$$3y < -8x + 12$$
$$3(0) < -8(0) + 12$$
$$0 < 12$$

True

Shade the region that contains the point $(0,0)$.

25. Graph the line $y + 5 = 7$ using a solid line. Choose the test point $(0,0)$.

$$y + 5 \leq 7$$
$$(0) + 5 \leq 7$$
$$5 \leq 7$$

True

Shade the region that contains the point $(0,0)$.

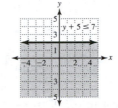

27. Graph the line $-3x = 6$ using a dashed line. Choose the test point $(0,0)$.

$$-3x > 6$$
$$-3(0) > 6$$
$$0 > 6$$

False

Shade the region that does not contain the point $(0,0)$.

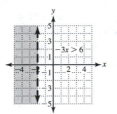

29. Graph the line $y = -\dfrac{5}{2}x + \dfrac{7}{2}$ using a solid line. Choose the test point $(0,0)$.

$$y \geq -\frac{5}{2}x + \frac{7}{2}$$
$$0 \geq -\frac{5}{2}(0) + \frac{7}{2}$$
$$0 \geq \frac{7}{2}$$

False

Shade the region that does not contain the point $(0,0)$.

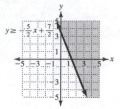

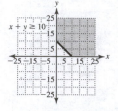

31. The ordered pair $(-3, 4)$ is a solution because $-10 < -4$.

$$2x - y < -4$$
$$2(-3) - (4) < -4$$
$$-10 < -4$$

The ordered pair $(0, 4)$ is not a solution because $-4 = -4$.

$$2x - y < -4$$
$$2(0) - (4) < -4$$
$$-4 < -4$$

The ordered pair $(6, 3)$ is not a solution because $9 > -4$.

$$2x - y < -4$$
$$2(6) - 3 < -4$$
$$9 < -4$$

33. No, because the point $(2, 3)$ would lie in one half-plane or the other.

35. Answers will vary; one example is: The origin is not a wise choice in this case because the result is $0 < 0$, which only indicates that the origin is not a solution. It does not give insight to which set of points is a solution.

37. no

39. Answers will vary; one example is: $(0, 0)$.

41. $x + y \geq 10$

Graph the equation $x + y = 10$ using a solid line.

Choose the test point $(0, 0)$.

$$x + y \geq 10$$
$$0 + 0 \geq 10$$
$$0 \geq 10$$

False

Shade the region in the first quadrant that does not contain $(0, 0)$. We only shade in the first quadrant because the number of sales cannot be negative.

43. Answers will vary; one example is: There are six times more red and white spools than blue spools and the storage capacity is 4,500 spools total.

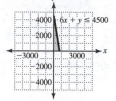

45. Prepare We must write and graph a linear inequality that represents the number of CDs and cassettes that Chant Music must sell per month given the condition that they must sell more than 3,250 units total.

Plan Let x represent the number of CDs and y represent the number of cassettes that Chant Music must sell per month.

Process
$$x + y > 3,250$$

Graph the equation $x + y = 3,250$ with a dashed line.

Choose the test point $(0, 0)$.

$$x + y > 3,250$$
$$0 + 0 > 3,250$$
$$0 > 3,250$$

False

Shade the region that does not contain $(0, 0)$.

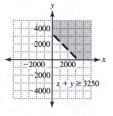

Ponder Do our answers seem reasonable? Yes. It is quite reasonable that Chant Music can sell an average of 271 CDs and cassettes per month.

47. Graph the equation $\frac{32}{25}x + \frac{8}{5}y = 4$ using a solid line.

Choose the test point $(0, 0)$.

$$\frac{32}{25}x+\frac{8}{5}y\geq 4$$

$$\frac{32}{25}(0)+\frac{8}{5}(0)\geq 4$$

$$0\geq 4$$

False

Shade the region that does not contain the point $(0,0)$.

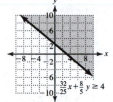

49. The slope of the line is 2 and the y-intercept is $(0,2)$. Therefore, the equation that represents the line is $y=2x+2$. Because the line is dashed, we must use either < or >. Because the use of < would cause the origin to satisfy the inequality, $y<2x+2$, we should choose $y<2x+2$ for the inequality.

3.6 Exercises

1. A <u>linear</u> <u>function</u> may be written in the form $f(x) = mx + b$.

3. A special type of relation in which every element of the <u>domain</u> is paired to a unique element of the <u>range</u>, is called a <u>function</u>.

5. The set that the independent variable comes from is called the <u>domain</u>.

7. The relationship is a state to the state's flower. The relation is a function.

Domain $= \{$Texas, Iowa, California, Florida$\}$

Range $= \left\{\begin{array}{l}\text{Bluebonnet, Wild Rose, Golden Poppy,}\\ \text{Orange Blossom}\end{array}\right\}$

9. The relationship is a city to its sport team name. This relation is not a function.

11. The relationship is a letter to its number corresponding to the order of the alphabet. The relation is a function.

Domain $= \{$a, b, c, d, e, ..., z$\}$

Range $= \{$1, 2, 3, 4, 5, ..., 26$\}$

13. The relationship is an animal to its breed. This relationship is not a function.

15. relation

17. function

19. function

21. neither

23. function

25. relation

27. $D = (-\infty, \infty), R = (-\infty, \infty)$

$f(x) = 5x$	$f(x) = 5x$	$f(x) = 5x$
$f(-1) = 5(-1)$	$f(0) = 5(0)$	$f(1) = 5(1)$
$= -5$	$= 0$	$= 5$
$(-1, -5)$	$(0, 0)$	$(1, 5)$

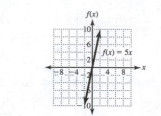

29. $D = (-\infty, \infty), R = (-\infty, \infty)$

$g(x) = x - 3$	$g(x) = x - 3$	$g(x) = x - 3$
$g(-1) = (-1) - 3$	$g(0) = (0) - 3$	$g(1) = (1) - 3$
$= -4$	$= -3$	$= -2$
$(-1, -4)$	$(0, -3)$	$(1, -2)$

31. $D = (-\infty, \infty), R = (-\infty, \infty)$

$h(x) = -2x + 7$	$h(x) = -2x + 7$	$h(x) = -2x + 7$
$h(-1) = -2(-1) + 7$	$h(0) = -2(0) + 7$	$h(1) = -2(1) + 7$
$= 9$	$= 7$	$= 5$
$(-1, 9)$	$(0, 7)$	$(1, 5)$

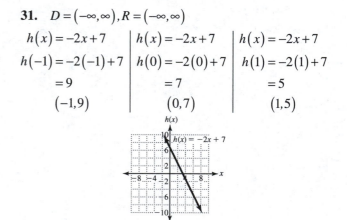

33. $D = (-\infty, \infty), R = (-\infty, \infty)$

$f(x) = \frac{2}{3}x - 1$	$f(x) = \frac{2}{3}x - 1$	$f(x) = \frac{2}{3}x - 1$
$f(-3) = \frac{2}{3}(-3) - 1$	$f(0) = \frac{2}{3}(0) - 1$	$f(3) = \frac{2}{3}(3) - 1$
$= -3$	$= -1$	$= 1$
$(-3, -3)$	$(0, -1)$	$(3, 1)$

35. $D = (-\infty, \infty), R = \{3\}$

$f(x) = 3$	$f(x) = 3$	$f(x) = 3$
$f(-1) = 3$	$f(0) = 3$	$f(1) = 3$
$(-1,3)$	$(0,3)$	$(1,3)$

37.

$f(x) = 5x$ $f(x) = 5x$ $f(x) = 5x$

$f(-3) = 5(-3)$ $f\left(\dfrac{1}{5}\right) = 5\left(\dfrac{1}{5}\right)$ $f(r) = 5(r)$

$\quad = -15$ $\qquad = 1$ $\quad = 5r$

$(-3,-15)$ $\left(\dfrac{1}{5},1\right)$ $(r,5r)$

39.

$g(x) = x - 3$ $g(x) = x - 3$ $g(x) = x - 3$

$g(0) = (0) - 3$ $g(-2) = (-2) - 3$ $g(c) = (c) - 3$

$\quad = -3$ $\quad = -5$ $\quad = c - 3$

$(0,-3)$ $(-2,-5)$ $(c,c-3)$

41.

$h(x) = -2x + 7$ $h(x) = -2x + 7$ $h(x) = -2x + 7$

$h(-5) = -2(-5) + 7$ $h(10) = -2(10) + 7$ $h(s) = -2(s) + 7$

$\qquad = 17$ $\qquad = -13$ $\qquad = -2s + 7$

$(-5,17)$ $(10,-13)$ $(s,-2s+7)$

43. $f(t) = \dfrac{t^2 - 1}{t}$ $f(t) = \dfrac{t^2 - 1}{t}$ $f(t) = \dfrac{t^2 - 1}{t}$

$f(3) = \dfrac{(3)^2 - 1}{(3)}$ $f(1) = \dfrac{(1)^2 - 1}{(1)}$ $f(0.5) = \dfrac{(0.5)^2 - 1}{(0.5)}$

$\quad = \dfrac{8}{3}$ $\quad = 0$ $\quad = -1.5$

$\left(3, \dfrac{8}{3}\right)$ $(1,0)$ $(0.5,-1.5)$

113

45.
$$f(x) = -5x^2 + 2x - 3$$
$$f(-6) = -5(-6)^2 + 2(-6) - 3$$
$$= -195$$
$$(-6, -195)$$

$$f(x) = -5x^2 + 2x - 3$$
$$f\left(\frac{1}{2}\right) = -5\left(\frac{1}{2}\right)^2 + 2\left(\frac{1}{2}\right) - 3$$
$$= -\frac{13}{4}$$
$$\left(\frac{1}{2}, -\frac{13}{4}\right)$$

$$f(x) = -5x^2 + 2x - 3$$
$$f(0.1) = -5(0.1)^2 + 2(0.1) - 3$$
$$= -2.85$$
$$(0.1, -2.85)$$

$$f(x) = -5x^2 + 2x - 3$$
$$f(a) = -5(a)^2 + 2(a) - 3$$
$$= -5a^2 + 2a - 3$$
$$\left(a, -5a^2 + 2a - 3\right)$$

47.
$$g(x) = 4x^3 - x + 4$$
$$g(-2) = 4(-2)^3 - (-2) + 4$$
$$= -26$$
$$(-2, -26)$$

$$g(x) = 4x^3 - x + 4$$
$$g(0.2) = 4(0.2)^3 - (0.2) + 4$$
$$= 3.832$$
$$(0.2, 3.832)$$

$$g(x) = 4x^3 - x + 4$$
$$g(t) = 4(t)^3 - (t) + 4$$
$$= 4t^3 - t + 4$$
$$\left(t, 4t^3 - t + 4\right)$$

49.
$$h(x) = |x + 13|$$
$$h(0) = |(0) + 13|$$
$$= 13$$
$$(0, 13)$$

$$h(x) = |x + 13|$$
$$h(-13) = |(-13) + 13|$$
$$= 0$$
$$(-13, 0)$$

$$h(x) = |x + 13|$$
$$h(-14) = |(-14) + 13|$$
$$= 1$$
$$(-14, 1)$$

51.
$$h(x) = 5 - 2x^2$$
$$h(-5) = 5 - 2(-5)^2$$
$$= -45$$
$$(-5, -45)$$

$$h(x) = 5 - 2x^2$$
$$h\left(\frac{3}{4}\right) = 5 - 2\left(\frac{3}{4}\right)^2$$
$$= \frac{31}{8}$$
$$\left(\frac{3}{4}, \frac{31}{8}\right)$$

$$h(x) = 5 - 2x^2$$
$$h(n) = 5 - 2(n)^2$$
$$= 5 - 2n^2$$
$$\left(n, 5 - 2n^2\right)$$

53. Answers will vary; one example is: A relation can pair up the independent variable with different values of the dependent variable, while a function can pair up different values of the dependent variable with one value of the independent variable.

55. Answers will vary; one example is: The graph of any linear function is a straight line.

57.
$$J(x) = -3x + 50,000$$
$$J(2,314) = -3(2,314) + 50,000$$
$$= 43,058$$

There are 43,058 green and other color jellybeans.

59.
$$C(x) = \frac{5}{3}x$$
$$C(51) = \frac{5}{3}(51)$$
$$= 85$$

There are 85 unscented candles.

$$C(1) = \frac{5}{3} \text{ and } C(2) = \frac{10}{3}$$

Domain $= \{x \mid x \geq 0 \text{ and } x \text{ is a multiple of } 3\}$

61. Prepare We need to write a linear function that represents the relationship between a person's age and their maximum heart rate. We will then use the function to determine the maximum heart rate of a person of age 25.

Plan We will use the ordered pairs $(20,194)$ and $(50,173)$ along with the slope formula to write the linear function.

Process Let x represent the person's age in years.

$$m = \frac{194-173}{20-50}$$
$$= \frac{21}{-30}$$
$$= -0.7$$

$$y = mx + b$$
$$194 = -0.7(20) + b$$
$$194 = -14 + b$$
$$208 = b$$

$$f(x) = -0.7x + 208$$

$$f(25) = -0.7(25) + 208$$
$$= 190.5$$

The maximum hear rate for a 25 year old is 190.5 bpm.

Ponder Does our answer seem reasonable? Yes, because 25 is between 20 and 50, and because maximum heart rate decreases with age, it seems reasonable that the heart rate of a 25 year old would be 190.5 bpm.

63. a) $P = 4s$

b) Answers will vary; one example is: $P(s)$.

c) $P(s) = 4s$

65. a) $h(t) = -16t^2 + 4,800$
$$h(0) = -16(0)^2 + 4,800$$
$$= 4,800$$
The initial height of the missile is 4,800 feet.

b) $h(10) = -16(10)^2 + 4,800$
$$= -1,600 + 4,800$$
$$= 3,200$$
The height of the missile at 10 seconds is 3,200 feet.

c) $h(15) = -16(15)^2 + 4,800$
$$= -3,600 + 4,800$$
$$= 1,200$$
The height of the missile at 15 seconds is 1,200 feet.

Chapter 3 Review Problem Set

1. This is a linear equation.

    $$x = \frac{3}{4}y + 2$$

    $$x - \frac{3}{4}y = \frac{3}{4}y - \frac{3}{4}y + 2$$

    $$x - \frac{3}{4}y = 2$$

2. This is not a linear equation because it cannot be rewritten in standard form.

3. This is not a linear equation because the exponent on y is 2

4. $$5x - y = -3$$
    $$5(0) - (-3) = -3$$
    $$0 + 3 = -3$$
    $$3 = -3$$

    The ordered pair $(0, -3)$ is not a solution.

5. $$y = 4x - 3$$
    $$(0) = 4(-3) - 3$$
    $$0 = -12 - 3$$
    $$0 = -15$$

    The ordered pair $(-3, 0)$ is not a solution.

6. $$y = 4x + 2$$
    $$(6) = 4(-2) + 2$$
    $$6 = -8 + 2$$
    $$6 = -6$$

    The ordered pair $(-2, 6)$ is not a solution.

7. $$3x - 2y = 1$$
    $$3\left(-\frac{1}{3}\right) - 2(1) = 1$$
    $$-1 - 2 = 1$$
    $$-3 = 1$$

    The ordered pair $\left(-\frac{1}{3}, 1\right)$ is not a solution.

8. $$-4x + 2y = 10$$
    $$-4\left(-\frac{1}{2}\right) + 2(6) = 10$$
    $$2 + 12 = 10$$
    $$14 = 10$$

    The ordered pair $\left(-\frac{1}{2}, 6\right)$ is not a solution.

9. $$3x - 2y = 10$$
    $$3(3) - 2y = 10$$
    $$9 - 2y = 10$$
    $$-2y = 1$$
    $$y = -\frac{1}{2}$$

    The ordered pair $\left(3, -\frac{1}{2}\right)$ is a solution.

10. $$2x + 3y = -6$$
    $$2(2) + 3y = -6$$
    $$4 + 3y = -6$$
    $$3y = -10$$
    $$y = -\frac{10}{3}$$

    The ordered pair $\left(2, -\frac{10}{3}\right)$ is a solution.

11. $$\frac{1}{4}x + y = 6$$
    $$\frac{1}{4}x + (3) = 6$$
    $$\frac{1}{4}x = 3$$
    $$x = 12$$

    The ordered pair $(12, 3)$ is a solution.

12. $$\frac{1}{2}x - y = 4$$
    $$\frac{1}{2}x - (2) = 4$$
    $$\frac{1}{2}x = 6$$
    $$x = 12$$

    The ordered pair $(12, 2)$ is a solution.

13.

$x = -3$	$x = 0$	$x = 3$
$x + 3y = 6$	$x + 3y = 6$	$x + 3y = 6$
$(-3) + 3y = 6$	$(0) + 3y = 6$	$(3) + 3y = 6$
$3y = 9$	$3y = 6$	$3y = 3$
$y = 3$	$y = 2$	$y = 1$
$(-3, 3)$	$(0, 2)$	$(3, 1)$

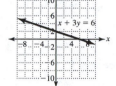

14.

$x = -1$	$x = 0$	$x = 1$
$2x + y = 8$	$2x + y = 8$	$2x + y = 8$
$2(-1) + y = 8$	$2(0) + y = 8$	$2(1) + y = 8$
$-2 + y = 8$	$0 + y = 8$	$2 + y = 8$
$y = 10$	$y = 8$	$y = 6$
$(-1, 10)$	$(0, 8)$	$(1, 6)$

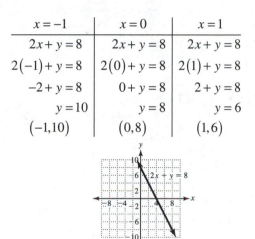

15.

$x = -1$	$x = 0$	$x = 1$
$-2x + y = 8$	$-2x + y = 8$	$-2x + y = 8$
$-2(-1) + y = 8$	$-2(0) + y = 8$	$-2(1) + y = 8$
$2 + y = 8$	$0 + y = 8$	$-2 + y = 8$
$y = 6$	$y = 8$	$y = 10$
$(-1, 6)$	$(0, 8)$	$(1, 10)$

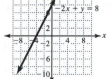

16.

$x = -1$	$x = 0$	$x = 1$
$4x - 2y = 8$	$4x - 2y = 8$	$4x - 2y = 8$
$4(-1) - 2y = 8$	$4(0) - 2y = 8$	$4(1) - 2y = 8$
$-4 - 2y = 8$	$0 - 2y = 8$	$4 - 2y = 8$
$-2y = 12$	$-2y = 8$	$-2y = 4$
$y = -6$	$y = -4$	$y = -2$
$(-1, -6)$	$(0, -4)$	$(2, 3)$

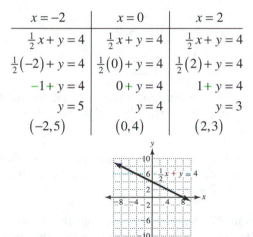

17.

$x = -2$	$x = 0$	$x = 2$
$\frac{1}{2}x + y = 4$	$\frac{1}{2}x + y = 4$	$\frac{1}{2}x + y = 4$
$\frac{1}{2}(-2) + y = 4$	$\frac{1}{2}(0) + y = 4$	$\frac{1}{2}(2) + y = 4$
$-1 + y = 4$	$0 + y = 4$	$1 + y = 4$
$y = 5$	$y = 4$	$y = 3$
$(-2, 5)$	$(0, 4)$	$(2, 3)$

18.

$x = -2$	$x = 0$	$x = 2$
$-\frac{1}{2}x - y = 6$	$-\frac{1}{2}x - y = 6$	$-\frac{1}{2}x - y = 6$
$-\frac{1}{2}(-2) - y = 6$	$-\frac{1}{2}(0) - y = 6$	$-\frac{1}{2}(2) - y = 6$
$1 - y = 6$	$0 - y = 6$	$-1 - y = 6$
$-y = 5$	$-y = 6$	$-y = 7$
$y = -5$	$y = -6$	$y = -7$
$(-2, -5)$	$(0, -6)$	$(2, -7)$

19. Prepare We must determine the y values that are related to each of the given x values and then use these values to make a T table.

Plan We will use the given equation to substitute the given x values and solve for the corresponding y values.

Process

$$-180x + y = 500 \qquad -180x + y = 500$$
$$-180(2) + y = 500 \qquad -180(5) + y = 500$$
$$-360 + y = 500 \qquad -900 + y = 500$$
$$y = 860 \qquad y = 1{,}400$$

$$-180x + y = 500$$
$$-180(10) + y = 500$$
$$-1{,}800 + y = 500$$
$$y = 2{,}300$$

x	y
2	860
5	1,400
10	2,300

Ponder Are our results correct? A quick check of the arithmetic will show that the answers are correct.

20. Prepare We must determine the y values that are related to each of the given x values and then use these values to make a T table.

Plan We will use the given equation to substitute the given x values and solve for the corresponding y values.

Process

$$-30x + y = 250 \qquad -30x + y = 250$$
$$-30(3) + y = 250 \qquad -30(7) + y = 250$$
$$-90 + y = 250 \qquad -210 + y = 250$$
$$y = 340 \qquad y = 460$$

$$-30x + y = 250$$
$$-30(15) + y = 250$$
$$-450 + y = 250$$
$$y = 700$$

x	y
3	340
7	460
15	700

Ponder Are our results correct? A quick check of the arithmetic will show that the answers are correct.

21. Let $x = 0$, and solve for y.
$$2x + 3y = 6$$
$$2(0) + 3y = 6$$
$$3y = 6$$
$$y = 2$$
The y-intercept is $(0, 2)$.

Let $y = 0$, and solve for x.
$$2x + 3y = 6$$
$$2x + 3(0) = 6$$
$$2x = 6$$
$$x = 3$$
The x-intercept is $(3, 0)$.

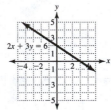

22. Let $x = 0$, and solve for y.
$$2x + 4y = 8$$
$$2(0) + 4y = 8$$
$$4y = 8$$
$$y = 2$$
The y-intercept is $(0, 2)$.

Let $y = 0$, and solve for x.
$$2x + 4y = 8$$
$$2x + 4(0) = 8$$
$$2x = 8$$
$$x = 4$$
The x-intercept is $(4, 0)$.

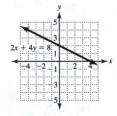

23. Let $x = 0$, and solve for y.
$$x - 3y = 0$$
$$(0) - 3y = 0$$
$$-3y = 0$$
$$y = 0$$
The y-intercept is $(0, 0)$.

Let $y = 0$, and solve for x.

$$x - 3y = 0$$
$$x - 3(0) = 0$$
$$x = 0$$

The x-intercept is $(0,0)$.

Find another point by setting $x = 3$.

$$x - 3y = 0$$
$$3 - 3y = 0$$
$$-3y = -3$$
$$y = 1$$

Plot the point $(3,1)$.

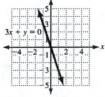

24. Let $x = 0$, and solve for y.

$$3x + y = 0$$
$$3(0) + y = 0$$
$$0 + y = 0$$
$$y = 0$$

The y-intercept is $(0,0)$.

Let $y = 0$, and solve for x.

$$3x + y = 0$$
$$3x + (0) = 0$$
$$3x = 0$$
$$x = 0$$

The x-intercept is $(0,0)$.

Find another point by setting $x = 1$.

$$3x + y = 0$$
$$3(1) + y = 0$$
$$3 + y = 0$$
$$y = -3$$

Plot the point $(1,-3)$.

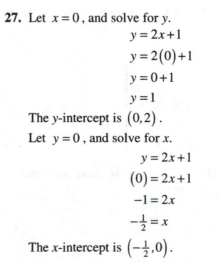

25. Let $x = 0$, and solve for y.

$$y = x + 4$$
$$y = (0) + 4$$
$$y = 4$$

The y-intercept is $(0,4)$.

Let $y = 0$, and solve for x.

$$y = x + 4$$
$$(0) = x + 4$$
$$-4 = x$$

The x-intercept is $(-4,0)$.

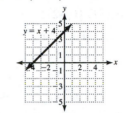

26. Let $x = 0$, and solve for y.

$$y = -x + 2$$
$$y = -(0) + 2$$
$$y = 2$$

The y-intercept is $(0,2)$.

Let $y = 0$, and solve for x.

$$y = -x + 2$$
$$(0) = -x + 2$$
$$x = 2$$

The x-intercept is $(2,0)$.

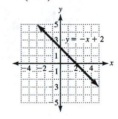

27. Let $x = 0$, and solve for y.

$$y = 2x + 1$$
$$y = 2(0) + 1$$
$$y = 0 + 1$$
$$y = 1$$

The y-intercept is $(0,2)$.

Let $y = 0$, and solve for x.

$$y = 2x + 1$$
$$(0) = 2x + 1$$
$$-1 = 2x$$
$$-\tfrac{1}{2} = x$$

The x-intercept is $\left(-\tfrac{1}{2},0\right)$.

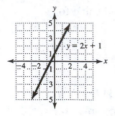

28. Let $x = 0$, and solve for y.

$$y = 3x - 2$$
$$y = 3(0) - 2$$
$$y = -2$$

The y-intercept is $(0, -2)$.

Let $y = 0$, and solve for x.

$$y = 3x - 2$$
$$(0) = 3x - 2$$
$$2 = 3x$$
$$\frac{2}{3} = x$$

The x-intercept is $\left(\frac{2}{3}, 0\right)$.

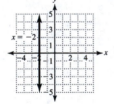

29. The graph of $x = -2$ is a vertical line with x-intercept $(-2, 0)$.

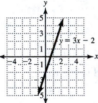

30. The graph of $x = 4$ is a vertical line with x-intercept $(4, 0)$.

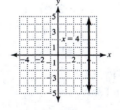

31. The graph of $y = 2$ is a horizontal line with y-intercept $(0, 2)$.

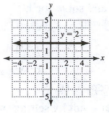

32. The graph of $y = -1$ is a horizontal line with y-intercept $(0, -1)$.

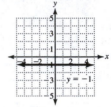

33. The graph of $x = \frac{2}{3}$ is a vertical line with x-intercept $\left(\frac{2}{3}, 0\right)$.

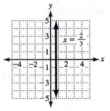

34. The graph of $y = \frac{5}{2}$ is a horizontal line with y-intercept $\left(0, \frac{5}{2}\right)$.

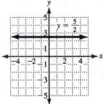

35. vertical

36. neither

37. horizontal

38. vertical

39. neither

40. neither

41. Prepare   We are asked to use the given linear equation, representing the number bird houses and planters that can be made in one 1,200 work week, to answer problems a) through d).

Plan We will answers the questions by using the techniques learned in this section concerning the intercepts of a line.

Process

a) Let $x = 0$, then $y = 10$. The y-intercept is $(0,10)$. There is no x-intercept.

b) If Wooden Creations builds no birdhouses, they will have to pay for 10 hours of labor.

c) If $x = 10$, then $y = 40$. Plot the point $(10,40)$.

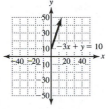

Ponder Does our answer seem reasonable? Yes. It seems reasonable that as the number of birdhouses produced goes up, that the number of labor hours needed will go up.

42. **Prepare** We are asked to use the given linear equation, representing the number bird houses and planters that can be made in one 1,200 work week, to answer problems a) through d).

Plan We will answers the questions by using the techniques learned in this section concerning the intercepts of a line.

Process

a) Let $x = 0$, then $y = 100$. The y-intercept is $(0,100)$. There is no x-intercept.

b) John makes \$100, even if it does not snow.

c) If $x = 10$, then $y = 200$. Plot the point $(10,200)$.

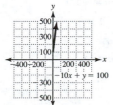

Ponder Does our answer seem reasonable? Yes. It seems reasonable that as the number of labor hours goes up that the charges will also go up.

43. zero

44. positive

45. undefined

46. negative

47. $m = \dfrac{\text{rise}}{\text{run}}$
$= \dfrac{-4}{3}$
$= -\dfrac{4}{3}$

48. $m = \dfrac{\text{rise}}{\text{run}}$
$= \dfrac{-4}{0}$
undefined

49. $m = \dfrac{\text{rise}}{\text{run}}$
$= \dfrac{0}{3}$
$= 0$

50. $m = \dfrac{\text{rise}}{\text{run}}$
$= \dfrac{3}{4}$

51. $m = \dfrac{y_2 - y_1}{x_2 - x_1}$
$= \dfrac{4-9}{13-3}$
$= \dfrac{-5}{10}$
$= -\dfrac{1}{2}$

52. $m = \dfrac{y_2 - y_1}{x_2 - x_1}$
$= \dfrac{3-12}{20-2}$
$= \dfrac{-9}{18}$
$= -\dfrac{1}{2}$

53. $m = \dfrac{y_2 - y_1}{x_2 - x_1}$

$= \dfrac{12 - 5}{3 - (-4)}$

$= \dfrac{7}{7}$

$= 1$

54. $m = \dfrac{y_2 - y_1}{x_2 - x_1}$

$= \dfrac{7 - (-1)}{9 - 5}$

$= \dfrac{8}{4}$

$= 2$

55. $m = \dfrac{y_2 - y_1}{x_2 - x_1}$

$= \dfrac{5 - 2}{-2 - 0}$

$= \dfrac{3}{-2}$

$= -\dfrac{3}{2}$

56. $m = \dfrac{y_2 - y_1}{x_2 - x_1}$

$= \dfrac{-5 - 9}{0 - 6}$

$= \dfrac{-14}{-6}$

$= \dfrac{7}{3}$

57. $m = \dfrac{y_2 - y_1}{x_2 - x_1}$

$= \dfrac{7 - (-2)}{5 - 5}$

$= \dfrac{9}{0}$

undefined

58. $m = \dfrac{y_2 - y_1}{x_2 - x_1}$

$= \dfrac{-6 - 9}{3 - 3}$

$= \dfrac{-15}{0}$

undefined

59. $m = \dfrac{y_2 - y_1}{x_2 - x_1}$

$= \dfrac{4 - 4}{-8 - 4}$

$= \dfrac{0}{-12}$

$= 0$

60. $m = \dfrac{y_2 - y_1}{x_2 - x_1}$

$= \dfrac{8 - 8}{0 - (-5)}$

$= \dfrac{0}{5}$

$= 0$

61.   Slope: $m = 5$

y-intercept: $(0, 2)$

62.   Slope: $m = -3$

y-intercept: $(0, 0)$

63.   Slope: $m = \dfrac{2}{3}$

y-intercept: $(0, 9)$

64.   Slope: $m = \dfrac{3}{4}$

y-intercept: $(0, -8)$

65.   Slope: $m = -5$

y-intercept: $(0, 10)$

66.   Slope: $m = 3$

y-intercept: $(0, -9)$

67.   Slope: $m = \dfrac{2}{3}$

y-intercept: $(0, 4)$

68.   Slope: $m = 3$

        y-intercept: $(0, -5)$

69.   Slope: $m = \dfrac{3}{2}$

        y-intercept: $(0, -7)$

70.   Slope: $m = \dfrac{5}{3}$

        y-intercept: $(0, 2)$

71.   Slope: $m = 0$

        y-intercept: $(0, 5)$

72.   Slope: $m = 0$

        y-intercept: $(0, -2)$

73.   Slope: $m = 3$

        y-intercept: $(0, -1)$

74.   Slope: $m = 2$

        y-intercept: $(0, 3)$

75.   Slope: $m = -2$

        y-intercept: $(0, 0)$

76.   Slope: $m = \dfrac{3}{4}$

        y-intercept: $(0, 0)$

77.   Slope: $m = -\dfrac{2}{3}$

        y-intercept: $(0, 4)$

78.   Slope: $m = -\dfrac{1}{4}$

        y-intercept: $(0, -3)$

79.   Slope: $m = \dfrac{2}{3}$

        y-intercept: $(0, -4)$

80.   Slope: $m = -2$

        y-intercept: $(0, 5)$

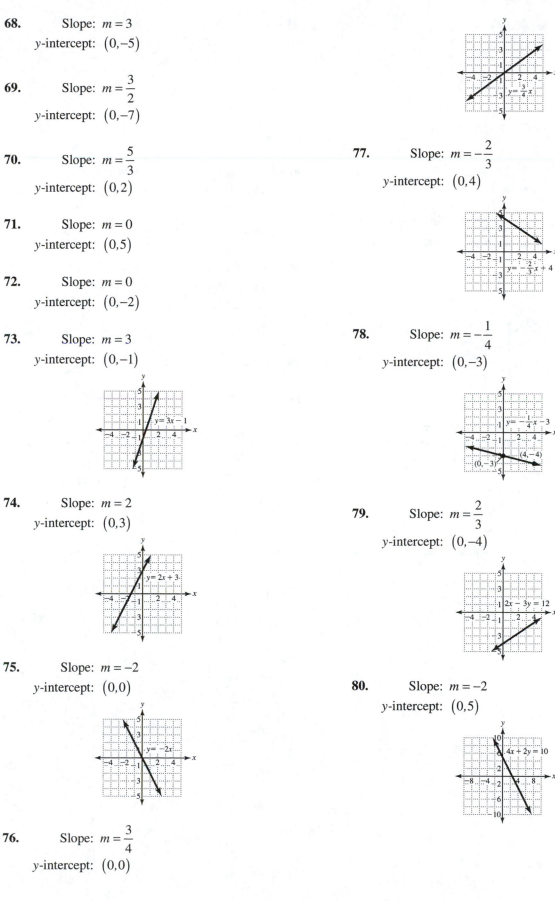

81. a) $(1, 28)$ and $(3, 68)$

b)

$$m = \frac{y_2 - y_2}{x_2 - x_1}$$

$$= \frac{68 - 28}{3 - 1}$$

$$= \frac{40}{2}$$

$$= 20$$

c) The y-intercept is $(0, 8)$, and represents the cost of the company operating with no production.

d)

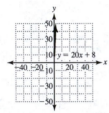

e) We can estimate using the graph that the cost to build five swings is $108. We can also let $x = 5$ and use the equation to determine the cost.

$$y = 20x + 8$$

$$y = 20(5) + 8$$

$$y = 108$$

82. $y = mx + b$

$$y = \left(\frac{1}{3}\right)x + (5)$$

$$y = \frac{1}{3}x + 5$$

83. $y = mx + b$

$$y = \left(\frac{2}{5}\right)x + (-2)$$

$$y = \frac{2}{5}x - 2$$

84. $y = mx + b$

$y = (-4)x + (1)$

$y = -4x + 1$

85. $y = 5$

86. $y = -2$

87. $y = mx + b$ $y = mx + b$

$(4) = (2)(-1) + b$ $y = 2x + 6$

$4 = -2 + b$

$6 = b$

88. $y = mx + b$ $y = mx + b$

$(4) = (-3)(1) + b$ $y = -3x + 7$

$4 = -3 + b$

$7 = b$

89. $x = 4$

90. $y = 5$

91. $m = \dfrac{y_2 - y_1}{x_2 - x_1}$ $b = -3$ $y = mx + b$

$= \dfrac{-3 - 3}{0 - 2}$ $y = 3x - 3$

$= \dfrac{-6}{-2}$

$= 3$

92. $m = \dfrac{y_2 - y_1}{x_2 - x_1}$ $b = 1$ $y = mx + b$

$= \dfrac{-2 - 1}{6 - 0}$ $y = -\dfrac{1}{2}x + 1$

$= \dfrac{-3}{6}$

$= -\dfrac{1}{2}$

93.
$$m = \frac{y_2 - y_1}{x_2 - x_1}$$

$$= \frac{-3-5}{1-(-1)}$$

$$= \frac{-8}{2}$$

$$= -4$$

$y = mx + b$

$5 = (-4)(-1) + b$

$5 = 4 + b$

$1 = b$

$y = mx + b$

$y = -4x + 1$

94.
$$m = \frac{y_2 - y_1}{x_2 - x_1}$$

$$= \frac{8-(-2)}{1-2}$$

$$= \frac{10}{-1}$$

$$= -10$$

$y = mx + b$

$-2 = (-10)(2) + b$

$-2 = -20 + b$

$18 = b$

$y = mx + b$

$y = -10x + 18$

95.
$$m = \frac{y_2 - y_1}{x_2 - x_1}$$

$$= \frac{4-4}{3-(-2)}$$

$$= \frac{0}{5}$$

$$= 0$$

$y = mx + b$

$y = 0x + 4$

$y = 4$

96.
$$m = \frac{y_2 - y_1}{x_2 - x_1}$$

$$= \frac{5-(-1)}{6-6}$$

$$= \frac{6}{0}$$

undefined

$x = 6$

97. The slope of L_1 is $m = \frac{2}{3}$. The slope of L_2 is $m = -\frac{3}{2}$. The lines are perpendicular.

98. The slope of L_1 is $m = -3$. The slope of L_2 is $m = 3$. The lines are neither parallel nor perpendicular.

99. The slope of L_1 is $m = 2$. The slope of L_2 is $m = \frac{1}{2}$. The lines are neither parallel nor perpendicular.

100. The slope of L_1 is $m = 2$. The slope of L_2 is $m = -2$. The lines are neither parallel nor perpendicular.

101. m is undefined

$x = -2$

102. $m = 0$ and $b = -6$

$y = mx + b$

$y = (0)x + (-6)$

$y = -6$

103. $m = \frac{2}{3}$ and $b = 2$

$y = mx + b$

$y = \left(\frac{2}{3}\right)x + (2)$

$3y = 2x + 6$

$2x - 3y = -6$

104.
$m = -\frac{1}{4}$ and $b = -1$

$y = mx + b$

$y = \left(-\frac{1}{4}\right)x + (-1)$

$4y = -x - 4$

$x + 4y = -4$

105. $m = -2$

$y = mx + b$

$(-3) = (-2)(6) + b$

$-3 = -12 + b$

$9 = b$

$y = mx + b$

$y = (-2)x + (9)$

$2x + y = 9$

106. $m = -\dfrac{1}{3}$ $y = mx + b$

$$(1) = \left(-\dfrac{1}{3}\right)(-2) + b$$

$$1 = \dfrac{2}{3} + b$$

$$\dfrac{1}{3} = b$$

$$y = mx + b$$

$$y = \left(-\dfrac{1}{3}\right)x + \left(\dfrac{1}{3}\right)$$

$$3y = -x + 1$$

$$x + 3y = 1$$

107.

$$y = mx + b \qquad\qquad y = mx + b$$
$$(4) = (-3)(-5) + b \qquad y = -3x - 11$$
$$4 = 15 + b \qquad\qquad 3x + y = -11$$
$$-11 = b$$

108. $x = -\dfrac{2}{5}$

109.

$$y = mx + b$$

$$y = -\dfrac{3}{2}x + 9$$

$$2y = -3x + 18$$

$$3x + 2y = 18$$

110. $m = 0$ and $b = -2$

$$y = mx + b$$

$$y = (0)x + (-2)$$

$$y = -2$$

111.

$$y = mx + b \qquad\qquad y = mx + b$$
$$(0) = (-3)(-4) + b \qquad y = -3x - 12$$
$$0 = 12 + b \qquad\qquad 3x + y = -12$$
$$-12 = b$$

112. $m = \dfrac{y_2 - y_1}{x_2 - x_1}$ $b = -16$ $y = mx + b$

$$= \dfrac{-16 - 0}{0 - 4} \qquad\qquad y = 4x - 16$$

$$= \dfrac{-16}{-4}$$

$$= 4 \qquad\qquad\qquad 4x - y = 16$$

113.
a) If we consider the ground to be $y = 0$ feet high, the balloon is 6 feet at time $x = 0$. Therefore, the ordered pair is $(0, 6)$. If the balloon climbs at a rate of 3 feet per second, then after 5 seconds, the balloon has risen 15 feet, making its total height 21 feet. Therefore, the ordered pair is $(5, 21)$.

b) The rate at which the balloon is climbing is 3 feet per second, so the slope is $m = 3$. The initial height of the balloon is 6 feet, so the y-intercept is $(0, 6)$.

c) $y = 3x + 6$

d) Let $y = 28.5$.

$$y = 3x + 6$$
$$28.5 = 3x + 6$$
$$22.5 = 3x$$
$$7.5 = x$$

It will take approximately 7.5 seconds.

114.
a) If we consider the ground to be $y = 0$ feet high, the helicopter is 150 feet at time $x = 0$. Therefore, the ordered pair is $(0, 150)$. If the helicopter climbs at a rate of 150 feet per minute, then after 3 minutes, the helicopter has risen 450 feet, making its total height 600 feet. Therefore, the ordered pair is $(3, 600)$.

b) The rate at which the helicopter is climbing is 150 feet per minute, so the slope is $m = 150$. The initial height of the balloon is 150 feet, so the y-intercept is $(0, 150)$.

c) $y = 150x + 150$

d) Let $y = 525$.

$$y = 150x + 150$$
$$525 = 150x + 150$$
$$375 = 150x$$
$$2.5 = x$$

It will take approximately 2.5 minutes.

115. Graph the line $y = -\dfrac{2}{3}x + 4$ using a solid line.

Choose the test point $(0,0)$.

$$y \geq -\frac{2}{3}x + 4$$

$$(0) \geq -\frac{2}{3}(0) + 4$$

$$0 \geq 4$$

False

Shade the region that does not contain the point $(0,0)$.

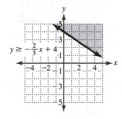

116. Graph the line $y = x$ using a dashed line.

Choose the test point $(0,1)$.

$$y < x$$

$$1 < 0$$

False

Shade the region that does not contain the point $(0,1)$.

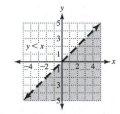

117. Graph the line $-8x + 10y = 40$ using a solid line.

Choose the test point $(0,0)$.

$$-8x + 10y \leq 40$$

$$-8(0) + 10(0) \leq 40$$

$$0 \leq 40$$

True

Shade the region that contains the point $(0,0)$.

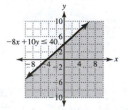

118. Graph the line $-2x - 5y = -20$ using a dashed line.

Choose the test point $(0,0)$.

$$-2x - 5y > -20$$

$$-2(0) - 5(0) > -20$$

$$0 > -20$$

True

Shade the region that contains the point $(0,0)$.

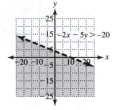

119. Graph the line $-3y = -3x - 6$ using a solid line.

Choose the test point $(0,0)$.

$$-3y \leq -3x - 6$$

$$-3(0) \leq -3(0) - 6$$

$$0 \leq -6$$

False

Shade the region that does not contain the point $(0,0)$.

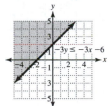

120. Graph the line $-5y = x + 5$ using a dashed line.

Choose the test point $(0,0)$.

$$-5y > x + 5$$

$$-5(0) > 0 + 5$$

$$0 > 5$$

False

Shade the region that does not contain the point $(0,0)$.

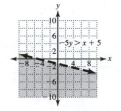

121. Graph the line $x = 3$ using a solid line. Choose the test point $(0,0)$.

$$x \geq 3$$
$$0 \geq 3$$
False

Shade the region that does not contain the point $(0,0)$.

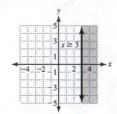

122. Graph the line $-2x = 8$ using a dashed line. Choose the test point $(0,0)$.

$$-2x < 8$$
$$-2(0) < 8$$
$$0 < 8$$
True

Shade the region that contains the point $(0,0)$.

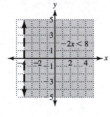

123. Graph the line $y = \dfrac{2}{3}$ using a dashed line. Choose the test point $(0,0)$.

$$y < \frac{2}{3}$$
$$0 < \frac{2}{3}$$
True

Shade the region that contains the point $(0,0)$.

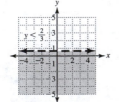

124. Graph the line $4y = -12$ using a solid line. Choose the test point $(0,0)$.

$$4y \geq -12$$
$$4(0) \geq -12$$
$$0 \geq -12$$
True

Shade the region that contains the point $(0,0)$.

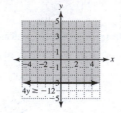

125. $2l + 2w \leq 1,000$

Graph the line $2l + 2w = 1,000$ using a solid line. Choose the test point $(0,0)$.

$$2(0) + 2(0) \leq 1,000$$
$$0 \leq 1,000$$
True

Shade the region that contains the point $(0,0)$.

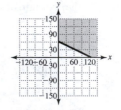

126. $x + 2y \geq 125$

Graph the line $x + 2y = 125$ using a solid line. Choose the test point $(0,0)$.

$$0 + 2(0) \geq 125$$
$$0 \geq 125$$
False

Shade the region that does not contain the point $(0,0)$.

127. A special type of relation in which every element of the <u>domain</u> is paired to a unique element of the <u>range</u>, is called a <u>function</u>.

128. The relationship is the title of a novel or movie to its format. This relation is not a fuction.

129. The relationship is a zoo to the state in which it is located. The relation is a function.

$$\text{Domain} = \left\{ \begin{array}{l} \text{Bronx Zoo, Philadelphia Zoo,} \\ \text{Honolulu Zoo, San Diego Zoo} \end{array} \right\}$$

$$\text{Range} = \left\{ \begin{array}{l} \text{New York, Pennsylvania,} \\ \text{Hawaii, California} \end{array} \right\}$$

130. yes

131. yes

132. no

133. yes

134. slope: $m = 3$

y-intercept: $(0,2)$

$\text{Domain} = (-\infty, \infty)$

$\text{Range} = (-\infty, \infty)$

135.
$g(x) = \dfrac{2}{3} - x$

$g(0) = \dfrac{2}{3} - (0)$

$= \dfrac{2}{3}$

$\left(0, \dfrac{2}{3}\right)$

$g(x) = \dfrac{2}{3} - x$

$g\left(\dfrac{7}{3}\right) = \dfrac{2}{3} - \left(\dfrac{7}{3}\right)$

$= -\dfrac{5}{3}$

$\left(\dfrac{7}{3}, -\dfrac{5}{3}\right)$

$g(x) = \dfrac{2}{3} - x$

$g(s) = \dfrac{2}{3} - (s)$

$= \dfrac{2}{3} - s$

$\left(s, -\dfrac{2}{3} - s\right)$

136.
$h(x) = -\dfrac{1}{4}x - 6$

$h(-16) = -\dfrac{1}{4}(-16) - 6$

$= -2$

$(-16, -2)$

$h(x) = -\dfrac{1}{4}x - 6$

$h(1) = -\dfrac{1}{4}(1) - 6$

$= -\dfrac{25}{4}$

$\left(1, -\dfrac{25}{4}\right)$

$h(x) = -\dfrac{1}{4}x - 6$

$h(t) = -\dfrac{1}{4}(t) - 6$

$= -\dfrac{1}{4}t - 6$

$\left(t, -\dfrac{1}{4}t - 6\right)$

137.
$f(x) = 2x^2 - x - 1$

$f(0) = 2(0)^2 - (0) - 1$

$= -1$

$(0, -1)$

$f(x) = 2x^2 - x - 1$

$f(-3) = 2(-3)^2 - (-3) - 1$

$= 20$

$(-3, 20)$

$f(x) = 2x^2 - x - 1$

$f(0.1) = 2(0.1)^2 - (0.1) - 1$

$= -1.08$

$(0.1, -1.08)$

$f(x) = 2x^2 - x - 1$

$f(b) = 2(b)^2 - (b) - 1$

$= 2b^2 - b - 1$

$\left(b, 2b^2 - b - 1\right)$

138.
$P(x) = -4x + 65{,}000$

$P(1{,}823) = -4(1{,}823) + 65{,}000$

$= 57{,}708$

There are 57,708 number 4 and other lead pencils.

CHAPTER 3 TEST

1. b, d, h

2. b, g, h

3. f

4. a, b, c, d, e, g, h, i

5. b, d, e, g, h, i

6. A function is a relationship between two sets such that an element of the first set is paired uniquely with one element of the second set.

7. a) $\dfrac{1}{2}x + 7y = -11$

$\dfrac{1}{2}(6) + 7y = -11$

$3 + 7y = -11$

$3 - 3 + 7y = -11 - 3$

$7y = -14$

$\dfrac{7y}{7} = \dfrac{-14}{7}$

$y = -2$

Yes, $(6, -2)$ is a solution to the equation.

b) $\dfrac{1}{2}x + 7y = -11$

$\dfrac{1}{2}x + 7(0) = -11$

$\dfrac{1}{2}x + 0 = -11$

$\dfrac{1}{2}x = -11$

$\dfrac{2}{1}\left(\dfrac{1}{2}x\right) = 2(-11)$

$x = -22$

Yes, $(-22, 0)$ is a solution to the equation.

8. $m = \dfrac{y_2 - y_1}{x_2 - x_1}$

$= \dfrac{-4 - 8}{-11 - (-5)}$

$= \dfrac{-4 - 8}{-11 + 5}$

$= \dfrac{-12}{-6}$

$= 2$

9. Write the equation in slope-intercept form.

$$-6x + 4y = -40$$
$$-6x + 6x + 4y = 6x - 40$$
$$4y = 6x - 40$$
$$\dfrac{4y}{4} = \dfrac{6x}{4} - \dfrac{40}{4}$$
$$y = \dfrac{3}{2}x - 10$$

Identify $m = \dfrac{3}{2}$ and $b = -10$. The slope is $\dfrac{3}{2}$ and the y-intercept is $(0, -10)$.

10. Create a t-table using $x = -2$, $x = 0$, and $x = 2$.

$x = -2$	$x = 0$	$x = 2$
$f(x) = \dfrac{3}{2}x$	$f(x) = \dfrac{3}{2}x$	$f(x) = \dfrac{3}{2}x$
$f(-2) = \dfrac{3}{2}(-2)$	$f(0) = \dfrac{3}{2}(0)$	$f(2) = \dfrac{3}{2}(2)$
$f(-2) = -3$	$f(0) = 0$	$f(2) = 3$
$(-2, -3)$	$(0, 0)$	$(2, 3)$

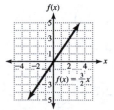

11. To find the y intercept, set $x = 0$ and solve for y.

$$3x + 5y = -15$$
$$3(0) + 5y = -15$$
$$5y = -15$$
$$\frac{5y}{5} = \frac{-15}{5}$$
$$y = -3$$

The y-intercept is $(0, -3)$. To find the x-intercept, set $y = 0$ and solve for x.

$$3x + 5y = -15$$
$$3x + 5(0) = -15$$
$$3x = -15$$
$$\frac{3x}{3} = \frac{-15}{3}$$
$$x = -5$$

The x-intercept is $(-5, 0)$.

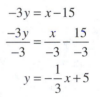

12. Rewrite the equation is slope-intercept form.

$$-3y = x - 15$$
$$\frac{-3y}{-3} = \frac{x}{-3} - \frac{15}{-3}$$
$$y = -\frac{1}{3}x + 5$$

The slope is $-\dfrac{1}{3}$ and the y-intercept is $(0, 5)$.

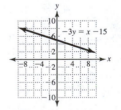

13. Write the equation in standard form.

$$x + 0y = -5$$

The graph is a vertical line with x-intercept $(-5, 0)$.

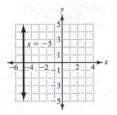

14. Use the intercept method. To find the y-intercept, set $x = 0$ and solve for y.

$$-2x + 3y = -18$$
$$-2(0) + 3y = -18$$
$$3y = -18$$
$$\frac{3y}{3} = \frac{-18}{3}$$
$$y = -6$$

The y-intercept is $(0, -6)$. To find the x-intercept, set $y = 0$ and solve for x.

$$-2x + 3y = -18$$
$$-2x + 3(0) = -18$$
$$-2x = -18$$
$$\frac{-2x}{-2} = \frac{-18}{-2}$$
$$x = 9$$

The x-intercept is $(9, 0)$.

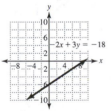

15. Graph the line $y = -3x - 2$ using the slope- intercept method and using a dashed line. Choose the test point $(0, 0)$.

$$y < -3x - 2$$
$$(0) < -3(0) - 2$$
$$0 < -2$$

False

Shade the region that does not contain the point $(0, 0)$.

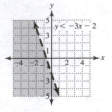

16. Substitute $m = -\dfrac{4}{5}$, $x = -2$, and $y = 6$ into the equation $y = mx + b$.

$$(6) = \left(-\dfrac{4}{5}\right)(-2) + b$$

$$6 = \dfrac{8}{5} + b$$

$$6 - \dfrac{8}{5} = b$$

$$\dfrac{22}{5} = b$$

The equation of the line is $y = -\dfrac{4}{5}x + \dfrac{22}{5}$.

17. The slope is undefined, so the line is vertical. The variable x must always equal 11 and y may be any number. Therefore, the equation is $x = 11$.

18. Determine the slope.

$$m = \dfrac{y_2 - y_1}{x_2 - x_1}$$

$$= \dfrac{(-4) - (6)}{(3) - (-1)}$$

$$= \dfrac{-4 - 6}{3 + 1}$$

$$= \dfrac{-10}{4}$$

$$= -\dfrac{5}{2}$$

Let $(x, y) = (-1, 6)$.

$$y = mx + b$$

$$(6) = \left(-\dfrac{5}{2}\right)(-1) + b$$

$$6 = \dfrac{5}{2} + b$$

$$\dfrac{7}{2} = b$$

$$y = -\dfrac{5}{2}x + \dfrac{7}{2}$$

19. The slope of L_2 is 2. Write L_1 in slope-intercept form.

$$2x - 3y = 6$$

$$2x - 2x - 3y = -2x + 6$$

$$-3y = -2x + 6$$

$$\dfrac{-3y}{-3} = \dfrac{-2x}{-3} + \dfrac{6}{-3}$$

$$y = \dfrac{2}{3}x - 2$$

The slope of L_1 is $\dfrac{2}{3}$, which is neither equal to nor the negative reciprocal of the slope of L_2. Therefore, the lines are neither parallel nor perpendicular.

20. Both lines are horizontal with different y-intercepts. Therefore, the lines are parallel.

21. Write the equation $2x - 3y = 5$ in slope-intercept form.

$$2x - 3y = 5$$

$$2x - 2x - 3y = -2x + 5$$

$$-3y = -2x + 5$$

$$\dfrac{-3y}{-3} = \dfrac{-2x}{-3} + \dfrac{5}{-3}$$

$$y = \dfrac{2}{3}x - \dfrac{5}{3}$$

The slope of $2x - 3y = 5$ is $\dfrac{2}{3}$. The new line is to be perpendicular to this line so its slope will be $-\dfrac{3}{2}$.

Substitute $y = 3$, $x = -6$, and $m = -\dfrac{3}{2}$ into the $y = mx + b$ to determine b.

$$y = mx + b$$

$$(3) = \left(-\frac{3}{2}\right)(-6) + b$$

$$3 = 9 + b$$

$$-6 = b$$

The equation is $y = -\frac{3}{2}x - 6$.

22. The relation is not a function because the number -1 is related to more than one number, one of which is not an element of the set B.

23. The relation is a function. Each number from the set A is related to exactly one number from the set B.

24. a)

$$f(x) = -\frac{3}{4}x + 6$$

$$f(-16) = -\frac{3}{4}(-16) + 6$$

$$= 12 + 6$$

$$= 18$$

b)

$$f(x) = -\frac{3}{4}x + 6$$

$$f(0) = -\frac{3}{4}(0) + 6$$

$$= 0 + 6$$

$$= 6$$

c)

$$f(x) = -\frac{3}{4}x + 6$$

$$f(s) = -\frac{3}{4}(s) + 6$$

$$= -\frac{3}{4}s + 6$$

25. **Prepare**   We are to use the given function to determine the number of pounds of carrots and other ingredients that would be in the mix if there are 3,000 pounds of lettuce. Then, determine how many pounds of lettuce given 2,000 pounds of carrots and other ingredients.

Plan   For a), since x represents the number of pounds of lettuce in the mix, substitute 3,000 for x in the function. For b), since $V(x)$ represents the number of pounds of carrots and other ingredients, substitute 2,000 for $V(x)$ in the function.

Process

a) $V(3000) = \frac{1}{3}(3000)$

$$= 1000$$

There are 1,000 pounds of carrots and other ingredients in the mix.

b) $V(x) = \frac{1}{3}x$

$$2000 = \frac{1}{3}x$$

$$6000 = x$$

There are 6,000 pounds of lettuce.

Ponder   Are our answers reasonable? Yes, because 3,000 is 3 times more than 1,000 and 6,000 is 3 times more than 2,000.

Chapters 1-3 Cumulative Review

1. Prepare, Plan, Process, Ponder

2. a) $\{0\}$

b) $\left\{-\sqrt{49}, -5, 0\right\}$

c) $\left\{-\sqrt{49}, -5, -2.6, \dfrac{-5}{3}, 0, 2.3498235..., \pi, 13\dfrac{1}{2}\right\}$

3. $\dfrac{5}{12} \cdot 5\dfrac{2}{5} = \dfrac{5}{12} \cdot \dfrac{27}{5}$

$\quad = \dfrac{{}^1\cancel{5} \cdot {}^1\cancel{3} \cdot 9}{{}_1\cancel{3} \cdot 4 \cdot {}_1\cancel{5}}$

$\quad = \dfrac{9}{4}$

4. $\dfrac{18}{7} \div 9 = \dfrac{18}{7} \div \dfrac{9}{1}$

$\quad = \dfrac{18 \cdot 1}{7 \cdot 9}$

$\quad = \dfrac{2 \cdot {}^1\cancel{9} \cdot 1}{7 \cdot {}_1\cancel{9}}$

$\quad = \dfrac{2}{7}$

5. $\dfrac{2}{3} + \dfrac{5}{8} + \dfrac{7}{6} = \dfrac{2 \cdot 8}{3 \cdot 8} + \dfrac{5 \cdot 3}{8 \cdot 3} + \dfrac{7 \cdot 4}{6 \cdot 4}$

$\quad = \dfrac{16}{24} + \dfrac{15}{24} + \dfrac{28}{24}$

$\quad = \dfrac{59}{24}$

6. $12\dfrac{1}{5} - 6\dfrac{2}{3} = \dfrac{61}{5} - \dfrac{20}{3}$

$\quad = \dfrac{61 \cdot 3}{5 \cdot 3} - \dfrac{20 \cdot 5}{3 \cdot 5}$

$\quad = \dfrac{183}{15} - \dfrac{100}{15}$

$\quad = \dfrac{83}{15}$

7. Commutative Property of Addition

8. $\dfrac{4^2 - 2(1-6) + |-2|}{-3(2)^2 - 1(2)} = \dfrac{4^2 - 2(-5) + 2}{-3(4) - 1(2)}$

$\quad = \dfrac{16 - 2(-5) + 2}{-12 - 1(2)}$

$\quad = \dfrac{16 + 10 + 2}{-12 - 2}$

$\quad = \dfrac{28}{-14}$

$\quad = -2$

9. $\dfrac{b^2 - 4ac}{2a} = \dfrac{(4)^2 - 4(-3)(-1)}{2(-3)}$

$\quad = \dfrac{16 - 4(-3)(-1)}{-6}$

$\quad = \dfrac{16 - 12}{-6}$

$\quad = \dfrac{4}{-6}$

$\quad = -\dfrac{2}{3}$

10. a) 14 mg

b) $60 \text{ mg} - 1 \text{ mg} = 59 \text{ mg}$

c) $20 \text{ mg} + 60 \text{ mg} + 1 \text{ mg} + 19 \text{ mg} + 14 \text{ mg} = 114 \text{ mg}$

11. $4x + 10 - 8x = x - 5 + 2x$

$\quad -4x + 10 = 3x - 5$

$\quad -7x + 10 = -5$

$\quad -7x = -15$

$\quad x = \dfrac{15}{7}$

Solution Set: $\left\{\dfrac{15}{7}\right\}$

12. $3 + 5(4x - 1) = 10x + 16$

$\quad 3 + 20x - 5 = 10x + 16$

$\quad 20x - 2 = 10x + 16$

$\quad 10x - 2 = 16$

$\quad 10x = 18$

$\quad x = \dfrac{9}{5}$

Solution Set: $\left\{\dfrac{9}{5}\right\}$

13.
$$\frac{3}{5}x + \frac{1}{2} = x + 10x$$
$$\frac{3}{5}x + \frac{1}{2} = 11x$$
$$\frac{10}{1}\left(\frac{3}{5}x + \frac{1}{2}\right) = 10(11x)$$
$$6x + 5 = 110x$$
$$5 = 104x$$
$$x = \frac{5}{104}$$

Solution Set: $\left\{\dfrac{5}{104}\right\}$

14.
$$F = \frac{9}{5}C + 32$$
$$F - 32 = \frac{9}{5}C$$
$$\frac{5}{9}(F - 32) = C$$

15.
$$\frac{x}{4} + \frac{2x}{3} \le \frac{1}{6}$$
$$\frac{12}{1}\left(\frac{x}{4} + \frac{2x}{3}\right) \le \frac{12}{1}\left(\frac{1}{6}\right)$$
$$3x + 8x \le 2$$
$$11x \le 2$$
$$x \le \frac{2}{11}$$
$$\left(-\infty, \frac{2}{11}\right]$$

16. $-8 < 3x + 1 < 28$
$$-9 < 3x < 27$$
$$\frac{-9}{3} < \frac{3x}{3} < \frac{27}{3}$$
$$-3 < x < 9$$
$$(-3, 9)$$

17. $6 - 7x > 20 \quad$ or $\quad 2x \ge 0$
$$-7x > 14 \quad \text{or} \quad x \ge 0$$
$$x < -2 \quad \text{or} \quad x \ge 0$$
$$(-\infty, -2) \cup [0, \infty)$$

18. Let x represent the unknown number.
$$2(x + 6) = x - 15$$
$$2x + 12 = x - 15$$
$$x + 12 = -15$$
$$x = -27$$
The number is -27.

19.
$$I = Prt$$
$$1{,}251.25 = (5{,}500)(0.065)t$$
$$1{,}251.25 = 357.5t$$
$$3.5 = t$$
It will take 3.5 years.

20. **Prepare** We are asked to determine how many gallons of each type of gasoline Walter purchased.

Plan We will set up and solve a linear equation with one variable using the information given in the problem.

Process Let x represent the number of gallons that Walter purchased at \$3.29 per gallon.

$$3.29x + 2.99(16 - x) = 52.34$$
$$3.29x + 47.84 - 2.99x = 52.34$$
$$0.30x + 47.84 = 52.34$$
$$0.30x = 4.5$$
$$x = 15$$

Walter buys 15 gallons of gasoline for his car and 1 gallon of gasoline for his lawn mower and hedger.

Ponder Does our answer seem reasonable? Yes. Walter spent:
$$\$3.29(15) + \$2.99(1) = \$49.35 + \$2.99 = \$52.34$$

21.
$$5x - y = 6$$
$$5\left(\frac{2}{5}\right) - (-3) = 6$$
$$2 + 3 = 6$$
$$5 = 6$$

The ordered pair $\left(\dfrac{2}{5}, -3\right)$ is not a solution.

22.   Slope: undefined

x-intercept: $(6,0)$

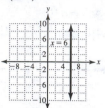

23.   Slope: $m = 1$

y-intercept: $(0,-3)$

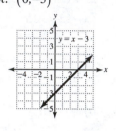

24.   Let $x = 0$ and solve for y.
$$-3x + 6y = 12$$
$$-3(0) + 6y = 12$$
$$6y = 12$$
$$y = 2$$
The y-intercept is $(0,2)$.

Let $y = 0$ and solve for x.
$$-3x + 6y = 12$$
$$-3x + 6(0) = 12$$
$$-3x = 12$$
$$x = -4$$
The x-intercept is $(-4,0)$.

25.   Graph the equation $4y = -3x + 8$ using a dashed line. Use the test point $(0,0)$.
$$4y > -3x + 8$$
$$4(0) > -3(0) + 8$$
$$0 > 8$$
False

Shade the region that does not contain the point $(0,0)$.

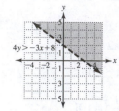

26. $y = mx + b$
$$(0) = \left(\frac{-2}{7}\right)(3) + b$$
$$0 = -\frac{6}{7} + b$$
$$\frac{6}{7} = b$$

$y = \left(-\frac{2}{7}\right)x + \left(\frac{6}{7}\right)$
$$7y = \frac{7}{1}\left(-\frac{2}{7}x + \frac{6}{7}\right)$$
$$7y = -2x + 6$$
$$2x + 7y = 6$$

27. $m = \dfrac{y_2 - y_1}{x_2 - x_1}$
$$= \frac{8-4}{3-(-1)}$$
$$= \frac{4}{4}$$
$$= 1$$

$y = mx + b$
$$(4) = (1)(-1) + b$$
$$4 = -1 + b$$
$$5 = b$$

$$y = mx + b$$
$$y = (1)x + (5)$$
$$y = x + 5$$
$$x - y = -5$$

28. $m = 3$

$y = mx + b$
$$(3) = (3)(2) + b$$
$$3 = 6 + b$$
$$-3 = b$$

$$y = mx + b$$
$$y = (3)x + (-3)$$
$$y = 3x - 3$$
$$3x - y = 3$$

29.a.   At time $t = 0$, the anchor has not yet dropped, therefore, the depth of the anchor is 0 feet. The ordered pair is $(0,0)$. Because the anchor is descending at a rate of 5 feet per second, the depth of the anchor after 18 seconds is $(-5)(18) = -90$ feet. The ordered pair is $(18,-90)$.

29.b. The slope is the rate at which the anchor descends. Therefore, the slope is $m = -5$. The y-intercept is $(0,0)$.

29.c. $y = mx + b$

$y = (-5)x + (0)$

$y = -5x$

29.d. $\qquad y = mx + b$

$(-115) = -5x$

$x = 23$

It takes the anchor 23 seconds to descend to a depth of 115 feet.

30. $\qquad$ Slope: $m = \dfrac{1}{3}$

y-intercept: $(0,-2)$

Domain: $(-\infty, \infty)$

Range: $(-\infty, \infty)$

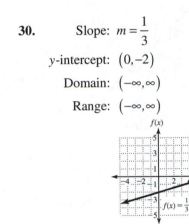

Chapter 4

4.1 Exercises

1. When two linear equations in two variables are considered together they are called a <u>system</u> <u>of</u> <u>equations</u>.

3. If the graph of a linear system in two variables produces intersecting lines, there is a <u>unique</u> solution to the system.

5. A linear system in two variables that has one or more solutions is called <u>consistent</u>.

7. A consistent, dependent linear system in two variables has <u>infinitely</u> <u>many</u> solutions.

9.
$$2x - 3y = 11$$
$$2(4) - 3(-1) = 11$$
$$8 + 3 = 11$$
$$11 = 11$$
True

$$-3x + 5y = -17$$
$$-3(4) + 5(-1) = -17$$
$$-12 - 5 = -17$$
$$-17 = -17$$
True

The ordered pair $(4, -1)$ is a solution to the system.

11.
$$-x + 3y = 6$$
$$-(-3) + 3(1) = 6$$
$$3 + 3 = 6$$
$$6 = 6$$
True

$$x - 3y = 0$$
$$(-3) - 3(1) = 0$$
$$-3 - 3 = 0$$
$$-6 = 0$$
False

The ordered pair $(-3, 1)$ is not a solution to the system.

13.
$$0.3x - 0.5y = -0.8$$
$$0.3(1) - 0.5(-1) = -0.8$$
$$0.3 + 0.5 = -0.8$$
$$0.8 = -0.8$$
False

The ordered pair $(1, -1)$ is not a solution to the system.

15.
$$\frac{2}{3}x + \frac{1}{4}y = 4$$
$$\frac{2}{3}(6) + \frac{1}{4}(0) = 4$$
$$4 + 0 = 4$$
$$4 = 4$$
True

$$\frac{1}{2}x - \frac{3}{5}y = 3$$
$$\frac{1}{2}(6) - \frac{3}{5}(0) = 3$$
$$3 - 0 = 3$$
$$3 = 3$$
True

The ordered pair $(6, 0)$ is a solution to the system.

17. c, e, h

19. a, f

21. The slope-intercept form of L_1 is $y = -x + 2$. The slope of L_1 is $m = -1$ and the y-intercept is $(0, 2)$. The slope-intercept form of L_2 is $y = -2x + 1$. The slope of L_2 is $m = -2$ and the y-intercept is $(0, 1)$.

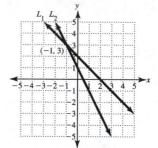

The solution set is $\{(-1, 3)\}$.

23. The slope-intercept form of L_1 is $y = x - 3$. The slope of L_1 is $m = 1$ and the y-intercept is $(0, -3)$.

The slope-intercept form of L_2 is $y = \frac{1}{2}x - 4$. The slope of L_2 is $m = \frac{1}{2}$ and the y-intercept is $(0 - 4)$.

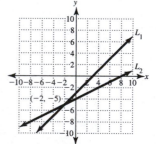

The solution set is $\{(-2, -5)\}$.

25. The slope-intercept form of L_1 is $y = \frac{1}{2}x - 2$. The slope of L_1 is $m = \frac{1}{2}$ and the y-intercept is $(0, -2)$.

The slope-intercept form of L_2 is $y = \frac{1}{2}x - 4$. The slope of L_2 is $m = \frac{1}{2}$ and the y-intercept is $(0, -4)$.

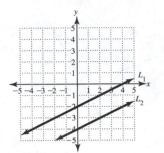

There is no solution.

27. The slope-intercept form of L_1 is $y = -\dfrac{2}{5}x + 2$.

The slope of L_1 is $m = -\dfrac{2}{5}$ and the y-intercept is $(0, 2)$. The slope-intercept form of L_2 is $y = -x + 2$. The slope of L_2 is $m = -1$ and the y-intercept is $(0, 2)$.

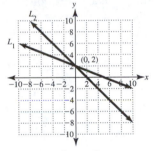

The solution set is $\{(0, 2)\}$.

29. The slope-intercept form of L_1 is $y = \dfrac{1}{2}x - 2$. The slope of L_1 is $m = \dfrac{1}{2}$ and the y-intercept is $(0, -2)$. The slope-intercept form of L_2 is $y = \dfrac{1}{2}x - 2$. The slope of L_2 is $m = \dfrac{1}{2}$ and the y-intercept is $(0, -2)$.

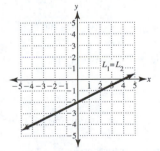

The system has infinitely many solutions.

31. The slope-intercept form of L_1 is $y = 6x + 2$. The slope of L_1 is $m = 6$ and the y-intercept is $(0, 2)$. The graph of L_2 is a vertical line with x-intercept $(-1, 0)$.

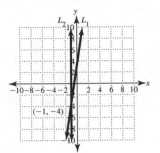

The solution set is $\{(-1, -4)\}$.

33. The slope-intercept form of L_1 is $y = \dfrac{3}{2}x + \dfrac{3}{2}$. The slope of L_1 is $m = \dfrac{3}{2}$ and the y-intercept is $\left(0, \dfrac{3}{2}\right)$. The slope-intercept form of L_2 is $y = -3x + 6$. The slope of L_2 is $m = -3$ and the y-intercept is $(0, 6)$.

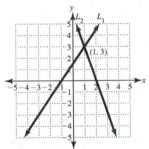

The solution set is $\{(1, 3)\}$.

35. The graph of L_1 is a vertical line with x-intercept $(3, 0)$. The graph of L_2 is a horizontal line with y-intercept $(0, -2)$.

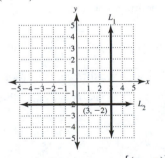

The solution set to the system is $\{(3, -2)\}$.

37. The slope-intercept form of L_1 is $y = -3x - 3$. The slope of L_1 is $m = -3$ and the y-intercept is $(0, -3)$. The slope-intercept form of L_2 is $y = -3x - 3$. The slope of L_2 is $m = -3$ and the y-intercept is $(0, -3)$.

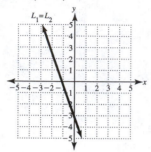

The system has infinitely many solutions.

39. The slope-intercept form of L_1 is $y = -\dfrac{1}{2}x + 3$.

The slope of L_1 is $m = -\dfrac{1}{2}$ and the y-intercept is $(0, 3)$. The slope-intercept form of L_2 is $y = -\dfrac{1}{2}x + \dfrac{5}{2}$. The slope of L_2 is $m = -\dfrac{1}{2}$ and the y-intercept is $\left(0, \dfrac{5}{2}\right)$.

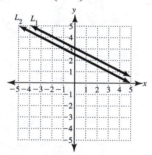

The system has no solution.

41. The slope-intercept form of L_1 is $y = -\dfrac{1}{3}x$. The slope of L_1 is $m = -\dfrac{1}{3}$ and the y-intercept is $(0, 0)$. The slope-intercept form of L_2 is $y = 2x$. The slope of L_2 is $m = 2$ and the y-intercept is $(0, 0)$.

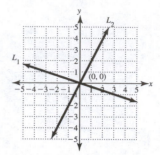

The solution set is $\{(0, 0)\}$.

43. A linear equation involves one equation, one variable, and thus one solution. A linear system of equations, however, involves two equations, two variables, and solutions that can range from a point of intersection if the lines intersect, no solution if the lines are parallel, and an infinite number of solutions if the lines coincide.

45. Solutions that contain fractions, especially small ones, are difficult to solve using the graphing method.

47. No system of equations can have exactly two solutions. If the lines intersect they will do so in only one point. If the system is consistent and dependent, there are infinitely many solutions, not exactly two solutions.

49. a) The system is consistent and independent.

   b) The lines are intersecting.

51. a) The system is inconsistent.

   b) The lines are parallel.

53. a) The system is consistent and dependent.

   b) The lines are coinciding.

55. a) The system is inconsistent.

   b) The lines are parallel.

57. a) The system is consistent and dependent.

   b) The lines are coinciding.

59. a) The system is consistent and independent.

   b) The lines are intersecting.

61. Prepare We need to write and graph the system of linear equations given the information in the problem and then decide whether the Swensons should use their regular sitter or the church's childcare.

Plan The given information will allow us to write the equations in slope-intercept form. We will also graph the equations using the slope and y-intercept.

Process Let x represent the number of children and y represent the total amount for the childcare. The total amount for the regular sitter is given by L_1: $y = 8x + 14$ and the amount for the church's childcare is given by L_2: $y = 5x + 20$. The slope and y-intercept of L_1 are $m = 8$ and $(0, 14)$, respectively. The slope and y-intercept of L_2 are $m = 5$ and $(0, 20)$, respectively.

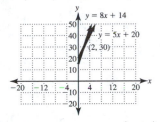

The point of intersection is $(2, 30)$, which is the solution to the system. Therefore, for a couple with more than 2 children, the church's childcare is the better choice. The Swensons should use the church fund-raiser.

Ponder Does the answer seem reasonable? Yes. With more people to watch the children, it seems reasonable that the price would be better if you have more children.

63. The slope-intercept form of L_1 is $y = -2x + 6$. The slope of L_1 is $m = -2$ and the y-intercept is $(0, 6)$. The slope-intercept from of L_2 is $y = 2x + 2$. The slope of L_2 is $m = 2$ and the y-intercept is $(0, 2)$.

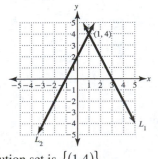

The solution set is $\{(1, 4)\}$.

65. The graph of L_1 is a horizontal line with y-intercepts $\left(0, \dfrac{3}{2}\right)$. The slope-intercept from of L_2 is $y = -x + 3$. The slope of L_2 is $m = -1$ and the y-intercept is $(0, 3)$.

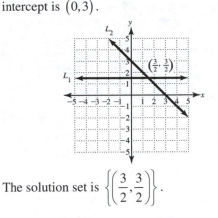

The solution set is $\left\{\left(\dfrac{3}{2}, \dfrac{3}{2}\right)\right\}$.

67. The slope-intercept form of L_1 is $y = -4x + \dfrac{5}{2}$. The slope of L_1 is $m = -4$ and the y-intercept is $\left(0, \dfrac{5}{2}\right)$.

The slope-intercept from of L_2 is $y = 2x - \dfrac{1}{2}$. The slope of L_2 is $m = 2$ and the y-intercept is $\left(0, -\dfrac{1}{2}\right)$.

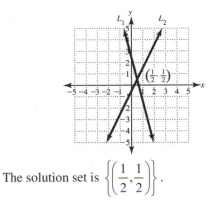

The solution set is $\left\{\left(\dfrac{1}{2}, \dfrac{1}{2}\right)\right\}$.

4.2 Exercises

1. When using the substitution method we solve <u>one</u> equation for a <u>variable</u>.

3. A solution to a linear system of equations should be stated as an <u>ordered</u> <u>pair</u> using set notation.

5. If a linear system of equations has no solutions, we will be left with a <u>false</u> arithmetic statement.

7. Solve the first equation for x to obtain $x = -3y + 5$. Substitute $x = -3y + 5$ into the second equation and solve for y.
$$2x - y = 3$$
$$2(-3y + 5) - y = 3$$
$$-6y + 10 - y = 3$$
$$-7y = -7$$
$$y = 1$$
Substitute $y = 1$ into $x = -3y + 5$ to find x.
$$x = -3y + 5$$
$$x = -3(1) + 5$$
$$x = -3 + 5$$
$$x = 2$$
The solution set is $\{(2,1)\}$.

9. Solve the first equation for y to obtain $y = -2x + 4$. Substitute $y = -2x + 4$ into the second equation and solve for x.
$$5x + 3y = 9$$
$$5x + 3(-2x + 4) = 9$$
$$5x - 6x + 12 = 9$$
$$-x = -3$$
$$x = 3$$
Substitute $x = 3$ into $y = -2x + 4$ to find y.
$$y = -2x + 4$$
$$y = -2(3) + 4$$
$$y = -6 + 4$$
$$y = -2$$
The solution set is $\{(3,-2)\}$.

11. Solve the first equation for y to obtain $y = -x + 5$. Substitute $y = -x + 5$ into the second equation and solve for x.
$$2x - 3y = 0$$
$$2x - 3(-x + 5) = 0$$
$$2x + 3x - 15 = 0$$
$$5x = 15$$
$$x = 3$$
Substitute $x = 3$ into $y = -x + 5$ to find y.
$$y = -x + 5$$
$$y = -(3) + 5$$
$$y = 2$$
The solution set is $\{(3,2)\}$.

13. Solve the second equation for y to obtain $y = 5x + 2$. Substitute $y = 5x + 2$ into the first equation and solve for x.
$$2x - 4y = 10$$
$$2x - 4(5x + 2) = 10$$
$$2x - 20x - 8 = 10$$
$$-18x = 18$$
$$x = -1$$
Substitute $x = -1$ into $y = 5x + 2$ to find y.
$$y = 5x + 2$$
$$y = 5(-1) + 2$$
$$y = -5 + 2$$
$$y = -3$$
The solution set is $\{(-1,-3)\}$.

15. Solve the first equation for x to obtain $x = 2y - 3$. Substitute $x = 2y - 3$ into the second equation and solve for y.
$$6x - 5y = 10$$
$$6(2y - 3) - 5y = 10$$
$$12y - 18 - 5y = 10$$
$$7y = 28$$
$$y = 4$$
Substitute $y = 4$ into $x = 2y - 3$ to find x.
$$x = 2y - 3$$
$$x = 2(4) - 3$$
$$x = 8 - 3$$
$$x = 5$$
The solution set is $\{(5,4)\}$.

17. Solve the first equation for x to obtain $x = 7y + 8$. Substitute $x = 7y + 8$ into the second equation and solve for y.

$$4x + 8y = 8$$
$$4(7y + 8) + 8y = 8$$
$$28y + 32 + 8y = 8$$
$$36y = -24$$
$$y = -\frac{2}{3}$$

Substitute $y = -\frac{2}{3}$ into $x = 7y + 8$ to find x.

$$x = 7y + 8$$
$$x = 7\left(-\frac{2}{3}\right) + 8$$
$$x = -\frac{14}{3} + \frac{24}{3}$$
$$x = \frac{10}{3}$$

The solution set is $\left\{\left(\frac{10}{3}, -\frac{2}{3}\right)\right\}$.

19. Solve the first equation for y to obtain $y = 3x + 5$. Substitute $y = 3x + 5$ into the second equation and solve for x.

$$-5x + 2y = 8$$
$$-5x + 2(3x + 5) = 8$$
$$-5x + 6x + 10 = 8$$
$$x = -2$$

Substitute $x = -2$ into $y = 3x + 5$ to find y.

$$y = 3x + 5$$
$$y = 3(-2) + 5$$
$$y = -6 + 5$$
$$y = -1$$

The solution set is $\{(-2, -1)\}$.

21. Solve the second equation for y to obtain $y = 7x - 2$. Substitute $y = 7x - 2$ into the first equation and solve for x.

$$5x - 5y = 10$$
$$5x - 5(7x - 2) = 10$$
$$5x - 35x + 10 = 10$$
$$-30x = 0$$
$$x = 0$$

Substitute $x = 0$ into $y = 7x - 2$ to find y.

$$y = 7x - 2$$
$$y = 7(0) - 2$$
$$y = 0 - 2$$
$$y = -2$$

The solution set is $\{(0, -2)\}$.

23. The first equation is already solved for x. Substitute $x = 6y - 2$ into the second equation and solve for y.

$$-3x + 8y = -4$$
$$-3(6y - 2) + 8y = -4$$
$$-18y + 6 + 8y = -4$$
$$-10y = -10$$
$$y = 1$$

Substitute $y = 1$ into $x = 6y - 2$ to find x.

$$x = 6y - 2$$
$$x = 6(1) - 2$$
$$x = 6 - 2$$
$$x = 4$$

The solution set is $\{(4, 1)\}$.

25. The first equation is already solved for y. Substitute $y = -2x - 1$ into the second equation and solve for x.

$$-3x - 4y = -11$$
$$-3x - 4(-2x - 1) = -11$$
$$-3x + 8x + 4 = -11$$
$$5x = -15$$
$$x = -3$$

Substitute $x = -3$ into $y = -2x - 1$ to find y.

$$y = -2x - 1$$
$$y = -2(-3) - 1$$
$$y = 6 - 1$$
$$y = 5$$

The solution set is $\{(-3, 5)\}$.

27. The second equation is already solved for y. Substitute $y = 3x$ into the first equation and solve for x.

$$x + y = 12$$
$$x + (3x) = 12$$
$$4x = 12$$
$$x = 3$$

Substitute $x = 3$ into $y = 3x$ to find y.

$$y = 3x$$
$$y = 3(3)$$
$$y = 9$$

The solution set is $\{(3,9)\}$.

29. The second equation is already solved for y. Substitute $y = -2x + 5$ into the first equation and solve for x.
$$-3x - y = -3$$
$$-3x - (-2x + 5) = -3$$
$$-3x + 2x - 5 = -3$$
$$-x = 2$$
$$x = -2$$
Substitute $x = -2$ into $y = -2x + 5$ to find y.
$$y = -2x + 5$$
$$y = -2(-2) + 5$$
$$y = 4 + 5$$
$$y = 9$$
The solution set is $\{(-2,9)\}$.

31. Solve the second equation for y to obtain $y = 6x - 15$. Substitute $y = 6x - 15$ into the first equation and solve for x.
$$7x = 2y + 10$$
$$7x = 2(6x - 15) + 10$$
$$7x = 12x - 30 + 10$$
$$-5x = -20$$
$$x = 4$$
Substitute $x = 4$ into $y = 6x - 15$ to find y.
$$y = 6x - 15$$
$$y = 6(4) - 15$$
$$y = 24 - 15$$
$$y = 9$$
The solution set is $\{(4,9)\}$.

33. Solve the second equation for y to obtain $y = -\dfrac{3}{2}x + 1$. Substitute $y = -\dfrac{3}{2}x + 1$ into the first equation and solve for x.
$$4x + 3y = 1$$
$$4x + 3\left(-\frac{3}{2}x + 1\right) = 1$$
$$4x - \frac{9}{2}x + 3 = 1$$
$$-\frac{1}{2}x = -2$$
$$x = 4$$
Substitute $x = 4$ into $y = -\dfrac{3}{2}x + 1$ to find y.

$$y = -\frac{3}{2}x + 1$$
$$y = -\frac{3}{2}(4) + 1$$
$$y = -6 + 1$$
$$y = -5$$
The solution set is $\{(4,-5)\}$.

35. Solve the second equation for x to obtain $x = -\dfrac{3}{2}y + 2$. Substitute $x = -\dfrac{3}{2}y + 2$ into the first equation and solve for y.
$$2x - 5y = 4$$
$$2\left(-\frac{3}{2}y + 2\right) - 5y = 4$$
$$-3y + 4 - 5y = 4$$
$$-8y = 0$$
$$y = 0$$
Substitute $y = 0$ into $x = -\dfrac{3}{2}y + 2$ to find x.
$$x = -\frac{3}{2}y + 2$$
$$x = -\frac{3}{2}(0) + 2$$
$$x = 0 + 2$$
$$x = 2$$
The solution set is $\{(2,0)\}$.

37. Solve the second equation for y to obtain $y = 2x - 3$. Substitute $y = 2x - 3$ into the first equation and solve for x.
$$4x - 2y = 6$$
$$4x - 2(2x - 3) = 6$$
$$4x - 4x + 6 = 6$$
$$6 = 6$$
$$\text{True}$$
The solution set is $\{(x, y) \mid 4x - 2y = 6\}$.

39. Solve the first equation for y to obtain $y = -3x + 5$. Substitute $y = -3x + 5$ into the second equation and solve for x.
$$9x + 3y = 10$$
$$9x + 3(-3x + 5) = 10$$
$$9x - 9x + 15 = 10$$
$$15 = 10$$
$$\text{False}$$
The solution set is $\{\ \}$.

41. Solve the first equation for x to obtain $x = 4y + 2$. Substitute $x = 4y + 2$ into the second equation and solve for y.

$$2x - 8y = 4$$
$$2(4y + 2) - 8y = 4$$
$$8y + 4 - 8y = 4$$
$$4 = 4$$
True

The solution set is $\{(x, y) \mid 2x - 8y = 4\}$.

43. The second equation is already solved for y. Substitute $y = 3x - 18$ into the first equation and solve for x.

$$x - \frac{1}{3}y = 6$$
$$x - \frac{1}{3}(3x - 18) = 6$$
$$x - x + 6 = 6$$
$$6 = 6$$
True

The solution set is $\{(x, y) \mid y = 3x - 18\}$.

45. Solve the second equation for y to obtain $y = 2x - 6$. Substitute $y = 2x - 6$ into the first equation and solve for x.

$$6x - 3y = 12$$
$$6x - 3(2x - 6) = 12$$
$$6x - 6x + 18 = 12$$
$$18 = 12$$
False

The solution set is $\{\ \}$.

47. Solve the first equation for y to obtain $y = 8x - 2$. Substitute $y = 8x - 2$ into the second equation and solve for x.

$$4x + 2y = 6$$
$$4x + 2(8x - 2) = 6$$
$$4x + 16x - 4 = 6$$
$$20x = 10$$
$$x = \frac{1}{2}$$

Substitute $x = \frac{1}{2}$ into $y = 8x - 2$ to find y.

$$y = 8x - 2$$
$$y = 8\left(\frac{1}{2}\right) - 2$$
$$y = 4 - 2$$
$$y = 2$$

The solution set is $\left\{\left(\frac{1}{2}, 2\right)\right\}$.

49. Solve the second equation for x to obtain $x = -8y + 2$. Substitute $x = -8y + 2$ into the first equation and solve for y.

$$3x - 11y = -1$$
$$3(-8y + 2) - 11y = -1$$
$$-24y + 6 - 11y = -1$$
$$-35y = -7$$
$$y = \frac{1}{5}$$

Substitute $y = \frac{1}{5}$ into $x = -8y + 2$ to find x.

$$x = -8y + 2$$
$$x = -8\left(\frac{1}{5}\right) + 2$$
$$x = -\frac{8}{5} + \frac{10}{5}$$
$$x = \frac{2}{5}$$

The solution set is $\left\{\left(\frac{2}{5}, \frac{1}{5}\right)\right\}$.

51. Solve the first equation for y to obtain $y = 3x - 6$. Substitute $y = 3x - 6$ into the second equation and solve for x.

$$6x + 5y = -23$$
$$6x + 5(3x - 6) = -23$$
$$6x + 15x - 30 = -23$$
$$21x = 7$$
$$x = \frac{1}{3}$$

Substitute $x = \frac{1}{3}$ into $y = 3x - 6$ to find y.

$$y = 3x - 6$$
$$y = 3\left(\frac{1}{3}\right) - 6$$
$$y = 1 - 6$$
$$y = -5$$

The solution set is $\left\{\left(\frac{1}{3}, -5\right)\right\}$.

145

53. The first equation is already solved for y. Substitute $y = 2x + 5$ into the second equation and solve for x.

$$y = 3x - 2$$
$$(2x + 5) = 3x - 2$$
$$-x = -7$$
$$x = 7$$

Substitute $x = 7$ into $y = 2x + 5$ to find y.

$$y = 2x + 5$$
$$y = 2(7) + 5$$
$$y = 14 + 5$$
$$y = 19$$

The solution set is $\{(7, 19)\}$.

55. The substitution method is a faster and less tedious method for solving systems of equations than the graphing method.

57. If the variables cancel after the substitution and the remaining numbers form a false statement (for example, $0 = 5$), then the system does not have a solution.

59. Check to see that the lines have the same slope and the same y-intercept.

61. a) The system is consistent and independent.

  b) The lines are intersecting.

63. a) The system is consistent and dependent.

  b) The lines are coinciding.

65. a) The system is inconsistent.

  b) The lines are parallel.

67. a) The system is consistent and independent.

  b) The lines are intersecting.

69. a) The system is inconsistent.

  b) The lines are parallel.

71. a) The system is consistent and dependent.

  b) The lines are coinciding.

73. Prepare We are asked to determine the age of Mr. Friedman and his violin.

Plan We will set up a system of two linear equations in two variables and solve it using the substitution method.

Process Let x represent Mr. Friedman's age and let y represent the age of the violin. Then we can write the system:

$$\begin{cases} x = 3y \\ x + y = 64 \end{cases}$$

$$x + y = 64$$
$$(3y) + y = 64$$
$$4y = 64$$
$$y = 16$$

$$x = 3y$$
$$x = 3(16)$$
$$x = 48$$

Mr. Friedman is 48 years old and his violin is 16 years old.

Ponder Does our answer seem reasonable? Yes. We can check to see that our answers fits the conditions of the problem. Mr. Friedman is indeed 3 times as old as his violin, because $48 = 3(16)$, and the sum of his age and the violin's age is 64, $48 + 16 = 64$.

75. Multiply both sides of the first equation by 5 to obtain:

$$5\left(\frac{x}{5} + \frac{y}{5}\right) = 5(2)$$
$$x + y = 10$$

Multiply both sides of the second equation by 15 to obtain:

$$15\left(\frac{1}{3}x + \frac{2}{5}y\right) = 15(3)$$
$$5x + 6y = 45$$

Solve $x + y = 10$ for y to obtain $y = 10 - x$ and substitute $10 - x$ into the second equation for y.

$$5x + 6y = 45$$
$$5x + 6(10 - x) = 45$$
$$-x + 60 = 45$$
$$x = 15$$

Substitute $x = 15$ into $y = 10 - x$ to find y.

$$y = 10 - x$$
$$y = 10 - 15$$
$$y = -5$$

The solution set is $\{(15,-5)\}$.

77. Multiply both sides of the first equation by 10 to obtain:

$$10(0.4x-0.3y)=10(1.3)$$
$$4x-3y=13$$

Multiply both sides of the second equation by 10 to obtain:

$$10(0.5x+0.2y)=10(-0.1)$$
$$5x+2y=-1$$

Solve $5x+2y=-1$ for y to obtain $y=-\dfrac{5}{2}x-\dfrac{1}{2}$

and substitute $-\dfrac{5}{2}x-\dfrac{1}{2}$ into the first equation for y.

$$4x-3y=13$$
$$4x-3\left(-\dfrac{5}{2}x-\dfrac{1}{2}\right)=13$$
$$4x+\dfrac{15}{2}x+\dfrac{3}{2}=13$$
$$8x+15x+3=26$$
$$23x=23$$
$$x=1$$

Substitute $x=1$ into $y=-\dfrac{5}{2}x-\dfrac{1}{2}$ to find y.

$$y=-\dfrac{5}{2}x-\dfrac{1}{2}$$
$$y=-\dfrac{5}{2}(1)-\dfrac{1}{2}$$
$$y=-3$$

The solution set is $\{(1,-3)\}$.

79. Multiply both sides of the first equation by 12 to obtain:

$$12\left(\dfrac{2}{3}x+\dfrac{1}{4}y\right)=12(4)$$
$$8x+3y=48$$

Multiply both sides of the second equation by 10 to obtain:

$$10\left(\dfrac{1}{2}x-\dfrac{3}{5}y\right)=10(3)$$
$$5x-6y=30$$

Solve $5x-6y=30$ for x to obtain $x=\dfrac{6}{5}y+6$ and

substitute $\dfrac{6}{5}y+6$ into the first equation for x.

$$8x+3y=48$$
$$8\left(\dfrac{6}{5}y+6\right)+3y=48$$
$$\dfrac{48}{5}y+48+3y=48$$
$$\dfrac{48}{5}y+3y=0$$
$$y=0$$

Substitute $y=0$ into $x=\dfrac{6}{5}y+6$ to find x.

$$x=\dfrac{6}{5}y+6$$
$$x=\dfrac{6}{5}(0)+6$$
$$x=6$$

The solution set is $\{(6,0)\}$.

4.3 Exercises

1. The first step in solving a system if equations using the elimination method is to write both equations in <u>standard</u> <u>form</u>, which is $Ax + By = C$.

3. The solution to a system of equations should be stated as an ordered pair using <u>set</u> <u>notation</u>.

5. Variables can be eliminated if they have <u>opposite</u> coefficients.

7. Eliminate y by adding Equation 1 and Equation 2.

    $$\text{Equation 1} \quad \begin{cases} x + y = 5 \\ x - y = 3 \end{cases}$$
    $$\text{Equation 2}$$
    $$\overline{\qquad\qquad 2x = 8}$$
    $$x = 4$$

    Substitute $x = 4$ into Equation 1 and solve for y.
    $$x + y = 5$$
    $$(4) + y = 5$$
    $$y = 1$$
    The solution set is $\{(4, 1)\}$.

9. Eliminate x by adding Equation 1 and Equation 2.

    $$\text{Equation 1} \quad \begin{cases} x + 4y = 27 \\ -x + y = 3 \end{cases}$$
    $$\text{Equation 2}$$
    $$\overline{\qquad\qquad 5y = 30}$$
    $$y = 6$$

    Substitute $y = 6$ into Equation 1 and solve for x.
    $$x + 4y = 27$$
    $$x + 4(6) = 27$$
    $$x = 3$$
    The solution set is $\{(3, 6)\}$.

11. Eliminate y by adding Equation 1 and Equation 2.

    $$\text{Equation 1} \quad \begin{cases} x + 3y = 13 \\ x - 3y = -17 \end{cases}$$
    $$\text{Equation 2}$$
    $$\overline{\qquad\qquad 2x = -4}$$
    $$x = -2$$

    Substitute $x = -2$ into Equation 1 and solve for y.
    $$x + 3y = 13$$
    $$(-2) + 3y = 13$$
    $$y = 5$$
    The solution set is $\{(-2, 5)\}$.

13. Eliminate x by adding Equation 1 and Equation 2.

    $$\text{Equation 1} \quad \begin{cases} 7x + y = 14 \\ -7x + y = -14 \end{cases}$$
    $$\text{Equation 2}$$
    $$\overline{\qquad\qquad 2y = 0}$$
    $$y = 0$$

    Substitute $y = 0$ into Equation 1 and solve for x.
    $$7x + y = 14$$
    $$7x + (0) = 14$$
    $$x = 2$$
    The solution set is $\{(2, 0)\}$.

15. Rewrite Equation 2 as $-2x + y = 8$. Eliminate y by adding Equation 1 and Equation 2.

    $$\text{Equation 1} \quad \begin{cases} 2x - y = 10 \\ -2x + y = 8 \end{cases}$$
    $$\text{Equation 2}$$
    $$\overline{\qquad\qquad 0 = 18}$$

    The solution set is $\{\ \}$.

17. Eliminate x by adding Equation 1 and -1 times Equation 2.

    $$\text{Equation 1} \quad \begin{cases} x + y = 5 \\ -x - 5y = -1 \end{cases}$$
    $$-1(\text{Equation 2})$$
    $$\overline{\qquad\qquad -4y = 4}$$
    $$y = -1$$

    Substitute $y = -1$ into Equation 1 and solve for x.
    $$x + y = 5$$
    $$x + (-1) = 5$$
    $$x = 6$$
    The solution set is $\{(6, -1)\}$.

19. Eliminate y by adding Equation 1 and -1 times Equation 2.

    $$\text{Equation 1} \quad \begin{cases} 2x + 4y = -4 \\ -5x - 4y = 10 \end{cases}$$
    $$-1(\text{Equation 2})$$
    $$\overline{\qquad\qquad -3x = 6}$$
    $$x = -2$$

    Substitute $x = -2$ into Equation 1 and solve for y.
    $$2x + 4y = -4$$
    $$2(-2) + 4y = -4$$
    $$y = 0$$
    The solution set is $\{(-2, 0)\}$.

21. Eliminate y by adding -1 times Equation 1 and Equation 2.

$$\begin{array}{l} -1(\text{Equation 1}) \\ \text{Equation 2} \end{array} \left\{ \begin{array}{l} -2x+6y=-8 \\ 3x-6y=3 \end{array} \right.$$
$$x=-5$$

Substitute $x=-5$ into Equation 1 and solve for y.
$$2x-6y=8$$
$$2(-5)-6y=8$$
$$y=-3$$

The solution set is $\{(-5,-3)\}$.

23. Eliminate x by adding -1 times Equation 1 and Equation 2.

$$\begin{array}{l} -1(\text{Equation 1}) \\ \text{Equation 2} \end{array} \left\{ \begin{array}{l} 6x+y=17 \\ -6x+9y=-27 \end{array} \right.$$
$$10y=-10$$
$$y=-1$$

Substitute $y=-1$ into Equation 1 and solve for x.
$$-6x-y=-17$$
$$-6x-(-1)=-17$$
$$x=3$$

The solution set to is $\{(3,-1)\}$.

25. Eliminate x by adding -1 times Equation 1 and Equation 2.

$$\begin{array}{l} -1(\text{Equation 1}) \\ \text{Equation 2} \end{array} \left\{ \begin{array}{l} -x-\dfrac{3}{2}y=-5 \\ x+\dfrac{3}{2}y=7 \end{array} \right.$$
$$0=2$$

The solution set is $\{\ \}$.

27. Eliminate x by adding 3 times Equation 1 and Equation 2.

$$\begin{array}{l} 3(\text{Equation 1}) \\ \text{Equation 2} \end{array} \left\{ \begin{array}{l} 3x+15y=-12 \\ -3x-2y=12 \end{array} \right.$$
$$13y=0$$
$$y=0$$

Substitute $y=0$ into Equation 1 and solve for x.
$$x+5y=-4$$
$$x+5(0)=-4$$
$$x=-4$$

The solution set is $\{(-4,0)\}$.

29. Eliminate x by adding -6 times Equation 1 and 2 times Equation 2.

$$\begin{array}{l} -6(\text{Equation 1}) \\ 2(\text{Equation 2}) \end{array} \left\{ \begin{array}{l} -12x-30y=-114 \\ 12x+8y=48 \end{array} \right.$$
$$-22y=-66$$
$$y=3$$

Substitute $y=3$ into Equation 1 and solve for x.
$$2x+5y=19$$
$$2x+5(3)=19$$
$$x=2$$

The solution set is $\{(2,3)\}$.

31. Eliminate y by adding Equation 1 and -2 times Equation 2.

$$\begin{array}{l} \text{Equation 1} \\ -2(\text{Equation 2}) \end{array} \left\{ \begin{array}{l} 4.5x+6y=6 \\ -15x-6y=-48 \end{array} \right.$$
$$-10.5x=-42$$
$$x=4$$

Substitute $x=4$ into Equation 1 and solve for y.
$$4.5x+6y=6$$
$$4.5(4)+6y=6$$
$$y=-2$$

The solution set is $\{(4,-2)\}$.

33. Eliminate y by adding -2 times Equation 1 and Equation 2.

$$\begin{array}{l} -2(\text{Equation 1}) \\ \text{Equation 2} \end{array} \left\{ \begin{array}{l} -10x+8y=-32 \\ 10x-8y=32 \end{array} \right.$$
$$0=0$$

The solution set is $\{(x,y)\,|\,5x-4y=16\}$.

35. Eliminate y by adding -2 times Equation 1 and Equation 2.

$$\begin{array}{l} -2(\text{Equation 1}) \\ \text{Equation 2} \end{array} \left\{ \begin{array}{l} -8x+10y=-6 \\ 8x-10y=-6 \end{array} \right.$$
$$0=12$$

The solution set is $\{\ \}$.

37. Eliminate x by adding 3 times Equation 1 and 2 times Equation 2.

$$\begin{array}{l} 3(\text{Equation 1}) \\ 2(\text{Equation 2}) \end{array} \left\{ \begin{array}{l} 6x+9y=-21 \\ -6x-8y=14 \end{array} \right.$$
$$y=-7$$

Substitute $y=-7$ into Equation 1 and solve for x.

$$2x+3y=-7$$
$$2x+3(-7)=-7$$
$$x=7$$

The solution set is $\{(7,-7)\}$.

39. Eliminate y by adding Equation 1 and 2 times Equation 2.

$$\begin{array}{ll} \text{Equation 1} & \\ 2(\text{Equation 2}) & \end{array} \left\{ \begin{array}{l} 8x-4y=-4 \\ -12x+4y=56 \end{array} \right.$$
$$-4x=52$$
$$x=-13$$

Substitute $x=-13$ into Equation 1 and solve for y.
$$8x-4y=-4$$
$$8(-13)-4y=-4$$
$$y=-25$$

The solution set is $\{(-13,-25)\}$.

41. Eliminate y by adding -3 times Equation 1 and 2 times Equation 2.

$$\begin{array}{ll} -3(\text{Equation 1}) & \\ 2(\text{Equation 2}) & \end{array} \left\{ \begin{array}{l} -15x-6y=-21 \\ 14x+6y=20 \end{array} \right.$$
$$-x=-1$$
$$x=1$$

Substitute $x=1$ into $5x+2y=7$ and solve for y.
$$5x+2y=7$$
$$5(1)+2y=7$$
$$y=1$$

The solution set is $\{(1,1)\}$.

43. Eliminate x by adding $-\dfrac{5}{2}$ times Equation 1 and

$\dfrac{1}{5}$ times Equation 2.

$$\begin{array}{ll} -\dfrac{5}{2}(\text{Equation 1}) & \\ \dfrac{1}{5}(\text{Equation 2}) & \end{array} \left\{ \begin{array}{l} -2x-3y=-5 \\ 2x+3y=5 \end{array} \right.$$
$$0=0$$

The solution set is $\{(x,y)\,|\,4x+6y=10\}$.

45. Eliminate y by adding 5 times Equation 1 and 3 times Equation 2.

$$\begin{array}{ll} 5(\text{Equation 1}) & \\ 3(\text{Equation 2}) & \end{array} \left\{ \begin{array}{l} 20x-15y=-55 \\ -18x+15y=54 \end{array} \right.$$
$$2x=-1$$
$$x=-\frac{1}{2}$$

Substitute $x=-\dfrac{1}{2}$ into Equation 1 and solve for y.
$$4x-3y=-11$$
$$4\left(-\frac{1}{2}\right)-3y=-11$$
$$y=3$$

The solution set is $\left\{\left(-\dfrac{1}{2},3\right)\right\}$.

47. Eliminate x by adding -12 times Equation 1 and 16 times Equation 2.

$$\begin{array}{ll} -12(\text{Equation 1}) & \\ 16(\text{Equation 2}) & \end{array} \left\{ \begin{array}{l} -4x+3y=-24 \\ 4x-2y=32 \end{array} \right.$$
$$y=8$$

Substitute $y=8$ into Equation 1 and solve for x.
$$\frac{x}{3}-\frac{y}{4}=2$$
$$\frac{x}{3}-\frac{(8)}{4}=2$$
$$x=12$$

The solution set is $\{(12,8)\}$.

49. Eliminate y by adding 50 times Equation 1 and 40 times Equation 2.

$$\begin{array}{ll} 50(\text{Equation 1}) & \\ 40(\text{Equation 2}) & \end{array} \left\{ \begin{array}{l} 15x-20y=150 \\ 24x+20y=-72 \end{array} \right.$$
$$39x=78$$
$$x=2$$

Substitute $x=2$ into Equation 1 and solve for y.
$$0.3x-0.4y=3.0$$
$$0.3(2)-0.4y=3.0$$
$$y=-6$$

The solution set is $\{(2,-6)\}$.

51. The Elimination Method is sometimes called the Addition Method because when eliminating a variable, the goal is to make either the x or the y terms sum to zero, thus allowing the remaining variable to be determined.

53. This system is ideal for the Substitution Method. By plugging the first equation into the second, it is possible to solve for x, then solve for y.

150

55. a) consistent/dependent
b) coinciding lines

57. a) consistent/independent
b) intersecting lines

59. a) inconsistent
b) parallel lines

61. a) consistent/independent
b) intersecting lines

63. a) consistent/dependent
b) coinciding lines

65. a) inconsistent
b) parallel lines

67. Prepare   We are asked to use the given information to determine the number of each type of raffle ticket sold by the Princeton Hospital Guild to raise money for the children's ward.

Plan   The two unknowns are the number of raffle tickets sold for the Hummer and the number of raffle tickets sold for lesser prizes. Let's assign a different variable to each unknown, write a system of linear equations, and solve the system by the Elimination Method.

Process   Let x represent the number of raffle tickets sold for the Hummer and y represent the number of raffle tickets sold for the lesser prizes. A total of 5,000 tickets were sold for the raffle, which we will indicate in the first equation.

$$\text{Equation 1: } x + y = 5,000$$

The total proceeds for the raffle were \$41,000, which we will indicate in the second equation.

$$\text{Equation 2: } 10x + 5y = 41,000$$

We can now solve the system of equations by the Elimination Method.

$$\begin{cases} x + y = 5,000 \\ 10x + 5y = 41,000 \end{cases}$$

Eliminate y by adding -5 times Equation 1 and Equation 2.

$$\begin{array}{r} -5(\text{Equation 1}) \\ \text{Equation 2} \end{array} \begin{cases} -5x - 5y = -25,000 \\ 10x + 5y = 41,000 \end{cases}$$
$$\overline{5x = 16,000}$$
$$x = 3,200$$

Substitute $x = 3,200$ into Equation 1 and solve for y.

$$x + y = 5,000$$
$$(3,200) + y = 5,000$$
$$y = 1,800$$

There were 3,200 raffle tickets sold for the Hummer and 1,800 raffle tickets sold for the lesser prizes.

Ponder   Do our answers seem reasonable? We can check to see if our answers satisfy the conditions of the problem.   There were $3,200 + 1,800 = 5,000$ tickets sold and $\$10(3,200) + \$5(1,800) = \$41,000$ worth of tickets sold.   Therefore, our answer is reasonable.

69. Eliminate x by adding -18 times Equation 1 and 4 times Equation 2.

$$\begin{array}{r} -18(\text{Equation 1}) \\ 4(\text{Equation 2}) \end{array} \begin{cases} -12x - 90y = -432 \\ 12x - y = 68 \end{cases}$$
$$\overline{-91y = -364}$$
$$y = 4$$

Substitute $y = 4$ into Equation 2 and solve for x.

$$3x - \frac{1}{4}y = 17$$
$$3x - \frac{1}{4}(4) = 17$$
$$x = 6$$

The solution set is $\{(6, 4)\}$.

71. Eliminate y by adding 6 times Equation 1 and 12 times Equation 2.

$$\begin{array}{r} 6(\text{Equation 1}) \\ 12(\text{Equation 2}) \end{array} \begin{cases} -144x + 3y = 126 \\ 24x - 3y = -26 \end{cases}$$
$$\overline{-120x = 100}$$
$$x = -\frac{5}{6}$$

Substitute $x = -\frac{5}{6}$ into Equation 1 and solve for y.

$$-24x + \frac{1}{2}y = 21$$
$$-24\left(-\frac{5}{6}\right) + \frac{1}{2}y = 21$$
$$y = 2$$

The solution set is $\left\{\left(-\frac{5}{6}, 2\right)\right\}$.

73. Eliminate x by adding 400 times Equation 1 and 10 times Equation 2.

$$\begin{array}{r} 400(\text{Equation 1}) \\ 10(\text{Equation 2}) \end{array} \begin{cases} 4x - 80y = 6,000 \\ -4x + 0.3y = 1,970 \end{cases}$$
$$\overline{-79.7y = 7,970}$$
$$y = -100$$

Substitute $y = -100$ into Equation 1 and solve for x.

$$0.01x - 0.2y = 15$$
$$0.01x - 0.2(-100) = 15$$
$$x = -500$$

The solution set is $\{(-500, -100)\}$.

4.4 Exercises

1. The solution of a linear equation in three variables is an <u>ordered</u> <u>triple</u>.

3. The graph of a linear equation in three variables is a <u>plane</u>, not a line.

5. If the graph of a linear system of equations in three variables produces three planes with a common line of intersection there are <u>infinite</u> solutions.

7.a.
$$x - 4y + z = 12$$
$$(2) - 4(-3) + (-2) = 12$$
$$12 = 12$$
True

$$3x + y - z = -2$$
$$3(2) + (-3) - (-2) = -2$$
$$5 = -2$$
False

The ordered triple $(2, -3, -2)$ is not a solution to the system.

7.b.
$$x - 4y + z = 12$$
$$(1) - 4(-2) + (3) = 12$$
$$12 = 12$$
True

$$3x + y - z = -2$$
$$3(1) + (-2) - (3) = -2$$
$$-2 = -2$$
True

$$2x - y + 2z = 6$$
$$2(1) - (-2) + 2(3) = 6$$
$$10 = 6$$
False

The ordered triple $(1, -2, 3)$ is not a solution to the system.

7.c.
$$x - 4y + z = 12$$
$$(0) - 4(-2) + (4) = 12$$
$$12 = 12$$
True

$$3x + y - z = -2$$
$$3(0) + (-2) - (4) = -2$$
$$-6 = -2$$
False

The ordered triple $(0, -2, 4)$ is not a solution to the system.

9. Solve Equation 3 for z.
$$2z = 4$$
$$z = 2$$
Substitute $z = 2$ into Equation 2 and solve for y.
$$2y + 3z = 12$$
$$2y + 3(2) = 12$$
$$y = 3$$
Substitute $y = 3$ and $z = 2$ into Equation 1 and solve for x.
$$5x + 3y - 2z = 10$$
$$5x + 3(3) - 2(2) = 10$$
$$x = 1$$
The solution set is $\{(1, 3, 2)\}$.

11. Eliminate z by adding Equation 1 and Equation 3.

Equation 1 $\quad \begin{cases} 4x - 5y - z = 7 \\ 3x - y + z = 6 \end{cases}$
Equation 3

Equation 4 $\qquad 7x - 6y = 13$

Eliminate z by adding Equation 1 and Equation 2.

Equation 1 $\quad \begin{cases} 4x - 5y - z = 7 \\ x + y + z = 2 \end{cases}$
Equation 2

Equation 5 $\qquad 5x - 4y = 9$

Eliminate y by adding 4 times Equation 4 and -6 times Equation 5.

$\begin{matrix} 4(\text{Equation 4}) \\ -6(\text{Equation 5}) \end{matrix} \begin{cases} 28x - 24y = 52 \\ -30x + 24y = -54 \end{cases}$

$$-2x = -2$$
$$x = 1$$

Substitute $x = 1$ into Equation 4 and solve for y.
$$7x - 6y = 13$$
$$7(1) - 6y = 13$$
$$y = -1$$

Substitute $x=1$ and $y=-1$ into Equation 1 and solve for z.

$$4x-5y-z=7$$
$$4(1)-5(-1)-z=7$$
$$z=2$$

The solution set is $\{(1,-1,2)\}$.

13. Eliminate z by adding Equation 1 and -2 times Equation 2.

$$\begin{array}{ll} \text{Equation 1} & x+y+4z=1 \\ -2(\text{Equation 2}) & -2x+2y-4z=-8 \\ \hline \text{Equation 4} & -x+3y=-7 \end{array}$$

Eliminate z by adding Equation 1 and 2 times Equation 3.

$$\begin{array}{ll} \text{Equation 1} & x+y+4z=1 \\ 2(\text{Equation 3}) & 6x+2y-4z=0 \\ \hline \text{Equation 5} & 7x+3y=1 \end{array}$$

Eliminate y by adding Equation 4 and -1 times Equation 5.

$$\begin{array}{ll} \text{Equation 4} & -x+3y=-7 \\ -1(\text{Equation 5}) & -7x-3y=-1 \\ \hline & -8x=-8 \\ & x=1 \end{array}$$

Substitute $x=1$ into Equation 4 and solve for y.

$$-x+3y=-7$$
$$-(1)+3y=-7$$
$$y=-2$$

Substitute $x=1$ and $y=-2$ into Equation 1 and solve for z.

$$x+y+4z=1$$
$$(1)+(-2)+4z=1$$
$$z=\frac{1}{2}$$

The solution set is $\left\{\left(1,-2,\frac{1}{2}\right)\right\}$.

15. Eliminate z by adding 3 times Equation 1 and -1 times Equation 3.

$$\begin{array}{ll} 3(\text{Equation 1}) & 3x+6y-12z=3 \\ -1(\text{Equation 3}) & -3x-6y+12z=-4 \\ \hline & 0=-1 \end{array}$$

The solution set is $\{\ \}$.

17. Eliminate y by adding 2 times Equation 1 and Equation 2.

$$\begin{array}{ll} 2(\text{Equation 1}) & 6x-2y=16 \\ \text{Equation 2} & 2y+z=-18 \\ \hline \text{Equation 4} & 6x+z=-2 \end{array}$$

Eliminate z by adding Equation 3 and 2 times Equation 4.

$$\begin{array}{ll} \text{Equation 3} & -5x-2z=11 \\ 2(\text{Equation 2}) & 12x+2z=-4 \\ \hline & 7x=7 \\ & x=1 \end{array}$$

Substitute $x=1$ into Equation 1 and solve for y.

$$3x-y=8$$
$$3(1)-y=8$$
$$y=-5$$

Substitute $y=-5$ into Equation 2 and solve for z.

$$2y+z=-18$$
$$2(-5)+z=-18$$
$$z=-8$$

The solution set is $\{(1,-5,-8)\}$.

19. Eliminate z by adding 2 times Equation 1 and Equation 2.

$$\begin{array}{ll} 2(\text{Equation 1}) & 2x-10y+4z=16 \\ \text{Equation 2} & -2x+10y-4z=-16 \\ \hline & 0=0 \end{array}$$

The solution set is $\{(x,y,z)\,|\,x-5y+2z=8\}$.

21. Eliminate z by adding 9 times Equation 1 and Equation 3.

$$\begin{array}{ll} 9(\text{Equation 1}) & 54y-9z=0 \\ \text{Equation 3} & 6x+9z=15 \\ \hline \text{Equation 4} & 6x+54y=15 \end{array}$$

Eliminate x by adding -3 times Equation 2 and 2 times Equation 4.

$$\begin{array}{ll} -3(\text{Equation 2}) & -12x-24y=12 \\ 2(\text{Equation 4}) & 12x+108y=30 \\ \hline & 84y=42 \\ & y=\frac{1}{2} \end{array}$$

Substitute $y=\frac{1}{2}$ into Equation 2 and solve for x.

$$4x+8y=-4$$
$$4x+8\left(\frac{1}{2}\right)=-4$$
$$x=-2$$

Substitute $y = \dfrac{1}{2}$ into Equation 1 and solve for z.

$$6y - z = 0$$

$$6\left(\dfrac{1}{2}\right) - z = 0$$

$$z = 3$$

The solution set is $\left\{\left(-2, \dfrac{1}{2}, 3\right)\right\}$.

23. Eliminate z by adding Equation 1 and Equation 2.

Equation 1 $\begin{cases} 2x + 2y + z = 2 \\ -x + y - z = 4 \end{cases}$
Equation 2

Equation 4 $x + 3y = 6$

Eliminate z by adding Equation 2 and Equation 3.

Equation 2 $\begin{cases} -x + y - z = 4 \\ 3x + 5y + z = 6 \end{cases}$
Equation 3

Equation 5 $2x + 6y = 10$

Eliminate y by adding -2 times Equation 4 and Equation 5.

$3(\text{Equation 4})$ $\begin{cases} -2x - 6y = -12 \\ 2x + 6y = 10 \end{cases}$
Equation 5

$$\underline{\hspace{3cm}}$$
$$0 = -2$$

The solution set is $\{ \ \}$.

25. Eliminate z by adding -4 times Equation 1 and 3 times Equation 2.

$-4(\text{Equation 1})$ $\begin{cases} -8x + 36y - 12z = -44 \\ 18x - 15y + 12z = 24 \end{cases}$
$3(\text{Equation 2})$

Equation 4 $10x + 21y = -20$

Eliminate z by adding 2 times Equation 1 and 3 times Equation 3.

$2(\text{Equation 1})$ $\begin{cases} 4x - 18y + 6z = 22 \\ 9x + 21y - 6z = -48 \end{cases}$
$3(\text{Equation 3})$

Equation 5 $13x + 3y = -26$

Eliminate y by adding Equation 4 and -7 times Equation 5.

Equation 4 $\begin{cases} 10x + 21y = -20 \\ -91x - 21y = 182 \end{cases}$
$-7(\text{Equation 5})$

$$\underline{\hspace{3cm}}$$
$$-81x = 162$$
$$x = -2$$

Substitute $x = -2$ into Equation 4 and solve for y.

$$10x + 21y = -20$$
$$10(-2) + 21y = -20$$
$$y = 0$$

Substitute $x = -2$ and $y = 0$ into Equation 1 and solve for z.

$$2x - 9y + 3z = 11$$
$$2(-2) - 9(0) + 3z = 11$$
$$z = 5$$

The solution set is $\{(-2, 0, 5)\}$.

27. Eliminate y by adding Equation 1 and Equation 2.

Equation 1 $\begin{cases} x - 3y + z = 2 \\ x + 2y - z = 1 \end{cases}$
Equation 2

Equation 4 $2x - y = 3$

Eliminate y by adding Equation 2 and Equation 3.

Equation 2 $\begin{cases} x + 2y - z = 1 \\ -7x + y + z = -10 \end{cases}$
Equation 3

Equation 5 $-6x + 3y = -9$

Eliminate y by adding 3 times Equation 4 and Equation 5.

$3(\text{Equation 4})$ $\begin{cases} 6x - 3y = 9 \\ -6x + 3y = -9 \end{cases}$
Equation 5

$$\underline{\hspace{3cm}}$$
$$0 = 0$$

The solution set is $\{(x, y, z) \mid x - 3y + z = 2\}$.

29. Eliminate y by adding Equation 1 and -1 times Equation 2.

Equation 1 $\begin{cases} x + 2y \quad = 10 \\ -2y - z = -5 \end{cases}$
$-1(\text{Equation 2})$

Equation 4 $x - z = 5$

Eliminate z by adding Equation 3 and 2 times Equation 4.

Equation 3 $\begin{cases} x + 2z = -4 \\ 2x - 2z = 10 \end{cases}$
$2(\text{Equation 4})$

$$\underline{\hspace{3cm}}$$
$$3x = 6$$
$$x = 2$$

Substitute $x = 2$ into Equation 1 and solve for y.

$$x + 2y = 10$$
$$(2) + 2y = 10$$
$$y = 4$$

Substitute $x = 2$ into Equation 3 and solve for z.

$$x + 2z = -4$$
$$(2) + 2z = -4$$
$$z = -3$$

The solution set is $\{(2, 4, -3)\}$.

31. Eliminate z by adding Equation 1 and Equation 2.

Equation 1 $\begin{cases} -9x + 16y - z = 18 \\ 7x - 4y + z = 10 \end{cases}$
Equation 2

Equation 4 $-2x + 12y = 28$

Eliminate z by adding Equation 2 and Equation 3.

$$\text{Equation 2} \quad \begin{cases} 7x - 4y + z = 10 \\ \text{Equation 3} \quad -6x - 2y - z = 4 \end{cases}$$

$$\text{Equation 5} \qquad\qquad x - 6y = 14$$

Eliminate y by adding Equation 4 and 2 times Equation 5.

$$\begin{array}{r} \text{Equation 4} \quad \begin{cases} -2x + 12y = 28 \\ 2(\text{Equation 5}) \quad 2x - 12y = 28 \end{cases} \\ \hline 0 = 56 \end{array}$$

The solution set is $\{\ \}$.

33. Answers will vary; one example is: Eliminate any variables that share equal coefficients with opposite signs first when solving a linear system in three variables.

35. Answers will vary; one example is: A linear system in three variables has no solution when all variables reduce to zero and a false statement such as $0 = -28$ remains.

37. Answers will vary; one example is: The graph of a system in three variables with no solution is three parallel and non-coincidental planes when graphed in three dimensions.

39. Answers will vary; one example is: The ordered triple $(2, 2, 0)$ is a solution to the dependent system because by definition, if a system is dependent, then any triple that satisfies one equation will satisfy all equations.

41. Let x represent the first angle, y represent the second angle, and z represent the third angle.
$$\begin{cases} x + y + z = 180 \\ z = 2x - 10 \\ y = 2z \end{cases}$$

Rewrite Equation 2 and Equation 3 to obtain the system:
$$\begin{cases} x + y + z = 180 \\ 2x - z = 10 \\ y - 2z = 0 \end{cases}$$

Eliminate z by adding Equation 1 and Equation 2.

$$\begin{array}{r} \text{Equation 1} \quad \begin{cases} x + y + z = 180 \\ \text{Equation 2} \quad 2x \qquad - z = 10 \end{cases} \\ \hline \text{Equation 4} \qquad 3x + y = 190 \end{array}$$

Eliminate z by adding 2 times Equation 1 and Equation 3.

$$\text{Equation 1} \quad \begin{cases} 2x + 2y + 2z = 360 \\ \text{Equation 2} \qquad\qquad y - 2z = 0 \end{cases}$$

$$\text{Equation 5} \qquad 2x + 3y = 360$$

Eliminate y by adding -3 times Equation 4 and Equation 5.

$$\begin{array}{r} -3(\text{Equation 4}) \quad \begin{cases} -9x - 3y = -570 \\ \text{Equation 5} \quad 2x + 3y = 360 \end{cases} \\ \hline -7x = -210 \\ x = 30 \end{array}$$

Substitute $x = 30$ into Equation 2 and solve for z.
$$2x - z = 10$$
$$2(30) - z = 10$$
$$z = 50$$

Substitute $z = 50$ into Equation 3 and solve for y.
$$y - 2z = 0$$
$$y - 2(50) = 0$$
$$y = 100$$

The first angle is $30°$, the second is $100°$, and the third is $50°$.

43. **Prepare** We are asked to determine how many of each type of souvenir that Fan Icon, Inc. hopes to sell.

Plan Assign a different variable to each unknown and write a system of equations representing the problem. Solve the system by the Elimination Method.

Process Let x represent the number of T-shirts sold, y represent the number of pins sold, and z represent the number of posters sold.
$$\begin{cases} x + y + z = 23{,}100 \\ 15x + 6y + 12z = 260{,}100 \\ y = z + 1{,}600 \end{cases}$$

Rewrite Equation 3 to obtain the system:
$$\begin{cases} x + y + z = 23{,}100 \\ 15x + 6y + 12z = 260{,}100 \\ y - z = 1{,}600 \end{cases}$$

Eliminate x by adding -15 times Equation 1 and Equation 2.

$$\begin{array}{r} -15(\text{Equation 1}) \quad \begin{cases} -15x - 15y - 15z = -346{,}500 \\ \text{Equation 2} \quad 15x + 6y + 12z = 260{,}100 \end{cases} \\ \hline \text{Equation 4} \qquad -9y - 3z = -86{,}400 \end{array}$$

Eliminate z by adding -3 times Equation 3 and Equation 4.

$$-3 \text{(Equation 3)} \quad \begin{cases} -3y + 3z = -4,800 \\ -9y - 3z = -86,400 \end{cases}$$
$$\text{Equation 4}$$

$$-12y = -91,200$$
$$y = 7,600$$

Substitute $y = 7,600$ into Equation 3 and solve for z.

$$y - z = 1,600$$
$$(7,600) - z = 1,600$$
$$z = 6,000$$

Substitute $y = 7,600$ and $z = 6,000$ into Equation 1 and solve for x.

$$x + y + z = 23,100$$
$$x + (7,600) + (6,000) = 23,100$$
$$x = 9,500$$

Fan Icon, Inc. is expected to sell 9,500 T-shirts, 7,600 pins, and 6,000 posters.

Ponder Do our answers seem reasonable? We can check to see if our answers satisfy the conditions of the problem. The total number of souvenirs sold is $9,500 + 7,600 + 6,000 = 23,100$. The total sales for all souvenirs is:

$$\$15(9,500) + \$6(7,600) + \$12(6,000) = \$260,100.$$

Therefore, our answers are reasonable.

4.5 Exercises

1. When writing a system of equations in this section, we translate the information into either two equations with <u>two</u> unknowns or <u>three</u> equations with three <u>unknowns</u>.

3. We can solve a system of equations using the <u>Graphing</u>, <u>Substitution</u>, or <u>Elimination</u> Method.

5. Eliminate y by adding -3 times Equation 1 and Equation 2.

$$\begin{array}{c} -3\,(\text{Equation 1}) \\ \text{Equation 2} \end{array} \begin{cases} -9x-3y=-45 \\ 2x+3y=3 \end{cases}$$
$$-7x=-42$$
$$x=6$$

Substitute $x=6$ into Equation 1 and solve for y.
$$3x+y=15$$
$$3(6)+y=15$$
$$y=-3$$
The solution set is $\{(6,-3)\}$.

7. Eliminate x by adding 2 times Equation 1 and Equation 2.

$$\begin{array}{c} 2\,(\text{Equation 1}) \\ \text{Equation 2} \end{array} \begin{cases} -2x+8y=20 \\ 2x+6y=8 \end{cases}$$
$$14y=28$$
$$y=2$$

Substitute $y=2$ into Equation 1 and solve for x.
$$-x+4y=10$$
$$-x+4(2)=10$$
$$x=-2$$
The solution set is $\{(-2,2)\}$.

9. Substitute $x=3y$ into Equation 1 and solve for y.

$$y=\frac{2}{3}x-3$$
$$y=\frac{2}{3}(3y)-3$$
$$y=3$$
Substitute $y=3$ into Equation 2 and solve for x.
$$x=3y$$
$$x=3(3)$$
$$x=9$$
The solution set is $\{(9,3)\}$.

11. Eliminate y by adding 5 times Equation 1 and -3 times Equation 2.

$$\begin{array}{c} 5\,(\text{Equation 1}) \\ -3\,(\text{Equation 2}) \end{array} \begin{cases} 20x-15y=80 \\ -21x+15y=-96 \end{cases}$$
$$-x=-16$$
$$x=16$$

Substitute $x=16$ into Equation 1 and solve for y.
$$4x-3y=16$$
$$4(16)-3y=16$$
$$y=16$$
The solution set is $\{(16,16)\}$.

13. Eliminate x by adding Equation 1 and -2 times Equation 2.

$$\begin{array}{c} \text{Equation 1} \\ -2\,(\text{Equation 2}) \end{array} \begin{cases} 8x+4y=9 \\ -8x-4y=-10 \end{cases}$$
$$0=-1$$
The solution set is $\{\ \}$.

15. Solve Equation 2 for x.
$$x+2=5$$
$$x=3$$
Substitute $x=3$ into Equation 1 and solve for y.
$$4x+4y=18$$
$$4(3)+4y=18$$
$$y=\frac{3}{2}$$
The solution set is $\left\{\left(3,\frac{3}{2}\right)\right\}$.

17. Eliminate y by adding 40 times Equation 1 and -12 times Equation 2.

$$\begin{array}{c} 40\,(\text{Equation 1}) \\ -12\,(\text{Equation 2}) \end{array} \begin{cases} 60x+8y=-120 \\ -3x-8y=-108 \end{cases}$$
$$57x=-228$$
$$x=-4$$

Substitute $x=-4$ into Equation 1 and solve for y.
$$\frac{3}{2}x+\frac{1}{5}y=-3$$
$$\frac{3}{2}(-4)+\frac{1}{5}y=-3$$
$$y=15$$
The solution set is $\{(-4,15)\}$.

19. Eliminate y by adding 6 times Equation 1 and 4 times Equation 2.

$$6(\text{Equation 1}) \quad \begin{cases} 36x - 24y = 12 \\ 4(\text{Equation 2}) \quad \underline{-36x + 24y = -12} \\ \qquad\qquad\quad 0 = 0 \end{cases}$$

The solution set is $\{(x, y) \mid 6x - 4y = 2\}$.

21. Eliminate y by adding 250 times Equation 1 and 810 times Equation 2.

$$\begin{aligned} 250(\text{Equation 1}) \quad & \begin{cases} 925x + 2{,}025y = 4{,}050 \\ 810(\text{Equation 2}) \quad \underline{7{,}614x - 2{,}025y = -4{,}050} \\ \qquad\qquad 8{,}539x = 0 \\ \qquad\qquad\quad\ x = 0 \end{cases} \end{aligned}$$

Substitute $x = 0$ into Equation 1 and solve for y.

$$3.7x + 8.1y = 16.2$$
$$3.7(0) + 8.1y = 16.2$$
$$y = 2$$

The solution set is $\{(0, 2)\}$.

23. Substitute $x = 4$ into Equation 2 and solve for y.

$$4x + 3y = 7$$
$$4(4) + 3y = 7$$
$$y = -3$$

Substitute $x = 4$ and $y = -3$ into Equation 1 and solve for z.

$$-3x - 2y + 5z = 19$$
$$-3(4) - 2(-3) + 5z = 19$$
$$z = 5$$

The solution set is $\{(4, -3, 5)\}$.

25. Eliminate y by adding 3 times Equation 1 and 2 times Equation 2.

$$\begin{aligned} 3(\text{Equation 1}) \quad & \begin{cases} 6x + 6y - 9z = -3 \\ 2(\text{Equation 2}) \quad \underline{2x - 6y \quad\ = -10} \end{cases} \end{aligned}$$

Equation 4 $\qquad\quad 8x - 9z = -13$

Eliminate x by adding -8 times Equation 3 and Equation 4.

$$\begin{aligned} -8(\text{Equation 3}) \quad & \begin{cases} -8x - 16z = -112 \\ \text{Equation 4} \quad \underline{\ \ 8x - 9z = -13} \\ \qquad\qquad -25z = -125 \\ \qquad\qquad\quad\ z = 5 \end{cases} \end{aligned}$$

Substitute $z = 5$ into Equation 3 and solve for x.

$$x + 2z = 14$$
$$x + 2(5) = 14$$
$$x = 4$$

Substitute $x = 4$ into Equation 2 and solve for y.

$$x - 3y = -5$$
$$(4) - 3y = -5$$
$$y = 3$$

The solution set is $\{(4, 3, 5)\}$.

27. Eliminate c by adding Equation 1 and Equation 2.

$$\begin{aligned} \text{Equation 1} \quad & \begin{cases} a + 2b - c = 0 \\ \text{Equation 2} \quad \underline{a - 5b + c = -9} \end{cases} \end{aligned}$$

Equation 4 $\qquad 2a - 3b = -9$

Eliminate c by adding 2 times Equation 1 and Equation 3.

$$\begin{aligned} 2(\text{Equation 1}) \quad & \begin{cases} 2a + 4b - 2c = 0 \\ \text{Equation 3} \quad \underline{\ \ 4a + b + 2c = 15} \end{cases} \end{aligned}$$

Equation 5 $\qquad\quad 6a + 5b = 15$

Eliminate b by adding 5 times Equation 4 and 3 times Equation 5.

$$\begin{aligned} 5(\text{Equation 4}) \quad & \begin{cases} 10a - 15b = -45 \\ 3(\text{Equation 5}) \quad \underline{18a + 15b = 45} \\ \qquad\qquad 28a = 0 \\ \qquad\qquad\ a = 0 \end{cases} \end{aligned}$$

Substitute $a = 0$ into Equation 4 and solve for b.

$$2a - 3b = -9$$
$$2(0) - 3b = -9$$
$$b = 3$$

Substitute $a = 0$ and $b = 3$ into Equation 1 and solve for c.

$$a + 2b - c = 0$$
$$(0) + 2(3) - c = 0$$
$$c = 6$$

The solution set is $\{(0, 3, 6)\}$.

29. a) Let x represent the smaller integer. Then the larger integer is $3x - 21$. Because the sum of the two integers is 71, we can write the equation:

$$(\text{smaller integer}) + (\text{larger integer}) = 71$$
$$(x) + (3x - 21) = 71$$

Solve the equation.

$$x + 3x - 21 = 71$$
$$4x - 21 = 71$$
$$4x = 92$$
$$x = 23$$

The smaller integer is 23 and the larger integer is $3(23) - 21 = 48$.

b) Let x represent the smaller integer and let y represent the larger integer. Write the system of equations:

$$\begin{cases} x + y = 71 \\ y = 3x - 21 \end{cases}$$

Substitute $y = 3x - 21$ into Equation 1 and solve for x.

$$x + y = 71$$
$$x + (3x - 21) = 71$$
$$4x = 92$$
$$x = 23$$

Substitute $x = 23$ into Equation 2 and solve for y.

$$y = 3x - 21$$
$$y = 3(23) - 21$$
$$y = 48$$

The two integers are 23 and 48.

After applying systems of equations, it is easier to identify two variables and set up two equations. The substitution method works well with these equations.

31. The Substitution Method, because each equation is solved for one of the variables.

33. Let x and y represent the two integers. The system of equations is:

$$\begin{cases} x + y = 462 \\ x - y = 206 \end{cases}$$

Eliminate y by adding Equation 1 and Equation 2.

$$\begin{array}{rr} \text{Equation 1} & \begin{cases} x + y = 462 \\ \text{Equation 2} & x - y = 206 \end{cases} \\ \hline & 2x = 668 \\ & x = 334 \end{array}$$

Substitute $x = 334$ into Equation 1 and solve for y.

$$x + y = 462$$
$$(334) + y = 462$$
$$y = 128$$

The two integers are 128 and 334.

35. Let y represent the smaller integer and x represent the larger integer. The system of equations is:

$$\begin{cases} x + y = -26 \\ x - y = 58 \end{cases}$$

Eliminate y by adding Equation 1 to Equation 2.

$$\begin{array}{rr} \text{Equation 1} & \begin{cases} x + y = -26 \\ \text{Equation 2} & x - y = 58 \end{cases} \\ \hline & 2x = 32 \\ & x = 16 \end{array}$$

Substitute $x = 16$ into Equation 1 and solve for y.

$$x + y = -26$$
$$(16) + y = -26$$
$$y = -42$$

The two integers are -42 and 16.

37. Let y represent the smaller number and x represent the larger number. The system of equations is:

$$\begin{cases} x = 8y \\ 2y + 3 = x \end{cases}$$

Substitute $x = 8y$ into Equation 2 and solve for y.

$$2y + 3 = x$$
$$2y + 3 = (8y)$$
$$-6y = -3$$
$$y = \frac{1}{2}$$

Substitute $y = \frac{1}{2}$ into Equation 1 and solve for x.

$$x = 8y$$
$$x = 8\left(\frac{1}{2}\right)$$
$$x = 4$$

The two numbers are $\frac{1}{2}$ and 4.

39. Let x represent the smaller integer and y represent the larger integer. The system of equations is:

$$\begin{cases} 4(x + y) = -28 \\ 3x + 2y = -19 \end{cases}$$

Rewrite the system as follows.

$$\begin{cases} 4x + 4y = -28 \\ 3x + 2y = -19 \end{cases}$$

Eliminate y by adding Equation 1 and -2 times Equation 2.

$$\begin{array}{rr} \text{Equation 1} & \begin{cases} 4x + 4y = -28 \\ -2(\text{Equation 2}) & -6x - 4y = 38 \end{cases} \\ \hline & -2x = 10 \\ & x = -5 \end{array}$$

Substitute $x = -5$ into Equation 1 and solve for y.

$$4x + 4y = -28$$
$$4(-5) + 4y = -28$$
$$y = -2$$

The two integers are -5 and -2.

41. Let x represent the first of the two consecutive even integers and let y represent the second. The system of equations is:

$$\begin{cases} x + y = 234 \\ y = x + 2 \end{cases}$$

Substitute $y = x + 2$ into Equation 1 and solve for x.

$$x+y=234$$
$$x+(x+2)=234$$
$$2x=232$$
$$x=116$$

Substitute $x=116$ into Equation 2 and solve for y.

$$y=x+2$$
$$y=(116)+2$$
$$y=118$$

The two consecutive even integers are 116 and 118.

43. Let n represent the number of nickels, d the number of dimes, and q the number quarters that Nanci found. The system of equations is:

$$\begin{cases} n+d+q=26 \\ 0.05n+0.10d+0.25q=4.20 \\ d=2n+2 \end{cases}$$

Rewrite the system.

$$\begin{cases} n+d+q=26 \\ 0.05n+0.10d+0.25q=4.20 \\ -2n+d=2 \end{cases}$$

Eliminate q by adding 25 times Equation 1 and -100 times Equation 2.

$$\begin{array}{l} 25(\text{Equation 1}) \\ -100(\text{Equation 2}) \end{array} \begin{cases} 25n+25d+25q=650 \\ -5n-10d-25q=-420 \end{cases}$$

$$\text{Equation 4} \qquad 20n+15d=230$$

Eliminate n by adding 10 times Equation 3 and Equation 4.

$$\begin{array}{l} 10(\text{Equation 3}) \\ \text{Equation 4} \end{array} \begin{cases} -20n+10d=20 \\ 20n+15d=230 \end{cases}$$

$$25d=250$$
$$d=10$$

Substitute $d=10$ into Equation 3 and solve for n.

$$-2n+d=2$$
$$-2n+(10)=2$$
$$-2n=-8$$
$$n=4$$

Substitute $d=10$ and $n=4$ into Equation 1 and solve for q.

$$n+d+q=26$$
$$(4)+(10)+q=26$$
$$q=12$$

There are 4 nickels, 10 dimes, and 12 quarters.

45. Prepare We must determine how many \$40 tickets and how many \$30 tickets were sold for the concert.

Plan Because there are two unknowns, we will set up and solve a system of two equations with two unknowns.

Process Let $c=$ the number of tickets sold for covered seats. Let $u=$ the number of tickets sold for uncovered seats. Because a total of 775 people attended the concert, one equation is $c+u=775$. The total amount received from the sale of tickets for covered seats is given by the expression $40c$, while the total amount received from the sale of tickets for uncovered seats is $30u$. Therefore, another equation is $40c+30u=27,750$. The system is:

$$\begin{cases} c+u=775 \\ 40c+30u=27,750 \end{cases}$$

Eliminate u by adding -30 times Equation 1 and Equation 2.

$$\begin{array}{l} -30(\text{Equation 1}) \\ \text{Equation 2} \end{array} \begin{cases} -30c-30u=-23,250 \\ 40c+30u=27,750 \end{cases}$$

$$10c=4,500$$
$$c=450$$

Substitute $c=450$ into Equation 1 and solve for u.

$$c+u=775$$
$$(450)+u=775$$
$$u=325$$

There were 450 tickets sold for covered seats and 325 tickets sold for uncovered seats.

Ponder Does our answer seem reasonable? We can check to see if our answers satisfy the conditions of the problem. First, $450+325=775$, which was the total number of people at the concert. The sale of tickets for covered seats was $450(\$40)=\$18,000$. The sale of tickets for uncovered seats was $325(\$30)=\$9,750$. The total ticket sales was $\$18,000+\$9,750=\$27,750$. Our answer is correct.

47. Prepare We must determine the amount that Junior Garcia deposited in each of two accounts.

Plan Because there are two unknowns, we will set up and solve a system of two equations with two unknowns.

Process Let $x=$ the amount deposited at 5% interest. Let $y=$ the amount deposited at 3%.

	Principal	Rate	Time	Interest
5%	x	0.05	1 year	$0.05x$
3%	y	0.03	1 year	$0.03y$

Because the total amount deposited is $8,500, one equation is $x + y = 8,500$. Because the total interest earned at 5% is $0.05x$ and the total interest earned at 3% is $0.03y$, the total interest earned from both deposits is $0.05x + 0.03y = 375$. The system of equations is:

$$\begin{cases} x + y = 8,500 \\ 0.05x + 0.03y = 375 \end{cases}$$

Eliminate y by adding -3 times Equation 1 and 100 times Equation 2.

$$\begin{array}{l} -3(\text{Equation 1}) \\ 100(\text{Equation 2}) \end{array} \begin{cases} -3x - 3y = -25,500 \\ 5x + 3y = 37,500 \end{cases}$$

$$2x = 12,000$$
$$x = 6,000$$

Substitute $x = 6,000$ into Equation 1 and solve for y.

$$x + y = 8,500$$
$$(6,000) + y = 8,500$$
$$y = 2,500$$

Junior Garcia deposited $6,000 at 5% and $2,500 at 3%.

Ponder Does our answer seem reasonable? First, we see that $6,000 + 2,500 = 8,500$, which was the total amount deposited at both interest rates. Next, the interest earned at 5% was:

$$0.05(\$6,000) = \$300$$

and the interest earned at 3% was:

$$0.03(\$2,500) = \$75$$

The total interest earned was $300 + \$75 = \$375$. Our answer is correct.

49. **Prepare** We must determine the number of pounds of fish and the number of pounds of chips that James and Peter prepared.

Plan Because there are two unknowns, we will set up and solve a system of two equations with two unknowns.

Process Let $c =$ the number of pounds of chips made and let $f =$ the number pounds of fish made. Because the total weight of the serving of fish and chips was 25.65 pounds, one equation is $c + f = 25.65$. Because the chips weighed 2.15 pounds more than the chips, another equation is $c = f + 2.15$. The system of equations is:

$$\begin{cases} c + f = 25.65 \\ c = f + 2.15 \end{cases}$$

Substitute $c = f + 2.15$ into Equation 1 and solve for f.

$$c + f = 25.65$$
$$(f + 2.15) + f = 25.65$$
$$2f = 23.5$$
$$f = 11.75$$

Substitute $f = 11.75$ into Equation 2 and solve for c.

$$c = f + 2.15$$
$$c = (11.75) + 2.15$$
$$c = 13.90$$

The serving consisted of 11.75 pounds of fish and 13.9 pounds of chips.

Ponder Does our answer seem reasonable? We can check to see if our answer satisfies the conditions of the problem. First, the total weight of the serving was $13.9 + 11.75 = 25.65$ pounds. Second, the difference in the weight of the chips and fish is $13.9 - 11.75 = 2.15$ pounds. Therefore, our answer is correct.

51. **Prepare** We must determine length and the girth of the world's heaviest snake in inches.

Plan Because there are two unknowns, we will set up and solve a system of two equations with two unknowns. The solution to the system will be in meters. We must then convert these measurements to inches.

Process Let $g =$ the girth and let $l =$ the length of the snake. Because the sum of the snake's length and girth was 9 meters, one equation is $g + l = 9$. Because the length was 12 times the girth, another equation is $l = 12g$. The system of equations is:

$$\begin{cases} g + l = 9 \\ l = 12g \end{cases}$$

Substitute $l = 12g$ into Equation 1 and solve for g.

$$g + l = 9$$
$$g + (12g) = 9$$
$$13g = 9$$
$$g \approx 0.69$$

Substitute $g = 0.69$ into Equation 2 and solve for l.

$$l = 12g$$
$$l \approx 12(0.69)$$
$$l \approx 8.28$$

Convert 0.69 meter to inches.

$$0.69(39) \approx 27$$

Convert 8.28 meters to inches.

$$8.28(39) \approx 323$$

The snake was approximately 323 inches long and had a girth of approximately 27 inches.

Ponder   Does our answer seem reasonable? Because 323 inches is approximately 27 feet, it seems reasonable that the snake was this long. Many Burmese Pythons have been found that are 20 feet in length.

53. **Prepare**   We must determine the number of pounds of almonds and the number of pounds of cashews that Caroline purchased.

Plan   Because there are two unknowns, we will set up and solve a system of two equations with two unknowns.

Process   Let $a =$ the number of pounds of almonds purchased and let $c =$ the number of pounds of cashews purchased.

	Almonds	Cashews	Mixture
Amount (pounds)	a	c	7
Price/Pound	$5	$8	
Total Price	$5a$	$8c$	$44

The system of equations is:
$$\begin{cases} a+c = 7 \\ 5a+8c = 44 \end{cases}$$

Eliminate a by adding -5 times Equation 1 and Equation 2.

$$\begin{matrix} -5(\text{Equation 1}) \\ \text{Equation 2} \end{matrix} \begin{cases} -5a-5c = -35 \\ 5a+8c = 44 \end{cases}$$

$$3c = 9$$
$$c = 3$$

Substitute $c = 3$ into Equation 1 and solve for a.
$$a+c = 7$$
$$a+(3) = 7$$
$$a = 4$$

Caroline purchased 4 pounds of almonds and 3 pounds of cashews.

Ponder   Does our answer seem reasonable? We can check to see if our answer satisfies the conditions of the problem. First, the sum of the weights of the nuts is $4+3 = 7$ pounds. Next, the cost of the almonds was $4($5) = 20 and the cost of the cashews was $3($8) = 24. The total cost was $20+$24 = 44. Therefore, our answer is correct.

55. **Prepare**   We must determine the number of liters of 50% orange juice concentrate and the number of liters of 30% orange juice concentrate the Kid's Club should purchase.

Plan   Because there are two unknowns, we will set up and solve a system of two equations with two unknowns.

Process   Let $x =$ the number of liters of 50% concentrate purchased and let $y =$ the number of liters of 30% concentrate purchased.

	50% Orange Juice	30% Orange Juice	45% Mixture
Amount (liters)	x	y	20
Percent Orange Juice	0.50	0.30	0.45
Amount of Orange Juice	$0.50x$	$0.30y$	$0.45(20)$

The system of equations is:
$$\begin{cases} x+y = 20 \\ 0.50x+0.30y = 9 \end{cases}$$

Eliminate y by adding -3 times Equation 1 and 10 times Equation 2.

$$\begin{matrix} -3(\text{Equation 1}) \\ 10(\text{Equation 2}) \end{matrix} \begin{cases} -3x-3y = -60 \\ 5x+3y = 90 \end{cases}$$

$$2x = 30$$
$$x = 15$$

Substitute $x = 15$ into Equation 1 and solve for y.
$$x+y = 20$$
$$(15)+y = 20$$
$$y = 5$$

The Kid's Club purchased 15 liters of 50% concentrate and 5 liters of 30% concentrate.

Ponder   Does our answer seem reasonable? We can check to see if our answer satisfies the conditions of the problem. First, the sum of the volumes of the orange juice concentrate is $15+5 = 20$ liters. Next, the amount of orange juice in 15 liters of the 50% concentrate is $0.50(15) = 7.5$ liters, and the amount of orange juice in 5 liters of the 30% concentrate is $0.30(5) = 1.5$ liters. The total liters of orange juice in the mixture is $0.45(20) = 9$ liters. Therefore, our answer is correct.

57. Prepare We must determine the number of pounds of 16% molasses-covered oat feed and the number of pounds of 7% molasses-covered oat feed Heidi should mix to make a 30 pound mixture containing 10% molasses-covered oats.

Plan Because there are two unknowns, we will set up and solve a system of two equations with two unknowns.

Process Let $x =$ the number of pounds of 16% molasses-covered oat feed needed and let $y =$ the number of pounds of 7% molasses-covered oat feed needed for the mixture.

	16% oats	7% oats	10% Mixture
Amount (pounds)	x	y	30
Percent oats	0.16	0.07	0.10
Amount of oats	$0.16x$	$0.07y$	$0.10(30)$

The system of equations is:
$$\begin{cases} x + y = 30 \\ 0.16x + 0.07y = 3 \end{cases}$$
Eliminate y by adding -7 times Equation 1 and 100 times Equation 2.
$$\begin{aligned} -7(\text{Equation 1}) \\ 100(\text{Equation 2}) \end{aligned} \begin{cases} -7x - 7y = -210 \\ 16x + 7y = 300 \end{cases}$$
$$9x = 90$$
$$x = 10$$
Substitute $x = 10$ into Equation 1 and solve for y.
$$x + y = 30$$
$$(10) + y = 30$$
$$y = 20$$
Heidi should mix 10 pounds of 16% molasses-covered oat feed with 20 pound of 7% molasses-covered oat feed.

Ponder Does our answer seem reasonable? We can check to see if our answer satisfies the conditions of the problem. First, the sum of the weights of the two types of feed is $10 + 20 = 30$ pounds. Next, the number of pound of oats in 10 pounds of the 16% oat feed is $0.16(10) = 1.6$ pounds, and the number of pounds of oats in 20 pounds of the 7% oat feed is $0.07(20) = 1.4$ pounds. The total number of pounds of oats in the mixture is $0.10(30) = 3$ pounds. Therefore, our answer is correct.

59. Prepare We must determine the speed of the boat in still water and the speed of the river's current.

Plan Because there are two unknowns, we will set up and solve a system of two equations with two unknowns.

Process Let s represent the speed of the boat in still water and let c represent the speed of the river's current.

	Distance (miles)	Rate (mph)	Time (hours)
Upstream	33	$s - c$	$1\frac{1}{2} = \frac{3}{2}$
Downstream	57	$s + c$	$1\frac{1}{2} = \frac{3}{2}$

Using the formula $D = RT$, we can write the equation for the boat's trip upstream; $33 = (s - c)\left(\frac{3}{2}\right)$. We can also write the equation for the boat's trip downstream; $57 = (s + c)\left(\frac{3}{2}\right)$. The system of equations is:
$$\begin{cases} 3s - 3c = 66 \\ 3s + 3c = 114 \end{cases}$$
Eliminate c by adding Equation 1 and Equation 2 .
$$\begin{aligned} \text{Equation 1} \\ \text{Equation 2} \end{aligned} \begin{cases} 3s - 3c = 66 \\ 3s + 3c = 114 \end{cases}$$
$$6s = 180$$
$$s = 30$$
Substitute $s = 30$ into Equation 1 and solve for c.
$$3s - 3c = 66$$
$$3(30) - 3c = 66$$
$$-3c = -24$$
$$c = 8$$
The speed of the boat in still water is 30 mph and the speed of the river's current is 8 mph.

Ponder Does our answer seem reasonable? We can use the formula $D = RT$ to check our results. The boat travels 30 mph in still water and the current is 8 mph, therefore the speed of the boat upstream is $30 - 8 = 22$ mph. The distance traveled by the boat in $1\frac{1}{2}$ hours upstream is $22\left(1\frac{1}{2}\right) = 33$ miles. The speed of the boat downstream is $30 + 8 = 38$ mph. The distance traveled by the boat downstream in $1\frac{1}{2}$ hours is $38\left(1\frac{1}{2}\right) = 57$ miles. Therefore, our answers are correct.

61. Prepare We must determine how long it will take Johanna to catch Katherine.

Plan Because there are two unknowns, we will set up and solve a system of two equations with two unknowns.

Process Let K represent Katherine's travel time and let J represent Johanna's travel time.

	Distance (miles)	Rate (mph)	Time (hours)
Katherine	$4K$	4	K
Johanna	$16J$	16	J

When Johanna catches Katherine, they will have traveled the same distance, therefore, one equation is $4K = 16J$. If we divide both sides by 4, this equation becomes $K = 4J$. Because Katherine leaves 1.5 hours before Johanna, another equation is $K = J + 1.5$. The system of equations is:

$$\begin{cases} K = 4J \\ K = J + 1.5 \end{cases}$$

Substitute $K = 4J$ into Equation 2 and solve for J

$$K = J + 1.5$$
$$(4J) = J + 1.5$$
$$3J = 1.5$$
$$J = 0.5$$

Substitute $J = 0.5$ into Equation 1 and solve for K.
$$K = 4J$$
$$K = 4(0.5)$$
$$K = 2$$

It will take Johanna 0.5 hour or 30 minutes to catch Katherine.

Ponder Does our answer seem reasonable? We can use the formula $D = RT$ to check our results. Katherine walks at a rate of 4 mph for 2 hours for a total distance of 8 miles. Johanna drives at a rate of 16 mph for 0.5 hour for a total distance of 8 miles. Therefore, our answer is correct.

63. Prepare We must determine the measure of two supplementary angles.

Plan Because there are two unknowns, we will set up and solve a system of two equations with two unknowns.

Process Let x and y represent the two angles. Because the angles are supplementary, their sum is 180, therefore, one equation is $x + y = 180$. Because one angle is three times the measure of the

other, another equation is $x = 3y$. The system of equations is:

$$\begin{cases} x + y = 180 \\ x = 3y \end{cases}$$

Substitute $x = 3y$ into Equation 1 and solve for y.
$$x + y = 180$$
$$(3y) + y = 180$$
$$4y = 180$$
$$y = 45$$

Substitute $y = 45$ into Equation 2 and solve for x.
$$x = 3y$$
$$x = 3(45)$$
$$x = 135$$

The measures of the two angles are $45°$ and $135°$.

Ponder Does our answer seem reasonable? The measures of the two angles satisfy the conditions of the problem. That is, their sum is $45 + 135 = 180$ and one of the angles is 3 time the other, $135 = 3(45)$. Therefore, our answers are correct.

65. Prepare We must determine the length and the width of the world's largest rectangular floating island.

Plan Because there are two unknowns, we will set up and solve a system of two equations with two unknowns.

Process Let $l =$ the length of the island and let $w =$ the width of the island. Because the perimeter of the island is 2,242 meters, we can use the perimeter formula $P = 2l + 2w$ to write the equation $2,242 = 2l + 2w$. Because the length is 879 meters longer than the width, we can write the equation $l = w + 879$. The system of equations is:

$$\begin{cases} 2l + 2w = 2,242 \\ l = w + 879 \end{cases}$$

Substitute $l = w + 879$ into Equation 1 and solve for w.
$$2l + 2w = 2,242$$
$$2(w + 879) + 2w = 2,242$$
$$4w = 484$$
$$w = 121$$

Substitute $w = 121$ into Equation 2 and solve for l.
$$l = w + 879$$
$$l = (121) + 879$$
$$l = 1,000$$

The length of the island is 1,000 meters and the width of the island is 121 meters.

Ponder Does our answer seem reasonable? We can check to see if our answer satisfies the conditions of the problem. First, the perimeter is $P = 2(1,000) + 2(121) = 2,242$ meters. Next, the difference between the length and the width is $1,000 - 121 = 879$ meters. Therefore, our answers are correct.

67. Prepare We must determine the amount that Alix invested at each of three interest rates.

Plan Because there are three unknowns, we will set up and solve a system of three equations with three unknowns.

Process Let $x =$ the amount deposited at 4.5% interest. Let $y =$ the amount deposited at 3%. Let $z =$ the amount invested at 5%.

	Principal	Rate	Time	Interest
4.5%	x	0.045	1 year	$0.045x$
3%	y	0.03	1 year	$0.03y$
5%	z	0.05	1 year	$0.05z$

Because the total amount deposited is $10,000, one equation is $x + y + z = 10,000$. Because the amount invested at 3% is $100 less than twice the amount invested at 5%, another equation is $y = 2z - 100$, or $y - 2z = -100$. Because the total interest earned at 4.5% is $0.045x$, the total interest earned at 3% is $0.03y$, and the total interest earned at 5% is $0.05z$, the total interest earned from all three investments is $0.045x + 0.03y + 0.05z = 438.5$. The system of equations is:

$$\begin{cases} x + y + z = 10,000 \\ 0.045x + 0.03y + 0.05z = 438.5 \\ y - 2z = -100 \end{cases}$$

Eliminate x by adding -4.5 times Equation 1 and 100 times Equation 2.

$$\begin{array}{ll} -4.5(\text{Equation 1}) & \begin{cases} -4.5x - 4.5y - 4.5z = -45,000 \\ 4.5x + 3y + 5z = 43,850 \end{cases} \\ 100(\text{Equation 2}) & \end{array}$$

$$\text{Equation 4} \qquad -1.5y + 0.5z = -1,150$$

Eliminate z by adding Equation 3 and 4 times Equation 4

$$\begin{array}{ll} \text{Equation 3} & \begin{cases} y - 2z = -100 \\ -6y + 2z = -4,600 \end{cases} \\ 4(\text{Equation 4}) & \end{array}$$

$$-5y = -4,700$$
$$y = 940$$

Substitute $y = 940$ into Equation 3 and solve for z.

$$y - 2z = -100$$
$$(940) - 2z = -100$$
$$z = 520$$

Substitute $y = 940$ and $z = 520$ into Equation 1 and solve for x.

$$x + y + z = 10,000$$
$$x + (940) + (520) = 10,000$$
$$x = 8,540$$

Alix invested $8,540 at 4.5%, $940 at 3%, and $520 at 5%.

Ponder Does our answer seem reasonable? First, we see that $8,540 + 940 + 520 = 10,000$, which was the total amount invested at each interest rate. Next, the interest earned at 4.5% was:

$$0.045(\$8,540) = \$384.30$$

The interest earned at 3% was:

$$0.03(\$940) = \$28.20$$

The interest earned at 5% was:

$$0.05(\$520) = \$26$$

The total interest earned was $\$384.30 + \$28.20 + \$26 = \$438.50$. Our answer is correct.

69. Prepare We must determine how many points, rebounds, and assists Tim Duncan had for the 2003-2004 basketball season.

Plan Because there are three unknowns, we will set up and solve a system of three equations with three unknowns.

Process Let $x =$ the points Tim scored. Let $y =$ the rebounds Tim had. Let $z =$ number of assists Tim had. Because Tim's total number of points, rebounds, and assists was 2,383, one equation is $x + y + z = 2,383$. Because the number of rebounds for the season was seven less than three times the number of assists, another equation is $y = 3z - 7$ or $y - 3z = -7$. Because the number of points was 274 more than twice the number of rebounds, another equation is $x = 2y + 274$ or $x - 2y = 274$. The system of equation is:

$$\begin{cases} x + y + z = 2,383 \\ y - 3z = -7 \\ x - 2y = 274 \end{cases}$$

Eliminate y by adding Equation 1 and -1 times Equation 2.

$$\begin{array}{ll} \text{Equation 1} & \begin{cases} x + y + z = 2,383 \\ -y + 3z = 7 \end{cases} \\ -1(\text{Equation 2}) & \end{array}$$

$$\text{Equation 4} \qquad x + 4z = 2,390$$

Eliminate y by adding 2 times Equation 1 and Equation 3.

$$2(\text{Equation 1}) \quad \begin{cases} 2x+2y+2z = 4,766 \\ x-2y \quad\quad = 274 \end{cases}$$
$$\text{Equation 3}$$
$$\overline{\text{Equation 5} \quad\quad 3x+2z = 5,040}$$

Eliminate z by adding Equation 4 and -2 times Equation 5.

$$\begin{array}{ll} \text{Equation 4} & \begin{cases} x+4z = 2,390 \\ -6x-4z = -10,080 \end{cases} \\ -2(\text{Equation 5}) & \end{array}$$
$$\overline{\quad\quad\quad -5x = -7,690}$$
$$x = 1,538$$

Substitute $x = 1,538$ into Equation 4 and solve for z.

$$x+4z = 2,390$$
$$(1,538)+4z = 2,390$$
$$4z = 852$$
$$z = 213$$

Substitute $x = 1,538$ and $z = 213$ into Equation 1 and solve for y.

$$x+y+z = 2,383$$
$$(1,538)+y+(213) = 2,383$$
$$y = 632$$

Tim scored 1,538 points, had 632 rebounds, and had 213 assists during the 2003-2004 season.

Ponder Does our answer seem reasonable? We can check to see if our answer satisfies the conditions of the problem. Because the sum of our results is $1,538+632+213 = 2,383$, we can say that our answer is reasonable.

71. Prepare We must determine the number of ounces of cornmeal, ant poison, and corn oil contained in a 16 ounce mixture of Moe's fire ant remedy.

Plan Because there are three unknowns, we will set up and solve a system of three equations with three unknowns.

Process Let $x =$ the number of ounces of cornmeal. Let $y =$ the number of ounces of ant poison. Let $z =$ the number of ounces of corn oil. Because the total number of ounces is 16, one equation is $x+y+z = 16$. Because the number of ounces of cornmeal is ten times the number of ounces of corn oil, another equation is $x = 10z$ or $x-10z = 0$. Because the number of ounces of ant poison is four ounces more than the number of ounces of corn oil, the third equation is $y = z+4$ or $y-z = 4$. The system of equations is:

$$\begin{cases} x+y+z = 16 \\ x-10z = 0 \\ y-z = 4 \end{cases}$$

Eliminate y by adding Equation 1 and -1 times Equation 2.

$$\begin{array}{ll} \text{Equation 1} & \begin{cases} x+y+\ z = 16 \\ -x \quad\quad +10z = 0 \end{cases} \\ -1(\text{Equation 2}) & \end{array}$$
$$\overline{\text{Equation 4} \quad\quad y+11z = 16}$$

Eliminate z by adding 11 times Equation 3 and Equation 4.

$$\begin{array}{ll} 11(\text{Equation 3}) & \begin{cases} 11y-11z = 44 \\ y+11z = 16 \end{cases} \\ \text{Equation 4} & \end{array}$$
$$\overline{\quad\quad\quad 12y = 60}$$
$$y = 5$$

Substitute $y = 5$ into Equation 4 and solve for z.

$$y+11z = 16$$
$$(5)+11z = 16$$
$$11z = 11$$
$$z = 1$$

Substitute $y = 5$ and $z = 1$ into Equation 1 and solve for x.

$$x+y+z = 16$$
$$x+(5)+(1) = 16$$
$$x = 10$$

The fire ant remedy contains 10 ounces of cornmeal, 5 ounces of ant poison, and 1 ounce of corn oil.

Ponder Does our answer seem reasonable? We can check to see if our answer satisfies the conditions of the problem. Because the sum of our results is $10+5+1 = 16$, we can say that our answer is reasonable.

4.6 Exercises

1. A <u>system</u> of <u>linear inequalities</u> is when two linear inequalities in two variables are considered together.

3. The are <u>infinitely</u> <u>many</u> solutions to a system of linear inequalities, provided the lines intersect.

5. For the system $\begin{cases} x - 3y < -2 \\ 4x + y \geq 10 \end{cases}$, the graph of the first line is <u>dashed</u>.

7. The solution to a system of linear inequalities is the <u>intersection</u> of the two inequalities' solution sets.

9. False. It does not lie in the double shaded region.

11. True

13. True

15. False. This point lies on the dashed line, so it is not a solution.

17. The slope-intercept form of L_1 is $y = -x + 4$, which has slope $m = -1$ and y-intercept $(0, 4)$. Graph L_1 with a dashed line. The slope-intercept form of L_2 is $y = x + 2$, which has slope $m = 1$ and y-intercept $(0, 2)$. Graph L_2 with a dashed line.
    $L_1 : x + y < 4$
    Test Point $(0, 0)$: $0 + 0 < 4$
    $\qquad\qquad\qquad\qquad 0 < 4$
    $\qquad\qquad\qquad\qquad$ True
    Shade the region that contains the origin.
    $L_2 : x - y > -2$
    Test Point $(0, 0)$: $0 - 0 > -2$
    $\qquad\qquad\qquad\qquad 0 > -2$
    $\qquad\qquad\qquad\qquad$ True
    Shade the region that contains the origin.

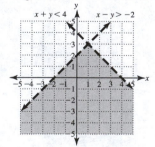

19. The slope-intercept form of L_1 is $y = -x + 4$, which has slope $m = -1$ and y-intercept $(0, 4)$. Graph L_1 with a dashed line. The slope-intercept form of L_2 is $y = -x + 2$, which has slope $m = -1$ and y-intercept $(0, 2)$. Graph L_2 with a solid line.
    $L_1 : x + y < 4$
    Test Point $(0, 0)$: $0 + 0 < 4$
    $\qquad\qquad\qquad\qquad 0 < 4$
    $\qquad\qquad\qquad\qquad$ True
    Shade the region that contains the origin.
    $L_2 : x + y \geq 2$
    Test Point $(0, 0)$: $0 + 0 \geq 2$
    $\qquad\qquad\qquad\qquad 0 \geq 2$
    $\qquad\qquad\qquad\qquad$ False
    Shade the region that does not contain the origin.

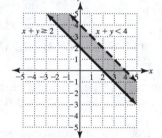

21. The slope-intercept form of L_1 is $y = 2x - 3$, which has slope $m = 2$ and y-intercept $(0, -3)$. Graph L_1 with a solid line. The slope-intercept form of L_2 is $y = -\dfrac{1}{3}x + 2$, which has slope $m = -\dfrac{1}{3}$ and y-intercept $(0, 2)$. Graph L_2 with a dashed line.
    $L_1 : 2x - y \leq 3$
    Test Point $(0, 0)$: $2(0) - 0 \leq 3$
    $\qquad\qquad\qquad\qquad 0 \leq 3$
    $\qquad\qquad\qquad\qquad$ True
    Shade the region that contains the origin.
    $L_2 : x + 3y > 6$
    Test Point $(0, 0)$: $0 + 3(0) > 6$
    $\qquad\qquad\qquad\qquad 0 > 6$
    $\qquad\qquad\qquad\qquad$ False
    Shade the region that does not contain the origin.

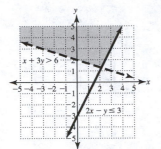

23. The slope-intercept form of L_1 is $y = \frac{1}{5}x - 1$,

which has slope $m = \frac{1}{5}$ and y-intercept $(0,-1)$.

Graph L_1 with a solid line. The slope-intercept

form of L_2 is $y = \frac{3}{2}x + 3$, which has slope $m = \frac{3}{2}$

and y-intercept $(0,3)$. Graph L_2 with a solid line.

$L_1: -x + 5y \geq -5$

Test Point $(0,0)$: $-0 + 5(0) \geq -5$

$0 \geq -5$

True

Shade the region that contains the origin.

$L_2: 3x - 2y \geq -6$

Test Point $(0,0)$: $3(0) - 2(0) \geq -6$

$0 \geq -6$

True

Shade the region that contains the origin.

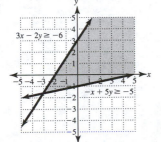

25. The slope-intercept form of L_1 is $y = \frac{1}{2}x + 3$,

which has slope $m = \frac{1}{2}$ and y-intercept $(0,3)$.

Graph L_1 with a solid line. The slope-intercept

form of L_2 is $y = \frac{1}{2}x - 1$, which has slope $m = \frac{1}{2}$

and y-intercept $(0,-1)$. Graph L_2 with a dashed

line.

$L_1: x - 2y \leq -6$

Test Point $(0,0)$: $0 - 2(0) \leq -6$

$0 \leq -6$

False

Shade the region that does not contain the origin.

$L_2: -4x + 8y < -8$

Test Point $(0,0)$: $-4(0) + 8(0) < -8$

$0 < -8$

False

Shade the region that does not contain the origin.

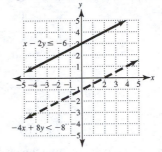

27. The slope-intercept form of L_1 is $y = -2x - 3$, which

has slope $m = -2$ and y-intercept $(0,-3)$. Graph L_1

with a solid line. The slope-intercept form of L_2 is

$y = \frac{1}{3}x - \frac{4}{3}$, which has slope $m = \frac{1}{3}$ and y-intercept

$\left(0, -\frac{4}{3}\right)$. Graph L_2 with a dashed line.

$L_1: 12x + 6y \leq -18$

Test Point $(0,0)$: $12(0) + 6(0) \leq -18$

$0 \leq -18$

False

Shade the region that does not contain the origin.

$L_2: -3x + 9y > -12$

Test Point $(0,0)$: $-3(0) + 9(0) > -12$

$0 > -12$

True

Shade the region that contains the origin.

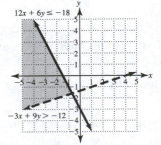

29. The slope-intercept form of L_1 is $y = 2x+1$, which has slope $m = 2$ and y-intercept $(0,1)$. Graph L_1 with a dashed line. The slope-intercept form of L_2 is $y = \frac{1}{6}x - \frac{1}{2}$, which has slope $m = \frac{1}{6}$ and y-intercept $\left(0, -\frac{1}{2}\right)$. Graph L_2 with a solid line.

$L_1: -2x + y < 1$

Test Point $(0,0)$: $-2(0) + 0 < 1$

$\qquad\qquad\qquad\qquad 0 < 1$

$\qquad\qquad\qquad\qquad\qquad$ True

Shade the region that contains the origin.

$L_2: x - 6y \le 3$

Test Point $(0,0)$: $0 - 6(0) \le 3$

$\qquad\qquad\qquad\qquad 0 \le 3$

$\qquad\qquad\qquad\qquad\qquad$ True

Shade the region that contains the origin.

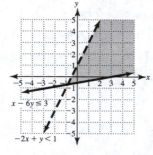

31. The slope-intercept form of L_1 is $y = \frac{1}{2}x + \frac{3}{2}$, which has slope $m = \frac{1}{2}$ and y-intercept $\left(0, \frac{3}{2}\right)$. Graph L_1 with a dashed line. L_2 is as vertical line with x-intercept $(-3, 0)$. Graph L_2 with a solid line.

$L_1: 7x - 14y < -21$

Test Point $(0,0)$: $7(0) - 14(0) < -21$

$\qquad\qquad\qquad\qquad 0 < -21$

$\qquad\qquad\qquad\qquad\qquad$ False

Shade the region that does not contain the origin.

$L_2: x \ge -3$

Test Point $(0,0)$: $0 \ge -3$

$\qquad\qquad\qquad\qquad\qquad$ False

Shade the region that does not contain the origin.

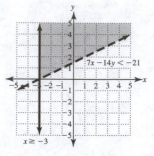

33. L_1 is a horizontal line with y-intercept $(0,2)$. Graph L_1 with a dashed line. The slope-intercept form of L_2 is $y = \frac{1}{2}x - 1$, which has slope $m = \frac{1}{2}$ and y-intercept $(0, -1)$. Graph L_2 with a dashed line.

$L_1: y > 2$

Test Point $(0,0)$: $0 > 2$

$\qquad\qquad\qquad\qquad\qquad$ False

Shade the region that does not contain the origin.

$L_2: \frac{1}{2}x - y < 1$

Test Point $(0,0)$: $\frac{1}{2}(0) - 0 < 1$

$\qquad\qquad\qquad\qquad 0 < 1$

$\qquad\qquad\qquad\qquad\qquad$ True

Shade the region that contains the origin.

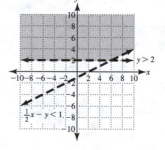

35. The slope-intercept form of L_1 is $y = \frac{2}{3}x$, which has slope $m = \frac{2}{3}$ and y-intercept $(0,0)$. Graph L_1 with a solid line. The slope-intercept form of L_2 is $y = \frac{3}{2}x$, which has slope $m = \frac{3}{2}$ and y-intercept $(0,0)$. Graph L_2 with a dashed line.

$L_1 : y - \dfrac{2}{3}x \le 0$

Test Point $(1,0)$: $0 - \dfrac{2}{3}(1) \le 0$

$-\dfrac{2}{3} \le 0$

True

Shade the region that contains $(1,0)$.

$L_2 : 2y > 3x$

Test Point $(1,0)$: $2(0) > 3(1)$

$0 > 3$

False

Shade the region that does not contain $(1,0)$

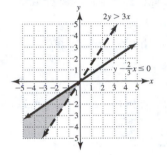

37. The slope of L_1 is $m = \dfrac{2}{3}$ and its y-intercept is

$\left(0, \dfrac{1}{3}\right)$. Graph L_1 with a solid line. The slope of

L_2 is $m = -3$ and its y-intercept $(0,5)$. Graph L_2 with a dashed line.

$L_1 : y \ge \dfrac{2}{3}x + \dfrac{1}{3}$

Test Point $(0,0)$: $0 \ge \dfrac{2}{3}(0) + \dfrac{1}{3}$

$0 \ge \dfrac{1}{3}$

False

Shade the region that does not contain the origin.

$L_2 : y < -3x + 5$

Test Point $(0,0)$: $0 < -3(0) + 5$

$0 < 5$

True

Shade the region that contains the origin.

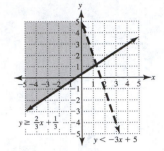

39. L_1 is a vertical line with x-intercept $(5,0)$. Graph L_1 with a solid line. L_2 is a horizontal line with y-intercept $(0,0)$. Graph L_2 with a dashed line.

$L_1 : x \le 5$

Test Point $(0,0)$: $0 \le 5$

True

Shade the region that contains the origin.

$L_2 : y < 0$

Test Point $(0,-1)$: $-1 < 0$

True

Shade the region that contains $(0,-1)$.

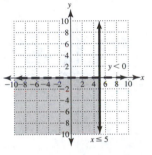

41. L_1 is a horizontal line with y-intercept $(0,3)$. Graph L_1 with a solid line. L_2 is a horizontal line with y-intercept $(0,-1)$. Graph L_2 with a dashed line.

$L_1 : y \ge 3$

Test Point $(0,0)$: $0 \ge 3$

False

Shade the region that does not contain the origin.

$L_2 : y < -1$

Test Point $(0,0)$: $0 < -1$

False

Shade the region that does not contain the origin.

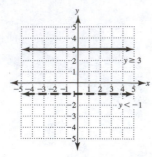

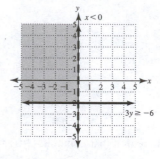

43. L_1 is a vertical line with x-intercept $(0,0)$. Graph L_1 with a solid line. L_2 is a horizontal line with y-intercept $(0,0)$. Graph L_2 with a solid line.

$L_1 : x \geq 0$

Test Point $(1,0)$: $1 \geq 0$

   True

Shade the region that contains $(1,0)$.

$L_2 : y \geq 0$

Test Point $(0,1)$: $1 \geq 0$

   True

Shade the region that contains $(0,1)$.

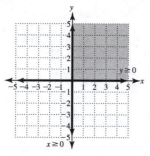

45. L_1 is a vertical line with x-intercept $(0,0)$. Graph L_1 with a dashed line. L_2 is a horizontal line with y-intercept $(0,-2)$. Graph L_2 with a solid line.

$L_1 : x < 0$

Test Point $(1,0)$: $1 < 0$

   False

Shade the region that does not contain $(1,0)$.

$L_2 : 3y \geq -6$

Test Point $(0,0)$: $3(0) \geq -6$

   $0 \geq -6$

   True

Shade the region that contains the origin.

47. The slope-intercept form of L_1 is $y = x+3$, which has slope $m=1$ and y-intercept $(0,3)$. Graph L_1 with a solid line. The slope-intercept form of L_2 is $y = -x+1$, which has slope $m=-1$ and y-intercept $(0,1)$. Graph L_2 with a dashed line.

$L_1 : x \leq y - 3$

Test Point $(0,0)$: $0 \leq 0 - 3$

   $0 \leq -3$

   False

Shade the region that does not contain the origin.

$L_2 : y - 1 > -x$

Test Point $(0,0)$: $0 - 1 > -(0)$

   $-1 > 0$

   False

Shade the region that does not contain the origin.

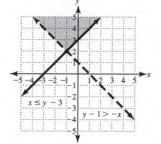

49. The slope-intercept form of L_1 is $y = -x+4$, which has slope $m=-1$ and y-intercept $(0,4)$. Graph L_1 with a dashed line. The slope-intercept form of L_2 is $y = x+2$, which has slope $m=1$ and y-intercept $(0,2)$. Graph L_2 with a dashed line. L_3 is a vertical line with x-intercept $(-1,0)$. Graph L_3 with a solid line.

$L_1 : x + y < 4$

Test Point $(0,0)$: $0 + 0 < 4$

   $0 < 4$

   True

Shade the region that contains the origin.

$L_2 : x - y > -2$

Test Point $(0,0)$: $0 - 0 > -2$

$0 > -2$

True

Shade the region that contains the origin.

$L_3 : x \geq -1$

Test Point $(0,0)$: $0 \geq -1$

True

Shade the region that contains the origin.

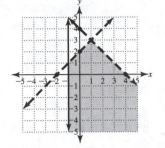

51. The slope of L_1 is $m = 2$ and its y-intercept is $(0,1)$. Graph L_1 with a dashed line. The slope-intercept form of L_2 is $y = \dfrac{1}{6}x - \dfrac{1}{2}$, which has slope $m = \dfrac{1}{6}$ and y-intercept $\left(0, -\dfrac{1}{2}\right)$. Graph L_2 with a solid line. L_3 is a vertical line with x-intercept $(2,0)$. Graph L_3 with a solid line.

$L_1 : y < 2x + 1$

Test Point $(0,0)$: $0 < 2(0) + 1$

$0 < 1$

True

Shade the region that contains the origin.

$L_2 : x - 6y \leq 3$

Test Point $(0,0)$: $0 - 6(0) \leq 3$

$0 \leq 3$

True

Shade the region that contains the origin.

$L_3 : x \leq 2$

Test Point $(0,0)$: $0 \leq 2$

True

Shade the region that contains the origin.

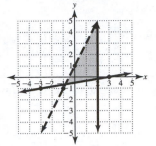

53. The slope-intercept form of L_1 is $y = -\dfrac{2}{3}x + 2$, which has slope $m = -\dfrac{2}{3}$ and y-intercept $(0,2)$. Graph L_1 with a dashed line. The slope-intercept form of L_2 is $y = 2x - 4$, which has slope $m = 2$ and y-intercept $(0,-4)$. Graph L_2 with a solid line. L_3 is a horizontal line with y-intercept $(0,2)$. Graph L_3 with a solid line.

$L_1 : 2x + 3y < 6$

Test Point $(0,0)$: $2(0) + 3(0) < 6$

$0 < 6$

True

Shade the region that contains the origin.

$L_2 : 4x - 2y \geq 8$

Test Point $(0,0)$: $4(0) - 2(0) \geq 8$

$0 \geq 8$

False

Shade the region that does not contain the origin.

$L_3 : y \leq 2$

Test Point $(0,0)$: $0 \leq 2$

True

Shade the region that contains the origin.

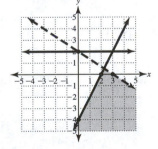

55. The slope-intercept form of L_1 is $y = -3x + 6$, which has slope $m = -3$ and y-intercept $(0,6)$. Graph L_1 with a dashed line. L_2 is a vertical line with x-intercept $(2,0)$. Graph L_2 with a solid line. L_3 is a horizontal line with y-intercept $(0,6)$. Graph L_3 with a solid line.

$L_1 : 3x + y < 6$

Test Point $(0,0)$: $3(0) + 0 < 6$

$0 < 6$

True

Shade the region that contains the origin.

$L_2 : x \leq 2$

Test Point $(0,0)$: $0 \leq 2$

True

Shade the region that contains the origin.

$L_3 : y \leq 6$

Test Point $(0,0)$: $0 \leq 6$

True

Shade the region that contains the origin.

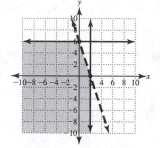

57. The slope-intercept form of L_1 is $y = x$, which has slope $m = 1$ and y-intercept $(0,0)$. Graph L_1 with a dashed line. L_2 is a vertical line with x-intercept $(3,0)$. Graph L_2 with a solid line. L_3 is a vertical line with x-intercept $(-2,0)$. Graph L_3 with a dashed line.

$L_1 : x < y$

Test Point $(0,1)$: $0 < 1$

True

Shade the region that contains $(0,1)$.

$L_2 : x \leq 3$

Test Point $(0,0)$: $0 \leq 3$

True

Shade the region that contains the origin.

$L_3 : x > -2$

Test Point $(0,0)$: $0 > -2$

True

Shade the region that contains the origin.

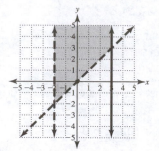

59. A graph of a system of linear inequalities would contain a dashed line if the equation for that line contains a less than but not equal sign.

61. The y-intercept of the solid line is $(0,2)$. The slope of the solid line is $m = \dfrac{-3}{6} = -\dfrac{1}{2}$. Therefore, the equation of the solid line is $y = -\dfrac{1}{2}x + 2$. Because the line is solid, we will used either $\leq$ or $\geq$. Based on the graph, the test point $(0,0)$ will satisfy the inequality. Therefore, the inequality should be $y \leq -\dfrac{1}{2} + 2$. The y-intercept of the dashed line is $\left(0, -\dfrac{5}{2}\right)$. The slope of the dashed line is $m = \dfrac{1}{2}$. Therefore, the equation of the dashed line is $y = \dfrac{1}{2}x - \dfrac{5}{2}$. Using the same reasoning as above, we can determine that the inequality should be $y > \dfrac{1}{2}x - \dfrac{5}{2}$.

63.

$$\begin{cases} x \leq 0 \\ y \leq 0 \end{cases}$$

65. Yes, it is possible that a solution point may satisfy one of the inequalities in a system without being a solution point to the system itself. This scenario can occur if the solution point lies outside the common area of both inequalities.

67. Prepare We are to write and solve a system of linear inequalities that satisfies the condition of the problem.

Plan Set up a system of linear inequalities and solve by graphing.
Let $x =$ the number of king-sized quilts made.
Let $y =$ the number of twin size quilts made.

Because the number of quilts made cannot be negative, there are automatically two inequalities for our system. That is, $x \geq 0$ and $y \geq 0$. Because the maximum number of quilts that can be made is 50, we can write the inequality $x + y \leq 50$. Because it takes 5 hours to make one king-sized quilt, it would take $5x$ hours to make x king-sized quilts. Likewise, it would take $2y$ hours to make y twin size quilts. The maximum number of hours allowed to make all quilts is 300. Therefore, the final inequality is $5x + 2y \leq 300$.

Process Write the linear system of inequalities and solve.

$$\begin{cases} x + y \leq 50 \\ 5x + 2y \leq 300 \\ x \geq 0 \\ y \geq 0 \end{cases}$$

Notice that the last two inequalities keep us within Quadrant I of the xy-plane. Therefore, we will graph the first two inequalities and only shade the first quadrant.

To graph the first two inequalities, we can sketch the intercepts for each and use the origin for the test point. The origin satisfies both inequalities. The shaded region of our graph represents the number of quilts the company can produce in one week under the given constraints.

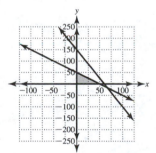

Ponder Does our answers seem reasonable? Yes. The shaded region of our graph is technically named the feasibility region because it satisfies all the production constraints of the company. That is, the number of quilts produced and the hours of labor do not exceed the constraints for the problem.

69. The slope-intercept form of L_1 is $y = -\dfrac{3}{4}x + \dfrac{9}{4}$, which has slope $m = -\dfrac{3}{4}$ and y-intercept $\left(0, \dfrac{9}{4}\right)$.

Graph L_1 with a dashed line. The slope-intercept form of L_2 is $y = x - 1$, which has slope $m = 1$

and y-intercept $(0, -1)$. Graph L_2 with a dashed line.

$$L_1 : \frac{1}{2}x + \frac{2}{3}y > \frac{3}{2}$$

Test Point $(0,0)$: $\dfrac{1}{2}(0) + \dfrac{2}{3}(0) > \dfrac{3}{2}$

$$0 > \frac{3}{2}$$

False

Shade the region that does not contain the origin.

$L_2 : x - y < 1$

Test Point $(0,0)$: $0 - 0 < 1$

$$0 < 1$$

True

Shade the region that contains the origin.

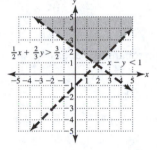

71. The slope-intercept form of L_1 is $y = 5x - 2$, which has slope $m = 5$ and y-intercept $(0, -2)$. Graph L_1 with a dashed line. The slope-intercept form of L_2 is $y = x$, which has slope $m = 1$ and y-intercept $(0, 0)$. Graph L_2 with a dashed line.

$L_1 : 0.5x - 0.1y < 0.2$

Test Point $(0,0)$: $0.5(0) - 0.1(0) < 0.2$

$$0 < 0.2$$

True

Shade the region that contains the origin.

$L_2 : -x + y < 0$

Test Point $(0,1)$: $-0 + 1 < 0$

$$1 < 0$$

False

Shade the region that does not contain $(0,1)$.

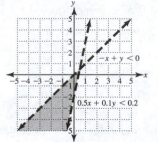

73. The slope-intercept form of L_1 is $y = -3x + \dfrac{1}{4}$,

which has slope $m = -3$ and y-intercept $\left(0, \dfrac{1}{4}\right)$.

Graph L_1 with a dashed line. The slope-intercept

form of L_2 is $y = -\dfrac{1}{18}x$, which has slope

$m = -\dfrac{1}{18}$ and y-intercept $(0,0)$. Graph L_2 with a

solid line.

$L_1: -2y < 6x - \dfrac{1}{2}$

Test Point $(0,0)$: $-2(0) < 6(0) - \dfrac{1}{2}$

$$0 < -\dfrac{1}{2}$$

False

Shade the region that does not contain the origin.

$L_2: 6y \geq -\dfrac{1}{3}x$

Test Point $(0,1)$: $6(1) \geq -\dfrac{1}{3}(0)$

$$6 \geq 0$$

True

Shade the region that contains $(0,1)$.

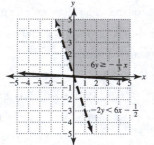

75. The slope-intercept form of L_1 is $y = -x + 2$,
which has slope $m = -1$ and y-intercept $(0,2)$.
Graph L_1 with a solid line. The slope-intercept
form of L_2 is $y = -x + 4$, which has slope $m = -1$
and y-intercept $(0,4)$. Graph L_2 with a dashed
line. L_3 is a horizontal line with y-intercept $(0,1)$.
Graph L_3 with a dashed line.

$L_1: x + y \geq 2$

Test Point $(0,0)$: $0 + 0 \geq 2$

$$0 \geq 2$$

False

Shade the region that does not contain the origin.

$L_2: x + y < 4$

Test Point $(0,0)$: $0 + 0 < 4$

$$0 < 4$$

True

Shade the region that contains the origin.

$L_3: y > 1$

Test Point $(0,0)$: $0 > 1$

False

Shade the region that does not contain the origin.

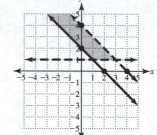

Chapter 4 Review Problem Set

1.

$$x - 4y = 14 \qquad\qquad -2x + 5y = -22$$
$$(6) - 4(-2) = 14 \qquad -2(6) + 5(-2) = -22$$
$$6 + 8 = 14 \qquad\qquad -12 - 10 = -22$$
$$14 = 14 \qquad\qquad -22 = -22$$
$$\text{True} \qquad\qquad\qquad \text{True}$$

The ordered pair $(6, -2)$ is a solution to the system.

2.

$$2x - y = -38 \qquad\qquad x - 8y = -47$$
$$2(-7) - (-5) = -38 \qquad (-7) - 8(-5) = -47$$
$$-14 + 5 = -38 \qquad\qquad -7 + 40 = -47$$
$$-9 = -38 \qquad\qquad\qquad 33 = -47$$
$$\text{False} \qquad\qquad\qquad \text{False}$$

The ordered pair $(-7, -5)$ is not a solution to the system.

3.

$$0.3x - 1.4y = 3.4 \qquad -1.6x + 0.8y = -1.6$$
$$0.3(2) - 1.4(-2) = 3.4 \quad -1.6(2) + 0.8(-2) = -1.6$$
$$0.6 + 2.8 = 3.4 \qquad\qquad -3.2 - 1.6 = -1.6$$
$$3.4 = 3.4 \qquad\qquad\qquad -4.8 = -1.6$$
$$\text{True} \qquad\qquad\qquad\quad \text{False}$$

The ordered pair $(2, -2)$ is not a solution to the system.

4.

$$\frac{2}{5}x - \frac{3}{4}y = -6 \qquad\qquad \frac{1}{2}x + \frac{5}{8}y = 5$$
$$\frac{2}{5}(0) - \frac{3}{4}(8) = -6 \qquad \frac{1}{2}(0) + \frac{5}{8}(8) = 5$$
$$0 - 6 = -6 \qquad\qquad\qquad 0 + 5 = 5$$
$$-6 = -6 \qquad\qquad\qquad\quad 5 = 5$$
$$\text{True} \qquad\qquad\qquad\qquad \text{True}$$

The ordered pair $(0, 8)$ is a solution to the system.

5. The slope of L_1 is $m = -1$ and the y-intercept is $(0, 3)$. The slope of L_2 is $m = -2$ and the y-intercept is $(0, 4)$.

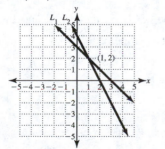

6. The slope-intercept form of L_1 is $y = -x + 3$. The slope of L_1 is $m = -1$ and the y-intercept is $(0, 3)$. The slope-intercept form of L_2 is $y = x - 5$. The slope of L_2 is $m = 1$ and the y-intercept is $(0, -5)$.

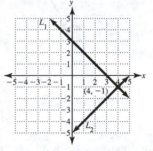

The solution set is $\{(4, -1)\}$.

7. The slope-intercept form of L_1 is $y = -x - 2$. The slope of L_1 is $m = -1$ and the y-intercept is $(0, -2)$. The slope-intercept form of L_2 is $y = 2x + 1$. The slope of L_2 is $m = 2$ and the y-intercept is $(0, 1)$.

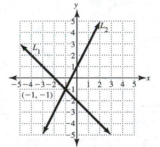

The solution set is $\{(-1, -1)\}$.

8. The slope of L_1 is $m = \frac{2}{3}$ and the y-intercept is $(0, 1)$. The slope-intercept form of L_2 is $y = \frac{1}{2}x + 2$. The slope of L_2 is $m = \frac{1}{2}$ and the y-intercept is $(0, 2)$.

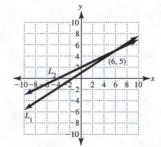

The solution set is $\{(1, 2)\}$.

The solution set is $\{(6,5)\}$.

9. The slope-intercept form of L_1 and L_2 is $y = 2x - 6$. The slope of L_1 and L_2 is $m = 2$ and the y-intercept is $(0, -6)$.

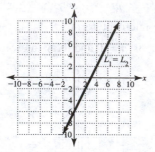

The solution set is $\{(x, y) \mid 2x - y = 6\}$.

10. The slope-intercept form of L_1 is $y = \dfrac{5}{4}x - \dfrac{1}{2}$.

    The slope of L_1 is $m = \dfrac{5}{4}$ and the y-intercept is $\left(0, -\dfrac{1}{2}\right)$. The slope-intercept form of L_2 is $y = \dfrac{3}{2}x$. The slope of L_2 is $m = \dfrac{3}{2}$ and the y-intercept is $(0, 0)$.

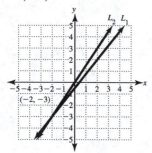

The solution set is $\{(-2, -3)\}$

11. The slope of L_1 is $m = \dfrac{1}{2}$ and the y-intercept is $(0, 3)$. The slope-intercept form of L_2 is $y = \dfrac{1}{2}x - 3$. The slope of L_2 is $m = \dfrac{1}{2}$ and the y-intercept is $(0, -3)$.

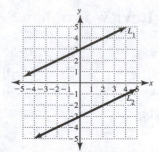

The solution is $\{\ \}$.

12. The slope-intercept form of L_1 is $y = -2x + 4$. The slope of L_1 is $m = -2$ and the y-intercept is $(0, 4)$. The slope of L_2 is $m = 0$ and the y-intercept is $(0, 4)$.

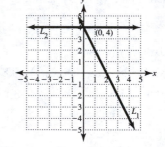

The solution set is $\{(0, 4)\}$.

13. The slope of L_1 is undefined and the x-intercept is $(-2, 0)$. The slope of L_2 is $m = 0$ and the y-intercept is $(0, 5)$.

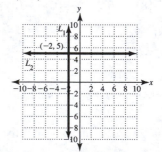

The solution set is $\{(-2, 5)\}$.

14. The slope of L_1 is undefined and the x-intercept is $(0, 0)$. The slope of L_2 is $m = 3$ and the y-intercept is $(0, 4)$.

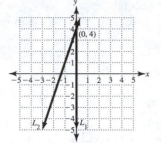

The solution set is $\{(0,4)\}$.

15. Solve the second equation for x to obtain $x = 3y - 7$. Substitute $x = 3y - 7$ into the first equation and solve for y.
$$2x + 2y = 18$$
$$2(3y - 7) + 2y = 18$$
$$6y - 14 + 2y = 18$$
$$8y = 32$$
$$y = 4$$
Substitute $y = 4$ into $x = 3y - 7$ to find x.
$$x = 3y - 7$$
$$x = 3(4) - 7$$
$$x = 12 - 7$$
$$x = 5$$
The solution set is $\{(5, 4)\}$.

16. Solve the first equation for y to obtain $y = -6x + 1$. Substitute $y = -6x + 1$ into the second equation and solve for x.
$$-4x - 2y = 10$$
$$-4x - 2(-6x + 1) = 10$$
$$-4x + 12x - 2 = 10$$
$$8x = 12$$
$$x = \frac{3}{2}$$
Substitute $x = \frac{3}{2}$ into $y = -6x + 1$ to find y.
$$y = -6x + 1$$
$$y = -6\left(\frac{3}{2}\right) + 1$$
$$y = -9 + 1$$
$$y = -8$$
The solution set is $\left\{\left(\frac{3}{2}, -8\right)\right\}$.

17. Solve the second equation for x to obtain $x = 5y$. Substitute $x = 5y$ into the first equation and solve for y.

$$x + y = 8$$
$$(5y) + y = 8$$
$$6y = 8$$
$$y = \frac{4}{3}$$
Substitute $y = \frac{4}{3}$ into $x = 5y$ to find x.
$$x = 5y$$
$$x = 5\left(\frac{4}{3}\right)$$
$$x = \frac{20}{3}$$
The solution set is $\left\{\left(\frac{20}{3}, \frac{4}{3}\right)\right\}$.

18. Substitute $y = \frac{1}{3}x - 4$ into the first equation and solve for x.
$$x - 3y = 12$$
$$x - 3\left(\frac{1}{3}x - 4\right) = 12$$
$$x - x + 12 = 12$$
$$12 = 12$$
The solution set is $\left\{(x, y) \mid y = \frac{1}{3}x - 4\right\}$.

19. Substitute $x = 4y - 1$ into the second equation and solve for y.
$$2x + 8y = -2$$
$$2(4y - 1) + 8y = -2$$
$$8y - 2 + 8y = -2$$
$$16y = 0$$
$$y = 0$$
Substitute $y = 0$ into $x = 4y - 1$ to find x.
$$x = 4y - 1$$
$$x = 4(0) - 1$$
$$x = -1$$
The solution set is $\{(-1, 0)\}$.

20. Solve the second equation for y to obtain $y = -4x$. Substitute $y = -4x$ into the first equation and solve for x.
$$7x + 3y = 10$$
$$7x + 3(-4x) = 10$$
$$7x - 12x = 10$$
$$-5x = 10$$
$$x = -2$$

179

Substitute $x = -2$ into $y = -4x$ to find y.
$$y = -4x$$
$$y = -4(-2)$$
$$y = 8$$
The solution set is $\{(-2, 8)\}$.

21. Solve the first equation for y to obtain $y = 5x - 19$. Substitute $y = 5x - 19$ into the second equation and solve for x.
$$2x - 5y = -20$$
$$2x - 5(5x - 19) = -20$$
$$2x - 25x + 95 = -20$$
$$-23x = -115$$
$$x = 5$$
Substitute $x = 5$ into $y = 5x - 19$ to find y.
$$y = 5x - 19$$
$$y = 5(5) - 19$$
$$y = 6$$
The solution set is $\{(5, 6)\}$.

22. Solve the second equation for y to obtain $y = -5x - 24$. Substitute $y = -5x - 24$ into the first equation and solve for x.
$$2x - 3y = 4$$
$$2x - 3(-5x - 24) = 4$$
$$2x + 15x + 72 = 4$$
$$17x = -68$$
$$x = -4$$
Substitute $x = -4$ into $y = -5x - 24$ to find y.
$$y = -5x - 24$$
$$y = -5(-4) - 24$$
$$y = -4$$
The solution set is $\{(-4, -4)\}$.

23. Substitute $y = 2x + 4$ into the second equation and solve for x.
$$y = -3x + 9$$
$$(2x + 4) = -3x + 9$$
$$5x = 5$$
$$x = 1$$
Substitute $x = 1$ into $y = 2x + 4$ to find y.
$$y = 2x + 4$$
$$y = 2(1) + 4$$
$$y = 6$$
The solution set is $\{(1, 6)\}$.

24. Solve the second equation for x to obtain $x = 6$. Substitute $x = 6$ into the first equation and solve for y.
$$4x - 7y = 10$$
$$4(6) - 7y = 10$$
$$-7y = -14$$
$$y = 2$$
The solution set is $\{(6, 2)\}$.

25. Solve the second equation for y to obtain $y = -2x + 5$. Substitute $y = -2x + 5$ into the first equation and solve for x.
$$4x - 2y = 10$$
$$4x - 2(-2x + 5) = 10$$
$$8x = 20$$
$$x = \frac{5}{2}$$
Substitute $x = \frac{5}{2}$ into $y = -2x + 5$ to find y.
$$y = -2x + 5$$
$$y = -2\left(\frac{5}{2}\right) + 5$$
$$y = 0$$
The solution set is $\left\{\left(\frac{5}{2}, 0\right)\right\}$.

26. Solve the second equation for y to obtain $y = 2x - 4$. Substitute $y = 2x - 4$ into the first equation and solve for x.
$$4x - 2y = 8$$
$$4x - 2(2x - 4) = 8$$
$$8 = 8$$
$$\text{True}$$
The solution set is $\{(x, y) \mid y = 2x - 4\}$.

27. Eliminate y by adding Equation 1 and Equation 2.

$$\begin{array}{ll} \text{Equation 1} & \{x + y = 19 \\ \text{Equation 2} & \{x - y = -8 \\ \hline & 2x = 11 \\ & x = \dfrac{11}{2} \end{array}$$

Substitute $x = \frac{11}{2}$ into Equation 1 and solve for y.

$$x + y = 19$$

$$\left(\frac{11}{2}\right) + y = 19$$

$$y = \frac{27}{2}$$

The solution set is $\left\{\left(\frac{11}{2}, \frac{27}{2}\right)\right\}$.

28. Eliminate y by adding Equation 1 and Equation 2.

$$\begin{array}{l} \text{Equation 1} \\ \text{Equation 2} \end{array} \left\{ \begin{array}{l} x + 5y = -19 \\ 3x - 5y = 23 \end{array} \right.$$

$$4x = 4$$

$$x = 1$$

Substitute $x = 1$ into Equation 1 and solve for y.

$$x + 5y = -19$$

$$(1) + 5y = -19$$

$$y = -4$$

The solution set is $\{(1, -4)\}$.

29. Eliminate x by adding Equation 1 and Equation 2.

$$\begin{array}{l} \text{Equation 1} \\ \text{Equation 2} \end{array} \left\{ \begin{array}{l} 8x + y = 6 \\ -8x + y = -6 \end{array} \right.$$

$$2y = 0$$

$$y = 0$$

Substitute $y = 0$ into Equation 1 and solve for x.

$$8x + y = 6$$

$$8x + (0) = 6$$

$$x = \frac{3}{4}$$

The solution set is $\left\{\left(\frac{3}{4}, 0\right)\right\}$.

30. Eliminate x by adding Equation 1 and 2 times Equation 2.

$$\begin{array}{l} \text{Equation 1} \\ 2(\text{Equation 2}) \end{array} \left\{ \begin{array}{l} 6x + y = -15 \\ -6x + 8y = -12 \end{array} \right.$$

$$9y = -27$$

$$y = -3$$

Substitute $y = -3$ into Equation 1 and solve for x.

$$6x + y = -15$$

$$6x + (-3) = -15$$

$$x = -2$$

The solution set is $\{(-2, -3)\}$.

31. Eliminate x by adding Equation 1 and -2 times Equation 2.

$$\begin{array}{l} \text{Equation 1} \\ -2(\text{Equation 2}) \end{array} \left\{ \begin{array}{l} 2x - 8y = 14 \\ -2x + 8y = -24 \end{array} \right.$$

$$0 = -10$$

The solution set is $\{\ \}$.

32. Eliminate y by adding Equation 1 and -1 times Equation 2.

$$\begin{array}{l} \text{Equation 1} \\ -1(\text{Equation 2}) \end{array} \left\{ \begin{array}{l} 3x + 5y = 14 \\ -7x - 5y = -6 \end{array} \right.$$

$$-4x = 8$$

$$x = -2$$

Substitute $x = -2$ into Equation 1 and solve for y.

$$3x + 5y = 14$$

$$3(-2) + 5y = 14$$

$$y = 4$$

The solution set is $\{(-2, 4)\}$.

33. Eliminate y by adding 4 times Equation 1 and Equation 2.

$$\begin{array}{l} 4(\text{Equation 1}) \\ \text{Equation 2} \end{array} \left\{ \begin{array}{l} -20x + 8y = 88 \\ -3x - 8y = 4 \end{array} \right.$$

$$-23x = 92$$

$$x = -4$$

Substitute $x = -4$ into Equation 1 and solve for y.

$$-5x + 2y = 22$$

$$-5(-4) + 2y = 22$$

$$y = 1$$

The solution set is $\{(-4, 1)\}$.

34. Eliminate y by adding Equation 1 and 16 times Equation 2.

$$\begin{array}{l} \text{Equation 1} \\ 1.6(\text{Equation 2}) \end{array} \left\{ \begin{array}{l} 0.4x - 3.2y = -6.4 \\ 24x + 3.2y = 201.6 \end{array} \right.$$

$$24.4x = 195.2$$

$$x = 8$$

Substitute $x = 8$ into Equation 1 and solve for y.

$$0.4x - 3.2y = -6.4$$

$$0.4(8) - 3.2y = -6.4$$

$$y = 3$$

The solution set is $\{(8, 3)\}$.

35. Rewrite Equation 1 as $2x - 5y = 11$. Eliminate x by adding Equation 1 and -1 times Equation 2.

$$\text{Equation 1} \quad \begin{cases} 2x - 5y = 11 \\ -2x + 11y = -5 \end{cases}$$
$$-1(\text{Equation 2})$$

$$6y = 6$$
$$y = 1$$

Substitute $y = 1$ into Equation 1 and solve for x.
$$2x = 5y + 11$$
$$2x = 5(1) + 11$$
$$x = 8$$
The solution set is $\{(8, 1)\}$.

36. Rewrite Equation 2 as $8x - 14y = 10$. Eliminate x by adding -2 times Equation 1 and Equation 2.

$$-2(\text{Equation 1}) \quad \begin{cases} -8x + 14y = -10 \\ 8x - 14y = 10 \end{cases}$$
$$\text{Equation 2}$$

$$0 = 0$$
The solution set is $\{(x, y) \mid 4x - 7y = 5\}$.

37. Eliminate y by adding 3 times Equation 1 and Equation 2.

$$3(\text{Equation 1}) \quad \begin{cases} 36x - 12y = 27 \\ 18x + 12y = 9 \end{cases}$$
$$\text{Equation 2}$$

$$54x = 36$$
$$x = \frac{2}{3}$$

Substitute $x = \frac{2}{3}$ into Equation 1 and solve for y.

$$12x - 4y = 9$$
$$12\left(\frac{2}{3}\right) - 4y = 9$$
$$y = -\frac{1}{4}$$

The solution set is $\left\{\left(\frac{2}{3}, -\frac{1}{4}\right)\right\}$.

38. Eliminate x by adding 5 times Equation 1 and 3 times Equation 2.

$$5(\text{Equation 1}) \quad \begin{cases} 15x - 25y = 100 \\ -15x - 12y = 48 \end{cases}$$
$$3(\text{Equation 2})$$

$$-37y = 148$$
$$y = -4$$

Substitute $y = -4$ into Equation 1 and solve for x.
$$3x - 5y = 20$$
$$3x - 5(-4) = 20$$
$$x = 0$$
The solution set is $\{(0, -4)\}$.

39. Eliminate y by adding 12 times Equation 1 and 24 times Equation 2.

$$12(\text{Equation 1}) \quad \begin{cases} 3x - 6y = 60 \\ 4x + 6y = 24 \end{cases}$$
$$24(\text{Equation 2})$$

$$7x = 84$$
$$x = 12$$

Substitute $x = 12$ into Equation 1 and solve for y.

$$\frac{x}{4} - \frac{y}{2} = 5$$
$$\frac{(12)}{4} - \frac{y}{2} = 5$$
$$y = -4$$

The solution set is $\{(12, -4)\}$.

40. Eliminate y by adding 18 times Equation 1 and -24 times Equation 2.

$$18(\text{Equation 1}) \quad \begin{cases} 3x + 6y = 54 \\ -8x - 6y = -24 \end{cases}$$
$$-24(\text{Equation 2})$$

$$-5x = 30$$
$$x = -6$$

Substitute $x = -6$ into Equation 1 and solve for y.

$$\frac{1}{6}x + \frac{1}{3}y = 3$$
$$\frac{1}{6}(-6) + \frac{1}{3}y = 3$$
$$y = 12$$

The solution set is $\{(-6, 12)\}$.

41.
$$2x + y - z = -1$$
$$2(2) + (-3) - (-2) = -1$$
$$4 - 3 + 2 = -1$$
$$3 = -1$$

False

The ordered triple $(2, -3, -2)$ is not a solution.

42.
$$x - 2y - z = 3$$
$$(2) - 2(2) - (-1) = 3$$
$$2 - 4 + 1 = 3$$
$$-1 = 3$$

False

The ordered triple $(2, 2, -1)$ is not a solution.

43. Solve Equation 3 for z.
$$2z = 4$$
$$z = 2$$
Substitute $z = 2$ into Equation 2 and solve for y.

182

$$2y+5z=8$$
$$2y+5(2)=8$$
$$y=-1$$

Substitute $y=-1$ and $z=2$ into Equation 1 and solve for x.

$$3x-2y-z=5$$
$$3x-2(-1)-(2)=5$$
$$x=\frac{5}{3}$$

The solution set is $\left\{\left(\frac{5}{3},-1,2\right)\right\}$.

44. Eliminate z by adding Equation 1 and Equation 2.

$$\begin{array}{ll}\text{Equation 1} & \left\{\begin{array}{l}x+y+z=6\end{array}\right.\\\text{Equation 2} & \left.\begin{array}{l}2x+3y-z=7\end{array}\right.\end{array}$$

$$\begin{array}{ll}\text{Equation 4} & 3x+4y=13\end{array}$$

Eliminate z by adding Equation 2 and Equation 3.

$$\begin{array}{ll}\text{Equation 2} & \left\{\begin{array}{l}2x+3y-z=7\end{array}\right.\\\text{Equation 3} & \left.\begin{array}{l}-3x+y+z=-6\end{array}\right.\end{array}$$

$$\begin{array}{ll}\text{Equation 5} & -x+4y=1\end{array}$$

Eliminate y by adding Equation 4 and -1 times Equation 5.

$$\begin{array}{ll}\text{Equation 4} & \left\{\begin{array}{l}3x+4y=13\end{array}\right.\\-1(\text{Equation 5}) & \left.\begin{array}{l}x-4y=-1\end{array}\right.\end{array}$$
$$4x=12$$
$$x=3$$

Substitute $x=3$ into Equation 4 and solve for y.

$$3x+4y=13$$
$$3(3)+4y=13$$
$$y=1$$

Substitute $x=3$ and $y=1$ into Equation 1 and solve for z.

$$x+y+z=6$$
$$(3)+(1)+z=6$$
$$z=2$$

The solution set is $\{(3,1,2)\}$.

45. Eliminate z by adding 2 times Equation 1 and Equation 2.

$$\begin{array}{ll}2(\text{Equation 1}) & \left\{\begin{array}{l}6x+8z=-8\end{array}\right.\\\text{Equation 2} & \left.\begin{array}{l}5y-8z=11\end{array}\right.\end{array}$$

$$\begin{array}{ll}\text{Equation 4} & 6x+5y=3\end{array}$$

Eliminate x by adding 6 times Equation 3 and Equation 4.

$$\begin{array}{ll}6(\text{Equation 3}) & \left\{\begin{array}{l}-6x+12y=48\end{array}\right.\\\text{Equation 4} & \left.\begin{array}{l}6x+5y=3\end{array}\right.\end{array}$$
$$17y=51$$
$$y=3$$

Substitute $y=3$ into Equation 3 and solve for x.

$$-x+2y=8$$
$$-x+2(3)=8$$
$$x=-2$$

Substitute $x=-2$ into Equation 1 and solve for z.

$$3x+4z=-4$$
$$3(-2)+4z=-4$$
$$z=\frac{1}{2}$$

The solution set is $\left\{\left(-2,3,\frac{1}{2}\right)\right\}$.

46. Eliminate z by adding Equation 1 and -2 times Equation 2.

$$\begin{array}{ll}\text{Equation 1} & \left\{\begin{array}{l}-7x+y+4z=-15\end{array}\right.\\-2(\text{Equation 2}) & \left.\begin{array}{l}-2x+2y-4z=-12\end{array}\right.\end{array}$$

$$\begin{array}{ll}\text{Equation 4} & -9x+3y=-27\end{array}$$

Eliminate z by adding Equation 1 and Equation 3.

$$\begin{array}{ll}\text{Equation 1} & \left\{\begin{array}{l}-7x+y+4z=-15\end{array}\right.\\\text{Equation 3} & \left.\begin{array}{l}x+y-4z=-3\end{array}\right.\end{array}$$

$$\begin{array}{ll}\text{Equation 5} & -6x+2y=-18\end{array}$$

Eliminate y by adding 2 times Equation 4 and -3 times Equation 5.

$$\begin{array}{ll}2(\text{Equation 4}) & \left\{\begin{array}{l}-18x+6y=-54\end{array}\right.\\-3(\text{Equation 5}) & \left.\begin{array}{l}18x-6y=54\end{array}\right.\end{array}$$
$$0=0$$

The solution set is $\{(x,y,z)\,|\,x-y+2z=6\}$.

47. Eliminate z by adding 2 times Equation 1 and Equation 2.

$$\begin{array}{ll}2(\text{Equation 1}) & \left\{\begin{array}{l}2x-4y-2z=0\end{array}\right.\\\text{Equation 2} & \left.\begin{array}{l}2x+y+2z=1\end{array}\right.\end{array}$$

$$\begin{array}{ll}\text{Equation 4} & 4x-3y=1\end{array}$$

Eliminate z by adding Equation 1 and Equation 3.

$$\begin{array}{ll}\text{Equation 1} & \left\{\begin{array}{l}x-2y-z=0\end{array}\right.\\\text{Equation 3} & \left.\begin{array}{l}3x-y+z=2\end{array}\right.\end{array}$$

$$\begin{array}{ll}\text{Equation 5} & 4x-3y=2\end{array}$$

Eliminate y by adding Equation 4 and -1 times Equation 5.

$$\begin{array}{ll}\text{Equation 4} & \left\{\begin{array}{l}4x-3y=1\end{array}\right.\\-1(\text{Equation 5}) & \left.\begin{array}{l}-4x+3y=-2\end{array}\right.\end{array}$$
$$0=-1$$

The solution set is $\{\ \}$.

48. Eliminate z by adding 3 times Equation 1 and 2 times Equation 2.

$$\begin{array}{ll} 3(\text{Equation 1}) & \left\{\begin{array}{l} 15x-12y-6z=-6 \\ 4x-6y+6z=-30 \end{array}\right. \\ 2(\text{Equation 2}) & \end{array}$$

$$\underline{\hspace{5cm}}$$

Equation 4 $19x-18y=-36$

Eliminate z by adding Equation 1 and 2 times Equation 3.

$$\begin{array}{ll} \text{Equation 1} & \left\{\begin{array}{l} 5x-4y-2z=-2 \\ 6x+4y+2z=2 \end{array}\right. \\ 2(\text{Equation 3}) & \end{array}$$

$$\underline{\hspace{5cm}}$$

$$11x=0$$
$$x=0$$

Substitute $x=0$ into Equation 4 and solve for y.

$$19x-18y=-36$$
$$19(0)-18y=-36$$
$$y=2$$

Substitute $x=0$ and $y=2$ into Equation 1 and solve for z.

$$5x-4y-2z=-2$$
$$5(0)-4(2)-2z=-2$$
$$z=-3$$

The solution set is $\{(0,2,-3)\}$.

49. Let x represent the first angle, y represent the second angle, and z represent the third angle.

$$\left\{\begin{array}{l} x+y+z=180 \\ z=y-20 \\ y=2x \end{array}\right.$$

Rewrite Equation 2 and Equation 3 to obtain the system:

$$\left\{\begin{array}{l} x+y+z=180 \\ y-z=20 \\ 2x-y=0 \end{array}\right.$$

Eliminate z by adding Equation 1 and Equation 2.

$$\begin{array}{ll} \text{Equation 1} & \left\{\begin{array}{l} x+y+z=180 \\ y-z=20 \end{array}\right. \\ \text{Equation 2} & \end{array}$$

$$\underline{\hspace{5cm}}$$

Equation 4 $x+2y=200$

Eliminate y by adding 2 times Equation 3 and Equation 4.

$$\begin{array}{ll} 2(\text{Equation 3}) & \left\{\begin{array}{l} 4x-2y=0 \\ x+2y=200 \end{array}\right. \\ \text{Equation 4} & \end{array}$$

$$\underline{\hspace{5cm}}$$

$$5x=200$$
$$x=40$$

Substitute $x=40$ into Equation 3 and solve for y.

$$2x-y=0$$
$$2(40)-y=0$$
$$y=80$$

Substitute $y=80$ into Equation 2 and solve for z.

$$y-z=20$$
$$(80)-z=20$$
$$z=60$$

The first angle is $40°$, the second is $80°$, and the third is $60°$.

50. Prepare We are asked to determine how many of each type of bag that Fan Icon, Inc. hopes to sell.

Plan Assign a different variable to each unknown and write a system of equations representing the problem. Solve the system by the Elimination Method.

Process Let x represent the number of backpacks sold, y represent the number of carryall bags sold, and z represent the number of deluxe totes sold.

$$\left\{\begin{array}{l} x+y+z=18{,}500 \\ 25x+18y+22z=396{,}200 \\ y=x+800 \end{array}\right.$$

Rewrite Equation 3 to obtain the system:

$$\left\{\begin{array}{l} x+y+z=18{,}500 \\ 25x+18y+22z=396{,}200 \\ -x+y=800 \end{array}\right.$$

Eliminate z by adding -22 times Equation 1 and Equation 2.

$$\begin{array}{ll} -22(\text{Equation 1}) & \left\{\begin{array}{l} -22x-22y-22z=-407{,}000 \\ 25x+18y+22z=396{,}200 \end{array}\right. \\ \text{Equation 2} & \end{array}$$

$$\underline{\hspace{5cm}}$$

Equation 4 $3x-4y=-10{,}800$

Eliminate x by adding 3 times Equation 3 and Equation 4.

$$\begin{array}{ll} 3(\text{Equation 3}) & \left\{\begin{array}{l} -3x+3y=2{,}400 \\ 3x-4y=-10{,}800 \end{array}\right. \\ \text{Equation 4} & \end{array}$$

$$\underline{\hspace{5cm}}$$

$$-y=-8{,}400$$
$$y=8{,}400$$

Substitute $y=8{,}400$ into Equation 3 and solve for x.

$$-x+y=800$$
$$-x+(8{,}400)=800$$
$$x=7{,}600$$

Substitute $x=7{,}600$ and $y=8{,}400$ into Equation 1 and solve for z.

$$x+y+z=18{,}500$$
$$(7{,}600)+(8{,}400)+z=18{,}500$$
$$z=2{,}500$$

Fan Icon, Inc. is expected to sell 7,600 backpacks, 8,400 carryall bags, and 2,500 deluxe totes.

Ponder Do our answers seem reasonable? We can check to see if our answers satisfy the conditions of the problem. The total number of bags sold is $7,600 + 8,400 + 2,500 = 18,500$. The total sales is:

$$\$25(7,600) + \$18(8,400) + \$22(2,500) = \$396,200.$$

Therefore, our answers are reasonable.

51. Eliminate y by adding 2 times Equation 1 and Equation 2.

$$\begin{array}{ll} 3(\text{Equation 1}) & \left\{ 8x - 2y = -2 \right. \\ \text{Equation 2} & \left. 3x + 2y = 24 \right. \end{array}$$
$$\overline{\qquad 11x = 22}$$
$$x = 2$$

Substitute $x = 2$ into Equation 1 and solve for y.
$$4x - y = -1$$
$$4(2) - y = -1$$
$$y = 9$$

The solution set is $\{(2, 9)\}$.

52. Substitute $y = -3x$ into Equation 1 and solve for x.
$$x - y = 12$$
$$x - (-3x) = 12$$
$$x = 3$$

Substitute $x = 3$ into Equation 2 and solve for y.
$$y = -3x$$
$$y = -3(3)$$
$$y = -9$$

The solution set is $\{(3, -9)\}$.

53. Eliminate y by adding -2 times Equation 1 and Equation 2.

$$\begin{array}{ll} -2(\text{Equation 1}) & \left\{ -x - 8y = -16 \right. \\ \text{Equation 2} & \left. x + 8y = 10 \right. \end{array}$$
$$\overline{\qquad 0 = -6}$$

The solution set is $\{\ \}$.

54. Eliminate x by adding 10 times Equation 1 and -30 times Equation 2.

$$\begin{array}{ll} 10(\text{Equation 1}) & \left\{ 12x + y = -38 \right. \\ -30(\text{Equation 2}) & \left. -12x + 111y = -186 \right. \end{array}$$
$$\overline{\qquad 112y = -224}$$
$$y = -2$$

Substitute $y = -2$ into Equation 1 and solve for x.

$$1.2x + 0.1y = -3.8$$
$$1.2x + 0.1(-2) = -3.8$$
$$x = -3$$

The solution set is $\{(-3, -2)\}$.

55. Substitute $x = 2y + 8$ into Equation 1 and solve for y.
$$2x + y = -4$$
$$2(2y + 8) + y = -4$$
$$y = -4$$

Substitute $y = -4$ into Equation 2 and solve for x.
$$x = 2y + 8$$
$$x = 2(-4) + 8$$
$$x = 0$$

The solution set is $\{(0, -4)\}$.

56. Substitute $y = \dfrac{1}{2}x + 2$ into Equation 1 and solve for x.

$$y = \frac{2}{3}x - 1$$
$$\left(\frac{1}{2}x + 2\right) = \frac{2}{3}x - 1$$
$$x = 18$$

Substitute $x = 18$ into Equation 2 and solve for y.

$$y = \frac{1}{2}x + 2$$
$$y = \frac{1}{2}(18) + 2$$
$$y = 11$$

The solution set is $\{(18, 11)\}$.

57. Solve the first equation for x to obtain $x = -2$. Substitute $x = -2$ into the second equation and solve for y.

$$4x - 2y = -2$$
$$4(-2) - 2y = -2$$
$$y = -3$$

The solution set is $\{(-2, -3)\}$.

58. Eliminate x by adding -2 times Equation 1 and Equation 2.

$$\begin{array}{ll} -2(\text{Equation 1}) & \left\{ -x - 6y = -10 \right. \\ \text{Equation 2} & \left. x + 6y = 10 \right. \end{array}$$
$$\overline{\qquad 0 = 0}$$

The solution set is $\{(x, y) \mid x + 6y = 10\}$.

59. Eliminate x by adding 12 times Equation 1 and -6 times Equation 2.

$$\begin{array}{ll} 12(\text{Equation 1}) & \left\{ \begin{array}{l} 3x+4y=48 \\ -3x+3y=-6 \end{array} \right. \\ -6(\text{Equation 2}) & \end{array}$$
$$7y=42$$
$$y=6$$

Substitute $y=6$ into Equation 1 and solve for x.

$$\frac{x}{4}+\frac{y}{3}=4$$
$$\frac{x}{4}+\frac{6}{3}=4$$
$$x=8$$

The solution set is $\{(8,6)\}$.

60. Eliminate y by adding 4 times Equation 1 and 5 times Equation 2.

$$\begin{array}{ll} 4(\text{Equation 1}) & \left\{ \begin{array}{l} 36x-20y=12 \\ -30x+20y=-10 \end{array} \right. \\ 5(\text{Equation 2}) & \end{array}$$
$$6x=2$$
$$x=\frac{1}{3}$$

Substitute $x=\frac{1}{3}$ into Equation 1 and solve for y.

$$9x-5y=3$$
$$9\left(\frac{1}{3}\right)-5y=3$$
$$y=0$$

The solution set is $\left\{\left(\frac{1}{3},0\right)\right\}$.

61. Substitute $x=4$ into Equation 2 and solve for y.
$$4x+2y=10$$
$$4(4)+2y=10$$
$$y=-3$$
Substitute $x=4$ and $y=-3$ into Equation 1 and solve for z.
$$2x+y-3z=-1$$
$$2(4)+(-3)-3z=-1$$
$$z=2$$
The solution set is $\{(4,-3,2)\}$.

62. Eliminate y by adding Equation 1 and Equation 2.

$$\begin{array}{ll} \text{Equation 1} & \left\{ \begin{array}{l} 2x+3y-2z=-2 \\ x-3y \quad\;\; =2 \end{array} \right. \\ \text{Equation 2} & \end{array}$$
$$\text{Equation 4} \qquad 3x-2z=0$$

Eliminate z by adding 2 times Equation 3 and 3 times Equation 4.

$$\begin{array}{ll} 2(\text{Equation 3}) & \left\{ \begin{array}{l} 2x+6z=22 \\ 9x-6z=0 \end{array} \right. \\ 3(\text{Equation 4}) & \end{array}$$
$$11x=22$$
$$x=2$$

Substitute $x=2$ into Equation 2 and solve for y.
$$x-3y=2$$
$$(2)-3y=2$$
$$y=0$$
Substitute $x=2$ and $y=0$ into Equation 1 and solve for z.
$$2x+3y-2z=-2$$
$$2(2)+3(0)-2z=-2$$
$$z=3$$
The solution set is $\{(2,0,3)\}$.

63. Eliminate x by adding -2 time Equation 1 and Equation 2.

$$\begin{array}{ll} -2(\text{Equation 1}) & \left\{ \begin{array}{l} -2x+4y-2z=-14 \\ 2x-y+5z=-1 \end{array} \right. \\ \text{Equation 2} & \end{array}$$
$$\text{Equation 4} \qquad\quad 3y+3z=-15$$

Eliminate x by adding Equation 2 and -2 times Equation 3.

$$\begin{array}{ll} \text{Equation 2} & \left\{ \begin{array}{l} 2x-y+5z=-1 \\ -2x+2y-2z=-4 \end{array} \right. \\ -2(\text{Equation 3}) & \end{array}$$
$$\text{Equation 5} \qquad\quad y+3z=-5$$

Eliminate y by adding Equation 4 and -3 times Equation 5.

$$\begin{array}{ll} \text{Equation 4} & \left\{ \begin{array}{l} 3y+3z=-15 \\ -3y-9z=15 \end{array} \right. \\ -3(\text{Equation 5}) & \end{array}$$
$$-6z=0$$
$$z=0$$

Substitute $z=0$ into Equation 5 and solve for y.
$$y+3z=-5$$
$$y+3(0)=-5$$
$$y=-5$$
Substitute $y=-5$ and $z=0$ into Equation 1 and solve for x.
$$x-2y+z=7$$
$$x-2(-5)+(0)=7$$
$$x=-3$$
The solution set is $\{(-3,-5,0)\}$.

64. Eliminate a by adding -3 time Equation 1 and Equation 2.

$$\begin{array}{ll} -3\,(\text{Equation 1}) & \begin{cases} -3a-3b-3c=0 \\ \end{cases} \\ \text{Equation 2} & \phantom{\begin{cases}\end{cases}} 3a+5b+4c=5 \\ \hline \text{Equation 4} & 2b+c=5 \end{array}$$

Eliminate a by adding Equation 2 and Equation 3.

$$\begin{array}{ll} \text{Equation 2} & \begin{cases} 3a+5b+4c=5 \\ \end{cases} \\ \text{Equation 3} & \phantom{\begin{cases}\end{cases}} -3a-6b-5c=-2 \\ \hline \text{Equation 5} & -b-c=3 \end{array}$$

Eliminate c by adding Equation 4 and Equation 5.

$$\begin{array}{ll} \text{Equation 4} & \begin{cases} 2b+c=5 \\ \end{cases} \\ \text{Equation 5} & \phantom{\begin{cases}\end{cases}} -b-c=3 \\ \hline & b=8 \end{array}$$

Substitute $b=8$ into Equation 4 and solve for c.

$$2b+c=5$$
$$2(8)+c=5$$
$$c=-11$$

Substitute $b=8$ and $c=-11$ into Equation 1 and solve for a.

$$a+b+c=0$$
$$a+(8)+(-11)=0$$
$$a=3$$

The solution set is $\{(3,8,-11)\}$.

65. Let x and y represent the two numbers. The system of equations is:

$$\begin{cases} x+y=491 \\ x-y=141 \end{cases}$$

Eliminate y by adding Equation 1 and Equation 2.

$$\begin{array}{ll} \text{Equation 1} & \begin{cases} x+y=491 \\ \end{cases} \\ \text{Equation 2} & \phantom{\begin{cases}\end{cases}} x-y=141 \\ \hline & 2x=632 \\ & x=316 \end{array}$$

Substitute $x=316$ into Equation 1 and solve for y.

$$x+y=491$$
$$(316)+y=491$$
$$y=175$$

The two numbers are 316 and 175.

66. Let x represent the greatest integer, y represent the middle integer, and z represent the least integer. The system of equations is:

$$\begin{cases} x+y+z=4 \\ 3z+x+2y=-11 \\ z+3x-y=30 \end{cases}$$

Rewrite the system as follows:

$$\begin{cases} x+y+z=4 \\ x+2y+3z=-11 \\ 3x-y+z=30 \end{cases}$$

Eliminate z by adding -3 times Equation 1 and Equation 2.

$$\begin{array}{ll} -3\,(\text{Equation 1}) & \begin{cases} -3x-3y-3z=-12 \\ \end{cases} \\ \text{Equation 2} & \phantom{\begin{cases}\end{cases}} x+2y+3z=-11 \\ \hline \text{Equation 4} & -2x-y=-23 \end{array}$$

Eliminate z by adding Equation 2 and -3 times Equation 3.

$$\begin{array}{ll} \text{Equation 2} & \begin{cases} x+2y+3z=-11 \\ \end{cases} \\ -3\,(\text{Equation 3}) & \phantom{\begin{cases}\end{cases}} -9x+3y-3z=-90 \\ \hline \text{Equation 5} & -8x+5y=-101 \end{array}$$

Eliminate y by adding 5 times Equation 4 and Equation 5.

$$\begin{array}{ll} 5\,(\text{Equation 4}) & \begin{cases} -10x-5y=-115 \\ \end{cases} \\ \text{Equation 5} & \phantom{\begin{cases}\end{cases}} -8x+5y=-101 \\ \hline & -18x=-216 \\ & x=12 \end{array}$$

Substitute $x=12$ into Equation 4 and solve for y.

$$-2x-y=-23$$
$$-2(12)-y=-23$$
$$y=-1$$

Substitute $x=12$ and $y=-1$ into Equation 1 and solve for z.

$$x+y+z=4$$
$$(12)+(-1)+z=4$$
$$z=-7$$

The greatest number is 12, the middle number is -1, and the least number is -7.

67. Prepare We are to determine the heights of the Gateway to the West Arch and the world's tallest flagpole.

Plan There are two unknowns and two conditions, so we will set up a system of two equations with two unknowns.

Process Let $x=$ the height of the Gateway to the West Arch.
Let $y=$ height of the world's tallest flagpole.
The system of equations is:

$$\begin{cases} x=y+105 \\ x+y=1{,}155 \end{cases}$$

Substitute $x=y+105$ into Equation 2 and solve for y.

$$x + y = 1{,}155$$
$$(y + 105) + y = 1{,}155$$
$$y = 525$$

Substitute $y = 525$ into Equation 1 and solve for x.

$$x = y + 105$$
$$x = (525) + 105$$
$$x = 630$$

The Gateway to the West Arch is 630 feet tall and the world's tallest flagpole is 525 feet tall.

Ponder Are our answers correct? We can check to see if they satisfy the condition of the problem. First, the sum of the heights is $525 + 630 = 1{,}155$ feet. Next, the difference in their heights is $630 - 525 = 105$ feet. Therefore, our answers are correct.

68. Prepare We are to determine the age of Samantha and her cousin.

Plan There are two unknowns and two conditions, so we will set up a system of two equations with two unknowns.

Process Let $x =$ Samantha's age.
Let $y =$ Samantha's cousin's age.
The system of equations is:
$$\begin{cases} x = 2y - 4 \\ x + y = 20 \end{cases}$$

Substitute $x = 2y - 4$ into Equation 2 and solve for y.

$$x + y = 20$$
$$(2y - 4) + y = 20$$
$$y = 8$$

Substitute $y = 8$ into Equation 1 and solve for x.

$$x = 2y - 4$$
$$x = 2(8) - 4$$
$$x = 12$$

Samantha is 12 years old and Samantha's cousin is 8 years old.

Ponder Are our answers correct? We can check to see if they satisfy the condition of the problem. First, the sum of the ages is $12 + 8 = 20$ years. Next, twice Samantha's cousin's age is 16 and Samantha is 4 years younger than 16. Therefore, our answers are correct.

69. Prepare We are to determine how much money Mr. Mai invested in each of two accounts.

Plan There are two unknowns and two conditions, so we will set up a system of two equations with two unknowns.

Process Let $x =$ the amount invested at 7% interest.
Let $y =$ the amount invested at $8\frac{1}{2}\%$ interest.

	Principal	Rate	Time	Interest
7%	x	0.07	1	$0.07x$
$8\frac{1}{2}\%$	y	0.085	1	$0.085y$

The system of equations is:
$$\begin{cases} x + y = 5{,}000 \\ 0.07x + 0.085y = 384.50 \end{cases}$$

Solve Equation 1 for x to obtain $x = 5{,}000 - y$. Substitute $x = 5{,}000 - y$ into Equation 2 and solve for y.

$$0.07x + 0.085y = 384.5$$
$$0.07(5{,}000 - y) + 0.085y = 384.5$$
$$0.015y = 34.5$$
$$y = 2{,}300$$

Substitute $y = 2{,}300$ into Equation 1 and solve for x.

$$x + y = 5{,}000$$
$$x + (2{,}300) = 5{,}000$$
$$x = 2{,}700$$

Mr. Mai deposited $2,700 at 7% interest and $2,300 at $8\frac{1}{2}\%$ interest.

Ponder Are our answers correct? We can check to see if our answers fit the conditions of the problem. First, the sum of the amounts deposited at the two interest rates is $\$2{,}700 + \$2{,}300 = \$5{,}000$. Next, the interest earned on the $2,700 is $\$2{,}700(0.07) = \$189$, and the interest earned on the $2,300 is $\$2{,}300(0.085) = \$195.50$. The sum of the interest from the two deposits is $\$189 + \$195.50 = \$384.50$. Therefore, our answers are correct.

70. Prepare We are to determine the cost of each ream of paper and each ink cartridge.

Plan There are two unknowns and two conditions, so we will set up a system of two equations with two unknowns.

Process Let $x =$ the cost of a ream of paper.
Let $y =$ the cost of an ink cartridge.
The system of equations is:

$$\begin{cases} 8x+4y=112 \\ 5x+3y=80.50 \end{cases}$$

Eliminate y by adding 3 times Equation 1 and -4 times Equation 2.

$$\begin{array}{l} 3(\text{Equation 1}) \\ -4(\text{Equation 2}) \end{array} \begin{cases} 24x+12y=336 \\ -20x-12y=-322 \end{cases}$$

$$4x=14$$
$$x=3.5$$

Substitute $x=3.5$ into Equation 1 and solve for y.

$$8x+4y=112$$
$$8(3.5)+4y=112$$
$$4y=84$$
$$y=21$$

The cost of a ream of paper is $3.50 and the cost of an ink cartridge is $21.

Ponder Are our answers correct? We can check to see of our answers satisfy the conditions of the problem. Jason purchased eight reams of paper, which cost $8(\$3.50)=\$28$. He also purchased four ink cartridges, which cost $4(\$21)=\$84$. Therefore, Jason spent a total of $\$28+\$84=\$112$. Jason's wife purchased five reams of paper, which cost $5(\$3.50)=\$17.50$. She also purchased three ink cartridges, which cost $3(\$21)=\$63$. Therefore, Jason's wife spent a total of $\$17.50+\$63=\$80.50$. Our answers are correct.

71. Prepare We are to determine the number of gallons of 20% salt solution that should be mixed with 20 gallons of 15% salt solution to make an 18% salt solution.

Plan We will set up and solve a system of two equations with two unknowns.

Process Let $x=$ the number of gallons of 20% salt solution.
Let $y=$ the number of gallons of 18% salt solution.

	20% Salt	15% Salt	18% Salt
Amount (gallons)	x	20	y
Percent Salt	0.20	0.15	0.18
Amount of Salt	$0.20x$	$0.15(20)=3$	$0.18y$

The system of equations is:

$$\begin{cases} x+20=y \\ 0.20x+3=0.18y \end{cases}$$

Substitute $y=x+20$ into Equation 2 and solve for x.

$$0.20x+3=0.18y$$
$$0.20x+3=0.18(x+20)$$
$$0.02x=0.6$$
$$x=30$$

Thirty gallons of the 20% salt solution are needed for the mixture.

Ponder Do our answers seem reasonable? Yes, it is reasonable that we would need more 20% solution than 15% solution to make an 18% solution.

72. Prepare We must determine the amount of time it will take Cynthia to catch up with Ricardo.

Plan We will set up and solve a system of two equations with two unknowns.

Process Let $d=$ the distance that both Ricardo and Cynthia travel.
Let $t=$ the amount of time it takes Cynthia to catch up with Ricardo.

	Distance	Rate	Time
Ricardo	d	55 mph	$y+1$ hrs.
Cynthia	d	65 mph	y hrs.

The system of equations is:

$$\begin{cases} d=55(y+1) \\ d=65y \end{cases}$$

Substitute $d=65y$ into Equation 1 and solve for y.

$$d=55(y+1)$$
$$(65y)=55(y+1)$$
$$10y=55$$
$$y=5.5$$

It takes Cynthia 5 hours and 30 minutes to catch up with Ricardo.

Ponder Does our answers seem reasonable? In 5.5 hours, Cynthia will have traveled $65(5.5)=357.5$ miles. In 6.5 hours, Ricardo will have traveled $55(6.5)=357.5$ miles. Because the distances are the same, our answer is reasonable.

73. Prepare We are to determine the number of each type of coin Latonya has in her jar.

Plan There are two unknowns, so we will set up a system of two equations with two unknowns.

Process Let $n=$ the number of nickels in the jar.

Let $q =$ the number of quarters in the jar.

	Number of Coins	Value
	n	$0.05n$
	q	$0.25q$
Total	$n+q$	$4.40

The system of equations is:
$$\begin{cases} n = 2q+4 \\ 0.05n + 0.25q = 4.40 \end{cases}$$
Substitute $n = 2q+4$ into Equation 2 and solve for q.
$$0.05n + 0.25q = 4.40$$
$$0.05(2q+4) + 0.25q = 4.40$$
$$0.35q = 4.2$$
$$q = 12$$
Substitute $q = 12$ into Equation 1 and solve for n.
$$n = 2q+4$$
$$n = 2(12)+4$$
$$n = 28$$
There were 28 nickels and 12 quarters in the jar.

Ponder Do our answers seem reasonable? Yes. The value of 12 quarters is $3.00 and the value of 28 nickels is $1.40. The total value is $4.40.

74. Prepare We are to determine the measures of two supplementary angles.

Plan There are two unknowns, so we will set up and solve a system of two equation with two unknowns.

Process Let x represent the measure of one of the angles and let y represent the measure of the other angle. The system of equations is:
$$\begin{cases} x + y = 180 \\ y = 4x \end{cases}$$
Substitute $y = 4x$ into Equation 1 and solve for x.
$$x + y = 180$$
$$x + (4x) = 180$$
$$5x = 180$$
$$x = 36$$
Substitute $x = 36$ into Equation 2 and solve for y.
$$y = 4x$$
$$y = 4(36)$$
$$y = 144$$
The measures of the two angles are $36°$ and $144°$.

Ponder Does our answer seem reasonable? Yes. The sum of the two angles is $180°$ and the $144 = 4(36)$. Therefore, our answers are correct.

75. Prepare We are to determine the length and the width of a rectangular swimming pool.

Plan There are two unknowns, so we will set up and solve a system of two equations with two unknowns.

Process Let $l =$ the length of the swimming pool. Let $w =$ the width of the swimming pool. The system of equations is:
$$\begin{cases} 2l + 2w = 1,110 \\ w = l - 405 \end{cases}$$
Substitute $w = l - 405$ into Equation 1 and solve for l.
$$2l + 2w = 1,110$$
$$2l + 2(l - 405) = 1,110$$
$$4l = 1,920$$
$$l = 480$$
Substitute $l = 480$ into Equation 2 and solve for w.
$$w = l - 405$$
$$w = (480) - 405$$
$$w = 75$$
The length of the pool is 480 meters and the width of the pool is 75 meters.

Ponder Does our answer seem reasonable? Yes. The perimeter of the pool is $2(480) + 2(75) = 1,110$.

76. Prepare We are to determine the amount Lola invested at each of three different interest rates.

Plan There are three unknowns, so we will set up and solve a system of three equations with three unknowns.

Process Let $x =$ the amount invested at 8%. Let $y =$ the amount invested at 9%. Let $z =$ the amount invested at 10%.

	Principal	Rate	Time	Interest
8%	x	0.08	1 year	$0.08x$
9%	y	0.09	1 year	$0.09y$
10%	z	0.10	1 year	$0.10z$

The system of equations is:
$$\begin{cases} x + y + z = 25,000 \\ 0.08x + 0.09y + 0.10z = 2,200 \\ z = 0.5x + 2,000 \end{cases}$$
Rewrite the system as:

$$\begin{cases} x+y+z=25,000 \\ 0.08x+0.09y+0.10z=2,200 \\ -0.5x+z=2,000 \end{cases}$$

Eliminate y by adding -9 times Equation 1 and 100 times Equation 2.

$$\begin{array}{l} -9(\text{Equation 1}) \\ 100(\text{Equation 2}) \end{array} \begin{cases} -9x-9y-9z=-225,000 \\ 8x+9y+10z=220,000 \end{cases}$$

$$\begin{array}{ll} \text{Equation 4} & -x+z=-5,000 \end{array}$$

Eliminate z by adding Equation 3 and -1 times Equation 4.

$$\begin{array}{l} \text{Equation 3} \\ -1(\text{Equation 4}) \end{array} \begin{cases} -0.5x+z=2,000 \\ x-z=5,000 \end{cases}$$

$$0.5x=7,000$$
$$x=14,000$$

Substitute $x=14,000$ into Equation 4 and solve for z.

$$-x+z=-5,000$$
$$-(14,000)+z=-5,000$$
$$z=9,000$$

Substitute $x=14,000$ and $z=9,000$ into Equation 1 and solve for y.

$$x+y+z=25,000$$
$$(14,000)+y+(9,000)=25,000$$
$$y=2,000$$

Lola invested \$14,000 at 8%, \$2,000 at 9%, and \$9,000 at 10%.

Ponder Does our answer seem reasonable? Yes. First, the sum of the investments is \$25,000. Next, we compute the interest for each investment.

Interest at 8%: $0.08(\$14,000)=\$1,120$

Interest at 9%: $0.09(\$2,000)=\$180$

Interest at 10%: $0.10(\$9,000)=\$900$

The sum of the interest from the three investments is \$2,200.

77. The slope-intercept form of L_1 is $y=-x+4$, which has slope $m=-1$ and y-intercept $(0,4)$. Graph L_1 with a solid line. The slope-intercept form of L_2 is $y=x+2$, which has slope $m=1$ and y-intercept $(0,2)$. Graph L_2 with a dashed line.

$L_1: x+y\le 4$

Test Point $(0,0)$: $\quad 0+0\le 4$

$$0\le 4$$

True

Shade the region that contains the origin.

$L_2: x-y>-2$

Test Point $(0,0)$: $\quad 0-0>-2$

$$0>-2$$

True

Shade the region that contains the origin.

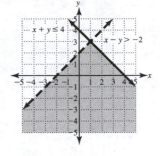

78. The slope-intercept form of L_1 is $y=2x-6$, which has slope $m=2$ and y-intercept $(0,-6)$. Graph L_1 with a dashed line. The slope-intercept form of L_2 is $y=-x+3$, which has slope $m=-1$ and y-intercept $(0,3)$. Graph L_2 with a solid line.

$L_1: 2x-y>6$

Test Point $(0,0)$: $\quad 2(0)-0>6$

$$0>6$$

False

Shade the region that does not contain the origin.

$L_2: x+y\ge 3$

Test Point $(0,0)$: $\quad 0+0\ge 3$

$$0\ge 3$$

False

Shade the region that does not contain the origin.

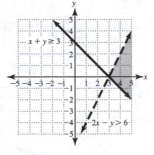

79. The slope-intercept form of L_1 is $y=\dfrac{1}{2}x-1$, which has slope $m=\dfrac{1}{2}$ and y-intercept $(0,-1)$. Graph L_1 with a dashed line. L_2 is a vertical line with x-intercept $(-2,0)$. Graph L_2 with a dashed line.

$L_1: -5x + 10y < -10$

Test Point $(0,0)$: $-5(0) + 10(0) < -10$

$$0 < -10$$

False

Shade the region that does not contain the origin.

$L_2: 3x > -6$

Test Point $(0,0)$: $3(0) > -6$

$$0 > -6$$

True

Shade the region that contains the origin.

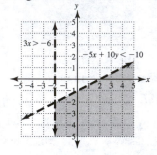

80. L_1 is a horizontal line with y-intercept $(0,2)$. Graph L_1 with a solid line. The slope-intercept for of L_2 is $y = \dfrac{3}{4}x - 3$, which has a slope $m = \dfrac{3}{4}$ and y-intercept $(0,-3)$. Graph L_2 with a solid line.

$L_1: -2y \geq 4$

Test Point $(0,0)$: $-2(0) \geq 4$

$$0 \geq 4$$

False

Shade the region that does not contain the origin.

$L_2: 3x - 4y \geq 12$

Test Point $(0,0)$: $3(0) - 4(0) \geq 12$

$$0 \geq 12$$

False

Shade the region that does not contain the origin.

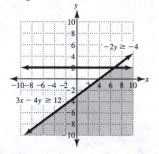

81. The slope-intercept form of L_1 is $y = x$, which has slope $m = 1$ and y-intercept $(0,0)$. Graph L_1 with a solid line. The slope-intercept form of L_2 is

$y = \dfrac{1}{2}x + \dfrac{1}{2}$, which has slope $m = \dfrac{1}{2}$ and y-intercept $\left(0, \dfrac{1}{2}\right)$. Graph L_2 with a solid line.

$L_1: x \leq y$

Test Point $(0,1)$: $0 \leq 1$

True

Shade the region that contains $(0,1)$.

$L_2: 2x \geq 4y - 2$

Test Point $(0,0)$: $2(0) \geq 4(0) - 2$

$$0 \geq -2$$

True

Shade the region that contains the origin.

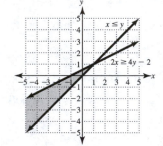

82. L_1 is a vertical line with x-intercept $(3,0)$. Graph L_1 with a dashed line. L_2 is a horizontal line with y-intercept $(0,1)$. Graph L_2 with a solid line.

$L_1: x > 3$

Test Point $(0,0)$: $0 > 3$

False

Shade the region that does not contain the origin.

$L_2: y \leq 1$

Test Point $(0,0)$: $0 \leq 1$

True

Shade the region that contains the origin.

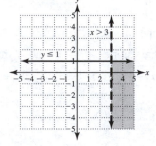

83. The slope-intercept form of L_1 is $y = -x$, which has slope $m = -1$ and y-intercept $(0,0)$. Graph L_1 with a dashed line. The slope-intercept form of L_2 is

$y = x - 2$, which has slope $m = 1$ and y-intercept $(0, -2)$. Graph L_2 with a dashed line.

$L_1 : x + y < 0$

Test Point $(0, 1)$: $0 + 1 < 0$

$1 < 0$

False

Shade the region that does not contain $(0, 1)$.

$L_2 : x - y > 2$

Test Point $(0, 0)$: $0 - 0 > 2$

$0 > 2$

False

Shade the region that does not contain the origin.

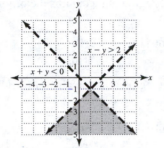

84. The slope-intercept form of L_1 is $y = x$, which has slope $m = 1$ and y-intercept $(0, 0)$. Graph L_1 with a dashed line. The slope-intercept form of L_2 is $y = x + 3$, which has slope $m = 1$ and y-intercept $(0, 3)$. Graph L_2 with a dashed line.

$L_1 : y < x$

Test Point $(0, 1)$: $1 < 0$

False

Shade the region that does not contain $(0, 1)$.

$L_2 : y > x + 3$

Test Point $(0, 0)$: $0 > 0 + 3$

$0 > 3$

False

Shade the region that does not contain the origin.

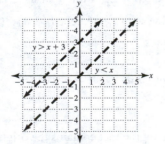

85. The slope-intercept form of L_1 is $y = \dfrac{1}{3}x - 1$, which has slope $m = \dfrac{1}{3}$ and y-intercept $(0, -1)$. Graph L_1 with a solid line. The slope-intercept form of L_2 is $y = -\dfrac{1}{5}x + 1$, which has slope $m = -\dfrac{1}{5}$ and y-intercept $(0, 1)$. Graph L_2 with a dashed line.

$L_1 : 3y \geq x - 3$

Test Point $(0, 0)$: $3(0) \geq 0 - 3$

$0 \geq -3$

True

Shade the region that contains the origin.

$L_2 : -5y > x - 5$

Test Point $(0, 0)$: $-5(0) > 0 - 5$

$0 > -5$

True

Shade the region that contains the origin.

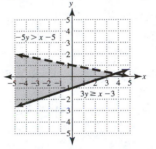

86. The slope-intercept form of L_1 is $y = \dfrac{1}{2}x - 7$, which has slope $m = \dfrac{1}{2}$ and y-intercept $(0, -7)$. Graph L_1 with a dashed line. The slope-intercept form of L_2 is $y = -\dfrac{8}{3}x - 4$, which has slope $m = -\dfrac{8}{3}$ and y-intercept $(0, -4)$. Graph L_2 with a solid line.

$L_1 : \dfrac{1}{2}x - y < 7$

Test Point $(0, 0)$: $\dfrac{1}{2}(0) - 0 < 7$

$0 < 7$

True

Shade the region that contains the origin.

$L_2 : \dfrac{2}{3}x + \dfrac{1}{4}y \geq -1$

Test Point $(0, 0)$: $\dfrac{2}{3}(0) + \dfrac{1}{4}(0) \geq -1$

$0 \geq -1$

True

Shade the region that contains the origin.

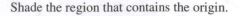
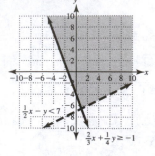

87. The slope-intercept form of L_1 is $y = -x+1$, which has slope $m = -1$ and y-intercept $(0,1)$. Graph L_1 with a dashed line. The slope-intercept form of L_2 is $y = -2x+4$, which has slope $m = -2$ and y-intercept $(0,4)$. Graph L_2 with a solid line. L_3 is a vertical line with x-intercept $(3,0)$. Graph L_3 with a solid line.

$L_1 : x+y>1$

Test Point $(0,0)$: $0+0>1$

$0>1$

False

Shade the region that does not contain the origin.

$L_2 : 2x+y \le 4$

Test Point $(0,0)$: $2(0)+0 \le 4$

$0 \le 4$

True

Shade the region that contains the origin.

$L_3 : x \le 3$

Test Point $(0,0)$: $0 \le 3$

True

Shade the region that contains the origin.

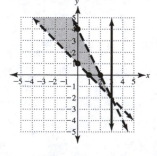

88. The slope-intercept form of L_1 is $y = -\dfrac{4}{3}x+4$, which has slope $m = -\dfrac{4}{3}$ and y-intercept $(0,4)$. Graph L_1 with a dashed line. L_2 is vertical line with x-intercept $(0,0)$. Graph L_2 with a solid line. L_3 is a horizontal line with y-intercept $(0,0)$. Graph L_3 with a solid line.

$L_1 : 4x+3y<12$

Test Point $(0,0)$: $4(0)+3(0)<12$

$0<12$

True

Shade the region that contains the origin.

$L_2 : x \ge 0$

Test Point $(1,0)$: $1 \ge 0$

True

Shade the region that contains $(1,0)$.

$L_3 : y \ge 0$

Test Point $(0,1)$: $1 \ge 0$

True

Shade the region that contains $(0,1)$.

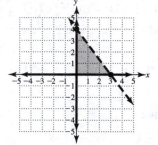

89. The slope-intercept form of L_1 is $y = \dfrac{2}{3}x-2$, which has slope $m = \dfrac{2}{3}$ and y-intercept $(0,-2)$. Graph L_1 with a solid line. L_2 is vertical line with x-intercept $(2,0)$. Graph L_2 with a dashed line. L_3 is a vertical line with x-intercept $(-3,0)$. Graph L_3 with a solid line.

$L_1 : 2x-3y \le 6$

Test Point $(0,0)$: $2(0)-3(0) \le 6$

$0 \le 6$

True

Shade the region that contains the origin.

$L_2 : x>2$

Test Point $(0,0)$: $0>2$

False

Shade the region that does not contain the origin.

$L_3 : x + 3 \leq 0$

Test Point $(0,0)$: $0 + 3 \leq 0$

$3 \leq 0$

False

Shade the region that does not contain the origin.

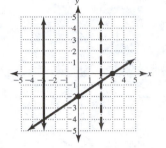

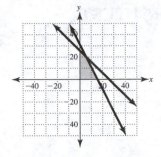

Ponder Does our answers seem reasonable? Yes. The shaded region of our graph is technically named the feasibility region because it satisfies all the production constraints of the company. That is, the number of gowns produced and the hours of labor do not exceed the constraints for the problem.

90. **Prepare** We are to write and solve a system of linear inequalities that satisfies the conditions of the problem.

Plan Set up a system of linear inequalities and solve by graphing.

Let $x =$ the number of full length gowns made.

Let $y =$ the number of shorter gowns made.

Because the number of gowns made cannot be negative, there are automatically two inequalities for our system. That is, $x \geq 0$ and $y \geq 0$. Because the maximum number of gowns that can be made is 25, we can write the inequality $x + y \leq 25$. Because it takes 20 hours to make a full length gown, it would take $20x$ hours to make x full length gowns. Likewise, it would take $10y$ hours to make y short gowns. The maximum number of hours allowed to make all of the gowns is 300. Therefore, the final inequality is $20x + 10y \leq 300$.

Process Write the linear system of inequalities and solve.

$$\begin{cases} x + y \leq 25 \\ 20x + 10y \leq 300 \\ x \geq 0 \\ y \geq 0 \end{cases}$$

Notice that the last two inequalities keep us within Quadrant I of the xy-plane. Therefore, we will graph the first two inequalities and only shade the first quadrant.

To graph the first two inequalities, we can sketch the intercepts for each and use the origin for the test point. The origin satisfies both inequalities. The shaded region of our graph represents the number of quilts the company can produce in one week under the given constraints.

CHAPTER 4 TEST

1. b, e, g

2. c, e, h

3. c, d, e, h

4. c, e, h

5. a, f

6. Substitute $x = -3$ and $y = \dfrac{1}{5}$ into the equation $2x - 5y = -5$.

$$2x - 5y = -5$$
$$2(-3) - 5\left(\dfrac{1}{5}\right) = -5$$
$$-6 - 1 = -5$$
$$-7 = -5$$

False

The point $\left(-3, \dfrac{1}{5}\right)$ is not a solution to the system.

7. Substitute $x = -4$, $y = -1$, and $z = 0$ into each equation.

$$x + y + z = -5$$
$$(-4) + (-1) + (0) = -5$$
$$-5 = -5$$

True

$$2x - 3y + 5z = -5$$
$$2(-4) - 3(-1) + (0) = -5$$
$$-8 - (-3) = -5$$
$$-5 = -5$$

True

$$-3x + 4y - 6z = 8$$
$$-3(-4) + 4(-1) - 6(0) = 8$$
$$12 + (-4) = 8$$
$$8 = 8$$

True

The point $(-4, -1, 0)$ is a solution to the system.

8. Graph L_1 using the intercept method. The intercepts are $(2, 0)$ and $(0, 2)$. Graph L_2 using the slope-intercept method. The slope-intercept form of L_2 is $y = \dfrac{3}{4}x - 5$.

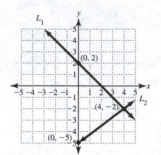

The solution set is $\{(4, -2)\}$.

9. Solve equation 1 for x to get $x = -6y - 2$. Substitute $x = -6y - 2$ into Equation 2.

$$-2x + 3y = 14$$
$$-2(-6y - 2) + 3y = 14$$
$$12y + 4 + 3y = 14$$
$$15y = 10$$
$$y = \dfrac{2}{3}$$

Substitute $y = \dfrac{2}{3}$ into $x = -6y - 2$ to find x.

$$x = -6y - 2$$
$$x = -6\left(\dfrac{2}{3}\right) - 2$$
$$x = -4 - 2$$
$$x = -6$$

The solution set is $\left\{\left(-6, \dfrac{2}{3}\right)\right\}$.

10. Substitute $x = \dfrac{3}{2}y + 6$ into Equation 1.

$$\dfrac{2}{3}x - y = -3$$
$$\dfrac{2}{3}\left(\dfrac{3}{2}y + 6\right) - y = -3$$
$$y + 4 - y = -3$$
$$4 = -3$$

False

The solution set is $\{\ \}$.

11. Eliminate y by adding -1 times Equation 1 with Equation 2.

$$\begin{array}{l} -1(\text{Equation 1}) \\ \text{Equation 2} \end{array} \begin{cases} -6x - y = -4 \\ -14x + y = 14 \end{cases}$$

$$-20x = 10$$

$$x = -\frac{1}{2}$$

Substitute $x = -\frac{1}{2}$ into Equation 1 to find y.

$$6x + y = 4$$

$$6\left(-\frac{1}{2}\right) + y = 4$$

$$-3 + y = 4$$

$$y = 7$$

The solution set is $\left\{\left(-\frac{1}{2}, 7\right)\right\}$.

12. Eliminate x by adding Equation 1 with -2 times Equation 2.

$$\begin{array}{l} \text{Equation 1} \\ -2(\text{Equation 2}) \end{array} \begin{cases} 2x + 3y = 12 \\ -2x - 3y = -12 \end{cases}$$

$$0 = 0$$

The solution set is $\{(x, y) \mid 2x + 3y = 12\}$.

13. Eliminate z by adding Equation 1 with Equation 2.

$$\begin{array}{l} \text{Equation 1} \\ \text{Equation 2} \end{array} \begin{cases} x + y + z = 0 \\ 2x + y - z = 2 \end{cases}$$

$$\text{Equation 4} \quad 3x + 2y = 2$$

Eliminate z by adding 2 times Equation 1 with Equation 3.

$$\begin{array}{l} 2(\text{Equation 1}) \\ \text{Equation 3} \end{array} \begin{cases} 2x + 2y + 2z = 0 \\ -3x + 2y - 2z = 10 \end{cases}$$

$$\text{Equation 5} \quad -x + 4y = 10$$

Eliminate x by adding Equation 4 with 3 times Equation 5.

$$\begin{array}{l} \text{Equation 4} \\ 3(\text{Equation 5}) \end{array} \begin{cases} 3x + 2y = 2 \\ -3x + 12y = 30 \end{cases}$$

$$14y = 32$$

$$y = \frac{16}{7}$$

Substitute $y = \frac{16}{7}$ into Equation 4 to find x.

$$3x + 2y = 2$$

$$3x + 2\left(\frac{16}{7}\right) = 2$$

$$3x + \frac{32}{7} = 2$$

$$3x = \frac{14}{7} - \frac{32}{7}$$

$$3x = -\frac{18}{7}$$

$$\frac{1}{3}(3x) = \frac{1}{3}\left(-\frac{18}{7}\right)$$

$$x = -\frac{6}{7}$$

Substitute $x = -\frac{6}{7}$ and $y = \frac{16}{7}$ into Equation 1 to find z.

$$x + y + z = 0$$

$$\left(-\frac{6}{7}\right) + \left(\frac{16}{7}\right) + z = 0$$

$$\frac{10}{7} + z = 0$$

$$z = -\frac{10}{7}$$

The solution set is $\left\{\left(-\frac{6}{7}, \frac{16}{7}, -\frac{10}{7}\right)\right\}$.

14. Use the substitution method. Substitute $y = \frac{8}{5}x + 9$ into $y = 3x - 2$.

$$y = 3x - 2$$

$$\frac{8}{5}x + 9 = 3x - 2$$

$$5\left(\frac{8}{5}x + 9\right) = 5(3x - 2)$$

$$8x + 45 = 15x - 10$$

$$-7x = -55$$

$$x = \frac{55}{7}$$

Substitute $x = \frac{55}{7}$ into $y = 3x - 2$ to find y.

$$y = 3x - 2$$

$$y = 3\left(\frac{55}{7}\right) - 2$$

$$y = \frac{165}{7} - \frac{14}{7}$$

$$y = \frac{151}{7}$$

The solution set is $\left\{\left(\dfrac{55}{7}, \dfrac{151}{7}\right)\right\}$.

15. Use the method of elimination. Eliminate x by adding 100 times Equation 1 with 10 times Equation 2.

$$\begin{array}{r} 100(\text{Equation 1}) \\ 10(\text{Equation 2}) \end{array} \left\{ \begin{array}{r} -10x + 10y = -21 \\ 10x - 10y = -20 \\ \hline 0 = -41 \end{array} \right.$$

The solution set is $\{\ \}$.

16. Use the method of substitution. Solve Equation 2 for y to get $y = 6z - 3$. Substitute $y = 6z - 3$ into Equation 3.

$$x + 3y = -5$$
$$x + 3(6z - 3) = -5$$
$$x + 18z - 9 = -5$$
$$x + 18z = 4$$

Solve $x + 18z = 4$ for x to get $x = -18z + 4$. Substitute $x = -18z + 4$ for x in Equation 1.

$$2x + 4z = -8$$
$$2(-18z + 4) + 4z = -8$$
$$-36z + 8 + 4z = -8$$
$$-32z = -16$$
$$z = \dfrac{1}{2}$$

Substitute $z = \dfrac{1}{2}$ into $x = -18z + 4$ to find x.

$$x = -18z + 4$$
$$x = -18\left(\dfrac{1}{2}\right) + 4$$
$$x = -9 + 4$$
$$x = -5$$

Substitute $z = \dfrac{1}{2}$ into $y = 6z - 3$ to find y.

$$y = 6z - 3$$
$$y = 6\left(\dfrac{1}{2}\right) - 3$$
$$y = 3 - 3$$
$$y = 0$$

The solution set is $\left\{\left(-5, 0, \dfrac{1}{2}\right)\right\}$.

17.a. The shaded region for L_1 is not the same as that of $2x < -y - 2$. To see this is the case, choose the test point $(0,0)$ from the shaded region of L_1 and test it in $2x < -y - 2$.

$$2x < -y - 2$$
$$2(0) < -(0) - 2$$
$$0 < -2$$
$$\text{False}$$

The shaded region for $2x < -y - 2$ would be opposite that of L_1, therefore, the statement is false.

17.b. Since $(-1, 0)$ lies on the dashed line, it is not a solution. Since $(1,1)$ is not on a line nor in the shaded region, it is not a solution. Therefore, the statement is true.

18. Graph L_1 using the intercept method and a solid line. The intercepts are $(0,3)$ and $(-3,0)$. Choose the test point $(0,0)$.

$$-x + y \le 3$$
$$-(0) + (0) \le 3$$
$$0 \le 3$$
$$\text{True}$$

Use arrows to indicate the shaded region containing the point $(0,0)$. Graph L_2 using the intercept method and a dashed line. The intercepts are $(0,5)$ and $(5,0)$. Choose the test point $(0,0)$.

$$x + y > 5$$
$$(0) + (0) > 5$$
$$0 > 5$$
$$\text{False}$$

Use arrows to indicate the shaded region that does not contain $(0,0)$. Shade the solution region.

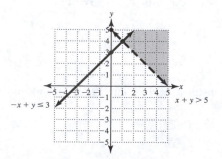

19. Graph the vertical line L_1 using a solid line. Shade the region to the right of the line. Graph the vertical line L_2 using a dashed line. Shade the region to the left of the line.

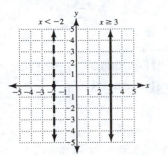

20. Graph L_1 using the slope-intercept method and a solid line. The slope is 1 and the y-intercept is $(0,0)$. Choose the test point $(1,-1)$.

$$x - y \geq 0$$
$$(1) - (-1) \geq 0$$
$$2 \geq 0$$
$$\text{True}$$

Use arrows to indicate the shaded region that contains the point $(1,-1)$. Graph L_2 using the intercept method and a solid line. The intercepts are $(0,10)$ and $(4,0)$. Choose the test point $(0,0)$.

$$5x + 2y \leq 20$$
$$5(0) + 2(0) \leq 20$$
$$0 \leq 20$$
$$\text{True}$$

Use arrows to indicate the shaded region that contains the point $(0,0)$. Graph the horizontal line L_3 using a dashed line. Use arrows to indicate the shaded region above the line.

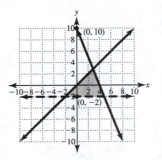

21. Let x be the lesser integer and y be the greater integer. Write the system of equations.

$$\begin{cases} x + y = 18 \\ 3x + 2y = -20 \end{cases}$$

Solve the system using the method of elimination. Add -2 Equation 1 with Equation 2 to eliminate y.

$$\begin{array}{ll} -2(\text{Equation 1}) & \begin{cases} -2x - 2y = -36 \\ 3x + 2y = -20 \end{cases} \\ \text{Equation 2} & \overline{} \\ & \qquad\quad x = -56 \end{array}$$

The lesser integer is -56.

22. Let x be the number of memorial stones and y be the number of steps. Write the system of equations.

$$\begin{cases} x + y = 1094 \\ y = 6x - 292 \end{cases}$$

Solve the system using the substitution method. Substitute $y = 6x - 292$ into equation 2.

$$x + y = 1094$$
$$x + (6x - 292) = 1094$$
$$7x - 292 = 1094$$
$$7x = 1386$$
$$x = 198$$

There are 198 memorial stones.

23. Prepare We must find the number of each type of seat in Majestic Theatre.

Plan Since there are three unknowns, we must set up and solve a system of three equations.

Process Let x be the number of orchestra seats, y be the number of mezzanine seats, and z be the number of balcony seats. Write the system of equations.

$$\begin{cases} x + y + z = 2310 \\ 75x + 70y + 60z = 158020 \\ x = 5y - 360 \end{cases}$$

Solve the system using the method of elimination. Eliminate z from Equation 1 and Equation 2.

$$\begin{array}{ll} -60(\text{Equation 1}) & \begin{cases} -60x - 60y - 60z = -138600 \\ 75x + 70y + 60z = 158020 \end{cases} \\ \text{Equation 2} & \overline{} \\ \text{Equation 4} & \quad 15x + 10y = 19420 \end{array}$$

Eliminate y from Equation 3 and Equation 4. First rewrite Equation 3 as $x - 5y = -360$.

$$\begin{array}{ll} 2(\text{Equation 3}) & \begin{cases} 2x - 10y = -720 \\ 15x + 10y = 19420 \end{cases} \\ \text{Equation 4} & \overline{} \\ & \quad 17x = 18700 \\ & \quadx = 1100 \end{array}$$

Substitute $x = 1100$ into Equation 3 to find y.

$$x = 5y - 360$$
$$1100 = 5y - 360$$
$$1460 = 5y$$
$$292 = y$$

Substitute $x = 1100$ and $y = 292$ into Equation 1 to find z.

$$x + y + z = 2310$$
$$(1100) + (292) + z = 2310$$
$$1392 + z = 2310$$
$$z = 918$$

There are 1,100 orchestra seats, 292 mezzanine seats, and 918 balcony seats.

Ponder Is this answer reasonable? Since the sum of the seats is 2,310, the answer seems reasonable.

24. Prepare We are to determine the amount invested at 3.5%.

Plan Because there are two unknowns, we must set up and solve a system of two equations.

Process Let x be the amount invested at 3.5% and y be the amount invested at 5%. Write the system of equations.

Account	Principal	Rate	Time	Interest
3.5%	x	0.035	1 year	$0.035x$
5%	y	0.05	1 year	$0.05y$

$$\begin{cases} x + y = 1000 \\ 0.035x + 0.05y = 44 \end{cases}$$

Solve by eliminating y.

$$\begin{array}{l} -50(\text{Equation 3}) \\ 1000(\text{Equation 4}) \end{array} \begin{cases} -50x - 50y = -50000 \\ 35x + 50y = 44000 \end{cases}$$
$$-15x = -6000$$
$$x = 400$$

Maura invested $400 at 3.5% APR.

Ponder Is this result reasonable? It seems reasonable that $400 of the $1,000 was invested at 3.5%.

25. Prepare We are to determine the rate of the river's current.

Plan There are two unknowns. They are the rate of the river current and the rate of the boat. We must set up and solve a system of two equations.

Process Let r be the rate of the river's current and s be the rate of the boat. Write the system of equations.

Direction	Rate	Time	Distance
upstream	$s - r$	3	$3(s - r) = 6$
downstream	$s + r$	1	$s + r = 6$

$$\begin{cases} 3(s - r) = 6 \\ s + r = 6 \end{cases}$$

Solve by eliminating s.

$$\begin{array}{l} -1(\text{Equation 3}) \\ 3(\text{Equation 4}) \end{array} \begin{cases} -3s + 3r = -6 \\ 3s + 3r = 18 \end{cases}$$
$$6r = 12$$
$$r = 2$$

The rate of the river's current is 2 miles per hour.

Ponder   Is the result reasonable?   It seems reasonable that the rate of the river's current is 2 miles per hour.

Chapter 5

5.1 Exercises

1. c, e

3. c, f

5. d

7. $5^{-3} = \dfrac{1}{5^3}$

$\qquad = \dfrac{1}{125}$

9. $24^{-1} = \dfrac{1}{24^1}$

$\qquad = \dfrac{1}{24}$

11. $\left(\dfrac{1}{3}\right)^{-4} = \left(\dfrac{3}{1}\right)^{4}$

$\qquad = 3 \cdot 3 \cdot 3 \cdot 3$

$\qquad = 81$

13. $\left(\dfrac{7}{8}\right)^{-1} = \left(\dfrac{8}{7}\right)^{1}$

$\qquad = \dfrac{8}{7}$

15. $(-1)^{-8} = \dfrac{1}{(-1)^8}$

$\qquad = \dfrac{1}{1}$

$\qquad = 1$

17. $(-10)^{-3} = \dfrac{1}{(-10)^3}$

$\qquad = \dfrac{1}{-1000}$

$\qquad = -\dfrac{1}{1000}$

19. $-2^{-4} = -1 \cdot 2^{-4}$

$\qquad = -1 \cdot \dfrac{1}{2^4}$

$\qquad = -1 \cdot \dfrac{1}{16}$

$\qquad = -\dfrac{1}{16}$

21. $x^7 \cdot x^{-2} \cdot x = x^{7+(-2)+1}$

$\qquad = x^6$

23. $6^{-4} \cdot 6^4 = 6^{-4+4}$

$\qquad = 6^0$

$\qquad = 1$

25. $y^{-12} \cdot y^{-8} = y^{-12+(-8)}$

$\qquad = y^{-20}$

$\qquad = \dfrac{1}{y^{20}}$

27. $\left(a^{-6}\right)^3 = a^{(-6)3}$

$\qquad = a^{-18}$

$\qquad = \dfrac{1}{a^{18}}$

29. $\left(8^{-2}\right)^{-1} = 8^{(-2)(-1)}$

$\qquad = 8^2$

$\qquad = 64$

31. $\left[(-3)^2\right]^2 = (-3)^{2(2)}$

$\qquad = (-3)^4$

$\qquad = 81$

33. $\left(5y^7\right)^{-3} = 5^{-3}\left(y^7\right)^{-3}$

$\qquad = 5^{-3}\, y^{-21}$

$\qquad = \dfrac{1}{5^3} \cdot \dfrac{1}{y^{21}}$

$\qquad = \dfrac{1}{125 y^{21}}$

35. $\left(-6a^5b^3\right)^2 = (-6)^2\left(a^5\right)^2\left(b^3\right)^2$

$\qquad = 36a^{10}b^6$

37. $\left(3a^5bc^{-5}\right)^3 = 3^3\left(a^5\right)^3\left(b^1\right)^3\left(c^{-5}\right)^3$

$\qquad = 27a^{15}b^3c^{-15}$

$\qquad = 27a^{15}b^3 \cdot \dfrac{1}{c^{15}}$

$\qquad = \dfrac{27a^{15}b^3}{c^{15}}$

39. $\dfrac{a^{15}}{a^{12}} = a^{15-12}$

$\qquad = a^3$

41. $\dfrac{5^5 x^4}{5^3 x^{-2}} = 5^{5-3}x^{4-(-2)}$

$\qquad = 5^2 x^6$

$\qquad = 25x^6$

43. $\dfrac{-8x^{-5}}{x^{-3}} = -8x^{-5-(-3)}$

$\qquad = -8x^{-2}$

$\qquad = -8 \cdot \dfrac{1}{x^2}$

$\qquad = -\dfrac{8}{x^2}$

45. $\left(\dfrac{4x^7}{5y^3}\right)^3 = \dfrac{\left(4x^7\right)^3}{\left(5y^3\right)^3}$

$\qquad = \dfrac{4^3\left(x^7\right)^3}{5^3\left(y^3\right)^3}$

$\qquad = \dfrac{64x^{21}}{125y^9}$

47. $\left(\dfrac{-2a^{-6}b}{a^8b^{-4}}\right)^4 = \dfrac{\left(-2a^{-6}b\right)^4}{\left(a^8b^{-4}\right)^4}$

$\qquad = \dfrac{(-2)^4\left(a^{-6}\right)^4 b^4}{\left(a^8\right)^4\left(b^{-4}\right)^4}$

$\qquad = \dfrac{16a^{-24}b^4}{a^{32}b^{-16}}$

$\qquad = 16a^{-24-32}b^{4-(-16)}$

$\qquad = 16a^{-56}b^{20}$

$\qquad = \dfrac{16b^{20}}{a^{56}}$

49. $\left(\dfrac{ab^{-1}c^0}{-6a^7c^{-2}}\right)^{-1} = \dfrac{\left(ab^{-1}c^0\right)^{-1}}{\left(-6a^7c^{-2}\right)^{-1}}$

$\qquad = \dfrac{a^{-1}\left(b^{-1}\right)^{-1}\left(c^0\right)^{-1}}{(-6)^{-1}\left(a^7\right)^{-1}\left(c^{-2}\right)^{-1}}$

$\qquad = \dfrac{a^{-1}bc^0}{(-6)^{-1}a^{-7}c^2}$

$\qquad = -6a^{-1-(-7)}bc^{0-2}$

$\qquad = -6a^6bc^{-2}$

$\qquad = \dfrac{-6a^6b}{c^2}$

51. $\dfrac{14a^{-6}}{5b^{-11}} = \dfrac{14b^{11}}{5a^6}$

53. $\dfrac{-5a^{-9}b^4}{12c^{-6}} = \dfrac{-5b^4c^6}{12a^9}$

55. $\dfrac{x^{-5}y^0z^8}{3^{-2}a} = \dfrac{3^2 y^0 z^8}{ax^5}$

$\qquad = \dfrac{9z^8}{ax^5}$

57. $\left(3x^5y\right)^4\left(-x^6y^{-2}\right) = 3^4\left(x^5\right)^4 y^4\left(-x^6y^{-2}\right)$

$\qquad = 81x^{20}y^4\left(-x^6y^{-2}\right)$

$\qquad = -81x^{26}y^2$

59. $\dfrac{8a^{16}b^{-2}}{12a^{-9}b^{-4}} = \dfrac{8}{12}a^{16-(-9)}b^{-2-(-4)}$

$\qquad = \dfrac{\overset{2}{\cancel{8}}}{\underset{3}{\cancel{12}}}a^{25}b^2$

$\qquad = \dfrac{2a^{25}b^2}{3}$

61. $\dfrac{2^4 x^8}{2^{-3}x^{-8}} = 2^{4-(-3)}x^{8-(-8)}$

$\qquad = 2^7 x^{16}$

$\qquad = 128x^{16}$

63. $\left(6a^8bc^{-2}\right)\left(\dfrac{1}{2}a^{-1}b^5\right)^4 = \left(6a^8bc^{-2}\right)\left(\dfrac{1}{2}\right)^4\left(a^{-1}\right)^4\left(b^5\right)^4$

$\qquad = \left(6a^8bc^{-2}\right)\left(\dfrac{1}{16}\right)a^{-4}b^{20}$

$\qquad = 6 \cdot \dfrac{1}{16}a^4b^{21}c^{-2}$

$\qquad = \dfrac{\overset{3}{\cancel{6}}a^4b^{21}}{\underset{8}{\cancel{16}}c^2}$

$\qquad = \dfrac{3a^4b^{21}}{8c^2}$

65. $\left(-2x^0y^4z^{-8}\right)^{-5} = (-2)^{-5}\left(x^0\right)^{-5}\left(y^4\right)^{-5}\left(z^{-8}\right)^{-5}$

$\qquad = (-2)^{-5}x^0y^{-20}z^{40}$

$\qquad = \dfrac{x^0z^{40}}{(-2)^5 y^{20}}$

$\qquad = -\dfrac{z^{40}}{32y^{20}}$

67. $\left(-a^6b^{-8}c^2\right)\left(-2a^7b^{-1}\right)^5 = \left(-a^6b^{-8}c^2\right)(-2)^5\left(a^7\right)^5\left(b^{-1}\right)^5$

$\qquad = \left(-a^6b^{-8}c^2\right)(-32)a^{35}b^{-5}$

$\qquad = 32a^{41}b^{-13}c^2$

$\qquad = \dfrac{32a^{41}c^2}{b^{13}}$

69. $\left(-7x^5y^{-2}z\right)^3\left(9x^{-4}z^2\right)^0 = (-7)^3\left(x^5\right)^3\left(y^{-2}\right)^3 z^3 \cdot 1$

$\qquad = -343x^{15}y^{-6}z^3$

$\qquad = -\dfrac{343x^{15}z^3}{y^6}$

71. Answers will vary; for example: To multiply two numbers using the product rule the bases must be the same. $3^3 = 27$, $4^4 = 256$, and $27 \cdot 256 = 6,912$. The incorrect answer would give $35,831,808$.

73. Answers will vary; for example: A negative exponent means moving a factor from the numerator to the denominator or vice versa.

75. Answers will vary; for example: You can multiply each term three times or use the product-to-a-power rule, $\left(-4a^5\right)^3 = -64a^{15}$. The product-to-a-power rule is much easier.

77. No. All exponents are positive and there are no other operations to perform.

79. $A = LW$

$$= \left(8x^2\right)\left(2x\right)$$

$$= 16x^{2+1}$$

$$= 16x^3 \text{ units}^2$$

81. $A = \pi r^2$

$$= \pi\left(2a^3\right)^2$$

$$= \pi\left(2\right)^2\left(a^3\right)^2$$

$$= 4\pi a^6 \text{ units}^2$$

83. $A = LWH$

$$= \left(2.5x^2\right)\left(2.5x^2\right)\left(2.5x^2\right)$$

$$= 15.625x^{2+2+2}$$

$$= 15.625x^6 \text{ units}^3$$

85. Prepare Using the given compound interest formula and the information regarding the new artist, we must determine how much money will be in her savings account after one year.

Plan For the compound interest formula, determine the values for P, r, n, and t, and then substitute them into the formula. Evaluate the formula to find the accumulated value A.

Process The principal amount to be invested is $P = \$20,000$. The simple annual interest rate is $r = 4\% = 0.04$. The interest is compounded quarterly, which means that $n = 4$. The time is $t = 1$ year.

$$A = P\left(1 + \frac{r}{n}\right)^{nt}$$

$$= \left(20,000\right)\left(1 + \frac{0.04}{4}\right)^{4(1)}$$

$$= \left(20,000\right)\left(1.01\right)^4$$

$$\approx 20,812.08$$

The new artist would have \$20,812.08 in the account after one year.

Ponder Does our answer seem reasonable? Yes, because simple interest of 4% on \$20,000 for one year would be \$800 using the simple interest formula $I = Prt$. Therefore, the new artist should make more if the investment is compounded quarterly, instead of just once.

87. Prepare Using the given compound interest formula and the information regarding the newlyweds, we must determine how much money will be in their certificate after five years.

Plan For the compound interest formula, determine the values for P, r, n, and t, and then substitute them into the formula. Evaluate the formula to find the accumulated value A.

Process The principal amount to be invested is $P = \$1,000$. The simple annual interest rate is $r = 8\% = 0.08$. The interest is compounded quarterly, which means that $n = 12$. The time is $t = 5$ years.

$$A = P\left(1 + \frac{r}{n}\right)^{nt}$$

$$= \left(1,000\right)\left(1 + \frac{0.08}{12}\right)^{12(5)}$$

$$= \left(1,000\right)\left(1.00\overline{6}\right)^{60}$$

$$\approx 1,489.85$$

The newlyweds would have \$1,489.85 in the certificate after five years.

Ponder Does our answer seem reasonable? Yes, because simple interest of 8% on \$1,000 for five years would be \$400 using the simple interest formula $I = Prt$. Therefore, the newlyweds should make more if the investment is compounded monthly, instead of just once.

89. $\left(\dfrac{-25x^{-4}y^{12}z^{-8}}{35x^{-16}y^{-20}z^6}\right)^{-2} = \left(\dfrac{\overset{7}{\cancel{35}}x^{-16}y^{-20}z^6}{-5\,\cancel{25}x^{-4}y^{12}z^{-8}}\right)^2$

$$= \left(-\frac{7}{5}x^{-12}y^{-32}z^{14}\right)^2$$

$$= \left(-\frac{7}{5}\right)^2\left(x^{-12}\right)^2\left(y^{-32}\right)^2\left(z^{14}\right)^2$$

$$= \frac{49}{25}x^{-24}y^{-64}z^{28}$$

$$= \frac{49z^{28}}{25x^{24}y^{64}}$$

91.
$$\frac{7x^{-5}y^0z^{14}}{\left(-7x^{16}y^{-8}z^{-2}\right)^2} = \frac{7x^{-5}y^0z^{14}}{(-7)^2\left(x^{16}\right)^2\left(y^{-8}\right)^2\left(z^{-2}\right)^2}$$
$$= \frac{{}^1\cancel{7}x^{-5}y^0z^{14}}{{}_7\cancel{49}x^{32}y^{-16}z^{-4}}$$
$$= \frac{1}{7}x^{-37}y^{16}z^{18}$$
$$= \frac{y^{16}z^{18}}{7x^{37}}$$

93.
$$\frac{\left(-3r^{-2}s^3t^{-1}\right)\left(4r^{-5}s^{-2}t^0\right)^2}{20r^7s^0t^3}$$
$$= \frac{\left(-3r^{-2}s^3t^{-1}\right)(4)^2\left(r^{-5}\right)^2\left(s^{-2}\right)^2\left(t^0\right)^2}{20r^7s^0t^3}$$
$$= \frac{\left(-3r^{-2}s^3t^{-1}\right)16r^{-10}s^{-4}t^0}{20r^7s^0t^3}$$
$$= \frac{{}^{-12}\cancel{-48}r^{-12}s^{-1}t^{-1}}{{}_5\cancel{20}r^7s^0t^3}$$
$$= -\frac{12}{5}r^{-19}s^{-1}t^{-4}$$
$$= -\frac{12}{5r^{19}st^4}$$

5.2 Exercises

1. A large number such as 125,000, when written in scientific notation, has a 5th power of 10.

3. When converting from scientific notation to standard notation, we move the decimal point to the left when the power of 10 is negative.

5. yes

7. no; $8.75(10^1)$

9. yes

11. no; $9(10^7)$

13. $375,000 = 3.75(10^5)$

15. $0.0000014 = 1.4(10^{-6})$

17. $2,691,000,000 = 2.691(10^9)$

19. $0.0000259 = 2.59(10^{-5})$

21. $5.2(10^5) = 520,000$

23. $5(10^6) = 5,000,000$

25. $3.71(10^0) = 3.71$

27. $7.2(10^{-7}) = 0.00000072$

29. $1.109(10^{-1}) = 0.1109$

31. $4.928(10^1) = 49.28$

33. $2(10^4) \cdot 3(10^2) = 6(10^6)$ Scientific Notation
$= 6,000,000$ Standard Notation

35. $3(10^{-5}) \cdot 2(10^{-4}) = 6(10^{-9})$ Scientific Notation
$= 0.000000006$ Standard Notation

37. $8(10^3) \cdot 6(10^5) = 48(10^8)$
$= 4.8(10^1)(10^8)$
$= 4.8(10^9)$ Scientific Notation
$= 48,000,000,000$ Standard Notation

39. $\dfrac{18(10^5)}{3(10^2)} = 6(10^3)$ Scientific Notation
$= 6,000$ Standard Notation

41. $\dfrac{4(10^{-4})}{16(10^2)} = 0.25(10^{-6})$
$= 2.5(10^{-1})(10^{-6})$
$= 2.5(10^{-7})$ Scientific Notation
$= 0.0000025$ Standard Notation

43. $(12,000)(14,000,000) = 1.2(10^4) \cdot 1.4(10^7)$
$= 1.68(10^{11})$ Scientific Notation
$= 168,000,000,000$ Standard Notation

45. $(2,360,000)(0.004) = 2.36(10^6) \cdot 4(10^{-3})$
$= 9.44(10^3)$ Scientific Notation
$= 9,440$ Standard Notation

206

47. $$\frac{(12,000)(45,000)}{0.0005} = \frac{1.2(10^4) \cdot \overset{0.9}{\cancel{4.5}}(10^4)}{{}_1\cancel{5}(10^{-4})}$$

$$= \frac{1.08(10^8)}{(10^{-4})}$$

$$= 1.08(10^{12}) \qquad \text{Scientific Notation}$$

$$= 1,080,000,000,000 \qquad \text{Standard Notation}$$

49. $$\frac{(20,000)(0.012)}{(300)(0.0002)} = \frac{\overset{1}{\cancel{2}}(10^4) \cdot \overset{0.4}{\cancel{1.2}}(10^{-2})}{{}_1\cancel{3}(10^2) \cdot {}_1\cancel{2}(10^{-4})}$$

$$= \frac{0.4(10^2)}{(10^{-2})}$$

$$= 0.4(10^4)$$

$$= 4(10^{-1})(10^4)$$

$$= 4(10^3) \qquad \text{Scientific Notation}$$

$$= 4,000 \qquad \text{Standard Notation}$$

51. Answers will vary; for example: Create a number that is greater than or equal to 1 and less than 10 by moving the decimal point. If the original number is between 0 and 1 the exponent will be negative, otherwise it is positive.

53. Answers will vary; for example: If the number is greater than 1, use a positive exponent. If the number is between 0 and 1, use a negative exponent.

55. $\$15,000,000 = \$1.5(10^7)$

$$\frac{1}{4} \cdot 1.5(10^7) = \$0.375(10^7)$$

$$= \$3.75(10^{-1})(10^7)$$

$$= \$3.75(10^6)$$

57. $60(\$407.08) = \$24,424.80$

$$= \$2.44248(10^4)$$

59. $2.368(10^5) = 236,800 \ \text{km}^2$

61. $A = s^2$

$$= \left[2.3(10^6)\right]^2$$

$$= (2.3^2)(10^6)^2$$

$$= 5.29(10^{12}) \ \text{mm}^2 \qquad \text{Scientific Notation}$$

$$= 5,290,000,000,000 \ \text{mm}^2 \qquad \text{Standard Notation}$$

63. **Prepare** Using scientific notation, the number of seats in the theater and the average cost per ticket, we must determine the total dollar amount of the ticket sales. We must then determine the amount given to each charity.

Plan Convert the number of seats and the average ticket price to scientific notation and multiply to find the total dollar amount of the ticket sales. Then divide the total amount by 5 to determine the amount given to each charity.

Process
$5,100 \cdot \$195$

$$= 5.1(10^3) \cdot \$1.95(10^2)$$

$$= \$9.945(10^5) \qquad \text{Scientific Notation}$$

$$= \$994,500 \qquad \text{Standard Notation}$$

$$\frac{\$9.945\left(10^5\right)}{5} = \$1.989\left(10^5\right)$$

$$= \$1.989\left(10^5\right) \quad \text{Scientific Notation}$$

$$= \$198,900 \quad\quad \text{Standard Notation}$$

Ponder Do our answers seem reasonable? Yes. A simple check of arithmetic will show our answers to be correct.

65. $2.1\left(10^8\right) + 1.9\left(10^7\right) = 2.1\left(10^8\right) + 0.19\left(10^8\right)$

$$= 2.29\left(10^8\right)$$

67. $3.1\left(10^7\right) \cdot 4.2\left(10^5\right) = 13.02\left(10^{12}\right)$

$$= 1.302\left(10^1\right)\left(10^{12}\right)$$

$$= 1.302\left(10^{13}\right)$$

69. $\dfrac{(93,000,000)(0.0000000005)}{(0.0155)(3,000,000,000,000)}$

$$= \frac{9.3\left(10^7\right) \cdot 5\left(10^{-10}\right)}{1.55\left(10^{-2}\right) \cdot 3\left(10^{12}\right)}$$

$$= \frac{46.5\left(10^{-3}\right)}{4.65\left(10^{10}\right)}$$

$$= \frac{4.65\left(10^1\right)\left(10^{-3}\right)}{4.65\left(10^{10}\right)}$$

$$= \frac{4.65\left(10^{-2}\right)}{4.65\left(10^{10}\right)}$$

$$= 1\left(10^{-12}\right)$$

71. $\dfrac{\left[3.02\left(10^{-7}\right)\right]\left[8.5\left(10^{12}\right)\right]}{5,134,000} = \dfrac{25.67\left(10^5\right)}{5.134\left(10^6\right)}$

$$= 5\left(10^{-1}\right)$$

5.3 Exercises

1. The <u>sum</u> of the exponents on all the variables of a term is called the <u>degree</u> of the term.

3. A polynomial with one term is a <u>monomial</u>.

5. In the term $-5a^3b^2$, negative 5 is called the <u>numerical</u> <u>coefficient</u>.

7. $\dfrac{5}{a}$ is not a <u>polynomial or monomial</u> because the variable has a negative exponent.

9. When adding polynomials, we combine <u>like</u> <u>terms</u>.

11. The degree of the polynomial is 2.

13. The degree of the polynomial is 6.

15. This is not a polynomial because of the negative exponent.

17. The degree of the monomial is 0.

19. This is not a polynomial because of the negative exponent.

21. $\left(-8a^2+5a-6\right)+\left(14a^2+10a-2\right)$

$=-8a^2+5a-6+14a^2+10a-2$

$=-8a^2+14a^2+5a+10a-6-2$

$=6a^2+15a-8$

23. $\left(4x^2-1\right)+\left(6x^3-3x^2-10\right)$

$=4x^2-1+6x^3-3x^2-10$

$=6x^3+4x^2-3x^2-1-10$

$=6x^3+x^2-11$

25. $\left(\dfrac{2}{3}x^5+\dfrac{1}{6}x^2-\dfrac{1}{2}\right)+\left(\dfrac{1}{2}x^5-\dfrac{2}{3}x^2-\dfrac{5}{6}\right)$

$=\dfrac{2}{3}x^5+\dfrac{1}{6}x^2-\dfrac{1}{2}+\dfrac{1}{2}x^5-\dfrac{2}{3}x^2-\dfrac{5}{6}$

$=\dfrac{2}{3}x^5+\dfrac{1}{2}x^5+\dfrac{1}{6}x^2-\dfrac{2}{3}x^2-\dfrac{1}{2}-\dfrac{5}{6}$

$=\dfrac{7}{6}x^5-\dfrac{1}{2}x^2-\dfrac{4}{3}$

27. $\left(5.6a^4-2.1a+8.4\right)+\left(2.9a^4-4.8a-5.7\right)$

$=5.6a^4-2.1a+8.4+2.9a^4-4.8a-5.7$

$=5.6a^4+2.9a^4-2.1a-4.8a+8.4-5.7$

$=8.5a^4-6.9a+2.7$

29. $\left(5x^2-8xy+5y+2y^2\right)+\left(-3x^2-13xy-2y^2\right)$

$=5x^2-8xy+5y+2y^2-3x^2-13xy-2y^2$

$=5x^2-3x^2-8xy-13xy+5y+2y^2-2y^2$

$=2x^2-21xy+5y$

31. $\left(9x^2-5x+3\right)-\left(4x^2-3x+2\right)$

$=9x^2-5x+3-4x^2+3x-2$

$=9x^2-4x^2-5x+3x+3-2$

$=5x^2-2x+1$

33. $\left(3y^3+4y\right)-\left(6y^2+4y-12\right)$

$=3y^3+4y-6y^2-4y+12$

$=3y^3-6y^2+4y-4y+12$

$=3y^3-6y^2+12$

35. $\left(\dfrac{3}{4}x^4+\dfrac{2}{3}x^2-\dfrac{1}{2}\right)-\left(\dfrac{1}{3}x^4-\dfrac{5}{6}x^2-3\right)$

$=\dfrac{3}{4}x^4+\dfrac{2}{3}x^2-\dfrac{1}{2}-\dfrac{1}{3}x^4+\dfrac{5}{6}x^2+3$

$=\dfrac{3}{4}x^4-\dfrac{1}{3}x^4+\dfrac{2}{3}x^2+\dfrac{5}{6}x^2-\dfrac{1}{2}+3$

$=\dfrac{5}{12}x^4+\dfrac{3}{2}x^2+\dfrac{5}{2}$

37. $\left(9.2a^5-4.3a^2+6.6a\right)-\left(3.2a^5-1.2a^2+7.5a\right)$

$=9.2a^5-4.3a^2+6.6a-3.2a^5+1.2a^2-7.5a$

$=9.2a^5-3.2a^5-4.3a^2+1.2a^2+6.6a-7.5a$

$=6a^5-3.1a^2-0.9a$

39. $\left(4a^5b^4+7a^2b^2+2ab^5\right)-\left(-13a^5b^4+a^2b^2-5ab^5\right)$

$=4a^5b^4+7a^2b^2+2ab^5+13a^5b^4-a^2b^2+5ab^5$

$=4a^5b^4+13a^5b^4+2ab^5+5ab^5+7a^2b^2-a^2b^2$

$=17a^5b^4+7ab^5+6a^2b^2$

41. $\left(3x^4 - 14x^2\right) + \left(5x^3 - 2x^2 + x\right) - \left(8x^4 - 6x^2 + x\right)$

$= 3x^4 - 14x^2 + 5x^3 - 2x^2 + x - 8x^4 + 6x^2 - x$

$= 3x^4 - 8x^4 + 5x^3 - 14x^2 - 2x^2 + 6x^2 + x - x$

$= -5x^4 + 5x^3 - 10x^2$

43. $\left(\dfrac{1}{2}x^2 + \dfrac{2}{5}y^2\right) - \left(\dfrac{4}{3}x^2 + \dfrac{1}{3}y^2\right) + \left(\dfrac{5}{6}x^2 - \dfrac{2}{3}y^2\right)$

$= \dfrac{1}{2}x^2 + \dfrac{2}{5}y^2 - \dfrac{4}{3}x^2 - \dfrac{1}{3}y^2 + \dfrac{5}{6}x^2 - \dfrac{2}{3}y^2$

$= \dfrac{1}{2}x^2 - \dfrac{4}{3}x^2 + \dfrac{5}{6}x^2 + \dfrac{2}{5}y^2 - \dfrac{1}{3}y^2 - \dfrac{2}{3}y^2$

$= -\dfrac{3}{5}y^2$

45. $\left(3.2a^2 - 5a + 1\right) + \left(-6.2a + 8\right) - \left(2.5a^2 + 7.3a + 3\right)$

$= 3.2a^2 - 5a + 1 - 6.2a + 8 - 2.5a^2 - 7.3a - 3$

$= 3.2a^2 - 2.5a^2 - 5a - 6.2a - 7.3a + 1 + 8 - 3$

$= 0.7a^2 - 18.5a + 6$

47. $\left(4x^2 + 3x - 9\right) + \left(-8x^2 + 6x + 1\right) - \left(6x^2 - 5x + 2\right)$

$= 4x^2 + 3x - 9 - 8x^2 + 6x + 1 - 6x^2 + 5x - 2$

$= 4x^2 - 8x^2 - 6x^2 + 3x + 6x + 5x - 9 + 1 - 2$

$= -10x^2 + 14x - 10$

49. $-8x^3 + 5x^2 - x + 15 = -8(-1)^3 + 5(-1)^2 - (-1) + 15$

$= -8(-1) + 5(1) + 1 + 15$

$= 8 + 5 + 1 + 15$

$= 29$

51. $6x^4 - 3x^3 + 7x - 11 = 6(-1)^4 - 3(-1)^3 + 7(-1) - 11$

$= 6(1) - 3(-1) - 7 - 11$

$= 6 + 3 - 7 - 11$

$= -9$

53. $16x^5 + 4x^2 - 8 = 16\left(\dfrac{1}{2}\right)^5 + 4\left(\dfrac{1}{2}\right)^2 - 8$

$= 16\left(\dfrac{1}{32}\right) + 4\left(\dfrac{1}{4}\right) - 8$

$= \dfrac{1}{2} + 1 - 8$

$= -\dfrac{13}{2}$

55. $-x^3 + 1.2x^2 + 10 = -(-0.3)^3 + 1.2(-0.3)^2 + 10$

$= -(-0.027) + 1.2(0.09) + 10$

$= 0.027 + 0.108 + 10$

$= 10.135$

57. $P(-1) = -3(-1)^4 - 4(-1)^3 + (-1) - 7$

$= -3(1) - 4(-1) - 1 - 7$

$= -3 + 4 - 1 - 7$

$= -7$

59. $P(-2) = \dfrac{1}{2}(-2)^4 + 6(-2)^3 - (-2)^2 + 10(-2) - 8$

$= \dfrac{1}{2}(16) + 6(-8) - 4 - 20 - 8$

$= 8 - 48 - 4 - 20 - 8$

$= -72$

61. $4x^8$

63. Answers will vary; for example: To determine the degree of a term, add the exponents of all variables.

65. Perimeter $= \left(-2x^2 - 5x + 10\right) + \left(-2x^2 - 5x + 10\right) + \left(3x^2 - 5x + 12\right) + \left(3x^2 - 5x + 12\right)$

$= -2x^2 - 5x + 10 - 2x^2 - 5x + 10 + 3x^2 - 5x + 12 + 3x^2 - 5x + 12$

$= -2x^2 - 2x^2 + 3x^2 + 3x^2 - 5x - 5x - 5x - 5x + 10 + 10 + 12 + 12$

$= 2x^2 - 20x + 44$ units

67. Perimeter $= \left(-a^2+2a+9\right)+\left(-a^2+2a+9\right)+\left(5a^2-3a-12\right)$

$$= -a^2+2a+9-a^2+2a+9+5a^2-3a-12$$

$$= -a^2-a^2+5a^2+2a+2a-3a+9+9-12$$

$$= 3a^2+a+6 \text{ units}$$

69. Prepare We are to write the cost, revenue, and profit functions for Image Entertainment based on the given information. Then, we must evaluate the profit function for two specific values of the independent variable and explain what the outcomes would mean to Image Entertainment.

Plan Write the cost function, given the fixed costs of $175,000 and cost per T-shirt of $6. Write the revenue function, given the selling price of each T-shirt is $25. Write the profit function, given the equation $P(x)=R(x)-C(x)$. Then, evaluate the profit function for $x=9,210$ and $x=9,211$, and determine what the outcomes would mean to the company.

Process

a) $C(x)=6x+175,000$

b) $R(x)=25x$

c) $P(x)=R(x)-C(x)$

$$= 25x-\left(6x+175,000\right)$$

$$= 19x-175,000$$

d) $P(9,210)=19(9,210)-175,000$

$$= 174,990-175,000$$

$$= -10$$

e) $P(9,211)=19(9,211)-175,000$

$$= 175,009-175,000$$

$$= 9$$

The company has to sell at least 9,211 T-shirts before it sees a profit instead of a loss.

Ponder Do our answers seem reasonable? Yes, based on the profit function. It is not unreasonable for a large music company to have to sell a minimum of 9,211 T-shirts before making a profit.

71. a) $\left(10x+30\right)+\left(15x-x^2\right)+\left(x^2+4x+5\right)$

$$= 10x+30+15x-x^2+x^2+4x+5$$

$$= -x^2+x^2+15x+10x+4x+30+5$$

$$= 29x+35$$

a) The degree of the polynomial is 1. The terms are $29x$ and 35. The numerical coefficients are 29 and 35.

b) $29x+35=180$

c) $29x+35=180$

$$29x=145$$

$$x=5$$

$$\left(15x-x^2\right)=15(5)-(5)^2$$

$$= 50°$$

$$\left(10x+30\right)=10(5)+30$$

$$= 80°$$

$$\left(x^2+4x+5\right)=(5)^2+4(5)+5$$

$$= 25+20+5$$

$$= 50°$$

73. $P\left(-\dfrac{1}{2}\right)$

$$= -8\left(-\dfrac{1}{2}\right)^4-4\left(-\dfrac{1}{2}\right)^3+2\left(-\dfrac{1}{2}\right)^2-\left(-\dfrac{1}{2}\right)-5$$

$$= -8\left(\dfrac{1}{16}\right)-4\left(-\dfrac{1}{8}\right)+2\left(\dfrac{1}{4}\right)+\dfrac{1}{2}-5$$

$$= -\dfrac{1}{2}+\dfrac{1}{2}+\dfrac{1}{2}+\dfrac{1}{2}-5$$

$$= -4$$

75. $\left(\dfrac{2}{3}x^2-2.08\right)+\left(-6x^2+0.7x+\dfrac{7}{10}\right)-\left(\dfrac{5}{6}x^2+\dfrac{2}{5}x-1.5\right)$

$$= \dfrac{2}{3}x^2-2.08-6x^2+0.7x+\dfrac{7}{10}-\dfrac{5}{6}x^2-\dfrac{2}{5}x+1.5$$

$$= \dfrac{2}{3}x^2-6x^2-\dfrac{5}{6}x^2+0.7x-0.4x+0.7+1.5-2.08$$

$$= -\dfrac{37}{6}x^2+0.3x+0.12$$

5.4 Exercises

1. a, i

3. f, h, k

5. c, d

7. $-2x^3\left(3x^2y\right) = (-2)(3)x^{3+2}y$

$\qquad = -6x^5y$

9. $\left(-6a^2b^2\right)\left(-2a^3b^5\right) = (-6)(-2)a^{2+3}b^{2+5}$

$\qquad = 12a^5b^7$

11. $\left(-\dfrac{2}{3}xy^2z^3\right)\left(6x^7yz^2\right) = \left(-\dfrac{2}{3}\right)(6)x^{1+7}y^{2+1}z^{3+2}$

$\qquad = -4x^8y^3z^5$

13. $\left(1.3xy^{13}z^5\right)\left(0.4x^2y^3z^2\right) = (1.3)(0.4)x^{1+2}y^{13+3}z^{5+2}$

$\qquad = 0.52x^3y^{16}z^7$

15. $5x(x-5) = (5x)(x) - (5x)(5)$

$\qquad = 5x^{1+1} - 25x$

$\qquad = 5x^2 - 25x$

17. $-3x^2(2x+1) = \left(-3x^2\right)(2x) + \left(-3x^2\right)(1)$

$\qquad = -6x^{2+1} - 3x^2$

$\qquad = -6x^3 - 3x^2$

19. $-3s^4\left(30s^2-4\right) = \left(-3s^4\right)\left(30s^2\right) - \left(-3s^4\right)(4)$

$\qquad = -90s^{4+2} + 12s^4$

$\qquad = -90s^6 + 12s^4$

21. $10x^3\left(2x^2-3x\right) = \left(10x^3\right)\left(2x^2\right) - \left(10x^3\right)(3x)$

$\qquad = 20x^{3+2} - 30x^{3+1}$

$\qquad = 20x^5 - 30x^4$

23. $8x^2y^5\left(-xy^3-9y^2\right)$

$\qquad = \left(8x^2y^5\right)\left(-xy^3\right) - \left(8x^2y^5\right)\left(9y^2\right)$

$\qquad = -8x^{2+1}y^{5+3} - 72x^2y^{5+2}$

$\qquad = -8x^3y^8 - 72x^2y^7$

25. $-22a^2b\left(-3a^{10}b^3+5ab^6\right)$

$\qquad = \left(-22a^2b\right)\left(-3a^{10}b^3\right) + \left(-22a^2b\right)\left(5ab^6\right)$

$\qquad = 66a^{2+10}b^{1+3} - 110a^{2+1}b^{1+6}$

$\qquad = 66a^{12}b^4 - 110a^3b^7$

27. $6h^7\left(\dfrac{1}{3}h^2+\dfrac{2}{3}\right) = \left(6h^7\right)\left(\dfrac{1}{3}h^2\right) + \left(6h^7\right)\left(\dfrac{2}{3}\right)$

$\qquad = 2h^{7+2} + 4h^7$

$\qquad = 2h^9 + 4h^7$

29. $\dfrac{5}{6}r^6\left(\dfrac{1}{10}r^7s-36r^2\right)$

$\qquad = \left(\dfrac{5}{6}r^6\right)\left(\dfrac{1}{10}r^7s\right) - \left(\dfrac{5}{6}r^6\right)\left(36r^2\right)$

$\qquad = \dfrac{1}{12}r^{6+7}s - 30r^{6+2}$

$\qquad = \dfrac{1}{12}r^{13}s - 30r^8$

31. $(x+2)(x+5) = x(x+5) + 2(x+5)$

$\qquad = x^2 + 5x + 2x + 10$

$\qquad = x^2 + 7x + 10$

33. $\left(x-\dfrac{1}{2}\right)(x-4) = x(x-4) - \dfrac{1}{2}(x-4)$

$\qquad = x^2 - 4x - \dfrac{1}{2}x + 2$

$\qquad = x^2 - \dfrac{9}{2}x + 2$

35. $(x-4)(2x+1) = x(2x+1) - 4(2x+1)$

$\qquad = 2x^2 + x - 8x - 4$

$\qquad = 2x^2 - 7x - 4$

37. $(6x+11)(10x-7) = 6x(10x-7) + 11(10x-7)$

$\qquad = 60x^2 - 42x + 110x - 77$

$\qquad = 60x^2 + 68x - 77$

39. $(4x-y)(3x-2y) = 4x(3x-2y) - y(3x-2y)$

$\qquad = 12x^2 - 8xy - 3xy + 2y^2$

$\qquad = 12x^2 - 11xy + 2y^2$

41. $\left(8a+\dfrac{1}{5}b\right)(3a+10b)$

$=8a(3a+10b)+\dfrac{1}{5}b(3a+10b)$

$=24a^2+80ab+\dfrac{3}{5}ab+2b^2$

$=24a^2+\dfrac{403}{5}ab+2b^2$

43. $\left(r-\dfrac{1}{2}\right)\left(r+\dfrac{2}{3}\right)=r\left(r+\dfrac{2}{3}\right)-\dfrac{1}{2}\left(r+\dfrac{2}{3}\right)$

$=r^2+\dfrac{2}{3}r-\dfrac{1}{2}r-\dfrac{1}{3}$

$=r^2+\dfrac{1}{6}r-\dfrac{1}{3}$

45. $\left(2r^2-5s^3\right)\left(r^2+12s^3\right)$

$=2r^2\left(r^2+12s^3\right)-5s^3\left(r^2+12s^3\right)$

$=2r^4+24r^2s^3-5r^2s^3-60s^6$

$=2r^4+19r^2s^3-60s^6$

47. $10x\left(2x^2-x+5\right)$

$=(10x)\left(2x^2\right)-(10x)(x)+(10x)(5)$

$=20x^{1+2}-10x^{1+1}+50x$

$=20x^3-10x^2+50x$

49. $-8s^3\left(s^2-3s+1\right)$

$=\left(-8s^3\right)\left(s^2\right)-\left(-8s^3\right)(3s)+\left(-8s^3\right)(1)$

$=-8s^{3+2}+24s^{3+1}-8s^3$

$=-8s^5+24s^4-8s^3$

51. $-25ab^5\left(-3a^2+2ab-4a^3b^5\right)=\left(-25ab^5\right)\left(-3a^2\right)+\left(-25ab^5\right)(2ab)-\left(-25ab^5\right)\left(4a^3b^5\right)$

$=75a^{1+2}b^5-50a^{1+1}b^{5+1}+100a^{1+3}b^{5+5}$

$=75a^3b^5-50a^2b^6+100a^4b^{10}$

53. $\left(-\dfrac{2}{5}xy^3\right)\left(\dfrac{1}{2}x^5y+xy^2+\dfrac{2}{5}\right)=\left(-\dfrac{2}{5}xy^3\right)\left(\dfrac{1}{2}x^5y\right)+\left(-\dfrac{2}{5}xy^3\right)\left(xy^2\right)+\left(-\dfrac{2}{5}xy^3\right)\left(\dfrac{2}{5}\right)$

$=-\dfrac{1}{5}x^{1+5}y^{3+1}-\dfrac{2}{5}x^{1+1}y^{3+2}-\dfrac{4}{25}xy^3$

$=-\dfrac{1}{5}x^6y^4-\dfrac{2}{5}x^2y^5-\dfrac{4}{25}xy^3$

55. $(x+3)\left(x^2+x+8\right)$

$=x\left(x^2+x+8\right)+3\left(x^2+x+8\right)$

$=x^3+x^2+8x+3x^2+3x+24$

$=x^3+x^2+3x^2+8x+3x+24$

$=x^3+4x^2+11x+24$

57. $(x-1)\left(2x^2-xy+5y^2\right)$

$=x\left(2x^2-xy+5y^2\right)-1\left(2x^2-xy+5y^2\right)$

$=2x^3-x^2y+5xy^2-2x^2+xy-5y^2$

59. $(x-2)\left(3x^2-2xy+y^2\right)$

$=x\left(3x^2-2xy+y^2\right)-2\left(3x^2-2xy+y^2\right)$

$=3x^3-2x^2y+xy^2-6x^2+4xy-2y^2$

61. $(2x-y)\left(5x^2+10xy-3y^2\right)$

$=2x\left(5x^2+10xy-3y^2\right)-y\left(5x^2+10xy-3y^2\right)$

$=10x^3+20x^2y-6xy^2-5x^2y-10xy^2+3y^3$

$=10x^3+20x^2y-5x^2y-6xy^2-10xy^2+3y^3$

$=10x^3+15x^2y-16xy^2+3y^3$

63.

$$
\begin{array}{r}
x^2+2xy+y^2 \\
\times\quad x^2-3xy+2y^2 \\
\hline
2x^2y^2+4xy^3+2y^4 \\
-3x^3y-6x^2y^2-3xy^3 \\
+\quad x^4+2x^3y+x^2y^2 \\
\hline
x^4-x^3y\ -3x^2y^2\ +xy^3+2y^4
\end{array}
$$

65.

$$-2a^2 + ab - 12b^2$$
$$\times \qquad 3a^2 - 5ab + b^2$$
$$\overline{\qquad -2a^2b^2 + \quad ab^3 - 12b^4}$$
$$10a^3b - 5a^2b^2 + 60ab^3$$
$$+ \quad -6a^4 + 3a^3b - 36a^2b^2$$
$$\overline{-6a^4 + 13a^3b - 43a^2b^2 + 61ab^3 - 12b^4}$$

67. Answers will vary; for example: To multiply two monomials, multiply the coefficients, then multiply any variables with exponents using the exponent rules.

69. $(2x-5)^3$

$$= (2x-5)(2x-5)(2x-5)$$
$$= \big[(2x-5)(2x-5)\big](2x-5)$$
$$= \big[2x(2x-5)-5(2x-5)\big](2x-5)$$
$$= \big[4x^2 - 10x - 10x + 25\big](2x-5)$$
$$= \big(4x^2 - 20x + 25\big)(2x-5)$$
$$= 4x^2(2x-5) - 20x(2x-5) + 25(2x-5)$$
$$= 8x^3 - 20x^2 - 40x^2 + 100x + 50x - 125$$
$$= 8x^3 - 60x^2 + 150x - 125$$

71. Total Area = Outer Area − Inner Area

$$= \big[(x+3)(x+3)\big] - \big[x \cdot x\big]$$
$$= x(x+3) + 3(x+3) - x^2$$
$$= x^2 + 3x + 3x + 9 - x^2$$
$$= x^2 - x^2 + 3x + 3x + 9$$
$$= 6x + 9$$

73. Total Area = Outer Area − Inner Area

$$= \big[(5x+3)(2x-1)\big] - \big[4(x \cdot x)\big]$$
$$= 5x(2x-1) + 3(2x-1) - 4x^2$$
$$= 10x^2 - 5x + 6x - 3 - 4x^2$$
$$= 10x^2 - 4x^2 - 5x + 6x - 3$$
$$= 6x^2 + x - 3$$

75. Prepare We need to determine the polynomial that represents the exact area of the shaded region. We then need to determine the approximate area for $x = 8$ and $\pi \approx 3.14$. Finally, we need to give an example of a real life situation this problem could represent.

Plan To calculate the area of the shaded region, we need to subtract the area of the circular region from the area of the square. The area of a circle is given by $A = \pi r^2$ and the area of a square is given by $A = s^2$.

Process

a) Total Area = Area of Square − Area of Circle

$$= s^2 - \pi r^2$$
$$= (2x+5)^2 - \pi\left(\frac{1}{4}x\right)^2$$
$$= 4x^2 + 20x + 25 - \frac{1}{16}\pi x^2$$
$$= \frac{(64-\pi)}{16}x^2 + 20x + 25$$

b) Total Area = Area of Square − Area of Circle

$$= \frac{(64-\pi)}{16}x^2 + 20x + 25$$
$$\approx \frac{(64-3.14)}{16}(8)^2 + 20(8) + 25$$
$$= 428.44 \ \text{m}^2$$

c) Answers will vary; for example: This polynomial could be used to find the area of a deck around a circular hot tub.

Ponder Do our answers seem reasonable? Yes. The area of the shaded region is smaller than the area of the whole square, therefore, our answer seems reasonable.

77. $-\dfrac{1}{2}x^2yz^5\left(\dfrac{4}{5}x^3yz^3+\dfrac{1}{3}x^2y^2z\right)+\dfrac{3}{5}x^5y^2z^8-\dfrac{5}{6}x^4y^3z^6$

$=\left(-\dfrac{1}{2}x^2yz^5\right)\left(\dfrac{4}{5}x^3yz^3\right)+\left(-\dfrac{1}{2}x^2yz^5\right)\left(\dfrac{1}{3}x^2y^2z\right)+\dfrac{3}{5}x^5y^2z^8-\dfrac{5}{6}x^4y^3z^6$

$=-\dfrac{2}{5}x^{2+3}y^{1+1}z^{5+3}-\dfrac{1}{6}x^{2+2}y^{1+2}z^{5+1}+\dfrac{3}{5}x^5y^2z^8-\dfrac{5}{6}x^4y^3z^6$

$=-\dfrac{2}{5}x^5y^2z^8-\dfrac{1}{6}x^4y^3z^6+\dfrac{3}{5}x^5y^2z^8-\dfrac{5}{6}x^4y^3z^6$

$=-\dfrac{2}{5}x^5y^2z^8+\dfrac{3}{5}x^5y^2z^8-\dfrac{1}{6}x^4y^3z^6-\dfrac{5}{6}x^4y^3z^6$

$=\dfrac{1}{5}x^5y^2z^8-x^4y^3z^6$

79. $\left(1.2x^2-3xy+5y^2\right)\left(0.3x^2+xy+2y^2\right)$

$=1.2x^2\left(0.3x^2+xy+2y^2\right)-3xy\left(0.3x^2+xy+2y^2\right)+5y^2\left(0.3x^2+xy+2y^2\right)$

$=0.36x^4+1.2x^3y+2.4x^2y^2-0.9x^3y-3x^2y^2-6xy^3+1.5x^2y^2+5xy^3+10y^4$

$=0.36x^4+1.2x^3y-0.9x^3y+2.4x^2y^2-3x^2y^2+1.5x^2y^2-6xy^3+5xy^3+10y^4$

$=0.36x^4+0.3x^3y+0.9x^2y^2-xy^3+10y^4$

5.5 Exercises

1. A special way to multiply two binomials is to use the <u>FOIL</u> method.

3. A verbal way to help in squaring a binomial can be stated as follows?   "Take the first term in the binomial and <u>square</u> it.   Add to this <u>twice</u> the product of the two terms (within the binomial, including the signs), then <u>add</u> the square of the last term."

5. $(x+3)^2 = (x)^2 + 2(x \cdot 3) + (3)^2$
    $= x^2 + 6x + 9$
    h

7. $(x-7)^2 = (x)^2 + 2(x \cdot (-7)) + (-7)^2$
    $= x^2 - 14x + 49$
    b

9. $(x+4)(x+7) = x(x) + x(7) + 4x + 4(7)$
    $= x^2 + 7x + 4x + 28$
    $= x^2 + 11x + 28$

11. $(2x+1)(x-3) = 2x(x) + 2x(-3) + 1x + 1(-3)$
    $= 2x^2 - 6x + x - 3$
    $= 2x^2 - 5x - 3$

13. $(0.1x - 0.1y)(2x - 9y) = 0.1x(2x) + 0.1x(-9y) + (-0.1y)(2x) + (-0.1y)(-9y)$
    $= 0.2x^2 - 0.9xy - 0.2xy + 0.9y^2$
    $= 0.2x^2 - 1.1xy + 0.9y^2$

15. $(8a+b)(-3a-b)$
    $= 8a(-3a) + 8a(-b) + b(-3a) + b(-b)$
    $= -24a^2 - 8ab - 3ab - b^2$
    $= -24a^2 - 11ab - b^2$

17. $(a+b)(x-y) = a(x) + a(-y) + b(x) + b(-y)$
    $= ax - ay + bx - by$

19. $(x+h)^2 = (x+h)(x+h)$
    $= x(x) + x(h) + h(x) + h(h)$
    $= x^2 + xh + xh + h^2$
    $= x^2 + 2xh + h^2$

21. $(x^2 - 3)(4x + 15y)$
    $= x^2(4x) + x^2(15y) + (-3)(4x) + (-3)(15y)$
    $= 4x^3 + 15x^2 y - 12x - 45y$

23. $(x^3 - 2x^2)(x^2 + 3x)$
    $= x^3(x^2) + x^3(3x) + (-2x^2)(x^2) + (-2x^2)(3x)$
    $= x^5 + 3x^4 - 2x^4 - 6x^3$
    $= x^5 + x^4 - 6x^3$

25. $\left(\dfrac{2}{3}a + \dfrac{6}{7}\right)\left(\dfrac{15}{7}a - \dfrac{1}{14}\right)$
    $= \dfrac{2}{3}a\left(\dfrac{15}{7}a\right) + \dfrac{2}{3}a\left(-\dfrac{1}{14}\right) + \dfrac{6}{7}\left(\dfrac{15}{7}a\right) + \dfrac{6}{7}\left(-\dfrac{1}{14}\right)$
    $= \dfrac{10}{7}a^2 - \dfrac{1}{21}a + \dfrac{90}{49}a - \dfrac{3}{49}$
    $= \dfrac{10}{7}a^2 + \dfrac{263}{147}a - \dfrac{3}{49}$

27. $(x+4)^2 = (x)^2 + 2(x \cdot 4) + (4)^2$
    $= x^2 + 8x + 16$

29. $(y+12)^2 = (y)^2 + 2(y \cdot 12) + (12)^2$
    $= y^2 + 24y + 144$

31. $(a+4b)^2 = (a)^2 + 2(a \cdot 4b) + (4b)^2$
    $= a^2 + 8ab + 16b^2$

33. $(10a+7b)^2 = (10a)^2 + 2(10a \cdot 7b) + (7b)^2$
    $= 100a^2 + 140ab + 49b^2$

35. $(x-2)^2 = (x)^2 + 2(x \cdot (-2)) + (-2)^2$
    $= x^2 - 4x + 4$

37. $(a-10)^2 = (a)^2 + 2(a \cdot (-10)) + (-10)^2$
    $= a^2 - 20a + 100$

39. $(2x-7)^2 = (2x)^2 + 2(2x \cdot (-7)) + (-7)^2$
$$= 4x^2 - 28x + 49$$

41. $\left(\frac{1}{2}x+3\right)^2 = \left(\frac{1}{2}x\right)^2 + 2\left(\frac{1}{2}x \cdot 3\right) + (3)^2$
$$= \frac{1}{4}x^2 + 3x + 9$$

43. $\left(x+\frac{2}{3}\right)^2 = (x)^2 + 2\left(x \cdot \frac{2}{3}\right) + \left(\frac{2}{3}\right)^2$
$$= x^2 + \frac{4}{3}x + \frac{4}{9}$$

45. $\left(a-\frac{1}{6}b\right)^2 = (a)^2 + 2\left(a \cdot \left(-\frac{1}{6}b\right)\right) + \left(-\frac{1}{6}b\right)^2$
$$= a^2 - \frac{1}{3}ab + \frac{1}{36}b^2$$

47. $(3x^2+2x)^2 = (3x^2)^2 + 2(3x^2 \cdot 2x) + (2x)^2$
$$= 9x^4 + 12x^3 + 4x^2$$

49. $(2a^3 - 3b^2)^2$
$$= (2a^3)^2 + 2(2a^3 \cdot (-3b^2)) + (-3b^2)^2$$
$$= 4a^6 - 12a^3b^2 + 9b^4$$

51. $(x-10)(x+10) = (x)^2 - (10)^2$
$$= x^2 - 100$$

53. $(x+y)(x-y) = (x)^2 - (y)^2$
$$= x^2 - y^2$$

55. $(3a-b)(3a+b) = (3a)^2 - (b)^2$
$$= 9a^2 - b^2$$

57. $(9a+12b)(9a-12b) = (9a)^2 - (12b)^2$
$$= 81a^2 - 144b^2$$

59. $\left(x+\frac{1}{3}\right)\left(x-\frac{1}{3}\right) = (x)^2 - \left(\frac{1}{3}\right)^2$
$$= x^2 - \frac{1}{9}$$

61. $\left(\frac{1}{2}x+y\right)\left(\frac{1}{2}x-y\right) = \left(\frac{1}{2}x\right)^2 - (y)^2$
$$= \frac{1}{4}x^2 - y^2$$

63. $(x^2+5y)(x^2-5y) = (x^2)^2 - (5y)^2$
$$= x^4 - 25y^2$$

65. $(2x+3)^2 = (2x)^2 + 2(2x \cdot 3) + (3)^2$
$$= 4x^2 + 12x + 9$$

67. $(5x-2y)(5x+2y) = (5x)^2 - (2y^2)$
$$= 25x^2 - 4y^2$$

69. $\left(\frac{1}{2}x-\frac{1}{2}\right)^2$
$$= \left(\frac{1}{2}x\right)^2 + 2\left(\frac{1}{2}x \cdot \left(-\frac{1}{2}\right)\right) + \left(-\frac{1}{2}\right)^2$$
$$= \frac{1}{4}x^2 - \frac{1}{2}x + \frac{1}{4}$$

71. $(5a+2b)(3a+11b)$
$$= 5a(3a) + 5a(11b) + 2b(3a) + 2b(11b)$$
$$= 15a^2 + 55ab + 6ab + 22b^2$$
$$= 15a^2 + 61ab + 22b^2$$

73. $\left(\frac{2}{3}a-\frac{1}{2}b\right)\left(\frac{2}{3}a+\frac{1}{2}b\right) = \left(\frac{2}{3}a\right)^2 - \left(\frac{1}{2}b\right)^2$
$$= \frac{4}{9}a^2 - \frac{1}{4}b^2$$

75. $(6x-5y)^2 = (6x)^2 + 2(6x \cdot (-5y)) + (-5y)^2$
$$= 36x^2 - 60xy + 25y^2$$

77. $\left(\frac{1}{2}x+6\right)(4x-12)$
$$= \frac{1}{2}x(4x) + \frac{1}{2}x(-12) + 6(4x) + 6(-12)$$
$$= 2x^2 - 6x + 24x - 72$$
$$= 2x^2 + 18x - 72$$

79. $(x+0.2)^2 = (x)^2 + 2(x \cdot 0.2) + (0.2)^2$
$$= x^2 + 0.4x + 0.04$$

81. Answers will vary; for example: $(x+y)^2 \neq x^2 + y^2$ because you must account for the outer and inner terms. The correct answers is $x^2 + 2xy + y^2$.

83. Answers will vary; for example: The outer and inner terms cancel because the outer product $-12xy$ when added to the inner product $12xy$ gives 0.

85. $A = s^2$

$= (3x-4)^2$

$= (3x)^2 + 2(3x \cdot (-4)) + (-4)^2$

$= 9x^2 - 24x + 16 \text{ units}^2$

87. Prepare First we must write a polynomial that represents the total area of the window. Next, we must determine the numerical value of the area of the window. Finally, we must determine the cost of the glass for the window.

Plan Use the diagram and the formulas $A = \dfrac{1}{2}bh$ and $A = lw$ to write the polynomial. Substitute $x = 3$ into the polynomial to find the numerical value of the area. Determine the cost by multiplying the area by the price per square inch of the glass, $0.50.

Process

$$\text{Total Area} = (\text{Area of Triangle}) + (\text{Area of Rectangle})$$

$$= \frac{1}{2}bh + lw$$

$$= \frac{1}{2}(x^2 - 2x)(x+3) + (x^2 + 2x)(x^2 - 2x)$$

$$= \frac{1}{2}(x^2(x) + x^2(3) + (-2x)(x) + (-2x)(3)) + (x^2)^2 - (2x)^2$$

$$= \frac{1}{2}(x^3 + 3x^2 - 2x^2 - 6x) + x^4 - 4x^2$$

$$= \frac{1}{2}(x^3 + x^2 - 6x) + x^4 - 4x^2$$

$$= \frac{1}{2}x^3 + \frac{1}{2}x^2 - 3x + x^4 - 4x^2$$

$$= x^4 + \frac{1}{2}x^3 + \frac{1}{2}x^2 - 4x^2 - 3x$$

$$= x^4 + \frac{1}{2}x^3 - \frac{7}{2}x^2 - 3x \text{ in}^2$$

$$\text{Total Area} = x^4 + \frac{1}{2}x^3 - \frac{7}{2}x^2 - 3x$$

$$= (3)^4 + \frac{1}{2}(3)^3 - \frac{7}{2}(3)^2 - 3(3)$$

$$= 81 + \frac{27}{2} - \frac{63}{2} - 9$$

$$= 54 \text{ in}^2$$

$$\text{Total Price} = (\text{Price Per Square Inch}) \times (\text{Total Area})$$

$$= \$0.50(54)$$

$$= \$27$$

Ponder Do our answers seem reasonable? Yes. Substituting $x = 3$ into $x^2 - 2x$, we see that the base of the window is 3 inches. Substituting $x = 3$ into $x^2 + 2x$, we see that the height of the rectangular portion of the window is 15 inches. Substituting $x = 3$ into $x+3$, we see that the height of the triangular portion of the window is 6 inches. The total area of the window is $\frac{1}{2}(3)(6) + (3)(15) = 54$ square inches.

89. $\left(\dfrac{4}{7}a^2 + \dfrac{2}{3}b^3\right)^2 = \left(\dfrac{4}{7}a^2\right)^2 + 2\left(\dfrac{4}{7}a^2 \cdot \dfrac{2}{3}b^3\right) + \left(\dfrac{2}{3}b^3\right)^2$

$\qquad\qquad\qquad = \dfrac{16}{49}a^4 + \dfrac{16}{21}a^2b^3 + \dfrac{4}{9}b^6$

91. $\left(r^2s^2 - \dfrac{1}{4}\right)^2 = \left(r^2s^2\right)^2 + 2\left(r^2s^2 \cdot \left(-\dfrac{1}{4}\right)\right) + \left(-\dfrac{1}{4}\right)^2$

$\qquad\qquad\quad = r^4s^4 - \dfrac{1}{2}r^2s^2 + \dfrac{1}{16}$

93. $\left[(x+2)+5\right]\left[(x+2)-5\right] = (x+2)^2 - (5)^2$

$\qquad\qquad\qquad\qquad = (x)^2 + 2(x\cdot 2) + (2)^2 - 25$

$\qquad\qquad\qquad\qquad = x^2 + 4x + 4 - 25$

$\qquad\qquad\qquad\qquad = x^2 + 4x - 21$

95. $(1.2x - 3.4y)(0.3x^2 + 2.1y^3) = 1.2x(0.3x^2) + 1.2x(2.1y^3) + (-3.4y)(0.3x^2) + (-3.4y)(2.1y^3)$

$\qquad\qquad\qquad\qquad\qquad = 0.36x^3 + 2.52xy^3 - 1.02x^2y - 7.14y^4$

$\qquad\qquad\qquad\qquad\qquad = 0.36x^3 - 1.02x^2y + 2.52xy^3 - 7.14y^4$

97. $\left[2a+(b-2c)\right]\left[2a-(b-2c)\right] = (2a)^2 - (b-2c)^2$

$\qquad\qquad\qquad\qquad\qquad = 4a^2 - \left[(b)^2 + 2(b\cdot(-2c)) + (-2c)^2\right]$

$\qquad\qquad\qquad\qquad\qquad = 4a^2 - \left[b^2 - 4bc + 4c^2\right]$

$\qquad\qquad\qquad\qquad\qquad = 4a^2 - b^2 + 4bc - 4c^2$

5.6 Exercises

1. When performing long division, <u>divide</u>, multiply, <u>subtract</u> and bring down are the four actions that repeat until the quotient and remainder are found.

3. When dividing a polynomial by a monomial, use the <u>Distributive</u> Property to <u>divide</u> each term of the numerator by the <u>denominator</u>.

5. In the division problem $\frac{2x^2+7x-25}{2x-3} = x+5+\frac{-10}{2x-3}$, the $2x^2+7x-25$ is called the dividend, $2x-3$ is called the divisor, $x+5$ is called the <u>quotient</u>, and -10 is called the remainder.

7. When a dividend has a missing x^3 term, use 0 or $0x^3$ as a placeholder when performing long division.

9. $\dfrac{12x^3y^4z}{-4x^2yz^2} = -3x^{3-2}y^{4-1}z^{1-2}$

$= -3x^1y^3z^{-1}$

$= \dfrac{-3xy^3}{z}$

11. $25a^7b^3 \div \left(5ab^6\right) = 5a^{7-1}b^{3-6}$

$= 5a^6b^{-3}$

$= \dfrac{5a^6}{b^3}$

13. $\dfrac{12x^3+24x^2}{6x^2} = \dfrac{12x^3}{6x^2} + \dfrac{24x^2}{6x^2}$

$= 2x^{3-2} + 4x^{2-2}$

$= 2x^1 + 4x^0$

$= 2x+4$

15. $\dfrac{6b^5-24b^2+12b}{-12b} = \dfrac{6b^5}{-12b} - \dfrac{24b^2}{-12b} + \dfrac{12b}{-12b}$

$= -\dfrac{1}{2}b^{5-1} + 2b^{2-1} - b^{1-1}$

$= -\dfrac{1}{2}b^4 + 2b^1 - b^0$

$= -\dfrac{1}{2}b^4 + 2b - 1$

17. $\dfrac{28a^5b^2-21a^2b-7ab^4}{14a^2b^3}$

$= \dfrac{28a^5b^2}{14a^2b^3} - \dfrac{21a^2b}{14a^2b^3} - \dfrac{7ab^4}{14a^2b^3}$

$= 2a^{5-2}b^{2-3} - \dfrac{3}{2}a^{2-2}b^{1-3} - \dfrac{1}{2}a^{1-2}b^{4-3}$

$= 2a^3b^{-1} - \dfrac{3}{2}a^0b^{-2} - \dfrac{1}{2}a^{-1}b^1$

$= \dfrac{2a^3}{b} - \dfrac{3}{2b^2} - \dfrac{b}{2a}$

19. $\dfrac{-12x^4-30x^3-40x^2+22x+75}{5x^2}$

$= \dfrac{-12x^4}{5x^2} - \dfrac{30x^3}{5x^2} - \dfrac{40x^2}{5x^2} + \dfrac{22x}{5x^2} + \dfrac{75}{5x^2}$

$= -\dfrac{12}{5}x^{4-2} - 6x^{3-2} - 8x^{2-2} + \dfrac{22}{5}x^{1-2} + \dfrac{15}{x^2}$

$= -\dfrac{12}{5}x^2 - 6x^1 - 8x^0 + \dfrac{22}{5}x^{-1} + \dfrac{15}{x^2}$

$= -\dfrac{12}{5}x^2 - 6x + \dfrac{22}{5x} + \dfrac{15}{x^2} - 8$

21. $\left(x^2+7x+10\right) \div \left(x+5\right) = x+2$

$$\begin{array}{r} x+2 \\ x+5 \overline{\smash{\big)}\ x^2+7x+10} \\ \underline{-\left(x^2+5x\right)} \\ 2x+10 \\ \underline{-\left(2x+10\right)} \\ 0 \end{array}$$

23. $\left(6x^2+x-12\right) \div \left(3x-4\right) = 2x+3$

$$\begin{array}{r} 2x+3 \\ 3x-4 \overline{\smash{\big)}\ 6x^2+x-12} \\ \underline{-\left(6x^2-8x\right)} \\ 9x-12 \\ \underline{-\left(9x-12\right)} \\ 0 \end{array}$$

25. $\left(2x^2 + x - 11\right) \div \left(x - 3\right) = 2x + 7 + \dfrac{10}{x-3}$

$$
\begin{array}{r}
2x+7 \\
x-3 \overline{\smash{\big)}\ 2x^2 + x - 11} \\
\underline{-\left(2x^2 - 6x\right)} \\
7x - 11 \\
\underline{-\left(7x - 21\right)} \\
10
\end{array}
$$

27. $\left(x^3 - 1\right) \div \left(x - 1\right) = x^2 + x + 1$

$$
\begin{array}{r}
x^2 + x + 1 \\
x-1 \overline{\smash{\big)}\ x^3 + 0x^2 + 0x - 1} \\
\underline{-\left(x^3 - x^2\right)} \\
x^2 + 0x \\
\underline{-\left(x^2 - x\right)} \\
x - 1 \\
\underline{-\left(x - 1\right)} \\
0
\end{array}
$$

29. $\left(2x^3 + 7x^2 - 10x - 47\right) \div \left(2x + 7\right) = x^2 - 5 + \dfrac{-12}{2x+7}$

$$
\begin{array}{r}
x^2 - 5 \\
2x+7 \overline{\smash{\big)}\ 2x^3 + 7x^2 - 10x - 47} \\
\underline{-\left(2x^3 + 7x^2\right)} \\
-10x - 47 \\
\underline{-\left(-10x - 35\right)} \\
-12
\end{array}
$$

31. $\left(-65a + 6a^2 + 50\right) \div \left(6a - 6\right) = a - 10$

$$
\begin{array}{r}
a - 10 \\
6a-6 \overline{\smash{\big)}\ 6a^2 - 65a + 50} \\
\underline{-\left(6a^2 - 5a\right)} \\
-60a + 50 \\
\underline{-\left(-60a + 50\right)} \\
0
\end{array}
$$

33. $\left(5y^2 + 2y^3 + 47 - 11y\right) \div \left(2y - 1\right)$

$= y^2 + 3y - 4 + \dfrac{43}{2y-1}$

$$
\begin{array}{r}
y^2 + 3y - 4 \\
2y-1 \overline{\smash{\big)}\ 2y^3 + 5y^2 - 11y + 47} \\
\underline{-\left(2y^3 - y^2\right)} \\
6y^2 - 11y \\
\underline{-\left(6y^2 - 3y\right)} \\
-8y + 47 \\
\underline{-\left(-8y + 4\right)} \\
43
\end{array}
$$

35. $\left(8b^3 - 1\right) \div \left(2b - 1\right) = 4b^2 + 2b + 1$

$$
\begin{array}{r}
4b^2 + 2b + 1 \\
2b-1 \overline{\smash{\big)}\ 8b^3 + 0b^2 + 0b - 1} \\
\underline{-\left(8b^3 - 4b^2\right)} \\
4b^2 + 0b \\
\underline{-\left(4b^2 - 2b\right)} \\
2b - 1 \\
\underline{-\left(2b - 1\right)} \\
0
\end{array}
$$

37. $\left(64x^3 - 85\right) \div \left(4x + 3\right) = 16x^2 - 12x + 9 + \dfrac{-112}{4x+3}$

$$
\begin{array}{r}
16x^2 - 12x + 9 \\
4x+3 \overline{\smash{\big)}\ 64x^3 + 0x^2 + 0x - 85} \\
\underline{-\left(64x^3 + 48x^2\right)} \\
-48x^2 + 0x \\
\underline{-\left(-48x^2 - 36x\right)} \\
36x - 85 \\
\underline{-\left(36x + 27\right)} \\
-112
\end{array}
$$

39. $\dfrac{4x^3 + x - 7}{2x - 7} = 2x^2 + 7x + 25 + \dfrac{168}{2x - 7}$

$$
\begin{array}{r}
2x^2 + 7x + 25 \\
2x-7 \overline{)4x^3 + 0x^2 + x - 7} \\
\underline{-\left(4x^3 - 14x^2\right)} \\
14x^2 + x \\
\underline{-\left(14x^2 - 49x\right)} \\
50x - 7 \\
\underline{-\left(50x - 175\right)} \\
168
\end{array}
$$

41. $\dfrac{14a^4 - a^3 + 11a^2 + 20a}{7a + 3} = 2a^3 - a^2 + 2a + 2 + \dfrac{-6}{7a + 3}$

$$
\begin{array}{r}
2a^3 - a^2 + 2a + 2 \\
7a+3 \overline{)14a^4 - a^3 + 11a^2 + 20a + 0} \\
\underline{-\left(14a^4 + 6a^3\right)} \\
-7a^3 + 11a^2 \\
\underline{-\left(-7a^3 - 3a^2\right)} \\
14a^2 + 20a \\
\underline{-\left(14a^2 + 6a\right)} \\
14a + 0 \\
\underline{-\left(14a + 6\right)} \\
-6
\end{array}
$$

43. $\dfrac{-6x^3 + 23x^2 - 36x + 35}{2x^2 - 3x + 5} = -3x + 7$

$$
\begin{array}{r}
-3x + 7 \\
2x^2 - 3x + 5 \overline{)-6x^3 + 23x^2 - 36x + 35} \\
\underline{-\left(-6x^3 + 9x^2 - 15x\right)} \\
14x^2 - 21x + 35 \\
\underline{-\left(14x^2 - 21x + 35\right)} \\
0
\end{array}
$$

45. $\dfrac{15y^4 - 41y^2 - 18}{5y^2 - 2} = 3y^2 - 7 + \dfrac{-32}{5y^2 - 2}$

$$
\begin{array}{r}
3y^2 - 7 \\
5y^2 + 0y - 2 \overline{)15y^4 + 0y^3 - 41y^2 + 0y - 18} \\
\underline{-\left(15y^4 + 0y^3 - 6y^2\right)} \\
-35y^2 + 0y - 18 \\
\underline{-\left(-35y^2 + 0y + 14\right)} \\
-32
\end{array}
$$

47. $\left(27a^3 + 125b^3\right) \div \left(3a + 5b\right) = 9a^2 - 15ab + 25b^2$

$$
\begin{array}{r}
9a^2 - 15ab + 25b^2 \\
3a+5b \overline{)27a^3 + 0a^2b + 0ab^2 + 125b^3} \\
\underline{-\left(27a^3 + 45a^2b\right)} \\
-45a^2b + 0ab^2 \\
\underline{-\left(-45a^2b - 75ab^2\right)} \\
75ab^2 + 125b^3 \\
\underline{-\left(75ab^2 + 125b^3\right)} \\
0
\end{array}
$$

49. $\dfrac{3a^3 - 10a^2 - 46a - 35}{a^2 - 5a - 7} = 3a + 5$

$$
\begin{array}{r}
3a + 5 \\
a^2 - 5a - 7 \overline{)3a^3 - 10a^2 - 46a - 35} \\
\underline{-\left(3a^3 - 15a^2 - 21a\right)} \\
5a^2 - 25a - 35 \\
\underline{-\left(5a^2 - 25a - 35\right)} \\
0
\end{array}
$$

51. $\dfrac{2x^4+x^3+6x-17}{2x^2+3x-1}=x^2-x+2+\dfrac{-x-15}{2x^2+3x-1}$

$$2x^2+3x-1\overline{)2x^4+x^3+0x^2+6x-17}$$

with quotient x^2-x+2

$$\underline{-\left(2x^4+3x^3-x^2\right)}$$
$$-2x^3+x^2+6x$$
$$\underline{-\left(-2x^3-3x^2+x\right)}$$
$$4x^2+5x-17$$
$$\underline{-\left(4x^2+6x-2\right)}$$
$$-x-15$$

53. $\dfrac{25x^4-9}{5x^2-3}=5x^2+3$

$$5x^2+0x-3\overline{)25x^4+0x^3+0x^2+0x-9}$$

with quotient $5x^2+3$

$$\underline{-\left(25x^4+0x^3-15x^2\right)}$$
$$15x^2+0x-9$$
$$\underline{-\left(15x^2+0x-9\right)}$$
$$0$$

55. This statement is incorrect because the remainder $\frac{-11}{10x+7}$ should be added to the quotient $6x-5$. The correct answer is $6x-5-\frac{11}{10x-7}$.

57. The error results from incorrectly dividing $-\frac{5b}{5b^3}$. The correct answer is $-4b-2b^3+\frac{1}{b^2}$.

59. Answers will vary; for example: It is important to write the dividend and divisor in descending order to keep work organized when subtracting terms from the dividend.

61. Height $=\dfrac{\text{Total Area}}{\text{Base}}=4x-18$ units

$$\tfrac{1}{2}x+5\overline{)2x^2+11x-90}$$

with quotient $4x-18$

$$\underline{-\left(2x^2+20x\right)}$$
$$-9x-90$$
$$\underline{-(-9x-90)}$$
$$0$$

63. $D=RT$

$$\frac{D}{R}=\frac{RT}{R}$$

$$T=\frac{D}{R}$$

$$T=\frac{3x^2-19x-40}{3x+5}=x-8$$

$$3x+5\overline{)3x^2-19x-40}$$

with quotient $x-8$

$$\underline{-\left(3x^2+5x\right)}$$
$$24x-40$$
$$\underline{-(24x-40)}$$
$$0$$

65. Prepare Determine the average cost function for Image Entertainment, and then find the average cost of producing 500 boxed sets of CD's per week.

Plan Find the average cost function $\overline{C}(x)=\frac{C(x)}{x}$ by dividing the cost function by x, and then, using substitution, let $x=500$ and determine the average cost of producing 500 boxed sets of CD's per week.

Process Average Cost Function:

$$\overline{C}(x)=\frac{C(x)}{x}$$

$$\overline{C}(x)=\frac{0.003x^3-0.9x^2+90x+3{,}000}{x}$$

$$\overline{C}(x)=\frac{0.003x^3}{x}-\frac{0.9x^2}{x}+\frac{90x}{x}+\frac{3{,}000}{x}$$

$$\overline{C}(x)=0.003x^2-0.9x+90+\frac{3{,}000}{x}$$

Average Cost of Producing 500 Units

$$\overline{C}(500)=0.003(500)^2-0.9(500)+90+\frac{3{,}000}{500}$$

$$=0.003(250{,}000)-450+90+6$$

$$=750-450+90+6$$

$$=396$$

The average cost of producing 500 boxed sets of CD's is $396.

Ponder Does our answer seem reasonable? This is a hard question to answer, unless you are comfortable working with cost functions. Therefore, let's check our answer mathematically by determining the cost for producing 500 units and then dividing by 500 to determine the average cost.

$$C(500) = 0.003(500)^3 - 0.9(500)^2 + 90(500) + 3,000$$
$$= 198,000$$

Therefore, the average cost to produce 500 units is given by:

$$\overline{C}(500) = \frac{C(500)}{500}$$
$$= \frac{198,000}{500}$$
$$= 396$$

67. $A = \dfrac{1}{2}h(a+b)$

$h = \dfrac{2A}{a+b}$

$h = \dfrac{2x^3 + 6x^2 + 2x - 10}{x^2 + 4x + 5}$

$$
\begin{array}{r}
2x - 2 \\
x^2+4x+5 \overline{\smash{)}\ 2x^3 + 6x^2 + 2x - 10} \\
\underline{-\left(2x^3 + 8x^2 + 10x\right)} \\
-2x^2 - 8x - 10 \\
\underline{-\left(-2x^2 - 8x - 10\right)} \\
0
\end{array}
$$

69. $\dfrac{8x^3 + 3x^5 - x^4 + 92 + 8x - 14x^2}{3x^2 + 2 - x}$

$= x^3 + 2x - 4 + \dfrac{100}{3x^2 - x + 2}$

$$
\begin{array}{r}
x^3 + 2x - 4 \\
3x^2-x+2 \overline{\smash{)}\ 3x^5 - x^4 + 8x^3 - 14x^2 + 8x + 92} \\
\underline{-\left(3x^5 - x^4 + 2x^3\right)} \\
6x^3 - 14x^2 + 8x \\
\underline{-\left(6x^3 - 2x^2 + 4x\right)} \\
-12x^2 + 4x + 92 \\
\underline{-\left(-12x^2 + 4x - 8\right)} \\
100
\end{array}
$$

71. $\left(18x^2 - 81xy + 55y^2\right) \div (3x - 11y) = 6x - 5y$

$$
\begin{array}{r}
6x - 5y \\
3x-11y \overline{\smash{)}\ 18x^2 - 81xy + 55y^2} \\
\underline{-\left(18x^2 - 66xy\right)} \\
-15xy + 55y^2 \\
\underline{-\left(-15xy + 55y^2\right)} \\
0
\end{array}
$$

Chapter 5 Review Problem Set

1. $2^{-3} = \dfrac{1}{2^3}$

$= \dfrac{1}{8}$

2. $\left(\dfrac{5}{2}\right)^{-1} = \left(\dfrac{2}{5}\right)^1$

$= \dfrac{2}{5}$

3. $-4^{-2} = -1 \cdot 4^{-2}$

$= -1 \cdot \dfrac{1}{4^2}$

$= -1 \cdot \dfrac{1}{16}$

$= \dfrac{-1}{16}$

4. $(-3)^{-4} = \dfrac{1}{(-3)^4}$

$= \dfrac{1}{81}$

5. $y^6 \cdot y^{-10} \cdot y^{-8} = y^{6+(-10)+(-8)}$

$= y^{-12}$

$= \dfrac{1}{y^{12}}$

6. $b \cdot b^5 \cdot b^7 = b^{1+5+7}$

$= b^{13}$

7. $5^{-3} \cdot 5 = 5^{-3+1}$

$= 5^{-2}$

$= \dfrac{1}{5^2}$

$= \dfrac{1}{25}$

8. $8^6 \cdot 8^{-6} = 8^{6+(-6)}$

$= 8^0$

$= 1$

9. $\left(x^4\right)^3 = x^{4(3)}$

$= x^{12}$

10. $\left(7^{-1}\right)^{-2} = 7^{(-1)(-2)}$

$= 7^2$

$= 49$

11. $\left(12^{-2}\right)^{-1} = 12^{(-2)(-1)}$

$= 12^2$

$= 144$

12. $\left[(-2)^2\right]^{-3} = (-2)^{2(-3)}$

$= (-2)^{-6}$

$= \dfrac{1}{(-2)^6}$

$= \dfrac{1}{64}$

13. $\left(6x^5\right)^2 = 6^2\left(x^5\right)^2$

$= 36x^{10}$

14. $\left(4a^{-9}\right)^3 = 4^3\left(a^{-9}\right)^3$

$= 64a^{-27}$

$= 64 \cdot \dfrac{1}{a^{27}}$

$= \dfrac{64}{a^{27}}$

15. $\left(-4a^{-8}bc^5\right)^2 = (-4)^2\left(a^{-8}\right)^2\left(b^1\right)^2\left(c^5\right)^2$

$= 16a^{-16}b^2c^{10}$

$= 16 \cdot \dfrac{1}{a^{16}} \cdot b^2c^{10}$

$= \dfrac{16b^2c^{10}}{a^{16}}$

16. $\left(10x^5yz^2\right)^{-2} = 10^{-2}\left(x^5\right)^{-2}\left(y^1\right)^{-2}\left(z^2\right)^{-2}$

$= 10^{-2}x^{-10}y^{-2}z^{-4}$

$= \dfrac{1}{10^2} \cdot \dfrac{1}{x^{10}} \cdot \dfrac{1}{y^2} \cdot \dfrac{1}{z^4}$

$= \dfrac{1}{100x^{10}y^2z^4}$

17. $\dfrac{2^4}{2^{-1}} = 2^{4-(-1)}$

$\qquad = 2^5$

$\qquad = 32$

18. $\dfrac{8^5 x^6}{8^3 x^{-3}} = 8^{5-3} x^{6-(-3)}$

$\qquad = 8^2 x^9$

$\qquad = 64 x^9$

19. $\dfrac{-7x^{-5}}{x^{-2}} = -7x^{-5-(-2)}$

$\qquad = -7x^{-3}$

$\qquad = -7 \cdot \dfrac{1}{x^3}$

$\qquad = -\dfrac{7}{x^3}$

20. $\dfrac{-14b^{-8}}{b^{-2}} = -14b^{-8-(-2)}$

$\qquad = -14b^{-6}$

$\qquad = -14 \cdot \dfrac{1}{b^6}$

$\qquad = -\dfrac{14}{b^6}$

21. $\left(\dfrac{7x^5}{8x}\right)^2 = \dfrac{\left(7x^5\right)^2}{(8x)^2}$

$\qquad = \dfrac{7^2 \left(x^5\right)^2}{8^2 x^2}$

$\qquad = \dfrac{49 x^{10}}{64 x^2}$

$\qquad = \dfrac{49}{64} x^{10-2}$

$\qquad = \dfrac{49}{64} x^8$

22. $\left(\dfrac{9a^8}{5a^{-2}}\right)^2 = \dfrac{\left(9a^8\right)^2}{\left(5a^{-2}\right)^2}$

$\qquad = \dfrac{9^2 \left(a^8\right)^2}{5^2 \left(a^{-2}\right)^2}$

$\qquad = \dfrac{81 a^{16}}{25 a^{-4}}$

$\qquad = \dfrac{81}{25} a^{16-(-4)}$

$\qquad = \dfrac{81}{25} a^{20}$

23. $\left(\dfrac{6xy^{-5}}{x^4 y^2 z}\right)^2 = \dfrac{\left(6xy^{-5}\right)^2}{\left(x^4 y^2 z\right)^2}$

$\qquad = \dfrac{6^2 x^2 \left(y^{-5}\right)^2}{\left(x^4\right)^2 \left(y^2\right)^2 z^2}$

$\qquad = \dfrac{36 x^2 y^{-10}}{x^8 y^4 z^2}$

$\qquad = 36 x^{2-8} y^{-10-4} z^{-2}$

$\qquad = 36 x^{-6} y^{-14} z^{-2}$

$\qquad = \dfrac{36}{x^6 y^{14} z^2}$

24. $\left(\dfrac{a^{12} bc^{-2}}{5a^7 b^{-4}}\right)^3 = \dfrac{\left(a^{12} bc^{-2}\right)^3}{\left(5a^7 b^{-4}\right)^3}$

$\qquad = \dfrac{\left(a^{12}\right)^3 b^3 \left(c^{-2}\right)^3}{5^3 \left(a^7\right)^3 \left(b^{-4}\right)^3}$

$\qquad = \dfrac{a^{36} b^3 c^{-6}}{125 a^{21} b^{-12}}$

$\qquad = \dfrac{1}{125} a^{36-21} b^{3-(-12)} c^{-6}$

$\qquad = \dfrac{1}{125} a^{15} b^{15} c^{-6}$

$\qquad = \dfrac{a^{15} b^{15}}{125 c^6}$

25. $\left(\dfrac{6a^{-13}}{13b^{-4}}\right) = \dfrac{6b^4}{13a^{13}}$

26. $\left(\dfrac{-14x^{-3}}{5y^{-10}}\right) = -\dfrac{14y^{10}}{5x^3}$

27. $\left(\dfrac{7^{-2}x^5y^{-3}}{a^{-4}}\right) = \dfrac{a^4x^5}{7^2y^3}$

$\qquad = \dfrac{a^4x^5}{49y^3}$

28. $\left(\dfrac{a^{-5}b^0}{(-2)^{-3}c^7}\right) = \dfrac{(-2)^3}{a^5c^7}$

$\qquad = -\dfrac{8}{a^5c^7}$

29. $\left(-4a^8bc^{-3}\right)\left(\dfrac{1}{2}ab^6c^{-5}\right)^3$

$= \left(-4a^8bc^{-3}\right)\left(\dfrac{1}{2}\right)^3 a^3\left(b^6\right)^3\left(c^{-5}\right)^3$

$= \left(-4a^8bc^{-3}\right)\dfrac{1}{8}a^3b^{18}c^{-15}$

$= -\dfrac{1}{2}a^{8+3}b^{1+18}c^{-3+(-15)}$

$= -\dfrac{1}{2}a^{11}b^{19}c^{-18}$

$= -\dfrac{a^{11}b^{19}}{2c^{18}}$

30. $\left(\dfrac{2}{3}x^0y^{-4}z^7\right)\left(6x^5y^2z^{-3}\right)^2$

$= \left(\dfrac{2}{3}x^0y^{-4}z^7\right)(6)^2\left(x^5\right)^2\left(y^2\right)^2\left(z^{-3}\right)^2$

$= \left(\dfrac{2}{3}x^0y^{-4}z^7\right)36x^{10}y^4z^{-6}$

$= 24x^{0+10}y^{-4+4}z^{7+(-6)}$

$= 24x^{10}y^0z^1$

$= 24x^{10}z$

31. $\left(\dfrac{14x^5y^0z^{-1}}{6x^{-9}y^4z^8}\right)^{-2} = \left(\dfrac{\overset{7}{\cancel{14}}}{\underset{3}{\cancel{6}}}x^{5-(-9)}y^{0-4}z^{-1-8}\right)^{-2}$

$= \left(\dfrac{7}{3}x^{14}y^{-4}z^{-9}\right)^{-2}$

$= \left(\dfrac{7}{3}\right)^{-2}\left(x^{14}\right)^{-2}\left(y^{-4}\right)^{-2}\left(z^{-9}\right)^{-2}$

$= \left(\dfrac{3}{7}\right)^2 x^{-28}y^8z^{18}$

$= \dfrac{9y^8z^{18}}{49x^{28}}$

32. $\left(\dfrac{-10ab^{-6}c^4}{15a^{-5}b^{-2}c^{-1}}\right)^{-3} = \left(-\dfrac{\overset{2}{\cancel{10}}}{\underset{3}{\cancel{15}}}a^{1-(-5)}b^{-6-(-2)}c^{4-(-1)}\right)^{-3}$

$= \left(-\dfrac{2}{3}a^6b^{-4}c^5\right)^{-3}$

$= \left(-\dfrac{2}{3}\right)^{-3}\left(a^6\right)^{-3}\left(b^{-4}\right)^{-3}\left(c^5\right)^{-3}$

$= \left(-\dfrac{3}{2}\right)^3 a^{-18}b^{12}c^{-15}$

$= -\dfrac{27b^{12}}{8a^{18}c^{15}}$

33. Prepare Using the given compound interest formula and the information regarding Keisha, we must determine how much money will be in her savings account after one year.

Plan For the compound interest formula, determine the values for P, r, n, and t, and then substitute them into the formula. Evaluate the formula to find the accumulated value A.

Process The principal amount to be invested is $P = \$200$. The simple annual interest rate is $r = 4\% = 0.04$. The interest is compounded quarterly, which means that $n = 4$. The time is $t = 1$ year.

$$A = P\left(1 + \dfrac{r}{n}\right)^{nt}$$

$$= (200)\left(1 + \dfrac{0.04}{4}\right)^{4(1)}$$

$$= (200)(1.01)^4$$

$$\approx 208.12$$

Keisha will have \$208.12 in the savings account after one year.

Ponder Does our answer seem reasonable? Yes, because simple interest of 4% on $200 for one year would be $8 using the simple interest formula $I = Prt$. Therefore, Keisha should make more if the investment is compounded quarterly, instead of just once.

34. Prepare Using the given compound interest formula and the information regarding Marvin, we must determine how much money he will owe at the end of the year.

Plan For the compound interest formula, determine the values for P, r, n, and t, and then substitute them into the formula. Evaluate the formula to find the accumulated value A.

Process The principal amount to be borrowed is $P = \$1,000$. The simple annual interest rate is $r = 12\% = 0.12$. The interest is compounded semi-annually, which means that $n = 2$. The time is $t = 1$ year.

$$A = P\left(1 + \frac{r}{n}\right)^{nt}$$

$$= (1,000)\left(1 + \frac{0.12}{2}\right)^{2(1)}$$

$$= (1,000)(1.06)^2$$

$$= 1,123.60$$

Marvin will owe a total of $1,123.60 after one year.

Ponder Does our answer seem reasonable? Yes, because simple interest of 12% on $1,000 for one year would be $120 using the simple interest formula $I = Prt$. Therefore, Marvin should owe more if the amount borrowed is compounded semi-annually, instead of just once.

35. no; $6.85(10^1)$

36. yes

37. no; $1.4(10^4)$

38. no; $6.6(10^{-4})$

39. $4,400,000 = 4.4(10^6)$

40. $18,460,000 = 1.846(10^7)$

41. $0.000056 = 5.6(10^{-5})$

42. $0.00111 = 1.11(10^{-3})$

43. $1.8(10^5) = 180,000$

44. $6.6(10^4) = 66,000$

45. $7.1(10^{-6}) = 0.0000071$

46. $2.63(10^{-2}) = 0.0263$

47. $8(10^3) \cdot 6(10^{-5}) = 48(10^{-2})$

$$= 4.8(10^1)(10^{-2})$$

$$= 4.8(10^{-1}) \qquad \text{Scientific Notation}$$

$$= 0.48 \qquad \text{Standard Notation}$$

48. $\dfrac{16(10^8)}{8(10^{-2})} = 2(10^{10}) \qquad \text{Scientific Notation}$

$$= 20,000,000,000 \quad \text{Standard Notation}$$

49. $(18,400,000)(0.0003)$

$$= 1.84(10^7) \cdot 3(10^{-4})$$

$$= 5.52(10^3) \qquad \text{Scientific Notation}$$

$$= 5,520 \qquad \text{Standard Noation}$$

50. $\dfrac{(12,000)(4,000)}{0.0003}$

$$= \frac{1.2(10^4) \cdot 4(10^3)}{3(10^{-4})}$$

$$= \frac{4.8(10^7)}{3(10^{-4})}$$

$$= 1.6(10^{11}) \qquad \text{Scientific Notation}$$

$$= 160,000,000,000 \quad \text{Standard Noation}$$

51. $\dfrac{(1,200)(24,000)}{(0.0003)(0.003)}$

$= \dfrac{1.2(10^3) \cdot 2.4(10^4)}{3(10^{-4}) \cdot 3(10^{-3})}$

$= \dfrac{2.88(10^7)}{9(10^{-7})}$

$= 0.32(10^{14})$

$= 3.2(10^{-1})(10^{14})$

$= 3.2(10^{13})$ Scientific Notation

$= 32,000,000,000,000$ Standard Noation

52. $(4,020,000)(14,000,000)$

$= 4.02(10^6) \cdot 1.4(10^7)$

$= 5.628(10^{13})$ Scientific Notation

$= 56,280,000,000,000$ Standard Noation

53. $2.59(10^4) \cdot 3.0(10^2)$

$= 7.77(10^6)$ Scientific Notation

$= 7,770,000$ Standard Notation

54. $A = \dfrac{1}{2}bh$

$= \dfrac{1}{2} \cdot 4.31(10^5) \cdot 2(10^3)$

$= 4.31(10^8) \ \text{ft}^2$ Scientific Notation

$= 431,000,000 \ \text{ft}^2$ Standard Noation

55. The polynomial is a trinomial with degree 5.

56. $-3y^7$

57. $(5x^4 - 3x^3 - x^2) + (-9x^4 + 3x^3 - 6x^2 + 5)$

$= 5x^4 - 3x^3 - x^2 - 9x^4 + 3x^3 - 6x^2 + 5$

$= 5x^4 - 9x^4 - 3x^3 + 3x^3 - x^2 - 6x^2 + 5$

$= -4x^4 - 7x^2 + 5$

58. $(6x^4 + 4xy - y^4) + (-7x^5 + 8y^4)$

$= 6x^4 + 4xy - y^4 - 7x^5 + 8y^4$

$= -7x^5 + 6x^4 + 4xy - y^4 + 8y^4$

$= -7x^5 + 6x^4 + 4xy + 7y^4$

59. $(x^2 - y^2) + (x^2 - 3x - y^2)$

$= x^2 - y^2 + x^2 - 3x - y^2$

$= x^2 + x^2 - 3x - y^2 - y^2$

$= 2x^2 - 3x - 2y^2$

60. $(-8x^2 - 10xy + y^2 - 2) + (6x^2 - 10xy + 5y^2)$

$= -8x^2 - 10xy + y^2 - 2 + 6x^2 - 10xy + 5y^2$

$= -8x^2 + 6x^2 - 10xy - 10xy + 5y^2 + y^2 - 2$

$= -2x^2 - 20xy + 6y^2 - 2$

61. $(12a^3 - 5a^2 + a - 15) - (2a^3 - 8a^2 - 4a + 7)$

$= 12a^3 - 5a^2 + a - 15 - 2a^3 + 8a^2 + 4a - 7$

$= 12a^3 - 2a^3 - 5a^2 + 8a^2 + a + 4a - 15 - 7$

$= 10a^3 + 3a^2 + 5a - 22$

62. $(2x^2y + 5xy - y^2) - (8x^2y - xy - 5y^2)$

$= 2x^2y + 5xy - y^2 - 8x^2y + xy + 5y^2$

$= 2x^2y - 8x^2y + 5xy + xy + 5y^2 - y^2$

$= -6x^2y + 6xy + 4y^2$

63. $\left(\dfrac{2}{3}x^2 + \dfrac{1}{5}x + \dfrac{5}{6}\right) - \left(\dfrac{1}{2}x^2 - \dfrac{2}{3}x + \dfrac{1}{3}\right)$

$= \dfrac{2}{3}x^2 + \dfrac{1}{5}x + \dfrac{5}{6} - \dfrac{1}{2}x^2 + \dfrac{2}{3}x - \dfrac{1}{3}$

$= \dfrac{2}{3}x^2 - \dfrac{1}{2}x^2 + \dfrac{1}{5}x + \dfrac{2}{3}x + \dfrac{5}{6} - \dfrac{1}{3}$

$= \dfrac{1}{6}x^2 + \dfrac{13}{15}x + \dfrac{1}{2}$

64. $(15.1y^3 + 6.8y^2 - 9.4) - (8.2y^3 - 5.17y^2 + 5.5y - 3.4)$

$= 15.1y^3 + 6.8y^2 - 9.4 - 8.2y^3 + 5.17y^2 - 5.5y + 3.4$

$= 15.1y^3 - 8.2y^3 + 6.8y^2 + 5.17y^2 - 5.5y - 9.4 + 3.4$

$= 6.9y^3 + 11.97y^2 - 5.5y - 6$

65. $-14y^3 + 3y^2 - 4y + 5$

$= -14(-1)^3 + 3(-1)^2 - 4(-1) + 5$

$= -14(-1) + 3(1) + 4 + 5$

$= 14 + 3 + 4 + 5$

$= 26$

66. $P(-3) = 2(-3)^3 - (-3)^2 + 5(-3) + 7$

$\qquad = 2(-27) - 9 - 15 + 7$

$\qquad = -54 - 9 - 15 + 7$

$\qquad = -71$

67. Perimeter $= a + b + c$

$\qquad = (5x^2 - 7) + (-3x^2 + 10x + 30) + (-x^2 + 8x - 5)$

$\qquad = 5x^2 - 7 - 3x^2 + 10x + 30 - x^2 + 8x - 5$

$\qquad = 5x^2 - 3x^2 - x^2 + 10x + 8x + 30 - 5 - 7$

$\qquad = x^2 + 18x + 18$

68. Perimeter $= (6x^2 - 4x + 8) + \left(\dfrac{1}{2}x^2 + 3x + 4\right) + \left(\dfrac{1}{2}x^2 + 3x + 4\right) + (5x)$

$\qquad = 6x^2 - 4x + 8 + \dfrac{1}{2}x^2 + 3x + 4 + \dfrac{1}{2}x^2 + 3x + 4 + 5x$

$\qquad = 6x^2 + \dfrac{1}{2}x^2 + \dfrac{1}{2}x^2 - 4x + 3x + 3x + 5x + 8 + 4 + 4$

$\qquad = 7x^2 + 7x + 16$

69. $(-3x^2 y^5)(x^3 y) = -3x^{2+3} y^{5+1}$

$\qquad = -3x^5 y^6$

70. $\dfrac{2}{3} x^2 y (9x^6 y^5) = \left(\dfrac{2}{3}\right)(9) x^{2+6} y^{1+5}$

$\qquad = 6x^8 y^6$

71. $-6a^2 b^3 (4ab^5 + 5b - 2)$

$\qquad = (-6a^2 b^3)(4ab^5) + (-6a^2 b^3)(5b) - (-6a^2 b^3)(2)$

$\qquad = -24a^{2+1} b^{3+5} - 30a^2 b^{3+1} + 12a^2 b^3$

$\qquad = -24a^3 b^8 - 30a^2 b^4 + 12a^2 b^3$

72. $1.5a^2 (3a^5 + 4.2a^2)$

$\qquad = (1.5a^2)(3a^5) + (1.5a^2)(4.2a^2)$

$\qquad = 4.5a^{2+5} + 6.3a^{2+2}$

$\qquad = 4.5a^7 + 6.3a^4$

73. $(x+5)(x-3) = x(x-3) + 5(x-3)$

$\qquad = x^2 - 3x + 5x - 15$

$\qquad = x^2 + 2x - 15$

74. $(3x - y)(2x + 9) = 3x(2x+9) - y(2x+9)$

$\qquad = 6x^2 + 27x - 2xy - 9y$

75. $(x+2)(x^2 - x + 1) = x(x^2 - x + 1) + 2(x^2 - x + 1)$

$\qquad = x^3 - x^2 + x + 2x^2 - 2x + 2$

$\qquad = x^3 - x^2 + 2x^2 + x - 2x + 2$

$\qquad = x^3 + x^2 - x + 2$

76. $(a-1)(4a^2 - ab + 3b^2)$

$\qquad = a(4a^2 - ab + 3b^2) - 1(4a^2 - ab + 3b^2)$

$\qquad = 4a^3 - a^2 b + 3ab^2 - 4a^2 + ab - 3b^2$

$\qquad = 4a^3 - 4a^2 - a^2 b + 3ab^2 + ab - 3b^2$

77. $(3a^2 - b)(5a^2 + 2ab - b^2)$

$\qquad = 3a^2 (5a^2 + 2ab - b^2) - b(5a^2 + 2ab - b^2)$

$\qquad = 15a^4 + 6a^3 b - 3a^2 b^2 - 5a^2 b - 2ab^2 + b^3$

78. $\left(x^2-3x+5\right)\left(-2x^2+7x-4\right)=x^2\left(-2x^2+7x-4\right)-3x\left(-2x^2+7x-4\right)+5\left(-2x^2+7x-4\right)$

$$=-2x^4+7x^3-4x^2+6x^3-21x^2+12x-10x^2+35x-20$$
$$=-2x^4+7x^3+6x^3-4x^2-21x^2-10x^2+12x+35x-20$$
$$=-2x^4+13x^3-35x^2+47x-20$$

79. $\left(5a^2-ab-2b^2\right)\left(-2a^2+3ab-b^2\right)=5a^2\left(-2a^2+3ab-b^2\right)-ab\left(-2a^2+3ab-b^2\right)-2b^2\left(-2a^2+3ab-b^2\right)$

$$=-10a^4+15a^3b-5a^2b^2+2a^3b-3a^2b^2+ab^3+4a^2b^2-6ab^3+2b^4$$
$$=-10a^4+15a^3b+2a^3b-5a^2b^2-3a^2b^2+4a^2b^2+ab^3-6ab^3+2b^4$$
$$=-10a^4+17a^3b-4a^2b^2-5ab^3+2b^4$$

80. Area = Area of Rectangle − Area of Squares

$$=\left(3x^2+5x-2\right)\left(-x^2+7x+3\right)-\left[x\cdot x+x\cdot x\right]$$
$$=3x^2\left(-x^2+7x+3\right)+5x\left(-x^2+7x+3\right)-2\left(-x^2+7x+3\right)-\left[x^2+x^2\right]$$
$$=-3x^4+21x^3+9x^2-5x^3+35x^2+15x+2x^2-14x-6-2x^2$$
$$=-3x^4+21x^3-5x^3+9x^2+35x^2+2x^2-2x^2+15x-14x-6$$
$$=-3x^4+16x^3+44x^2+x-6$$

81. $(x+5)(x+9)=x(x)+x(9)+5(x)+5(9)$
$$=x^2+9x+5x+45$$
$$=x^2+14x+45$$

82. $(4x-1)(x+3)$
$$=4x(x)+4x(3)+(-1)(x)+(-1)(3)$$
$$=4x^2+12x-x-3$$
$$=4x^2+11x-3$$

83. $(6x-5y)(7x-2y)$
$$=6x(7x)+6x(-2y)+(-5y)(7x)+(-5y)(-2y)$$
$$=42x^2-12xy-35xy+10y^2$$
$$=42x^2-47xy+10y^2$$

84. $(10a+b)(8a-9b)$
$$=10a(8a)+10a(-9b)+b(8a)+b(-9b)$$
$$=80a^2-90ab+8ab-9b^2$$
$$=80a^2-82ab-9b^2$$

85. $\left(\dfrac{3}{4}a-7\right)(8a+16)$

$$=\frac{3}{4}a(8a)+\frac{3}{4}a(16)+(-7)(8a)+(-7)(16)$$
$$=6a^2+12a-56a-112$$
$$=6a^2-44a-112$$

86. $(2x+3y)(a-b)$
$$=2x(a)+2x(-b)+3y(a)+3y(-b)$$
$$=2ax-2bx+3ay-3by$$

87. $(x+a)^2=(x+a)(x+a)$
$$=x(x)+x(a)+a(x)+a(a)$$
$$=x^2+ax+ax+a^2$$
$$=x^2+2ax+a^2$$

88. $\left(\dfrac{1}{2}x+3\right)\left(\dfrac{4}{5}x+2\right)$

$$=\frac{1}{2}x\left(\frac{4}{5}x\right)+\frac{1}{2}x(2)+3\left(\frac{4}{5}x\right)+3(2)$$
$$=\frac{2}{5}x^2+x+\frac{12}{5}x+6$$
$$=\frac{2}{5}x^2+\frac{17}{5}x+6$$

89. $(x+5)^2 = (x)^2 + 2(x \cdot 5) + (5)^2$
$\quad = x^2 + 10x + 25$

90. $(y+13)^2 = (y)^2 + 2(y \cdot 13) + (13)^2$
$\quad = y^2 + 26y + 169$

91. $(2x+7y)^2 = (2x)^2 + 2(2x \cdot 7y) + (7y)^2$
$\quad = 4x^2 + 28xy + 49y^2$

92. $(x-3)^2 = (x)^2 + 2(x \cdot (-3)) + (-3)^2$
$\quad = x^2 - 6x + 9$

93. $(2y-1)^2 = (2y)^2 + 2(2y \cdot (-1)) + (-1)^2$
$\quad = 4y^2 - 4y + 1$

94. $(5a-8b)^2 = (5a)^2 + 2(5a \cdot (-8b)) + (-8b)^2$
$\quad = 25a^2 - 80ab + 64b^2$

95. $\left(\dfrac{1}{3}x+4\right)^2 = \left(\dfrac{1}{3}x\right)^2 + 2\left(\dfrac{1}{3}x \cdot 4\right) + (4)^2$
$\quad = \dfrac{1}{9}x^2 + \dfrac{8}{3}x + 16$

96. $\left(\dfrac{1}{2}x-\dfrac{3}{5}\right)^2 = \left(\dfrac{1}{2}x\right)^2 + 2\left(\dfrac{1}{2}x \cdot \left(-\dfrac{3}{5}\right)\right) + \left(-\dfrac{3}{5}\right)^2$
$\quad = \dfrac{1}{4}x^2 - \dfrac{3}{5}x + \dfrac{9}{25}$

97. $(3x^2-7x)^2 = (3x^2)^2 + 2(3x^2 \cdot (-7x)) + (-7x)^2$
$\quad = 9x^4 - 42x^3 + 49x^2$

98. $\left(a+\dfrac{1}{7}b\right)^2 = (a)^2 + 2\left(a \cdot \dfrac{1}{7}b\right) + \left(\dfrac{1}{7}b\right)^2$
$\quad = a^2 + \dfrac{2}{7}ab + \dfrac{1}{49}b^2$

99. Area $= \dfrac{1}{2}bh$
$\quad = \dfrac{1}{2}(5x+3)(5x+3)$
$\quad = \dfrac{1}{2}(5x+3)^2$
$\quad = \dfrac{1}{2}\left[(5x)^2 + 2(5x \cdot 3) + (3)^2\right]$
$\quad = \dfrac{1}{2}(25x^2 + 30x + 9)$
$\quad = \dfrac{25}{2}x^2 + 15x + \dfrac{9}{2}$

100. **Prepare** We are to determine a polynomial that represents the amount of outdoor carpet still needed to cover the patio. Using the value $x=2$, we must then determine the numerical value of the area. Finally, given that the carpet costs $5 per square foot, we must determine how much the remainder of the carpet will cost.

Plan We can subtract the area of the carpet that Mr. Sejnowski already has from the total area of the patio. We can then substitute the value 2 for x in the polynomial to determine the numerical value of the area. Finally, we can multiply the numerical value of the area by 5 to determine the cost of the remainder of the carpet that needs to be purchased.

Process

$$\text{Area} = (6x-3)^2 - (3x+1)^2$$
$$= (6x)^2 + 2(6x \cdot (-3)) + (-3)^2 - \left[(3x)^2 + 2(3x \cdot 1) + (1)^2\right]$$
$$= 36x^2 - 36x + 9 - \left[9x^2 + 6x + 1\right]$$
$$= 36x^2 - 36x + 9 - 9x^2 - 6x - 1$$
$$= 36x^2 - 9x^2 - 36x - 6x + 9 - 1$$
$$= 27x^2 - 42x + 8$$

$$\text{Numerical Area} = 27x^2 - 42x + 8$$
$$= 27(2)^2 - 42(2) + 8$$
$$= 27(4) - 84 + 8$$
$$= 108 - 84 + 8$$
$$= 32$$

$$\text{Cost} = \text{Area} \times \text{Cost per Square Foot}$$
$$= 32(5)$$
$$= 160$$

The polynomial that represents the area is $27x^2 - 42x + 8$, the numerical area is 32 square feet, and the cost for the 32 square feet of carpet is \$160.

Ponder Do our answers seem reasonable? If we substitute $x = 2$ into the polynomial $6x - 3$, we get $6(2) - 3 = 9$, therefore, the area of the whole patio is 81 square feet. If we substitute $x = 2$ into the polynomial $3x + 1$, we get $3(2) + 1 = 7$, therefore, the area of the portion of the patio that is already carpeted is 49 square feet. Because $81 - 49$ is 32, our answer is correct.

101. $\dfrac{124a^3bc^5}{-93a^2bc^7} = -\dfrac{\overset{4}{\cancel{124}}}{\underset{3}{\cancel{93}}}a^{3-2}b^{1-1}c^{5-7}$

$$= -\dfrac{4}{3}a^1b^0c^{-2}$$

$$= -\dfrac{4a}{3c^2}$$

102. $\dfrac{34x^3y^2 - 17x^5y}{17x^2y} = \dfrac{34x^3y^2}{17x^2y} - \dfrac{17x^5y}{17x^2y}$

$$= 2x^{3-2}y^{2-1} - x^{5-2}y^{1-1}$$
$$= 2xy - x^3y^0$$
$$= 2xy - x^3$$

103. $\dfrac{-70x^2y^6z^3 + 55x^5y^3z^2 - 20xyz}{-10x^5y^3z^2} = \dfrac{-70x^2y^6z^3}{-10x^5y^3z^2} + \dfrac{55x^5y^3z^2}{-10x^5y^3z^2} - \dfrac{20xyz}{-10x^5y^3z^2}$

$$= 7x^{2-5}y^{6-3}z^{3-2} - \dfrac{11}{2}x^{5-5}y^{3-3}z^{2-2} + 2x^{1-5}y^{1-3}z^{1-2}$$

$$= 7x^{-3}y^3z^1 - \dfrac{11}{2}x^0y^0z^0 + 2x^{-4}y^{-2}z^{-1}$$

$$= \dfrac{7y^3z}{x^3} - \dfrac{11}{2} + \dfrac{2}{x^4y^2z}$$

104. $\dfrac{-12x^4 + 6x^3 + 10x^2 - 16}{6x^4} = \dfrac{-12x^4}{6x^4} + \dfrac{6x^3}{6x^4} + \dfrac{10x^2}{6x^4} - \dfrac{16}{6x^4}$

$$= -2x^{4-4} + x^{3-4} + \dfrac{5}{3}x^{2-4} - \dfrac{8}{3x^4}$$

$$= -2x^0 + x^{-1} + \dfrac{5}{3}x^{-2} - \dfrac{8}{3x^4}$$

$$= -2 + \dfrac{1}{x} + \dfrac{5}{3x^2} - \dfrac{8}{3x^4}$$

105. $\left(x^2+10x+21\right)\div(x+3)=x+7$

$$
\begin{array}{r}
x+7 \\
x+3\overline{)x^2+10x+21} \\
-\left(x^2+3x\right) \\
\hline
7x+21 \\
-(7x+21) \\
\hline
0
\end{array}
$$

106. $\left(32x^2-4x-56\right)\div(4x-5)=8x+9-\dfrac{11}{4x-5}$

$$
\begin{array}{r}
8x+9 \\
4x-5\overline{)32x^2-4x-56} \\
-\left(32x^2-40x\right) \\
\hline
36x-56 \\
-(36x-45) \\
\hline
-11
\end{array}
$$

107. $\left(30x^3-35x^2+6x+83\right)\div\left(5x^2+1\right)$

$$
=6x-7+\frac{90}{5x^2+1}
$$

$$
\begin{array}{r}
6x-7 \\
5x^2+0x+1\overline{)30x^3-35x^2+6x+83} \\
-\left(30x^3+\ 0x^2+\ 6x\right) \\
\hline
-35x^2+0x+83 \\
-\left(-35x^2+0x-\ 7\right) \\
\hline
90
\end{array}
$$

108. $\left(x^3-8\right)\div(x-2)=x^2+2x+4$

$$
\begin{array}{r}
x^2+2x+4 \\
x-2\overline{)x^3+0x^2+0x-8} \\
-\left(x^3-2x^2\right) \\
\hline
2x^2+0x \\
-\left(2x^2-4x\right) \\
\hline
4x-8 \\
-(4x-8) \\
\hline
0
\end{array}
$$

109. $\left(16x^3-8x^2-12\right)\div\left(4x^2-1\right)=4x-2+\dfrac{4x-14}{4x^2-1}$

$$
\begin{array}{r}
4x-2 \\
4x^2+0x-1\overline{)16x^3-8x^2+0x-12} \\
-\left(16x^3+0x^2-4x\right) \\
\hline
-8x^2+4x-12 \\
-\left(8x^2+0x+\ 2\right) \\
\hline
4x-14
\end{array}
$$

110. $\left(3x^3+18x^2-5x-30\right)\div(x+6)=3x^2-5$

$$
\begin{array}{r}
3x^2-5 \\
x+6\overline{)3x^3+18x^2-5x-30} \\
-\left(3x^3+18x^2\right) \\
\hline
-5x-30 \\
-(-5x-30) \\
\hline
0
\end{array}
$$

111. $b=\text{Total Area}\div h$

$$
=\left(2x^2+11x-6\right)\div\left(\frac{1}{3}x+2\right)
$$

$$
=6x-3
$$

$$
\begin{array}{r}
6x-3 \\
\frac{1}{3}x+2\overline{)2x^2+11x-6} \\
-\left(2x^2+12x\right) \\
\hline
-x-6 \\
-(-x-6) \\
\hline
0
\end{array}
$$

CHAPTER 5 TEST

1. The negative exponent rule states that if $b \in R$, $b \neq 0$, and $n \in N$, then $b^{-n} = \left(\dfrac{1}{b}\right)^n = \dfrac{1}{\underline{b^n}}$.

2. The degree of the term $-4x^3yz^5$ is $\underline{9}$ which is the $\underline{\text{sum}}$ of all the $\underline{\text{exponents}}$ on the variables.

3. The $\underline{\text{degree}}$ of the $\underline{\text{polynomial}}$ $13x^4 - x^3 + 5x^2 + x - 11$ is $\underline{4}$. It has $\underline{5}$ terms. The second term is $\underline{-x^3}$ and has a numerical coefficient of $\underline{-1}$.

4. The special product of two binomials can be achieved through the acronym $\underline{\text{FOIL}}$ which stands for the product of the $\underline{\text{first}}$ terms, plus the $\underline{\text{product}}$ of the outer terms, plus the product of the $\underline{\text{inner}}$ terms, $\underline{\text{plus}}$ the product of the $\underline{\text{last}}$ terms.

5.a. $\left(\dfrac{4}{5}\right)^{-2} = \left(\dfrac{5}{4}\right)^2$

$= \dfrac{5}{4} \cdot \dfrac{5}{4}$

$= \dfrac{25}{16}$

5.b. $-3^{-4} = -1 \cdot 3^{-4}$

$= -1 \cdot \dfrac{1}{3^4}$

$= -1 \cdot \dfrac{1}{81}$

$= -\dfrac{1}{81}$

6. $\left(12a^2b^{-1}c^3\right)^2 = (12)^2\left(a^2\right)^2\left(b^{-1}\right)^2\left(c^3\right)^2$

$= 144a^4b^{-2}c^6$

$= \dfrac{144a^4}{1} \cdot \dfrac{1}{b^2} \cdot \dfrac{c^6}{1}$

$= \dfrac{144a^4c^6}{b^2}$

7. $\dfrac{-10x^0y^{-3}z^4}{55x^{12}y^6z^{-18}} = -\dfrac{\overset{2}{\cancel{10}}}{\underset{11}{\cancel{55}}}x^{0-12}y^{-3-6}z^{4-(-18)}$

$= -\dfrac{2}{11}x^{-12}y^{-9}z^{22}$

$= -\dfrac{2}{11} \cdot \dfrac{1}{x^{12}} \cdot \dfrac{1}{y^9} \cdot \dfrac{z^{22}}{1}$

$= -\dfrac{2z^{22}}{11x^{12}y^9}$

8. $\left(\dfrac{24r^{-2}s^5}{28t^{-7}}\right)^{-1} = \left(\dfrac{28t^{-7}}{24r^{-2}s^5}\right)^1$

$= \dfrac{\overset{7}{\cancel{28}}r^2}{\underset{6}{\cancel{24}}t^7s^5}$

$= \dfrac{7r^2}{6t^7s^5}$

9. $\left(-8x^4y^{-10}z^{-6}\right)\left(6x^{15}y^{-8}z^2\right)^{-3}$

$= \left(-8x^4y^{-10}z^{-6}\right)(6)^{-3}\left(x^{15}\right)^{-3}\left(y^{-8}\right)^{-3}\left(z^2\right)^{-3}$

$= \left(-8x^4y^{-10}z^{-6}\right)\left(6^{-3}x^{-45}y^{24}z^{-6}\right)$

$= -\dfrac{8}{1} \cdot \dfrac{1}{6^3}x^{4+(-45)}y^{-10+24}z^{-6+(-6)}$

$= -\dfrac{8}{6^3}x^{-41}y^{14}z^{-12}$

$= -\dfrac{\overset{1}{\cancel{8}}}{\underset{27}{\cancel{216}}} \cdot \dfrac{1}{x^{41}} \cdot \dfrac{y^{14}}{1} \cdot \dfrac{1}{z^{12}}$

$= -\dfrac{y^{14}}{27x^{41}z^{12}}$

10. $\left(\dfrac{3}{5}a^{-12}b^{8}c^{-1}\right)^{-3}\left(6a^{20}b^{-4}c^{-9}\right)^{2}$

$=\left(\dfrac{3}{5}\right)^{-3}\left(a^{-12}\right)^{-3}\left(b^{8}\right)^{-3}\left(c^{-1}\right)^{-3}(6)^{2}\left(a^{20}\right)^{2}\left(b^{-4}\right)^{2}\left(c^{-9}\right)^{2}$

$=\left(\dfrac{5}{3}\right)^{3}\left(a^{36}\right)\left(b^{-24}\right)\left(c^{3}\right)(36)\left(a^{40}\right)\left(b^{-8}\right)\left(c^{-18}\right)$

$=\left(\dfrac{125}{27}\right)\left(\dfrac{36}{1}\right)a^{36+40}b^{-24+(-8)}c^{3+(-18)}$

$=\left(\dfrac{125\cdot \overset{4}{\cancel{36}}}{\underset{3}{\cancel{27}}\cdot 1}\right)a^{76}b^{-32}c^{-15}$

$=\dfrac{500}{3}\cdot\dfrac{a^{76}}{1}\cdot\dfrac{1}{b^{32}}\cdot\dfrac{1}{c^{15}}$

$=\dfrac{500a^{76}}{3b^{32}c^{15}}$

11. Standard Notation: 50,150,000
Scientific Notation: $5.015\left(10^{7}\right)$

12. $\dfrac{6.8\left(10^{9}\right)(0.00000801)}{340,000,000,000}=\dfrac{6.8\left(10^{9}\right)8.01\left(10^{-6}\right)}{3.4\left(10^{11}\right)}$

$=\dfrac{\overset{2}{\cancel{6.8}}\left(10^{9}\right)8.01\left(10^{-6}\right)}{\underset{1}{\cancel{3.4}}\left(10^{11}\right)}$

$=\dfrac{2(8.01)\left(10^{3}\right)}{\left(10^{11}\right)}$

$=16.02\left(10^{3-11}\right)$

$=1.602\left(10^{1}\right)\left(10^{-8}\right)$

$=1.602\left(10^{-7}\right)$

15. $\left(6x^{3}-17x^{2}+x-5\right)+\left(-7x^{3}+5x^{2}-9x-12\right)-\left(-8x^{2}-x+32\right)$

$=6x^{3}-7x^{3}-17x^{2}+5x^{2}+8x^{2}+x-9x+x-5-12-32$

$=-x^{3}-4x^{2}-7x-49$

16. $(2x-5y)(7x+3y)=2x(7x+3y)-5y(7x+3y)$

$=14x^{2}+6xy-35xy-15y^{2}$

$=14x^{2}-29xy-15y^{2}$

Standard Notation: 0.0000001602
Scientific Notation: $1.602\left(10^{-7}\right)$

13.a. $\dfrac{1}{2}x^{3}+x^{-2}$ is not a polynomial because -2 cannot be an exponent of a polynomial.

13.b. i. $10x^{3}y^{2}z-x^{6}yz+3x^{2}yz^{4}$ is a polynomial because all exponents are positive.

ii. The polynomial has three terms, $10x^{3}y^{2}z$, $-x^{6}yz$, $3x^{2}yz^{4}$, so it is a trinomial.

iii. The term $-x^{6}yz$ has a degree of 8, which is the sum of the exponents of x, y, and z. This is the largest degree of the three terms, so the degree of the polynomial is 8.

iv. The terms of the polynomial are, $10x^{3}y^{2}z$, which has a coefficient of 10, $-x^{6}yz$, which has a coefficient of -1, and $3x^{2}yz^{4}$, which has a coefficient of 3.

14. $-3x^{2}+5x-10=-3(-2)^{2}+5(-2)-10$

$=-3(4)+5(-2)-10$

$=-12+5(-2)-10$

$=-12+(-10)-10$

$=-22-10$

$=-32$

17. $(x+4)(2x^2-5x-3)=x(2x^2-5x-3)+4(2x^2-5x-3)$

$$=2x^3-5x^2-3x+8x^2-20x-12$$
$$=2x^3-5x^2+8x^2-3x-20x-12$$
$$=2x^3+3x^2-23x-12$$

18. $\left(x-\dfrac{1}{2}\right)^2=(x)^2-2\left(x\cdot\dfrac{1}{2}\right)+\left(\dfrac{1}{2}\right)^2$

$$=x^2-x+\dfrac{1}{4}$$

19. $(6x-7)(6x+7)=(6x)^2-(7)^2$

$$=36x^2-49$$

20. $(3x+5y)^2=(3x)^2+2(3x\cdot5y)+(5y^2)$

$$=9x^2+30xy+25y^2$$

21. $\dfrac{-15a^3-7a^2+15a}{-5a^2}=\dfrac{-15a^3}{-5a^2}-\dfrac{7a^2}{-5a^2}+\dfrac{15a}{-5a^2}$

$$=3a^{3-2}+\dfrac{7}{5}a^{2-2}-3a^{1-2}$$

$$=3a+\dfrac{7}{5}a^0-3a^{-1}$$

$$=3a+\dfrac{7}{5}-\dfrac{3}{1}\cdot\dfrac{1}{a}$$

$$=3a+\dfrac{7}{5}-\dfrac{3}{a}$$

22.a. $(10x^2-x-29)\div(2x-3)=5x+7+\dfrac{-8}{2x-3}$

$$\require{enclose}
\begin{array}{r}
5x+7 \\
2x-3 \enclose{longdiv}{10x^2-x-29} \\
\end{array}$$

$$\dfrac{-(10x^2-15x)}{}$$
$$14x-29$$
$$\dfrac{-(14x-21)}{-8}$$

22.b. $(8x^3-27)\div(2x-3)=4x^2+6x+9$

$$\begin{array}{r}
4x^2+6x+9 \\
2x-3 \enclose{longdiv}{8x^3+0x^2+0x-27} \\
\end{array}$$

$$\dfrac{-(8x^3-12x^2)}{}$$
$$12x^2+0x$$
$$\dfrac{-(12x^2-18x)}{}$$
$$18x-27$$
$$\dfrac{-(18x-27)}{0}$$

23. Let P represent the perimeter of the figure.

$$
\begin{array}{rcl}
a^2-2ab+ & 5b^2 \\
a^2-2ab+ & 5b^2 \\
-2a^2 & +28b^2 \\
-2a^2 & +28b^2 \\
a^2 & +b^2 \\
+\quad a^2 & +b^2 \\
\hline
& -4ab+68b^2
\end{array}
$$

The perimeter is $P=-4ab+68b^2$ units.

24. Let V represent the volume of the figure.

$$V=x^2(5x-5)(-x^2+7x+8)$$

$$=(5x^3-5x^2)(-x^2+7x+8)$$

$$=5x^3(-x^2+7x+8)-5x^2(-x^2+7x+8)$$

$$=-5x^5+35x^4+40x^3+5x^4-35x^3-40x^2$$

$$=-5x^5+35x^4+5x^4+40x^3-35x^3-40x^2$$

$$=-5x^5+40x^4+5x^3-40x^2$$

The volume of the figure is
$V=-5x^5+40x^4+5x^3-40x^2$ cubic units.

25. Prepare We are to write the cost, revenue, and profit functions for Image Entertainment based on the given information. Then, we must evaluate the profit function for two specific values of the independent variable and explain what the outcomes would mean to Image Entertainment.

Plan Write the cost function, given the fixed costs of $1,250 and cost per poster of $1.10. That is, fixed costs added to the cost to produce each poster, where x is the number of posters. Write the revenue function, given the selling price of $12 for each poster. Write the profit function, given the equation $P(x) = R(x) - C(x)$. Then, evaluate the profit function for $x = 114$ and $x = 115$, and determine what the outcomes would mean to the company.

Process
(a) The cost function is the fixed costs added to the cost to produce each poster, $1.10x$, where x is the number of posters.

Cost Function: $C(x) = 1.10x + 1250$, $x \geq 0$

(b) The revenue function is the selling price of each poster times the number of posters sold.

Revenue Function: $R(x) = 12x$

(c) Profit Function:

$$P(x) = R(x) - C(x)$$
$$P(x) = 12x - (1.10x + 1250)$$
$$= 12x - 1.10x - 1250$$
$$P(x) = 10.90x - 1250$$

(d) $P(114) = 10.90(114) - 1250$
$$= -7.40$$

$P(115) = 10.90(115) - 1250$
$$= 3.50$$

Image Entertainment must sell at least 115 posters before it makes a positive profit, otherwise, the company loses money.

Ponder Do our answers seem reasonable? Yes, based on the profit function. It is not unreasonable for a large music company to have to sell a minimum of 115 posters before making a profit.

Chapter 6

6.1 Exercises

1. The goal of factoring is to go from a sum or difference to a <u>product</u>.

3. GCF stands for <u>Greatest</u> <u>Common</u> <u>Factor</u>.

5. When a polynomial has four terms, we try to factor <u>by</u> <u>grouping</u>.

7. $6x^2 - 5$

9. $y^6 + x^5$

11. $6a^2b^5$

13. $3a + 1$

15. y

17. 5

19. $x^3y^5z^2$

21. $12s^2$

23. $2 - 5c$

25. The GCF is 5.
$$5x - 10 = 5(x - 2)$$

27. The GCF is x.
$$x^3 + 6x = x(x^2 + 6)$$

29. The GCF is $7t$.
$$14t^3 - 7t = 7t(2t^2 - 1)$$

31. The GCF is $6a^3$.
$$6a^3 + 12a^4 = 6a^3(1 + 2a)$$

33. The GCF is $6abc$.
$$24abcd + 18abc = 6abc(4d + 3)$$

35. The GCF is $5s^2t^3$.
$$50s^5t^3 - 35s^2t^8 = 5s^2t^3(10s^3 - 7t^5)$$

37. The GCF is 6.
$$6a - 18c + 12 = 6(a - 3c + 2)$$

39. The GCF is $8a^2b^7c^2$.
$$a^4b^7c^2 - a^2b^8c^6 = a^2b^7c^2(a^2 - bc^4)$$

41. The GCF is $20a^3c^2$.
$$80a^6b^9c^2 + 60a^3c^4 = 20a^3c^2(4a^3b^9 + 3c^2)$$

43. The GCF is 3.
$$3x^2 - 18x - 3 = 3(x^2 - 6x - 1)$$

45. The GCF is b^2.
$$5b^2 + 3a^2b^2 + 2b^3 = b^2(5 + 3a^2 + 2b)$$

47. The GCF is $8x^2$.
$$24x^5 + 40x^3 - 8x^2 = 8x^2(3x^3 + 5x - 1)$$

49. The GCF is $2a^3$.
$$6a^{10} - 20a^5 + 14a^3 = 2a^3(3a^7 - 10a^2 + 7)$$

51. The GCF is $7x^2y$.
$$7x^4y^4 + 7x^3y^3 + 35x^2y = 7x^2y(x^2y^3 + xy^2 + 5)$$

53. The GCF is 8.
$$16x - 40b + 24c - 64 = 8(2x - 5b + 3c - 8)$$

55. The GCF is $6x$.
$$18x^4 + 12x^3 - 24x^2 + 6x = 6x(3x^3 + 2x^2 - 4x + 1)$$

57. The GCF is $2ab$.
$$16a^3b^2 + 8a^2b^2 + 6a^2b - 10ab^2$$
$$= 2ab(8a^2b + 4ab + 3a - 5b)$$

59. The GCF is $a - 1$.
$$5x(a - 1) + 3(a - 1) = (a - 1)(5x + 3)$$

61. The GCF is $x - 8$.
$$9(x - 8) + 7a(x - 8) = (x - 8)(9 + 7a)$$

63. The GCF is $x+7$.

$$2a(x+7)-3b(x+7)=(x+7)(2a-3b)$$

65. The GCF is $2x+y$.

$$6x(2x+y)-11y(2x+y)=(2x+y)(6x-11y)$$

67. The GCF is $3y+5$.

$$2x(3y+5)+(3y+5)=(3y+5)(2x+1)$$

69. $x^2+bx+ax+ab=x(x+b)+a(x+b)$
$$=(x+b)(x+a)$$

71. $ax+3a+bx+3b=a(x+3)+b(x+3)$
$$=(x+3)(a+b)$$

73. $3xy+3x+y+1=3x(y+1)+(y+1)$
$$=(y+1)(3x+1)$$

75. $2ab+8a-3b-12=2a(b+4)-3(b+4)$
$$=(b+4)(2a-3)$$

77. $ax+ay-x-y=a(x+y)-(x+y)$
$$=(x+y)(a-1)$$

79. $3bs-3bt-s+t=3b(s-t)-(s-t)$
$$=(s-t)(3b-1)$$

81. $5ax+5x+5ay+5y=5(ax+x+ay+y)$
$$=5\left[x(a+1)+y(a+1)\right]$$
$$=5(a+1)(x+y)$$

83. $2pm-4p+12m-24=2(pm-2p+6m-12)$
$$=2\left[p(m-2)+6(m-2)\right]$$
$$=2(m-2)(p+6)$$

85. $5vg-40g-5v+40=5(vg-8g-v+8)$
$$=5\left[g(v-8)-(v-8)\right]$$
$$=5(v-8)(g-1)$$

87. $60s+12t+120as+24at=12(5s+t+10as+2at)$
$$=12\left[(5s+t)+2a(5s+t)\right]$$
$$=12(5s+t)(1+2a)$$

89. $6a^3x+3a^3+8a^2x+4a^2$
$$=a^2(6ax+3a+8x+4)$$
$$=a^2\left[3a(2x+1)+4(2x+1)\right]$$
$$=a^2(2x+1)(3a+4)$$

91. $18ax^3-6x^3+54ax^2y-18x^2y$
$$=6x^2(3ax-x+9ay-3y)$$
$$=6x^2\left[x(3a-1)+3y(3a-1)\right]$$
$$=6x^2(3a-1)(x+3y)$$

93. $6a-6b-12ab+12b^2=6(a-b-2ab+2b^2)$
$$=6\left[(a-b)-2b(a-b)\right]$$
$$=6(a-b)(1-2b)$$

95. $8ax^3+12bx^3-8ax^2-12bx^2$
$$=4x^2(2ax+3bx-2a-3b)$$
$$=4x^2\left[x(2a+3b)-(2a+3b)\right]$$
$$=4x^2(2a+3b)(x-1)$$

97. Answers will vary; one example is: To find the GCF look for the largest term that is common to all terms of the polynomial. The GCF can be a combination of coefficients and variables with exponents.

99. Answers will vary; one example is: $6x^3+9x^2$.

101. $2a+4b+8+ab=8+2a+4b+ab$
$$=2(4+a)+b(4+a)$$
$$=(4+a)(2+b)$$

103. $ac-2d-ad+2c=ac-ad+2c-2d$
$$=a(c-d)+2(c-d)$$
$$=(c-d)(a+2)$$

105. $a^2b^4+a^2b^3c+a^2b^2c^2+a^2b^3c$
$$=a^2b^2(b^2+bc+c^2+bc)$$
$$=a^2b^2(b^2+bc+bc+c^2)$$
$$=a^2b^2\left[b(b+c)+c(b+c)\right]$$
$$=a^2b^2(b+c)(b+c)$$

107. $as^2 + 4bs^2 - 2cs^2 + at + 4bt - 2ct$

$= s^2(a + 4b - 2c) + t(a + 4b - 2c)$

$= (a + 4b - 2c)(s^2 + t)$

6.2 Exercises

1. The <u>sum</u> of squares is not factorable using only integer factors.

3. If a polynomial is not factorable using only integer factors, we say the polynomial is <u>prime</u>.

5. difference of squares

7. sum of cubes

9. difference of cubes

11. $x^2 - 25 = (x)^2 - (5)^2$
$= (x+5)(x-5)$

13. $81 - a^2 = (9)^2 - (a)^2$
$= (9+a)(9-a)$

15. prime

17. $4x^2 - 9 = (2x)^2 - (3)^2$
$= (2x+3)(2x-3)$

19. $64 - 49t^2 = (8)^2 - (7t)^2$
$= (8+7t)(8-7t)$

21. prime

23. $x^2y^2 - 64 = (xy)^2 - (8)^2$
$= (xy+8)(xy-8)$

25. $81a^2 - 25b^2 = (9a)^2 - (5b)^2$
$= (9a+5b)(9a-5b)$

27. prime

29. $x^3 + y^3 = (x)^3 + (y)^3$
$= (x+y)(x^2 - xy + y^2)$

31. $a^3 - b^3 = (a)^3 - (b)^3$
$= (a-b)(a^2 + ab + b^2)$

33. $x^3 + 8 = (x)^3 + (2)^3$
$= (x+2)(x^2 - 2x + 2^2)$
$= (x+2)(x^2 - 2x + 4)$

35. $27a^3 - 1 = (3a)^3 - (1)^3$
$= (3a-1)((3a)^2 + (3a)(1) + 1^2)$
$= (3a-1)(9a^2 + 3a + 1)$

37. $8x^3 + y^3 = (2x)^3 + (y)^3$
$= (2x+y)((2x)^2 - (2x)(y) + y^2)$
$= (2x+y)(4x^2 - 2xy + y^2)$

39. $27 + a^3 = (3)^3 + (a)^3$
$= (3+a)(3^2 - 3a + a^2)$
$= (3+a)(9 - 3a + a^2)$

41. $1 + 64x^3 = (1)^3 + (4x)^3$
$= (1+4x)(1^2 - (1)(4x) + (4x)^2)$
$= (1+4x)(1 - 4x + 16x^2)$

43. $125x^3 - 64y^3 = (5x)^3 - (4y)^3$
$= (5x-4y)((5x)^2 + (5x)(4y) + (4y)^2)$
$= (5x-4y)(25x^2 + 20xy + 16y^2)$

45. $8a^3 + 27b^3 = (2a)^3 + (3b)^3$
$= (2a+3b)((2a)^2 - (2a)(3b) + (3b)^2)$
$= (2a+3b)(4a^2 - 6ab + 9b^2)$

47. $2x^2 - 50 = 2(x^2 - 25)$
$= 2((x)^2 - (5)^2)$
$= 2(x+5)(x-5)$

49. $3a^2 + 27 = 3(a^2 + 9)$

51. $2m^3 + 16 = 2(m^3 + 8)$

$$= 2((m)^3 + (2)^3)$$
$$= 2(m+2)(m^2 - 2m + 2^2)$$
$$= 2(m+2)(m^2 - 2m + 4)$$

53. $a^3 - ab^2 = a(a^2 - b^2)$

$$= a(a+b)(a-b)$$

55. $4s^2 - 36t^2 = 4(s^2 - 9t^2)$

$$= 4((s)^2 - (3t)^2)$$
$$= 4(s+3t)(s-3t)$$

57. $a^3b + b^4 = b(a^3 + b^3)$

$$= b(a+b)(a^2 - ab + b^2)$$

59. $x^3 + 100x = x(x^2 + 100)$

61. $3x^3 - 12y^3 = 3(x^3 - 4y^3)$

63. $9 - 9x^4 = 9(1 - x^4)$

$$= 9((1)^2 - (x^2)^2)$$
$$= 9(1+x^2)(1-x^2)$$
$$= 9(1+x^2)((1)^2 - (x)^2)$$
$$= 9(1+x^2)(1+x)(1-x)$$

65. $8x - 8 + xy^3 - y^3 = 8(x-1) + y^3(x-1)$

$$= (x-1)(8 + y^3)$$
$$= (x-1)((2)^3 + (y)^3)$$
$$= (x-1)(2+y)(2^2 - 2y + y^2)$$
$$= (x-1)(2+y)(4 - 2y + y^2)$$

67. Answers will vary; one example is: The sum of squares is not factorable using only integer factors because there are only the following three possibilities, none of which work: $(a+b)(a+b)$, $(a-b)(a-b)$, and $(a+b)(a-b)$.

69. Answers will vary; one example is: An example of a difference of squares is the binomial $x^2 - 4$. An example of a difference of cubes is the binomial $x^3 - 8$.

71. a) $(2x-3y)^2 - (5x+4y)^2 = ((2x-3y)+(5x+4y))((2x-3y)-(5x+4y))$

$$= (7x+y)(-3x-7y)$$

b) $(2x-3y)^2 - (5x+4y)^2 = ((2x)^2 - (2)(2x)(3y) + (3y)^2) - ((5x)^2 + (2)(5x)(4y) + (4y)^2)$

$$= (4x^2 - 12xy + 9y^2) - (25x^2 + 40xy + 16y^2)$$
$$= -21x^2 - 52xy - 7y^2$$

c) The two answers are equal because (a) is the factored form of (b).

73. $\dfrac{4}{9}x^2 - \dfrac{1}{25}y^2 = \left(\dfrac{2}{3}x\right)^2 - \left(\dfrac{1}{5}y\right)^2$

$$= \left(\dfrac{2}{3}x + \dfrac{1}{5}y\right)\left(\dfrac{2}{3}x - \dfrac{1}{5}y\right)$$

75. $(x+y)^2 - 16 = (x+y)^2 - (4)^2$

$$= (x+y+4)(x+y-4)$$

77. $(x+5)^2 - (x-5)^2$

$$= ((x+5)+(x-5))((x+5)-(x-5))$$
$$= (2x)(10)$$
$$= 20x$$

6.3 Exercises

1. When we factor a trinomial using the AC Method, we rewrite the trinomial as <u>four</u> terms and <u>factor</u> <u>by</u> <u>grouping</u>.

3. The Educated Guess-and-Test Method used to factor trinomials is preferred when the <u>product</u> <u>AC</u> is very large and has a long list of <u>factors</u>.

5. The product of binomial factors $(x-2)(3y+5)$ equals $(3y+5)(x-2)$ because <u>multiplication</u> is <u>commutative</u>.

7. $3x-2$

9. $4a-5$

11. $5y-4$

13. $5-3m$

15. $A=2$, $C=3$, and $AC=6$
The factors of 6 that add to 7 are 1 and 6.
$$2x^2+7x+3=2x^2+x+6x+3$$
$$=x(2x+1)+3(2x+1)$$
$$=(2x+1)(x+3)$$

17. $A=3$, $C=8$, and $AC=24$
The factors of 24 that add to 14 are 12 and 2.
$$3a^2+14a+8=3a^2+12a+2a+8$$
$$=3a(a+4)+2(a+4)$$
$$=(a+4)(3a+2)$$

19. $A=5$, $C=6$, and $AC=30$
The factors of 30 that add to 17 are 15 and 2.
$$5y^2+17y+6=5y^2+15y+2y+6$$
$$=5y(y+3)+2(y+3)$$
$$=(y+3)(5y+2)$$

21. $A=2$, $C=-12$, and $AC=-24$
The factors of -24 that add to 5 are -3 and 8.
$$2x^2+5x-12=2x^2+8x-3x-12$$
$$=2x(x+4)-3(x+4)$$
$$=(x+4)(2x-3)$$

23. $A=3$, $C=-5$, and $AC=-15$
There are no factors of -15 that add to 4, therefore the trinomial is prime.

25. $A=7$, $C=-10$, and $AC=-70$
The factors of -70 that add to -9 are 5 and -14.
$$7a^2-9a-10=7a^2-14a+5a-10$$
$$=7a(a-2)+5(a-2)$$
$$=(a-2)(7a+5)$$

27. $A=6$, $C=-5$, and $AC=-30$
The factors of -30 that add to 7 are 10 and -3.
$$6t^2+7t-5=6t^2+10t-3t-5$$
$$=2t(3t+5)-(3t+5)$$
$$=(3t+5)(2t-1)$$

29. $A=5$, $C=6$, and $AC=30$
The factors of 30 that add to -17 are -2 and -15.
$$5y^2-17y+6=5y^2-15y-2y+6$$
$$=5y(y-3)-2(y-3)$$
$$=(y-3)(5y-2)$$

31. $A=7$, $C=6$, and $AC=42$
The factors of 42 that add to -17 are -14 and -3.
$$7y^2-17y+6=7y^2-14y-3y+6$$
$$=7y(y-2)-3(y-2)$$
$$=(y-2)(7y-3)$$

33. $A=6$, $C=3$, and $AC=18$
The factors of 18 that add to -11 are -9 and -2.
$$6b^2-11b+3=6b^2-9b-2b+3$$
$$=3b(2b-3)-(2b-3)$$
$$=(2b-3)(3b-1)$$

35. $A=12$, $C=6$, and $AC=72$
The factors of 72 that add to 17 are 8 and 9.
$$12y^2+17y+6=12y^2+8y+9y+6$$
$$=4y(3y+2)+3(3y+2)$$
$$=(3y+2)(4y+3)$$

37. $A=20$, $C=-6$, and $AC=-120$
The factors of -120 that add to -7 are -15 and 8.
$$20a^2-7a-6=20a^2-15a+8a-6$$
$$=5a(4a-3)+2(4a-3)$$
$$=(4a-3)(5a+2)$$

39. $A = 18$, $C = 10$, and $AC = 180$

The factors of 180 that add to -27 are -15 and -12.

$$18a^2 - 27a + 10 = 18a^2 - 15a - 12a + 10$$
$$= 3a(6a - 5) - 2(6a - 5)$$
$$= (6a - 5)(3a - 2)$$

41. $A = 15$, $C = -2$, and $AC = -30$

The factors of -30 that add to -7 are -10 and 3.

$$15x^2 - 7xy - 2y^2 = 15x^2 - 10xy + 3xy - 2y^2$$
$$= 5x(3x - 2y) + y(3x - 2y)$$
$$= (3x - 2y)(5x + y)$$

43. $A = 12$, $C = 15$, and $AC = 180$

The factors of 180 that add to 28 are 18 and 10.

$$12a^2 + 28ab + 15b^2 = 12a^2 + 18ab + 10ab + 15b^2$$
$$= 6a(2a + 3b) + 5b(2a + 3b)$$
$$= (2a + 3b)(6a + 5b)$$

45. The factors of 5 are 1 and 5. The factors of 10 are 1, 2, 5, and 10.

$$5x^2 + 27x + 10 = (5x + 2)(x + 5)$$

47. The factors of 6 are 1, 2, 3, and 6. The factors of 10 are 1, 2, 5, and 10.

$$6a^2 + 19a + 10 = (2a + 5)(3a + 2)$$

49. The factors of 8 are 1, 2, 4, and 8. The factors of 3 are 1 and 3.

$$8x^2 - 2x - 3 = (2x + 1)(4x - 3)$$

51. The factors of 5 are 1 and 5. The factors of 6 are 1, 2, 3, and 6.

$$5b^2 - 7b - 6 = (5b + 3)(b - 2)$$

53. The factors of 6 are 1, 2, 3, and 6. The factors of 5 are 1 and 5.

$$6a^2 - 13a + 5 = (2a - 1)(3a - 5)$$

55. The factors of 12 are 1, 2, 3, 4, 6, and 12. The factors of 10 are 1, 2, 5, and 10.

$$12y^2 - 23y + 10 = (4y - 5)(3y - 2)$$

57. The factors 16 are 1, 2, 4, 8 and 16. The factors of 18 are 1, 2, 3, 6, 9, and 18. The polynomial is prime.

59. The factors of 48 are 1, 2, 3, 4, 6, 8, 12, 16, 24, and 48. The factors of 15 are 1, 3, 5, and 15.

$$48a^2 - 22a - 15 = (8a + 3)(6a - 5)$$

61. The factors of 16 are 1, 2, 4, 8, and 16. The factors of 45 are 1, 3, 5, 9, 15, and 45.

$$16b^2 - 62b - 45 = (8b + 5)(2b - 9)$$

63. The factors of 4 are 1, 2, and 4. The factors of 6 are 1, 2, 3, and 6.

$$4y^2 - 25y + 6 = (4y - 1)(y - 6)$$

65. The factors of 36 are 1, 2, 3, 4, 6, 9, 12, 18, and 36. The factors of 25 are 1, 5, and 25.

$$36c^2 + 60c + 25 = (6c + 5)(6c + 5)$$
$$= (6c + 5)^2$$

67. The factors of 42 are 1, 2, 3, 6, 7, 14, 21, and 42. The factors of 10 are 1, 2, 5, and 10.

$$42y^2 + 47y + 10 = (7y + 2)(6y + 5)$$

69. The factors of 16 are 1, 2, 4, 8, and 16. The factors of 35 are 1, 5, 7, and 35.

$$16x^2 + 54xy + 35y^2 = (8x + 7y)(2x + 5y)$$

71. The factors of 64 are 1, 2, 4, 8, 16, 32, and 64. The factors of 9 are 1, 3, and 9.

$$64s^2 - 48st + 9t^2 = (8s - 3t)(8s - 3t)$$
$$= (8s - 3t)^2$$

73. The factors of 24 are 1, 2, 3, 4, 6, 8, 12 and 24. The factors of 25 are 1, 5, and 25.

$$24x^2 + 50xy - 25y^2 = (12x - 5y)(2x + 5y)$$

75. $A = 6$, $C = 9$, and $AC = 54$

There are no factors of 54 that add to by 5, therefore the trinomial is prime.

77. $5a^3 + 17a^2 + 6a = a(5a^2 + 17a + 6)$

$$= a(5a^2 + 15a + 2a + 6)$$
$$= a[5a(a + 3) + 2(a + 3)]$$
$$= a(a + 3)(5a + 2)$$

79. $4b^2 + 26b + 40 = 2(2b^2 + 13b + 20)$

$$= 2(2b^2 + 8b + 5b + 20)$$
$$= 2[2b(b + 4) + 5(b + 4)]$$
$$= 2(b + 4)(2b + 5)$$

81. $18c^2 + 60c - 48 = 6(3c^2 + 10c - 8)$

$$= 6(3c^2 + 12c - 2c - 8)$$
$$= 6[3c(c+4) - 2(c+4)]$$
$$= 6(c+4)(3c-2)$$

83. $2a^3b + 13a^2b^2 + 6ab^3 = ab(2a^2 + 13ab + 6b^2)$

$$= ab(2a^2 + 12ab + ab + 6b^2)$$
$$= ab[2a(a+6b) + b(a+6b)]$$
$$= ab(a+6b)(2a+b)$$

85. $60b^2 - 21b - 18 = 3(20b^2 - 7b - 6)$

$$= 3(5b+2)(4b-3)$$

87. $40t^2 - 78t + 36 = 2(20t^2 - 39t + 18)$

$$= 2(5t-6)(4t-3)$$

89. $8y^3 + 8y^2 - 6y = 2y(4y^2 + 4y - 3)$

$$= 2y(4y^2 - 2y + 6y - 3)$$
$$= 2y[2y(2y-1) + 3(2y-1)]$$
$$= 2y(2y-1)(2y+3)$$

91. $12x^3 - 34x^2y + 24xy^2$

$$= 2x(6x^2 - 17xy + 12y^2)$$
$$= 2x(6x^2 - 9xy - 8xy + 12y^2)$$
$$= 2x[3x(2x-3y) - 4y(2x-3y)]$$
$$= 2x(2x-3y)(3x-4y)$$

93. To find the polynomial whose factors are $(2x+7)$ and $(8x-11)$, we must multiply the factors.

$$(2x+7)(8x-11) = (2x+7)8x - (2x+7)11$$
$$= 16x^2 + 56x - 22x - 77$$
$$= 16x^2 + 34x - 77$$

95. Answers will vary; one example is: If either A or C is a prime number it is easier to use the AC Method, because there are fewer factors.

97. $7.2x^2 + 5.4x - 5.6 = 2(3.6x^2 + 2.7x - 2.8)$

$$= 2(1.2x - 0.7)(3x + 4)$$

99. $16x^4 - 8x^2y^2 + y^4$

$$= 16x^4 - 4x^2y^2 - 4x^2y^2 + y^4$$
$$= 4x^2(4x^2 - y^2) - y^2(4x^2 - y^2)$$
$$= (4x^2 - y^2)(4x^2 - y^2)$$
$$= (2x+y)(2x-y)(2x+y)(2x-y)$$
$$= (2x+y)^2(2x-y)^2$$

101. $64x^6 + 16x^3y^3 + y^6 = 64x^6 + 8x^3y^3 + 8x^3y^3 + y^6$

$$= 8x^3(8x^3 + y^3) + y^3(8x^3 + y^3)$$
$$= (8x^3 + y^3)(8x^3 + y^3)$$
$$= (2x+y)(4x^2 - 2xy + y^2)(2x+y)(4x^2 - 2xy + y^2)$$
$$= (2x+y)^2(4x^2 - 2xy + y^2)^2$$

103. a) $18x^2 + 37x - 20 = (2x+5)(9x-4)$

The width of the rectangle is $W = 9x - 4$ units.

b)

$$
\begin{array}{r}
9x-4 \\
2x+5 \overline{\smash{\big)}\ 18x^2 + 37x - 20} \\
-\left(18x^2 + 45x\right) \\
\hline
-8x - 20 \\
-\quad(-8x - 20) \\
\hline
0
\end{array}
$$

The width of the rectangle is $W = 9x - 4$ units.

c) The results are equal

d) When the polynomial is divided by one of the two binomial factors, the quotient is the other factor.

6.4 Exercises

1. It is usually easier to factor trinomials of the form $Ax^2 + Bx + C$ where $A = 1$ using the Educated Guess & Test Method.

3. When factoring a trinomial without a GCF, we first check to see of it is a perfect square trinomial.

5. In a perfect square trinomial, the middle term must be twice the product of what is being squared.

7. $x + 2$

9. $a + 18b$

11. $x^2 + 14x + 49$ is a perfect square trinomial.

13. No, the middle term would equal $-36ab$ if the trinomial was a perfect square.

15. The factors of 24 that sum to 11 are 3 and 8.
$$x^2 + 11x + 24 = (x+3)(x+8)$$

17. The factors of 50 that sum to 15 are 5 and 10.
$$a^2 + 15a + 50 = (a+5)(a+10)$$

19. The factors of 10 that sum to -11 are -1 and -10.
$$x^2 - 11x + 10 = (x-1)(x-10)$$

21. The factors of 32 that sum to -12 are -4 and -8.
$$y^2 - 12y + 32 = (y-4)(y-8)$$

23. The factors of 16 that differ by 6 are 2 and 8.
$$x^2 + 6x - 16 = (x-2)(x+8)$$

25. The factors of 6 that differ by 1 are 2 and 3.
$$x^2 + x - 6 = (x-2)(x+3)$$

27. The factors of 9 that sum to 6 are 3 and 3.
$$y^2 + 6y + 9 = (y+3)^2$$

29. The factors of 4 that sum to -4 are -2 and -2.
$$x^2 - 4x + 4 = (x-2)^2$$

31. The factors of 36 that differ by 5 are 4 and 9.
$$t^2 + 5t - 36 = (t-4)(t+9)$$

33. The factors of 18 that sum to -11 are -2 and -9.
$$h^2 - 11h + 18 = (h-2)(h-9)$$

35. The factors of 32 that differ by 4 are 4 and 8.
$$k^2 - 4k - 32 = (k+4)(k-8)$$

37. The factors of 24 that differ by 10 are 2 and 12.
$$s^2 - 10s - 24 = (s+2)(s-12)$$

39. The factors of 1 that sum to 2 are 1 and 1.
$$a^2 + 2ab + b^2 = (a+b)^2$$

41. The factors of 6 that sum to 5 are 2 and 3.
$$a^2 + 5ab + 6b^2 = (a+2b)(a+3b)$$

43. The factors of 48 that differ by 2 are 6 and 8.
$$s^2 + 2st - 48t^2 = (s-6t)(s+8t)$$

45. The factors of 28 that differ by 12 are 2 and 14.
$$p^2 + 12pq - 28q^2 = (p-2q)(p+14q)$$

47. The factors of 36 that sum to -15 are -3 and -12.
$$b^2 - 15ba + 36a^2 = (b-3a)(b-12a)$$

49. The factors of 12 that sum to 7 are 3 and 4.
$$x^4 + 7x^2 + 12 = (x^2+3)(x^2+4)$$

51. $x^2 + 8x + 16 = (x)^2 + 2(4)(x) + (4)^2$
$$= (x+4)^2$$

53. $c^2 - 4c + 4 = (c)^2 - 2(2)(c) + (2)^2$
$$= (c-2)^2$$

55. $b^2 - 10b - 25$ is not a perfect square trinomial because the last term is negative, therefore the trinomial is prime.

57. $t^2 + 2t + 1 = (t)^2 + 2(1)(t) + (1)^2$
$$= (t+1)^2$$

59. $a^2 - 18a + 81 = (a)^2 - 2(9)(a) + (9)^2$
$$= (a-9)^2$$

61. The middle term of $x^2 - xy + y^2$ would have to equal $-2xy$ for it to be a perfect square trinomial, therefore it is prime.

63. $4s^2 - 36s + 81 = (2s)^2 - 2(2s)(9) + (9)^2$
$= (2s - 9)^2$

65. $36x^2 + 12x + 1 = (6x)^2 + 2(6x)(1) + (1)^2$
$= (6x + 1)^2$

67. $4a^2 + 4ab + b^2 = (2a)^2 + 2(2a)(b) + (b)^2$
$= (2a + b)^2$

69. The middle term of $16c^2 - 12c + 9$ would have to equal $-24c$ for it to be a perfect square trinomial, therefore it is prime.

71. $9t^2 + 30t + 25 = (3t)^2 + 2(3t)(5) + (5)^2$
$= (3t + 5)^2$

73. $49p^2 - 28pq + 4q^2 = (7p)^2 - 2(7p)(2a) + (2q)^2$
$= (7p - 2q)^2$

75. $25a^2 + 20ab + 4b^2 = (5a)^2 + 2(5a)(2b) + (2b)^2$
$= (5a + 2b)^2$

77. $a^2b^2 + 6ab + 9 = (ab)^2 + 2(ab)(3) + (3)^2$
$= (ab + 3)^2$

79. $81x^4 - 18x^2 + 1 = (9x^2)^2 - 2(9x^2)(1) + (1)^2$
$= (9x^2 - 1)^2$
$= \left[(3x + 1)(3x - 1)\right]^2$
$= (3x + 1)^2(3x - 1)^2$

81. $2x^3 + 8x^2 + 6x = 2x(x^2 + 4x + 3)$
$= 2x(x + 1)(x + 3)$

83. $3x^2 - 6x + 3 = 3(x^2 - 2x + 1)$
$= 3(x - 1)^2$

85. $4x^2 + 20x - 200 = 4(x^2 + 5x - 50)$
$= 4(x - 5)(x + 10)$

87. $4a^4 - 4a^3 + a^2 = a^2(4a^2 - 4a + 1)$
$= a^2(2a - 1)^2$

89. $a^4 - 15a^3 + 56a^2 = a^2(a^2 - 15a + 56)$
$= a^2(a - 7)(a - 8)$

91. $2a^3 + 20a^2 + 50a = 2a(a^2 + 10a + 25)$
$= 2a(a + 5)^2$

93. $4a^3 + 4a^2 - 8a = 4a(a^2 + a - 2)$
$= 4a(a - 1)(a + 2)$

95. $2a^4b^3 + 6a^3b^3 - 260a^2b^3 = 2a^2b^3(a^2 + 3a - 130)$
$= 2a^2b^3(a - 10)(a + 13)$

97. $18x^3 + 60x^2y + 50xy^2 = 2x(9x^2 + 30xy + 25y^2)$
$= 2x(3x + 5y)^2$

99. Answers will vary; one example is:
$16x^2 + 40xy + 25y^2 = (4x + 5y)^2$.

101. Answers will vary; one example is:
$x^2 - 9x + 20 = (x - 4)(x - 5)$.

103. Not necessarily. For example:
$\left(x + \dfrac{1}{2}\right)^2 = x^2 + x + \dfrac{1}{4}$.

105.a. $4x^2 + 12x + 9 = (2x + 3)^2$
The length of each side of the square is $2x + 3$ units.

105.b. $2x + 3 = 2(15) + 3$
$= 33$
The length of each side of the square is 33 feet.
$Area = 33^2$
$= 1089$
The area of the square is 1089 square feet.

107. $\dfrac{1}{5}x^2 + \dfrac{12}{5}x + 4 = \dfrac{1}{5}(x^2 + 12x + 20)$
$= \dfrac{1}{5}(x + 2)(x + 10)$

109. $x^4 - x^2 - 12 = \left(x^2 - 4\right)\left(x^2 + 3\right)$

$\qquad\qquad\quad = (x+2)(x-2)\left(x^2+3\right)$

111. $y^2\left(y+1\right) + 5y\left(y+1\right) + 4\left(y+1\right) = \left(y+1\right)\left(y^2 + 5y + 4\right)$

$\qquad\qquad\qquad\qquad\qquad\qquad\quad = \left(y+1\right)\left(y+1\right)\left(y+4\right)$

6.5 Exercises

1. $10x^2 + 5x - 15 = 5(2x+3)(x-1)$

c, n

3. $3x^2 - 3 = 3(x+1)(x-1)$

a, c, h

5. o

7. $14x^3 + 4x^2 = 2x^2(7x+2)$

g

9. $x^2 + 6x + 9 = (x+3)^2$

b

11. $2x^3 + 12x^2 + 18x = 2x(x^2+6x+9)$

$$= 2x(x+3)^2$$

13. $a^2 + 2ab - 15b^2 = (a-3b)(a+5b)$

15. $48a^4b - 108a^2b = 12a^2b(4a^2-9)$

$$= 12a^2b(2a+3)(2a-3)$$

17. Prime

19. $x^8y^2 + 8x^5y^2 = x^5y^2(x^3+8)$

$$= x^5y^2(x+2)(x^2-2x+4)$$

21. $24x^2 + 16x - 30 = 2(12x^2+8x-15)$

$$= 2(6x-5)(2x+3)$$

23. $4x^3 + 9x^2 + 24x = x(4x^2+9x+24)$

25. $18ax - 6ay + 9bx - 3by$

$$= 3(6ax - 2ay + 3bx - by)$$

$$= 3[2a(3x-y) + b(3x-y)]$$

$$= 3(3x-y)(2a+b)$$

27. $4x^3 + 10x^2 + 6x = 2x(2x^2+5x+3)$

$$= 2x(2x+3)(x+1)$$

29. $9 - 9b^4 = 9(1-b^4)$

$$= 9(1+b^2)(1-b^2)$$

$$= 9(1+b^2)(1+b)(1-b)$$

31. Prime

33. $2x^3 - 72x = 2x(x^2-36)$

$$= 2x(x+6)(x-6)$$

35. $x^4 + 5x^2 - 36 = (x^2+9)(x^2-4)$

$$= (x^2+9)(x+2)(x-2)$$

37. $5x^2 + 7x + 2 = (5x+2)(x+1)$

39. Prime

41. $6x^2 - 44x + 14 = 2(3x^2-22x+7)$

$$= 2(3x-1)(x-7)$$

43. $5y^3 + 2y^2 + 9y = y(5y^2+2y+9)$

45. $2a^3 - 16 = 2(a^3-8)$

$$= 2(a-2)(a^2+2a+4)$$

47. $108b^2 - 36b + 3 = 3(36b^2-12b+1)$

$$= 3(6b-1)^2$$

49. $125x^3 + 27y^3 = (5x+3y)(25x^2-15xy+9y^2)$

51. $3(x+y) + a(x+y) = (x+y)(3+a)$

53. Prime

55. $2ax^2 + bx^2 - 4ay - 2by = x^2(2a+b) - 2y(2a+b)$

$$= (2a+b)(x^2-2y)$$

57. Prime

59. $8x^2 + 23xy - 3y^2 = (8x-y)(x+3y)$

251

61. $w^2 - 36z^2 = (w + 6z)(w - 6z)$

63. $30x^3 y^3 + 192x^2 y^4 - 72xy^5$
$= 6xy^3 \left(5x^2 + 32xy - 12y^2 \right)$

65. $6 + 3h + 2k + hk = 3(2 + h) + k(2 + h)$
$= (2 + h)(3 + k)$

67. $s^7 - s^6 t - 2s^5 t^2 = s^5 \left(s^2 - st - 2t^2 \right)$
$= s^5 (s + t)(s - 2t)$

69. Prime

71. $2p^2 + 11pq + 5q^2 = (2p + q)(p + 5q)$

73. $2ab - 8a - b + 4 = 2a(b - 4) - (b - 4)$
$= (b - 4)(2a - 1)$

75. $3x^2 (y - 1) - 2(y - 1) = (y - 1)\left(3x^2 - 2 \right)$

77. $6x^4 y^9 z^6 + 14x^5 y^4 z^8 = 2x^4 y^4 z^6 \left(3y^5 + 7xz^2 \right)$

79. $42x^2 + 47x + 10 = (7x + 2)(6x + 5)$

81. $5rt - 7ru - 5st + 7su = r(5t - 7u) - s(5t - 7u)$
$= (5t - 7u)(r - s)$

83. Prime

85. $5t^7 + 20t^5 - 105t^3 = 5t^3 \left(t^4 + 4t^2 - 21 \right)$
$= 5t^3 \left(t^2 - 3 \right)\left(t^2 + 7 \right)$

87. $x^2 (x - 3) - (x - 3) = (x - 3)\left(x^2 - 1 \right)$
$= (x - 3)(x + 1)(x - 1)$

89. $x^2 - 4x - 32 = (x + 4)(x - 8)$

91. The last term is missing from the incorrectly factored form. The correct answer is $5ab(3a + 2b + 1)$.

93. There should be a "+" sign between $x(2a + 3)$ and $5(2a + 3)$.

95. $2ax^2 + 4x^2 - 7ax - 14x - 3a - 6$
$= 2x^2 (a + 2) - 7x(a + 2) - 3(a + 2)$
$= (a + 2)\left(2x^2 - 7x - 3 \right)$

97. $(x - 8)^2 - (x + 3)^2$
$= \left[(x - 8) + (x + 3) \right]\left[(x - 8) - (x + 3) \right]$
$= (2x - 5)(-11)$
$= -11(2x - 5)$

99. $4(x - 1)^2 + 7(x - 1) - 2$
$= \left[4(x - 1) - 1 \right]\left[(x - 1) + 2 \right]$
$= (4x - 5)(x + 1)$

101. $x^6 - 64$
$= \left(x^3 + 8 \right)\left(x^3 - 8 \right)$
$= (x + 2)\left(x^2 - 2x + 4 \right)(x - 2)\left(x^2 + 2x + 4 \right)$

103. $\dfrac{6}{7} x^2 + \dfrac{26}{7} x - \dfrac{20}{7} = \dfrac{2}{7}\left(3x^2 + 13x - 10 \right)$
$= \dfrac{2}{7}(3x - 2)(x + 5)$

6.6 Exercises

1. We use the Zero Factor Property to <u>solve</u> nonlinear <u>equations</u>.

3. Using the Zero Factor Property, the solution set of the equation $x(x-5)=0$ is $\{0,5\}$.

5. Before using the Zero Factor Property to solve $(3x+2)(x+1)=4$, we must set the equation equal to <u>zero</u>, use FOIL, and then <u>solve</u>.

7. $P(x)=3x^2+5x-12$ is called a <u>polynomial</u> <u>function</u> or a quadratic function.

9. $x(x+7)=0$

$$x=0 \quad \text{or} \quad x+7=0$$
$$x=0 \quad \text{or} \quad x=-7$$

The solution set is $\{-7,0\}$.

11. $3x(x-5)=0$

$$3x=0 \quad \text{or} \quad x-5=0$$
$$x=0 \quad \text{or} \quad x=5$$

The solution set is $\{0,5\}$.

13. $(x+3)(x+5)=0$

$$x+3=0 \quad \text{or} \quad x+5=0$$
$$x=-3 \quad \text{or} \quad x=-5$$

The solution set is $\{-5,-3\}$.

15. $(x-9)(x+6)=0$

$$x-9=0 \quad \text{or} \quad x+6=0$$
$$x=9 \quad \text{or} \quad x=-6$$

The solution set is $\{-6,9\}$.

17. $(2x-3)(x-7)=0$

$$2x-3=0 \quad \text{or} \quad x-7=0$$
$$x=\frac{3}{2} \quad \text{or} \quad x=7$$

The solution set is $\left\{\frac{3}{2},7\right\}$.

19. $x^2-25=0$

$$(x+5)(x-5)=0$$
$$x+5=0 \quad \text{or} \quad x-5=0$$
$$x=-5 \quad \text{or} \quad x=5$$

The solution set is $\{-5,5\}$.

21. $y^2=36$

$$y^2-36=0$$
$$(y+6)(y-6)=0$$
$$y+6=0 \quad \text{or} \quad y-6=0$$
$$y=-6 \quad \text{or} \quad y=6$$

The solution set is $\{-6,6\}$.

23. $x^2-5x=0$

$$x(x-5)=0$$
$$x=0 \quad \text{or} \quad x-5=0$$
$$x=0 \quad \text{or} \quad x=5$$

The solution set is $\{0,5\}$.

25. $4c^2=9$

$$4c^2-9=0$$
$$(2c+3)(2c-3)=0$$
$$2c+3=0 \quad \text{or} \quad 2c-3=0$$
$$c=-\frac{3}{2} \quad \text{or} \quad c=\frac{3}{2}$$

The solution set is $\left\{-\frac{3}{2},\frac{3}{2}\right\}$.

27. $25k^2=4$

$$25k^2-4=0$$
$$(5k+2)(5k-2)=0$$
$$5k+2=0 \quad \text{or} \quad 5k-2=0$$
$$k=-\frac{2}{5} \quad \text{or} \quad k=\frac{2}{5}$$

The solution set is $\left\{-\frac{2}{5},\frac{2}{5}\right\}$.

29. $x^2+5x+6=0$

$$(x+2)(x+3)=0$$
$$x+2=0 \quad \text{or} \quad x+3=0$$
$$x=-2 \quad \text{or} \quad x=-3$$

The solution set is $\{-3,-2\}$.

31. $y^2=2y+15$

$$y^2-2y-15=0$$
$$(y+3)(y-5)=0$$
$$y+3=0 \quad \text{or} \quad y-5=0$$
$$y=-3 \quad \text{or} \quad y=5$$

The solution set is $\{-3,5\}$.

33.
$$8b^2 + 33b = -4$$
$$8b^2 + 33b + 4 = 0$$
$$(8b+1)(b+4) = 0$$
$$8b+1 = 0 \quad \text{or} \quad b+4 = 0$$
$$b = -\frac{1}{8} \quad \text{or} \quad b = -4$$

The solution set is $\left\{-4, -\frac{1}{8}\right\}$.

35.
$$4x^2 + 7 = 11x$$
$$4x^2 - 11x + 7 = 0$$
$$(4x-7)(x-1) = 0$$
$$4x-7 = 0 \quad \text{or} \quad x-1 = 0$$
$$x = \frac{7}{4} \quad \text{or} \quad x = 1$$

The solution set is $\left\{1, \frac{7}{4}\right\}$.

37. $x^2 - 6x + 9 = 0$
$$(x-3)^2 = 0$$
$$x-3 = 0$$
$$x = 3$$

The solution set is $\{3\}$.

39.
$$12k^2 - 5k = 2$$
$$12k^2 - 5k - 2 = 0$$
$$(4k+1)(3k-2) = 0$$
$$4k+1 = 0 \quad \text{or} \quad 3k-2 = 0$$
$$k = -\frac{1}{4} \quad \text{or} \quad k = \frac{2}{3}$$

The solution set is $\left\{-\frac{1}{4}, \frac{2}{3}\right\}$.

41.
$$4a^2 + 20a = -25$$
$$4a^2 + 20a + 25 = 0$$
$$(2a+5)(2a+5) = 0$$
$$2a+5 = 0$$
$$a = -\frac{5}{2}$$

The solution set is $\left\{-\frac{5}{2}\right\}$.

43. $(x-7)(x+5) = -20$
$$x^2 - 2x - 35 = -20$$
$$x^2 - 2x - 15 = 0$$
$$(x+3)(x-5) = 0$$
$$x+3 = 0 \quad \text{or} \quad x-5 = 0$$
$$x = -3 \quad \text{or} \quad x = 5$$

The solution set is $\{-3,5\}$.

45.a.
$$P(0) = 4(0)^2 - 2(0)$$
$$= 4(0) - 2(0)$$
$$= 0 + 0$$
$$= 0$$

45.b.
$$P(-2) = 4(-2)^2 - 2(-2)$$
$$= 4(4) - 2(-2)$$
$$= 16 + 4$$
$$= 20$$

45.c.
$$P\left(\frac{3}{2}\right) = 4\left(\frac{3}{2}\right)^2 - 2\left(\frac{3}{2}\right)$$
$$= 4\left(\frac{9}{4}\right) - 2\left(\frac{3}{2}\right)$$
$$= 9 - 3$$
$$= 6$$

47.a.
$$P(0) = -6(0)^2 - (0) + 5$$
$$= -6(0) - (0) + 5$$
$$= 0 - 0 + 5$$
$$= 5$$

47.b.
$$P(1) = -6(1)^2 - (1) + 5$$
$$= -6(1) - (1) + 5$$
$$= -6 - 1 + 5$$
$$= -2$$

47.c.
$$P\left(\frac{2}{3}\right) = -6\left(\frac{2}{3}\right)^2 - \left(\frac{2}{3}\right) + 5$$
$$= -6\left(\frac{4}{9}\right) - \left(\frac{2}{3}\right) + 5$$
$$= -\frac{8}{3} - \frac{2}{3} + 5$$
$$= -\frac{10}{3} + 5$$
$$= \frac{5}{3}$$

49. Answers will vary; one example is: The two binomials are not set equal to zero, therefore the Zero Factor Property cannot be used to simplify the binomials.

51. Answers will vary; one example is: $x(x-8)=0$.

53. Area $= LW$

$$12 = (x-2)(x-1)$$
$$12 = x^2 - 3x + 2$$
$$x^2 - 3x - 10 = 0$$
$$(x+2)(x-5) = 0$$
$$x+2 = 0 \quad \text{or} \quad x-5 = 0$$
$$x = -2 \quad \text{or} \quad x = 5$$

The width is 3 feet and the length is 4 feet.

55. Let $c =$ the length of the ladder.

$$6^2 + 8^2 = c^2$$
$$100 = c^2$$
$$c^2 - 100 = 0$$
$$(c+10)(c-10) = 0$$
$$c+10 = 0 \quad \text{or} \quad c-10 = 0$$
$$c = -10 \quad \text{or} \quad c = 10$$

The length of the ladder is 10 feet.

57.
$$x^2 + (x+1)^2 = (x+2)^2$$
$$x^2 + x^2 + 2x + 1 = x^2 + 4x + 4$$
$$x^2 - 2x - 3 = 0$$
$$(x+1)(x-3) = 0$$
$$x+1 = 0 \quad \text{or} \quad x-3 = 0$$
$$x = -1 \quad \text{or} \quad x = 3$$

The lengths of the sides are 3 units, 4 units, and 5 units.

59. Let $w =$ the width of the garden, then the length is $l = 4w$.

$$\text{Area} = lw$$
$$25 = (4w)(w)$$
$$25 = 4w^2$$
$$4w^2 - 25 = 0$$
$$(2w+5)(2w-5) = 0$$
$$2w+5 = 0 \quad \text{or} \quad 2w-5 = 0$$
$$w = -\frac{5}{2} \quad \text{or} \quad w = \frac{5}{2}$$

The length of the garden is 10 feet and the width is 2.5 feet.

61. Let $x =$ the number.

$$x + x^2 = 72$$
$$x^2 + x - 72 = 0$$
$$(x-8)(x+9) = 0$$
$$x-8 = 0 \quad \text{or} \quad x+9 = 0$$
$$x = 8 \quad \text{or} \quad x = -9$$

The number can be either 8 or -9.

63. Let $x =$ the first rational number, then the second rational number is $9x$

$$(x)(9x) = 49$$
$$9x^2 = 49$$
$$9x^2 - 49 = 0$$
$$(3x+7)(3x-7) = 0$$
$$3x+7 = 0 \quad \text{or} \quad 3x-7 = 0$$
$$x = -\frac{7}{3} \quad \text{or} \quad x = \frac{7}{3}$$

The two rational numbers are $-\frac{7}{3}$ and -21 or $\frac{7}{3}$ and 21.

65. Prepare We are to determine how long it will take the rocket to return to the ground after it is launched.

Plan We will solve the equation $h(t) = 0$ for t, using the Zero Factor Property.

Process

$$h(t) = -16t^2 + 160t$$
$$-16t^2 + 160t = 0$$
$$-16t(t-10) = 0$$
$$-16t = 0 \quad \text{or} \quad t-10 = 0$$
$$t = 0 \quad \text{or} \quad t = 10$$

The rocket blaster will return to the ground 10 seconds after it is launched.

Ponder Does our answer seem reasonable? Yes, it is quite reasonable for a firecracker to stay in the air for 10 seconds.

67. $(x^2 - 9)(x^2 - 25) = 0$

$$x^2 - 9 = 0 \quad \text{or} \quad x^2 - 25 = 0$$
$$(x+3)(x-3) = 0 \quad \text{or} \quad (x+5)(x-5) = 0$$
$$x+3 = 0 \quad \text{or} \quad x-3 = 0 \quad \text{or} \quad x+5 = 0 \quad \text{or} \quad x-5 = 0$$
$$x = -3 \quad \text{or} \quad x = 3 \quad \text{or} \quad x = -5 \quad \text{or} \quad x = 5$$

The solution set is $\{-5, -3, 3, 5\}$.

69.

$$12x^3 + 12x^2 = 9x$$

$$12x^3 + 12x^2 - 9x = 0$$

$$3x\left(4x^2 + 4x - 3\right) = 0$$

$$3x(2x+3)(2x-1) = 0$$

$$3x = 0 \quad \text{or} \quad 2x+3 = 0 \quad \text{or} \quad 2x-1 = 0$$

$$x = 0 \quad \text{or} \quad x = -\frac{3}{2} \quad \text{or} \quad x = \frac{1}{2}$$

The solution set is $\left\{-\frac{3}{2}, 0, \frac{1}{2}\right\}$.

71.

$$2a^2 + 8a - 48 = 12a$$

$$2a^2 - 4a - 48 = 0$$

$$2\left(a^2 - 2a - 24\right) = 0$$

$$2(a+4)(a-6) = 0$$

$$a+4 = 0 \quad \text{or} \quad a-6 = 0$$

$$a = -4 \quad \text{or} \quad a = 6$$

The solution set is $\{-4, 6\}$.

Chapter 6 Review Problem Set

1. $2 - 5a^2b^2$

2. $2a - 1$

3. $3x^4y^9z^2$

4. $2 - 5x$

5. The GCF is $5a^3b^6c^2$.
$$25a^5b^6c^2 + 70a^3b^8c^2 = 5a^3b^6c^2\left(5a^2 + 14b^2\right)$$

6. The GCF is 2.
$$6r - 8s + 12t = 2(3r - 4s + 6t)$$

7. The GCF is 4.
$$4y^2 + 16y - 4 = 4\left(y^2 + 4y - 1\right)$$

8. The GCF is r^3.
$$8r^8 + 11r^5 - 3r^3 = r^3\left(8r^5 + 11r^2 - 3\right)$$

9. The GCF is $x + 5y$.
$$3x(x + 5y) - 11y(x + 5y) = (x + 5y)(3x - 11y)$$

10. The GCF is $9k + 1$.
$$5h(9k + 1) + (9k + 1) = (9k + 1)(5h + 1)$$

11. $ac + ad + bc + bd = a(c + d) + b(c + d)$
$$= (c + d)(a + b)$$

12. $x^2 + 2xy + 5x + 10y = x(x + 2y) + 5(x + 2y)$
$$= (x + 2y)(x + 5)$$

13. $5rt - 8r + 5st - 8s = r(5t - 8) + s(5t - 8)$
$$= (5t - 8)(r + s)$$

14. $3xy + 3y + x + 1 = 3y(x + 1) + (x + 1)$
$$= (x + 1)(3y + 1)$$

15. $6ab - b - 12a + 2 = b(6a - 1) - 2(6a - 1)$
$$= (6a - 1)(b - 2)$$

16. $st + 4s - t - 4 = s(t + 4) - (t + 4)$
$$= (t + 4)(s - 1)$$

17. $49 - x^2 = (7)^2 - (x)^2$
$$= (7 + x)(7 - x)$$

18. Prime

19. $16c^2 - 1 = (4c)^2 - (1)^2$
$$= (4c + 1)(4c - 1)$$

20. $64 - 25x^2 = (8)^2 - (5x)^2$
$$= (8 + 5x)(8 - 5x)$$

21. Prime

22. $4x^2y^2 - 9a^2b^2 = (2xy)^2 - (3ab)^2$
$$= (2xy + 3ab)(2xy - 3ab)$$

23. $x^2 + y^3 = (x)^3 + (y)^3$
$$= (x + y)\left(x^2 - xy + y^2\right)$$

24. $1 - c^3 = (1)^3 - (c)^3$
$$= (1 - c)\left(1^2 + (1)(c) + c^2\right)$$
$$= (1 - c)\left(1 + c + c^2\right)$$

25. $8x^3 - y^3 = (2x)^3 - (y)^3$
$$= (2x - y)\left((2x)^2 + (2x)(y) + y^2\right)$$
$$= (2x - y)\left(4x^2 + 2xy + y^2\right)$$

26. $64b^3 + a^3 = (4b)^3 + (a)^3$
$$= (4b + a)\left((4b)^2 - (4b)(a) + a^2\right)$$
$$= (4b + a)\left(16b^2 - 4ab + a^2\right)$$

27. $27 - 8x^3 = (3)^3 - (2x)^3$
$$= (3 - 2x)\left((3)^2 + (3)(2x) + (2x)^2\right)$$
$$= (3 - 2x)\left(9 + 6x + 4x^2\right)$$

28. $8a^3 + 125b^3 = (2a)^3 + (5b)^3$

$$= (2a + 5b)\left((2a)^2 - (2a)(5b) + (5b)^2\right)$$

$$= (2a + 5b)\left(4a^2 - 10ab + 25b^2\right)$$

29. $2x - 3$

30. $8a + b$

31. $A = 3,\ C = 10,\ AC = 30$

The factors of 30 whose sum is 17 are 2 and 15.

$$3x^2 + 17x + 10 = 3x^2 + 2x + 15x + 10$$

$$= x(3x + 2) + 5(3x + 2)$$

$$= (3x + 2)(x + 5)$$

32. $A = 2,\ C = 4,\ AC = 8$

The factors of 8 whose sum is -9 are -1 and -8.

$$2x^2 - 9x + 4 = 2x^2 - x - 8x + 4$$

$$= x(2x - 1) - 4(2x - 1)$$

$$= (2x - 1)(x - 4)$$

33. $A = 8,\ C = 3,\ AC = 24$

The factors of 24 that differ by 10 are 2 and 12.

$$8a^2 - 10x - 3 = 8a^2 + 2a - 12a - 3$$

$$= 2a(4a + 1) - 3(4a + 1)$$

$$= (4a + 1)(2a - 3)$$

34. Prime

35. $A = 6,\ C = 5,\ AC = 30$

The factors of 30 whose sum is -13 are -3 and -10.

$$6b^2 - 13b + 5 = 6b^2 - 3b - 10b + 5$$

$$= 3b(2b - 1) - 5(2b - 1)$$

$$= (2b - 1)(3b - 5)$$

36. $A = 8,\ C = 3,\ AC = 24$

The factors of 24 that differ by 2 are 4 and 6.

$$8x^2 + 2xy - 3y^2 = 8x^2 - 4xy + 6xy - 3y^2$$

$$= 4x(2x - y) + 3y(2x - y)$$

$$= (2x - y)(4x + 3y)$$

37. The factors of 30 are 1, 2, 3, 5, 6, 10, 15, and 30. The factors of 4 are 1, 2, and 4.

$$30x^2 + 29x + 4 = (6x + 1)(5x + 4)$$

38. The factors of 20 are 1, 2, 4, 5, 10, and 20. The factors of 5 are 1 and 5.

$$20y^2 - 21y - 5 = (5y + 1)(4y - 5)$$

39. The factors of 18 are 1, 2, 3, 6, 9, and 18. The factors of 3 are 1 and 3.

$$18x^2 + 25x - 3 = (9x - 1)(2x + 3)$$

40. Prime

41. The factors of 48 are 1, 2, 3, 4, 6, 8, 12, 16, 24, and 48. The factors of 15 are 1, 3, 5, and 15.

$$48a^2 - 16a - 15 = (12a + 5)(4a - 3)$$

42. The factors of 56 are 1, 2, 4, 7, 8, 14, 28, and 56. The factors of 9 are 1, 3, and 9.

$$56x^2 + 3xy - 9y^2 = (8x - 3y)(7x + 3y)$$

43.
$$Area = bh$$

$$2x^2 - xv - v^2 = (x - v)(2x + v)$$

The height is $2x + v$.

44.
$$Volume = LWH$$

$$12x^3 - 22x^2 + 8x = 2x\left(6x^2 - 11x + 4\right)$$

$$= 2x(2x - 1)(3x - 4)$$

The width is $3x - 4$.

45. No, the middle term would equal $48x$ if the polynomial were a perfect square trinomial.

46. Yes, the polynomial is a trinomial.

47. The factors of 16 whose sum is 10 are 2 and 8.

$$x^2 + 10x + 16 = (x + 2)(x + 8)$$

48. The factors of 28 whose sum is 11 are 4 and 7.

$$y^2 - 11y + 28 = (y - 4)(y - 7)$$

49. There are no factors of 4 whose sum is 2. Therefore, the polynomial is prime.

50. The factors of 36 that differ by 5 are 4 and 9.

$$h^2 + 5h - 36 = (h - 4)(h + 9)$$

51. The factors of 6 whose sum is 7 are 1 and 6.

$$a^2 + 7ab + 6b^2 = (a + b)(a + 6b)$$

52. The factors of 15 whose sum is 8 are 3 and 5.

$$x^4 + 8x^2 + 15 = (x^2 + 3)(x^2 + 5)$$

53. $a^2 + 20a + 100 = a^2 + 2(a)(10) + 10^2$
$$= (a+10)^2$$

54. $9b^2 - 24b + 16 = (3b)^2 - 2(3b)(4) + 4^2$
$$= (3b-4)^2$$

55. $25y^2 + 10y + 1 = (5y)^2 + 2(5y)(1) + 1^2$
$$= (5y+1)^2$$

56. $x^2 + 4xy + 4y^2 = x^2 + 2(x)(2y) + (2y)^2$
$$= (x+2y)^2$$

57. $x^2y^2 - 18xy + 81 = (xy)^2 - 2(xy)(9) + 9^2$
$$= (xy-9)^2$$

58. $16x^4 - 8x^2 + 1 = (4x^2)^2 - 2(4x)(1) + 1^2$
$$= (4x^2 - 1)^2$$
$$= [(2x+1)(2x-1)]^2$$
$$= (2x+1)^2(2x-1)^2$$

59. $x^4 + x = x(x^3 + 1)$
$$= x(x+1)(x^2 - x + 1)$$

60. $12x^2 + 32x + 20 = 4(3x^2 + 8x + 5)$
$$= 4(3x+5)(x+1)$$

61. $2s^3t^2 - 12s^2t^2 + 10st^2 = 2st^2(s^2 - 6s + 5)$
$$= 2st^2(s-1)(s-5)$$

62. Prime

63. $8x^2 - 8xy - 6y^2 = 2(4x^2 - 4xy - 3y^2)$
$$= 2(2x+y)(2x-3y)$$

64. $15x^2 - 6x + 9 = 3(5x^2 - 2x + 3)$

65. $ax^2 - 3abx + 2a^2x - 6a^2b$
$$= a(x^2 - 3bx + 2ax - 6ab)$$
$$= a[x(x-3b) + 2a(x-3b)]$$
$$= a(x-3b)(x+2a)$$

66. Prime

67. $h(6x-5) - 5(6x-5) = (6x-5)(h-5)$

68. $6a^3 - 5a^2 - 4a = a(6a^2 - 5a - 4)$
$$= a(3a-4)(2a+1)$$

69. $y^2 + 13y - 30 = (y-2)(y+15)$

70. $8 - k^3 = 2^3 - k^3$
$$= (2-k)(2^2 + 2k + k^2)$$
$$= (2-k)(4 + 2k + k^2)$$

71. Prime

72. $5b^3 - 7b^2 - 6b = b(5b^2 - 7b - 6)$
$$= b(5b+3)(b-2)$$

73. $9a^2 - 48ab + 64b^2 = (3a)^2 - 2(3a)(8b) + (8b)^2$
$$= (3a-8b)^2$$

74. $27x^2 - 18x + 3 = 3(9x^2 - 6x + 1)$
$$= 3[(3x)^2 - 2(3x)(1) + 1^2]$$
$$= 3(3x-1)^2$$

75. $x^4 - 101x^2 + 100 = (x^2 - 100)(x^2 - 1)$
$$= (x^2 - 10^2)(x^2 - 1^2)$$
$$= (x+10)(x-10)(x+1)(x-1)$$

76. $x^5 - 4x^3 - x^2 + 4$
$$= x^3(x^2 - 4) - (x^2 - 4)$$
$$= (x^2 - 4)(x^3 - 1)$$
$$= (x+2)(x-2)(x-1)(x^2 + x + 1)$$

259

77. Prime

78. $16m^2 + 50mn - 21n^2 = (8m - 3n)(2m + 7n)$

79. $11z^2 - 33z = 11z(z - 3)$

80. $2a(x + 5) + (x + 5) = (x + 5)(2a + 1)$

81. $x(x - 5) = 0$

$\qquad x = 0 \quad$ or $\quad x - 5 = 0$

$\qquad x = 0 \quad$ or $\qquad x = 5$

The solution set is $\{0, 5\}$.

82. $x(2x + 7) = 0$

$\qquad x = 0 \quad$ or $\quad 2x + 7 = 0$

$\qquad x = 0 \quad$ or $\qquad x = -\dfrac{7}{2}$

The solution set is $\left\{-\dfrac{7}{2}, 0\right\}$.

83. $(x - 2)(x + 8) = 0$

$\qquad x - 2 = 0 \quad$ or $\quad x + 8 = 0$

$\qquad x = 2 \quad$ or $\qquad x = -8$

The solution set is $\{-8, 2\}$.

84. $(x - 5)(2x - 1) = 0$

$\qquad x - 5 = 0 \quad$ or $\quad 2x - 1 = 0$

$\qquad x = 5 \quad$ or $\qquad x = \dfrac{1}{2}$

The solution set is $\left\{\dfrac{1}{2}, 5\right\}$.

85. $x^2 - 49 = 0$

$\qquad (x + 7)(x - 7) = 0$

$\qquad x + 7 = 0 \quad$ or $\quad x - 7 = 0$

$\qquad x = -7 \quad$ or $\qquad x = 7$

The solution set is $\{-7, 7\}$.

86. $y^2 = 64$

$\qquad y^2 - 64 = 0$

$\qquad (y + 8)(y - 8) = 0$

$\qquad y + 8 = 0 \quad$ or $\quad y - 8 = 0$

$\qquad y = -8 \quad$ or $\qquad y = 8$

The solution set is $\{-8, 8\}$.

87. $a^2 - 5a = 0$

$\qquad a(a - 5) = 0$

$\qquad a = 0 \quad$ or $\quad a - 5 = 0$

$\qquad a = 0 \quad$ or $\qquad a = 5$

The solution set is $\{0, 5\}$.

88. $b^2 = 7b$

$\qquad b^2 - 7b = 0$

$\qquad b(b - 7) = 0$

$\qquad b = 0 \quad$ or $\quad b - 7 = 0$

$\qquad b = 0 \quad$ or $\qquad b = 7$

The solution set is $\{0, 7\}$.

89. $16h^2 = 25$

$\qquad 16h^2 - 25 = 0$

$\qquad (4h + 5)(4h - 5) = 0$

$\qquad 4h + 5 = 0 \quad$ or $\quad 4h - 5 = 0$

$\qquad x = -\dfrac{5}{4} \quad$ or $\qquad x = \dfrac{5}{4}$

The solution set is $\left\{-\dfrac{5}{4}, \dfrac{5}{4}\right\}$.

90. $9c^2 - 4 = 0$

$\qquad (3c + 2)(3c - 2) = 0$

$\qquad 3c + 2 = 0 \quad$ or $\quad 3c - 2 = 0$

$\qquad c = -\dfrac{2}{3} \quad$ or $\qquad c = \dfrac{2}{3}$

The solution set is $\left\{-\dfrac{2}{3}, \dfrac{2}{3}\right\}$.

91. $x^2 - 6x = -8$

$\qquad x^2 - 6x + 8 = 0$

$\qquad (x - 2)(x - 4) = 0$

$\qquad x - 2 = 0 \quad$ or $\quad x - 4 = 0$

$\qquad x = 2 \quad$ or $\qquad x = 4$

The solution set is $\{2, 4\}$.

92. $6x^2 - 2 = x$

$\qquad 6x^2 - x - 2 = 0$

$\qquad (3x - 2)(2x + 1) = 0$

$\qquad 3x - 2 = 0 \quad$ or $\quad 2x + 1 = 0$

$\qquad x = \dfrac{2}{3} \quad$ or $\qquad x = -\dfrac{1}{2}$

The solution set is $\left\{-\dfrac{1}{2},\dfrac{2}{3}\right\}$.

93.
$$12y^2 = 3 - 5y$$
$$12y^2 + 5y - 3 = 0$$
$$(3y-1)(4y+3) = 0$$
$$3y - 1 = 0 \quad \text{or} \quad 4y + 3 = 0$$
$$x = \frac{1}{3} \quad \text{or} \quad y = -\frac{3}{4}$$

The solution set is $\left\{-\dfrac{3}{4},\dfrac{1}{3}\right\}$.

94. $4b^2 - 28b + 49 = 0$
$$(2b-7)^2 = 0$$
$$2b - 7 = 0$$
$$b = \frac{7}{2}$$

The solution set is $\left\{\dfrac{7}{2}\right\}$.

95. $(a-3)^2 = 1$
$$a^2 - 6a + 8 = 0$$
$$(a-4)(a-2) = 0$$
$$a - 4 = 0 \quad \text{or} \quad a - 2 = 0$$
$$a = 4 \quad \text{or} \quad a = 2$$

The solution set is $\{2,4\}$.

96. $(x+2)(x-6) = 20$
$$x^2 - 4x - 32 = 0$$
$$(x+4)(x-8) = 0$$
$$x + 4 = 0 \quad \text{or} \quad x - 8 = 0$$
$$x = -4 \quad \text{or} \quad x = 8$$

The solution set is $\{-4,8\}$.

97. $(x-1)(x+9) = 11$
$$x^2 + 8x - 20 = 0$$
$$(x-2)(x+10) = 0$$
$$x - 2 = 0 \quad \text{or} \quad x + 10 = 0$$
$$x = 2 \quad \text{or} \quad x = -10$$

The solution set is $\{-10,2\}$.

98. $3x^3 + 2x^2 - 5x = 0$
$$x(3x^2 + 2x - 5) = 0$$
$$x(3x+5)(x-1) = 0$$
$$x = 0 \quad \text{or} \quad 3x + 5 = 0 \quad \text{or} \quad x - 1 = 0$$
$$x = 0 \quad \text{or} \quad x = -\frac{5}{3} \quad \text{or} \quad x = 1$$

The solution set is $\left\{-\dfrac{5}{3},0,1\right\}$.

99. a) $P(0) = 8(0)^2 - 6(0) + 5$
$$= 8(0) - 6(0) + 5$$
$$= 0 + 0 + 5$$
$$= 5$$

b) $P(-2) = 8(-2)^2 - 6(-2) + 5$
$$= 8(4) - 6(-2) + 5$$
$$= 32 + 12 + 5$$
$$= 49$$

c) $P\left(\dfrac{3}{2}\right) = 8\left(\dfrac{3}{2}\right)^2 - 6\left(\dfrac{3}{2}\right) + 5$
$$= 8\left(\frac{9}{4}\right) - 6\left(\frac{3}{2}\right) + 5$$
$$= 18 - 9 + 5$$
$$= 14$$

100. a) $P(0) = -4(0)^2 + 8(0) - 1$
$$= -4(0) + 8(0) - 1$$
$$= 0 + 0 - 1$$
$$= -1$$

b) $P(-3) = -4(-3)^2 + 8(-3) - 1$
$$= -4(9) + 8(-3) - 1$$
$$= -36 - 24 - 1$$
$$= -61$$

c) $P\left(\dfrac{1}{4}\right) = -4\left(\dfrac{1}{4}\right)^2 + 8\left(\dfrac{1}{4}\right) - 1$
$$= -4\left(\frac{1}{16}\right) + 8\left(\frac{1}{4}\right) - 1$$
$$= -\frac{1}{4} + 2 - 1$$
$$= \frac{3}{4}$$

101. Let $l =$ the length of the rectangle.   Then the width of the rectangle is $w = l - 1$.

$$Area = lw$$
$$20 = l(l-1)$$
$$l^2 - l - 20 = 0$$
$$(l+4)(l-5) = 0$$
$$l + 4 = 0 \quad \text{or} \quad l - 5 = 0$$
$$l = -4 \quad \text{or} \qquad l = 5$$

The length of the rectangle is 5 feet and the width is 4 feet.

102. Let $x =$ the unknown number.

$$x(x-3) = 28$$
$$x^2 - 3x - 28 = 0$$
$$(x+4)(x-7) = 0$$
$$x + 4 = 0 \quad \text{or} \quad x - 7 = 0$$
$$x = -4 \quad \text{or} \qquad x = 7$$

There are two possible solutions; the number -4 or the number 7.

103. Let $x =$ the unknown number.

$$x + x^2 = 56$$
$$x^2 + x - 56 = 0$$
$$(x-7)(x+8) = 0$$
$$x - 7 = 0 \quad \text{or} \quad x + 8 = 0$$
$$x = 7 \quad \text{or} \qquad x = -8$$

There are two possible solutions; the number -7 or the number 8.

104. Prepare We must determine how long the calf is out of the water.

Plan We will solve the equation $h(t) = 0$ using the Zero Factor Property.

Process

$$h(t) = -16t^2 + 18t$$
$$-16t^2 + 18t = 0$$
$$-2t(8t - 9) = 0$$
$$-2t = 0 \quad \text{or} \quad 8t - 9 = 0$$
$$t = 0 \quad \text{or} \qquad t = 1.125$$

The calf is out of the water for 1.125 seconds.

Ponder   Does our answer seem reasonable? Yes, it is quite reasonable for the calf to remain out of the water for 1.125 seconds.

CHAPTER 6 TEST

1. $4a^2 - 9b^2 = (2a + 3b)(2a - 3b)$

f

2. $a^2 - 14ab + 49b^2 = (a - 7b)^2$

g

3. $3a^3 - 15a^2b + 18ab^2 = 3a(a - 2b)(a - 3b)$

a, d

4. $a^2 + 49b^2$ is prime.

j

5. $8a^3 + 27b^3 = (2a + 3b)(4a^2 - 6ab + 9b^2)$

f

6. $A = 5$, $C = -12$, and $AC = -60$. The factors of -60 that differ by 11 are 15 and -4.

$$5x^2 + 11x - 12 = 5x^2 + 15x - 4x - 12$$
$$= 5x(x + 3) - 4(x + 3)$$
$$= (x + 3)(5x - 4)$$

7. The factors of 15 are 1, 3, 5, and 15. The factors of 24 are 1, 2, 3, 4, 5, 8, 12, and 24.

$$15x^2 + 38x + 24 = (3x + 4)(5x + 6)$$

8. $4y^3 - 9y = y(4y^2 - 9)$

$$= y((2y)^2 - (3)^2)$$
$$= y(2y + 3)(2y - 3)$$

9. $80x^2 - 34x - 90 = 2(40x^2 - 17x - 45)$

10. $12a^2 - 94ab + 70b^2 = 2(6a^2 - 47ab + 35b^2)$

$$= 2(6a - 5b)(a - 7b)$$

11. $8r^3 - 1 = (2r)^3 - (1)^3$

$$= (2r - 1)((2r)^2 + (2r)(1) + (1)^2)$$
$$= (2r - 1)(4r^2 + 2r + 1)$$

12. $A = 2$, $C = 5$, and $AC = 10$. There are no factors of 10 whose product is 10 and whose sum is -6.

Therefore, $2x^2 - 6x + 5$ is prime.

13. $2ax - 2x + 3ay - 3y = 2x(a - 1) + 3y(a - 1)$

$$= (a - 1)(2x + 3y)$$

14. $a^4 - 8a^3 - 20a^2 = a^2(a^2 - 8a - 20)$

$$= a^2(a + 2)(a - 10)$$

15. The GCF is $6a^2b^3c$.

$$24a^4b^3c + 36a^3b^3c + 54a^2b^5c = 6a^2b^3c(4a^2 + 6a + 9b^2)$$

16. $36y^2 - 3y - 105 = 3(12y^2 - y - 35)$

$$= 3(3y + 5)(4y - 7)$$

17. $18r^3 - 24r^2 + 8r = 2r(9r^2 - 12r + 4)$

$$= 2r((3r)^2 - 2(3r)(2) + (2)^2)$$
$$= 2r(3r - 2)^2$$

18. $(2x + 3)(x - 1) = 0$

$$
\begin{array}{lll}
2x + 3 = 0 & or & x - 1 = 0 \\
2x + 3 - 3 = 0 - 3 & & x - 1 + 1 = 0 + 1 \\
2x = -3 & & x = 1 \\
\dfrac{2x}{2} = \dfrac{-3}{2} & & \\
x = -\dfrac{3}{2} & &
\end{array}
$$

The solution set is $\left\{ -\dfrac{3}{2}, 1 \right\}$.

19.

$$x^3 = 9x$$
$$x^3 - 9x = 9x - 9x$$
$$x^3 - 9x = 0$$
$$x(x^2 - 9) = 0$$
$$x(x + 3)(x - 3) = 0$$

$$
\begin{array}{lll}
x = 0 \quad or & x + 3 = 0 & or \quad x - 3 = 0 \\
& x + 3 - 3 = 0 - 3 & x - 3 + 3 = 0 + 3 \\
& x = -3 & x = 3
\end{array}
$$

The solution set is $\{-3, 0, 3\}$

20.
$$8x^2 - 10x + 8 = 5$$
$$8x^2 - 10x + 8 - 5 = 5 - 5$$
$$8x^2 - 10x + 3 = 0$$
$$(2x-1)(4x-3) = 0$$

$$2x - 1 = 0 \qquad or \qquad 4x - 3 = 0$$
$$2x - 1 + 1 = 0 + 1 \qquad 4x - 3 + 3 = 0 + 3$$
$$2x = 1 \qquad\qquad 4x = 3$$
$$\frac{2x}{2} = \frac{1}{2} \qquad\qquad \frac{4x}{4} = \frac{3}{4}$$
$$x = \frac{1}{2} \qquad\qquad x = \frac{3}{4}$$

The solution set is $\left\{\dfrac{1}{2}, \dfrac{3}{4}\right\}$.

21.
$$(x+2)(x-3) = 14$$
$$x^2 - 3x + 2x - 6 = 14$$
$$x^2 - x - 6 = 14$$
$$x^2 - x - 6 - 14 = 14 - 14$$
$$x^2 - x - 20 = 0$$
$$(x+4)(x-5) = 0$$

$$x + 4 = 0 \qquad or \qquad x - 5 = 0$$
$$x + 4 - 4 = 0 - 4 \qquad x - 5 + 5 = 0 + 5$$
$$x = -4 \qquad\qquad x = 5$$

The solution set is $\{-4, 5\}$.

22. a) $P(x) = -3x^2 + 7x - 2$
$$P(0) = -3(0)^2 + 7(0) - 2$$
$$P(0) = 0 + 0 - 2$$
$$P(0) = -2$$

b) $P(x) = -3x^2 + 7x - 2$
$$P(-4) = -3(-4)^2 + 7(-4) - 2$$
$$P(-4) = -3(16) + (-28) - 2$$
$$P(-4) = -48 + (-28) - 2$$
$$P(-4) = -76 - 2$$
$$P(-4) = -78$$

c) $P(x) = -3x^2 + 7x - 2$
$$P\left(\frac{1}{3}\right) = -3\left(\frac{1}{3}\right)^2 + 7\left(\frac{1}{3}\right) - 2$$
$$P\left(\frac{1}{3}\right) = -3\left(\frac{1}{9}\right) + \frac{7}{3} - 2$$
$$P\left(\frac{1}{3}\right) = -\frac{1}{3} + \frac{7}{3} - 2$$
$$P\left(\frac{1}{3}\right) = \frac{6}{3} - 2$$
$$P\left(\frac{1}{3}\right) = 2 - 2$$
$$P\left(\frac{1}{3}\right) = 0$$

23. *Total Area* $= 2x^2 + x - 21$
$$= 2x(x-3) + 7(x-3)$$
$$= (x-3)(2x+7)$$

Since the total area is b times h, and since $h = x - 3$, we must have $b = 2x + 7$.

24. Let x be the number, then $(x+5)^2 = x + 17$.
$$(x+5)^2 = x + 17$$
$$x^2 + 10x + 25 = x + 17$$
$$x^2 + 9x + 8 = 0$$
$$(x+1)(x+8) = 0$$

$$x + 1 = 0 \qquad or \qquad x + 8 = 0$$
$$x + 1 - 1 = 0 - 1 \qquad x + 8 - 8 = 0 - 8$$
$$x = -1 \qquad\qquad x = -8$$

The two numbers that satisfy the conditions are -1 -8.

25. Prepare We are to determine the amount of time it will take the egg carton to reach the ground after it is dropped.

Plan We must solve the equation $49 = 16t^2$ for t.

Process
$$49 = 16t^2$$
$$49 - 16t^2 = 0$$
$$(7)^2 - (4t)^2 = 0$$
$$(7+4t)(7-4t) = 0$$

$$7 + 4t = 0 \qquad or \qquad 7 - 4t = 0$$
$$4t = -7 \qquad\qquad -4t = -7$$
$$t = -\frac{7}{4} \qquad\qquad t = \frac{7}{4}$$
$$t = -1.75 \qquad\qquad t = 1.75$$

Since time is positive, use the solution 1.75. That is, it takes the egg carton 1.75 seconds to reach the ground.

Ponder Is the result reasonable? I seems reasonable that it would take the egg carton 1.75 seconds to cover a distance of 49 feet.

Chapters 4-6 Cumulative Review

1.
$$x - 3y = 16 \qquad -4x + 2y = -6$$
$$(1) - 3(-5) = 16 \qquad -4(1) + 2(-5) = 16$$
$$1 + 15 = 16 \qquad -4 - 10 = 16$$
$$16 = 16 \qquad -14 = 16$$
$$\text{True} \qquad\qquad \text{False}$$

The ordered pair $(1, -5)$ is not a solution.

2. The slope of L_1 is $m = \dfrac{1}{2}$ and the y-intercept is $(0, -4)$. The slope-intercept from of L_2 is $y = -3x + 3$. The slope of L_2 is $m = -3$ and the y-intercept is $(0, 3)$.

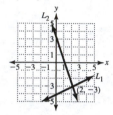

The solution set to the system is $\{(2, -3)\}$.

3. Solve the second equation for x to obtain $x = 4y + 2$. Substitute $x = 4y + 2$ into the first equation and solve for y.
$$2x + 6y = 11$$
$$2(4y + 2) + 6y = 11$$
$$8y + 4 + 6y = 11$$
$$14y = 7$$
$$y = \frac{1}{2}$$

Substitute $y = \dfrac{1}{2}$ into $x = 4y + 2$ to find x.
$$x = 4y + 2$$
$$x = 4\left(\frac{1}{2}\right) + 2$$
$$x = 4$$

The solution set is $\left\{\left(4, \dfrac{1}{2}\right)\right\}$.

4. Eliminate y by adding Equation 1 and 18 times Equation 2.
$$\begin{array}{ll} \text{Equation 1} & \left\{\begin{array}{l} 6x - 18y = 12 \\ -6x + 18y = -12 \end{array}\right. \\ 18(\text{Equation 2}) & \end{array}$$
$$\overline{\qquad\qquad 0 = 0 \qquad\qquad}$$

The solution set is $\{(x, y) \mid 6x - 18y = 12\}$.

5. Substitute $y = 4x + 2$ into the second equation and solve for x.
$$5x - 2y = 5$$
$$5x - 2(4x + 2) = 5$$
$$5x - 8x - 4 = 5$$
$$-3x = 9$$
$$x = -3$$
Substitute $x = -3$ into $y = 4x + 2$ to find y.
$$y = 4x + 2$$
$$y = 4(-3) + 2$$
$$y = -10$$
The solution set is $\{(-3, -10)\}$.

6. Eliminate y by adding 2 times Equation 1 and Equation 2.
$$\begin{array}{ll} 2(\text{Equation 1}) & \left\{\begin{array}{l} -4x + 6y = 30 \\ 4x - 6y = 42 \end{array}\right. \\ \text{Equation 2} & \end{array}$$
$$\overline{\qquad\qquad 0 = 72 \qquad\qquad}$$

The solution set is $\{\ \}$.

7. Eliminate z by adding Equation 1 and -1 times Equation 2.
$$\begin{array}{ll} \text{Equation 1} & \left\{\begin{array}{l} x + 2y + z = -6 \\ -3x + 4y - z = -16 \end{array}\right. \\ -1(\text{Equation 2}) & \end{array}$$
$$\overline{\text{Equation 4} \qquad -2x + 6y = -22}$$
Eliminate z by adding Equation 1 and Equation 3.
$$\begin{array}{ll} \text{Equation 1} & \left\{\begin{array}{l} x + 2y + z = -6 \\ 2x + y - z = -1 \end{array}\right. \\ \text{Equation 3} & \end{array}$$
$$\overline{\text{Equation 5} \qquad 3x + 3y = -7}$$
Eliminate y by adding Equation 4 and -2 times Equation 5.
$$\begin{array}{ll} \text{Equation 4} & \left\{\begin{array}{l} -2x + 6y = -22 \\ -6x - 6y = 14 \end{array}\right. \\ -2(\text{Equation 5}) & \end{array}$$
$$\overline{\qquad\qquad -8x = -8}$$
$$x = 1$$
Substitute $x = 1$ into Equation 4 and solve for y.
$$-2x + 6y = -22$$
$$-2(1) + 6y = -22$$
$$y = -\frac{10}{3}$$
Substitute $x = 1$ and $y = -\dfrac{10}{3}$ into Equation 1 and solve for z.

$$x + 2y + z = -6$$

$$(1) + 2\left(-\frac{10}{3}\right) + z = -6$$

$$z = -\frac{1}{3}$$

The solution set to the system is $\left\{\left(1, -\frac{10}{3}, -\frac{1}{3}\right)\right\}$.

8. Let x and y represent the two unknown numbers. The system of equations is

$$\begin{cases} x + y = 430 \\ x - y = 46 \end{cases}$$

Eliminate y by adding Equation 1 and Equation 2.

Equation 1 $\begin{cases} x + y = 430 \\ x - y = 46 \end{cases}$
Equation 2

$$\overline{2x = 476}$$

$$x = 238$$

Substitute $x = 238$ into Equation 1 and solve for y.

$$x + y = 430$$

$$(238) + y = 430$$

$$y = 192$$

The two numbers are 192 and 238.

9. **Prepare** We are to determine the amount Ms. Hogan deposited in each account.

Plan Because there are two unknowns, we must set up and solve a system of two equations.

Process Let x be the amount invested at 5% and y be the amount invested at 7.5%. Write the system of equations.

Account	Principal	Rate	Time	Interest
5%	x	0.05	1 year	0.05x
7.5%	y	0.075	1 year	0.075y

$$\begin{cases} x + y = 5,000 \\ 0.05x + 0.075y = 306.25 \end{cases}$$

Eliminate y by adding −50 times Equation 1 and 1,000 times Equation 2.

$-50(\text{Equation 1})$ $\begin{cases} -50x - 50y = -250,000 \\ 50x + 75y = 306,250 \end{cases}$
$1,000(\text{Equation 2})$

$$\overline{25y = 56,250}$$

$$y = 2,250$$

Substitute $y = 2,250$ into Equation 1 and solve for y.

$$x + y = 5,000$$

$$x + (2,250) = 5,000$$

$$x = 2,750$$

Ms. Hogan invested $2,750 at 5% and $2,250 at 7.5%.

Ponder Does our answer seem reasonable? Yes. We can check to see that our results satisfy the conditions of the problem. First, the sum of the two amounts is $2,250 + 2,750 = 5,000$. Finally, the interest earned at 5% is $2,750(0.05) = 137.50$ and the interest earned at 7.5% is $2,250(0.075) = 168.75$. The sum of the interest from the two accounts is $137.50 + 168.75 = 306.25$. Therefore, our answers are correct.

10. Graph L_1 using the slope-intercept method and a solid line. The slope is $m = -1$ and the y-intercept is $(0,3)$. Choose the test point $(0,0)$.

$$x + y \leq 3$$

$$(0) + (0) \leq 3$$

$$0 \leq 3$$

True

Use arrows to indicate the shaded region that contains the point $(0,0)$. Graph L_2 using the slope-intercept method and a dashed line. The slope is $m = 1$ and the y-intercept is $(0,0)$. Choose the test point $(1,0)$.

$$x > y$$

$$1 > 0$$

True

Use arrows to indicate the shaded region that contains the point $(1,0)$. Shade the region where the shaded regions for each graph overlap.

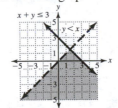

11. $\left(\frac{2}{5}\right)^{-3} = \left(\frac{5}{2}\right)^3$

$$= \frac{5}{2} \cdot \frac{5}{2} \cdot \frac{5}{2}$$

$$= \frac{125}{8}$$

12. $\left(\dfrac{18a^{10}b^{-5}}{15a^{-2}b^{-8}c^3}\right)^2 = \dfrac{\left(\overset{6}{\cancel{18}}a^{10}b^{-5}\right)^2}{\left(\underset{5}{\cancel{15}}a^{-2}b^{-8}c^3\right)^2}$

$ = \dfrac{6^2\left(a^{10}\right)^2\left(b^{-5}\right)^2}{5^2\left(a^{-2}\right)^2\left(b^{-8}\right)^2\left(c^3\right)^2}$

$ = \dfrac{36a^{20}b^{-10}}{25a^{-4}b^{-16}c^6}$

$ = \dfrac{36}{25}a^{24}b^6c^{-6}$

$ = \dfrac{36a^{24}b^6}{25c^6}$

13. $\left(4x^{-2}y^0z^8\right)^{-3}\left(6x^{-10}y^5z\right)^2$

$= 4^{-3}\left(x^{-2}\right)^{-3}\left(y^0\right)^{-3}\left(z^8\right)^{-3}\cdot 6^2\left(x^{-10}\right)^2\left(y^5\right)^2 z^2$

$= 4^{-3}x^6y^0z^{-24}\cdot 36x^{-20}y^{10}z^2$

$= \dfrac{36}{4^3}x^{-14}y^{10}z^{-22}$

$= \dfrac{\overset{9}{\cancel{36}}\,y^{10}}{\underset{16}{\cancel{64}}\,x^{14}z^{22}}$

$= \dfrac{9y^{10}}{16x^{14}z^{22}}$

14. $690{,}000{,}000{,}000$ Standard Notation

$6.9\left(10^{11}\right)$ Scientific Notation

15. $-5x^3-14x^2+x-4 = -5(-2)^3-14(-2)^2+(-2)-4$

$ = -5(-8)-14(4)-2-4$

$ = 40-56-2-4$

$ = -22$

16. $\left(-18y^2+7y-15\right)-\left(8y^2-2\right)+\left(4y^2+12y-10\right)$

$= -18y^2+7y-15-8y^2+2+4y^2+12y-10$

$= -18y^2-8y^2+4y^2+7y+12y-15+2-10$

$= -22y^2+19y-23$

17. $(8x-7y)(3x+4y) = 8x(3x+4y)-7y(3x+4y)$

$ = 24x^2+32xy-21xy-28y^2$

$ = 24x^2+11xy-28y^2$

18. $(2x+5)^2 = (2x)^2+2(2x)(5)+5^2$

$ = 4x^2+20x+25$

19. $\left(12a^2-5a-9\right)\div(3a-2) = 4a+1-\dfrac{7}{3a-2}$

$\begin{array}{r} 4a+1 \\ 3a-2\,\overline{\smash{)}12a^2-5a-9} \\ -\,\underline{\left(12a^2-8a\right)} \\ 3a-9 \\ -\,\underline{\left(3a-2\right)} \\ -7 \end{array}$

20. a) $P = 2L+2W$

$ = 2(4x-1)+2\left(3x^2+12x-5\right)$

$ = 8x-2+6x^2+24x-10$

$ = 6x^2+8x+24x-2-10$

$ = 6x^2+32x-12 \quad \text{units}$

b) $A = LW$

$ = (4x-1)\left(3x^2+12x-5\right)$

$ = 4x\left(3x^2+12x-5\right)-1\left(3x^2+12x-5\right)$

$ = 12x^3+48x^2-20x-3x^2-12x+5$

$ = 12x^3+48x^2-3x^2-20x-12x+5$

$ = 12x^3-45x^2-32x+5 \quad \text{units}^2$

21. $3x^4-24x = 3x\left(x^3-8\right)$

$ = 3x(x-2)\left(x^2+2x+2^2\right)$

$ = 3x(x-2)\left(x^2+2x+4\right)$

22. $8a^2x+48a^2b-5bx-30b^2$

$= \left(8a^2x+48a^2b\right)-\left(5bx+30b^2\right)$

$= 8a^2(x+6b)-5b(x+6b)$

$= (x+6b)\left(8a^2-5b\right)$

23. $y^4-2y^2-3 = y^4-3y^2+y^2-3$

$ = \left(y^4-3y^2\right)+\left(y^2-3\right)$

$ = y^2\left(y^2-3\right)+\left(y^2-3\right)$

$ = \left(y^2-3\right)\left(y^2+1\right)$

24. $25k^2 - 5k - 12 = 25k^2 - 20k + 15k - 12$

$$= \left(25k^2 - 20k\right) + \left(15k - 12\right)$$

$$= 5k\left(5k - 4\right) + 3\left(5k - 4\right)$$

$$= \left(5k - 4\right)\left(5k + 3\right)$$

25. The GCF is $3a^2bc^3$.

$$18a^3b^2c^4 + 15a^2bc^3 - 9a^5b^2c^5$$

$$= 3a^2bc^3\left(6abc + 5 - 3a^3bc^2\right)$$

26. $49x^2 + 42x + 9 = \left(7x\right)^2 + 2\left(7x\right)\left(3\right) + 3^2$

$$= \left(7x + 3\right)^2$$

27.
$$y^3 - 16y = 0$$

$$y\left(y^2 - 16\right) = 0$$

$$y\left(y + 4\right)\left(y - 4\right) = 0$$

$y = 0$ or $y + 4 = 0$ or $y - 4 = 0$

$y = 0$ or $y = -4$ or $y = 4$

Solution Set: $\{-4, 0, 4\}$

28.
$$\left(x + 3\right)\left(x - 2\right) = 14$$

$$x^2 + x - 20 = 0$$

$$\left(x + 5\right)\left(x - 4\right) = 0$$

$x + 5 = 0$ or $x - 4 = 0$

$x = -5$ $x = 4$

Solution Set: $\{-5, 4\}$

29. Let x represent the number.

$$\left(3x - 1\right)^2 = 9$$

$$9x^2 - 6x - 8 = 0$$

$$\left(3x + 2\right)\left(3x - 4\right) = 0$$

$3x + 2 = 0$ or $3x - 4 = 0$

$x = -\dfrac{2}{3}$ or $x = \dfrac{4}{3}$

There are two numbers that satisfy the conditions.

They are $-\dfrac{2}{3}$ and $\dfrac{4}{3}$.

30. Prepare We are to determine the amount of time it will take the bottle rocket to return to the ground after it is fired.

Plan We will use the given equation and substitute 0 for h in the equation and solve for t, because when the rocket returns to the ground, its height is 0 feet.

Process

$$h = -16t^2 + 32t$$

$$0 = -16t^2 + 32t$$

$$0 = -16t\left(t - 2\right)$$

$-16t = 0$ or $t - 2 = 0$

$t = 0$ or $t = 2$

It will take the rocket 2 seconds to come down and hit the ground.

Ponder Does our answer seem reasonable? Yes, it seems reasonable that a bottle rocket could stay in the air for 2 seconds.

Chapter 7

7.1 Exercises

1. $\frac{x^2-4}{2x^2-7x+15}$ is an example of a <u>rational</u> expression because the numerator and denominator are <u>polynomials</u>.

3. Rational expressions are not <u>defined</u> for any values that cause the denominator to be <u>zero</u>.

5. A rational expression is simplified when the numerator and denominator have no common <u>factors</u> other than <u>1</u>.

7. $\frac{18x^7y^6}{24xy^6} = \frac{\overset{3}{\cancel{18}}\,\overset{1}{\cancel{x}}\,x^6\,\overset{1}{\cancel{y^6}}}{\underset{4}{\cancel{24}}\,\underset{1}{\cancel{x}}\,\underset{1}{\cancel{y^6}}}$

$= \frac{3x^6}{4}$

9. $\frac{-6a^2y^{14}}{24a^6y^8} = \frac{\overset{-1}{\cancel{-6}}\,\overset{1}{\cancel{a^2}}\,y^6\,\overset{1}{\cancel{y^8}}}{\underset{4}{\cancel{24}}\,\underset{1}{\cancel{a^2}}\,a^4\,\underset{1}{\cancel{y^8}}}$

$= -\frac{y^6}{4a^4}$

11. $\frac{6(h-5)}{18(h-5)} = \frac{\overset{1}{\cancel{6}}\,\overset{1}{\cancel{(h-5)}}}{\underset{3}{\cancel{18}}\,\underset{1}{\cancel{(h-5)}}}$

$= \frac{1}{3}$

13. $\frac{(a+2)(5a-3)}{(a+4)(5a-3)} = \frac{(a+2)\,\overset{1}{\cancel{(5a-3)}}}{(a+4)\,\underset{1}{\cancel{(5a-3)}}}$

$= \frac{(a+2)}{(a+4)}$

15. $\frac{y}{y^2+2y} = \frac{y}{y(y+2)}$

$= \frac{\overset{1}{\cancel{y}}}{\underset{1}{\cancel{y}}(y+2)}$

$= \frac{1}{y+2}$

17. $\frac{y^2-4}{7y-14} = \frac{(y+2)(y-2)}{7(y-2)}$

$= \frac{(y+2)\,\overset{1}{\cancel{(y-2)}}}{7\,\underset{1}{\cancel{(y-2)}}}$

$= \frac{y+2}{7}$

19. $\frac{8x+32}{4x^2-64} = \frac{8(x+4)}{4(x^2-16)}$

$= \frac{8(x+4)}{4(x+4)(x-4)}$

$= \frac{\overset{2}{\cancel{8}}\,\overset{1}{\cancel{(x+4)}}}{\underset{1}{\cancel{4}}\,\underset{1}{\cancel{(x+4)}}(x-4)}$

$= \frac{2}{x-4}$

21. $\frac{2y+3}{6y^2+7y-3} = \frac{(2y+3)}{(2y+3)(3y-1)}$

$= \frac{\overset{1}{\cancel{(2y+3)}}}{\underset{1}{\cancel{(2y+3)}}(3y-1)}$

$= \frac{1}{3y-1}$

23. $\frac{2x^2+5x+3}{2x^2+11x+12} = \frac{(2x+3)(x+1)}{(2x+3)(x+4)}$

$= \frac{\overset{1}{\cancel{(2x+3)}}(x+1)}{\underset{1}{\cancel{(2x+3)}}(x+4)}$

$= \frac{x+1}{x+4}$

25. $\frac{9x^2-25}{5-3x} = \frac{(3x+5)(3x-5)}{(5-3x)}$

$= \frac{(3x+5)(-1)\,\overset{1}{\cancel{(5-3x)}}}{\underset{1}{\cancel{(5-3x)}}}$

$= -3x-5$

27. $\dfrac{-x-4y}{6x+24y} = \dfrac{(-1)^{\overset{1}{}}\cancel{(x+4y)}}{6_{\overset{}{1}}\cancel{(x+4y)}}$

$= -\dfrac{1}{6}$

29. $\dfrac{3z^2-2z+10}{-10+2z-3z^2} = \dfrac{(-1)^{\overset{1}{}}\cancel{\left(-10+2z-3z^2\right)}}{{}_{\overset{}{1}}\cancel{\left(-10+2z-3z^2\right)}}$

$= -1$

31. $\dfrac{9-c}{c^2-81} = \dfrac{(-1)^{\overset{1}{}}\cancel{(c-9)}}{(c+9)_{\overset{}{1}}\cancel{(c-9)}}$

$= -\dfrac{1}{c+9}$

33. $\dfrac{y^2-14y+49}{49-y^2} = \dfrac{(y-7)(y-7)}{(7+y)(7-y)}$

$= \dfrac{(y-7)(-1)^{\overset{1}{}}\cancel{(7-y)}}{(7+y)_{\overset{}{1}}\cancel{(7-y)}}$

$= \dfrac{-y+7}{y+7}$

35. $\dfrac{p^3-8}{2-p} = \dfrac{(p-2)\left(p^2+2p+4\right)}{(2-p)}$

$= \dfrac{(-1)^{\overset{1}{}}\cancel{(2-p)}\left(p^2+2p+4\right)}{{}_{\overset{}{1}}\cancel{(2-p)}}$

$= -p^2-2p-4$

37. $\dfrac{12b^2-4b^3}{b-3} = \dfrac{4b^2(3-b)}{(b-3)}$

$= \dfrac{4b^2(-1)^{\overset{1}{}}\cancel{(b-3)}}{{}_{\overset{}{1}}\cancel{(b-3)}}$

$= -4b^2$

39. $\dfrac{4xy+6y^2}{2x^2+xy-3y^2} = \dfrac{2y(2x+3y)}{(x-y)(2x+3y)}$

$= \dfrac{2y^{\overset{1}{}}\cancel{(2x+3y)}}{(x-y)_{\overset{}{1}}\cancel{(2x+3y)}}$

$= \dfrac{2y}{x-y}$

41. $\dfrac{36-y^2}{y^2-12y+36} = \dfrac{(6+y)(6-y)}{(y-6)(y-6)}$

$= \dfrac{(6+y)(-1)^{\overset{1}{}}\cancel{(y-6)}}{(y-6)_{\overset{}{1}}\cancel{(y-6)}}$

$= \dfrac{-6-y}{y-6}$

43. $\dfrac{ab+6a-b^2-6b}{12+2b} = \dfrac{(b+6)(a-b)}{2(6+b)}$

$= \dfrac{^{\overset{1}{}}\cancel{(b+6)}\,(a-b)}{2_{\overset{}{1}}\cancel{(b+6)}}$

$= \dfrac{a-b}{2}$

45. $\dfrac{5m^2n^3-5m^2n^2-10m^2n}{5n^2-9n-2} = \dfrac{5m^2n\left(n^2-n-2\right)}{(5n+1)(n-2)}$

$= \dfrac{5m^2n(n+1)(n-2)}{(5n+1)(n-2)}$

$= \dfrac{5m^2n(n+1)^{\overset{1}{}}\cancel{(n-2)}}{(5n+1)_{\overset{}{1}}\cancel{(n-2)}}$

$= \dfrac{5m^2n^2+5m^2n}{5n+1}$

47. $\dfrac{2y-y^2}{4y^2-13y+10} = \dfrac{y(2-y)}{(4y-5)(y-2)}$

$= \dfrac{y(-1)(y-2)}{(4y-5)(y-2)}$

$= \dfrac{y(-1)^{\overset{1}{}}\cancel{(y-2)}}{(4y-5)_{\overset{}{1}}\cancel{(y-2)}}$

$= \dfrac{-y}{4y-5}$

49. $\dfrac{10x^2-11x-6}{15x-10x^2} = \dfrac{(5x+2)(2x-3)}{5x(3-2x)}$

$= \dfrac{(5x+2)(-1)(3-2x)}{5x(3-2x)}$

$= \dfrac{(5x+2)(-1)^{\overset{1}{}}\cancel{(3-2x)}}{5x_{\overset{}{1}}\cancel{(3-2x)}}$

$= \dfrac{-5x-2}{5x}$

51. $\dfrac{4a^3b^2 - 18a^2b^2 - 10ab^2}{5b + 10 - ab - 2a}$

$= \dfrac{2ab^2\left(2a^2 - 9a - 5\right)}{(b+2)(5-a)}$

$= \dfrac{2ab^2(2a+1)(a-5)}{(b+2)(5-a)}$

$= \dfrac{2ab^2(2a+1)\,{}^1\cancel{(a-5)}}{(b+2)(-1)\,{}_1\cancel{(a-5)}}$

$= \dfrac{-4a^2b^2 - 2ab^2}{b+2}$

53. $\dfrac{8x^3 - 125y^3}{10y - 4x}$

$= \dfrac{(2x-5y)\left(4x^2 + 10xy + 25y^2\right)}{2(5y - 2x)}$

$= \dfrac{(-1)(5y-2x)\left(4x^2 + 10xy + 25y^2\right)}{2(5y - 2x)}$

$= \dfrac{(-1)\,{}^1\cancel{(5y-2x)}\left(4x^2 + 10xy + 25y^2\right)}{2\,{}_1\cancel{(5y-2x)}}$

$= \dfrac{-4x^2 - 10xy - 25y^2}{2}$

55. $\dfrac{12x^2y + 12xy^2 + 3y^3}{12ax + 36bx + 6ay + 18by}$

$= \dfrac{3y\left(4x^2 + 4xy + y^2\right)}{6(2ax + 6bx + ay + 3by)}$

$= \dfrac{3y(2x+y)(2x+y)}{6(a+3b)(2x+y)}$

$= \dfrac{{}^1\cancel{3}y(2x+y)\,{}^1\cancel{(2x+y)}}{{}_2\cancel{6}(a+3b)\,{}_1\cancel{(2x+y)}}$

$= \dfrac{2xy + y^2}{2a + 6b}$

57. $\dfrac{a^3 - 3a^2 - 4a + 12}{a^3 + 2a^2 - 9a - 18} = \dfrac{(a-3)\left(a^2 - 4\right)}{(a+2)\left(a^2 - 9\right)}$

$= \dfrac{(a-3)(a+2)(a-2)}{(a+2)(a+3)(a-3)}$

$= \dfrac{{}^1\cancel{(a-3)}\,{}^1(a+2)(a-2)}{{}_1(a+2)(a+3)\,{}_1\cancel{(a-3)}}$

$= \dfrac{a-2}{a+3}$

59. $\dfrac{x^5 - 16x^3}{x^2y + 12xy + 32y} = \dfrac{x^3\left(x^2 - 16\right)}{y\left(x^2 + 12x + 32\right)}$

$= \dfrac{x^3(x+4)(x-4)}{y(x+4)(x+8)}$

$= \dfrac{x^3\,{}^1\cancel{(x+4)}(x-4)}{y\,{}_1\cancel{(x+4)}(x+8)}$

$= \dfrac{x^4 - 4x^3}{xy + 8y}$

61. An undefined rational expression has a denominator that equals zero.

63. To reduce a rational expression to -1, the absolute values of the terms in the numerator must equal those in the denominator, but all their signs must be opposite.

65. $\dfrac{32a^3bx^3 + 24a^2b^2x^3 - 200a^3bx - 150a^2b^2x}{48a^2x + 36abx + 120a^2 + 90ab}$

$= \dfrac{2a^2bx\left(16ax^2 + 12bx^2 - 100a - 75b\right)}{6a(8ax + 6bx + 20a + 15b)}$

$= \dfrac{2a^2bx(4a+3b)\left(4x^2 - 25\right)}{6a(4a+3b)(2x+5)}$

$= \dfrac{2a^2bx(4a+3b)(2x+5)(2x-5)}{6a(4a+3b)(2x+5)}$

$= \dfrac{{}^1\cancel{2}\,{}^1\cancel{a}\,abx\,{}^1\cancel{(4a+3b)}\,{}^1\cancel{(2x+5)}(2x-5)}{{}_3\cancel{6}\,{}_1\cancel{a}\,{}_1\cancel{(4a+3b)}\,{}_1\cancel{(2x+5)}}$

$= \dfrac{2abx^2 - 5abx}{3}$

67. $\dfrac{(a+b)^2-(c+d)^2}{(c+d)^2-(a+b)^2}=\dfrac{(-1)^{\overset{1}{}}\Big[\cancel{(c+d)^2-(a+b)^2}\Big]}{\underset{1}{\cancel{(c+d)^2-(a+b)^2}}}$

$\qquad\qquad\qquad\quad=-1$

69. $\dfrac{48-6t^3}{?}=\dfrac{6\left(8-t^3\right)}{?}$

$\qquad\qquad=\dfrac{6(2-t)\left(4+2t+t^2\right)}{?}$

The denominator should be $6t^2+12t+24$.

7.2 Exercises

1. When multiplying rational expressions, $\frac{a}{b} \cdot \frac{c}{d} = \frac{ac}{bd}$,

where $b, d \neq 0$.

3. When multiplying or dividing rational expressions we <u>do</u> <u>not</u> need to find a common denominator.

5. $\dfrac{4a^2b^3}{5} \cdot \dfrac{25}{14ab^4} = \dfrac{\overset{5}{\cancel{25}} \cdot \overset{2}{\cancel{4}} \overset{a}{\cancel{a^2}} \overset{1}{\cancel{b^3}}}{\underset{1}{\cancel{5}} \cdot \underset{7}{\cancel{14}} \underset{1}{\cancel{a}} \underset{b}{\cancel{b^4}}}$

$= \dfrac{10a}{7b}$

7. $\dfrac{a+b}{9ab^3} \cdot \dfrac{3a^2b}{a-b} = \dfrac{\overset{1}{\cancel{3}} \overset{a}{\cancel{a^2}} \overset{1}{\cancel{b}} (a+b)}{\underset{3}{\cancel{9}} \underset{1}{\cancel{a}} \underset{b^2}{\cancel{b^3}} (a-b)}$

$= \dfrac{a^2 + ab}{3ab^2 - 3b^3}$

9. $\dfrac{x^2 - 4y^2}{8xy^2} \cdot \dfrac{2x^2y}{x+2y} = \dfrac{(x+2y)(x-2y)}{8xy^2} \cdot \dfrac{2x^2y}{x+2y}$

$= \dfrac{\overset{1}{\cancel{2}} \overset{x}{\cancel{x^2}} \overset{1}{\cancel{y}} (x+2y)(x-2y)}{\underset{4}{\cancel{8}} \underset{1}{\cancel{x}} \underset{y}{\cancel{y^2}} \underset{1}{(x+2y)}}$

$= \dfrac{x^2 - 2xy}{4y}$

11. $\dfrac{s^3 + 8}{s+4} \cdot \dfrac{s^2 + 4s}{s^2 - 2s + 4}$

$= \dfrac{(s+2)(s^2 - 2s + 4)}{(s+4)} \cdot \dfrac{s(s+4)}{(s^2 - 2s + 4)}$

$= \dfrac{s \overset{1}{\cancel{(s+4)}} (s+2) \overset{1}{\cancel{(s^2 - 2s + 4)}}}{\underset{1}{\cancel{(s+4)}} \underset{1}{\cancel{(s^2 - 2s + 4)}}}$

$= s^2 + 2s$

13. $\dfrac{4x^2 - 9}{2x^2 + 5x - 12} \cdot \dfrac{x^2 + 7x + 12}{2x^2 + 9x + 9}$

$= \dfrac{(2x+3)(2x-3)}{(2x-3)(x+4)} \cdot \dfrac{(x+3)(x+4)}{(2x+3)(x+3)}$

$= \dfrac{\overset{1}{\cancel{(2x+3)}} \overset{1}{\cancel{(2x-3)}} \overset{1}{\cancel{(x+3)}} \overset{1}{\cancel{(x+4)}}}{\underset{1}{\cancel{(2x-3)}} \underset{1}{\cancel{(x+4)}} \underset{1}{\cancel{(2x+3)}} \underset{1}{\cancel{(x+3)}}}$

$= 1$

15. $\dfrac{16 - 2c}{4c^2d^3} \div \dfrac{c^2 + 8c}{6c^5d} = \dfrac{16 - 2c}{4c^2d^3} \cdot \dfrac{6c^5d}{c^2 + 8c}$

$= \dfrac{2(8-c)}{4c^2d^3} \cdot \dfrac{6c^5d}{c(c+8)}$

$= \dfrac{\overset{3}{\cancel{12}} \overset{c^2}{\cancel{c^5}} \overset{1}{\cancel{d}} (8-c)}{\underset{1}{\cancel{4}} \underset{1}{\cancel{c^3}} \underset{d^2}{\cancel{d^3}} (c+8)}$

$= \dfrac{24c^2 - 3c^3}{cd^2 + 8d^2}$

17. $\dfrac{y+2}{y^2 - 16} \div \dfrac{y^2 - 4}{y^2 - 6y + 8}$

$= \dfrac{y+2}{y^2 - 16} \cdot \dfrac{y^2 - 6y + 8}{y^2 - 4}$

$= \dfrac{(y+2)}{(y+4)(y-4)} \cdot \dfrac{(y-4)(y-2)}{(y+2)(y-2)}$

$= \dfrac{\overset{1}{\cancel{(y+2)}} \overset{1}{\cancel{(y-4)}} \overset{1}{\cancel{(y-2)}}}{(y+4) \underset{1}{\cancel{(y-4)}} \underset{1}{\cancel{(y+2)}} \underset{1}{\cancel{(y-2)}}}$

$= \dfrac{1}{y+4}$

19. $\dfrac{15b^2+7b-2}{15b^2-28b+5} \div \dfrac{9b^2+21b+10}{9b^2-25}$

$= \dfrac{15b^2+7b-2}{15b^2-28b+5} \cdot \dfrac{9b^2-25}{9b^2+21b+10}$

$= \dfrac{(5b-1)(3b+2)}{(5b-1)(3b-5)} \cdot \dfrac{(3b+5)(3b-5)}{(3b+5)(3b+2)}$

$= \dfrac{\cancel{(5b-1)}^{1} \ \cancel{(3b+2)}^{1} \ \cancel{(3b+5)}^{1} \ \cancel{(3b-5)}^{1}}{\cancel{(5b-1)}_{1} \ \cancel{(3b-5)}_{1} \ \cancel{(3b+5)}_{1} \ \cancel{(3b+2)}_{1}}$

$= 1$

21. $\dfrac{24-2x-x^2}{x^2+2x-8} \div \dfrac{x^2+2x-24}{3x^2+10x-8}$

$= \dfrac{24-2x-x^2}{x^2+2x-8} \cdot \dfrac{3x^2+10x-8}{x^2+2x-24}$

$= \dfrac{(-1)(x^2+2x-24)}{(x-2)(x+4)} \cdot \dfrac{(x+4)(3x-2)}{(x^2+2x-24)}$

$= \dfrac{(-1)\,\cancel{(x^2+2x-24)}^{1}\,\cancel{(x+4)}^{1}(3x-2)}{(x-2)\,\cancel{(x+4)}_{1}\,\cancel{(x^2+2x-24)}_{1}}$

$= \dfrac{-3x+2}{x-2}$

23. $\dfrac{a^2-4b^2}{3a^2+5ab-2b^2} \div \dfrac{3a^2-5ab-2b^2}{9a^2-6ab+b^2}$

$= \dfrac{a^2-4b^2}{3a^2+5ab-2b^2} \cdot \dfrac{9a^2-6ab+b^2}{3a^2-5ab-2b^2}$

$= \dfrac{(a+2b)(a-2b)}{(3a-b)(a+2b)} \cdot \dfrac{(3a-b)(3a-b)}{(3a+b)(a-2b)}$

$= \dfrac{\cancel{(a+2b)}^{1}\,\cancel{(a-2b)}^{1}\,\cancel{(3a-b)}^{1}(3a-b)}{\cancel{(3a-b)}_{1}\,\cancel{(a+2b)}_{1}(3a+b)\,\cancel{(a-2b)}_{1}}$

$= \dfrac{3a-b}{3a+b}$

25. $\dfrac{16-y^2}{8-27y-20y^2} \cdot \dfrac{10y^2+16y}{8y^2-32y}$

$= \dfrac{(-1)(y^2-16)}{(-1)(20y^2+27y-8)} \cdot \dfrac{2y(5y+8)}{8y(y-4)}$

$= \dfrac{(-1)(y+4)(y-4)}{(-1)(5y+8)(4y-1)} \cdot \dfrac{2y(5y+8)}{8y(y-4)}$

$= \dfrac{\cancel{(-1)}^{1}(y+4)\,\cancel{(y-4)}^{1}\,\cancel{(2y)}^{1}\,\cancel{(5y+8)}^{1}}{\cancel{(-1)}_{1}\,\cancel{(5y+8)}_{1}(4y-1)\,\cancel{(8y)}_{4}\,\cancel{(y-4)}_{1}}$

$= \dfrac{y+4}{16y-4}$

27. $\dfrac{(x+3)^2(x-2)}{(x-2)^4(x-4)} \div \dfrac{x^2+6x+9}{x^2-4x+4}$

$= \dfrac{(x+3)^2(x-2)}{(x-2)^4(x-4)} \cdot \dfrac{x^2-4x+4}{x^2+6x+9}$

$= \dfrac{(x+3)^2(x-2)}{(x-2)^4(x-4)} \cdot \dfrac{(x-2)^2}{(x+3)^2}$

$= \dfrac{\cancel{(x+3)^2}^{1}\,\cancel{(x-2)}^{1}\,\cancel{(x-2)^2}^{1}}{\cancel{(x-2)^4}_{x-2}(x-4)\,\cancel{(x+3)^2}_{1}}$

$= \dfrac{1}{(x-2)(x-4)}$

29. $\dfrac{15a^2b^3}{2a^5} \cdot \dfrac{6a^3b}{21b^6} \div \dfrac{9a}{7b^3} = \dfrac{15a^2b^3}{2a^5} \cdot \dfrac{6a^3b}{21b^6} \cdot \dfrac{7b^3}{9a}$

$= \dfrac{15 \cdot 6 \cdot 7 a^5 b^7}{2 \cdot 21 \cdot 9 a^6 b^6}$

$= \dfrac{\cancel{15}^{5} \cdot \cancel{6}^{\,} \cdot \cancel{7}^{1} a^5 b^7}{\cancel{2} \cdot \cancel{21} \cdot \cancel{9} a^6 b^6}$

$= \dfrac{5b}{3a}$

31. $\dfrac{4x^2-9y^2}{2x^2+5xy} \cdot \dfrac{8x^2y}{4x-6y} \div \dfrac{2x+3y}{4x^2-25y^2}$

$= \dfrac{4x^2-9y^2}{2x^2+5xy} \cdot \dfrac{8x^2y}{4x-6y} \cdot \dfrac{4x^2-25y^2}{2x+3y}$

$= \dfrac{(2x+3y)(2x-3y)}{x(2x+5y)} \cdot \dfrac{8x^2y}{2(2x-3y)} \cdot \dfrac{(2x+5y)(2x-5y)}{2x+3y}$

$= \dfrac{\overset{4}{\cancel{8}}\,\overset{x}{\cancel{x^2}}\,y\,\cancel{(2x+3y)}\,\cancel{(2x-3y)}\,\cancel{(2x+5y)}(2x-5y)}{\underset{1}{\cancel{2}}\,\underset{1}{\cancel{x}}\,\cancel{(2x+5y)}\,\cancel{(2x-3y)}\,\cancel{(2x+3y)}}$

$= 8x^2y - 20xy^2$

33. $\dfrac{ax+x+4a+4}{3ax+4x-6a-8} \cdot \dfrac{9a^2+9a-4}{3a^2+2a-1} \div \left(x^2+8x+16\right)$

$= \dfrac{ax+x+4a+4}{3ax+4x-6a-8} \cdot \dfrac{9a^2+9a-4}{3a^2+2a-1} \cdot \dfrac{1}{x^2+8x+16}$

$= \dfrac{(a+1)(x+4)}{(3a+4)(x-2)} \cdot \dfrac{(3a-1)(3a+4)}{(a+1)(3a-1)} \cdot \dfrac{1}{(x+4)^2}$

$= \dfrac{\cancel{(a+1)}\,\cancel{(x+4)}\,\cancel{(3a-1)}\,\cancel{(3a+4)}}{(3a+4)(x-2)\cancel{(a+1)}\,\cancel{(3a-1)}\,\cancel{(x+4)^2}}$

$= \dfrac{1}{x^2+2x-8}$

35. $\dfrac{6x-12}{3x^2y} \div \left(\dfrac{x^3-8}{2x^3y+2y} \cdot \dfrac{x^2-x+1}{x^2+2x+4} \right)$

$= \dfrac{6x-12}{3x^2y} \cdot \dfrac{2x^3y+2y}{x^3-8} \cdot \dfrac{x^2+2x+4}{x^2-x+1}$

$= \dfrac{6(x-2)}{3x^2y} \cdot \dfrac{2y(x+1)\left(x^2-x+1\right)}{(x-2)\left(x^2+2x+4\right)} \cdot \dfrac{x^2+2x+4}{x^2-x+1}$

$= \dfrac{\overset{4}{\cancel{12}}\,\cancel{y}\,\cancel{(x-2)}(x+1)\cancel{\left(x^2-x+1\right)}\cancel{\left(x^2+2x+4\right)}}{\cancel{3}\,x^2\,\cancel{y}\,\cancel{(x-2)}\cancel{\left(x^2+2x+4\right)}\cancel{\left(x^2-x+1\right)}}$

$= \dfrac{4x+4}{x^2}$

37. $\dfrac{6a}{ab^2} \cdot \dfrac{6ac^2}{6ac^2} = \dfrac{36a^2c^2}{6a^2b^2c^2}$

39. $\dfrac{-3x}{x-5} \cdot \dfrac{x}{x} = \dfrac{-3x^2}{x(x-5)}$

41. $\dfrac{h-2}{h+3} \cdot \dfrac{h+3}{h+3} = \dfrac{h^2+h-6}{(h+3)^2}$

43. $\dfrac{5-2y}{3y+2} \cdot \dfrac{y-5}{y-5} = \dfrac{-2y^2+15y-25}{(3y+2)(y-5)}$

45. $\dfrac{2x+3}{x+6} \cdot \dfrac{x-6}{x-6} = \dfrac{2x^2-9x-18}{x^2-36}$

47. $\dfrac{10x}{x-2} \cdot \dfrac{-3}{-3} = \dfrac{-30x}{6-3x}$

49. To divide out common factors in a division problem involving rational expressions, the division must be converted to multiplication by the reciprocal. Once all expressions are factored, the common factors can be divided out.

51. To divide rational expressions, first write the division step(s) as multiplication by the reciprocal. Next, factor each numerator and denominator completely then divide out common factors. Last, multiply all numerators then multiply all denominators and write in lowest terms.

53. To build up $\dfrac{x^2-5x+6}{x-3} = \dfrac{?}{3-x}$, multiply the numerator and denominator by $\dfrac{-1}{-1}$ to get $\dfrac{-x^2+5x-6}{3-x}$.

55. $\dfrac{3ax-ay-3bx+by}{3a^2x-18ax+24x} \div \dfrac{b-a}{2x-3y} \cdot \dfrac{6x^3-24x}{6x^2-11xy+3y^2} = \dfrac{3ax-ay-3bx+by}{3a^2x-18ax+24x} \cdot \dfrac{2x-3y}{b-a} \cdot \dfrac{6x^3-24x}{6x^2-11xy+3y^2}$

$= \dfrac{(3x-y)(-1)(b-a)}{3x(a-4)(a-2)} \cdot \dfrac{2x-3y}{b-a} \cdot \dfrac{6x(x+2)(x-2)}{(2x-3y)(3x-y)}$

$= \dfrac{\overset{2}{\cancel{6}}\,\overset{1}{\cancel{x}}\,\overset{1}{\cancel{(3x-y)}}(-1)\overset{1}{\cancel{(b-a)}}\overset{1}{\cancel{(2x-3y)}}(x+2)(x-2)}{\underset{1}{\cancel{3}}\,\underset{1}{\cancel{x}}(a-4)(a-2)\underset{1}{\cancel{(b-a)}}\underset{1}{\cancel{(2x-3y)}}\underset{1}{\cancel{(3x-y)}}}$

$= \dfrac{-2x^2+8}{a^2-6a+8}$

57. $\dfrac{9x^2-16}{6a^2+13ab-5b^2} \div \dfrac{15-11x+2x^2}{15a-5b-6ax+2bx} \div \dfrac{8-10x+3x^2}{6-5x+x^2} = \dfrac{9x^2-16}{6a^2+13ab-5b^2} \cdot \dfrac{15a-5b-6ax+2bx}{15-11x+2x^2} \cdot \dfrac{6-5x+x^2}{8-10x+3x^2}$

$= \dfrac{(3x+4)(3x-4)}{(3a-b)(2a+5b)} \cdot \dfrac{(3a-b)(-1)(2x-5)}{(x-3)(2x-5)} \cdot \dfrac{(x-3)(x-2)}{(x-2)(3x-4)}$

$= \dfrac{(3x+4)\overset{1}{\cancel{(3x-4)}}\overset{1}{\cancel{(3a-b)}}(-1)\overset{1}{\cancel{(2x-5)}}\overset{1}{\cancel{(x-3)}}\overset{1}{\cancel{(x-2)}}}{\underset{1}{\cancel{(3a-b)}}(2a+5b)\underset{1}{\cancel{(x-3)}}\underset{1}{\cancel{(2x-5)}}\underset{1}{\cancel{(x-2)}}\underset{1}{\cancel{(3x-4)}}}$

$= \dfrac{-3x-4}{2a+5b}$

7.3 Exercises

1. Rational expressions need to have a <u>common</u> <u>denominator</u> before we can add or subtract them.

3. When finding the LCD of rational expressions, we <u>factor</u> all denominators <u>completely</u>.

5. b

7. c

9. e

11. $\dfrac{11x+24}{8}-\dfrac{3x}{8}=\dfrac{11x+24-(3x)}{8}$

$\quad\quad = \dfrac{8x+24}{8}$

$\quad\quad = \dfrac{\overset{1}{\cancel{8}}(x+3)}{\underset{1}{\cancel{8}}}$

$\quad\quad = x+3$

13. $\dfrac{x^2+8x}{x+7}+\dfrac{x^2+6x}{x+7}=\dfrac{x^2+8x+x^2+6x}{x+7}$

$\quad\quad = \dfrac{2x^2+14x}{x+7}$

$\quad\quad = \dfrac{2x\,\overset{1}{\cancel{(x+7)}}}{\underset{1}{\cancel{(x+7)}}}$

$\quad\quad = 2x$

15. $\dfrac{2a^2}{a^2-36}-\dfrac{7a+30}{a^2-36}=\dfrac{2a^2-(7a+30)}{a^2-36}$

$\quad\quad = \dfrac{2a^2-7a-30}{a^2-36}$

$\quad\quad = \dfrac{(2a+5)\,\overset{1}{\cancel{(a-6)}}}{(a+6)\,\underset{1}{\cancel{(a-6)}}}$

$\quad\quad = \dfrac{2a+5}{a+6}$

17. $\dfrac{2x^2+8x+7}{x^2+8x+12}+\dfrac{x^2+2x+1}{x^2+8x+12}$

$\quad = \dfrac{2x^2+8x+7+x^2+2x+1}{x^2+8x+12}$

$\quad = \dfrac{3x^2+10x+8}{x^2+8x+12}$

$\quad = \dfrac{(3x+4)\,\overset{1}{\cancel{(x+2)}}}{(x+6)\,\underset{1}{\cancel{(x+2)}}}$

$\quad = \dfrac{3x+4}{x+6}$

19. $\dfrac{x^3}{x^2+x+1}-\dfrac{1}{x^2+x+1}$

$\quad = \dfrac{x^3-1}{x^2+x+1}$

$\quad = \dfrac{(x-1)(x^2+x+1)}{(x^2+x+1)}$

$\quad = \dfrac{(x-1)\,\overset{1}{\cancel{(x^2+x+1)}}}{\underset{1}{\cancel{(x^2+x+1)}}}$

$\quad = x-1$

21. $3ab^4 = 3^1 a^1 b^4$

$\quad 12a^4b^3c = 2^2\cdot 3^1 a^4 b^3 c^1$

$\quad\quad LCD = 2^2\cdot 3^1 a^4 b^4 c^1$

$\quad\quad\quad = 12a^4b^4c$

23. $LCD = x(x-5)$

25. $a^2-4=(a+2)(a-2)$

$\quad a+2=(a+2)$

$\quad LCD=(a+2)(a-2)$

27. $9x^2+12x+4=(3x+2)^2$

$\quad 2-3x=(-1)(3x-2)$

$\quad\quad LCD=-(3x-2)(3x+2)^2$

29. $LCD=(m-2)(m+9)$

31. $\text{LCD} = 5x^3 y^5$

$$\frac{6x}{5x^2 y} + \frac{7y^2}{x^3 y^5} = \frac{xy^4 (6x)}{xy^4 (5x^2 y)} + \frac{5(7y^2)}{5(x^3 y^5)}$$

$$= \frac{6x^2 y^4}{5x^3 y^5} + \frac{35y^2}{5x^3 y^5}$$

$$= \frac{6x^2 y^4 + 35y^2}{5x^3 y^5}$$

$$= \frac{\overset{1}{\cancel{y^2}} (6x^2 y^2 + 35)}{5x^3 \underset{y^3}{\cancel{y^5}}}$$

$$= \frac{6x^2 y^2 + 35}{5x^3 y^3}$$

33. $\text{LCD} = 8a^2 b^2$

$$\frac{5a^2 b}{8a^2 b^2} - \frac{9a}{4ab^2} = \frac{5a^2 b}{8a^2 b^2} - \frac{2a(9a)}{2a(4ab^2)}$$

$$= \frac{5a^2 b}{8a^2 b^2} - \frac{18a^2}{8a^2 b^2}$$

$$= \frac{5a^2 b - 18a^2}{8a^2 b^2}$$

$$= \frac{\overset{1}{\cancel{a^2}} (5b - 18)}{8 \underset{1}{\cancel{a^2}} b^2}$$

$$= \frac{5b - 18}{8b^2}$$

35. $\text{LCD} = c(c+2)$

$$\frac{4c}{c+2} + \frac{3}{c} = \frac{c(4c)}{c(c+2)} + \frac{3(c+2)}{c(c+2)}$$

$$= \frac{4c^2}{c(c+2)} + \frac{3c+6}{c(c+2)}$$

$$= \frac{4c^2 + 3c + 6}{c(c+2)}$$

37. $\text{LCD} = x - 5$

$$8 - \frac{x+2}{x-5} = \frac{8(x-5)}{x-5} - \frac{x+2}{x-5}$$

$$= \frac{8x - 40}{x-5} - \frac{x+2}{x-5}$$

$$= \frac{8x - 40 - (x+2)}{x-5}$$

$$= \frac{7x - 42}{x-5}$$

39. $\text{LCD} = (y+3)(y-3)$

$$\frac{5}{y+3} + \frac{2}{y-3} = \frac{5(y-3)}{(y+3)(y-3)} + \frac{2(y+3)}{(y-3)(y+3)}$$

$$= \frac{5y - 15}{(y+3)(y-3)} + \frac{2y + 6}{(y+3)(y-3)}$$

$$= \frac{7y - 9}{(y+3)(y-3)}$$

41. $\text{LCD} = (x-2)(x+3)$

$$\frac{4x-1}{x-2} - \frac{2x}{x+3} = \frac{(4x-1)(x+3)}{(x-2)(x+3)} - \frac{2x(x-2)}{(x+3)(x-2)}$$

$$= \frac{4x^2 + 11x - 3}{(x-2)(x+3)} - \frac{2x^2 - 4x}{(x-2)(x+3)}$$

$$= \frac{4x^2 + 11x - 3 - (2x^2 - 4x)}{(x-2)(x+3)}$$

$$= \frac{2x^2 + 15x - 3}{(x-2)(x+3)}$$

43. $\text{LCD} = (2x-5)(x+1)$

$$\frac{x+1}{2x-5} + \frac{x-2}{x+1} = \frac{(x+1)(x+1)}{(2x-5)(x+1)} + \frac{(x-2)(2x-5)}{(x+1)(2x-5)}$$

$$= \frac{x^2 + 2x + 1}{(2x-5)(x+1)} + \frac{2x^2 - 9x + 10}{(2x-5)(x+1)}$$

$$= \frac{3x^2 - 7x + 11}{(2x-5)(x+1)}$$

45. $\text{LCD} = (m+3)(m-3)$

$$\frac{6}{m+3} + \frac{36}{m^2-9} = \frac{6(m-3)}{(m+3)(m-3)} + \frac{36}{(m+3)(m-3)}$$

$$= \frac{6m-18}{(m+3)(m-3)} + \frac{36}{(m+3)(m-3)}$$

$$= \frac{6m+18}{(m+3)(m-3)}$$

$$= \frac{\overset{1}{6\cancel{(m+3)}}}{\cancel{(m+3)}(m-3)}$$

$$= \frac{6}{m-3}$$

47. $\text{LCD} = (x-2)(x-3)$

$$\frac{2}{x-2} + \frac{x}{x^2-5x+6}$$

$$= \frac{2(x-3)}{(x-2)(x-3)} + \frac{x}{(x-2)(x-3)}$$

$$= \frac{2x-6}{(x-2)(x-3)} + \frac{x}{(x-2)(x-3)}$$

$$= \frac{3x-6}{(x-2)(x-3)}$$

$$= \frac{\overset{1}{3\cancel{(x-2)}}}{\cancel{(x-2)}(x-3)}$$

$$= \frac{3}{x-3}$$

49. $\text{LCD} = (x-2)(x+1)(x-4)$

$$\frac{x+1}{x^2-x-2} + \frac{x-2}{x^2-6x+8}$$

$$= \frac{x+1}{(x-2)(x+1)} + \frac{x-2}{(x-2)(x-4)}$$

$$= \frac{(x+1)(x-4)}{(x-2)(x+1)(x-4)} + \frac{(x-2)(x+1)}{(x-2)(x-4)(x+1)}$$

$$= \frac{x^2-3x-4}{(x-2)(x+1)(x-4)} + \frac{x^2-x-2}{(x-2)(x-4)(x+1)}$$

$$= \frac{2x^2-4x-6}{(x-2)(x+1)(x-4)}$$

$$= \frac{\overset{1}{(2x-6)\cancel{(x+1)}}}{(x-2)\cancel{(x+1)}(x-4)}$$

$$= \frac{2x-6}{(x-2)(x-4)}$$

51. $LCD = (x+4)(3x+2)$

$$\frac{x}{x+4} - \frac{x+14}{3x^2+14x+8} + \frac{4}{3x+2} = \frac{x}{x+4} - \frac{x+14}{(x+4)(3x+2)} + \frac{4}{3x+2}$$

$$= \frac{x(3x+2)}{(x+4)(3x+2)} - \frac{x+14}{(x+4)(3x+2)} + \frac{4(x+4)}{(3x+2)(x+4)}$$

$$= \frac{3x^2+2x}{(x+4)(3x+2)} - \frac{x+14}{(x+4)(3x+2)} + \frac{4x+16}{(3x+2)(x+4)}$$

$$= \frac{3x^2+2x-(x+14)+4x+16}{(x+4)(3x+2)}$$

$$= \frac{3x^2+5x+2}{(x+4)(3x+2)}$$

$$= \frac{(x+1)\overset{1}{\cancel{(3x+2)}}}{(x+4)\underset{1}{\cancel{(3x+2)}}}$$

$$= \frac{x+1}{x+4}$$

53. $LCD = x(x+4)$

$$\frac{5x+2}{x+4} - \frac{2}{x} + \frac{x+20}{x^2+4x}$$

$$= \frac{5x+2}{x+4} - \frac{2}{x} + \frac{x+20}{x(x+4)}$$

$$= \frac{x(5x+2)}{x(x+4)} - \frac{2(x+4)}{x(x+4)} + \frac{x+20}{x(x+4)}$$

$$= \frac{5x^2+2x}{x(x+4)} - \frac{2x+8}{x(x+4)} + \frac{x+20}{x(x+4)}$$

$$= \frac{5x^2+2x-(2x+8)+x+20}{x(x+4)}$$

$$= \frac{5x^2+x+12}{x(x+4)}$$

55. $LCD = y-6$

$$\frac{y-2}{y-6} + \frac{4}{6-y} = \frac{y-2}{y-6} + \frac{-4}{y-6}$$

$$= \frac{y-2+(-4)}{y-6}$$

$$= \frac{\overset{1}{\cancel{(y-6)}}}{\underset{1}{\cancel{(y-6)}}}$$

$$= 1$$

57. $LCD = a-4$

$$\frac{a^2}{a-4} + \frac{16}{4-a} = \frac{a^2}{a-4} + \frac{-16}{a-4}$$

$$= \frac{a^2+(-16)}{a-4}$$

$$= \frac{a^2-16}{a-4}$$

$$= \frac{(a+4)\overset{1}{\cancel{(a-4)}}}{\underset{1}{\cancel{(a-4)}}}$$

$$= a+4$$

59. $\text{LCD} = 4x(x-4)$

$$\frac{4}{x^2-4x} - \frac{x}{4x-16} = \frac{4}{x(x-4)} - \frac{x}{4(x-4)}$$

$$= \frac{4(4)}{4x(x-4)} - \frac{x(x)}{4x(x-4)}$$

$$= \frac{16}{4x(x-4)} - \frac{x^2}{4x(x-4)}$$

$$= \frac{16-x^2}{4x(x-4)}$$

$$= \frac{-1(x+4)\cancel{(x-4)}^{1}}{4x\,\cancel{(x-4)}_{1}}$$

$$= \frac{-x-4}{4x}$$

61. $\text{LCD} = (x+1)(x-1)$

$$\frac{10x}{x^2-1} - \frac{5}{x+1} - \frac{7}{1-x}$$

$$= \frac{10x}{(x+1)(x-1)} - \frac{5(x-1)}{(x+1)(x-1)} - \frac{-7(x+1)}{(x-1)(x+1)}$$

$$= \frac{10x}{(x+1)(x-1)} - \frac{5x-5}{(x+1)(x-1)} - \frac{-7x-7}{(x-1)(x+1)}$$

$$= \frac{10x-(5x-5)-(-7x-7)}{(x+1)(x-1)}$$

$$= \frac{12x+12}{(x+1)(x-1)}$$

$$= \frac{12\cancel{(x+1)}^{1}}{\cancel{(x+1)}_{1}(x-1)}$$

$$= \frac{12}{x-1}$$

63. $\text{LCD} = 3y(2y+3)$

$$\frac{2y-5}{6y+9} + \frac{1}{y} - \frac{4}{2y^2+3y}$$

$$= \frac{2y-5}{3(2y+3)} + \frac{1}{y} - \frac{4}{y(2y+3)}$$

$$= \frac{y(2y-5)}{3y(2y+3)} + \frac{(1)3(2y+3)}{3y(2y+3)} - \frac{3(4)}{3y(2y+3)}$$

$$= \frac{2y^2-5y}{3y(2y+3)} + \frac{6y+9}{3y(2y+3)} - \frac{12}{3y(2y+3)}$$

$$= \frac{2y^2+y-3}{3y(2y+3)}$$

$$= \frac{(y-1)\cancel{(2y+3)}^{1}}{3y\,\cancel{(2y+3)}_{1}}$$

$$= \frac{y-1}{3y}$$

65. $\text{LCD} = x-5$

$$\frac{x-3}{x-5} + \frac{2}{5-x} + 1 = \frac{x-3}{x-5} + \frac{-2}{x-5} + 1$$

$$= \frac{x-3}{x-5} + \frac{-2}{x-5} + \frac{x-5}{x-5}$$

$$= \frac{2x-10}{x-5}$$

$$= \frac{2\cancel{(x-5)}^{1}}{\cancel{(x-5)}_{1}}$$

$$= 2$$

67. $\text{LCD} = (a-4)(a+1)(2a+3)$

$$\frac{a}{a^2-3a-4} - \frac{a-2}{2a^2+5a+3}$$

$$= \frac{a}{(a-4)(a+1)} - \frac{a-2}{(a+1)(2a+3)}$$

$$= \frac{a(2a+3)}{(a-4)(a+1)(2a+3)} - \frac{(a-4)(a-2)}{(a-4)(a+1)(2a+3)}$$

$$= \frac{2a^2+3a}{(a-4)(a+1)(2a+3)} - \frac{a^2-6a+8}{(a-4)(a+1)(2a+3)}$$

$$= \frac{2a^2+3a-\left(a^2-6a+8\right)}{(a-4)(a+1)(2a+3)}$$

$$= \frac{a^2+9a-8}{(a-4)(a+1)(2a+3)}$$

69. $\text{LCD} = (3y+1)(3y-1)^2$

$$\frac{4y}{9y^2-6y+1}+\frac{2}{9y^2-1}$$

$$=\frac{4y}{(3y-1)^2}+\frac{2}{(3y+1)(3y-1)}$$

$$=\frac{4y(3y+1)}{(3y+1)(3y-1)^2}+\frac{2(3y-1)}{(3y+1)(3y-1)^2}$$

$$=\frac{12y^2+4y}{(3y+1)(3y-1)^2}+\frac{6y-2}{(3y+1)(3y-1)^2}$$

$$=\frac{12y^2+10y-2}{(3y+1)(3y-1)^2}$$

71. $\text{LCD} = (3x-y)(x+y)(x-y)$

$$\frac{6x}{3x^2+2xy-y^2}-\frac{y}{x^2-y^2}$$

$$=\frac{6x}{(3x-y)(x+y)}-\frac{y}{(x+y)(x-y)}$$

$$=\frac{6x(x-y)}{(3x-y)(x+y)(x-y)}-\frac{y(3x-y)}{(3x-y)(x+y)(x-y)}$$

$$=\frac{6x^2-6xy}{(3x-y)(x+y)(x-y)}-\frac{3xy-y^2}{(3x-y)(x+y)(x-y)}$$

$$=\frac{6x^2-6xy-\left(3xy-y^2\right)}{(3x-y)(x+y)(x-y)}$$

$$=\frac{6x^2-9xy+y^2}{(3x-y)(x+y)(x-y)}$$

73. $\left(\dfrac{x}{x^2-9}+\dfrac{2}{x+3}\right)\div\dfrac{x-2}{x+3}$

$$=\left(\frac{x}{(x+3)(x-3)}+\frac{2(x-3)}{(x+3)(x-3)}\right)\cdot\frac{x+3}{x-2}$$

$$=\left(\frac{x}{(x+3)(x-3)}+\frac{2x-6}{(x+3)(x-3)}\right)\cdot\frac{x+3}{x-2}$$

$$=\frac{3x-6}{(x+3)(x-3)}\cdot\frac{x+3}{x-2}$$

$$=\frac{3\,\overset{1}{\cancel{(x-2)}}\,\overset{1}{\cancel{(x+3)}}}{\underset{1}{\cancel{(x+3)}}\,(x-3)\,\underset{1}{\cancel{(x-2)}}}$$

$$=\frac{3}{x-3}$$

75. $\left(\dfrac{3a}{a+3}+1\right)\div\left(\dfrac{2a}{a+1}+6\right)$

$$=\left(\frac{3a}{a+3}+\frac{a+3}{a+3}\right)\div\left(\frac{2a}{a+1}+\frac{6(a+1)}{a+1}\right)$$

$$=\frac{4a+3}{a+3}\div\left(\frac{2a}{a+1}+\frac{6a+6}{a+1}\right)$$

$$=\frac{4a+3}{a+3}\div\frac{8a+6}{a+1}$$

$$=\frac{4a+3}{a+3}\cdot\frac{a+1}{8a+6}$$

$$=\frac{\overset{1}{\cancel{(4a+3)}}\,(a+1)}{(a+3)(2)\,\underset{1}{\cancel{(4a+3)}}}$$

$$=\frac{a+1}{2a+6}$$

77. Answers will vary; for example: To find the LCD of a rational expression, factor each denominator completely. Multiply each unique factor raised to the highest power found in either denominator to determine the LCD.

79. The term "building up" a rational expression refers to the process of creating an equivalent rational expression with the LCD as the denominator.

81. To add $\frac{x}{x+3}+\frac{2}{3-x}$, first multiply the second rational expression by $\frac{-1}{-1}$ to obtain $\frac{-2}{x-3}$. Now that both rational expressions have the same denominator, add them to obtain the answer $\frac{x-2}{x-3}$.

83. $\left(\dfrac{4x}{x-5}+\dfrac{x-25}{5-x}\right)\left(\dfrac{x+5}{5x}+\dfrac{4x-7}{4x}\right)$

$$=\left(\frac{4x}{x-5}-\frac{x-25}{x-5}\right)\left(\frac{4(x+5)}{20x}+\frac{5(4x-7)}{20x}\right)$$

$$=\left(\frac{4x-(x-25)}{x-5}\right)\left(\frac{4x+20+20x-35}{20x}\right)$$

$$=\left(\frac{3x+25}{x-5}\right)\left(\frac{24x-15}{20x}\right)$$

$$=\frac{(3x+25)(24x-15)}{20x(x-5)}$$

$$=\frac{3(3x+25)(8x-5)}{20x(x-5)}$$

85. $\dfrac{2}{3y-1}+\left(\dfrac{y}{3y-1}\right)^2-1$

$=\dfrac{2}{3y-1}+\dfrac{y^2}{(3y-1)^2}-1$

$=\dfrac{2(3y-1)}{(3y-1)^2}+\dfrac{y^2}{(3y-1)^2}-\dfrac{(3y-1)^2}{(3y-1)^2}$

$=\dfrac{6y-2}{(3y-1)^2}+\dfrac{y^2}{(3y-1)^2}-\dfrac{9y^2-6y+1}{(3y-1)^2}$

$=\dfrac{6y-2+y^2-\left(9y^2-6y+1\right)}{(3y-1)^2}$

$=\dfrac{-8y^2+12y-3}{(3y-1)^2}$

87. $\dfrac{6b^2}{2b^2-14b+24}\div\left(\dfrac{3b}{b^2-11b+28}-\dfrac{4b}{b^2-10b+21}\right)$

$=\dfrac{6b^2}{2(b-4)(b-3)}\div\left(\dfrac{3b}{(b-7)(b-4)}-\dfrac{4b}{(b-7)(b-3)}\right)$

$=\dfrac{6b^2}{2(b-4)(b-3)}\div\left(\dfrac{3b(b-3)}{(b-7)(b-3)(b-4)}-\dfrac{4b(b-4)}{(b-7)(b-3)(b-4)}\right)$

$=\dfrac{6b^2}{2(b-4)(b-3)}\div\left(\dfrac{3b^2-9b}{(b-7)(b-3)(b-4)}-\dfrac{4b^2-16b}{(b-7)(b-3)(b-4)}\right)$

$=\dfrac{6b^2}{2(b-4)(b-3)}\div\left(\dfrac{3b^2-9b-\left(4b^2-16b\right)}{(b-7)(b-3)(b-4)}\right)$

$=\dfrac{6b^2}{2(b-4)(b-3)}\div\left(\dfrac{-b^2+7b}{(b-7)(b-3)(b-4)}\right)$

$=\dfrac{6b^2}{2(b-4)(b-3)}\cdot\dfrac{(b-7)(b-3)(b-4)}{-b(b-7)}$

$=\dfrac{\overset{-3}{\cancel{6}}\,\overset{b}{\cancel{b^2}}\,\overset{1}{\cancel{(b-7)}}\,\overset{1}{\cancel{(b-3)}}\,\overset{1}{\cancel{(b-4)}}}{\underset{1\ \ 1}{\cancel{2}\,\cancel{b}}\,\underset{1}{\cancel{(b-4)}}\,\underset{1}{\cancel{(b-3)}}\,\underset{1}{\cancel{(b-7)}}}$

$=-3b$

7.4 Exercises

1. The shorthand procedure for dividing a polynomial by a <u>binomial</u> of the form $(x-k)$, where $k \in R$, is called <u>synthetic</u> <u>division</u>.

3. When dividing polynomials we write both polynomials in <u>descending</u> order, adding <u>zero</u> for any missing powers of the variable.

5. A rational expression that has a numerator containing one or more fractions is called a <u>complex</u> fraction.

7. Method <u>1</u> is the preferred choice for simplifying a complex fraction that has single fractions in the numerator and denominator.

9. To simplify a complex fraction, multiply by the numerator by the <u>reciprocal</u> of the denominator or multiply each term in the numerator and denominator by the <u>least</u> <u>common</u> <u>denominator</u> of all the denominators.

11. $(x^2 + 10x + 21) \div (x+3) = x+7$

$$
\begin{array}{r|rrr}
-3 & 1 & 10 & 21 \\
   & \Downarrow & -3 & -21 \\
\hline
   & 1 & 7 & \underline{|0}
\end{array}
$$

13. $(3x^2 - 7x - 32) \div (x-5) = 3x + 8 + \dfrac{8}{x-5}$

$$
\begin{array}{r|rrr}
5 & 3 & -7 & -32 \\
  & \Downarrow & 15 & 40 \\
\hline
  & 3 & 8 & \underline{|8}
\end{array}
$$

15. $(-65b + 6b^2 + 50) \div (b-10) = 6b - 5$

$$
\begin{array}{r|rrr}
10 & 6 & -65 & 50 \\
   & \Downarrow & 60 & -50 \\
\hline
   & 6 & -5 & \underline{|0}
\end{array}
$$

17. $(x^3 + 2x^2 - 3x + 2) \div (x+1) = x^2 + x - 4 + \dfrac{6}{x+1}$

$$
\begin{array}{r|rrrr}
-1 & 1 & 2 & -3 & 2 \\
   & \Downarrow & -1 & -1 & 4 \\
\hline
   & 1 & 1 & -4 & \underline{|6}
\end{array}
$$

19. $(3y^3 + 7y^2 - 4y + 1) \div (y+3) = 3y^2 - 2y + 2 - \dfrac{5}{y+3}$

$$
\begin{array}{r|rrrr}
-3 & 3 & 7 & -4 & 1 \\
   & \Downarrow & -9 & 6 & -6 \\
\hline
   & 3 & -2 & 2 & \underline{|-5}
\end{array}
$$

21. $(2a^3 - a^2 - 12) \div (a-2) = 2a^2 + 3a + 6$

$$
\begin{array}{r|rrrr}
2 & 2 & -1 & 0 & -12 \\
  & \Downarrow & 4 & 6 & 12 \\
\hline
  & 2 & 3 & 6 & \underline{|0}
\end{array}
$$

23. $(x^4 - 7x^3 + 17x^2 - 22x + 8) \div (x-4)$

$= x^3 - 3x^2 + 5x - 2$

$$
\begin{array}{r|rrrrr}
4 & 1 & -7 & 17 & -22 & 8 \\
  & \Downarrow & 4 & -12 & 20 & -8 \\
\hline
  & 1 & -3 & 5 & -2 & \underline{|0}
\end{array}
$$

25. $(a^5 + a^3 - a) \div (a+1)$

$= a^4 - a^3 + 2a^2 - 2a + 1 - \dfrac{1}{a+1}$

$$
\begin{array}{r|rrrrrr}
-1 & 1 & 0 & 1 & 0 & -1 & 0 \\
   & \Downarrow & -1 & 1 & -2 & 2 & -1 \\
\hline
   & 1 & -1 & 2 & -2 & 1 & \underline{|-1}
\end{array}
$$

27. $(2x^3 - 9x^2 + x + 3) \div \left(x + \dfrac{1}{2}\right) = 2x^2 - 10x + 6$

$$
\begin{array}{r|rrrr}
-\dfrac{1}{2} & 2 & -9 & 1 & 3 \\
              & \Downarrow & -1 & 5 & -3 \\
\hline
              & 2 & -10 & 6 & \underline{|0}
\end{array}
$$

29. $(3x^3 + 16x^2 - 18x + 4) \div \left(x - \dfrac{2}{3}\right)$

$= 3x^2 + 18x - 6$

$$
\begin{array}{r|rrrr}
\dfrac{2}{3} & 3 & 16 & -18 & 4 \\
             & \Downarrow & 2 & 12 & -4 \\
\hline
             & 3 & 18 & -6 & \underline{|0}
\end{array}
$$

31. $\dfrac{\dfrac{x^3}{y^5}}{\dfrac{x^4}{y^8}} = \left(\dfrac{x^3}{y^5}\right) \div \left(\dfrac{x^4}{y^8}\right)$

$= \left(\dfrac{x^3}{y^5}\right) \cdot \left(\dfrac{y^8}{x^4}\right)$

$= \dfrac{\overset{1}{\cancel{x^3}}\ \overset{y^3}{\cancel{y^8}}}{\underset{x}{\cancel{x^4}}\ \underset{1}{\cancel{y^5}}}$

$= \dfrac{y^3}{x}$

33. $\dfrac{\dfrac{2ab^3}{a^2}}{\dfrac{6a^2b}{b^2}} = \left(\dfrac{2ab^3}{a^2}\right) \div \left(\dfrac{6a^2b}{b^2}\right)$

$= \left(\dfrac{2ab^3}{a^2}\right) \cdot \left(\dfrac{b^2}{6a^2b}\right)$

$= \dfrac{\overset{1}{\cancel{2}}\ \overset{1}{\cancel{a}}\ \overset{b^4}{\cancel{b^5}}}{\underset{3}{\cancel{6}}\ \underset{a^3}{\cancel{a^4}}\ \underset{1}{\cancel{b}}}$

$= \dfrac{b^4}{3a^3}$

35. $\dfrac{\dfrac{12}{x+6}}{\dfrac{15}{x^2-36}} = \left(\dfrac{12}{x+6}\right) \div \left(\dfrac{15}{x^2-36}\right)$

$= \left(\dfrac{12}{x+6}\right) \cdot \left(\dfrac{x^2-36}{15}\right)$

$= \dfrac{12}{(x+6)} \cdot \dfrac{(x+6)(x-6)}{15}$

$= \dfrac{\overset{4}{\cancel{12}}\ \overset{1}{\cancel{(x+6)}}\ (x-6)}{\underset{5}{\cancel{15}}\ \underset{1}{\cancel{(x+6)}}}$

$= \dfrac{4x-24}{5}$

37. $\dfrac{\dfrac{x+4y}{x^2+5xy+6y^2}}{\dfrac{x+3y}{x^2+6xy+8y^2}}$

$= \left(\dfrac{x+4y}{x^2+5xy+6y^2}\right) \div \left(\dfrac{x+3y}{x^2+6xy+8y^2}\right)$

$= \left(\dfrac{x+4y}{x^2+5xy+6y^2}\right) \cdot \left(\dfrac{x^2+6xy+8y^2}{x+3y}\right)$

$= \dfrac{(x+4y)}{(x+3y)(x+2y)} \cdot \dfrac{(x+2y)(x+4y)}{(x+3y)}$

$= \dfrac{(x+4y)\ \overset{1}{\cancel{(x+2y)}}\ (x+4y)}{(x+3y)\ \underset{1}{\cancel{(x+2y)}}\ (x+3y)}$

$= \dfrac{(x+4y)^2}{(x+3y)^2}$

39. $\dfrac{\dfrac{x}{x-3y}}{\dfrac{y}{x^2-9y^2}} = \left(\dfrac{x}{x-3y}\right) \div \left(\dfrac{y}{x^2-9y^2}\right)$

$= \left(\dfrac{x}{x-3y}\right) \cdot \left(\dfrac{x^2-9y^2}{y}\right)$

$= \dfrac{x}{(x-3y)} \cdot \dfrac{(x+3y)(x-3y)}{y}$

$= \dfrac{x(x+3y)\ \overset{1}{\cancel{(x-3y)}}}{y\ \underset{1}{\cancel{(x-3y)}}}$

$= \dfrac{x^2+3xy}{y}$

41.
$$\frac{8-\dfrac{2}{b}}{4-\dfrac{1}{b}} = \left(8-\frac{2}{b}\right) \div \left(4-\frac{1}{b}\right)$$

$$= \left(\frac{8}{1}\cdot\frac{b}{b}-\frac{2}{b}\right) \div \left(\frac{4}{1}\cdot\frac{b}{b}-\frac{1}{b}\right)$$

$$= \left(\frac{8b-2}{b}\right) \div \left(\frac{4b-1}{b}\right)$$

$$= \left(\frac{8b-2}{b}\right) \cdot \left(\frac{b}{4b-1}\right)$$

$$= \frac{2\cancel{b}\,\cancel{(4b-1)}}{\cancel{b}\,\cancel{(4b-1)}}$$

$$= 2$$

43.
$$\frac{\dfrac{5}{x}+\dfrac{5}{y}}{\dfrac{5}{x}-\dfrac{5}{y}} = \frac{\left(\dfrac{5}{x}+\dfrac{5}{y}\right)\cdot\dfrac{xy}{1}}{\left(\dfrac{5}{x}-\dfrac{5}{y}\right)\cdot\dfrac{xy}{1}}$$

$$= \frac{\left(\dfrac{5}{\cancel{x}}\cdot\dfrac{\cancel{x}\,y}{1}\right)+\left(\dfrac{5}{\cancel{y}}\cdot\dfrac{x\,\cancel{y}}{1}\right)}{\left(\dfrac{5}{\cancel{x}}\cdot\dfrac{\cancel{x}\,y}{1}\right)-\left(\dfrac{5}{\cancel{y}}\cdot\dfrac{x\,\cancel{y}}{1}\right)}$$

$$= \frac{5y+5x}{5y-5x}$$

$$= \frac{\cancel{5}\,(y+x)}{\cancel{5}\,(y-x)}$$

$$= \frac{y+x}{y-x}$$

45.
$$\frac{\dfrac{2}{a^2}-\dfrac{5}{3a}}{\dfrac{7}{a}+\dfrac{1}{a^2}} = \frac{\left(\dfrac{2}{a^2}-\dfrac{5}{3a}\right)\cdot\dfrac{3a^2}{1}}{\left(\dfrac{7}{a}+\dfrac{1}{a^2}\right)\cdot\dfrac{3a^2}{1}}$$

$$= \frac{\left(\dfrac{2}{\cancel{a^2}}\cdot\dfrac{3\cancel{a^2}}{1}\right)-\left(\dfrac{5}{\cancel{3}\cancel{a}}\cdot\dfrac{\cancel{3}\,\cancel{a}\,a}{1}\right)}{\left(\dfrac{7}{\cancel{a}}\cdot\dfrac{3\cancel{a^2}^{\,a}}{1}\right)+\left(\dfrac{1}{\cancel{a^2}}\cdot\dfrac{3\cancel{a^2}}{1}\right)}$$

$$= \frac{6-5a}{21a+3}$$

47.
$$\frac{\dfrac{2}{3x}+\dfrac{4}{y^2}}{\dfrac{x}{6x^2 y}} = \frac{\left(\dfrac{2}{3x}+\dfrac{4}{y^2}\right)\cdot\dfrac{6x^2 y^2}{1}}{\left(\dfrac{x}{6x^2 y}\right)\cdot\dfrac{6x^2 y^2}{1}}$$

$$= \frac{\left(\dfrac{2}{\cancel{3}\cancel{x}}\cdot\dfrac{\cancel{6}^{2}\,\cancel{x^2}^{\,x}\,y^2}{1}\right)+\left(\dfrac{4}{\cancel{y^2}}\cdot\dfrac{6x^2\,\cancel{y^2}^{\,1}}{1}\right)}{\dfrac{x}{\cancel{6}\,\cancel{x^2}\,\cancel{y}}\cdot\dfrac{\cancel{6}\,\cancel{x^2}\,\cancel{y^2}^{\,y}}{1}}$$

$$= \frac{4xy^2+24x^2}{xy}$$

$$= \frac{\cancel{x}\left(4y^2+24x\right)}{\cancel{x}\,y}$$

$$= \frac{4y^2+24x}{y}$$

49. $\dfrac{a+\dfrac{1}{b}}{\dfrac{1}{a}+b} = \dfrac{\left(a+\dfrac{1}{b}\right)}{\left(\dfrac{1}{a}+b\right)}\cdot\dfrac{\dfrac{ab}{1}}{\dfrac{ab}{1}}$

$= \dfrac{\left(\dfrac{a}{1}\cdot\dfrac{ab}{1}\right)+\left(\dfrac{1}{\cancel{b}}\cdot\dfrac{a\cancel{b}}{1}\right)}{\left(\dfrac{1}{a}\cdot\dfrac{ab}{1}\right)+\left(\dfrac{b}{1}\cdot\dfrac{ab}{1}\right)}$

$= \dfrac{a^2b+a}{b+ab^2}$

$= \dfrac{a\,\cancel{(ab+1)}}{b\,\cancel{(1+ab)}}$

$= \dfrac{a}{b}$

51. $\dfrac{\dfrac{3}{s}+\dfrac{4}{t}}{\dfrac{9t^2-16s^2}{st}} = \dfrac{\left(\dfrac{3}{s}+\dfrac{4}{t}\right)}{\left(\dfrac{9t^2-16s^2}{st}\right)}\cdot\dfrac{\dfrac{st}{1}}{\dfrac{st}{1}}$

$= \dfrac{\left(\dfrac{3}{\cancel{s}}\cdot\dfrac{\cancel{s}t}{1}\right)+\left(\dfrac{4}{\cancel{t}}\cdot\dfrac{s\cancel{t}}{1}\right)}{\dfrac{9t^2-16s^2}{\cancel{st}}\cdot\dfrac{\cancel{st}}{1}}$

$= \dfrac{\cancel{(3t+4s)}}{\cancel{(3t+4s)}\,(3t-4s)}$

$= \dfrac{1}{3t-4s}$

53. $\dfrac{\dfrac{3}{y}+1}{y-\dfrac{9}{y}} = \dfrac{\left(\dfrac{3}{y}+1\right)}{\left(y-\dfrac{9}{y}\right)}\cdot\dfrac{\dfrac{y}{1}}{\dfrac{y}{1}}$

$= \dfrac{\dfrac{3}{\cancel{y}}\cdot\dfrac{\cancel{y}}{1}+1(y)}{y(y)-\dfrac{9}{\cancel{y}}\cdot\dfrac{\cancel{y}}{1}}$

$= \dfrac{3+y}{y^2-9}$

$= \dfrac{\cancel{(y+3)}}{\cancel{(y+3)}\,(y-3)}$

$= \dfrac{1}{y-3}$

55. $\dfrac{\dfrac{5x}{y}-\dfrac{2y}{x}-9}{16+\dfrac{5x}{y}+\dfrac{3y}{x}} = \dfrac{\left(\dfrac{5x}{y}-\dfrac{2y}{x}-9\right)}{\left(16+\dfrac{5x}{y}+\dfrac{3y}{x}\right)}\cdot\dfrac{\dfrac{xy}{1}}{\dfrac{xy}{1}}$

$= \dfrac{\dfrac{5x}{\cancel{y}}\cdot\dfrac{x\cancel{y}}{1}-\dfrac{2y}{\cancel{x}}\cdot\dfrac{\cancel{x}y}{1}-9(xy)}{16(xy)+\dfrac{5x}{\cancel{y}}\cdot\dfrac{x\cancel{y}}{1}+\dfrac{3y}{\cancel{x}}\cdot\dfrac{\cancel{x}y}{1}}$

$= \dfrac{5x^2-9xy-2y^2}{5x^2+16xy+3y^2}$

$= \dfrac{\cancel{(5x+y)}\,(x-2y)}{\cancel{(5x+y)}\,(x+3y)}$

$= \dfrac{x-2y}{x+3y}$

57.
$$\frac{x^{-1}-y^{-1}}{x^{-1}y^{-1}}=\frac{\dfrac{1}{x}-\dfrac{1}{y}}{\dfrac{1}{xy}}$$

$$=\frac{\left(\dfrac{1}{x}-\dfrac{1}{y}\right)\dfrac{xy}{1}}{\left(\dfrac{1}{xy}\right)\dfrac{xy}{1}}$$

$$=\frac{\dfrac{1}{\cancel{x}}\cdot\dfrac{\cancel{x}\,y}{1}-\dfrac{1}{\cancel{y}}\cdot\dfrac{x\,\cancel{y}}{1}}{\dfrac{1}{\cancel{xy}}\cdot\dfrac{\cancel{xy}}{1}}$$

$$=y-x$$

59.
$$\frac{a^{-2}-b^{-2}}{b^{-1}-a^{-1}}=\frac{\dfrac{1}{a^2}-\dfrac{1}{b^2}}{\dfrac{1}{b}-\dfrac{1}{a}}$$

$$=\frac{\left(\dfrac{1}{a^2}-\dfrac{1}{b^2}\right)\dfrac{a^2b^2}{1}}{\left(\dfrac{1}{b}-\dfrac{1}{a}\right)\dfrac{a^2b^2}{1}}$$

$$=\frac{\dfrac{1}{\cancel{a^2}}\cdot\dfrac{\cancel{a^2}\,b^2}{1}-\dfrac{1}{\cancel{b^2}}\cdot\dfrac{a^2\,\cancel{b^2}}{1}}{\dfrac{1}{\cancel{b}}\cdot\dfrac{a^2\,\cancel{b^2}^{\,a}}{1}-\dfrac{1}{\cancel{a}}\cdot\dfrac{\cancel{a^2}^{\,b}b^2}{1}}$$

$$=\frac{b^2-a^2}{a^2b-ab^2}$$

$$=\frac{(b+a)(-1)\cancel{(a-b)}}{ab\,\cancel{(a-b)}}$$

$$=\frac{-b-a}{ab}$$

61. The degree of the quotient is always one less than the degree of the dividend when dividing by synthetic division because the divisor is a linear factor of the form $(x-k)$.

63. Use Method 1 to simplify complex fractions with a single fraction in the numerator and/or denominator, and use Method 2 to simplify complex fractions with more than one fraction in the numerator and/or denominator.

65.
$$\frac{\dfrac{4x}{y}-\dfrac{2y}{x}-7}{3+\dfrac{4x}{y}+\dfrac{13y}{x}}=\frac{\left(\dfrac{4x}{y}-\dfrac{2y}{x}-7\right)\dfrac{xy}{1}}{\left(3+\dfrac{4x}{y}+\dfrac{13y}{x}\right)\dfrac{xy}{1}}$$

$$=\frac{\dfrac{4x}{\cancel{y}}\cdot\dfrac{x\,\cancel{y}}{1}-\dfrac{2y}{\cancel{x}}\cdot\dfrac{\cancel{x}\,y}{1}-7(xy)}{3(xy)+\dfrac{4x}{\cancel{y}}\cdot\dfrac{x\,\cancel{y}}{1}+\dfrac{13y}{\cancel{x}}\cdot\dfrac{\cancel{x}\,y}{1}}$$

$$=\frac{4x^2-7xy-2y^2}{4x^2+3xy+13y^2}$$

67. The Identity Property of Multiplication is used to simplify complex fractions by multiplying the fraction by a special form of 1.

69.
$$\frac{\dfrac{1}{y}}{\dfrac{1}{y}+1}=\frac{\left(\dfrac{1}{y}\right)\dfrac{y}{1}}{\left(\dfrac{1}{y}+1\right)\dfrac{y}{1}}$$

$$=\frac{\dfrac{1}{\cancel{y}}\cdot\dfrac{\cancel{y}}{1}}{\dfrac{1}{\cancel{y}}\cdot\dfrac{\cancel{y}}{1}+1(y)}$$

$$=\frac{1}{1+y}$$

71. $\dfrac{\frac{1}{x}+\frac{1}{y}}{\frac{1}{x^2}-\frac{1}{y^2}} = \dfrac{\left(\frac{1}{x}+\frac{1}{y}\right)\frac{x^2y^2}{1}}{\left(\frac{1}{x^2}-\frac{1}{y^2}\right)\frac{x^2y^2}{1}}$

$= \dfrac{\frac{1}{\cancel{x}}\cdot\frac{\cancel{x}^{\;x}y^2}{1}+\frac{1}{\cancel{y}}\cdot\frac{x^2\cancel{y}^{\;y}}{1}}{\frac{1}{\cancel{x}^2}\cdot\frac{\cancel{x}^2y^2}{1}-\frac{1}{\cancel{y}^2}\cdot\frac{x^2\cancel{y}^2}{1}}$

$= \dfrac{xy^2+x^2y}{y^2-x^2}$

$= \dfrac{xy\,\cancel{(y+x)}^{\;1}}{\cancel{(y+x)}\,(y-x)}$

$= \dfrac{xy}{y-x}$

73. $\left(3a^3+\dfrac{11}{2}a^2-3a-5\right)\div(a+2)$

$= 3a^2-\dfrac{1}{2}a-2-\dfrac{1}{a+2}$

$\begin{array}{r|rrrr} -2 & 3 & \frac{11}{2} & -3 & -5 \\ & \Downarrow & -6 & 1 & 4 \\ \hline & 3 & -\frac{1}{2} & -2 & \underline{|-1} \end{array}$

75. $\left(12x^3-\dfrac{13}{2}x^2-7x+4\right)\div\left(x-\dfrac{2}{3}\right)$

$= 12x^2+\dfrac{3}{2}x-6$

$\begin{array}{r|rrrr} \frac{2}{3} & 12 & -\frac{13}{2} & -7 & 4 \\ & \Downarrow & 8 & 1 & -4 \\ \hline & 12 & \frac{3}{2} & -6 & \underline{|0} \end{array}$

77. $\left(-16-32x+x^2-6x^3+27x^4\right)\div\left(x+\dfrac{4}{9}\right)$

$= 27x^3-18x^2+9x-36$

$\begin{array}{r|rrrrr} -\frac{4}{9} & 27 & -6 & 1 & -32 & -16 \\ & \Downarrow & -12 & 8 & -4 & 16 \\ \hline & 27 & -18 & 9 & -36 & \underline{|0} \end{array}$

79. $x-\dfrac{x}{x-\frac{y}{x}} = x-\dfrac{x}{x-\frac{y}{x}}\cdot\dfrac{\frac{x}{1}}{\frac{x}{1}}$

$= x-\dfrac{x(x)}{x(x)-\frac{y}{\cancel{x}}\cdot\frac{\cancel{x}}{1}}$

$= x-\dfrac{x^2}{x^2-y}$

$= x\cdot\dfrac{x^2-y}{x^2-y}-\dfrac{x^2}{x^2-y}$

$= \dfrac{x^3-xy}{x^2-y}-\dfrac{x^2}{x^2-y}$

$= \dfrac{x^3-xy-x^2}{x^2-y}$

81. $2+\dfrac{2}{2+\frac{2}{2+\frac{2}{x}}} = 2+\dfrac{2}{2+\frac{2(x)}{\left(2+\frac{2}{x}\right)x}}$

$= 2+\dfrac{2}{2+\frac{2x}{2x+2}}$

$= 2+\dfrac{2(2x+2)}{\left(2+\frac{2x}{2x+2}\right)(2x+2)}$

$= 2+\dfrac{4x+4}{2(2x+2)+2x}$

$= 2+\dfrac{4x+4}{4x+4+2x}$

$= 2\cdot\dfrac{6x+4}{6x+4}+\dfrac{4x+4}{6x+4}$

$= \dfrac{12x+8}{6x+4}+\dfrac{4x+4}{6x+4}$

$= \dfrac{16x+12}{6x+4}$

$= \dfrac{\cancel{2}^{\;1}(8x+6)}{\cancel{2}^{\;1}(3x+2)}$

$= \dfrac{8x+6}{3x+2}$

83. $\dfrac{9x^{-1}+6y^{-1}-3x^{-1}y^{-1}}{12x^{-1}+8y^{-1}-4x^{-1}y^{-1}}$

$$=\dfrac{\dfrac{9}{x}+\dfrac{6}{y}-\dfrac{3}{xy}}{\dfrac{12}{x}+\dfrac{8}{y}-\dfrac{4}{xy}}$$

$$=\dfrac{\dfrac{9}{x}+\dfrac{6}{y}-\dfrac{3}{xy}}{\dfrac{12}{x}+\dfrac{8}{y}-\dfrac{4}{xy}}\cdot\dfrac{\dfrac{xy}{1}}{\dfrac{xy}{1}}$$

$$=\dfrac{\dfrac{9}{\cancel{x}}\cdot\dfrac{\overset{1}{\cancel{x}}\,y}{1}+\dfrac{6}{\cancel{y}}\cdot\dfrac{x\,\overset{1}{\cancel{y}}}{1}-\dfrac{3}{\cancel{xy}}\cdot\dfrac{\overset{1}{\cancel{xy}}}{1}}{\dfrac{12}{\cancel{x}}\cdot\dfrac{\underset{1}{\cancel{x}}\,y}{1}+\dfrac{8}{\cancel{y}}\cdot\dfrac{x\,\underset{1}{\cancel{y}}}{1}-\dfrac{4}{\cancel{xy}}\cdot\dfrac{\underset{1}{\cancel{xy}}}{1}}$$

$$=\dfrac{9y+6x-3}{12y+8x-4}$$

$$=\dfrac{3\,\overset{1}{\cancel{(3y+2x-1)}}}{4\,\underset{1}{\cancel{(3y+2x-1)}}}$$

$$=\dfrac{3}{4}$$

7.5 Exercises

1. If $P(x)$ and $Q(x)$ are both polynomials, then $R(x) = \dfrac{P(x)}{Q(x)}$, $Q(x) \neq 0$ is called a <u>rational</u> <u>function</u>.

3. When variables occur in the denominator of a rational equation, we must check the solution(s) for <u>extraneous</u> solutions.

5. $\left(\dfrac{3}{y}+1\right)\left(y-\dfrac{9}{y}\right)$ is an example of an algebraic <u>expression</u>.

7. $D = (-\infty, \infty)$

9. $5 + t = 0$
$t = -5$
$D = \{t \mid t \neq -5\}$

11. $3x = 0$
$x = 0$
$D = \{x \mid x \neq 0\}$

13. $t^2 + 7t - 8 = 0$
$(t+8)(t-1) = 0$
$t + 8 = 0 \quad \text{or} \quad t - 1 = 0$
$t = -8 \qquad\qquad t = 1$
$D = \{t \mid t \neq -8 \text{ and } t \neq 1\}$

15. $D = (-\infty, \infty)$

17.
$$\frac{5}{14} - \frac{2}{x} = \frac{3}{x}$$
$$\frac{14x}{1}\left(\frac{5}{14} - \frac{2}{x}\right) = \frac{14x}{1}\left(\frac{3}{x}\right)$$
$$\frac{\cancel{14}x}{1} \cdot \frac{5}{\cancel{14}} - \frac{14\cancel{x}}{1} \cdot \frac{2}{\cancel{x}} = \frac{14\cancel{x}}{1} \cdot \frac{3}{\cancel{x}}$$
$$5x - 28 = 42$$
$$5x = 70$$
$$x = 14$$
Solution Set: $\{14\}$

19.
$$\frac{5}{x} - \frac{1}{3} = \frac{13}{3x}$$
$$\frac{3x}{1}\left(\frac{5}{x} - \frac{1}{3}\right) = \frac{3x}{1}\left(\frac{13}{3x}\right)$$
$$\frac{3\cancel{x}}{1} \cdot \frac{5}{\cancel{x}} - \frac{\cancel{3}x}{1} \cdot \frac{1}{\cancel{3}} = \frac{\cancel{3}\cancel{x}}{1} \cdot \frac{13}{\cancel{3}\cancel{x}}$$
$$15 - x = 13$$
$$-x = -2$$
$$x = 2$$
Solution Set: $\{2\}$

21.
$$\frac{4}{x+3} + \frac{6}{x} = \frac{8}{x}$$
$$\frac{x(x+3)}{1}\left(\frac{4}{x+3} + \frac{6}{x}\right) = \frac{x(x+3)}{1}\left(\frac{8}{x}\right)$$
$$\frac{x\cancel{(x+3)}}{1} \cdot \frac{4}{\cancel{(x+3)}} + \frac{\cancel{x}(x+3)}{1} \cdot \frac{6}{\cancel{x}} = \frac{\cancel{x}(x+3)}{1} \cdot \frac{8}{\cancel{x}}$$
$$4x + 6x + 18 = 8x + 24$$
$$2x = 6$$
$$x = 3$$
Solution Set: $\{3\}$

23.
$$\frac{11x}{8} = \frac{3}{x} + \frac{5}{2x}$$
$$\frac{8x}{1}\left(\frac{11x}{8}\right) = \frac{8x}{1}\left(\frac{3}{x} + \frac{5}{2x}\right)$$
$$\frac{\cancel{8}x}{1} \cdot \frac{11x}{\cancel{8}} = \frac{8\cancel{x}}{1} \cdot \frac{3}{\cancel{x}} + \frac{\cancel{8}\cancel{x}}{1} \cdot \frac{5}{\cancel{2}\cancel{x}}$$
$$11x^2 = 24 + 20$$
$$11x^2 - 44 = 0$$
$$11(x+2)(x-2) = 0$$
$$x + 2 = 0 \quad \text{or} \quad x - 2 = 0$$
$$x = -2 \qquad\qquad x = 2$$
Solution Set: $\{-2, 2\}$

25.

$$\frac{3x}{x-1} = \frac{2x}{x+2}$$

$$\frac{\overset{1}{\cancel{(x-1)}}(x+2)}{1} \cdot \frac{3x}{\cancel{(x-1)}_1} = \frac{(x-1)\overset{1}{\cancel{(x+2)}}}{1} \cdot \frac{2x}{\cancel{(x+2)}_1}$$

$$3x^2 + 6x = 2x^2 - 2x$$

$$x^2 + 8x = 0$$

$$x(x+8) = 0$$

$$x = 0 \quad \text{or} \quad x + 8 = 0$$

$$x = -8$$

Solution Set: $\{-8, 0\}$

27.

$$\frac{2}{x^2 - 3x} = \frac{4}{x^2 - 9}$$

$$\frac{2}{x(x-3)} = \frac{4}{(x+3)(x-3)}$$

$$\frac{\overset{1}{\cancel{x}}(x+3)\overset{1}{\cancel{(x-3)}}}{1} \cdot \frac{2}{\cancel{x}\,\cancel{(x-3)}_1} = \frac{x\overset{1}{\cancel{(x+3)}}\overset{1}{\cancel{(x-3)}}}{1} \cdot \frac{4}{\cancel{(x+3)}\,\cancel{(x-3)}}$$

$$2x + 6 = 4x$$

$$-2x = -6$$

$$\cancel{x = 3}$$

Solution Set: $\{\ \}$

29.

$$\frac{6}{t-4} - \frac{7}{t} = \frac{4}{t^2 - 4t}$$

$$\frac{6}{t-4} - \frac{7}{t} = \frac{4}{t(t-4)}$$

$$\frac{t(t-4)}{1}\left(\frac{6}{t-4} - \frac{7}{t}\right) = \frac{t(t-4)}{1}\left(\frac{4}{t(t-4)}\right)$$

$$\frac{t\overset{1}{\cancel{(t-4)}}}{1} \cdot \frac{6}{\cancel{(t-4)}_1} - \frac{\overset{1}{\cancel{t}}(t-4)}{1} \cdot \frac{7}{\cancel{t}_1} = \frac{\overset{1}{\cancel{t}}\overset{1}{\cancel{(t-4)}}}{1} \cdot \frac{4}{\cancel{t}\,\cancel{(t-4)}}$$

$$6t - (7t - 28) = 4$$

$$-t + 28 = 4$$

$$-t = -24$$

$$t = 24$$

Solution Set: $\{24\}$

31.

$$\frac{5}{x-4}-\frac{16}{x+4}=\frac{18}{x^2-16}$$

$$\frac{5}{x-4}-\frac{16}{x+4}=\frac{18}{(x+4)(x-4)}$$

$$\frac{(x+4)(x-4)}{1}\left(\frac{5}{x-4}-\frac{16}{x+4}\right)=\frac{(x+4)(x-4)}{1}\left(\frac{18}{(x+4)(x-4)}\right)$$

$$\frac{(x+4)\cancel{(x-4)}^{1}}{1}\cdot\frac{5}{\cancel{(x-4)}_{1}}-\frac{(x+4)(x-4)}{1}\cdot\frac{16}{\cancel{(x+4)}_{1}}=\frac{\cancel{(x+4)}^{1}\cancel{(x-4)}^{1}}{1}\cdot\frac{18}{\cancel{(x+4)}_{1}\cancel{(x-4)}_{1}}$$

$$5x+20-(16x-64)=18$$

$$-11x+84=18$$

$$-11x=-66$$

$$x=6$$

Solution Set: $\{6\}$

33.

$$\frac{8}{x^2-4}=1+\frac{2}{x-2}$$

$$\frac{8}{(x+2)(x-2)}=1+\frac{2}{x-2}$$

$$\frac{(x+2)(x-2)}{1}\left(\frac{8}{(x+2)(x-2)}\right)=\frac{(x+2)(x-2)}{1}\left(1+\frac{2}{x-2}\right)$$

$$\frac{\cancel{(x+2)}^{1}\cancel{(x-2)}^{1}}{1}\cdot\frac{8}{\cancel{(x+2)}_{1}\cancel{(x-2)}_{1}}=(x+2)(x-2)\cdot1+\frac{(x+2)\cancel{(x-2)}^{1}}{1}\cdot\frac{2}{\cancel{(x-2)}_{1}}$$

$$8=x^2-4+(2x+4)$$

$$8=x^2+2x$$

$$x^2+2x-8=0$$

$$(x+4)(x-2)=0$$

$$x+4=0 \quad\text{or}\quad x-2=0$$

$$x=-4 \qquad\qquad \cancel{x=2}$$

Solution Set: $\{-4\}$

35.

$$\frac{3x}{x+2}+\frac{4}{x+4}=3$$

$$\frac{(x+2)(x+4)}{1}\left(\frac{3x}{x+2}+\frac{4}{x+4}\right)=(x+2)(x+4)(3)$$

$$\frac{\cancel{(x+2)}^{1}(x+4)}{1}\cdot\frac{3x}{\cancel{(x+2)}_{1}}+\frac{(x+2)\cancel{(x+4)}^{1}}{1}\cdot\frac{4}{\cancel{(x+4)}_{1}}=(x+2)(x+4)(3)$$

$$3x^2+12x+4x+8=3x^2+18x+24$$

$$-2x=16$$

$$x=-8$$

Solution Set: $\{-8\}$

37.

$$\frac{2}{x+6} - 3 = \frac{3}{x+2}$$

$$\frac{(x+6)(x+2)}{1}\left(\frac{2}{x+6} - 3\right) = \frac{(x+6)(x+2)}{1}\left(\frac{3}{x+2}\right)$$

$$\frac{\cancel{(x+6)}(x+2)}{1} \cdot \frac{2}{\cancel{(x+6)}} - (x+6)(x+2)(3) = \frac{(x+6)\cancel{(x+2)}}{1} \cdot \frac{3}{\cancel{(x+2)}}$$

$$2x + 4 - \left(3x^2 + 24x + 36\right) = 3x + 18$$

$$-3x^2 - 22x - 32 = 3x + 18$$

$$3x^2 + 25x + 50 = 0$$

$$(x+5)(3x+10) = 0$$

$$x + 5 = 0 \quad \text{or} \quad 3x + 10 = 0$$

$$x = -5 \qquad\qquad x = -\frac{10}{3}$$

Solution Set: $\left\{-5, -\frac{10}{3}\right\}$

39.

$$\frac{3}{2} + \frac{2}{2x-4} = \frac{1}{x-2}$$

$$\frac{2(x-2)}{1}\left(\frac{3}{2} + \frac{2}{2(x-2)}\right) = \frac{2(x-2)}{1}\left(\frac{1}{x-2}\right)$$

$$\frac{\cancel{2}(x-2)}{1} \cdot \frac{3}{\cancel{2}} + \frac{\cancel{2}\,\cancel{(x-2)}}{1} \cdot \frac{2}{\cancel{2}\,\cancel{(x-2)}} = \frac{2\,\cancel{(x-2)}}{1} \cdot \frac{1}{\cancel{(x-2)}}$$

$$3x - 6 + 2 = 2$$

$$3x = 6$$

$$\cancel{x = 2}$$

Solution Set: $\{\ \}$

41.

$$\frac{x^2}{x^2-1} + \frac{3}{x+1} = \frac{5}{x-1}$$

$$\frac{(x+1)(x-1)}{1}\left(\frac{x^2}{(x+1)(x-1)} + \frac{3}{x+1}\right) = \frac{(x+1)(x-1)}{1}\left(\frac{5}{x-1}\right)$$

$$\frac{\cancel{(x+1)}\,\cancel{(x-1)}}{1} \cdot \frac{x^2}{\cancel{(x+1)}\,\cancel{(x-1)}} + \frac{\cancel{(x+1)}(x-1)}{1} \cdot \frac{3}{\cancel{(x+1)}} = \frac{(x+1)\,\cancel{(x-1)}}{1} \cdot \frac{5}{\cancel{(x-1)}}$$

$$x^2 + 3x - 3 = 5x + 5$$

$$x^2 - 2x - 8 = 0$$

$$(x-4)(x+2) = 0$$

$$x - 4 = 0 \quad \text{or} \quad x + 2 = 0$$

$$x = 4 \qquad\qquad x = -2$$

Solution Set: $\{-2, 4\}$

43.

$$\frac{x+2}{4x^2-11x-3}-\frac{3}{4x+1}=\frac{2}{x-3}$$

$$\frac{(4x+1)(x-3)}{1}\left(\frac{x+2}{(4x+1)(x-3)}-\frac{3}{4x+1}\right)=\frac{(4x+1)(x-3)}{1}\left(\frac{2}{x-3}\right)$$

$$\frac{\cancel{(4x+1)}\ \cancel{(x-3)}}{1}\cdot\frac{x+2}{\cancel{(4x+1)}\ \cancel{(x-3)}}-\frac{\cancel{(4x+1)}\ (x-3)}{1}\cdot\frac{3}{\cancel{(4x+1)}}=\frac{(4x+1)\ \cancel{(x-3)}}{1}\cdot\frac{2}{\cancel{(x-3)}}$$

$$x+2-(3x-9)=8x+2$$

$$-2x+11=8x+2$$

$$-10x=-9$$

$$x=\frac{9}{10}$$

Solution Set: $\left\{\dfrac{9}{10}\right\}$

45.

$$\frac{3x}{6x^2+x-12}=\frac{5}{2x+3}-\frac{4}{3x-4}$$

$$\frac{(2x+3)(3x-4)}{1}\left(\frac{3x}{(2x+3)(3x-4)}\right)=\frac{(2x+3)(3x-4)}{1}\left(\frac{5}{2x+3}-\frac{4}{3x-4}\right)$$

$$\frac{\cancel{(2x+3)}\ \cancel{(3x-4)}}{1}\cdot\frac{3x}{\cancel{(2x+3)}\ \cancel{(3x-4)}}=\frac{\cancel{(2x+3)}\ (3x-4)}{1}\cdot\frac{5}{\cancel{(2x+3)}}-\frac{(2x+3)\ \cancel{(3x-4)}}{1}\cdot\frac{4}{\cancel{(3x-4)}}$$

$$3x=15x-20-(8x+12)$$

$$3x=7x-32$$

$$-4x=-32$$

$$x=8$$

Solution Set: $\{8\}$

47. Expression

$$\frac{x+2}{2x}+\frac{1-x}{x^2}=\frac{x^2+2x}{2x^2}+\frac{2-2x}{2x^2}$$

$$=\frac{x^2+2}{2x^2}$$

49. Equation

$$\frac{x-3}{x+5}=\frac{5}{2x-3}$$

$$\frac{\cancel{(x+5)}\ (2x-3)}{1}\cdot\frac{(x-3)}{\cancel{(x+5)}}=\frac{(x+5)\ \cancel{(2x-3)}}{1}\cdot\frac{5}{\cancel{(2x-3)}}$$

$$2x^2-9x+9=5x+25$$

$$2x^2-14x-16=0$$

$$2(x-8)(x+1)=0$$

$$x-8=0\quad\text{or}\quad x+1=0$$

$$x=8\qquad\qquad x=-1$$

Solution Set: $\{-1,8\}$

51. Equation

$$\frac{x}{4}+\frac{5}{24}=\frac{x^2}{3}$$

$$\frac{\overset{6}{\cancel{24}}}{1}\cdot\frac{x}{\cancel{4}}+\frac{\overset{1}{\cancel{24}}}{1}\cdot\frac{5}{\cancel{24}}=\frac{\overset{8}{\cancel{24}}}{1}\cdot\frac{x^2}{\cancel{3}}$$

$$6x+5=8x^2$$

$$8x^2-6x-5=0$$

$$(2x+1)(4x-5)=0$$

$$2x+1=0 \quad \text{or} \quad 4x-5=0$$

$$x=-\frac{1}{2} \qquad x=\frac{5}{4}$$

Solution Set: $\left\{-\dfrac{1}{2},\dfrac{5}{4}\right\}$

53. Expression

$$\frac{x-3}{2x^2+8x}+\frac{7}{x^2-16}$$

$$=\frac{(x-3)(x-4)}{2x(x+4)(x-4)}+\frac{7(2x)}{2x(x+4)(x-4)}$$

$$=\frac{x^2-7x+12+14x}{2x(x+4)(x-4)}$$

$$=\frac{x^2+7x+12}{2x(x+4)(x-4)}$$

$$=\frac{(x+3)\overset{1}{\cancel{(x+4)}}}{2x\,\cancel{(x+4)}\,(x-4)}$$

$$=\frac{x+3}{2x^2-8x}$$

55. $A=\dfrac{h(a+b)}{2}$

$$A=\frac{ah+bh}{2}$$

$$2A=\frac{\overset{1}{\cancel{2}}}{1}\cdot\frac{ah+bh}{\cancel{2}}$$

$$2A=ah+bh$$

$$ah=2A-bh$$

$$a=\frac{2A-bh}{h}$$

57.

$$\frac{1}{f}=\frac{1}{a}+\frac{1}{b}$$

$$\frac{abf}{1}\left(\frac{1}{f}\right)=\frac{abf}{1}\left(\frac{1}{a}+\frac{1}{b}\right)$$

$$\frac{ab\cancel{f}}{1}\cdot\frac{1}{\cancel{f}}=\frac{\cancel{a}bf}{1}\cdot\frac{1}{\cancel{a}}+\frac{a\cancel{b}f}{1}\cdot\frac{1}{\cancel{b}}$$

$$ab=bf+af$$

$$ab-af=bf$$

$$a(b-f)=bf$$

$$a=\frac{bf}{b-f}$$

59. $P=\dfrac{A}{1+rt}$

$$P(1+rt)=\frac{A}{\cancel{(1+rt)}}\cdot\frac{\overset{1}{\cancel{(1+rt)}}}{1}$$

$$P+Prt=A$$

$$Prt=A-P$$

$$t=\frac{A-P}{Pr}$$

61.

$$\frac{P_1V_1}{T_1}=\frac{P_2V_2}{T_2}$$

$$\frac{\overset{1}{\cancel{T_1}}T_2}{1}\cdot\frac{P_1V_1}{\cancel{T_1}}=\frac{T_1\overset{1}{\cancel{T_2}}}{1}\cdot\frac{P_2V_2}{\cancel{T_2}}$$

$$P_1T_2V_1=P_2T_1V_2$$

$$T_2=\frac{P_2T_1V_2}{P_1V_1}$$

63. To find the domain of a rational function, set the denominator equal to zero. The domain will be the set of all real numbers except those values for which the denominator equals zero.

65. Answers will vary; for example: An algebraic expression does not have an equals sign and simplifies to a single rational expression. An example of an algebraic expression is $\frac{x+3}{2x^2-8x}+\frac{7}{x^2-16}$. An algebraic equation contains an equals sign and simplifies to a real number solution. An example of an algebraic equation is $\frac{2}{x}+\frac{3}{7}=\frac{5}{x}$.

67. Let x represent the first number, then $4x$ is the second number. The equation is $\dfrac{1}{x}+\dfrac{1}{4x}=\dfrac{5}{12}$.

$$\frac{1}{x}+\frac{1}{4x}=\frac{5}{12}$$

$$\frac{12x}{1}\left(\frac{1}{x}+\frac{1}{4x}\right)=\frac{12x}{1}\left(\frac{5}{12}\right)$$

$$\frac{\overset{1}{\cancel{12}}\,x}{1}\cdot\frac{1}{\cancel{x}}+\frac{\overset{3}{\cancel{12}}\,\overset{1}{\cancel{x}}}{1}\cdot\frac{1}{\cancel{4}\,\cancel{x}}=\frac{\cancel{12}\,x}{1}\cdot\frac{5}{\cancel{12}}$$

$$12+3=5x$$

$$5x=15$$

$$x=3$$

If $x=3$, then $4x=12$. The two numbers are 3 and 12.

69. Let x represent the first number, then $x+2$ is the second number. The equation is $\dfrac{1}{x}+\dfrac{1}{x+2}=\dfrac{5}{12}$.

$$\frac{1}{x}+\frac{1}{x+2}=\frac{5}{12}$$

$$\frac{12x(x+2)}{1}\left(\frac{1}{x}+\frac{1}{x+2}\right)=\frac{12x(x+2)}{1}\left(\frac{5}{12}\right)$$

$$\frac{12\,\cancel{x}\,(x+2)}{1}\cdot\frac{1}{\cancel{x}}+\frac{12x\,\cancel{(x+2)}}{1}\cdot\frac{1}{\cancel{(x+2)}}=\frac{\cancel{12}\,x(x+2)}{1}\cdot\frac{5}{\cancel{12}}$$

$$12x+24+12x=5x^2+10x$$

$$5x^2-14x-24=0$$

$$(5x+6)(x-4)=0$$

$$5x+6=0 \quad \text{or} \quad x-4=0$$

$$x=-\frac{6}{5} \qquad\qquad x=4$$

If $x=-\dfrac{6}{5}$, then $x+2=\dfrac{4}{5}$. If $x=4$, then $x+2=6$.

The two numbers are $-\dfrac{6}{5}$ and $\dfrac{4}{5}$, or 4 and 6.

71. Prepare   We need to use the function $C(a)=\frac{a}{a+12}\cdot A$ to convert an adult's daily dosage of erythromycin to a child's dosage.

Plan We first replace the A in the formula with the adult dosage of 500 mg. Therefore, the rational function becomes $C(a)=\frac{500a}{a+12}$, and the independent variable is the child's age. In this case, the child's age is $a=12$, and we will evaluate the function at $C(12)$.

Process Evaluate $C(12)$.

$$C(12)=\frac{500(12)}{(12)+12}$$

$$=\frac{6,000}{24}$$

$$=250$$

Therefore, the child's daily dosage is 250 mg.

Ponder Does are answer seem reasonable? Based on our formula, yes. Also, we would certainly expect a child's dosage to be considerably smaller than an adult's for the same medicine.

73.
$$\frac{x^2-6x+9}{x^2+2x+1}-\frac{2(x-3)}{x+1}=3$$

$$\frac{(x+1)^2}{1}\left(\frac{x^2-6x+9}{(x+1)^2}-\frac{2(x-3)}{x+1}\right)=(x+1)^2(3)$$

$$\frac{\cancel{(x+1)^2}^{\,1}}{1}\cdot\frac{x^2-6x+9}{\cancel{(x+1)^2}_{\,1}}-\frac{\cancel{(x+1)^2}^{\,(x+1)}}{1}\cdot\frac{2(x-3)}{\cancel{(x+1)}_{\,1}}=(x+1)^2(3)$$

$$x^2-6x+9-2(x+1)(x-3)=3(x+1)^2$$

$$x^2-6x+9-2(x^2-2x-3)=3x^2+6x+3$$

$$-x^2-2x+15=3x^2+6x+3$$

$$4x^2+8x-12=0$$

$$4(x+3)(x-1)=0$$

$$x+3=0 \quad \text{or} \quad x-1=0$$

$$x=-3 \qquad\qquad x=1$$

Solution Set: $\{-3,1\}$

75.
$$x^2-5x=\frac{10}{x+5}\div\frac{15}{x^2-25}$$

$$x^2-5x=\frac{10}{x+5}\cdot\frac{x^2-25}{15}$$

$$x^2-5x=\frac{\cancel{10}^{\,2}}{\cancel{(x+5)}_{\,1}}\cdot\frac{\cancel{(x+5)}(x-5)}{\cancel{15}_{\,3}}$$

$$x^2-5x=\frac{2}{3}x-\frac{10}{3}$$

$$3(x^2-5x)=3\left(\frac{2}{3}x-\frac{10}{3}\right)$$

$$3x^2-15x=2x-10$$

$$3x^2-17x+10=0$$

$$(3x-2)(x-5)=0$$

$$3x-2=0 \quad \text{or} \quad x-5=0$$

$$x=\frac{2}{3} \qquad\qquad \cancel{x=5}$$

Solution Set: $\left\{\frac{2}{3}\right\}$

7.6 Exercises

1. When solving a work problem we used the formula work = rate•time , where work is 1 <u>complete job</u>.

3. The equation $y = kx$ is an example of <u>direct</u> variation, where k is the <u>constant</u> of variation.

5. If y varies jointly with x and z and inversely with q, the variation equation is expressed as $y = \frac{kxz}{q}$.

7. $T = ku^3$

9. $G = \frac{kab}{c}$

11. $F = \frac{k}{jc}$

13. $c = \frac{k}{d}$

$4 = \frac{k}{8}$

$k = 32$

15. $X = kyz^2$

$24 = k(3)(4)^2$

$24 = 48k$

$k = \frac{1}{2}$

17. $w = kb$ $w = \frac{7}{4}b$

$21 = k(12)$ $w = \frac{7}{4}(28)$

$k = \frac{7}{4}$ $= 49$

19. $A = kbc$ $A = 2bc$

$625 = k(12.5)(25)$ $A = 2(15)(78.5)$

$625 = 312.5k$ $= 2,355$

$k = 2$

21. If the boat is traveling downstream add the current, and if the boat is traveling upstream subtract the current.

23. With two people working together, the time to complete the job can never be more than the fastest rate of any individual working alone.

25. The "1" in the work formula represents one complete job or task.

27. A direct variation equals a constant multiplied by a variable, while an inverse variation equals a constant divided by a variable.

29. Any variable that is said to "vary inversely" belongs in the denominator of an inverse variation equation.

31. If a and b are both doubled, then C must be quadrupled if C varies jointly with a and b.

33. $D = kt$ $D = 52t$

$78 = k\left(1\frac{1}{2}\right)$ $D = 52(4)$

$k = 52$ $= 208$

Alan travels 208 miles in 4 hours.

35. $P = kb$ $P = 6.2b$

$806 = k(130)$ $P = 6.2(270)$

$k = 6.2$ $= 1,674$

The store can expect to make $1,674.

37. $D = kt^2$ $D = 16t^2$

$64 = k(2)^2$ $D = 16(3)^2$

$k = 16$ $= 144$

The coin will fall 144 feet in 3 seconds.

39. $h = \frac{kA}{b}$ $h = \frac{2A}{b}$

$8 = \frac{k(24)}{6}$ $h = \frac{2(36)}{9}$

$k = 2$ $= 8$

The height of the triangle is 8 millimeters.

41. Prepare We will use the distance formula, $D = RT$. However, because we know that Fabian's trip upstream took the same amount of time as his trip downstream, we will use the formula in a different form.

Plan Solve the distance formula for T, that is, $T = \frac{D}{R}$, and fill in a chart with what we know. Let $T_U =$ the time to travel upstream, and $T_D =$ the time to travel downstream. That is, $T_U = T_D$. Let $s =$ the speed of the current.

	D	R	T
Upstream	14 miles	$12-s$ (mph)	$T_U = \dfrac{14}{12-s}$
Downstream	34 miles	$12+s$ (mph)	$T_D = \dfrac{34}{12+s}$

Process Write the equation.

$$T_U = T_D$$
$$\frac{14}{12-s} = \frac{34}{12+s}$$
$$14(12+s) = 34(12-s)$$
$$168+14s = 408-34s$$
$$48s = 240$$
$$s = 5$$

The speed of current is 5 miles per hour.

Ponder Does our answer seem reasonable? Yes. It seems reasonable that a river's current is 5 mph. We can us the speed of the current to check to see if it took the same amount of time to travel upstream as it took to travel downstream.

43. **Prepare** We will use the distance formula, $D = RT$. However, because we know that the total trip took 5 hours, we will use the formula in a different form.

Plan Solve the distance formula for T, that is, $T = \frac{D}{R}$, and fill in a chart with what we know. Let $T_t =$ the time traveled with a tailwind, and $T_h =$ the time to traveled with a head wind. That is, $T_t + T_h = 5$. Let $s =$ the speed of the wind.

	D	R	T
Tailwind	390 miles	$120+s$ (mph)	$T_t = \dfrac{390}{120+s}$
Headwind	220 miles	$120-s$ (mph)	$T_h = \dfrac{220}{120-s}$

Process Write the equation.

$$T_t + T_h = 5$$
$$\frac{390}{120+s} + \frac{220}{120-s} = 5$$
$$390(120-s) + 220(120+s) = 5(120-s)(120+s)$$
$$46,800 - 390s + 26,400 + 220s = 72,000 - 5s^2$$
$$5s^2 - 170s + 1,200 = 0$$
$$5(s-24)(s-10) = 0$$
$$s-24 = 0 \quad \text{or} \quad s-10 = 0$$
$$s = 24 \qquad\qquad s = 10$$

The speed of the wind is 24 miles per hour or 10 miles per hour.

Ponder Does our answer seem reasonable? Yes. It seems reasonable that the strength of the wind could be either 10 mph or 24 mph. We could check the answer by finding the rates of the plane and see if the total trip was made in 5 hours.

45. Prepare We will use the distance formula, $D = RT$. However, because we know that the round trip took 4 hours, we will use the formula in a different form.

Plan Solve the distance formula for T, that is, $T = \frac{D}{R}$, and fill in a chart with what we know. Let $T_U =$ the time to travel upstream, and $T_D =$ the time to travel downstream. That is, $T_U + T_D = 4$. Let $s =$ the speed if the river's current.

	D	R	T
Upstream	18 miles	$12 - s$ (mph)	$T_U = \dfrac{18}{12 - s}$
Downstream	18 miles	$12 + s$ (mph)	$T_D = \dfrac{18}{12 + s}$

Process Write the equation.

$$T_U + T_D = 4$$
$$\frac{18}{12 - s} + \frac{18}{12 + s} = 4$$
$$18(12 + s) + 18(12 - s) = 4(12 + s)(12 - s)$$
$$216 + 18s + 216 - 18s = 576 - 4s^2$$
$$4s^2 - 144 = 0$$
$$4(s + 6)(s - 6) = 0$$
$$s + 6 = 0 \quad \text{or} \quad s - 6 = 0$$
$$\cancel{s = -6} \qquad\qquad s = 6$$

The speed of the river's current is 6 miles per hour.

Ponder Does our answer seem reasonable? Yes. It seems reasonable that the speed of the river's current is 6 mph. We could check the answer by finding the rates up and downstream and seeing that the times are the same.

47. Prepare We will use the distance formula, $D = RT$. However, because we know that the time traveled each way was the same, we will use the formula in a different form.

Plan Solve the distance formula for T, that is, $T = \frac{D}{R}$, and fill in a chart with what we know. Let $T_t =$ the time to Johnson's girlfriend's house , and $T_f =$ the time from Johnson's girlfriend's house. That is, $T_t = T_f$. Let $x =$ the speed to his girlfriend's house.

	D	R	T
To	250 miles	x (mph)	$T_t = \dfrac{250}{x}$
From	225 miles	$x - 5$ (mph)	$T_f = \dfrac{225}{x - 5}$

Process Write the equation.

$$T_t = T_f$$

$$\frac{250}{x} = \frac{225}{x-5}$$

$$250(x-5) = 225x$$

$$25x = 1,250$$

$$x = 50$$

The speed of Johnson's car to his girlfriend's house was 50 mph. The speed of Johnson's car from his girlfriend's house was 45 mph.

Ponder Does our answer seem reasonable? Yes, it seems reasonable that he traveled at a rate of 50 mph on his first trip and 45 mph on his second trip. We can check our answers by seeing if these speeds produce trips of equal time lengths.

49. **Prepare** We will use the distance formula, $D = RT$. However, because we know that the truck left 6 hours earlier than the plane, we will use the formula in a different form.

Plan Solve the distance formula for T, that is, $T = \frac{D}{R}$, and fill in a chart with what we know. Let T_p = the time the plane traveled, and T_T = the time the truck traveled. That is, $T_T - T_P = 6$. Let x = the speed of the truck.

	D	R	T
Plane	450 miles	$3x$ (mph)	$T_P = \dfrac{450}{3x}$
Truck	450 miles	x (mph)	$T_T = \dfrac{450}{x}$

Process Write the equation.

$$T_T - T_P = 6$$

$$\frac{450}{x} - \frac{450}{3x} = 6$$

$$450 - 150 = 6x$$

$$300 = 6x$$

$$50 = x$$

The speed of the plane was 150 mph.

Ponder Does our answer seem reasonable? Yes. It seems reasonable that a plane could travel at a rate of 150 mph. We could also check our answer using the facts stated in the problem.

51. **Prepare** We will use the distance formula, $D = RT$. However, because we know that total time for the combined trips was 4 hours, we will use the formula in a different form.

Plan Solve the distance formula for T, that is, $T = \frac{D}{R}$, and fill in a chart with what we know. Let T_p = the time the plane traveled, and T_C = the time the car traveled. That is, $T_C + T_P = 4$. Let x = the speed of the car.

	D	R	T
Plane	240 miles	$3x$ (mph)	$T_P = \dfrac{240}{3x}$
Car	80 miles	x (mph)	$T_C = \dfrac{80}{x}$

Process Write the equation.

303

$$T_C + T_P = 4$$

$$\frac{80}{x} + \frac{240}{3x} = 4$$

$$80 + 80 = 4x$$

$$160 = 4x$$

$$40 = x$$

The speed of the car was 40 mph.

Ponder Does our answer seem reasonable? Yes. It seems reasonable that a car could travel at a rate of 40 mph. We could also check our answer using the facts stated in the problem.

53. **Prepare** We will use the work equation along with Gabby's and Jada's individual work rates to see how long it would take for them to complete the job together.

Plan It takes Gabby 4 hours to do the job alone, therefore, Gabby's rate is $\frac{1}{4}$ of the job per hour. It takes Jada 6 hours to do the job alone, therefore, Jada's rate is $\frac{1}{6}$ of the job per hour. Let $t =$ the time it takes for Gabby and Jada to do the job together.

Process Write the equation.

$$\left(\begin{array}{c} \text{Time} \\ \text{Worked} \end{array} \right)\left(\begin{array}{c} \text{Gabby's} \\ \text{Rate} \end{array} \right) + \left(\begin{array}{c} \text{Time} \\ \text{Worked} \end{array} \right)\left(\begin{array}{c} \text{Jada's} \\ \text{Rate} \end{array} \right) = 1$$

$$t\left(\frac{1}{4}\right) + t\left(\frac{1}{6}\right) = 1$$

$$\frac{t}{4} + \frac{t}{6} = 1$$

$$3t + 2t = 12$$

$$5t = 12$$

$$t = \frac{12}{5}$$

It takes Gabby and Jada $\frac{12}{5}$ hours or 2 hours and 24 minutes to do the job together.

Ponder Does our answer seem reasonable? Yes. If it takes Gabby 4 hours to do the job alone, it seems reasonable that it would take less time working along side Jada.

55. **Prepare** We will use the work equation along with Lyle's and Mark's individual work rates to see how long it would take for each of them to do the job alone.

Plan Let t represent the amount of time (in days) it takes Lyle to complete the job alone. Lyle's rate is $\frac{1}{t}$ of the job per day. It takes Mark $3t$ days to do the job alone, therefore, Mark's rate is $\frac{1}{3t}$ of the job per day. It takes 3 days for Lyle and Mark to do the job together.

Process Write the equation.

$$\left(\begin{array}{c}\text{Time} \\ \text{Worked}\end{array}\right)\left(\begin{array}{c}\text{Lyle's} \\ \text{Rate}\end{array}\right) + \left(\begin{array}{c}\text{Time} \\ \text{Worked}\end{array}\right)\left(\begin{array}{c}\text{Mark's} \\ \text{Rate}\end{array}\right) = 1$$

$$3\left(\frac{1}{t}\right) + 3\left(\frac{1}{3t}\right) = 1$$

$$\frac{3}{t} + \frac{1}{t} = 1$$

$$3 + 1 = t$$

$$4 = t$$

It takes Lyle 4 days to do the job alone, and it takes Mark 12 days to do the job alone.

Ponder Does our answer seem reasonable? Yes. If it takes Lyle and Mark 3 days to do the job together, it seems reasonable that it would take each of them longer alone.

57. **Prepare** We will use the work equation along with Remy's, Sissy's, and Jack's individual work rates to see how long it would take for them to complete the job together.

Plan It takes Remy 8 minutes to do the job alone, therefore, Remy's rate is $\frac{1}{8}$ of the job per minute. It takes Sissy 24 minutes to do the job alone, therefore, Sissy's rate is $\frac{1}{24}$ of the job per minute. It takes Jack 16 minutes to do the job alone, therefore, Jack's rate is $\frac{1}{16}$ of the job per minute. Let $t =$ the time it takes for Remy, Sissy, and Jack to do the job together.

Process Write the equation.

$$\left(\begin{array}{c}\text{Time} \\ \text{Worked}\end{array}\right)\left(\begin{array}{c}\text{Remy's} \\ \text{Rate}\end{array}\right) + \left(\begin{array}{c}\text{Time} \\ \text{Worked}\end{array}\right)\left(\begin{array}{c}\text{Sissy's} \\ \text{Rate}\end{array}\right) + \left(\begin{array}{c}\text{Time} \\ \text{Worked}\end{array}\right)\left(\begin{array}{c}\text{Jack's} \\ \text{Rate}\end{array}\right) = 1$$

$$t\left(\frac{1}{8}\right) + t\left(\frac{1}{24}\right) + t\left(\frac{1}{16}\right) = 1$$

$$6t + 2t + 3t = 48$$

$$11t = 48$$

$$t = \frac{48}{11}$$

It takes Remy, Sissy, and Jack $\frac{48}{11}$ minutes to do the job together.

Ponder Does our answer seem reasonable? Yes. If it takes Remy 8 minutes to do the job alone, it seems reasonable that it would take less time working with Sissy and Jack.

59. **Prepare** We will use the work equation along with Jimmy's, Wayne's, and Joseph's individual work rates to see how long it would take for them to complete the job alone.

Plan Let $t =$ the time it takes for Jimmy to do the job alone. Jimmy's rate is $\frac{1}{t}$ of the job per day. It takes Wayne $2t$ days to do the job alone, therefore, Wayne's rate is $\frac{1}{2t}$ of the job per day. It takes Joseph $t-1$ days to do the job alone, therefore, Joseph's rate is $\frac{1}{t-1}$ of the job per day. Jimmy works for a total of 3 days. Wayne and Joseph work for a total of 5 days.

Process Write the equation.

$$\left(\begin{array}{c}\text{Time}\\\text{Worked}\end{array}\right)\left(\begin{array}{c}\text{Jimmy's}\\\text{Rate}\end{array}\right)+\left(\begin{array}{c}\text{Time}\\\text{Worked}\end{array}\right)\left(\begin{array}{c}\text{Wayne's}\\\text{Rate}\end{array}\right)+\left(\begin{array}{c}\text{Time}\\\text{Worked}\end{array}\right)\left(\begin{array}{c}\text{Joseph's}\\\text{Rate}\end{array}\right)=1$$

$$3\left(\frac{1}{t}\right)+5\left(\frac{1}{2t}\right)+5\left(\frac{1}{t-1}\right)=1$$

$$6(t-1)+5(t-1)+5(2t)=2t(t-1)$$

$$6t-6+5t-5+10t=2t^2-2t$$

$$21t-11=2t^2-2t$$

$$2t^2-23t+11=0$$

$$(2t-1)(t-11)=0$$

$$2t-1=0 \quad \text{or} \quad t-11=0$$

$$t\neq\frac{1}{2} \qquad t=11$$

It takes Jimmy 11 days to do the job alone, Wayne 22 days to do the job alone, and Joseph 10 days to do the job alone.

Ponder Does our answer seem reasonable? Yes. The time it takes Jimmy, working alone, should be considerably longer than the time it would take if he was working with the other two men. Also, Joseph, the most experienced of the three, is the fastest at 10 days, so all three working together should be faster than Joseph working alone.

Chapter 7 Review Problem Set

1. $\dfrac{18x^7y^5}{32xy^5} = \dfrac{\overset{9}{\cancel{18}}\,\cancel{x}\,x^6\,\overset{1}{\cancel{y^5}}}{\underset{16}{\cancel{32}}\,\underset{1}{\cancel{x}}\,\underset{1}{\cancel{y^5}}}$

$= \dfrac{9x^6}{16}$

2. $\dfrac{-8a^{10}y^{16}}{20a^{18}y^{12}} = \dfrac{\overset{-2}{\cancel{-8}}\,\overset{1}{\cancel{a^{10}}}\,\overset{1}{\cancel{y^{12}}}\,y^4}{\underset{5}{\cancel{20}}\,\underset{1}{\cancel{a^{10}}}\,a^8\,\underset{1}{\cancel{y^{12}}}}$

$= -\dfrac{2y^4}{5a^8}$

3. $\dfrac{6(c-5)}{24(c-5)} = \dfrac{\overset{1}{\cancel{6}}\,\overset{1}{\cancel{(c-5)}}}{\underset{4}{\cancel{24}}\,\underset{1}{\cancel{(c-5)}}}$

$= \dfrac{1}{4}$

4. $\dfrac{(3s-t)(s+3)}{(3s-t)(s+6)} = \dfrac{\overset{1}{\cancel{(3s-t)}}(s+3)}{\underset{1}{\cancel{(3s-t)}}(s+6)}$

$= \dfrac{s+3}{s+6}$

5. $\dfrac{a}{a^2-6a} = \dfrac{\overset{1}{\cancel{a}}}{\underset{1}{\cancel{a}}(a-6)}$

$= \dfrac{1}{a-6}$

6. $\dfrac{4y^2-16y}{y^2-16} = \dfrac{4y\,\overset{1}{\cancel{(y-4)}}}{(y+4)\,\underset{1}{\cancel{(y-4)}}}$

$= \dfrac{4y}{y+4}$

7. $\dfrac{6x+18}{3x^2-27} = \dfrac{6(x+3)}{3(x^2-9)}$

$= \dfrac{\overset{2}{\cancel{6}}\,\overset{1}{\cancel{(x+3)}}}{\underset{1}{\cancel{3}}\,\underset{1}{\cancel{(x+3)}}(x-3)}$

$= \dfrac{2}{x-3}$

8. $\dfrac{b^2-21b+54}{b^2-17b-18} = \dfrac{\overset{1}{\cancel{(b-18)}}(b-3)}{\underset{1}{\cancel{(b-18)}}(b+1)}$

$= \dfrac{b-3}{b+1}$

9. $\dfrac{4y^2-25}{5-2y} = \dfrac{(2y+5)(2y-5)}{(5-2y)}$

$= \dfrac{(2y+5)(-1)\,\overset{1}{\cancel{(5-2y)}}}{\underset{1}{\cancel{(5-2y)}}}$

$= -2y-5$

10. $\dfrac{81-a^2}{a^2-18a+81} = \dfrac{(9+a)(9-a)}{(a-9)(a-9)}$

$= \dfrac{(9+a)(-1)\,\overset{1}{\cancel{(a-9)}}}{(a-9)\,\underset{1}{\cancel{(a-9)}}}$

$= \dfrac{-9-a}{a-9}$

11. $\dfrac{p^3-64}{4-p} = \dfrac{(p-4)(p^2+4p+16)}{(4-p)}$

$= \dfrac{(-1)\,\overset{1}{\cancel{(4-p)}}(p^2+4p+16)}{\underset{1}{\cancel{(4-p)}}}$

$= -p^2-4p-16$

307

12. $\dfrac{6xy+9y^2}{2x^2+xy-3y^2}=\dfrac{3y(2x+3y)}{(x-y)(2x+3y)}$

$=\dfrac{3y\,\cancel{(2x+3y)}^{1}}{(x-y)\,\cancel{(2x+3y)}}$

$=\dfrac{3y}{x-y}$

13. $\dfrac{8s^3-27t^3}{6t-4s}=\dfrac{(2s-3t)(4s^2+6st+9t^2)}{2(3t-2s)}$

$=\dfrac{(-1)\,\cancel{(3t-2s)}^{1}\,(4s^2+6st+9t^2)}{2\,\cancel{(3t-2s)}_{1}}$

$=\dfrac{-4s^2-6st-9t^2}{2}$

14. $\dfrac{x^2+5xy-xy-5y^2}{3x^2+3xy-60y^2}=\dfrac{(x+5y)(x-y)}{(x+5y)(3x-12y)}$

$=\dfrac{\cancel{(x+5y)}^{1}\,(x-y)}{\cancel{(x+5y)}_{1}\,(3x-12y)}$

$=\dfrac{x-y}{3x-12y}$

15. $\dfrac{6m^2n^3-6m^2n^2-12m^2n}{6n^2m-11mn-2m}=\dfrac{6m^2n(n^2-n-2)}{m(6n^2-11n-2)}$

$=\dfrac{6\,\cancel{m^2}^{m}\,n(n+1)\,\cancel{(n-2)}^{1}}{\cancel{m}_{1}\,(6n+1)\,\cancel{(n-2)}_{1}}$

$=\dfrac{6mn^2+6mn}{6n+1}$

16. $\dfrac{a^3+3a^2-9a-27}{2a^3-4a^2-18a+36}=\dfrac{(a+3)(a^2-9)}{2(a^3-2a^2-9a+18)}$

$=\dfrac{(a+3)(a+3)(a-3)}{2(a-2)(a^2-9)}$

$=\dfrac{(a+3)\,\cancel{(a+3)}^{1}\,\cancel{(a-3)}^{1}}{2(a-2)\,\cancel{(a+3)}_{1}\,\cancel{(a-3)}_{1}}$

$=\dfrac{a+3}{2a-4}$

17. $\dfrac{4x^3y^2}{5}\cdot\dfrac{30}{14xy^4}=\dfrac{\cancel{30}^{6}\cdot 4\,\cancel{x^3}^{x^2}\,\cancel{y^2}^{1}}{\cancel{5}_{1}\cdot\cancel{14}_{7}\,\cancel{x}_{1}\,\cancel{y^4}_{y^2}}$

$=\dfrac{12x^2}{7y^2}$

18. $\dfrac{16x^2-y^2}{8x^3y^2}\cdot\dfrac{36x^8y^5}{8x+2y}$

$=\dfrac{(4x+y)(4x-y)}{8x^3y^2}\cdot\dfrac{36x^8y^5}{2(4x+y)}$

$=\dfrac{\cancel{36}^{9}\,\cancel{x^8}^{x^5}\,\cancel{y^5}^{y^3}\,\cancel{(4x+y)}^{1}\,(4x-y)}{\cancel{16}_{4}\,\cancel{x^3}_{1}\,\cancel{y^2}_{1}\,\cancel{(4x+y)}_{1}}$

$=\dfrac{36x^6y^3-9x^5y^4}{4}$

19. $\dfrac{a^2-2a+4}{8a+a^2}\cdot\dfrac{a+8}{a^3+8}$

$=\dfrac{(a^2-2a+4)}{a(8+a)}\cdot\dfrac{(a+8)}{(a+2)(a^2-2a+4)}$

$=\dfrac{\cancel{(a^2-2a+4)}^{1}\,\cancel{(a+8)}^{1}}{a\,\cancel{(a+8)}_{1}\,(a+2)\,\cancel{(a^2-2a+4)}_{1}}$

$=\dfrac{1}{a^2+2a}$

20. $\dfrac{4x^2-25}{2x^2+15x+25} \cdot \dfrac{x^2+3x-10}{2x^2-7x+6}$

$= \dfrac{(2x+5)(2x-5)}{(2x+5)(x+5)} \cdot \dfrac{(x+5)(x-2)}{(2x-3)(x-2)}$

$= \dfrac{\cancel{(2x+5)}^{1}(2x-5)\cancel{(x+5)}^{1}\cancel{(x-2)}^{1}}{\cancel{(2x+5)}_{1}\cancel{(x+5)}_{1}(2x-3)\cancel{(x-2)}_{1}}$

$= \dfrac{2x-5}{2x-3}$

21. $\dfrac{14-2a}{2a^2b^3} \div \dfrac{a^2+7a}{7a^5b} = \dfrac{14-2a}{2a^2b^3} \cdot \dfrac{7a^5b}{a^2+7a}$

$= \dfrac{2(7-a)}{2a^2b^3} \cdot \dfrac{7a^5b}{a(a+7)}$

$= \dfrac{\cancel{14}^{7}\cancel{a^5}^{a^2}\cancel{b}^{1}(7-a)}{\cancel{2}_{1}\cancel{a^3}_{1}\cancel{b^3}_{b^2}(a+7)}$

$= \dfrac{49a^2-7a^3}{ab^2+7b^2}$

22. $\dfrac{y^2-16}{y^2-4} \div \dfrac{y^2+8y+16}{4y-8}$

$= \dfrac{y^2-16}{y^2-4} \cdot \dfrac{4y-8}{y^2+8y+16}$

$= \dfrac{(y+4)(y-4)}{(y+2)(y-2)} \cdot \dfrac{4(y-2)}{(y+4)(y+4)}$

$= \dfrac{4\cancel{(y+4)}^{1}(y-4)\cancel{(y-2)}^{1}}{(y+2)\cancel{(y-2)}_{1}\cancel{(y+4)}_{1}(y+4)}$

$= \dfrac{4y-16}{(y+2)(y+4)}$

23. $\dfrac{10x^2+13x-3}{20x^2+11x-3} \div \dfrac{4x^2-9}{8x^2-6x-9}$

$= \dfrac{10x^2+13x-3}{20x^2+11x-3} \cdot \dfrac{8x^2-6x-9}{4x^2-9}$

$= \dfrac{(2x+3)(5x-1)}{(4x+3)(5x-1)} \cdot \dfrac{(2x-3)(4x+3)}{(2x+3)(2x-3)}$

$= \dfrac{\cancel{(2x+3)}^{1}\cancel{(5x-1)}^{1}\cancel{(2x-3)}^{1}\cancel{(4x+3)}^{1}}{\cancel{(4x+3)}_{1}\cancel{(5x-1)}_{1}\cancel{(2x+3)}_{1}\cancel{(2x-3)}_{1}}$

$= 1$

24. $\dfrac{9-h^2}{12-23h-2h^2} \div \dfrac{h^3-3h^2}{2h^2+24h}$

$= \dfrac{9-h^2}{12-23h-2h^2} \cdot \dfrac{2h^2+24h}{h^3-3h^2}$

$= \dfrac{(-1)(3+h)(h-3)}{(-1)(h+12)(2h-1)} \cdot \dfrac{2h(h+12)}{h^2(h-3)}$

$= \dfrac{\cancel{(-1)}^{1}2\cancel{h}^{1}(3+h)\cancel{(h-3)}^{1}\cancel{(h+12)}^{1}}{\cancel{(-1)}_{1}\cancel{h^2}_{h}\cancel{(h+12)}_{1}(2h-1)\cancel{(h-3)}_{1}}$

$= \dfrac{6+2h}{2h^2-h}$

25. $\dfrac{24x^7}{7xy^5} \cdot \dfrac{18x^4}{14y^8} = \dfrac{\cancel{24}^{12}\cdot18\,\cancel{x^{11}}^{x^{10}}}{7\cdot\cancel{14}^{7}\,\cancel{x}^{1}y^{13}}$

$= \dfrac{216x^{10}}{49y^{13}}$

26. $\dfrac{x^2-8x+16}{x^2+4x+4} \div \dfrac{(x-4)^2(x+2)}{(x+2)^3(x+8)}$

$= \dfrac{(x-4)^2}{(x+2)^2} \cdot \dfrac{(x+2)^3(x+8)}{(x-4)^2(x+2)}$

$= \dfrac{\cancel{(x-4)^2}^{1}\cancel{(x+2)^3}^{1}(x+8)}{\cancel{(x+2)^3}_{1}\cancel{(x-4)^2}_{1}}$

$= x+8$

27. $\dfrac{9a^2-25}{9a^2+21a+10} \div \dfrac{15a^2+7a-2}{15a^2-28a+5}$

$= \dfrac{9a^2-25}{9a^2+21a+10} \cdot \dfrac{15a^2-28a+5}{15a^2+7a-2}$

$= \dfrac{(3a+5)(3a-5)}{(3a+5)(3a+2)} \cdot \dfrac{(3a-5)(5a-1)}{(3a+2)(5a-1)}$

$= \dfrac{\cancel{(3a+5)}^{1}(3a-5)^2\cancel{(5a-1)}^{1}}{\cancel{(3a+5)}_{1}(3a+2)^2\cancel{(5a-1)}_{1}}$

$= \dfrac{(3a-5)^2}{(3a+2)^2}$

28. $\dfrac{2y^2+11dy+5d^2}{20y^2-3y-2} \div \dfrac{cy-y+5cd-5d}{5cy-2c-5y+2}$

$= \dfrac{2y^2+11dy+5d^2}{20y^2-3y-2} \cdot \dfrac{5cy-2c-5y+2}{cy-y+5cd-5d}$

$= \dfrac{(2y+d)(y+5d)}{(4y+1)(5y-2)} \cdot \dfrac{(5y-2)(c-1)}{(c-1)(y+5d)}$

$= \dfrac{(2y+d)\,\overset{1}{\cancel{(y+5d)}}\,\overset{1}{\cancel{(5y-2)}}\,\overset{1}{\cancel{(c-1)}}}{(4y+1)\,\underset{1}{\cancel{(5y-2)}}\,\underset{1}{\cancel{(c-1)}}\,\underset{1}{\cancel{(y+5d)}}}$

$= \dfrac{2y+d}{4y+1}$

29. $\dfrac{15a^3b}{6b^6} \cdot \dfrac{14a^2b^3}{21a^5} \div \dfrac{10a}{9b^3} = \dfrac{15a^3b}{6b^6} \cdot \dfrac{14a^2b^3}{21a^5} \cdot \dfrac{9b^3}{10a}$

$= \dfrac{\overset{5}{\cancel{15}}\cdot\overset{2}{\cancel{14}}\cdot\overset{3}{\cancel{9}}\,\overset{1}{\cancel{a^5}}\,\overset{b}{\cancel{b^7}}}{\underset{2}{\cancel{6}}\cdot\underset{3}{\cancel{21}}\cdot\underset{2}{\cancel{10}}\,\underset{a}{\cancel{a^6}}\,\underset{1}{\cancel{b^6}}}$

$= \dfrac{3b}{2a}$

30. $\dfrac{4x^2+13x+3}{2x^2+7x-4} \cdot \dfrac{2x^2+5x-3}{4x^2-7x-2} \div (x^2+6x+9)$

$= \dfrac{4x^2+13x+3}{2x^2+7x-4} \cdot \dfrac{2x^2+5x-3}{4x^2-7x-2} \cdot \dfrac{1}{x^2+6x+9}$

$= \dfrac{(x+3)(4x+1)}{(x+4)(2x-1)} \cdot \dfrac{(x+3)(2x-1)}{(x-2)(4x+1)} \cdot \dfrac{1}{(x+3)^2}$

$= \dfrac{\overset{1}{\cancel{(x+3)^2}}\,\overset{1}{\cancel{(4x+1)}}\,\overset{1}{\cancel{(2x-1)}}}{(x+4)\,\underset{1}{\cancel{(2x-1)}}\,(x-2)\,\underset{1}{\cancel{(4x+1)}}\,\underset{1}{\cancel{(x+3)^2}}}$

$= \dfrac{1}{(x+4)(x-2)}$

31. $\dfrac{8x}{x^2y} = \dfrac{8x}{x^2y} \cdot \dfrac{8xy^2z^3}{8xy^2z^3}$

$= \dfrac{64x^2y^2z^3}{8x^3y^3z^3}$

32. $\dfrac{a+2}{a-6} = \dfrac{(a+2)}{(a-6)} \cdot \dfrac{(a+6)}{(a+6)}$

$= \dfrac{a^2+8a+12}{a^2-36}$

33. $\dfrac{3x}{x-5} = \dfrac{3x}{(x-5)} \cdot \dfrac{-2}{-2}$

$= \dfrac{-6x}{10-2x}$

34. $\dfrac{b-1}{b-3} = \dfrac{(b-1)}{(b-3)} \cdot \dfrac{(b-3)}{(b-3)}$

$= \dfrac{b^2-4b+3}{(b-3)^2}$

35. $\dfrac{15x+20}{4} - \dfrac{3x}{4} = \dfrac{15x+20-(3x)}{4}$

$= \dfrac{12x+20}{4}$

$= \dfrac{\overset{1}{\cancel{4}}(3x+5)}{\underset{1}{\cancel{4}}}$

$= 3x+5$

36. $\dfrac{x^2+12x}{x+8} + \dfrac{x^2+4x}{x+8} = \dfrac{x^2+12x+x^2+4x}{x+8}$

$= \dfrac{2x^2+16x}{x+8}$

$= \dfrac{2x\,\overset{1}{\cancel{(x+8)}}}{\underset{1}{\cancel{(x+8)}}}$

$= 2x$

37. $\dfrac{5c^2+12c-3}{c^2+7c+12} - \dfrac{2c^2-9c-39}{c^2+7c+12}$

$= \dfrac{5c^2+12c-3-(2c^2-9c-39)}{c^2+7c+12}$

$= \dfrac{5c^2+12c-3-2c^2+9c+39}{c^2+7c+12}$

$= \dfrac{3c^2+21c+36}{c^2+7c+12}$

$= \dfrac{3\,\overset{1}{\cancel{(c^2+7c+12)}}}{\underset{1}{\cancel{(c^2+7c+12)}}}$

$= 3$

38. $\dfrac{b^3}{b^2-2b+4}+\dfrac{8}{b^2-2b+4}$

$=\dfrac{b^3+8}{b^2-2b+4}$

$=\dfrac{(b+2)\overset{1}{\cancel{\left(b^2-2b+4\right)}}}{\underset{1}{\cancel{\left(b^2-2b+4\right)}}}$

$=b+2$

39. $3ab^4=3^1a^1b^4$

$\quad15a^3b^2c=3^1\cdot5^1a^3b^2c^1$

$\quad\quad\text{LCD}=3^1\cdot5^1a^3b^4c^1$

$\quad\quad\quad=15a^3b^4c$

40. $\text{LCD}=z(z-7)$

41. $x-3=(x-3)$

$\quad x^2-9=(x+3)(x-3)$

$\quad\quad\text{LCD}=(x+3)(x-3)$

42. $9y^2+12y+4=(3y+2)^2$

$\quad\quad2-3y=(2-3y)$

$\quad\quad\quad\text{LCD}=(3y+2)^2(2-3y)$

43. $\text{LCD}=6x^2y^5$

$\dfrac{4x^2}{xy^5}+\dfrac{6y}{6x^2y^3}=\dfrac{6x\left(4x^2\right)}{6x\left(xy^5\right)}+\dfrac{y^2\left(6y\right)}{y^2\left(6x^2y^3\right)}$

$=\dfrac{24x^3}{6x^2y^5}+\dfrac{6y^3}{6x^2y^5}$

$=\dfrac{24x^3+6y^3}{6x^2y^5}$

$=\dfrac{\overset{1}{\cancel{6}}\left(4x^3+y^3\right)}{\underset{1}{\cancel{6}}\,x^2y^5}$

$=\dfrac{4x^3+y^3}{x^2y^5}$

44. $\text{LCD}=10a^4b^3$

$\dfrac{2a^2b}{5ab^3}+\dfrac{3b}{10a^4b^2}=\dfrac{2a^3\left(2a^2b\right)}{2a^3\left(5ab^3\right)}+\dfrac{b\left(3b\right)}{b\left(10a^4b^2\right)}$

$=\dfrac{4a^5b}{10a^4b^3}+\dfrac{3b^2}{10a^4b^3}$

$=\dfrac{4a^5b+3b^2}{10a^4b^3}$

$=\dfrac{\overset{1}{\cancel{b}}\left(4a^5+3b\right)}{10a^4\,\underset{b^2}{\cancel{b^3}}}$

$=\dfrac{4a^5+3b}{10a^4b^2}$

45. $\text{LCD}=c-9$

$2-\dfrac{c+2}{c-9}=\dfrac{2(c-9)}{c-9}-\dfrac{c+2}{c-9}$

$=\dfrac{2c-18}{c-9}-\dfrac{c+2}{c-9}$

$=\dfrac{2c-18-(c+2)}{c-9}$

$=\dfrac{2c-18-c-2}{c-9}$

$=\dfrac{c-20}{c-9}$

46. $\text{LCD}=c(c+4)$

$\dfrac{4c}{c+4}-\dfrac{1}{c}=\dfrac{c(4c)}{c(c+4)}-\dfrac{1(c+4)}{c(c+4)}$

$=\dfrac{4c^2}{c(c+4)}-\dfrac{c+4}{c(c+4)}$

$=\dfrac{4c^2-(c+4)}{c(c+4)}$

$=\dfrac{4c^2-c-4}{c(c+4)}$

47. $\text{LCD} = (x-6)(x+1)(x-3)$

$$\frac{x}{x^2-5x-6}+\frac{2}{x-3}$$

$$=\frac{x}{(x-6)(x+1)}+\frac{2}{x-3}$$

$$=\frac{x(x-3)}{(x-6)(x+1)(x-3)}+\frac{2(x-6)(x+1)}{(x-6)(x+1)(x-3)}$$

$$=\frac{x^2-3x}{(x-6)(x+1)(x-3)}+\frac{2x^2-10x-12}{(x-6)(x+1)(x-3)}$$

$$=\frac{x^2-3x+2x^2-10x-12}{(x-6)(x+1)(x-3)}$$

$$=\frac{3x^2-13x-12}{(x-6)(x+1)(x-3)}$$

48. $\text{LCD} = (x-2)(x+3)$

$$\frac{3}{x-2}+\frac{5}{x+3}=\frac{3(x+3)}{(x-2)(x+3)}+\frac{5(x-2)}{(x+3)(x-2)}$$

$$=\frac{3x+9}{(x-2)(x+3)}+\frac{5x-10}{(x-2)(x+3)}$$

$$=\frac{3x+9+5x-10}{(x-2)(x+3)}$$

$$=\frac{8x-1}{(x-2)(x+3)}$$

49. $\text{LCD} = (x+4)(x-3)(x+2)$

$$\frac{4x+2}{x^2+x-12}-\frac{3x+8}{x^2+6x+8}$$

$$=\frac{4x+2}{(x+4)(x-3)}-\frac{3x+8}{(x+4)(x+2)}$$

$$=\frac{(4x+2)(x+2)}{(x+4)(x-3)(x+2)}-\frac{(3x+8)(x-3)}{(x+4)(x+2)(x-3)}$$

$$=\frac{4x^2+10x+4}{(x+4)(x-3)(x+2)}-\frac{3x^2-x-24}{(x+4)(x+2)(x-3)}$$

$$=\frac{4x^2+10x+4-\left(3x^2-x-24\right)}{(x+4)(x-3)(x+2)}$$

$$=\frac{4x^2+10x+4-3x^2+x+24}{(x+4)(x-3)(x+2)}$$

$$=\frac{x^2+11x+28}{(x+4)(x-3)(x+2)}$$

$$=\frac{\overset{1}{\cancel{(x+4)}}(x+7)}{\underset{1}{\cancel{(x+4)}}(x-3)(x+2)}$$

$$=\frac{x+7}{(x-3)(x+2)}$$

50. $\text{LCD} = (x-4)(x-5)$

$$\frac{x-8}{x^2-9x+20}+\frac{3}{x-5}=\frac{x-8}{(x-4)(x-5)}+\frac{3}{x-5}$$

$$=\frac{x-8}{(x-4)(x-5)}+\frac{3(x-4)}{(x-5)(x-4)}$$

$$=\frac{x-8}{(x-4)(x-5)}+\frac{3x-12}{(x-4)(x-5)}$$

$$=\frac{x-8+3x-12}{(x-4)(x-5)}$$

$$=\frac{4x-20}{(x-4)(x-5)}$$

$$=\frac{4\overset{1}{\cancel{(x-5)}}}{(x-4)\underset{1}{\cancel{(x-5)}}}$$

$$=\frac{4}{x-4}$$

51. LCD $= x(x-2)$

$$\frac{5}{x} + \frac{x-6}{x^2-2x} + \frac{2}{x-2}$$

$$= \frac{5}{x} + \frac{x-6}{x(x-2)} + \frac{2}{x-2}$$

$$= \frac{5(x-2)}{x(x-2)} + \frac{x-6}{x(x-2)} + \frac{2x}{x(x-2)}$$

$$= \frac{5x-10}{x(x-2)} + \frac{x-6}{x(x-2)} + \frac{2x}{x(x-2)}$$

$$= \frac{5x-10+x-6+2x}{x(x-2)}$$

$$= \frac{8x-16}{x(x-2)}$$

$$= \frac{8\,\cancel{(x-2)}^{1}}{x\,\cancel{(x-2)}_{1}}$$

$$= \frac{8}{x}$$

52. LCD $= (y+1)(y-1)$

$$\frac{2}{y-1} + \frac{12y}{y^2-1} - \frac{6}{y+1}$$

$$= \frac{2}{y-1} + \frac{12y}{(y+1)(y-1)} - \frac{6}{y+1}$$

$$= \frac{2(y+1)}{(y-1)(y+1)} + \frac{12y}{(y+1)(y-1)} - \frac{6(y-1)}{(y+1)(y-1)}$$

$$= \frac{2y+2}{(y-1)(y+1)} + \frac{12y}{(y+1)(y-1)} - \frac{6y-6}{(y+1)(y-1)}$$

$$= \frac{2y+2+12y-(6y-6)}{(y+1)(y-1)}$$

$$= \frac{2y+2+12y-6y+6}{(y+1)(y-1)}$$

$$= \frac{8y+8}{(y+1)(y-1)}$$

$$= \frac{8\,\cancel{(y+1)}^{1}}{\cancel{(y+1)}_{1}(y-1)}$$

$$= \frac{8}{y-1}$$

53. LCD $= (x+2)(2x+3)$

$$\frac{x}{x+2} - \frac{2x+6}{2x^2+7x+6} + \frac{2}{2x+3}$$

$$= \frac{x}{x+2} - \frac{2x+6}{(x+2)(2x+3)} + \frac{2}{2x+3}$$

$$= \frac{x(2x+3)}{(x+2)(2x+3)} - \frac{2x+6}{(x+2)(2x+3)} + \frac{2(x+2)}{(2x+3)(x+2)}$$

$$= \frac{2x^2+3x}{(x+2)(2x+3)} - \frac{2x+6}{(x+2)(2x+3)} + \frac{2x+4}{(2x+3)(x+2)}$$

$$= \frac{2x^2+3x-(2x+6)+2x+4}{(x+2)(2x+3)}$$

$$= \frac{2x^2+3x-2x-6+2x+4}{(x+2)(2x+3)}$$

$$= \frac{2x^2+3x-2}{(x+2)(2x+3)}$$

$$= \frac{(2x-1)(x+2)}{(x+2)(2x+3)}$$

$$= \frac{(2x-1)\,\cancel{(x+2)}^{1}}{\cancel{(x+2)}_{1}(2x+3)}$$

$$= \frac{2x-1}{2x+3}$$

54. $\left(\dfrac{2x}{x^2-16} + \dfrac{2}{x+4}\right) \div \dfrac{x-2}{x+4}$

$$= \left(\frac{2x}{(x+4)(x-4)} + \frac{2}{x+4}\right) \cdot \frac{x+4}{x-2}$$

$$= \left(\frac{2x}{(x+4)(x-4)} + \frac{2(x-4)}{(x+4)(x-4)}\right) \cdot \frac{x+4}{x-2}$$

$$= \left(\frac{2x}{(x+4)(x-4)} + \frac{2x-8}{(x+4)(x-4)}\right) \cdot \frac{x+4}{x-2}$$

$$= \left(\frac{2x+2x-8}{(x+4)(x-4)}\right) \cdot \frac{x+4}{x-2}$$

$$= \frac{4(x-2)}{(x+4)(x-4)} \cdot \frac{(x+4)}{(x-2)}$$

$$= \frac{4\,\cancel{(x-2)}^{1}\,\cancel{(x+4)}^{1}}{\cancel{(x+4)}_{1}(x-4)\,\cancel{(x-2)}_{1}}$$

$$= \frac{4}{x-4}$$

55. $\left(3x^2 - 2x - 8\right) \div (x-2) = 3x + 4$

$$2 \begin{array}{|rrr} 3 & -2 & -8 \\ & 6 & 8 \\ \hline 3 & 4 & \underline{|0} \end{array}$$

56. $\left(2x^3 + 11x^2 + 8x - 14\right) \div (x+3)$

$= 2x^2 + 5x - 7 + \dfrac{7}{x+3}$

$$-3 \begin{array}{|rrrr} 2 & 11 & 8 & -14 \\ & -6 & -15 & 21 \\ \hline 2 & 5 & -7 & \underline{|7} \end{array}$$

57. $\left(20c^3 + 160\right) \div (c+2) = 20c^2 - 40c + 80$

$$-2 \begin{array}{|rrrr} 20 & 0 & 0 & 160 \\ & -40 & 80 & -160 \\ \hline 20 & -40 & 80 & \underline{|0} \end{array}$$

58. $\left(y^6 + y^4 - y\right) \div (y-1)$

$= y^5 + y^4 + 2y^3 + 2y^2 + 2y + 1 + \dfrac{1}{y-1}$

$$1 \begin{array}{|rrrrrrr} 1 & 0 & 1 & 0 & 0 & -1 & 0 \\ & 1 & 1 & 2 & 2 & 2 & 1 \\ \hline 1 & 1 & 2 & 2 & 2 & 1 & \underline{|1} \end{array}$$

59. $\left(x^4 - 8x^3 + 12 + 16x^2 - 26x\right) \div (x-6)$

$= x^3 - 2x^2 + 4x - 2$

$$6 \begin{array}{|rrrrr} 1 & -8 & 16 & -26 & 12 \\ & 6 & -12 & 24 & -12 \\ \hline 1 & -2 & 4 & -2 & \underline{|0} \end{array}$$

60. $\left(2a^3 + 7a^2 - 5a - 4\right) \div \left(a + \dfrac{1}{2}\right)$

$= 2a^2 + 6a - 8$

$$-\dfrac{1}{2} \begin{array}{|rrrr} 2 & 7 & -5 & -4 \\ & -1 & -3 & 4 \\ \hline 2 & 6 & -8 & \underline{|0} \end{array}$$

61. $\dfrac{\dfrac{4ab^4}{a^2}}{\dfrac{6a^2b}{b^2}} = \left(\dfrac{4ab^4}{a^2}\right) \div \left(\dfrac{6a^2b}{b^2}\right)$

$= \left(\dfrac{4ab^4}{a^2}\right) \cdot \left(\dfrac{b^2}{6a^2b}\right)$

$= \dfrac{\overset{2}{\cancel{4}}\, \overset{1}{\cancel{a}}\, \overset{b^5}{\cancel{b^6}}}{\underset{3}{\cancel{6}}\, \underset{a^3}{\cancel{a^4}}\, \underset{1}{\cancel{b}}}$

$= \dfrac{2b^5}{3a^3}$

62. $\dfrac{\dfrac{x^2+4}{x}}{\dfrac{x+2}{x^2}} = \left(\dfrac{x^2+4}{x}\right) \div \left(\dfrac{x+2}{x^2}\right)$

$= \dfrac{x^2+4}{x} \cdot \dfrac{x^2}{x+2}$

$= \dfrac{\left(x^2+4\right)\overset{x}{\cancel{x^2}}}{\underset{1}{\cancel{x}}(x+2)}$

$= \dfrac{x^3+4x}{x+2}$

63. $\dfrac{\dfrac{12}{x+4}}{\dfrac{18}{x^2-16}} = \left(\dfrac{12}{x+4}\right) \div \left(\dfrac{18}{x^2-16}\right)$

$= \dfrac{12}{x+4} \cdot \dfrac{x^2-16}{18}$

$= \dfrac{12}{x+4} \cdot \dfrac{(x+4)(x-4)}{18}$

$= \dfrac{\overset{2}{\cancel{12}}\,(x+4)(x-4)}{\underset{3}{\cancel{18}}\,(x+4)}$

$= \dfrac{2x-8}{3}$

64.
$$\frac{\dfrac{x+2y}{x^2+4xy+4y^2}}{\dfrac{x+4y}{x^2+7xy+10y^2}}$$

$$=\left(\frac{x+2y}{x^2+4xy+4y^2}\right)\div\left(\frac{x+4y}{x^2+7xy+10y^2}\right)$$

$$=\frac{x+2y}{x^2+4xy+4y^2}\cdot\frac{x^2+7xy+10y^2}{x+4y}$$

$$=\frac{x+2y}{(x+2y)^2}\cdot\frac{(x+2y)(x+5y)}{x+4y}$$

$$=\frac{\overset{1}{\cancel{(x+2y)^2}}(x+5y)}{\underset{1}{\cancel{(x+2y)^2}}(x+4y)}$$

$$=\frac{x+5y}{x+4y}$$

65.
$$\frac{\dfrac{1}{xy}}{\dfrac{1}{x}+\dfrac{1}{y}}=\frac{\left(\dfrac{1}{xy}\right)}{\left(\dfrac{1}{x}+\dfrac{1}{y}\right)}\cdot\frac{\dfrac{xy}{1}}{\dfrac{xy}{1}}$$

$$=\frac{\dfrac{1}{\cancel{xy}}\cdot\dfrac{\cancel{xy}}{1}}{\left(\dfrac{1}{\cancel{x}}\cdot\dfrac{\cancel{x}\,y}{1}\right)+\left(\dfrac{1}{\cancel{y}}\cdot\dfrac{x\,\cancel{y}}{1}\right)}$$

$$=\frac{1}{y+x}$$

66.
$$\frac{\dfrac{4a^2-9b^2}{ab}}{\dfrac{3}{a}+\dfrac{2}{b}}=\frac{\left(\dfrac{4a^2-9b^2}{ab}\right)}{\left(\dfrac{3}{a}+\dfrac{2}{b}\right)}\cdot\frac{\dfrac{ab}{1}}{\dfrac{ab}{1}}$$

$$=\frac{\dfrac{4a^2-9b^2}{\cancel{ab}}\cdot\dfrac{\cancel{ab}}{1}}{\left(\dfrac{3}{\cancel{a}}\cdot\dfrac{\cancel{a}\,b}{1}\right)+\left(\dfrac{2}{\cancel{b}}\cdot\dfrac{a\,\cancel{b}}{1}\right)}$$

$$=\frac{(2a+3b)(2a-3b)}{(3b+2a)}$$

$$=2a-3b$$

67.
$$\frac{\dfrac{4x^2}{3y}+\dfrac{y}{x^2}}{\dfrac{3}{4x}-\dfrac{2x}{y}}=\frac{\left(\dfrac{4x^2}{3y}+\dfrac{y}{x^2}\right)}{\left(\dfrac{3}{4x}-\dfrac{2x}{y}\right)}\cdot\frac{\dfrac{12x^2y}{1}}{\dfrac{12x^2y}{1}}$$

$$=\frac{\left(\dfrac{4x^2}{\cancel{3y}}\cdot\dfrac{\overset{4}{\cancel{12}}\,x^2\,\cancel{y}}{1}\right)+\left(\dfrac{y}{\cancel{x^2}}\cdot\dfrac{12\,\cancel{x^2}\,y}{1}\right)}{\left(\dfrac{3}{\cancel{4x}}\cdot\dfrac{\overset{3}{\cancel{12}}\,\overset{x}{\cancel{x^2}}\,y}{1}\right)-\left(\dfrac{2x}{\cancel{y}}\cdot\dfrac{12x^2\,\cancel{y}}{1}\right)}$$

$$=\frac{16x^4+12y^2}{9xy-24x^3}$$

68.
$$\frac{\dfrac{4x}{y}-\dfrac{2y}{x}-7}{3+\dfrac{4x}{y}+\dfrac{13y}{x}}=\frac{\left(\dfrac{4x}{y}-\dfrac{2y}{x}-7\right)}{\left(3+\dfrac{4x}{y}+\dfrac{13y}{x}\right)}\cdot\frac{\dfrac{xy}{1}}{\dfrac{xy}{1}}$$

$$=\frac{\dfrac{4x}{\cancel{y}}\cdot\dfrac{x\,\cancel{y}}{1}-\dfrac{2y}{\cancel{x}}\cdot\dfrac{\cancel{x}\,y}{1}-7(xy)}{3(xy)+\dfrac{4x}{\cancel{y}}\cdot\dfrac{x\,\cancel{y}}{1}+\dfrac{13y}{\cancel{x}}\cdot\dfrac{\cancel{x}\,y}{1}}$$

$$=\frac{4x^2-7xy-2y^2}{4x^2+3xy+13y^2}$$

69.
$$\frac{x+x^{-1}}{x^{-1}+3x^{-2}}=\frac{x+\dfrac{1}{x}}{\dfrac{1}{x}+\dfrac{3}{x^2}}$$

$$=\frac{\left(x+\dfrac{1}{x}\right)}{\left(\dfrac{1}{x}+\dfrac{3}{x^2}\right)}\cdot\frac{\dfrac{x^2}{1}}{\dfrac{x^2}{1}}$$

$$=\frac{x(x^2)+\dfrac{1}{\cancel{x}}\cdot\dfrac{\overset{x}{\cancel{x^2}}}{1}}{\dfrac{1}{\cancel{x}}\cdot\dfrac{\overset{x}{\cancel{x^2}}}{1}+\dfrac{3}{\cancel{x^2}}\cdot\dfrac{\cancel{x^2}}{1}}$$

$$=\frac{x^3+x}{x+3}$$

315

70. $\dfrac{x+2}{\dfrac{4}{x}-x} = \dfrac{(x+2)\dfrac{x}{1}}{\left(\dfrac{4}{x}-x\right)\dfrac{x}{1}}$

$= \dfrac{\dfrac{(x+2)x}{1}}{\dfrac{4}{\cancel{x}}\cdot\dfrac{\cancel{x}}{1}-x(x)}$

$= \dfrac{x(x+2)}{4-x^2}$

$= \dfrac{x\,\cancel{(x+2)}}{\cancel{(2+x)}\,(2-x)}$

$= \dfrac{x}{2-x}$

71. $\dfrac{\dfrac{1}{x}+\dfrac{1}{y}}{\dfrac{1}{x}\cdot\dfrac{1}{y}} = \dfrac{\left(\dfrac{1}{x}+\dfrac{1}{y}\right)\dfrac{xy}{1}}{\left(\dfrac{1}{xy}\right)\dfrac{xy}{1}}$

$= \dfrac{\dfrac{1}{\cancel{x}}\cdot\dfrac{\cancel{x}\,y}{1}+\dfrac{1}{\cancel{y}}\cdot\dfrac{x\,\cancel{y}}{1}}{\dfrac{1}{\cancel{xy}}\cdot\dfrac{\cancel{xy}}{1}}$

$= y+x$

72. $\dfrac{\dfrac{1}{x}+\dfrac{1}{y}}{\dfrac{1}{x}} = \dfrac{\left(\dfrac{1}{x}+\dfrac{1}{y}\right)\dfrac{xy}{1}}{\left(\dfrac{1}{x}\right)\dfrac{xy}{1}}$

$= \dfrac{\dfrac{1}{\cancel{x}}\cdot\dfrac{\cancel{x}\,y}{1}+\dfrac{1}{\cancel{y}}\cdot\dfrac{x\,\cancel{y}}{1}}{\dfrac{1}{\cancel{x}}\cdot\dfrac{\cancel{x}\,y}{1}}$

$= \dfrac{y+x}{y}$

73. $D=(-\infty,\infty)$

74. $x+4=0$

$x=-4$

$D=\{x\,|\,x\neq -4\}$

75. $5t=0$

$t=0$

$D=\{t\,|\,t\neq 0\}$

76. $t^2+5t-6=0$

$(t+6)(t-1)=0$

$t+6=0 \quad\text{or}\quad t-1=0$

$t=-6 \qquad\qquad t=1$

$D=\{t\,|\,t\neq -6 \text{ and } t\neq 1\}$

77. $\dfrac{2}{x}+\dfrac{3}{4}=\dfrac{5}{x}$

$\dfrac{4x}{1}\left(\dfrac{2}{x}+\dfrac{3}{4}\right)=\dfrac{4x}{1}\left(\dfrac{5}{x}\right)$

$\dfrac{4\cancel{x}}{1}\cdot\dfrac{2}{\cancel{x}}+\dfrac{\cancel{4}\,x}{1}\cdot\dfrac{3}{\cancel{4}}=\dfrac{4\cancel{x}}{1}\cdot\dfrac{5}{\cancel{x}}$

$8+3x=20$

$3x=12$

$x=4$

Solution Set: $\{4\}$

78. $\dfrac{7}{x}+\dfrac{2}{x+3}=\dfrac{6}{x}$

$\dfrac{x(x+3)}{1}\left(\dfrac{7}{x}+\dfrac{2}{x+3}\right)=\dfrac{x(x+3)}{1}\left(\dfrac{6}{x}\right)$

$\dfrac{\cancel{x}\,(x+3)}{1}\cdot\dfrac{7}{\cancel{x}}+\dfrac{x\,\cancel{(x+3)}}{1}\cdot\dfrac{2}{\cancel{(x+3)}}=\dfrac{\cancel{x}\,(x+3)}{1}\cdot\dfrac{6}{\cancel{x}}$

$7x+21+2x=6x+18$

$9x+21=6x+18$

$3x=-3$

$x=-1$

Solution Set: $\{-1\}$

79.

$$\frac{x}{x-2}+\frac{1}{2}=\frac{2}{x-2}$$

$$\frac{2(x-2)}{1}\left(\frac{x}{x-2}+\frac{1}{2}\right)=\frac{2(x-2)}{1}\left(\frac{2}{x-2}\right)$$

$$\frac{2\,\overset{1}{\cancel{(x-2)}}}{1}\cdot\frac{x}{\cancel{(x-2)}_{1}}+\frac{\overset{1}{\cancel{2}}(x-2)}{1}\cdot\frac{1}{\cancel{2}_{1}}=\frac{2\,\overset{1}{\cancel{(x-2)}}}{1}\cdot\frac{2}{\cancel{(x-2)}_{1}}$$

$$2x+x-2=4$$

$$3x=6$$

$$\cancel{x=2}$$

Solution Set: $\{\ \}$

80.

$$\frac{5y}{y+5}=\frac{3y+10}{2y}$$

$$\frac{2y(y+5)}{1}\cdot\frac{5y}{(y+5)}=\frac{2y(y+5)}{1}\cdot\frac{3y+10}{2y}$$

$$\frac{2y\,\overset{1}{\cancel{(y+5)}}}{1}\cdot\frac{5y}{\cancel{(y+5)}_{1}}=\frac{\overset{1}{\cancel{2y}}(y+5)}{1}\cdot\frac{3y+10}{\cancel{2y}_{1}}$$

$$10y^2=3y^2+25y+50$$

$$7y^2-25y-50=0$$

$$(y-5)(7y+10)=0$$

$$y-5=0\quad\text{or}\quad 7y+10=0$$

$$y=5\qquad\qquad y=-\frac{10}{7}$$

Solution Set: $\left\{-\dfrac{10}{7},5\right\}$

81.

$$\frac{2}{x^2}+\frac{5}{3x}=\frac{25}{3}$$

$$\frac{3x^2}{1}\left(\frac{2}{x^2}+\frac{5}{3x}\right)=\frac{3x^2}{1}\left(\frac{25}{3}\right)$$

$$\frac{3\,\overset{1}{\cancel{x^2}}}{1}\cdot\frac{2}{\cancel{x^2}_{1}}+\frac{\overset{1}{\cancel{3}}\,\overset{x}{\cancel{x^2}}}{1}\cdot\frac{5}{\cancel{3}_{1}\,\cancel{x}_{1}}=\frac{\overset{1}{\cancel{3}}\,x^2}{1}\cdot\frac{25}{\cancel{3}_{1}}$$

$$6+5x=25x^2$$

$$25x^2-5x-6=0$$

$$(5x-3)(5x+2)=0$$

$$5x-3=0\quad\text{or}\quad 5x+2=0$$

$$x=\frac{3}{5}\qquad\qquad x=-\frac{2}{5}$$

Solution Set: $\left\{-\dfrac{2}{5},\dfrac{3}{5}\right\}$

82.

$$\frac{5}{b+4}+\frac{2b+1}{b}=\frac{b+11}{b^2+4b}$$

$$\frac{5}{b+4}+\frac{2b+1}{b}=\frac{b+11}{b(b+4)}$$

$$\frac{\cancel{b}\,\cancel{(b+4)}}{1}\cdot\frac{5}{\cancel{(b+4)}}+\frac{\cancel{b}\,(b+4)}{1}\cdot\frac{2b+1}{\cancel{b}}=\frac{\cancel{b}\,\cancel{(b+4)}}{1}\cdot\frac{b+11}{\cancel{b}\,\cancel{(b+4)}}$$

$$5b+2b^2+9b+4=b+11$$

$$2b^2+13b-7=0$$

$$(2b-1)(b+7)=0$$

$$2b-1=0 \quad\text{or}\quad b+7=0$$

$$x=\frac{1}{2} \qquad\qquad x=-7$$

Solution Set: $\left\{-7,\dfrac{1}{2}\right\}$

83.

$$\frac{3x}{x+2}+\frac{6}{x-6}=4$$

$$\frac{(x+2)(x-6)}{1}\left(\frac{3x}{x+2}+\frac{6}{x-6}\right)=4(x+2)(x-6)$$

$$\frac{\cancel{(x+2)}\,(x-6)}{1}\cdot\frac{3x}{\cancel{(x+2)}}+\frac{(x+2)\,\cancel{(x-6)}}{1}\cdot\frac{6}{\cancel{(x-6)}}=4(x+2)(x-6)$$

$$3x^2-18x+6x+12=4x^2-16x-48$$

$$x^2-4x-60=0$$

$$(x-10)(x+6)=0$$

$$x-10=0 \quad\text{or}\quad x+6=0$$

$$x=10 \qquad\qquad x=-6$$

Solution Set: $\{-6,10\}$

84.

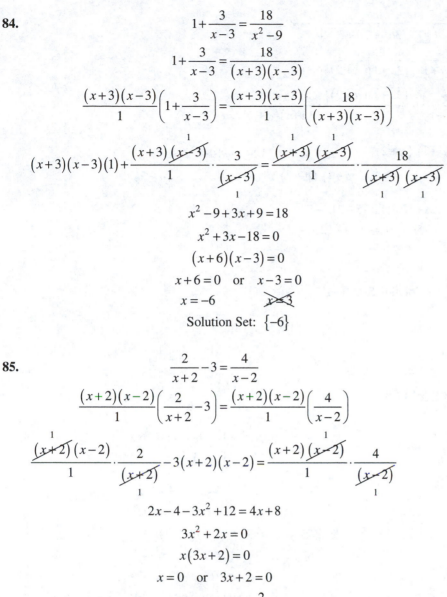

$$1 + \frac{3}{x-3} = \frac{18}{x^2 - 9}$$

$$1 + \frac{3}{x-3} = \frac{18}{(x+3)(x-3)}$$

$$\frac{(x+3)(x-3)}{1}\left(1 + \frac{3}{x-3}\right) = \frac{(x+3)(x-3)}{1}\left(\frac{18}{(x+3)(x-3)}\right)$$

$$(x+3)(x-3)(1) + \frac{(x+3)\,\cancel{(x-3)}^{\,1}}{1} \cdot \frac{3}{\cancel{(x-3)}_{\,1}} = \frac{\cancel{(x+3)}^{\,1}\,\cancel{(x-3)}^{\,1}}{1} \cdot \frac{18}{\cancel{(x+3)}_{\,1}\,\cancel{(x-3)}_{\,1}}$$

$$x^2 - 9 + 3x + 9 = 18$$

$$x^2 + 3x - 18 = 0$$

$$(x+6)(x-3) = 0$$

$$x + 6 = 0 \quad \text{or} \quad x - 3 = 0$$

$$x = -6 \qquad \qquad \cancel{x = 3}$$

Solution Set: $\{-6\}$

85.

$$\frac{2}{x+2} - 3 = \frac{4}{x-2}$$

$$\frac{(x+2)(x-2)}{1}\left(\frac{2}{x+2} - 3\right) = \frac{(x+2)(x-2)}{1}\left(\frac{4}{x-2}\right)$$

$$\frac{\cancel{(x+2)}^{\,1}(x-2)}{1} \cdot \frac{2}{\cancel{(x+2)}_{\,1}} - 3(x+2)(x-2) = \frac{(x+2)\,\cancel{(x-2)}^{\,1}}{1} \cdot \frac{4}{\cancel{(x-2)}_{\,1}}$$

$$2x - 4 - 3x^2 + 12 = 4x + 8$$

$$3x^2 + 2x = 0$$

$$x(3x+2) = 0$$

$$x = 0 \quad \text{or} \quad 3x + 2 = 0$$

$$x = -\frac{2}{3}$$

Solution Set: $\left\{-\frac{2}{3}, 0\right\}$

86.

$$\frac{5}{3a+1} = \frac{4a-5}{3a^2+7a+2} - \frac{7}{a+2}$$

$$\frac{5}{3a+1} = \frac{4a-5}{(3a+1)(a+2)} - \frac{7}{a+2}$$

$$\frac{(3a+1)(a+2)}{1}\left(\frac{5}{3a+1}\right) = \frac{(3a+1)(a+2)}{1}\left(\frac{4a-5}{(3a+1)(a+2)} - \frac{7}{a+2}\right)$$

$$\frac{\overset{1}{\cancel{(3a+1)}}(a+2)}{1}\cdot\frac{5}{\cancel{(3a+1)}} = \frac{\overset{1}{\cancel{(3a+1)}}\overset{1}{\cancel{(a+2)}}}{1}\cdot\frac{4a-5}{\cancel{(3a+1)}\cancel{(a+2)}} - \frac{(3a+1)\overset{1}{\cancel{(a+2)}}}{1}\cdot\frac{7}{\cancel{(a+2)}}$$

$$5a+10 = 4a-5-21a-7$$

$$5a+10 = -17a-12$$

$$22a = -22$$

$$a = -1$$

Solution Set: $\{-1\}$

87. Expression

$$\left(\frac{a}{b}+2\right) \div \left(\frac{a}{b}+1\right) = \left(\frac{a}{b}+\frac{2b}{b}\right) \div \left(\frac{a}{b}+\frac{b}{b}\right)$$

$$= \left(\frac{a+2b}{b}\right) \div \left(\frac{a+b}{b}\right)$$

$$= \frac{a+2b}{\cancel{b}} \cdot \frac{\overset{1}{\cancel{b}}}{a+b}$$

$$= \frac{a+2b}{a+b}$$

88. Expression

$$\frac{14-x}{3x} + \frac{x}{2x^2} = \frac{28x-2x^2}{6x^2} + \frac{3x}{6x^2}$$

$$= \frac{31x-2x^2}{6x^2}$$

$$= \frac{\overset{1}{\cancel{x}}(31-2x)}{6\cancel{x^2}}$$

$$= \frac{31-2x}{6x}$$

89. Equation

$$\frac{14}{3x} - \frac{x}{6} = \frac{1}{2}$$

$$\frac{6x}{1}\left(\frac{14}{3x} - \frac{x}{6}\right) = \frac{6x}{1}\left(\frac{1}{2}\right)$$

$$\frac{\overset{2}{\cancel{6x}}}{1}\cdot\frac{14}{\cancel{3x}} - \frac{\overset{1}{\cancel{6}}x}{1}\cdot\frac{x}{\cancel{6}} = \frac{\overset{3}{\cancel{6}}x}{1}\cdot\frac{1}{\cancel{2}}$$

$$28-x^2 = 3x$$

$$x^2+3x-28 = 0$$

$$(x+7)(x-4) = 0$$

$$x+7 = 0 \quad \text{or} \quad x-4 = 0$$

$$x = -7 \qquad\qquad x = 4$$

Solution Set: $\{-7, 4\}$

320

90. Equation

$$\frac{2x+1}{x} + \frac{5}{x+4} = \frac{x+11}{x^2+4x}$$

$$\frac{2x+1}{x} + \frac{5}{x+4} = \frac{x+11}{x(x+4)}$$

$$\frac{x(x+4)}{1}\left(\frac{2x+1}{x} + \frac{5}{x+4}\right) = \frac{x(x+4)}{1}\left(\frac{x+11}{x(x+4)}\right)$$

$$\frac{\overset{1}{\cancel{x}}(x+4)}{1} \cdot \frac{2x+1}{\underset{1}{\cancel{x}}} + \frac{x\overset{1}{\cancel{(x+4)}}}{1} \cdot \frac{5}{\underset{1}{\cancel{(x+4)}}} = \frac{\overset{1}{\cancel{x}}\,\overset{1}{\cancel{(x+4)}}}{1} \cdot \frac{x+11}{\underset{1}{\cancel{x}}\,\underset{1}{\cancel{(x+4)}}}$$

$$2x^2 + 9x + 4 + 5x = x + 11$$

$$2x^2 + 13x - 7 = 0$$

$$(2x-1)(x+7) = 0$$

$$2x - 1 = 0 \quad \text{or} \quad x + 7 = 0$$

$$x = \frac{1}{2} \qquad x = -7$$

Solution Set: $\left\{-7, \dfrac{1}{2}\right\}$

91.
$$y = \frac{kx}{z}$$

$$z(y) = \frac{\overset{1}{\cancel{z}}}{1} \cdot \frac{kx}{\underset{1}{\cancel{z}}}$$

$$yz = kx$$

$$x = \frac{yz}{k}$$

92.
$$p = \frac{s}{1+rt}$$

$$p(1+rt) = \frac{s}{\underset{1}{\cancel{(1+rt)}}} \cdot \frac{\overset{1}{\cancel{(1+rt)}}}{1}$$

$$p + prt = s$$

$$prt = s - p$$

$$r = \frac{s-p}{pt}$$

93.
$$s = \frac{a}{1-r}$$

$$s(1-r) = \frac{a}{\underset{1}{\cancel{(1-r)}}} \cdot \frac{\overset{1}{\cancel{(1-r)}}}{1}$$

$$s - rs = a$$

$$rs = s - a$$

$$r = \frac{s-a}{s}$$

94. Let x represent the first number, then $4x$ is the second number. The equation is $\dfrac{1}{x} + \dfrac{1}{4x} = \dfrac{5}{16}$.

$$\frac{1}{x} + \frac{1}{4x} = \frac{5}{16}$$

$$\frac{16x}{1}\left(\frac{1}{x} + \frac{1}{4x}\right) = \frac{16x}{1}\left(\frac{5}{16}\right)$$

$$\frac{16\overset{1}{\cancel{x}}}{1} \cdot \frac{1}{\underset{1}{\cancel{x}}} + \frac{\overset{4}{\cancel{16}}\,\overset{1}{\cancel{x}}}{1} \cdot \frac{1}{\underset{1}{\cancel{4}}\,\underset{1}{\cancel{x}}} = \frac{\overset{1}{\cancel{16}}\,x}{1} \cdot \frac{5}{\underset{1}{\cancel{16}}}$$

$$16 + 4 = 5x$$

$$5x = 20$$

$$x = 4$$

If $x = 4$, then $4x = 16$. The two numbers are 4 and 16.

95. Let x represent the first number, then $x+2$ is the second number. The equation is $\dfrac{1}{x}+\dfrac{1}{x+2}=\dfrac{7}{24}$.

$$\frac{1}{x}+\frac{1}{x+2}=\frac{7}{24}$$

$$\frac{24x(x+2)}{1}\left(\frac{1}{x}+\frac{1}{x+2}\right)=\frac{24x(x+2)}{1}\left(\frac{7}{24}\right)$$

$$\frac{24x(x+2)}{1}\cdot\frac{1}{x}+\frac{24x(x+2)}{1}\cdot\frac{1}{(x+2)}=\frac{24x(x+2)}{1}\cdot\frac{7}{24}$$

$$24x+48+24x=7x^2+14x$$

$$7x^2-34x-48=0$$

$$(x-6)(7x+8)=0$$

$$x-6=0 \quad\text{or}\quad 7x+8=0$$

$$x=6 \qquad \cancel{x=-\frac{8}{7}}$$

If $x=6$, then $x+2=8$. The two numbers are 6 and 8.

96. Prepare   We need to use the function $C(a)=\frac{a}{a+12}\cdot A$ to convert an adult's daily dosage of doxycycline to a child's dosage.

Plan We first replace the A in the formula with the adult daily dosage of 200 mg. Therefore, the rational function becomes $C(a)=\frac{200a}{a+12}$, and the independent variable is the child's age. In this case, the child's age is $a=13$, and we will evaluate the function at $C(13)$.

Process Evaluate $C(13)$.

$$C(13)=\frac{200(13)}{(13)+12}$$

$$=\frac{2{,}600}{25}$$

$$=104$$

Therefore, the child's daily dosage is 104 mg.

Ponder Does are answer seem reasonable? Based on our formula, yes. Also, we would certainly expect a child's dosage to be considerably smaller than an adult's for the same medicine.

97. $U=kr^3$

98. $T=\dfrac{ksp}{\sqrt{n}}$

99. $a=\dfrac{k}{b}$

$6=\dfrac{k}{9}$

$k=54$

100. $Y=kxw^2$

$352=k(2)(4)^2$

$k=11$

101. $q=kt \qquad q=11t$

$132=k(12) \qquad q=11(40)$

$\quad k=11 \qquad\qquad =440$

102. $x=\dfrac{kR^2}{y} \qquad x=\dfrac{6R^2}{y}$

$30=\dfrac{k(10)^2}{20} \qquad x=\dfrac{6(4)^2}{24}$

$\quad k=6 \qquad\qquad\quad =4$

103. $W=kg^2l \qquad W=\dfrac{1}{800}g^2l$

$784=k(70^2)(128) \qquad W=\dfrac{1}{800}(44)^2(60)$

$\quad k=\dfrac{1}{800} \qquad\qquad\quad =145.2$

The shark weighs 145.2 pounds.

104. $F=kIA \qquad F=\dfrac{1}{41{,}000}IA$

$2=k(10)(8{,}200) \qquad F=\dfrac{1}{41{,}000}(40)(4{,}100)$

$k=\dfrac{1}{41{,}000} \qquad\qquad =4$

Shaker Heights Little League need 4 floodlights.

105. $B=\dfrac{kw}{h^2} \qquad B=\dfrac{726w}{h}$

$22=\dfrac{k(132)}{(66)^2} \qquad B=\dfrac{726(325)}{(85)^2}$

$k=726 \qquad\qquad \approx 32.7$

Shaquille O'Neal's BMI is approximately 32.7.

106. $s=\dfrac{k}{t} \qquad s=\dfrac{100}{t}$

$30=\dfrac{k}{3\frac{1}{3}} \qquad s=\dfrac{100}{2\frac{1}{2}}$

$k=100 \qquad\qquad =40$

Carol is riding at a speed of 40 miles per hour.

107. **Prepare** We will use the distance formula, $D = RT$. However, because we know that Violet's trip upstream took the same amount of time as her trip downstream, we will use the formula in a different form.

Plan Solve the distance formula for T, that is, $T = \frac{D}{R}$, and fill in a chart with what we know. Let T_U = the time to travel upstream, and T_D = the time to travel downstream. That is, $T_U = T_D$. Let s = the speed of Violet's new fishing boat.

	D	R	T
Upstream	8 miles	$s - 4$ (mph)	$T_U = \dfrac{8}{s-4}$
Downstream	24 miles	$s + 4$ (mph)	$T_D = \dfrac{24}{s+4}$

Process Write the equation.

$$T_U = T_D$$
$$\frac{8}{s-4} = \frac{24}{s+4}$$
$$8(s+4) = 24(s-4)$$
$$8s + 32 = 24s - 96$$
$$128 = 16s$$
$$8 = s$$

The speed of Violet's new fishing boat in still water is 8 miles per hour.

Ponder Does our answer seem reasonable? Yes. It is very reasonable for a fishing boat to be able to travel 8 mph in still water.

108. **Prepare** We will use the distance formula, $D = RT$. However, because we know that the total trip took 5 hours, we will use the formula in a different form.

Plan Solve the distance formula for T, that is, $T = \frac{D}{R}$, and fill in a chart with what we know. Let T_t = the time the plane spent flying with a tailwind and T_h = the time the plane spent flying with a headwind. That is, $T_t + T_h = 5$. Let s = the speed of the wind.

	D	R	T
Tailwind	470 miles	$200 + s$ (mph)	$T_t = \dfrac{470}{200+s}$
Headwind	495 miles	$200 - s$ (mph)	$T_h = \dfrac{495}{200-s}$

Process Write the equation.

$$T_t + T_h = 5$$
$$\frac{470}{200+s} + \frac{495}{200-s} = 5$$
$$470(200-s) + 495(200+s) = 5(200+s)(200-s)$$
$$94{,}000 - 470s + 99{,}000 + 495s = 200{,}000 - 5s^2$$
$$5s^2 + 25s - 7{,}000 = 0$$
$$5(s-35)(s+40) = 0$$
$$s - 35 = 0 \quad \text{or} \quad s + 40 = 0$$
$$s = 35 \qquad \cancel{s = -40}$$

The average speed of the wind was 35 miles per hour.

Ponder Does our answer seem reasonable? It seems reasonable that a plane would experience winds of 35 mph at altitude.

109. **Prepare** We will use the work equation along with Salvatore's and Salvatore's assistant's individual work rates to see how long it would take for Salvatore to complete the job alone.

Plan Let t = Salvatore's time to finish the job alone. Then $6t$ = the assistant's time to finish the job alone. Therefore, Salvatore's rate is $\frac{1}{t}$ of the job per minute and the assistant's rate is $\frac{1}{6t}$ of the job per minute. Salvatore and his assistant both worked for 12 minutes.

Process Write the equation.

$$\left(\begin{matrix} \text{Time} \\ \text{Worked} \end{matrix}\right)\left(\begin{matrix} \text{Salvatore's} \\ \text{Rate} \end{matrix}\right) + \left(\begin{matrix} \text{Time} \\ \text{Worked} \end{matrix}\right)\left(\begin{matrix} \text{Assistant's} \\ \text{Rate} \end{matrix}\right) = 1$$

$$12\left(\frac{1}{t}\right) + 12\left(\frac{1}{6t}\right) = 1$$

$$12 + 2 = t$$

$$14 = t$$

It will take Salvatore 14 minutes to complete the job alone.

Ponder Does our answer seem reasonable? Yes, it seems reasonable that it would only take Salvatore slightly longer to do the job himself as compare to doing the job with his assistant.

110. **Prepare** We will use the work equation along with Federico's, Raquel's, and Timothy's individual work rates to determine how long it will take them stack and carry luggage the required distance.

Plan Federico's time alone is 2 minutes, therefore his rate is $\frac{1}{2}$ of the job per minute. Raquel's time alone is 4 minutes, therefore her rate is $\frac{1}{4}$ of the job per minute. Timothy's time alone is 9 minutes, therefore his rate is $\frac{1}{9}$ of the job per minute. Let t = the time it takes Federico, Raquel, and Timothy to stack and carry the luggage together.

Process Write the equation.

$$\left(\begin{matrix} \text{Time} \\ \text{Worked} \end{matrix}\right)\left(\begin{matrix} \text{Federico's} \\ \text{Rate} \end{matrix}\right) + \left(\begin{matrix} \text{Time} \\ \text{Worked} \end{matrix}\right)\left(\begin{matrix} \text{Raquel's} \\ \text{Rate} \end{matrix}\right) + \left(\begin{matrix} \text{Time} \\ \text{Worked} \end{matrix}\right)\left(\begin{matrix} \text{Timothy's} \\ \text{Rate} \end{matrix}\right) = 1$$

$$t\left(\frac{1}{2}\right) + t\left(\frac{1}{4}\right) + t\left(\frac{1}{9}\right) = 1$$

$$18t + 9t + 4t = 36$$

$$31t = 36$$

$$t = \frac{36}{31}$$

It will take them $\frac{36}{31}$ minutes to stack and carry the luggage together.

Ponder Does the answer seem reasonable? Yes, it seems reasonable that it would take less time for them to stack and carry luggage together than it would for each of them to do it alone.

CHAPTER 7 TEST

1. $\dfrac{x^2-16}{x+4}$ is an algebraic expression.

$$\frac{x^2-16}{x+4}=\frac{\overset{1}{\cancel{(x+4)}}(x-4)}{\underset{1}{\cancel{x+4}}}$$
$$=x-4$$

d

2. $\dfrac{x^2-16}{x+4}=x$ is an equation.

Excluded Value: -4

LCD: $x+4$

$$\frac{x^2-16}{x+4}=x$$
$$\frac{\overset{1}{\cancel{x+4}}}{1}\left(\frac{x^2-16}{\underset{1}{\cancel{x+4}}}\right)=(x+4)(x)$$
$$x^2-16=x^2+4x$$
$$-16=4x$$
$$\cancel{-4=x}$$

Solution set: $\{\ \}$

j

3. $\dfrac{x+1}{3x+2}+\dfrac{4}{x}$ is an algebraic expression.

LCD: $x(3x+2)$

$$\frac{x+1}{3x+2}+\frac{4}{x}=\frac{x(x+1)}{x(3x+2)}+\frac{(3x+2)(4)}{(3x+2)(x)}$$
$$=\frac{x^2+x}{x(3x+2)}+\frac{12x+8}{x(3x+2)}$$
$$=\frac{x^2+x+12x+8}{x(3x+2)}$$
$$=\frac{x^2+13x+8}{x(3x+2)}$$

c

4. $\dfrac{3x^3+9x^2}{x}\div\dfrac{x+3}{x^2-16}$ is an algebraic expression.

$$\frac{3x^3+9x^2}{x}\div\frac{x+3}{x^2-16}=\frac{3x^3+9x^2}{x}\cdot\frac{x^2-16}{x+3}$$
$$=\frac{3\overset{1}{\cancel{x}}\cdot x\overset{1}{\cancel{(x+3)}}}{\underset{1}{\cancel{x}}}\cdot\frac{(x+4)(x-4)}{\underset{1}{\cancel{x+3}}}$$
$$=3x(x+4)(x-4)$$
$$=3x^3-48x$$

i

5. $\dfrac{2ax+3bx-2ay-3by}{2a^2-7ab-15b^2}=\dfrac{x(2a+3b)-y(2a+3b)}{(2a+3b)(a-5b)}$
$$=\frac{\overset{1}{\cancel{(2a+3b)}}(x-y)}{\underset{1}{\cancel{(2a+3b)}}(a-5b)}$$
$$=\frac{x-y}{a-5b}$$

6. $\dfrac{x+6}{40x^2y^8}\cdot\dfrac{-10x^5y^3}{x-6}$
$$=\frac{x+6}{\underset{4}{\cancel{40}}\underset{1}{\cancel{x^2}}\underset{1}{\cancel{y^3}}y^5}\cdot\frac{\overset{-1}{\cancel{-10}}\,\overset{1}{\cancel{x^2}}x^3\,\overset{1}{\cancel{y^3}}}{x-6}$$
$$=\frac{-x^3(x+6)}{4y^5(x-6)}$$

7. $\dfrac{6}{x+3}+\dfrac{2x^2}{x+3}-\dfrac{21-x}{x+3}=\dfrac{6+2x^2-21+x}{x+3}$
$$=\frac{2x^2+x-15}{x+3}$$
$$=\frac{(2x-5)\overset{1}{\cancel{(x+3)}}}{\underset{1}{\cancel{x+3}}}$$
$$=2x-5$$

8. $\dfrac{64-y^2}{y^2-7y-8}\div\dfrac{5y^2-2y^3}{5y^2-2y}$
$$=\frac{64-y^2}{y^2-7y-8}\cdot\frac{5y^2-2y}{5y^2-2y^3}$$
$$=\frac{(8+y)\overset{-1}{\cancel{(8-y)}}}{\underset{1}{\cancel{(y-8)}}(y+1)}\cdot\frac{\overset{1}{\cancel{y}}(5y-2)}{\underset{1}{\cancel{y}}\,y(5-2y)}$$
$$=-\frac{(8+y)(5y-2)}{y(y+1)(5-2y)}$$

325

9. LCD: $(t+2)(t+4)$

$$\frac{t-1}{t+2}+\frac{t}{t+4}+\frac{2t}{t^2+6t+8}=\frac{(t-1)(t+4)}{(t+2)(t+4)}+\frac{t(t+2)}{(t+2)(t+4)}+\frac{2t}{(t+2)(t+4)}$$

$$=\frac{t^2+3t-4}{(t+2)(t+4)}+\frac{t^2+2t}{(t+2)(t+4)}+\frac{2t}{(t+2)(t+4)}$$

$$=\frac{t^2+3t-4+t^2+2t+2t}{(t+2)(t+4)}$$

$$=\frac{2t^2+7t-4}{(t+2)(t+4)}$$

$$=\frac{(2t-1)\overset{1}{(t+4)}}{(t+2)\underset{1}{(t+4)}}$$

$$=\frac{2t-1}{t+2}$$

10. $\dfrac{7a+2}{7-a}+\dfrac{a^2+5a}{a-7}-\dfrac{3a+12}{a-7}=\dfrac{(-1)(7a+2)}{a-7}+\dfrac{a^2+5a}{a-7}-\dfrac{3a+12}{a-7}$

$$=\frac{-7a-2+a^2+5a-3a-12}{a-7}$$

$$=\frac{a^2-5a-14}{a-7}$$

$$=\frac{\overset{1}{(a-7)}(a+2)}{\underset{1}{a-7}}$$

$$=a+2$$

11. $\dfrac{\dfrac{x^2-25}{6}}{\dfrac{x-5}{36}}=\dfrac{x^2-25}{6}\div\dfrac{x-5}{36}$

$$=\frac{x^2-25}{6}\cdot\frac{36}{x-5}$$

$$=\frac{(x+5)\overset{1}{(x-5)}}{\underset{1}{6}}\cdot\frac{\overset{6}{36}}{\underset{1}{x-5}}$$

$$=6(x+5)$$

$$=6x+30$$

12. $\dfrac{\dfrac{5}{y^2} - \dfrac{14}{xy} - \dfrac{3}{x^2}}{\dfrac{5}{y^2} - \dfrac{4}{xy} - \dfrac{1}{x^2}} = \dfrac{\dfrac{x^2 y^2}{1}\left(\dfrac{5}{y^2} - \dfrac{14}{xy} - \dfrac{3}{x^2}\right)}{\dfrac{x^2 y^2}{1}\left(\dfrac{5}{y^2} - \dfrac{4}{xy} - \dfrac{1}{x^2}\right)}$

$$= \dfrac{\dfrac{x^2 \,\cancel{y^2}^{\,1}}{1}\cdot\dfrac{5}{\cancel{y^2}_{\,1}} - \dfrac{\cancel{x}^1 x \,\cancel{y}^1 y}{1}\cdot\dfrac{14}{\cancel{x}_1\,\cancel{y}_1} - \dfrac{\cancel{x^2}^{\,1} y^2}{1}\cdot\dfrac{3}{\cancel{x^2}_{\,1}}}{\dfrac{x^2 \,\cancel{y^2}^{\,1}}{1}\cdot\dfrac{5}{\cancel{y^2}_{\,1}} - \dfrac{\cancel{x}^1 x \,\cancel{y}^1 y}{1}\cdot\dfrac{4}{\cancel{x}_1\,\cancel{y}_1} - \dfrac{\cancel{x^2}^{\,1} y^2}{1}\cdot\dfrac{1}{\cancel{x^2}_{\,1}}}$$

$$= \dfrac{5x^2 - 14xy - 3y^2}{5x^2 - 4xy - y^2}$$

$$= \dfrac{\cancel{(5x+y)}^{\,1}(x-3y)}{\cancel{(5x+y)}_{\,1}(x-y)}$$

$$= \dfrac{x-3y}{x-y}$$

13. $\dfrac{-4a^3 b + 36ab^2 - 6ab}{-6ab}$

$$= \dfrac{-4a^3 b}{-6ab} + \dfrac{36ab^2}{-6ab} - \dfrac{6ab}{-6ab}$$

$$= \dfrac{\cancel{-4}^{\,2}\,\cancel{a}^1 a a^2\,\cancel{b}}{\cancel{-6}_{\,3}\,\cancel{a}_1\,\cancel{b}} + \dfrac{\cancel{36}^{\,6}\,\cancel{a}b b}{-1\,\cancel{6}\,\cancel{a}b} - \dfrac{\cancel{6ab}^{\,1}}{-1\,\cancel{6ab}}$$

$$= \dfrac{2}{3}a^2 - 6b + 1$$

14.

$$\begin{array}{r|rrrr} 4 & 2 & -5 & 0 & -25 \\ & & 8 & 12 & 48 \\ \hline & 2 & 3 & 12 & \underline{|23} \end{array}$$

$$\dfrac{2x^3 - 5x^2 - 25}{x-4} = 2x^2 + 3x + 12 + \dfrac{23}{x-4}$$

15.

$$\begin{array}{r|rrrr} -\dfrac{1}{2} & 6 & -13 & 12 & 2 \\ & & -3 & 8 & -10 \\ \hline & 6 & -16 & 20 & \underline{|-8} \end{array}$$

$$\dfrac{6x^3 - 13x^2 + 12x + 2}{x + \dfrac{1}{2}} = 6x^2 - 16x + 20 + \dfrac{-8}{x + \dfrac{1}{2}}$$

16.
a) To find the excluded values, set the denominator equal to zero and solve for x.
$$3x - 5 = 0$$
$$3x - 5 + 5 = 0 + 5$$
$$3x = 5$$
$$\dfrac{3x}{3} = \dfrac{5}{3}$$
$$x = \dfrac{5}{3}$$

The domain for f is $D = \left\{ x \mid x \neq \dfrac{5}{3} \right\}$.

b) To find the excluded values, set the denominator equal to zero and solve for x.
$$2x^2 - 5x - 3 = 0$$
$$(2x + 1)(x - 3) = 0$$

$\begin{aligned} 2x + 1 &= 0 \qquad & or \qquad x - 3 &= 0 \\ 2x + 1 - 1 &= 0 - 1 & x - 3 + 3 &= 0 + 3 \\ 2x &= -1 & x &= 3 \\ \dfrac{2x}{2} &= \dfrac{-1}{2} & & \\ x &= -\dfrac{1}{2} & & \end{aligned}$

The domain for f is $\left\{ x \mid x \neq -\dfrac{1}{2} \text{ and } x \neq 3 \right\}$

17. Excluded Values: $x = -5$ and $x = 1$

LCD: $(x+5)(x-1)$

$$\frac{x+3}{x+5} = \frac{x}{x-1}$$

$$\frac{\overset{1}{\cancel{(x+5)}}(x-1)}{1}\left(\frac{x+3}{\underset{1}{\cancel{x+5}}}\right) = \frac{(x+5)\overset{1}{\cancel{(x-1)}}}{1}\left(\frac{x}{\underset{1}{\cancel{x-1}}}\right)$$

$$(x-1)(x-3) = (x+5)x$$
$$x^2 + 2x - 3 = x^2 + 5x$$
$$-3x = 3$$
$$x = -1$$

The solution set is $\{-1\}$.

18. Excluded Value: $x = 6$

LCD: $x-6$

$$\frac{x}{x-6} + 3 = \frac{6}{x-6}$$

$$\frac{x-6}{1}\left(\frac{x}{x-6} + 3\right) = \frac{\overset{1}{\cancel{x-6}}}{1}\left(\frac{6}{\underset{1}{\cancel{x-6}}}\right)$$

$$\frac{\overset{1}{\cancel{x-6}}}{1}\left(\frac{x}{\underset{1}{\cancel{x-6}}}\right) + \frac{x-6}{1}\left(\frac{3}{1}\right) = 6$$

$$x + (x-6)3 = 6$$
$$x + 3x - 18 = 6$$
$$4x = 24$$
$$\cancel{x = 6}$$

The solution set is $\{\ \}$.

19. Excluded Values: $n = \frac{1}{3}$ and $n = 0$.

LCD: $n(3n-1)$

$$\frac{3n}{3n-1} = \frac{1}{3n-1} - \frac{1}{n}$$

$$\frac{n\overset{1}{\cancel{(3n-1)}}}{1}\left(\frac{3n}{\underset{1}{\cancel{3n-1}}}\right) = \frac{n(3n-1)}{1}\left(\frac{1}{3n-1} - \frac{1}{n}\right)$$

$$3n^2 = \frac{n\overset{1}{\cancel{(3n-1)}}}{1}\left(\frac{1}{\underset{1}{\cancel{3n-1}}}\right) - \frac{\overset{1}{\cancel{n}}(3n-1)}{1}\left(\frac{1}{\underset{1}{\cancel{n}}}\right)$$

$$3n^2 = n - (3n-1)$$
$$3n^2 + 2n - 1 = 0$$
$$(3n-1)(n+1) = 0$$
$$3n-1 = 0 \quad or \quad n+1 = 0$$
$$3n = 1 \qquad\qquad n = -1$$
$$\cancel{n = \frac{1}{3}}$$

The solution set is $\{-1\}$.

20. Excluded Values: $t = 1$ and $t = -2$

LCD: $(t-1)(t+2)$

$$\frac{5}{t-1} - \frac{8}{t+2} = \frac{t+2}{t^2+t-2}$$

$$\frac{(t-1)(t+2)}{1}\left(\frac{5}{t-1} - \frac{8}{t+2}\right) = \frac{\overset{1}{\cancel{(t-1)(t+2)}}}{1}\left(\frac{t+2}{\underset{1}{\cancel{(t-1)(t+2)}}}\right)$$

$$\frac{\overset{1}{\cancel{(t-1)}}(t+2)}{1}\left(\frac{5}{\underset{1}{\cancel{t-1}}}\right) - \frac{(t-1)\overset{1}{\cancel{(t+2)}}}{1}\left(\frac{8}{\underset{1}{\cancel{t+2}}}\right) = t+2$$

$$5(t+2) - 8(t-1) = t+2$$
$$-3t + 18 = t+2$$
$$-4t = -16$$
$$t = 4$$

The solution set is $\{4\}$.

21.
$$y = kx$$
$$1200 = k(50)$$
$$\frac{1200}{50} = k$$
$$k = 24$$

$$y = 24x$$
$$y = 24\left(\frac{1}{2}\right)$$
$$y = 12$$

22. Let t be the time to complete the task and n be the number of workers assigned to the task.
$$t = \frac{k}{n}$$
$$6 = \frac{k}{8}$$
$$(6)(8) = k$$
$$k = 48$$

$$t = \frac{48}{n}$$
$$t = \frac{48}{10}$$
$$t = 4.8$$

It takes 4.8 hours or 4 hours and 48 minutes for 10 workers to complete the task.

23.
$$S = \frac{kpg}{t^2}$$
$$200 = \frac{k(10)(2)}{(16)^2}$$
$$200 = \frac{20k}{256}$$
$$(200)(256) = 20k$$
$$51200 = 20k$$
$$\frac{51200}{20} = k$$
$$k = 2560$$

$$S = \frac{2560pg}{t^2}$$
$$S = \frac{2560(6)(3)}{(10)^2}$$
$$S = 460.8$$

24. Prepare We are to determine how fast Major Dahlgren jogs.

Plan Let T_w = Major Dahlgren's time walking and T_j = Major Dahlgren's time jogging. The total morning exercise routine took 1 hour.
$$T_w + T_j = 1$$
Let r = the rate at which Major Dahlgren walks.

	Distance	Rate	Time
Walking	1 mile	r	$\dfrac{1}{r}$
Jogging	4 miles	$r+3$	$\dfrac{4}{r+3}$

Process Write and solve the equation.
$$T_w + T_j = 1$$
$$\frac{1}{r} + \frac{4}{r+3} = 1$$
$$\frac{r(r+3)}{1}\left(\frac{1}{r} + \frac{4}{r+3}\right) = \frac{r(r+3)}{1}(1)$$
$$\frac{\cancel{r}(r+3)}{1}\left(\frac{1}{\cancel{r}}\right) + \frac{r\,\cancel{(r+3)}}{1}\left(\frac{4}{\cancel{r+3}}\right) = r(r+3)$$
$$r + 3 + 4r = r^2 + 3r$$
$$r^2 - 2r - 3 = 0$$
$$(r-3)(r+1) = 0$$
$$r - 3 = 0 \quad or \quad r + 1 = 0$$
$$r = 3 \qquad\qquad r = -1$$

The Major walks at a rate of 3 miles per hour, so he jogs at a rate of 6 miles per hour.

Ponder Is the result reasonable? It seems reasonable that the major could jog at a rate of 6 miles per hour.

25. Prepare We are to determine how long it would take each person to assemble an iPod alone.

Plan Let t = the time it takes Wendy to assemble an iPod, then $2t$ = the time it takes Prudence to assemble an iPod. The rate at which Wendy can assemble an iPod is $\dfrac{1}{t}$ of the job per minute. The rate at which Prudence can assemble an iPod is $\dfrac{1}{2t}$ of the job per minute.

Process Write and solve the equation.

$$\left(\begin{array}{c}\text{Time}\\\text{Worked}\end{array}\right)\left(\begin{array}{c}\text{Prudence's}\\\text{Rate}\end{array}\right)+\left(\begin{array}{c}\text{Time}\\\text{Worked}\end{array}\right)\left(\begin{array}{c}\text{Wendy's}\\\text{Rate}\end{array}\right)=1$$

$$3\left(\frac{1}{2t}\right)+3\left(\frac{1}{t}\right)=1$$

$$\frac{3}{2t}+\frac{3}{t}=1$$

$$\frac{2t}{1}\left(\frac{3}{2t}+\frac{3}{t}\right)=2t\,(1)$$

$$\frac{{}^1\cancel{2t}}{1}\left(\frac{3}{{}_1\cancel{2t}}\right)+\frac{2^1\cancel{t}}{1}\left(\frac{3}{{}_1\cancel{t}}\right)=2t$$

$$3+6=2t$$

$$9=2t$$

$$4.5=t$$

It takes Wendy 4.5 minutes to assemble an iPod and it takes Prudence 9 minutes to assemble an iPod.

Ponder Does this answer seem reasonable? It seems reasonable that an experienced person can assemble an iPod in 4.5 minutes and a beginner can assemble an iPod in 9 minutes.

Chapter 8

8.1 Exercises

1. Finding the square root of a number is the reverse process of <u>squaring</u> a number.

3. If x is any real number, then $\sqrt{x^2}$ equals $\underline{|x|}$.

5. The principal square root of a is denoted by $\underline{\sqrt{a}}$.

7. Simplified radical form means there are no <u>perfect squares</u> as factors of the radicand.

9. The square root of a product is equal to the <u>product</u> of the square roots.

11. $\sqrt{81} = 9$

13. $\sqrt{144} = 12$

15. $-\sqrt{64} = (-1)\sqrt{64}$
$= (-1)8$
$= -8$

17. $-\sqrt{0} = (-1)\sqrt{0}$
$= (-1)0$
$= 0$

19. $-\sqrt{\dfrac{1}{9}} = (-1)\sqrt{\dfrac{1}{9}}$
$= (-1)\dfrac{1}{3}$
$= -\dfrac{1}{3}$

21. $-\sqrt{\dfrac{144}{49}} = (-1)\sqrt{\dfrac{144}{49}}$
$= (-1)\dfrac{12}{7}$
$= -\dfrac{12}{7}$

23. $\sqrt{0.16} = 0.4$

25. $-\sqrt{0.09} = (-1)\sqrt{0.09}$
$= (-1)0.3$
$= -0.3$

27. $\sqrt{12} = \sqrt{4 \cdot 3}$
$= \sqrt{4} \cdot \sqrt{3}$
$= 2\sqrt{3}$

29. $\sqrt{24} = \sqrt{4 \cdot 6}$
$= \sqrt{4} \cdot \sqrt{6}$
$= 2\sqrt{6}$

31. $\sqrt{40} = \sqrt{4 \cdot 10}$
$= \sqrt{4} \cdot \sqrt{10}$
$= 2\sqrt{10}$

33. $\sqrt{200} = \sqrt{100 \cdot 2}$
$= \sqrt{100} \cdot \sqrt{2}$
$= 10\sqrt{2}$

35. $\sqrt{98} = \sqrt{49 \cdot 2}$
$= \sqrt{49} \cdot \sqrt{2}$
$= 7\sqrt{2}$

37. $\sqrt{150} = \sqrt{25 \cdot 6}$
$= \sqrt{25} \cdot \sqrt{6}$
$= 5\sqrt{6}$

39. $\sqrt{90} = \sqrt{9 \cdot 10}$
$= \sqrt{9} \cdot \sqrt{10}$
$= 3\sqrt{10}$

41. $\sqrt{315} = \sqrt{9 \cdot 35}$
$= \sqrt{9} \cdot \sqrt{35}$
$= 3\sqrt{35}$

43. $\sqrt{720} = \sqrt{144 \cdot 5}$
$= \sqrt{144} \cdot \sqrt{5}$
$= 12\sqrt{5}$

45. $\sqrt{1,200} = \sqrt{400 \cdot 3}$
$= \sqrt{400} \cdot \sqrt{3}$
$= 20\sqrt{3}$

331

47. $\sqrt{(5x)^2} = |5x|$
$$= |5||x|$$
$$= 5|x|$$

49. $\sqrt{(100a)^2} = |100a|$
$$= |100||a|$$
$$= 100|a|$$

51. $-\sqrt{100a^2} = (-1)\sqrt{100} \cdot \sqrt{a^2}$
$$= -10|a|$$

53. $\sqrt{\dfrac{a^2}{b^2}} = \left|\dfrac{a}{b}\right|$

55. $-\sqrt{\dfrac{16}{25m^2}} = (-1)\sqrt{\dfrac{16}{25}} \cdot \sqrt{\dfrac{1}{m^2}}$
$$= -\dfrac{4}{5} \cdot \left|\dfrac{1}{m}\right|$$
$$= -\dfrac{4}{5|m|}$$

57. $\sqrt{(x+5)^2} = |x+5|$

59. $\sqrt{(3g+2h)^2} = |3g+2h|$

61. $\sqrt{a^2 - 10a + 25} = \sqrt{(a-5)^2}$
$$= |a-5|$$

63. $\sqrt{9a^2 + 12ab + 4b^2} = \sqrt{(3a+2b)^2}$
$$= |3a+2b|$$

65. $\sqrt{x^{12}} = x^6$

67. $\sqrt{h^{64}} = h^{32}$

69. $\sqrt{x^{13}} = \sqrt{x^{12} \cdot x}$
$$= \sqrt{x^{12}} \cdot \sqrt{x}$$
$$= x^6 \sqrt{x}$$

71. $\sqrt{a^{25}} = \sqrt{a^{24} \cdot a}$
$$= \sqrt{a^{24}} \cdot \sqrt{a}$$
$$= a^{12} \sqrt{a}$$

73. $\sqrt{c^{81}} = \sqrt{c^{80} \cdot c}$
$$= \sqrt{c^{80}} \cdot \sqrt{c}$$
$$= c^{40} \sqrt{c}$$

75. $\sqrt{12x^6} = \sqrt{4x^6 \cdot 3}$
$$= \sqrt{4x^6} \cdot \sqrt{3}$$
$$= 2x^3 \sqrt{3}$$

77. $\sqrt{36s^7} = \sqrt{36s^6 \cdot s}$
$$= \sqrt{36s^6} \cdot \sqrt{s}$$
$$= 6s^3 \sqrt{s}$$

79. $\sqrt{24b^9} = \sqrt{4b^8 \cdot 6b}$
$$= \sqrt{4b^8} \cdot \sqrt{6b}$$
$$= 2b^4 \sqrt{6b}$$

81. $\sqrt{20a^8 b^{15}} = \sqrt{4a^8 b^{14} \cdot 5b}$
$$= \sqrt{4a^8 b^{14}} \cdot \sqrt{5b}$$
$$= 2a^4 b^7 \sqrt{5b}$$

83. $\sqrt{80c^7 d^{17}} = \sqrt{16c^6 d^{16} \cdot 5cd}$
$$= \sqrt{16c^6 d^{16}} \cdot \sqrt{5cd}$$
$$= 4c^3 d^8 \sqrt{5cd}$$

85. $\sqrt{180x^{18} y^{19}} = \sqrt{36x^{18} y^{18} \cdot 5y}$
$$= \sqrt{36x^{18} y^{18}} \cdot \sqrt{5y}$$
$$= 6x^9 y^9 \sqrt{5y}$$

87. $\sqrt{210a^6 b^{15} c} = \sqrt{a^6 b^{14} \cdot 210bc}$
$$= \sqrt{a^6 b^{14}} \cdot \sqrt{210bc}$$
$$= a^3 b^7 \sqrt{210bc}$$

89. $\sqrt{(x+5)^3} = \sqrt{(x+5)^2 (x+5)}$
$$= \sqrt{(x+5)^2} \cdot \sqrt{x+5}$$
$$= (x+5)\sqrt{x+5}$$

91. $8\sqrt{3} - 12\sqrt{3} + \sqrt{3} = (8 - 12 + 1)\sqrt{3}$

$\qquad = -3\sqrt{3}$

93. $\sqrt{5x} + \sqrt{5x} - 6\sqrt{5x} = (1 + 1 - 6)\sqrt{5x}$

$\qquad = -4\sqrt{5x}$

95. $5\sqrt{6} - 2\sqrt{6} + 12\sqrt{10} = (5 - 2)\sqrt{6} + 12\sqrt{10}$

$\qquad = 3\sqrt{6} + 12\sqrt{10}$

97. $8\sqrt{14} + 22 - 5\sqrt{14} = 8\sqrt{14} - 5\sqrt{14} + 22$

$\qquad = (8 - 5)\sqrt{14} + 22$

$\qquad = 3\sqrt{14} + 22$

99. $\sqrt{8} - \sqrt{2} = \sqrt{4 \cdot 2} - \sqrt{2}$

$\qquad = \sqrt{4}\sqrt{2} - \sqrt{2}$

$\qquad = 2\sqrt{2} - \sqrt{2}$

$\qquad = (2 - 1)\sqrt{2}$

$\qquad = \sqrt{2}$

101. $-8\sqrt{5} - \sqrt{45} = -8\sqrt{5} - \sqrt{9 \cdot 5}$

$\qquad = -8\sqrt{5} - \sqrt{9}\sqrt{5}$

$\qquad = -8\sqrt{5} - 3\sqrt{5}$

$\qquad = (-8 - 3)\sqrt{5}$

$\qquad = -11\sqrt{5}$

103. $12\sqrt{3a^2} - 4\sqrt{27a^2} = 12\sqrt{a^2 \cdot 3} - 4\sqrt{9a^2 \cdot 3}$

$\qquad = 12\sqrt{a^2}\sqrt{3} - 4\sqrt{9a^2}\sqrt{3}$

$\qquad = 12a\sqrt{3} - 4 \cdot 3a\sqrt{3}$

$\qquad = 12a\sqrt{3} - 12a\sqrt{3}$

$\qquad = (12a - 12a)\sqrt{3}$

$\qquad = 0\sqrt{3}$

$\qquad = 0$

105. $4\sqrt{20a} + 6\sqrt{45a} = 4\sqrt{4 \cdot 5a} + 6\sqrt{9 \cdot 5a}$

$\qquad = 4\sqrt{4}\sqrt{5a} + 6\sqrt{9}\sqrt{5a}$

$\qquad = 4 \cdot 2\sqrt{5a} + 6 \cdot 3\sqrt{5a}$

$\qquad = 8\sqrt{5a} + 18\sqrt{5a}$

$\qquad = (8 + 18)\sqrt{5a}$

$\qquad = 26\sqrt{5a}$

107. $9\sqrt{6} - \sqrt{24} + 3\sqrt{54} = 9\sqrt{6} - \sqrt{4 \cdot 6} + 3\sqrt{9 \cdot 6}$

$\qquad = 9\sqrt{6} - \sqrt{4}\sqrt{6} + 3\sqrt{9}\sqrt{6}$

$\qquad = 9\sqrt{6} - 2\sqrt{6} + 3 \cdot 3\sqrt{6}$

$\qquad = 9\sqrt{6} - 2\sqrt{6} + 9\sqrt{6}$

$\qquad = (9 - 2 + 9)\sqrt{6}$

$\qquad = 16\sqrt{6}$

109. $\sqrt{27} + 5\sqrt{48} - 11\sqrt{12}$

$\qquad = \sqrt{9 \cdot 3} + 5\sqrt{16 \cdot 3} - 11\sqrt{4 \cdot 3}$

$\qquad = \sqrt{9}\sqrt{3} + 5\sqrt{16}\sqrt{3} - 11\sqrt{4}\sqrt{3}$

$\qquad = 3\sqrt{3} + 5 \cdot 4\sqrt{3} - 11 \cdot 2\sqrt{3}$

$\qquad = 3\sqrt{3} + 20\sqrt{3} - 22\sqrt{3}$

$\qquad = (3 + 20 - 22)\sqrt{3}$

$\qquad = \sqrt{3}$

111. An irrational number contains a radical, while a simplified rational number contains no radicals. The integer 2 is a rational number, while $\sqrt{2}$ is an irrational number.

113. For real numbers, $\sqrt{x^2}$ can be $-x$ or x; therefore, the absolute value symbol must be used to note that there are two solutions to the square root $\sqrt{x^2}$.

115. $\qquad a^2 + b^2 = c^2$

$\qquad (6)^2 + (12)^2 = c^2$

$\qquad 36 + 144 = c^2$

$\qquad 180 = c^2$

$\qquad c^2 - 180 = 0$

$\qquad (c + \sqrt{180})(c - \sqrt{180}) = 0$

$\qquad c + \sqrt{180} = 0 \quad \text{or} \quad c - \sqrt{180} = 0$

$\qquad \cancel{c = -\sqrt{180}} \qquad c = \sqrt{180}$

$\qquad c = \sqrt{180}$

$\qquad = \sqrt{36 \cdot 5}$

$\qquad = \sqrt{36}\sqrt{5}$

$\qquad = 6\sqrt{5}$

117.

$$a^2 + b^2 = c^2$$
$$a^2 + (16)^2 = (30)^2$$
$$a^2 + 256 = 900$$
$$a^2 - 644 = 0$$
$$\left(a + \sqrt{644}\right)\left(a - \sqrt{644}\right) = 0$$
$$a + \sqrt{644} = 0 \quad \text{or} \quad a - \sqrt{644} = 0$$
$$\cancel{a = -\sqrt{644}} \qquad a = \sqrt{644}$$

$$a = \sqrt{644}$$
$$= \sqrt{4 \cdot 161}$$
$$= \sqrt{4}\sqrt{161}$$
$$= 2\sqrt{161}$$

119. Prepare We need to determine how far up the wall the 20-foot ladder will reach.

Plan Keeping in mind that the base of the ladder is 8 feet from the house and that the building creates a right angle with the ground, we can use the Pythagorean theorem.

Process The unknown is the height the ladder can reach given the circumstances, so we can let $h =$ the height the ladder will reach (in feet) up the side of the building. Therefore, $a^2 + b^2 = c^2$ becomes the equation $a^2 + h^2 = c^2$, with $a = 4$, $c = 20$, and h unknown.

$$a^2 + h^2 = c^2$$
$$(8)^2 + h^2 = (20)^2$$
$$64 + h^2 = 400$$
$$h^2 - 336 = 0$$
$$\left(h + \sqrt{336}\right)\left(h - \sqrt{336}\right) = 0$$
$$h + \sqrt{336} = 0 \quad \text{or} \quad h - \sqrt{336} = 0$$
$$\cancel{h = -\sqrt{336}} \qquad h = \sqrt{336}$$

Because the height of the ladder up the side of the building cannot be negative, simplify only the positive square root.

$$h = \sqrt{336}$$
$$= \sqrt{16 \cdot 21}$$
$$= \sqrt{16} \cdot \sqrt{21}$$
$$= 4\sqrt{21} \text{ feet}$$

Therefore, the ladder will reach $4\sqrt{21}$, or approximately 18.33 feet up the side of the house.

Ponder Does our answer seem reasonable? Yes. It is reasonable that a 20-foot ladder could reach 18 feet up a wall when its base is set 8 feet from the wall.

121. Prepare We need to determine the length of a rectangle given its width and its diagonal.

Plan The diagonal (hypotenuse), the length, and the width of a rectangle form a right triangle, therefore, we can use the Pythagorean theorem to find the length.

Process Let $l =$ the measure of the length, $w =$ the measure of the width, and $d =$ the measure of the diagonal. Then $l^2 + w^2 = d^2$.

$$l^2 + w^2 = d^2$$
$$l^2 + (10)^2 = (16)^2$$
$$l^2 + 100 = 256$$
$$l^2 - 156 = 0$$
$$\left(l + \sqrt{156}\right)\left(l - \sqrt{156}\right) = 0$$
$$l + \sqrt{156} = 0 \quad \text{or} \quad l - \sqrt{156} = 0$$
$$\cancel{l = -\sqrt{156}} \qquad l = \sqrt{156}$$

Because the measure of the length is positive, we will only simplify $l = \sqrt{156}$.

$$l = \sqrt{156}$$
$$= \sqrt{4 \cdot 39}$$
$$= \sqrt{4} \cdot \sqrt{39}$$
$$= 2\sqrt{39} \text{ mm}$$

Therefore, the length of the rectangle is $2\sqrt{39}$, or approximately 12.49 mm.

Ponder Does our answer seem reasonable? Yes. Because a leg of a right triangle must be shorter than the hypotenuse, it is reasonable that the length is 12.49 mm.

123.
$$\sqrt{648x^4 y^{24} z} = \sqrt{324x^4 y^{24} \cdot 2z}$$
$$= \sqrt{324x^4 y^{24}} \cdot \sqrt{2z}$$
$$= 18x^2 y^{12}\sqrt{2z}$$

125. $5x\sqrt{300yz^2} - 2z\sqrt{108x^2 y}$

$= 5x\sqrt{100z^2 \cdot 3y} - 2z\sqrt{36x^2 \cdot 3y}$

$= 5x\sqrt{100z^2}\sqrt{3y} - 2z\sqrt{36x^2}\sqrt{3y}$

$= 5x \cdot 10z\sqrt{3y} - 2z \cdot 6x\sqrt{3y}$

$= 50xz\sqrt{3y} - 12xz\sqrt{3y}$

$= \left(50xz - 12xz\right)\sqrt{3y}$

$= 38xz\sqrt{3y}$

127. $-5\sqrt{50} - \sqrt{27} + 4\sqrt{18} - 2\sqrt{36}$

$= -5\sqrt{25 \cdot 2} - \sqrt{9 \cdot 3} + 4\sqrt{9 \cdot 2} - 2(6)$

$= -5\sqrt{25}\sqrt{2} - \sqrt{9}\sqrt{3} + 4\sqrt{9}\sqrt{2} - 12$

$= -5 \cdot 5\sqrt{2} - 3\sqrt{3} + 4 \cdot 3\sqrt{2} - 12$

$= -25\sqrt{2} - 3\sqrt{3} + 12\sqrt{2} - 12$

$= -3\sqrt{3} - 25\sqrt{2} + 12\sqrt{2} - 12$

$= -3\sqrt{3} + \left(-25 + 12\right)\sqrt{2} - 12$

$= -3\sqrt{3} - 13\sqrt{2} - 12$

129. $5\sqrt{36x^4} + 2x\sqrt{x^2} - 8x^2$

$= 5 \cdot 6x^2 + 2x \cdot x - 8x^2$

$= 30x^2 + 2x^2 - 8x^2$

$= \left(30 + 2 - 8\right)x^2$

$= 24x^2$

8.2 Exercises

1. We need like radicals to perform the arithmetic operations of <u>addition</u> and <u>subtraction</u>.

3. The process of eliminating a radical from the denominator is called <u>rationalizing</u> the denominator.

5. The radical expressions $\left(\sqrt{3}+\sqrt{5}\right)$ and $\left(\sqrt{3}-\sqrt{5}\right)$ are called <u>conjugates</u>.

7.
$$\begin{aligned}
\sqrt{7}\cdot\sqrt{14} &= \sqrt{7\cdot14}\\
&= \sqrt{7\cdot7\cdot2}\\
&= \sqrt{49\cdot2}\\
&= \sqrt{49}\cdot\sqrt{2}\\
&= 7\sqrt{2}
\end{aligned}$$

9.
$$\begin{aligned}
\sqrt{3}\cdot\sqrt{21} &= \sqrt{3\cdot21}\\
&= \sqrt{3\cdot3\cdot7}\\
&= \sqrt{9\cdot7}\\
&= \sqrt{9}\cdot\sqrt{7}\\
&= 3\sqrt{7}
\end{aligned}$$

11.
$$\begin{aligned}
\sqrt{6}\cdot\sqrt{10} &= \sqrt{6\cdot10}\\
&= \sqrt{2\cdot3\cdot2\cdot5}\\
&= \sqrt{4\cdot15}\\
&= \sqrt{4}\cdot\sqrt{15}\\
&= 2\sqrt{15}
\end{aligned}$$

13.
$$\begin{aligned}
\sqrt{12}\cdot\sqrt{15} &= \sqrt{12\cdot15}\\
&= \sqrt{2\cdot2\cdot3\cdot3\cdot5}\\
&= \sqrt{36\cdot5}\\
&= \sqrt{36}\cdot\sqrt{5}\\
&= 6\sqrt{5}
\end{aligned}$$

15.
$$\begin{aligned}
\sqrt{6a}\cdot\sqrt{2a} &= \sqrt{6a\cdot2a}\\
&= \sqrt{2\cdot3\cdot a\cdot2\cdot a}\\
&= \sqrt{4a^2\cdot3}\\
&= \sqrt{4a^2}\cdot\sqrt{3}\\
&= 2a\sqrt{3}
\end{aligned}$$

17.
$$\begin{aligned}
\sqrt{5x}\cdot\sqrt{10x} &= \sqrt{5x\cdot10x}\\
&= \sqrt{5\cdot x\cdot2\cdot5\cdot x}\\
&= \sqrt{25x^2\cdot2}\\
&= \sqrt{25x^2}\cdot\sqrt{2}\\
&= 5x\sqrt{2}
\end{aligned}$$

19.
$$\begin{aligned}
\sqrt{14x^3}\cdot\sqrt{7x^2} &= \sqrt{14x^3\cdot7x^2}\\
&= \sqrt{2\cdot7\cdot x^2\cdot x\cdot7x^2}\\
&= \sqrt{49x^4\cdot2x}\\
&= \sqrt{49x^4}\cdot\sqrt{2x}\\
&= 7x^2\sqrt{2x}
\end{aligned}$$

21.
$$\begin{aligned}
4\sqrt{15}\cdot2\sqrt{10} &= 4\cdot2\cdot\sqrt{15}\cdot\sqrt{10}\\
&= 8\sqrt{15\cdot10}\\
&= 8\sqrt{3\cdot5\cdot2\cdot5}\\
&= 8\sqrt{25\cdot6}\\
&= 8\sqrt{25}\cdot\sqrt{6}\\
&= 8\cdot5\sqrt{6}\\
&= 40\sqrt{6}
\end{aligned}$$

23.
$$\begin{aligned}
\left(-2\sqrt{6}\right)\left(5\sqrt{15}\right) &= -2\cdot(5)\sqrt{6}\cdot\sqrt{15}\\
&= -10\sqrt{6\cdot15}\\
&= -10\sqrt{2\cdot3\cdot3\cdot5}\\
&= -10\sqrt{9\cdot10}\\
&= -10\sqrt{9}\cdot\sqrt{10}\\
&= -10(3)\sqrt{10}\\
&= -30\sqrt{10}
\end{aligned}$$

25.
$$\begin{aligned}
\left(2\sqrt{35x}\right)\left(\sqrt{21x}\right) &= 2\cdot\sqrt{35x}\cdot\sqrt{21x}\\
&= 2\sqrt{35x\cdot21x}\\
&= 2\sqrt{5\cdot7x\cdot3\cdot7x}\\
&= 2\sqrt{49x^2\cdot15}\\
&= 2\sqrt{49x^2}\cdot\sqrt{15}\\
&= 2(7x)\sqrt{15}\\
&= 14x\sqrt{15}
\end{aligned}$$

27. $\left(\sqrt{48}\right)\left(\sqrt{27}\right) = \sqrt{16\cdot 3}\left(\sqrt{9\cdot 3}\right)$

$\qquad = \sqrt{16}\cdot\sqrt{9}\cdot\sqrt{3}\cdot\sqrt{3}$

$\qquad = 4\cdot 3\sqrt{9}$

$\qquad = 12\cdot 3$

$\qquad = 36$

29. $\left(-\sqrt{8x}\right)\left(4\sqrt{12x}\right) = -1\cdot 4\sqrt{8x}\cdot\sqrt{12x}$

$\qquad = -4\sqrt{8x\cdot 12x}$

$\qquad = -4\sqrt{2\cdot 2\cdot 2x\cdot 2\cdot 2\cdot 3x}$

$\qquad = -4\sqrt{16x^2\cdot 6}$

$\qquad = -4\sqrt{16x^2}\cdot\sqrt{6}$

$\qquad = -4(4x)\sqrt{6}$

$\qquad = -16x\sqrt{6}$

31. $\left(\sqrt{12x}\right)^2 = \sqrt{12x}\cdot\sqrt{12x}$

$\qquad = \sqrt{144x^2}$

$\qquad = 12x$

33. $\left(5\sqrt{6}\right)^2 = 5^2\left(\sqrt{6}\right)^2$

$\qquad = 25\sqrt{6}\cdot\sqrt{6}$

$\qquad = 25\sqrt{36}$

$\qquad = 25\cdot 6$

$\qquad = 150$

35. $\left(3\sqrt{14a}\right)^2 = 3^2\left(\sqrt{14a}\right)^2$

$\qquad = 9\sqrt{14a}\cdot\sqrt{14a}$

$\qquad = 9\sqrt{196a^2}$

$\qquad = 9\cdot 14a$

$\qquad = 126a$

37. $\sqrt{2}\left(\sqrt{2}+\sqrt{5}\right) = \sqrt{2}\cdot\sqrt{2}+\sqrt{2}\cdot\sqrt{5}$

$\qquad = \sqrt{4}+\sqrt{10}$

$\qquad = 2+\sqrt{10}$

39. $\sqrt{6}\left(4\sqrt{7}-\sqrt{6}\right) = \sqrt{6}\cdot 4\sqrt{7}-\sqrt{6}\cdot\sqrt{6}$

$\qquad = 4\sqrt{42}-\sqrt{36}$

$\qquad = 4\sqrt{42}-6$

41. $\sqrt{x}\left(\sqrt{x}+\sqrt{2}\right) = \sqrt{x}\cdot\sqrt{x}+\sqrt{x}\cdot\sqrt{2}$

$\qquad = \sqrt{x^2}+\sqrt{2x}$

$\qquad = x+\sqrt{2x}$

43. $2\sqrt{2}\left(\sqrt{14}-\sqrt{18}\right) = 2\sqrt{2}\cdot\sqrt{14}-2\sqrt{2}\cdot\sqrt{18}$

$\qquad = 2\sqrt{28}-2\sqrt{36}$

$\qquad = 2\sqrt{4\cdot 7}-2\cdot 6$

$\qquad = 2\cdot 2\sqrt{7}-12$

$\qquad = 4\sqrt{7}-12$

45. $4\sqrt{2}\left(2\sqrt{18}+\sqrt{2}\right) = 4\sqrt{2}\cdot 2\sqrt{18}+4\sqrt{2}\cdot\sqrt{2}$

$\qquad = 8\sqrt{36}+4\sqrt{4}$

$\qquad = 8\cdot 6+4\cdot 2$

$\qquad = 48+8$

$\qquad = 56$

47. $\left(\sqrt{2}-\sqrt{3}\right)\left(\sqrt{10}+\sqrt{15}\right)$

$\qquad = \sqrt{2}\cdot\sqrt{10}+\sqrt{2}\cdot\sqrt{15}-\sqrt{3}\cdot\sqrt{10}-\sqrt{3}\cdot\sqrt{15}$

$\qquad = \sqrt{20}+\sqrt{30}-\sqrt{30}-\sqrt{45}$

$\qquad = \sqrt{4\cdot 5}-\sqrt{9\cdot 5}$

$\qquad = 2\sqrt{5}-3\sqrt{5}$

$\qquad = -\sqrt{5}$

49. $\left(5\sqrt{7x}-8\right)\left(5+\sqrt{14x}\right)$

$\qquad = 5\sqrt{7x}\cdot 5+5\sqrt{7x}\cdot\sqrt{14x}-8\cdot 5-8\cdot\sqrt{14x}$

$\qquad = 25\sqrt{7x}+5\sqrt{98x^2}-40-8\sqrt{14x}$

$\qquad = 25\sqrt{7x}+5\sqrt{49x^2\cdot 2}-40-8\sqrt{14x}$

$\qquad = 25\sqrt{7x}+35x\sqrt{2}-40-8\sqrt{14x}$

51. $\left(2\sqrt{12}+7\right)\left(2\sqrt{12}-7\right) = \left(2\sqrt{12}\right)^2-(7)^2$

$\qquad = 2^2\left(\sqrt{12}\right)^2-49$

$\qquad = 4\sqrt{12}\cdot\sqrt{12}-49$

$\qquad = 4\sqrt{144}-49$

$\qquad = 48-49$

$\qquad = -1$

53. $\left(3+7\sqrt{2}\right)^2 = (3)^2 + 2\left(3\cdot 7\sqrt{2}\right)+\left(7\sqrt{2}\right)^2$

$\qquad = 9 + 42\sqrt{2} + 49\sqrt{4}$

$\qquad = 9 + 42\sqrt{2} + 49\cdot 2$

$\qquad = 9 + 42\sqrt{2} + 98$

$\qquad = 107 + 42\sqrt{2}$

55. $\left(\sqrt{5}-8\sqrt{15}\right)^2 = \left(\sqrt{5}\right)^2 - 2\left(\sqrt{5}\cdot 8\sqrt{15}\right)+\left(8\sqrt{15}\right)^2$

$\qquad = \sqrt{25} - 16\sqrt{75} + 64\sqrt{225}$

$\qquad = 5 - 16\sqrt{25\cdot 3} + 64\cdot 15$

$\qquad = 5 - 16\cdot 5\sqrt{3} + 960$

$\qquad = 965 - 80\sqrt{3}$

57. $\dfrac{\sqrt{50}}{\sqrt{2}} = \sqrt{\dfrac{50}{2}}$

$\qquad = \sqrt{25}$

$\qquad = 5$

59. $\dfrac{\sqrt{2}}{\sqrt{72}} = \sqrt{\dfrac{2}{72}}$

$\qquad = \sqrt{\dfrac{1}{36}}$

$\qquad = \dfrac{1}{6}$

61. $\dfrac{3\sqrt{500}}{\sqrt{5}} = 3\sqrt{\dfrac{500}{5}}$

$\qquad = 3\sqrt{100}$

$\qquad = 3\cdot 10$

$\qquad = 30$

63. $\dfrac{\sqrt{18a^5}}{\sqrt{3a^3}} = \sqrt{\dfrac{18a^5}{3a^3}}$

$\qquad = \sqrt{6a^2}$

$\qquad = \sqrt{a^2\cdot 6}$

$\qquad = \sqrt{a^2}\cdot\sqrt{6}$

$\qquad = a\sqrt{6}$

65. $\dfrac{\sqrt{72y^{10}}}{\sqrt{2y^2}} = \sqrt{\dfrac{72y^{10}}{2y^2}}$

$\qquad = \sqrt{36y^8}$

$\qquad = 6y^4$

67. $\dfrac{20\sqrt{8}}{2\sqrt{2}} = 10\sqrt{\dfrac{8}{2}}$

$\qquad = 10\sqrt{4}$

$\qquad = 10\cdot 2$

$\qquad = 20$

69. $\dfrac{7}{\sqrt{3}} = \dfrac{7}{\sqrt{3}}\cdot\dfrac{\sqrt{3}}{\sqrt{3}}$

$\qquad = \dfrac{7\sqrt{3}}{\sqrt{9}}$

$\qquad = \dfrac{7\sqrt{3}}{3}$

71. $\dfrac{1}{\sqrt{x}} = \dfrac{1}{\sqrt{x}}\cdot\dfrac{\sqrt{x}}{\sqrt{x}}$

$\qquad = \dfrac{\sqrt{x}}{\sqrt{x^2}}$

$\qquad = \dfrac{\sqrt{x}}{x}$

73. $\sqrt{\dfrac{2}{7}} = \dfrac{\sqrt{2}}{\sqrt{7}}\cdot\dfrac{\sqrt{7}}{\sqrt{7}}$

$\qquad = \dfrac{\sqrt{14}}{\sqrt{49}}$

$\qquad = \dfrac{\sqrt{14}}{7}$

75. $\dfrac{\sqrt{6}}{\sqrt{10}} = \dfrac{\sqrt{6}}{\sqrt{10}}\cdot\dfrac{\sqrt{10}}{\sqrt{10}}$

$\qquad = \dfrac{\sqrt{60}}{\sqrt{100}}$

$\qquad = \dfrac{\sqrt{4\cdot 15}}{10}$

$\qquad = \dfrac{2\sqrt{15}}{10}$

$\qquad = \dfrac{\sqrt{15}}{5}$

338

77. $\sqrt{\dfrac{7}{18x}} = \dfrac{\sqrt{7}}{\sqrt{18x}}$

$= \dfrac{\sqrt{7}}{\sqrt{9 \cdot 2x}}$

$= \dfrac{\sqrt{7}}{3\sqrt{2x}} \cdot \dfrac{\sqrt{2x}}{\sqrt{2x}}$

$= \dfrac{\sqrt{14x}}{3\sqrt{4x^2}}$

$= \dfrac{\sqrt{14x}}{3 \cdot 2x}$

$= \dfrac{\sqrt{14x}}{6x}$

79. $\dfrac{\sqrt{24}}{5\sqrt{36}} = \dfrac{\sqrt{4 \cdot 6}}{5 \cdot 6}$

$= \dfrac{2\sqrt{6}}{30}$

$= \dfrac{\sqrt{6}}{15}$

81. $\dfrac{\sqrt{5b^4}}{\sqrt{18a^5}} = \dfrac{\sqrt{b^4 \cdot 5}}{\sqrt{9a^4 \cdot 2a}}$

$= \dfrac{b^2\sqrt{5}}{3a^2\sqrt{2a}}$

$= \dfrac{b^2\sqrt{5}}{3a^2\sqrt{2a}} \cdot \dfrac{\sqrt{2a}}{\sqrt{2a}}$

$= \dfrac{b^2\sqrt{10a}}{3a^2\sqrt{4a^2}}$

$= \dfrac{b^2\sqrt{10a}}{6a^3}$

83. $\dfrac{2}{5+\sqrt{7}} = \left(\dfrac{2}{5+\sqrt{7}}\right)\left(\dfrac{5-\sqrt{7}}{5-\sqrt{7}}\right)$

$= \dfrac{2(5-\sqrt{7})}{(5)^2 - (\sqrt{7})^2}$

$= \dfrac{2(5-\sqrt{7})}{25-7}$

$= \dfrac{\overset{1}{2}(5-\sqrt{7})}{\underset{9}{18}}$

$= \dfrac{5-\sqrt{7}}{9}$

85. $\dfrac{\sqrt{3}}{\sqrt{3}-\sqrt{7}} = \left(\dfrac{\sqrt{3}}{\sqrt{3}-\sqrt{7}}\right)\left(\dfrac{\sqrt{3}+\sqrt{7}}{\sqrt{3}+\sqrt{7}}\right)$

$= \dfrac{\sqrt{3}(\sqrt{3}+\sqrt{7})}{(\sqrt{3})^2 - (\sqrt{7})^2}$

$= \dfrac{\sqrt{9}+\sqrt{21}}{3-7}$

$= -\dfrac{3+\sqrt{21}}{4}$

87. $\dfrac{1+\sqrt{5}}{\sqrt{3}-\sqrt{6}} = \left(\dfrac{1+\sqrt{5}}{\sqrt{3}-\sqrt{6}}\right)\left(\dfrac{\sqrt{3}+\sqrt{6}}{\sqrt{3}+\sqrt{6}}\right)$

$= \dfrac{1 \cdot \sqrt{3} + 1 \cdot \sqrt{6} + \sqrt{5} \cdot \sqrt{3} + \sqrt{5} \cdot \sqrt{6}}{(\sqrt{3})^2 - (\sqrt{6})^2}$

$= \dfrac{\sqrt{3}+\sqrt{6}+\sqrt{15}+\sqrt{30}}{\sqrt{9}-\sqrt{36}}$

$= \dfrac{\sqrt{3}+\sqrt{6}+\sqrt{15}+\sqrt{30}}{3-6}$

$= -\dfrac{\sqrt{3}+\sqrt{6}+\sqrt{15}+\sqrt{30}}{3}$

89. $\dfrac{\sqrt{18}}{\sqrt{3}+\sqrt{14}} = \dfrac{\sqrt{9 \cdot 2}}{\sqrt{3}+\sqrt{14}}$

$= \dfrac{3\sqrt{2}}{\sqrt{3}+\sqrt{14}}$

$= \left(\dfrac{3\sqrt{2}}{\sqrt{3}+\sqrt{14}}\right)\left(\dfrac{\sqrt{3}-\sqrt{14}}{\sqrt{3}-\sqrt{14}}\right)$

$= \dfrac{3\sqrt{2}(\sqrt{3}-\sqrt{14})}{(\sqrt{3})^2 - (\sqrt{14})^2}$

$= \dfrac{3\sqrt{6}-3\sqrt{28}}{\sqrt{9}-\sqrt{196}}$

$= \dfrac{3\sqrt{6}-3\sqrt{4 \cdot 7}}{3-14}$

$= -\dfrac{3\sqrt{6}-3 \cdot 2\sqrt{7}}{11}$

$= -\dfrac{3\sqrt{6}-6\sqrt{7}}{11}$

91. Simplifying and then multiplying the radicals is one method to work exercise 27. It is easy to see that $\sqrt{48}$ is divisible by $\sqrt{16}$ and $\sqrt{27}$ is divisible by $\sqrt{9}$. The problem simplifies to $4\sqrt{3} \cdot 3\sqrt{3}$, which equals 36.

93. Rationalizing a denominator involves creating an equivalent fraction with no radicals in the denominator by multiplying the fraction by a special form of 1.

95. A radical is simplified when no perfect square factors remain as radicands; there are no radicals in the denominator, and no fractions under the radical symbol.

97. To add $\sqrt{2}$ and $\sqrt{8}$ it is necessary to reduce $\sqrt{8}$ to $2\sqrt{2}$. Now that $\sqrt{2}$ and $2\sqrt{2}$ share a common radical, they can be added together to form $3\sqrt{2}$. To multiply $\sqrt{2}$ and $\sqrt{8}$, it is not necessary to reduce $\sqrt{8}$ first. The two radicals multiply to give $\sqrt{16}$, which equals 4.

99. $A = L \cdot W$

$$A = \left(7 + 4\sqrt{6}\right)\left(5 + 3\sqrt{2}\right)$$
$$= 7 \cdot 5 + 7 \cdot 3\sqrt{2} + 4\sqrt{6} \cdot 5 + 4\sqrt{6} \cdot 3\sqrt{2}$$
$$= 35 + 21\sqrt{2} + 20\sqrt{6} + 12\sqrt{12}$$
$$= 35 + 21\sqrt{2} + 20\sqrt{6} + 12\sqrt{4 \cdot 3}$$
$$= 35 + 21\sqrt{2} + 20\sqrt{6} + 12 \cdot 2\sqrt{3}$$
$$= 35 + 21\sqrt{2} + 20\sqrt{6} + 24\sqrt{3} \ \text{cm}^2$$

101. $L = \dfrac{A}{W}$

$$L = \frac{8}{6 + \sqrt{2}}$$
$$= \frac{8}{6 + \sqrt{2}} \cdot \frac{6 - \sqrt{2}}{6 - \sqrt{2}}$$
$$= \frac{8\left(6 - \sqrt{2}\right)}{\left(6\right)^2 - \left(\sqrt{2}\right)^2}$$
$$= \frac{8\left(6 - \sqrt{2}\right)}{36 - \sqrt{4}}$$
$$= \frac{8\left(6 - \sqrt{2}\right)}{36 - 2}$$
$$= \frac{\overset{4}{\cancel{8}}\left(6 - \sqrt{2}\right)}{\underset{17}{\cancel{34}}}$$
$$= \frac{24 - 4\sqrt{2}}{17} \ \text{ft.}$$

103. **Prepare** We need to determine the speed of the accident vehicle that left 200 feet of skid marks.

Plan $S =$ the unknown speed of the accident vehicle, $s = 36$ mph (the speed of the test vehicle), $D = 200$ feet (the length of the skid marks at the accident scene), $d = 75$ feet (the length of the skid marks left by the test vehicle).

Process Substitute the values into the formula and solve for S.

$$S = s\sqrt{\frac{D}{d}}$$
$$= 36\sqrt{\frac{200}{75}}$$
$$= 36\sqrt{\frac{8}{3}}$$
$$= 36 \frac{\sqrt{8}}{\sqrt{3}} \cdot \frac{\sqrt{3}}{\sqrt{3}}$$
$$= \frac{\overset{12}{\cancel{36}}}{1} \cdot \frac{2\sqrt{6}}{\underset{1}{\cancel{3}}}$$
$$= 24\sqrt{6}$$

The vehicle involved in the accident was traveling $24\sqrt{6}$ mph, or approximately 59 mph.

Ponder Does our answer seem reasonable? Yes. The skid marks left by the test vehicle were significantly shorter than the skid marks at the scene of the accident, and the test vehicle was traveling at a slower speed. Suffice it to say that a vehicle traveling at a higher rate of speed will leave significantly longer skid marks.

105. $\left(5\sqrt{6} + 8\sqrt{2}\right)^2$

$$= \left(5\sqrt{6}\right)^2 + 2\left(5\sqrt{6}\right)\left(8\sqrt{2}\right) + \left(8\sqrt{2}\right)^2$$
$$= 25 \cdot 6 + 80\sqrt{12} + 64 \cdot 2$$
$$= 150 + 80\sqrt{4 \cdot 3} + 128$$
$$= 278 + 160\sqrt{3}$$

107. $\dfrac{3\sqrt{6}+\sqrt{5}}{4\sqrt{2}-\sqrt{8}}$

$=\dfrac{3\sqrt{6}+\sqrt{5}}{4\sqrt{2}-\sqrt{8}}\cdot\dfrac{4\sqrt{2}+\sqrt{8}}{4\sqrt{2}+\sqrt{8}}$

$=\dfrac{3\sqrt{6}\cdot4\sqrt{2}+3\sqrt{6}\cdot\sqrt{8}+\sqrt{5}\cdot4\sqrt{2}+\sqrt{5}\cdot\sqrt{8}}{\left(4\sqrt{2}\right)^2-\left(\sqrt{8}\right)^2}$

$=\dfrac{12\sqrt{12}+3\sqrt{48}+4\sqrt{10}+\sqrt{40}}{32-8}$

$=\dfrac{24\sqrt{3}+12\sqrt{3}+4\sqrt{10}+2\sqrt{10}}{24}$

$=\dfrac{36\sqrt{3}+6\sqrt{10}}{24}$

$=\dfrac{\overset{1}{\cancel{6}}\left(6\sqrt{3}+\sqrt{10}\right)}{\underset{4}{\cancel{24}}}$

$=\dfrac{6\sqrt{3}+\sqrt{10}}{4}$

109. $\dfrac{2\sqrt{x}-\sqrt{5}}{\sqrt{x}+\sqrt{3}}$

$=\dfrac{2\sqrt{x}-\sqrt{5}}{\sqrt{x}+\sqrt{3}}\cdot\dfrac{\sqrt{x}-\sqrt{3}}{\sqrt{x}-\sqrt{3}}$

$=\dfrac{2\sqrt{x}\cdot\sqrt{x}-2\sqrt{x}\cdot\sqrt{3}-\sqrt{5}\cdot\sqrt{x}+\sqrt{5}\cdot\sqrt{3}}{\left(\sqrt{x}\right)^2-\left(\sqrt{3}\right)^2}$

$=\dfrac{2\sqrt{x^2}-2\sqrt{3x}-\sqrt{5x}+\sqrt{15}}{x-3}$

$=\dfrac{2x-2\sqrt{3x}-\sqrt{5x}+\sqrt{15}}{x-3}$

111. $\left(6\sqrt{3}-2\sqrt{7a}\right)^2$

$=\left(6\sqrt{3}\right)^2-2\left(6\sqrt{3}\right)\left(2\sqrt{7a}\right)+\left(2\sqrt{7a}\right)^2$

$=36\cdot3-24\sqrt{21a}+4\cdot7a$

$=108-24\sqrt{21a}+28a$

113. $\left(5-3\sqrt{2}+x\right)\left(2+4\sqrt{2}+6x\right)$

$=5\left(2+4\sqrt{2}+6x\right)-3\sqrt{2}\left(2+4\sqrt{2}+6x\right)+x\left(2+4\sqrt{2}+6x\right)$

$=10+20\sqrt{2}+30x-6\sqrt{2}-12\sqrt{4}-18x\sqrt{2}+2x+4x\sqrt{2}+6x^2$

$=6x^2+30x+2x-18x\sqrt{2}+4x\sqrt{2}+20\sqrt{2}-6\sqrt{2}-24+10$

$=6x^2+32x-14x\sqrt{2}+14\sqrt{2}-14$

115. $\dfrac{8\sqrt{8x^8}}{3\sqrt{27y^5}}=\dfrac{8\sqrt{4x^8\cdot2}}{3\sqrt{9y^4\cdot3y}}$

$=\dfrac{16x^4\sqrt{2}}{9y^2\sqrt{3y}}\cdot\dfrac{\sqrt{3y}}{\sqrt{3y}}$

$=\dfrac{16x^4\sqrt{6y}}{9y^2\sqrt{9y^2}}$

$=\dfrac{16x^4\sqrt{6y}}{27y^3}$

117. $\sqrt{\dfrac{200a}{48a^2b}}=\sqrt{\dfrac{25a}{6a^2b}}$

$=\dfrac{\sqrt{25a}}{\sqrt{6a^2b}}$

$=\dfrac{5\sqrt{a}}{a\sqrt{6b}}\cdot\dfrac{\sqrt{6b}}{\sqrt{6b}}$

$=\dfrac{5\sqrt{6ab}}{a\sqrt{36b^2}}$

$=\dfrac{5\sqrt{6ab}}{6ab}$

8.3 Exercises

1. A <u>radical</u> <u>equation</u> is an equation that contains a variable in the radicand.

3. When solving equations involving radicals, the goal is to <u>isolate</u> the radical on one side of the equation and apply the <u>Squaring</u> <u>Property</u> of <u>Equality</u> to eliminate the radical.

5. In the radical equation $\sqrt{2x} + 5 = 8$, the first step in solving it would be to <u>isolate</u> $\sqrt{2x}$ by <u>subtracting</u> 5 from both sides of the equation.

7. When applying the Squaring Property of Equality to solve equations involving radicals, <u>extraneous</u> solution(s) may be introduced.

9. $$\sqrt{x+11} = 16$$
    $$\left(\sqrt{x+11}\right)^2 = (16)^2$$
    $$x + 11 = 256$$
    $$x = 245$$
    Solution Set: $\{245\}$

11. $$\sqrt{3x+1} = 100$$
    $$\left(\sqrt{3x+1}\right)^2 = (100)^2$$
    $$3x + 1 = 10,000$$
    $$3x = 9,999$$
    $$x = 3,333$$
    Solution Set: $\{3,333\}$

13. $$\sqrt{8x-7} = 7$$
    $$\left(\sqrt{8x-7}\right)^2 = (7)^2$$
    $$8x - 7 = 49$$
    $$8x = 56$$
    $$x = 7$$
    Solution Set: $\{7\}$

15. $$2 + \sqrt{6x} = 14$$
    $$\sqrt{6x} = 12$$
    $$\left(\sqrt{6x}\right)^2 = (12)^2$$
    $$6x = 144$$
    $$x = 24$$
    Solution Set: $\{24\}$

17. $$\sqrt{82-x} - 6 = 4$$
    $$\sqrt{82-x} = 10$$
    $$\left(\sqrt{82-x}\right)^2 = (10)^2$$
    $$82 - x = 100$$
    $$x = -18$$
    Solution Set: $\{-18\}$

19. $$\sqrt{-6x} + 188 = 200$$
    $$\sqrt{-6x} = 12$$
    $$\left(\sqrt{-6x}\right)^2 = (12)^2$$
    $$-6x = 144$$
    $$x = -24$$
    Solution Set: $\{-24\}$

21. $$\sqrt{2x+3} + 5 = 0$$
    $$\sqrt{2x+3} = -5$$
    $$\left(\sqrt{2x+3}\right)^2 = (-5)^2$$
    $$2x + 3 = 25$$
    $$2x = 22$$
    $$\cancel{x = 11}$$
    Solution Set: $\{\ \}$

23. $$\sqrt{8-4x} = -6$$
    $$\left(\sqrt{8-4x}\right)^2 = (-6)^2$$
    $$8 - 4x = 36$$
    $$-4x = 28$$
    $$\cancel{x = -7}$$
    Solution Set: $\{\ \}$

25. $$\sqrt{6x+1} = \sqrt{8x-17}$$
    $$\left(\sqrt{6x+1}\right)^2 = \left(\sqrt{8x-17}\right)^2$$
    $$6x + 1 = 8x - 17$$
    $$-2x = -18$$
    $$x = 9$$
    Solution Set: $\{9\}$

27.
$$\sqrt{15+4x} = \sqrt{20-2x}$$
$$\left(\sqrt{15+4x}\right)^2 = \left(\sqrt{20-2x}\right)^2$$
$$15+4x = 20-2x$$
$$6x = 5$$
$$x = \frac{5}{6}$$
Solution Set: $\left\{\frac{5}{6}\right\}$

29.
$$\sqrt{x^2-x} = \sqrt{5-5x}$$
$$\left(\sqrt{x^2-x}\right)^2 = \left(\sqrt{5-5x}\right)^2$$
$$x^2-x = 5-5x$$
$$x^2+4x-5 = 0$$
$$(x-1)(x+5) = 0$$
$$x-1=0 \quad \text{or} \quad x+5=0$$
$$x=1 \qquad\qquad x=-5$$
Solution Set: $\{-5,1\}$

31.
$$\sqrt{3x^2} = \sqrt{x^2-x}$$
$$\left(\sqrt{3x^2}\right)^2 = \left(\sqrt{x^2-x}\right)^2$$
$$3x^2 = x^2-x$$
$$2x^2+x = 0$$
$$x(2x+1) = 0$$
$$x=0 \quad \text{or} \quad 2x+1=0$$
$$x = -\frac{1}{2}$$
Solution Set: $\left\{-\frac{1}{2},0\right\}$

33.
$$x-6 = \sqrt{-7x+72}$$
$$(x-6)^2 = \left(\sqrt{-7x+72}\right)^2$$
$$x^2-12x+36 = -7x+72$$
$$x^2-5x-36 = 0$$
$$(x-9)(x+4) = 0$$
$$x-9=0 \quad \text{or} \quad x+4=0$$
$$x=9 \qquad\qquad \cancel{x=-4}$$
Solution Set: $\{9\}$

35.
$$x-1 = \sqrt{1-5x}$$
$$(x-1)^2 = \left(\sqrt{1-5x}\right)^2$$
$$x^2-2x+1 = 1-5x$$
$$x^2+3x = 0$$
$$x(x+3) = 0$$
$$\cancel{x=0} \quad \text{or} \quad x+3=0$$
$$\cancel{x=-3}$$
Solution Set: $\{\ \}$

37.
$$\sqrt{x}+3 = \sqrt{9+19x}$$
$$\left(\sqrt{x}+3\right)^2 = \left(\sqrt{9+19x}\right)^2$$
$$x+6\sqrt{x}+9 = 9+19x$$
$$6\sqrt{x} = 18x$$
$$\sqrt{x} = 3x$$
$$\left(\sqrt{x}\right)^2 = (3x)^2$$
$$x = 9x^2$$
$$0 = 9x^2-x$$
$$0 = x(9x-1)$$
$$x=0 \quad \text{or} \quad 9x-1=0$$
$$x = \frac{1}{9}$$
Solution Set: $\left\{0,\frac{1}{9}\right\}$

39.
$$x-6 = \sqrt{26-x}$$
$$(x-6)^2 = \left(\sqrt{26-x}\right)^2$$
$$x^2-12x+36 = 26-x$$
$$x^2-11x+10 = 0$$
$$(x-1)(x-10) = 0$$
$$x-1=0 \quad \text{or} \quad x-10=0$$
$$\cancel{x=1} \qquad\qquad x=10$$
Solution Set: $\{10\}$

41.
$$x+3=\sqrt{-3x-11}$$
$$(x+3)^2=\left(\sqrt{-3x-11}\right)^2$$
$$x^2+6x+9=-3x-11$$
$$x^2+9x+20=0$$
$$(x+4)(x+5)=0$$
$$x+4=0 \quad \text{or} \quad x+5=0$$
$$\cancel{x=-4} \qquad \cancel{x=-5}$$

Solution Set: $\{\ \}$

43.
$$\sqrt{x}+8=\sqrt{64-55x}$$
$$\left(\sqrt{x}+8\right)^2=\left(\sqrt{64-55x}\right)^2$$
$$x+16\sqrt{x}+64=64-55x$$
$$16\sqrt{x}=-56x$$
$$\sqrt{x}=-\frac{7}{2}x$$
$$\left(\sqrt{x}\right)^2=\left(-\frac{7}{2}x\right)^2$$
$$x=\frac{49}{4}x^2$$
$$0=\frac{49}{4}x^2-x$$
$$0=x\left(\frac{49}{4}x-1\right)$$
$$x=0 \quad \text{or} \quad \frac{49}{4}x-1=0$$
$$\cancel{x=\frac{4}{49}}$$

Solution Set: $\{0\}$

45. The Squaring Property of Equality states that squaring both sides of an equation results in an equivalent equation. This property is commonly used to eliminate radicals from radical equations.

47. Applying the Squaring Property of Equality prior to isolating the radical produces a complex equation that requires the use of the squaring property a second time. By isolating the variable first, the property is only needed one time and the algebra is much simpler.

49. Prepare Using the given formula, we are to determine the length (in feet) of the pendulum in the clock tower of the downtown square, given that it completes one full cycle in 4 seconds.

Plan Using the formula $t=2\pi\sqrt{\dfrac{L}{g}}$, we will substitute in the known values and solve for the unknown length L. $t=4$ seconds, $g=32$ feet/second squared, and $L=$ Unknown.

Process Substituting the known values yields the equation $4=2\pi\sqrt{\dfrac{L}{32}}$.

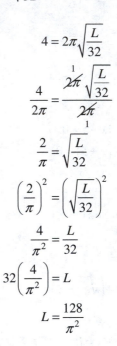

$$4=2\pi\sqrt{\frac{L}{32}}$$

$$\frac{4}{2\pi}=\frac{\overset{1}{\cancel{2\pi}}\sqrt{\dfrac{L}{32}}}{\underset{1}{\cancel{2\pi}}}$$

$$\frac{2}{\pi}=\sqrt{\frac{L}{32}}$$

$$\left(\frac{2}{\pi}\right)^2=\left(\sqrt{\frac{L}{32}}\right)^2$$

$$\frac{4}{\pi^2}=\frac{L}{32}$$

$$32\left(\frac{4}{\pi^2}\right)=L$$

$$L=\frac{128}{\pi^2}$$

The length of the pendulum in the clock tower is exactly $\dfrac{128}{\pi^2}$ feet, or approximately 12.97 feet.

Ponder Does the answer seem reasonable? Yes. The clock in a tower would be quite large, so it seems reasonable for the pendulum to be about 13 feet long.

51.

$$\sqrt{x+1}+3=\sqrt{4x+4}$$

$$\left(\sqrt{x+1}+3\right)^2=\left(\sqrt{4x+4}\right)^2$$

$$x+1+6\sqrt{x+1}+9=4x+4$$

$$6\sqrt{x+1}=3x-6$$

$$\left(6\sqrt{x+1}\right)^2=\left(3x-6\right)^2$$

$$36\left(x+1\right)=9x^2-36x+36$$

$$36x+36=9x^2-36x+36$$

$$0=9x^2-72x$$

$$0=9x\left(x-8\right)$$

$$9x=0 \quad \text{or} \quad x-8=0$$

$$\cancel{x=0} \qquad x=8$$

Solution Set: $\{8\}$

53.

$$\sqrt{\sqrt{x}}=\sqrt{x-2}$$

$$\left(\sqrt{\sqrt{x}}\right)^2=\left(\sqrt{x-2}\right)^2$$

$$\sqrt{x}=x-2$$

$$\left(\sqrt{x}\right)^2=\left(x-2\right)^2$$

$$x=x^2-4x+4$$

$$0=x^2-5x+4$$

$$0=\left(x-1\right)\left(x-4\right)$$

$$x-1=0 \quad \text{or} \quad x-4=0$$

$$\cancel{x=1} \qquad x=4$$

Solution Set: $\{4\}$

55.

$$\sqrt{x}=\sqrt{\sqrt{2-x}}$$

$$\left(\sqrt{x}\right)^2=\left(\sqrt{\sqrt{2-x}}\right)^2$$

$$x=\sqrt{2-x}$$

$$\left(x\right)^2=\left(\sqrt{2-x}\right)^2$$

$$x^2=2-x$$

$$x^2+x-2=0$$

$$\left(x+2\right)\left(x-1\right)=0$$

$$x+2=0 \quad \text{or} \quad x-1=0$$

$$\cancel{x=-2} \qquad x=1$$

Solution Set: $\{1\}$

8.4 Exercises

1. In an isosceles right triangle, the measure of the largest angle is <u>90°</u> and the measure of the sum of the other two angles is <u>90°</u> .

3. In a 30°-60°-90° triangle, the length of the hypotenuse is <u>twice</u> the length of the shortest leg.

5. The distance between the two points $(3,-2)$ and $(-5,7)$ is given by the formula $d = \sqrt{(-5-\underline{3})^2 + (7-\underline{-2})^2}$.

7. b

9. a

11. $d = \sqrt{(x_2 - x_1)^2 + (y_2 - y_1)^2}$

$= \sqrt{(-4-4)^2 + (-1-5)^2}$

$= \sqrt{(-8)^2 + (-6)^2}$

$= \sqrt{64+36}$

$= \sqrt{100}$

$= 10$

13. $d = \sqrt{(x_2 - x_1)^2 + (y_2 - y_1)^2}$

$= \sqrt{(-6-(-2))^2 + (3-(-3))^2}$

$= \sqrt{(-4)^2 + (6)^2}$

$= \sqrt{16+36}$

$= \sqrt{52}$

$= \sqrt{4 \cdot 13}$

$= 2\sqrt{13}$

15. $d = \sqrt{(x_2 - x_1)^2 + (y_2 - y_1)^2}$

$= \sqrt{(-3-5)^2 + (0-(-8))^2}$

$= \sqrt{(-8)^2 + (8)^2}$

$= \sqrt{64+64}$

$= \sqrt{128}$

$= \sqrt{64 \cdot 2}$

$= 8\sqrt{2}$

17. $d = \sqrt{(x_2 - x_1)^2 + (y_2 - y_1)^2}$

$= \sqrt{(0-(-1))^2 + (2-0)^2}$

$= \sqrt{(1)^2 + (2)^2}$

$= \sqrt{1+4}$

$= \sqrt{5}$

19. $d = \sqrt{(x_2 - x_1)^2 + (y_2 - y_1)^2}$

$= \sqrt{(-0.1-0.2)^2 + (-1.3-(-0.9))^2}$

$= \sqrt{(-0.3)^2 + (-0.4)^2}$

$= \sqrt{0.09+0.16}$

$= \sqrt{0.25}$

$= 0.5$

21. a) The square root of five times a number
    b) The square root of the product of 5 and a number
    c) The square root of the sum of 5 and a number
    d) The sum of the square root of 5 and a number

23. The relationship between the sides of a 45°-45°-90° triangle is such that the hypotenuse is $\sqrt{2}$ times longer than the lengths of the legs.

25. Let x represent the unknown number. The equation is $\sqrt{x+4} = \sqrt{7x}$.

$$\sqrt{x+4} = \sqrt{7x}$$
$$\left(\sqrt{x+4}\right)^2 = \left(\sqrt{7x}\right)^2$$
$$x+4 = 7x$$
$$4 = 6x$$
$$\frac{2}{3} = x$$

The number is $\frac{2}{3}$.

27. Let x represent the unknown number. The equation is $\sqrt{5x-4} = \sqrt{2+3x}$.

$$\sqrt{5x-4} = \sqrt{2+3x}$$
$$\left(\sqrt{5x-4}\right)^2 = \left(\sqrt{2+3x}\right)^2$$
$$5x-4 = 2+3x$$
$$2x = 6$$
$$x = 3$$

The number is 3 .

29. Let x represent the unknown number. The equation is $x+3 = \sqrt{x+3}$.

$$x+3 = \sqrt{x+3}$$
$$(x+3)^2 = \left(\sqrt{x+3}\right)^2$$
$$x^2+6x+9 = x+3$$
$$x^2+5x+6 = 0$$
$$(x+2)(x+3) = 0$$
$$x+2 = 0 \quad \text{or} \quad x+3 = 0$$
$$x = -2 \qquad\qquad x = -3$$

The number is either -3 or -2.

31. Let x represent the unknown number. The equation is $x+3 = \sqrt{2x+14}$.

$$x+3 = \sqrt{2x+14}$$
$$(x+3)^2 = \left(\sqrt{2x+14}\right)^2$$
$$x^2+6x+9 = 2x+14$$
$$x^2+4x-5 = 0$$
$$(x+5)(x-1) = 0$$
$$x+5 = 0 \quad \text{or} \quad x-1 = 0$$
$$\cancel{x=-5} \qquad\qquad x = 1$$

The number is 1.

33. Let x represent the unknown number. The equation is $x-2 = \sqrt{7x-26}$.

$$x-2 = \sqrt{7x-26}$$
$$(x-2)^2 = \left(\sqrt{7x-26}\right)^2$$
$$x^2-4x+4 = 7x-26$$
$$x^2-11x+30 = 0$$
$$(x-5)(x-6) = 0$$
$$x-5 = 0 \quad \text{or} \quad x-6 = 0$$
$$x = 5 \qquad\qquad x = 6$$

The number is either 5 or 6.

35. Let h represent the length of the hypotenuse.

$$h = x\sqrt{2}$$
$$= 5\sqrt{6}\left(\sqrt{2}\right)$$
$$= 5\sqrt{12}$$
$$= 5\sqrt{4\cdot 3}$$
$$= 10\sqrt{3}$$

The length of the hypotenuse is $10\sqrt{3}$ feet.

37. Let l represent the length of the legs.

$$l = \frac{6\sqrt{18}}{\sqrt{2}}$$
$$= 6\sqrt{\frac{18}{2}}$$
$$= 6\sqrt{9}$$
$$= 6\cdot 3$$
$$= 18$$

The length of the legs is 18 meters.

39. Let l represent the length of the longer leg.

$$l = a\sqrt{3}$$
$$= 2\sqrt{6}\left(\sqrt{3}\right)$$
$$= 2\sqrt{18}$$
$$= 2\sqrt{9\cdot 2}$$
$$= 6\sqrt{2}$$

The length of the longer leg is $6\sqrt{2}$ meters.

Let h represent the length of the hypotenuse.

$$h = 2a$$
$$= 2\left(2\sqrt{6}\right)$$
$$= 4\sqrt{6}$$

The length of the hypotenuse is $4\sqrt{6}$ meters.

41. Let l represent the length of the shorter leg.

$$l = \frac{6\sqrt{3}}{2}$$
$$= 3\sqrt{3}$$

The length of the shorter leg is $3\sqrt{3}$ feet.

Let L represent the length of the longer leg.

$$L = l\sqrt{3}$$
$$= 3\sqrt{3}\left(\sqrt{3}\right)$$
$$= 3\sqrt{9}$$
$$= 3\cdot 3$$
$$= 9$$

The length of the longer leg is 9 feet.

43. Prepare We need to determine how many pints of paint the cheerleaders will need to paint their megaphones by using the given information and the formula for the surface area of a right circular cone.

Plan To determine how many pints of paint the cheerleaders will need, we must find the total surface area of all 9 megaphones. Then we can divide the total surface area by the surface area that 1 pint of paint will cover. The radius of each megaphone is $r = 6$ inches. The height of each megaphone is $h = 36$ inches.

Process

$$SA = \pi r \sqrt{r^2 + h^2}$$
$$= \pi(6)\sqrt{(6)^2 + (36)^2}$$
$$= 6\pi\sqrt{1,332} \text{ square inches}$$

We need to estimate the surface area in order to divide it by 1,800 square inches.

$$6\pi\sqrt{1,332} = 6\pi \cdot 6\sqrt{37}$$
$$= 36\pi\sqrt{37}$$
$$\approx 688 \text{ square inches}$$

Because there are 9 megaphones, the total surface area is 688 times 9 square inches, which equals 6,192 square inches. To determine how many pints of paint will be needed, divide 6,192 by 1,800, which equals 3.44. Therefore, the cheerleaders will need 4 pints of paint.

Ponder Does our answer seem reasonable? Yes. If our arithmetic is correct, each megaphone has a surface area of roughly 700 square inches. If one pint of paint would cover 1,800 square inches, then one pint of paint would be enough for roughly two megaphones. Because there are 9 megaphones, that would be roughly 4 pints of paint.

45. Prepare We need to determine how long it takes Jane's camera to hit the ground.

Plan Using the formula and the information $d = 1,728$ feet, we will solve for the time t.

Process

$$t = \sqrt{\frac{d}{16}}$$
$$= \sqrt{\frac{1,728}{16}}$$
$$= \sqrt{108}$$
$$= 6\sqrt{3}$$

It will take $6\sqrt{3}$, or approximately 10.40 seconds, for the camera to hit the ground.

Ponder Does our answer seem reasonable? Yes. It seems reasonable that it would take a little over 10 seconds for an object to fall 1,728 feet.

47. Prepare Using the given formula, we are to determine the radius of the time capsule with a surface area of 12 square feet.

Plan Use the formula $r = \sqrt{\dfrac{S}{4\pi}}$ and the fact that $S = 12$ square feet.

Process

$$r = \sqrt{\frac{S}{4\pi}}$$
$$= \sqrt{\frac{12}{4\pi}}$$
$$= \sqrt{\frac{3}{\pi}}$$
$$= \frac{\sqrt{3\pi}}{\pi}$$
$$\approx 0.98 \text{ ft.}$$

The radius of the time capsule is approximately 0.98 foot.

Ponder Does our answer seem reasonable? Yes. This is a reasonable radius for a time capsule. A quick check of our arithmetic will also show our answer is correct.

49. $d = \sqrt{(x_2 - x_1)^2 + (y_2 - y_1)^2}$
$$= \sqrt{\left(\frac{1}{2} - 1\right)^2 + \left(1 - \frac{2}{3}\right)^2}$$
$$= \sqrt{\left(-\frac{1}{2}\right)^2 + \left(\frac{1}{3}\right)^2}$$
$$= \sqrt{\frac{1}{4} + \frac{1}{9}}$$
$$= \sqrt{\frac{13}{36}}$$
$$= \frac{\sqrt{13}}{6}$$

51. Let l represent the length of the shorter leg.

$$l = \frac{\frac{\sqrt{6}}{5}}{\sqrt{3}}$$

$$= \frac{\sqrt{6}}{5\sqrt{3}} \cdot \frac{\sqrt{3}}{\sqrt{3}}$$

$$= \frac{\sqrt{18}}{15}$$

$$= \frac{3\sqrt{2}}{15}$$

$$= \frac{\sqrt{2}}{5}$$

The length of the shorter leg is $\dfrac{\sqrt{2}}{5}$ cm.

Let h represent the length of the hypotenuse.

$$h = 2l$$

$$= 2\left(\frac{\sqrt{2}}{5}\right)$$

$$= \frac{2\sqrt{2}}{5}$$

The length of the hypotenuse is $\dfrac{2\sqrt{2}}{5}$ cm.

53. The distance between $(-2,-3)$ and $(0,1)$ is:

$$d = \sqrt{(x_2 - x_1)^2 + (y_2 - y_1)^2}$$

$$= \sqrt{(0-(-2))^2 + (1-(-3))^2}$$

$$= \sqrt{(-2)^2 + (4)^2}$$

$$= \sqrt{4+16}$$

$$= \sqrt{20}$$

$$= \sqrt{4 \cdot 5}$$

$$= 2\sqrt{5}$$

The distance between $(2,5)$ and $(0,1)$ is:

$$d = \sqrt{(x_2 - x_1)^2 + (y_2 - y_1)^2}$$

$$= \sqrt{(0-(2))^2 + (1-(5))^2}$$

$$= \sqrt{(-2)^2 + (-4)^2}$$

$$= \sqrt{4+16}$$

$$= \sqrt{20}$$

$$= \sqrt{4 \cdot 5}$$

$$= 2\sqrt{5}$$

Because the distances are the same, $(0,1)$ is the midpoint.

8.5 Exercises

1. If $a > 0$, then $\sqrt[n]{a}$ is the <u>principal</u> $\underline{n^{th}}$ root of a.

3. If $a < 0$, and n is odd, then $\sqrt[n]{a}$ exists and is a <u>negative</u> <u>principal</u> <u>root</u>.

5. When rewriting $a^{\frac{m}{n}}$ as an equivalent radical expression, m is the <u>power</u>.

7. $\sqrt[3]{8} = 2$

9. $\sqrt[4]{81} = 3$

11. $\sqrt[4]{-81}$ is not a real number

13. $\sqrt[3]{-\dfrac{1}{8}} = -\dfrac{1}{2}$

15. $-\sqrt[4]{256} = (-1)\sqrt[4]{256}$
$\qquad = (-1)4$
$\qquad = -4$

17. $-\sqrt[3]{-\dfrac{125}{27}} = (-1)\sqrt[3]{-\dfrac{125}{27}}$
$\qquad = (-1)\left(-\dfrac{5}{3}\right)$
$\qquad = \dfrac{5}{3}$

19. $\sqrt[3]{81} = \sqrt[3]{27 \cdot 3}$
$\qquad = \sqrt[3]{27} \cdot \sqrt[3]{3}$
$\qquad = 3\sqrt[3]{3}$

21. $\sqrt[4]{32x^8} = \sqrt[4]{16x^8 \cdot 2}$
$\qquad = \sqrt[4]{16x^8} \cdot \sqrt[4]{2}$
$\qquad = 2x^2\sqrt[4]{2}$

23. $\sqrt[5]{128a^{10}b^{12}} = \sqrt[5]{32a^{10}b^{10} \cdot 4b^2}$
$\qquad = \sqrt[5]{32a^{10}b^{10}} \cdot \sqrt[5]{4b^2}$
$\qquad = 2a^2b^2\sqrt[5]{4b^2}$

25. $\sqrt[3]{-ch^{27}k^{24}} = \sqrt[3]{-h^{27}k^{24} \cdot c}$
$\qquad = \sqrt[3]{-h^{27}k^{24}} \cdot \sqrt[3]{c}$
$\qquad = -h^9k^8\sqrt[3]{c}$

27. $\sqrt[3]{\dfrac{1}{3}} = \dfrac{\sqrt[3]{1}}{\sqrt[3]{3}}$
$\qquad = \dfrac{1}{\sqrt[3]{3}} \cdot \dfrac{\sqrt[3]{9}}{\sqrt[3]{9}}$
$\qquad = \dfrac{\sqrt[3]{9}}{\sqrt[3]{27}}$
$\qquad = \dfrac{\sqrt[3]{9}}{3}$

29. $\sqrt[4]{\dfrac{2}{x^3}} = \dfrac{\sqrt[4]{2}}{\sqrt[4]{x^3}} \cdot \dfrac{\sqrt[4]{x}}{\sqrt[4]{x}}$
$\qquad = \dfrac{\sqrt[4]{2x}}{\sqrt[4]{x^4}}$
$\qquad = \dfrac{\sqrt[4]{2x}}{x}$

31. $7\sqrt[5]{10} - \sqrt[5]{10} + 4\sqrt[5]{10} = (7 - 1 + 4)\sqrt[5]{10}$
$\qquad = 10\sqrt[5]{10}$

33. $2\sqrt[5]{160a} + \sqrt[5]{5a} = 2\sqrt[5]{32 \cdot 5a} + \sqrt[5]{a}$
$\qquad = 2 \cdot 2\sqrt[5]{5a} + \sqrt[5]{5a}$
$\qquad = 4\sqrt[5]{5a} + \sqrt[5]{5a}$
$\qquad = (4 + 1)\sqrt[5]{5a}$
$\qquad = 5\sqrt[5]{5a}$

35. $\sqrt[3]{16} + 12\sqrt[3]{2} - \sqrt[3]{54} = \sqrt[3]{8 \cdot 2} + 12\sqrt[3]{2} - \sqrt[3]{27 \cdot 2}$
$\qquad = 2\sqrt[3]{2} + 12\sqrt[3]{2} - 3\sqrt[3]{2}$
$\qquad = (2 + 12 - 3)\sqrt[3]{2}$
$\qquad = 11\sqrt[3]{2}$

37. $\sqrt[4]{81} + \sqrt[4]{48} - 7\sqrt[4]{3} = 3 + \sqrt[4]{16 \cdot 3} - 7\sqrt[4]{3}$
$\qquad = 3 + 2\sqrt[4]{3} - 7\sqrt[4]{3}$
$\qquad = 3 + (2 - 7)\sqrt[4]{3}$
$\qquad = 3 - 5\sqrt[4]{3}$

39. $\sqrt[3]{250} + 2\sqrt[4]{5} = \sqrt[3]{125 \cdot 2} + 2\sqrt[4]{5}$
$\qquad = 5\sqrt[3]{2} + 2\sqrt[4]{5}$

41. $\sqrt[6]{16} \cdot \sqrt[6]{12} = \sqrt[6]{192}$
$\qquad = \sqrt[6]{64 \cdot 3}$
$\qquad = 2\sqrt[6]{3}$

43. $\sqrt[3]{25x^2} \cdot \sqrt[3]{30x^2} = \sqrt[3]{750x^4}$

$\qquad = \sqrt[3]{125x^3 \cdot 6x}$

$\qquad = 5x\sqrt[3]{6x}$

45. $\left(\sqrt[3]{18xy^2}\right)^2 = \sqrt[3]{18xy^2} \cdot \sqrt[3]{18xy^2}$

$\qquad = \sqrt[3]{324x^2 y^4}$

$\qquad = \sqrt[3]{27y^3 \cdot 12x^2 y}$

$\qquad = 3y\sqrt[3]{12x^2 y}$

47. $\sqrt[3]{9}\left(\sqrt[3]{3} - \sqrt[3]{24}\right) = \sqrt[3]{9} \cdot \sqrt[3]{3} - \sqrt[3]{9} \cdot \sqrt[3]{24}$

$\qquad = \sqrt[3]{27} - \sqrt[3]{216}$

$\qquad = 3 - 6$

$\qquad = -3$

49. $\sqrt{7} = 7^{\frac{1}{2}}$

51. $\sqrt[3]{5} = 5^{\frac{1}{3}}$

53. $-\sqrt{6} = (-1)6^{\frac{1}{2}}$

$\qquad = -6^{\frac{1}{2}}$

55. $\sqrt[3]{\dfrac{1}{4}} = \left(\dfrac{1}{4}\right)^{\frac{1}{3}}$

57. $49^{\frac{1}{2}} = \sqrt{49}$

$\qquad = 7$

59. $(-8)^{\frac{1}{3}} = \sqrt[3]{-8}$

$\qquad = -2$

61. $(-100)^{\frac{1}{2}} = \sqrt{-100}$

$\qquad$ not a real number

63. $-625^{\frac{1}{4}} = (-1)625^{\frac{1}{4}}$

$\qquad = (-1)\sqrt[4]{625}$

$\qquad = (-1)5$

$\qquad = -5$

65. $\left(\dfrac{4}{9}\right)^{\frac{1}{2}} = \sqrt{\dfrac{4}{9}}$

$\qquad = \dfrac{2}{3}$

67. $16^{\frac{3}{2}} = \left(\sqrt{16}\right)^3$

$\qquad = (4)^3$

$\qquad = 64$

69. $(-32)^{\frac{2}{5}} = \left(\sqrt[5]{-32}\right)^2$

$\qquad = (-2)^2$

$\qquad = 4$

71. $27^{\frac{3}{2}} = \left(\sqrt{27}\right)^3$

$\qquad = \left(\sqrt{9 \cdot 3}\right)^3$

$\qquad = \left(3\sqrt{3}\right)^3$

$\qquad = 3\sqrt{3} \cdot 3\sqrt{3} \cdot 3\sqrt{3}$

$\qquad = 27\sqrt{27}$

$\qquad = 27\sqrt{9 \cdot 3}$

$\qquad = 27 \cdot 3\sqrt{3}$

$\qquad = 81\sqrt{3}$

73. $8^{\frac{2}{3}} = \left(\sqrt[3]{8}\right)^2$

$\qquad = (2)^2$

$\qquad = 4$

75. $\left(\dfrac{8}{27}\right)^{\frac{2}{3}} = \left(\sqrt[3]{\dfrac{8}{27}}\right)^2$

$\qquad = \left(\dfrac{2}{3}\right)^2$

$\qquad = \dfrac{4}{9}$

77. $3^{\frac{1}{2}} \cdot 3^{\frac{5}{2}} = 3^{\frac{1}{2} + \frac{5}{2}}$

$\qquad = 3^{\frac{6}{2}}$

$\qquad = 3^3$

$\qquad = 27$

351

79. $x^{\frac{2}{3}} \cdot x^{\frac{10}{3}} = x^{\frac{2}{3}+\frac{10}{3}}$

$\qquad = x^{\frac{12}{3}}$

$\qquad = x^4$

81. $\left(4^{\frac{3}{5}}\right)^5 = 4^3$

$\qquad = 64$

83. $\left(8x^{\frac{1}{3}}\right)^{\frac{2}{3}} = 8^{\frac{2}{3}} x^{\frac{2}{9}}$

$\qquad = 4x^{\frac{2}{9}}$

85. $\dfrac{a^{\frac{3}{5}}}{a^{\frac{1}{5}}} = a^{\frac{3}{5}-\frac{1}{5}}$

$\qquad = a^{\frac{2}{5}}$

87. $25^{-\frac{3}{2}} = \dfrac{1}{25^{\frac{3}{2}}}$

$\qquad = \dfrac{1}{\left(\sqrt{25}\right)^3}$

$\qquad = \dfrac{1}{5^3}$

$\qquad = \dfrac{1}{125}$

89. $\left(36x^{-\frac{2}{3}}\right)^{-\frac{1}{2}} = 36^{-\frac{1}{2}} x^{\frac{1}{3}}$

$\qquad = \dfrac{x^{\frac{1}{3}}}{36^{\frac{1}{2}}}$

$\qquad = \dfrac{x^{\frac{1}{3}}}{\sqrt{36}}$

$\qquad = \dfrac{x^{\frac{1}{3}}}{6}$

91. $\dfrac{a^{-8}b}{a^{\frac{1}{2}}b^{\frac{2}{5}}} = a^{-8-\frac{1}{2}} b^{1-\frac{2}{5}}$

$\qquad = a^{-\frac{17}{2}} b^{\frac{3}{5}}$

$\qquad = \dfrac{b^{\frac{3}{5}}}{a^{\frac{17}{2}}}$

93. $\sqrt[6]{4^3} = 4^{\frac{3}{6}}$

$\qquad = 4^{\frac{1}{2}}$

$\qquad = \sqrt{4}$

$\qquad = 2$

95. To simplify $25^{\frac{1}{2}}$, take the square root of 25 raised to the power 1. Because $25^1 = 25$, the square root of 25 is 5.

97. $s = \sqrt{\dfrac{p(1-p)}{n}}$

$\qquad = \sqrt{\dfrac{0.2(1-0.2)}{100}}$

$\qquad = \sqrt{\dfrac{0.16}{100}}$

$\qquad = \sqrt{0.0016}$

$\qquad = 0.04$

99. $s = \sqrt[3]{V}$

$\qquad = \sqrt[3]{216}$

$\qquad = 6$ ft.

101. $\sqrt[5]{4a^5b^7} - 8ab\sqrt[5]{4b^2} = \sqrt[5]{a^5b^5 \cdot 4b^2} - 8ab\sqrt[5]{4b^2}$

$\qquad = ab\sqrt[5]{4b^2} - 8ab\sqrt[5]{4b^2}$

$\qquad = (ab - 8ab)\sqrt[5]{4b^2}$

$\qquad = -7ab\sqrt[5]{4b^2}$

103. $\left(5\sqrt[3]{4} + \sqrt[3]{12}\right)\left(\sqrt[3]{2} - 2\sqrt[3]{6}\right)$

$\qquad = 5\sqrt[3]{4} \cdot \sqrt[3]{2} - 5\sqrt[3]{4} \cdot 2\sqrt[3]{6} + \sqrt[3]{12} \cdot \sqrt[3]{2} - \sqrt[3]{12} \cdot 2\sqrt[3]{6}$

$\qquad = 5\sqrt[3]{8} - 10\sqrt[3]{24} + \sqrt[3]{24} - 2\sqrt[3]{72}$

$\qquad = 5 \cdot 2 - 10\sqrt[3]{8 \cdot 3} + \sqrt[3]{8 \cdot 3} - 2\sqrt[3]{8 \cdot 9}$

$\qquad = 10 - 20\sqrt[3]{3} + 2\sqrt[3]{3} - 4\sqrt[3]{9}$

$\qquad = 10 - (20-2)\sqrt[3]{3} - 4\sqrt[3]{9}$

$\qquad = 10 - 18\sqrt[3]{3} - 4\sqrt[3]{9}$

105. $(-8)^{-\frac{2}{3}} = \dfrac{1}{(-8)^{\frac{2}{3}}}$

$\qquad\qquad = \dfrac{1}{\left(\sqrt[3]{-8}\right)^2}$

$\qquad\qquad = \dfrac{1}{(-2)^2}$

$\qquad\qquad = \dfrac{1}{4}$

107. $\dfrac{x^{\frac{3}{4}} y^{-\frac{1}{2}}}{x^{\frac{2}{3}} y^6} = x^{\frac{3}{4}-\frac{2}{3}} y^{-\frac{1}{2}-6}$

$\qquad\qquad = x^{\frac{1}{12}} y^{-\frac{13}{2}}$

$\qquad\qquad = \dfrac{x^{\frac{1}{12}}}{y^{\frac{13}{2}}}$

8.6 Exercises

1. $g(x) = \sqrt[3]{5x - 12}$ is an example of a <u>radical</u> <u>function</u>.

3. To solve the equation $\sqrt[5]{3x + 7} = \sqrt[5]{8x - 18}$, we apply the <u>power</u> rule.

5. The first step in solving the radical equation $5 + \sqrt[4]{8x} = 7$ would be to <u>isolate</u> $\sqrt[4]{8x}$ by <u>subtracting</u> 5 from both sides of the equation.

7. When solving the radical equation $\sqrt[4]{x + 5} = -3$, one possible solution is $x = 76$. This is called an <u>extraneous</u> <u>solution</u> because it does not check.

9. b

11. c

13. $x - 5 \geq 0$
$$x \geq 5$$
$$D_f = [5, \infty)$$

15. $D_g = (-\infty, \infty)$

17. $6 - 12x \geq 0$
$$-12x \geq -6$$
$$x \leq \frac{1}{2}$$
$$D_g = \left(-\infty, \frac{1}{2}\right]$$

19. $D_f = (-\infty, \infty)$

21. $\sqrt[4]{x + 23} = 2$
$$\left(\sqrt[4]{x + 23}\right)^4 = (2)^4$$
$$x + 23 = 16$$
$$x = -7$$
Solution Set: $\{-7\}$

23. $\sqrt[6]{3x + 1} = 1$
$$\left(\sqrt[6]{3x + 1}\right)^6 = (1)^6$$
$$3x + 1 = 1$$
$$3x = 0$$
$$x = 0$$
Solution Set: $\{0\}$

25. $\sqrt[3]{x - 5} = 3$
$$\left(\sqrt[3]{x - 5}\right)^3 = (3)^3$$
$$x - 5 = 27$$
$$x = 32$$
Solution Set: $\{32\}$

27. $\sqrt[3]{36 - 5x} = 5$
$$\left(\sqrt[3]{36 - 5x}\right)^3 = (5)^3$$
$$36 - 5x = 125$$
$$-5x = 89$$
$$x = -\frac{89}{5}$$
Solution Set: $\left\{-\frac{89}{5}\right\}$

29. $\sqrt[4]{-6x} = 2$
$$\left(\sqrt[4]{-6x}\right)^4 = (2)^4$$
$$-6x = 16$$
$$x = -\frac{8}{3}$$
Solution Set: $\left\{-\frac{8}{3}\right\}$

31. $21 + \sqrt[3]{49x} = 30$
$$\sqrt[3]{49x} = 9$$
$$\left(\sqrt[3]{49x}\right)^3 = (9)^3$$
$$49x = 729$$
$$x = \frac{729}{49}$$
Solution Set: $\left\{\frac{729}{49}\right\}$

33. $\sqrt[3]{5 - 4x} - 9 = -8$
$$\sqrt[3]{5 - 4x} = 1$$
$$\left(\sqrt[3]{5 - 4x}\right)^3 = (1)^3$$
$$5 - 4x = 1$$
$$-4x = -4$$
$$x = 1$$
Solution Set: $\{1\}$

35. $\sqrt[5]{10x-12}+2=0$

$\sqrt[5]{10x-12}=-2$

$\left(\sqrt[5]{10x-12}\right)^5=(-2)^5$

$10x-12=-32$

$10x=-20$

$x=-2$

Solution Set: $\{-2\}$

37. $\sqrt[4]{7,470-11x}=-10$

$\left(\sqrt[4]{7,470-11x}\right)^4=(-10)^4$

$7,470-11x=10,000$

$-11x=2,530$

$\cancel{x=-230}$

Solution Set: $\{\ \}$

39. $\sqrt[5]{5x+15}=\sqrt[5]{2x^2+12}$

$\left(\sqrt[5]{5x+15}\right)^5=\left(\sqrt[5]{2x^2+12}\right)^5$

$5x+15=2x^2+12$

$0=2x^2-5x-3$

$0=(2x+1)(x-3)$

$2x+1=0$ or $x-3=0$

$x=-\dfrac{1}{2}$ $x=3$

Solution Set: $\left\{-\dfrac{1}{2},3\right\}$

41. $\sqrt[3]{2x+7}-\sqrt[3]{4x+6}=0$

$\left(\sqrt[3]{2x+7}\right)^3=\left(\sqrt[3]{4x+6}\right)^3$

$2x+7=4x+6$

$-2x=-1$

$x=\dfrac{1}{2}$

Solution Set: $\left\{\dfrac{1}{2}\right\}$

43. $\sqrt[4]{5x-15}=\sqrt[4]{3x-x^2}$

$\left(\sqrt[4]{5x-15}\right)^4=\left(\sqrt[4]{3x-x^2}\right)^4$

$5x-15=3x-x^2$

$x^2+2x-15=0$

$(x+5)(x-3)=0$

$x+5=0$ or $x-3=0$

$\cancel{x=-5}$ $x=3$

Solution Set: $\{3\}$

45. $\sqrt[4]{2x^2-4x}-\sqrt[4]{2x}=0$

$\sqrt[4]{2x^2-4x}=\sqrt[4]{2x}$

$\left(\sqrt[4]{2x^2-4x}\right)^4=\left(\sqrt[4]{2x}\right)^4$

$2x^2-4x=2x$

$2x^2-6x=0$

$2x(x-3)=0$

$2x=0$ or $x-3=0$

$x=0$ $x=3$

Solution Set: $\{0,3\}$

47. $1+\sqrt[3]{4x^2}=9$

$\sqrt[3]{4x^2}=8$

$\left(\sqrt[3]{4x^2}\right)^3=(8)^3$

$4x^2=512$

$4x^2-512=0$

$\left(2x+\sqrt{512}\right)\left(2x-\sqrt{512}\right)=0$

$2x+\sqrt{512}=0$ or $2x-\sqrt{512}=0$

$x=-\dfrac{\sqrt{512}}{2}$ $x=\dfrac{\sqrt{512}}{2}$

$x=-\dfrac{16\sqrt{2}}{2}$ $x=\dfrac{16\sqrt{2}}{2}$

$x=-8\sqrt{2}$ $x=8\sqrt{2}$

Solution Set: $\left\{-8\sqrt{2},8\sqrt{2}\right\}$

49. $\sqrt[5]{3+80x}=3$

$\left(\sqrt[5]{3+80x}\right)^5=(3)^5$

$3+80x=243$

$80x=240$

$x=3$

Solution Set: $\{3\}$

51. $\sqrt[3]{x^2+2x}-2=0$

$\sqrt[3]{x^2+2x}=2$

$\left(\sqrt[3]{x^2+2x}\right)^3=(2)^3$

$x^2+2x=8$

$x^2+2x-8=0$

$(x+4)(x-2)=0$

$x+4=0$ or $x-2=0$

$x=-4$ $x=2$

Solution Set: $\{-4,2\}$

53. Answers will vary; for example: To determine if a potential solution is extraneous, plug the solution into the original problem to verify that it creates a true statement.

55. Answers will vary; for example: Because the fourth root of a real number is not a negative number.

57. Answers will vary; for example: To find the excluded values and determine the domain of a radical function $f(x)=\sqrt{2x-5}$, create an inequality with the radicand set greater than or equal to zero.

59. Let x represent the unknown number. The equation is $\sqrt[4]{x+1}=\sqrt[4]{2x-2}$.

$\sqrt[4]{x+1}=\sqrt[4]{2x-2}$

$\left(\sqrt[4]{x+1}\right)^4=\left(\sqrt[4]{2x-2}\right)^4$

$x+1=2x-2$

$3=x$

The number is 3.

61. Let x represent the unknown number. The equation is $\sqrt[6]{7x}=\sqrt[6]{3+x}$.

$\sqrt[6]{7x}=\sqrt[6]{3+x}$

$\left(\sqrt[6]{7x}\right)^6=\left(\sqrt[6]{3+x}\right)^6$

$7x=3+x$

$6x=3$

$x=\dfrac{1}{2}$

The number is $\frac{1}{2}$.

63. Let x represent the unknown number. The equation is $\sqrt[3]{2x}=\sqrt[3]{x+4}$.

$\sqrt[3]{2x}=\sqrt[3]{x+4}$

$\left(\sqrt[3]{2x}\right)^3=\left(\sqrt[3]{x+4}\right)^3$

$2x=x+4$

$x=4$

The number is 4.

65. Let x represent the unknown number. The equation is $\sqrt[4]{1+x}=\sqrt[4]{2x+1}$.

$\sqrt[4]{1+x}=\sqrt[4]{2x+1}$

$\left(\sqrt[4]{1+x}\right)^4=\left(\sqrt[4]{2x+1}\right)^4$

$1+x=2x+1$

$0=x$

The number is 0.

67. $\left(24x-2x^2\right)^{1/3}-x=0$

$\left(24x-2x^2\right)^{1/3}=x$

$\sqrt[3]{24x-2x^2}=x$

$\left(\sqrt[3]{24x-2x^2}\right)^3=x^3$

$24x-2x^2=x^3$

$0=x^3+2x^2-24x$

$0=x(x+6)(x-4)$

$x=0$ or $x+6=0$ or $x-4=0$

$x=-6$ $x=4$

Solution Set: $\{-6,0,4\}$

Chapter 8 Review Problem Set

1. $\sqrt{25} = 5$

2. $-\sqrt{49} = (-1)\sqrt{49}$
$= (-1)7$
$= -7$

3. $\sqrt{\dfrac{100}{9}} = \dfrac{10}{3}$

4. $\sqrt{-\dfrac{1}{81}}$ is not a real number

5. $\sqrt{20} = \sqrt{4 \cdot 5}$
$= \sqrt{4} \cdot \sqrt{5}$
$= 2\sqrt{5}$

6. $\sqrt{72} = \sqrt{36 \cdot 2}$
$= \sqrt{36} \cdot \sqrt{2}$
$= 6\sqrt{2}$

7. $\sqrt{450} = \sqrt{225 \cdot 2}$
$= \sqrt{225} \cdot \sqrt{2}$
$= 15\sqrt{2}$

8. $\sqrt{216} = \sqrt{36 \cdot 6}$
$= \sqrt{36} \cdot \sqrt{6}$
$= 6\sqrt{6}$

9. $\sqrt{(15x)^2} = |15x|$
$= |15||x|$
$= 15|x|$

10. $-\sqrt{(144a)^2} = (-1)\sqrt{(144a)^2}$
$= (-1)|12a|$
$= (-1)|12||a|$
$= -12|a|$

11. $\sqrt{(2x+5)^2} = |2x+5|$

12. $\sqrt{x^2 - 12x + 36} = \sqrt{(x-6)^2}$
$= |x-6|$

13. $\sqrt{x^{16}} = x^8$

14. $\sqrt{y^{21}} = \sqrt{y^{20} \cdot y}$
$= \sqrt{y^{20}} \cdot \sqrt{y}$
$= y^{10}\sqrt{y}$

15. $\sqrt{18a^7b^{10}} = \sqrt{9a^6b^{10} \cdot 2a}$
$= \sqrt{9a^6b^{10}} \cdot \sqrt{2a}$
$= 3a^3b^5\sqrt{2a}$

16. $\sqrt{120x^{12}y^9z} = \sqrt{4x^{12}y^8 \cdot 30yz}$
$= \sqrt{4x^{12}y^8} \cdot \sqrt{30yz}$
$= 2x^6y^4\sqrt{30yz}$

17. $7\sqrt{7} - 14\sqrt{7} + \sqrt{7} = (7 - 14 + 1)\sqrt{7}$
$= -6\sqrt{7}$

18. $\sqrt{27} + 5\sqrt{3} = \sqrt{9 \cdot 3} + 5\sqrt{3}$
$= \sqrt{9}\sqrt{3} + 5\sqrt{3}$
$= 3\sqrt{3} + 5\sqrt{3}$
$= (3 + 5)\sqrt{3}$
$= 8\sqrt{3}$

19. $18\sqrt{2a^2} - 6\sqrt{18a^2} = 18\sqrt{a^2 \cdot 2} - 6\sqrt{9a^2 \cdot 2}$
$= 18\sqrt{a^2}\sqrt{2} - 6\sqrt{9a^2}\sqrt{2}$
$= 18a\sqrt{2} - 6 \cdot 3a\sqrt{2}$
$= 18a\sqrt{2} - 18a\sqrt{2}$
$= (18a - 18a)\sqrt{2}$
$= 0\sqrt{2}$
$= 0$

20. $9y\sqrt{20x}+\sqrt{45x}-8y\sqrt{5x}$

$=9y\sqrt{4\cdot5x}+\sqrt{9\cdot5x}-8y\sqrt{5x}$

$=9y\sqrt{4}\sqrt{5x}+\sqrt{9}\sqrt{5x}-8y\sqrt{5x}$

$=9y\cdot2\sqrt{5x}+3\sqrt{5x}-8y\sqrt{5x}$

$=18y\sqrt{5x}+3\sqrt{5x}-8y\sqrt{5x}$

$=(18y+3-8y)\sqrt{5x}$

$=(10y+3)\sqrt{5x}$

$=10y\sqrt{5x}+3\sqrt{5x}$

21. Prepare We need to determine the length of the diagonal of a rectangle given its length and width.

Plan Because the length, width, and diagonal of a rectangle form a right triangle, we can use the Pythagorean theorem to find the length of the diagonal.

Process Let $c=$ the length of the diagonal, $a=$ the width of the rectangle, and $b=$ the length of the rectangle. Given that $a=2$ and $b=6$, the equation becomes $(2)^2+(6)^2=c^2$.

$$(2)^2+(6)^2=c^2$$
$$40=c^2$$
$$0=c^2-40$$
$$0=\left(c+\sqrt{40}\right)\left(c-\sqrt{40}\right)$$
$$c+\sqrt{40}=0 \quad\text{or}\quad c-\sqrt{40}=0$$
$$\cancel{c=-\sqrt{40}} \qquad c=\sqrt{40}$$

Because the diagonal of a rectangle cannot be negative, simplify only the positive square root.

$$c=\sqrt{40}$$
$$=\sqrt{4\cdot10}$$
$$=\sqrt{4}\cdot\sqrt{10}$$
$$=2\sqrt{10}\ \text{feet}$$

Therefore, the length of the diagonal is $2\sqrt{10}$ feet.

Ponder Does our answer seem reasonable? Yes. Because the diagonal of a rectangle should be longer than the length and the width, it is reasonable that the diagonal could be $2\sqrt{10}\approx6.32$ feet.

22. Prepare We need to determine how far the base of the 10-foot ladder is from the wall of the house.

Plan Keeping in mind that the ladder is resting against the house at a height of 8 feet from the ground and that the wall of the house creates a right angle with the ground, we can use the Pythagorean theorem.

Process The unknown is the distance of the base of the ladder from the wall of the house, so we can let $d=$ that distance (in feet). Therefore, $a^2+b^2=c^2$ becomes the equation $a^2+d^2=c^2$, with $a=8$, $c=10$, and d unknown.

$$a^2+d^2=c^2$$
$$(8)^2+d^2=(10)^2$$
$$64+d^2=100$$
$$d^2-36=0$$
$$(d+6)(d-6)=0$$
$$d+6=0 \quad\text{or}\quad d-6=0$$
$$\cancel{d=-6} \qquad\qquad d=6$$

Because the distance of the base of the ladder from the wall of the house cannot be negative, we take the distance to be 6 feet, that is, the distance of the base of the ladder from the wall of the house is 6 feet.

Ponder Does our answer seem reasonable? Yes. It is reasonable that you would have to set a 10-foot ladder 6 feet from the wall of the house for it to reach 8 feet up the wall.

23. $\sqrt{7}\cdot\sqrt{21}=\sqrt{7\cdot21}$

$=\sqrt{7\cdot7\cdot3}$

$=\sqrt{49\cdot3}$

$=\sqrt{49}\cdot\sqrt{3}$

$=7\sqrt{3}$

24. $\sqrt{12a^2}\cdot\sqrt{15a^2}=\sqrt{12a^2\cdot15a^2}$

$=\sqrt{4a^2\cdot3\cdot5\cdot3a^2}$

$=\sqrt{36a^4\cdot5}$

$=\sqrt{36a^4}\cdot\sqrt{5}$

$=6a^2\sqrt{5}$

25. $\left(2\sqrt{18x}\right)\left(-5\sqrt{8x}\right) = 2\cdot(-5)\sqrt{18x}\cdot\sqrt{8x}$

$\qquad\qquad = -10\sqrt{18x\cdot 8x}$

$\qquad\qquad = -10\sqrt{144x^2}$

$\qquad\qquad = -10\cdot 12x$

$\qquad\qquad = -120x$

26. $\left(5\sqrt{6}\right)^2 = 5^2\left(\sqrt{6}\right)^2$

$\qquad\qquad = 25\sqrt{6}\cdot\sqrt{6}$

$\qquad\qquad = 25\sqrt{36}$

$\qquad\qquad = 25\cdot 6$

$\qquad\qquad = 150$

27. $\sqrt{6}\left(\sqrt{10}-\sqrt{6}\right) = \sqrt{6}\cdot\sqrt{10}-\sqrt{6}\cdot\sqrt{6}$

$\qquad\qquad = \sqrt{60}-\sqrt{36}$

$\qquad\qquad = \sqrt{4\cdot 15}-6$

$\qquad\qquad = 2\sqrt{15}-6$

28. $3\sqrt{2}\left(\sqrt{14}+2\sqrt{6}\right) = 3\sqrt{2}\cdot\sqrt{14}+3\sqrt{2}\cdot 2\sqrt{6}$

$\qquad\qquad = 3\sqrt{28}+6\sqrt{12}$

$\qquad\qquad = 3\sqrt{4\cdot 7}+6\sqrt{4\cdot 3}$

$\qquad\qquad = 3\cdot 2\sqrt{7}+6\cdot 2\sqrt{3}$

$\qquad\qquad = 6\sqrt{7}+12\sqrt{3}$

29. $\left(3\sqrt{2}+4\sqrt{6}\right)\left(5\sqrt{3}-8\sqrt{6}\right)$

$= 3\sqrt{2}\cdot 5\sqrt{3}-3\sqrt{2}\cdot 8\sqrt{6}+4\sqrt{6}\cdot 5\sqrt{3}-4\sqrt{6}\cdot 8\sqrt{6}$

$= 15\sqrt{6}-24\sqrt{12}+20\sqrt{18}-32\sqrt{36}$

$= 15\sqrt{6}-24\sqrt{4\cdot 3}+20\sqrt{9\cdot 2}-32(6)$

$= 15\sqrt{6}-24\cdot 2\sqrt{3}+20\cdot 3\sqrt{2}-192$

$= 15\sqrt{6}-48\sqrt{3}+60\sqrt{2}-192$

30. $\left(4+7\sqrt{5}\right)^2 = (4)^2+2\left(4\cdot 7\sqrt{5}\right)+\left(7\sqrt{5}\right)^2$

$\qquad\qquad = 16+56\sqrt{5}+49\sqrt{25}$

$\qquad\qquad = 16+56\sqrt{5}+49\cdot 5$

$\qquad\qquad = 16+56\sqrt{5}+245$

$\qquad\qquad = 261+56\sqrt{5}$

31. $\dfrac{\sqrt{147}}{\sqrt{3}} = \sqrt{\dfrac{147}{3}}$

$\qquad\quad = \sqrt{49}$

$\qquad\quad = 7$

32. $\dfrac{2\sqrt{600}}{\sqrt{6}} = 2\sqrt{\dfrac{600}{6}}$

$\qquad\quad = 2\sqrt{100}$

$\qquad\quad = 2\cdot 10$

$\qquad\quad = 20$

33. $\dfrac{\sqrt{18x^7}}{\sqrt{3x^5}} = \sqrt{\dfrac{18x^7}{3x^5}}$

$\qquad\quad = \sqrt{6x^2}$

$\qquad\quad = \sqrt{x^2\cdot 6}$

$\qquad\quad = x\sqrt{6}$

34. $\dfrac{20\sqrt{18}}{4\sqrt{3}} = 5\sqrt{\dfrac{18}{3}}$

$\qquad\quad = 5\sqrt{6}$

35. $\dfrac{5}{\sqrt{2}} = \dfrac{5}{\sqrt{2}}\cdot\dfrac{\sqrt{2}}{\sqrt{2}}$

$\qquad = \dfrac{5\sqrt{2}}{\sqrt{4}}$

$\qquad = \dfrac{5\sqrt{2}}{2}$

36. $\dfrac{2}{\sqrt{y}} = \dfrac{2}{\sqrt{y}}\cdot\dfrac{\sqrt{y}}{\sqrt{y}}$

$\qquad = \dfrac{2\sqrt{y}}{\sqrt{y^2}}$

$\qquad = \dfrac{2\sqrt{y}}{y}$

37. $\sqrt{\dfrac{7}{5}} = \dfrac{\sqrt{7}}{\sqrt{5}}\cdot\dfrac{\sqrt{5}}{\sqrt{5}}$

$\qquad = \dfrac{\sqrt{35}}{\sqrt{25}}$

$\qquad = \dfrac{\sqrt{35}}{5}$

38. $\dfrac{\sqrt{6}}{\sqrt{15}} = \dfrac{\sqrt{6}}{\sqrt{15}} \cdot \dfrac{\sqrt{15}}{\sqrt{15}}$

$= \dfrac{\sqrt{90}}{\sqrt{225}}$

$= \dfrac{\sqrt{9 \cdot 10}}{15}$

$= \dfrac{\overset{1}{\cancel{3}}\sqrt{10}}{\underset{5}{\cancel{15}}}$

$= \dfrac{\sqrt{10}}{5}$

39. $\dfrac{\sqrt{24}}{3\sqrt{28}} = \dfrac{\sqrt{4 \cdot 6}}{3\sqrt{4 \cdot 7}}$

$= \dfrac{2\sqrt{6}}{3 \cdot 2\sqrt{7}}$

$= \dfrac{2\sqrt{6}}{6\sqrt{7}} \cdot \dfrac{\sqrt{7}}{\sqrt{7}}$

$= \dfrac{2\sqrt{42}}{6\sqrt{49}}$

$= \dfrac{2\sqrt{42}}{6 \cdot 7}$

$= \dfrac{\overset{1}{\cancel{2}}\sqrt{42}}{\underset{21}{\cancel{42}}}$

$= \dfrac{\sqrt{42}}{21}$

40. $\dfrac{\sqrt{7a^2}}{\sqrt{18b^3}} = \dfrac{\sqrt{a^2 \cdot 7}}{\sqrt{9b^2 \cdot 2b}}$

$= \dfrac{a\sqrt{7}}{3b\sqrt{2b}}$

$= \dfrac{a\sqrt{7}}{3b\sqrt{2b}} \cdot \dfrac{\sqrt{2b}}{\sqrt{2b}}$

$= \dfrac{a\sqrt{14b}}{3b\sqrt{4b^2}}$

$= \dfrac{a\sqrt{14b}}{3b \cdot 2b}$

$= \dfrac{a\sqrt{14b}}{6b^2}$

41. $\dfrac{5}{2+\sqrt{7}} = \left(\dfrac{5}{2+\sqrt{7}}\right)\left(\dfrac{2-\sqrt{7}}{2-\sqrt{7}}\right)$

$= \dfrac{5\left(2-\sqrt{7}\right)}{\left(2\right)^2 - \left(\sqrt{7}\right)^2}$

$= \dfrac{10 - 5\sqrt{7}}{4 - 7}$

$= \dfrac{10 - 5\sqrt{7}}{-3}$

42. $\dfrac{1+\sqrt{5}}{\sqrt{2}-\sqrt{6}} = \left(\dfrac{1+\sqrt{5}}{\sqrt{2}-\sqrt{6}}\right)\left(\dfrac{\sqrt{2}+\sqrt{6}}{\sqrt{2}+\sqrt{6}}\right)$

$= \dfrac{1 \cdot \sqrt{2} + 1 \cdot \sqrt{6} + \sqrt{5} \cdot \sqrt{2} + \sqrt{5} \cdot \sqrt{6}}{\left(\sqrt{2}\right)^2 - \left(\sqrt{6}\right)^2}$

$= \dfrac{\sqrt{2} + \sqrt{6} + \sqrt{10} + \sqrt{30}}{\sqrt{4} - \sqrt{36}}$

$= \dfrac{\sqrt{2} + \sqrt{6} + \sqrt{10} + \sqrt{30}}{2 - 6}$

$= \dfrac{\sqrt{2} + \sqrt{6} + \sqrt{10} + \sqrt{30}}{-4}$

43. $\sqrt{-16 + 5x} = 7$

$\left(\sqrt{-16 + 5x}\right)^2 = \left(7\right)^2$

$-16 + 5x = 49$

$5x = 65$

$x = 13$

Solution Set: $\{13\}$

44. $\sqrt{x^2 - 8x} = \sqrt{-24 - 18x}$

$\left(\sqrt{x^2 - 8x}\right)^2 = \left(\sqrt{-24 - 18x}\right)^2$

$x^2 - 8x = -24 - 18x$

$x^2 + 10x + 24 = 0$

$\left(x + 4\right)\left(x + 6\right) = 0$

$x + 4 = 0 \quad \text{or} \quad x + 6 = 0$

$x = -4 \qquad\qquad x = -6$

Solution Set: $\{-6, -4\}$

45. $20 + \sqrt{5 - 10x} = 15$

$\sqrt{5 - 10x} = -5$

$\left(\sqrt{5 - 10x}\right)^2 = (-5)^2$

$5 - 10x = 25$

$-10x = 20$

$\cancel{x = -2}$

Solution Set: $\{\ \}$

46. $2x - 1 = \sqrt{x^2 - 3x + 1}$

$(2x - 1)^2 = \left(\sqrt{x^2 - 3x + 1}\right)^2$

$4x^2 - 4x + 1 = x^2 - 3x + 1$

$3x^2 - x = 0$

$x(3x - 1) = 0$

$\cancel{x = 0} \quad \text{or} \quad 3x - 1 = 0$

$\cancel{x = \dfrac{1}{3}}$

Solution Set: $\{\ \}$

47. $\sqrt{2x^2 - 3x} - \sqrt{x^2 + 2x - 4} = 0$

$\sqrt{2x^2 - 3x} = \sqrt{x^2 + 2x - 4}$

$\left(\sqrt{2x^2 - 3x}\right)^2 = \left(\sqrt{x^2 + 2x - 4}\right)^2$

$2x^2 - 3x = x^2 + 2x - 4$

$x^2 - 5x + 4 = 0$

$(x - 1)(x - 4) = 0$

$x - 1 = 0 \quad \text{or} \quad x - 4 = 0$

$\cancel{x = 1} \qquad\qquad x = 4$

Solution Set: $\{4\}$

48. $8 - x = \sqrt{-x + 10}$

$(8 - x)^2 = \left(\sqrt{-x + 10}\right)^2$

$64 - 16x + x^2 = -x + 10$

$x^2 - 15x + 54 = 0$

$(x - 6)(x - 9) = 0$

$x - 6 = 0 \quad \text{or} \quad x - 9 = 0$

$x = 6 \qquad\qquad \cancel{x = 9}$

Solution Set: $\{6\}$

49. $\sqrt{x} + 1 = \sqrt{x + 13}$

$\left(\sqrt{x} + 1\right)^2 = \left(\sqrt{x + 13}\right)^2$

$x + 2\sqrt{x} + 1 = x + 13$

$2\sqrt{x} = 12$

$\sqrt{x} = 6$

$\left(\sqrt{x}\right)^2 = (6)^2$

$x = 36$

Solution Set: $\{36\}$

50. $2\sqrt{x^2 - 4} + 3 = \sqrt{x^2 - 1} + 3$

$2\sqrt{x^2 - 4} = \sqrt{x^2 - 1}$

$\left(2\sqrt{x^2 - 4}\right)^2 = \left(\sqrt{x^2 - 1}\right)^2$

$4(x^2 - 4) = x^2 - 1$

$3x^2 - 15 = 0$

$3\left(x + \sqrt{5}\right)\left(x - \sqrt{5}\right) = 0$

$x + \sqrt{5} = 0 \quad \text{or} \quad x - \sqrt{5} = 0$

$x = -\sqrt{5} \qquad\qquad x = \sqrt{5}$

Solution Set: $\left\{-\sqrt{5}, \sqrt{5}\right\}$

51. $d = \sqrt{(x_2 - x_1)^2 + (y_2 - y_1)^2}$

$= \sqrt{(-10 - (-4))^2 + (10 - 2)^2}$

$= \sqrt{(-6)^2 + (-8)^2}$

$= \sqrt{36 + 64}$

$= \sqrt{100}$

$= 10$

52. $d = \sqrt{(x_2 - x_1)^2 + (y_2 - y_1)^2}$

$= \sqrt{(-4 - 0)^2 + (1 - 8)^2}$

$= \sqrt{(-4)^2 + (-7)^2}$

$= \sqrt{16 + 49}$

$= \sqrt{65}$

53. Let l represent the length of the legs.

$$l = \frac{3\sqrt{10}}{\sqrt{2}}$$

$$= 3\sqrt{\frac{10}{2}}$$

$$= 3\sqrt{5}$$

The length of the legs is $3\sqrt{5}$ centimeters.

54. Let l represent the length of the shorter leg.

$$l = \frac{10}{2}$$

$$= 5$$

The length of the shorter leg is 5 yards.

Let L represent the length of the longer leg.

$$L = l\sqrt{3}$$

$$= 5\left(\sqrt{3}\right)$$

$$= 5\sqrt{3}$$

The length of the longer leg is $5\sqrt{3}$ yards.

55. Let x represent the unknown number. The equation is $\sqrt{7x} = \sqrt{4+4x}$.

$$\sqrt{7x} = \sqrt{4+4x}$$

$$\left(\sqrt{7x}\right)^2 = \left(\sqrt{4+4x}\right)^2$$

$$7x = 4+4x$$

$$3x = 4$$

$$x = \frac{4}{3}$$

The number is $\frac{4}{3}$.

56. Let x represent the unknown number. The equation is $7+x = \sqrt{9x+73}$.

$$7+x = \sqrt{9x+73}$$

$$(7+x)^2 = \left(\sqrt{9x+73}\right)^2$$

$$49+14x+x^2 = 9x+73$$

$$x^2+5x-24 = 0$$

$$(x+8)(x-3) = 0$$

$$x+8 = 0 \quad \text{or} \quad x-3 = 0$$

$$\cancel{x = -8} \qquad x = 3$$

The number is 3.

57. Let h represent the length of the hypotenuse.

$$h = x\sqrt{2}$$

$$= 3\sqrt{6}\left(\sqrt{2}\right)$$

$$= 3\sqrt{12}$$

$$= 3\sqrt{4 \cdot 3}$$

$$= 6\sqrt{3}$$

The length of the hypotenuse is $6\sqrt{3}$ centimeters.

58. Let l represent the length of the shorter leg.

$$l = \frac{\sqrt{6}}{2}$$

The length of the shorter leg is $\dfrac{\sqrt{6}}{2}$ inches.

Let L represent the length of the longer leg.

$$L = l\sqrt{3}$$

$$= \frac{\sqrt{6}}{2}\left(\sqrt{3}\right)$$

$$= \frac{\sqrt{18}}{2}$$

$$= \frac{\sqrt{9 \cdot 2}}{2}$$

$$= \frac{3\sqrt{2}}{2}$$

The length of the longer leg is $\dfrac{3\sqrt{2}}{2}$ inches.

59. The distance between $(-5,-3)$ and $(0,2)$ is:

$$d = \sqrt{(x_2-x_1)^2+(y_2-y_1)^2}$$

$$= \sqrt{(0-(-5))^2+(2-(-3))^2}$$

$$= \sqrt{(5)^2+(5)^2}$$

$$= \sqrt{25+25}$$

$$= \sqrt{50}$$

$$= \sqrt{25 \cdot 2}$$

$$= 5\sqrt{2}$$

The distance between $(5,7)$ and $(0,2)$ is:

$$d = \sqrt{(x_2 - x_1)^2 + (y_2 - y_1)^2}$$
$$= \sqrt{(0 - (5))^2 + (2 - (7))^2}$$
$$= \sqrt{(-5)^2 + (-5)^2}$$
$$= \sqrt{25 + 25}$$
$$= \sqrt{50}$$
$$= \sqrt{25 \cdot 2}$$
$$= 5\sqrt{2}$$

Because the distances are the same, $(0, 2)$ is the midpoint.

60. Prepare We need to determine, using the given information and formula for surface area, how much profit Bloomfield Academy will make selling princess hats.

Plan We need to determine how much fabric was purchased to make the hats by finding the total surface area of the 25 hats and dividing the total surface area by the area of one sheet of fabric and then multiply the result by the cost per sheet. We then need to compute the revenue from selling 25 hats and subtract the cost to determine the profit.

Process First compute the surface area of one hat given that $r = 6$ inches and $h = 18$ inches.

$$SA = \pi r \sqrt{r^2 + h^2}$$
$$= \pi(6)\sqrt{(6)^2 + (18)^2}$$
$$= 6\pi\sqrt{360}$$
$$= 36\pi\sqrt{10}$$
$$\approx 357.65 \text{ in.}^2$$

Therefore, the surface area of 25 hats would be approximately $25(357.65) = 8{,}941.25$ square inches. The number of sheets of fabric needed would be $8{,}941.25 \div 576 \approx 16$ sheets. The cost of 16 sheets of fabric would be $16(\$9) = \$144$. The revenue from selling 25 hats would be $25(\$10) = \$250$. The profit would be $\$250 - \$144 = \$106$.

Ponder Does our answer seem reasonable? Yes. It seems reasonable that the profit would be roughly half the revenue.

61. $\sqrt[3]{27} = 3$

62. $\sqrt[4]{-16}$ is not a real number

63. $\sqrt[4]{-625}$ is not a real number

64. $-\sqrt[5]{\dfrac{1}{32}} = (-1)\sqrt[5]{\dfrac{1}{32}}$
$$= (-1)\frac{1}{2}$$
$$= -\frac{1}{2}$$

65. $\sqrt[3]{32} = \sqrt[3]{8 \cdot 4}$
$$= \sqrt[3]{8} \cdot \sqrt[3]{4}$$
$$= 2\sqrt[3]{4}$$

66. $\sqrt[4]{32a^{12}} = \sqrt[4]{16a^{12} \cdot 2}$
$$= \sqrt[4]{16a^{12}} \cdot \sqrt[4]{2}$$
$$= 2a^3\sqrt[4]{2}$$

67. $\sqrt[3]{-54x^{12}y^{10}} = \sqrt[3]{-27x^{12}y^9 \cdot 2y}$
$$= \sqrt[3]{-27x^{12}y^9} \cdot \sqrt[3]{2y}$$
$$= -3x^4y^3\sqrt[3]{2y}$$

68. $\sqrt[4]{\dfrac{1}{2}} = \dfrac{\sqrt[4]{1}}{\sqrt[4]{2}} \cdot \dfrac{\sqrt[4]{8}}{\sqrt[4]{8}}$
$$= \frac{\sqrt[4]{8}}{\sqrt[4]{16}}$$
$$= \frac{\sqrt[4]{8}}{2}$$

69. $7\sqrt[4]{16} - \sqrt[4]{16} + 9\sqrt[4]{16} = 7 \cdot 2 - 2 + 9 \cdot 2$
$$= 14 - 2 + 18$$
$$= 30$$

70. $5\sqrt[3]{54} + 10\sqrt[3]{2} - \sqrt[3]{16} = 5\sqrt[3]{27 \cdot 2} + 10\sqrt[3]{2} - \sqrt[3]{8 \cdot 2}$
$$= 15\sqrt[3]{2} + 10\sqrt[3]{2} - 2\sqrt[3]{2}$$
$$= (15 + 10 - 2)\sqrt[3]{2}$$
$$= 23\sqrt[3]{2}$$

71. $\sqrt[3]{50x^2} \cdot \sqrt[3]{20x^2} = \sqrt[3]{1{,}000x^4}$
$$= \sqrt[3]{1000x^3 \cdot x}$$
$$= 10x\sqrt[3]{x}$$

72. $\sqrt[3]{4}\left(\sqrt[3]{2}+\sqrt[3]{16}\right)=\sqrt[3]{4}\cdot\sqrt[3]{2}+\sqrt[3]{4}\cdot\sqrt[3]{16}$

$$=\sqrt[3]{8}+\sqrt[3]{64}$$

$$=2+4$$

$$=6$$

73. $\sqrt{13}=13^{\frac{1}{2}}$

74. $\sqrt{\dfrac{1}{5}}=\left(\dfrac{1}{5}\right)^{\frac{1}{2}}$

75. $\sqrt[3]{25}=25^{\frac{1}{3}}$

76. $-\sqrt[4]{3}=(-1)\sqrt[4]{3}$

$$=(-1)3^{\frac{1}{4}}$$

$$=-3^{\frac{1}{4}}$$

77. $81^{\frac{1}{2}}=\sqrt{81}$

$$=9$$

78. $(-27)^{\frac{1}{3}}=\sqrt[3]{-27}$

$$=-3$$

79. $25^{\frac{3}{2}}=\left(\sqrt{25}\right)^{3}$

$$=(5)^{3}$$

$$=125$$

80. $(-8)^{\frac{5}{3}}=\left(\sqrt[3]{-8}\right)^{5}$

$$=(-2)^{5}$$

$$=-32$$

81. $x^{\frac{2}{3}}\cdot x^{\frac{10}{3}}=x^{\frac{2}{3}+\frac{10}{3}}$

$$=x^{\frac{12}{3}}$$

$$=x^{4}$$

82. $\left(6^{\frac{2}{3}}\right)^{3}=6^{2}$

$$=36$$

83. $\dfrac{a^{\frac{6}{5}}}{a^{\frac{2}{5}}}=a^{\frac{6}{5}-\frac{2}{5}}$

$$=a^{\frac{4}{5}}$$

84. $16^{-\frac{3}{2}}=\dfrac{1}{16^{\frac{3}{2}}}$

$$=\dfrac{1}{\left(\sqrt{16}\right)^{3}}$$

$$=\dfrac{1}{4^{3}}$$

$$=\dfrac{1}{64}$$

85. $x-8\geq 0$

$$x\geq 8$$

$$D_{f}=[8,\infty)$$

86. $D_{g}=(-\infty,\infty)$

87. $6-3x\geq 0$

$$-3x\geq -6$$

$$x\leq 2$$

$$D_{g}=(-\infty,2]$$

88. $\sqrt{3x+19}=7$

$$\left(\sqrt{3x+19}\right)^{2}=(7)^{2}$$

$$3x+19=49$$

$$3x=30$$

$$x=10$$

Solution Set: $\{10\}$

89. $\sqrt[3]{x-14}-4=0$

$$\sqrt[3]{x-14}=4$$

$$\left(\sqrt[3]{x-14}\right)^{3}=(4)^{3}$$

$$x-14=64$$

$$x=78$$

Solution Set: $\{78\}$

90. $\sqrt[4]{-3x}=3$

$$\left(\sqrt[4]{-3x}\right)^{4}=(3)^{4}$$

$$-3x=81$$

$$x=-27$$

Solution Set: $\{-27\}$

91. $\sqrt{4-4x} - 7 = -1$

$\sqrt{4-4x} = 6$

$\left(\sqrt{4-4x}\right)^2 = (6)^2$

$4 - 4x = 36$

$-32 = 4x$

$-8 = x$

Solution Set: $\{-8\}$

92. $\sqrt[5]{7x-12} + 3 = 0$

$\sqrt[5]{7x-12} = -3$

$\left(\sqrt[5]{7x-12}\right)^5 = (-3)^5$

$7x - 12 = -243$

$7x = -231$

$x = -33$

Solution Set: $\{-33\}$

93. $\sqrt{7x-28} = \sqrt{4x-x^2}$

$\left(\sqrt{7x-28}\right)^2 = \left(\sqrt{4x-x^2}\right)^2$

$7x - 28 = 4x - x^2$

$x^2 + 3x - 28 = 0$

$(x+7)(x-4) = 0$

$x + 7 = 0$ or $x - 4 = 0$

$\cancel{x = -7}$ $x = 4$

Solution Set: $\{4\}$

94. $\sqrt[4]{2x^2 - x} - \sqrt[4]{x} = 0$

$\sqrt[4]{2x^2 - x} = \sqrt[4]{x}$

$\left(\sqrt[4]{2x^2 - x}\right)^4 = \left(\sqrt[4]{x}\right)^4$

$2x^2 - x = x$

$2x^2 - 2x = 0$

$2x(x-1) = 0$

$2x = 0$ or $x - 1 = 0$

$x = 0$ $x = 1$

Solution Set: $\{0,1\}$

95. $3 + \sqrt[3]{16a^2} = 7$

$\sqrt[3]{16a^2} = 4$

$\left(\sqrt[3]{16a^2}\right)^3 = (4)^3$

$16a^2 = 64$

$16a^2 - 64 = 0$

$16(a+2)(a-2) = 0$

$a + 2 = 0$ or $a - 2 = 0$

$a = -2$ $a = 2$

Solution Set: $\{-2, 2\}$

96. Let x represent the unknown number. The equation is $\sqrt[4]{x+5} = \sqrt[4]{5x-7}$.

$\sqrt[4]{x+5} = \sqrt[4]{5x-7}$

$\left(\sqrt[4]{x+5}\right)^4 = \left(\sqrt[4]{5x-7}\right)^4$

$x + 5 = 5x - 7$

$12 = 4x$

$3 = x$

The number is 3.

97. Let x represent the unknown number. The equation is $\sqrt[3]{2+2x} = \sqrt[3]{x+5}$.

$\sqrt[3]{2+2x} = \sqrt[3]{x+5}$

$\left(\sqrt[3]{2+2x}\right)^3 = \left(\sqrt[3]{x+5}\right)^3$

$2 + 2x = x + 5$

$x = 3$

The number is 3.

98. Let x represent the unknown number. The equation is $\sqrt[6]{1+x} = \sqrt[6]{7x-19}$.

$\sqrt[6]{1+x} = \sqrt[6]{7x-19}$

$\left(\sqrt[6]{1+x}\right)^6 = \left(\sqrt[6]{7x-19}\right)^6$

$1 + x = 7x - 19$

$20 = 6x$

$\dfrac{10}{3} = x$

The number is $\frac{10}{3}$.

CHAPTER 8 TEST

1. f

2. a

3. b

4. d

5. $\left(-128x^{21}y^{-7}\right)^{-3/7} = (-128)^{-3/7}\left(x^{21}\right)^{-3/7}\left(y^{-7}\right)^{-3/7}$

$\qquad = \left((-2)^7\right)^{-3/7}\left(x^{21}\right)^{-3/7}\left(y^{-7}\right)^{-3/7}$

$\qquad = (-2)^{7(-3/7)}\,x^{21(-3/7)}\,y^{-7(-3/7)}$

$\qquad = (-2)^{-3}\,x^{-9}\,y^{3}$

$\qquad = \dfrac{y^3}{(-2)^3\,x^9}$

$\qquad = \dfrac{-y^3}{8x^9}$

6. $\sqrt{343} = \sqrt{49\cdot 7}$

$\qquad = \sqrt{49}\,\sqrt{7}$

$\qquad = 7\sqrt{7}$

7. $-\sqrt{80x^3y^5} = -\sqrt{16x^2y^4\cdot 5xy}$

$\qquad = -\sqrt{16x^2y^4}\,\sqrt{5xy}$

$\qquad = -4xy^2\sqrt{5xy}$

8. $\sqrt[3]{-56a^3b^8c} = \sqrt[3]{-8a^3b^6\cdot 7b^2c}$

$\qquad = \sqrt[3]{-8a^3b^6}\,\sqrt[3]{7b^2c}$

$\qquad = -2ab^2\sqrt[3]{7b^2c}$

9. $\sqrt{16z^2} = 4|z|$

10. $2\sqrt{18} + 4\sqrt{2} - 5\sqrt{32} = 2\sqrt{9\cdot 2} + 4\sqrt{2} - 5\sqrt{16\cdot 2}$

$\qquad = 2\sqrt{9}\,\sqrt{2} + 4\sqrt{2} - 5\sqrt{16}\,\sqrt{2}$

$\qquad = 2\cdot 3\sqrt{2} + 4\sqrt{2} - 5\cdot 4\sqrt{2}$

$\qquad = 6\sqrt{2} + 4\sqrt{2} - 20\sqrt{2}$

$\qquad = (6+4-20)\sqrt{2}$

$\qquad = -10\sqrt{2}$

11. $-\sqrt[3]{192y} + 2\sqrt[3]{24y} - \sqrt[3]{3y}$

$\qquad = -\sqrt[3]{64\cdot 3y} + 2\sqrt[3]{8\cdot 3y} - \sqrt[3]{3y}$

$\qquad = -\sqrt[3]{64}\sqrt[3]{3y} + 2\sqrt[3]{8}\sqrt[3]{3y} - \sqrt[3]{3y}$

$\qquad = -4\sqrt[3]{3y} + 2\cdot 2\sqrt[3]{3y} - \sqrt[3]{3y}$

$\qquad = -4\sqrt[3]{3y} + 4\sqrt[3]{3y} - \sqrt[3]{3y}$

$\qquad = (-4+4-1)\sqrt[3]{3y}$

$\qquad = -\sqrt[3]{3y}$

12. $\left(-4\sqrt{8}\right)\left(3\sqrt{10}\right) = -12\sqrt{8\cdot 10}$

$\qquad = -12\sqrt{80}$

$\qquad = -12\sqrt{16\cdot 5}$

$\qquad = -12\sqrt{16}\sqrt{5}$

$\qquad = -12\cdot 4\sqrt{5}$

$\qquad = -48\sqrt{5}$

13. $\left(\sqrt{6}+3\sqrt{5}\right)\left(\sqrt{3}-\sqrt{5}\right)$

$\qquad = \sqrt{6}\sqrt{3} - \sqrt{6}\sqrt{5} + 3\sqrt{5}\sqrt{3} - 3\sqrt{5}\sqrt{5}$

$\qquad = \sqrt{18} - \sqrt{30} + 3\sqrt{15} - 3\sqrt{25}$

$\qquad = \sqrt{9\cdot 2} - \sqrt{30} + 3\sqrt{15} - 3\cdot 5$

$\qquad = \sqrt{9}\sqrt{2} - \sqrt{30} + 3\sqrt{15} - 15$

$\qquad = 3\sqrt{2} - \sqrt{30} + 3\sqrt{15} - 15$

14. $\dfrac{\sqrt{80a^{25}}}{\sqrt{5a^{21}}} = \sqrt{\dfrac{80a^{25}}{5a^{21}}}$

$\qquad = \sqrt{16a^4}$

$\qquad = 4a^2$

15. $\dfrac{-10\sqrt{3}}{\sqrt{5}} = \dfrac{-10\sqrt{3}}{\sqrt{5}}\cdot 1$

$\qquad = \dfrac{-10\sqrt{3}}{\sqrt{5}}\cdot\dfrac{\sqrt{5}}{\sqrt{5}}$

$\qquad = \dfrac{-10\sqrt{15}}{\sqrt{25}}$

$\qquad = \dfrac{-10\sqrt{15}}{5}$

$\qquad = -2\sqrt{15}$

16. $\dfrac{5\sqrt[3]{3}}{\sqrt[3]{4}} = \dfrac{5\sqrt[3]{3}}{\sqrt[3]{4}} \cdot 1$

$\qquad = \dfrac{5\sqrt[3]{3}}{\sqrt[3]{4}} \cdot \dfrac{\sqrt[3]{2}}{\sqrt[3]{2}}$

$\qquad = \dfrac{5\sqrt[3]{6}}{\sqrt[3]{8}}$

$\qquad = \dfrac{5\sqrt[3]{6}}{2}$

17. $\dfrac{6\sqrt{2}}{2-\sqrt{3}} = \left(\dfrac{6\sqrt{2}}{2-\sqrt{3}}\right)\left(\dfrac{2+\sqrt{3}}{2+\sqrt{3}}\right)$

$\qquad = \dfrac{6\sqrt{2}\left(2+\sqrt{3}\right)}{(2)^2 - \left(\sqrt{3}\right)^2}$

$\qquad = \dfrac{12\sqrt{2}+6\sqrt{6}}{4-\sqrt{9}}$

$\qquad = \dfrac{12\sqrt{2}+6\sqrt{6}}{4-3}$

$\qquad = 12\sqrt{2}+6\sqrt{6}$

18. $\sqrt[4]{8}\left(7\sqrt[4]{2}-3\sqrt[4]{32}\right) = \sqrt[4]{8}\cdot 7\sqrt[4]{2}-\sqrt[4]{8}\cdot 3\sqrt[4]{32}$

$\qquad = 7\sqrt[4]{16}-3\sqrt[4]{256}$

$\qquad = 7\cdot 2 - 3\cdot 4$

$\qquad = 14-12$

$\qquad = 2$

19. $f(x) = \sqrt{2x-3}$

$\qquad 2x-3 \geq 0$

$\qquad 2x \geq 3$

$\qquad x \geq \dfrac{3}{2}$

The domain is $D_f = \left[\dfrac{3}{2}, \infty\right)$ or $D_f = \left\{x \,|\, x \geq \dfrac{3}{2}\right\}$.

20. $3+\sqrt{11-4x} = 7$

$\qquad \sqrt{11-4x} = 4$

$\qquad \left(\sqrt{11-4x}\right)^2 = (4)^2$

$\qquad 11-4x = 16$

$\qquad -4x = 5$

$\qquad x = -\dfrac{5}{4}$

Check

$3+\sqrt{11-4\left(-\dfrac{5}{4}\right)} = 7$

$3+\sqrt{11+5} = 7$

$3+\sqrt{16} = 7$

$3+4 = 7$

$7 = 7$

True

The solution set is $\left\{-\dfrac{5}{4}\right\}$.

21. $\sqrt{x^2-6x} = \sqrt{18-3x}$

$\qquad \left(\sqrt{x^2-6x}\right)^2 = \left(\sqrt{18-3x}\right)^2$

$\qquad x^2-6x = 18-3x$

$\qquad x^2-3x-18 = 0$

$\qquad (x+3)(x-6) = 0$

$\qquad x+3=0 \quad or \quad x-6=0$

$\qquad x=-3 \qquad\qquad x=6$

Check

$x=-3 \quad \sqrt{(-3)^2-6(-3)} = \sqrt{18-3(-3)}$

$\sqrt{9+18} = \sqrt{18+9}$

$\sqrt{27} = \sqrt{27}$

True

$x=6 \quad \sqrt{(6)^2-6(6)} = \sqrt{18-3(6)}$

$\sqrt{36-36} = \sqrt{36-36}$

$\sqrt{0} = \sqrt{0}$

$0 = 0$

True

The solution set is $\{-3, 6\}$.

22. $\sqrt[3]{3x-6} + \sqrt[3]{13-2x} = 0$

$\qquad \sqrt[3]{3x-6} = -\sqrt[3]{13-2x}$

$\qquad \left(\sqrt[3]{3x-6}\right)^3 = \left(-\sqrt[3]{13-2x}\right)^3$

$\qquad 3x-6 = -(13-2x)$

$\qquad 3x-6 = -13+2x$

$\qquad x = -7$

Check

$$\sqrt[3]{3(-7)-6} + \sqrt[3]{13-2(-7)} = 0$$
$$\sqrt[3]{-21-6} + \sqrt[3]{13+14} = 0$$
$$\sqrt[3]{-27} + \sqrt[3]{27} = 0$$
$$-3+3 = 0$$
$$0 = 0$$
True

The solution set is $\{-7\}$.

23.
$$x-1 = \sqrt{-4x+9}$$
$$(x-1)^2 = \left(\sqrt{-4x+9}\right)^2$$
$$x^2 - 2x + 1 = -4x + 9$$
$$x^2 + 2x - 8 = 0$$
$$(x-2)(x+4) = 0$$
$$x-2 = 0 \quad or \quad x+4 = 0$$
$$x = 2 \qquad\qquad x = -4$$

Check
$$x = 2 \quad (2)-1 = \sqrt{-4(2)+9}$$
$$1 = \sqrt{-8+9}$$
$$1 = \sqrt{1}$$
$$1 = 1$$
True

$$x = -4 \quad (-4)-1 = \sqrt{-4(-4)+9}$$
$$-5 = \sqrt{16+9}$$
$$-5 = \sqrt{25}$$
$$-5 = 5$$
False

The solution set is $\{2\}$.

24. Let c = the length of the hypotenuse, then $2x^2 = c^2$.

$$2x^2 = c^2$$
$$2\left(4\sqrt{10}\right)^2 = c^2$$
$$2(16 \cdot 10) = c^2$$
$$320 = c^2$$
$$0 = c^2 - 320$$
$$0 = \left(c + \sqrt{320}\right)\left(c - \sqrt{320}\right)$$
$$c = -\sqrt{320} \quad or \quad c = \sqrt{320}$$
$$c = \sqrt{64} \cdot \sqrt{5}$$
$$c = 8\sqrt{5}$$

The length of the hypotenuse is $8\sqrt{5}$ yards.

25. **Prepare** We are to find the length of the guy wire needed and determine if Duncan Works must purchase additional wire for the job.

Plan We can use the Pythagorean Theorem to determine g, and then see if 20 feet will be enough wire.

Process
$$8^2 + 22^2 = g^2$$
$$64 + 484 = g^2$$
$$548 = g^2$$
$$0 = g^2 - 548$$
$$0 = \left(g + \sqrt{548}\right)\left(g - \sqrt{548}\right)$$
$$g + \sqrt{548} = 0 \quad or \quad g - \sqrt{548} = 0$$
$$g = \cancel{-\sqrt{548}} \qquad g = \sqrt{548}$$
$$g = \sqrt{4} \cdot \sqrt{137}$$
$$g = 2\sqrt{137}$$
$$g \approx 23.4 \text{ feet}$$

Duncan Works will need approximately 23.4 feet of wire and must purchase additional wire.

Ponder Is the result reasonable? Since g is the hypotenuse, it is the longest side, and so it must be greater than 22 feet. Therefore, the result is reasonable.

Chapter 9

9.1 Exercises

1. Given the function $\{(4,6),(8,6),(10,6),(15,6)\}$, the <u>domain</u> is given by $\{4,8,10,15\}$.

3. A graph represents a function if, and only if, every <u>vertical</u> line intersects the graph at most <u>once</u>.

5. Yes, because each element of the domain is paired with at most one element of the range.
$D = \{2,4,5,6,8\}$, $R = \{-3,5,7,9\}$

7. Yes, because each element of the domain is paired with at most one element of the range.
$D = \{2,4,5,6,8\}$, $R = \{-3,0,1,5\}$

9. No, because the number 2 from the domain is paired with eight different numbers.

11. $f(x) = 5x + 6$
$f(10) = 5(10) + 6$
$\quad = 50 + 6$
$\quad = 56$
$(10,56)$

13. $g(x) = \dfrac{2}{3}x - \dfrac{3}{5}$
$g(-6) = \dfrac{2}{3}(-6) - \dfrac{3}{5}$
$\quad = -4 - \dfrac{3}{5}$
$\quad = -4\dfrac{3}{5}$
$\left(-6, -4\tfrac{3}{5}\right)$

15. $g(t) = -t^2 - t + 4$
$g(-2) = -(-2)^2 - (-2) + 4$
$\quad = -(4) + 2 + 4$
$\quad = 2$
$(-2,2)$

17. $h(x) = 8x^2 - 6x$
$h\left(\dfrac{-1}{3}\right) = 8\left(\dfrac{-1}{3}\right)^2 - 6\left(\dfrac{-1}{3}\right)$
$\quad = 8\left(\dfrac{1}{9}\right) + 2$
$\quad = \dfrac{8}{9} + 2$
$\quad = \dfrac{26}{9}$
$\left(\dfrac{-1}{3}, \dfrac{26}{9}\right)$

19. $f(x) = 3x^3 + 4x^2 - 8x + 12$
$f(2) = 3(2)^3 + 4(2)^2 - 8(2) + 12$
$\quad = 3(8) + 4(4) - 16 + 12$
$\quad = 24 + 16 - 16 + 12$
$\quad = 36$
$(2,36)$

21. $g(x) = |5x - 20|$
$g(-1) = |5(-1) - 20|$
$\quad = |-5 - 20|$
$\quad = |-25|$
$\quad = 25$
$(-1,25)$

23. $h(s) = \dfrac{4s^2 - 6}{s^2 - 5s + 8}$
$h(-3) = \dfrac{4(-3)^2 - 6}{(-3)^2 - 5(-3) + 8}$
$\quad = \dfrac{4(9) - 6}{9 + 15 + 8}$
$\quad = \dfrac{36 - 6}{32}$
$\quad = \dfrac{30}{32}$
$\quad = \dfrac{15}{16}$
$\left(-3, \tfrac{15}{16}\right)$

25. $f(x) = \dfrac{2x^2 - 3x + 1}{0.4 + x}$

$f(0.3) = \dfrac{2(0.3)^2 - 3(0.3) + 1}{0.4 + (0.3)}$

$= \dfrac{2(0.09) - 0.9 + 1}{0.7}$

$= \dfrac{0.18 - 0.9 + 1}{0.7}$

$= \dfrac{0.28}{0.7}$

$= 0.4$

$(0.3, 0.4)$

27. $f(x) = \sqrt[3]{4 - 18x}$

$f\left(\dfrac{2}{3}\right) = \sqrt[3]{4 - 18\left(\dfrac{2}{3}\right)}$

$= \sqrt[3]{4 - 12}$

$= \sqrt[3]{-8}$

$= -2$

$\left(\tfrac{2}{3}, -2\right)$

29. $g(x) = -x^2 + 14x - 25$

$g(t) = -(t)^2 + 14(t) - 25$

$= -t^2 + 14t - 25$

31. $f(x) = -5x + 20$

$f(x - 8) = -5(x - 8) + 20$

$= -5x + 40 + 20$

$= -5x + 60$

33. $h(x) = 2x^2 + x - 1$

$h(x + 3) = 2(x + 3)^2 + (x + 3) - 1$

$= 2(x^2 + 6x + 9) + x + 2$

$= 2x^2 + 12x + 18 + x + 2$

$= 2x^2 + 13x + 20$

35. $f(x) = x^2 - 4$

$f(a + h) = (a + h)^2 - 4$

$= a^2 + 2ah + h^2 - 4$

37. $g(v) = 5 - 12v$

$g\left(\dfrac{1}{2b}\right) = 5 - 12\left(\dfrac{1}{2b}\right)$

$= 5 - \dfrac{6}{b}$

39. $\dfrac{f(a + h) - f(a)}{h} = \dfrac{[4(a + h) + 7] - [4(a) + 7]}{h}$

$= \dfrac{4a + 4h + 7 - 4a - 7}{h}$

$= \dfrac{4 \cancel{h}^{1}}{\cancel{h}_{1}}$

$= 4$

41. $\dfrac{f(a + h) - f(a)}{h} = \dfrac{\left[4(a + h)^2\right] - \left[4(a)^2\right]}{h}$

$= \dfrac{4a^2 + 8ah + 4h^2 - 4a^2}{h}$

$= \dfrac{8ah + 4h^2}{h}$

$= \dfrac{\cancel{h}^{1}(8a + 4h)}{\cancel{h}_{1}}$

$= 8a + 4h$

43. $\dfrac{f(a + h) - f(a)}{h}$

$= \dfrac{\left[2(a + h)^2 - (a + h)\right] - \left[2(a)^2 - (a)\right]}{h}$

$= \dfrac{2a^2 + 4ah + 2h^2 - a - h - 2a^2 + a}{h}$

$= \dfrac{4ah + 2h^2 - h}{h}$

$= \dfrac{\cancel{h}^{1}(4a + 2h - 1)}{\cancel{h}_{1}}$

$= 4a + 2h - 1$

45. This graph does not represent a function, since any there is a vertical line that intersects the graph twice.

47. This graph does represent a function, since any vertical line drawn would intersect the graph at most once.

49. This graph does not represent a function, since there is a vertical line that intersects the graph twice.

51. This graph does represent a function, since any vertical line drawn would intersect the graph at most once.

53. Answers will vary; for example: To find $f(5)$ for any function $f(x)$, simply substitute 5 for each x in the function and perform the necessary operations.

55. $f(2) = 10$

57. $x = 11$

59. Answers will vary; for example:

Function   Not a function

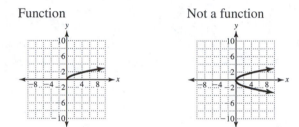

61. Answers will vary; for example: Any vertical line will not represent a function because for each x there are infinite y values.

63. a) yes
  b) $y = -3$
  c) $x = 0$ or $x = 4$

65. a) no
  b) $y = 0$
  c) $x = -2$ or $x = 2$

67. $v(h) = \sqrt{64h}$

   $v(9) = \sqrt{64(9)}$

   $ = 24$

   The velocity of the brick is 24 ft/sec.

69. a) $h(2) = -16(2)^2 + 64(2) + 80$

   $ = -16(4) + 128 + 80$

   $ = -64 + 128 + 80$

   $ = 144$ ft.

  b) $h(3) = -16(3)^2 + 64(3) + 80$

   $ = -16(9) + 192 + 80$

   $ = -144 + 192 + 80$

   $ = 128$ ft.

  c) $h(5) = -16(5)^2 + 64(5) + 80$

   $ = -16(25) + 320 + 80$

   $ = -400 + 320 + 80$

   $ = 0$ ft.

  d) The rock initially ascended to its maximum height at 2 seconds, but began to descend between 2 and 3 seconds and eventually struck the ground at 5 seconds.

71. Prepare We are asked to plot seven data points in the form $(\text{year, number of visitors})$, where the number of visitors is given in millions. If the relationship is linear, we will write a linear function to represent the data and estimate the number of visitors to the park in 2025.

Plan We will plot the seven data points on the plane and determine if there appears to be a linear relationship.

Process Plot the points $(0, 43.5)$, $(1, 40.8)$, $(2, 43)$, $(3, 45)$, $(4, 48)$, $(5, 50.9)$, and $(6, 53.1)$.

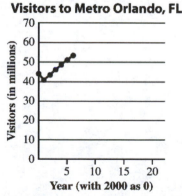

Visitors to Metro Orlando, FL

The relationship does appear to be linear. Let's choose two out of the seven data points to estimate a linear function to represent the set of data. Find the slope between $(x_1, y_1) = (1, 40.8)$ and $(x_2, y_2) = (6, 53.1)$. Using the slope formula yields:

371

$$m = \frac{y_2 - y_1}{x_2 - x_1}$$
$$= \frac{53.1 - 40.8}{6 - 1}$$
$$= \frac{12.3}{5}$$
$$= 2.46$$

Find the equation of the line containing the point $(x_1, y_1) = (1, 40.8)$ with slope $m = 2.46$. Using the point-slope formula and then solving for y yields:

$$y - y_1 = m(x - x_1)$$
$$y - (40.8) = 2.46(x - (1))$$
$$y = 2.46x + 38.34$$
$$f(x) = 2.46x + 38.34$$

Use the function to estimate the number of visitors to the park in 2025. That is, the year 2025 corresponds to an x-value of 25. Find $f(25)$.

$$f(25) = 2.46(25) + 38.34$$
$$= 99.84$$

Approximately 100 million visitors can be expected in Orlando, Florida in 2025 if this relationship continues.

Ponder Does the linear function and estimate for 2025 seem reasonable? Yes. Based on the seven data points provided.

73. $y = 2$

75. $x = 1,\ x = 3,\ x = 11$

77. $D = [-8, \infty)$

9.2 Exercises

1. The sum of two functions g and h with overlapping domains is defined as $(g+h)(x) = g(x)+h(x)$.

3. The <u>composition</u> of two functions g and h is defined as $(g \circ h)(x) = g(h(x))$.

5. The domain of $(g \circ h)(x)$ is the set of all x in the domain of <u>h</u> such that <u>$h(x)$</u> is in the domain of <u>g</u>.

7. $(f+g)(x) = f(x)+g(x)$
$= \left(x^2+2\right)+(5+x)$
$= x^2+x+7$
$D = (-\infty,\infty)$

9. $(g+h)(x) = g(x)+h(x)$
$= (5+x)+(3x-1)$
$= 4x+4$
$D = (-\infty,\infty)$

11. $(h-g)(x) = h(x)-g(x)$
$= (3x-1)-(5+x)$
$= 3x-1-5-x$
$= 2x-6$
$D = (-\infty,\infty)$

13. $(f-g)(x) = f(x)-g(x)$
$= \left(x^2+2\right)-(5+x)$
$= x^2+2-5-x$
$= x^2-x-3$
$D = (-\infty,\infty)$

15. $(f \cdot h)(x) = f(x) \cdot h(x)$
$= \left(x^2+2\right)(3x-1)$
$= 3x^3-x^2+6x-2$
$D = (-\infty,\infty)$

17. $(g \cdot h)(x) = g(x) \cdot h(x)$
$= (5+x)(3x-1)$
$= 15x-5+3x^2-x$
$= 3x^2+14x-5$
$D = (-\infty,\infty)$

19. $\left(\dfrac{f}{h}\right)(x) = \dfrac{f(x)}{h(x)}$
$= \dfrac{x^2+2}{3x-1}$
<u>Domain</u>
$3x-1=0$
$3x=1$
$x = \dfrac{1}{3}$
$D = \left\{x \mid x \neq \tfrac{1}{3}\right\}$

21. $\left(\dfrac{g}{h}\right)(x) = \dfrac{g(x)}{h(x)}$
$= \dfrac{5+x}{3x-1}$
<u>Domain</u>
$3x-1=0$
$3x=1$
$x = \dfrac{1}{3}$
$D = \left\{x \mid x \neq \tfrac{1}{3}\right\}$

23. $\left(\dfrac{f}{g}\right)(t) = \dfrac{f(t)}{g(t)}$
$= \dfrac{\dfrac{3}{t+2}}{\dfrac{5}{t^2-4}}$
$= \left(\dfrac{3}{t+2}\right) \div \left(\dfrac{5}{t^2-4}\right)$
$= \dfrac{3}{\overset{1}{\cancel{(t+2)}}} \cdot \dfrac{\overset{}{\cancel{(t+2)}}(t-2)}{5}$
$= \dfrac{3t-6}{5}$

<u>Domain</u>

$$t^2 - 4 = 0$$

$$(t+2)(t-2) = 0$$

$$t + 2 = 0 \quad \text{or} \quad t - 2 = 0$$

$$t = -2 \quad \text{or} \quad t = 2$$

$$D = \{t \mid t \neq -2 \text{ and } t \neq 2\}$$

25. $\left(\dfrac{f}{g}\right)(t) = \dfrac{3t-6}{5}$

$\left(\dfrac{f}{g}\right)(0) = \dfrac{3(0)-6}{5}$

$= -\dfrac{6}{5}$

27. $(g+f)(t) = g(t) + f(t)$

$= \left(\dfrac{5}{t^2-4}\right) + \left(\dfrac{3}{t+2}\right)$

$= \dfrac{5}{(t+2)(t-2)} + \dfrac{3(t-2)}{(t+2)(t-2)}$

$= \dfrac{5+3t-6}{(t+2)(t-2)}$

$= \dfrac{3t-1}{t^2-4}$

<u>Domain</u>

$$t^2 - 4 = 0$$

$$(t+2)(t-2) = 0$$

$$t + 2 = 0 \quad \text{or} \quad t - 2 = 0$$

$$t = -2 \quad \text{or} \quad t = 2$$

$$D = \{t \mid t \neq -2 \text{ and } t \neq 2\}$$

29. $(g+f)(t) = \dfrac{3t-1}{t^2-4}$

$(g+f)(0) = \dfrac{3(0)-1}{(0)^2-4}$

$= \dfrac{0-1}{0-4}$

$= \dfrac{1}{4}$

31. $(g+f)(t) = \dfrac{3t-1}{t^2-4}$

$(g+f)(2)$ is undefined

33. $(g \cdot f)(t) = g(t) \cdot f(t)$

$= \left(\dfrac{5}{t^2-4}\right)\left(\dfrac{3}{t+2}\right)$

$= \dfrac{15}{t^3+2t^2-4t-8}$

<u>Domain</u>

$$t^2 - 4 = 0$$

$$(t+2)(t-2) = 0$$

$$t + 2 = 0 \quad \text{or} \quad t - 2 = 0$$

$$t = -2 \quad \text{or} \quad t = 2$$

$$D = \{t \mid t \neq -2 \text{ and } t \neq 2\}$$

35. $(g \cdot f)(t) = \dfrac{15}{t^3+2t^2-4t-8}$

$(g \cdot f)(-4) = \dfrac{15}{(-4)^3+2(-4)^2-4(-4)-8}$

$= \dfrac{15}{-64+2(16)+16-8}$

$= \dfrac{15}{-64+32+16-8}$

$= \dfrac{15}{-24}$

$= -\dfrac{5}{8}$

37. $(h+h)\left(\dfrac{1}{4}\right) = h\left(\dfrac{1}{4}\right) + h\left(\dfrac{1}{4}\right)$

$= 2\left(\dfrac{1}{4}\right) + 2\left(\dfrac{1}{4}\right)$

$= \dfrac{1}{2} + \dfrac{1}{2}$

$= 1$

39. $(f \circ g)(t) = f(g(t))$

$= f(3t^2+2)$

$= 5(3t^2+2)$

$= 15t^2+10$

$D = (-\infty, \infty)$

374

41. $(g \circ h)(t) = g(h(t))$

$\quad = g(\sqrt{t-2})$

$\quad = 3(\sqrt{t-2})^2 + 2$

$\quad = 3(t-2) + 2$

$\quad = 3t - 4$

$\quad$ <u>Domain</u>

$\quad t - 2 \geq 0$

$\quad t \geq 2$

$\quad D = [2, \infty)$

43. $(f \circ g)(t) = 15t^2 + 10$

$(f \circ g)(2) = 15(2)^2 + 10$

$\quad = 15(4) + 10$

$\quad = 60 + 10$

$\quad = 70$

45. $(g \circ g)(1) = g(g(1))$

$\quad = g(3(1)^2 + 2)$

$\quad = 3(5)^2 + 2$

$\quad = 3(25) + 2$

$\quad = 77$

47. $(f \circ h)(a) = f(h(a))$

$\quad = f(\sqrt{(a)-2})$

$\quad = 5(\sqrt{a-2})$

$\quad = 5\sqrt{a-2}$

$\quad D = [2, \infty)$

49. $(f \circ g)(t) = 15t^2 + 10$

$(f \circ g)(0.2) = 15(0.2)^2 + 10$

$\quad = 15(0.04) + 10$

$\quad = 0.6 + 10$

$\quad = 10.6$

51. Answers will vary; for example: To find $(g \circ f)(x)$, substitute $f(x)$ into every x in the function $g(x)$, then simplify.

53. Answers will vary; for example: $f(x) = 2x$ and $g(x) = \frac{\sqrt{x+3}}{2}$.

55. Prepare We are to discuss the domain of the Navajo Canyon Helicopter Rides' profit function and determine why the company has a two rider minimum policy.

Plan We can use the cost and revenue functions to write the profit function, and then discuss its domain. We must also determine why the company requires at least two riders. We can determine this by evaluating the profit function for $x = 1$.

Process

$$P(x) = R(x) - C(x)$$
$$= (180x) - (30x + 250)$$
$$= 150x - 250$$

$$P(1) = 150(1) - 250$$
$$= -100$$

Because x represents the number of riders and the company will only take a minimum of two riders and a maximum of six riders, the domain is $D = \{2,3,4,5,6\}$.   Allowing only one rider would cause the company to lose money. This is a very good reason for having a two rider minimum.

Ponder Does our conclusion seem reasonable? The conclusion is reasonable because a company would make a positive profit for 2, 3, 4, 5, or 6, riders. It also seems reasonable that a typical helicopter could hold at most six passengers along with the pilot.

57. $(g+f)(-1) = g(-1) + f(-1)$

$\quad = -1 + 3$

$\quad = 2$

59. $(f-g)(0) = f(0) - g(0)$

$\quad = 2 - (-2)$

$\quad = 4$

61. $(f \cdot g)(1) = f(1) \cdot g(1)$

$\quad = (-1)(-1)$

$\quad = 1$

63. $\left(\dfrac{g}{f}\right)(-3) = \dfrac{g(-3)}{f(-3)}$

$\qquad\qquad = \dfrac{1}{-1}$

$\qquad\qquad = -1$

65. $(g \cdot g)(-2) = g(-2) \cdot g(-2)$

$\qquad\qquad = 0 \cdot 0$

$\qquad\qquad = 0$

67. $\left(\dfrac{f}{g}\right)(-2) = \dfrac{f(-2)}{g(-2)}$

$\qquad\qquad = \dfrac{2}{0}$

$\qquad\qquad$ undefined

9.3 Exercises

1. The <u>graph</u> of the function f is the set of all ordered pairs $\left(x, \underline{f(x)}\right)$ such that x is in the <u>domain</u> of f.

3. The function $g(x) = c$ is called the <u>constant</u> function.

5. The square root function can be represented by $f(x) = \sqrt{x}$.

7. $f(x) = x^2 - 4$

x	$f(x)$	$(x, f(x))$
-1	$(-1)^2 - 4 = -3$	$(-1, -3)$
0	$(0)^2 - 4 = -4$	$(0, -4)$
1	$(1)^2 - 4 = -3$	$(1, -3)$

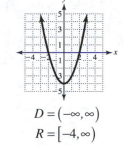

$$D = (-\infty, \infty)$$
$$R = [-4, \infty)$$

9. $g(x) = \sqrt{x+2}$

x	$g(x)$	$(x, g(x))$
-2	$\sqrt{(-2)+2} = 0$	$(-2, 0)$
-1	$\sqrt{(-1)+2} = 1$	$(-1, 1)$
2	$\sqrt{(2)+2} = 2$	$(2, 2)$

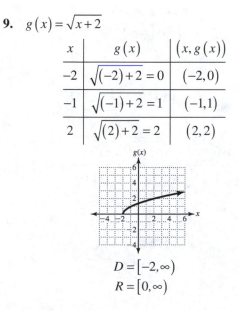

$$D = [-2, \infty)$$
$$R = [0, \infty)$$

11. $h(x) = |x|$

x	$h(x)$	$(x, h(x))$
-1	$|-1| = 1$	$(-1, 1)$
0	$|0| = 0$	$(0, 0)$
1	$|1| = 1$	$(1, 1)$

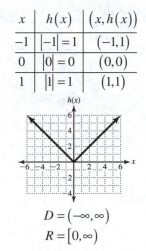

$$D = (-\infty, \infty)$$
$$R = [0, \infty)$$

13. $f(x) = 4$

x	$f(x)$	$(x, f(x))$
-1	4	$(-1, 4)$
0	4	$(0, 4)$
1	4	$(1, 4)$

$$D = (-\infty, \infty)$$
$$R = \{4\}$$

15. $g(x) = x + 2$

x	$g(x)$	$(x, g(x))$
-1	$(-1) + 2 = 1$	$(-1, 1)$
0	$(0) + 2 = 2$	$(0, 2)$
1	$(1) + 2 = 3$	$(1, 3)$

$$D = (-\infty, \infty)$$
$$R = (-\infty, \infty)$$

17. $h(x) = \sqrt{x}$

x	$h(x)$	$(x, h(x))$
0	$\sqrt{(0)} = 0$	$(0,0)$
1	$\sqrt{(1)} = 1$	$(1,1)$
4	$\sqrt{(4)} = 2$	$(4,2)$

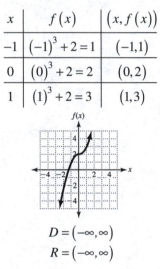

$D = [0, \infty)$

$R = [0, \infty)$

19. $f(x) = x^3 + 2$

x	$f(x)$	$(x, f(x))$
-1	$(-1)^3 + 2 = 1$	$(-1,1)$
0	$(0)^3 + 2 = 2$	$(0,2)$
1	$(1)^3 + 2 = 3$	$(1,3)$

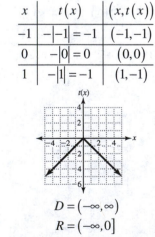

$D = (-\infty, \infty)$

$R = (-\infty, \infty)$

21. $t(x) = -|x|$

x	$t(x)$	$(x, t(x))$
-1	$-|-1| = -1$	$(-1,-1)$
0	$-|0| = 0$	$(0,0)$
1	$-|1| = -1$	$(1,-1)$

$D = (-\infty, \infty)$

$R = (-\infty, 0]$

23. $g(x) = x^3 + 1$

x	$g(x)$	$(x, g(x))$
-1	$(-1)^3 + 1 = 0$	$(-1,0)$
0	$(0)^3 + 1 = 1$	$(0,1)$
1	$(1)^3 + 1 = 2$	$(1,2)$

$D = (-\infty, \infty)$

$R = (-\infty, \infty)$

25. $f(x) = |x| + 2$

x	$f(x)$	$(x, f(x))$
-1	$|-1| + 2 = 3$	$(-1,3)$
0	$|0| + 2 = 2$	$(0,2)$
1	$|1| + 2 = 3$	$(1,3)$

$D = (-\infty, \infty)$

$R = [2, \infty)$

27. $g(x) = \sqrt{1-x}$

x	$g(x)$	$(x, g(x))$
-3	$\sqrt{1-(-3)} = 2$	$(-3,2)$
0	$\sqrt{1-(0)} = 1$	$(0,1)$
1	$\sqrt{1-(1)} = 0$	$(1,0)$

$D = (-\infty, 1]$

$R = [0, \infty)$

29. $h(x) = x^2 + 1$

x	$h(x)$	$(x, h(x))$
-1	$(-1)^2 + 1 = 2$	$(-1, 2)$
0	$(0)^2 + 1 = 1$	$(0, 1)$
1	$(1)^2 + 1 = 2$	$(1, 2)$

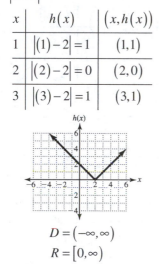

$D = (-\infty, \infty)$

$R = [1, \infty)$

31. $h(x) = |x - 2|$

x	$h(x)$	$(x, h(x))$
1	$|(1) - 2| = 1$	$(1, 1)$
2	$|(2) - 2| = 0$	$(2, 0)$
3	$|(3) - 2| = 1$	$(3, 1)$

$D = (-\infty, \infty)$

$R = [0, \infty)$

33. $s(x) = \dfrac{5}{2}$

x	$s(x)$	$(x, s(x))$
-1	$\frac{5}{2}$	$(-1, \frac{5}{2})$
0	$\frac{5}{2}$	$(0, \frac{5}{2})$
1	$\frac{5}{2}$	$(1, \frac{5}{2})$

$D = (-\infty, \infty)$

$R = \left\{ \frac{5}{2} \right\}$

35. $f(x) = \dfrac{1}{2x}$

x	$f(x)$	$(x, f(x))$
-2	$\dfrac{1}{2(-2)} = -\dfrac{1}{4}$	$(-2, -\frac{1}{4})$
-1	$\dfrac{1}{2(-1)} = -\dfrac{1}{2}$	$(-1, -\frac{1}{2})$
$-\frac{1}{2}$	$\dfrac{1}{2(-\frac{1}{2})} = -1$	$(-\frac{1}{2}, -1)$
$\frac{1}{2}$	$\dfrac{1}{2(\frac{1}{2})} = 1$	$(\frac{1}{2}, 1)$
1	$\dfrac{1}{2(1)} = \dfrac{1}{2}$	$(1, \frac{1}{2})$
2	$\dfrac{1}{2(2)} = \dfrac{1}{4}$	$(2, \frac{1}{4})$

$D = (-\infty, 0) \cup (0, \infty)$

$R = (-\infty, 0) \cup (0, \infty)$

37. Answers will vary; for example: An example of a constant function is $f(x) = 4$. When graphed, this function is a horizontal line that intersects the y-axis at 4.

39. Answers will vary; for example: To graph an unfamiliar function, create an x, $f(x)$ table and plot points.

41. Answers will vary; for example: The graph of $f(x) = |3x|$ has the same domain and range as $f(x) = |x|$, but has a more positive slope in quadrant I and a more negative slope in quadrant II.

43. Prepare We will plot the data using ordered pairs (distance, elevation). The actual destination is not relevant to the problem; however, we will use the graph to determine the elevation of a backpacker at 15 miles. We are looking for a graph that resembles one of the six basic graphs.

Plan   Plot the nine ordered pairs $(0,6860)$, $(1.5,5720)$, ..., $(19.2,6860)$.

Determine if the graph resembles one of the six basic graphs, and if so, state which one. Use the graph to approximate the elevation of a backpacker at 15 miles.

Process   The graph has more of a **V**-shape than a **U**-shape; therefore, the graph resembles the absolute value function $f(x) = |x|$. Using the graph, the backpacker would be at an elevation of approximately 4,250 feet after 15 miles of hiking.

Bright Angel Trail Elevation vs. Distance

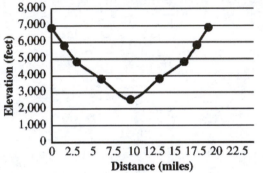

Ponder   Does the graph and the elevation seem reasonable? The **V**-shape of the graph seems reasonable because as the hikers traveled the first 10 miles, they descended into the canyon. The next 10 miles the backpackers hiked out of the canyon, and reached the same elevation coming out as they did going in.

45. $x^2 + y^2 = 9$

x	y	(x,y)
-3	0	$(-3,0)$
-1	$-2\sqrt{2}$ or $2\sqrt{2}$	$\left(-1,-2\sqrt{2}\right)$ or $\left(-1,2\sqrt{2}\right)$
0	-3 or 3	$(0,-3)$ or $(0,3)$
1	$-2\sqrt{2}$ or $2\sqrt{2}$	$\left(1,-2\sqrt{2}\right)$ or $\left(1,2\sqrt{2}\right)$
3	0	$(3,0)$

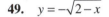

This graph does not represent a function, because there is a vertical line that would intersect the graph more than once.

47. $x = y^2 + 1$

x	y	(x,y)
1	0	$(1,0)$
2	-1 or 1	$(2,-1)$ or $(2,1)$
5	-2 or 2	$(5,-2)$ or $(5,2)$

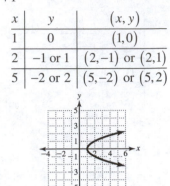

This graph does not represent a function, because there is a vertical line that would intersect the graph more than once.

49. $y = -\sqrt{2-x}$

x	y	(x,y)
2	0	$(2,0)$
1	-1	$(1,-1)$
-2	-2	$(-2,2)$

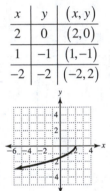

This graph does represent a function, since any vertical line drawn would intersect the graph at most once.

9.4 Exercises

1. The vertex of a parabola that opens upward is called the <u>minimum</u> point.

3. A vertical translation that does not change the basic shape of a graph is also known as a <u>rigid</u> transformation.

5. The equation of the function $g(x)$ that is a reflection of the graph of $h(x)$ about the y-axis is given by $g(x) = \underline{h(-x)}$.

7. If the graph of a function shifts to the left, it is called a <u>horizontal</u> translation.

9. c

11. a

13. e

15. This is the graph of $y = x$ shifted up 2 units.

$y = x$	$f(x) = x + 2$
$(-1,-1)$	$(-1,1)$
$(0,0)$	$(0,2)$
$(1,1)$	$(1,3)$

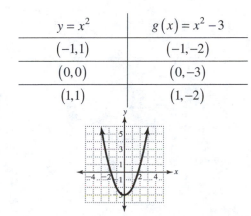

17. This is the graph of $y = x^2$ shifted down 3 units.

$y = x^2$	$g(x) = x^2 - 3$
$(-1,1)$	$(-1,-2)$
$(0,0)$	$(0,-3)$
$(1,1)$	$(1,-2)$

19. This is the graph of $y = |x|$ shifted to the left 1 unit.

$y = |x|$	$k(x) = |x+1|$
$(-1,1)$	$(-2,1)$
$(0,0)$	$(-1,0)$
$(1,1)$	$(0,1)$

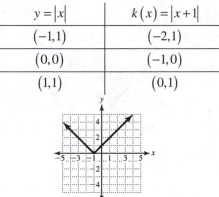

21. This is the graph of $y = \sqrt{x}$ shifted to the right 3 units.

$y = \sqrt{x}$	$h(x) = \sqrt{x-3}$
$(0,0)$	$(3,0)$
$(1,1)$	$(4,1)$
$(4,2)$	$(7,2)$

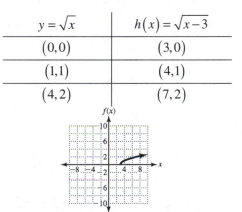

23. This is the graph of $y = x^3$ shifted down 2 units.

$y = x^3$	$r(x) = x^3 - 2$
$(-1,-1)$	$(-1,-3)$
$(0,0)$	$(0,-2)$
$(1,1)$	$(1,-1)$

25. This is the graph of $y = |x|$ shifted up 3 units.

$y = |x|$	$p(x) = |x| + 3$
$(-1, 1)$	$(-1, 4)$
$(0, 0)$	$(0, 3)$
$(1, 1)$	$(1, 4)$

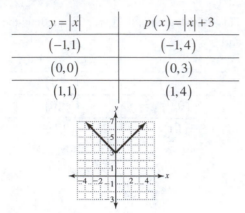

27. This is the graph of $y = x^2$ shifted to the right 3 units.

$y = x^2$	$f(x) = (x - 3)^2$
$(-1, 1)$	$(2, 1)$
$(0, 0)$	$(3, 0)$
$(1, 1)$	$(4, 1)$

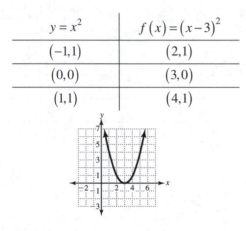

29. This is the graph of $y = \sqrt{x}$ shifted to the right 2 units and then shifted up 3 units.

$y = \sqrt{x}$	$g(x) = \sqrt{x - 2} + 3$
$(0, 0)$	$(2, 3)$
$(1, 1)$	$(3, 4)$
$(4, 2)$	$(6, 5)$

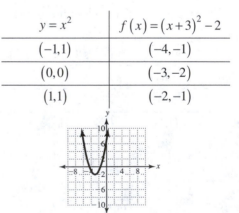

31. This is the graph of $y = |x|$ shifted to the left $\frac{1}{2}$ unit and then shifted up 2 units.

$y = |x|$	$s(x) = 2 + \left|x + \frac{1}{2}\right|$
$(-1, 1)$	$\left(-\frac{3}{2}, 3\right)$
$(0, 0)$	$\left(-\frac{1}{2}, 2\right)$
$(1, 1)$	$\left(\frac{1}{2}, 3\right)$

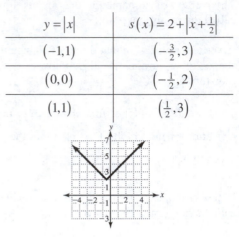

33. This is the graph of $y = x^3$ shifted to the right 1 unit and then shifted down 2 units.

$y = x^3$	$h(x) = (x - 1)^3 - 2$
$(-1, -1)$	$(0, -3)$
$(0, 0)$	$(1, -2)$
$(1, 1)$	$(2, -1)$

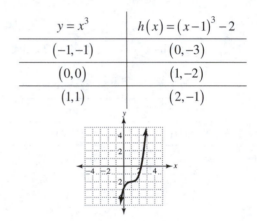

35. This is the graph of $y = x^2$ shifted to the left 3 units and then shifted down 2 units.

$y = x^2$	$f(x) = (x + 3)^2 - 2$
$(-1, 1)$	$(-4, -1)$
$(0, 0)$	$(-3, -2)$
$(1, 1)$	$(-2, -1)$

37. This is the graph of the function $y = \sqrt{x}$ shifted to the right 2 units and then reflected about the *x*-axis.

$y = \sqrt{x}$	$g(x) = -\sqrt{x-2}$
$(0,0)$	$(2,0)$
$(1,1)$	$(3,-1)$
$(4,2)$	$(6,-2)$

39. This is the graph of the function $y = |x|$ shifted to the left 3 units and then reflected about the *x*-axis.

$y = |x|$	$h(x) = -|x+3|$
$(-1,1)$	$(-4,-1)$
$(0,0)$	$(-3,0)$
$(1,1)$	$(-2,-1)$

41. This is the graph of the function $y = |x|$ reflected about the *x*-axis and then shifted up 4 units.

$y = |x|$	$m(x) = -|x|+4$
$(-1,1)$	$(-1,3)$
$(0,0)$	$(0,4)$
$(1,1)$	$(1,3)$

43. This is the graph of the function $y = x$ reflected about the *x*-axis and then shifted up 4 units.

$y = x$	$f(x) = -x+4$
$(-1,-1)$	$(-1,5)$
$(0,0)$	$(0,4)$
$(1,1)$	$(1,3)$

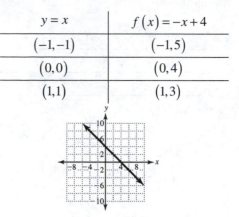

45. This is the graph of the function $y = \sqrt{x}$ reflected about the *y*-axis and then shifted down 2 units.

$y = \sqrt{x}$	$g(x) = \sqrt{-x}-2$
$(0,0)$	$(0,-2)$
$(1,1)$	$(-1,-1)$
$(4,2)$	$(-4,0)$

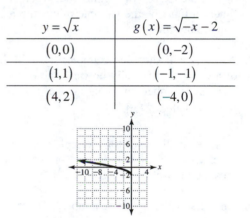

47. This is the graph of the function $y = |x|$ shifted to the left 1 unit, reflected about the *x*-axis, and then shifted up 1 unit.

$y = |x|$	$t(x) = -|x+1|+1$
$(-1,1)$	$(-2,0)$
$(0,0)$	$(-1,1)$
$(1,1)$	$(0,0)$

49. This is the graph of $y = \sqrt{x}$ shifted to the right 2 units, reflected about the x-axis, and then shifted up two units.

$y = \sqrt{x}$	$h(x) = 2 - \sqrt{x-2}$
$(0,0)$	$(2,2)$
$(1,1)$	$(3,1)$
$(4,2)$	$(6,0)$

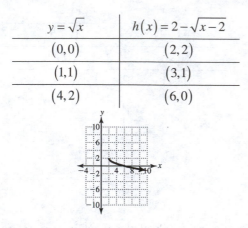

51. Answers will vary; for example: To shift the graph of a function to the right, the argument of the function must be the variable minus the number of units to be shifted.

53. Answers will vary; for example: To shift the graph of a function vertically upward, the equation must add the number of units to be shifted to the function value $f(x)$.

55. Answers will vary; for example: To reflect the graph of a function about the y-axis, the argument must be multiplied by a negative 1.

57. Answers will vary; for example: To graph one of the basic functions with a combination of translations, first perform the horizontal translation, and then perform the vertical translation.

59. This is the function f shifted up 1 unit.

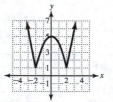

61. This is the function f shifted to the right 2 units.

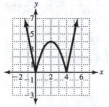

63. This is the function f reflected about the x-axis.

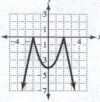

65. This is the function f shifted to the left 2 units and then shifted down 1 unit.

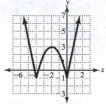

Chapter 9 Review Problem Set

1. Yes, because each element of the domain is paired with at most one element of the range.
$D = \{1,3,5,7,8\}$, $R = \{-2,4,8,9\}$

2. Yes, because each element of the domain is paired with at most one element of the range.
$D = \{1,3,5,7,8\}$, $R = \{-7\}$

3. Yes, because each element of the domain is paired with at most one element of the range.
$D = \{1,3,5,7,8\}$, $R = \{-7,0,1,4,8\}$

4. Yes, because each element of the domain is paired with at most one element of the range.
$D = \{1,3,5,7,8\}$, $R = \{0,4,9\}$

5. No, because the number 5 from the domain is paired with seven different numbers.

6. Yes, because each element of the domain is paired with at most one element of the range.
$D = \{1,3,5,7,8\}$, $R = \{4\}$

7. $f(x) = 4x^3 - 3x^2 - 11x + 2$

$f(2) = 4(2)^3 - 3(2)^2 - 11(2) + 2$

$\quad = 4(8) - 3(4) - 22 + 2$

$\quad = 32 - 12 - 22 + 2$

$\quad = 0$

$(2,0)$

8. $h(s) = \dfrac{s^2 - 4}{s^2 - 3s + 8}$

$h(-4) = \dfrac{(-4)^2 - 4}{(-4)^2 - 3(-4) + 8}$

$\quad = \dfrac{16 - 4}{16 + 12 + 8}$

$\quad = \dfrac{12}{36}$

$\quad = \dfrac{1}{3}$

$\left(-4, \tfrac{1}{3}\right)$

9. $f(x) = \sqrt[3]{5 - 24x}$

$f\left(\dfrac{4}{3}\right) = \sqrt[3]{5 - 24\left(\dfrac{4}{3}\right)}$

$\quad = \sqrt[3]{5 - 32}$

$\quad = \sqrt[3]{-27}$

$\quad = -3$

$\left(\tfrac{4}{3}, -3\right)$

10. $g(x) = |3x + 10|$

$g(-6) = |3(-6) + 10|$

$\quad = |-18 + 10|$

$\quad = |-8|$

$\quad = 8$

$(-6, 8)$

11. $f(x) = -8x + 13$

$f(x - 4) = -8(x - 4) + 13$

$\quad = -8x + 32 + 13$

$\quad = -8x + 45$

12. $h(x) = 3x^2 - x - 5$

$h(x + 2) = 3(x + 2)^2 - (x + 2) - 5$

$\quad = 3(x^2 + 4x + 4) - x - 7$

$\quad = 3x^2 + 12x + 12 - x - 7$

$\quad = 3x^2 + 11x + 5$

13. $g(t) = 1 + 12t$

$g\left(\dfrac{1}{6-c}\right) = 1 + 12\left(\dfrac{1}{6-c}\right)$

$\quad = 1 + \dfrac{12}{6-c}$

$\quad = \dfrac{6-c}{6-c} + \dfrac{12}{6-c}$

$\quad = \dfrac{18-c}{6-c}$

14. $\dfrac{f(a+h)-f(a)}{h}=\dfrac{\left[3(a+h)+5\right]-\left[3(a)+5\right]}{h}$

$=\dfrac{3a+3h+5-3a-5}{h}$

$=\dfrac{3\overset{1}{\cancel{h}}}{\underset{1}{\cancel{h}}}$

$=3$

15. This graph does represent a function, since any vertical line drawn would intersect the graph at most once.

16. This graph does not represent a function, since there is a vertical line that intersects the graph twice.

17. This graph does not represent a function, since there is a vertical line that intersects the graph twice.

18. This graph does not represent a function, since there is a vertical line that intersects the graph twice.

19. $(f+g)(x)=f(x)+g(x)$

$=\left(2x^2+5\right)+(x-12)$

$=2x^2+x-7$

$D=(-\infty,\infty)$

20. $(f-g)(x)=f(x)-g(x)$

$=\left(2x^2+5\right)-(x-12)$

$=2x^2-x+17$

$D=(-\infty,\infty)$

21. $(g-f)(x)=g(x)-f(x)$

$=(x-12)-\left(2x^2+5\right)$

$=-2x^2+x-17$

$D=(-\infty,\infty)$

22. $(g\cdot f)(x)=g(x)\cdot f(x)$

$=(x-12)\left(2x^2+5\right)$

$=2x^3+5x-24x^2-60$

$=2x^3-24x^2+5x-60$

$D=(-\infty,\infty)$

23. $\left(\dfrac{f}{g}\right)(x)=\dfrac{f(x)}{g(x)}$

$=\dfrac{2x^2+5}{x-12}$

$D=\{x\,|\,x\neq 12\}$

24. $\left(\dfrac{g}{f}\right)(x)=\dfrac{g(x)}{f(x)}$

$=\dfrac{x-12}{2x^2+5}$

$D=(-\infty,\infty)$

25. $(g+f)(x)=g(x)+f(x)$

$=\dfrac{x}{x^2-9}+\dfrac{8}{x+3}$

$=\dfrac{x}{(x+3)(x-3)}+\dfrac{8(x-3)}{(x+3)(x-3)}$

$=\dfrac{x+8x-24}{(x+3)(x-3)}$

$=\dfrac{9x-24}{x^2-9}$

$D=\{x\,|\,x\neq -3 \text{ and } x\neq 3\}$

$(g+f)(0)=\dfrac{9(0)-24}{(0)^2-9}$

$=\dfrac{8}{3}$

26. $(g+f)(x)=g(x)+f(x)$

$=\dfrac{x}{x^2-9}+\dfrac{8}{x+3}$

$=\dfrac{x}{(x+3)(x-3)}+\dfrac{8(x-3)}{(x+3)(x-3)}$

$=\dfrac{x+8x-24}{(x+3)(x-3)}$

$=\dfrac{9x-24}{x^2-9}$

$D=\{x\,|\,x\neq -3 \text{ and } x\neq 3\}$

$(g+f)(3)$ is undefined

27. $(f-g)(x) = f(x) - g(x)$

$$= \frac{8}{x+3} - \frac{x}{x^2-9}$$

$$= \frac{8(x-3)}{(x+3)(x-3)} - \frac{x}{(x+3)(x-3)}$$

$$= \frac{8x-24-x}{(x+3)(x-3)}$$

$$= \frac{7x-24}{x^2-9}$$

$$D = \{x \mid x \neq -3 \text{ and } x \neq 3\}$$

$$(f-g)(2) = \frac{7(2)-24}{(2)^2-9}$$

$$= \frac{14-24}{4-9}$$

$$= \frac{-10}{-5}$$

$$= 2$$

28. $(g-f)(x) = g(x) - f(x)$

$$= \frac{x}{x^2-9} - \frac{8}{x+3}$$

$$= \frac{x}{(x+3)(x-3)} - \frac{8(x-3)}{(x+3)(x-3)}$$

$$= \frac{x-8x+24}{(x+3)(x-3)}$$

$$= \frac{-7x+24}{x^2-9}$$

$$D = \{x \mid x \neq -3 \text{ and } x \neq 3\}$$

$$(g-f)(2) = \frac{-7(2)+24}{(2)^2-9}$$

$$= \frac{-14+24}{4-9}$$

$$= \frac{10}{-5}$$

$$= -2$$

29. $(g \cdot f)(x) = g(x) \cdot f(x)$

$$= \left(\frac{x}{x^2-9}\right)\left(\frac{8}{x+3}\right)$$

$$= \frac{8x}{(x+3)^2(x-3)}$$

$$D = \{x \mid x \neq -3 \text{ and } x \neq 3\}$$

$$(g \cdot f)(4) = \frac{8(4)}{((4)+3)^2((4)-3)}$$

$$= \frac{32}{(7)^2(1)}$$

$$= \frac{32}{49}$$

30. $(f \cdot g)(x) = f(x) \cdot g(x)$

$$= \left(\frac{8}{x+3}\right)\left(\frac{x}{x^2-9}\right)$$

$$= \frac{8x}{(x+3)^2(x-3)}$$

$$D = \{x \mid x \neq -3 \text{ and } x \neq 3\}$$

$$(f \cdot g)(2) = \frac{8(2)}{((2)+3)^2((2)-3)}$$

$$= \frac{16}{(5)^2(-1)}$$

$$= -\frac{16}{25}$$

31. $\left(\dfrac{f}{g}\right)(x) = \dfrac{f(x)}{g(x)}$

$$= \frac{\dfrac{8}{x+3}}{\dfrac{x}{x^2-9}}$$

$$= \left(\frac{8}{x+3}\right)\left(\frac{x^2-9}{x+3}\right)$$

$$= \left(\frac{8}{\cancel{(x+3)}}\right)\left(\frac{\cancel{(x+3)}(x-3)}{x+3}\right)$$

$$= \frac{8x-24}{x+3}$$

$$D = \{x \mid x \neq -3 \text{ and } x \neq 0 \text{ and } x \neq 3\}$$

32. $\left(\dfrac{g}{f}\right)(x) = \dfrac{g(x)}{f(x)}$

$= \dfrac{\dfrac{x}{x^2-9}}{\dfrac{8}{x+3}}$

$= \left(\dfrac{x}{x^2-9}\right)\left(\dfrac{x+3}{8}\right)$

$= \left(\dfrac{x}{(x+3)(x-3)}\right)\left(\dfrac{(x+3)}{8}\right)$

$= \dfrac{x}{8x-24}$

$D = \{x \mid x \neq -3 \text{ and } x \neq 3\}$

33. $\left(\dfrac{g}{f}\right)(x) = \dfrac{x}{8x-24}$

$D = \{x \mid x \neq -3 \text{ and } x \neq 3\}$

$\left(\dfrac{g}{f}\right)(3)$ is not defined

34. $\left(\dfrac{f}{g}\right)(x) = \dfrac{8x-24}{x+3}$

$D = \{x \mid x \neq -3 \text{ and } x \neq 0 \text{ and } x \neq 3\}$

$\left(\dfrac{f}{g}\right)(0)$ is not defined

35. $(f \circ g)(t) = f\big(g(t)\big)$

$= f\big(3t^2+2\big)$

$= 5\big(3t^2+2\big)$

$= 15t^2+10$

$D = (-\infty, \infty)$

36. $(g \circ f)(t) = g\big(f(t)\big)$

$= g(5t)$

$= 3(5t)^2+2$

$= 3 \cdot 25t^2+2$

$= 75t^2+2$

$D = (-\infty, \infty)$

37. $(g \circ g)(t) = g\big(g(t)\big)$

$= g\big(3t^2+2\big)$

$= 3\big(3t^2+2\big)^2+2$

$= 3\big(9t^4+12t^2+4\big)+2$

$= 27t^4+36t^2+12+2$

$= 27t^4+36t^2+14$

$D = (-\infty, \infty)$

38. $(f \circ f)(t) = f\big(f(t)\big)$

$= f(5t)$

$= 5(5t)$

$= 25t$

$D = (-\infty, \infty)$

39. $(g \circ g)(t) = 27t^4+36t^2+14$

$(g \circ g)(1) = 27(1)^4+36(1)^2+14$

$= 27+36+14$

$= 77$

40. $(g \circ f)(t) = 75t^2+2$

$(g \circ f)(1) = 75(1)^2+2$

$= 75+2$

$= 77$

41. $(h \circ g)(6) = h\big(g(6)\big)$

$= h\big(3(6)^2+2\big)$

$= h\big(3(36)+2\big)$

$= h(108+2)$

$= h(110)$

$= \sqrt{(110)-2}$

$= \sqrt{108}$

$= 6\sqrt{3}$

42. $(f \circ f)(3) = f(f(3))$

$= f(5(3))$

$= f(15)$

$= 5(15)$

75

43. $f(x) = 4$

x	$f(x)$	$(x, f(x))$
-1	4	$(-1, 4)$
0	4	$(0, 4)$
1	4	$(1, 4)$

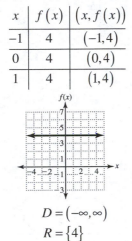

$D = (-\infty, \infty)$
$R = \{4\}$

44. $f(x) = x + 3$

x	$f(x)$	$(x, f(x))$
-1	$(-1) + 3 = 2$	$(-1, 2)$
0	$(0) + 3 = 3$	$(0, 3)$
1	$(1) + 3 = 4$	$(1, 4)$

$D = (-\infty, \infty)$
$R = (-\infty, \infty)$

45. $f(x) = 3x$

x	$f(x)$	$(x, f(x))$
-1	$3(-1) = -3$	$(-1, -3)$
0	$3(0) = 0$	$(0, 0)$
1	$3(1) = 3$	$(1, 3)$

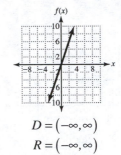

$D = (-\infty, \infty)$
$R = (-\infty, \infty)$

46. $g(x) = \sqrt{x-3}$

x	$g(x)$	$(x, g(x))$
3	$\sqrt{(3) - 3} = 0$	$(3, 0)$
4	$\sqrt{(4) - 3} = 1$	$(4, 1)$
7	$\sqrt{(7) - 3} = 2$	$(7, 2)$

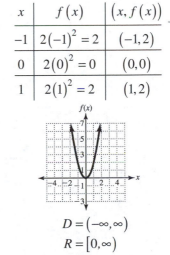

$D = [3, \infty)$
$R = [0, \infty)$

47. $f(x) = 2x^2$

x	$f(x)$	$(x, f(x))$
-1	$2(-1)^2 = 2$	$(-1, 2)$
0	$2(0)^2 = 0$	$(0, 0)$
1	$2(1)^2 = 2$	$(1, 2)$

$D = (-\infty, \infty)$
$R = [0, \infty)$

48. $h(x) = |x+2|$

x	$h(x)$	$(x, h(x))$
−3	$|(-3)+2| = 1$	$(-3, 1)$
−2	$|(-2)+2| = 0$	$(-2, 0)$
−1	$|(-1)+2| = 1$	$(-1, 1)$

$D = (-\infty, \infty)$

$R = [0, \infty)$

49. $h(x) = 2|x|$

x	$h(x)$	$(x, h(x))$
−1	$2|-1| = 2$	$(-1, 2)$
0	$2|0| = 0$	$(0, 0)$
1	$2|1| = 2$	$(1, 2)$

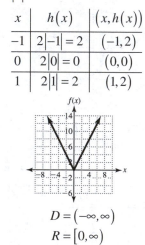

$D = (-\infty, \infty)$

$R = [0, \infty)$

50. $g(x) = 2x^3$

x	$g(x)$	$(x, g(x))$
−1	$2(-1)^3 = -2$	$(-1, -2)$
0	$2(0)^3 = 0$	$(0, 0)$
1	$2(1)^3 = 2$	$(1, 2)$

$D = (-\infty, \infty)$

$R = (-\infty, \infty)$

51. $g(x) = |2x|$

x	$g(x)$	$(x, g(x))$
−1	$|2(-1)| = 2$	$(-1, 2)$
0	$|2(0)| = 0$	$(0, 0)$
1	$|2(1)| = 2$	$(1, 2)$

$D = (-\infty, \infty)$

$R = [0, \infty)$

52. $g(x) = -\dfrac{1}{2}x^2$

x	$g(x)$	$(x, g(x))$
−2	$-\frac{1}{2}(-2)^2 = 2$	$(-2, -2)$
0	$-\frac{1}{2}(0)^2 = 2$	$(0, 0)$
2	$-\frac{1}{2}(2)^2 = 2$	$(2, -2)$

$D = (-\infty, \infty)$

$R = (-\infty, 0]$

53. $h(x) = \sqrt{x+3}$

x	$h(x)$	$(x, h(x))$
−3	$\sqrt{(-3)+3} = 0$	$(-3, 0)$
−2	$\sqrt{(-2)+3} = 1$	$(-2, 1)$
1	$\sqrt{(1)+3} = 2$	$(1, 2)$

$D = [-3, \infty)$

$R = [0, \infty)$

54. $h(x) = (x-2)^2$

x	$h(x)$	$(x, h(x))$
1	$((1)-2)^2 = 1$	$(1,1)$
2	$((2)-2)^2 = 0$	$(2,0)$
3	$((3)-2)^2 = 1$	$(3,1)$

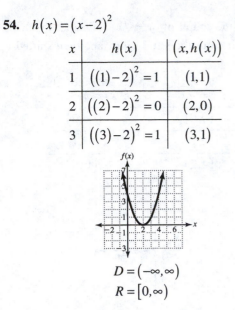

$$D = (-\infty, \infty)$$
$$R = [0, \infty)$$

55. This is the graph of $y = x^2$ shifted up 2 units.

$y = x^2$	$f(x) = x^2 + 2$
$(-1,1)$	$(-1,3)$
$(0,0)$	$(0,2)$
$(1,1)$	$(1,3)$

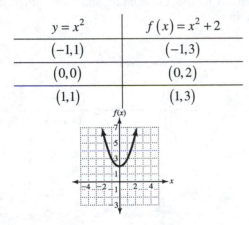

56. This is the graph of $y = |x|$ shifted to the right 3 units.

$y = |x|$	$f(x) = |x-3|$
$(-1,1)$	$(2,1)$
$(0,0)$	$(3,0)$
$(1,1)$	$(4,1)$

57. This is the graph of $y = x^3$ shifted down 1 unit.

$y = x^3$	$g(x) = x^3 - 1$
$(-1,1)$	$(-1,-2)$
$(0,0)$	$(0,-1)$
$(1,1)$	$(1,0)$

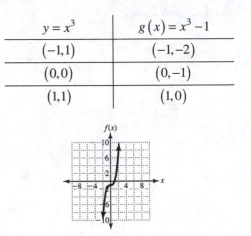

58. This is the graph of $y = \sqrt{x}$ shifted to the right 1 unit and then shifted up 2 units.

$y = \sqrt{x}$	$g(x) = \sqrt{x-1} + 2$
$(0,0)$	$(1,2)$
$(1,1)$	$(2,3)$
$(4,2)$	$(5,4)$

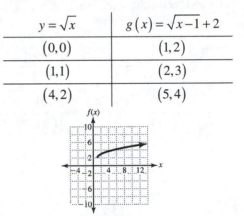

59. This is the graph of $y = |x|$ shifted to the left 3 units and then shifted down 3 units.

$y = |x|$	$k(x) = |x+3| - 3$
$(-1,1)$	$(-4,-2)$
$(0,0)$	$(-3,-3)$
$(1,1)$	$(-2,-2)$

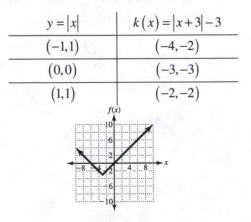

60. This is the graph of $y = |x|$ reflected about the x-axis and then shifted up 1 unit.

$y = |x|$	$k(x) = -|x| + 1$
$(-1, 1)$	$(-1, 0)$
$(0, 0)$	$(0, 1)$
$(1, 1)$	$(1, 0)$

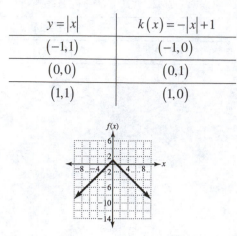

61. This is the graph of $y = x$ reflected about the x-axis and then shifted up 3 units.

$y = x$	$h(x) = -x + 3$
$(-1, -1)$	$(-1, 4)$
$(0, 0)$	$(0, 3)$
$(1, 1)$	$(1, 2)$

62. This is the graph of $y = \sqrt{x}$ reflected about the y-axis and then shifted down 2 units.

$y = \sqrt{x}$	$h(x) = \sqrt{-x} - 2$
$(0, 0)$	$(0, -2)$
$(1, 1)$	$(-1, -1)$
$(4, 2)$	$(-4, 0)$

63. This is the graph of $y = \sqrt{x}$ reflected about the x-axis, shifted to the left 3 units, and then shifted up 2 units.

$y = \sqrt{x}$	$r(x) = 2 - \sqrt{x + 3}$
$(0, 0)$	$(-3, 2)$
$(1, 1)$	$(-2, 1)$
$(4, 2)$	$(1, 0)$

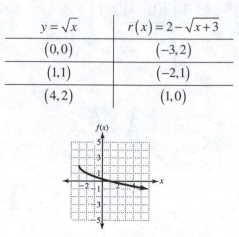

64. This is the graph of $y = |x|$ reflected about the x-axis, shifted to the left 2 units, and then shifted down 2 units.

$y = |x|$	$s(x) = -|x + 2| - 2$
$(-1, 1)$	$(-3, -3)$
$(0, 0)$	$(-2, -2)$
$(1, 1)$	$(-1, -3)$

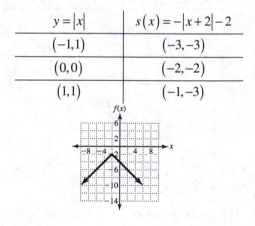

CHAPTER 9 TEST

1. a, f

2. b, e

3. c, i, g

4. d, f

5. j, g

6. a) This is a function from the set X to the set Y.
The domain is $D = \{-2, -1, 0, 1, 2, 3\}$
The range is $R = \{-6, 0, 5, 23\}$

b) This is a function from the set X to the set Y.
The domain is $D = \{-2, -1, 0, 1, 2, 3\}$.
The range is $R = \{-4, 5, 11\}$.

7. $h(x) = 9x^2 - 6x + 5$

$h\left(-\dfrac{1}{3}\right) = 9\left(-\dfrac{1}{3}\right)^2 - 6\left(-\dfrac{1}{3}\right) + 5$

$\qquad = 9\left(\dfrac{1}{9}\right) - 6\left(-\dfrac{1}{3}\right) + 5$

$\qquad = 1 + 2 + 5$

$\qquad = 8$

The ordered pair is $\left(-\dfrac{1}{3}, 8\right)$.

8. $g(t) = \sqrt[3]{7x^3 + 8}$

$g(2) = \sqrt[3]{7(2)^3 + 8}$

$\qquad = \sqrt[3]{7(8) + 8}$

$\qquad = \sqrt[3]{56 + 8}$

$\qquad = \sqrt[3]{64}$

$\qquad = 4$

The ordered pair is $(2, 4)$

9. $\dfrac{f(a+h) - f(a)}{h} = \dfrac{[5(a+h) - 12] - [5(a) - 12]}{h}$

$\qquad = \dfrac{[5a + 5h - 12] - 5a + 12}{h}$

$\qquad = \dfrac{5h}{h}$

$\qquad = 5$

10. a) This graph does not represent a function because it does not pass the vertical line test.

b) This graph does not represent a function because it does not pass the vertical line test.

11. $(f - h)(x) = f(x) - h(x)$

$\qquad = (6x - 10) - (2x + 5)$

$\qquad = 6x - 10 - 2x - 5$

$\qquad = 4x - 15$

The domain of $f - h$ is $D = (-\infty, \infty)$.

12. $(g \cdot f)(x) = g(x) \cdot f(x)$

$\qquad = \left(x^2 - 3\right)(6x - 10)$

$\qquad = 6x^3 - 10x^2 - 18x + 30$

The domain of $g \cdot f$ is $D = (-\infty, \infty)$.

13. $\left(\dfrac{g}{h}\right)(x) = \dfrac{g(x)}{h(x)}$

$\qquad = \dfrac{x^2 - 3}{2x + 5}$

Domain

$\qquad\qquad 2x + 5 = 0$

$\qquad\qquad 2x = -5$

$\qquad\qquad x = -\dfrac{5}{2}$

The domain of $\dfrac{g}{h}$ is $D = \left\{x \;\middle|\; x \neq -\dfrac{5}{2}\right\}$.

14. $(f - g)(t) = f(t) - g(t)$

$\qquad = \left(\dfrac{2}{t+3}\right) - \left(\dfrac{7}{t^2 - 9}\right)$

$\qquad = \dfrac{2(t-3)}{(t+3)(t-3)} - \dfrac{7}{(t+3)(t-3)}$

$\qquad = \dfrac{2t - 6 - 7}{(t+3)(t-3)}$

$\qquad = \dfrac{2t - 13}{t^2 - 9}$

Domain

$\qquad\qquad t^2 - 9 = 0$

$\qquad\qquad t^9 = 0$

$\qquad\qquad t = -3 \quad or \quad t = 3$

The domain of $f - g$ is $D = \{t \mid t \neq -3 \text{ and } t \neq 3\}$.

15. $\left(\dfrac{g}{f}\right)(t) = \dfrac{g(t)}{f(t)}$

$$= \dfrac{\dfrac{7}{t^2-9}}{\dfrac{2}{t+3}}$$

$$= \dfrac{7}{t^2-9} \cdot \dfrac{t+3}{2}$$

$$= \dfrac{7}{\underset{1}{\cancel{(t+3)}}(t-3)} \cdot \dfrac{\overset{1}{\cancel{t+3}}}{2}$$

$$= \dfrac{7}{2t-6}$$

The domain of $\dfrac{g}{f}$ is $D = \{t \mid t \neq -3 \text{ and } t \neq 3\}$.

$\left(\dfrac{g}{f}\right)(-3)$ is undefined because -3 is not in the domain.

16. $(f \circ g)(t) = f(g(t))$

$$= 6(-4t^2) + 1$$

$$= -24t^2 + 1$$

The domain is $D = (-\infty, \infty)$

17. $(h \circ g)(t) = h(g(t))$

$$= \left|(-4t^2) - 3\right|$$

$$= \left|-4t^2 - 3\right|$$

The domain is $D = (-\infty, \infty)$.

$(h \circ g)(-2) = \left|-4(-2)^2 - 3\right|$

$$= \left|-4(4) - 3\right|$$

$$= \left|-16 - 3\right|$$

$$= \left|-19\right|$$

$$= 19$$

18. $(g \circ f)(t) = g(f(t))$

$$= -4(6t + 1)^2$$

$$= -4(36t^2 + 12t + 1)$$

$$= -144t^2 - 48t - 4$$

The domain is $D = (-\infty, \infty)$.

19. $h(x) = 3\sqrt{x+2} - 1$

x	$f(x)$	$(x, f(x))$
-2	-1	$(-2, -1)$
-1	2	$(-1, 2)$
2	5	$(2, 5)$

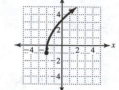

Domain $= [-2, \infty)$, Range $= [-1, \infty)$

20. $g(x) = x^3 + 2$

The basic graph is $f(x) = x^3$.

The translation is a vertical shift up 2 units.

$f(x) = x^3$	$g(x) = x^3 + 2$
$(-1, -1)$	$(-1, 1)$
$(0, 0)$	$(0, 2)$
$(1, 1)$	$(1, 3)$

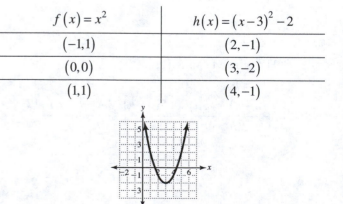

21. $h(x) = (x-3)^2 - 2$

The basic graph is $f(x) = x^2$.

The translation is a vertical shift down 2 units and a horizontal shift right 3 units.

$f(x) = x^2$	$h(x) = (x-3)^2 - 2$
$(-1, 1)$	$(2, -1)$
$(0, 0)$	$(3, -2)$
$(1, 1)$	$(4, -1)$

22. $f(x) = -|x| + 3$

The basic graph is $y = |x|$.

There is a reflection about the x-axis and a vertical shift up 3 units.

$y = |x|$	$f(x) = -|x| + 3$
$(-1, 1)$	$(-1, 2)$
$(0, 0)$	$(0, 3)$
$(1, 1)$	$(1, 2)$

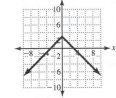

23. $f(L) = 2\pi \sqrt{\dfrac{L}{32}}$

$f(4) = 2\pi \sqrt{\dfrac{4}{32}}$

$\quad = 2\pi \sqrt{\dfrac{1}{8}}$

$\quad = \dfrac{2\pi}{\sqrt{8}}$

$\quad = \dfrac{2\pi}{2\sqrt{2}}$

$\quad = \dfrac{\pi}{\sqrt{2}} \cdot \dfrac{\sqrt{2}}{\sqrt{2}}$

$\quad = \dfrac{\pi\sqrt{2}}{2}$

$\quad \approx 2.22$

The time it would take to complete one full cycle $\dfrac{\pi\sqrt{2}}{2}$ seconds, or approximately 2.22 seconds.

24. a) $h(t) = -16t^2 + 16t + 32$

$h(1) = -16(1)^2 + 16(1) + 32$

$\quad = 32$

The height of the penny at $t = 1$ second is 32 feet.

b) $h(t) = -16t^2 + 16t + 32$

$h(1.5) = -16(1.5)^2 + 16(1.5) + 32$

$\quad = -36 + 24 + 32$

$\quad = 20$

The height of the penny at $t = 1.5$ seconds is 20 feet.

c) $h(t) = -16t^2 + 16t + 32$

$h(2) = -16(2)^2 + 16(2) + 32$

$\quad = -64 + 32 + 32$

$\quad = 0$

The height of the penny at $t = 2$ seconds is 0 feet.

d) The penny achieves a height of 32 feet at 1 second and continues to fall to the surface of the water at 2 seconds.

25. Prepare We must determine why the company has a minimum of 6 backpackers policy.

Plan We can determine the profit function and evaluate it for the values $x = 5$ and $x = 6$.

Process

$P(x) = R(x) - C(x)$

$\quad = \left(100x^2\right) - \left(210x + 1610\right)$

$\quad = 100x^2 - 210x - 1610$

$P(5) = 100(5)^2 - 210(5) - 1610$

$\quad = -160$

$P(6) = 100(6)^2 - 210(6) - 1610$

$\quad = 730$

If the company were to allow less than 6 backpackers, it would lose money. Therefore, the domain is $[6, 18]$.

Ponder The conclusion is reasonable because a company would want to make a positive profit.

Chapters 7-9 Cumulative Review

1. $\dfrac{3ax+6ab+bx+2b^2}{2ax+4ab-x^2-2bx} = \dfrac{\overset{1}{\cancel{(x+2b)}}\,(3a+b)}{\underset{1}{\cancel{(x+2b)}}\,(2a-x)}$

$$= \dfrac{3a+b}{2a-x}$$

2. $\dfrac{9b^2-24ab+16a^2}{4a^2-3ab} = \dfrac{\overset{1}{\cancel{(4a-3b)}}\,(4a-3b)}{a\,\underset{1}{\cancel{(4a-3b)}}}$

$$= \dfrac{4a-3b}{a}$$

3. $\dfrac{x^2}{x+3}\cdot\dfrac{x^2-4x-21}{x^2-5x}\div\dfrac{x^2-49}{x^2-10x+25}$

$$= \dfrac{x^2}{x+3}\cdot\dfrac{x^2-4x-21}{x^2-5x}\cdot\dfrac{x^2-10x+25}{x^2-49}$$

$$= \dfrac{x^2}{x+3}\cdot\dfrac{(x-7)(x+3)}{x(x-5)}\cdot\dfrac{(x-5)(x-5)}{(x+7)(x-7)}$$

$$= \dfrac{\overset{x}{\cancel{x^2}}\,\overset{1}{\cancel{(x-7)}}\,\overset{1}{\cancel{(x+3)}}\,\overset{1}{\cancel{(x-5)}}\,(x-5)}{\underset{1}{\cancel{x}}\,\underset{1}{\cancel{(x+3)}}\,\underset{1}{\cancel{(x-5)}}\,(x+7)\,\underset{1}{\cancel{(x-7)}}}$$

$$= \dfrac{x^2-5x}{x+7}$$

4. $\dfrac{a^2+a-7}{a^2+3a-10}+\dfrac{a^2+5a-13}{a^2+3a-10}$

$$= \dfrac{a^2+a-7+a^2+5a-13}{a^2+3a-10}$$

$$= \dfrac{2a^2+6a-20}{a^2+3a-10}$$

$$= \dfrac{2\,\overset{1}{\cancel{(a^2+3a-10)}}}{\underset{1}{\cancel{(a^2+3a-10)}}}$$

$$= 2$$

5. $\dfrac{x-2}{x^2+2x-8}-\dfrac{x+4}{x^2-16}$

$$= \dfrac{x-2}{(x-2)(x+4)}-\dfrac{x+4}{(x+4)(x-4)}$$

$$= \dfrac{(x-2)(x-4)}{(x-2)(x+4)(x-4)}-\dfrac{(x-2)(x+4)}{(x-2)(x+4)(x-4)}$$

$$= \dfrac{x^2-6x+8}{(x-2)(x+4)(x-4)}-\dfrac{x^2+2x-8}{(x-2)(x+4)(x-4)}$$

$$= \dfrac{x^2-6x+8-\left(x^2+2x-8\right)}{(x-2)(x+4)(x-4)}$$

$$= \dfrac{x^2-6x+8-x^2-2x+8}{(x-2)(x+4)(x-4)}$$

$$= \dfrac{-8x+16}{(x-2)(x+4)(x-4)}$$

$$= \dfrac{-8\,\overset{1}{\cancel{(x-2)}}}{\underset{1}{\cancel{(x-2)}}\,(x+4)(x-4)}$$

$$= -\dfrac{8}{(x+4)(x-4)}$$

6. $\dfrac{y}{y-3}-\dfrac{2}{y+4}-\dfrac{14}{y^2+y-12}$

$$= \dfrac{y}{y-3}-\dfrac{2}{y+4}-\dfrac{14}{(y-3)(y+4)}$$

$$= \dfrac{y(y+4)}{(y-3)(y+4)}-\dfrac{2(y-3)}{(y-3)(y+4)}-\dfrac{14}{(y-3)(y+4)}$$

$$= \dfrac{y^2+4y}{(y-3)(y+4)}-\dfrac{2y-6}{(y-3)(y+4)}-\dfrac{14}{(y-3)(y+4)}$$

$$= \dfrac{y^2+4y-(2y-6)-(14)}{(y-3)(y+4)}$$

$$= \dfrac{y^2+4y-2y+6-14}{(y-3)(y+4)}$$

$$= \dfrac{y^2+2y-8}{(y-3)(y+4)}$$

$$= \dfrac{(y-2)\,\overset{1}{\cancel{(y+4)}}}{(y-3)\,\underset{1}{\cancel{(y+4)}}}$$

$$= \dfrac{y-2}{y-3}$$

7. $\dfrac{\dfrac{1}{2}+\dfrac{1}{a}}{\dfrac{4}{a^2}-1}=\dfrac{\dfrac{1}{2}+\dfrac{1}{a}}{\dfrac{4}{a^2}-1}\cdot\dfrac{\dfrac{2a^2}{1}}{\dfrac{2a^2}{1}}$

$$=\dfrac{\dfrac{\cancel{2}^{\,1}\,a^2}{1}\cdot\dfrac{1}{\cancel{2}^{\,1}}+\dfrac{2\,\cancel{a^2}^{\,a}}{1}\cdot\dfrac{1}{\cancel{a}^{\,1}}}{\dfrac{2\,\cancel{a^2}^{\,1}}{1}\cdot\dfrac{4}{\cancel{a^2}^{\,1}}-2a^2\cdot1}$$

$$=\dfrac{a^2+2a}{8-2a^2}$$

$$=\dfrac{a\,\cancel{(a+2)}^{\,1}}{2\,\cancel{(2+a)}_{\,1}\,(2-a)}$$

$$=\dfrac{a}{2(2-a)}$$

8.

$$\dfrac{-7}{2x+8}=\dfrac{16}{8x-12}$$

$$\dfrac{-7}{2(x+4)}=\dfrac{16}{4(2x-3)}$$

$$\dfrac{\cancel{4}^{\,2}\,\cancel{(x+4)}^{\,1}\,(2x-3)}{1}\cdot\dfrac{-7}{\cancel{2}_{\,1}\,\cancel{(x+4)}_{\,1}}=\dfrac{16}{\cancel{4}_{\,1}\,\cancel{(2x-3)}_{\,1}}\cdot\dfrac{\cancel{4}^{\,1}\,(x+4)\,\cancel{(2x-3)}^{\,1}}{1}$$

$$-28x+42=16x+64$$

$$-44x=22$$

$$x=-\dfrac{1}{2}$$

Solution Set: $\left\{-\dfrac{1}{2}\right\}$

9.
$$\frac{2y^2}{y+1}+1=\frac{2}{y+1}$$

$$\frac{y+1}{1}\left(\frac{2y^2}{y+1}+1\right)=\frac{y+1}{1}\left(\frac{2}{y+1}\right)$$

$$\frac{\cancel{y+1}^{1}}{1}\cdot\frac{2y^2}{\cancel{y+1}_{1}}+(y+1)1=\frac{\cancel{y+1}^{1}}{1}\cdot\frac{2}{\cancel{y+1}_{1}}$$

$$2y^2+y+1=2$$
$$2y^2+y-1=0$$
$$(2y-1)(y+1)=0$$
$$2y-1=0 \quad\text{or}\quad y+1=0$$
$$y=\frac{1}{2} \qquad \cancel{y=-1}$$

Solution Set: $\left\{\dfrac{1}{2}\right\}$

10. Let $t=$ the amount of time it takes Laurie to complete the job by herself. It takes Salli $t-12$ minutes to complete the job by herself.

$$\left(\begin{matrix}\text{Time}\\\text{Worked}\end{matrix}\right)\left(\begin{matrix}\text{Laurie's}\\\text{Rate}\end{matrix}\right)+\left(\begin{matrix}\text{Time}\\\text{Worked}\end{matrix}\right)\left(\begin{matrix}\text{Salli's}\\\text{Rate}\end{matrix}\right)=1$$

$$8\left(\frac{1}{t}\right)+8\left(\frac{1}{t-12}\right)=1$$

$$8(t-12)+8t=t(t-12)$$
$$8t-96+8t=t^2-12t$$
$$0=t^2-28t+96$$
$$0=(t-4)(t-24)$$
$$t-4=0 \quad\text{or}\quad t-24=0$$
$$\cancel{t=4} \qquad\qquad t=24$$

It takes Laurie 24 minutes to complete the job alone.

11. $\sqrt{180a^{17}b^{10}}=\sqrt{36a^{16}b^{10}\cdot 5a}$
$$=\sqrt{36a^{16}b^{10}}\cdot\sqrt{5a}$$
$$=6a^8b^5\sqrt{5a}$$

12. $2\sqrt{27}-10\sqrt{75}+\sqrt{48}=2\sqrt{9\cdot3}-10\sqrt{25\cdot3}+\sqrt{16\cdot3}$
$$=2\cdot3\sqrt{3}-10\cdot5\sqrt{3}+4\sqrt{3}$$
$$=6\sqrt{3}-50\sqrt{3}+4\sqrt{3}$$
$$=(6-50+4)\sqrt{3}$$
$$=-40\sqrt{3}$$

13. $\left(3+5\sqrt{6}\right)^2=(3)^2+2(3)\left(5\sqrt{6}\right)+\left(5\sqrt{6}\right)^2$
$$=9+30\sqrt{6}+25(6)$$
$$=159+30\sqrt{6}$$

14. $\dfrac{1}{4+\sqrt{7}}=\dfrac{1}{4+\sqrt{7}}\cdot\dfrac{4-\sqrt{7}}{4-\sqrt{7}}$
$$=\frac{4-\sqrt{7}}{(4)^2-\left(\sqrt{7}\right)^2}$$
$$=\frac{4-\sqrt{7}}{16-7}$$
$$=\frac{4-\sqrt{7}}{9}$$

15. $3+\sqrt{-8+4x}=7$
$$\sqrt{-8+4x}=4$$
$$\left(\sqrt{-8+4x}\right)^2=(4)^2$$
$$-8+4x=16$$
$$4x=24$$
$$x=6$$
Solution Set: $\{6\}$

16. $\sqrt{x^2-7x}=\sqrt{5x-20}$
$$\left(\sqrt{x^2-7x}\right)^2=\left(\sqrt{5x-20}\right)^2$$
$$x^2-7x=5x-20$$
$$x^2-12x+20=0$$
$$(x-10)(x-2)=0$$
$$x-10=0 \quad\text{or}\quad x-2=0$$
$$x=10 \qquad\qquad \cancel{x=2}$$
Solution Set: $\{10\}$

17. $\sqrt[5]{5t+4}=2$
$$\left(\sqrt[5]{5t+4}\right)^5=(2)^5$$
$$5t+4=32$$
$$5t=28$$
$$t=\frac{28}{5}$$
Solution Set: $\left\{\dfrac{28}{5}\right\}$

18. $\sqrt[3]{-24a^8b^{27}} = \sqrt[3]{-8a^6b^{27}\cdot 3a^2}$

$\qquad = \sqrt[3]{-8a^6b^{27}}\cdot\sqrt[3]{3a^2}$

$\qquad -2a^2b^9\sqrt[3]{3a^2}$

19. $\sqrt[4]{100x^3}\cdot\sqrt[4]{200x^5} = \sqrt[4]{20,000x^8}$

$\qquad = \sqrt[4]{10,000x^8\cdot 2}$

$\qquad = \sqrt[4]{10,000x^8}\cdot\sqrt[4]{2}$

$\qquad = 10x^2\sqrt[4]{2}$

20. $49^{\frac{3}{2}} = \left(\sqrt{49}\right)^3$

$\qquad = (7)^3$

$\qquad = 343$

21. $g(-2) = -(-2)^2 + 12(-2) + 25$

$\qquad = -4 - 24 + 25$

$\qquad = -3$

22. $h(a-3) = -5(a-3) + 2$

$\qquad = -5a + 15 + 2$

$\qquad = -5a + 17$

23. This graph does represent a function, since any vertical line drawn would intersect the graph at most once.

24. $(f-g)(x) = (x-2) - \left(\dfrac{5}{x^2-1}\right)$

$\qquad = \dfrac{(x-2)(x^2-1)}{x^2-1} - \dfrac{5}{x^2-1}$

$\qquad = \dfrac{x^3-2x^2-x+2}{x^2-1} - \dfrac{5}{x^2-1}$

$\qquad = \dfrac{x^3-2x^2-x-3}{x^2-1}$

$\qquad\quad$ Domain

$\qquad\quad x^2-1=0$

$\qquad\quad (x+1)(x-1)=0$

$\qquad x+1=0 \quad$ or $\quad x-1=0$

$\qquad\quad x=-1 \;$ or $\qquad x=1$

$\qquad D = \{x\in R\,|\,x\neq -1, x\neq 1\}$

25. $(g\cdot f)(4) = g(4)\cdot f(4)$

$\qquad = \left(\dfrac{5}{(4)^2-1}\right)\big((4)-2\big)$

$\qquad = \dfrac{5}{15}(2)$

$\qquad = \dfrac{2}{3}$

$\qquad\quad$ Domain

$\qquad\quad x^2-1=0$

$\qquad\quad (x+1)(x-1)=0$

$\qquad x+1=0 \quad$ or $\quad x-1=0$

$\qquad\quad x=-1 \;$ or $\qquad x=1$

$\qquad D = \{x\in R\,|\,x\neq -1, x\neq 1\}$

26. $\left(\dfrac{f}{g}\right)(-4) = \dfrac{f(-4)}{g(4)}$

$\qquad = \dfrac{(-4)-2}{\dfrac{5}{(-4)^2-1}}$

$\qquad = \dfrac{-6}{\dfrac{1}{3}}$

$\qquad = \dfrac{-6}{1}\cdot\dfrac{3}{1}$

$\qquad = -18$

$\qquad\quad$ Domain

$\qquad\quad x^2-1=0$

$\qquad\quad (x+1)(x-1)=0$

$\qquad x+1=0 \quad$ or $\quad x-1=0$

$\qquad\quad x=-1 \;$ or $\qquad x=1$

$\qquad D = \{x\in R\,|\,x\neq -1, x\neq 1\}$

27. $(g\circ f)(x) = g(f(x))$

$\qquad = g(6x-2)$

$\qquad = |(6x-2)+4|$

$\qquad = |6x+2|$

$\qquad D = (-\infty,\infty)$

28. $f(x) = x^2 - 1$

x	$f(x)$	(x, y)
-1	1	$(-1, 1)$
0	-1	$0, -1$
1	1	$(1, 1)$

$D = (-\infty, \infty), \quad R = [-1, \infty)$

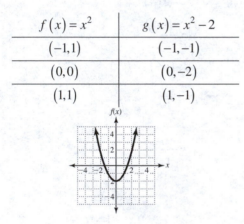

29. Shift the base graph $f(x) = x^2$ vertically down 2 units.

$f(x) = x^2$	$g(x) = x^2 - 2$
$(-1, 1)$	$(-1, -1)$
$(0, 0)$	$(0, -2)$
$(1, 1)$	$(1, -1)$

30. Shift the base graph $f(x) = |x|$ horizontally to the left 1 unit.

$f(x) = |x|$	$k(x) = |x + 1|$
$(-1, 1)$	$(-2, 1)$
$(0, 0)$	$(-1, 0)$
$(1, 1)$	$(0, 1)$

Chapter 10

10.1 Exercises

1. The imaginary unit i is equal to $\underline{\sqrt{-1}}$.

3. Any number that can be written in the form $a+bi$, where a and b are real numbers, is called a <u>complex</u> <u>number</u>.

5. For the complex number $a+bi$, a is called the <u>real</u> <u>part</u>.

7. True

9. $\sqrt{-36} = i\sqrt{36}$
$\phantom{\sqrt{-36}} = 6i$

11. $\sqrt{-1} = i\sqrt{1}$
$\phantom{\sqrt{-1}} = i$

13. $\sqrt{-2.9} = i\sqrt{2.9}$

15. $\sqrt{-54} = i\sqrt{54}$
$\phantom{\sqrt{-54}} = i\sqrt{9 \cdot 6}$
$\phantom{\sqrt{-54}} = i\sqrt{9} \cdot \sqrt{6}$
$\phantom{\sqrt{-54}} = 3i\sqrt{6}$

17. $\sqrt{-\dfrac{75}{49}} = i\sqrt{\dfrac{75}{49}}$
$\phantom{\sqrt{-\dfrac{75}{49}}} = \dfrac{i\sqrt{75}}{\sqrt{49}}$
$\phantom{\sqrt{-\dfrac{75}{49}}} = \dfrac{i\sqrt{25 \cdot 3}}{7}$
$\phantom{\sqrt{-\dfrac{75}{49}}} = \dfrac{i\sqrt{25} \cdot \sqrt{3}}{7}$
$\phantom{\sqrt{-\dfrac{75}{49}}} = \dfrac{5i\sqrt{3}}{7}$

19. $-\sqrt{-375} = -i\sqrt{375}$
$\phantom{-\sqrt{-375}} = -i\sqrt{25 \cdot 15}$
$\phantom{-\sqrt{-375}} = -i\sqrt{25} \cdot \sqrt{15}$
$\phantom{-\sqrt{-375}} = -5i\sqrt{15}$

21. $(12+5i)+(7-13i) = (12+7)+(5-13)i$
$ = 19-8i$

23. $(10-7i)-(8-i) = 10-7i-8+i$
$ = (10-8)+(-7+1)i$
$ = 2-6i$

25. $(20+4i)+(15-4i) = (20+15)+(4-4)i$
$ = 35+0i$

27. $\left(8\sqrt{6}+7i\right)+\left(-7\sqrt{6}-3i\right) = \left(8\sqrt{6}-7\sqrt{6}\right)+(7-3)i$
$\phantom{\left(8\sqrt{6}+7i\right)+\left(-7\sqrt{6}-3i\right)} = \sqrt{6}+4i$

29. $16i-(2-8i) = 16i-2+8i$
$ = -2+(16+8)i$
$ = -2+24i$

31. $\left(\dfrac{3}{2}+\dfrac{1}{3}i\right)+\left(\dfrac{4}{3}-\dfrac{5}{6}i\right) = \left(\dfrac{3}{2}+\dfrac{4}{3}\right)+\left(\dfrac{1}{3}-\dfrac{5}{6}\right)i$
$\phantom{\left(\dfrac{3}{2}+\dfrac{1}{3}i\right)+\left(\dfrac{4}{3}-\dfrac{5}{6}i\right)} = \dfrac{17}{6}-\dfrac{1}{2}i$

33. $(5i)(5i) = 25i^2$
$ = 25(-1)$
$ = -25+0i$

35. $(-0.3i)(0.11i) = -0.033i^2$
$ = -0.033(-1)$
$ = 0.033+0i$

37. $6i(6-9i) = 6i(6)-6i(9i)$
$ = 36i-54i^2$
$ = 36i-54(-1)$
$ = 54+36i$

39. $12i\left(\dfrac{2}{3}+\dfrac{1}{2}i\right) = 12i\left(\dfrac{2}{3}\right)+12i\left(\dfrac{1}{2}i\right)$
$\phantom{12i\left(\dfrac{2}{3}+\dfrac{1}{2}i\right)} = 8i+6i^2$
$\phantom{12i\left(\dfrac{2}{3}+\dfrac{1}{2}i\right)} = 8i+6(-1)$
$\phantom{12i\left(\dfrac{2}{3}+\dfrac{1}{2}i\right)} = -6+8i$

41. $(3-5i)(7+i) = 21+3i-35i-5i^2$
$$= 21-32i-5(-1)$$
$$= 21-32i+5$$
$$= 26-32i$$

43. $(9-4i)(9+4i) = (9)^2 - (4i)^2$
$$= 81-16i^2$$
$$= 81-16(-1)$$
$$= 81+16$$
$$= 97+0i$$

45. $(5+3i)^2 = (5)^2 + 2(5 \cdot 3i) + (3i)^2$
$$= 25+30i+9i^2$$
$$= 25+30i+9(-1)$$
$$= 25+30i-9$$
$$= 16+30i$$

47. $\dfrac{24-18i}{6} = \dfrac{24}{6} - \dfrac{18}{6}i$
$$= 4-3i$$

49. $\dfrac{-12+6i}{3i} = \left(\dfrac{-12+6i}{3i}\right)\left(\dfrac{i}{i}\right)$
$$= \dfrac{-12i+6i^2}{3i^2}$$
$$= \dfrac{-12i+6(-1)}{3(-1)}$$
$$= \dfrac{-12i-6}{-3}$$
$$= \dfrac{-6-12i}{-3}$$
$$= \dfrac{-6}{-3} + \dfrac{-12}{-3}i$$
$$= 2+4i$$

51. $\dfrac{1-2i}{2i} = \left(\dfrac{1-2i}{2i}\right)\left(\dfrac{i}{i}\right)$
$$= \dfrac{i-2i^2}{2i^2}$$
$$= \dfrac{i-2(-1)}{2(-1)}$$
$$= \dfrac{i+2}{-2}$$
$$= \dfrac{2+i}{-2}$$
$$= \dfrac{2}{-2} + \dfrac{1}{-2}i$$
$$= -1 - \dfrac{1}{2}i$$

53. $\dfrac{2i}{8-4i} = \left(\dfrac{2i}{8-4i}\right)\left(\dfrac{8+4i}{8+4i}\right)$
$$= \dfrac{16i+8i^2}{(8)^2 - (4i)^2}$$
$$= \dfrac{16i+8(-1)}{64-16i^2}$$
$$= \dfrac{16i-8}{64-16(-1)}$$
$$= \dfrac{-8+16i}{80}$$
$$= -\dfrac{1}{10} + \dfrac{1}{5}i$$

55. $\dfrac{12-i}{1+3i} = \left(\dfrac{12-i}{1+3i}\right)\left(\dfrac{1-3i}{1-3i}\right)$
$$= \dfrac{(12-i)(1-3i)}{(1)^2 - (3i)^2}$$
$$= \dfrac{12-36i-i+3i^2}{1-9i^2}$$
$$= \dfrac{12-36i-i+3(-1)}{1-9(-1)}$$
$$= \dfrac{9-37i}{10}$$
$$= \dfrac{9}{10} - \dfrac{37}{10}i$$

57. $\dfrac{5+i}{3-2i} = \left(\dfrac{5+i}{3-2i}\right)\left(\dfrac{3+2i}{3+2i}\right)$

$= \dfrac{(5+i)(3+2i)}{(3)^2-(2i)^2}$

$= \dfrac{15+10i+3i+2i^2}{9-4i^2}$

$= \dfrac{15+10i+3i+2(-1)}{9-4(-1)}$

$= \dfrac{13+13i}{13}$

$= 1+i$

59. $\dfrac{2+2i}{1+3i} = \left(\dfrac{2+2i}{1+3i}\right)\left(\dfrac{1-3i}{1-3i}\right)$

$= \dfrac{(2+2i)(1-3i)}{(1)^2-(3i)^2}$

$= \dfrac{2-6i+2i-6i^2}{1-9i^2}$

$= \dfrac{2-6i+2i-6(-1)}{1-9(-1)}$

$= \dfrac{8-4i}{10}$

$= \dfrac{4}{5}-\dfrac{2}{5}i$

61. Answers will vary; for example: Every real number is complex, such as $16+0i$, but the complex number $16+3i$ is not a real number because it has an imaginary component.

63. Answers will vary; for example: The sum of two complex numbers is always complex because any number, real or complex, can be written in the complex form $a+bi$.

65. Answers will vary; for example: When a complex number is multiplied by its conjugate, the imaginary component disappears.

67. Answers will vary; for example: It is not possible, because any number n can be written as $n+0i$.

69. $(2+3i)^3 = (2+3i)(2+3i)(2+3i)$

$= \left(4+6i+6i+9i^2\right)(2+3i)$

$= \left(4+12i+9(-1)\right)(2+3i)$

$= (-5+12i)(2+3i)$

$= -10-15i+24i+36i^2$

$= -10+9i+36(-1)$

$= -46+9i$

71. $(3+2i)^2 + (8-i)^2$

$= (3)^2 + 2(3)(2i) + (2i)^2 + (8)^2 - 2(8)(i) + (i)^2$

$= 9+12i+4i^2+64-16i+i^2$

$= 9+12i+4(-1)+64-16i+(-1)$

$= 68-4i$

73. $\dfrac{(5+2i)^2}{(3-3i)^2} = \dfrac{(5)^2+2(5)(2i)+(2i)^2}{(3)^2-2(3)(3i)+(3i)^2}$

$= \dfrac{25+20i+4i^2}{9-18i+9i^2}$

$= \dfrac{25+20i+4(-1)}{9-18i+9(-1)}$

$= \dfrac{21+20i}{-18i}$

$= \left(\dfrac{21+20i}{-18i}\right)\left(\dfrac{i}{i}\right)$

$= \dfrac{21i+20i^2}{-18i^2}$

$= \dfrac{21i+20(-1)}{-18(-1)}$

$= \dfrac{-20+21i}{18}$

$= -\dfrac{10}{9}+\dfrac{7}{6}i$

10.2 Exercises

1. A quadratic equation written in standard form is $\underline{ax^2 + bx + c = 0}$.

3. To solve a quadratic equation of the form $ax^2 + bx + c = 0$ by completing the square, the leading coefficient $\underline{a}$ must equal $\underline{one}$.

5. When the radicand is negative after applying the Square Root Property, there will be $\underline{no}$ $\underline{real}$ number solutions.

7. We create a perfect square trinomial by taking $\underline{half}$ of the linear term's coefficient and $\underline{squaring}$ it.

9. $(3x - 2)(x + 5) = 0$

$3x - 2 = 0$ or $x + 5 = 0$

$x = \dfrac{2}{3}$ or $x = -5$

Solution Set: $\left\{ -5, \dfrac{2}{3} \right\}$

11. $x(2x + 1) = 0$

$x = 0$ or $2x + 1 = 0$

$x = 0$ or $x = -\dfrac{1}{2}$

Solution Set: $\left\{ -\dfrac{1}{2}, 0 \right\}$

13. $3p^2 + 2p - 40 = 0$

$(3p - 10)(p + 4) = 0$

$3p - 10 = 0$ or $p + 4 = 0$

$p = \dfrac{10}{3}$ or $p = -4$

Solution Set: $\left\{ -4, \dfrac{10}{3} \right\}$

15. $2x^2 - 7x = 15$

$2x^2 - 7x - 15 = 0$

$(2x + 3)(x - 5) = 0$

$2x + 3 = 0$ or $x - 5 = 0$

$x = -\dfrac{3}{2}$ or $x = 5$

Solution Set: $\left\{ -\dfrac{3}{2}, 5 \right\}$

17. $x^2 = 144$

$x = -\sqrt{144}$ or $x = \sqrt{144}$

$x = -12$ or $x = 12$

Solution Set: $\{ -12, 12 \}$

19. $x^2 = \dfrac{9}{16}$

$x = -\sqrt{\dfrac{9}{16}}$ or $x = \sqrt{\dfrac{9}{16}}$

$x = -\dfrac{3}{4}$ or $x = \dfrac{3}{4}$

Solution Set: $\left\{ -\dfrac{3}{4}, \dfrac{3}{4} \right\}$

21. $s^2 = 48$

$s = -\sqrt{48}$ or $s = \sqrt{48}$

$s = -4\sqrt{3}$ or $s = 4\sqrt{3}$

Solution Set: $\left\{ -4\sqrt{3}, 4\sqrt{3} \right\}$

23. $x^2 = -64$

$x = -\sqrt{-64}$ or $x = \sqrt{-64}$

$x = -8i$ or $x = 8i$

Solution Set: $\{ 0 - 8i, 0 + 8i \}$

25. $3x^2 + 150 = 0$

$3x^2 = -150$

$x^2 = -50$

$x = -\sqrt{-50}$ or $x = \sqrt{-50}$

$x = -5i\sqrt{2}$ or $x = 5i\sqrt{2}$

Solution Set: $\left\{ 0 - 5i\sqrt{2}, 0 + 5i\sqrt{2} \right\}$

27. $5y^2 - 100 = 0$

$5y^2 = 100$

$y^2 = 20$

$y = -\sqrt{20}$ or $y = \sqrt{20}$

$y = -2\sqrt{5}$ or $y = 2\sqrt{5}$

Solution Set: $\left\{ -2\sqrt{5}, 2\sqrt{5} \right\}$

29.
$$(x-1)^2 = 25$$
$$x-1 = -\sqrt{25} \quad \text{or} \quad x-1 = \sqrt{25}$$
$$x-1 = -5 \quad \text{or} \quad x-1 = 5$$
$$x = -4 \quad \text{or} \quad x = 6$$
Solution Set: $\{-4, 6\}$

31.
$$(x+7)^2 = -16$$
$$x+7 = -\sqrt{-16} \quad \text{or} \quad x+7 = \sqrt{-16}$$
$$x+7 = -4i \quad \text{or} \quad x+7 = 4i$$
$$x = -7-4i \quad \text{or} \quad x = -7+4i$$
Solution Set: $\{-7-4i, -7+4i\}$

33.
$$(4x-5)^2 = 1$$
$$4x-5 = -\sqrt{1} \quad \text{or} \quad 4x-5 = \sqrt{1}$$
$$4x-5 = -1 \quad \text{or} \quad 4x-5 = 1$$
$$4x = 4 \quad \text{or} \quad 4x = 6$$
$$x = 1 \quad \text{or} \quad x = \frac{3}{2}$$
Solution Set: $\left\{1, \frac{3}{2}\right\}$

35.
$$(5k+4)^2 - 19 = 0$$
$$(5k+4)^2 = 19$$
$$5k+4 = -\sqrt{19} \quad \text{or} \quad 5k+4 = \sqrt{19}$$
$$5k = -4-\sqrt{19} \quad \text{or} \quad 5k = -4+\sqrt{19}$$
$$k = \frac{-4-\sqrt{19}}{5} \quad \text{or} \quad k = \frac{-4+\sqrt{19}}{5}$$
Solution Set: $\left\{\dfrac{-4-\sqrt{19}}{5}, \dfrac{-4+\sqrt{19}}{5}\right\}$

37.
$$(4x-8)^2 = -32$$
$$4x-8 = -\sqrt{-32} \quad \text{or} \quad 4x-8 = \sqrt{-32}$$
$$4x-8 = -4i\sqrt{2} \quad \text{or} \quad 4x-8 = 4i\sqrt{2}$$
$$4x = 8-4i\sqrt{2} \quad \text{or} \quad 4x = 8+4i\sqrt{2}$$
$$x = \frac{8-4i\sqrt{2}}{4} \quad \text{or} \quad x = \frac{8+4i\sqrt{2}}{4}$$
$$x = \frac{\overset{1}{\cancel{4}}\left(2-i\sqrt{2}\right)}{\underset{1}{\cancel{4}}} \quad \text{or} \quad x = \frac{\overset{1}{\cancel{4}}\left(2+i\sqrt{2}\right)}{\underset{1}{\cancel{4}}}$$
$$x = 2-i\sqrt{2} \quad \text{or} \quad x = 2+i\sqrt{2}$$
Solution Set: $\{2-i\sqrt{2}, 2+i\sqrt{2}\}$

39.
$$(6x+15)^2 = 18$$
$$6x+15 = -\sqrt{18} \quad \text{or} \quad 6x+15 = \sqrt{18}$$
$$6x+15 = -3\sqrt{2} \quad \text{or} \quad 6x+15 = 3\sqrt{2}$$
$$6x = -15-3\sqrt{2} \quad \text{or} \quad 6x = -15+3\sqrt{2}$$
$$x = \frac{-15-3\sqrt{2}}{6} \quad \text{or} \quad x = \frac{-15+3\sqrt{2}}{6}$$
$$x = \frac{\overset{1}{\cancel{3}}\left(-5-\sqrt{2}\right)}{\underset{2}{\cancel{6}}} \quad \text{or} \quad x = \frac{\overset{1}{\cancel{3}}\left(-5+\sqrt{2}\right)}{\underset{2}{\cancel{6}}}$$
$$x = \frac{-5-\sqrt{2}}{2} \quad \text{or} \quad x = \frac{-5+\sqrt{2}}{2}$$
Solution Set: $\left\{\dfrac{-5-\sqrt{2}}{2}, \dfrac{-5+\sqrt{2}}{2}\right\}$

41.
$$\left(\frac{1}{2}\cdot(-18)\right)^2 = (-9)^2$$
$$= 81$$

43.
$$\left(\frac{1}{2}\cdot 15\right)^2 = \left(\frac{15}{2}\right)^2$$
$$= \frac{225}{4}$$

45.
$$\left(\frac{1}{2}\cdot\frac{5}{3}\right)^2 = \left(\frac{5}{6}\right)^2$$
$$= \frac{25}{36}$$

47.
$$x^2 + 10x - 11 = 0$$
$$x^2 + 10x = 11$$
$$x^2 + 10x + 25 = 11 + 25$$
$$(x+5)^2 = 36$$
$$x+5 = -\sqrt{36} \quad \text{or} \quad x+5 = \sqrt{36}$$
$$x+5 = -6 \quad \text{or} \quad x+5 = 6$$
$$x = -11 \quad \text{or} \quad x = 1$$
Solution Set: $\{-11, 1\}$

49.
$$x^2 + 6x + 8 = 0$$
$$x^2 + 6x = -8$$
$$x^2 + 6x + 9 = -8 + 9$$
$$(x+3)^2 = 1$$
$$x + 3 = -\sqrt{1} \quad \text{or} \quad x + 3 = \sqrt{1}$$
$$x + 3 = -1 \quad \text{or} \quad x + 3 = 1$$
$$x = -4 \quad \text{or} \quad x = -2$$
Solution Set: $\{-4, -2\}$

51.
$$x^2 - 12x = 0$$
$$x^2 - 12x + 36 = 0 + 36$$
$$(x-6)^2 = 36$$
$$x - 6 = -\sqrt{36} \quad \text{or} \quad x - 6 = \sqrt{36}$$
$$x - 6 = -6 \quad \text{or} \quad x - 6 = 6$$
$$x = 0 \quad \text{or} \quad x = 12$$
Solution Set: $\{0, 12\}$

53.
$$q^2 + 8q + 20 = 0$$
$$q^2 + 8q = -20$$
$$q^2 + 8q + 16 = -20 + 16$$
$$(q+4)^2 = -4$$
$$q + 4 = -\sqrt{-4} \quad \text{or} \quad q + 4 = \sqrt{-4}$$
$$q + 4 = -2i \quad \text{or} \quad q + 4 = 2i$$
$$q = -4 - 2i \quad \text{or} \quad q = -4 + 2i$$
Solution Set: $\{-4 - 2i, -4 + 2i\}$

55.
$$x^2 + 10x + 60 = 10$$
$$x^2 + 10x = -50$$
$$x^2 + 10x + 25 = -50 + 25$$
$$(x+5)^2 = -25$$
$$x + 5 = -\sqrt{-25} \quad \text{or} \quad x + 5 = \sqrt{-25}$$
$$x + 5 = -5i \quad \text{or} \quad x + 5 = 5i$$
$$x = -5 - 5i \quad \text{or} \quad x = -5 + 5i$$
Solution Set: $\{-5 - 5i, -5 + 5i\}$

57.
$$x^2 + 4x = 20$$
$$x^2 + 4x + 4 = 20 + 4$$
$$(x+2)^2 = 24$$
$$x + 2 = -\sqrt{24} \quad \text{or} \quad x + 2 = \sqrt{24}$$
$$x + 2 = -2\sqrt{6} \quad \text{or} \quad x + 2 = 2\sqrt{6}$$
$$x = -2 - 2\sqrt{6} \quad \text{or} \quad x = -2 + 2\sqrt{6}$$
Solution Set: $\{-2 - 2\sqrt{6}, -2 + 2\sqrt{6}\}$

59.
$$x^2 + 14x + 9 = 10$$
$$x^2 + 14x = 1$$
$$x^2 + 14x + 49 = 1 + 49$$
$$(x+7)^2 = 50$$
$$x + 7 = -\sqrt{50} \quad \text{or} \quad x + 7 = \sqrt{50}$$
$$x + 7 = -5\sqrt{2} \quad \text{or} \quad x + 7 = 5\sqrt{2}$$
$$x = -7 - 5\sqrt{2} \quad \text{or} \quad x = -7 + 5\sqrt{2}$$
Solution Set: $\{-7 - 5\sqrt{2}, -7 + 5\sqrt{2}\}$

61.
$$x^2 - 8x + 24 = 0$$
$$x^2 - 8x = -24$$
$$x^2 - 8x + 16 = -24 + 16$$
$$(x-4)^2 = -8$$
$$x - 4 = -\sqrt{-8} \quad \text{or} \quad x - 4 = \sqrt{-8}$$
$$x - 4 = -2i\sqrt{2} \quad \text{or} \quad x - 4 = 2i\sqrt{2}$$
$$x = 4 - 2i\sqrt{2} \quad \text{or} \quad x = 4 + 2i\sqrt{2}$$
Solution Set: $\{4 - 2i\sqrt{2}, 4 + 2i\sqrt{2}\}$

63.
$$w^2 + 3w + 2 = 0$$
$$w^2 + 3w = -2$$
$$w^2 + 3w + \frac{9}{4} = -2 + \frac{9}{4}$$
$$\left(w + \frac{3}{2}\right)^2 = \frac{1}{4}$$
$$w + \frac{3}{2} = -\sqrt{\frac{1}{4}} \quad \text{or} \quad w + \frac{3}{2} = \sqrt{\frac{1}{4}}$$
$$w + \frac{3}{2} = -\frac{1}{2} \quad \text{or} \quad w + \frac{3}{2} = \frac{1}{2}$$
$$w = -2 \quad \text{or} \quad w = -1$$
Solution Set: $\{-2, -1\}$

65.
$$x^2 + 2x + 30 = 1$$
$$x^2 + 2x = -29$$
$$x^2 + 2x + 1 = -29 + 1$$
$$(x+1)^2 = -28$$
$$x+1 = -\sqrt{-28} \quad \text{or} \quad x+1 = \sqrt{-28}$$
$$x+1 = -2i\sqrt{7} \quad \text{or} \quad x+1 = 2i\sqrt{7}$$
$$x = -1 - 2i\sqrt{7} \quad \text{or} \quad x = -1 + 2i\sqrt{7}$$
Solution Set: $\left\{-1 - 2i\sqrt{7}, -1 + 2i\sqrt{7}\right\}$

67.
$$2x^2 + 24x + 22 = 0$$
$$\frac{2x^2}{2} + \frac{24x}{2} + \frac{22}{2} = \frac{0}{2}$$
$$x^2 + 12x + 11 = 0$$
$$x^2 + 12x = -11$$
$$x^2 + 12x + 36 = -11 + 36$$
$$(x+6)^2 = 25$$
$$x+6 = -\sqrt{25} \quad \text{or} \quad x+6 = \sqrt{25}$$
$$x+6 = -5 \quad \text{or} \quad x+6 = 5$$
$$x = -11 \quad \text{or} \quad x = -1$$
Solution Set: $\{-11, -1\}$

69.
$$3x^2 - 18x + 12 = 0$$
$$\frac{3x^2}{3} - \frac{18x}{3} + \frac{12}{3} = \frac{0}{3}$$
$$x^2 - 6x + 4 = 0$$
$$x^2 - 6x = -4$$
$$x^2 - 6x + 9 = -4 + 9$$
$$(x-3)^2 = 5$$
$$x-3 = -\sqrt{5} \quad \text{or} \quad x-3 = \sqrt{5}$$
$$x = 3 - \sqrt{5} \quad \text{or} \quad x = 3 + \sqrt{5}$$
Solution Set: $\left\{3 - \sqrt{5}, 3 + \sqrt{5}\right\}$

71.
$$4x^2 + 8x + 20 = 0$$
$$\frac{4x^2}{4} + \frac{8x}{4} + \frac{20}{4} = \frac{0}{4}$$
$$x^2 + 2x + 5 = 0$$
$$x^2 + 2x = -5$$
$$x^2 + 2x + 1 = -5 + 1$$
$$(x+1)^2 = -4$$
$$x+1 = -\sqrt{-4} \quad \text{or} \quad x+1 = \sqrt{-4}$$
$$x+1 = -2i \quad \text{or} \quad x+1 = 2i$$
$$x = -1 - 2i \quad \text{or} \quad x = -1 + 2i$$
Solution Set: $\{-1 - 2i, -1 + 2i\}$

73.
$$2x^2 + 6x - 10 = 12$$
$$\frac{2x^2}{2} + \frac{6x}{2} - \frac{10}{2} = \frac{12}{2}$$
$$x^2 + 3x - 5 = 6$$
$$x^2 + 3x = 11$$
$$x^2 + 3x + \frac{9}{4} = 11 + \frac{9}{4}$$
$$\left(x + \frac{3}{2}\right)^2 = \frac{53}{4}$$
$$x + \frac{3}{2} = -\sqrt{\frac{53}{4}} \quad \text{or} \quad x + \frac{3}{2} = \sqrt{\frac{53}{4}}$$
$$x + \frac{3}{2} = -\frac{\sqrt{53}}{2} \quad \text{or} \quad x + \frac{3}{2} = \frac{\sqrt{53}}{2}$$
$$x = \frac{-3 - \sqrt{53}}{2} \quad \text{or} \quad x = \frac{-3 + \sqrt{53}}{2}$$
Solution Set: $\left\{\dfrac{-3 - \sqrt{53}}{2}, \dfrac{-3 + \sqrt{53}}{2}\right\}$

75.

$$9x^2 + 36x + 37 = 0$$

$$\frac{9x^2}{9} + \frac{36x}{9} + \frac{37}{9} = \frac{0}{9}$$

$$x^2 + 4x + \frac{37}{9} = 0$$

$$x^2 + 4x = -\frac{37}{9}$$

$$x^2 + 4x + 4 = -\frac{37}{9} + 4$$

$$(x+2)^2 = -\frac{1}{9}$$

$$x + 2 = -\sqrt{-\frac{1}{9}} \quad \text{or} \quad x + 2 = \sqrt{-\frac{1}{9}}$$

$$x + 2 = -\frac{1}{3}i \quad \text{or} \quad x + 2 = \frac{1}{3}i$$

$$x = -2 - \frac{1}{3}i \quad \text{or} \quad x = -2 + \frac{1}{3}i$$

Solution Set: $\left\{ -2 - \frac{1}{3}i, -2 + \frac{1}{3}i \right\}$

77.

$$2m^2 + 10m + 10 = 0$$

$$\frac{2m^2}{2} + \frac{10m}{2} + \frac{10}{2} = \frac{0}{2}$$

$$m^2 + 5m + 5 = 0$$

$$m^2 + 5m = -5$$

$$m^2 + 5m + \frac{25}{4} = -5 + \frac{25}{4}$$

$$\left(m + \frac{5}{2} \right)^2 = \frac{5}{4}$$

$$m + \frac{5}{2} = -\sqrt{\frac{5}{4}} \quad \text{or} \quad m + \frac{5}{2} = \sqrt{\frac{5}{4}}$$

$$m + \frac{5}{2} = -\frac{\sqrt{5}}{2} \quad \text{or} \quad m + \frac{5}{2} = \frac{\sqrt{5}}{2}$$

$$m = \frac{-5 - \sqrt{5}}{2} \quad \text{or} \quad m = \frac{-5 + \sqrt{5}}{2}$$

Solution Set: $\left\{ \frac{-5 - \sqrt{5}}{2}, \frac{-5 + \sqrt{5}}{2} \right\}$

79.

$$4x^2 + 20x + 29 = 0$$

$$\frac{4x^2}{4} + \frac{20x}{4} + \frac{29}{4} = \frac{0}{4}$$

$$x^2 + 5x + \frac{29}{4} = 0$$

$$x^2 + 5x = -\frac{29}{4}$$

$$x^2 + 5x + \frac{25}{4} = -\frac{29}{4} + \frac{25}{4}$$

$$\left(x + \frac{5}{2} \right)^2 = -1$$

$$x + \frac{5}{2} = -\sqrt{-1} \quad \text{or} \quad x + \frac{5}{2} = \sqrt{-1}$$

$$x + \frac{5}{2} = -i \quad \text{or} \quad x + \frac{5}{2} = i$$

$$x = -\frac{5}{2} - i \quad \text{or} \quad x = -\frac{5}{2} + i$$

Solution Set: $\left\{ -\frac{5}{2} - i, -\frac{5}{2} + i \right\}$

81. Answers will vary; for example: The coefficient a cannot equal zero in the standard form of a quadratic equation or the equation ceases to be quadratic and becomes linear.

83. Answers will vary; for example: Use the Square Root Property to solve quadratic equations when the squared term can be isolated from the constant term.

85. Answers will vary; for example: Any quadratic equation can be expected to have two solutions: either two real or two complex solutions. It is also possible that there may be only one real solution if both linear factors are identical.

87. Answers will vary; for example: To complete the square when $a \neq 1$, divide all terms by a so that a will equal 1.

89. Let x represent the unknown number. The equation is $5x^2 - 30 = 0$.

$$5x^2 - 30 = 0$$

$$5x^2 = 30$$

$$x^2 = 6$$

$$x = -\sqrt{6} \quad \text{or} \quad x = \sqrt{6}$$

The two numbers are $-\sqrt{6}$ and $\sqrt{6}$.

91. Let x represent the unknown number. The equation is $(x+7)^2 = 15$.

$$(x+7)^2 = 15$$
$$x+7 = -\sqrt{15} \quad \text{or} \quad x+7 = \sqrt{15}$$
$$x = -7-\sqrt{15} \quad \text{or} \quad x = -7+\sqrt{15}$$

The two numbers are $-7-\sqrt{15}$ and $-7+\sqrt{15}$.

93. Let x represent the unknown number. The equation is $x^2 + 5x = 6$.

$$x^2 + 5x = 6$$
$$x^2 + 5x + \frac{25}{4} = 6 + \frac{25}{4}$$
$$\left(x+\frac{5}{2}\right)^2 = \frac{49}{4}$$
$$x+\frac{5}{2} = -\sqrt{\frac{49}{4}} \quad \text{or} \quad x+\frac{5}{2} = \sqrt{\frac{49}{4}}$$
$$x+\frac{5}{2} = -\frac{7}{2} \quad \text{or} \quad x+\frac{5}{2} = \frac{7}{2}$$
$$x = -6 \quad \text{or} \quad x = 1$$

The two numbers are -6 and 1.

95. Prepare We need to find the time it takes Pierre to return to the ground, once he is propelled from the slingshot, using the formula and given information.

Plan We set the function $h(t) = 0$, since returning to the ground represents a height of 0. We will solve the resulting equation by completing the square.

Process

$$-16t^2 + 8t + 5 = 0$$
$$\frac{-16t^2}{-16} + \frac{8t}{-16} + \frac{5}{-16} = \frac{0}{-16}$$
$$t^2 - \frac{1}{2}t - \frac{5}{16} = 0$$
$$t^2 - \frac{1}{2}t = \frac{5}{16}$$
$$t^2 - \frac{1}{2}t + \frac{1}{16} = \frac{5}{16} + \frac{1}{16}$$
$$\left(t-\frac{1}{4}\right)^2 = \frac{6}{16}$$

$$t-\frac{1}{4} = -\sqrt{\frac{6}{16}} \quad \text{or} \quad t-\frac{1}{4} = \sqrt{\frac{6}{16}}$$
$$t-\frac{1}{4} = -\frac{\sqrt{6}}{4} \quad \text{or} \quad t-\frac{1}{4} = \frac{\sqrt{6}}{4}$$
$$t = \cancel{\frac{1}{4}-\frac{\sqrt{6}}{4}} \quad \text{or} \quad t = \frac{1}{4}+\frac{\sqrt{6}}{4}$$

Therefore, it would take Pierre exactly $\frac{1}{4}+\frac{\sqrt{6}}{4}$ seconds, or approximately 0.86 seconds to return to the ground.

Ponder Does our answer seem reasonable? Yes. If we substitute 0.86 into the formula for t, we get a height of 0.0464 feet, which is roughly a height of 0.

97.
$$\left(\frac{1}{3}x+4\right)^2 = 12$$
$$\frac{1}{3}x+4 = -\sqrt{12} \quad \text{or} \quad \frac{1}{3}x+4 = \sqrt{12}$$
$$\frac{1}{3}x+4 = -2\sqrt{3} \quad \text{or} \quad \frac{1}{3}x+4 = 2\sqrt{3}$$
$$\frac{1}{3}x = -4-2\sqrt{3} \quad \text{or} \quad \frac{1}{3}x = -4+2\sqrt{3}$$
$$x = -12-6\sqrt{3} \quad \text{or} \quad x = -12+6\sqrt{3}$$

Solution Set: $\left\{-12-6\sqrt{3}, -12+6\sqrt{3}\right\}$

99.
$$\left(\frac{2}{3}x-4\right)^2 + 9 = 0$$
$$\left(\frac{2}{3}x-4\right)^2 = -9$$
$$\frac{2}{3}x-4 = -\sqrt{-9} \quad \text{or} \quad \frac{2}{3}x-4 = \sqrt{-9}$$
$$\frac{2}{3}x-4 = -3i \quad \text{or} \quad \frac{2}{3}x-4 = 3i$$
$$\frac{2}{3}x = 4-3i \quad \text{or} \quad \frac{2}{3}x = 4+3i$$
$$x = 6-\frac{9}{2}i \quad \text{or} \quad x = 6+\frac{9}{2}i$$

Solution Set: $\left\{6-\frac{9}{2}i, 6+\frac{9}{2}i\right\}$

101.

$$\frac{3}{5}x^2 - 6x - 3 = 0$$

$$\frac{5}{3}\left(\frac{3}{5}x^2 - 6x - 3\right) = \frac{5}{3}(0)$$

$$x^2 - 10x - 5 = 0$$

$$x^2 - 10x = 5$$

$$x^2 - 10x + 25 = 5 + 25$$

$$(x-5)^2 = 30$$

$$x - 5 = -\sqrt{30} \quad \text{or} \quad x - 5 = \sqrt{30}$$

$$x = 5 - \sqrt{30} \quad \text{or} \quad x = 5 + \sqrt{30}$$

Solution Set: $\left\{5 - \sqrt{30}, 5 + \sqrt{30}\right\}$

103.

$$\frac{1}{8}x^2 + \frac{1}{2}x + \frac{3}{2} = 0$$

$$\frac{8}{1}\left(\frac{1}{8}x^2 + \frac{1}{2}x + \frac{3}{2}\right) = \frac{8}{1}(0)$$

$$x^2 + 4x + 12 = 0$$

$$x^2 + 4x = -12$$

$$x^2 + 4x + 4 = -12 + 4$$

$$(x+2)^2 = -8$$

$$x + 2 = -\sqrt{-8} \quad \text{or} \quad x + 2 = \sqrt{-8}$$

$$x + 2 = -2i\sqrt{2} \quad \text{or} \quad x + 2 = 2i\sqrt{2}$$

$$x = -2 - 2i\sqrt{2} \quad \text{or} \quad x = -2 + 2i\sqrt{2}$$

Solution Set: $\left\{-2 - 2i\sqrt{2}, -2 + 2i\sqrt{2}\right\}$

105.

$$(2x-3)(x+2) = 9$$

$$2x^2 + x - 6 = 9$$

$$2x^2 + x - 15 = 0$$

$$\frac{2x^2}{2} + \frac{x}{2} - \frac{15}{2} = \frac{0}{2}$$

$$x^2 + \frac{1}{2}x - \frac{15}{2} = 0$$

$$x^2 + \frac{1}{2}x = \frac{15}{2}$$

$$x^2 + \frac{1}{2}x + \frac{1}{16} = \frac{15}{2} + \frac{1}{16}$$

$$\left(x + \frac{1}{4}\right)^2 = \frac{121}{16}$$

$$x + \frac{1}{4} = -\sqrt{\frac{121}{16}} \quad \text{or} \quad x + \frac{1}{4} = \sqrt{\frac{121}{16}}$$

$$x + \frac{1}{4} = -\frac{11}{4} \quad \text{or} \quad x + \frac{1}{4} = \frac{11}{4}$$

$$x = -3 \quad \text{or} \quad x = \frac{5}{2}$$

Solution Set: $\left\{-3, \frac{5}{2}\right\}$

10.3 Exercises

1. The Quadratic Formula is given by $x = \frac{-b \pm \sqrt{b^2 - 4ac}}{2a}$.

3. We can determine the number and type of solutions to $ax^2 + bx + c = 0$ by examining the <u>discriminant</u>, which is the radicand of the Quadratic Formula.

5. Before identifying the values for a, b, and c we must write the quadratic equation in <u>standard</u> <u>form</u>.

7. If $b^2 - 4ac > 0$, there are <u>two</u> <u>real</u> solutions.

9. $2x^2 + x - 3 = 0$

$a = 2,\ b = 1,\ c = -3$

$$x = \frac{-b \pm \sqrt{b^2 - 4ac}}{2a}$$

$$= \frac{-1 \pm \sqrt{(1)^2 - 4(2)(-3)}}{2(2)}$$

$$= \frac{-1 \pm \sqrt{1 + 24}}{4}$$

$$= \frac{-1 \pm \sqrt{25}}{4}$$

$$= \frac{-1 \pm 5}{4}$$

Solution Set: $\left\{ -\frac{3}{2}, 1 \right\}$

11. $2x^2 + 7x + 3 = 0$

$a = 2,\ b = 7,\ c = 3$

$$x = \frac{-b \pm \sqrt{b^2 - 4ac}}{2a}$$

$$= \frac{-7 \pm \sqrt{(7)^2 - 4(2)(3)}}{2(2)}$$

$$= \frac{-7 \pm \sqrt{49 - 24}}{4}$$

$$= \frac{-7 \pm \sqrt{25}}{4}$$

$$= \frac{-7 \pm 5}{4}$$

Solution Set: $\left\{ -3, -\frac{1}{2} \right\}$

13. $3x^2 + 2x = 5$

$3x^2 + 2x - 5 = 0$

$a = 3,\ b = 2,\ c = -5$

$$x = \frac{-b \pm \sqrt{b^2 - 4ac}}{2a}$$

$$= \frac{-2 \pm \sqrt{(2)^2 - 4(3)(-5)}}{2(3)}$$

$$= \frac{-2 \pm \sqrt{4 + 60}}{6}$$

$$= \frac{-2 \pm \sqrt{64}}{6}$$

$$= \frac{-2 \pm 8}{6}$$

Solution Set: $\left\{ -\frac{5}{3}, 1 \right\}$

15. $4t^2 + 9 = 0$

$a = 4,\ b = 0,\ c = 9$

$$t = \frac{-b \pm \sqrt{b^2 - 4ac}}{2a}$$

$$= \frac{-0 \pm \sqrt{(0)^2 - 4(4)(9)}}{2(4)}$$

$$= \frac{\pm \sqrt{0 - 144}}{8}$$

$$= \frac{\pm \sqrt{-144}}{8}$$

$$= \frac{\pm 12i}{8}$$

Solution Set: $\left\{ 0 - \frac{3}{2}i, 0 + \frac{3}{2}i \right\}$

17. $2x^2 - 2x + 5 = 0$

$a = 2,\ b = -2,\ c = 5$

$$x = \frac{-b \pm \sqrt{b^2 - 4ac}}{2a}$$

$$= \frac{-(-2) \pm \sqrt{(-2)^2 - 4(2)(5)}}{2(2)}$$

$$= \frac{2 \pm \sqrt{4 - 40}}{4}$$

$$= \frac{2 \pm \sqrt{-36}}{4}$$

$$= \frac{2 \pm 6i}{4}$$

Solution Set: $\left\{ \dfrac{1}{2} - \dfrac{3}{2}i,\ \dfrac{1}{2} + \dfrac{3}{2}i \right\}$

19. $3x^2 - x + 1 = 0$

$a = 3,\ b = -1,\ c = 1$

$$x = \frac{-b \pm \sqrt{b^2 - 4ac}}{2a}$$

$$= \frac{-(-1) \pm \sqrt{(-1)^2 - 4(3)(1)}}{2(3)}$$

$$= \frac{1 \pm \sqrt{1 - 12}}{6}$$

$$= \frac{1 \pm \sqrt{-11}}{6}$$

$$= \frac{1 \pm i\sqrt{11}}{6}$$

Solution Set: $\left\{ \dfrac{1}{6} - \dfrac{\sqrt{11}}{6}i,\ \dfrac{1}{6} + \dfrac{\sqrt{11}}{6}i \right\}$

21. $x^2 + 9 = 3x$

$x^2 - 3x + 9 = 0$

$a = 1,\ b = -3,\ c = 9$

$$x = \frac{-b \pm \sqrt{b^2 - 4ac}}{2a}$$

$$= \frac{-(-3) \pm \sqrt{(-3)^2 - 4(1)(9)}}{2(1)}$$

$$= \frac{3 \pm \sqrt{9 - 36}}{2}$$

$$= \frac{3 \pm \sqrt{-27}}{2}$$

$$= \frac{3 \pm 3i\sqrt{3}}{2}$$

Solution Set: $\left\{ \dfrac{3}{2} - \dfrac{3\sqrt{3}}{2}i,\ \dfrac{3}{2} + \dfrac{3\sqrt{3}}{2}i \right\}$

23. $6y^2 + 5y = 0$

$a = 6,\ b = 5,\ c = 0$

$$y = \frac{-b \pm \sqrt{b^2 - 4ac}}{2a}$$

$$= \frac{-5 \pm \sqrt{(5)^2 - 4(6)(0)}}{2(6)}$$

$$= \frac{-5 \pm \sqrt{25 - 0}}{12}$$

$$= \frac{-5 \pm \sqrt{25}}{12}$$

$$= \frac{-5 \pm 5}{12}$$

Solution Set: $\left\{ -\dfrac{5}{6},\ 0 \right\}$

25. $4h^2 - 6h = -1$

$4h^2 - 6h + 1 = 0$

$a = 4,\ b = -6,\ c = 1$

$$h = \frac{-b \pm \sqrt{b^2 - 4ac}}{2a}$$

$$= \frac{-(-6) \pm \sqrt{(-6)^2 - 4(4)(1)}}{2(4)}$$

$$= \frac{6 \pm \sqrt{36 - 16}}{8}$$

$$= \frac{6 \pm \sqrt{20}}{8}$$

$$= \frac{6 \pm 2\sqrt{5}}{8}$$

Solution Set: $\left\{ \dfrac{3 - \sqrt{5}}{4},\ \dfrac{3 + \sqrt{5}}{4} \right\}$

27. $6x^2 - 4x + 2 = 0$

$a = 6,\ b = -4,\ c = 2$

$$x = \frac{-b \pm \sqrt{b^2 - 4ac}}{2a}$$

$$= \frac{-(-4) \pm \sqrt{(-4)^2 - 4(6)(2)}}{2(6)}$$

$$= \frac{4 \pm \sqrt{16 - 48}}{12}$$

$$= \frac{4 \pm \sqrt{-32}}{12}$$

$$= \frac{4 \pm 4i\sqrt{2}}{12}$$

Solution Set: $\left\{ \dfrac{1}{3} - \dfrac{\sqrt{2}}{3}i, \dfrac{1}{3} + \dfrac{\sqrt{2}}{3}i \right\}$

29. $5y^2 = 9y + 2$

$5y^2 - 9y - 2 = 0$

$a = 5,\ b = -9,\ c = -2$

$$y = \frac{-b \pm \sqrt{b^2 - 4ac}}{2a}$$

$$= \frac{-(-9) \pm \sqrt{(-9)^2 - 4(5)(-2)}}{2(5)}$$

$$= \frac{9 \pm \sqrt{81 + 40}}{10}$$

$$= \frac{9 \pm \sqrt{121}}{10}$$

$$= \frac{9 \pm 11}{10}$$

Solution Set: $\left\{ -\dfrac{1}{5}, 2 \right\}$

31. $8x^2 + 2x - 1 = 0$

$a = 8,\ b = 2,\ c = -1$

$b^2 - 4ac = (2)^2 - 4(8)(-1)$

$\qquad = 4 + 32$

$\qquad = 36$

Because $b^2 - 4ac = 36$ and $36 > 0$, there are two real solutions to the equation.

33. $4x^2 + 2x + 3 = 0$

$a = 4,\ b = 2,\ c = 3$

$b^2 - 4ac = (2)^2 - 4(4)(3)$

$\qquad = 4 - 48$

$\qquad = -44$

Because $b^2 - 4ac = -44$ and $-44 < 0$, there are two complex solutions to the equation.

35. $4x^2 - 4x + 7 = 6$

$4x^2 - 4x + 1 = 0$

$a = 4,\ b = -4,\ c = 1$

$b^2 - 4ac = (-4)^2 - 4(4)(1)$

$\qquad = 16 - 16$

$\qquad = 0$

Because $b^2 - 4ac = 0$, there is one real solution to the equation.

37. $4s^2 = 4s + 1$

$4s^2 - 4s - 1 = 0$

$a = 4,\ b = -4,\ c = -1$

$b^2 - 4ac = (-4)^2 - 4(4)(-1)$

$\qquad = 16 + 16$

$\qquad = 32$

Because $b^2 - 4ac = 32$ and $32 > 0$, there are two real solutions to the equation.

39. $x^2 + 7x + 12 = 0$

$(x + 3)(x + 4) = 0$

$x + 3 = 0$ or $x + 4 = 0$

$x = -3$ or $x = -4$

Solution Set: $\{-4, -3\}$

41. $x^2 + 6x + 13 = 0$

$x^2 + 6x = -13$

$x^2 + 6x + 9 = -13 + 9$

$(x + 3)^2 = -4$

$x + 3 = -\sqrt{-4}$ or $x + 3 = \sqrt{-4}$

$x + 3 = -2i$ or $x + 3 = 2i$

$x = -3 - 2i$ or $x = -3 + 2i$

Solution Set: $\{-3 - 2i, -3 + 2i\}$

43.
$$8x^2 + 2x - 3 = 0$$
$$(2x-1)(4x+3) = 0$$
$$2x - 1 = 0 \quad \text{or} \quad 4x + 3 = 0$$
$$x = \frac{1}{2} \quad \text{or} \quad x = -\frac{3}{4}$$
Solution Set: $\left\{-\frac{3}{4}, \frac{1}{2}\right\}$

45.
$$(2x+5)^2 + 3 = 12$$
$$(2x+5)^2 = 9$$
$$2x + 5 = -\sqrt{9} \quad \text{or} \quad 2x + 5 = \sqrt{9}$$
$$2x + 5 = -3 \quad \text{or} \quad 2x + 5 = 3$$
$$2x = -8 \quad \text{or} \quad 2x = -2$$
$$x = -4 \quad \text{or} \quad x = -1$$
Solution Set: $\{-4, -1\}$

47.
$$3x^2 + 30x = 24$$
$$\frac{3x^2}{3} + \frac{30x}{3} = \frac{24}{3}$$
$$x^2 + 10x = 8$$
$$x^2 + 10x + 25 = 8 + 25$$
$$(x+5)^2 = 33$$
$$x + 5 = -\sqrt{33} \quad \text{or} \quad x + 5 = \sqrt{33}$$
$$x = -5 - \sqrt{33} \quad \text{or} \quad x = -5 + \sqrt{33}$$
Solution Set: $\left\{-5 - \sqrt{33}, -5 + \sqrt{33}\right\}$

49. $9k^2 + 16 = 0$
$$a = 9, \ b = 0, \ c = 16$$
$$k = \frac{-b \pm \sqrt{b^2 - 4ac}}{2a}$$
$$= \frac{-0 \pm \sqrt{(0)^2 - 4(9)(16)}}{2(9)}$$
$$= \frac{\pm\sqrt{0 - 576}}{18}$$
$$= \frac{\pm\sqrt{-576}}{18}$$
$$= \frac{\pm 24i}{18}$$
Solution Set: $\left\{0 - \frac{4}{3}i, 0 + \frac{4}{3}i\right\}$

51.
$$(x+3)(x-5) = 10$$
$$x^2 - 2x - 15 = 10$$
$$x^2 - 2x = 25$$
$$x^2 - 2x + 1 = 25 + 1$$
$$(x-1)^2 = 26$$
$$x - 1 = -\sqrt{26} \quad \text{or} \quad x - 1 = \sqrt{26}$$
$$x = 1 - \sqrt{26} \quad \text{or} \quad 1 + \sqrt{26}$$
Solution Set: $\left\{1 - \sqrt{26}, 1 + \sqrt{26}\right\}$

53.
$$\left(\frac{1}{2}x - 5\right)^2 = -18$$
$$\frac{1}{2}x - 5 = -\sqrt{-18} \quad \text{or} \quad \frac{1}{2}x - 5 = \sqrt{-18}$$
$$\frac{1}{2}x - 5 = -3i\sqrt{2} \quad \text{or} \quad \frac{1}{2}x - 5 = 3i\sqrt{2}$$
$$\frac{1}{2}x = 5 - 3i\sqrt{2} \quad \text{or} \quad \frac{1}{2}x = 5 + 3i\sqrt{2}$$
$$x = 10 - 6i\sqrt{2} \quad \text{or} \quad x = 10 + 6i\sqrt{2}$$
Solution Set: $\left\{10 - 6i\sqrt{2}, 10 + 6i\sqrt{2}\right\}$

55.
$$2x^2 + 4x + 10 = 0$$
$$\frac{2x^2}{2} + \frac{4x}{2} + \frac{10}{2} = \frac{0}{2}$$
$$x^2 + 2x + 5 = 0$$
$$x^2 + 2x = -5$$
$$x^2 + 2x + 1 = -5 + 1$$
$$(x+1)^2 = -4$$
$$x + 1 = -\sqrt{-4} \quad \text{or} \quad x + 1 = \sqrt{-4}$$
$$x + 1 = -2i \quad \text{or} \quad x + 1 = 2i$$
$$x = -1 - 2i \quad \text{or} \quad x = -1 + 2i$$
Solution Set: $\{-1 - 2i, -1 + 2i\}$

57. $g^2 + 4 = 3g$

$g^2 - 3g + 4 = 0$

$a = 1,\ b = -3,\ c = 4$

$g = \dfrac{-b \pm \sqrt{b^2 - 4ac}}{2a}$

$= \dfrac{-(-3) \pm \sqrt{(-3)^2 - 4(1)(4)}}{2(1)}$

$= \dfrac{3 \pm \sqrt{9 - 16}}{2}$

$= \dfrac{3 \pm \sqrt{-7}}{2}$

$= \dfrac{3 \pm i\sqrt{7}}{2}$

Solution Set: $\left\{ \dfrac{3}{2} - \dfrac{\sqrt{7}}{2}i, \dfrac{3}{2} + \dfrac{\sqrt{7}}{2}i \right\}$

59, $4y^2 + 8y + 12 = 0$

$\dfrac{4y^2}{4} + \dfrac{8y}{4} + \dfrac{12}{4} = \dfrac{0}{4}$

$y^2 + 2y + 3 = 0$

$y^2 + 2y = -3$

$y^2 + 2y + 1 = -3 + 1$

$(y + 1)^2 = -2$

$y + 1 = -\sqrt{-2}$ or $y + 1 = \sqrt{-2}$

$y + 1 = -i\sqrt{2}$ or $y + 1 = i\sqrt{2}$

$y = -1 - i\sqrt{2}$ or $y = -1 + i\sqrt{2}$

Solution Set: $\left\{ -1 - i\sqrt{2}, -1 + i\sqrt{2} \right\}$

61. $\dfrac{1}{12}x^2 + \dfrac{1}{4}x + \dfrac{1}{8} = 0$

$\dfrac{12}{1}\left(\dfrac{1}{12}x^2 + \dfrac{1}{4}x + \dfrac{1}{8} \right) = 12(0)$

$x^2 + 3x + \dfrac{3}{2} = 0$

$x^2 + 3x = -\dfrac{3}{2}$

$x^2 + 3x + \dfrac{9}{4} = -\dfrac{3}{2} + \dfrac{9}{4}$

$\left(x + \dfrac{3}{2} \right)^2 = \dfrac{3}{4}$

$x + \dfrac{3}{2} = -\sqrt{\dfrac{3}{4}}$ or $x + \dfrac{3}{2} = \sqrt{\dfrac{3}{4}}$

$x + \dfrac{3}{2} = -\dfrac{\sqrt{3}}{2}$ or $x + \dfrac{3}{2} = \dfrac{\sqrt{3}}{2}$

$x = \dfrac{-3 - \sqrt{3}}{2}$ or $x = \dfrac{-3 + \sqrt{3}}{2}$

Solution Set: $\left\{ \dfrac{-3 - \sqrt{3}}{2}, \dfrac{-3 + \sqrt{3}}{2} \right\}$

63. $x + \dfrac{18}{x} = 11$

$\dfrac{x}{1}\left(x + \dfrac{18}{x} \right) = x(11)$

$x^2 + 18 = 11x$

$x^2 - 11x + 18 = 0$

$(x - 2)(x - 9) = 0$

$x - 2 = 0$ or $x - 9 = 0$

$x = 2$ or $x = 9$

Solution Set: $\{2, 9\}$

65. $\dfrac{6}{m} = \dfrac{m - 4}{m + 4}$

$\dfrac{m(m + 4)}{1}\left(\dfrac{6}{m} \right) = \dfrac{m(m + 4)}{1}\left(\dfrac{m - 4}{m + 4} \right)$

$6(m + 4) = m(m - 4)$

$6m + 24 = m^2 - 4m$

$0 = m^2 - 10m - 24$

$0 = (m - 12)(m + 2)$

$m - 12 = 0$ or $m + 2 = 0$

$m = 12$ or $m = -2$

Solution Set: $\{-2, 12\}$

67. $\dfrac{4x}{x - 4} - \dfrac{1}{x} = \dfrac{8x - 1}{x}$

$\dfrac{x(x - 4)}{1}\left(\dfrac{4x}{x - 4} - \dfrac{1}{x} \right) = \dfrac{x(x - 4)}{1}\left(\dfrac{8x - 1}{x} \right)$

$4x^2 - (x - 4) = (x - 4)(8x - 1)$

$4x^2 - x + 4 = 8x^2 - 33x + 4$

$0 = 4x^2 - 32x$

$0 = 4x(x - 8)$

$4x = 0$ or $x - 8 = 0$

$\cancel{x = 0}$ or $x = 8$

Solution Set: $\{8\}$

69.
$$\frac{2x}{x-2}+\frac{4}{x+2}=\frac{6}{x^2-4}$$

$$\frac{(x-2)(x+2)}{1}\left(\frac{2x}{x-2}+\frac{4}{x+2}\right)=\frac{(x-2)(x+2)}{1}\left(\frac{6}{x^2-4}\right)$$

$$2x(x+2)+4(x-2)=6$$

$$2x^2+4x+4x-8=6$$

$$2x^2+8x-14=0$$

$$\frac{2x^2}{2}+\frac{8x}{2}-\frac{14}{2}=\frac{0}{2}$$

$$x^2+4x-7=0$$

$$x^2+4x=7$$

$$x^2+4x+4=7+4$$

$$(x+2)^2=11$$

$$x+2=-\sqrt{11}\quad\text{or}\quad x+2=\sqrt{11}$$

$$x=-2-\sqrt{11}\quad\text{or}\quad x=-2+\sqrt{11}$$

Solution Set: $\left\{-2-\sqrt{11},-2+\sqrt{11}\right\}$

71.
$$\frac{2x}{x-1}+\frac{4}{x}=\frac{x^2-11}{x^2-x}$$

$$\frac{x(x-1)}{1}\left(\frac{2x}{x-1}+\frac{4}{x}\right)=\frac{x(x-1)}{1}\left(\frac{x^2-11}{x^2-x}\right)$$

$$2x^2+4(x-1)=x^2-11$$

$$2x^2+4x-4=x^2-11$$

$$x^2+4x+7=0$$

$$a=1,\ b=4,\ c=7$$

$$x=\frac{-b\pm\sqrt{b^2-4ac}}{2a}$$

$$=\frac{-4\pm\sqrt{(4)^2-4(1)(7)}}{2(1)}$$

$$=\frac{-4\pm\sqrt{16-28}}{2}$$

$$=\frac{-4\pm\sqrt{-12}}{2}$$

$$=\frac{-4\pm2i\sqrt{3}}{2}$$

Solution Set: $\left\{-2-i\sqrt{3},-2+i\sqrt{3}\right\}$

73. Answers will vary; for example: The Quadratic Formula can be used to solve any quadratic equation.

75. Answers will vary; for example: The solutions to a quadratic equation will be rational if b^2-4ac equals zero or a perfect square. If b^2-4ac does not equal a perfect square and is greater than zero, the solutions will be irrational.

77. $a=3k,\ b=-6,\ c=1$

$$b^2-4ac=0$$

$$(-6)^2-4(3k)(1)=0$$

$$36-12k=0$$

$$-12k=-36$$

$$k=3$$

79. Let x represent the distance from the base of the pole that the guy wire is attached to the ground. The equation is $x^2+10^2=25^2$.

$$x^2+10^2=25^2$$

$$x^2+100=625$$

$$x^2=525$$

$$x=-\sqrt{525}\quad\text{or}\quad x=\sqrt{525}$$

$$x=-5\sqrt{21}\quad\text{or}\quad x=5\sqrt{21}$$

The distance from the base of the pole that the guy wire is attached to the ground is $5\sqrt{21}$, or approximately 22.91 feet.

81. Prepare We need to determine how far Diego and Samantha walk on the high wires, using the Pythagorean theorem.

Plan Let's use the Pythagorean theorem with $a = x$, $b = x - 7$ and $c = 13$ (feet) to solve for x. Then, we can find how far Diego walks by substituting this value into $(x - 7)$.

Process Let $x =$ the length of wire Samantha walks and $(x - 7) =$ Diego's length of wire.

$$a^2 + b^2 = c^2$$
$$x^2 + (x - 7)^2 = (13)^2$$
$$x^2 + x^2 - 14x + 49 = 169$$
$$2x^2 - 14x - 120 = 0$$
$$\frac{2x^2}{2} - \frac{14x}{2} - \frac{120}{2} = \frac{0}{2}$$
$$x^2 - 7x - 60 = 0$$
$$(x - 12)(x + 5) = 0$$
$$x - 12 = 0 \quad \text{or} \quad x + 5 = 0$$
$$x = 12 \quad \text{or} \quad \cancel{x = -5}$$

Substituting 12 for x we get $x - 7 = 12 - 7 = 5$. Therefore, Samantha travels 12 feet on the high wire and Diego travels 5 feet on the high wire.

Ponder Do the lengths seem reasonable? Yes, because we know from geometry that the hypotenuse of a right triangle is the longest side. Therefore, Samantha and Diego should each walk less than 13 feet. We can also check our answers by substituting them into the Pythagorean theorem.

$$a^2 + b^2 = c^2$$
$$(12)^2 + (5)^2 = (13)^2$$
$$144 + 25 = 169$$
$$169 = 169$$
$$\text{True}$$

83. Let $x =$ the length of the shortest side. Then $(x + 1) =$ the length of the longer leg and $(x + 2) =$ the length of the hypotenuse.

$$a^2 + b^2 = c^2$$
$$(x)^2 + (x + 1)^2 = (x + 2)^2$$
$$x^2 + x^2 + 2x + 1 = x^2 + 4x + 4$$
$$x^2 - 2x - 3 = 0$$
$$(x - 3)(x + 1) = 0$$
$$x - 3 = 0 \quad \text{or} \quad x + 1 = 0$$
$$x = 3 \quad \text{or} \quad \cancel{x = -1}$$

If $x = 3$, then $x + 1 = 3 + 1 = 4$ and $x + 2 = 3 + 2 = 5$. Therefore, the length of the three sides are 3, 4 and 5 units.

10.4 Exercises

1. An equation that is *quadratic in form* reduces to a <u>quadratic equation</u> once we begin to simplify it.

3. When solving the equation $2(w+4)^2 + 11(w+4) - 21 = 0$, we could use substitution and let $u = \underline{(w+4)}$ and $u^2 = \underline{(w+4)^2}$.

5.
$$4p^4 + 11p^2 - 3 = 0$$
$$(4p^2 - 1)(p^2 + 3) = 0$$
$$4p^2 - 1 = 0 \quad \text{or} \quad p^2 + 3 = 0$$
$$p^2 = \frac{1}{4} \quad \text{or} \quad p^2 = -3$$
$$p = \pm\sqrt{\frac{1}{4}} \quad \text{or} \quad p = \pm\sqrt{-3}$$
$$p = \pm\frac{1}{2} \quad \text{or} \quad p = \pm i\sqrt{3}$$
Solution Set: $\left\{ 0 - i\sqrt{3}, 0 + i\sqrt{3}, -\frac{1}{2}, \frac{1}{2} \right\}$

7.
$$s^4 + 21s^2 - 100 = 0$$
$$(s^2 - 4)(s^2 + 25) = 0$$
$$s^2 - 4 = 0 \quad \text{or} \quad s^2 + 25 = 0$$
$$s^2 = 4 \quad \text{or} \quad s^2 = -25$$
$$s = \pm\sqrt{4} \quad \text{or} \quad s = \pm\sqrt{-25}$$
$$s = \pm 2 \quad \text{or} \quad s = \pm 5i$$
Solution Set: $\{0 - 5i, 0 + 5i, -2, 2\}$

9.
$$6r^4 + 11r^2 = 10$$
$$6r^4 + 11r^2 - 10 = 0$$
$$(2r^2 + 5)(3r^2 - 2) = 0$$
$$2r^2 + 5 = 0 \quad \text{or} \quad 3r^2 - 2 = 0$$
$$r^2 = \frac{-5}{2} \quad \text{or} \quad r^2 = \frac{2}{3}$$
$$r = \pm\sqrt{\frac{-5}{2}} \quad \text{or} \quad r = \pm\sqrt{\frac{2}{3}}$$
$$r = \pm\frac{\sqrt{10}}{2}i \quad \text{or} \quad r = \pm\frac{\sqrt{6}}{3}$$
Solution Set: $\left\{ 0 - \frac{\sqrt{10}}{2}i, 0 + \frac{\sqrt{10}}{2}i, -\frac{\sqrt{6}}{3}, \frac{\sqrt{6}}{3} \right\}$

11. Let $u = (w+4)$ and $u^2 = (w+4)^2$.

$$2(w+4)^2 + 11(w+4) - 21 = 0$$
$$2u^2 + 11u - 21 = 0$$
$$(2u - 3)(u + 7) = 0$$
$$2u - 3 = 0 \quad \text{or} \quad u + 7 = 0$$
$$u = \frac{3}{2} \quad \text{or} \quad u = -7$$

$w + 4 = \frac{3}{2}$ or $w + 4 = -7$

$w = -\frac{5}{2}$ or $w = -11$

Solution Set: $\left\{ -11, -\frac{5}{2} \right\}$

13. Let $u = (t+1)$ and $u^2 = (t+1)^2$.

$$4(t+1)^2 + 20(t+1) + 25 = 0$$
$$4u^2 + 20u + 25 = 0$$
$$(2u + 5)^2 = 0$$
$$2u + 5 = 0$$
$$u = -\frac{5}{2}$$

$t + 1 = -\frac{5}{2}$

$t = -\frac{7}{2}$

Solution Set: $\left\{ -\frac{7}{2} \right\}$

15. Let $u = x^{-1}$ and $u^2 = x^{-2}$.

$$4x^{-2} + 17x^{-1} - 15 = 0$$
$$4u^2 + 17u - 15 = 0$$
$$(u + 5)(4u - 3) = 0$$
$$u + 5 = 0 \quad \text{or} \quad 4u - 3 = 0$$
$$u = -5 \quad \text{or} \quad u = \frac{3}{4}$$

$x^{-1} = -5$ or $x^{-1} = \frac{3}{4}$

$\frac{1}{x} = -5$ or $\frac{1}{x} = \frac{3}{4}$

$-5x = 1$ or $3x = 4$

$x = -\frac{1}{5}$ or $x = \frac{4}{3}$

Solution Set: $\left\{ -\frac{1}{5}, \frac{4}{3} \right\}$

17. Let $u = y^{-1}$ and $u^2 = y^{-2}$.

$$8y^{-2} - 2y^{-1} - 3 = 0$$
$$8u^2 - 2u - 3 = 0$$
$$(2u + 1)(4u - 3) = 0$$
$$2u + 1 = 0 \quad \text{or} \quad 4u - 3 = 0$$
$$u = -\frac{1}{2} \quad \text{or} \quad u = \frac{3}{4}$$

$y^{-1} = -\frac{1}{2}$ or $y^{-1} = \frac{3}{4}$

$\frac{1}{y} = -\frac{1}{2}$ or $\frac{1}{y} = \frac{3}{4}$

$y = -2$ or $3y = 4$

$y = -2$ or $y = \frac{4}{3}$

Solution Set: $\left\{ -2, \frac{4}{3} \right\}$

19. Let $u = x^3$ and $u^2 = x^6$.

$$x^6 = 35x^3 - 216$$
$$u^2 = 35u - 216$$
$$u^2 - 35u + 216 = 0$$
$$(u-27)(u-8) = 0$$
$$u-27 = 0 \quad \text{or} \quad u-8 = 0$$
$$u = 27 \quad \text{or} \quad u = 8$$

$$x^3 = 27 \qquad\qquad x^3 = 8$$
$$x^3 - 27 = 0 \qquad\qquad x^3 - 8 = 0$$
$$(x-3)(x^2 + 3x + 9) = 0 \qquad (x-2)(x^2 + 2x + 4) = 0$$

$x-3 = 0$ or $\qquad x^2 + 3x + 9 = 0$ $\qquad$ or $\quad x-2 = 0$ or $\qquad x^2 + 2x + 4 = 0$

$x = 3 \qquad\qquad x^2 + 3x = -9 \qquad\qquad\qquad x = 2 \qquad\qquad x^2 + 2x = -4$

$$x^2 + 3x + \frac{9}{4} = -9 + \frac{9}{4}$$

$$x^2 + 2x + 1 = -4 + 1$$

$$\left(x + \frac{3}{2}\right)^2 = -\frac{27}{4}$$

$$(x+1)^2 = -3$$

$x + \dfrac{3}{2} = -\sqrt{-\dfrac{27}{4}}$ or $x + \dfrac{3}{2} = \sqrt{-\dfrac{27}{4}}$ $\qquad$ $x+1 = -\sqrt{-3}$ or $x+1 = \sqrt{-3}$

$x + \dfrac{3}{2} = -\dfrac{3i\sqrt{3}}{2}$ or $x + \dfrac{3}{2} = \dfrac{3i\sqrt{3}}{2}$ $\qquad$ $x+1 = -i\sqrt{3}$ or $x+1 = i\sqrt{3}$

$x = -\dfrac{3}{2} - \dfrac{3i\sqrt{3}}{2}$ or $x = -\dfrac{3}{2} + \dfrac{3i\sqrt{3}}{2}$ $\qquad$ $x = -1 - i\sqrt{3}$ or $x = -1 + i\sqrt{3}$

Solution Set: $\left\{ -1 - i\sqrt{3}, -1 + i\sqrt{3}, -\dfrac{3}{2} - \dfrac{3\sqrt{3}}{2}i, -\dfrac{3}{2} + \dfrac{3\sqrt{3}}{2}i, 2, 3 \right\}$

21. Let $u = (y+6)$ and $u^2 = (y+6)^2$.

$$3(y+6)^2 - 6(y+6) = 0$$
$$3u^2 - 6u = 0$$
$$3u(u-2) = 0$$
$$3u = 0 \quad \text{or} \quad u-2 = 0$$
$$u = 0 \quad \text{or} \quad u = 2$$

$$y+6 = 0 \quad \text{or} \quad y+6 = 2$$
$$y = -6 \quad \text{or} \quad y = -4$$

Solution Set: $\{-6, -4\}$

23. Let $u = t^{\frac{1}{2}}$ and $u^2 = t$.

$$t + t^{\frac{1}{2}} - 20 = 0$$
$$u^2 + u - 20 = 0$$
$$(u+5)(u-4) = 0$$
$$u+5 = 0 \quad \text{or} \quad u-4 = 0$$
$$u = -5 \quad \text{or} \quad u = 4$$

$$t^{\frac{1}{2}} = -5 \quad \text{or} \quad t^{\frac{1}{2}} = 4$$
$$\cancel{t = 25} \quad \text{or} \quad t = 16$$

Solution Set: $\{16\}$

419

25. Answers will vary; for example: An equation is *quadratic in form* if it can be simplified, rewritten as a quadratic equation and solved using one of the four methods.

27. Answers will vary; for example: When solving $4(y+3)^2 - 8(y+3) = 0$ using substitution, let u^2 equal the factor being squared (in this case $(y+3)^2$), and let u equal the factor raised to the power 1 (in this case $(y+3)$).

29. Answers will vary; for example: In the perimeter formula, $P = 2l + 2w$, we may be given the perimeter and width and need to solve for the length.

31. $A = \pi r^2$

$$\frac{A}{\pi} = \frac{\pi r^2}{\pi}$$

$$r^2 = \frac{A}{\pi}$$

$$r = \sqrt{\frac{A}{\pi}}$$

$$r = \frac{\sqrt{\pi A}}{\pi}$$

33. $V = \frac{1}{3}\pi r^2 h$

$$3V = 3\left(\frac{1}{3}\pi r^2 h\right)$$

$$3V = \pi r^2 h$$

$$\frac{3V}{\pi h} = \frac{\pi r^2 h}{\pi h}$$

$$r^2 = \frac{3V}{\pi h}$$

$$r = \sqrt{\frac{3V}{\pi h}}$$

$$r = \frac{\sqrt{3V\pi h}}{\pi h}$$

35. $a^2 + b^2 = c^2$

$$a^2 - a^2 + b^2 = c^2 - a^2$$

$$b^2 = c^2 - a^2$$

$$b = \sqrt{c^2 - a^2}$$

37. $t = 2\pi\sqrt{\frac{L}{g}}$

$$\frac{t}{2\pi} = \frac{2\pi}{2\pi}\sqrt{\frac{L}{g}}$$

$$\frac{t}{2\pi} = \sqrt{\frac{L}{g}}$$

$$\left(\frac{t}{2\pi}\right)^2 = \left(\sqrt{\frac{L}{g}}\right)^2$$

$$\frac{t^2}{4\pi^2} = \frac{L}{g}$$

$$g\frac{t^2}{4\pi^2} = L$$

$$g = \frac{4\pi^2 L}{t^2}$$

39. $S = \pi r\sqrt{r^2 + h^2}$

$$\frac{S}{\pi r} = \frac{\pi r}{\pi r}\sqrt{r^2 + h^2}$$

$$\frac{S}{\pi r} = \sqrt{r^2 + h^2}$$

$$\left(\frac{S}{\pi r}\right)^2 = \left(\sqrt{r^2 + h^2}\right)^2$$

$$\frac{S^2}{\pi^2 r^2} = r^2 + h^2$$

$$\frac{S^2}{\pi^2 r^2} - r^2 = r^2 - r^2 + h^2$$

$$\frac{S^2 - \pi^2 r^4}{\pi^2 r^2} = h^2$$

$$h = \frac{\sqrt{S^2 - \pi^2 r^4}}{\pi r}$$

41. Prepare It takes Willamena and Nadine 1 minute to handle 5 orders together. We are to determine how long it would take each of them alone if it takes Willamena 2 minutes longer than Nadine to handle 5 orders.

Plan We will use the work equation and Willamena's and Nadine's individual work rates to determine how long it will take each of them to handle 5 orders alone.

	Time to handle 5 orders alone	Individual rates
Willamena	x minutes	$\frac{1}{x}$ of the 5 orders per minute
Nadine	$x - 2$ minutes	$\frac{1}{x-2}$ of the 5 orders per minute

Process Write the equation, remembering that the women worked together for 1 minute to handle 5 orders.

$$\left(\genfrac{}{}{0pt}{}{time}{worked}\right)\left(\genfrac{}{}{0pt}{}{Willamena's}{rate}\right)+\left(\genfrac{}{}{0pt}{}{time}{worked}\right)\left(\genfrac{}{}{0pt}{}{Nadine's}{rate}\right)=1$$

$$(1)\left(\frac{1}{x}\right)+(1)\left(\frac{1}{x-2}\right)=1$$

$$x-2+x=x(x-2)$$

$$2x-2=x^2-2x$$

$$0=x^2-4x+2$$

$$x^2-4x+2=0$$

$$a=1,\ b=-4,\ c=2$$

$$x=\frac{-b\pm\sqrt{b^2-4ac}}{2a}$$

$$x=\frac{-(-4)\pm\sqrt{(-4)^2-4(1)(2)}}{2(1)}$$

$$x=\frac{4\pm\sqrt{16-8}}{2}$$

$$x=\frac{4\pm\sqrt{8}}{2}$$

$$x=\frac{4\pm2\sqrt{2}}{2}$$

$$x=2\pm\sqrt{2}$$

$$x=2-\sqrt{2}\quad\text{or}\quad x=2+\sqrt{2}$$
$$x\approx2-1.4\qquad x\approx2+1.4$$
$$x\approx0.6\qquad\ \ x\approx3.4$$

Notice that $x\approx0.6$ minute is not a plausible answer, because $x-2$, Nadine's time, would be negative. Therefore, the only possible answer is $x\approx3.4$ minutes for Willamena to handle 5 orders and $x-2\approx1.4$ minutes for Nadine to handle 5 orders.

Ponder Does the answers seem reasonable: Yes, it is reasonable to assume that if it takes them 1 minute to handle 5 orders together, it would not take them much longer individually.

43. Prepare Gabe and Cael work for 3 hours together on the job and then Gabe finished the job alone in 2 more hours. We are to determine how long it would take each of them alone if it takes Cael 1 hour longer than Gabe to do the job alone.

Plan We will use the work equation and Cael's and Gabe's individual work rates to determine how long it will take each of them to do the job alone.

	Time to do the job alone	Individual rates
Cael	x hours	$\frac{1}{x}$ of the job done per hour
Gabe	$x-1$ hours	$\frac{1}{x-1}$ of the job done per hour

Process Write the equation, remembering that the men worked together for 3 hours and then Gabe finished the job alone in 2 more hours.

$$\left(\genfrac{}{}{0pt}{}{time}{worked}\right)\left(\genfrac{}{}{0pt}{}{Cael's}{rate}\right)+\left(\genfrac{}{}{0pt}{}{time}{worked}\right)\left(\genfrac{}{}{0pt}{}{Gabe's}{rate}\right)=1$$

$$(3)\left(\frac{1}{x}\right)+(5)\left(\frac{1}{x-1}\right)=1$$

$$3(x-1)+5x=x(x-1)$$

$$3x-3+5x=x^2-x$$

$$0=x^2-9x+3$$

$$x^2-9x+3=0$$

$$a=1,\ b=-9,\ c=3$$

$$x=\frac{-b\pm\sqrt{b^2-4ac}}{2a}$$

$$x=\frac{-(-9)\pm\sqrt{(-9)^2-4(1)(3)}}{2(1)}$$

$$x=\frac{9\pm\sqrt{81-12}}{2}$$

$$x=\frac{9\pm\sqrt{69}}{2}$$

$$x=\frac{9-\sqrt{69}}{2}\quad\text{or}\quad x=\frac{9+\sqrt{69}}{2}$$
$$x\approx\frac{9-8.3}{2}\qquad x\approx\frac{9+8.3}{2}$$
$$x\approx0.175\qquad x\approx8.65$$

Notice that $x\approx0.175$ hour is not a plausible answer, because $x-1$, Gabes's time, would be negative. Therefore, the only possible answers is $x\approx8.65$ hours for Cael to do the job alone and $x-1\approx7.65$ hours for Gabe to do the job alone.

Ponder Does the answers seem reasonable: Yes, because Gabe has more experience than Cael it is reasonable that it would take Gabe less time than Cael to do the job alone.

45. Prepare We are to determine the rate at which Lucy jogs.

Plan Solve the distance formula for T to obtain $T = \frac{D}{R}$, and fill in a chart with what we know. Let T_0 = the time Lucy spent walking, T_1 = the time Lucy spent jogging, and r = Lucy walking rate. Then $T_0 + T_1 = 1\frac{1}{6}$.

	D	R	T
Walking	2 miles	r	$T_0 = \frac{2}{r}$ hours
Jogging	4 miles	$r+2$	$T_1 = \frac{4}{r+2}$ hours

Process Write and solve the equation.

$$T_0 + T_1 = 1\frac{1}{6}$$

$$\frac{2}{r} + \frac{4}{r+2} = \frac{7}{6}$$

$$2 \cdot 6(r+2) + 4(6r) = 7r(r+2)$$

$$12r + 24 + 24r = 7r^2 + 14r$$

$$0 = 7r^2 - 22r - 24$$

$$7r^2 - 22r - 24 = 0$$

$$(r-4)(7r+6) = 0$$

$$r - 4 = 0 \quad \text{or} \quad 7r + 6 = 0$$

$$r = 4 \quad \text{or} \quad r = \cancel{-\frac{6}{7}}$$

Because the rate cannot be negative, Lucy's walking rate is 4 mile per hour.

Ponder Does the answer seem reasonable? It is very reasonable for a person to be able to wald at a rate of 4 miles per hour.

47.

$$S = 2x^2 + 4xh$$

$$0 = 2x^2 + (4h)x - S$$

$$a = 2,\ b = 4h,\ c = -S$$

$$x = \frac{-(4h) + \sqrt{(4h)^2 - 4(2)(-S)}}{2(2)}$$

$$= \frac{-4h + \sqrt{16h^2 + 8S}}{4}$$

$$= \frac{-4h + \sqrt{4(4h^2 + 2S)}}{4}$$

$$= \frac{-4h + 2\sqrt{4h^2 + 2S}}{4}$$

$$= \frac{-2h + \sqrt{4h^2 + 2S}}{2}$$

49. Let $u = x^{\frac{3}{2}}$ and $u^2 = x^3$.

$$3x^3 + 11x^{\frac{3}{2}} - 4 = 0$$

$$3u^2 + 11u - 4 = 0$$

$$(u+4)(3u-1) = 0$$

$$u + 4 = 0 \quad \text{or} \quad 3u - 1 = 0$$

$$u = -4 \quad \text{or} \quad u = \frac{1}{3}$$

$$x^{\frac{3}{2}} = -4 \qquad \text{or} \qquad x^{\frac{3}{2}} = \frac{1}{3}$$

$$\sqrt{x^3} = -4 \qquad \sqrt{x^3} = \frac{1}{3}$$

$$x^3 = 16 \qquad x^3 = \frac{1}{9}$$

$$\cancel{x = \sqrt[3]{16}} \qquad x^3 = \frac{1}{9}$$

$$x = \sqrt[3]{\frac{1}{9}}$$

$$x = \frac{\sqrt[3]{3}}{3}$$

Solution Set: $\left\{ \dfrac{\sqrt[3]{3}}{3} \right\}$

51. Let $u = \sqrt[3]{t}$ and $u^2 = \sqrt[3]{t^2}$.

$$8 = 215\sqrt[3]{t} + 27\sqrt[3]{t^2}$$

$$8 = 215u + 27u^2$$

$$27u^2 + 215u - 8 = 0$$

$$(u+8)(27u-1) = 0$$

$$u + 8 = 0 \quad \text{or} \quad 27u - 1 = 0$$

$$u = -8 \quad \text{or} \quad u = \frac{1}{27}$$

$$\sqrt[3]{t} = -8 \quad \text{or} \quad \sqrt[3]{t} = \frac{1}{27}$$

$$\left(\sqrt[3]{t}\right)^3 = (-8)^3 \quad \text{or} \quad \left(\sqrt[3]{t}\right)^3 = \left(\frac{1}{27}\right)^3$$

$$t = -512 \quad \text{or} \quad t = \frac{1}{19{,}683}$$

Solution Set: $\left\{ -512, \dfrac{1}{19{,}683} \right\}$

53. Let $u = y^{-3}$ and $u^2 = y^{-6}$.

$$216y^{-6} - 485y^{-3} - 64 = 0$$

$$216u^2 - 485u - 64 = 0$$

$$(8u+1)(27u-64) = 0$$

$$8u + 1 = 0 \quad \text{or} \quad 27u - 64 = 0$$

$$u = -\frac{1}{8} \quad \text{or} \quad u = \frac{64}{27}$$

$$y^{-3} = -\frac{1}{8} \quad \text{or} \quad y^{-3} = \frac{64}{27}$$

$$\frac{1}{y^3} = -\frac{1}{8} \quad \text{or} \quad \frac{1}{y^3} = \frac{64}{27}$$

$$y^3 = -8 \qquad y^3 = \frac{27}{64}$$

$$y = -2 \qquad y = \frac{3}{4}$$

Solution Set: $\left\{ -2, \dfrac{3}{4} \right\}$

10.5 Exercises

1. A quadratic inequality involving "less than" can be written in the form $ax^2 + bx + c < 0$, where a, b, and c are real numbers with $a \neq 0$.

3. A boundary value will have a <u>bracket</u> when it satisfies the original inequality.

5. To solve a quadratic inequality, we use boundary values on the real line to create <u>test</u> <u>regions</u>.

7. $(x+2)(x-6) > 0$

Boundary Values

$(x+2)(x-6) = 0$

$x + 2 = 0$ or $x - 6 = 0$

$x = -2$ or $x = 6$

Region A $(-\infty, -2)$	Region B $(-2, 6)$	Region C $(6, \infty)$
Test Point: $x = -3$ $(x+2)(x-6) > 0$ $(-)(-) > 0$ $(+) > 0$ True: Shade Region A	Test Point: $x = 0$ $(x+2)(x-6) > 0$ $(+)(-) > 0$ $(-) > 0$ False: Do Not Shade Region B	Test Point: $x = 7$ $(x+2)(x-6) > 0$ $(+)(+) > 0$ $(+) > 0$ True: Shade Region C

The solution set is $(-\infty, -2) \cup (6, \infty)$.

9. $(r+2)(r+5) < 0$

Boundary Values

$(r+2)(r+5) = 0$

$r + 2 = 0$ or $r + 5 = 0$

$r = -2$ or $r = -5$

Region A $(-\infty, -5)$	Region B $(-5, -2)$	Region C $(-2, \infty)$
Test Point: $r = -6$ $(r+2)(r+5) < 0$ $(-)(-) < 0$ $(+) < 0$ False: Do Not Shade Region A	Test Point: $r = -3$ $(r+2)(r+5) < 0$ $(-)(+) < 0$ $(-) < 0$ True: Shade Region B	Test Point: $r = 0$ $(r+2)(r+5) < 0$ $(+)(+) < 0$ $(+) < 0$ False: Do Not Shade Region C

The solution set is $(-5, -2)$.

423

11. $x^2 + 7x - 18 \leq 0$

$(x+9)(x-2) \leq 0$

<u>Boundary Values</u>

$(x+9)(x-2) = 0$

$x + 9 = 0 \quad \text{or} \quad x - 2 = 0$

$x = -9 \quad \text{or} \quad x = 2$

Region A $(-\infty, -9)$	Region B $(-9, 2)$	Region C $(2, \infty)$
Test Point: $x = -10$ $(x+9)(x-2) \leq 0$ $(-)(-) \leq 0$ $(+) \leq 0$ False: Do Not Shade Region A	Test Point: $x = 0$ $(x+9)(x-2) \leq 0$ $(+)(-) \leq 0$ $(-) \leq 0$ True: Shade Region B	Test Point: $x = 3$ $(x+9)(x-2) \leq 0$ $(+)(+) \leq 0$ $(+) \leq 0$ False: Do Not Shade Region C

The solution set is $[-9, 2]$.

13. $x^2 - 4x > 0$

$x(x-4) > 0$

<u>Boundary Values</u>

$x(x-4) = 0$

$x = 0 \quad \text{or} \quad x - 4 = 0$

$x = 4$

Region A $(-\infty, 0)$	Region B $(0, 4)$	Region C $(4, \infty)$
Test Point: $x = -1$ $x(x-4) > 0$ $(-)(-) > 0$ $(+) > 0$ True: Shade Region A	Test Point: $x = 1$ $x(x-4) > 0$ $(+)(-) > 0$ $(-) > 0$ False: Do Not Shade Region B	Test Point: $x = 5$ $x(x-4) > 0$ $(+)(+) > 0$ $(+) > 0$ True: Shade Region C

The solution set is $(-\infty, 0) \cup (4, \infty)$.

15. $2x^2 - 9x - 5 \geq 0$

$(2x+1)(x-5) \geq 0$

<u>Boundary Values</u>

$(2x+1)(x-5) = 0$

$2x + 1 = 0 \quad \text{or} \quad x - 5 = 0$

$x = -\dfrac{1}{2} \quad \text{or} \quad x = 5$

Region A $\left(-\infty, -\frac{1}{2}\right)$	Region B $\left(-\frac{1}{2}, 5\right)$	Region C $(5, \infty)$
Test Point: $x = -1$ $(2x+1)(x-5) \geq 0$ $(-)(-) \geq 0$ $(+) \geq 0$ True: Shade Region A	Test Point: $x = 0$ $(2x+1)(x-5) \geq 0$ $(+)(-) \geq 0$ $(-) \geq 0$ False: Do Not Shade Region B	Test Point: $x = 6$ $(2x+1)(x-5) \geq 0$ $(+)(+) \geq 0$ $(+) \geq 0$ True: Shade Region C

The solution set is $\left(-\infty, -\dfrac{1}{2}\right] \cup [5, \infty)$.

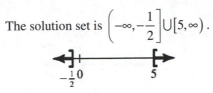

17. $y^2 + 5y \leq -6$

$y^2 + 5y + 6 \leq 0$

$(y+2)(y+3) \leq 0$

Boundary Values
$(y+2)(y+3) = 0$

$y + 2 = 0$ or $y + 3 = 0$

$y = -2$ or $y = -3$

Region A $(-\infty, -3)$	Region B $(-3, -2)$	Region C $(-2, \infty)$
Test Point: $y = -4$ $(y+2)(y+3) \leq 0$ $(-)(-) \leq 0$ $(+) \leq 0$ False: Do Not Shade Region A	Test Point: $y = -2.5$ $(y+2)(y+3) \leq 0$ $(-)(+) \leq 0$ $(-) \leq 0$ True: Shade Region B	Test Point: $y = 0$ $(y+2)(y+3) \leq 0$ $(+)(+) \leq 0$ $(+) \leq 0$ False: Do Not Shade Region C

The solution set is $[-3, -2]$.

19. $5x^2 - 2x > 0$

$x(5x - 2) > 0$

Boundary Values
$x(5x - 2) = 0$

$x = 0$ or $5x - 2 = 0$

$x = \dfrac{2}{5}$

Region A $(-\infty, 0)$	Region B $\left(0, \frac{2}{5}\right)$	Region C $\left(\frac{2}{5}, \infty\right)$
Test Point: $x = -1$ $x(5x-2) > 0$ $(-)(-) > 0$ $(+) > 0$ True: Shade Region A	Test Point: $x = \frac{1}{5}$ $x(5x-2) > 0$ $(+)(-) > 0$ $(-) > 0$ False: Do Not Shade Region B	Test Point: $x = 1$ $x(5x-2) > 0$ $(+)(+) > 0$ $(+) > 0$ True: Shade Region C

The solution set is $(-\infty, 0) \cup \left(\frac{2}{5}, \infty\right)$.

21. $x^2 - 9 < 0$
$(x+3)(x-3) < 0$

<u>Boundary Values</u>
$(x+3)(x-3) = 0$
$x + 3 = 0 \quad \text{or} \quad x - 3 = 0$
$x = -3 \quad \text{or} \quad x = 3$

Region A $(-\infty, -3)$	Region B $(-3, 3)$	Region C $(3, \infty)$
Test Point: $x = -4$ $(x+3)(x-3) < 0$ $(-)(-) < 0$ $(+) < 0$ False: Do Not Shade Region A	Test Point: $x = 0$ $(x+3)(x-3) < 0$ $(+)(-) < 0$ $(-) < 0$ True: Shade Region B	Test Point: $x = 4$ $(x+3)(x-3) < 0$ $(+)(+) < 0$ $(+) < 0$ False: Do Not Shade Region C

The solution set is $(-3, 3)$.

23. $9n^2 \geq 4$
$9n^2 - 4 \geq 0$
$(3n+2)(3n-2) \geq 0$

<u>Boundary Values</u>
$(3n+2)(3n-2) = 0$
$3n + 2 = 0 \quad \text{or} \quad 3n - 2 = 0$
$n = -\frac{2}{3} \quad \text{or} \quad n = \frac{2}{3}$

Region A $\left(-\infty, -\frac{2}{3}\right)$	Region B $\left(-\frac{2}{3}, \frac{2}{3}\right)$	Region C $\left(\frac{2}{3}, \infty\right)$
Test Point: $n = -1$	Test Point: $n = 0$	Test Point: $n = 1$
$(3n+2)(3n-1) \geq 0$	$(3n+2)(3n-1) \geq 0$	$(3n+2)(3n-1) \geq 0$
$(-)(-) \geq 0$	$(+)(-) \geq 0$	$(+)(+) \geq 0$
$(+) \geq 0$	$(-) \geq 0$	$(+) \geq 0$
True: Shade Region A	False: Do Not Shade Region B	True: Shade Region C

The solution set is $\left(-\infty, -\frac{2}{3}\right] \cup \left[\frac{2}{3}, \infty\right)$.

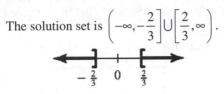

25. $\dfrac{1}{p+6} < 0$

<u>Boundary Value</u>
$$p + 6 = 0$$
$$p = -6$$

Region A $(-\infty, -6)$	Region B $(-6, \infty)$
Test Point: $p = -7$	Test Point: $p = 0$
$\dfrac{1}{p+6} < 0$	$\dfrac{1}{p+6} < 0$
$\dfrac{(+)}{(-)} < 0$	$\dfrac{(+)}{(+)} < 0$
$(-) < 0$	$(+) < 0$
True: Shade Region A	False: Do Not Shade Region B

The solution set is $(-\infty, -6)$.

27. $\dfrac{x-4}{x+2} > 0$

<u>Boundary Values</u>
$$x - 4 = 0 \quad \text{or} \quad x + 2 = 0$$
$$x = 4 \quad \text{or} \quad x = -2$$

Region A $(-\infty,-2)$	Region B $(-2,4)$	Region C $(4,\infty)$
Test Point: $x=-3$	Test Point: $x=0$	Test Point: $x=5$
$\dfrac{x-4}{x+2}>0$	$\dfrac{x-4}{x+2}>0$	$\dfrac{x-4}{x+2}>0$
$\dfrac{(-)}{(-)}>0$	$\dfrac{(-)}{(+)}>0$	$\dfrac{(+)}{(+)}>0$
$(+)>0$	$(-)>0$	$(+)>0$
True: Shade Region A	False: Do Not Shade Region B	True: Shade Region C

The solution set is $(-\infty,-2)\cup(4,\infty)$.

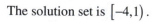

29. $\dfrac{k+4}{k-1}\le 0$

Boundary Values

$$k+4=0 \quad \text{or} \quad k-1=0$$
$$k=-4 \quad \text{or} \quad k=1$$

Region A $(-\infty,-4]$	Region B $[-4,1)$	Region C $(1,\infty)$
Test Point: $k=-5$	Test Point: $k=0$	Test Point: $k=2$
$\dfrac{k+4}{k-1}\le 0$	$\dfrac{k+4}{k-1}\le 0$	$\dfrac{k+4}{k-1}\le 0$
$\dfrac{(-)}{(-)}\le 0$	$\dfrac{(+)}{(-)}\le 0$	$\dfrac{(+)}{(+)}\le 0$
$(+)\le 0$	$(-)\le 0$	$(+)\le 0$
False: Do Not Shade Region A	True: Shade Region B	False: Do Not Shade Region C

The solution set is $[-4,1)$.

31. $\dfrac{x}{x-2}\ge 0$

Boundary Values

$$x=0 \quad \text{or} \quad x-2=0$$
$$x=2$$

Region A $(-\infty,0]$	Region B $[0,2)$	Region C $(2,\infty)$
Test Point: $x=-1$	Test Point: $x=1$	Test Point: $x=3$
$\dfrac{x}{x-2}\geq 0$	$\dfrac{x}{x-2}\geq 0$	$\dfrac{x}{x-2}\geq 0$
$\dfrac{(-)}{(-)}\geq 0$	$\dfrac{(+)}{(-)}\geq 0$	$\dfrac{(+)}{(+)}\geq 0$
$(+)\geq 0$	$(-)\geq 0$	$(+)\geq 0$
True: Shade Region A	False: Do Not Shade Region B	True: Shade Region C

The solution set is $(-\infty,0]\cup(2,\infty)$.

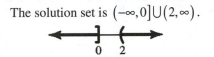

33. $\dfrac{2x+1}{x+3}>1$

$\dfrac{2x+1}{x+3}-1>0$

$\dfrac{2x+1}{x+3}-\dfrac{x+3}{x+3}>0$

$\dfrac{x-2}{x+3}>0$

<u>Boundary Values</u>

$x-2=0$ or $x+3=0$

$x=2$ or $x=-3$

Region A $(-\infty,-3)$	Region B $(-3,2)$	Region C $(2,\infty)$
Test Point: $x=-4$	Test Point: $x=0$	Test Point: $x=3$
$\dfrac{x-2}{x+3}>0$	$\dfrac{x-2}{x+3}>0$	$\dfrac{x-2}{x+3}>0$
$\dfrac{(-)}{(-)}>0$	$\dfrac{(-)}{(+)}>0$	$\dfrac{(+)}{(+)}>0$
$(+)>0$	$(-)>0$	$(+)>0$
True: Shade Region A	False: Do Not Shade Region B	True: Shade Region C

The solution set is $(-\infty,-3)\cup(2,\infty)$.

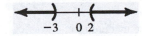

429

35.
$$\frac{4x+5}{x+4} \leq 2$$

$$\frac{4x+5}{x+4} - 2 \leq 0$$

$$\frac{4x+5}{x+4} - \frac{2(x+4)}{x+4} \leq 0$$

$$\frac{2x-3}{x+4} \leq 0$$

<u>Boundary Values</u>

$$2x-3=0 \quad \text{or} \quad x+4=0$$

$$x = \frac{3}{2} \quad \text{or} \quad x = -4$$

Region A $(-\infty, -4)$	Region B $\left(-4, \frac{3}{2}\right]$	Region C $\left[\frac{3}{2}, \infty\right)$
Test Point: $x = -5$	Test Point: $x = 0$	Test Point: $x = 2$
$\dfrac{2x-3}{x+4} \leq 0$	$\dfrac{2x-3}{x+4} \leq 0$	$\dfrac{2x-3}{x+4} \leq 0$
$\dfrac{(-)}{(-)} \leq 0$	$\dfrac{(-)}{(+)} \leq 0$	$\dfrac{(+)}{(+)} \leq 0$
$(+) \leq 0$	$(-) \leq 0$	$(+) \leq 0$
False: Do Not Shade Region A	True: Shade Region B	False: Do Not Shade Region C

The solution set is $\left(-4, \dfrac{3}{2}\right]$.

37. $ax^2 + bx + c \leq 0$

$ax^2 + bx + c > 0$

$ax^2 + bx + c \geq 0$

39. Answers will vary; for example: To find the boundary values of a quadratic inequality, set the quadratic expression equal to zero and solve for the variable.

41. Answers will vary; for example: For the rational inequality $\frac{x+6}{x-6} \leq 0$, there is a bracket at -6 because zero can be in the numerator and satisfy the inequality; however, there is an parentheses at 6 because there cannot be a zero in the denominator.

43. Let x represent the unknown number(s). The inequality is $\dfrac{x}{x-2} \geq 0$.

<u>Boundary Values</u>

$$x = 0 \quad \text{or} \quad x - 2 = 0$$

$$x = 2$$

Region A $(-\infty, 0]$	Region B $[0, 2)$	Region C $(2, \infty)$
Test Point: $x = -1$	Test Point: $x = 1$	Test Point: $x = 3$
$\dfrac{x}{x-2} \geq 0$	$\dfrac{x}{x-2} \geq 0$	$\dfrac{x}{x-2} \geq 0$
$\dfrac{(-)}{(-)} \geq 0$	$\dfrac{(+)}{(-)} \geq 0$	$\dfrac{(+)}{(+)} \geq 0$
$(+) \geq 0$	$(-) \geq 0$	$(+) \geq 0$
True: Shade Region A	False: Do Not Shade Region B	True: Shade Region C

The solution set is $(-\infty, 0] \cup (2, \infty)$.

45. Let x represent the unknown number(s). The inequality is $x + 10\left(\dfrac{1}{x}\right) > 7$.

$$x + 10\left(\frac{1}{x}\right) > 7$$

$$\frac{x^2}{x} + \frac{10}{x} - \frac{7x}{x} > 0$$

$$\frac{x^2 - 7x + 10}{x} > 0$$

$$\frac{(x-2)(x-5)}{x} > 0$$

<u>Boundary Values</u>

$x - 2 = 0$ or $x - 5 = 0$ or $x = 0$

$x = 2$ or $x = 5$ or $x = 0$

Region A $(-\infty, 0)$	Region B $(0, 2)$	Region C $(2, 5)$	Region D $(5, \infty)$
Test Point: $x = -1$	Test Point: $x = 1$	Test Point: $x = 3$	Test Point: $x = 6$
$\dfrac{(x-2)(x-5)}{x} > 0$	$\dfrac{(x-2)(x-5)}{x} > 0$	$\dfrac{(x-2)(x-5)}{x} > 0$	$\dfrac{(x-2)(x-5)}{x} > 0$
$\dfrac{(-)(-)}{(-)} > 0$	$\dfrac{(-)(-)}{(+)} > 0$	$\dfrac{(+)(-)}{(+)} > 0$	$\dfrac{(+)(+)}{(+)} > 0$
$(-) > 0$	$(+) > 0$	$(-) > 0$	$(+) > 0$
False: Do Not Shade Region A	True: Shade Region B	False: Do Not Shade Region C	True: Shade Region D

The solution set is $(0, 2) \cup (5, \infty)$.

47. $(x+1)(x-2)(x+3) > 0$

<u>Boundary Values</u>

$x+1 = 0$ or $x-2 = 0$ or $x+3 = 0$

$x = -1$ or $x = 2$ or $x = -3$

Region A $(-\infty, -3)$	Region B $(-3, -1)$	Region C $(-1, 2)$	Region D $(2, \infty)$
Test Point: $x = -4$ $(x+1)(x-2)(x+3) > 0$ $(-)(-)(-) > 0$ $(-) > 0$ False: Do Not Shade Region A	Test Point: $x = -2$ $(x+1)(x-2)(x+3) > 0$ $(-)(-)(+) > 0$ $(+) > 0$ True: Shade Region B	Test Point: $x = 0$ $(x+1)(x-2)(x+3) > 0$ $(+)(-)(+) > 0$ $(-) > 0$ False: Do Not Shade Region C	Test Point: $x = 3$ $(x+1)(x-2)(x+3) > 0$ $(+)(+)(+) > 0$ $(+) > 0$ True: Shade Region D

The solution set is $(-3, -1) \cup (2, \infty)$.

$$\longleftarrow \overset{(\qquad)}{\underset{-3 \quad -1 \quad 0}{\hspace{1cm}}} \quad \overset{(}{\underset{2}{\hspace{0.5cm}}} \longrightarrow$$

49. $d^2 + 6d + 9 \geq 0$

$(d+3)^2 \geq 0$

<u>Boundary Values</u>

$d + 3 = 0$

$d = -3$

Region A $(-\infty, -3]$	Region C $[-3, \infty)$
Test Point: $d = -4$ $(d+3)^2 \geq 0$ $(-)^2 \geq 0$ $(+) \geq 0$ True: Shade Region A	Test Point: $d = -2$ $(d+3)^2 \geq 0$ $(+)^2 \geq 0$ $(+) \geq 0$ True: Shade Region C

The solution set is $(-\infty, \infty)$.

$$\longleftarrow \underset{0}{\hspace{2cm}} \longrightarrow$$

51. $\dfrac{(x-3)(x+1)}{x+4} < 0$

<u>Boundary Values</u>

$x-3 = 0$ or $x+1 = 0$ or $x+4 = 0$

$x = 3$ or $x = -1$ or $x = -4$

Region A $(-\infty,-4)$	Region B $(-4,-1)$	Region C $(-1,3)$	Region D $(3,\infty)$
Test Point: $x=-5$	Test Point: $x=-2$	Test Point: $x=0$	Test Point: $x=4$
$\dfrac{(x-3)(x+1)}{x+4}<0$	$\dfrac{(x-3)(x+1)}{x+4}<0$	$\dfrac{(x-3)(x+1)}{x+4}<0$	$\dfrac{(x-3)(x+1)}{x+4}<0$
$\dfrac{(-)(-)}{(-)}<0$	$\dfrac{(-)(-)}{(+)}<0$	$\dfrac{(-)(+)}{(+)}<0$	$\dfrac{(+)(+)}{(+)}<0$
$(-)<0$	$(+)<0$	$(-)<0$	$(+)<0$
True: Shade Region A	False: Do Not Shade Region B	True: Shade Region C	False: Do Not Shade Region D

The solution set is $(-\infty,-4)\cup(-1,3)$.

Chapter 10 Review Problem Set

1. $\sqrt{-49} = i\sqrt{49}$
$= 7i$

2. $\sqrt{-1} = i\sqrt{1}$
$= i$

3. $\sqrt{-150} = i\sqrt{150}$
$= i\sqrt{25 \cdot 6}$
$= i\sqrt{25} \cdot \sqrt{6}$
$= 5i\sqrt{6}$

4. $-\sqrt{-72} = -i\sqrt{72}$
$= -i\sqrt{36 \cdot 2}$
$= -i\sqrt{36} \cdot \sqrt{2}$
$= -6i\sqrt{2}$

5. $(-12+8i)+(7-12i) = (-12+7)+(8-12)i$
$= -5 - 4i$

6. $\left(10\sqrt{2}-17i\right)-\left(5\sqrt{2}-i\right) = 10\sqrt{2}-17i-5\sqrt{2}+i$
$= \left(10\sqrt{2}-5\sqrt{2}\right)+(-17+1)i$
$= 5\sqrt{2}-16i$

7. $(20+4i)+(15-4i) = (20+15)+(4-4)i$
$= 35 + 0i$

8. $\left(\dfrac{3}{2}+\dfrac{1}{3}i\right)-\left(\dfrac{2}{3}-\dfrac{4}{9}i\right) = \dfrac{3}{2}+\dfrac{1}{3}i-\dfrac{2}{3}+\dfrac{4}{9}i$
$= \left(\dfrac{3}{2}-\dfrac{2}{3}\right)+\left(\dfrac{1}{3}+\dfrac{4}{9}\right)i$
$= \dfrac{5}{6}+\dfrac{7}{9}i$

9. $(12i)(12i) = 144i^2$
$= 144(-1)$
$= -144 + 0i$

10. $6i(10-4i) = 6i(10)-6i(4i)$
$= 60i - 24i^2$
$= 60i - 24(-1)$
$= 24 + 60i$

11. $(4+11i)(8-3i) = 32-12i+88i-33i^2$
$= 32+76i-33(-1)$
$= 32+76i+33$
$= 65+76i$

12. $(7+5i)^2 = (7)^2+2(7\cdot 5i)+(5i)^2$
$= 49+70i+25i^2$
$= 49+70i+25(-1)$
$= 49+70i-25$
$= 24+70i$

13. $\dfrac{8-12i}{2} = \dfrac{8}{2}-\dfrac{12}{2}i$
$= 4 - 6i$

14. $\dfrac{10+8i}{2i} = \left(\dfrac{10+8i}{2i}\right)\left(\dfrac{i}{i}\right)$
$= \dfrac{10i+8i^2}{2i^2}$
$= \dfrac{10i+8(-1)}{2(-1)}$
$= \dfrac{-8+10i}{-2}$
$= \dfrac{-8}{-2}+\dfrac{10}{-2}i$
$= 4 - 5i$

15. $\dfrac{7i}{3+5i} = \left(\dfrac{7i}{3+5i}\right)\left(\dfrac{3-5i}{3-5i}\right)$
$= \dfrac{21i-35i^2}{(3)^2-(5i)^2}$
$= \dfrac{21i-35(-1)}{9-25i^2}$
$= \dfrac{35+21i}{9-25(-1)}$
$= \dfrac{35+21i}{34}$
$= \dfrac{35}{34}+\dfrac{21}{34}i$

16. $\dfrac{9i}{4-5i} = \left(\dfrac{9i}{4-5i}\right)\left(\dfrac{4+5i}{4+5i}\right)$

$= \dfrac{36i+45i^2}{(4)^2-(5i)^2}$

$= \dfrac{36i+45(-1)}{16-25i^2}$

$= \dfrac{-45+36i}{16-25(-1)}$

$= \dfrac{-45+36i}{41}$

$= -\dfrac{45}{41}+\dfrac{36}{41}i$

17. $\dfrac{2+6i}{3-3i} = \left(\dfrac{2+6i}{3-3i}\right)\left(\dfrac{3+3i}{3+3i}\right)$

$= \dfrac{(2+6i)(3+3i)}{(3)^2-(3i)^2}$

$= \dfrac{6+6i+18i+18i^2}{9-9i^2}$

$= \dfrac{6+6i+18i+18(-1)}{9-9(-1)}$

$= \dfrac{-12+24i}{18}$

$= -\dfrac{2}{3}+\dfrac{4}{3}i$

18. $\dfrac{5+3i}{3+2i} = \left(\dfrac{5+3i}{3+2i}\right)\left(\dfrac{3-2i}{3-2i}\right)$

$= \dfrac{(5+3i)(3-2i)}{(3)^2-(2i)^2}$

$= \dfrac{15-10i+9i-6i^2}{9-4i^2}$

$= \dfrac{15-10i+9i-6(-1)}{9-4(-1)}$

$= \dfrac{21-i}{13}$

$= \dfrac{21}{13}-\dfrac{1}{13}i$

19. $(4x+3)(x-6)=0$

$4x+3=0 \quad\text{or}\quad x-6=0$

$x=-\dfrac{3}{4} \quad\text{or}\quad x=6$

Solution Set: $\left\{-\dfrac{3}{4},6\right\}$

20. $d(5d-3)=0$

$d=0 \quad\text{or}\quad 5d-3=0$

$d=0 \quad\text{or}\quad d=\dfrac{3}{5}$

Solution Set: $\left\{0,\dfrac{3}{5}\right\}$

21. $x^2-16+48=0$

$(x-12)(x-4)=0$

$x-12=0 \quad\text{or}\quad x-4=0$

$x=12 \quad\text{or}\quad x=4$

Solution Set: $\{4,12\}$

22. $x^2=81$

$x=-\sqrt{81} \quad\text{or}\quad x=\sqrt{81}$

$x=-9 \quad\text{or}\quad x=9$

Solution Set: $\{-9,9\}$

23. $x^2=\dfrac{25}{9}$

$x=-\sqrt{\dfrac{25}{9}} \quad\text{or}\quad x=\sqrt{\dfrac{25}{9}}$

$x=-\dfrac{5}{3} \quad\text{or}\quad x=\dfrac{5}{3}$

Solution Set: $\left\{-\dfrac{5}{3},\dfrac{5}{3}\right\}$

24. $x^2=72$

$x=-\sqrt{72} \quad\text{or}\quad x=\sqrt{72}$

$x=-6\sqrt{2} \quad\text{or}\quad x=6\sqrt{2}$

Solution Set: $\left\{-6\sqrt{2},6\sqrt{2}\right\}$

25. $x^2=-144$

$x=-\sqrt{-144} \quad\text{or}\quad x=\sqrt{-144}$

$x=-12i \quad\text{or}\quad x=12i$

Solution Set: $\{0-12i,0+12i\}$

26. $2h^2-100=0$

$2h^2=100$

$h^2=50$

$h=-\sqrt{50} \quad\text{or}\quad h=\sqrt{50}$

$h=-5\sqrt{2} \quad\text{or}\quad h=5\sqrt{2}$

Solution Set: $\left\{-5\sqrt{2},5\sqrt{2}\right\}$

27.
$$(x-2)^2 = 36$$
$$x-2 = -\sqrt{36} \quad \text{or} \quad x-2 = \sqrt{36}$$
$$x-2 = -6 \quad \text{or} \quad x-2 = 6$$
$$x = -4 \quad \text{or} \quad x = 8$$
Solution Set: $\{-4, 8\}$

28.
$$(x+1)^2 = -25$$
$$x+1 = -\sqrt{-25} \quad \text{or} \quad x+1 = \sqrt{-25}$$
$$x+1 = -5i \quad \text{or} \quad x+1 = 5i$$
$$x = -1-5i \quad \text{or} \quad x = -1+5i$$
Solution Set: $\{-1-5i, -1+5i\}$

29.
$$(s+2)^2 + 4 = 0$$
$$(s+2)^2 = -4$$
$$s+2 = -\sqrt{-4} \quad \text{or} \quad s+2 = \sqrt{-4}$$
$$s+2 = -2i \quad \text{or} \quad s+2 = 2i$$
$$s = -2-2i \quad \text{or} \quad s = -2+2i$$
Solution Set: $\{-2-2i, -2+2i\}$

30.
$$(2x-5)^2 - 13 = 0$$
$$(2x-5)^2 = 13$$
$$2x-5 = -\sqrt{13} \quad \text{or} \quad 2x-5 = \sqrt{13}$$
$$2x = 5-\sqrt{13} \quad \text{or} \quad 2x = 5+\sqrt{13}$$
$$x = \frac{5-\sqrt{13}}{2} \quad \text{or} \quad x = \frac{5+\sqrt{13}}{2}$$
Solution Set: $\left\{\dfrac{5-\sqrt{13}}{2}, \dfrac{5+\sqrt{13}}{2}\right\}$

31.
$$(7x-2)^2 - 15 = 0$$
$$(7x-2)^2 = 15$$
$$7x-2 = -\sqrt{15} \quad \text{or} \quad 7x-2 = \sqrt{15}$$
$$7x = 2-\sqrt{15} \quad \text{or} \quad 7x = 2+\sqrt{15}$$
$$x = \frac{2-\sqrt{15}}{7} \quad \text{or} \quad x = \frac{2+\sqrt{15}}{7}$$
Solution Set: $\left\{\dfrac{2-\sqrt{15}}{7}, \dfrac{2+\sqrt{15}}{7}\right\}$

32.
$$(4x-8)^2 = -28$$
$$4x-8 = -\sqrt{-28} \quad \text{or} \quad 4x-8 = \sqrt{-28}$$
$$4x-8 = -2i\sqrt{7} \quad \text{or} \quad 4x-8 = 2i\sqrt{7}$$
$$4x = 8-2i\sqrt{7} \quad \text{or} \quad 4x = 8+2i\sqrt{7}$$
$$x = \frac{8-2i\sqrt{7}}{4} \quad \text{or} \quad x = \frac{8+2i\sqrt{7}}{4}$$
Solution Set: $\left\{2-\dfrac{\sqrt{7}}{2}i, 2+\dfrac{\sqrt{7}}{2}i\right\}$

33.
$$(4x-6)^2 = -20$$
$$4x-6 = -\sqrt{-20} \quad \text{or} \quad 4x-6 = \sqrt{-20}$$
$$4x-6 = -2i\sqrt{5} \quad \text{or} \quad 4x-6 = 2i\sqrt{5}$$
$$4x = 6-2i\sqrt{5} \quad \text{or} \quad 4x = 6+2i\sqrt{5}$$
$$x = \frac{6-2i\sqrt{5}}{4} \quad \text{or} \quad x = \frac{6+2i\sqrt{5}}{4}$$
Solution Set: $\left\{\dfrac{3}{2}-\dfrac{\sqrt{5}}{2}i, \dfrac{3}{2}+\dfrac{\sqrt{5}}{2}i\right\}$

34. $\left(\dfrac{1}{2}\cdot(-16)\right)^2 = (-8)^2$
$$= 64$$

35. $\left(\dfrac{1}{2}\cdot(13)\right)^2 = \left(\dfrac{13}{2}\right)^2$
$$= \frac{169}{4}$$

36. $\left(\dfrac{1}{2}\cdot\left(\dfrac{7}{3}\right)\right)^2 = \left(\dfrac{7}{6}\right)^2$
$$= \frac{49}{36}$$

37.
$$x^2 + 4x + 12 = 0$$
$$x^2 + 4x = -12$$
$$x^2 + 4x + 4 = -12 + 4$$
$$(x+2)^2 = -8$$
$$x+2 = -\sqrt{-8} \quad \text{or} \quad x+2 = \sqrt{-8}$$
$$x+2 = -2i\sqrt{2} \quad \text{or} \quad x+2 = 2i\sqrt{2}$$
$$x = -2-2i\sqrt{2} \quad \text{or} \quad x = -2+2i\sqrt{2}$$
Solution Set: $\{-2-2i\sqrt{2}, -2+2i\sqrt{2}\}$

38.

$$r^2 - 10r + 21 = 0$$
$$r^2 - 10r = -21$$
$$r^2 - 10r + 25 = -21 + 25$$
$$(r-5)^2 = 4$$
$$r - 5 = -\sqrt{4} \quad \text{or} \quad r - 5 = \sqrt{4}$$
$$r - 5 = -2 \quad \text{or} \quad r - 5 = 2$$
$$r = 3 \quad \text{or} \quad r = 7$$
Solution Set: $\{3, 7\}$

39.

$$x^2 + 2x = 8$$
$$x^2 + 2x + 1 = 8 + 1$$
$$(x+1)^2 = 9$$
$$x + 1 = -\sqrt{9} \quad \text{or} \quad x + 1 = \sqrt{9}$$
$$x + 1 = -3 \quad \text{or} \quad x + 1 = 3$$
$$x = -4 \quad \text{or} \quad x = 2$$
Solution Set: $\{-4, 2\}$

40.

$$x^2 - 8x = 0$$
$$x^2 - 8x + 16 = 0 + 16$$
$$(x-4)^2 = 16$$
$$x - 4 = -\sqrt{16} \quad \text{or} \quad x - 4 = \sqrt{16}$$
$$x - 4 = -4 \quad \text{or} \quad x - 4 = 4$$
$$x = 0 \quad \text{or} \quad x = 8$$
Solution Set: $\{0, 8\}$

41.

$$x^2 - 12x + 16 = 20$$
$$x^2 - 12x = 4$$
$$x^2 - 12x + 36 = 4 + 36$$
$$(x-6)^2 = 40$$
$$x - 6 = -\sqrt{40} \quad \text{or} \quad x - 6 = \sqrt{40}$$
$$x - 6 = -2\sqrt{10} \quad \text{or} \quad x - 6 = 2\sqrt{10}$$
$$x = 6 - 2\sqrt{10} \quad \text{or} \quad x = 6 + 2\sqrt{10}$$
Solution Set: $\{6 - 2\sqrt{10}, 6 + 2\sqrt{10}\}$

42.

$$x^2 - 6x + 34 = 0$$
$$x^2 - 6x = -34$$
$$x^2 - 6x + 9 = -34 + 9$$
$$(x-3)^2 = -25$$
$$x - 3 = -\sqrt{-25} \quad \text{or} \quad x - 3 = \sqrt{-25}$$
$$x - 3 = -5i \quad \text{or} \quad x - 3 = 5i$$
$$x = 3 - 5i \quad \text{or} \quad x = 3 + 5i$$
Solution Set: $\{3 - 5i, 3 + 5i\}$

43.

$$p^2 + 10p + 35 = -10$$
$$p^2 + 10p = -45$$
$$p^2 + 10p + 25 = -45 + 25$$
$$(p+5)^2 = -20$$
$$p + 5 = -\sqrt{-20} \quad \text{or} \quad p + 5 = -\sqrt{-20}$$
$$p + 5 = -2i\sqrt{5} \quad \text{or} \quad p + 5 = -2i\sqrt{5}$$
$$x = -5 - 2i\sqrt{5} \quad \text{or} \quad x = -5 - 2i\sqrt{5}$$
Solution Set: $\{-5 - 2i\sqrt{5}, -5 + 2i\sqrt{5}\}$

44.

$$x^2 + 3x - 6 = 0$$
$$x^2 + 3x = 6$$
$$x^2 + 3x + \frac{9}{4} = 6 + \frac{9}{4}$$
$$\left(x + \frac{3}{2}\right)^2 = \frac{33}{4}$$
$$x + \frac{3}{2} = -\sqrt{\frac{33}{4}} \quad \text{or} \quad x + \frac{3}{2} = \sqrt{\frac{33}{4}}$$
$$x + \frac{3}{2} = -\frac{\sqrt{33}}{2} \quad \text{or} \quad x + \frac{3}{2} = \frac{\sqrt{33}}{2}$$
$$x = -\frac{3}{2} - \frac{\sqrt{33}}{2} \quad \text{or} \quad x = \frac{-3}{2} + \frac{\sqrt{33}}{2}$$
Solution Set: $\left\{\dfrac{-3 - \sqrt{33}}{2}, \dfrac{-3 + \sqrt{33}}{2}\right\}$

45.
$$x^2 + 7x + 2 = 0$$
$$x^2 + 7x = -2$$
$$x^2 + 7x + \frac{49}{4} = -2 + \frac{49}{4}$$
$$\left(x + \frac{7}{2}\right)^2 = \frac{41}{4}$$
$$x + \frac{7}{2} = -\sqrt{\frac{41}{4}} \quad \text{or} \quad x + \frac{7}{2} = \sqrt{\frac{41}{4}}$$
$$x + \frac{7}{2} = -\frac{\sqrt{41}}{2} \quad \text{or} \quad x + \frac{7}{2} = \frac{\sqrt{41}}{2}$$
$$x = -\frac{7}{2} - \frac{\sqrt{41}}{2} \quad \text{or} \quad x = -\frac{7}{2} + \frac{\sqrt{41}}{2}$$
Solution Set: $\left\{\dfrac{-7-\sqrt{41}}{2}, \dfrac{-7+\sqrt{41}}{2}\right\}$

46.
$$2x^2 - 16x + 48 = 0$$
$$\frac{2x^2}{2} - \frac{16x}{2} + \frac{48}{2} = \frac{0}{2}$$
$$x^2 - 8x + 24 = 0$$
$$x^2 - 8x = -24$$
$$x^2 - 8x + 16 = -24 + 16$$
$$(x-4)^2 = -8$$
$$x - 4 = -\sqrt{-8} \quad \text{or} \quad x - 4 = \sqrt{-8}$$
$$x - 4 = -2i\sqrt{2} \quad \text{or} \quad x - 4 = 2i\sqrt{2}$$
$$x = 4 - 2i\sqrt{2} \quad \text{or} \quad x = 4 + 2i\sqrt{2}$$
Solution Set: $\left\{4 - 2i\sqrt{2}, 4 + 2i\sqrt{2}\right\}$

47.
$$2q^2 - 12q + 72 = 0$$
$$\frac{2q^2}{2} - \frac{12q}{2} + \frac{72}{2} = \frac{0}{2}$$
$$x^2 - 6x + 36 = 0$$
$$x^2 - 6x = -36$$
$$x^2 - 6x + 9 = -36 + 9$$
$$(x-3)^2 = -27$$
$$x - 3 = -\sqrt{-27} \quad \text{or} \quad x - 3 = \sqrt{-27}$$
$$x - 3 = -3i\sqrt{3} \quad \text{or} \quad x - 3 = 3i\sqrt{3}$$
$$x = 3 - 3i\sqrt{3} \quad \text{or} \quad x = 3 + 3i\sqrt{3}$$
Solution Set: $\left\{3 - 3i\sqrt{3}, 3 + 3i\sqrt{3}\right\}$

48.
$$4x^2 + 12x - 8 = 0$$
$$\frac{4x^2}{4} + \frac{12x}{4} - \frac{8}{4} = \frac{0}{4}$$
$$x^2 + 3x - 2 = 0$$
$$x^2 + 3x = 2$$
$$x^2 + 3x + \frac{9}{4} = 2 + \frac{9}{4}$$
$$\left(x + \frac{3}{2}\right)^2 = \frac{17}{4}$$
$$x + \frac{3}{2} = -\sqrt{\frac{17}{4}} \quad \text{or} \quad x + \frac{3}{2} = \sqrt{\frac{17}{4}}$$
$$x + \frac{3}{2} = -\frac{\sqrt{17}}{2} \quad \text{or} \quad x + \frac{3}{2} = \frac{\sqrt{17}}{2}$$
$$x = -\frac{3}{2} - \frac{\sqrt{17}}{2} \quad \text{or} \quad x = -\frac{3}{2} + \frac{\sqrt{17}}{2}$$
Solution Set: $\left\{\dfrac{-3-\sqrt{17}}{2}, \dfrac{-3+\sqrt{17}}{2}\right\}$

49. Let x represent the unknown number. The equation is $5x^2 - 50 = 0$.
$$5x^2 - 50 = 0$$
$$5x^2 = 50$$
$$x^2 = 10$$
$$x = -\sqrt{10} \quad \text{or} \quad x = \sqrt{10}$$
The two numbers are $-\sqrt{10}$ and $\sqrt{10}$.

50. Let x represent the unknown number. The equation is $36 = (5 + 2x)^2$.
$$(2x+5)^2 = 36$$
$$2x + 5 = -\sqrt{36} \quad \text{or} \quad 2x + 5 = \sqrt{36}$$
$$2x + 5 = -6 \quad \text{or} \quad 2x + 5 = 6$$
$$2x = -11 \quad \text{or} \quad 2x = 1$$
$$x = -\frac{11}{2} \quad \text{or} \quad x = \frac{1}{2}$$
The two numbers are $-\frac{11}{2}$ and $\frac{1}{2}$.

51. Let x represent the unknown number. The equation is $(3x+2)^2 = 9$.

$$(3x+2)^2 = 9$$
$$3x+2 = -\sqrt{9} \quad \text{or} \quad 3x+2 = \sqrt{9}$$
$$3x+2 = -3 \quad \text{or} \quad 3x+2 = 3$$
$$3x = -5 \quad \text{or} \quad 3x = 1$$
$$x = -\frac{5}{3} \quad \text{or} \quad x = \frac{1}{3}$$

The two numbers are $-\frac{5}{3}$ and $\frac{1}{3}$.

52. Let x represent the unknown number. The equation is $x^2 + 7x = -6$.

$$x^2 + 7x = -6$$
$$x^2 + 7x + \frac{49}{4} = -6 + \frac{49}{4}$$
$$\left(x + \frac{7}{2}\right)^2 = \frac{25}{4}$$
$$x + \frac{7}{2} = -\sqrt{\frac{25}{4}} \quad \text{or} \quad x + \frac{7}{2} = \sqrt{\frac{25}{4}}$$
$$x + \frac{7}{2} = -\frac{5}{2} \quad \text{or} \quad x + \frac{7}{2} = \frac{5}{2}$$
$$x = -6 \quad \text{or} \quad x = -1$$

The two numbers are -6 and -1.

53. Let x represent the unknown number. The equation is $13 = 12x + x^2$.

$$x^2 + 12x = 13$$
$$x^2 + 12x + 36 = 13 + 36$$
$$(x+6)^2 = 49$$
$$x+6 = -\sqrt{49} \quad \text{or} \quad x+6 = \sqrt{49}$$
$$x+6 = -7 \quad \text{or} \quad x+6 = 7$$
$$x = -13 \quad \text{or} \quad x = 1$$

The two numbers are -13 and 1.

54. Prepare We need to find the time it takes Pierre's cousin Michel to return to the ground, once he is propelled from the cannon, using the formula and given information.

Plan We set the function $h(t) = 0$, since returning to the ground represents a height of 0. We will solve the resulting equation by completing the square.

Process

$$-16t^2 + 32t + 4 = 0$$
$$\frac{-16t^2}{-16} + \frac{32t}{-16} + \frac{4}{-16} = \frac{0}{-16}$$
$$t^2 - 2t - \frac{1}{4} = 0$$
$$t^2 - 2t = \frac{1}{4}$$
$$t^2 - 2t + 1 = \frac{1}{4} + 1$$
$$(t-1)^2 = \frac{5}{4}$$
$$t-1 = -\sqrt{\frac{5}{4}} \quad \text{or} \quad t-1 = \sqrt{\frac{5}{4}}$$
$$t-1 = -\frac{\sqrt{5}}{2} \quad \text{or} \quad t-1 = \frac{\sqrt{5}}{2}$$
$$t = 1 - \frac{\sqrt{5}}{2} \quad \text{or} \quad t = 1 + \frac{\sqrt{5}}{2}$$

Therefore, it would take Pierre's cousin Michel exactly $1 + \frac{\sqrt{5}}{2}$ seconds, or approximately 2.12 seconds to return to the ground.

Ponder Does our answer seem reasonable? Yes. If we substitute 2.12 into the formula for t, we get a height of -0.0704 feet, which is roughly a height of 0.

55. $6x^2 + 5x - 4 = 0$

$a = 6,\ b = 5,\ c = -4$

$$x = \frac{-b \pm \sqrt{b^2 - 4ac}}{2a}$$
$$= \frac{-5 \pm \sqrt{(5)^2 - 4(6)(-4)}}{2(6)}$$
$$= \frac{-5 \pm \sqrt{25 + 96}}{12}$$
$$= \frac{-5 \pm \sqrt{121}}{12}$$
$$= \frac{-5 \pm 11}{12}$$

Solution Set: $\left\{-\frac{4}{3}, \frac{1}{2}\right\}$

56. $2w^2 - 3w - 1 = 0$

$a = 2, \; b = -3, \; c = -1$

$$w = \frac{-b \pm \sqrt{b^2 - 4ac}}{2a}$$

$$= \frac{-(-3) \pm \sqrt{(-3)^2 - 4(2)(-1)}}{2(2)}$$

$$= \frac{3 \pm \sqrt{9+8}}{4}$$

$$= \frac{3 \pm \sqrt{17}}{4}$$

Solution Set: $\left\{ \dfrac{3 - \sqrt{17}}{4}, \dfrac{3 + \sqrt{17}}{4} \right\}$

57. $4x^2 - 2 = 8x$

$4x^2 - 8x - 2 = 0$

$a = 4, \; b = -8, \; c = -2$

$$x = \frac{-b \pm \sqrt{b^2 - 4ac}}{2a}$$

$$= \frac{-(-8) \pm \sqrt{(-8)^2 - 4(4)(-2)}}{2(4)}$$

$$= \frac{8 \pm \sqrt{64 + 32}}{8}$$

$$= \frac{8 \pm \sqrt{96}}{8}$$

$$= \frac{8 \pm 4\sqrt{6}}{8}$$

Solution Set: $\left\{ \dfrac{2 - \sqrt{6}}{2}, \dfrac{2 + \sqrt{6}}{2} \right\}$

58. $4m^2 + 25 = 0$

$a = 4, \; b = 0, \; c = 25$

$$m = \frac{-b \pm \sqrt{b^2 - 4ac}}{2a}$$

$$= \frac{-0 \pm \sqrt{(0)^2 - 4(4)(25)}}{2(4)}$$

$$= \frac{\pm \sqrt{-400}}{8}$$

$$= \frac{\pm 20i}{8}$$

Solution Set: $\left\{ 0 - \dfrac{5}{2}i, 0 + \dfrac{5}{2}i \right\}$

59. $2x^2 - 6x = 1$

$2x^2 - 6x - 1 = 0$

$a = 2, \; b = -6, \; c = -1$

$$x = \frac{-b \pm \sqrt{b^2 - 4ac}}{2a}$$

$$= \frac{-(-6) \pm \sqrt{(-6)^2 - 4(2)(-1)}}{2(2)}$$

$$= \frac{6 \pm \sqrt{36 + 8}}{4}$$

$$= \frac{6 \pm \sqrt{44}}{4}$$

$$= \frac{6 \pm 2\sqrt{11}}{4}$$

Solution Set: $\left\{ \dfrac{3 - \sqrt{11}}{2}, \dfrac{3 + \sqrt{11}}{2} \right\}$

60. $3x^2 - 7x - 6 = 0$

$a = 3, \; b = -7, \; c = -6$

$$x = \frac{-b \pm \sqrt{b^2 - 4ac}}{2a}$$

$$= \frac{-(-7) \pm \sqrt{(-7)^2 - 4(3)(-6)}}{2(3)}$$

$$= \frac{7 \pm \sqrt{49 + 72}}{6}$$

$$= \frac{7 \pm \sqrt{121}}{6}$$

$$= \frac{7 \pm 11}{6}$$

Solution Set: $\left\{ -\dfrac{2}{3}, 3 \right\}$

61. $(x + 4)(x - 2) = 1$

$x^2 + 2x - 8 = 1$

$x^2 + 2x - 9 = 0$

$a = 1, \; b = 2, \; c = -9$

$$x = \frac{-b \pm \sqrt{b^2 - 4ac}}{2a}$$

$$= \frac{-2 \pm \sqrt{(2)^2 - 4(1)(-9)}}{2(1)}$$

$$= \frac{-2 \pm \sqrt{4 + 36}}{2}$$

$$= \frac{-2 \pm \sqrt{40}}{2}$$

$$= \frac{-2 \pm 2\sqrt{10}}{2}$$

Solution Set: $\left\{ -1 - \sqrt{10}, -1 + \sqrt{10} \right\}$

62. $6y^2 + 8y + 4 = 0$

$a = 6, \ b = 8, \ c = 4$

$$y = \frac{-b \pm \sqrt{b^2 - 4ac}}{2a}$$

$$= \frac{-8 \pm \sqrt{(8)^2 - 4(6)(4)}}{2(6)}$$

$$= \frac{-8 \pm \sqrt{64 - 96}}{12}$$

$$= \frac{-8 \pm \sqrt{-32}}{12}$$

$$= \frac{-8 \pm 4i\sqrt{2}}{12}$$

Solution Set: $\left\{ -\dfrac{2}{3} - \dfrac{\sqrt{2}}{3}i, -\dfrac{2}{3} + \dfrac{\sqrt{2}}{3}i \right\}$

63. $\dfrac{1}{3}x^2 + \dfrac{1}{2}x - \dfrac{5}{3} = 0$

$$\frac{6}{1}\left(\frac{1}{3}x^2 + \frac{1}{2}x - \frac{5}{3} \right) = 6(0)$$

$2x^2 + 3x - 10 = 0$

$a = 2, \ b = 3, \ c = -10$

$$y = \frac{-b \pm \sqrt{b^2 - 4ac}}{2a}$$

$$= \frac{-3 \pm \sqrt{(3)^2 - 4(2)(-10)}}{2(2)}$$

$$= \frac{-3 \pm \sqrt{9 + 80}}{4}$$

$$= \frac{-3 \pm \sqrt{89}}{4}$$

Solution Set: $\left\{ \dfrac{-3 - \sqrt{89}}{4}, \dfrac{-3 + \sqrt{89}}{4} \right\}$

64. $y^2 + 8y + 15 = 0$

$a = 1, \ b = 8, \ c = 15$

$$b^2 - 4ac = (8)^2 - 4(1)(15)$$

$$= 64 - 60$$

$$= 4$$

Because $b^2 - 4ac = 4$ and $4 > 0$, there are two real solutions to the equation.

65. $2x^2 + 4x + 3 = 0$

$a = 2, \ b = 4, \ c = 3$

$$b^2 - 4ac = (4)^2 - 4(2)(3)$$

$$= 16 - 24$$

$$= -8$$

Because $b^2 - 4ac = -8$ and $-8 < 0$, there are two complex solutions to the equation.

66. $4x^2 - 4x + 5 = 4$

$4x^2 - 4x + 1 = 0$

$a = 4, \ b = -4, \ c = 1$

$$b^2 - 4ac = (-4)^2 - 4(4)(1)$$

$$= 16 - 16$$

$$= 0$$

Because $b^2 - 4ac = 0$, there is one real solution to the equation.

67. $7x = 20 - 6x^2$

$6x^2 + 7x - 20 = 0$

$a = 6, \ b = 7, \ c = -20$

$$b^2 - 4ac = (7)^2 - 4(6)(-20)$$

$$= 49 + 480$$

$$= 529$$

Because $b^2 - 4ac = 529$ and $529 > 0$, there are two real solutions to the equation.

68. $(n + 5)(2n - 3) = 0$

$n + 5 = 0 \quad \text{or} \quad 2n - 3 = 0$

$n = -5 \quad \text{or} \quad n = \dfrac{3}{2}$

Solution Set: $\left\{ -5, \dfrac{3}{2} \right\}$

69. $3x^2 - 19x = 40$

$3x^2 - 19x - 40 = 0$

$(3x+5)(x-8) = 0$

$3x+5 = 0$ or $x-8 = 0$

$x = -\dfrac{5}{3}$ or $x = 8$

Solution Set: $\left\{ -\dfrac{5}{3}, 8 \right\}$

70. $(x-5)^2 = 49$

$x-5 = -\sqrt{49}$ or $x-5 = \sqrt{49}$

$x-5 = -7$ or $x-5 = 7$

$x = -2$ or $x = 12$

Solution Set: $\{-2, 12\}$

71. $x^2 = -60$

$x = -\sqrt{-60}$ or $x = \sqrt{-60}$

$x = -2i\sqrt{15}$ or $x = 2i\sqrt{15}$

Solution Set: $\left\{ 0 - 2i\sqrt{15}, 0 + 2i\sqrt{15} \right\}$

72. $k^2 - 2k + 6 = 18$

$k^2 - 2k = 12$

$k^2 - 2k + 1 = 12 + 1$

$(k-1)^2 = 13$

$k-1 = -\sqrt{13}$ or $k-1 = \sqrt{13}$

$k = 1 - \sqrt{13}$ or $k = 1 + \sqrt{13}$

Solution Set: $\left\{ 1 - \sqrt{13}, 1 + \sqrt{13} \right\}$

73. $3x^2 + 15x + 15 = 0$

$\dfrac{3x^2}{3} + \dfrac{15x}{3} + \dfrac{15}{3} = \dfrac{0}{3}$

$x^2 + 5x + 5 = 0$

$x^2 + 5x = -5$

$x^2 + 5x + \dfrac{25}{4} = -5 + \dfrac{25}{4}$

$\left(x + \dfrac{5}{2} \right)^2 = \dfrac{5}{4}$

$x + \dfrac{5}{2} = -\sqrt{\dfrac{5}{4}}$ or $x + \dfrac{5}{2} = \sqrt{\dfrac{5}{4}}$

$x + \dfrac{5}{2} = -\dfrac{\sqrt{5}}{2}$ or $x + \dfrac{5}{2} = \dfrac{\sqrt{5}}{2}$

$x = -\dfrac{5}{2} - \dfrac{\sqrt{5}}{2}$ or $x = -\dfrac{5}{2} + \dfrac{\sqrt{5}}{2}$

Solution Set: $\left\{ \dfrac{-5 - \sqrt{5}}{2}, \dfrac{-5 + \sqrt{5}}{2} \right\}$

74. $x^2 - 8x + 25 = 0$

$x^2 - 8x = -25$

$x^2 - 8x + 16 = -25 + 16$

$(x-4)^2 = -9$

$x-4 = -\sqrt{-9}$ or $x-4 = \sqrt{-9}$

$x-4 = -3i$ or $x-4 = 3i$

$x = 4 - 3i$ or $x = 4 + 3i$

Solution Set: $\{4 - 3i, 4 + 3i\}$

75. $(x-4)(x+2) = 16$

$x^2 - 2x - 8 = 16$

$x^2 - 2x - 24 = 0$

$(x-6)(x+4) = 0$

$x-6 = 0$ or $x+4 = 0$

$x = 6$ or $x = -4$

Solution Set: $\{-4, 6\}$

76. $3x^2 + 3x = 1$

$3x^2 + 3x - 1 = 0$

$a = 3,\ b = 3,\ c = -1$

$y = \dfrac{-b \pm \sqrt{b^2 - 4ac}}{2a}$

$= \dfrac{-3 \pm \sqrt{(3)^2 - 4(3)(-1)}}{2(3)}$

$= \dfrac{-3 \pm \sqrt{9 + 12}}{6}$

$= \dfrac{-3 \pm \sqrt{21}}{6}$

Solution Set: $\left\{ \dfrac{-3 - \sqrt{21}}{6}, \dfrac{-3 + \sqrt{21}}{6} \right\}$

77. $5y^2 - 2y + 3 = 0$

$a = 5, \ b = -2, \ c = 3$

$$y = \frac{-b \pm \sqrt{b^2 - 4ac}}{2a}$$

$$= \frac{-(-2) \pm \sqrt{(-2)^2 - 4(5)(3)}}{2(5)}$$

$$= \frac{2 \pm \sqrt{4 - 60}}{10}$$

$$= \frac{2 \pm \sqrt{-56}}{10}$$

$$= \frac{2 \pm 2i\sqrt{14}}{10}$$

Solution Set: $\left\{ \dfrac{1}{5} - \dfrac{\sqrt{14}}{5}i, \dfrac{1}{5} + \dfrac{\sqrt{14}}{5}i \right\}$

78. $3x^2 + 6x + 5 = 0$

$a = 3, \ b = 6, \ c = 5$

$$y = \frac{-b \pm \sqrt{b^2 - 4ac}}{2a}$$

$$= \frac{-6 \pm \sqrt{(6)^2 - 4(3)(5)}}{2(3)}$$

$$= \frac{-6 \pm \sqrt{36 - 60}}{6}$$

$$= \frac{-6 \pm \sqrt{-24}}{6}$$

$$= \frac{-6 \pm 2i\sqrt{6}}{6}$$

Solution Set: $\left\{ -1 - \dfrac{\sqrt{6}}{3}i, -1 + \dfrac{\sqrt{6}}{3}i \right\}$

79. $(2x + 1)^2 = x$

$4x^2 + 4x + 1 = x$

$4x^2 + 3x + 1 = 0$

$a = 4, \ b = 3, \ c = 1$

$$y = \frac{-b \pm \sqrt{b^2 - 4ac}}{2a}$$

$$= \frac{-3 \pm \sqrt{(3)^2 - 4(4)(1)}}{2(4)}$$

$$= \frac{-3 \pm \sqrt{9 - 16}}{8}$$

$$= \frac{-3 \pm \sqrt{-7}}{8}$$

$$= \frac{-3 \pm i\sqrt{7}}{8}$$

Solution Set: $\left\{ -\dfrac{3}{8} - \dfrac{\sqrt{7}}{8}i, -\dfrac{3}{8} + \dfrac{\sqrt{7}}{8}i \right\}$

80. $\qquad p + \dfrac{14}{p} = 9$

$$\frac{p}{1}\left(p + \frac{14}{p} \right) = p(9)$$

$$p^2 + 14 = 9p$$

$$p^2 - 9p + 14 = 0$$

$$(p - 7)(p - 2) = 0$$

$p - 7 = 0 \quad \text{or} \quad p - 2 = 0$

$p = 7 \quad \text{or} \quad p = 2$

Solution Set: $\{2, 7\}$

81. $\qquad 2x = \dfrac{3}{x + 2}$

$$2x(x + 2) = \frac{x + 2}{1}\left(\frac{3}{x + 2} \right)$$

$$2x^2 + 4x = 3$$

$$2x^2 + 4x - 3 = 0$$

$a = 2, \ b = 4, \ c = -3$

$$y = \frac{-b \pm \sqrt{b^2 - 4ac}}{2a}$$

$$= \frac{-4 \pm \sqrt{(4)^2 - 4(2)(-3)}}{2(2)}$$

$$= \frac{-4 \pm \sqrt{16 + 24}}{4}$$

$$= \frac{-4 \pm \sqrt{40}}{4}$$

$$= \frac{-4 \pm 2\sqrt{10}}{4}$$

Solution Set: $\left\{ \dfrac{-2 - \sqrt{10}}{2}, \dfrac{-2 + \sqrt{10}}{2} \right\}$

82.
$$\frac{2x}{x-2}-\frac{1}{x}=\frac{4x-1}{x}$$

$$\frac{x(x-2)}{1}\left(\frac{2x}{x-2}-\frac{1}{x}\right)=\frac{x(x-2)}{1}\left(\frac{4x-1}{x}\right)$$

$$2x^2-(x-2)=(x-2)(4x-1)$$

$$2x^2-x+2=4x^2-9x+2$$

$$0=2x^2-8x$$

$$0=2x(x-4)$$

$$2x=0 \quad \text{or} \quad x-4=0$$

$$\cancel{x=0} \quad \text{or} \quad x=4$$

Solution Set: $\{4\}$

83.
$$\frac{4}{x}+\frac{2x}{x-1}=\frac{x^2-3x-12}{x^2-x}$$

$$\frac{x(x-1)}{1}\left(\frac{4}{x}+\frac{2x}{x-1}\right)=\frac{x(x-1)}{1}\left(\frac{x^2-3x-12}{x^2-x}\right)$$

$$4(x-1)+2x^2=x^2-3x-12$$

$$4x-4+2x^2=x^2-3x-12$$

$$x^2+7x+8=0$$

$$a=1,\ b=7,\ c=8$$

$$y=\frac{-b\pm\sqrt{b^2-4ac}}{2a}$$

$$=\frac{-7\pm\sqrt{(7)^2-4(1)(8)}}{2(1)}$$

$$=\frac{-7\pm\sqrt{49-32}}{2}$$

$$=\frac{-7\pm\sqrt{17}}{2}$$

Solution Set: $\left\{\dfrac{-7-\sqrt{17}}{2},\dfrac{-7+\sqrt{17}}{2}\right\}$

84.
$$\frac{x^2-5}{x^2-x}=\frac{2x}{x}+\frac{4}{x}$$

$$\frac{x(x-1)}{1}\left(\frac{x^2-5}{x^2-x}\right)=\frac{x(x-1)}{1}\left(\frac{2x}{x}+\frac{4}{x}\right)$$

$$x^2-5=2x(x-1)+4(x-1)$$

$$x^2-5=2x^2-2x+4x-4$$

$$0=x^2+2x+1$$

$$0=(x+1)^2$$

$$x+1=0$$

$$x=-1$$

Solution Set: $\{-1\}$

85. Let x represent the distance from the base of the pole that the guy rope is attached to the ground. The equation is $x^2+3^2=6^2$.

$$x^2+3^2=6^2$$

$$x^2+9=36$$

$$x^2=27$$

$$x=-\sqrt{27} \quad \text{or} \quad x=\sqrt{27}$$

$$\cancel{x=-3\sqrt{3}} \quad \text{or} \quad x=3\sqrt{3}$$

The distance from the base of the pole that the guy rope is attached to the ground is $3\sqrt{3}$, or approximately 5.20 feet.

86. Prepare We need to determine how fare the two high-wire performers walk on the high wires, using the Pythagorean theorem.

Plan Let's use the Pythagorean theorem with $a=x$, $b=2x+2$ and $c=13$ (feet) to solve for x. Then, we can find how far the other performer walks by substituting this value into $(2x+2)$.

Process Let $x=$ the length of wire the first performer walks and $(2x+2)=$ length of wire the second performer walks.

$$a^2+b^2=c^2$$

$$x^2+(2x+2)^2=(13)^2$$

$$x^2+4x^2+8x+4=169$$

$$5x^2+8x-165=0$$

$$(x-5)(5x+33)=0$$

$$x-5=0 \quad \text{or} \quad 5x+33=0$$

$$x=5 \quad \text{or} \quad \cancel{x=-\frac{33}{5}}$$

Substituting 5 for x we get $2x+2=10+2=12$. Therefore, the first performer travels 5 feet on the high wire and the second performer travels 12 feet on the high wire.

Ponder Do the lengths seem reasonable? Yes, because we know from geometry that the hypotenuse of a right triangle is the longest side. Therefore, the two performers should each walk less than 13 feet. We can also check our answers by substituting them into the Pythagorean theorem.

$$a^2+b^2=c^2$$

$$(5)^2+(12)^2=(13)^2$$

$$25+144=169$$

$$169=169$$

True

87.
$$p^4 + 21p^2 - 100 = 0$$
$$\left(p^2 - 4\right)\left(p^2 + 25\right) = 0$$
$$p^2 - 4 = 0 \quad \text{or} \quad p^2 + 25 = 0$$
$$p^2 = 4 \quad \text{or} \quad p^2 = -25$$
$$p = \pm\sqrt{4} \quad \text{or} \quad p = \pm\sqrt{-25}$$
$$p = \pm 2 \quad \text{or} \quad p = \pm 5i$$
Solution Set: $\{0 - 5i, 0 + 5i, -2, 2\}$

88.
$$27t^4 - 39t^2 + 4 = 0$$
$$\left(3t^2 - 4\right)\left(9t^2 - 1\right) = 0$$
$$3t^2 - 4 = 0 \quad \text{or} \quad 9t^2 - 1 = 0$$
$$t^2 = \frac{4}{3} \quad \text{or} \quad t^2 = \frac{1}{9}$$
$$t = \pm\sqrt{\frac{4}{3}} \quad \text{or} \quad t = \pm\sqrt{\frac{1}{9}}$$
$$t = \pm\frac{2\sqrt{3}}{3} \quad \text{or} \quad t = \pm\frac{1}{3}$$
Solution Set: $\left\{-\frac{2\sqrt{3}}{3}, -\frac{1}{3}, \frac{1}{3}, \frac{2\sqrt{3}}{3}\right\}$

89.
$$6s^4 - 13s^2 - 28 = 0$$
$$\left(2s^2 - 7\right)\left(3s^2 + 4\right) = 0$$
$$2s^2 - 7 = 0 \quad \text{or} \quad 3s^2 + 4 = 0$$
$$s^2 = \frac{7}{2} \quad \text{or} \quad s^2 = -\frac{4}{3}$$
$$s = \pm\sqrt{\frac{7}{2}} \quad \text{or} \quad s = \pm\sqrt{-\frac{4}{3}}$$
$$s = \pm\frac{\sqrt{14}}{2} \quad \text{or} \quad s = \pm\frac{2i\sqrt{3}}{3}$$
Solution Set: $\left\{0 - \frac{2i\sqrt{3}}{3}, 0 + \frac{2i\sqrt{3}}{3}, -\frac{\sqrt{14}}{2}, \frac{\sqrt{14}}{2}\right\}$

90.
$$s^4 + 63s^2 - 64 = 0$$
$$\left(s^2 - 1\right)\left(s^2 + 64\right) = 0$$
$$s^2 - 1 = 0 \quad \text{or} \quad s^2 + 64 = 0$$
$$s^2 = 1 \quad \text{or} \quad s^2 = -64$$
$$s = \pm\sqrt{1} \quad \text{or} \quad s = \pm\sqrt{-64}$$
$$s = \pm 1 \quad \text{or} \quad s = \pm 8i$$
Solution Set: $\{0 - 8i, 0 + 8i, -1, 1\}$

91. Let $u = y^{-1}$ and $u^2 = y^{-2}$.
$$42y^{-2} + 13y^{-1} = 40$$
$$42u^2 + 13u = 40$$
$$42u^2 + 13u - 40 = 0$$
$$\left(6u - 5\right)\left(7u + 8\right) = 0$$
$$6u - 5 = 0 \quad \text{or} \quad 7u + 8 = 0$$
$$u = \frac{5}{6} \quad \text{or} \quad u = -\frac{8}{7}$$

$$y^{-1} = \frac{5}{6} \quad \text{or} \quad y^{-1} = -\frac{8}{7}$$
$$\frac{1}{y} = \frac{5}{6} \quad \text{or} \quad \frac{1}{y} = -\frac{8}{7}$$
$$5y = 6 \quad \text{or} \quad 8y = -7$$
$$y = \frac{6}{5} \quad \text{or} \quad y = -\frac{7}{8}$$
Solution Set: $\left\{-\frac{7}{8}, \frac{6}{5}\right\}$

92. Let $u = x^3$ and $u^2 = x^6$.

$$x^6 - 7x^3 - 8 = 0$$
$$u^2 - 7u - 8 = 0$$
$$(u - 8)(u + 1) = 0$$
$$u - 8 = 0 \quad \text{or} \quad u + 1 = 0$$
$$u = 8 \quad \text{or} \quad u = -1$$

$$x^3 = 8 \qquad\qquad x^3 = -1$$
$$x^3 - 8 = 0 \qquad\qquad x^3 + 1 = 0$$
$$(x - 2)(x^2 + 2x + 4) = 0 \qquad (x + 1)(x^2 - x + 1) = 0$$

$$x - 2 = 0 \quad \text{or} \quad x^2 + 2x + 4 = 0 \qquad \text{or} \quad x + 1 = 0 \quad \text{or} \quad x^2 - x + 1 = 0$$

$$x = 2 \qquad x = \frac{-2 \pm \sqrt{2^2 - 4(1)(4)}}{2(1)} \qquad\qquad x = -1 \qquad x = \frac{-(-1) \pm \sqrt{(-1)^2 - 4(1)(1)}}{2(1)}$$

$$= \frac{-2 \pm \sqrt{-12}}{2} \qquad\qquad\qquad = \frac{1 \pm \sqrt{-3}}{2}$$

$$= -1 \pm i\sqrt{3} \qquad\qquad\qquad = \frac{1 \pm i\sqrt{3}}{2}$$

Solution Set: $\left\{ -1 - i\sqrt{3}, -1 + i\sqrt{3}, \dfrac{1 - i\sqrt{3}}{2}, \dfrac{1 + i\sqrt{3}}{2}, -1, 2 \right\}$

93. Let $u = (w + 7)$ and $u^2 = (x + 7)^2$.

$$6(w + 7)^2 - 13(w + 7) - 8 = 0$$
$$6u^2 - 13u - 8 = 0$$
$$(2u + 1)(3u - 8) = 0$$
$$2u + 1 = 0 \quad \text{or} \quad 3u - 8 = 0$$
$$u = -\frac{1}{2} \quad \text{or} \quad u = \frac{8}{3}$$

$$w + 7 = -\frac{1}{2} \quad \text{or} \quad w + 7 = \frac{8}{3}$$
$$w = -\frac{15}{2} \quad \text{or} \quad w = -\frac{13}{3}$$

Solution Set: $\left\{ -\dfrac{15}{2}, -\dfrac{13}{3} \right\}$

94. Let $u = (y - 5)$ and $u^2 = (y - 5)^2$.

$$20(y - 5)^2 - 19(y - 5) - 6 = 0$$
$$20u^2 - 19u - 6 = 0$$
$$(4u + 1)(5u - 6) = 0$$
$$4u + 1 = 0 \quad \text{or} \quad 5u - 6 = 0$$
$$u = -\frac{1}{4} \quad \text{or} \quad u = \frac{6}{5}$$

$$y - 5 = -\frac{1}{4} \quad \text{or} \quad y - 5 = \frac{6}{5}$$
$$y = \frac{19}{4} \quad \text{or} \quad y = \frac{31}{5}$$

Solution Set: $\left\{ \dfrac{19}{4}, \dfrac{31}{5} \right\}$

95. $S = 4\pi r^2$

$$\frac{S}{4\pi} = \frac{4\pi r^2}{4\pi}$$

$$r^2 = \frac{S}{4\pi}$$

$$r = \sqrt{\frac{S}{4\pi}}$$

$$r = \frac{\sqrt{\pi S}}{2\pi}$$

96. $x^2 + y^2 = r^2$

$$x^2 - x^2 + y^2 = r^2 - x^2$$

$$y^2 = r^2 - x^2$$

$$y = \sqrt{r^2 - x^2}$$

97. $S = 2\pi r (h + r)$

$$S = 2\pi rh + 2\pi r^2$$

$$0 = (2\pi)r^2 + (2\pi h)r - S$$

$$a = 2\pi,\ b = 2\pi h,\ c = -S$$

$$x = \frac{-(2\pi h) + \sqrt{(2\pi h)^2 - 4(2\pi)(-S)}}{2(2\pi)}$$

$$= \frac{-2\pi h + \sqrt{4\pi^2 h^2 + 8\pi S}}{4\pi}$$

$$= \frac{-2\pi h + \sqrt{4(\pi^2 h^2 + 2\pi S)}}{4\pi}$$

$$= \frac{-2\pi h + 2\sqrt{\pi^2 h^2 + 2\pi S}}{4\pi}$$

$$= \frac{-\pi h + \sqrt{\pi^2 h^2 + 2\pi S}}{2\pi}$$

98. $T = \sqrt{\dfrac{2D}{g}}$

$$(T)^2 = \left(\sqrt{\frac{2D}{g}}\right)^2$$

$$T^2 = \frac{2D}{g}$$

$$T^2 g = 2D$$

$$\frac{T^2 g}{2} = \frac{2D}{2}$$

$$\frac{T^2 g}{2} = D$$

99. Prepare It takes Robert and Sammy 4 hours to do the landscaping job together. We are to determine how long it would take it would take each of them to do the job alone if it takes Robert 1 hour less than Sammy to do the job alone.

Plan We will use the work equation and Robert's and Sammy's individual work rates to determine how long it will take each of them to do the job alone.

	Time to do the job alone	Individual rates
Sammy	x hours	$\frac{1}{x}$ of the job per hour
Robert	$x - 1$ hour	$\frac{1}{x-1}$ of the job per hour

Process Write the equation, remembering that the men worked together for 4 hours to complete the job.

$$\left(\begin{matrix}\text{time}\\\text{worked}\end{matrix}\right)\left(\begin{matrix}\text{Sammy's}\\\text{rate}\end{matrix}\right) + \left(\begin{matrix}\text{time}\\\text{worked}\end{matrix}\right)\left(\begin{matrix}\text{Robert's}\\\text{rate}\end{matrix}\right) = 1$$

$$(4)\left(\frac{1}{x}\right) + (4)\left(\frac{1}{x-1}\right) = 1$$

$$4(x-1) + 4x = x(x-1)$$

$$4x - 4 + 4x = x^2 - x$$

$$0 = x^2 - 9x + 4$$

$$x^2 - 9x + 4 = 0$$

$$a = 1,\ b = -9,\ c = 4$$

$$x = \frac{-b \pm \sqrt{b^2 - 4ac}}{2a}$$

$$x = \frac{-(-9) \pm \sqrt{(-9)^2 - 4(1)(4)}}{2(1)}$$

$$x = \frac{9 \pm \sqrt{81 - 16}}{2}$$

$$x = \frac{9 \pm \sqrt{65}}{2}$$

$$x = \frac{9 - \sqrt{65}}{2} \quad \text{or} \quad x = \frac{9 + \sqrt{65}}{2}$$

$$x \approx \frac{9 - 8.1}{2} \qquad\qquad x \approx \frac{9 + 8.1}{2}$$

$$x \approx 0.45 \qquad\qquad\qquad x \approx 8.55$$

Notice that $x \approx 0.45$ hour is not a plausible answer, because $x-1$, Robert's time, would be negative. Therefore, the only possible answer is $x \approx 8.55$ hours for Sammy to do the job alone and $x-1 \approx 7.55$ hours for Robert to do the job alone.

Ponder Does the answers seem reasonable: Yes, it is reasonable to assume that if it takes them 4 hours to do the job together, it would take them longer individually.

100. Prepare We are to determine the rate at which Tony and Selma were driving prior to sundown.

Plan Solve the distance formula for T to obtain $T = \frac{D}{R}$, and fill in a chart with what we know. Let $T_0 =$ the time they spent driving before sundown, $T_1 =$ the time they spent driving in the dark, and $r =$ the speed in the before sundown. Then $T_0 + T_1 = 2\frac{1}{2}$.

	D	R	T
Day	35 miles	r	$T_0 = \frac{35}{r}$ hours
Night	120 miles	$r-10$	$T_1 = \frac{120}{r-10}$ hours

$$T_0 + T_1 = 2\tfrac{1}{2}$$
$$\frac{35}{r} + \frac{120}{r-10} = \frac{5}{2}$$
$$35 \cdot 2(r-10) + 120(2r) = 5r(r-10)$$
$$70r - 700 + 240r = 5r^2 - 50r$$
$$0 = 5r^2 - 360r + 700$$
$$5r^2 - 360r + 700 = 0$$
$$5(r-70)(r-2) = 0$$
$$r - 70 = 0 \quad \text{or} \quad r-2 = 0$$
$$r = 70 \quad \text{or} \quad \cancel{r=2}$$

Because the rate cannot be negative, Tony and Selma's speed before dark was 70 miles per hour.

Ponder Does the answer seem reasonable? It is very reasonable for a person to have to slow down to 60 miles per hour when driving in the dark.

448

101. $(d+4)(d-2)>0$

Boundary Values
$$(d+4)(d-2)=0$$
$$d+4=0 \quad \text{or} \quad d-2=0$$
$$d=-4 \quad \text{or} \quad d=2$$

Region A $(-\infty,-4)$	Region B $(-4,2)$	Region C $(2,\infty)$
Test Point: $d=-5$ $(d+4)(d-2)>0$ $(-)(-)>0$ $(+)>0$ True: Shade Region A	Test Point: $d=0$ $(d+4)(d-2)>0$ $(+)(-)>0$ $(-)>0$ False: Do Not Shade Region B	Test Point: $d=3$ $(d+4)(d-2)>0$ $(+)(+)>0$ $(+)>0$ True: Shade Region C

The solution set is $(-\infty,-4)\cup(2,\infty)$.

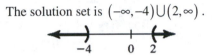

102. $(x+5)(x+3)<0$

Boundary Values
$$(x+5)(x+3)=0$$
$$x+5=0 \quad \text{or} \quad x+3=0$$
$$x=-5 \quad \text{or} \quad x=-3$$

Region A $(-\infty,-5)$	Region B $(-5,-3)$	Region C $(-3,\infty)$
Test Point: $x=-6$ $(x+5)(x+3)<0$ $(-)(-)<0$ $(+)<0$ False: Do Not Shade Region A	Test Point: $x=-4$ $(x+5)(x+3)<0$ $(+)(-)<0$ $(-)<0$ True: Shade Region B	Test Point: $x=0$ $(x+5)(x+3)<0$ $(+)(+)<0$ $(+)<0$ False: Do Not Shade Region C

The solution set is $(-5,-3)$.

103. $y^2+6y-16>0$
$(y+8)(y-2)>0$

Boundary Values
$$(y+8)(y-2)=0$$
$$y+8=0 \quad \text{or} \quad y-2=0$$
$$y=-8 \quad \text{or} \quad y=2$$

449

Region A $(-\infty,-8)$	Region B $(-8,2)$	Region C $(2,\infty)$
Test Point: $y=-9$ $(y+8)(y-2)>0$ $(-)(-)>0$ $(+)>0$ True: Shade Region A	Test Point: $y=0$ $(y+8)(y-2)>0$ $(+)(-)>0$ $(-)>0$ False: Do Not Shade Region B	Test Point: $y=3$ $(y+8)(y-2)>0$ $(+)(+)>0$ $(+)>0$ True: Shade Region C

The solution set is $(-\infty,-8)\cup(2,\infty)$.

104. $x^2-2x-24\le 0$

$(x+4)(x-6)\le 0$

Boundary Values

$(x+4)(x-6)=0$

$x+4=0$ or $x-6=0$

$x=-4$ or $x=6$

Region A $(-\infty,-4]$	Region B $[-4,6]$	Region C $[6,\infty)$
Test Point: $x=-5$ $(x+4)(x-6)\le 0$ $(-)(-)\le 0$ $(+)\le 0$ False: Do Not Shade Region A	Test Point: $x=0$ $(x+4)(x-6)\le 0$ $(+)(-)\le 0$ $(-)\le 0$ True: Shade Region B	Test Point: $x=7$ $(x+4)(x-6)\le 0$ $(+)(+)\le 0$ $(+)\le 0$ False: Do Not Shade Region C

The solution set is $[-4,6]$.

105. $h^2-3h>0$

$h(h-3)>0$

Boundary Values

$h(h-3)=0$

$h=0$ or $h-3=0$

$h=3$

Region A $(-\infty, 0)$	Region B $(0, 3)$	Region C $(3, \infty)$
Test Point: $h = -1$ $h(h-3) > 0$ $(-)(-) > 0$ $(+) > 0$ True: Shade Region A	Test Point: $h = 1$ $h(h-3) > 0$ $(+)(-) > 0$ $(-) > 0$ False: Do Not Shade Region B	Test Point: $h = 4$ $h(h-3) > 0$ $(+)(+) > 0$ $(+) > 0$ True: Shade Region C

The solution set is $(-\infty, 0) \cup (3, \infty)$.

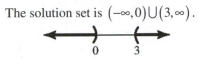

106. $2x^2 + 9x - 5 \geq 0$

$(2x-1)(x+5) \geq 0$

<u>Boundary Values</u>

$(2x-1)(x+5) = 0$

$2x - 1 = 0 \quad \text{or} \quad x + 5 = 0$

$x = \dfrac{1}{2} \quad \text{or} \quad x = -5$

Region A $(-\infty, -5]$	Region B $\left[-5, \frac{1}{2}\right]$	Region C $\left[\frac{1}{2}, \infty\right)$
Test Point: $x = -6$ $(2x-1)(x+5) \geq 0$ $(-)(-) \geq 0$ $(+) \geq 0$ True: Shade Region A	Test Point: $x = 0$ $(2x-1)(x+5) \geq 0$ $(-)(+) \geq 0$ $(-) \geq 0$ False: Do Not Shade Region B	Test Point: $x = 1$ $(2x-1)(x+5) \geq 0$ $(+)(+) \geq 0$ $(+) \geq 0$ True: Shade Region C

The solution set is $(-\infty, -5] \cup \left[\dfrac{1}{2}, \infty\right)$.

107. $s^2 + 5s \leq 14$

$s^2 + 5s - 14 \leq 0$

$(s+7)(s-2) \leq 0$

<u>Boundary Values</u>

$(s+7)(s-2) = 0$

$s + 7 = 0 \quad \text{or} \quad s - 2 = 0$

$s = -7 \quad \text{or} \quad s = 2$

451

Region A $(-\infty, -7]$	Region B $[-7, 2]$	Region C $[2, \infty)$
Test Point: $s = -8$	Test Point: $s = 0$	Test Point: $s = 3$
$(s+7)(s-2) \le 0$	$(s+7)(s-2) \le 0$	$(s+7)(s-2) \le 0$
$(-)(-) \le 0$	$(+)(-) \le 0$	$(+)(+) \le 0$
$(+) \le 0$	$(-) \le 0$	$(+) \le 0$
False: Do Not Shade Region A	True: Shade Region B	False: Do Not Shade Region C

The solution set is $[-7, 2]$.

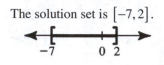

108. $x^2 - 4 < 0$

$(x+2)(x-2) < 0$

<u>Boundary Values</u>
$(x+2)(x-2) = 0$
$x+2 = 0 \quad \text{or} \quad x-2 = 0$
$x = -2 \quad \text{or} \quad x = 2$

Region A $(-\infty, -2)$	Region B $(-2, 2)$	Region C $(2, \infty)$
Test Point: $x = -3$	Test Point: $x = 0$	Test Point: $x = 3$
$(x+2)(x-2) < 0$	$(x+2)(x-2) < 0$	$(x+2)(x-2) < 0$
$(-)(-) < 0$	$(+)(-) < 0$	$(+)(+) < 0$
$(+) < 0$	$(-) < 0$	$(+) < 0$
False: Do Not Shade Region A	True: Shade Region B	False: Do Not Shade Region C

The solution set is $(-2, 2)$.

109. $4z^2 \ge 9$

$4z^2 - 9 \ge 0$

$(2z+3)(2z-3) \ge 0$

<u>Boundary Values</u>
$(2z+3)(2z-3) = 0$
$2z+3 = 0 \quad \text{or} \quad 2z-3 = 0$
$z = -\dfrac{3}{2} \quad \text{or} \quad z = \dfrac{3}{2}$

452

Region A $\left(-\infty, -\frac{3}{2}\right]$	Region B $\left[-\frac{3}{2}, \frac{3}{2}\right]$	Region C $\left[\frac{3}{2}, \infty\right)$
Test Point: $z = -2$ $(2z+3)(2z-3) \geq 0$ $(-)(-) \geq 0$ $(+) \geq 0$ True: Shade Region A	Test Point: $z = 0$ $(2z+3)(2z-3) \geq 0$ $(+)(-) \geq 0$ $(-) \geq 0$ False: Do Not Shade Region B	Test Point: $z = 2$ $(2z+3)(2z-3) \geq 0$ $(+)(+) \geq 0$ $(+) \geq 0$ True: Shade Region C

The solution set is $\left(-\infty, -\frac{3}{2}\right] \cup \left[\frac{3}{2}, \infty\right)$.

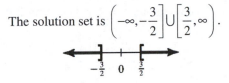

110. $\dfrac{1}{x+5} < 0$

<u>Boundary Value</u>
$$x + 5 = 0$$
$$x = -5$$

Region A $(-\infty, -5)$	Region B $(-5, \infty)$
Test Point: $x = -6$ $\dfrac{1}{x+5} < 0$ $\dfrac{(+)}{(-)} < 0$ $(-) < 0$ True: Shade Region A	Test Point: $x = 0$ $\dfrac{1}{x+5} < 0$ $\dfrac{(+)}{(+)} < 0$ $(+) < 0$ False: Do Not Shade Region B

The solution set is $(-\infty, -5)$.

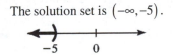

111. $\dfrac{1}{g-6} > 0$

<u>Boundary Value</u>
$$g - 6 = 0$$
$$g = 6$$

453

Region A $(-\infty, 6)$	Region B $(6, \infty)$
Test Point: $g = 5$	Test Point: $g = 7$
$\dfrac{1}{g-6} > 0$	$\dfrac{1}{g-6} > 0$
$\dfrac{(+)}{(-)} > 0$	$\dfrac{(+)}{(+)} > 0$
$(-) > 0$	$(+) > 0$
False: Do Not Shade Region A	True: Shade Region B

The solution set is $(6, \infty)$.

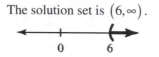

112. $\dfrac{y+2}{y-4} > 0$

Boundary Values

$y + 2 = 0 \quad \text{or} \quad y - 4 = 0$

$y = -2 \quad \text{or} \quad y = 4$

Region A $(-\infty, -2)$	Region B $(-2, 4)$	Region C $(4, \infty)$
Test Point: $y = -3$	Test Point: $y = 0$	Test Point: $y = 5$
$\dfrac{y+2}{y-4} > 0$	$\dfrac{y+2}{y-4} > 0$	$\dfrac{y+2}{y-4} > 0$
$\dfrac{(-)}{(-)} > 0$	$\dfrac{(+)}{(-)} > 0$	$\dfrac{(+)}{(+)} > 0$
$(+) > 0$	$(-) > 0$	$(+) > 0$
True: Shade Region A	False: Do Not Shade Region B	True: Shade Region C

The solution set is $(-\infty, -2) \cup (4, \infty)$.

113 $\dfrac{x+3}{x-5} \le 0$

Boundary Values

$x + 3 = 0 \quad \text{or} \quad x - 5 = 0$

$x = -3 \quad \text{or} \quad x = 5$

454

Region A $(-\infty,-3]$	Region B $[-3,5)$	Region C $(5,\infty)$
Test Point: $x=-4$	Test Point: $x=0$	Test Point: $x=6$
$\dfrac{x+3}{x-5}\le 0$	$\dfrac{x+3}{x-5}\le 0$	$\dfrac{x+3}{x-5}\le 0$
$\dfrac{(-)}{(-)}\le 0$	$\dfrac{(+)}{(-)}\le 0$	$\dfrac{(+)}{(+)}\le 0$
$(+)\le 0$	$(-)\le 0$	$(+)\le 0$
False: Do Not Shade Region A	True: Shade Region B	False: Do Not Shade Region C

The solution set is $[-3,5)$.

$\xleftarrow{\qquad} \underset{-3\quad 0\quad 5}{[\;+\;)} \xrightarrow{\qquad}$

114. $\dfrac{t}{t+3}\ge 0$

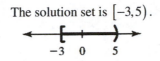

Boundary Values

$t=0$ or $t+3=0$

$t=-3$

Region A $(-\infty,-3)$	Region B $(-3,0]$	Region C $[0,\infty)$
Test Point: $t=-4$	Test Point: $t=-1$	Test Point: $t=3$
$\dfrac{t}{t+3}\ge 0$	$\dfrac{t}{t+3}\ge 0$	$\dfrac{t}{t+3}\ge 0$
$\dfrac{(-)}{(-)}\ge 0$	$\dfrac{(-)}{(+)}\ge 0$	$\dfrac{(+)}{(+)}\ge 0$
$(+)\ge 0$	$(-)\ge 0$	$(+)\ge 0$
True: Shade Region A	False: Do Not Shade Region B	True: Shade Region C

The solution set is $(-\infty,-3)\cup[0,\infty)$.

$\xleftarrow{\qquad} \underset{-3\quad 0}{)\quad [} \xrightarrow{\qquad}$

115. $\dfrac{2x-1}{x+3}>1$

$\dfrac{2x-1}{x+3}-1>0$

$\dfrac{2x-1}{x+3}-\dfrac{x+3}{x+3}>0$

$\dfrac{x-4}{x+3}>0$

Boundary Values

$x-4=0$ or $x+3=0$

$x=4$ or $x=-3$

455

Region A $(-\infty, -3)$	Region B $(-3, 4)$	Region C $(4, \infty)$
Test Point: $x = -4$	Test Point: $x = 0$	Test Point: $x = 5$
$\dfrac{x-4}{x+3} > 0$	$\dfrac{x-4}{x+3} > 0$	$\dfrac{x-4}{x+3} > 0$
$\dfrac{(-)}{(-)} > 0$	$\dfrac{(-)}{(+)} > 0$	$\dfrac{(+)}{(+)} > 0$
$(+) > 0$	$(-) > 0$	$(+) > 0$
True: Shade Region A	False: Do Not Shade Region B	True: Shade Region C

The solution set is $(-\infty, -3) \cup (4, \infty)$.

116.

$$\frac{3x+4}{x-3} > 2$$

$$\frac{3x+4}{x-3} - 2 > 0$$

$$\frac{3x+4}{x-3} - \frac{2(x-3)}{x-3} > 0$$

$$\frac{x+10}{x-3} > 0$$

<u>Boundary Values</u>

$$x + 10 = 0 \quad \text{or} \quad x - 3 = 0$$

$$x = -10 \quad \text{or} \quad x = 3$$

Region A $(-\infty, -10)$	Region B $(-10, 3)$	Region C $(3, \infty)$
Test Point: $x = -11$	Test Point: $x = 0$	Test Point: $x = 4$
$\dfrac{x+10}{x-3} > 0$	$\dfrac{x+10}{x-3} > 0$	$\dfrac{x+10}{x-3} > 0$
$\dfrac{(-)}{(-)} > 0$	$\dfrac{(+)}{(-)} > 0$	$\dfrac{(+)}{(+)} > 0$
$(+) > 0$	$(-) > 0$	$(+) > 0$
True: Shade Region A	False: Do Not Shade Region B	True: Shade Region C

The solution set is $(-\infty, -10) \cup (3, \infty)$.

CHAPTER 10 TEST

1. $\sqrt{-147} = i\sqrt{147}$

$\qquad = i\sqrt{49\cdot3}$

$\qquad = i\sqrt{49}\cdot\sqrt{3}$

$\qquad = 7i\sqrt{3}$

2. $(-10+6i)-(4-3i)=(-10-4)+(6+3)i$

$\qquad\qquad\qquad\qquad = -14+9i$

3. $20i\left(\dfrac{3}{4}-\dfrac{1}{5}i\right)=20i\left(\dfrac{3}{4}\right)-20i\left(\dfrac{1}{5}i\right)$

$\qquad\qquad = \dfrac{\overset{5}{\cancel{20}}i}{1}\left(\dfrac{3}{\underset{1}{\cancel{4}}}\right)-\dfrac{\overset{4}{\cancel{20}}i}{1}\left(\dfrac{i}{\underset{1}{\cancel{5}}}\right)$

$\qquad\qquad = 15i-4i^2$

$\qquad\qquad = 15i-4(-1)$

$\qquad\qquad = 15i+4$

$\qquad\qquad = 4+15i$

4. $\dfrac{-1+3i}{2+i}=\left(\dfrac{-1+3i}{2+i}\right)\left(\dfrac{2-i}{2-i}\right)$

$\qquad = \dfrac{(-1+3i)(2-i)}{(2)^2-(i)^2}$

$\qquad = \dfrac{-2+i+6i-3i^2}{4-i^2}$

$\qquad = \dfrac{-2+7i-3(-1)}{4-(-1)}$

$\qquad = \dfrac{1+7i}{5}$

$\qquad = \dfrac{1}{5}+\dfrac{7}{5}i$

5. $\qquad 10x^2-x-3=0$

$\quad (2x+1)(5x-3)=0$

$\qquad 2x+1=0 \quad$ or $\quad 5x-3=0$

$\qquad\quad 2x=-1 \quad$ or $\qquad 5x=3$

$\qquad\quad x=-\dfrac{1}{2} \quad$ or $\qquad x=\dfrac{3}{5}$

The solution set is $\left\{-\dfrac{1}{2},\dfrac{3}{5}\right\}$.

6. $(x+3)^2+24=0$

$\qquad (x+3)^2=-24$

$\qquad x+3=-\sqrt{-24} \quad$ or $\quad x+3=\sqrt{-24}$

$\qquad x+3=-2i\sqrt{6} \quad$ or $\quad x+3=2i\sqrt{6}$

$\qquad x=-3-2i\sqrt{6} \quad$ or $\qquad x=-3+2i\sqrt{6}$

The solution set is $\left\{-3-2i\sqrt{6},-3+2i\sqrt{6}\right\}$.

7. $\qquad n^2-4n=1$

$\qquad n^2-4n-1=0$

$\qquad a=1,\ b=-4,\ c=-1$

$\qquad n=\dfrac{-b\pm\sqrt{b^2-4ac}}{2a}$

$\qquad\quad = \dfrac{-(-4)\pm\sqrt{(-4)^2-4(1)(-1)}}{2(1)}$

$\qquad\quad = \dfrac{4\pm\sqrt{16+4}}{2}$

$\qquad\quad = \dfrac{4\pm\sqrt{20}}{2}$

$\qquad\quad = \dfrac{4\pm2\sqrt{5}}{2}$

$\qquad\quad = 2\pm\sqrt{5}$

The solution set is $\left\{2-\sqrt{5},2+\sqrt{5}\right\}$.

8. $\quad x^2-2x-35=0$

$\qquad x^2-2x=35$

$\qquad x^2-2x+1=35+1$

$\qquad (x-1)^2=36$

$\qquad x-1=-\sqrt{36} \quad$ or $\quad x-1=\sqrt{36}$

$\qquad x-1=-6 \quad$ or $\quad x-1=6$

$\qquad\quad x=-5 \quad$ or $\qquad x=7$

The solution set is $\left\{-5,7\right\}$.

9. $\quad x^2-15=0$

$\qquad x^2=15$

$\qquad x=-\sqrt{15} \quad$ or $\quad x=\sqrt{15}$

The solution set is $\left\{-\sqrt{15},\sqrt{15}\right\}$

10. $3w^2 + 2w = -1$

$3w^2 + 2w + 1 = 0$

$a = 3, \ b = 2, \ c = 1$

$$w = \frac{-b \pm \sqrt{b^2 - 4ac}}{2a}$$

$$= \frac{-(2) \pm \sqrt{(2)^2 - 4(3)(1)}}{2(3)}$$

$$= \frac{-2 \pm \sqrt{4 - 12}}{6}$$

$$= \frac{-2 \pm \sqrt{-8}}{6}$$

$$= \frac{-2 \pm 2i\sqrt{2}}{6}$$

$$= \frac{-1 \pm i\sqrt{2}}{3}$$

The solution set is $\left\{ \dfrac{-1 + i\sqrt{2}}{3}, \dfrac{-1 + i\sqrt{2}}{3} \right\}$.

11. $20x^2 + 40x + 200 = 0$

$20(x^2 + 2x + 10) = 0$

$x^2 + 2x + 10 = 0$

$x^2 + 2x = -10$

$x^2 + 2x + 1 = -10 + 1$

$(x + 1)^2 = -9$

$x + 1 = -\sqrt{-9} \quad or \quad x + 1 = \sqrt{-9}$

$x + 1 = -3i \qquad\qquad x + 1 = 3i$

$x = -1 - 3i \qquad\qquad x = -1 + 3i$

The solution set is $\{-1 - 3i, -1 + 3i\}$.

12. $5x^2 - 9x + 6 = 0$

$a = 5, \ b = -9, \ c = 6$

$b^2 - 4ac = (-9)^2 - 4(5)(6)$

$= 81 - 120$

$= -39$

Because $b^2 - 4ac = -39$ and $-39 < 0$, there are two complex solutions to the equation.

13. Excluded Value: $x = 0$

LCD: x

$$x + \frac{16}{x} = 10$$

$$x\left(x + \frac{16}{x}\right) = x(10)$$

$$x^2 + 16 = 10x$$

$$x^2 - 10x + 16 = 0$$

$$(x - 2)(x - 8) = 0$$

$x - 2 = 0 \quad or \quad x - 8 = 0$

$x = 2 \quad or \qquad x = 8$

The solution set is $\{2, 8\}$.

14. Excluded Values: $x = 0$ and $x = 5$

LCD: $x(x - 5)$

$$\frac{5x}{x - 5} - \frac{1}{x} = \frac{10x - 1}{x}$$

$$\frac{x(x - 5)}{1}\left(\frac{5x}{x - 5} - \frac{1}{x}\right) = \frac{x(x - 5)}{1}\left(\frac{10x - 1}{x}\right)$$

$$5x^2 - (x - 5) = (x - 5)(10x - 1)$$

$$5x^2 - x + 5 = 10x^2 - 51x + 5$$

$$5x^2 - 50x = 0$$

$$5x(x - 10) = 0$$

$5x = 0 \qquad or \quad x - 10 = 0$

$\cancel{x = 0} \quad or \qquad x = 10$

The solution set is $\{10\}$.

15. $4p^4 + 11p^2 - 225 = 0$

$(4p^2 - 25)(p^2 + 9) = 0$

$4p^2 - 25 = 0 \quad or \quad p^2 + 9 = 0$

$4p^2 = 25 \qquad\qquad p^2 = -9$

$$p^2 = \frac{25}{4}$$

$p = -\sqrt{\dfrac{25}{4}} \ or \ p = \sqrt{\dfrac{25}{4}} \ or \ p = -\sqrt{-9} \ or \ p = \sqrt{-9}$

$p = -\dfrac{5}{2} \ or \ p = \dfrac{5}{2} \ or \ p = -3i \ or \ p = 3i$

The solution set is $\left\{ -\dfrac{5}{2}, \dfrac{5}{2}, -3i, 3i \right\}$.

16. Let $u = (t+3)$, then $u^2 = (t+3)^2$.

$$2(t+3)^2 - 17(t+3) + 21 = 0$$

$$2u^2 - 17u + 21 = 0$$

$$(2u - 3)(u - 7) = 0$$

$$2u - 3 = 0 \quad \text{or} \quad u - 7 = 0$$

$$u = \frac{3}{2} \quad \text{or} \quad u = 7$$

$$t + 3 = \frac{3}{2} \quad \text{or} \quad t + 3 = 7$$

$$t = -\frac{3}{2} \quad \text{or} \quad t = 4$$

The solution set is $\left\{ -\frac{3}{2}, 4 \right\}$.

17.

$$V = \pi r^2 h$$

$$\frac{V}{\pi h} = \frac{\pi r^2 h}{\pi h}$$

$$\frac{V}{\pi h} = r^2$$

$$\sqrt{\frac{V}{\pi h}} = r$$

$$\frac{\sqrt{V}}{\sqrt{\pi h}} = r$$

$$\frac{\sqrt{V}}{\sqrt{\pi h}} \cdot \frac{\sqrt{\pi h}}{\sqrt{\pi h}} = r$$

$$\frac{\sqrt{V \pi h}}{\pi h} = r$$

18.

$$S = s\sqrt{\frac{D}{d}}$$

$$\frac{S}{s} = \sqrt{\frac{D}{d}}$$

$$\left(\frac{S}{s} \right)^2 = \frac{D}{d}$$

$$\frac{S^2 d}{s^2} = D$$

19. Let x be the unknown number.

$$3x^2 - 30 = 0$$

$$3x^2 = 30$$

$$x^2 = 10$$

$$x = -\sqrt{10} \quad \text{or} \quad x = \sqrt{10}$$

There are two possible numbers that satisfy the conditions, $-\sqrt{10}$ and $\sqrt{10}$.

20. Let x be the distance from the base of the pole at which the guy wire is attached.

$$x^2 + 10^2 = 24^2$$

$$x^2 + 100 = 576$$

$$x^2 = 476$$

$$x = 2\sqrt{119}$$

$$x \approx 21.8$$

The guy wire is attached to the ground $2\sqrt{119}$ feet or approximately 21.8 feet from the base of the pole.

21.

$$(x+1)^2 + x^2 = 5^2$$

$$x^2 + 2x + 1 + x^2 = 25$$

$$2x^2 + 2x - 24 = 0$$

$$2(x^2 + x - 12) = 0$$

$$x^2 + x - 12 = 0$$

$$(x+4)(x-3) = 0$$

$$x + 4 = 0 \quad \text{or} \quad x - 3 = 0$$

$$\cancel{x = -4} \qquad x = 3$$

The lengths of the sides are 3, 4 and 5 meters.

22. Prepare We are to determine the at which Rachid drives in the storm.

Plan Let $r =$ Rachid's speed from San Antonio to Austin, then $r - 35$ is his speed from Austin to San Antonio in the storm. If T_n is the time it takes to travel from San Antonio to Austin and T_s is the time it takes to travel from Austin to San Antonio, then the total time for both trips is $T_n + T_s = 3$.

	Distance	Rate	Time
San Antonio To Austin	70	R	$T_n = \dfrac{70}{r}$
Austin to San Antonio	70	$r - 35$	$T_s = \dfrac{70}{r-35}$

Process Write and solve the equation.

$$T_n + T_s = 3$$

$$\frac{70}{r} + \frac{70}{r-35} = 3$$

$$\frac{r(r-35)}{1}\left(\frac{70}{r} + \frac{70}{r-35} \right) = r(r-35)(3)$$

$$70(r-35) + 70r = 3r^2 - 105r$$

$$140r - 2450 = 3r^2 - 105r$$

$$3r^2 - 245r + 2450 = 0$$

$$(3r - 35)(r - 70) = 0$$

$$3r - 35 = 0 \quad \text{or} \quad r - 70 = 0$$

$$r = \frac{35}{3} \quad \text{or} \qquad r = 70$$

Since $r - 35$ is Rachid's speed in the storm, we should choose the solution $r = 70$. Therefore, Rachid's speed in the rain is 35 miles per hour.

Ponder Does this answer seem reasonable? It seems reasonable that Rachid had to slow down to 35 miles per hour in the storm.

23. $x^2 - x - 12 > 0$

$(x-4)(x+3) > 0$

Boundary Values

$(x-4)(x+3) = 0$

$x - 4 = 0 \quad \text{or} \quad x + 3 = 0$

$x = 4 \quad \text{or} \qquad x = -3$

Region A $(-\infty, -3)$	Region B $(-3, 4)$	Region C $(4, \infty)$
Test Point: $x = -4$	Test Point: $x = 0$	Test Point: $x = 5$
$(x-4)(x+3) > 0$	$(x-4)(x+3) > 0$	$(x-4)(x+3) > 0$
$(-)(-) > 0$	$(-)(+) > 0$	$(+)(+) > 0$
$(+) > 0$	$(-) > 0$	$(+) > 0$
True: Shade Region A	False: Do Not Shade Region B	True: Shade Region C

The solution set is $(-\infty, -3) \cup (4, \infty)$.

$$\underset{\substack{-3 \quad\ 0 \quad\ 4}}{\longleftrightarrow}$$

24. $2x^2 - 17x \le 0$

$x(2x - 17) \le 0$

Boundary Values

$x(2x - 17) = 0$

$x = 0 \quad \text{or} \quad 2x - 17 = 0$

$$x = \frac{17}{2}$$

Region A $(-\infty, 0)$	Region B $\left(0, \dfrac{17}{2}\right)$	Region C $\left(\dfrac{17}{2}, \infty\right)$
Test Point: $x = -1$	Test Point: $x = 1$	Test Point: $x = 9$
$x(2x-17) \le 0$	$x(2x-17) \le 0$	$x(2x-17) \le 0$
$(-)(-) \le 0$	$(+)(-) \le 0$	$(+)(+) \le 0$
$(+) \le 0$	$(-) \le 0$	$(+) \le 0$
False: Do Not Shade Region A	True: Shade Region B	False: Do Not Shade Region C

The solution set is $\left[0, \dfrac{17}{2}\right]$.

$$\underset{\substack{0 \qquad\quad \frac{17}{2}}}{\longleftrightarrow}$$

25. $\dfrac{x+5}{x+2} \ge 0$

Boundary Values

$x + 5 = 0 \quad \text{or} \quad x + 2 = 0$

$x = -5 \quad \text{or} \qquad x = -2$

Region A $(-\infty, -5)$	Region B $(-5, -2)$	Region C $(-2, \infty)$
Test Point: $x = -6$	Test Point: $x = -3$	Test Point: $x = 0$
$\dfrac{x+5}{x+2} \ge 0$	$\dfrac{x+5}{x+2} \ge 0$	$\dfrac{x+5}{x+2} \ge 0$
$\dfrac{(-)}{(-)} \ge 0$	$\dfrac{(+)}{(-)} \ge 0$	$\dfrac{(+)}{(+)} \ge 0$
$(+) \ge 0$	$(-) \ge 0$	$(+) \ge 0$
True: Shade Region A	False: Do Not Shade Region B	True: Shade Region C

The solution set is $(-\infty, -5] \cup (-2, \infty)$.

$$\underset{\substack{-5 \qquad -2\ \ 0}}{\longleftrightarrow}$$

Chapter 11

11.1 Exercises

1. A parabola can be "cut" from a right-circular cone and thus is an example of a <u>conic</u> <u>section</u>.

3. The graph representing the quadratic equation $x = ay^2 + by + c$ is a <u>horizontal</u> parabola.

5. If you "fold" a parabola along the <u>axis of symmetry</u>, the two halves will match.

7. i

9. d

11. i

13. $a = 1, b = 0, c = 3$

a) The equation is quadratic in x and $a = 1 > 0$; therefore, the parabola will open up.

b) The axis of symmetry is:
$$x = \frac{-b}{2a}$$
$$x = \frac{-(0)}{2(1)}$$
$$x = 0$$

c) Find the y-coordinate of the vertex by substituting $x = 0$ into the original equation.
$$y = x^2 + 3$$
$$y = (0)^2 + 3$$
$$y = 3$$
The vertex is $(0,3)$.

d) There are no x-intercepts because the vertex lies above the x-axis and the parabola opens up. The y-intercept is $(0,c) = (0,3)$.

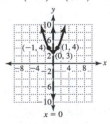

15. $a = \frac{1}{3}, b = 0, c = 0$

a) The equation is quadratic in x and $a = \frac{1}{3} > 0$; therefore, the parabola will open up.

b) The axis of symmetry is:

$$x = \frac{-b}{2a}$$
$$x = \frac{-(0)}{2\left(\frac{1}{3}\right)}$$
$$x = 0$$

c) Find the y-coordinate of the vertex by substituting $x = 0$ into the original equation.
$$y = \frac{1}{3}x^2$$
$$y = \frac{1}{3}(0)^2$$
$$y = 0$$
The vertex is $(0,0)$.

d) There is only one x-intercept because the vertex is located at the origin. The x-intercept is $(0,0)$. The y-intercept is $(0,c) = (0,0)$.

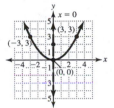

17. $a = -1, b = 0, c = 2$

a) The equation is quadratic in x and $a = -1 < 0$; therefore, the parabola will open down.

b) The axis of symmetry is:
$$x = \frac{-b}{2a}$$
$$x = \frac{-(0)}{2(-1)}$$
$$x = 0$$

c) Find the y-coordinate of the vertex by substituting $x = 0$ into the original equation.
$$y = -x^2 + 2$$
$$y = -(0)^2 + 2$$
$$y = 2$$
The vertex is $(0,2)$.

d) There are two x-intercepts because the vertex lies above the x-axis and the parabola opens down. To find the x-intercepts, set $y = 0$ and solve for x.

$$0 = -x^2 + 2$$
$$x^2 = 2$$
$$x = -\sqrt{2} \quad \text{or} \quad x = \sqrt{2}$$

The x-intercepts are $\left(-\sqrt{2}, 0\right)$ and $\left(\sqrt{2}, 0\right)$. The y-intercept is $(0, c) = (0, 2)$.

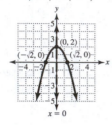

19. $a = 1, b = 1, c = 0$

a) The equation is quadratic in x and $a = 1 > 0$; therefore, the parabola will open up.

b) The axis of symmetry is:
$$x = \frac{-b}{2a}$$
$$x = \frac{-(1)}{2(1)}$$
$$x = -\frac{1}{2}$$

c) Find the y-coordinate of the vertex by substituting $x = -\frac{1}{2}$ into the original equation.
$$y = x^2 + x$$
$$y = \left(-\frac{1}{2}\right)^2 + \left(-\frac{1}{2}\right)$$
$$y = -\frac{1}{4}$$

The vertex is $\left(-\frac{1}{2}, -\frac{1}{4}\right)$.

d) There are two x-intercepts because the vertex lies below the x-axis and the parabola opens up. To find the x-intercepts, set $y = 0$ and solve for x.
$$0 = x^2 + x$$
$$0 = x(x+1)$$
$$x = 0 \quad \text{or} \quad x + 1 = 0$$
$$x = 0 \quad \text{or} \quad x = -1$$

The x-intercepts are $(-1, 0)$ and $(0, 0)$. The y-intercept is $(0, c) = (0, 0)$.

21. $a = 1, b = 2, c = -3$

a) The equation is quadratic in x and $a = 1 > 0$; therefore, the parabola will open up.

b) The axis of symmetry is:
$$x = \frac{-b}{2a}$$
$$x = \frac{-(2)}{2(1)}$$
$$x = -1$$

c) Find the y-coordinate of the vertex by substituting $x = -1$ into the original equation.
$$y = x^2 + 2x - 3$$
$$y = (-1)^2 + 2(-1) - 3$$
$$y = -4$$

The vertex is $(-1, -4)$.

d) There are two x-intercepts because the vertex lies below the x-axis and the parabola opens up. To find the x-intercepts, set $y = 0$ and solve for x.
$$0 = x^2 + 2x - 3$$
$$0 = (x+3)(x-1)$$
$$x + 3 = 0 \quad \text{or} \quad x - 1 = 0$$
$$x = -3 \quad \text{or} \quad x = 1$$

The x-intercepts are $(-3, 0)$ and $(1, 0)$. The y-intercept is $(0, c) = (0, -3)$.

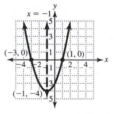

23. $a = -1, b = 6, c = -9$

a) The equation is quadratic in x and $a = -1 < 0$; therefore, the parabola will open down.

b) The axis of symmetry is:
$$x = \frac{-b}{2a}$$
$$x = \frac{-(6)}{2(-1)}$$
$$x = 3$$

c) Find the y-coordinate of the vertex by substituting $x = 3$ into the original equation.
$$y = -x^2 + 6x - 9$$
$$y = -(3)^2 + 6(3) - 9$$
$$y = 0$$

The vertex is $(3, 0)$.

d) There is only one x-intercept because the vertex is located on the x-axis. The x-intercept is $(3,0)$. The y-intercept is $(0,c)=(0,-9)$.

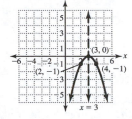

25. $a=1, b=0, c=2$

a) The equation is quadratic in y and $a=1>0$; therefore, the parabola will open right.

b) The axis of symmetry is:
$$y=\frac{-b}{2a}$$
$$y=\frac{-(0)}{2(1)}$$
$$y=0$$

c) Find the x-coordinate of the vertex by substituting $y=0$ into the original equation.
$$x=y^2+2$$
$$x=(0)^2+2$$
$$x=2$$
The vertex is $(2,0)$.

d) The x-intercept is $(c,0)=(2,0)$. There are no y-intercepts because the vertex lies to the right of the y-axis and the parabola opens right.

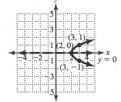

27. $a=-1, b=0, c=-1$

a) The equation is quadratic in y and $a=-1<0$; therefore, the parabola will open left.

b) The axis of symmetry is:
$$y=\frac{-b}{2a}$$
$$y=\frac{-(0)}{2(-1)}$$
$$y=0$$

c) Find the x-coordinate of the vertex by substituting $y=0$ into the original equation.

$$x=-y^2-1$$
$$x=-(0)^2-1$$
$$x=-1$$
The vertex is $(-1,0)$.

d) The x-intercept is $(c,0)=(-1,0)$. There are no y-intercepts because the vertex lies to the left of the y-axis and the parabola opens left.

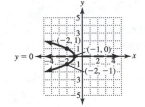

29. $a=1, b=-3, c=0$

a) The equation is quadratic in y and $a=1>0$; therefore, the parabola will open right.

b) The axis of symmetry is:
$$y=\frac{-b}{2a}$$
$$y=\frac{-(-3)}{2(1)}$$
$$y=\frac{3}{2}$$

c) Find the x-coordinate of the vertex by substituting $y=\frac{3}{2}$ into the original equation.
$$x=y^2-3y$$
$$x=\left(\frac{3}{2}\right)^2-3\left(\frac{3}{2}\right)$$
$$x=-\frac{9}{4}$$
The vertex is $\left(-\frac{9}{4},\frac{3}{2}\right)$.

d) The x-intercept is $(c,0)=(0,0)$. There are two y-intercepts because the vertex lies to the left of the y-axis and the parabola opens to the right. To find the y-intercepts, set $x=0$ and solve for y.
$$0=y^2-3y$$
$$0=y(y-3)$$
$$y=0 \quad\text{or}\quad y-3=0$$
$$y=0 \quad\text{or}\quad y=3$$
The y-intercepts are $(0,0)$ and $(0,3)$.

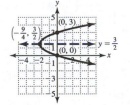

31. $a = -2$, $b = 4$, $c = 0$

a) The equation is quadratic in y and $a = -2 < 0$; therefore, the parabola will open left.

b) The axis of symmetry is:

$$y = \frac{-b}{2a}$$

$$y = \frac{-(4)}{2(-2)}$$

$$y = 1$$

c) Find the x-coordinate of the vertex by substituting $y = 1$ into the original equation.

$$x = -2y^2 + 4y$$

$$x = -2(1)^2 + 4(1)$$

$$x = 2$$

The vertex is $(2, 1)$.

d) The x-intercept is $(c, 0) = (0, 0)$. There are two y-intercepts because the vertex lies to the right of the y-axis and the parabola opens to the left. To find the y-intercepts, set $x = 0$ and solve for y.

$$0 = -2y^2 + 4y$$

$$0 = -2y(y - 2)$$

$$-2y = 0 \quad \text{or} \quad y - 2 = 0$$

$$y = 0 \quad \text{or} \quad y = 2$$

The y-intercepts are $(0, 0)$ and $(0, 2)$.

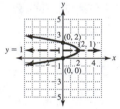

33. $a = 1$, $b = -3$, $c = 2$

a) The equation is quadratic in y and $a = 1 > 0$; therefore, the parabola will open right.

b) The axis of symmetry is:

$$y = \frac{-b}{2a}$$

$$y = \frac{-(-3)}{2(1)}$$

$$y = \frac{3}{2}$$

c) Find the x-coordinate of the vertex by substituting $y = \frac{3}{2}$ into the original equation.

$$x = y^2 - 3y + 2$$

$$x = \left(\frac{3}{2}\right)^2 - 3\left(\frac{3}{2}\right) + 2$$

$$x = -\frac{1}{4}$$

The vertex is $\left(-\frac{1}{4}, \frac{3}{2}\right)$.

d) The x-intercept is $(c, 0) = (2, 0)$. There are two y-intercepts because the vertex lies to the left of the y-axis and the parabola opens to the right. To find the y-intercepts, set $x = 0$ and solve for y.

$$0 = y^2 - 3y + 2$$

$$0 = (y - 1)(y - 2)$$

$$y - 1 = 0 \quad \text{or} \quad y - 2 = 0$$

$$y = 1 \quad \text{or} \quad y = 2$$

The y-intercepts are $(0, 1)$ and $(0, 2)$.

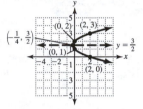

35. $a = -1$, $b = 4$, $c = -4$

a) The equation is quadratic in y and $a = -1 < 0$; therefore, the parabola will open left.

b) The axis of symmetry is:

$$y = \frac{-b}{2a}$$

$$y = \frac{-(4)}{2(-1)}$$

$$y = 2$$

c) Find the x-coordinate of the vertex by substituting $y = 2$ into the original equation.

$$x = -y^2 + 4y - 4$$

$$x = -(2)^2 + 4(2) - 4$$

$$x = 0$$

The vertex is $(0, 2)$.

d) The x-intercept is $(c, 0) = (-4, 0)$. There is only one y-intercept because the vertex is located on the y-axis. The y-intercept is $(0, 2)$.

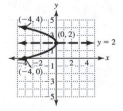

37. $a = 1, h = 2, k = 1$

The equation is quadratic in x and $a = 1 > 0$; therefore, the parabola opens up. The vertex is $(h, k) = (2, 1)$. The axis of symmetry is $x = h$. That is, $x = 2$. There are no x-intercepts because the vertex is above the x-axis and the graph opens up. To find the y-intercept, set $x = 0$ and solve for y.

$$y = (x - 2)^2 + 1$$
$$y = (0 - 2)^2 + 1$$
$$y = (-2)^2 + 1$$
$$y = 5$$

The y-intercept is $(0, 5)$. We can use symmetry to find a third point, $(4, 5)$

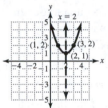

39. $a = 1, h = -3, k = 0$

The equation is quadratic in x and $a = 1 > 0$; therefore, the parabola opens up. The vertex is $(h, k) = (-3, 0)$. The axis of symmetry is $x = h$. That is, $x = -3$. There is only one x-intercept because the vertex lies on the x-axis. The x-intercept is $(-3, 0)$. To find the y-intercept, set $x = 0$ and solve for y.

$$y = (x + 3)^2$$
$$y = (0 + 3)^2$$
$$y = (3)^2$$
$$y = 9$$

The y-intercept is $(0, 9)$. We can use symmetry to find a third point, $(-6, 9)$.

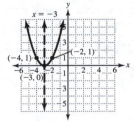

41. $a = -1, h = -2, k = 2$

The equation is quadratic in x and $a = -1 < 0$; therefore, the parabola opens down. The vertex is

$(h, k) = (-2, 2)$. The axis of symmetry is $x = h$. That is, $x = -2$. The x-intercepts will not have integer coordinates, so we will not use them to graph the function. To find the y-intercept, set $x = 0$ and solve for y.

$$y = -(x + 2)^2 + 2$$
$$y = -(0 + 2)^2 + 2$$
$$y = -(2)^2 + 2$$
$$y = -2$$

The y-intercept is $(0, -2)$. We can use symmetry to find a third point, $(-4, -2)$.

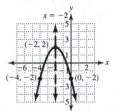

43. $a = 2, h = 1, k = -3$

The equation is quadratic in x and $a = 2 > 0$; therefore, the parabola opens up. The vertex is $(h, k) = (1, -3)$. The axis of symmetry is $x = h$. That is, $x = 1$. The x-intercepts will not have integer coordinates, so we will not use them to graph the function. To find the y-intercept, set $x = 0$ and solve for y.

$$y = 2(x - 1)^2 - 3$$
$$y = 2(0 - 1)^2 - 3$$
$$y = 2(-1)^2 - 3$$
$$y = -1$$

The y-intercept is $(0, -1)$. We can use symmetry to find a third point, $(2, -1)$.

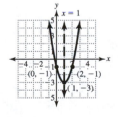

45. $a = -\frac{1}{2}, h = 2, k = 5$

The equation is quadratic in x and $a = -\frac{1}{2} < 0$; therefore, the parabola opens down. The vertex is $(h, k) = (2, 5)$. The axis of symmetry is $x = h$. That is, $x = 2$. The x-intercepts will not have integer coordinates, so we will not use them to graph the function. To find the y-intercept, set $x = 0$ and solve for y.

$$y = -\frac{1}{2}(x-2)^2 + 5$$

$$y = -\frac{1}{2}(0-2)^2 + 5$$

$$y = -\frac{1}{2}(-2)^2 + 5$$

$$y = 3$$

The y-intercept is $(0,3)$. We can use symmetry to find a third point, $(4,3)$.

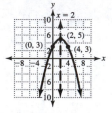

47. $a = 1, h = -5, k = -1$

The equation is quadratic in y and $a = 1 > 0$; therefore, the parabola opens right. The vertex is $(h,k) = (-5,-1)$. The axis of symmetry is $y = k$. That is, $y = -1$. The y-intercepts will not have integer coordinates, so we will not use them to graph the function. To find the x-intercept, set $y = 0$ and solve for x.

$$x = (y+1)^2 - 5$$

$$x = (0+1)^2 - 5$$

$$x = (1)^2 - 5$$

$$x = -4$$

The x-intercept is $(-4,0)$. We can use symmetry to find a third point, $(-4,-2)$.

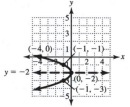

49. $a = 1, h = 0, k = 3$

The equation is quadratic in y and $a = 1 > 0$; therefore, the parabola opens right. The vertex is $(h,k) = (0,3)$. The axis of symmetry is $y = k$. That is, $y = 3$. There is only one y-intercept because the vertex lies on the y-axis. The y-intercept is $(0,3)$. To find the x-intercept, set $y = 0$ and solve for x.

$$x = (y-3)^2$$

$$x = (0-3)^2$$

$$x = (-3)^2$$

$$x = 9$$

The x-intercept is $(9,0)$. We can use symmetry to find a third point, $(9,6)$.

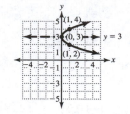

51. $a = -1, h = 0, k = -2$

The equation is quadratic in y and $a = -1 < 0$; therefore, the parabola opens left. The vertex is $(h,k) = (0,-2)$. The axis of symmetry is $y = k$. That is, $y = -2$. There is only one y-intercept because the vertex lies on the y-axis. The y-intercept is $(0,-2)$. To find the x-intercept, set $y = 0$ and solve for x.

$$x = -(y+2)^2$$

$$x = -(0+2)^2$$

$$x = -(2)^2$$

$$x = -4$$

The x-intercept is $(-4,0)$. We can use symmetry to find a third point, $(-4,-4)$.

53. $a = 3, h = 1, k = 1$

The equation is quadratic in y and $a = 3 > 0$; therefore, the parabola opens right. The vertex is $(h,k) = (1,1)$. The axis of symmetry is $y = k$. That is, $y = 1$. There are no y-intercepts because the vertex lies to the right of the y-axis and the parabola opens right. To find the x-intercept, set $y = 0$ and solve for x.

$$x = 3(y-1)^2 + 1$$

$$x = 3(0-1)^2 + 1$$

$$x = 3(-1)^2 + 1$$

$$x = 4$$

The x-intercept is $(4,0)$. We can use symmetry to find a third point, $(4,2)$.

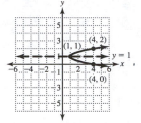

55. $a = \frac{3}{2}, h = -4, k = -2$

The equation is quadratic in y and $a = \frac{3}{2} > 0$; therefore, the parabola opens right. The vertex is $(h,k) = (-4,-2)$. The axis of symmetry is $y = k$. That is, $y = -2$. The y-intercepts will not have integer coordinates, so we will not use them to graph the function. To find the x-intercept, set $y = 0$ and solve for x.

$$x = \frac{3}{2}(y+2)^2 - 4$$

$$x = \frac{3}{2}(0+2)^2 - 4$$

$$x = \frac{3}{2}(2)^2 - 4$$

$$x = 2$$

The x-intercept is $(2,0)$. We can use symmetry to find a third point, $(2,-4)$.

57.
$$y = x^2 + 2x - 5$$

$$y + 5 = x^2 + 2x$$

$$y + 5 + 1 = x^2 + 2x + 1$$

$$y + 6 = (x+1)^2$$

a) $y = (x+1)^2 - 6$

$a = 1, h = -1, k = -6$

b) The vertex is $(h,k) = (-1,-6)$.

c) The axis of symmetry is $x = h$, that is $x = -1$.
d) Because $a = 1 > 0$, and the axis of symmetry is vertical, the graph opens up.

59.
$$y = -x^2 - 2x + 7$$

$$y - 7 = -x^2 - 2x$$

$$y - 7 = -(x^2 + 2x)$$

$$y - 7 - 1 = -(x^2 + 2x + 1)$$

$$y - 8 = -(x+1)^2$$

a) $y = -(x+1)^2 + 8$

$a = -1, h = -1, k = 8$

b) The vertex is $(h,k) = (-1,8)$.

c) The axis of symmetry is $x = h$, that is $x = -1$.
d) Because $a = -1 < 0$, and the axis of symmetry is vertical, the graph opens down.

61.
$$y = -3x^2 + 3x + 2$$

$$y - 2 = -3x^2 + 3x$$

$$y - 2 = -3(x^2 - x)$$

$$y - 2 - \frac{3}{4} = -3\left(x^2 - x + \frac{1}{4}\right)$$

$$y - \frac{11}{4} = -3\left(x - \frac{1}{2}\right)^2$$

a) $y = -3\left(x - \frac{1}{2}\right)^2 + \frac{11}{4}$

$a = -3, h = \frac{1}{2}, k = \frac{11}{4}$

b) The vertex is $(h,k) = \left(\frac{1}{2}, \frac{11}{4}\right)$.

c) The axis of symmetry is $x = h$, that is $x = \frac{1}{2}$.
d) Because $a = -3 < 0$, and the axis of symmetry is vertical, the graph opens down.

63.
$$y = \frac{1}{3}x^2 + 12x + 18$$

$$y - 18 = \frac{1}{3}x^2 + 12x$$

$$y - 18 = \frac{1}{3}(x^2 + 36x)$$

$$y - 18 + 108 = \frac{1}{3}(x^2 + 36x + 324)$$

$$y + 90 = \frac{1}{3}(x+18)^2$$

a) $y = \frac{1}{3}(x+18)^2 - 90$

$a = \frac{1}{3}, h = -18, k = -90$

467

b) The vertex is $(h,k)=(-18,-90)$.

c) The axis of symmetry is $x=h$, that is $x=-18$.

d) Because $a=\frac{1}{3}>0$, and the axis of symmetry is vertical, the graph opens up.

65. $$x=-y^2+7y+2$$
$$x-2=-y^2+7y$$
$$x-2=-\left(y^2-7y\right)$$
$$x-2-\frac{49}{4}=-\left(y^2-7y+\frac{49}{4}\right)$$
$$x-\frac{57}{4}=-\left(y-\frac{7}{2}\right)^2$$

a) $$x=-\left(y-\frac{7}{2}\right)^2+\frac{57}{4}$$
$$a=-1,\,h=\frac{57}{4},\,k=\frac{7}{2}$$

b) The vertex is $(h,k)=\left(\frac{57}{4},\frac{7}{2}\right)$.

c) The axis of symmetry is $y=k$, that is $y=\frac{7}{2}$.

d) Because $a=-1<0$, and the axis of symmetry is horizontal, the graph opens left.

67. $$x=3y^2+6y+5$$
$$x-5=3y^2+6y$$
$$x-5=3\left(y^2+2y\right)$$
$$x-5+3=3\left(y^2+2y+1\right)$$
$$x-2=3\left(y+1\right)^2$$

a) $$x=3\left(y+1\right)^2+2$$
$$a=3,\,h=2,\,k=-1$$

b) The vertex is $(h,k)=(2,-1)$.

c) The axis of symmetry is $y=h$, that is $y=-1$.

d) Because $a=3>0$, and the axis of symmetry is horizontal, the graph opens right.

69. $$x=-2y^2+4y-1$$
$$x+1=-2y^2+4y$$
$$x+1=-2\left(y^2-2y\right)$$
$$x+1-2=-2\left(y^2-2y+1\right)$$
$$x-1=-2\left(y-1\right)^2$$

a) $$x=-2\left(y-1\right)^2+1$$
$$a=-2,\,h=1,\,k=1$$

b) The vertex is $(h,k)=(1,1)$.

c) The axis of symmetry is $y=k$, that is $y=1$.

d) Because $a=-2<0$, and the axis of symmetry is horizontal, the graph opens left.

71. $$x=\frac{3}{2}y^2+6y+12$$
$$x-12=\frac{3}{2}y^2+6y$$
$$x-12=\frac{3}{2}\left(y^2+4y\right)$$
$$x-12+6=\frac{3}{2}\left(y^2+4y+4\right)$$
$$x-6=\frac{3}{2}\left(y+2\right)^2$$

a) $$x=\frac{3}{2}\left(y+2\right)^2+6$$
$$a=\frac{3}{2},\,h=6,\,k=-2$$

b) The vertex is $(h,k)=(6,-2)$.

c) The axis of symmetry is $y=k$, that is $y=-2$.

d) Because $a=\frac{3}{2}>0$, and the axis of symmetry is horizontal, the graph opens right.

73. It is not possible to determine the axis of symmetry for a parabola with a vertex of $(2,3)$ because the parabola can have either a horizontal or vertical axis that contains this vertex.

75. A parabola with two x-intercepts either has a vertex below the x-axis and is open up or has a vertex above the x-axis and is open down.

77. A graph of a quadratic equation is a function if it is either open up or open down. In either case, it would pass the vertical line test.

79. To determine the maximum height reached and the time it takes Hunter to reach this height, we must determine the vertex of the parabola.
$$a=-16,\,b=16$$
$$t=\frac{-b}{2a}$$
$$=\frac{-(16)}{2(-16)}$$
$$=0.5$$
It takes Hunter 0.5 second to reach his maximum height.
$$h=-16t^2+16t+10$$
$$=-16(0.5)^2+16(0.5)+10$$
$$=14$$
Hunter reached a maximum height of 14 feet.

81. The axis of symmetry of the tunnel is $x = 5$, and because the tunnel has a height of 8 meters, the vertex of the tunnel is $(5, 8)$. Therefore, we have $h = 5$ and $k = 8$. We can write $y = a(x-5)^2 + 8$. To find a, note that the y-intercept of the tunnel is $(0, 0)$.

$$y = a(x-5)^2 + 8$$
$$0 = a(0-5)^2 + 8$$
$$0 = 25a + 8$$
$$-\frac{8}{25} = a$$

The equation is $y = -\frac{8}{25}(x-5)^2 + 8$.

83. Prepare   We need to determine the maximum vertical height and horizontal length of one complete jump using the given quadratic equation.

Plan   The maximum value for a quadratic equation occurs at the vertex if the parabola opens down. Therefore, the maximum vertical height of one complete jump is the y-coordinate of the vertex. We will solve the given quadratic equation for y and use the form $y = ax^2 + bx + c$ to determine the vertex. The total horizontal length of one hop means we are looking for a height of 0 feet which would be represented by the x-intercepts. That is, we will set $y = 0$ and solve for x.

Process   Solve the given quadratic equation for y.
$$3x^2 - 120x + 100y = 0$$
$$100y = -3x^2 + 120x$$
$$\frac{100y}{100} = \frac{-3x^2}{100} + \frac{120x}{100}$$
$$y = -\frac{3}{100}x^2 + \frac{6}{5}x$$

To find the maximum vertical height of one jump, determine the vertex. First find the x-coordinate of the vertex, $x = \frac{-b}{2a}$. Identify $a = -\frac{3}{100}$ and $b = \frac{6}{5}$.

$$x = \frac{-b}{2a}$$
$$= \frac{-\frac{6}{5}}{2\left(-\frac{3}{100}\right)}$$
$$= \frac{\frac{6}{5}}{\frac{3}{50}}$$
$$= \frac{6}{5} \cdot \frac{50}{3}$$
$$= 20$$

Find y, when $x = 20$.
$$y = -\frac{3}{100}x^2 + \frac{6}{5}x$$
$$= -\frac{3}{100}(20)^2 + \frac{6}{5}(20)$$
$$= -\frac{3}{100}(400) + 24$$
$$= -12 + 24$$
$$= 12$$

Therefore, the maximum height of one jump is 12 inches.

To determine the horizontal length of one jump, set $y = 0$ in the given quadratic equation and solve for x.
$$3x^2 - 120x + 100y = 0$$
$$3x^2 - 120x + 100(0) = 0$$
$$3x^2 - 120x = 0$$
$$3x(x - 40) = 0$$
$$3x = 0 \quad \text{or} \quad x - 40 = 0$$
$$x = 0 \quad \text{or} \quad x = 40$$

Because 0 feet would be the beginning of the jump, the horizontal length of one complete jump is 40 inches.

Ponder   Do our answers seem reasonable? The vertical height of 12 inches for one jump seems reasonable for a frog. Because the frogs can jump up to 20 times their body length, it certainly seems reasonable for a 3 inch frog to be able to jump 40 inches, which is less than 20 times 3 inches.

85. Prepare We need to determine the maximum vertical height of the tunnel and its width at the base.

Plan The maximum value for a quadratic equation occurs at the vertex if the parabola opens down. Therefore, the maximum vertical height of the tunnel is the y-coordinate of the vertex. We will solve the given quadratic equation for y and use the form $y = ax^2 + bx + c$ to determine the vertex. The determine the width of the tunnel at the base we must look for a height of 0 feet which would be represented by the x-intercepts. That is, we will set $y = 0$ and solve for x.

Process Solve the given quadratic equation for y.

$$3x^2 - 48x + 16y = 0$$

$$16y = -3x^2 + 48x$$

$$\frac{16y}{16} = \frac{-3x^2}{16} + \frac{48x}{16}$$

$$y = -\frac{3}{16}x^2 + 3x$$

To find the maximum height of the tunnel, determine the vertex. First find the x-coordinate of the vertex, $x = \frac{-b}{2a}$. Identify $a = -\frac{3}{16}$ and $b = 3$.

$$x = \frac{-b}{2a}$$

$$= \frac{-3}{2\left(-\frac{3}{16}\right)}$$

$$= \frac{3}{\frac{3}{8}}$$

$$= 3 \cdot \frac{8}{3}$$

$$= 8$$

Find y, when $x = 8$.

$$y = -\frac{3}{16}x^2 + 3x$$

$$= -\frac{3}{16}(8)^2 + 3(8)$$

$$= -\frac{3}{16}(64) + 24$$

$$= -12 + 24$$

$$= 12$$

Therefore, the maximum height of the tunnel is 12 feet.

To determine the width of the tunnel at its base, set $y = 0$ in the given quadratic equation and solve for x.

$$3x^2 - 48x + 16y = 0$$

$$3x^2 - 48x + 16(0) = 0$$

$$3x^2 - 48x = 0$$

$$3x(x - 16) = 0$$

$$3x = 0 \quad \text{or} \quad x - 16 = 0$$

$$x = 0 \quad \text{or} \quad x = 16$$

Because 0 feet would mean that the tunnel had no width, the width of the tunnel at its base is 16 feet.

Ponder Do our answers seem reasonable? It seems reasonable that the tunnel below a footbridge could have a maximum height of 12 feet and its base could have a width of 16 feet.

87.

$$y = -x^2 + 5x - 2$$

$$y + 2 = -x^2 + 5x$$

$$y + 2 = -\left(x^2 - 5x\right)$$

$$y + 2 - \frac{25}{4} = -\left(x^2 - 5x + \frac{25}{4}\right)$$

$$y - \frac{17}{4} = -\left(x - \frac{5}{2}\right)^2$$

$$y = -\left(x - \frac{5}{2}\right)^2 + \frac{17}{4}$$

$$a = -1,\ h = \tfrac{5}{2},\ k = \tfrac{17}{4}$$

a) The vertex is $(h, k) = \left(\frac{5}{2}, \frac{17}{4}\right)$.

b) The axis of symmetry is $x = h$, that is $x = \frac{5}{2}$.

c) Because $a = -1 < 0$, and the axis of symmetry is vertical, the graph opens down.

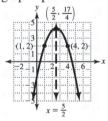

89.

$$x = y^2 + 3y + 3$$

$$x - 3 = y^2 + 3y$$

$$x - 3 + \frac{9}{4} = y^2 + 3y + \frac{9}{4}$$

$$x - \frac{3}{4} = \left(y + \frac{3}{2}\right)^2$$

$$x = \left(y + \frac{3}{2}\right)^2 + \frac{3}{4}$$

$$a = 1,\ h = \tfrac{3}{4},\ k = -\tfrac{3}{2}$$

a) The vertex is $(h,k)=\left(\frac{3}{4},-\frac{3}{2}\right)$.

b) The axis of symmetry is $y=k$, that is $y=-\frac{3}{2}$.

c) Because $a=1>0$, and the axis of symmetry is horizontal, the graph opens right.

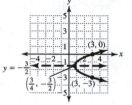

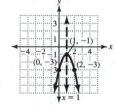

91.
$$y=-2x^2+4x-3$$
$$y+3=-2x^2+4x$$
$$y+3=-2\left(x^2-2x\right)$$
$$y+3-2=-2\left(x^2-2x+1\right)$$
$$y+1=-2(x-1)^2$$
$$y=-2(x-1)^2-1$$
$$a=-2, h=1, k=-1$$

a) The vertex is $(h,k)=(1,-1)$.

b) The axis of symmetry is $x=h$, that is $x=1$.

c) Because $a=-2<0$, and the axis of symmetry is vertical, the graph opens down.

93.
$$x=\frac{1}{3}y^2+6y+5$$
$$x-5=\frac{1}{3}y^2+6y$$
$$x-5=\frac{1}{3}\left(y^2+18y\right)$$
$$x-5+27=\frac{1}{3}\left(y^2+18y+81\right)$$
$$x+22=\frac{1}{3}(y+9)^2$$
$$x=\frac{1}{3}(y+9)^2-22$$
$$a=\tfrac{1}{3}, h=-22, k=-9$$

a) The vertex is $(h,k)=(-22,-9)$.

b) The axis of symmetry is $y=k$, that is $y=-9$.

c) Because $a=\tfrac{1}{3}>0$, and the axis of symmetry is horizontal, the graph opens right.

11.2 Exercises

1. The graph of $(x-h)^2 + (y-k)^2 = r^2$ is a <u>circle</u> with center (h,k) and radius <u>r</u>.

3. The set of all points (x, y) in the plane such that the sum of the distances from (x, y) to two fixed points is constant is called an <u>ellipse</u>.

5. The x-intercepts of an ellipse centered at the origin, given by the equation $\frac{x^2}{a^2} + \frac{y^2}{b^2} = 1$, are given by the ordered pairs $\underline{(a,0)}$ and $\underline{(-a,0)}$.

7. $x^2 + y^2 = 16$

$(x-0)^2 + (y-0)^2 = (4)^2$

$h = 0, k = 0, r = 4$

The center is $(h,k) = (0,0)$.

Plot points 4 units up, down, left, and right, from the center, and connect them.

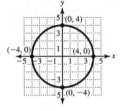

9. $(x-4)^2 + (y+3)^2 = 64$

$(x-4)^2 + (y-(-3))^2 = (8)^2$

$h = 4, k = -3, r = 8$

The center is $(h,k) = (4,-3)$.

Plot points 8 units up, down, left, and right, from the center, and connect them.

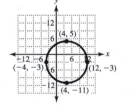

11. $x^2 + (y+3)^2 = 4$

$(x-0)^2 + (y-(-3))^2 = (2)^2$

$h = 0, k = -3, r = 2$

The center is $(h,k) = (0,-3)$.

Plot points 2 units up, down, left, and right, from the center, and connect them.

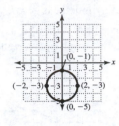

13. $(x-5)^2 + y^2 = 25$

$(x-5)^2 + (y-0)^2 = (5)^2$

$h = 5, k = 0, r = 5$

The center is $(h,k) = (5,0)$.

Plot points 5 units up, down, left, and right, from the center, and connect them.

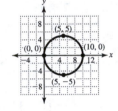

15. $(x+2)^2 + (y-3)^2 - 5 = 0$

$(x-(-2))^2 + (y-3)^2 = (\sqrt{5})^2$

$h = -2, k = 3, r = \sqrt{5}$

The center is $(h,k) = (-2,3)$.

Plot points $\sqrt{5}$, approximately 2.2, units up, down, left, and right, from the center, and connect them.

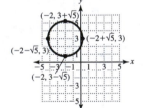

17. $(x-1)^2 + y^2 = 10$

$(x-1)^2 + (y-0)^2 = (\sqrt{10})^2$

$h = 1, k = 0, r = \sqrt{10}$

The center is $(h,k) = (1,0)$.

Plot points $\sqrt{10}$, approximately 3.2, units up, down, left, and right, from the center, and connect them.

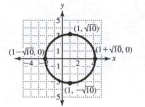

19. $h = -1,\ k = 6,\ r = 16$

$$\left(x-h\right)^2 + \left(y-k\right)^2 = r^2$$

$$\left(x-(-1)\right)^2 + \left(y-(6)\right)^2 = (16)^2$$

$$\left(x+1\right)^2 + \left(y-6\right)^2 = 256$$

21. $h = 0,\ k = -3,\ r^2 = 12$

$$\left(x-h\right)^2 + \left(y-k\right)^2 = r^2$$

$$\left(x-(0)\right)^2 + \left(y-(-3)\right)^2 = 12$$

$$x^2 + \left(y+3\right)^2 = 12$$

23. $h = 0,\ k = 0,\ r = \sqrt{3}$

$$\left(x-h\right)^2 + \left(y-k\right)^2 = r^2$$

$$\left(x-(0)\right)^2 + \left(y-(0)\right)^2 = \left(\sqrt{3}\right)^2$$

$$x^2 + y^2 = 3$$

25. $h = 2,\ k = -7,\ r = 2\sqrt{2}$

$$\left(x-h\right)^2 + \left(y-k\right)^2 = r^2$$

$$\left(x-(2)\right)^2 + \left(y-(-7)\right)^2 = \left(2\sqrt{2}\right)^2$$

$$\left(x-2\right)^2 + \left(y+7\right)^2 = 8$$

27. $h = -9,\ k = 0,\ r = 3\sqrt{5}$

$$\left(x-h\right)^2 + \left(y-k\right)^2 = r^2$$

$$\left(x-(-9)\right)^2 + \left(y-(0)\right)^2 = \left(3\sqrt{5}\right)^2$$

$$\left(x+9\right)^2 + y^2 = 45$$

29. $h = 5,\ k = 0,\ r = 5$

$$\left(x-h\right)^2 + \left(y-k\right)^2 = r^2$$

$$\left(x-(5)\right)^2 + \left(y-(0)\right)^2 = (5)^2$$

$$\left(x-5\right)^2 + y^2 = 25$$

31. $h = 3,\ k = 3,\ r = 3$

$$\left(x-h\right)^2 + \left(y-k\right)^2 = r^2$$

$$\left(x-(3)\right)^2 + \left(y-(3)\right)^2 = (3)^2$$

$$\left(x-3\right)^2 + \left(y-3\right)^2 = 9$$

33.
$$x^2 + y^2 + 6x + 8y - 11 = 0$$

$$\left(x^2 + 6x\right) + \left(y^2 + 8y\right) = 11$$

$$\left(x^2 + 6x + 9\right) + \left(y^2 + 8y + 16\right) = 11 + 9 + 16$$

$$\left(x+3\right)^2 + \left(y+4\right)^2 = 36$$

The center is $(-3, -4)$ and the radius is 6.

35.
$$x^2 + y^2 - 8x + 10y + 40 = 0$$

$$\left(x^2 - 8x\right) + \left(y^2 + 10y\right) = -40$$

$$\left(x^2 - 8x + 16\right) + \left(y^2 + 10y + 25\right) = -40 + 16 + 25$$

$$\left(x-4\right)^2 + \left(y+5\right)^2 = 1$$

The center is $(4, -5)$ and the radius is 1.

37.
$$x^2 + y^2 - 2x - 12y = 3$$

$$\left(x^2 - 2x\right) + \left(y^2 - 12y\right) = 3$$

$$\left(x^2 - 2x + 1\right) + \left(y^2 - 12y + 36\right) = 3 + 1 + 36$$

$$\left(x-1\right)^2 + \left(y-6\right)^2 = 40$$

The center is $(1, 6)$ and the radius is $2\sqrt{10}$.

39. The center is $(0, 0)$.

$a^2 = 16 \Rightarrow a = 4$

$b^2 = 9 \Rightarrow b = 3$

x-intercepts: $(-a, 0) = (-4, 0)$ and $(a, 0) = (4, 0)$

y-intercepts: $(0, -b) = (0, -3)$ and $(0, b) = (0, 3)$

Plot the four intercepts and connect with a smooth oval-shaped curve.

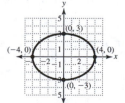

41. The center is $(0,0)$.

$a^2 = 9 \Rightarrow a = 3$

$b^2 = 25 \Rightarrow b = 5$

x-intercepts: $(-a,0) = (-3,0)$ and $(a,0) = (3,0)$

y-intercepts: $(0,-b) = (0,-5)$ and $(0,b) = (0,5)$

Plot the four intercepts and connect with a smooth oval-shaped curve.

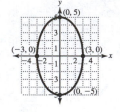

43. The center is $(0,0)$.

$a^2 = 36 \Rightarrow a = 6$

$b^2 = 4 \Rightarrow b = 2$

x-intercepts: $(-a,0) = (-6,0)$ and $(a,0) = (6,0)$

y-intercepts: $(0,-b) = (0,-2)$ and $(0,b) = (0,2)$

Plot the four intercepts and connect with a smooth oval-shaped curve.

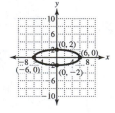

45. $x^2 + 4y^2 = 36$

$$\frac{x^2}{36} + \frac{4y^2}{36} = \frac{36}{36}$$

$$\frac{x^2}{36} + \frac{y^2}{9} = 1$$

The center is $(0,0)$.

$a^2 = 36 \Rightarrow a = 6$

$b^2 = 9 \Rightarrow b = 3$

x-intercepts: $(-a,0) = (-6,0)$ and $(a,0) = (6,0)$

y-intercepts: $(0,-b) = (0,-3)$ and $(0,b) = (0,3)$

Plot the four intercepts and connect with a smooth oval-shaped curve.

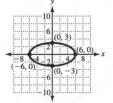

47. $9x^2 + 16y^2 = 144$

$$\frac{9x^2}{144} + \frac{16y^2}{144} = \frac{144}{144}$$

$$\frac{x^2}{16} + \frac{y^2}{9} = 1$$

The center is $(0,0)$.

$a^2 = 16 \Rightarrow a = 4$

$b^2 = 9 \Rightarrow b = 3$

x-intercepts: $(-a,0) = (-4,0)$ and $(a,0) = (4,0)$

y-intercepts: $(0,-b) = (0,-3)$ and $(0,b) = (0,3)$

Plot the four intercepts and connect with a smooth oval-shaped curve.

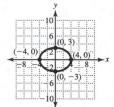

49. $8x^2 + 2y^2 = 32$

$$\frac{8x^2}{32} + \frac{2y^2}{32} = \frac{32}{32}$$

$$\frac{x^2}{4} + \frac{y^2}{16} = 1$$

The center is $(0,0)$.

$a^2 = 4 \Rightarrow a = 2$

$b^2 = 16 \Rightarrow b = 4$

x-intercepts: $(-a,0) = (-2,0)$ and $(a,0) = (2,0)$

y-intercepts: $(0,-b) = (0,-4)$ and $(0,b) = (0,4)$

Plot the four intercepts and connect with a smooth oval-shaped curve.

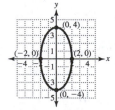

51. The center is $(h,k) = (1,-2)$.

$a^2 = 9 \Rightarrow a = 3$

$b^2 = 4 \Rightarrow b = 2$

To find the endpoints of the vertical axis, move up and down 2 units from the center. To find the endpoints of the horizontal axis, move left and right 3 units from the center.

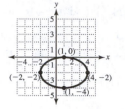

53. The center is $(h, k) = (2, -3)$.

$a^2 = 4 \Rightarrow a = 2$

$b^2 = 9 \Rightarrow b = 3$

To find the endpoints of the vertical axis, move up and down 3 units from the center. To find the endpoints of the horizontal axis, move left and right 2 units from the center.

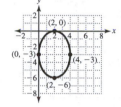

55. The center is $(h, k) = (-2, 0)$.

$a^2 = 25 \Rightarrow a = 5$

$b^2 = 4 \Rightarrow b = 2$

To find the endpoints of the vertical axis, move up and down 2 units from the center. To find the endpoints of the horizontal axis, move left and right 5 units from the center.

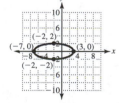

57. The center is $(h, k) = (0, 3)$.

$a^2 = 9 \Rightarrow a = 3$

$b^2 = 25 \Rightarrow b = 5$

To find the endpoints of the vertical axis, move up and down 5 units from the center. To find the endpoints of the horizontal axis, move left and right 3 units from the center.

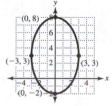

59. $a = 5, b = 4, (h, k) = (0, 0)$

$$\frac{x^2}{a^2} + \frac{y^2}{b^2} = 1$$

$$\frac{x^2}{(5)^2} + \frac{y^2}{(4)^2} = 1$$

$$\frac{x^2}{25} + \frac{y^2}{16} = 1$$

61. $a = 2, b = 5, (h, k) = (0, 0)$

$$\frac{x^2}{a^2} + \frac{y^2}{b^2} = 1$$

$$\frac{x^2}{(2)^2} + \frac{y^2}{(5)^2} = 1$$

$$\frac{x^2}{4} + \frac{y^2}{25} = 1$$

63. $a = 3, b = 5, (h, k) = (2, 0)$

$$\frac{(x-h)^2}{a^2} + \frac{(y-k)^2}{b^2} = 1$$

$$\frac{(x-(2))^2}{(3)^2} + \frac{(y-(0))^2}{(5)^2} = 1$$

$$\frac{(x-2)^2}{9} + \frac{y^2}{25} = 1$$

65. $a = 1, b = 2, (h, k) = (-3, 4)$

$$\frac{(x-h)^2}{a^2} + \frac{(y-k)^2}{b^2} = 1$$

$$\frac{(x-(-3))^2}{(1)^2} + \frac{(y-(4))^2}{(2)^2} = 1$$

$$\frac{(x+3)^2}{1} + \frac{(y-4)^2}{4} = 1$$

67. There are two squared terms and their coefficients equal, therefore, this equation represents a circle.

69. There is one squared term, therefore, this equation represents a parabola.

71. There are two squared terms and their coefficients have the same signs but are not equal, therefore, this equation represents an ellipse.

73. Answers will vary; for example: Find the center of the circle and plot it on the graph. Find the radius and use it to plots points to the left and right of the center, and up and down from the center and connect.

75. The foci of the ellipse are the points whose distance to all points, (x, y), on the ellipse sum to a constant.

77. $(x+3)^2 + (y-3)^2 = 4$

79. The graph is a point located at the origin.

81. $a = 4.5$, $b = 2.5$, $(h, k) = (0, 0)$

$$\frac{x^2}{a^2} + \frac{y^2}{b^2} = 1$$

$$\frac{x^2}{(4.5)^2} + \frac{y^2}{(2.5)^2} = 1$$

$$\frac{x^2}{20.25} + \frac{y^2}{6.25} = 1$$

83. Prepare   We need to determine the minimum length of the retrieving wand the trainers would need to reach the entire surface of the water with the barricade in place.

Plan   Determine the radius of the pool and then add 3 feet to the radius to account for the barricade.

Process   The circumference of the pool is described by the equation $x^2 + y^2 = 289$, where $r^2 = 289$. Therefore, $r = 17$ feet is the radius of the pool. After adding 3 feet, we find that the minimum length of the retrieving wand must be 20 feet.

Ponder   Does our answer seem reasonable? Yes. A simple quick check of our work will show that our answer is correct.

85. The diameter of the circle is 6 units, therefore, the radius is $r = 3$. The midpoint of the diameter is $(h, k) = (4, -1)$, which is the center of the circle.

$$(x-h)^2 + (y-k)^2 = r^2$$

$$(x-(4))^2 + (y-(-1))^2 = (3)^2$$

$$(x-4)^2 + (y+1)^2 = 9$$

87. We can determine the radius of the circle using the distance formula.

$$d = \sqrt{(x_2 - x_1)^2 + (y_2 - y_1)^2}$$

$$d = \sqrt{(-2-1)^2 + (1-4)^2}$$

$$d = \sqrt{(-3)^2 + (-3)^2}$$

$$d = \sqrt{18}$$

Use $(h, k) = (1, 4)$ and $r = \sqrt{18}$ to write the equation of the circle.

$$(x-h)^2 + (y-k)^2 = r^2$$

$$(x-(1))^2 + (y-(4))^2 = \left(\sqrt{18}\right)^2$$

$$(x-1)^2 + (y-4)^2 = 18$$

89.
$$\frac{(x-h)^2}{a^2} + \frac{(y-k)^2}{b^2} = 1$$

$$\frac{(x-(0))^2}{(2\sqrt{5})^2} + \frac{(y-(3))^2}{(3\sqrt{3})^2} = 1$$

$$\frac{x^2}{20} + \frac{(y-3)^2}{27} = 1$$

91. $a = 2$, $b = 3$, $(h, k) = (2, -3)$

$$\frac{(x-h)^2}{a^2} + \frac{(y-k)^2}{b^2} = 1$$

$$\frac{(x-(2))^2}{(2)^2} + \frac{(y-(-3))^2}{(3)^2} = 1$$

$$\frac{(x-2)^2}{4} + \frac{(y+3)^2}{9} = 1$$

11.3 Exercises

1. The set of all points such that the absolute value of the difference of the distances from each point to two fixed points is called a <u>hyperbola</u>.

3. The equations of a hyperbola centered at the origin are $\frac{x^2}{a^2} - \frac{y^2}{b^2} = 1$ and $\frac{y^2}{b^2} - \frac{x^2}{a^2} = 1$.

5. A hyperbola that opens left/right, given by the equation $\frac{x^2}{a^2} - \frac{y^2}{b^2} = 1$, has vertices $\underline{(-a,0)}$ and $\underline{(a,0)}$.

7. $a^2 = 9 \Rightarrow a = 3$

$b^2 = 9 \Rightarrow b = 3$

The vertices are $(-3,0)$ and $(3,0)$. The additional points are $(0,-3)$ and $(0,3)$.

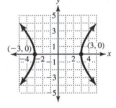

9. $a^2 = 4 \Rightarrow a = 2$

$b^2 = 25 \Rightarrow b = 5$

The vertices are $(0,-5)$ and $(0,5)$. The additional points are $(-2,0)$ and $(2,0)$.

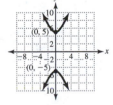

11. $a^2 = 36 \Rightarrow a = 6$

$b^2 = 9 \Rightarrow b = 3$

The vertices are $(-6,0)$ and $(6,0)$. The additional points are $(0,-3)$ and $(0,3)$.

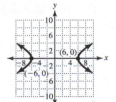

13. $a^2 = 4 \Rightarrow a = 2$

$b^2 = 9 \Rightarrow b = 3$

The vertices are $(0,-3)$ and $(0,3)$. The additional points are $(-2,0)$ and $(2,0)$.

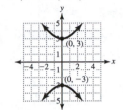

15. $x^2 - y^2 = 16$

$\frac{x^2}{16} - \frac{y^2}{16} = \frac{16}{16}$

$\frac{x^2}{16} - \frac{y^2}{16} = 1$

$a^2 = 16 \Rightarrow a = 4$

$b^2 = 16 \Rightarrow b = 4$

The vertices are $(-4,0)$ and $(4,0)$. The additional points are $(0,-4)$ and $(0,4)$.

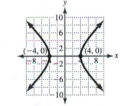

17. $y^2 - x^2 = 1$

$\frac{y^2}{1} - \frac{x^2}{1} = 1$

$a^2 = 1 \Rightarrow a = 1$

$b^2 = 1 \Rightarrow b = 1$

The vertices are $(0,-1)$ and $(0,1)$. The additional points are $(-1,0)$ and $(1,0)$.

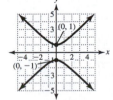

19. $25y^2 - 9x^2 = 225$

$$\frac{25y^2}{225} - \frac{9x^2}{225} = \frac{225}{225}$$

$$\frac{y^2}{9} - \frac{x^2}{25} = 1$$

$a^2 = 25 \Rightarrow a = 5$

$b^2 = 9 \Rightarrow b = 3$

The vertices are $(0,-3)$ and $(0,3)$. The additional points are $(-5,0)$ and $(5,0)$.

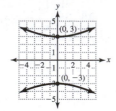

21. $9x^2 - 25y^2 = 225$

$$\frac{9x^2}{225} - \frac{25y^2}{225} = \frac{225}{225}$$

$$\frac{x^2}{25} - \frac{y^2}{9} = 1$$

$a^2 = 25 \Rightarrow a = 5$

$b^2 = 9 \Rightarrow b = 3$

The vertices are $(-5,0)$ and $(5,0)$. The additional points are $(0,-3)$ and $(0,3)$.

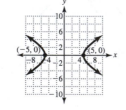

23. $x^2 - 4y^2 = 36$

$$\frac{x^2}{36} - \frac{4y^2}{36} = \frac{36}{36}$$

$$\frac{x^2}{36} - \frac{y^2}{9} = 1$$

$a^2 = 36 \Rightarrow a = 6$

$b^2 = 9 \Rightarrow b = 3$

The vertices are $(-6,0)$ and $(6,0)$. The additional points are $(0,-3)$ and $(0,3)$.

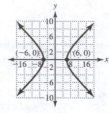

25. $a^2 = 4 \Rightarrow a = 2$

$b^2 = 25 \Rightarrow b = 5$

Center: $(2,-3)$

The hyperbola opens left and right because $(x-2)^2$ is positive. The vertices are 2 units to the left and the right of the center. The additional points are 5 units up and down from the center.

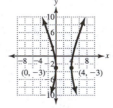

27. $a^2 = 16 \Rightarrow a = 4$

$b^2 = 9 \Rightarrow b = 3$

Center: $(2,2)$

The hyperbola opens up and down because $(y-2)^2$ is positive. The vertices are 3 units up and down from the center. The additional points are 4 units to the left and the right of the center.

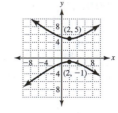

29. $a^2 = 9 \Rightarrow a = 3$

$b^2 = 9 \Rightarrow b = 3$

Center: $(-2,3)$

The hyperbola opens left and right because $(x+2)^2$ is positive. The vertices are 3 units to the left and the right of the center. The additional points are 3 units up and down from the center.

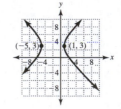

31. $(y+2)^2 - (x+3)^2 = 4$

$$\frac{(y+2)^2}{4} - \frac{(x+3)^2}{4} = \frac{4}{4}$$

$$\frac{(y+2)^2}{4} - \frac{(x+3)^2}{4} = 1$$

$a^2 = 4 \Rightarrow a = 2$

$b^2 = 4 \Rightarrow b = 2$

Center: $(-3,-2)$

The hyperbola opens up and down because $(y+2)^2$ is positive. The vertices are 2 units up and down from the center. The additional points are 2 units to the left and the right of the center.

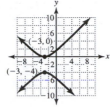

33. Center: $(0,0)$

$a = 2 \Rightarrow a^2 = 4$

$b = 5 \Rightarrow b^2 = 25$

$$\frac{x^2}{a^2} - \frac{y^2}{b^2} = 1$$

$$\frac{x^2}{4} - \frac{y^2}{25} = 1$$

35. Center: $(2,1)$

$a = 2 \Rightarrow a^2 = 4$

$b = 3 \Rightarrow b^2 = 9$

$$\frac{(y-k)^2}{b^2} - \frac{(x-h)^2}{a^2} = 1$$

$$\frac{(y-1)^2}{9} - \frac{(x-2)^2}{4} = 1$$

37. Center: $(-3,-2)$

$a = 2 \Rightarrow a^2 = 4$

$b = 3 \Rightarrow b^2 = 9$

$$\frac{(x-h)^2}{a^2} - \frac{(y-k)^2}{b^2} = 1$$

$$\frac{(x+3)^2}{4} - \frac{(y+2)^2}{9} = 1$$

39. There are two squared terms and their coefficients have opposite signs, therefore, this equation represents a hyperbola.

41. There are two squared terms and their coefficients have the same signs but are not equal, therefore, this equation represents an ellipse.

43. There are two squared terms and their coefficients have opposite signs, therefore, this equation represents a hyperbola.

45. There is one squared term, therefore, this equation represents a parabola.

47. There are two squared terms and their coefficients equal, therefore, this equation represents a circle.

49. There are no squared terms, therefore, this equation represents a straight line.

51. Circles have the same coefficients on x^2 and y^2. Ellipses have different positive coefficients on x^2 and y^2. Hyperbolas have coefficients with opposite signs on x^2 and y^2. Parabolas have only one squared term, and straight lines have no squared terms.

53. The equations of the asymptotes for a hyperbola are $y = -\frac{b}{a}x$ and $y = \frac{b}{a}x$. This equation works because $\pm b$ always represents the change in y from the center and $\pm a$ always represents the change in x from the center in the slope formula.

55. Answers will vary; for example: Take $\frac{1}{2}$ the distance between $(-2,-1)$ and $(-2,-7)$ to get $|b|$. Take $\frac{1}{2}$ the distance between $(0,-4)$ and $(-4,-4)$ to get $|a|$. Place the center of the hyperbola at $(-2,-4)$, square $|a|$ and $|b|$, and plug the numbers into the general hyperbola equation to obtain $\frac{(y+4)^2}{9} - \frac{(x+2)^2}{4} = 1$.

57. Center: $(-5,2)$

$a = 2\sqrt{2} \Rightarrow a^2 = 8$

$b = 6\sqrt{3} \Rightarrow b^2 = 108$

$$\frac{(x-h)^2}{a^2} - \frac{(y-k)^2}{b^2} = 1$$

$$\frac{(x+5)^2}{8} - \frac{(y-2)^2}{108} = 1$$

59. Center: $(0,0)$

$a = 4 \Rightarrow a^2 = 16$

$b = 1 \Rightarrow b^2 = 1$

$\dfrac{x^2}{a^2} - \dfrac{y^2}{b^2} = 1$

$\dfrac{x^2}{16} - \dfrac{y^2}{1} = 1$

61. $a^2 = 8 \Rightarrow a = 2\sqrt{2}$

$b^2 = 10 \Rightarrow b = \sqrt{10}$

The vertices are $\left(-2\sqrt{2},0\right)$ and $\left(2\sqrt{2},0\right)$. The additional points are $\left(0,-\sqrt{10}\right)$ and $\left(0,\sqrt{10}\right)$.

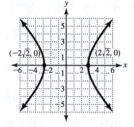

11.4 Exercises

1. Two or more equations considered together, where at least one of the equations is nonlinear, are called a system of nonlinear equations.

3. A system of nonlinear equations consisting of an ellipse and a circle can have at most four solutions.

5. An inequality of degree 2 or higher is called a nonlinear inequality.

7. $x^2 + y^2 = 25$ is a circle with center $(0,0)$ and radius $r = 5$. $-x + y = 5$ is a line with slope-intercept form $y = x + 5$. The slope is $m = 1$ and the y-intercept is $(0,5)$.

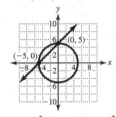

The solution set is $\{(-5,0),(0,5)\}$.

9. $y = -x^2 - 3$ is a parabola with vertex $(0,-3)$ and open down. $2x + y = -6$ is a line with slope-intercept form $y = -2x - 6$. The slope is $m = -2$ and the y-intercept is $(0,-6)$.

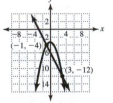

The solution set is $\{(-1,-4),(3,-12)\}$.

11. Rewrite $9x^2 - 4y^2 = 36$ as $\dfrac{x^2}{4} - \dfrac{y^2}{9} = 1$. This is a hyperbola centered at the origin with vertices $(-2,0)$ and $(2,0)$, and additional points $(0,-3)$ and $(0,3)$. $x = 1$ is a vertical line with x-intercept $(1,0)$.

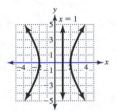

The solution set is $\{\ \}$.

13. Rewrite $y + 3 = 0$ as $y = -3$. This is a horizontal line with y-intercept $(0,-3)$. Rewrite $9x^2 + 4y^2 = 36$ as $\dfrac{x^2}{4} + \dfrac{y^2}{9} = 1$. This is an ellipse centered at the origin with x-intercepts $(-2,0)$ and $(2,0)$, and y-intercepts $(0,-3)$ and $(0,3)$.

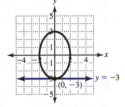

The solution set is $\{(0,-3)\}$.

15. $(x-2)^2 + y^2 = 4$ is a circle with center $(2,0)$ and radius $r = 2$. $x = \dfrac{1}{2}y^2$ is a parabola with vertex $(0,0)$ and open to the right.

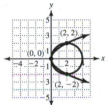

The solution set is $\{(0,0),(2,-2),(2,2)\}$.

17. Solve equation 2 for x to obtain the equation $x = -3y + 1$. Substitute $x = -3y + 1$ into equation 1 and solve for y.

$$x^2 + 2y^2 = 6$$
$$(-3y + 1)^2 + 2y^2 = 6$$
$$9y^2 - 6y + 1 + 2y^2 = 6$$
$$11y^2 - 6y - 5 = 0$$
$$(11y + 5)(y - 1) = 0$$
$$11y + 5 = 0 \quad \text{or} \quad y - 1 = 0$$
$$y = -\frac{5}{11} \quad \text{or} \quad y = 1$$

Solve for x

$$x = -3\left(-\frac{5}{11}\right) + 1 \ \bigg| \ x = -3(1) + 1$$
$$x = \frac{26}{11} \quad \bigg| \quad x = -2$$

481

The solution set is $\left\{(-2,1),\left(\frac{26}{11},-\frac{5}{11}\right)\right\}$.

19. Solve equation 2 for y to obtain the equation $y = -2x - 5$. Substitute $y = -2x - 5$ into equation 1 and solve for x.

$$x^2 + y^2 = 10$$
$$x^2 + (-2x - 5)^2 = 10$$
$$x^2 + 4x^2 + 20x + 25 = 10$$
$$5x^2 + 20x + 15 = 0$$
$$5(x + 1)(x + 3) = 0$$
$$x + 1 = 0 \quad \text{or} \quad x + 3 = 0$$
$$x = -1 \quad \text{or} \quad x = -3$$

$$\underline{\text{Solve for } y}$$

$$y = -2(-1) - 5 \; \Big| \; y = -2(-3) - 5$$
$$y = -3 \qquad \Big| \qquad y = 1$$

The solution set is $\left\{(-3,1),(-1,-3)\right\}$.

21. Eliminate y by adding 2 times Equation 1 and Equation 2.

$$\begin{array}{ll} 2(\text{Equation 1}) & \left\{ \begin{array}{l} 4x^2 - 2y^2 = 12 \\ x^2 + 2y^2 = 13 \end{array} \right. \\ \text{Equation 2} \end{array}$$
$$\overline{\qquad\qquad 5x^2 = 25}$$
$$x^2 = 5$$
$$x = \pm\sqrt{5}$$

Substitute $x = \pm\sqrt{5}$ into Equation 2 and solve for y.

$$x^2 + 2y^2 = 13$$
$$\left(\pm\sqrt{5}\right)^2 + 2y^2 = 13$$
$$5 + 2y^2 = 13$$
$$2y^2 = 8$$
$$y^2 = 4$$
$$y = \pm 2$$

$$\underline{\text{Solution Set}}$$

$$\left\{\left(-\sqrt{5},-2\right),\left(-\sqrt{5},2\right),\left(\sqrt{5},-2\right),\left(\sqrt{5},2\right)\right\}$$

23. Eliminate y by adding -1 times Equation 1 and Equation 2.

$$\begin{array}{ll} -1(\text{Equation 1}) & \left\{ \begin{array}{l} -x^2 - y^2 = -5 \\ x^2 + y^2 = 9 \end{array} \right. \\ \text{Equation 2} \end{array}$$
$$\overline{\qquad\qquad 0 = 4}$$

The solution set is $\left\{ \; \right\}$.

25. Eliminate x by adding Equation 1 and Equation 2.

$$\begin{array}{ll} \text{Equation 1} & \left\{ \begin{array}{l} y = -x^2 + 2x + 1 \\ y = x^2 - 2x + 1 \end{array} \right. \\ \text{Equation 2} \end{array}$$
$$\overline{\qquad\qquad 2y = 2}$$
$$y = 1$$

Substitute $y = 1$ into Equation 2 and solve for x.

$$y = x^2 - 2x + 1$$
$$(1) = x^2 - 2x + 1$$
$$0 = x^2 - 2x$$
$$0 = x(x - 2)$$
$$x = 0 \quad \text{or} \quad x - 2 = 0$$
$$x = 0 \quad \text{or} \qquad x = 2$$

$$\underline{\text{Solution Set}}$$
$$\left\{(0,1),(2,1)\right\}$$

27. Substitute $y = x^2$ into equation 2 and solve for x.

$$y = (x - 4)^2 + 8$$
$$\left(x^2\right) = (x - 4)^2 + 8$$
$$x^2 = x^2 - 8x + 16 + 8$$
$$0 = -8x + 24$$
$$8x = 24$$
$$x = 3$$

Substitute $x = 3$ into equation 1 and solve for y.

$$y = x^2$$
$$y = (3)^2$$
$$y = 9$$

$$\underline{\text{Solution Set}}$$
$$\left\{(3,9)\right\}$$

29. Eliminate $(x - 2)$ by adding Equation 1 and -4 times Equation 2.

$$\begin{array}{ll} \text{Equation 1} & \left\{ \begin{array}{l} 4(x-2)^2 + 9(y-2)^2 = 36 \\ -4(x-2)^2 - 4(y-2)^2 = -16 \end{array} \right. \\ -4(\text{Equation 2}) \end{array}$$
$$\overline{\qquad\qquad 5(y-2)^2 = 20}$$
$$(y-2)^2 = 4$$
$$y - 2 = -\sqrt{4} \quad \text{or} \quad y - 2 = \sqrt{4}$$
$$y - 2 = -2 \quad \text{or} \quad y - 2 = 2$$
$$y = 0 \qquad \text{or} \qquad y = 4$$

Solve for x

$$(x-2)^2+(y-2)^2=4 \quad \Big| \quad (x-2)^2+(y-2)^2=4$$
$$(x-2)^2+((0)-2)^2=4 \quad \Big| \quad (x-2)^2+((4)-2)^2=4$$
$$(x-2)^2+4=4 \quad \Big| \quad (x-2)^2+4=4$$
$$(x-2)^2=0 \quad \Big| \quad (x-2)^2=0$$
$$x-2=0 \quad \Big| \quad x-2=0$$
$$x=2 \quad \Big| \quad x=2$$

Solution Set

$$\{(2,0),(2,4)\}$$

31. Substitute $y=x^2+3$ into equation 2 and solve for x.

$$y=-x^2-2x-2$$
$$(x^2+3)=-x^2-2x-2$$
$$2x^2+2x+5=0$$
$$2x^2+2x=-5$$
$$\frac{2x^2}{2}+\frac{2x}{2}=\frac{-5}{2}$$
$$x^2+x=-\frac{5}{2}$$
$$x^2+x+\frac{1}{4}=-\frac{5}{2}+\frac{1}{4}$$
$$\left(x+\frac{1}{2}\right)^2=-\frac{9}{4}$$
$$x+\frac{1}{2}=-\sqrt{-\frac{9}{4}} \quad \text{or} \quad x+\frac{1}{2}=\sqrt{-\frac{9}{4}}$$
$$x+\frac{1}{2}=-\frac{3}{2}i \quad \text{or} \quad x+\frac{1}{2}=\frac{3}{2}i$$
$$x=-\frac{1}{2}-\frac{3}{2}i \quad \text{or} \quad x=-\frac{1}{2}+\frac{3}{2}i$$

The solution set is $\{\ \}$.

33. Eliminate y by adding Equation 1 and 4 times Equation 2.

$$\begin{array}{r} \text{Equation 1} \\ 4(\text{Equation 2}) \end{array} \left\{ \begin{array}{l} x^2+8y^2=8 \\ 12x^2-8y^2=96 \end{array} \right.$$
$$13x^2=104$$
$$x^2=8$$
$$x=\pm2\sqrt{2}$$

Substitute $x=\pm2\sqrt{2}$ into Equation 1 and solve for y.

$$x^2+8y^2=8$$
$$(\pm2\sqrt{2})^2+8y^2=8$$
$$8+8y^2=8$$
$$8y^2=0$$
$$y^2=0$$
$$y=0$$

Solution Set

$$\{(-2\sqrt{2},0),(2\sqrt{2},0)\}$$

35. Substitute $y=x+3$ into equation 1 and solve for x.

$$y=x^2-6x+13$$
$$(x+3)=x^2-6x+13$$
$$0=x^2-7x+10$$
$$0=(x-2)(x-5)$$
$$x-2=0 \quad \text{or} \quad x-5=0$$
$$x=2 \quad \text{or} \quad x=5$$

Solve for y

$$y=(2)+3 \quad \Big| \quad y=(5)+3$$
$$y=5 \quad \Big| \quad y=8$$

Solution Set

$$\{(5,8),(2,5)\}$$

37. Substitute $y=x^2-2$ into equation 1 and solve for x.

$$4y^2-4x^2=-8$$
$$4(x^2-2)^2-4x^2=-8$$
$$4x^4-16x^2+16-4x^2=-8$$
$$4x^4-20x^2+24=0$$
$$4(x^2-3)(x^2-2)=0$$
$$x^2-3=0 \quad \text{or} \quad x^2-2=0$$
$$x^2=3 \quad \text{or} \quad x^2=2$$
$$x=\pm\sqrt{3} \quad \text{or} \quad x=\pm\sqrt{2}$$

Solve for y

$$y=(\pm\sqrt{3})^2-2 \quad \Big| \quad y=(\pm\sqrt{2})^2-2$$
$$y=1 \quad \Big| \quad y=0$$

Solution Set

$$\{(-\sqrt{3},1),(\sqrt{3},1),(-\sqrt{2},0),(\sqrt{2},0)\}$$

39. Eliminate y by adding Equation 1 and 3 times Equation 2.

$$\begin{array}{r} \text{Equation 1} \\ 3(\text{Equation 2}) \end{array} \begin{cases} 5x^2 - 6y^2 = 9 \\ -9x^2 + 6y^2 = -45 \end{cases}$$

$$-4x^2 = -36$$
$$x^2 = 9$$
$$x = \pm 3$$

Substitute $x = \pm 3$ into Equation 1 and solve for y.

$$5x^2 - 6y^2 = 9$$
$$5(\pm 3)^2 - 6y^2 = 9$$
$$45 - 6y^2 = 9$$
$$-6y^2 = -36$$
$$y^2 = 6$$
$$y = \pm\sqrt{6}$$

Solution Set
$$\left\{ \left(-3, -\sqrt{6}\right), \left(-3, \sqrt{6}\right), \left(3, -\sqrt{6}\right), \left(3, \sqrt{6}\right) \right\}$$

41. Graph the parabola given by $y = x^2 - 1$. Use a solid line because of the $\leq$ symbol. The equation is quadratic in x and $a = 1 > 0$, which implies the parabola opens up. The x-intercepts are $(-1, 0)$ and $(1, 0)$. The y-intercept is $(0, -1)$. Choose the test point $(0, 0)$.

$$y \leq x^2 - 1$$
$$0 \leq (0)^2 - 1$$
$$0 \leq -1$$

False. Shade the region that does not contain the origin.

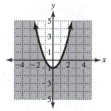

43. Graph the circle given by $x^2 + y^2 = 9$ using a dashed line because of the $<$ symbol. The center is $(0, 0)$ and the radius is $r = 3$. Choose the test point $(0, 0)$.

$$x^2 + y^2 < 9$$
$$(0)^2 + (0)^2 < 9$$
$$0 < 9$$

True. Shade the region that contains the origin.

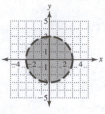

45. Graph the ellipse given by $\dfrac{x^2}{16} + \dfrac{y^2}{9} = 1$ using a solid line because of the $\geq$ symbol. The center is $(0, 0)$, the x-intercepts are $(-4, 0)$ and $(4, 0)$, and the y-intercepts are $(0, -3)$ and $(0, 3)$. Choose the test point $(0, 0)$.

$$\frac{x^2}{16} + \frac{y^2}{9} \geq 1$$
$$\frac{(0)^2}{16} + \frac{(0)^2}{9} \geq 1$$
$$0 \geq 1$$

False. Shade the region that does not contain the origin.

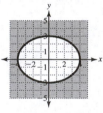

47. Graph the hyperbola given by $\dfrac{y^2}{4} - \dfrac{x^2}{25} = 1$ using a dashed line because of the $>$ symbol. The center is $(0, 0)$, the vertices are $(0, -2)$ and $(0, 2)$, and the additional points are $(-5, 0)$ and $(5, 0)$. Choose the test point $(0, 0)$.

$$\frac{y^2}{4} - \frac{x^2}{25} > 1$$
$$\frac{(0)^2}{4} - \frac{(0)^2}{25} > 1$$
$$0 > 1$$

False. Shade the region that does not contain the origin.

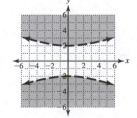

49. Graph the circle given by $x^2 + (y+3)^2 = 4$ using a solid line because of the $\geq$ symbol. The center is $(0,-3)$ and the radius is $r = 2$. Choose the test point $(0,0)$.

$$x^2 + (y+3)^2 \geq 4$$

$$(0)^2 + ((0)+3)^2 \geq 4$$

$$9 \geq 4$$

True. Shade the region that contains the origin.

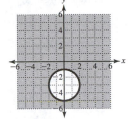

51. Graph the parabola given by $x = (y-2)^2 + 1$ using a dashed line because of the $>$ symbol. The equation is quadratic in y, and $a = 1 > 0$, which implies the parabola opens right. The vertex is $(1,2)$. The x-intercept is $(5,0)$. There are no y-intercepts. Choose the test point $(0,0)$.

$$x > (y-2)^2 + 1$$

$$(0) > ((0)-2)^2 + 1$$

$$0 > 5$$

False. Shade the region that does not contain the origin.

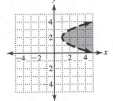

53. Rewrite the inequality to obtain the equation $\dfrac{x^2}{4} - \dfrac{y^2}{9} = 1$. Graph the hyperbola using a solid line because of the $\leq$ symbol. The center is $(0,0)$, the vertices are $(-2,0)$ and $(2,0)$, and the additional points are $(0,-3)$ and $(0,3)$. Choose the test point $(0,0)$.

$$\frac{x^2}{4} - \frac{y^2}{9} \leq 1$$

$$\frac{(0)^2}{4} - \frac{(0)^2}{9} \leq 1$$

$$0 \leq 1$$

True. Shade the region that contains the origin.

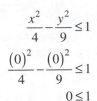

55. Rewrite the inequality to obtain the equation $\dfrac{x^2}{16} + \dfrac{y^2}{9} = 1$. Graph the ellipse using a dashed line because of the $<$ symbol. The center is $(0,0)$, the x-intercepts are $(-4,0)$ and $(4,0)$, and the y-intercepts are $(0,-3)$ and $(0,3)$. Choose the test point $(0,0)$.

$$\frac{x^2}{16} + \frac{y^2}{9} < 1$$

$$\frac{(0)^2}{16} + \frac{(0)^2}{9} < 1$$

$$0 < 1$$

True. Shade the region that contains the origin.

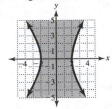

57. $y < \dfrac{2}{3}x - 2$

Graph the line $y = \dfrac{2}{3}x - 2$ using a dashed line. The slope is $m = \dfrac{2}{3}$ and the y-intercept is $(0,-2)$. Choose the test point $(0,0)$.

$$y < \frac{2}{3}x - 2$$

$$(0) < \frac{2}{3}(0) - 2$$

$$0 < -2$$

False: Use arrows to show the shaded region that does not contain the origin..

$$x \geq 2y^2 + 4y - 2$$

Graph the parabola $x = 2y^2 + 4y - 2$ using a solid line. The equation is quadratic in y and $a = 2 > 0$, which implies the parabola opens right. The vertex is $(-4, -1)$ and the x-intercept is $(-2, 0)$. The y-intercepts are $\left(0, -1 - \sqrt{2}\right)$ and $\left(0, -1 + \sqrt{2}\right)$. Choose the test point $(0, 0)$.

$$x \geq 2y^2 + 4y - 2$$
$$(0) \geq 2(0)^2 + 4(0) - 2$$
$$0 \geq -2$$

True: Use arrows to show the shaded region that contains the origin.
Finally, shade the region where the individual shaded regions overlap.

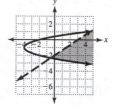

59. $y > 2x^2$

Graph the parabola $y = 2x^2$ using a dashed line. The vertex is $(0, 0)$. Choose the test point $(0, 1)$.

$$y > 2x^2$$
$$(1) > 2(0)^2$$
$$1 > 0$$

True: Use arrows to show the shaded region that contains the point $(0, 1)$

$$\frac{x^2}{4} + \frac{(y - 4)^2}{16} \leq 1$$

Graph the ellipse $\dfrac{x^2}{4} + \dfrac{(y - 4)^2}{16} = 1$ using a solid line. The center is $(0, 4)$. There are no x-intercepts. The y-intercepts are $(0, 0)$ and $(0, 8)$. Choose the test point $(0, 1)$.

$$\frac{x^2}{4} + \frac{(y - 4)^2}{16} \leq 1$$
$$\frac{(0)^2}{4} + \frac{((1) - 4)^2}{16} \leq 1$$
$$\frac{9}{16} \leq 1$$

True: Use arrows to show the shaded region that contains the point $(0, 1)$

Finally, shade the region where the individual shaded regions overlap.

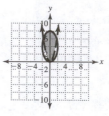

61. $x^2 + y^2 \leq 5$

Graph the circle $x^2 + y^2 = 5$ using a solid line. The center is $(0, 0)$ and the radius is $r = \sqrt{5}$. Choose the test point $(0, 0)$.

$$x^2 + y^2 \leq 5$$
$$(0)^2 + (0)^2 \leq 5$$
$$0 \leq 5$$

True: Use arrows to show the shaded region that contains the origin.

$$4x^2 - y^2 > 4$$

Graph the hyperbola $\dfrac{x^2}{1} - \dfrac{y^2}{4} = 1$ using a dashed line. The vertices are $(-1, 0)$ and $(1, 0)$. The additional points are $(0, -2)$ and $(0, 2)$. Choose the test point $(0, 0)$.

$$\frac{x^2}{1} - \frac{y^2}{4} > 1$$
$$\frac{(0)^2}{1} - \frac{(0)^2}{4} > 1$$
$$0 > 1$$

False: Use arrows to show the shaded region that does not contain the origin.
Finally, shade the region where the individual shaded regions overlap.

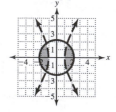

63. $y \leq -(x - 2)^2$

Graph the parabola $y = -(x - 2)^2$ using a solid line. The equation is quadratic in x and $a = -1 < 0$, which implies the graph opens down. The vertex is $(2, 0)$. The x-intercept is $(2, 0)$, and the y-intercept is $(0, -4)$. Choose the test point $(0, 0)$.

$$y \le -(x-2)^2$$
$$(0) \le -((0)-2)^2$$
$$0 \le -4$$

False: Use arrows to show the shaded region that does not contain the origin.

$$y > (x-1)^2 - 2$$

Graph the parabola $y = (x-1)^2 - 2$ using a dashed line. The equation is quadratic in x and $a = 1 > 0$, which implies the graph opens up. The vertex is $(1,-2)$. The x-intercepts are $(1-\sqrt{2},0)$ and $(1+\sqrt{2},0)$, and the y-intercept is $(0,-1)$. Choose the test point $(0,0)$.

$$y > (x-1)^2 - 2$$
$$(0) > ((0)-1)^2 - 2$$
$$0 > -1$$

True: Use arrows to show the shaded region that contains the origin.
Finally, shade the region where the individual shaded regions overlap.

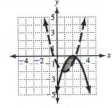

65. $x^2 + y^2 \ge 8$

Graph the circle $x^2 + y^2 = 8$ using a solid line.
The center is $(0,0)$ and the radius is $r = 2\sqrt{2}$

Choose the test point $(0,0)$.

$$x^2 + y^2 \ge 8$$
$$(0)^2 + (0)^2 \ge 8$$
$$0 \ge 8$$

False: Use arrows to show the shaded region that does not contain the origin.
$x + 3y > 2$

Graph the line $y = -\dfrac{1}{3}x + \dfrac{2}{3}$ using a dashed line.

The slope is $m = -\dfrac{1}{3}$ and the y-intercept is $\left(0,\dfrac{2}{3}\right)$.

Choose the test point $(0,0)$.

$$x + 3y > 2$$
$$(0) + 3(0) > 2$$
$$0 > 2$$

False: Use arrows to show the shaded region that does not contain the origin.
Finally, shade the region where the individual shaded regions overlap.

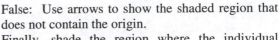

67. a)

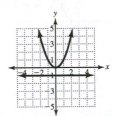

b)

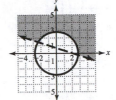
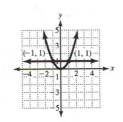

c)

69. a)

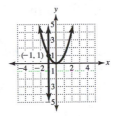

b)

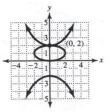
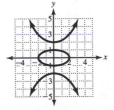

c)

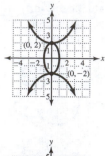

d)

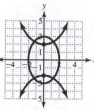

71. Let x and y represent the two numbers. The equations are $x^2 + y^2 = 100$ and $2x - 13 = y - 9$. We must solve the system:

$$\begin{cases} x^2 + y^2 = 100 \\ 2x - 13 = y - 9 \end{cases}$$

Rewrite equation 2 to obtain $y = 2x - 4$ and substitute this into equation 1 to solve for x.

$$x^2 + y^2 = 100$$
$$x^2 + (2x - 4)^2 = 100$$
$$x^2 + 4x^2 - 16x + 16 = 100$$
$$5x^2 - 16x - 84 = 0$$
$$(x - 6)(5x + 14) = 0$$
$$x - 6 = 0 \quad \text{or} \quad 5x + 14 = 0$$
$$x = 6 \quad \text{or} \quad x = -\frac{14}{5}$$

Solve for y

$$y = 2(6) - 4 \quad\bigg|\quad y = 2\left(-\frac{14}{5}\right) - 4$$
$$y = 8 \quad\bigg|\quad y = -\frac{48}{5}$$

Because the negative solutions do not satisfy the second condition of the problem, the two numbers are 6 and 8.

73. Let x and y represent the two numbers. The equations are $x^2 + y^2 = 13$ and $2x^2 + 3x^2 = 30$. We must solve the system:

$$\begin{cases} x^2 + y^2 = 13 \\ 2x^2 + 3y^2 = 30 \end{cases}$$

Eliminate y by adding -3 times Equation 1 and Equation 2.

$$\begin{array}{ll} -3(\text{Equation 1}) & \begin{cases} -3x^2 - 3y^2 = -39 \\ \text{Equation 2} \quad 2x^2 + 3y^2 = 30 \end{cases} \\ \hline & \quad\quad\quad -x^2 = -9 \\ & \quad\quad\quad\quad x^2 = 9 \\ & \quad\quad\quad\quad x = \pm 3 \end{array}$$

Substitute $x = \pm 3$ into Equation 1 and solve for y.

$$x^2 + y^2 = 13$$
$$(\pm 3)^2 + y^2 = 13$$
$$9 + y^2 = 13$$
$$y^2 = 4$$
$$y = \pm 2$$

Solution Set

$$\{(3, 2), (-3, 2), (3, -2), (-3, -2)\}$$

75. $y = -3$ is a horizontal line with y-intercept $(0, -3)$. Rewrite $x^2 + y + 3 = 0$ as $y = -x^2 - 3$. This is a parabola with vertex $(0, -3)$ and open down. There are no x-intercepts and the y-intercept is $(0, -3)$. $x^2 + y^2 = 9$ is a circle with center $(0, 0)$ and radius $r = 3$.

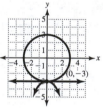

The solution set is $\{(0, -3)\}$.

77. $x > y$

Graph the line $y = x$ using a dashed line. The slope is $m = 1$ and the y-intercept is $(0, 0)$. Choose the test point $(0, 1)$.

$$x > y$$
$$0 > 1$$

False: Use arrows to show the shaded region that does not contain the point $(0, 1)$.

$$x^2 - 6x - y + 10 \leq 0$$

Graph the parabola $y = x^2 - 6x + 10$ using a solid line. The equation is quadratic in x and $a = 1 > 0$, which implies the graph opens up. The vertex is $(3, 1)$. There are no x-intercepts and the y-intercept is $(0, 10)$. Choose the test point $(0, 0)$.

$$x^2 - 6x - y + 10 \le 0$$

$$(0)^2 - 6(0) - (0) + 10 \le 0$$

$$10 \le 0$$

False: Use arrows to show the shaded region that does not contain the origin.

$$x^2 + y^2 - 25 < 0$$

Graph the circle $x^2 + y^2 = 25$ using a dashed line.

The center is $(0,0)$ and the radius is $r = 5$.

Choose the test point $(0,0)$.

$$x^2 + y^2 - 25 < 0$$

$$(0)^2 + (0)^2 - 25 < 0$$

$$-25 < 0$$

True: Use arrows to show the shaded region that contains the origin.

Finally, shade the region where the individual shaded regions overlap.

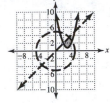

Chapter 11 Review Problem Set

1. $a = 1, b = 0, c = -4$

a) The equation is quadratic in x and $a = 1 > 0$; therefore, the parabola will open up.

b) The axis of symmetry is:

$$x = \frac{-b}{2a}$$

$$x = \frac{-(0)}{2(1)}$$

$$x = 0$$

c) Find the y-coordinate of the vertex by substituting $x = 0$ into the original equation.

$$y = x^2 - 4$$

$$y = (0)^2 - 4$$

$$y = -4$$

The vertex is $(0, -4)$.

d) There are two x-intercepts because the vertex lies below the x-axis and the parabola opens up. To find the x-intercepts, set $y = 0$ and solve for x.

$$0 = x^2 - 4$$

$$0 = (x + 2)(x - 2)$$

$$x + 2 = 0 \quad \text{or} \quad x - 2 = 0$$

$$x = -2 \quad \text{or} \quad x = 2$$

The x-intercepts are $(-2, 0)$ and $(2, 0)$.

e) The y-intercept is $(0, c) = (0, -4)$.

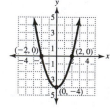

2. $a = 1, b = 0, c = -1$

a) The equation is quadratic in x and $a = 1 > 0$; therefore, the parabola will open up.

b) The axis of symmetry is:

$$x = \frac{-b}{2a}$$

$$x = \frac{-(0)}{2(1)}$$

$$x = 0$$

c) Find the y-coordinate of the vertex by substituting $x = 0$ into the original equation.

$$y = x^2 - 1$$

$$y = (0)^2 - 1$$

$$y = -1$$

The vertex is $(0, -1)$.

d) There are two x-intercepts because the vertex lies below the x-axis and the parabola opens up. To find the x-intercepts, set $y = 0$ and solve for x.

$$0 = x^2 - 1$$

$$0 = (x + 1)(x - 1)$$

$$x + 1 = 0 \quad \text{or} \quad x - 1 = 0$$

$$x = -1 \quad \text{or} \quad x = 1$$

The x-intercepts are $(-1, 0)$ and $(1, 0)$.

e) The y-intercept is $(0, c) = (0, -1)$.

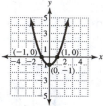

3. $a = -2, b = 8, c = 0$

a) The equation is quadratic in x and $a = -2 < 0$; therefore, the parabola will open down.

b) The axis of symmetry is:

$$x = \frac{-b}{2a}$$

$$x = \frac{-(8)}{2(-2)}$$

$$x = 2$$

c) Find the y-coordinate of the vertex by substituting $x = 2$ into the original equation.

$$y = -2x^2 + 8x$$

$$y = -2(2)^2 + 8(2)$$

$$y = 8$$

The vertex is $(2, 8)$.

d) There are two x-intercepts because the vertex lies above the x-axis and the parabola opens down. To find the x-intercepts, set $y = 0$ and solve for x.

$$0 = -2x^2 + 8x$$

$$0 = -2x(x - 4)$$

$$-2x = 0 \quad \text{or} \quad x - 4 = 0$$

$$x = 0 \quad \text{or} \quad x = 4$$

The x-intercepts are $(0, 0)$ and $(4, 0)$.

e) The y-intercept is $(0, c) = (0, 0)$.

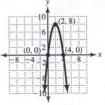

4. $a = -3, b = 6, c = 0$

a) The equation is quadratic in x and $a = -3 < 0$; therefore, the parabola will open down.

b) The axis of symmetry is:

$$x = \frac{-b}{2a}$$

$$x = \frac{-(6)}{2(-3)}$$

$$x = 1$$

c) Find the y-coordinate of the vertex by substituting $x = 1$ into the original equation.

$$y = -3x^2 + 6x$$

$$y = -3(1)^2 + 6(1)$$

$$y = 3$$

The vertex is $(1,3)$.

d) There are two x-intercepts because the vertex lies above the x-axis and the parabola opens down. To find the x-intercepts, set $y = 0$ and solve for x.

$$0 = -3x^2 + 6x$$

$$0 = -3x(x-2)$$

$$-3x = 0 \quad \text{or} \quad x - 2 = 0$$

$$x = 0 \quad \text{or} \quad x = 2$$

The x-intercepts are $(0,0)$ and $(2,0)$.

e) The y-intercept is $(0,c) = (0,0)$.

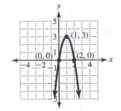

5. $a = 2, b = 0, c = 0$

a) The equation is quadratic in y and $a = 2 > 0$; therefore, the parabola will open right.

b) The axis of symmetry is:

$$y = \frac{-b}{2a}$$

$$y = \frac{-(0)}{2(2)}$$

$$y = 0$$

c) Find the x-coordinate of the vertex by substituting $y = 0$ into the original equation.

$$x = 2y^2$$

$$x = 2(0)^2$$

$$x = 0$$

The vertex is $(0,0)$.

d) The x-intercept is $(c,0) = (0,0)$.

e) There is only one y-intercept because the vertex is located at the origin. The y-intercept is $(0,0)$.

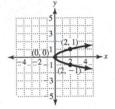

6. $a = \frac{1}{3}, b = 0, c = 0$

a) The equation is quadratic in y and $a = \frac{1}{3} > 0$; therefore, the parabola will open right.

b) The axis of symmetry is:

$$y = \frac{-b}{2a}$$

$$y = \frac{-(0)}{2\left(\dfrac{1}{3}\right)}$$

$$y = 0$$

c) Find the x-coordinate of the vertex by substituting $y = 0$ into the original equation.

$$x = \frac{1}{3}y^2$$

$$x = \frac{1}{3}(0)^2$$

$$x = 0$$

The vertex is $(0,0)$.

d) The x-intercept is $(c,0) = (0,0)$.

e) There is only one y-intercept because the vertex is located at the origin. The y-intercept is $(0,0)$.

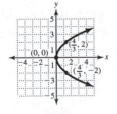

7. $a = -1, b = 4, c = -4$

a) The equation is quadratic in y and $a = -1 < 0$; therefore, the parabola will open left.

b) The axis of symmetry is:

$$y = \frac{-b}{2a}$$

$$y = \frac{-(4)}{2(-1)}$$

$$y = 2$$

c) Find the x-coordinate of the vertex by substituting $y = 2$ into the original equation.

$$x = -y^2 + 4y - 4$$

$$x = -(2)^2 + 4(2) - 4$$

$$x = 0$$

The vertex is $(0, 2)$.

d) The x-intercept is $(c, 0) = (-4, 0)$.

e) There is only one y-intercept because the vertex is located on the x-axis. The y-intercept is $(0, 2)$.

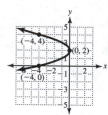

8. $a = -1$, $b = 2$, $c = -1$

a) The equation is quadratic in y and $a = -1 < 0$; therefore, the parabola will open left.

b) The axis of symmetry is:

$$y = \frac{-b}{2a}$$

$$y = \frac{-(2)}{2(-1)}$$

$$y = 1$$

c) Find the x-coordinate of the vertex by substituting $y = 1$ into the original equation.

$$x = -y^2 + 2y - 1$$

$$x = -(1)^2 + 2(1) - 1$$

$$x = 0$$

The vertex is $(0, 1)$.

d) The x-intercept is $(c, 0) = (-1, 0)$.

e) There is only one y-intercept because the vertex is located on the x-axis. The y-intercept is $(0, 1)$.

9. $a = 1$, $h = 4$, $k = -2$

The equation is quadratic in x and $a = 1 > 0$; therefore, the parabola opens up. The vertex is $(h, k) = (4, -2)$. The axis of symmetry is $x = h$. That is, $x = 4$. The x-intercepts will not have integer coordinates, so we will not use them to graph the function. To find the y-intercept, set $x = 0$ and solve for y.

$$y = (x - 4)^2 - 2$$

$$y = (0 - 4)^2 - 2$$

$$y = (-4)^2 - 2$$

$$y = 14$$

The y-intercept is $(0, 14)$. We can use symmetry to find a third point, $(8, 14)$.

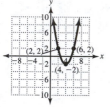

10. $a = 1$, $h = 2$, $k = -4$

The equation is quadratic in x and $a = 1 > 0$; therefore, the parabola opens up. The vertex is $(h, k) = (2, -4)$. The axis of symmetry is $x = h$. That is, $x = 2$. To find the x-intercepts, set $y = 0$ and solve for x.

$$0 = (x - 2)^2 - 4$$

$$4 = (x - 2)^2$$

$$x - 2 = -2 \quad \text{or} \quad x - 2 = 2$$

$$x = 0 \quad \text{or} \quad x = 4$$

The x-intercepts are $(0, 0)$ and $(4, 0)$.

To find the y-intercept, set $x = 0$ and solve for y.

$$y = (x - 2)^2 - 4$$

$$y = (0 - 2)^2 - 4$$

$$y = (-2)^2 - 4$$

$$y = 0$$

The y-intercept is $(0, 0)$.

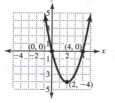

11. $a = -1, h = 4, k = -1$

The equation is quadratic in y and $a = -1 < 0$; therefore, the parabola opens left. The vertex is $(h,k) = (4,-1)$. The axis of symmetry is $y = k$. That is, $y = -1$. To find the y-intercepts, set $x = 0$ and solve for y.

$$x = -(y+1)^2 + 4$$
$$0 = -(y+1)^2 + 4$$
$$4 = (y+1)^2$$
$$y+1 = -2 \quad \text{or} \quad y+1 = 2$$
$$y = -3 \quad \text{or} \quad y = 1$$

The y-intercepts are $(0,-3)$ and $(0,1)$. To find the x-intercept, set $y = 0$ and solve for x.

$$x = -(y+1)^2 + 4$$
$$x = -(0+1)^2 + 4$$
$$x = -(1)^2 + 4$$
$$x = 3$$

The x-intercept is $(3,0)$.

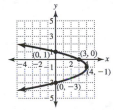

12. $a = -1, h = 2, k = -1$

The equation is quadratic in y and $a = -1 < 0$; therefore, the parabola opens left. The vertex is $(h,k) = (2,-1)$. The axis of symmetry is $y = k$. That is, $y = -1$. The y-intercepts will not have integer coordinates, so we will not use them to graph the function. To find the x-intercept, set $y = 0$ and solve for x.

$$x = -(y+1)^2 + 2$$
$$x = -(0+1)^2 + 2$$
$$x = -(1)^2 + 2$$
$$x = 1$$

The x-intercept is $(1,0)$. We can use symmetry to find a third point, $(1,-2)$.

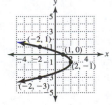

13.
$$y = x^2 - 6x + 2$$
$$y - 2 = x^2 - 6x$$
$$y - 2 + 9 = x^2 - 6x + 9$$
$$y + 7 = (x-3)^2$$
$$y = (x-3)^2 - 7$$
$$a = 1, h = 3, k = -7$$

a) The vertex is $(h,k) = (3,-7)$.

b) The axis of symmetry is $x = h$, that is $x = 3$.

c) Because $a = 1 > 0$, and the axis of symmetry is vertical, the graph opens up.

14.
$$y = -x^2 + 8x - 12$$
$$y + 12 = -x^2 + 8x$$
$$y + 12 = -(x^2 - 8x)$$
$$y + 12 - 16 = -(x^2 - 8x + 16)$$
$$y - 4 = -(x-4)^2$$
$$y = -(x-4)^2 + 4$$
$$a = -1, h = 4, k = 4$$

a) The vertex is $(h,k) = (4,4)$.

b) The axis of symmetry is $x = h$, that is $x = 4$.

c) Because $a = -1 < 0$, and the axis of symmetry is vertical, the graph opens down.

15.
$$y = 3x^2 - 6x + 8$$
$$y - 8 = 3x^2 - 6x$$
$$y - 8 = 3(x^2 - 2x)$$
$$y - 8 + 3 = 3(x^2 - 2x + 1)$$
$$y - 5 = 3(x-1)^2$$
$$y = 3(x-1)^2 + 5$$
$$a = 3, h = 1, k = 5$$

a) The vertex is $(h,k) = (1,5)$.

b) The axis of symmetry is $x = h$, that is $x = 1$.

c) Because $a = 3 > 0$, and the axis of symmetry is vertical, the graph opens up.

16.
$$x = y^2 - 4y + 1$$
$$x - 1 = y^2 - 4y$$
$$x - 1 + 4 = y^2 - 4y + 4$$
$$x + 3 = (y-2)^2$$
$$x = (y-2)^2 - 3$$
$$a = 1, h = -3, k = 2$$

a) The vertex is $(h,k)=(-3,2)$.

b) The axis of symmetry is $y=k$, that is $y=2$.

c) Because $a=1>0$, and the axis of symmetry is horizontal, the graph opens right.

17.
$$x=2y^2-4y+5$$
$$x-5=2y^2-4y$$
$$x-5=2(y^2-2y)$$
$$x-5+2=2(y^2-2y+1)$$
$$x-3=2(y-1)^2$$
$$x=2(y-1)^2+3$$
$$a=2,\ h=3,\ k=1$$

a) The vertex is $(h,k)=(3,1)$.

b) The axis of symmetry is $y=k$, that is $y=1$.

c) Because $a=2>0$, and the axis of symmetry is horizontal, the graph opens right.

18.
$$x=-3y^2-9y+4$$
$$x-4=-3y^2-9y$$
$$x-4=-3(y^2+3y)$$
$$x-4-\frac{27}{4}=-3\left(y^2+3y+\frac{9}{4}\right)$$
$$x-\frac{43}{4}=-3\left(y+\frac{3}{2}\right)^2$$
$$x=-3\left(y+\frac{3}{2}\right)^2+\frac{43}{4}$$
$$a=-3,\ h=\tfrac{43}{4},\ k=-\tfrac{3}{2}$$

a) The vertex is $(h,k)=\left(\frac{43}{4},-\frac{3}{2}\right)$.

b) The axis of symmetry is $y=k$, that is $y=-\frac{3}{2}$.

c) Because $a=-3<0$, and the axis of symmetry is horizontal, the graph opens left.

19. To find the maximum height of the rabbit's hop, we must find the y-coordinate of the vertex. To do this, we must first find the x-coordinate of the vertex.

Solve the equation for y.
$$3x^2-48x+16y=0$$
$$16y=-3x^2+48x$$
$$\frac{16y}{16}=\frac{-3x^2}{16}+\frac{48x}{16}$$
$$y=-\frac{3}{16}x^2+3x$$

Identify a, b, and c.
$$a=-\tfrac{3}{16},\ b=3,\ c=0$$

Determine the x-coordinate of the vertex.
$$x=\frac{-b}{2a}$$
$$=\frac{-(3)}{2\left(-\frac{3}{16}\right)}$$
$$=\frac{3}{\frac{3}{8}}$$
$$=3\cdot\frac{8}{3}$$
$$=8$$

Determine the y-coordinate of the vertex by substituting $x=8$ into the original equation and solve for y.
$$3x^2-48x+16y=0$$
$$3(8)^2-48(8)+16y=0$$
$$3(64)-384+16y=0$$
$$192-384+16y=0$$
$$16y=192$$
$$y=12$$

The maximum height of the jack rabbit's hop is 12 feet.

20. The vertex of the mirror is $(h,k)=(0,3)$. Therefore, we can write:
$$y=a(x-h)^2+k$$
$$y=a(x-0)^2+3$$
$$y=ax^2+3$$

To find a, we can use either of the x-intercepts, $(-1,0)$ or $(1,0)$.
$$y=ax^2+3$$
$$0=a(1)^2+3$$
$$0=a+3$$
$$a=-3$$

The equation is $y=-3x^2+3$.

21.
$$x^2+y^2=1$$
$$(x-0)^2+(y-0)^2=(1)^2$$
$$h=0,\ k=0,\ r=1$$

The center is $(h,k)=(0,0)$.

Plot points 1 unit up, down, left, and right, from the center, and connect them.

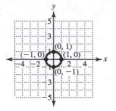

22. $x^2 + (y+2)^2 = 9$

$(x-0)^2 + (y-(-2))^2 = (3)^2$

$h = 0, k = -2, r = 3$

The center is $(h,k) = (0,-2)$.

Plot points 3 units up, down, left, and right, from the center, and connect them.

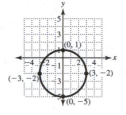

23. $(x-3)^2 + (y-1)^2 = 4$

$(x-3)^2 + (y-1)^2 = (2)^2$

$h = 3, k = 1, r = 2$

The center is $(h,k) = (3,1)$.

Plot points 2 units up, down, left, and right, from the center, and connect them.

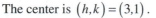
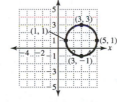

24. $(x+3)^2 + (y-4)^2 = 25$

$(x-(-3))^2 + (y-4)^2 = (5)^2$

$h = -3, k = 4, r = 5$

The center is $(h,k) = (-3,4)$.

Plot points 5 units up, down, left, and right, from the center, and connect them.

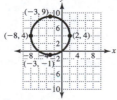

25. $h = -7, k = 3, r = 8$

$$(x-h)^2 + (y-k)^2 = r^2$$

$$(x-(-7))^2 + (y-(3))^2 = (8)^2$$

$$(x+7)^2 + (y-3)^2 = 64$$

26. $h = 4, k = 8, r = 10$

$$(x-h)^2 + (y-k)^2 = r^2$$

$$(x-(4))^2 + (y-(8))^2 = (10)^2$$

$$(x-4)^2 + (y-8)^2 = 100$$

27.

$$x^2 + y^2 + 6x + 8y - 11 = 0$$

$$(x^2 + 6x) + (y^2 + 8y) = 11$$

$$(x^2 + 6x + 9) + (y^2 + 8y + 16) = 11 + 9 + 16$$

$$(x+3)^2 + (y+4)^2 = 36$$

28.

$$x^2 + y^2 + 4x + 12y - 9 = 0$$

$$(x^2 + 4x) + (y^2 + 12y) = 9$$

$$(x^2 + 4x + 4) + (y^2 + 12y + 36) = 9 + 4 + 36$$

$$(x+2)^2 + (y+6)^2 = 49$$

29.

$$x^2 + y^2 - 8x + 10y + 40 = 0$$

$$(x^2 - 8x) + (y^2 + 10y) = -40$$

$$(x^2 - 8x + 16) + (y^2 + 10y + 25) = -40 + 16 + 25$$

$$(x-4)^2 + (y+5)^2 = 1$$

30.

$$x^2 + y^2 - 8x + 4y + 15 = 0$$

$$(x^2 - 8x) + (y^2 + 4y) = -15$$

$$(x^2 - 8x + 16) + (y^2 + 4y + 4) = -15 + 16 + 4$$

$$(x-4)^2 + (y+2)^2 = 5$$

31. The center is $(0,0)$.

$a^2 = 25 \Rightarrow a = 5$

$b^2 = 9 \Rightarrow b = 3$

x-intercepts: $(-a,0) = (-5,0)$ and $(a,0) = (5,0)$

y-intercepts: $(0,-b) = (0,-3)$ and $(0,b) = (0,3)$

Plot the four intercepts and connect with a smooth oval-shaped curve.

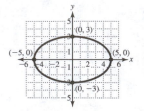

32. The center is $(0,0)$.

$a^2 = 4 \Rightarrow a = 2$
$b^2 = 25 \Rightarrow b = 5$

x-intercepts: $(-a,0) = (-2,0)$ and $(a,0) = (2,0)$

y-intercepts: $(0,-b) = (0,-5)$ and $(0,b) = (0,5)$

Plot the four intercepts and connect with a smooth oval-shaped curve.

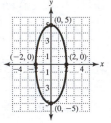

33. $4x^2 + y^2 = 16$

$$\frac{4x^2}{16} + \frac{y^2}{16} = \frac{16}{16}$$

$$\frac{x^2}{4} + \frac{y^2}{16} = 1$$

The center is $(0,0)$.

$a^2 = 4 \Rightarrow a = 2$
$b^2 = 16 \Rightarrow b = 4$

x-intercepts: $(-a,0) = (-2,0)$ and $(a,0) = (2,0)$

y-intercepts: $(0,-b) = (0,-4)$ and $(0,b) = (0,4)$

Plot the four intercepts and connect with a smooth oval-shaped curve.

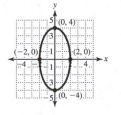

34. $16x^2 + y^2 = 64$

$$\frac{16x^2}{64} + \frac{y^2}{64} = \frac{64}{64}$$

$$\frac{x^2}{4} + \frac{y^2}{64} = 1$$

The center is $(0,0)$.

$a^2 = 4 \Rightarrow a = 2$

$b^2 = 64 \Rightarrow b = 8$

x-intercepts: $(-a,0) = (-2,0)$ and $(a,0) = (2,0)$

y-intercepts: $(0,-b) = (0,-8)$ and $(0,b) = (0,8)$

Plot the four intercepts and connect with a smooth oval-shaped curve.

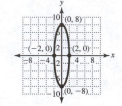

35. The center is $(h,k) = (2,3)$.

$a^2 = 49 \Rightarrow a = 7$
$b^2 = 36 \Rightarrow b = 6$

To find the endpoints of the vertical axis, move up and down 6 units from the center. To find the endpoints of the horizontal axis, move left and right 7 units from the center.

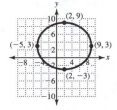

36. The center is $(h,k) = (1,2)$.

$a^2 = 36 \Rightarrow a = 6$
$b^2 = 9 \Rightarrow b = 3$

To find the endpoints of the vertical axis, move up and down 3 units from the center. To find the endpoints of the horizontal axis, move left and right 6 units from the center.

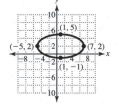

37. The center is $(h,k) = (-2,-4)$.

$a^2 = 36 \Rightarrow a = 6$
$b^2 = 4 \Rightarrow b = 2$

To find the endpoints of the vertical axis, move up and down 2 unit from the center. To find the endpoints of the horizontal axis, move left and right 6 units from the center.

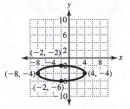

38. The center is $(h,k)=(1,2)$.

$a^2 = 9 \Rightarrow a = 3$

$b^2 = 49 \Rightarrow b = 7$

To find the endpoints of the vertical axis, move up and down 7 units from the center. To find the endpoints of the horizontal axis, move left and right 3 units from the center.

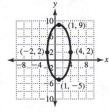

39. $a = 6, b = 3, (h,k)=(0,0)$

$$\frac{x^2}{a^2} + \frac{y^2}{b^2} = 1$$

$$\frac{x^2}{(6)^2} + \frac{y^2}{(3)^2} = 1$$

$$\frac{x^2}{36} + \frac{y^2}{9} = 1$$

40. $a = 1, b = 4, (h,k)=(0,0)$

$$\frac{x^2}{a^2} + \frac{y^2}{b^2} = 1$$

$$\frac{x^2}{(1)^2} + \frac{y^2}{(4)^2} = 1$$

$$\frac{x^2}{1} + \frac{y^2}{16} = 1$$

41. $a = 1, b = 3, (h,k)=(-2,6)$

$$\frac{(x-h)^2}{a^2} + \frac{(y-k)^2}{b^2} = 1$$

$$\frac{(x-(-2))^2}{(1)^2} + \frac{(y-(6))^2}{(3)^2} = 1$$

$$\frac{(x+2)^2}{1} + \frac{(y-6)^2}{9} = 1$$

42. $a = 5, b = 2, (h,k)=(4,-2)$

$$\frac{(x-h)^2}{a^2} + \frac{(y-k)^2}{b^2} = 1$$

$$\frac{(x-(4))^2}{(5)^2} + \frac{(y-(-2))^2}{(2)^2} = 1$$

$$\frac{(x-4)^2}{25} + \frac{(y+2)^2}{4} = 1$$

43. $h = 2, k = 4, r = 2\sqrt{5}$

$$(x-h)^2 + (y-k)^2 = r^2$$

$$(x-(2))^2 + (y-(4))^2 = (2\sqrt{5})^2$$

$$(x-2)^2 + (y-4)^2 = 20$$

44. $h = 2, k = 6, r = 2\sqrt{10}$

$$(x-h)^2 + (y-k)^2 = r^2$$

$$(x-(2))^2 + (y-(6))^2 = (2\sqrt{10})^2$$

$$(x-2)^2 + (y-6)^2 = 40$$

45. $a^2 = 9 \Rightarrow a = 3$

$b^2 = 16 \Rightarrow b = 4$

The vertices are $(0,-4)$ and $(0,4)$. The additional points are $(-3,0)$ and $(3,0)$.

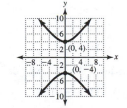

46. $a^2 = 4 \Rightarrow a = 2$

$b^2 = 25 \Rightarrow b = 5$

The vertices are $(-2,0)$ and $(2,0)$. The additional points are $(0,-5)$ and $(0,5)$.

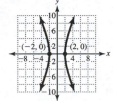

47. $a^2 = 9 \Rightarrow a = 3$

$b^2 = 25 \Rightarrow b = 5$

The vertices are $(0, -5)$ and $(0, 5)$. The additional points are $(-3, 0)$ and $(3, 0)$.

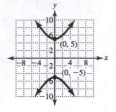

48. $a^2 = 4 \Rightarrow a = 2$

$b^2 = 16 \Rightarrow b = 4$

The vertices are $(0, -4)$ and $(0, 4)$. The additional points are $(-2, 0)$ and $(2, 0)$.

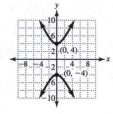

49. $9x^2 - 4y^2 = 36$

$\dfrac{9x^2}{36} - \dfrac{4y^2}{36} = \dfrac{36}{36}$

$\dfrac{x^2}{4} - \dfrac{y^2}{9} = 1$

$a^2 = 4 \Rightarrow a = 2$

$b^2 = 9 \Rightarrow b = 3$

The vertices are $(-2, 0)$ and $(2, 0)$. The additional points are $(0, -3)$ and $(0, 3)$.

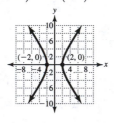

50. $4x^2 - 9y^2 = 36$

$\dfrac{4x^2}{36} - \dfrac{9y^2}{36} = \dfrac{36}{36}$

$\dfrac{x^2}{9} - \dfrac{y^2}{4} = 1$

$a^2 = 9 \Rightarrow a = 3$

$b^2 = 4 \Rightarrow b = 2$

The vertices are $(-3, 0)$ and $(3, 0)$. The additional points are $(0, -2)$ and $(0, 2)$.

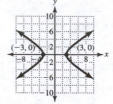

51. Center: $(0, 0)$

$a = 5 \Rightarrow a^2 = 25$

$b = 8 \Rightarrow b^2 = 64$

$\dfrac{x^2}{a^2} - \dfrac{y^2}{b^2} = 1$

$\dfrac{x^2}{25} - \dfrac{y^2}{64} = 1$

52. Center: $(-5, 4)$

$a = 3 \Rightarrow a^2 = 9$

$b = \sqrt{7} \Rightarrow b^2 = 7$

$\dfrac{(x-k)^2}{b^2} - \dfrac{(y-h)^2}{a^2} = 1$

$\dfrac{(x+5)^2}{9} - \dfrac{(y-4)^2}{7} = 1$

53. There are two squared terms and their coefficients have opposite signs, therefore, this equation represents a hyperbola.

54. There are two squared terms and their coefficients equal, therefore, this equation represents a circle.

55. There are two squared terms and their coefficients have the same signs but are not equal, therefore, this equation represents an ellipse.

56. There are no squared terms, therefore, this equation represents a straight line.

57. There is one squared term, therefore, this equation represents a parabola.

58. There are two squared terms and their coefficients equal, therefore, this equation represents a circle.

59. There is one squared term, therefore, this equation represents a parabola.

60. There are two squared terms and their coefficients have opposite signs, therefore, this equation represents a hyperbola.

61. $x^2 + y^2 = 16$ is a circle with center $(0,0)$ and radius $r = 4$. $y - x = -4$ is a line with slope-intercept form $y = x - 4$. The slope is $m = 1$ and the y-intercept is $(0,-4)$.

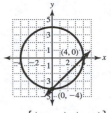

The solution set is $\{(0,-4),(4,0)\}$.

62. $y = x^2 - 2$ is a parabola with vertex $(0,-2)$ and open up. $2x - y = -1$ is a line with slope-intercept form $y = 2x + 1$. The slope is $m = 2$ and the y-intercept is $(0,1)$.

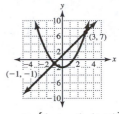

The solution set is $\{(-1,-1),(3,7)\}$.

63. $\dfrac{x^2}{4} + \dfrac{y^2}{9} = 1$ is an ellipse with center $(0,0)$, x-intercepts $(-2,0)$ and $(2,0)$, and y-intercepts $(0,-3)$ and $(0,3)$. $\dfrac{y^2}{9} - \dfrac{x^2}{16} = 1$ is a hyperbola with center $(0,0)$. The vertices are $(0,-3)$ and $(0,3)$. The additional points are $(-4,0)$ and $(4,0)$.

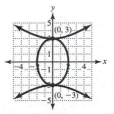

The solution set is $\{(0,-3),(0,3)\}$.

64. $x^2 + y^2 = 3$ is a circle with center $(0,0)$ and radius $r = \sqrt{3}$. Rewrite the second equation as $\dfrac{x^2}{9} - \dfrac{y^2}{12} = 1$. It is a hyperbola with center $(0,0)$. The vertices are $(-3,0)$ and $(3,0)$. The additional points are $\left(0,-2\sqrt{3}\right)$ and $\left(0,2\sqrt{3}\right)$.

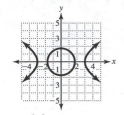

The solution set is $\{\ \}$.

65. Substitute $y = x^2 - 3$ into equation 1 and solve for x.

$$x^2 + y^2 = 9$$
$$x^2 + \left(x^2 - 3\right)^2 = 9$$
$$x^2 + x^4 - 6x^2 + 9 = 9$$
$$x^4 - 5x^2 = 0$$
$$x^2\left(x^2 - 5\right) = 0$$
$$x^2 = 0 \quad \text{or} \quad x^2 - 5 = 0$$
$$x = 0 \quad \text{or} \quad x = \pm\sqrt{5}$$

$$\underline{\text{Solve for } y}$$
$$y = (0)^2 - 3 \quad \Big| \quad y = \left(\pm\sqrt{5}\right)^2 - 3$$
$$y = -3 \quad \Big| \quad y = 2$$

$$\underline{\text{Solution Set}}$$
$$\left\{(0,-3),\left(-\sqrt{5},2\right),\left(\sqrt{5},2\right)\right\}$$

66. Eliminate y by adding -4 times Equation 1 and Equation 2.

$$\begin{array}{r} -4(\text{Equation 1}) \\ \text{Equation 2} \end{array} \left\{ \begin{array}{r} -4x^2 - 4y^2 = -16 \\ x^2 + 4y^2 = 16 \end{array} \right.$$
$$-3x^2 = 0$$
$$x^2 = 0$$
$$x = 0$$

Substitute $x = 0$ into Equation 1 and solve for y.
$$x^2 + y^2 = 4$$
$$(0)^2 + y^2 = 4$$
$$y^2 = 4$$
$$y = \pm 2$$

Solution Set

$$\left\{(0,-2),(0,2)\right\}$$

67. Substitute $y = 3$ into equation 2 and solve for x.

$$y = -\frac{1}{2}x^2 - 2x$$

$$(3) = -\frac{1}{2}x^2 - 2x$$

$$\frac{1}{2}x^2 + 2x + 3 = 0$$

$$\frac{1}{2}x^2 + 2x = -3$$

$$2\left(\frac{1}{2}x^2 + 2x\right) = 2(-3)$$

$$x^2 + 4x = -6$$

$$x^2 + 4x + 4 = -6 + 4$$

$$(x+2)^2 = -2$$

$$x + 2 = -\sqrt{-2} \quad \text{or} \quad x + 2 = \sqrt{-2}$$

$$x + 2 = -i\sqrt{2} \quad \text{or} \quad x + 2 = i\sqrt{2}$$

$$x = -2 - i\sqrt{2} \quad \text{or} \quad x = -2 + i\sqrt{2}$$

The solution set is $\{\ \}$.

68. Eliminate y by adding Equation 1 and Equation 2.

Equation 1 $\quad \begin{cases} 3x^2 - y^2 = 15 \\ -2x^2 + y^2 = -7 \end{cases}$
Equation 2

$$x^2 = 8$$

$$x = \pm 2\sqrt{2}$$

Substitute $x = \pm\sqrt{2}$ into Equation 1 and solve for y.

$$3x^2 - y^2 = 15$$

$$3\left(\pm 2\sqrt{2}\right)^2 - y^2 = 15$$

$$24 - y^2 = 15$$

$$y^2 = 9$$

$$y = \pm 3$$

Solution Set

$$\left\{\left(-2\sqrt{2}, -3\right), \left(-2\sqrt{2}, 3\right), \left(2\sqrt{2}, -3\right), \left(2\sqrt{2}, 3\right)\right\}$$

69. Substitute $x = -y^2 + 1$ into equation 2 and solve for y.

$$x = y^2 + 1$$

$$\left(-y^2 + 3\right) = y^2 + 1$$

$$-2y^2 = -2$$

$$y^2 = 1$$

$$y = \pm 1$$

Solve for x

$$x = (\pm 1)^2 + 1$$

$$x = 2$$

Solution Set

$$\left\{(2,-1),(2,1)\right\}$$

70. Substitute $y = 2x - 1$ into equation 1 and solve for x.

$$3x^2 + y^2 = 4$$

$$3x^2 + (2x - 1)^2 = 4$$

$$3x^2 + 4x^2 - 4x + 1 = 4$$

$$7x^2 - 4x - 3 = 0$$

$$(7x + 3)(x - 1) = 0$$

$$7x + 3 = 0 \quad \text{or} \quad x - 1 = 0$$

$$x = -\frac{3}{7} \quad \text{or} \quad x = 1$$

Solve for y

$$y = 2\left(-\frac{3}{7}\right) - 1 \quad \bigg| \quad y = 2(1) - 1$$

$$y = -\frac{13}{7} \quad \bigg| \quad y = 1$$

Solution Set

$$\left\{(1,1),\left(-\frac{3}{7},-\frac{13}{7}\right)\right\}$$

71. Rewrite the inequality to obtain the equation $\frac{x^2}{4} + \frac{y^2}{9} = 1$. Graph the ellipse using a dashed line because of the $<$ symbol. The center is $(0,0)$, the x-intercepts are $(-2,0)$ and $(2,0)$, and the y-intercepts are $(0,-3)$ and $(0,3)$. Choose the test point $(0,0)$.

$$\frac{x^2}{4} + \frac{y^2}{9} < 1$$

$$\frac{(0)^2}{4} + \frac{(0)^2}{9} < 1$$

$$0 < 1$$

True. Shade the region that contains the origin.

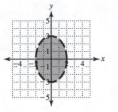

72. Graph the circle given by $x^2 + (y-2)^2 = 9$ using a dashed line because of the > symbol. The center is $(0,2)$ and the radius is $r = 3$. Choose the test point $(0,0)$.

$$x^2 + (y-2)^2 > 9$$
$$(0)^2 + ((0)-2)^2 > 9$$
$$4 > 9$$

False. Shade the region that does not contain the origin.

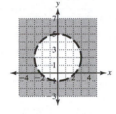

73. Graph the hyperbola given by $\dfrac{y^2}{25} - \dfrac{x^2}{9} = 1$ using a solid line because of the $\geq$ symbol. The center is $(0,0)$, the vertices are $(0,-5)$ and $(0,5)$, and the additional points are $(-3,0)$ and $(3,0)$. Choose the test point $(0,0)$.

$$\frac{y^2}{25} - \frac{x^2}{4} \geq 1$$
$$\frac{(0)^2}{25} - \frac{(0)^2}{4} \geq 1$$
$$0 \geq 1$$

False. Shade the region that does not contain the origin.

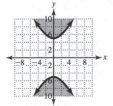

74. Graph the parabola given by $x = y^2 + 3$ using a solid line because of the $\leq$ symbol. The equation is quadratic in y, and $a = 1 > 0$, which implies the parabola opens right. The x-intercept is $(3,0)$. There are no y-intercepts. Choose the test point $(0,0)$.

$$x \leq y^2 + 3$$
$$(0) \leq (0)^2 + 3$$
$$0 \leq 3$$

True. Shade the region that contains the origin.

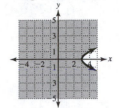

75. $y > x^2 + 4x - 2$

Graph the parabola $y = x^2 + 4x - 2$ using a dashed line. The equation is quadratic in x and $a = 1 > 0$, which implies the parabola opens up. The vertex is $(-2,-6)$ and the y-intercept is $(0,-2)$. The x-intercepts are not rational so we will not use them. Choose the test point $(0,0)$.

$$y > x^2 + 4x - 2$$
$$(0) > (0)^2 + 4(0) - 2$$
$$0 > -2$$

True: Use arrows to show the shaded region that contains the origin.

$$y < -\frac{3}{4}x - 3$$

Graph the line $y = -\frac{3}{4}x - 3$ using a dashed line. The slope is $m = -\frac{3}{4}$ and the y-intercept is $(0,-3)$. Choose the test point $(0,0)$.

$$y < -\frac{3}{4}x - 3$$
$$(0) < -\frac{3}{4}(0) - 3$$
$$0 < -3$$

False: Use arrows to show the shaded region that does not contain the origin.
Finally, shade the region where the individual shaded regions overlap.

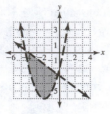

76. $4x^2 + y^2 \ge 16$

Graph the ellipse $\dfrac{x^2}{4} + \dfrac{y^2}{16} = 1$ using a solid line. The x-intercepts are $(-2,0)$ and $(2,0)$. The y-intercepts are $(0,-4)$ and $(0,4)$. Choose the test point $(0,0)$.

$$4x^2 + y^2 \ge 16$$
$$4(0)^2 + (0)^2 \ge 16$$
$$0 \ge 16$$

False: Use arrows to show the shaded region that does not contain the origin.

$9y^2 - 4x^2 < 36$

Graph the hyperbola $\dfrac{y^2}{4} - \dfrac{x^2}{9} < 1$ using a dashed line. The vertices are $(0,-2)$ and $(0,2)$. The additional points are $(-3,0)$ and $(0,3)$. Choose the test point $(0,0)$.

$$9y^2 - 4x^2 < 36$$
$$9(0)^2 - 4(0)^2 < 36$$
$$0 < 36$$

True: Use arrows to show the shaded region that contains the origin.

Finally, shade the region where the individual shaded regions overlap.

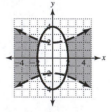

CHAPTER 11 TEST

1. e

2. g

3. f

4. i

5. h

6. c

7.
$$x^2 + y^2 + 10x - 6y + 16 = 0$$
$$\left(x^2 + 10x\right) + \left(y^2 - 6y\right) = -16$$
$$\left(x^2 + 10x + 25\right) + \left(y^2 - 6y + 9\right) = -16 + 25 + 9$$
$$(x+5)^2 + (y-3)^2 = 18$$
Center: $(-5, 3)$, Radius: $\sqrt{18} = 3\sqrt{2}$

8.
$$(x-h)^2 + (y-k)^2 = r^2$$
$$\left(x-(-1)\right)^2 + \left(y-(3)\right)^2 = \left(2\sqrt{3}\right)^2$$
$$(x+1)^2 + (y-3)^2 = 12$$
$$\left(x^2 + 2x + 1\right) + \left(y^2 - 6y + 9\right) = 12$$
$$x^2 + y^2 + 2x - 6y + 1 + 9 - 12 = 0$$
$$x^2 + y^2 + 2x - 6y - 2 = 0$$

9.
$$\frac{x^2}{a^2} + \frac{y^2}{b^2} = 1$$
$$\frac{x^2}{(3)^2} + \frac{y^2}{\left(2\sqrt{2}\right)^2} = 1$$
$$\frac{x^2}{9} + \frac{y^2}{8} = 1$$
$$72\left(\frac{x^2}{9} + \frac{y^2}{8}\right) = 72(1)$$
$$8x^2 + 9y^2 = 72$$
$$8x^2 + 9y^2 - 72 = 0$$

10.
$$\frac{y^2}{b^2} - \frac{x^2}{a^2} = 1$$
$$\frac{y^2}{(4)^2} - \frac{x^2}{(5)^2} = 1$$
$$\frac{y^2}{16} - \frac{x^2}{25} = 1$$
$$400\left(\frac{y^2}{16} - \frac{x^2}{25}\right) = 400(1)$$
$$25y^2 - 16x^2 = 400$$
$$-16x^2 + 25y^2 - 400 = 0$$

11. The equation $x^2 + y^2 = 2500$ is in standard form, therefore, $r^2 = 2500$ which implies $r = 50$. Let d represent the diameter of the rehearsal hall, then
$$d = 2r$$
$$= 2(50).$$
$$= 100$$
That is, the diameter of the rehearsal hall is 100 feet.

12. Let x and y be the two numbers. Then $x^2 + y^2 = 85$ and $3x^2 - y^2 = 59$. This is a system of equations that can be solved by elimination. Choose to eliminate y^2.

$$\begin{cases} x^2 + y^2 = 85 \\ 3x^2 - y^2 = 59 \end{cases}$$
$$4x^2 \quad\quad = 144$$
$$x^2 = 36$$
$$x = \pm 6$$

Now substitute $x = \pm 6$ for x in the first equation and solve for y.
$$x^2 + y^2 = 85$$
$$(\pm 6)^2 + y^2 = 85$$
$$y^2 = 49$$
$$y = \pm 7$$
There are four pairs of numbers that work.
$$\{(6,7),(6,-7),(-6,7),(-6,-7)\}$$

13. Prepare We are to write the equation of the parabolic satellite dish given the length of the base and the maximum height.

Plan We must determine the values of a, h, and k for the equation $y = a(x-h)^2 + k$.

Process Since the endpoints of the base of the parabola are 18 inches apart and since the left endpoint is at the origin, by symmetry, the x-coordinate of the vertex is 9. Since the maximum height of the parabola is 4, the y-coordinate of the vertex is 4. Therefore, $(h,k) = (9,4)$. We can use the fact that the left endpoint of the parabola is $(0,0)$, to find the value of a.

$$y = a(x-h)^2 + k$$
$$0 = a(0-9)^2 + 4$$
$$0 = a(81) + 4$$
$$-4 = 81a$$
$$-\frac{4}{81} = a$$

Therefore, the equation of the parabola in standard form is

$$y = -\frac{4}{81}(x-9)^2 + 4.$$

Ponder Is this equation reasonable? We can sketch the graph of the equation to see that it's reasonable.

14. Rewrite the equation to identify h, k, and r.

$$\left(x-(-2)\right)^2 + (y-3)^2 = (2)^2$$

The center is $(h,k) = (-2,3)$ and the radius is $r = 2$.

Plot the points $(-2,5)$, $(-2,1)$, $(-4,3)$, and $(0,3)$ That are 2 units up, down, left, and right from the center, respectively.

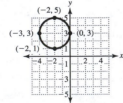

15. Rewrite the equation to identify a, h, and k.

$$y = -2\left(x-(-3)\right)^2 + 0$$

$a = -2 < 0$ implies the graph opens down. The vertex is $(h,k) = (-3,0)$. The axis of symmetry is the vertical line $x = h$, that is, $x = -3$. The vertex lies on the x-axis, therefore it is the only x-intercept. Let's find two additional points.

x	y	Solution
-2	-2	$(-2,-2)$
-4	-2	$(-4,-2)$

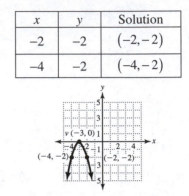

16. The x term is positive so the hyperbola will open left and right. Since $a^2 = 36 \Rightarrow a = 6$, the vertices are $(-a,0) = (-6,0)$ and $(a,0) = (6,0)$. Since $b^2 = 16 \Rightarrow b = 4$, the additional points are $(0,-b) = (0,-4)$ and $(0,b) = (0,4)$.

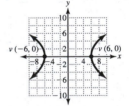

17. Rewrite the equation in standard form.

$$\frac{10x^2}{10} + \frac{y^2}{10} = \frac{10}{10}$$
$$\frac{x^2}{1} + \frac{y^2}{10} = 1$$

The center is $(0,0)$. Since $a^2 = 1 \Rightarrow a = 1$, the x-intercepts are $(-a,0) = (-1,0)$ and $(a,0) = (1,0)$. Since $b^2 = 10 \Rightarrow b = \sqrt{10}$, the y-intercepts are $(0,-b) = (0,-\sqrt{10})$ and $(0,b) = (0,\sqrt{10})$.

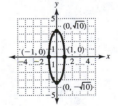

18. Identify $a = 3$, $b = -24$, and $c = 45$. The equation is quadratic in y and $a = 3 > 0$, so the graph is a parabola that opens right. The axis of symmetry is

$$y = \frac{-b}{2a}$$

$$y = \frac{-(-24)}{2(3)}$$

$$y = 4.$$

By substituting $y = 4$ into the equation,

$$x = 3(4)^2 - 24(4) + 45$$

$$x = 48 - 96 + 45$$

$$x = -3,$$

we find that the vertex is $(-3, 4)$.

$$x = 3(0)^2 - 24(0) + 45$$

$$x = 45$$

The x-intercept is $(45, 0)$. The y-intercepts are $(0, 5)$ and $(0, 3)$.

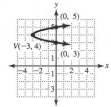

19. The center is $(h, k) = (2, 3)$. Since $a^2 = 9 \Rightarrow a = 3$, the endpoints of the horizontal axis are $(-1, 3)$ and $(5, 3)$. Since $b^2 = 4 \Rightarrow b = 2$, the endpoints of the vertical axis are $(2, 5)$ and $(2, 1)$.

20. Rewrite the equation to identify h, k, and r.

$$(x - 0)^2 + (y - 1)^2 = (3)^2$$

The center is $(h, k) = (0, 1)$ and the radius is $r = 3$. Plot the points $(0, 4)$, $(0, -2)$, $(-3, 1)$, and $(3, 1)$, that are 3 units up, down, left, and right from the center, respectively.

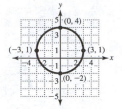

21. Graph the parabola given by the equation $y = x^2 + 4x$ using a solid line. The parabola opens up. Axis of Symmetry is $x = \frac{-b}{2a}$ or $x = \frac{-4}{2(1)} = -2$. Substitute $x = -2$ into y to find the vertex is $(-2, -4)$. The y-intercept is $(0, 0)$ and the x-intercepts are $(0, 0)$ and $(-4, 0)$. Choose the test point $(-2, 0)$.

$$y \geq x^2 + 4x$$

$$0 \geq (-2)^2 + 4(-2)$$

$$0 \geq -4$$

True

Shade the region containing $(-2, 0)$.

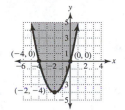

22. Graph the ellipse given by the equation $25x^2 + 4y^2 = 100$ using a dashed line. The equation in standard form is

$$\frac{x^2}{4} + \frac{y^2}{25} = 1.$$

The center is $(0, 0)$. The endpoints of the horizontal axis are $(-2, 0)$ and $(2, 0)$. The endpoints of the vertical axis are $(0, -5)$ and $(0, 5)$. Choose the test point $(0, 0)$.

$$25x^2 + 4y^2 > 100$$

$$25(0)^2 + 4(0)^2 > 100$$

$$0 > 100$$

False

Shade the region outside the ellipse.

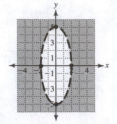

23. Graph the circle given by the equation $x^2 + y^2 = 8$. The center is $(0,0)$ and the radius is $r = 2\sqrt{2}$. Choose the test point $(0,0)$.

$$x^2 + y^2 \leq 8$$
$$(0)^2 + (0)^2 \leq 8$$
$$0 \leq 8$$

True

Use arrows to show the shaded region inside the circle. Graph the line given by the equation $-4x + 3y = -3$. The y-intercept is $(0,-1)$ and the slope is $m = \dfrac{4}{3}$. Choose the test point $(0,0)$.

$$-4x + 3y < -3$$
$$-4(0) + 3(0) < -3$$
$$0 < -3$$

False

Use arrows to show the shaded region below the line.

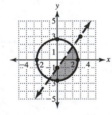

24. Use the method of substitution. Solve the equation $x^2 - y = 4$ for y to get $y = x^2 - 4$. Substitute the expression $x^2 - 4$ for y in the equation $x - 3y = 2$.

$$x - 3y = 2$$
$$x - 3(x^2 - 4) = 2$$
$$3x^2 - x - 10 = 0$$
$$(3x + 5)(x - 2) = 0$$
$$3x + 5 = 0 \quad \text{or} \quad x - 2 = 0$$
$$x = -\frac{5}{3} \qquad\qquad x = 2$$

Substitute $x = -\dfrac{5}{3}$ in $x - 3y = 2$.

$$x - 3y = 2$$
$$-\frac{5}{3} - 3y = 2$$
$$y = -\frac{11}{9}$$

Substitute $x = 2$ in $x - 3y = 2$.

$$x - 3y = 2$$
$$2 - 3y = 2$$
$$y = 0$$

The solution set is $\left\{ (2,0), \left(-\dfrac{5}{3}, -\dfrac{11}{9} \right) \right\}$.

25. Use the method of elimination to eliminate y^2.

$$2(\text{Eq1}) + \text{Eq2}$$

$$\begin{cases} 6x^2 - 2y^2 = -46 \\ -8x^2 + 2y^2 = 28 \end{cases}$$
$$\overline{ -2x^2 \qquad\quad = -18}$$
$$x^2 = 9$$
$$x = \pm 3$$

Substitute $x = \pm 3$ into $3x^2 - y^2 = -23$.

$$3x^2 - y^2 = -23$$
$$3(\pm 3)^2 - y^2 = -23$$
$$y^2 = 50$$
$$y = \pm 5\sqrt{2}$$

The solution set is

$$\left\{ \left(3, 5\sqrt{2}\right), \left(3, -5\sqrt{2}\right), \left(-3, 5\sqrt{2}\right), \left(-3, -5\sqrt{2}\right) \right\}.$$

Chapters 10-11 Cumulative Review

1. $(-2+7i)(3-5i) = -6+10i+21i-35i^2$
$$= -6+31i-35(-1)$$
$$= -6+31i+35$$
$$= 29+31i$$

2. $6+3i(5-10i) = 6+15i-30i^2$
$$= 6+15i-30(-1)$$
$$= 6+15i+30$$
$$= 36+15i$$

3. $\dfrac{-10+4i}{5i} = \dfrac{-10+4i}{5i} \cdot \dfrac{i}{i}$
$$= \dfrac{-10i+4i^2}{5i^2}$$
$$= \dfrac{-10i+4(-1)}{5(-1)}$$
$$= \dfrac{-10i-4}{-5}$$
$$= \dfrac{-4-10i}{-5}$$
$$= \dfrac{-4}{-5} + \dfrac{-10i}{-5}$$
$$= \dfrac{4}{5} + 2i$$

4. $\dfrac{-2+3i}{3+i} = \left(\dfrac{-2+3i}{3+i}\right)\left(\dfrac{3-i}{3-i}\right)$
$$= \dfrac{(-2+3i)(3-i)}{(3)^2-(i)^2}$$
$$= \dfrac{-6+2i+9i-3i^2}{9-(-1)}$$
$$= \dfrac{-6+11i-3(-1)}{10}$$
$$= \dfrac{-6+11i+3}{10}$$
$$= -\dfrac{3}{10} + \dfrac{11}{10}i$$

5. $\left(-\dfrac{1}{2}+3i\right)^2 = \left(-\dfrac{1}{2}\right)^2 + 2\left(-\dfrac{1}{2}\cdot 3i\right) + (3i)^2$
$$= \dfrac{1}{4} - 3i + 9i^2$$
$$= \dfrac{1}{4} - 3i + 9(-1)$$
$$= \dfrac{1}{4} - 3i - 9$$
$$= -\dfrac{35}{4} - 3i$$

6. $(x-4)^2 + 18 = 0$
$$(x-4)^2 = -18$$
$$x-4 = -\sqrt{-18} \quad \text{or} \quad x-4 = \sqrt{-18}$$
$$x-4 = -3i\sqrt{2} \quad \text{or} \quad x-4 = 3i\sqrt{2}$$
$$x = 4-3i\sqrt{2} \quad \text{or} \quad x = 4+3i\sqrt{2}$$
Solution Set: $\left\{4-3i\sqrt{2}, 4+3i\sqrt{2}\right\}$

7. $k^2 - 10k + 5 = 0$
$$k^2 - 10k = -5$$
$$k^2 - 10k + 25 = -5 + 25$$
$$(k-5)^2 = 20$$
$$k-5 = -\sqrt{20} \quad \text{or} \quad k-5 = \sqrt{20}$$
$$k-5 = -2\sqrt{5} \quad \text{or} \quad k-5 = 2\sqrt{5}$$
$$k = 5-2\sqrt{5} \quad \text{or} \quad k = 5+2\sqrt{5}$$
Solution Set: $\left\{5-2\sqrt{5}, 5+2\sqrt{5}\right\}$

8. $8x^2 - 8x = 1$

$8x^2 - 8x - 1 = 0$

$a = 8,\ b = -8,\ c = -1$

$$x = \frac{-b \pm \sqrt{b^2 - 4ac}}{2a}$$

$$= \frac{-(-8) \pm \sqrt{(-8)^2 - 4(8)(-1)}}{2(8)}$$

$$= \frac{8 \pm \sqrt{64 + 32}}{16}$$

$$= \frac{8 \pm \sqrt{96}}{16}$$

$$= \frac{2 \pm \sqrt{6}}{4}$$

Solution Set: $\left\{ \dfrac{2 - \sqrt{6}}{4}, \dfrac{2 + \sqrt{6}}{4} \right\}$

9. $5t^2 + 30 = 0$

$5t^2 = -30$

$t^2 = -6$

$t = -\sqrt{-6}$ or $t = \sqrt{6}$

$t = -i\sqrt{6}$ or $t = i\sqrt{6}$

$\left\{ -i\sqrt{6}, i\sqrt{6} \right\}$

10. $(x - 5)(3x + 4) = 0$

$x - 5 = 0$ or $3x + 4 = 0$

$x = 5$ or $x = -\dfrac{4}{3}$

$\left\{ -\dfrac{4}{3}, 5 \right\}$

11. $10x^2 + 3x - 4 = 0$

$(5x + 4)(2x - 1) = 0$

$5x + 4 = 0$ or $2x - 1 = 0$

$x = -\dfrac{4}{5}$ or $x = \dfrac{1}{2}$

$\left\{ -\dfrac{4}{5}, \dfrac{1}{2} \right\}$

12. $2p^2 - p + 5 = 0$

$a = 2,\ b = -1,\ c = 5$

$$x = \frac{-b \pm \sqrt{b^2 - 4ac}}{2a}$$

$$= \frac{-(-1) \pm \sqrt{(-1)^2 - 4(2)(5)}}{2(2)}$$

$$= \frac{1 \pm \sqrt{1 - 40}}{4}$$

$$= \frac{1 \pm \sqrt{-39}}{4}$$

$$= \frac{1 \pm i\sqrt{39}}{4}$$

Solution Set: $\left\{ \dfrac{1}{4} - \dfrac{\sqrt{39}}{4}i, \dfrac{1}{4} + \dfrac{\sqrt{39}}{4}i \right\}$

13. $y^4 + 12y^2 - 64 = 0$

$(y^2 - 4)(y^2 + 16) = 0$

$y^2 - 4 = 0$ or $y^2 + 16 = 0$

$y^2 = 4$ or $y^2 = -16$

$y = \pm 2$ or $y = \pm\sqrt{-16}$

$y = \pm 4i$

Solution Set: $\{-2, 2, -4i, 4i\}$

14. $\dfrac{2x}{x + 4} - \dfrac{8}{x^2 - 16} = \dfrac{8}{x - 4}$

$\dfrac{x^2 - 16}{1}\left(\dfrac{2x}{x + 4} - \dfrac{8}{x^2 - 16} \right) = \dfrac{x^2 - 16}{1}\left(\dfrac{8}{x - 4} \right)$

$2x(x - 4) - 8 = 8(x + 4)$

$2x^2 - 8x - 8 = 8x + 32$

$2x^2 - 16x - 40 = 0$

$2(x + 2)(x - 10) = 0$

$x + 2 = 0$ or $x - 10 = 0$

$x = -2$ or $x = 10$

Solution Set: $\{-2, 10\}$

15. $s^2 + 2s - 8 > 0$

$(s+4)(s-2) > 0$

Boundary Values

$(s+4)(s-2) = 0$

$s+4 = 0$ or $s-2 = 0$

$s = -4$ or $s = 2$

Region A $(-\infty, -4)$	Region B $(-4, 2)$	Region C $(2, \infty)$
Test Point: $x = -5$ $(s+4)(s-2) > 0$ $(-)(-) > 0$ $(+) > 0$ True: Shade Region A	Test Point: $x = 0$ $(s+4)(s-2) > 0$ $(+)(-) > 0$ $(-) > 0$ False: Do Not Shade Region B	Test Point: $x = 3$ $(s+4)(s-2) > 0$ $(+)(+) > 0$ $(+) > 0$ True: Shade Region C

The solution set is $(-\infty, -4) \cup (2, \infty)$.

16. $\dfrac{x+6}{x-4} \le 0$

Boundary Values

$x - 4 = 0$ or $x + 6 = 0$

$x = 4$ or $x = -6$

Region A $(-\infty, -6]$	Region B $[-6, 4)$	Region C $(4, \infty)$
Test Point: $x = -7$ $\dfrac{x-4}{x+6} \le 0$ $\dfrac{(-)}{(-)} \le 0$ $(+) \le 0$ False: Do Not Shade Region A	Test Point: $x = 0$ $\dfrac{x-4}{x+6} \le 0$ $\dfrac{(-)}{(+)} \le 0$ $(-) \le 0$ True: Shade Region B	Test Point: $x = 5$ $\dfrac{x-4}{x+6} \le 0$ $\dfrac{(+)}{(+)} \le 0$ $(+) \le 0$ False: Do Not Shade Region C

The solution set is $[-6, 4)$.

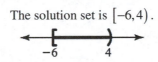

509

17. $a = 1$, $b = 4$, $c = 4$

a) The equation is quadratic in y and $a = 1 > 0$; therefore, the parabola will open right.

b) The axis of symmetry is:

$$y = \frac{-b}{2a}$$

$$y = \frac{-(4)}{2(1)}$$

$$y = -2$$

c) Find the x-coordinate of the vertex by substituting $y = -2$ into the original equation.

$$x = y^2 + 4y + 4$$

$$x = (-2)^2 + 4(-2) + 4$$

$$x = 0$$

The vertex is $(0, -2)$.

d) The x-intercept is $(c, 0) = (4, 0)$. There is only one y-intercept because the vertex lies on the y-axis. The y-intercept is $(0, -2)$.

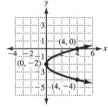

18. $a = -1$, $h = -3$, $k = 2$

The equation is quadratic in x and $a = -1 < 0$; therefore, the parabola opens down. The vertex is $(h, k) = (-3, 2)$. The axis of symmetry is $x = h$. That is, $x = -3$. To find the x-intercepts, set $y = 0$ and solve for x.

$$-(x+3)^2 + 2 = 0$$

$$(x+3)^2 = 2$$

$$x + 3 = -\sqrt{2} \quad \text{or} \quad x + 3 = \sqrt{2}$$

$$x = -3 - \sqrt{2} \quad \text{or} \quad x = -3 + \sqrt{2}$$

The x-intercepts are $\left(-3 - \sqrt{2}, 0\right)$ and $\left(-3 + \sqrt{2}, 0\right)$.

To find the y-intercept, set $x = 0$ and solve for y.

$$y = -(x+3)^2 + 2$$

$$y = -(0+3)^2 + 2$$

$$y = -(3)^2 + 2$$

$$y = -7$$

The y-intercept is $(0, -7)$. We can use symmetry to find a third point, $(-6, -7)$.

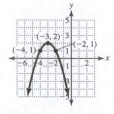

19. $r^2 = 16 \Rightarrow r = 4$, $h = 5$, $k = -\frac{1}{2}$

The radius is 4 and the center is $\left(5, -\frac{1}{2}\right)$.

20. $r^2 = 8 \Rightarrow r = 2\sqrt{2}$, $h = 0$, $k = 1$

The radius is $2\sqrt{2}$ and the center is $(0, 1)$.

21. $x^2 + 6x + y^2 - 2y + 9 = 0$

$$\left(x^2 + 6x\right) + \left(y^2 - 2y\right) = -9$$

$$\left(x^2 + 6x + 9\right) + \left(y^2 - 2y + 1\right) = -9 + 9 + 1$$

$$(x+3)^2 + (y-1)^2 = 1$$

$$h = -3, k = 1, r = 1$$

The center is $(h, k) = (-3, 1)$.

Plot points 1 unit up, down, left, and right, from the center, and connect them.

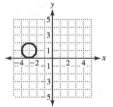

22. The center is $(h, k) = (-2, 1)$.

$$a^2 = 4 \Rightarrow a = 2$$

$$b^2 = 16 \Rightarrow b = 4$$

To find the endpoints of the vertical axis, move up and down 4 units from the center. To find the endpoints of the horizontal axis, move left and right 2 units from the center.

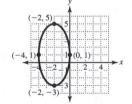

23. $a^2 = 25 \Rightarrow a = 5$

$b^2 = 1 \Rightarrow b = 1$

The vertices are $(-5, 0)$ and $(5, 0)$. The additional points are $(0, -1)$ and $(0, 1)$.

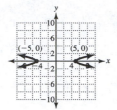

24. $a = 5$, $b = 2$, $(h,k) = (0,0)$

$$\frac{x^2}{a^2} + \frac{y^2}{b^2} = 1$$

$$\frac{x^2}{(5)^2} + \frac{y^2}{(2)^2} = 1$$

$$\frac{x^2}{25} + \frac{y^2}{4} = 1$$

25. There are no squared terms, therefore, this equation represents a straight line.

26. There are two squared terms and their coefficients have the same signs but are not equal, therefore, this equation represents an ellipse.

27. There are two squared terms and their coefficients equal, therefore, this equation represents a circle.

28. There are two squared terms and their coefficients have opposite signs, therefore, this equation represents a hyperbola.

29. Graph the parabola $y = -x^2 - 2x + 3$. Use a dashed line because of the $>$ symbol. The equation is quadratic in x and $a = -1 < 0$ which implies the parabola opens down. The x-intercepts are $(-3,0)$ and $(1,0)$. The y-intercept is $(0,3)$.

Finally, choose the test point $(0,0)$.

$$y > -x^2 - 2x + 3$$

$$0 > -(0)^2 - 2(0) + 3$$

$$0 > 3$$

False: shade the region that does not contain the origin.

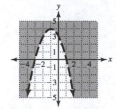

30. $\dfrac{x^2}{1} + \dfrac{y^2}{9} \geq 1$

Graph the ellipse $\dfrac{x^2}{1} + \dfrac{y^2}{9} = 1$ using a solid line. The center is $(0,0)$, the x-intercepts are $(-1,0)$ and $(1,0)$, and the y-intercepts are $(0,-3)$ and $(0,3)$. Choose the test point $(0,0)$.

$$\frac{x^2}{1} + \frac{y^2}{9} \geq 1$$

$$\frac{(0)^2}{1} + \frac{(0)^2}{9} \geq 1$$

$$0 \geq 1$$

False: Use arrows to show the shaded region outside the ellipse.

$$\frac{y^2}{4} - \frac{x^2}{1} \leq 1$$

Graph the hyperbola using a solid line. The center is $(0,0)$, the vertices are $(0,-2)$ and $(0,2)$, and the additional points are $(-1,0)$ and $(1,0)$. Choose the test point $(0,0)$.

$$\frac{y^2}{4} - \frac{x^2}{1} \leq 1$$

$$\frac{(0)^2}{4} - \frac{(0)^2}{1} \leq 1$$

$$0 \leq 1$$

True: Use arrows to show the shaded region between the curves of the hyperbola.
Finally, shade the region where the individual shaded regions overlap.

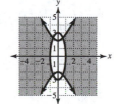

Chapter 12

12.1 Exercises

1. A function f is called one-to-one if every y value (output) corresponds to exactly one x value (input).

3. Every one-to-one function has an <u>inverse</u> function denoted by f^{-1} .

5. The graphs of f and f^{-1} are symmetric with respect to the line $y = x$.

7. The function is not one-to-one because it fails the horizontal line test.

9. The function is one-to-one because it passes the horizontal line test.

11. The function is one-to-one because it passes the horizontal line test.

13. The function is not one-to-one because it fails the horizontal line test.

15. The function is one-to-one because it passes the horizontal line test.

17. The function is not one-to-one because it fails the horizontal line test.

19. The function is not one-to-one because it fails the horizontal line test.

21.
$$(f \circ g)(x) = f(g(x)) \qquad (g \circ f)(x) = g(f(x))$$
$$= f\left(\frac{x}{8}\right) \qquad\qquad = g(8x)$$
$$= 8\left(\frac{x}{8}\right) \qquad\qquad = \frac{8x}{8}$$
$$= x \qquad\qquad\qquad = x$$

These functions are inverses.

23.
$$(f \circ g)(x) = f(g(x)) \qquad (g \circ f)(x) = g(f(x))$$
$$= f(x+2) \qquad\qquad = g(x-2)$$
$$= (x+2)-2 \qquad\quad = (x-2)+2$$
$$= x \qquad\qquad\qquad = x$$

These functions are inverses.

25.
$$(f \circ g)(x) = f(g(x))$$
$$= f(3-2x)$$
$$= 2(3-2x)+6$$
$$= 6-4x+6$$
$$= -4x+12$$

These functions are not inverses.

27.
$$(f \circ g)(x) = f(g(x)) \qquad (g \circ f)(x) = g(f(x))$$
$$= f\left(\sqrt[3]{x}\right) \qquad\qquad = g\left(x^3\right)$$
$$= \left(\sqrt[3]{x}\right)^3 \qquad\qquad = \sqrt[3]{x^3}$$
$$= x \qquad\qquad\qquad = x$$

These functions are inverses.

29.
$$(f \circ g)(x) = f(g(x))$$
$$= f\left(\sqrt[5]{x-3}\right)$$
$$= \left(\sqrt[5]{x-3}\right)^5 + 3$$
$$= x-3+3$$
$$= x$$

$$(g \circ f)(x) = g(f(x))$$
$$= g\left(x^5 + 3\right)$$
$$= \sqrt[5]{\left(x^5 + 3\right)-3}$$
$$= \sqrt[5]{x^5}$$
$$= x$$

These functions are inverses.

31.
$$f(x) = 4x+3$$
$$y = 4x+3$$
$$x = 4y+3$$
$$x-3 = 4y$$
$$\frac{x-3}{4} = y$$
$$f^{-1}(x) = \frac{x-3}{4}$$

The domain of f is the interval $(-\infty, \infty)$, which is the range of the inverse function. The range of f is the interval $(-\infty, \infty)$, which is the domain of the inverse function.

Verifications

$\left(f\circ f^{-1}\right)(x)$	$\left(f^{-1}\circ f\right)(x)$
$=f\left(f^{-1}(x)\right)$	$=f^{-1}\left(f(x)\right)$
$=f\left(\dfrac{x-3}{4}\right)$	$=f^{-1}\left(4x+3\right)$
$=4\left(\dfrac{x-3}{4}\right)+3$	$=\dfrac{(4x+3)-3}{4}$
$=x-3+3$	$=\dfrac{4x}{4}$
$=x$	$=x$

33. $h(x)=\dfrac{5-x}{3}$

$y=\dfrac{5-x}{3}$

$x=\dfrac{5-y}{3}$

$3x=5-y$

$3x-5=-y$

$y=-3x+5$

$h^{-1}(x)=-3x+5$

The domain of h is the interval $(-\infty,\infty)$, which is the range of the inverse function. The range of h is the interval $(-\infty,\infty)$, which is the domain of the inverse function.

Verifications

$\left(h\circ h^{-1}\right)(x)$	$\left(h^{-1}\circ h\right)(x)$
$=h\left(h^{-1}(x)\right)$	$=h^{-1}\left(h(x)\right)$
$=h(-3x+5)$	$=h^{-1}(4x+3)$
$=\dfrac{5-(-3x+5)}{3}$	$=-3\left(\dfrac{5-x}{3}\right)+5$
$=\dfrac{3x}{3}$	$=-5+x+5$
$=x$	$=x$

35. $f(x)=x^3-2$

$y=x^3-2$

$x=y^3-2$

$x+2=y^3$

$\sqrt[3]{x+2}=y$

$f^{-1}(x)=\sqrt[3]{x+2}$

The domain of f is the interval $(-\infty,\infty)$, which is the range of the inverse function. The range of f is the interval $(-\infty,\infty)$, which is the domain of the inverse function.

Verifications

$\left(f\circ f^{-1}\right)(x)$	$\left(f^{-1}\circ f\right)(x)$
$=f\left(f^{-1}(x)\right)$	$=f^{-1}\left(f(x)\right)$
$=f\left(\sqrt[3]{x+2}\right)$	$=f^{-1}\left(x^3-2\right)$
$=\left(\sqrt[3]{x+2}\right)^2-2$	$=\sqrt[3]{\left(x^3-2\right)+2}$
$=x+2-2$	$=\sqrt[3]{x^3}$
$=x$	$=x$

37. $f(x)=\sqrt{x-4}$

$y=\sqrt{x-4}$

$x=\sqrt{y-4}$

$x^2=y-4$

$x^2+4=y$

$f^{-1}(x)=x^2+4,\ x\ge0$

The domain of f is the interval $[4,\infty)$, which is the range of the inverse function. The range of f is the interval $[0,\infty)$, which is the domain of the inverse function.

Verifications

$\left(f\circ f^{-1}\right)(x)$	$\left(f^{-1}\circ f\right)(x)$
$=f\left(f^{-1}(x)\right)$	$=f^{-1}\left(f(x)\right)$
$=f\left(x^2+4\right)$	$=f^{-1}\left(\sqrt{x-4}\right)$
$=\sqrt{\left(x^2+4\right)-4}$	$=\left(\sqrt{x-4}\right)^2+4$
$=\sqrt{x^2}$	$=x-4+4$
$=x$	$=x$

39. $h(x)=(x-1)^3$

$y=(x-1)^3$

$x=(y-1)^3$

$\sqrt[3]{x}=y-1$

$\sqrt[3]{x}+1=y$

$h^{-1}(x)=\sqrt[3]{x}+1$

The domain of h is the interval $(-\infty,\infty)$, which is the range of the inverse function. The range of h is the interval $(-\infty,\infty)$, which is the domain of the inverse function.

Verifications

$\left(h\circ h^{-1}\right)(x)$	$\left(h^{-1}\circ h\right)(x)$
$= h\left(h^{-1}(x)\right)$	$= h^{-1}\left(h(x)\right)$
$= h\left(\sqrt[3]{x}+1\right)$	$= h^{-1}\left((x-1)^3\right)$
$= \left(\left(\sqrt[3]{x}+1\right)-1\right)^3$	$= \sqrt[3]{(x-1)^3}+1$
$= \left(\sqrt[3]{x}\right)^3$	$= x-1+1$
$= x$	$= x$

41. $g(x)=\dfrac{2}{x}$

$y=\dfrac{2}{x}$

$x=\dfrac{2}{y}$

$xy=\dfrac{2}{y}\cdot y$

$xy=2$

$y=\dfrac{2}{x}$

$g^{-1}(x)=\dfrac{2}{x},\ x\neq 0$

The domain of g is the interval $(-\infty,0)\cup(0,\infty)$, which is the range of the inverse function. The range of g is the interval $(-\infty,0)\cup(0,\infty)$, which is the domain of the inverse function.

Verifications

$\left(g\circ g^{-1}\right)(x)$	$\left(g^{-1}\circ g\right)(x)$
$= g\left(g^{-1}(x)\right)$	$= g^{-1}\left(g(x)\right)$
$= g\left(\dfrac{2}{x}\right)$	$= g^{-1}\left(\dfrac{2}{x}\right)$
$= \dfrac{2}{\frac{2}{x}}$	$= \dfrac{2}{\frac{2}{x}}$
$= \dfrac{2}{1}\cdot\dfrac{x}{2}$	$= \dfrac{2}{1}\cdot\dfrac{x}{2}$
$= x$	$= x$

43. $g(x)=\sqrt[3]{x+2}$

$y=\sqrt[3]{x+2}$

$x=\sqrt[3]{y+2}$

$x^3=y+2$

$x^3-2=y$

$g^{-1}(x)=x^3-2$

The domain of g is the interval $(-\infty,\infty)$, which is the range of the inverse function. The range of g is the interval $(-\infty,\infty)$, which is the domain of the inverse function.

Verifications

$\left(g\circ g^{-1}\right)(x)$	$\left(g^{-1}\circ g\right)(x)$
$= g\left(g^{-1}(x)\right)$	$= g^{-1}\left(g(x)\right)$
$= g\left(x^3-2\right)$	$= g^{-1}\left(\sqrt[3]{x+2}\right)$
$= \sqrt[3]{\left(x^3-2\right)+2}$	$= \left(\sqrt[3]{x+2}\right)^3-2$
$= \sqrt[3]{x^3}$	$= x+2-2$
$= x$	$= x$

45. $h(x)=\dfrac{1-x}{x}$

$y=\dfrac{1-x}{x}$

$x=\dfrac{1-y}{y}$

$xy=\dfrac{1-y}{y}\cdot y$

$xy=1-y$

$xy+y=1$

$y(x+1)=1$

$y=\dfrac{1}{x+1}$

$h^{-1}(x)=\dfrac{1}{x+1},\ x\neq -1$

The domain of h is the interval $(-\infty,0)\cup(0,\infty)$, which is the range of the inverse function. The range of h is the interval $(-\infty,-1)\cup(-1,\infty)$, which is the domain of the inverse function.

Verifications

$(h \circ h^{-1})(x)$	$(h^{-1} \circ h)(x)$
$= h(h^{-1}(x))$	$= h^{-1}(h(x))$
$= h\left(\dfrac{1}{x+1}\right)$	$= h^{-1}\left(\dfrac{1-x}{x}\right)$
$= \dfrac{1-\dfrac{1}{x+1}}{\dfrac{1}{x+1}}$	$= \dfrac{1}{\dfrac{1-x}{x}+1}$
$= \dfrac{x+1-1}{1}$	$= \dfrac{x}{1-x+x}$
$= x$	$= x$

47. The vertical line test determines if the graph represents a function. The horizontal line test is used to determine if a function is one-to-one.

49. Answers will vary; for example: To find the inverse of a function, first replace $f(x)$ with y. Then switch all x and y variables. Finally, solve algebraically for y.

51. $f(x)$ and $g(x)$ are inverses if $f(g(x)) = x$ and $g(f(x)) = x$.

53. Given the graph of a function, the graph of the inverse function will be a reflection across the line $y = x$.

55. a) $f(x) = x + 30$
$f(10) = (10) + 30$
$= 40$
He bought a size 40 for his wife.

55. b) $f(x) = x + 30$
$y = x + 30$
$x = y + 30$
$x - 30 = y$
$f^{-1}(x) = x - 30$

55. c) $f^{-1}(x) = x - 30$
$f^{-1}(45) = (45) - 30$
$= 15$
A Slovakian blouse of size 45 is a US size 15.

57. a) $f(x) = 400 + 0.06x$
$y = 400 + 0.06x$
$x = 400 + 0.06y$
$x - 400 = 0.06y$
$\dfrac{x - 400}{0.06} = y$
$f^{-1}(x) = \dfrac{x - 400}{0.06}$

x represents the weekly salary, and $f^{-1}(x)$ represents the total sales

57. b) $f^{-1}(x) = \dfrac{x - 400}{0.06}$
$f^{-1}(880) = \dfrac{(880) - 400}{0.06}$
$= 8,000$
Priscilla's total sales were $8,000.

59. a) $f(x) = 1.96x$
$y = 1.96x$
$x = 1.96y$
$\dfrac{x}{1.96} = y$
$f^{-1}(x) = \dfrac{x}{1.96}$

x represents the number of marks, and $f^{-1}(x)$ represents the number of Euros.

59. b) $f^{-1}(x) = \dfrac{x}{1.96}$
$f^{-1}(12,544) = \dfrac{12,544}{1.96}$
$= 6,400$
Frau Essig total received 6,400 Euros for 12,544 marks.

61. Because the graph passes the horizontal line test, the function is one-to-one.

$$f(x) = \frac{1}{8}x^3$$

$$y = \frac{1}{8}x^3$$

$$x = \frac{1}{8}y^3$$

$$8x = y^3$$

$$\sqrt[3]{8x} = y$$

$$2\sqrt[3]{x} = y$$

$$f^{-1}(x) = 2\sqrt[3]{x}$$

63. Because the graph does not pass the horizontal line test, the function is not one-to-one. We can restrict its domain to $x \geq 0$.

$$g(x) = \frac{1}{4}x^2$$

$$y = \frac{1}{4}x^2$$

$$x = \frac{1}{4}y^2$$

$$4x = y^2$$

$$\sqrt{4x} = y^2$$

$$2\sqrt{x} = y$$

$$g^{-1}(x) = 2\sqrt{x}, x \geq 0$$

65. Because the graph does not pass the horizontal line test, the function is not one-to-one. We can restrict its domain to $x \geq 2$.

$$f(x) = |x - 2|$$

$$y = |x - 2|$$

$$x = |y - 2|$$

$$x = y - 2$$

$$x + 2 = y$$

$$f^{-1}(x) = x + 2, x \geq 0$$

67. Because the graph does not pass the horizontal line test, the function is not one-to-one. We can restrict its domain to $x \geq 0$

$$h(x) = x^2 - 4$$

$$y = x^2 - 4$$

$$x = y^2 - 4$$

$$x + 4 = y^2$$

$$\sqrt{x + 4} = y$$

$$h^{-1}(x) = \sqrt{x + 4}, x \geq -4$$

12.2 Exercises

1. The function $f(x) = b^x$ is called an <u>exponential function</u>.

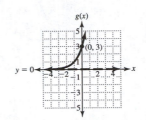

3. $a^x = b^x$ if and only if <u>$a = b$</u>, where $a, b > 0$, $a, b \neq 1$, and $x \neq 0$.

5. $f(x) = 4^x$

x	$f(x) = 4^x$
−2	$4^{-2} = \frac{1}{4^2} = \frac{1}{16}$
−1	$4^{-1} = \frac{1}{4}$
0	$4^0 = 1$
1	$4^1 = 4$
2	$4^2 = 16$

11. $f(x) = 2^{x-1}$

x	$f(x) = 2^{x-1}$
−2	$2^{-2-1} = 2^{-3} = \frac{1}{2^3} = \frac{1}{8}$
−1	$2^{-1-1} = 2^{-2} = \frac{1}{2^2} = \frac{1}{4}$
0	$2^{0-1} = 2^{-1} = \frac{1}{2}$
1	$2^{1-1} = 2^0 = 1$
2	$2^{2-1} = 2^1 = 2$

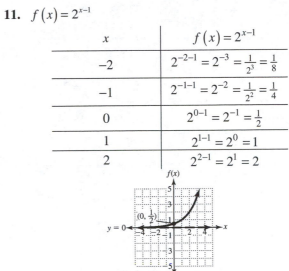

7. $f(x) = 2^x$

x	$f(x) = 2^x$
−2	$2^{-2} = \frac{1}{2^2} = \frac{1}{4}$
−1	$2^{-1} = \frac{1}{2}$
0	$2^0 = 1$
1	$2^1 = 2$
2	$2^2 = 4$

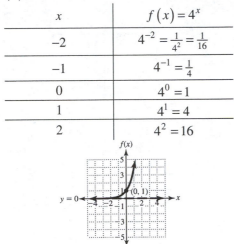

13. $y = 3^x + 1$

x	$y = 3^x + 1$
−2	$3^{-2} + 1 = \frac{1}{3^2} + 1 = 1\frac{1}{9}$
−1	$3^{-1} + 1 = \frac{1}{3} + 1 = 1\frac{1}{3}$
0	$3^0 + 1 = 1 + 1 = 2$
1	$3^1 + 1 = 4$
2	$3^2 = 9 + 1 = 10$

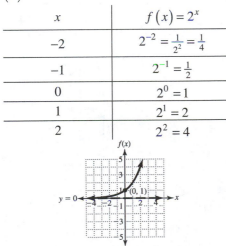

9. $g(x) = 3^{x+1}$

x	$g(x) = 3^{x+1}$
−2	$3^{-2+1} = 3^{-1} = \frac{1}{3}$
−1	$3^{-1+1} = 3^0 = 1$
0	$3^{0+1} = 3^1 = 3$
1	$3^{1+1} = 3^2 = 9$
2	$3^{2+1} = 3^3 = 27$

15. $f(x) = 2^x - 1$

x	$f(x) = 2^x - 1$
−2	$2^{-2} - 1 = \frac{1}{2^2} - 1 = -\frac{3}{4}$
−1	$2^{-1} - 1 = \frac{1}{2} - 1 = -\frac{1}{2}$
0	$2^0 - 1 = 1 - 1 = 0$
1	$2^1 - 1 = 1$
2	$2^2 = 4 - 1 = 3$

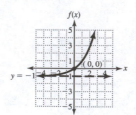

17. $f(x) = \left(\frac{1}{2}\right)^x$

x	$f(x) = \left(\frac{1}{2}\right)^x$
-2	$\left(\frac{1}{2}\right)^{-2} = 2^2 = 4$
-1	$\left(\frac{1}{2}\right)^{-1} = 2^1 = 2$
0	$\left(\frac{1}{2}\right)^{0} = 1$
1	$\left(\frac{1}{2}\right)^{1} = \frac{1}{2}$
2	$\left(\frac{1}{2}\right)^{2} = \frac{1}{4}$

19. $g(x) = 5^{-x}$

x	$g(x) = 5^{-x}$
-2	$5^{-(-2)} = 5^2 = 25$
-1	$5^{-(-1)} = 5^1 = 5$
0	$5^{-(0)} = 1$
1	$5^{-(1)} = \frac{1}{5}$
2	$5^{-(2)} = \frac{1}{5^2} = \frac{1}{25}$

21. $f(x) = -2^x$

x	$f(x) = -2^x$
-2	$-2^{-2} = -\frac{1}{2^2} = -\frac{1}{4}$
-1	$-2^{-1} = -\frac{1}{2}$
0	$-2^{0} = -1$
1	$-2^{1} = -2$
2	$-2^{2} = -4$

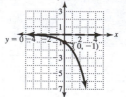

23. $h(x) = -\left(\frac{1}{4}\right)^x$

x	$h(x) = -\left(\frac{1}{4}\right)^x$
-2	$-\left(\frac{1}{4}\right)^{-2} = -4^2 = -16$
-1	$-\left(\frac{1}{4}\right)^{-1} = -4^1 = -4$
0	$-\left(\frac{1}{4}\right)^{0} = -1$
1	$-\left(\frac{1}{4}\right)^{1} = -\frac{1}{4}$
2	$-\left(\frac{1}{4}\right)^{2} = -\frac{1}{16}$

25.

$$f(-3) = 8e^{-3(-3)} \qquad f(0) = 8e^{-3(0)}$$
$$= 8e^9 \qquad\qquad = 8e^0$$
$$\approx 64,824.671 \qquad = 8$$

$$f(2) = 8e^{-3(2)}$$
$$= 8e^{-6}$$
$$\approx 0.020$$

27. $f(-2) = -4e^{2.3(-2)}$ $f(0) = -4e^{2.3(0)}$
$= -4e^{-4.6}$ $= -4e^0$
≈ -0.040 $= -4$

$f(1) = -4e^{2.3(1)}$
$= -4e^{2.3}$
≈ -39.897

29. $f(-4) = 2e^{\frac{-4}{2}}$ $f(0) = 2e^{\frac{0}{2}}$
$= 2e^{-2}$ $= 2e^0$
≈ 0.271 $= 2$

$f(2) = 2e^{\frac{2}{2}}$
$= 2e^1$
≈ 5.437

31. $f(-1) = 5e^{(-1)^2}$ $f(0) = 5e^{(0)^2}$
$= 5e^1$ $= 5e^0$
≈ 13.591 $= 5$

$f(3.4) = 5e^{(3.4)^2}$
$= 5e^{11.56}$
$\approx 524,100.067$

33. $2^x = 32$
$2^x = 2^5$
$x = 5$
Solution Set: $\{5\}$

35. $4^x = 256$
$4^x = 4^4$
$x = 4$
Solution Set: $\{4\}$

37. $16^x = 8$
$(2^4)^x = 2^3$
$2^{4x} = 2^3$
$4x = 3$
$x = \frac{3}{4}$

Solution Set: $\left\{\frac{3}{4}\right\}$

39. $8^x = \frac{1}{128}$
$(2^3)^x = \frac{1}{2^7}$
$2^{3x} = 2^{-7}$
$3x = -7$
$x = -\frac{7}{3}$
Solution Set: $\left\{-\frac{7}{3}\right\}$

41. $5^{2x+1} = 125$
$5^{2x+1} = 5^3$
$2x+1 = 3$
$2x = 2$
$x = 1$
Solution Set: $\{1\}$

43. $144 = 12^{5x}$
$12^2 = 12^{5x}$
$2 = 5x$
$\frac{2}{5} = x$
Solution Set: $\left\{\frac{2}{5}\right\}$

45. $3^{4x+2} = \frac{1}{81}$
$3^{4x+2} = \frac{1}{3^4}$
$3^{4x+2} = 3^{-4}$
$4x+2 = -4$
$4x = -6$
$x = -\frac{3}{2}$
Solution Set: $\left\{-\frac{3}{2}\right\}$

47.
$$8^x = 32^{x+1}$$
$$\left(2^3\right)^x = \left(2^5\right)^{x+1}$$
$$2^{3x} = 2^{5x+5}$$
$$3x = 5x + 5$$
$$-2x = 5$$
$$x = -\frac{5}{2}$$
Solution Set: $\left\{-\dfrac{5}{2}\right\}$

49.
$$25^{2x} = 125^{x-3}$$
$$\left(5^2\right)^{2x} = \left(5^3\right)^{x-3}$$
$$5^{4x} = 5^{3x-9}$$
$$4x = 3x - 9$$
$$x = -9$$
Solution Set: $\{-9\}$

51.
$$(2x+5)^3 = (5x-4)^3$$
$$2x+5 = 5x-4$$
$$-3x = -9$$
$$x = 3$$
Solution Set: $\{3\}$

53.
$$(2-3x)^4 = (3x+20)^4$$
$$2-3x = 3x+20$$
$$-6x = 18$$
$$x = -3$$
Solution Set: $\{-3\}$

55.
$$\left(\frac{2}{3}x+1\right)^3 = \left(2-\frac{3}{5}x\right)^3$$
$$\frac{2}{3}x+1 = 2-\frac{3}{5}x$$
$$\frac{19}{15}x = 1$$
$$x = \frac{15}{19}$$
Solution Set: $\left\{\dfrac{15}{19}\right\}$

57. A function is an exponential function when it has a variable in the exponent.

59. Both graphs approach the line $y = 0$, but $f(x)$ is increasing while $g(x)$ is decreasing.

61. Answers will vary; for example: To solve an exponential equation, manipulate the numbers to get a common base on both sides of the equation. Set exponents equal to each other and solve for the variable. Check the solution for validity, and write the solution using set notation.

63. $P = \$4,000$
$r = 0.06$
$t = 3$
$$A = Pe^{rt}$$
$$= 4,000e^{0.06(3)}$$
$$= 4,000e^{0.18}$$
$$\approx 4,788.87$$
After three years, Georgia will have $4,788.87.

65. $P = \$6,300$
$r = 0.08$
$t = 4$
$$A = Pe^{rt}$$
$$= 6,300e^{0.08(4)}$$
$$= 6,300e^{0.32}$$
$$\approx 8,675.90$$
After four years, Shane will owe $8,675.90.

67. Prepare We will use the continuous growth formula, $A = Pe^{rt}$, to approximate the population of Ethiopia eight years from now.

Plan Identify the unknowns in the growth model $A = Pe^{rt}$.
$P = 78,000,000$
$r = 0.02$
$t = 8$
Substitute these values into the growth formula and use a calculator to round to the nearest person.

Process
$$A = Pe^{rt}$$
$$= (78,000,000)e^{0.02(8)}$$
$$= (78,000,000)e^{0.16}$$
$$\approx 91,533,848$$

The population of Ethiopia will be approximately 91,533,848 eight years from now.

Ponder Does the answer seem reasonable? Yes. However, it is just an approximation, under normal conditions, and assumes a continuous growth model.

69. $\left(\dfrac{1}{8}\right)^x = 4$

$\left(\dfrac{1}{2^3}\right)^x = 2^2$

$\left(2^{-3}\right)^x = 2^2$

$2^{-3x} = 2^2$

$-3x = 2$

$x = -\dfrac{2}{3}$

Solution Set: $\left\{-\dfrac{2}{3}\right\}$

71. $\left(\dfrac{16}{9}\right)^x = \dfrac{64}{27}$

$\left(\left(\dfrac{4}{3}\right)^2\right)^x = \left(\dfrac{4}{3}\right)^3$

$\left(\dfrac{4}{3}\right)^{2x} = \left(\dfrac{4}{3}\right)^3$

$2x = 3$

$x = \dfrac{3}{2}$

Solution Set: $\left\{\dfrac{3}{2}\right\}$

12.3 Exercises

1. For all positive numbers b, where $b \neq 1$ and x is a positive real number, $y = \log_b (x)$ means the same as $\underline{b^y = x}$.

3. The inverse of the exponential function is the <u>logarithmic</u> <u>function</u> and is denoted by $f^{-1}(x) = \underline{\log_b (x)}$.

5. The function defined by $f(x) = \ln(x)$ is called the <u>natural</u> <u>logarithmic</u> <u>function</u>.

7. $5^2 = 25$

9. $3^3 = 27$

11. $5^4 = 625$

13. $2^{-3} = \dfrac{1}{8}$

15. $6^{-2} = \dfrac{1}{36}$

17. $16^{\frac{1}{2}} = 4$

19. $\log_6 (216) = 3$

21. $\log_2 (64) = 6$

23. $\log_4 \left(\dfrac{1}{16}\right) = -2$

25. $\log_5 \left(\dfrac{1}{125}\right) = -3$

27. $\log_{16} (4) = \dfrac{1}{2}$

29. $\log_{1,000} (10) = \dfrac{1}{3}$

31. $\log_3 (9) = y$ if and only if $3^y = 9$

$$3^y = 9$$
$$3^y = 3^2$$
$$y = 2$$

Therefore, $\log_3 (9) = 2$.

33. $\log_2 (32) = y$ if and only if $2^y = 32$

$$2^y = 32$$
$$2^y = 2^5$$
$$y = 5$$

Therefore, $\log_2 (32) = 5$.

35. $\log_4 \left(\dfrac{1}{16}\right) = y$ if and only if $4^y = \dfrac{1}{16}$

$$4^y = \dfrac{1}{16}$$
$$4^y = 4^{-2}$$
$$y = -2$$

Therefore, $\log_4 \left(\dfrac{1}{16}\right) = -2$.

37. $\log_2 \left(\dfrac{1}{16}\right) = y$ if and only if $2^y = \dfrac{1}{16}$

$$2^y = \dfrac{1}{16}$$
$$2^y = 2^{-4}$$
$$y = -4$$

Therefore, $\log_2 \left(\dfrac{1}{16}\right) = -4$.

39. $\log_{25} (5) = y$ if and only if $25^y = 5$

$$25^y = 5$$
$$25^y = 25^{\frac{1}{2}}$$
$$y = \dfrac{1}{2}$$

Therefore, $\log_{25} (5) = \dfrac{1}{2}$.

41. $\log_{125} (5) = y$ if and only if $125^y = 5$

$$125^y = 5$$
$$125^y = 125^{\frac{1}{3}}$$
$$y = \dfrac{1}{3}$$

Therefore, $\log_{125} (5) = \dfrac{1}{3}$.

43. $f(x) = \log_4(x)$

$x = 4^y$	y	Solutions (x, y)
$4^{-1} = \frac{1}{4}$	-1	$\left(\frac{1}{4}, -1\right)$
$4^0 = 1$	0	$(1, 0)$
$4^1 = 4$	1	$(4, 1)$

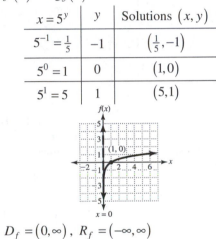

$D_f = (0, \infty)$, $R_f = (-\infty, \infty)$

45. $f(x) = \log_5(x)$

$x = 5^y$	y	Solutions (x, y)
$5^{-1} = \frac{1}{5}$	-1	$\left(\frac{1}{5}, -1\right)$
$5^0 = 1$	0	$(1, 0)$
$5^1 = 5$	1	$(5, 1)$

$D_f = (0, \infty)$, $R_f = (-\infty, \infty)$

47. $f(x) = \log_{\frac{1}{2}}(x)$

$x = \left(\frac{1}{2}\right)^y$	y	Solutions (x, y)
$\left(\frac{1}{2}\right)^{-1} = 2$	-1	$(2, -1)$
$\left(\frac{1}{2}\right)^0 = 1$	0	$(1, 0)$
$\left(\frac{1}{2}\right)^1 = \frac{1}{2}$	1	$\left(\frac{1}{2}, 1\right)$

$D_f = (0, \infty)$, $R_f = (-\infty, \infty)$

49. $\ln\left(\frac{1}{3}\right) \approx -1.099$

51. $\log(1,000) = 3.000$

53. $\ln(0.046) \approx -3.079$

55. $\log(-5)$ is undefined because $-5 \notin (0, \infty)$, the domain of the logarithm.

57. $\log\left(\sqrt{5} + 2\right) \approx 0.627$

59. $\ln\left(\frac{\pi + 6}{5}\right) \approx 0.603$

61. $\log_2(x) = 5$

$\qquad 2^5 = x$

$\qquad x = 32$

63. $\log_{10}(x) = -3$

$\qquad 10^{-3} = x$

$\qquad x = \dfrac{1}{1000}$

65. $\log_{27}(x) = \dfrac{1}{3}$

$\qquad 27^{\frac{1}{3}} = x$

$\qquad x = 3$

67. $\log_5(625) = y$

$\qquad 5^y = 625$

$\qquad 5^y = 5^4$

$\qquad y = 4$

69. $\log_3(81) = y$

$\qquad 3^y = 81$

$\qquad 3^y = 3^4$

$\qquad y = 4$

71. $\log_5\left(\dfrac{1}{25}\right) = y$

$\qquad 5^y = \dfrac{1}{25}$

$\qquad 5^y = 5^{-2}$

$\qquad y = -2$

73. $\log_a(81) = 4$

$a^4 = 81$

$a^4 = 3^4$

$a = 3$

75. $\log_a\left(\dfrac{1}{100}\right) = -2$

$a^{-2} = \dfrac{1}{100}$

$a^{-2} = \dfrac{1}{10^2}$

$a^{-2} = 10^{-2}$

$a = 10$

77. $\log_a(64) = -2$

$a^{-2} = 64$

$a^{-2} = 8^2$

$a^{-2} = \left(\dfrac{1}{8}\right)^{-2}$

$a = \dfrac{1}{8}$

79. $\ln(x) = 7$

$e^7 = x$

$x \approx 1,096.63$

81. $\log(x) = -0.12$

$10^{-0.12} = x$

$x \approx 0.76$

83. Take the base b of the logarithm raised to the other side of the equation y and set it equal to the argument x of the logarithm.

85. The base of a logarithmic function cannot equal one because 1 raised to any power will equal 1.

87. $L = 10\log_{10}\left(\dfrac{I}{I_0}\right)$

$L = 10\log_{10}\left(\dfrac{10^{-3}}{10^{-12}}\right)$

$L = 10\log_{10}\left(10^9\right)$

$L = 10(9)$

$L = 90$

The decibel level of heavy traffic is 90 dB.

89. Prepare We need to use the loudness equation $L = 10\log_{10}\left(\dfrac{I}{I_0}\right)$ to determine the decibel level of thunder, and if thunder could cause damage to a person's hearing.

Plan Identify the unknowns in the formula, substitute, and solve.

$L =$ Unknown decibel level of thunder

$I = 10^0$ sound intensity of thunder

$I_0 = 10^{-12}$ standard threshold of hearing

Process

$$L = 10\log_{10}\left(\dfrac{I}{I_0}\right)$$

$$L = 10\log_{10}\left(\dfrac{10^0}{10^{-12}}\right)$$

$$L = 10\log_{10}\left(10^{12}\right)$$

$$L = 10(12)$$

$$L = 120$$

The decibel level of thunder is 120 dB. Because noise levels higher than 80 dB can cause hearing damage, thunder could certainly damage someone's hearing.

Ponder Do our answers seem reasonable? Yes, because thunder is often very loud when one is close to the storm, and therefore a decibel level greater than 80 would be expected.

91. $\ln(k) = 5$

93. $10^q = \sqrt{2x}$

95. $f(x) = \log_3(x-4)$

$x = 3^y + 4$	y	Solutions (x, y)
$3^{-1} + 4 = \frac{13}{3}$	-1	$\left(\frac{13}{3}, -1\right)$
$3^0 + 4 = 5$	0	$(5, 0)$
$3^1 + 4 = 7$	1	$(7, 1)$

Vertical Asymptote: $x = 4$, x-intercept: $(5, 0)$

12.4 Exercises

1. $\log_3\left(\dfrac{5}{2}\right) = \log_3(5) - \log_3(2)$

h

3. $\log_3(10) = \log_3(2 \cdot 5)$

$= \log_3(2) + \log_3(5)$

g

5. $b^{\log_b(x)} = x$

c

7. $\log_{99}(99) = 1$

b

9. $\log_3(3) = 1$ property 2

11. $\log_5(1) = 0$ property 1

13. $\log_5(5^2) = 2$ property 3

15. $5^{\log_5(2)} = 2$ property 4

17. $\ln(e) = 1$ property 2

19. $\log_x x^{-3} = -3$ property 3

21. $10^{\log(5)} = 5$ property 4

23. $\ln(1) = 0$ property 1

25. $\log_5(2y) = \log_5(2) + \log_5(y)$

27. $\log_2(a^5) = 5\log_2(a)$

29. $\log_3\left(\dfrac{x}{2}\right) = \log_3(x) - \log_3(2)$

31. $\log_4(x + y)$

33. $\ln(xy) = \ln(x) + \ln(y)$

35. $\log_a(x^8) = 8\log_a(x)$

37. $\log_c\left(\dfrac{x}{y}\right) = \log_c(x) - \log_c(y)$

39. $\log_a(xyz) = \log_a(x) + \log_a(y) + \log_a(z)$

41. $\log_8(5 - y)$

43. $\log_3\left(\dfrac{4x}{5}\right) = \log_3(4x) - \log_3(5)$

$= \log_3(4) + \log_3(x) - \log_3(5)$

45. $\log_2\left(\dfrac{a^3}{b}\right) = \log_2(a^3) - \log_2(b)$

$= 3\log_2(a) - \log_2(b)$

47. $\ln\sqrt{2x} = \ln(2x)^{\frac{1}{2}}$

$= \dfrac{1}{2}\ln(2x)$

$= \dfrac{1}{2}\big[\ln(2) + \ln(x)\big]$

$= \dfrac{1}{2}\ln(2) + \dfrac{1}{2}\ln(x)$

49. $\log_2\big[5(a+b)\big] = \log_2(5) + \log_2(a+b)$

51. $\log_a\big[x^2(y-2)\big] = \log_a(x^2) + \log_a(y-2)$

$= 2\log_a(x) + \log_a(y-2)$

53. $\ln\left(\dfrac{a^2}{2+b}\right) = \ln(a^2) - \ln(2+b)$

$= 2\ln(a) - \ln(2+b)$

55. $\log_5(x) + \log_5(y) = \log_5(xy)$

57. $-8\log(a) = \log(a^{-8})$

59. $3\ln(x) + \ln(y) = \ln(x^3) + \ln(y)$

$= \ln(x^3y)$

61. $\log_3(10) - \log_3(5) = \log_3\left(\dfrac{10}{5}\right)$

$= \log_3(2)$

63. $2\log_2(4) + \log_2(5) = \log_2(4^2) + \log_2(5)$

$\qquad\qquad\qquad = \log_2(4^2 \cdot 5)$

$\qquad\qquad\qquad = \log_2(80)$

65. $\ln(x) - \ln(y+2) = \ln\left(\dfrac{x}{y+2}\right)$

67. $\log_7(8) + \log_7(3) - \log_7(2)$

$\qquad = \log_7(8 \cdot 3) - \log_7(2)$

$\qquad = \log_7\left(\dfrac{8 \cdot 3}{2}\right)$

$\qquad = \log_7(12)$

69. $5\log(8) + 5\log(y) = \log(8^5) + \log(y^5)$

$\qquad\qquad\qquad = \log(8^5 y^5)$

$\qquad\qquad\qquad = \log(32{,}768\, y^5)$

71. $\log_2(x+1) - \log_2(x-1) = \log_2\left(\dfrac{x+1}{x-1}\right)$

73. $4\log_a(x) + 5\log_a(y) - \log_a(z)$

$\qquad = \log_a(x^4) + \log_a(y^5) - \log_a(z)$

$\qquad = \log_a(x^4 y^5) - \log_a(z)$

$\qquad = \log_a\left(\dfrac{x^4 y^5}{z}\right)$

75. $\dfrac{1}{2}\log_b(x) + 2\log_b(y-1) = \log_b(x)^{\frac{1}{2}} + \log_b(y-1)^2$

$\qquad\qquad\qquad\qquad = \log_b\sqrt{x} + \log_b(y-1)^2$

$\qquad\qquad\qquad\qquad = \log_b\left[\sqrt{x}\,(y-1)^2\right]$

77. $\ln(a) + 5\ln(b) - \dfrac{1}{2}\ln(c) - 4\ln(d)$

$\qquad = \ln(a) + \ln(b^5) - \ln\left(c^{\frac{1}{2}}\right) - \ln(d^4)$

$\qquad = \ln(ab^5) - \ln\sqrt{c} - \ln(d^4)$

$\qquad = \ln\left(\dfrac{ab^5}{\sqrt{c}}\right) - \ln(d^4)$

$\qquad = \ln\left(\dfrac{ab^5}{d^4\sqrt{c}}\right)$

79. $\log_4(5) - \log_4(x+1) + \log_4(6)$

$\qquad = \log_4\left(\dfrac{5}{x+1}\right) + \log_4(6)$

$\qquad = \log_4\left(\dfrac{5}{x+1} \cdot 6\right)$

$\qquad = \log_4\left(\dfrac{30}{x+1}\right)$

81. $\ln(14) - 2\ln(7) + \ln(21)$

$\qquad = \ln(14) - \ln(7^2) + \ln(21)$

$\qquad = \ln\left(\dfrac{14}{7^2}\right) + \ln(21)$

$\qquad = \ln\left(\dfrac{14}{7^2} \cdot 21\right)$

$\qquad = \ln(6)$

83. $2\log_a(x) + \dfrac{1}{3}\log_a(x) - 5\log_a(x)$

$\qquad = \log_a(x^2) + \log_a\left(x^{\frac{1}{3}}\right) - \log_a(x^5)$

$\qquad = \log_a\left(x^2 \sqrt[3]{x}\right) - \log_a(x^5)$

$\qquad = \log_a\left(\dfrac{x^2\sqrt[3]{x}}{x^5}\right)$

$\qquad = \log_a\left(\dfrac{\sqrt[3]{x}}{x^3}\right)$

85. False. Only the logarithm of a product can be written as a sum of logarithms. Example:

$$\log(5 \cdot 3) = \log(5) + \log(3)$$

87. True. Example: $\log\left(\dfrac{5}{3}\right) = \log(5) - \log(3)$

89. $\log_b(15) = \log_b(5 \cdot 3)$

$\qquad\quad = \log_b(5) + \log_b(3)$

$\qquad\quad \approx 0.83 + 0.56$

$\qquad\quad = 1.39$

91. $\log_b(81) = \log_b(3^4)$

$\qquad\quad = 4\log_b(3)$

$\qquad\quad \approx 4(0.56)$

$\qquad\quad = 2.24$

93. $\log_b\left(\dfrac{9}{4}\right) = \log_b(9) - \log_b(4)$

$$= \log_b\left(3^2\right) - \log_b\left(2^2\right)$$
$$= 2\log_b(3) - 2\log_b(2)$$
$$\approx 2(0.56) - 2(0.36)$$
$$= 0.40$$

95. $\log_b\left(\dfrac{18}{25}\right) = \log_b(18) - \log_b(25)$

$$= \log_b(9 \cdot 2) - \log_b\left(5^2\right)$$
$$= \log_b(9) + \log_b(2) - 2\log_b(5)$$
$$= \log_b\left(3^2\right) + \log_b(2) - 2\log_b(5)$$
$$= 2\log_b(3) + \log_b(2) - 2\log_b(5)$$
$$\approx 2(0.56) + 0.36 - 2(0.83)$$
$$= -0.18$$

97. $\log_7\left[\dfrac{x(x+3)^2}{\sqrt{z-1}}\right]$

$$= \log_7\left[\dfrac{x(x+3)^2}{(z-1)^{\frac{1}{2}}}\right]$$
$$= \log_7\left(x(x+3)^2\right) - \log_7(z-1)^{\frac{1}{2}}$$
$$= \log_7(x) + \log_7(x+3)^2 - \log_7(z-1)^{\frac{1}{2}}$$
$$= \log_7(x) + 2\log_7(x+3) - \dfrac{1}{2}\log_7(z-1)$$

99. $\dfrac{1}{2}\log(2x+3) - 5\log(y) + \dfrac{2}{3}\log(z-4)$

$$= \log(2x+3)^{\frac{1}{2}} - \log\left(y^5\right) + \log(z-4)^{\frac{2}{3}}$$
$$= \log\left[\dfrac{(2x+3)^{\frac{1}{2}}}{y^5}\right] + \log(z-4)^{\frac{2}{3}}$$
$$= \log\left[\dfrac{(2x+3)^{\frac{1}{2}}}{y^5}\cdot(z-4)^{\frac{2}{3}}\right]$$
$$= \log\left[\dfrac{(2x+3)^{\frac{1}{2}}(z-4)^{\frac{2}{3}}}{y^5}\right]$$
$$= \log\left[\dfrac{\sqrt{2x+3}\,\sqrt[3]{(z-4)^2}}{y^5}\right]$$

12.5 Exercises

1. A logarithm with base 10 is called the <u>common</u> logarithm.

3. The formula $\log b(M) = \dfrac{\log_a(M)}{\log_b(M)}$ is called the <u>change</u>-of-<u>base</u> formula.

5. When solving logarithmic equations where two logarithms with the same base are set equal to one another, we set their arguments <u>equal</u> using the <u>one-to-one</u> logarithmic property.

7. $\log_8(27) = \dfrac{\ln(27)}{\ln(8)}$

≈ 1.5850

9. $\log_3(\sqrt{5}) = \dfrac{\ln(\sqrt{5})}{\ln(3)}$

≈ 0.7325

11. $\log_{\frac{1}{2}}(0.016) = \dfrac{\ln(0.016)}{\ln\left(\dfrac{1}{2}\right)}$

≈ 5.9658

13. $\log_{20}(\pi^2) = \dfrac{\ln(\pi^2)}{\ln(20)}$

≈ 0.7642

15. $\log_7(4) = \dfrac{\log(4)}{\log(7)}$

≈ 0.7124

17. $\log_{\sqrt{2}}(1{,}023) = \dfrac{\log(1{,}023)}{\log(\sqrt{2})}$

≈ 19.9972

19. $\log_{1.3}\left(\dfrac{2}{5}\right) = \dfrac{\log\left(\dfrac{2}{5}\right)}{\log(1.3)}$

≈ -3.4924

21. $\log_{1{,}000}(63.2) = \dfrac{\log(63.2)}{\log(1{,}000)}$

≈ 0.6002

23. $\quad 4^x = 11$

$\ln(4^x) = \ln(11)$

$x\ln(4) = \ln(11)$

$\dfrac{x\ln(4)}{\ln(4)} = \dfrac{\ln(11)}{\ln(4)}$

$x = \dfrac{\ln(11)}{\ln(4)}$

$x \approx 1.73$

25. $2^{3x} = 32$

$2^{3x} = 2^5$

$3x = 5$

$x = \dfrac{5}{3}$

$x \approx 1.67$

27. $\quad 3^{6x} = 489$

$\ln(3^{6x}) = \ln(489)$

$6x\ln(3) = \ln(489)$

$\dfrac{6x\ln(3)}{6\ln(3)} = \dfrac{\ln(489)}{6\ln(3)}$

$x = \dfrac{\ln(489)}{6\ln(3)}$

$x \approx 0.94$

29. $\quad 5^{3x-1} = 21$

$\ln(5^{3x-1}) = \ln(21)$

$(3x-1)\ln(5) = \ln(21)$

$3x\ln(5) - \ln(5) = \ln(21)$

$3x\ln(5) = \ln(21) + \ln(5)$

$\dfrac{3x\ln(5)}{3\ln(5)} = \dfrac{\ln(21) + \ln(5)}{3\ln(5)}$

$x = \dfrac{\ln(21) + \ln(5)}{3\ln(5)}$

$x \approx 0.96$

31. $\quad e^x = 1{,}008$

$\ln(e^x) = \ln(1{,}008)$

$x = \ln(1{,}008)$

$x \approx 6.92$

33.
$$e^{-3x} = 2.5$$
$$\ln\left(e^{-3x}\right) = \ln\left(2.5\right)$$
$$-3x = \ln\left(2.5\right)$$
$$x = \frac{\ln\left(2.5\right)}{-3}$$
$$x \approx -0.31$$

35.
$$e^{2x+3} = 9$$
$$\ln\left(e^{2x+3}\right) = \ln\left(9\right)$$
$$2x + 3 = \ln\left(9\right)$$
$$2x = \ln\left(9\right) - 3$$
$$x = \frac{\ln\left(9\right) - 3}{2}$$
$$x \approx -0.40$$

37.
$$8^{2x-1} = 9^{4x+3}$$
$$\ln\left(8^{2x-1}\right) = \ln\left(9^{4x+3}\right)$$
$$\left(2x-1\right)\ln\left(8\right) = \left(4x+3\right)\ln\left(9\right)$$
$$2x\ln\left(8\right) - \ln\left(8\right) = 4x\ln\left(9\right) + 3\ln\left(9\right)$$
$$2x\ln\left(8\right) - 4x\ln\left(9\right) = 3\ln\left(9\right) + \ln\left(8\right)$$
$$x\left[2\ln\left(8\right) - 4\ln\left(9\right)\right] = 3\ln\left(9\right) + \ln\left(8\right)$$
$$\frac{x\left[2\ln\left(8\right) - 4\ln\left(9\right)\right]}{2\ln\left(8\right) - 4\ln\left(9\right)} = \frac{3\ln\left(9\right) + \ln\left(8\right)}{2\ln\left(8\right) - 4\ln\left(9\right)}$$
$$x = \frac{3\ln\left(9\right) + \ln\left(8\right)}{2\ln\left(8\right) - 4\ln\left(9\right)}$$
$$x \approx -1.87$$

39.
$$10^{8-x} = e^{3x}$$
$$\ln\left(10^{8-x}\right) = \ln\left(e^{3x}\right)$$
$$\left(8-x\right)\ln\left(10\right) = 3x$$
$$8\ln\left(10\right) - x\ln\left(10\right) = 3x$$
$$8\ln\left(10\right) = 3x + x\ln\left(10\right)$$
$$8\ln\left(10\right) = x\left[3 + \ln\left(10\right)\right]$$
$$\frac{8\ln\left(10\right)}{3 + \ln\left(10\right)} = \frac{x\left[3 + \ln\left(10\right)\right]}{3 + \ln\left(10\right)}$$
$$\frac{8\ln\left(10\right)}{3 + \ln\left(10\right)} = x$$
$$x \approx 3.47$$

41.
$$\log_5\left(x+7\right) = 2$$
$$5^2 = x+7$$
$$x+7 = 25$$
$$x = 18$$

Check
$$\log_5\left(18+7\right) = 2$$
$$\log_5\left(25\right) = 2$$
$$2 = 2$$
The solution set is $\{18\}$.

43.
$$\log_6\left(2x-3\right) = \log_6\left(15-7x\right)$$
$$2x-3 = 15-7x$$
$$9x = 18$$
$$x = 2$$

Check
$$\log_6\left(2(2)-3\right) = \log_6\left(15-7(2)\right)$$
$$\log_6\left(1\right) = \log_6\left(1\right)$$
$$0 = 0$$
The solution set is $\{2\}$.

45.
$$\log\left(3x-10\right) = \log\left(4+10x\right)$$
$$3x-10 = 4+10x$$
$$-7x = 14$$
$$x = -2$$

Check
$$\log\left(3(-2)-10\right) = \log\left(4+10(-2)\right)$$
$$\log\left(-16\right) = \log\left(-16\right)$$
undefined
The solution set is $\{\ \}$.

47.
$$\log_3 x^2 = 4$$
$$3^4 = x^2$$
$$x^2 = 81$$
$$x = -\sqrt{81} \quad \text{or} \quad x = \sqrt{81}$$
$$x = -9 \quad \text{or} \quad x = 9$$

Check
$$\log_3\left(-9\right)^2 = 4 \qquad \log_3\left(9\right)^2 = 4$$
$$\log_3\left(81\right) = 4 \qquad \log_3\left(81\right) = 4$$
$$4 = 4 \qquad\qquad 4 = 4$$
The solution set is $\{-9, 9\}$.

49. $\log(x) + \log(x+21) = 2$

$\log[x(x+21)] = 2$

$10^2 = x(x+21)$

$x^2 + 21x - 100 = 0$

$(x+25)(x-4) = 0$

$x + 25 = 0$ or $x - 4 = 0$

$x = -25$ or $x = 4$

Check

$\log(-25) + \log(-25+21) = 2$

undefined

$\log(4) + \log(4+21) = 2$

$\log(4) + \log(25) = 2$

$\log(100) = 2$

$2 = 2$

The solution set is $\{4\}$.

Check

$\log_2\left(6 \cdot \dfrac{1}{3}\right) + \log_2\left(\dfrac{1}{3}+1\right) = \log_2\left(3 - \dfrac{1}{3}\right)$

$\log_2(2) + \log_2\left(\dfrac{4}{3}\right) = \log_2\left(\dfrac{8}{3}\right)$

$\log_2\left(2 \cdot \dfrac{4}{3}\right) = \log_2\left(\dfrac{8}{3}\right)$

$\log_2\left(\dfrac{8}{3}\right) = \log_2\left(\dfrac{8}{3}\right)$

$\log_2\left(6 \cdot -\dfrac{3}{2}\right) + \log_2\left(-\dfrac{3}{2}+1\right) = \log_2\left(3 - \left(-\dfrac{3}{2}\right)\right)$

$\log_2(-9) + \log_2\left(-\dfrac{1}{2}\right) = \log_2\left(\dfrac{9}{2}\right)$

undefined

The solution set is $\left\{\dfrac{1}{3}\right\}$.

51. $\ln(3x) - \ln(x-2) = \ln(5)$

$\ln\left(\dfrac{3x}{x-2}\right) = \ln(5)$

$\dfrac{3x}{x-2} = 5$

$3x = 5(x-2)$

$3x = 5x - 10$

$-2x = -10$

$x = 5$

Check

$\ln(3 \cdot 5) - \ln(5-2) = \ln(5)$

$\ln(15) - \ln(3) = \ln(5)$

$\ln(5) = \ln(5)$

The solution set is $\{5\}$.

53. $\log_2(6x) + \log_2(x+1) = \log_2(3-x)$

$\log_2[6x(x+1)] = \log_2(3-x)$

$6x(x+1) = 3 - x$

$6x^2 + 6x = 3 - x$

$6x^2 + 7x - 3 = 0$

$(3x-1)(2x+3) = 0$

$3x - 1 = 0$ or $2x + 3 = 0$

$x = \dfrac{1}{3}$ or $x = -\dfrac{3}{2}$

55. $\log_2(5x^2 - 36x + 15) = 3$

$2^3 = 5x^2 - 36x + 15$

$5x^2 - 36x + 7 = 0$

$(5x-1)(x-7) = 0$

$5x - 1 = 0$ or $x - 7 = 0$

$x = \dfrac{1}{5}$ or $x = 7$

Check

$\log_2\left(5\left(\dfrac{1}{5}\right)^2 - 36\left(\dfrac{1}{5}\right) + 15\right) = 3$

$\log_2\left(\dfrac{1}{5} - \dfrac{36}{5} + 15\right) = 3$

$\log_2(8) = 3$

$3 = 3$

$\log_2\left(5(7)^2 - 36(7) + 15\right) = 3$

$\log_2(245 - 252 + 15) = 3$

$\log_2(8) = 3$

$2 = 2$

The solution set is $\left\{\dfrac{1}{5}, 7\right\}$.

57. $\log_3(x) + \log_3(x-6) = 3$

$$\log_3[x(x-6)] = 3$$

$$3^3 = x(x-6)$$

$$x^2 - 6x - 27 = 0$$

$$(x-9)(x+3) = 0$$

$$x - 9 = 0 \quad \text{or} \quad x + 3 = 0$$

$$x = 9 \quad \text{or} \quad x = -3$$

Check

$$\log_3(9) + \log_3(9-6) = 3$$

$$\log_3(9) + \log_3(3) = 3$$

$$\log_3(27) = 3$$

$$3 = 3$$

$$\log_3(-3) + \log_3(-3-6) = 3$$

$$\log_3(-3) + \log_3(-9) = 3$$

undefined

The solution set is $\{9\}$.

59. $\log(x+18) - \log(2) = \log(x+3) + \log(x-3)$

$$\log\left[\frac{x+18}{2}\right] = \log[(x+3)(x-3)]$$

$$\frac{x+18}{2} = (x+3)(x-3)$$

$$x + 18 = 2(x+3)(x-3)$$

$$x + 18 = 2x^2 - 18$$

$$2x^2 - x - 36 = 0$$

$$(2x-9)(x+4) = 0$$

$$2x - 9 = 0 \quad \text{or} \quad x + 4 = 0$$

$$x = \frac{9}{2} \quad \text{or} \quad x = -4$$

Check

$$\log\left(\frac{9}{2}+18\right) - \log(2) = \log\left(\frac{9}{2}+3\right) + \log\left(\frac{9}{2}-3\right)$$

$$\log\left(\frac{45}{2}\right) - \log(2) = \log\left(\frac{15}{2}\right) + \log\left(\frac{3}{2}\right)$$

$$\log\left(\frac{45}{4}\right) = \log\left(\frac{45}{4}\right)$$

$$\log(-4+18) - \log(2) = \log(-4+3) + \log(-4-3)$$

$$\log(14) - \log(2) = \log(-1) + \log(-7)$$

undefined

The solution set is $\left\{\frac{9}{2}\right\}$.

61. Answers will vary; for example: The change of base formula can be used to evaluate logarithms with bases other than e and 10.

63. a) $\qquad 3^x = 7$

$$\log(3^x) = \log(7)$$

$$x\log(3) = \log(7)$$

$$\frac{x\log(3)}{\log(3)} = \frac{\log(7)}{\log(3)}$$

$$x = \frac{\log(7)}{\log(3)}$$

$$x \approx 1.7712$$

63. b) $\qquad 3^x = 7$

$$\ln(3^x) = \ln(7)$$

$$x\ln(3) = \ln(7)$$

$$\frac{x\ln(3)}{\ln(3)} = \frac{\ln(7)}{\ln(3)}$$

$$x = \frac{\ln(7)}{\ln(3)}$$

$$x \approx 1.7712$$

63. c) $\qquad 3^x = 7$

$$\log_3(3^x) = \log(7)$$

$$x = \log_3(7)$$

$$x = \frac{\log(7)}{\log(3)}$$

$$x \approx 1.7712$$

All answers give $x \approx 1.7712$. Parts a) and b) differ in the use of the natural log or common log to obtain the answers. In part c), taking the $\log_3$ of both sides results in $x = \log_3(7)$. From this solution it is necessary to use the change-of-base formula to obtain the solution.

65. The doubling growth formula uses time, rate (the time to double), and an initial amount to find a final amount.

67. $A_0 = 2.3$

$d = 23.4$

$t = 6$

$$A = A_0 2^{\frac{t}{d}}$$

$$= (2.3) 2^{\frac{6}{23.4}}$$

$$\approx 2.7$$

There will be 2.7 ng/ml of PSA in Mr. Jackson's blood 6 months after the surgery.

69. $A_0 = 2.1$

$d = 150$

$t = 185$

$$A = A_0 2^{\frac{t}{d}}$$

$$= (2.1) 2^{\frac{185}{150}}$$

$$\approx 4.9$$

There will be approximately 4.9 million online users in 185 days.

71. $P = \$5,250$

$r = 0.035$

$t = 18$

annually, $n = 1$ $A = P\left(1 + \dfrac{r}{n}\right)^{nt}$

$$= 5,250\left(1 + \frac{0.035}{1}\right)^{1(18)}$$

$$\approx \$9,751.82$$

semiannually, $n = 2$ $A = P\left(1 + \dfrac{r}{n}\right)^{nt}$

$$= 5,250\left(1 + \frac{0.035}{2}\right)^{2(18)}$$

$$\approx \$9,803.89$$

monthly, $n = 12$ $A = P\left(1 + \dfrac{r}{n}\right)^{nt}$

$$= 5,250\left(1 + \frac{0.035}{12}\right)^{12(18)}$$

$$\approx \$9,848.42$$

weekly, $n = 52$ $A = P\left(1 + \dfrac{r}{n}\right)^{nt}$

$$= 5,250\left(1 + \frac{0.035}{52}\right)^{52(18)}$$

$$\approx \$9,855.37$$

daily, $n = 365$ $A = P\left(1 + \dfrac{r}{n}\right)^{nt}$

$$= 5,250\left(1 + \frac{0.035}{365}\right)^{365(18)}$$

$$\approx \$9,857.15$$

73. $P = \$5,000$

$t = 8$

Patrick, $r = 0.0575$, $n = 12$

$$A = P\left(1 + \frac{r}{n}\right)^{nt}$$

$$= 5,000\left(1 + \frac{0.0575}{12}\right)^{12(8)}$$

$$\approx \$7,911.67$$

Sean, $r = 0.055$, $n = 52$

$$A = P\left(1 + \frac{r}{n}\right)^{nt}$$

$$= 5,000\left(1 + \frac{0.055}{52}\right)^{52(8)}$$

$$\approx \$7,761.73$$

Patrick made the wiser decision.

75. Prepare We will use the half-life decay formula to determine how many grams of U-238 will remain after 2 million years if the initial amount is 12 grams. The half-life of U-238 is 4.51 billion years.

Plan Identify the variables in the half-life decay formula $A = A_0 \left(\frac{1}{2}\right)^{\frac{t}{h}}$, then substitute the known values into the formula to determine how much U-238 will remain after 2 million years.

The known variables are $A_0 = 12$ grams, $t = 2,000,000$ years, and $h = 4,510,000,000$ years.

Process

$$A = A_0 \left(\frac{1}{2}\right)^{\frac{t}{h}}$$

$$= 12 \left(\frac{1}{2}\right)^{\frac{2,000,000}{4,510,00,000}}$$

$$\approx 11.9963$$

Approximately 11.9963 grams of U-238 will remain after 2 million years.

Ponder Does our answer seem reasonable? Yes, as 2 million years is very small compared to the half-life of U-238. Therefore, the majority of the 12 gram sample should remain.

77. Prepare We will use the half-life decay formula to determine how many grams of Am-241 will remain after 100 years if the initial amount is 0.24 pounds. The half-life of Am-241 is 432 years.

Plan Identify the variables in the half-life decay formula $A = A_0 \left(\frac{1}{2}\right)^{\frac{t}{h}}$, convert the 0.24 pounds to grams, then substitute the known values into the formula to determine how many grams of Am-241 will remain after 100 years. The known variables are $A_0 = 0.24$ pounds, $t = 100$ years, and $h = 432$ years. Multiply 0.24 by 454 to obtain 108.96 grams of Am-241.

Process

$$A = A_0 \left(\frac{1}{2}\right)^{\frac{t}{h}}$$

$$= 108.96 \left(\frac{1}{2}\right)^{\frac{100}{432}}$$

$$\approx 92.8077$$

Approximately 92.8077 grams of Am-241 will remain after 100 years.

Ponder Does our answer seem reasonable? Yes, because after 432 years only about 54 grams of the Am-241 would remain. Therefore, 92.8077 grams seems reasonable.

79.
$$e^{2x} - e^x - 12 = 0$$
$$\left(e^x + 3\right)\left(e^x - 4\right) = 0$$
$$e^x + 3 = 0 \quad \text{or} \quad e^x - 4 = 0$$
$$e^x = -3 \quad \text{or} \quad e^x = 4$$
$$\text{undefined} \quad \text{or} \quad x = \ln(4) \approx 1.39$$

81.
$$3xe^{-2x} - x^2 e^{-2x} = 0$$
$$xe^{-2x}(3 - x) = 0$$
$$x = 0 \quad \text{or} \quad \cancel{e^{-2x} = 0} \quad \text{or} \quad 3 - x = 0$$
$$x = 3$$

The solution set is $\{0, 3\}$.

83.
$$\log_7(x+2) + \log_7(x-2) = \log_7(2x)$$
$$\log_7\left[(x+2)(x-2)\right] = \log_7(2x)$$
$$\log_7\left(x^2 - 4\right) = \log_7(2x)$$
$$x^2 - 4 = 2x$$
$$x^2 - 2x - 4 = 0$$
$$x^2 - 2x = 4$$
$$x^2 - 2x + 1 = 4 + 1$$
$$(x-1)^2 = 5$$
$$x - 1 = -\sqrt{5} \quad \text{or} \quad x - 1 = \sqrt{5}$$
$$\cancel{x = 1 - \sqrt{5}} \quad \text{or} \quad x = 1 + \sqrt{5}$$

Chapter 12 Review Problem Set

1. The function is one-to-one because it passes the horizontal line test.

2. The function is not one-to-one because it fails the horizontal line test.

3. The function is not one-to-one because it fails the horizontal line test.

4. The function is one-to-one because it passes the horizontal line test.

5.
$$(f \circ g)(x) \qquad (g \circ f)(x)$$
$$= f(g(x))$$
$$= f\left(\frac{x+1}{2}\right) \qquad = g(f(x))$$
$$= g(2x-1)$$
$$= 2\left(\frac{x+1}{2}\right)-1 \quad = \frac{(2x-1)+1}{2}$$
$$= x+1-1 \qquad = \frac{2x}{2}$$
$$= x \qquad\qquad = x$$

These functions are inverses.

6.
$$(f \circ g)(x) \qquad (g \circ f)(x)$$
$$= g(f(x))$$
$$= f(g(x)) \qquad = g\left(\frac{x-5}{3}\right)$$
$$= f(3x+5)$$
$$= \frac{(3x+5)-5}{3} \quad = 3\left(\frac{x-5}{3}\right)+5$$
$$= \frac{3x}{3} \qquad\qquad = x-5+5$$
$$= x \qquad\qquad = x$$

These functions are inverses.

7.
$$f(x) = 3x+4$$
$$y = 3x+4$$
$$x = 3y+4$$
$$x-4 = 3y$$
$$\frac{x-4}{3} = y$$
$$f^{-1}(x) = \frac{x-4}{3}$$

The domain of f is the interval $(-\infty, \infty)$, which is the range of the inverse function. The range of f is the interval $(-\infty, \infty)$, which is the domain of the inverse function.

Verifications
$$(f \circ f^{-1})(x) \quad\Big|\quad (f^{-1} \circ f)(x)$$
$$= f(f^{-1}(x)) \quad\Big|\quad = f^{-1}(f(x))$$
$$= f\left(\frac{x-4}{3}\right) \quad\Big|\quad = f^{-1}(3x+4)$$
$$= 3\left(\frac{x-4}{3}\right)+4 \quad\Big|\quad = \frac{(3x+4)-4}{3}$$
$$= x-4+4 \quad\Big|\quad = \frac{3x}{3}$$
$$= x \quad\Big|\quad = x$$

8.
$$f(x) = \sqrt{x}$$
$$y = \sqrt{x}$$
$$x = \sqrt{y}$$
$$x^2 = y$$
$$f^{-1}(x) = x^2, \ x \geq 0$$

The domain of f is the interval $[0, \infty)$, which is the range of the inverse function. The range of f is the interval $[0, \infty)$, which is the domain of the inverse function.

Verifications
$$(f \circ f^{-1})(x) \quad\Big|\quad (f^{-1} \circ f)(x)$$
$$= f(f^{-1}(x)) \quad\Big|\quad = f^{-1}(f(x))$$
$$= f(x^2) \quad\Big|\quad = f^{-1}(\sqrt{x})$$
$$= \sqrt{x^2} \quad\Big|\quad = (\sqrt{x})^2$$
$$= x \quad\Big|\quad = x$$

9.
$$h(x) = (x+2)^2$$
$$y = (x+2)^2$$
$$x = (y+2)^2$$
$$\sqrt{x} = y+2$$
$$\sqrt{x}-2 = y$$
$$h^{-1}(x) = \sqrt{x}-2, \ x \geq 0$$

The domain of h is the interval $[-2, \infty)$, which is the range of the inverse function. The range of h is the interval $[0, \infty)$, which is the domain of the inverse function.

Verifications

$\left(f \circ f^{-1}\right)(x)$	$\left(f^{-1} \circ f\right)(x)$
$= f\left(f^{-1}(x)\right)$	$= f^{-1}\left(f(x)\right)$
$= f\left(\sqrt{x}-2\right)$	$= f^{-1}\left((x+2)^2\right)$
$= \left(\left(\sqrt{x}-2\right)+2\right)^2$	$= \sqrt{(x+2)^2}-2$
$= \left(\sqrt{x}\right)^2$	$= x+2-2$
$= x$	$= x$

10. $g(x) = \dfrac{1}{5-x}$

$y = \dfrac{1}{5-x}$

$x = \dfrac{1}{5-y}$

$x(5-y) = \dfrac{1}{5-y}(5-y)$

$5x - xy = 1$

$-xy = -5x + 1$

$y = \dfrac{-5x+1}{-x}$

$y = 5 - \dfrac{1}{x}$

$g^{-1}(x) = 5 - \dfrac{1}{x}, \ x \neq 0$

The domain of g is the interval $(-\infty,5) \cup (5,\infty)$, which is the range of the inverse function. The range of g is the interval $(-\infty,0) \cup (0,\infty)$, which is the domain of the inverse function.

Verifications

$\left(g \circ g^{-1}\right)(x)$	$\left(g^{-1} \circ g\right)(x)$
$= g\left(g^{-1}(x)\right)$	$= g^{-1}\left(g(x)\right)$
$= g\left(5-\dfrac{1}{x}\right)$	$= g^{-1}\left(\dfrac{1}{5-x}\right)$
$= \dfrac{1}{5-\left(5-\dfrac{1}{x}\right)}$	$= 5 - \dfrac{1}{\dfrac{1}{5-x}}$
$= \dfrac{1}{\dfrac{1}{x}}$	$= 5 - (5-x)$
$= x$	$= x$

11. $\{(5,-2),(2,-1),(3,0),(4,1)\}$

12. $f(x) = -\sqrt{x}$

$y = -\sqrt{x}$

$x = -\sqrt{y}$

$x^2 = y$

$f^{-1}(x) = x^2, \ x \leq 0$

13. $f(x) = -(x-2)^2$

$y = -(x-2)^2$

$x = -(y-2)^2$

$-x = (y-2)^2$

$\sqrt{-x} = y-2$

$\sqrt{-x} + 2 = y$

$f^{-1}(x) = \sqrt{-x} + 2, \ x \leq 0$

14. $f(x) = |x+2|$

$y = |x+2|$

$x = |y+2|$

$x = y+2$

$x - 2 = y$

$f^{-1}(x) = x - 2, \ x \geq 0$

15. a) $f(x) = 350 + 0.05x$

$y = 350 + 0.05x$

$x = 350 + 0.05y$

$x - 350 = 0.05y$

$\dfrac{x-350}{0.05} = y$

$f^{-1}(x) = \dfrac{x-350}{0.05}$

$f^{-1}(x)$ is Cameron's weekly sales, and x is the total weekly income.

15. b) $f^{-1}(427.50) = \dfrac{(427.50)-350}{0.05}$

$= 1,550.00$

Cameron's total sales for the week was $1,550.00.

16. a) $f(x) = 13.8x$

$y = 13.8x$

$x = 13.8y$

$\dfrac{x}{13.8} = y$

$f^{-1}(x) = \dfrac{x}{13.8}$

$f^{-1}(x)$ is the number of Euros and x is the number Austrian schillings.

16. b) $f^{-1}(634{,}800) = \dfrac{634{,}800}{13.8}$

$\qquad\qquad\quad = 46{,}000$

Dr. Alpern received 46,000 Euros.

17. $f(x) = 3^x$

x	$f(x) = 3^x$
-2	$3^{-2} = \frac{1}{3^2} = \frac{1}{9}$
-1	$3^{-1} = \frac{1}{3}$
0	$3^0 = 1$
1	$3^1 = 3$
2	$3^2 = 9$

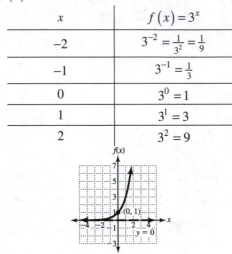

18. $f(x) = 3^{-x}$

x	$f(x) = 3^{-x}$
-2	$3^{-(-2)} = 3^2 = 9$
-1	$3^{-(-1)} = 3^1 = 3$
0	$3^{-(0)} = 3^0 = 1$
1	$3^{-(1)} = \frac{1}{3^1} = \frac{1}{3}$
2	$3^{-(2)} = \frac{1}{3^2} = \frac{1}{9}$

19. $f(x) = \left(\dfrac{1}{3}\right)^x$

x	$f(x) = \left(\frac{1}{3}\right)^x$
-2	$\left(\frac{1}{3}\right)^{-2} = 3^2 = 9$
-1	$\left(\frac{1}{3}\right)^{-1} = 3^1 = 3$
0	$\left(\frac{1}{3}\right)^{0} = 1$
1	$\left(\frac{1}{3}\right)^{1} = \frac{1}{3}$
2	$\left(\frac{1}{3}\right)^{2} = \frac{1}{9}$

20. $f(x) = 2^{x-2}$

x	$f(x) = 2^{x-2}$
-2	$2^{-2-2} = 2^{-4} = \frac{1}{2^4} = \frac{1}{16}$
-1	$2^{-1-2} = 2^{-3} = \frac{1}{2^3} = \frac{1}{8}$
0	$2^{0-2} = 2^{-2} = \frac{1}{2^2} = \frac{1}{4}$
1	$2^{1-2} = 2^{-1} = \frac{1}{2}$
2	$2^{2-2} = 2^0 = 1$

21. $f(-3) = -3e^{2.5(-3)}$ $\qquad$ $f(0) = -3e^{2.5(0)}$

$\qquad\quad = -3e^{-7.5}$ $\qquad\qquad\qquad = -3e^0$

$\qquad\quad \approx -0.002$ $\qquad\qquad\qquad\ = -3$

$f(2) = -3e^{2.5(2)}$

$\qquad = -3e^5$

$\qquad \approx -445.239$

22.

$f(-3) = 5e^{-4(-3)}$

$= 5e^{12}$

$\approx 813,773.957$

$f(0) = 5e^{-4(0)}$

$= 5e^0$

$= 5$

$f(2) = 5e^{-4(2)}$

$= 5e^{-8}$

≈ 0.002

23. $10^x = 1,000$

$10^x = 10^3$

$x = 3$

Solution Set: $\{3\}$

24. $8^x = 4$

$\left(2^3\right)^x = 2^2$

$2^{3x} = 2^2$

$3x = 2$

$x = \dfrac{2}{3}$

Solution Set: $\left\{\dfrac{2}{3}\right\}$

25. $3^x = \dfrac{1}{729}$

$3^x = \dfrac{1}{3^6}$

$3^x = 3^{-6}$

$x = -6$

Solution Set: $\{-6\}$

26. $8^{5x} = 16^{2x+1}$

$\left(2^3\right)^{5x} = \left(2^4\right)^{2x+1}$

$2^{15x} = 2^{8x+4}$

$15x = 8x + 4$

$7x = 4$

$x = \dfrac{4}{7}$

Solution Set: $\left\{\dfrac{4}{7}\right\}$

27. $\dfrac{1}{9} = 27^{2x}$

$\dfrac{1}{3^2} = \left(3^3\right)^{2x}$

$3^{-2} = 3^{6x}$

$-2 = 6x$

$-\dfrac{1}{3} = x$

Solution Set: $\left\{-\dfrac{1}{3}\right\}$

28. $\left(\dfrac{2}{3}x + 1\right)^3 = (5 - 6x)^3$

$\dfrac{2}{3}x + 1 = 5 - 6x$

$\dfrac{20}{3}x = 4$

$x = \dfrac{3}{5}$

Solution Set: $\left\{\dfrac{3}{5}\right\}$

29. $P = \$6,000$

$r = 0.06$

$t = 3$

$A = Pe^{rt}$

$= 6,000e^{0.06(3)}$

$= 6,000e^{0.18}$

$\approx 7,183.30$

After three years, Greg will have \$7,183.30.

30. $P = \$9,600$

$r = 0.04$

$t = 4$

$A = Pe^{rt}$

$= 9,600e^{0.04(4)}$

$= 9,600e^{0.16}$

$\approx 11,265.70$

After four years, Marsha will owe \$11,265.70.

31. $P = \$850$
$r = 0.125$
$t = 6$

$$A = Pe^{rt}$$
$$= 850e^{0.125(6)}$$
$$= 850e^{0.75}$$
$$\approx 1,799.45$$

After six years, Jan will owe $1,799.45.

32. Prepare   We will use the continuous growth formula, $A = Pe^{rt}$, to approximate the population of the world in 2020 given the population in 2010.

Plan Identify the unknowns in the growth model $A = Pe^{rt}$.
$P = 6.812$ billion
$r = 0.0106$
$t = 10$
Substitute these values into the growth formula and use a calculator to round to the nearest person.

Process
$$A = Pe^{rt}$$
$$= (6.812)e^{0.0106(10)}$$
$$= (6.812)e^{0.106}$$
$$\approx 7.573$$

The population of world will be approximately 7.573 billion in 2020.

Ponder   Does the answer seem reasonable? Yes. However, it is just an approximation, under normal conditions, and assumes a continuous growth model.

33. $2^5 = 32$

34. $9^{-2} = \dfrac{1}{81}$

35. $25^{\frac{1}{2}} = 5$

36. $4^1 = 4$

37. $\log_7 (2,401) = 4$

38. $\log_5 \left(\dfrac{1}{125} \right) = -3$

39. $\log_{64} (4) = \dfrac{1}{3}$

40. $\log_3 (243) = 5$

41. $\log_6 (36) = y$ if and only if $6^y = 36$
$$6^y = 36$$
$$6^y = 6^2$$
$$y = 2$$
Therefore, $\log_6 (36) = 2$.

42. $\log_3 \left(\dfrac{1}{27} \right) = y$ if and only if $3^y = \dfrac{1}{27}$
$$3^y = \dfrac{1}{27}$$
$$3^y = 3^{-3}$$
$$y = -3$$
Therefore, $\log_3 \left(\dfrac{1}{27} \right) = -3$.

43. $\log_8 (8) = y$ if and only if $8^y = 8$
$$8^y = 8$$
$$8^y = 8^1$$
$$y = 1$$
Therefore, $\log_8 (8) = 1$.

44. $\log_{1,000} (10) = y$ if and only if $1,000^y = 10$
$$1,000^y = 10$$
$$1,000^y = 1,000^{\frac{1}{3}}$$
$$y = \dfrac{1}{3}$$
Therefore, $\log_{1,000} (10) = \dfrac{1}{3}$.

45. $f(x) = \log_2 (x)$

$x = 2^y$	y	Solutions (x, y)
$2^{-1} = \frac{1}{2}$	-1	$\left(\frac{1}{2}, -1 \right)$
$2^0 = 1$	0	$(1, 0)$
$2^1 = 2$	1	$(2, 1)$

$D_f = (0, \infty)$, $R_f = (-\infty, \infty)$

46. $f(x) = \log_{\frac{1}{4}}(x)$

$x = \left(\frac{1}{4}\right)^y$	y	Solutions (x, y)
$\left(\frac{1}{4}\right)^{-1} = 4$	-1	$(4, -1)$
$\left(\frac{1}{4}\right)^0 = 1$	0	$(1, 0)$
$\left(\frac{1}{4}\right)^1 = \frac{1}{4}$	1	$\left(\frac{1}{4}, 1\right)$

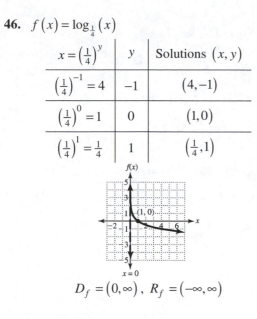

$D_f = (0, \infty), \ R_f = (-\infty, \infty)$

47. $\log(10,000) = 4.000$

48. $\ln\left(\frac{2}{5}\right) \approx -0.916$

49. $\log(-96)$ is undefined because $-96 \notin (0, \infty)$, the domain of the logarithm.

50. $\ln\left(\frac{\pi + 2}{5}\right) \approx 0.028$

51. $\log_2(x) = 4$

$2^4 = x$

$x = 16$

52. $\log_3(x) = -4$

$3^{-4} = x$

$x = \dfrac{1}{81}$

53. $\log_{625}(5) = y$

$625^y = 5$

$\left(5^4\right)^y = 5^1$

$5^{4y} = 5^1$

$4y = 1$

$y = \dfrac{1}{4}$

54. $\log_2\left(\dfrac{1}{32}\right) = y$

$2^y = \dfrac{1}{32}$

$2^y = \dfrac{1}{2^5}$

$2^y = 2^{-5}$

$y = -5$

55. $\log_b(100) = 2$

$b^2 = 100$

$b^2 = 10^2$

$b = 10$

56. $\log_b(1,000) = -3$

$b^{-3} = 1,000$

$b^{-3} = 10^3$

$b^{-3} = \left(\dfrac{1}{10}\right)^{-3}$

$b = \dfrac{1}{10}$

57. $\ln(x) = 8$

$e^8 = x$

$x \approx 2,980.96$

58. $\log(x) = 1.875$

$10^{1.875} = x$

$x \approx 74.99$

59. $L = 10\log_{10}\left(\dfrac{I}{I_0}\right)$

$L = 10\log_{10}\left(\dfrac{10^{-4}}{10^{-12}}\right)$

$L = 10\log_{10}\left(10^8\right)$

$L = 10(8)$

$L = 80$

The decibel level of the average home is 80 dB.

60. $L = 10\log_{10}\left(\dfrac{I}{I_0}\right)$

$L = 10\log_{10}\left(\dfrac{10^{-2}}{10^{-12}}\right)$

$L = 10\log_{10}\left(10^{10}\right)$

$L = 10(10)$

$L = 100$

The decibel level of a lawn mower is 100 dB.

61. $\log_6(4x) = \log_6(4) + \log_6(x)$

62. $\log_3\left(a^7\right) = 7\log_3(a)$

63. $\log_2\left(\dfrac{y}{3}\right) = \log_2(y) - \log_2(3)$

64. $\log(a+b)$

65. $\ln(xyz) = \ln(x) + \ln(y) + \ln(z)$

66. $\log_x\left(\sqrt{3a}\right) = \log_x(3a)^{\frac{1}{2}}$

$= \dfrac{1}{2}\log_x(3a)$

$= \dfrac{1}{2}\left[\log_x(3) + \log_x(a)\right]$

67. $\log_5\left[2(y-1)\right] = \log_5(2) + \log_5(y-1)$

68. $\log_a\left(\dfrac{x^5}{y+3}\right) = \log_a\left(x^5\right) - \log_a(y+3)$

$= 5\log_a(x) - \log_a(y+3)$

69. $\log_6(a) + \log_6(b) = \log_6(ab)$

70. $-5\log_b(x) = \log_b\left(x^{-5}\right)$

71. $4\log(x) + \log(3) = \log\left(x^4\right) + \log(3)$

$= \log\left(3x^4\right)$

72. $\ln(a) - \ln(b+5) = \ln\left(\dfrac{a}{b+5}\right)$

73. $\dfrac{1}{2}\log_a(x) + 2\log_a(x+3)$

$= \log_a\left(x^{\frac{1}{2}}\right) + \log_a(x+3)^2$

$= \log_a\left(\sqrt{x}\right) + \log_a(x+3)^2$

$= \log_a\left[\sqrt{x}(x+3)^2\right]$

74. $2\log(h) + 3\log(k) - \log(m)$

$= \log\left(h^2\right) + \log\left(k^3\right) - \log(m)$

$= \log\left(h^2k^3\right) - \log(m)$

$= \log\left(\dfrac{h^2k^3}{m}\right)$

75. $\ln(15) - \ln(27) + 2\ln(3)$

$= \ln(15) - \ln(27) + \ln\left(3^2\right)$

$= \ln\left(\dfrac{15}{27}\right) + \ln\left(3^2\right)$

$= \ln\left(\dfrac{5}{9}\cdot 9\right)$

$= \ln(5)$

76. $\ln(x) + 6\ln(y) - 2\ln(w) - \dfrac{1}{3}\ln(z)$

$= \ln(x) + \ln\left(y^6\right) - \ln\left(w^2\right) - \ln\left(z^{\frac{1}{3}}\right)$

$= \ln\left(xy^6\right) - \ln\left(w^2\right) - \ln\left(\sqrt[3]{z}\right)$

$= \ln\left(\dfrac{xy^6}{w^2}\right) - \ln\left(\sqrt[3]{z}\right)$

$= \ln\left(\dfrac{xy^6}{w^2\sqrt[3]{z}}\right)$

77. $\log_b(10) = \log_b(2\cdot 5)$

$= \log_b(2) + \log_b(5)$

$\approx 0.39 + 0.89$

$= 1.28$

78. $\log_b\left(\dfrac{9}{5}\right) = \log_b(9) - \log_b(5)$

$= \log_b\left(3^2\right) - \log_b(5)$

$= 2\log_b(3) - \log_b(5)$

$\approx 2(0.61) - 0.89$

$= 0.33$

79. $\log_b\left(\dfrac{25}{18}\right) = \log_b(25) - \log_b(18)$

$= \log_b\left(5^2\right) - \log_b\left(2 \cdot 3^2\right)$

$= 2\log_b(5) - \left[\log_b(2) + \log_b\left(3^2\right)\right]$

$= 2\log_b(5) - \left[\log_b(2) + 2\log_b(3)\right]$

$\approx 2(0.89) - \left[0.39 + 2(0.61)\right]$

$= 0.17$

80. $\log_b(45) = \log_b\left(5 \cdot 3^2\right)$

$= \log_b(5) + \log_b\left(3^2\right)$

$= \log_b(5) + 2\log_b(3)$

$\approx 0.89 + 2(0.61)$

$= 2.11$

81. $\log_8(23) = \dfrac{\ln(23)}{\ln(8)}$

≈ 1.5079

82. $\log_{\sqrt{3}}(145) = \dfrac{\ln(145)}{\ln\left(\sqrt{3}\right)}$

≈ 9.0600

83. $\log_{245}(0.23) = \dfrac{\ln(0.23)}{\ln(245)}$

≈ -0.2672

84. $\log_b\left(\pi^2\right) = \dfrac{\ln\left(\pi^2\right)}{\ln(b)}$

$= \dfrac{2\ln(\pi)}{\ln(b)}$

85. $\log_\pi(4,000) = \dfrac{\log(4,000)}{\log(\pi)}$

≈ 7.2454

86. $\log_{16}(42) = \dfrac{\log(42)}{\log(16)}$

≈ 1.3481

87. $\log_{\frac{1}{3}}(1.0008) = \dfrac{\log(1.0008)}{\log\left(\dfrac{1}{3}\right)}$

≈ -0.0007

88. $\log_{2,000}\left(e^3\right) = \dfrac{\log\left(e^3\right)}{\log(2,000)}$

≈ 0.3947

89. $2^x = 13$

$\ln\left(2^x\right) = \ln(13)$

$x\ln(2) = \ln(13)$

$\dfrac{x\ln(2)}{\ln(2)} = \dfrac{\ln(13)}{\ln(2)}$

$x = \dfrac{\ln(13)}{\ln(2)}$

$x \approx 3.70$

90. $3^{-4x} = 7$

$\ln\left(3^{-4x}\right) = \ln(7)$

$-4x\ln(3) = \ln(7)$

$\dfrac{-4x\ln(3)}{-4\ln(3)} = \dfrac{\ln(7)}{-4\ln(3)}$

$x = \dfrac{\ln(7)}{-4\ln(3)}$

$x \approx -0.44$

91. $6^{2x-5} = 41$

$\ln\left(6^{2x-5}\right) = \ln(41)$

$(2x-5)\ln(6) = \ln(41)$

$2x\ln(6) - 5\ln(6) = \ln(41)$

$2x\ln(6) = \ln(41) + 5\ln(6)$

$\dfrac{2x\ln(6)}{2\ln(6)} = \dfrac{\ln(41) + 5\ln(6)}{2\ln(6)}$

$x = \dfrac{\ln(41) + 5\ln(6)}{2\ln(6)}$

$x \approx 3.54$

92. $e^x = 22$

$\ln\left(e^x\right) = \ln(22)$

$x = \ln(22)$

$x \approx 3.09$

93.

$$e^{10-3x} = 18$$

$$\ln\left(e^{10-3x}\right) = \ln\left(18\right)$$

$$10 - 3x = \ln\left(18\right)$$

$$-3x = \ln\left(18\right) - 10$$

$$x = \frac{\ln\left(18\right) - 10}{-3}$$

$$x \approx 2.37$$

94.

$$4^x = 5^{3x}$$

$$\ln\left(4^x\right) = \ln\left(5^{3x}\right)$$

$$x\ln\left(4\right) = 3x\ln\left(5\right)$$

$$x\ln\left(4\right) - 3x\ln\left(5\right) = 0$$

$$x\left[\ln\left(4\right) - 3\ln\left(5\right)\right] = 0$$

$$\frac{x\left[\ln\left(4\right) - 3\ln\left(5\right)\right]}{\ln\left(4\right) - 3\ln\left(5\right)} = \frac{0}{\ln\left(4\right) - 3\ln\left(5\right)}$$

$$x = 0$$

95.

$$8^{6x-1} = 3^{2-x}$$

$$\ln\left(8^{6x-1}\right) = \ln\left(3^{2-x}\right)$$

$$\left(6x - 1\right)\ln\left(8\right) = \left(2 - x\right)\ln\left(3\right)$$

$$6x\ln\left(8\right) - \ln\left(8\right) = 2\ln\left(3\right) - x\ln\left(3\right)$$

$$6x\ln\left(8\right) + x\ln\left(3\right) = 2\ln\left(3\right) + \ln\left(8\right)$$

$$x\left[6\ln\left(8\right) + \ln\left(3\right)\right] = 2\ln\left(3\right) + \ln\left(8\right)$$

$$\frac{x\left[6\ln\left(8\right) + \ln\left(3\right)\right]}{6\ln\left(8\right) + \ln\left(3\right)} = \frac{2\ln\left(3\right) + \ln\left(8\right)}{6\ln\left(8\right) + \ln\left(3\right)}$$

$$x = \frac{2\ln\left(3\right) + \ln\left(8\right)}{6\ln\left(8\right) + \ln\left(3\right)}$$

$$x \approx 0.32$$

96.

$$10^{3x} = e^{2x+1}$$

$$\ln\left(10^{3x}\right) = \ln\left(e^{2x+1}\right)$$

$$3x\ln\left(10\right) = 2x + 1$$

$$3x\ln\left(10\right) - 2x = 1$$

$$x\left[3\ln\left(10\right) - 2\right] = 1$$

$$\frac{x\left[3\ln\left(10\right) - 2\right]}{3\ln\left(10\right) - 2} = \frac{1}{3\ln\left(10\right) - 2}$$

$$x = \frac{1}{3\ln\left(10\right) - 2}$$

$$x \approx 0.20$$

97.

$$\log_4\left(x + 5\right) = 3$$

$$4^3 = x + 5$$

$$x + 5 = 64$$

$$x = 59$$

<u>Check</u>

$$\log_4\left(59 + 5\right) = 3$$

$$\log_4\left(64\right) = 3$$

$$3 = 3$$

The solution set is $\left\{59\right\}$.

98.

$$\log_3\left(5x - 6\right) = \log_3\left(7x + 4\right)$$

$$5x - 6 = 7x + 4$$

$$-2x = 10$$

$$x = -5$$

<u>Check</u>

$$\log_3\left(5\left(-5\right) - 6\right) = \log_3\left(7\left(-5\right) + 4\right)$$

$$\log_6\left(-31\right) = \log_6\left(-31\right)$$

undefined

The solution set is $\left\{\ \right\}$.

99.

$$\log_5\left(x^2 + x + 5\right) = 2$$

$$5^2 = x^2 + x + 5$$

$$0 = x^2 + x - 20$$

$$0 = \left(x + 5\right)\left(x - 4\right)$$

$$x + 5 = 0 \quad \text{or} \quad x - 4 = 0$$

$$x = -5 \quad \text{or} \quad x = 4$$

<u>Check</u>

$$\log_5\left(\left(-5\right)^2 + \left(-5\right) + 5\right) = 2 \qquad \log_5\left(\left(4\right)^2 + \left(4\right) + 5\right) = 2$$

$$\log_5\left(25\right) = 2 \qquad\qquad\qquad \log_5\left(25\right) = 2$$

$$2 = 2 \qquad\qquad\qquad\qquad 2 = 2$$

The solution set is $\left\{-5, 4\right\}$.

100.

$$\ln\left(3x - 2\right) - \ln\left(5x^2\right) = 0$$

$$\ln\left(3x - 2\right) = \ln\left(5x^2\right)$$

$$3x - 2 = 5x^2$$

$$0 = 5x^2 - 3x + 2$$

$$b^2 - 4ac = \left(-3\right)^2 - 4\left(5\right)\left(2\right)$$

$$= 9 - 40$$

$$= -31$$

$$< 0$$

The solution set is $\left\{\ \right\}$.

101. $\log(x)+\log(x-5)=\log(3)+\log(5-x)$

$$\log[x(x-5)]=\log[3(5-x)]$$
$$x(x-5)=3(5-x)$$
$$x^2-5x=15-3x$$
$$x^2-2x-15=0$$
$$(x+3)(x-5)=0$$
$$x+3=0 \quad\text{or}\quad x-5=0$$
$$x=-3 \quad\text{or}\quad x=5$$

Check

$$\log(-3)+\log(-3-5)=\log(3)+\log(5-(-3))$$

undefined

$$\log(5)+\log(5-5)=\log(5)+\log(5-5)$$

undefined

The solution set is $\{\ \}$.

102. $\log_2(3x)+\log_2(x-5)=\log_2(2x^2-x-48)$

$$\log_2[3x(x-5)]=\log(2x^2-x-48)$$
$$3x(x-5)=2x^2-x-48$$
$$3x^2-15x=2x^2-x-48$$
$$x^2-14x+48=0$$
$$(x-6)(x-8)=0$$
$$x-6=0 \quad\text{or}\quad x-8=0$$
$$x=6 \quad\text{or}\quad x=8$$

Check

$$\log_2[3(6)]+\log_2(6-5)=\log_2[2(6)^2-(6)-48]$$
$$\log_2(18)+\log_2(1)=\log_2(18)$$
$$\log_2(18)=\log_2(18)$$

$$\log_2[3(8)]+\log_2(8-5)=\log_2[2(8)^2-(8)-48]$$
$$\log_2(24)+\log_2(3)=\log_2(72)$$
$$\log_2(72)=\log_2(72)$$

The solution set is $\{6,8\}$.

103. $A_0=12$

$d=3$

$t=18$

$$A=A_0 2^{\frac{t}{d}}$$
$$=12\cdot 2^{\frac{18}{3}}$$
$$=12\cdot 2^6$$
$$=768$$

There are 768 cells after 18 months.

104. $A_0=650$

$d=30$

$t=82$

$$A=A_0 2^{\frac{t}{d}}$$
$$=650\cdot 2^{\frac{82}{30}}$$
$$\approx 4{,}322$$

There are approximately 4,322 salmon after 82 days.

105. Prepare We will use the half-life decay formula to determine how many milligrams of an original amount of 0.0004 mg of the isotope ^{63}Ni will remain in the human body after 10 years. The half-life of ^{63}Ni is given as 100 years.

Plan Identify the variables in the half-life decay formula $A=A_0\left(\frac{1}{2}\right)^{\frac{t}{h}}$, then substitute the known values into the formula to determine how much ^{63}Ni remains in the body after 10 years. The known variables are $A_0=0.0004$ mg, $h=100$ years, and $t=10$ years.

Process

$$A=A_0\left(\frac{1}{2}\right)^{\frac{t}{h}}$$
$$=(0.0004)\left(\frac{1}{2}\right)^{\frac{10}{100}}$$
$$\approx 0.000373 \text{ mg}$$

Ponder Does our answer seem reasonable? Yes, as it would take 100 years for the amount of nickel-63 in the body to be reduced to 0.0002 mg. Therefore, after only 10 years, there should be between 0.0002 and 0.0004 milligrams of the substance left.

CHAPTER 12 TEST

1. c

2. e

3. f

4. b

5. a) Sketch a graph of f and apply the horizontal line test.
The graph passes the horizontal line test, so f is one-to-one.

b) Sketch a graph of f and apply the horizontal line test.
The graph is a parabola opening up and does not pass the horizontal line test, so f is not one-to-one.

6. $f(x) = \dfrac{2}{7}x + 3$

$y = \dfrac{2}{7}x + 3$

$x = \dfrac{2}{7}y + 3$

$x - 3 = \dfrac{2}{7}y$

$\dfrac{7}{2}(x-3) = y$

$\dfrac{7x-21}{2} = y$

$f^{-1}(x) = \dfrac{7x-21}{2}$

$\left(f \circ f^{-1}\right)(x) = f\left(f^{-1}(x)\right)$

$= \dfrac{\cancel{2}^{1}}{7}\left(\dfrac{7x-21}{\cancel{2}_{1}}\right) + 3$

$= \dfrac{7x-21}{7} + 3$

$= \dfrac{\cancel{7}^{1}x}{\cancel{7}_{1}} - \dfrac{\cancel{21}^{3}}{\cancel{7}_{1}} + 3$

$= x - 3 + 3$

$= x$

$\left(f^{-1} \circ f\right)(x) = f^{-1}\left(f(x)\right)$

$= \dfrac{7\left(\dfrac{2}{7}x+3\right)-21}{2}$

$= \dfrac{\cancel{7}^{1}\left(\dfrac{2}{\cancel{7}_{1}}x\right)+21-21}{2}$

$= \dfrac{2x+21-21}{2}$

$= \dfrac{\cancel{2}^{1}x}{\cancel{2}_{1}}$

$= x$

$D_f = R_{f^{-1}} = (-\infty, \infty)$

$R_f = D_{f^{-1}} = (-\infty, \infty)$

7. $f(x) = \sqrt{x-6}$

$y = \sqrt{x-6}, x \geq 6, y \geq 0$

$x = \sqrt{y-6}, y \geq 6, x \geq 0$

$x^2 = y - 6$

$x^2 + 6 = y$

$f^{-1}(x) = x^2 + 6, x \geq 0$

$\left(f \circ f^{-1}\right)(x) = f\left(f^{-1}(x)\right)$

$= \sqrt{\left(x^2+6\right)-6}$

$= \sqrt{x^2}$

$= x,\ x \geq 0$

$\left(f^{-1} \circ f\right)(x) = f^{-1}\left(f(x)\right)$

$= \left(\sqrt{x-6}\right)^2 + 6$

$= x - 6 + 6,\ x \geq 6$

$= x$

$D_f = R_{f^{-1}} = [6, \infty)$

$R_f = D_{f^{-1}} = [0, \infty)$

8.a. $7 = \log_2(128)$ if and only if $2^7 = 128$

8.b. $-2 = \log(0.01)$ if and only if $10^{-2} = 0.01$

9.a. $e^{\pi} = k$ if and only if $\ln(k) = \pi$

544

9.b. $3^{-2} = \dfrac{1}{9}$ if and only if $\log_3\left(\dfrac{1}{9}\right) = -2$

10.a. $\log_6(216) = y$ if and only if $6^y = 216$

$$6^y = 216$$
$$6^y = 6^3$$
$$y = 3$$

Therefore, $\log_6(216) = 3$.

10.b. $\log_2\left(\dfrac{1}{16}\right) = y$ if and only if $2^y = \dfrac{1}{16}$

$$2^y = \frac{1}{16}$$
$$2^y = \frac{1}{2^4}$$
$$2^y = 2^{-4}$$
$$y = -4$$

Therefore, $\log_2\left(\dfrac{1}{16}\right) = -4$.

11. $\log_{28}\left(\sqrt{15}\right) = \dfrac{\ln\left(\sqrt{15}\right)}{\ln(28)}$

$$\approx 0.4063$$

12. $\log_5\left(\sqrt{7x}\right) = \log_5\left[(7x)^{1/2}\right]$

$$= \log_5\left(7^{1/2}\, x^{1/2}\right)$$
$$= \log_5\left(7^{1/2}\right) + \log_5\left(x^{1/2}\right)$$
$$= \frac{1}{2}\log_5(7) + \frac{1}{2}\log_5(x)$$

13. $\log\left[a^2(b-c)^3\right] = \log\left(a^2\right) + \log(b-c)^3$

$$= 2\log(a) + 3\log(b-c)$$

14. $2\log_a(x) - \dfrac{1}{3}\log_a(y) = \log_a\left(x^2\right) - \log_a\left(y^{1/3}\right)$

$$= \log_a\left(\frac{x^2}{y^{1/3}}\right)$$
$$= \log_a\left(\frac{x^2}{\sqrt[3]{y}}\right)$$

15. $\ln(5x) + \ln(x+5) - 8\ln(y)$

$$= \ln(5x) + \ln(x+5) - \ln\left(y^8\right)$$
$$= \ln\left[5x(x+5)\right] - \ln\left(y^8\right)$$
$$= \ln\left(5x^2 + 25x\right) - \ln\left(y^8\right)$$
$$= \ln\left(\frac{5x^2 + 25x}{y^8}\right)$$

16. $5^{3x} = 625$

$$5^{3x} = 5^4$$
$$3x = 4$$
$$x = \frac{4}{3}$$

17. $e^{-3x} = 2.57$

$$\ln\left(e^{-3x}\right) = \ln(2.57)$$
$$-3x = \ln(2.57)$$
$$x = \frac{\ln(2.57)}{-3}$$
$$x \approx -0.315$$

18. $$7^{2x-1} = 3^x$$
$$\ln\left(7^{2x-1}\right) = \ln\left(3^x\right)$$
$$(2x-1)\ln(7) = x\ln(3)$$
$$2x\ln(7) - \ln(7) = x\ln(3)$$
$$2x\ln(7) - x\ln(3) = \ln(7)$$
$$x\left[2\ln(7) - \ln(3)\right] = \ln(7)$$
$$\frac{x\left[2\ln(7) - \ln(3)\right]}{2\ln(7) - \ln(3)} = \frac{\ln(7)}{2\ln(7) - \ln(3)}$$
$$x = \frac{\ln(7)}{2\ln(7) - \ln(3)}$$
$$x \approx 0.697$$

19. $\log_4(x+9) = 2$

$$4^2 = x+9$$
$$x+9 = 16$$
$$x = 7$$

<u>Check</u>
$$\log_4(7+9) = 2$$
$$\log_4(16) = 2$$
$$2 = 2$$
True

The solution set is $\{7\}$.

20. $\log\left(x^2-7x\right)=\log\left(21-3x\right)$

$$x^2-7x=21-3x$$
$$x^2-4x-21=0$$
$$(x-7)(x+3)=0$$
$$x-7=0 \quad or \quad x+3=0$$
$$\cancel{x=7} \qquad \qquad x=-3$$

Check

$x=7 \quad \log\left((7)^2-7(7)\right)=\log\left(21-3(7)\right)$
$$\log(49-49)=\log(21-21)$$
$$\log(0)=\log(0)$$
False

$x=-3 \quad \log\left((-3)^2-7(-3)\right)=\log\left(21-3(-3)\right)$
$$\log(9+21)=\log(21+9)$$
$$\log(30)=\log(30)$$
True

The solution set is $\{-3\}$.

21. $\log_8(x)+\log_8(-x+16)=2$
$$\log_8\left[x(-x+16)\right]=2$$
$$\log_8\left(-x^2+16x\right)=2$$
$$8^2=-x^2+16x$$
$$x^2-16x+64=0$$
$$(x-8)^2=0$$
$$x-8=0$$
$$x=8$$

Check

$$\log_8(8)+\log_8\left(-(8)+16\right)=2$$
$$1+\log_8(8)=2$$
$$1+1=2$$
$$2=2$$
True

The solution set is $\{8\}$.

22. $\ln(15x)-\ln(x+2)=\ln(x+6)$
$$\ln\left(\frac{15x}{x+2}\right)=\ln(x+6)$$
$$\frac{15x}{x+2}=x+6$$
$$15x=(x+2)(x+6)$$
$$15x=x^2+8x+12$$
$$x^2-7x+12=0$$
$$(x-3)(x-4)=0$$
$$x-3=0 \quad or \quad x-4=0$$
$$x=3 \qquad \qquad x=4$$

Check

$x=3 \quad \ln\left[15(3)\right]-\ln\left[(3)+2\right]=\ln\left[(3)+6\right]$
$$\ln(45)-\ln(5)=\ln(9)$$
$$\ln\left(\frac{45}{5}\right)=\ln(9)$$
$$\ln(9)=\ln(9)$$
True

$x=4 \quad \ln\left[15(4)\right]-\ln\left[(4)+2\right]=\ln\left[(4)+6\right]$
$$\ln(60)-\ln(6)=\ln(10)$$
$$\ln\left(\frac{60}{6}\right)=\ln(10)$$
$$\ln(10)=\ln(10)$$
True

The solution set is $\{3,4\}$.

23. $A_0=20$, $d=1.7$, $t=20$

$$A=A_0\,2^{t/d}$$
$$=(20)\,2^{20/1.7}$$
$$\approx 69,592$$

The population will be approximately 69,592.

24. $H^+=1.3\left(10^{-9}\right)$

$$pH=-\log\left[H^+\right]$$
$$=-\log\left[1.3\left(10^{-9}\right)\right]$$
$$\approx 8.89$$

The *pH* of ammonia is approximately 8.89

25. Prepare We are to determine how much of the radioactive material would remain in a patient after 5 days.

Plan Using $A = A_0 \left(\dfrac{1}{2} \right)^{t/h}$ and the given information, $A_0 = 5$, $h = 73$, and $t = 120$, we can determine how much radioactive material remains in the patient.

Process

$$A = A_0 \left(\frac{1}{2} \right)^{t/h}$$
$$= 5 \left(\frac{1}{2} \right)^{120/73}$$
$$\approx 1.6$$

There would be approximately 1.6 mCi of the radioactive material remaining in the patient after 5 days.

Ponder Is this result reasonable? After 73 hours, half of the 5 mCi (2.5 mCi) would be left in the patient. After 146 hours, half of the 2.5 mCi (1.25 mCi) would be left in the patient. Since 120 is between 73 and 146 and since 1.6 is between 1.25 and 2.5, the result seems reasonable.

Appendix A

Linear Equations and Inequalities in One Variable

1.
$$3(s-2)=4(s+3)-9$$
$$3((-4)-2)=4((-4)+3)-9$$
$$3(-6)=4(-1)-9$$
$$-18=-4-9$$
$$-18=-13$$
False

No, -4 is not a solution.

2.
$$8x+9=29-2x$$
$$8x+2x+9=29-2x+2x$$
$$10x+9=29$$
$$10x+9-9=29-9$$
$$10x=20$$
$$\frac{10x}{10}=\frac{20}{10}$$
$$x=2$$
Solution Set: $\{2\}$

3.
$$\frac{2}{7}x+3=5$$
$$\frac{2}{7}x+3-3=5-3$$
$$\frac{2}{7}x=2$$
$$\frac{7}{2}\left(\frac{2}{7}x\right)=\frac{7}{2}(2)$$
$$x=7$$
Solution Set: $\{7\}$

4.
$$\frac{x-5}{6}+\frac{3(x+1)}{4}=\frac{8}{3}$$
$$\frac{12}{1}\left(\frac{x-5}{6}+\frac{3(x+1)}{4}\right)=\frac{12}{1}\left(\frac{8}{3}\right)$$
$$\frac{12}{1}\left(\frac{x-5}{6}\right)+\frac{12}{1}\left(\frac{3(x+1)}{4}\right)=\frac{12}{1}\left(\frac{8}{3}\right)$$
$$2(x-5)+3(3(x+1))=32$$
$$2x-10+9x+9=32$$
$$11x-1=32$$
$$11x-1+1=32+1$$
$$11x=33$$
$$\frac{11x}{11}=\frac{33}{11}$$
$$x=3$$
Solution Set: $\{3\}$

5.
$$5x+0.6=2x+1.35$$
$$5x-2x+0.6=2x-2x+1.35$$
$$3x+0.6=1.35$$
$$3x+0.6-0.6=1.35-0.6$$
$$3x=0.75$$
$$\frac{3x}{3}=\frac{0.75}{3}$$
$$x=0.25$$
Solution Set: $\{0.25\}$

6.
$$3(m-2)=2(2m-5)$$
$$3m-6=4m-10$$
$$3m-4m-6=4m-4m-10$$
$$-m-6=-10$$
$$-m-6+6=-10+6$$
$$-m=-4$$
$$\frac{-m}{-1}=\frac{-4}{-1}$$
$$m=4$$
Solution Set: $\{4\}$

7.
$$2x - 1 = \frac{5}{7} - 4x$$
$$2x + 4x - 1 = \frac{5}{7} - 4x + 4x$$
$$6x - 1 = \frac{5}{7}$$
$$6x - 1 + 1 = \frac{5}{7} + 1$$
$$6x = \frac{12}{7}$$
$$\frac{1}{6}(6x) = \frac{1}{6}\left(\frac{12}{7}\right)$$
$$x = \frac{2}{7}$$
Solution Set: $\left\{\frac{2}{7}\right\}$

8.
$$7x - 19 = 23$$
$$7x - 19 + 19 = 23 + 19$$
$$7x = 42$$
$$\frac{7x}{7} = \frac{42}{7}$$
$$x = 6$$
Solution Set: $\{6\}$

9. $-5(y + 6) + 4y = 9(y - 2) - 4(2y + 1)$
$$-5y - 30 + 4y = 9y - 18 - 8y - 4$$
$$-y - 30 = y - 22$$
$$-y - y - 30 = y - y - 22$$
$$-2y - 30 = -22$$
$$-2y - 30 + 30 = -22 + 30$$
$$-2y = 8$$
$$\frac{-2y}{-2} = \frac{8}{-2}$$
$$y = -4$$
Solution Set: $\{-4\}$

10.
$$\frac{x - 4}{2} = \frac{2x + 3}{5}$$
$$\frac{10}{1}\left(\frac{x - 4}{2}\right) = \frac{10}{1}\left(\frac{2x + 3}{5}\right)$$
$$5(x - 4) = 2(2x + 3)$$
$$5x - 20 = 4x + 6$$
$$5x - 4x - 20 = 4x - 4x + 6$$
$$x - 20 = 6$$
$$x - 20 + 20 = 6 + 20$$
$$x = 26$$
Solution Set: $\{26\}$

11.
$$\frac{x}{3} - 4 = \frac{2x}{3} - 1$$
$$3\left(\frac{x}{3} - 4\right) = 3\left(\frac{2x}{3} - 1\right)$$
$$x - 12 = 2x - 3$$
$$x - 2x - 12 = 2x - 2x - 3$$
$$-x - 12 = -3$$
$$-x - 12 + 12 = -3 + 12$$
$$x = -9$$
Solution Set: $\{-9\}$

12. Let x represent the unknown number.
$$x + 8 = 2x - 7$$
$$x - 2x + 8 = 2x - 2x - 7$$
$$-x + 8 = -7$$
$$-x + 8 - 8 = -7 - 8$$
$$-x = -15$$
$$\frac{-x}{-1} = \frac{-15}{-1}$$
$$x = 15$$
The number is 15.

13. Let x represent the unknown number.
$$3x - 9 = 19 - 4x$$
$$3x + 4x - 9 = 19 - 4x + 4x$$
$$7x - 9 = 19$$
$$7x - 9 + 9 = 19 + 9$$
$$7x = 28$$
$$\frac{7x}{7} = \frac{28}{7}$$
$$x = 4$$
The number is 4.

14. $m(x+2) = 9$

$$\frac{m(x+2)}{m} = \frac{9}{m}$$

$$x + 2 = \frac{9}{m}$$

$$x + 2 - 2 = \frac{9}{m} - 2$$

$$x = \frac{9}{m} - 2$$

15. $S = P + Prt$

$$S - P = P - P + Prt$$

$$S - P = Prt$$

$$\frac{S-P}{Pt} = \frac{Prt}{Pt}$$

$$\frac{S-P}{Pt} = r$$

16. $I = \$2{,}522$

$P = \$9{,}700$

$r = 0.065$

$t = ?$

$I = Prt$

$2{,}522 = (9{,}700)(0.065)t$

$2{,}522 = 630.5t$

$$\frac{2{,}522}{630.5} = \frac{630.5t}{630.5}$$

$4 = t$

It will take 4 years to earn \$2,522.

17. Let x represent the number of liters of 30% acidic acid Marjorie needs to mix with 100% acidic acid to make 15.4 liters of 65% acidic acid. Then $15.4 - x$ in the number liters of 100% acidic acid needed.

$$0.30x + 1.00(15.4 - x) = 0.65(15.4)$$

$$0.3x + 15.4 - x = 10.01$$

$$-0.7x + 15.4 = 10.01$$

$$-0.7x + 15.4 - 15.4 = 10.01 - 15.4$$

$$-0.7x = -5.39$$

$$\frac{-0.7x}{-0.7} = \frac{-5.39}{-0.7}$$

$$x = 7.7$$

Marjorie will need 7.7 liters of 30% acidic acid.

18. $3x > 21$

$$\frac{3x}{3} > \frac{21}{3}$$

$$x > 7$$

$$(7, \infty)$$

19. $7 - 3m < -5$

$$7 - 7 - 3m < -5 - 7$$

$$-3m < -12$$

$$\frac{-3m}{-3} > \frac{-12}{-3}$$

$$m > 4$$

$$(4, \infty)$$

20. $9y - 5 \geq 19 + 3y$

$$9y - 3y - 5 \geq 19 + 3y - 3y$$

$$6y - 5 \geq 19$$

$$6y - 5 + 5 \geq 19 + 5$$

$$6y \geq 24$$

$$\frac{6y}{6} \geq \frac{24}{6}$$

$$y \geq 4$$

$$[4, \infty)$$

21. $2(y-2) \geq -4(y+4)$

$$2y - 4 \geq -4y - 16$$

$$2y + 4y - 4 \geq -4y + 4y - 16$$

$$6y - 4 \geq -16$$

$$6y - 4 + 4 \geq -16 + 4$$

$$6y \geq -12$$

$$\frac{6y}{6} \geq \frac{-12}{6}$$

$$y \geq -2$$

$$[-2, \infty)$$

22. $(-\infty, -3) \cup [5, \infty)$

23. $x \leq -2$ or $x > 5$

24.
$$3x + 5 \geq 2x + 3 \quad \text{or} \quad 5x - 6 < 4x + 3$$
$$3x - 2x + 5 \geq 2x - 2x + 3 \quad \text{or} \quad 5x - 4x - 6 < 4x - 4x + 3$$
$$x + 5 \geq 3 \quad \text{or} \quad x - 6 < 3$$
$$x + 5 - 5 \geq 3 - 5 \quad \text{or} \quad x - 6 + 6 < 3 + 6$$
$$x \geq -2 \quad \text{or} \quad x < 9$$
$$(\infty, \infty)$$

25.
$$-9 < 2x + 7 \leq 11$$
$$-9 - 7 < 2x + 7 - 7 \leq 11 - 7$$
$$-16 < 2x \leq 4$$
$$\frac{-16}{2} < \frac{2x}{2} \leq \frac{4}{2}$$
$$-8 < x \leq 2$$
$$(-8, 2]$$

Linear Equations and Inequalities in Two Variables

1.
$$2x - 9y = -4$$
$$2(7) - 9(2) = -4$$
$$14 - 18 = -4$$
$$-4 = -4$$
$$\text{True}$$

Yes, $(7,2)$ is a solution.

2. a) $\dfrac{3}{4}x + 2y = 6$

$$\dfrac{3}{4}(4) + 2y = 6$$

$$3 + 2y = 6$$

$$2y = 3$$

$$y = \dfrac{3}{2}$$

$$\left(4, \dfrac{3}{2}\right)$$

2. b) $\dfrac{3}{4}x + 2y = 6$

$$\dfrac{3}{4}x + 2(3) = 6$$

$$\dfrac{3}{4}x + 6 = 6$$

$$\dfrac{3}{4}x = 0$$

$$x = 0$$

$$(0,3)$$

3.

$x = 0$	$x = 1$	$x = 2$
$4x + y = 7$	$4x + y = 7$	$4x + y = 7$
$4(0) + y = 7$	$4(1) + y = 7$	$4(2) + y = 7$
$0 + y = 7$	$4 + y = 7$	$8 + y = 7$
$y = 7$	$y = 3$	$y = -1$
$(0,7)$	$(1,3)$	$(2,-1)$

4.

$x = -3$	$x = -1$	$x = 1$
$x - 2y = 3$	$x - 2y = 3$	$x - 2y = 3$
$(-3) - 2y = 3$	$(-1) - 2y = 3$	$(1) - 2y = 3$
$-2y = 6$	$-2y = 4$	$-2y = 2$
$y = -3$	$y = -2$	$y = -1$
$(-3,-3)$	$(-1,-2)$	$(1,-1)$

5.

$x = -1$	$x = 0$	$x = 1$
$3x - y = 4$	$3x - y = 4$	$3x - y = 4$
$3(-1) - y = 4$	$3(0) - y = 4$	$3(1) - y = 4$
$-3 - y = 4$	$0 - y = 4$	$3 - y = 4$
$-y = 7$	$-y = 4$	$-y = 1$
$y = -7$	$y = -4$	$y = -1$
$(-1,-7)$	$(0,-4)$	$(1,-1)$

6.

$x = -2$	$x = 1$	$x = 4$
$2x + 3y = 5$	$2x + 3y = 5$	$2x + 3y = 5$
$2(-2) + 3y = 5$	$2(1) + 3y = 5$	$2(4) + 3y = 5$
$-4 + 3y = 5$	$2 + 3y = 5$	$8 + 3y = 5$
$3y = 9$	$3y = 3$	$3y = -3$
$y = 3$	$y = 1$	$y = -1$
$(-2,3)$	$(1,1)$	$(4,-1)$

7.

$x=-1$	$x=0$	$x=1$
$y=-1$	$y=-1$	$y=-1$
$(-1,-1)$	$(0,-1)$	$(1,-1)$

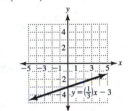

8. The graph of the equation $x=5y$ is neither vertical nor horizontal, because the equation contains both an x and a y.

9. $m=\dfrac{y_2-y_1}{x_2-x_1}$

$=\dfrac{0-5}{-1-3}$

$=\dfrac{-5}{-4}$

$=\dfrac{5}{4}$

10. $m=\dfrac{y_2-y_1}{x_2-x_1}$

$=\dfrac{5-(-2)}{7-0}$

$=\dfrac{7}{7}$

$=1$

11. Slope: $m=\dfrac{3}{2}$

y-intercept: $(0,2)$

12. $x-4y=6$

$-4y=-x+6$

$y=\dfrac{1}{4}x-\dfrac{3}{2}$

Slope: $m=\dfrac{1}{4}$

y-intercept: $\left(0,-\dfrac{3}{2}\right)$

13. $m=\dfrac{y_2-y_1}{x_2-x_1}$

$=\dfrac{4-(-4)}{-4-0}$

$=\dfrac{8}{-4}$

$=-2$

14. Slope: $m=\dfrac{1}{3}$

y-intercept: $(0,-3)$

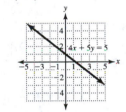

15. $4x+5y=5$

$5y=-4x+5$

$y=-\dfrac{4}{5}x+1$

Slope: $m=-\dfrac{4}{5}$

y-intercept: $(0,1)$

16. $y=mx+b$

$y=\left(\dfrac{2}{3}\right)x+(-2)$

$y=\dfrac{2}{3}x-2$

17. $m=\dfrac{y_2-y_1}{x_2-x_1}$ $\qquad y=mx+b$

$=\dfrac{7-3}{2-0}$ $\qquad y=(2)x+(3)$

$=\dfrac{4}{2}$ $\qquad y=2x+3$

$=2$

18. $m = \dfrac{y_2 - y_1}{x_2 - x_1}$ $\quad y = mx + b$

$\qquad = \dfrac{5 - 4}{3 - 1}$ $\quad (4) = \left(\dfrac{1}{2}\right)(1) + b$

$\qquad = \dfrac{1}{2}$ $\qquad 4 = \dfrac{1}{2} + b$

$\qquad\qquad\qquad\qquad \dfrac{7}{2} = b$

$\qquad\qquad y = \dfrac{1}{2}x + \dfrac{7}{2}$

19. The slope of L_1 is $\frac{2}{3}$ and the slope of L_2 is 4, therefore the lines are neither parallel nor perpendicular.

20. The slope of L_1 is $-\frac{3}{4}$ and the slope of L_2 is $-\frac{3}{4}$, therefore the lines are parallel.

21. $\quad y = mx + b$ $\qquad y = mx + b$

$\quad (-5) = (-1)(2) + b$ $\quad y = (-1)x + (-3)$

$\qquad -5 = -2 + b$ $\qquad y = -x - 3$

$\qquad -3 = b$ $\qquad x + y = -3$

22. $m = \dfrac{y_2 - y_1}{x_2 - x_1}$ $\qquad y = mx + b$

$\qquad = \dfrac{11 - 6}{-4 - (-2)}$ $\quad (6) = \left(-\dfrac{5}{2}\right)(-2) + b$

$\qquad = -\dfrac{5}{2}$ $\qquad 6 = 5 + b$

$\qquad\qquad\qquad\qquad 1 = b$

$\qquad\qquad y = mx + b$

$\qquad\qquad y = -\dfrac{5}{2}x + 1$

$\qquad\qquad 2y = -5x + 2$

$\qquad\qquad 5x + 2y = 2$

23. $m = \dfrac{2}{3}$ $\qquad y = mx + b$

$\qquad\qquad (5) = \left(\dfrac{2}{3}\right)(6) + b$

$\qquad\qquad 5 = 4 + b$

$\qquad\qquad 1 = b$

$\qquad\qquad y = mx + b$

$\qquad\qquad y = \dfrac{2}{3}x + 1$

$\qquad\qquad 3y = 2x + 3$

$\qquad\qquad -2x + 3y = 3$

24. Graph the line $x - 2y = -4$ using a solid line. Choose the test point $(0, 0)$.

$$x - 2y \geq -4$$
$$(0) - 2(0) \geq -4$$
$$0 \geq -4$$

True

Shade the region that contains the point $(0, 0)$.

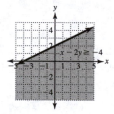

25. Graph the line $3x = -2y$ using a dashed line. Choose the test point $(0, 1)$.

$$3x < -2y$$
$$3(0) < -2(1)$$
$$0 < -2$$

False

Shade the region that does not contain the point $(0, 1)$.

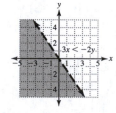

554

Integer Exponents

1. $\left(\dfrac{5}{3}\right)^{-3} = \left(\dfrac{3}{5}\right)^{3}$

$\quad = \dfrac{3}{5}\cdot\dfrac{3}{5}\cdot\dfrac{3}{5}$

$\quad = \dfrac{27}{125}$

2. $\left(\dfrac{7}{3}\right)^{2} = \dfrac{7}{3}\cdot\dfrac{7}{3}$

$\quad = \dfrac{49}{9}$

3. $n^{5}\cdot n^{4}\cdot n^{-2} = n^{5+4+(-2)}$

$\quad = n^{7}$

4. $\left(4a^{2}b^{9}\right)^{-2} = 4^{-2}\left(a^{2}\right)^{-2}\left(b^{9}\right)^{-2}$

$\quad = 4^{-2}a^{-4}b^{-18}$

$\quad = \dfrac{1}{4^{2}}\cdot\dfrac{1}{a^{4}}\cdot\dfrac{1}{b^{18}}$

$\quad = \dfrac{1}{16a^{4}b^{18}}$

5. $\dfrac{9x^{-5}}{24y^{-9}} = \dfrac{\overset{3}{\cancel{9}}\,y^{9}}{\underset{8}{\cancel{24}}\,x^{5}}$

$\quad = \dfrac{3y^{9}}{8x^{5}}$

6. $\dfrac{3^{2}x^{3}}{3^{-2}x^{6}} = 3^{2-(-2)}x^{3-6}$

$\quad = 3^{4}x^{-3}$

$\quad = 81\cdot\dfrac{1}{x^{3}}$

$\quad = \dfrac{81}{x^{3}}$

7. $\left(-8a^{2}bc^{-5}\right)^{-3} = (-8)^{-3}\left(a^{2}\right)^{-3}b^{-3}\left(c^{-5}\right)^{-3}$

$\quad = (-8)^{-3}a^{-6}b^{-3}c^{15}$

$\quad = \dfrac{1}{(-8)^{3}}\cdot\dfrac{1}{a^{6}}\cdot\dfrac{1}{b^{3}}\cdot c^{15}$

$\quad = -\dfrac{c^{15}}{512a^{6}b^{3}}$

8. $\left(4m^{3}n^{2}\right)\cdot\left(-6m^{-4}n^{6}\right) = -24m^{3+(-4)}n^{2+6}$

$\quad = -24m^{-1}n^{8}$

$\quad = -24\cdot\dfrac{1}{m}\cdot n^{8}$

$\quad = -\dfrac{24n^{8}}{m}$

9. $\left(9a^{3}b^{4}c^{-3}\right)\cdot\left(\dfrac{5}{3}ab^{-3}c\right) = \dfrac{\overset{15}{\cancel{45}}}{\underset{1}{\cancel{3}}}a^{3+1}b^{4+(-3)}c^{-3+1}$

$\quad = 15a^{4}bc^{-2}$

$\quad = 15a^{4}b\cdot\dfrac{1}{c^{2}}$

$\quad = \dfrac{15a^{4}b}{c^{2}}$

10. $\dfrac{4a^{-3}}{12b^{-5}} = \dfrac{\overset{1}{\cancel{4}}\,b^{5}}{\underset{3}{\cancel{12}}\,a^{3}}$

$\quad = \dfrac{b^{5}}{3a^{3}}$

11. $\dfrac{\left(4ab^{2}c^{-1}\right)^{-2}}{\left(2a^{-3}bc^{2}\right)^{-3}} = \dfrac{4^{-2}a^{-2}\left(b^{2}\right)^{-2}\left(c^{-1}\right)^{-2}}{2^{-3}\left(a^{-3}\right)^{-3}b^{-3}\left(c^{2}\right)^{-3}}$

$\quad = \dfrac{4^{-2}a^{-2}b^{-4}c^{2}}{2^{-3}a^{9}b^{-3}c^{-6}}$

$\quad = \dfrac{4^{-2}}{2^{-3}}a^{-2-9}b^{-4-(-3)}c^{2-(-6)}$

$\quad = \dfrac{2^{3}}{4^{2}}a^{-11}b^{-1}c^{8}$

$\quad = \dfrac{\overset{1}{\cancel{8}}}{\underset{2}{\cancel{16}}}\cdot\dfrac{1}{a^{11}}\cdot\dfrac{1}{b}\cdot c^{8}$

$\quad = \dfrac{c^{8}}{2a^{11}b}$

12. $\left(\dfrac{a^2}{2b^3}\right)^3 \cdot \left(\dfrac{3a}{4b^2}\right)^{-2} = \left(\dfrac{a^2}{2b^3}\right)^3 \cdot \left(\dfrac{4b^2}{3a}\right)^2$

$\qquad = \dfrac{\left(a^2\right)^3}{\left(2b^3\right)^3} \cdot \dfrac{\left(4b^2\right)^2}{\left(3a\right)^2}$

$\qquad = \dfrac{a^6}{8b^9} \cdot \dfrac{16b^4}{9a^2}$

$\qquad = \dfrac{\overset{2}{\cancel{16}}\, a^6 b^4}{\underset{9}{\cancel{72}}\, a^2 b^9}$

$\qquad = \dfrac{2}{9} a^{6-2} b^{4-9}$

$\qquad = \dfrac{2}{9} a^4 b^{-5}$

$\qquad = \dfrac{2}{9} \cdot a^4 \cdot \dfrac{1}{b^5}$

$\qquad = \dfrac{2a^4}{9b^5}$

13. $\left(15x^5 y^{-2} z^3\right)^0 = 1$

14. $V = lwh$

$\qquad = 5x \cdot \dfrac{3y^3}{z^4} \cdot x^2 y$

$\qquad = \dfrac{15x^{1+2} y^{3+1}}{z^4}$

$\qquad = \dfrac{15x^3 y^4}{z^4}$ cubic meters

15. $P = \$1{,}300;\ r = 0.0375;\ t = 2;\ n = 12$

$\qquad A = P\left(1 + \dfrac{r}{n}\right)^{nt}$

$\qquad = \$1{,}300\left(1 + \dfrac{0.0375}{12}\right)^{(12)(2)}$

$\qquad \approx \$1{,}401.09$

16. $\left(9a^{-3} b^2 c^7\right)^2 \cdot \left(7ab^9 c^{12}\right)^0 = 9^2 \left(a^{-3}\right)^2 \left(b^2\right)^2 \left(c^7\right)^2 \cdot 1$

$\qquad = 81 a^{-6} b^4 c^{14}$

$\qquad = \dfrac{81 b^4 c^{14}}{a^6}$

17. $\dfrac{3^{-3} y^5}{3^2 y^{-3}} = 3^{-3-2} y^{5-(-3)}$

$\qquad = 3^{-5} y^8$

$\qquad = \dfrac{y^8}{3^5}$

$\qquad = \dfrac{y^8}{243}$

18. $4{,}210{,}000 = 4.21(10)^6$

19. $0.000943 = 9.43(10)^{-4}$

20. $3.093(10)^{-5} = 0.00003093$

21. $7.14(10)^7 = 71{,}400{,}000$

22. $5\left(10^{-2}\right) \cdot 6\left(10^4\right) = 30\left(10^2\right)$

$\qquad = 3.0\left(10^1\right)\left(10^2\right)$

$\qquad = 3.0\left(10^3\right)$ Scientific Notation

$\qquad = 3{,}000$ Standard Notation

23. $\dfrac{6\left(10^7\right)}{8\left(10^{-2}\right)} = 0.75\left(10^9\right)$

$\qquad = 7.5\left(10^{-1}\right)\left(10^9\right)$

$\qquad = 7.5\left(10^8\right)$ Scientific Notation

$\qquad = 750{,}000{,}000$ Standard Notation

24. $(91{,}750{,}000)(0.000052)$

$\qquad = 9.175\left(10^7\right) \cdot 5.2\left(10^{-5}\right)$

$\qquad = 47.71\left(10^2\right)$

$\qquad = 4.771\left(10^1\right)\left(10^2\right)$

$\qquad = 4.771\left(10^3\right)$ Scientific Notation

$\qquad = 4{,}771$ Standard Notation

25. $84{,}190 = 8.419\left(10^4\right)$

Polynomials

1. 4

2. This is not a polynomial because $\frac{7}{b} = 7b^{-1}$, and by definition a polynomial cannot have a negative exponent.

3. $\left(4n^3 - 2n + 6\right) + \left(7n - 9\right) = 4n^3 - 2n + 6 + 7n - 9$
$$= 4n^3 - 2n + 7n + 6 - 9$$
$$= 4n^3 + 5n - 3$$

4. $\left(8x^4 - 5x^2 + x - 3\right) - \left(6x^2 + 2x - 4\right)$
$$= 8x^4 - 5x^2 + x - 3 - 6x^2 - 2x + 4$$
$$= 8x^4 - 5x^2 - 6x^2 + x - 2x - 3 + 4$$
$$= 8x^4 - 11x^2 - x + 1$$

5. $\left(\frac{2}{3}y^3 + \frac{1}{2}y^2 - y + 2\right) + \left(\frac{1}{6}y^3 - 3y^2 + \frac{1}{2}y - 5\right)$
$$= \frac{2}{3}y^3 + \frac{1}{2}y^2 - y + 2 + \frac{1}{6}y^3 - 3y^2 + \frac{1}{2}y - 5$$
$$= \frac{2}{3}y^3 + \frac{1}{6}y^3 + \frac{1}{2}y^2 - 3y^2 + \frac{1}{2}y - y + 2 - 5$$
$$= \frac{5}{6}y^3 - \frac{5}{2}y^2 - \frac{1}{2}y - 3$$

6. $\left(x^3 + 5x^2 - x + 2\right) - \left(2x^3 - 3\right) + \left(7x^2 - 9x + 6\right)$
$$= x^3 + 5x^2 - x + 2 - 2x^3 + 3 + 7x^2 - 9x + 6$$
$$= x^3 - 2x^3 + 5x^2 + 7x^2 - x - 9x + 2 + 3 + 6$$
$$= -x^3 + 12x^2 - 10x + 11$$

7. $9x^3 + 7x^2 - 10 = 9(0.5)^3 + 7(0.5)^2 - 10$
$$= 9(0.125) + 7(0.25) - 10$$
$$= 1.125 + 1.75 - 10$$
$$= -7.125$$

8. $A(x) = 15x^2 - 9x + 16$
$$A(2) = 15(2)^2 - 9(2) + 16$$
$$= 15(4) - 18 + 16$$
$$= 60 - 18 + 16$$
$$= 58$$

9. $a^3b^2 \cdot 3ab^3 = 3a^{3+1}b^{2+3}$
$$= 3a^4b^5$$

10. $9x^2\left(xy^3 - 6x^2y\right) = 9x^2 \cdot xy^3 - 9x^2 \cdot 6x^2y$
$$= 9x^{2+1}y^3 - 54x^{2+2}y$$
$$= 9x^3y^3 - 54x^4y$$

11. $(2x-1)(x+4) = 2x(x+4) - 1(x+4)$
$$= 2x^2 + 8x - x - 4$$
$$= 2x^2 + 7x - 4$$

12. $(5x+3)(x-7) = 5x(x-7) + 3(x-7)$
$$= 5x^2 - 35x + 3x - 21$$
$$= 5x^2 - 32x - 21$$

13. $(x-3)\left(x^2 - 5x + 6\right)$
$$= x\left(x^2 - 5x + 6\right) - 3\left(x^2 - 5x + 6\right)$$
$$= x^3 - 5x^2 + 6x - 3x^2 + 15x - 18$$
$$= x^3 - 5x^2 - 3x^2 + 6x + 15x - 18$$
$$= x^3 - 8x^2 + 21x - 18$$

14. $A = \frac{1}{2}bh$
$$= \frac{1}{2}(x+5)(2x-3)$$
$$= \frac{1}{2}\left[x(2x-3) + 5(2x-3)\right]$$
$$= \frac{1}{2}\left[2x^2 - 3x + 10x - 15\right]$$
$$= \frac{1}{2}\left[2x^2 + 7x - 15\right]$$
$$= x^2 + \frac{7}{2}x - \frac{15}{2} \text{ square feet}$$

15. $(3a-5)(b+2)$
$$= (3a)(b) + (3a)(2) + (-5)(b) + (-5)(2)$$
$$= 3ab + 6a - 5b - 10$$

16. $(y-4)(3y+7)$
$$= (y)(3y) + (y)(7) + (-4)(3y) + (-4)(7)$$
$$= 3y^2 + 7y - 12y - 28$$
$$= 3y^2 - 5y - 28$$

17. $(2a-5)^2 = (2a)^2 + 2(2a)(-5) + (-5)^2$
$$= 4a^2 - 20a + 25$$

18. $(2x+3y)^2 = (2x)^2 + 2(2x)(3y) + (3y)^2$
$$= 4x^2 + 12xy + 9y^2$$

19. $\left(y - \dfrac{1}{2}\right)\left(y + \dfrac{1}{2}\right) = (y)^2 - \left(\dfrac{1}{2}\right)^2$
$$= y^2 - \dfrac{1}{4}$$

20. $(2a+5b)(2a-5b) = (2a)^2 - (5b)^2$
$$= 4a^2 - 25b^2$$

21. $\dfrac{6y^3 + 18y^2 - 9y}{3y} = \dfrac{6y^3}{3y} + \dfrac{18y^2}{3y} - \dfrac{9y}{3y}$
$$= 2y^{3-1} + 6y^{2-1} - 3y^{1-1}$$
$$= 2y^2 + 6y^1 - 3y^0$$
$$= 2y^2 + 6y - 3(1)$$
$$= 2y^2 + 6y - 3$$

22. $(4a^2 - a - 3) \div (a - 1) = 4a + 3$

$$
\begin{array}{r}
4a+3 \\
a-1 \overline{\smash{)}4a^2 - a - 3} \\
\underline{-(4a^2 - 4a)} \\
3a - 3 \\
\underline{-(3a - 3)} \\
0
\end{array}
$$

23. $(2x^3 - x^2 - 25x - 12) \div (x + 3) = 2x^2 - 7x - 4$

$$
\begin{array}{r}
2x^2 - 7x - 4 \\
x+3 \overline{\smash{)}2x^3 - x^2 - 25x - 12} \\
\underline{-(2x^3 + 6x^2)} \\
-7x^2 - 25x \\
\underline{-(-7x^2 - 21x)} \\
-4x - 12 \\
\underline{-(-4x - 12)} \\
0
\end{array}
$$

24. $(64a^3 + 27) \div (4a + 3) = 16a^2 - 12a + 9$

$$
\begin{array}{r}
16a^2 - 12a + 9 \\
4a+3 \overline{\smash{)}64a^3 + 0a^2 + 0a + 27} \\
\underline{-(64a^3 + 48a^2)} \\
-48a^2 + 0a \\
\underline{-(-48a^2 - 36a)} \\
36a + 27 \\
\underline{-(36a + 27)} \\
0
\end{array}
$$

25. $(12z^4 - 11z^3 + 5z^2 + z - 9) \div (3z - 2)$

$$= 4z^3 - z^2 + z + 1 + \dfrac{-7}{3z - 2}$$

$$
\begin{array}{r}
4z^3 - z^2 + z + 1 \\
3z-2 \overline{\smash{)}12z^4 - 11z^3 + 5z^2 + z - 9} \\
\underline{-(12z^4 - 8z^3)} \\
-3z^3 + 5z^2 \\
\underline{-(-3z^3 + 2z^2)} \\
3z^2 + z \\
\underline{-(3z^2 - 2z)} \\
3z - 9 \\
\underline{-(3z - 2)} \\
-7
\end{array}
$$

Factoring Polynomials

1. The GCF is $3x$.
$$6x^3 + 18x^2y - 9x = 3x(2x^2 + 6xy - 3)$$

2. The GCF is $(2a-3)$.
$$2x(2a-3) - 9(2a-3) = (2a-3)(2x-9)$$

3. The GCF is 2.
$$4ax + 2ay - 6bx - 8by = 2(2ax + ay - 3bx - 4by)$$

4. $49 - 4x^2 = (7)^2 - (2x)^2$
$$= (7-2x)(7+2x)$$

5. prime

6. $8x^3 + 64y^3 = 8(x^3 + 8y^3)$
$$= 8\left[x^3 + (2y)^3\right]$$
$$= 8(x+2y)\left(x^2 - x\cdot 2y + (2y)^2\right)$$
$$= 8(x+2y)(x^2 - 2xy + 4y^2)$$

7. $5x^2y - 20y^3 = 5y(x^2 - 4y^2)$
$$= 5y(x-2y)(x+2y)$$

8. $8x^2 + 2x - 15 = 8x^2 + 12x - 10x - 15$
$$= 4x(2x+3) - 5(2x+3)$$
$$= (2x+3)(4x-5)$$

9. $21a^2 - 10ab - 16b^2 = 21a^2 - 24ab + 14ab - 16b^2$
$$= 3a(7a-8b) + 2b(7a-8b)$$
$$= (7a-8b)(3a+2b)$$

10. $10a^3b - 35a^3b^2 + 40a^4b^2 - 5a^3b^4$
$$= 5a^3b(2 - 7b + 8ab - b^3)$$

11. $x^2 - 7x + 12 = x^2 - 3x - 4x + 12$
$$= x(x-3) - 4(x-3)$$
$$= (x-3)(x-4)$$

12. $55x^2 - 84xy - 27y^2$
$$= 55x^2 + 15xy - 99xy - 27y^2$$
$$= 5x(11x+3y) - 9y(11x+3y)$$
$$= (11x+3y)(5x-9y)$$

13. prime

14. $x^2 - 5x - 84 = x^2 + 7x - 12x - 84$
$$= x(x+7) - 12(x+7)$$
$$= (x+7)(x-12)$$

15. $24a^2 + 52ab - 20b^2 = 4(6a^2 + 13ab - 5b^2)$
$$= 4(3a-b)(2a+5b)$$

16. $36at^2x + 12at^2y - 162bt^2x - 54bt^2y$
$$= 6t^2(6ax + 2ay - 27bx - 9by)$$
$$= 6t^2\left[2a(3x+y) - 9b(3x+y)\right]$$
$$= 6t^2(3x+y)(2a-9b)$$

17. $y^2 + 16y + 64 = y^2 + 8y + 8y + 64$
$$= y(y+8) + 8(y+8)$$
$$= (y+8)(y+8)$$
$$= (y+8)^2$$

18. $9z^4 - 81z^3 - 324z^2 = 9z^2(z^2 - 9z - 36)$
$$= 9z^2(z+3)(z-12)$$

19. prime

20. $48a^3 - 750 = 6(8a^3 - 125)$
$$= 6(2a-5)(4a^2 + 10a + 25)$$

21. $12hx + 3hy + 20kx + 5ky$
$$= 3h(4x+y) + 5k(4x+y)$$
$$= (4x+y)(3h+5k)$$

22. $3ax^3 - 9ax^2y - 12bx^3 + 36bx^2y$
$$= 3x^2(ax - 3ay - 4bx + 12by)$$
$$= 3x^2\left[a(x-3y) - 4b(x-3y)\right]$$
$$= 3x^2(x-3y)(a-4b)$$

23. $(x-2)(x+5)=0$

$x-2=0$ or $x+5=0$

$x=2$ or $x=-5$

Solution Set: $\{-5,2\}$

24. $2a^2+11a=21$

$2a^2+11a-21=0$

$(2a-3)(a+7)=0$

$2a-3=0$ or $a+7=0$

$a=\dfrac{3}{2}$ or $a=-7$

Solution Set: $\left\{-7,\dfrac{3}{2}\right\}$

25. Area $=$ length $\times$ width

$24=(x+2)(x-3)$

$24=x^2-x-6$

$0=x^2-x-30$

$0=(x+5)(x-6)$

$x+5=0$ or $x-6=0$

$\cancel{x=-5}$ or $x=6$

Because the dimensions of the rectangle must be positive, we will use 6 as the solution. Therefore, the dimensions of the rectangle are $x+2=8$ meters and $x-3=3$ meters.

Rational Expressions

1. $\dfrac{x^2-4x-12}{x-6} = \dfrac{\cancel{(x-6)}^{1}(x+2)}{\cancel{(x-6)}_{1}}$

$\qquad = x+2$

2. $\dfrac{x^2-4}{6a-2b-3ax+xb} = \dfrac{(x+2)(x-2)}{(3a-b)(2-x)}$

$\qquad = \dfrac{(x+2)\cancel{(x-2)}^{1}}{(3a-b)(-1)\cancel{(x-2)}_{1}}$

$\qquad = \dfrac{(x+2)}{(3a-b)(-1)}$

$\qquad = \dfrac{-x-2}{3a-b}$

3. $\dfrac{a^3-8}{a^2+2a+4} = \dfrac{(a-2)\cancel{(a^2+2a+4)}^{1}}{\cancel{(a^2+2a+4)}_{1}}$

$\qquad = a-2$

4. $\dfrac{y^2-64}{64+16y+y^2} = \dfrac{\cancel{(y+8)}^{1}(y-8)}{\cancel{(8+y)}_{1}(8+y)}$

$\qquad = \dfrac{y-8}{y+8}$

5. $\dfrac{x-2}{x+3} \div \dfrac{(x+5)(x-2)}{(x+3)(x-4)} = \dfrac{x-2}{x+3} \cdot \dfrac{(x+3)(x-4)}{(x+5)(x-2)}$

$\qquad = \dfrac{\cancel{(x-2)}^{1}\cancel{(x+3)}^{1}(x-4)}{\cancel{(x+3)}_{1}(x+5)\cancel{(x-2)}_{1}}$

$\qquad = \dfrac{x-4}{x+5}$

6. $\dfrac{(t-2)^2(t+3)}{(t-4)(t-5)} \cdot \dfrac{t^2-7t+10}{t^2-t-12}$

$\qquad = \dfrac{(t-2)^2(t+3)}{(t-4)(t-5)} \cdot \dfrac{(t-2)(t-5)}{(t-4)(t+3)}$

$\qquad = \dfrac{(t-2)^2\cancel{(t+3)}^{1}(t-2)\cancel{(t-5)}^{1}}{(t-4)\cancel{(t-5)}_{1}(t-4)\cancel{(t+3)}_{1}}$

$\qquad = \dfrac{(t-2)^3}{(t-4)^2}$

7. $\dfrac{a^2-9}{a^2+8a+16} \cdot \dfrac{a+4}{a-3} \div \dfrac{a^2-2a-15}{a^2+9a+20}$

$\qquad = \dfrac{a^2-9}{a^2+8a+16} \cdot \dfrac{a+4}{a-3} \cdot \dfrac{a^2+9a+20}{a^2-2a-15}$

$\qquad = \dfrac{(a+3)(a-3)}{(a+4)(a+4)} \cdot \dfrac{(a+4)}{(a-3)} \cdot \dfrac{(a+4)(a+5)}{(a-5)(a+3)}$

$\qquad = \dfrac{\cancel{(a+3)}^{1}\cancel{(a-3)}^{1}\cancel{(a+4)}^{1}\cancel{(a+4)}^{1}(a+5)}{\cancel{(a+4)}_{1}\cancel{(a+4)}_{1}\cancel{(a-3)}_{1}(a-5)\cancel{(a+3)}_{1}}$

$\qquad = \dfrac{a+5}{a-5}$

8. $\dfrac{3c+4}{c-2} - \dfrac{2c+3}{c-2} = \dfrac{3c+4-(2c+3)}{c-2}$

$\qquad = \dfrac{3c+4-2c-3}{c-2}$

$\qquad = \dfrac{c+1}{c-2}$

9. $\dfrac{7}{x-5} + \dfrac{3}{4} = \dfrac{4\cdot 7}{4(x-5)} + \dfrac{3(x-5)}{4(x-5)}$

$\qquad = \dfrac{28}{4(x-5)} + \dfrac{3x-15}{4(x-5)}$

$\qquad = \dfrac{28+3x-15}{4(x-5)}$

$\qquad = \dfrac{3x+13}{4(x-5)}$

10. $\dfrac{y}{2y-3}-\dfrac{2y^2+y-3}{4y^2-9}$

$=\dfrac{y}{2y-3}-\dfrac{\cancel{(2y+3)}(y-1)^{1}}{\cancel{(2y+3)}(2y-3)_{1}}$

$=\dfrac{y}{2y-3}-\dfrac{y-1}{2y-3}$

$=\dfrac{y-(y-1)}{2y-3}$

$=\dfrac{y-y+1}{2y-3}$

$=\dfrac{1}{2y-3}$

11. $\dfrac{\dfrac{x+3}{x^2+2x-35}}{\dfrac{x^2-2x-15}{x+7}}=\dfrac{\dfrac{(x+3)}{(x+7)(x-5)}}{\dfrac{(x-5)(x+3)}{(x+7)}}$

$=\dfrac{\dfrac{(x+3)}{(x+7)(x-5)}}{\dfrac{(x-5)(x+3)}{(x+7)}}\cdot\dfrac{\dfrac{(x+7)(x-5)}{1}}{\dfrac{(x+7)(x-5)}{1}}$

$=\dfrac{\dfrac{(x+3)\cancel{(x+7)}^{1}\cancel{(x-5)}^{1}}{\cancel{(x+7)}\cancel{(x-5)}}}{\dfrac{(x-5)(x+3)\cancel{(x+7)}^{1}(x-5)}{\cancel{(x+7)}}}$

$=\dfrac{\cancel{(x+3)}^{1}}{(x-5)\cancel{(x+3)}(x-5)}$

$=\dfrac{1}{(x-5)^2}$

12. $\dfrac{\dfrac{1}{2a}-\dfrac{4}{ab^2}}{\dfrac{3}{4b^2}+\dfrac{2}{a}}=\dfrac{\dfrac{1}{2a}-\dfrac{4}{ab^2}}{\dfrac{3}{4b^2}+\dfrac{2}{a}}\cdot\dfrac{\dfrac{4ab^2}{1}}{\dfrac{4ab^2}{1}}$

$=\dfrac{\dfrac{1}{\cancel{2a}}\cdot\dfrac{\cancel{4}\,\cancel{a}b^2}{1}-\dfrac{4}{\cancel{ab^2}}\cdot\dfrac{4\cancel{a}\,\cancel{b^2}}{1}}{\dfrac{3}{\cancel{4b^2}}\cdot\dfrac{\cancel{4}\,a\cancel{b^2}}{1}+\dfrac{2}{\cancel{a}}\cdot\dfrac{4\cancel{a}\,b^2}{1}}$

$=\dfrac{2b^2-16}{3a+8b^2}$

$=\dfrac{2(b^2-8)}{3a+8b^2}$

13. $\dfrac{4}{x}+\dfrac{1}{5}=\dfrac{7}{x}$

$\dfrac{5x}{1}\left(\dfrac{4}{x}+\dfrac{1}{5}\right)=\dfrac{5x}{1}\left(\dfrac{7}{x}\right)$

$\dfrac{20\cancel{x}}{\cancel{x}}+\dfrac{\cancel{5}x}{\cancel{5}}=\dfrac{35\cancel{x}}{\cancel{x}}$

$20+x=35$

$x=15$

Solution Set: $\{15\}$

14. $\dfrac{y}{7}=\dfrac{5}{y+2}$

$\dfrac{\cancel{7}(y+2)}{1}\left(\dfrac{y}{\cancel{7}}\right)=\dfrac{7\cancel{(y+2)}}{1}\left(\dfrac{5}{\cancel{y+2}}\right)$

$y^2+2y=35$

$y^2+2y-35=0$

$(y+7)(y-5)=0$

$y+7=0\quad\text{or}\quad y-5=0$

$y=-7\quad\text{or}\quad y=5$

Solution Set: $\{-7,5\}$

15.

$$2 - \frac{3}{x-3} = \frac{8}{x^2-9}$$

$$2 - \frac{3}{x-3} = \frac{8}{(x+3)(x-3)}$$

$$\frac{(x+3)(x-3)}{1}\left(2 - \frac{3}{x-3}\right) = \frac{(x+3)(x-3)}{1}\left(\frac{8}{(x+3)(x-3)}\right)$$

$$\frac{(x+3)(x-3)}{1} \cdot 2 - \frac{(x+3)\cancel{(x-3)}}{1} \cdot \frac{3}{\cancel{x-3}} = \frac{\cancel{(x+3)}\cancel{(x-3)}}{1}\left(\frac{8}{\cancel{(x+3)}\cancel{(x-3)}}\right)$$

$$2x^2 - 18 - 3x - 9 = 8$$

$$2x^2 - 3x - 35 = 0$$

$$(2x+7)(x-5) = 0$$

$$2x + 7 = 0 \quad \text{or} \quad x - 5 = 0$$

$$-\frac{7}{2} \quad \text{or} \quad x = 5$$

Solution Set: $\left\{-\frac{7}{2}, 5\right\}$

Beginning Algebra Review

1.
$$14 + 3x = -7$$
$$14 - 14 + 3x = -7 - 14$$
$$3x = -21$$
$$\frac{3x}{3} = \frac{-21}{3}$$
$$x = -7$$
Solution Set: $\{-7\}$

2.
$$5(5a - 2) = 4(a + 7) + 4$$
$$25a - 10 = 4a + 28 + 4$$
$$25a - 10 = 4a + 32$$
$$25a - 10 + 10 = 4a + 32 + 10$$
$$25a = 4a + 42$$
$$25a - 4a = 4a - 4a + 42$$
$$21a = 42$$
$$\frac{21a}{21} = \frac{42}{21}$$
$$a = 2$$
Solution Set: $\{2\}$

3. Let x represent the unknown number.
$$4x + 7 = 23$$
$$4x + 7 - 7 = 23 - 7$$
$$4x = 16$$
$$\frac{4x}{4} = \frac{16}{4}$$
$$x = 4$$
The number is 4.

4.
$$3x \leq -9$$
$$\frac{3x}{3} \leq \frac{-9}{3}$$
$$x \leq -3$$
$$(-\infty, -3]$$

5.
$$-19 \leq 6x - 7 < -1$$
$$-19 + 7 \leq 6x - 7 + 7 < -1 + 7$$
$$-12 \leq 6x < 6$$
$$\frac{-12}{6} \leq \frac{6x}{6} < \frac{6}{6}$$
$$-2 \leq x < 1$$
$$[-2, 1)$$

6. Let $y = 0$.
$$6x + 3(0) = 9$$
$$6x = 9$$
$$x = 1.5$$
The x-intercept is $(1.5, 0)$.
Let $x = 0$.
$$6(0) + 3y = 9$$
$$3y = 9$$
$$y = 3$$
The y-intercept is $(0, -3)$.

7. $m = \dfrac{y_2 - y_1}{x_2 - x_1}$
$$= \frac{9 - 15}{-2 - (-6)}$$
$$= \frac{-6}{4}$$
$$= -\frac{3}{2}$$

8. $m = \dfrac{y_2 - y_1}{x_2 - x_1}$ $y = mx + b$
$$= \frac{5 - 1}{4 - (-2)} \qquad (5) = \left(\frac{2}{3}\right)(4) + b$$
$$= \frac{4}{6} \qquad\qquad 5 = \frac{8}{3} + b$$
$$= \frac{2}{3} \qquad\qquad \frac{7}{3} = b$$
$$y = \frac{2}{3}x + \frac{7}{3}$$

9. $m = \dfrac{1}{2}$ $y = mx + b$
$$(-4) = \left(\frac{1}{2}\right)(2) + b$$
$$-4 = 1 + b$$
$$-5 = b$$

$$y = \frac{1}{2}x + (-5)$$
$$y = \frac{1}{2}x - 5$$
$$2y = x - 10$$
$$-x + 2y = -10$$
$$x - 2y = 10$$

10. $\left(3m^3 n^{-2}\right)^{-3} = 3^{-3}\left(m^3\right)^{-3}\left(n^{-2}\right)^{-3}$

$$= 3^{-3} m^{-9} n^6$$

$$= \frac{1}{3^3} \cdot \frac{1}{m^9} \cdot n^6$$

$$= \frac{n^6}{27m^9}$$

11. $\left(7x^4 y^2 z^{-3}\right) \cdot \left(-\frac{1}{14}x^{-2}y^3 z^3\right)$

$$= -\frac{7}{14}x^{4+(-2)}y^{2+3}z^{-3+3}$$

$$= -\frac{1}{2}x^2 y^5 z^0$$

$$= -\frac{1}{2}x^2 y^5 (1)$$

$$= -\frac{x^2 y^5}{2}$$

12. $\left(4a^2 b^{-3} c\right)^3 \cdot \left(2a^{-4} b^{-3} c^0\right)^{-2}$

$$= 4^3 \left(a^2\right)^3 \left(b^{-3}\right)^3 c^3 \cdot 2^{-2}\left(a^{-4}\right)^{-2}\left(b^{-3}\right)^{-2}\left(c^0\right)^{-2}$$

$$= 4^3 a^6 b^{-9} c^3 \cdot 2^{-2} a^8 b^6 c^0$$

$$= 4^3 \cdot 2^{-2} a^{6+8} b^{-9+6} c^{3+0}$$

$$= 4^3 \cdot 2^{-2} a^{14} b^{-3} c^3$$

$$= 4^3 \cdot \frac{1}{2^2} \cdot a^{14} \cdot \frac{1}{b^3} \cdot c^3$$

$$= \frac{\overset{16}{\cancel{64}} a^{14} c^3}{\underset{1}{\cancel{4}} b^3}$$

$$= \frac{16 a^{14} c^3}{b^3}$$

13. $5.2\left(10^{-4}\right) \cdot 6.8\left(10^9\right)$

$$= 35.36\left(10^5\right)$$

$$= 3.536\left(10^1\right)\left(10^5\right)$$

$$= 3.536\left(10^6\right) \qquad \text{Scientific Notation}$$

$$= 3,536,000 \qquad \text{Standard Notation}$$

14. $(149,060,000) \cdot (0.004)$

$$= 1.4906\left(10^8\right) \cdot 4\left(10^{-3}\right)$$

$$= 5.9624\left(10^5\right) \qquad \text{Scientific Notation}$$

$$= 596,240 \qquad \text{Standard Notation}$$

15. $\left(9a^3 - 14a^2 + 3a - 7\right) - \left(-8a^2 - 5a + 11\right)$

$$= 9a^3 - 14a^2 + 3a - 7 + 8a^2 + 5a - 11$$

$$= 9a^3 - 14a^2 + 8a^2 + 3a + 5a - 7 - 11$$

$$= 9a^3 - 6a^2 + 8a - 18$$

16. $mn^5 \cdot 4m^2 n^3 \div 2mn^4 = 4m^{1+2} n^{5+3} \div 2mn^4$

$$= 4m^3 n^8 \div 2mn^4$$

$$= \frac{\overset{2}{\cancel{4}} m^3 n^8}{\underset{1}{\cancel{2}} mn^4}$$

$$= 2m^{3-1} n^{8-4}$$

$$= 2m^2 n^4$$

17. $(9x - 3y)(a - 4b) = 9x(a - 4b) - 3y(a - 4b)$

$$= 9ax - 36bx - 3ay - 12by$$

18. $(x - 6y)(2x + 5y) = x(2x + 5y) - 6y(2x + 5y)$

$$= 2x^2 + 5xy - 12xy - 30y^2$$

$$= 2x^2 - 7xy - 30y^2$$

19. $\left(x^3 - 5x^2 + 13x - 17\right) \div (x - 2) = x^2 - 3x + 7 - \dfrac{3}{x-2}$

$$
\begin{array}{r}
x^2 - 3x + 7 \\
x-2\overline{)x^3 - 5x^2 + 13x - 17} \\
\underline{-\left(x^3 - 2x^2\right)} \\
-3x^2 + 13x \\
\underline{-\left(-3x^2 + 6x\right)} \\
7x - 17 \\
\underline{-(7x - 14)} \\
-3
\end{array}
$$

20. The GCF is $4a^4 b^2$.

$$12a^5 b^3 - 24a^6 b^2 + 20a^4 b^4 = 4a^4 b^2\left(3ab - 6a^2 + 5b^2\right)$$

21. $12b^2 + 29b - 8 = 12b^2 - 3b + 32b - 8$

$$= 3b(4b - 1) + 8(4b - 1)$$

$$= (4b - 1)(3b + 8)$$

22. $18ax - 45ay + 2hx - 5hy$

$\quad = 9a(2x - 5y) + h(2x - 5y)$

$\quad = (2x - 5y)(9a + h)$

23. $8ab^2x - 24b^3x + 4ab^2y - 12b^3y$

$\quad = 4b^2(2ax - 6bx + ay - 3by)$

$\quad = 4b^2[2x(a - 3b) + y(a - 3b)]$

$\quad = 4b^2(a - 3b)(2x + y)$

24. $x^2 + 4x - 117 = x^2 + 13x - 9x - 117$

$\qquad\qquad\quad = x(x + 13) - 9(x + 13)$

$\qquad\qquad\quad = (x + 13)(x - 9)$

25. $\qquad 2z^2 + 9z - 32 = 24$

$\qquad\quad 2z^2 + 9z - 56 = 0$

$\qquad\quad (2z - 7)(z + 8) = 0$

$\qquad 2z - 7 = 0 \quad \text{or} \quad z + 8 = 0$

$\qquad\quad z = \dfrac{7}{2} \quad \text{or} \quad z = -8$

$\qquad \text{Solution Set: } \left\{-8, \dfrac{7}{2}\right\}$